PRINCIPLES
OF ACCOUNTING

PRINCIPLES OF ACCOUNTING

SECOND EDITION

Belverd E. Needles, Jr.

Ph.D., C.P.A., C.M.A.
Professor of Accounting
Director,
School of Accountancy
DePaul University

Henry R. Anderson

Ph.D., C.P.A., C.M.A.
Professor of Accounting
Director,
School of Accounting
University of
Central Florida

James C. Caldwell

Ph.D., C.P.A.
Partner
Educational
Consulting Services
Arthur Andersen & Co.
Dallas/Fort Worth

Houghton Mifflin Company   Boston

Dallas   Geneva, Illinois   Hopewell, New Jersey   Palo Alto

To Marian Needles, and to Jennifer and Jeff
To Sue Anderson, and to Deborah, Howard, Harold, and Hugh
To Bonnie Caldwell, and to Stephanie, Susan, and Sharon

Cover photograph by David Wade

Printed in the U.S.A.

Library of Congress Catalog Card Number: 83-80989

ISBN: 0-395-34329-1

DEFGHIJ-RM-898765

Contents

Part Two   Extensions of the Basic Accounting Model

Micro-Tec Practice Set may be used after Chapter 7.

College Words and Sounds Store Practice Set may be used after Chapter 9.

Contents

Part Five Special Reports and Analyses of Accounting Information

Video-Games, Inc., Practice Set may be used after Chapter 18.

Part Six   Basic Concepts of Management Accounting

Part Seven   Accounting for Management Decision Making

Preface

Principles of Accounting, Second Edition, is a comprehensive first course in accounting for students who have had no previous training in accounting or business.
Designed for both majors and nonmajors, it is intended for use in the traditional
two-semester and two- or three-quarter sequences.

The textbook is part of a well-integrated package of materials for students and
instructors, including new ancillaries not found in the previous edition. Available
for students are the Study Guide, Working Papers (four sets), Electronic Working
Papers (new to the Second Edition), four traditional Practice Sets (one new to the
Second Edition), three computer-assisted Practice Sets (one new to the Second
Edition), and a Check List of Key Figures. Available for instructors are the In-
structor's Solutions Manual, Practice Sets Solutions Manuals, the Instructor's
Handbook (new to the Second Edition), Transparencies, Test Bank, Computer-
Assisted Test Bank, and preprinted Achievement Tests. All are described later in
this preface.

We wrote this book because we believe that the first course in accounting
should emphasize concepts and practices that will be useful to students throughout their careers, whether they are accounting majors or not. The learning
method of this book combines doing with understanding. Concepts take on
meaning when applied, and practices are most easily understood if related to a
conceptual foundation.

The success of the book has justified our confidence in the principal objectives
and features underlying the first edition. These objectives are (1) its design for the
student's first exposure to accounting, (2) its authoritative and practical basis,
(3) its contemporary emphasis, (4) its decision-making emphasis, and (5) its com-
pleteness as a flexible learning system.

Designed for the Student's First Exposure to Accounting

The text's intended audience has influenced the organization of the book in several ways. First, we have carefully planned the timing of new concepts and tech-

niques to facilitate learning. The pace enables the student to grasp and retain the material. For example, we have delayed the presentation of adjusting entries, recognized as one of the most difficult topics for beginning students, until Chapter 4. Second, we have taken special care, particularly in the early part of the book, to limit the number of difficult concepts or practices in each chapter. To aid comprehension of adjusting entries, for instance, we have devoted most of Chapter 4 to this topic. Third, the book presents accounting as one of the most important and fascinating professions in our society. Finally, we focus throughout on understanding rather than mere memorization.

To facilitate student learning, we use the sole proprietorship in the first half of the book to illustrate basic accounting concepts and techniques, but at important points in Chapters 1 and 9 we point out the relationship of proprietorship accounting to corporation accounting. In Chapter 9, for example, we introduce students to corporate financial statements by presenting excerpts from the General Mills annual report.

Authoritative and Practical Basis

This book presents accounting as it is practiced, but the concepts underlying each accounting practice are also carefully explained. Throughout, accounting terms and concepts are defined according to current pronouncements of the AICPA, APB, and FASB. As the basis for discussion, relevant APB Opinions, FASB Statements, SEC pronouncements, and other authoritative sources are often cited. Statements of Financial Accounting Standards Numbers 33 and 52 receive extensive treatment. In addition, the Statements of Financial Accounting Concepts Numbers 1, 2, and 3 of the FASB's Conceptual Framework Study form the theoretical underpinning of the book and are used to assess various accounting situations and controversies.

Contemporary Emphasis

The topical coverage is up-to-date and responsive to current trends in business and accounting. Taxation, inflation accounting, and international accounting are just three of the contemporary topics emphasized. Taxation is not an isolated subject but an important and integral part of the study of accounting. For this reason, rather than devoting just one chapter to taxation, we cover it at many places where it is relevant to the discussion. For example, the topic of taxation and LIFO inventories is included in the chapter on inventories (Chapter 11), and the Accelerated Cost Recovery System is discussed in the chapter on property, plant, and equipment (Chapter 13). Corporate income tax liability is covered in Chapter 17, and income tax allocation is covered in Chapter 18. The important topic of inflation accounting receives a thorough treatment in Chapter 14. The section of Chapter 20 that is devoted to international accounting should help schools meet the new accreditation standard of the American Assembly of Collegiate Schools of Business. Each of these topics, as well as others, may be supplemented by selected readings from the Study Guide that accompanies the text.

Decision-Making Emphasis

Another objective has been to present the contemporary business world and the real-life complexities of accounting in a clear, concise, easy-to-understand manner. Accounting is treated as an information system that helps management, investors, and creditors make economic decisions. Chapter 1 emphasizes this role of accounting. It describes the use of accounting by all segments of society and discusses the impact of the AICPA, APB, FASB, SEC, and IRS on generally accepted accounting principles. In addition to other questions, exercises, and problems, the chapter assignments include two new decision-oriented features in each chapter: an exercise on "Interpreting Accounting Information" and a "Financial (or Management) Decision Case." In each situation, the student is required to extract quantitative information from the exercise or case and make an interpretation or a decision.

Complete and Flexible Learning System

Organization

The organization of the book in seven parts is designed for schools using either a semester or a quarter sequence. Those using the two-semester or two-quarter sequence may cover three parts during the first term and four parts during the second. Those using the three quarter sequence may cover two parts in each of the first two quarters and three parts in the last quarter. If a shorter course is required, all or parts of Chapters 5, 7, 12, 14, 20, and 21 may be omitted or covered briefly without hindering comprehension of later chapters. For instructors who want to introduce students to the present and future value of money and/or individual income taxes, appendixes on these subjects, along with accounting examples and exercises, are provided at the end of the text.

Textbook Features

Learning Objectives Action-oriented objectives at the beginning of each chapter indicate in precise terms what the students should be able to do when they complete the chapter. The objectives are stated again in the margins beside pertinent text discussion. Then the end-of-chapter review clearly relates each objective to the content of the chapter. The end-of-chapter assignments are also keyed to specific learning objectives.

Real-World Applications Many chapters include graphs or tables illustrating the practice of actual businesses in relation to the topics of the chapter. In addition, most of the exercises on Interpreting Accounting Information are based on the published financial reports of real companies.

Key Terms and Glossary Throughout the book, key accounting terms are emphasized with bold color type and clearly defined in context. These terms are also assembled in a comprehensive glossary for easy reference.

Chapter Review A unique feature of each chapter is a special review section comprising (1) a Review of Learning Objectives that summarizes the main points of the chapter in relation to the objectives, (2) a Self-Test in Chapters 1 through 5 that reviews the basic concepts of these crucial early chapters, with end-of-chapter answers that provide immediate feedback to the students, and (3) in all chapters, a Review Problem with complete solution to demonstrate the chapter's major procedures before students tackle the exercises and problems.

Questions Discussion questions at the end of each chapter focus, for the most part, on major concepts and terms.

Classroom Exercises Classroom Exercises provide practice in applying concepts taught in the chapter and are very effective in illustrating lecture points. Each exercise is keyed to the learning objectives. In addition, transparencies are available for all exercise solutions.

Interpreting Accounting Information This feature asks the student to interpret published financial information (in Chapters 1–21) or internal management reports (in Chapters 22–28). Most are based on excerpts from actual annual reports or on published articles about well-known corporations or organizations. Among the companies included are K mart, Sears, U.S. Steel, Marathon Oil, Chrysler, Iowa Beef Processors, International Paper, Lockheed, and Federal Express. Each of these exercises requires students to demonstrate their ability to interpret published information by extracting data from what they read and by making a computation and interpretation.

A and B Problems We have included two sets of problems to provide maximum flexibility in homework assignments. In general, the problems are arranged in order of difficulty, with Problems A-1 or B-1 for each chapter being the simplest, and the last in the series the most comprehensive. A and B problems have been matched by topic, so that A-1 and B-1, for example, are equivalent in content and level of difficulty. In addition, all problems are keyed to the learning objectives. Difficulty ratings, time estimates, and solutions are available to the instructor. Transparencies of all solutions are also available.

Financial and Management Decision Cases Each chapter contains a case that emphasizes the usefulness of accounting information in making decisions. The business background and financial information for each case are presented in a decision context. The decision maker may be a manager, an investor, an analyst, or a creditor. In the role of decision maker, the student is asked to extract the relevant data from the case, make computations as necessary, and make a decision.

Appendixes At the end of the book, we have included appendixes on using present and future value, as well as compound interest and present value tables. Appendix C is an overview of income taxes for individuals.

Supplementary Learning Aids

The supplementary learning aids provide a variety of useful tools for the student. They consist of the Study Guide, Working Papers (four sets), Electronic Working Papers, four traditional Practice Sets, three computer-assisted Practice Sets, and a Check List of Key Figures.

Study Guide This learning aid is a chapter-by-chapter guide to help the student understand the concepts presented in the text. Each chapter begins with a summary, in numbered paragraph form, of the major concepts and applications in that chapter. Next, to test the students' basic knowledge of chapter content, we provide a matching test, a completion test, a true-false test of important relationships, and a multiple-choice test. Students are then asked to apply their knowledge in short exercises. Finally, a crossword puzzle every second chapter challenges the students' mastery of key terms. Answers to all tests, exercises, and puzzles are given at the end of the book. The Study Guide also includes twenty readings from professional journals and the popular press on career opportunities, the societal impact of accounting, key issues in accounting, and difficult concepts covered in the text.

Working Papers The working papers are designed to reduce pencil pushing by students. Each problem has an appropriate form, certain information is preprinted, and in some cases part of the answer is entered to provide a model for the student. Illustrative work sheet analyses for manufacturing companies using the periodic and perpetual inventory approaches, respectively, are provided at the beginning of the Working Papers. Students who are reading Chapters 22 and 23 in the text will be directed to these work sheet analyses.

Electronic Working Papers, by Paul C. Kircher and Robert F. Roan This accounting problems tutorial consists of computer software and a workbook to help students work selected problems from Chapters 1 through 21 of the text. Not only will students be able to do homework assignments and gain familiarity with the computer, but they will receive step-by-step guidance and feedback from the computer.

Traditional Practice Sets Each of the following practice sets is designed to introduce students to specific aspects of accounting.

1. *Micro-Tec.* This simple practice set, designed for use after Chapter 7, covers the basic accounting cycle for one month in a sole proprietorship merchandising company. It is available either as a workbook for the student or as a set of business documents.

2. *College Words and Sounds Store.* This practice set presents a realistic set of transactions and records for a small merchandising concern over a two-month period. Designed for use after Chapter 9, it introduces both a petty cash system and a voucher system. Like *Micro-Tec,* it is available either as a workbook or as a set of business documents.

3. *Video-Games, Inc.* This practice set demonstrates the corporate form of a wholesale business. In its early stages it also shows the purchase of a partnership

by the corporation. Designed for use after Chapter 18, it is available in workbook format.

4. *Aluma-Cylinder Company, Inc.,* by Henry R. Anderson and Carol A. Gordon. This practice set is a comprehensive simulation of a job order cost accounting system for a manufacturing firm. Designed for use after Chapter 23, it covers a three-month period in the life of the company. The practice set comes in workbook format.

Computer-Assisted Practice Sets Three computer-assisted, interactive practice sets are available. Although they stress transaction analysis, they also demonstrate the computer's ability to speed the flow of accounting data. They require no programming experience on the part of the student or the instructor and actually can be done manually if the instructor wishes. The three sets are as follows:

• *Cook's Solar Energy System,* by Donald E. Edwards and Ronald C. Kettering. For use after Chapter 3, this practice set covers the basic accounting cycle for one month in a sole proprietorship merchandising company.

• *Berger Automotive Company* and *Stormer Painting Company,* by Clairmont P. Carter and Douglas S. Platt. These two practice sets may be started at any point after Chapter 3 and continued throughout the course. Either set covers most of financial accounting. *Berger* covers the first year of an auto service proprietorship that grows into a corporation. *Stormer* covers the first year of a service company that changes into a merchandising company; later it changes from a proprietorship into a corporation.

Check List of Key Figures This aid for students is available free in quantity to instructors who request it. It consists of a key figure from the solution to each text problem so that students can know if they are on the right track. Each check list has a glued edge; thus students can affix it to their texts if they wish.

Instructor's Aids

Instructor's Handbook This new ancillary is a resource aid for the instructor in teaching the course. For each chapter the Handbook provides a list of the topic headings in the text, teaching hints by Raymond Green, lecture resource materials for each learning objective, learning objectives charts for end-of-chapter assignments, an analysis of the time and difficulty involved in solving each text problem, and finally a ten-minute quiz with answers.

Instructor's Solutions Manual The Instructor's Solutions Manual contains solutions to all questions, exercises, and problems in the text. Charts rate each problem as easy, medium, or difficult and suggest the time in minutes that an average student will need to solve it. Other charts show how each learning objective in the text is met by specific exercises and problems.

Test Bank and Achievement Tests The Test Bank, which is available both in printed form and as a computer program, offers a variety of testing material for each chapter. Short exercises and problems are included as well as true-false and multiple-choice items. Overall, the Test Bank totals more than a thousand items. A machine-scorable verion of the Test Bank is also available.

There are also thirteen preprinted Achievement Tests, each with an A version and a B version. Each test covers two or three chapters. As in the Test Bank, short problems are included along with briefer questions. Points are assigned to each item, giving a total score of 100 points for each test.

Transparencies More than 900 transparencies, free to adopters, provide solutions to all exercises and the A and B problems. Another 73 transparencies reproduce instructional charts and diagrams from the text.

Changes in the Second Edition

This new edition has benefited substantially from the suggestions of the many users and reviewers who have corresponded with us. In response to these comments, various organizational changes have been made.

Chapter 7 on "General Purpose External Financial Statements" has become Chapter 9, and Special Journals are now covered in Chapter 7. A new practice set, Micro-Tec, fits right after the new Chapter 7. The managerial accounting chapters have been restructured so that the material in Part Five is presented in three, instead of four, chapters. Chapter 29 has been dropped, and the subject of business income taxes has been integrated at appropriate points in the text. Personal income taxes are discussed in Appendix C. An "Interpreting Accounting Information" exercise has been added to each chapter. In the financial chapters (1–21), these contain published financial information, and in the managerial chapters (22–28), they contain managerial information. A Financial Decision Case has been added to each of the first twenty-one chapters and a Management Decision Case has been added to Chapters 22 through 28. New material on not-for-profit accounting has been added to Chapters 1, 3, 26, and 27.

All exercises and problems have been revised. Also, each exercise and problem is now keyed by number to a specific learning objective(s).

Changes in the content of specific chapters is described below.

Chapter 2. Accounting as an Information System. The section on qualitative standards has been moved to Chapter 9. Accounting measurement is now the focal point of the chapter. Terms such as *assets, liabilities,* and *equity* are defined using definitions from the FASB Statements of Financial Accounting Concepts. The illustrations in the chapter, including the example set of four basic financial statements at the end of the chapter, are part of a single integrated case, Shannon Realty. The income statement, the statement of owner's equity, and the balance sheet are now shown in a single figure with lines showing their relationships.

Chapter 3. The Double Entry System. The Section on T accounts has been moved to a point later in the chapter for more logical presentation. The chart of accounts is expanded. A new illustration shows the relationships of the owner's equity accounts.

Chapter 4. Business Income and Adjusting Entries. Revenues, expenses, and accrual accounting are defined using FASB Statements of Financial Accounting

Concepts. The concepts of deferrals and accruals are added to identify situations that require adjusting entries.

Chapter 5. Completing the Accounting Cycle. Following through on the Joan Miller Advertising case that was used in Chapters 3 and 4, the transactions are all identified by date and the entries and postings all show proper posting references as they would in practice. An explanation of reversing entries as the first step of the next accounting period is added here and applied to the Joan Miller case. Reversing entries are also added to the chapter assignments.

Chapter 6. Accounting for Merchandising Operations. Control of purchases discounts is introduced through the net method of recording purchases and the Purchases Discounts Lost account. A complete income statement for a merchandising company has been added. The chapter now gives the instructor the option of using the adjusting entry or the closing entry method of handling merchandise inventory on the work sheet and in the accounting records.

Chapter 7. Accounting Systems and Special-Purpose Journals. The discussion of computer data processing has been updated and given more prominence. The relationship of microcomputers to accounting systems is discussed.

Chapter 8. Internal Control and Merchandising Operations. The application of internal control has been broadened to include merchandising transactions.

Chapter 9. General-Purpose External Financial Statements. This chapter emphasizes the Conceptual Framework Statements of Financial Accounting Concepts of the FASB. The condensed multistep and single-step income statements are presented. The ratios of return on assets and return on equity are now based on average total assets and average owner's equity instead of end-of-year balances. The debt to equity ratio is now used instead of the capital structure ratio because the former is more widely used in practice. The financial statements of General Mills are presented.

Chapter 10. Short-Term Liquid Assets. The title has been changed to reflect the addition of a section on accounting for cash and short-term investments. Coverage of short-term investments has been expanded.

Chapter 11. Inventories. The ceiling and floor method of determining market value has been deleted because reviewers consider it appropriate for more advanced courses.

Chapter 12. Current Liabilities and Payroll Accounting. The topic of contingent liability has been introduced. The payroll section has been updated for changes in the payroll taxes. The topic of reversing entries was moved to Chapter 5.

Chapter 13. Property, Plant, and Equipment. The Accelerated Cost Recovery System (ACRS) has been added and discussed.

Chapter 14. Revenue and Expense Issues and Inflation Accounting. Discussion of accounting conventions that aid in the interpretation of financial statements has been moved to Chapter 9.

Chapter 16. Corporations: Organization and Contributed Capital. The section called "Other Stockholders' Equity Transactions," including retirement of stock, donation of stock, and donations by nonstockholders, has been moved to this chapter from Chapter 17.

Chapter 17. Retained Earnings and Corporate Income Statements. A discussion of corporate income taxes and their calculation has been inserted.

Chapter 18. Long-Term Liabilities. The section on accounting for bond investments has been moved to Chapter 20. This step simplifies and unifies the chapter, since it now deals only with liabilities. The procedure for determining the value of a bond using present value techniques has been added. The discussion of long-term leases has been expanded to show the journal entries for capital leases. A short and simple discussion of pensions and pension liabilities has been added. A section on financial reporting and income tax allocation has also been included.

Chapter 20. Intercompany Investments and International Accounting. The section on pooling of interests has been dropped, and one on accounting for bond investments is now included. The coverage of international accounting has been updated. It now includes a complete discussion and illustration of FASB's *Statement of Financial Accounting Standards No. 52*, "Foreign Currency Translation."

Chapter 21. Financial Statement Analysis. The chapter is organized around a complete financial analysis of Eastman Kodak. The ratios of receivable turnover, inventory turnover, asset turnover, return on assets, and return on equity are now based on average receivables, average inventory, average assets, and average owners' equity.

Chapter 22. Manufacturing Accounting: Cost Elements and Reporting. Chapters 22 and 23 from the first edition have been condensed and combined into a single chapter. The focus of the chapter is on management accounting and the unique elements of accounting for manufacturing operations including the preparation of financial statements for a manufacturing company. The appendix on manufacturing companies using the periodic inventory approach has been transferred to the Working Papers.

Chapter 23. Product Costing: The Job Order System. The appendix on the work sheet for manufacturing companies using the perpetual inventory method has been transferred to the Working Papers.

Chapter 24. Product Costing: The Process Cost Accounting System. This optional chapter now uses the average method rather than the FIFO method of accounting for process unit costs and work-in-process inventories.

Chapter 25. Basic Cost Planning and Control Tools. Sections on cost allocation and on accounting for joint production costs have been added.

Chapter 26. Budgetary Control: The Planning Function. This chapter on budgeting has been completely rewritten. "Principles of Budgeting" is a new section. The discussion of cash budgeting has been expanded significantly. The section on budgeting in not-for-profit organizations is also new.

Chapter 27. Cost Control Using Standard Costing. The complete presentation of standard costing now appears in one chapter. Cost control in not-for-profit organizations is new.

Appendix C. A new appendix, "An Overview of Income Taxes for Individuals," has been added to replace the discussion in Chapter 29 of the first edition. Assignment material is included. Taxes for businesses have been integrated into appropriate text chapters.

Acknowledgments

An introductory accounting text is a long and demanding project that cannot really succeed without the help of one's colleagues. We are grateful to a large number of professors and other professional colleagues as well as students for constructive comments that have led to improvements in the text. Unfortunately, space does not permit us to mention all those who have contributed to this volume.

Some of those who have been supportive and who have had an impact on our efforts are Hobart W. Adams (University of Akron), Albert J. Arsenault (Hillsborough Community College), Larry Bailey (Temple University), D. Dale Bandy (California State University, Fullerton), David Bayley (Santa Monica College), Mary M. Bethel (Georgia Southern College), Benedict Bombera (DePaul University), Jeri Brockett (University of Cincinnati), Montclair P. Carter (University of Lowell), Harold E. Caylor (Lakeland Community College), Erlinda Clark (California State University, Sacramento), Edwin Cohen (DePaul University), Jack Coleman (California State University, Fullerton), Pauline L. Corn (Virginia Polytechnic Institute and State University), James Davis (Bucks County Community College), Sherman H. Dearth (Mesa Community College), Joseph G. Doser (Truckee Meadows Community College), Christopher Dungan (University of Louisville), Kenneth O. Elvik (Iowa State University), Kenneth L. Fox (Kansas State University), David Gabhart (DePaul University), Lou Gilles (Coastal Carolina Community College), Joseph Goodman (Chicago State University), Carol A. Gordon (tax consultant), Raymond Green (Texas Tech University), Roy Gross (Dutchess Community College), James M. Hoyt (University of Nevada, Reno), Kara Johan (California State University, Fullerton), Alan P. Johnson (California State University, Hayward), Donna L. Randall Lacey (Bunker Hill Community College), Bill Lawrence (Austin Community College), Charles Lawrence (Purdue University), Tom and Clara Lelievre (University of Cincinnati), and W. Morley Lemon (McMaster University).

We would also like to thank Terry S. Lindenberg (Rock Valley College), Don MacGilvra (Shoreline Community College), Marcos Massoud (California State Polytechnic University), Mark McCarthy (DePaul University), Robert J. McCarter (CPA), James D. McEntire (Contra Costa College), Verda McKellips (Southwestern Oklahoma State University), William K. Meigs (Coastal Carolina Community College), Elizabeth Murphy (DePaul University), Dennis Neilson (University of San Francisco), Leo Newcombe (DePaul University), Steven Palmer (Appalachian State University), James W. Pfister (St. Petersburg Junior College), Marshall Pitman (DePaul University), Sharon L. Robinson (Frostburg State College), Robert Schaefer (Blinn College), Lee H. Schlorff (Bentley College), Talaat El Shazly (College of Charleston, SC), Jeffrey R. Shwartz (Montgomery College), Earl L. Smith (Oscar Rose Junior College), Charles C. Speer (Appalachian State University), Gary Sundem (Cornell University), Abe Tawil (Baruch College), G. Guy Wallace (University of North Carolina, Charlotte), Lee C. Wilson (Mesa Community College), and Victoria C. Zimelis (DePaul University).

We would also like to acknowledge the assistance of Arthur Young & Company, Boston, who reviewed the entire text and solutions manual to ascertain that the presentation is up-to-date and accurate. We are especially indebted to Bruce E. Bezanson, Elaine S. Coyne, William J. DeMartino, James D. Flynn, Susan T. Greene, Michael Kennedy, Thomas P. McDermott, Dean S. Rhodes, Patricia G. Smith, Lawrence D. Whitman, and Deborah J. Wuttke.

Without the help of these and others, this book would not be possible.

B.E.N.   H.R.A.   J.C.C.

ARTHUR YOUNG

ARTHUR YOUNG & COMPANY
ONE BOSTON PLACE
BOSTON, MASSACHUSETTS 02102

(617) 723-7570

Houghton Mifflin Company
College Division
One Beacon Street
Boston, MA 02108

We have reviewed the text of the second edition of PRINCIPLES OF ACCOUNTING by Needles, Anderson, and Caldwell, together with its accompanying Instructor's Solutions Manual, for the purpose of ascertaining that the material is accurate and up to date. Our review, among other things, was directed at this work's technical and mathematical accuracy, internal consistency, and the appropriateness and accuracy of references to professional and other pronouncements. This review was carried out during the composition process and before final page proof. We communicated to you our observations, suggestions, and recommendations and found that such changes that were needed, were made to our satisfaction. In our opinion, the material in this book is technically and mathematically accurate, internally consistent, and references to professional and other pronouncements are accurate and appropriate within the framework of introductory accounting concepts and techniques.

Arthur Young & Company

ARTHUR YOUNG & COMPANY
October 7, 1983

Part One

The Basic Accounting Model

Accounting is an information system for measuring, processing, and communicating information that is useful in making economic decisions.

Part I presents the fundamental concepts and techniques of the basic accounting system, including accounting for a complete cycle of business activities for a service enterprise.

Chapter 1 explores the nature and environment of accounting, with special emphasis on the users of accounting information, the roles of accountants in society, and the organizations that influence accounting practice.

Chapter 2 introduces the four basic financial statements, the concept of accounting measurement, and the effects of business transactions on financial position.

Chapter 3 continues the discussion of accounting measurement by focusing on the problems of recognition, valuation, and classification and how they are solved in the recording of business transactions.

In Chapter 4, the accounting concept of business income is defined, and the role of adjusting entries in its measurement is discussed and demonstrated.

Chapter 5 completes the accounting system with a presentation of the work sheet and closing entries.

Accounting in Business and Society

1. *Describe the role of accounting in making informed business and economic decisions.*

2. *Define accounting.*

3. *Recognize the many users of accounting information in society.*

4. *Recognize accounting as a profession with a wide career choice.*

5. *Describe the three basic forms of business organization.*

6. *Relate accounting theory and practice to generally accepted accounting principles (GAAP).*

7. *Recognize the organizations that influence generally accepted accounting principles.*

Your first accounting course begins with a general view of the accounting discipline and profession. In this chapter you will learn about the important roles that accountants play in society and about the organizations where they work. As a result of studying this chapter, you should be able to meet the learning objectives listed on the left.

Every individual or group in society must make economic decisions about the future. For example, the manager of a company needs to know which products have been unsuccessful. With this information, the manager can decide whether to stop selling them or to do something that will increase their appeal to customers. Other persons will want to find out if a firm is financially sound before accepting a job or investing money in the company. Similarly, nonprofit organizations need financial information. Federal, state, and local government units, for example, need financial information to levy taxes. Other nonprofit institutions such as churches and charities need meaningful and easily understood economic information before planning their social programs. Because of their financial knowledge, accountants are often asked to search through the available financial data for clues that will serve as guides to the future.

Accounting and Decision Making

The major reason for studying accounting is to acquire the knowledge and skills to participate in important economic decisions. The information accountants provide is the basis for such decisions both inside and outside the business enterprise.

*Objective 1
Describe the
role of account-
ing in making
informed
business and
economic
decisions*

is a tool and, like most tools, cannot be of much direct help to those who are unable or unwilling to use it or who misuse it. Its use can be learned, however, and [accounting] should provide information that can be used by all—nonprofessionals as well as professionals—who are willing to use it properly.[1]

The first step in this learning process is to understand how decisions are made and how accountants can contribute to the process.

To make a wise decision and carry it out effectively, the decision maker must answer the following questions:

What is the goal to be achieved? (Step 1)
What different ways are available to reach the goal? (Step 2)
Which alternative provides the best way to achieve the goal? (Step 3)
What action should be taken? (Step 4)
Was the goal achieved? (Step 5)

Figure 1-1 shows the steps that an individual or an institution follows in making a decision.

When the decision involves business and economic questions, accounting information is essential to the decision system because it provides quantitative information for three functions: planning, control, and evaluation. Figure 1-2 illustrates the role of accounting information in a decision system.

Planning is the process of formulating a course of action. It includes setting a goal, finding alternative ways of accomplishing the goal, and deciding which alternative is the best course of action. At this stage, the accountant should be able to present a clear statement of the financial alternatives. Accounting information dealing with projections of income and budgets of cash requirements would also be important in planning for the future.

Control is the process of seeing that plans are, in fact, carried out. In other words, do actions agree with plans? At this point, the accountant

Figure 1-1
A Decision
System

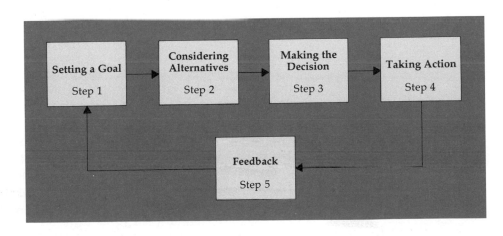

1. *Statement of Financial Accounting Concepts, No. 1,* "Objectives of Financial Reporting by Business Enterprises" (Stamford, Conn.: Financial Accounting Standards Board, 1978), p. 17.

Figure 1-2
A Decision
System and
Accounting
Information

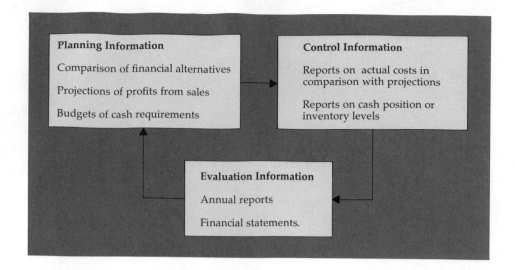

Planning Information

Comparison of financial alternatives

Projections of profits from sales

Budgets of cash requirements

Control Information

Reports on actual costs in comparison with projections

Reports on cash position or inventory levels

Evaluation Information

Annual reports

Financial statements.

might be expected to give information on actual costs, as compared with costs planned earlier.

Evaluation, which involves the whole decision system, is the process of studying the decision system to improve it. It asks the question, Was the original goal met (feedback)? If not, the reason could have been poor planning or control, or perhaps the wrong goal was chosen. Evaluation information may be given in annual reports and other financial statements based on accounting information.

For example, Jennifer Post, a student, had a certain amount of money to spend during the school year. She *planned* to make it through the year by developing a budget, or list of her expected expenditures. She *controlled* her spending by keeping track of her expenditures each month and was able to complete the year without running out of money. To determine how much money she would need for the next year, she *evaluated* each of the major categories of expenditures so that she could determine in which areas she could save money and in which areas she would have to spend more.

Accounting Defined

*Objective 2
Define
accounting*

Early definitions of accounting generally focused on the traditional record-keeping functions of the accountant. In 1941, for example, the American Institute of Certified Public Accountants (AICPA) defined accounting as "the art of recording, classifying, and summarizing in a significant manner and in terms of money, transactions and events which are, in part at least, of a financial character, and interpreting the results thereof."[2] The modern definition of accounting, however, is much

2. Committee on Accounting Terminology, *Accounting Terminology Bulletin Number 2* (New York: American Institute of Certified Public Accountants, 1953), p. 9.

Figure 1-3
Accounting as
an Information
System for
Business
Decisions

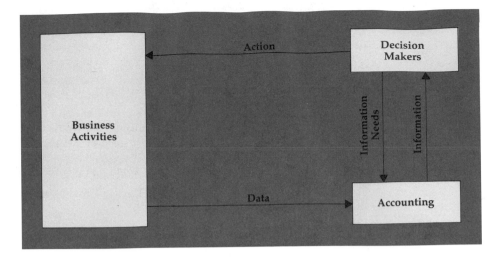

broader. In 1970, AICPA stated that the function of accountancy is "to provide quantitative information, primarily financial in nature, about economic entities that is intended to be useful in making economic decisions."[3] (An economic entity is a unit such as a business that has an independent existence.)

The modern accountant, therefore, is concerned not only with record keeping but also with a whole range of activities involving planning and problem solving; control and attention directing; and evaluation, review, and auditing. Today's accountant focuses on the ultimate needs of those who use accounting information, whether these users are inside or outside the business itself. So accounting "is not an end in itself."[4] Instead it is an information system that measures, processes, and communicates financial information about an identifiable economic entity. This information allows users to make "reasoned choices among alternative uses of scarce resources in the conduct of business and economic activities."[5]

This modern view of accounting is shown in Figure 1-3. In this view, accounting is seen as a service activity. It is a link between business activities and decision makers. First, accounting records data on business activities for future use. Second, through data processing, the data are stored until needed, then processed in such a way as to become useful information. Third, the information is communicated, through reports, to those who can use it in making decisions. One might say that data about business activities are the input to the accounting system, and useful information for decision makers is the output.

A distinction is traditionally made between accounting information that is provided for those people within the business and that which is provided for those outside the business. Usually, management accounting

3. *Statement of the Accounting Principles Board, No. 4,* "Basic Concepts and Accounting Principles Underlying Financial Statements of Business Enterprises" (New York: American Institute of Certified Public Accountants, 1970), par. 40.
4. *Statement of Financial Accounting Concepts, No. 1,* p. 5.
5. Ibid.

concerns accounting information used mainly by those within the business organization. **Financial accounting** refers to accounting information reported to and used by those outside the organization. The first five parts of this book focus on the traditional subjects of financial accounting: the preparation, reporting, analysis, and interpretation of accounting information in reports for external users. The last two parts focus on the traditional topics of management accounting. However, all accounting information, whether financial or managerial, is management information because both kinds are essential to management in making the decisions to achieve the goals of a business.

To avoid certain misunderstandings about accounting, it is important to clarify its relationship with bookkeeping, the computer, and management information systems.

Bookkeeping: An Accounting Process

People often fail to understand the difference between accounting and bookkeeping. **Bookkeeping**, which is a process of accounting, is the means of recording transactions and keeping records. Mechanical and repetitive, bookkeeping is only a small, simple part of accounting. Accounting, on the other hand, includes the design of an information system that meets user needs, as described earlier. The major goal of accounting is the analysis, interpretation, and use of information. Accountants look for important relationships in the figures they produce. They are interested in finding trends and studying the effects of different alternatives. Accounting includes systems design, budgeting, cost analysis, auditing, and income tax preparation or planning.

The Computer: An Accounting Tool

The **computer** is an electronic tool that can collect, organize, and communicate vast amounts of information with great speed. Accountants have been among the earliest and most enthusiastic users of computers. Before the age of computers, the millions of transactions of large organizations had to be recorded by hand. It often took months to produce financial reports that now take days or hours. Although it may appear that the computer is doing the accountant's job, it is in fact only a tool that is instructed to do the routine bookkeeping operations. It is important that the user of accounting information and the new accountant understand the processes underlying accounting. For this reason, most examples in this book are treated from the standpoint of manual accounting. You should remember, however, that most large accounting operations are now computerized.

Accounting and Management Information Systems

Most businesses use a large amount of nonfinancial information. Their marketing departments, for example, are interested in the style or packaging of competitors' products. Personnel departments keep health and employment records of employees. With the widespread use of the computer today, many of these varied information needs are being organized into what might be called a **management information system (MIS)**. The management information system consists of the interconnected subsystems that provide the information needed to run a business. The accounting information system is the most important subsystem because it plays the primary role of managing the flow of economic data to all parts of a business and to interested parties outside the business. Accounting is the financial hub of the management information system. It gives both management and outsiders a complete view of the business organization.

Decision Makers: The Users of Accounting Information

Accounting and accounting information are used more than commonly realized. Here are some questions we might ask about everyday activities that involve accounting:

Objective 3
Recognize the
many users of
accounting
information in
society

In going to school How much money will it take to get through the next school year? Will there be enough money for rent, food, and transportation next month? What is the correct way to balance a bank statement and checkbook?

In applying for a loan How should the financial statement for the bank be completed? How is the interest on a loan computed?

In taking a job Is the company financially sound? What is its future? What are its most successful products? Are they the most profitable? What are the company's benefit plans and retirement programs?

In making an investment Is this a good company to invest in? What is the risk? What is the possible return? What is the company's profit record? Is the company in a good cash position?

These are just a few of the many important uses of accounting. As a member of various groups in management and society, the student of business and accounting will use accounting daily as an aid in making difficult decisions.

The users of accounting can be divided roughly into three groups: (1) those who manage a business; (2) those outside a business enterprise who have direct financial interest in the business; and (3) those persons, groups, or agencies that have an indirect financial interest in the business. These groups are shown in Figure 1-4 (next page).

Management

Management is the group of people in a business who have overall responsibility for achieving the company's goals. Business enterprises have many goals. These goals include providing quality goods and services at low cost, creating new and improved products, increasing the number of jobs available, improving the environment, and accomplishing many other social tasks. To achieve any of these goals, of course, the company must be successful. Success and survival in a tough, competitive business environment require that management concentrate much of its effort on

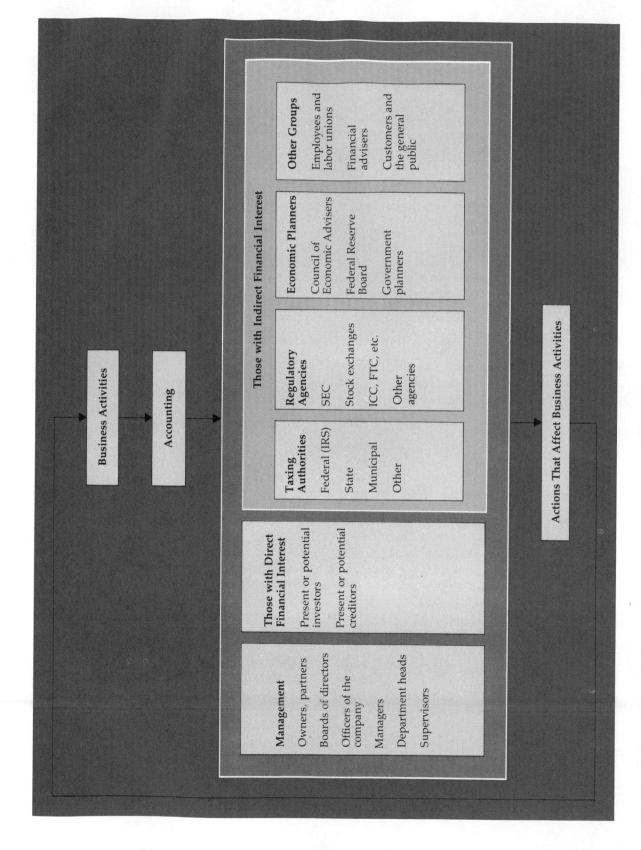

Business Activities

Accounting

Those with Direct Financial Interest

Present or potential investors

Present or potential creditors

Management

Owners, partners

Boards of directors

Officers of the company

Managers

Department heads

Supervisors

Those with Indirect Financial Interest

Taxing Authorities	Regulatory Agencies	Economic Planners	Other Groups
Federal (IRS)	SEC	Council of Economic Advisers	Employees and labor unions
State	Stock exchanges	Federal Reserve Board	Financial advisers
Municipal	ICC, FTC, etc.	Government planners	Customers and the general public
Other	Other agencies		

Actions That Affect Business Activities

Figure 1-4
The Users of
Accounting
Information

two major goals: profitability and liquidity. Profitability is the ability to make enough profit to attract and hold investment capital. Liquidity means having enough funds on hand to pay debts when they fall due.

Management at all levels is responsible for a company's successful operation. In a small business, the greatest responsibility is often with the owner, who also manages the company's operations. In a large corporation, the company's goals will be assigned to many people, from the board of directors and officers of the firm to the managers, department heads, and supervisors.

Managers must constantly decide what to do, how to do it, and whether the results match the original plans. Successful managers consistently make the right decisions on the basis of timely and valid information. Many of these decisions are based on the flow of accounting data and their analysis. For this reason, management is one of the most important users of accounting information, and a major function of accounting is to provide management with relevant and useful information. For example, here are some questions a manager might ask: What was the company's net income during the past quarter? Is the return to the owners adequate? Does the company have enough cash? What products are most profitable? What is the cost of manufacturing each product?

Users with a Direct Financial Interest

A major function of accounting is to measure and report information about how a business has performed. Most businesses periodically publish a set of general-purpose financial statements that report on their success in meeting objectives of profitability and liquidity. Though these statements show what has happened in the past, they are important guides to future success. Today there are many people outside the company who carefully study these financial reports.

Present or Potential Investors Those who are thinking of investing in a company are interested in the past success of the business and its potential earnings in the future. A thorough study of the company's financial statements will help potential investors judge the prospects for a profitable investment. After investing in a company, investors must continually review their commitment. Is the company performing as expected? Are earnings satisfactory? Are interest payments and other distributions protected by an adequate supply of cash (cash flow)? Is the company investing in projects that can be expected to be profitable? Are the methods of financing growth and expansion sound? These investor questions and many more can be answered by a study of the periodic financial statements.

Present or Potential Creditors Most companies must borrow money for both long- and short-term operating needs. The creditors, who lend the money, are interested mainly in whether the company will have the cash to pay the interest charges and repay the debt at the appropriate time. They will study the company's liquidity and cash flow as well as its profitability. Banks, finance companies, mortgage companies, securities firms,

insurance firms, individuals, and others who lend money expect to analyze a company's financial position before making a loan to that company.

Users with an Indirect Financial Interest

Society as a whole, through its government officials and public groups, has
in recent years become one of the biggest and most important users of
accounting information. Some of the users who need accounting information to make decisions on public issues include (1) taxing authorities, (2)
regulatory agencies, (3) economic planners, and (4) other groups.

Taxing Authorities Our governments are financed through the payment
of taxes. Under federal, state, and local laws, companies and individuals
pay many kinds of taxes. Among these levies are federal, state, and city
income taxes, social security and other payroll taxes, excise taxes, and
sales taxes. Each tax requires special tax returns and often a complex set
of records as well. Proper reporting is generally a matter of law and can
be very complicated. The Internal Revenue Code of the federal government, for instance, contains thousands of rules governing preparation of
the financial statements used in computing federal income taxes.

Regulatory Agencies Most companies must report to one or more regulatory agencies at the federal, state, and local levels. All public
corporations must report periodically to the Securities and Exchange
Commission. This body was set up by Congress to protect the public and
therefore regulates the issuing, buying, and selling of stocks in the United
States. Companies that are listed on stock exchanges, such as the New
York Stock Exchange, must also meet the special reporting requirements
of their exchange.

   Accounting reports are also important in other areas of governmental
regulation. The Interstate Commerce Commission regulates industries
such as trucking and railroads, and the Federal Aviation Administration
regulates airlines. All public utilities such as electric, gas, and telephone
companies are regulated and must defend their rates with accounting reports. Accounting is also involved in the new and broader regulations like
those of the Environmental Protection Agency, which is concerned with
the cost and speed of reducing environmental pollution.

Economic Planners Since the 1930s, the government's wish to take a
more active part in planning and forecasting economic activity has led to
greater use of accounting and accounting information. A system of accounting called national income accounting has been developed for the
whole economy. It deals with the total production, inventories, income,
dividends, taxes, and so forth of our economy. Planners who are members
of the President's Council of Economic Advisers or are connected with the
Federal Reserve System use this information to set economic policies and
judge economic programs.

Other Groups Employees, consumers, and the general public all have an
interest in the financial statements of businesses. Employees and labor

unions study the financial statements of corporations as part of their task of preparing for important labor negotiations. The amount and computation of income and costs are often important in these negotiations. Those who advise investors and creditors also have an indirect interest in the financial performance and prospects of a business. In this group are financial analysts and advisers, brokers, underwriters, lawyers, economists, and the financial press. Consumers' groups, customers, and the general public have become more curious about the financing and earnings of corporations as well as with the effects that corporations have on inflation, the environment, social problems, and the quality of life.

The Accounting Profession

Objective 4
Recognize
accounting as a
profession with
a wide career
choice

The accounting function is as old as the need to exchange things of value and keep track of the wealth. The commercial and trading revolution of the Renaissance was a great impetus to accounting, as was the Industrial Revolution later. The great growth of industry and government in the twentieth century has expanded the need for accountants even further.

Today, accounting offers interesting, challenging, well-paid, and socially satisfying careers. The profession can be divided into four broad fields: (1) management accounting, (2) public accounting, (3) government and other nonprofit accounting, and (4) accounting education.

Management Accounting

An accountant who is employed by a business is said to be in **management accounting.** A small business may have only one or a few people doing this work, though a medium-size or large company may have hundreds of accountants working under a chief accounting officer called a controller, treasurer, or financial vice president. Other positions that may be held by accountants at lower managerial levels are assistant controller, chief accountant, internal auditor, plant accountant, systems analyst, financial accountant, and cost accountant.

Because of their broad and intimate view of all aspects of a company's operations, management accountants often have an important effect on management decision making. According to most recent surveys, more top-level business executives have backgrounds in accounting and finance than in any other field. Just a few of the well-known companies whose presidents or chairmen of the board are (or have been) accountants are American Airlines, Chrysler, General Foods, International Business Machines, Caterpillar Tractor, General Motors, Kennecott Copper, Ford, General Electric, General Telephone and Electronics, Consolidated Edison, International Telephone and Telegraph, and 3-M.

The management accountant's main task is to give management the information it needs to make wise decisions. Management accountants also set up a system of internal control to increase efficiency and prevent fraud in their companies. They aid in profit planning, budgeting, and cost control. It is their duty to see that a company has good records, prepares proper financial reports, and complies with tax laws and government regulations. Management accountants also need to keep up with the latest developments in the uses of computers and in computer systems design.

Accountants provide many special reports for management decision making. This function requires the gathering of both historical and projected data. It is important for accountants to present the financial effects of alternative courses of action so that the best course can be selected. Examples of these special reports are evaluations of proposed new products, analyses of alternative plant sites, a proposed advertising campaign, a long-term financing plan, and a recommendation that a product, department, or service be dropped.

Management accountants may certify their professional competence and training by qualifying for the Certificate in Management Accounting (CMA), which is given by the Institute of Management Accounting of the National Association of Accountants. Under the CMA program, candidates must pass a number of examinations and meet educational and professional standards.

Some of the activities of management accountants are described in the next few paragraphs.

General Accounting　General accounting is the overall record keeping, preparation of financial statements and reports, and control of all business activities such as sales, expenses, receivables, inventories, and payment of bills. Much of what you will learn in this book falls under the heading of general accounting.

Cost Accounting　Cost accounting refers to the determination and control of costs. The cost accountant is interested in the costs of manufacturing products or providing services as well as in the costs of selling and distributing those products or services. It is important that the cost accountant collect, assemble, and interpret data in a way that helps management judge current operations and plan for the future.

Budgeting　Budgeting is the planning of the financial aspects of business operations. Budgets are important to management both in planning a course of action and in judging results. Many companies consider budgeting one of the most important duties of the accountant.

Tax Accounting　It is very important to plan business operations so that while they comply with the tax laws, the effect of taxes on profits is as small as possible. The success of many financial transactions depends on how well the tax accountant is able to handle the details of the tax laws.

Information Systems Design　Every business calls for an information system designed specifically for that business's needs. This system uses many forms, records, flow charts, manuals, controls, and reports. The design of systems has become more complex because the computer has made it possible to expand systems design to include all parts of the business, not just the financial records. Accountants who are specialists in systems design develop the systems and put them into operation.

Internal Auditing Most large companies have accountants who specialize in seeing that management's policies and procedures are properly followed. These accountants are also interested in protecting the company's assets. They are called internal auditors. Professionals who make a career in this field may qualify through a series of examinations for the Certificate in Internal Auditing (CIA) administered by the Institute of Internal Auditors.

Public Accounting

The field of **public accounting** offers services in auditing, taxes, and management consulting to the public for a fee. In the short time since about 1900, public accounting in this country has gained a stature similar to that of the older professions of law and medicine. **Certified public accountants (CPAs)** are licensed by all states for the same reason that lawyers and doctors are—to protect the public by ensuring a high quality of professional service.

To become a CPA, the applicant must meet rigorous requirements. These requirements vary from state to state but have certain characteristics in common. An applicant must be a person of integrity and have at least a high school education. Most states require four years of college (a few require five years), with a major in accounting. Further, the applicant must pass a difficult and comprehensive two and one-half-day examination in accounting practice, accounting theory, auditing, and business law. Although the examination is uniform in all states, some states also require an examination in an area such as economics. The examination is prepared by the American Institute of Certified Public Accountants and is given twice a year. Most states also require from one to five years' experience in the office of a certified public accountant, or acceptable equivalent experience. In some cases, additional education can be substituted for one or more years of accounting experience.

Certified public accountants offer their services to the public for a fee, just as doctors or lawyers do. Accounting firms are made up of partners, who must be CPAs, and staff accountants, many of whom are CPAs and hope to become partners someday. Accounting firms vary in size from large international firms with hundreds of partners and thousands of employees (see the table, next page) to small one- or two-person firms.

The work of the public accountant is varied, complex, and interesting. Most accounting firms organize themselves into several principal areas of specialization, which may include (1) auditing, (2) tax services, (3) management advisory services, and (4) small business services.

Auditing The most important and distinctive function of a certified public accountant is **auditing,** which is the examination and testing of financial statements. Society relies heavily on the auditing function, which is also called the attest function, for credible financial reports. All public corporations and many companies that apply for sizable loans must have their financial statements and records audited by an independent certified public accountant.

An audit's purpose is to give the auditor's professional opinion as to

Firm	Home Office	Some Major Clients
Arthur Andersen & Co.	Chicago	ITT, Texaco, United Airlines
Arthur Young & Co.	New York	Mobil, Sperry Corp., McDonald's
Coopers & Lybrand	New York	AT&T, Ford, Firestone
Deloitte, Haskins & Sells	New York	General Motors, Procter & Gamble
Ernst & Whinney	Cleveland	McDonnell Douglas, Coca-Cola
Peat, Marwick, Mitchell & Co.	New York	General Electric, Xerox
Price Waterhouse	New York	IBM, Exxon, DuPont
Touche Ross & Co.	New York	Chrysler, Boeing, Sears

whether the company's financial reports fairly present its financial position and operating results. Auditors check and test the accounting records and controls as necessary to satisfy themselves about the quality of the financial statements. Auditors must prove cash balances, watch physical inventories, and verify the amounts owed by customers. They must also decide if there are adequate controls and if the company's records are kept in accordance with accepted accounting practices. In the end, auditors must depend on their own judgment to reach an opinion about a company's financial reports. Their professional reputation is at stake because banks, investors, and creditors depend on the financial statements bearing the auditors' opinions in buying and selling the company's stocks, making loans, and giving credit.

Tax Services   In the area of tax services, public accountants not only prepare tax returns and make sure of compliance with tax laws; they also help plan business decisions to reduce the company's taxes in the future. Tax accounting work calls for much knowledge and skill regardless of the size of a business. Few business decisions are without tax effects.

Management Advisory Services   A growing and important part of most public accounting firms' practice is management advisory services, or consulting. With their intimate knowledge of a business's operations, auditors can make important suggestions for improvements and, as a matter of course, usually do. In the past, these recommendations have dealt mainly with accounting records, budgeting, and cost accounting. But in the last few years they have expanded into marketing, organizational planning, personnel and recruiting, production, systems, and many other business areas. The wide use of computers has led to the offering of services in systems design and control and to the use of mathematical and statistical decision models. All these different services combined make up management advisory services.

Small Business Services   Many small businesses look to their CPA for advice on operating their business and keeping their accounting records. Although small CPA firms have traditionally performed these functions, large firms are also establishing small business practice units. Among the types of services a CPA might provide are setting up or revising an accounting system, compiling monthly financial statements, preparing a budget of cash needs over the next year, and assisting the client in obtaining a bank loan.

Government and Other Nonprofit Accounting

Agencies and departments at all levels of government hire accountants to prepare reports so that officials can responsibly carry out their duties. Millions of income, payroll, and sales tax returns must be checked and audited. In the federal government, the Federal Bureau of Investigation and the Internal Revenue Service use thousands of accountants. The General Accounting Office audits government activities for Congress, using many auditors and other accounting specialists all over the world. Federal agencies such as the Securities and Exchange Commission, Interstate Commerce Commission, and Federal Communications Commission hire accountants, as do state agencies such as those dealing with public utilities regulation or tax collection.

Many other nonprofit enterprises besides the government employ accountants. Some of these organizations are hospitals, colleges, universities, and foundations. These institutions, like the government, are interested in compliance with the law and efficient use of public resources. They account for over 25 percent of the gross output of our economy. Clearly, the role of accountants in helping these organizations use their resources wisely is important to our society. Social accounting helps judge the impact of government and other human service programs by trying to answer questions about their cost and effectiveness. Some of these programs are welfare programs, housing subsidies, public education, and pollution control. Accountants working in these areas are looking for new ways to apply accounting techniques to pressing social problems.

Accounting Education

Training new accountants is a challenging and rewarding career, and today instructors of accounting are in great demand. Accounting instructors at the secondary level must have a college degree with a major in accounting and must meet state teacher certification requirements. One entry-level requirement for teaching at the college level is the master's degree. There is a growing trend to require a doctorate at the university level. In many schools, holding the CPA, CMA, or CIA certificate will help an instructor to advance professionally.

Forms of Business Organization

Accountants need to understand the three basic forms of business organization: sole proprietorships, partnerships, and corporations. Accountants recognize each form as an economic unit separate from its owners,

Table 1-1
Comparative
Features of
the Forms of
Business
Organization

	Sole Proprietorship	Partnership	Corporation
1. Legal status	Not a separate legal entity	Not a separate legal entity	Separate legal entity
2. Risk of ownership	Owner's personal resources at stake	Partners' resources at stake	Limited to investment in corporation
3. Duration or life	Limited by desire or death of owner	Limited by desire or death of each partner	Indefinite, possibly unlimited
4. Transferability of ownership	Sale by owner establishes new company	Changes in any partner's interest requires new partnership	Transferable by sale of stock
5. Accounting treatment	Separate economic unit	Separate economic unit	Separate economic unit

Objective 5
Describe the
three basic
forms of
business
organization

although legally only the corporation is considered separate from its owners. Other legal differences among the three forms are summarized in Table 1-1 and discussed briefly below. In this book, we first show accounting for the sole proprietorship because it is the simplest form of accounting. At critical points, however, we call attention to its essential differences from accounting for corporations and partnerships. Later, in Part IV, we deal specifically with partnership accounting and corporation accounting.

Sole Proprietorships

A **sole proprietorship** is a business formed by one person. This form of business gives the individual a means of controlling the business apart from his or her personal interests. Legally, however, the proprietorship is the same economic unit as the individual. The individual receives all profits or losses and is liable for all obligations of the proprietorship. Proprietorships represent the largest number of businesses in the United States, but typically they are the smallest in size. The life of a proprietorship ends when the owner wishes it to, or at the owner's death or incapacity.

Partnerships

A **partnership** is like a proprietorship in most ways except that it has more than one owner. A partnership is not a legal economic unit separate from the owners but an unincorporated association that brings together the talents and resources of two or more people. The partners share profits and losses of the partnership according to an agreed-upon formula. Generally, any partner can bind the partnership to another party and, if necessary, the personal resources of each partner can be called on to pay obligations of the partnership. In some cases, one or more partners may limit their liability, but at least one partner must have unlimited liability. A partnership must be dissolved if the ownership changes, as when a partner leaves or dies. If the business continues, a new proprietorship or partnership must be formed.

Corporations

A **corporation** is a business unit that is legally separate from its owners. The owners, whose ownership is represented by shares or stocks in the corporation, do not directly control the operations of the corporation. Instead they elect a board of directors who run the corporation for the benefit of the stockholders. In exchange for limited involvement in the corporation's actual operations, stockholders enjoy limited liability. That is, they are liable only for the amount paid for their shares. If they wish, stockholders can sell their shares to other persons without affecting corporate operations. Because of this limited liability, stockholders are often willing to invest in riskier, but potentially profitable, activities. Also, because ownership can be transferred without dissolving the corporation, the life of the corporation is unlimited and not subject to the whims or health of a proprietor or partner.

Corporations have several important advantages over proprietorships and partnerships (see Chapter 16) that make them very efficient in amassing capital for the formation and growth of very large companies. Even though corporations are fewer in number than the proprietorships and partnerships, they contribute much more to the U.S. economy in monetary terms (see the chart, next page). For example, in 1983, General Motors generated more revenues than all but thirteen of the world's countries.

Accounting Theory and Practice

Objective 6
Relate
accounting
theory and
practice to
generally
accepted
accounting
principles
(GAAP)

Accounting is usually defined in terms of practice, or actions. In accordance with our earlier definition of accounting as an information system that measures, processes, and communicates information, **accounting practice** consists of the procedures used to carry out those functions. Accounting actions, however, must be the logical result of a reasoning process. In other words, a framework of **accounting theory** must underlie the actions or practice of accountants. Accounting theory answers the question, Why? Accounting practice answers the question, How?

In this book, we have tried to present accounting practice as it is today. We have also tried to explain the reasons or theory on which the practice is based. The two—theory and practice—are part and parcel of the study of accounting. You should realize that accounting is a discipline that is always growing, changing, and improving. Just as in medicine, where years of research may be necessary before a new surgical method or life-saving drug can be introduced into medical practice, research and new

Number and
Receipts of U.S.
Proprietorships,
Partnerships,
and
Corporations,
1979

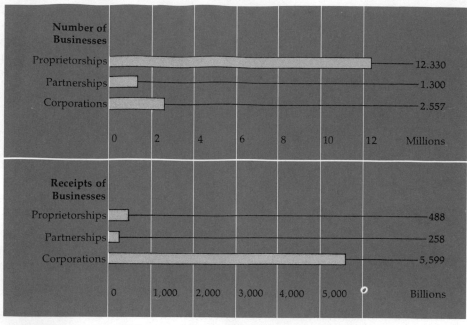

Source: U.S. Department of Commerce, Bureau of the Census, *Statistical Abstract of the United States,*
1982–1983, p. 528.

discoveries in accounting often take years to become common practice.
So you may sometimes hear of practices that seem inconsistent. In some
cases, we have pointed toward new directions in accounting. Your instructor may mention certain weaknesses in current theory or practice. To
help you understand how theory and practice have been and are developed, the following paragraphs examine the concept of generally accepted
accounting principles and the organizations that influence them.

Generally Accepted Accounting Principles

The term generally accepted accounting principles (GAAP) is used
widely and with several meanings in accounting literature. Perhaps the
best definition is the following: "Generally accepted accounting principles
encompass the conventions, rules, and procedures necessary to define
accepted accounting practice at a particular time."[6] In other words,
GAAP arise from wide agreement on the theory and practice of accounting at a particular time. Of course, these "principles" are not like the
unchangeable laws of nature found in chemistry or physics. They are
developed by accountants and businesses to serve the needs of decision
makers and can be changed as better methods are developed or as circumstances change.

6. *Statement of the Accounting Principles Board, No. 4,* par. 138.

Organizations Concerned with Accounting Practice

By definition, GAAP have wide support among practicing accountants and authoritative organizations concerned with accounting practice. The most important of these organizations are the American Institute of Certified Public Accountants, the Financial Accounting Standards Board, the Securities and Exchange Commission, the Internal Revenue Service, and the Government Accounting Standards Board. There are international and other groups as well.

American Institute of Certified Public Accountants The **American Institute of Certified Public Accountants (AICPA)** has been concerned with accounting practice longer than most groups. From 1938 to 1958 the AICPA's Committee on Accounting Procedures issued a series of pronouncements dealing with accounting principles, procedures, and terms. In 1959 the AICPA organized the Accounting Principles Board (APB) to replace the Committee on Accounting Procedures. The board published a number of APB Opinions on accounting practice. APB Opinions carry so much weight that since December 31, 1965, departures from them in accounting practice must be reported along with a company's financial statements.

Financial Accounting Standards Board The APB Opinions are still in effect and will be referred to often in this book. However, in 1973 the responsibility for developing and issuing rules on accounting practice was given to a new body called the Financial Accounting Foundation and, in particular, to an arm of the foundation called the **Financial Accounting Standards Board (FASB)**. This group is separate from the AICPA and issues Statements of Financial Accounting Standards. The group is governed by a board of trustees that includes the president of the AICPA and eight others elected by the AICPA.

Securities and Exchange Commission The **Securities and Exchange Commission (SEC)** is an agency of the U.S. government that has the legal power to set and enforce accounting practices for companies reporting to it. As such, it has great influence on accounting practice. Because the APB failed to solve some of the major problems in accounting practice, the SEC began to play a larger and more aggressive part in deciding rules of accounting. The FASB represents a major effort on the part of accountants to keep control over their profession and to limit the SEC to its traditional role of allowing the accounting profession to regulate itself. It appears certain that during the coming years, the SEC will keep putting pressure on the accounting profession to improve its accounting practice. The success or failure of the FASB will be important in determining how much influence the SEC will have on accounting in the future.

Internal Revenue Service The U.S. tax laws govern the assessment and collection of revenue for operating the government. Because a major source of the government's revenue is the income tax, the law specifies the rules for determining taxable income. These rules are interpreted and enforced by the Internal Revenue Service (IRS). In some cases, these rules may be in conflict with good accounting practice, but they are an important influence on practice. Income tax is a major cost of most profitable businesses and must be shown in the records. Businesses must use certain accounting practices simply because they are required by the tax law. Sometimes companies follow an accounting practice specified in the tax law to take advantage of rules that will help them financially. Cases where the tax law may affect accounting practice are noted throughout this book.

Government Accounting Standards Board Concern over the financial reporting of governmental units has resulted in increased attention to the development of accounting principles for these units. The Government Accounting Standards Board (GASB), which was established in 1983 under the same governing body as the Financial Accounting Standards Board, is responsible for issuing accounting standards for state and local governments. The GASB will undoubtedly have a great influence on financial reporting by these units.

International Organizations Worldwide cooperation in the development of accounting principles has made great strides in recent years. The International Accounting Standards Committee (IASC) has approved more than ten international standards; these have been translated into six languages. In 1977, the International Federation of Accountants (IFAC), now made up of sixty-three professional accounting bodies from forty-nine countries, was started to promote international agreement on accounting questions.

Other Organizations Concerned with Accounting The National Association of Accountants (NAA) is composed mainly of industrial accountants. This organization is engaged in education and research, with an emphasis on cost accounting and accounting for management decisions. The Financial Executives Institute (FEI) is made up of persons who hold the highest financial positions in large businesses. It is most interested in standards and research in financial accounting.

The American Accounting Association (AAA) was founded in 1935, succeeding the American Association of University Instructors in Accounting, which was started in 1916. This group has an academic and theoretical point of view. Its members have contributed greatly to the theoretical development of accounting.

Chapter Review

Review of Learning Objectives

1. Describe the role of accounting in making informed business and economic decisions.

Accounting is not an end in itself but is a tool to be used in providing information that is useful in making reasoned choices among alternative uses of scarce resources in the conduct of business and economic activities.

2. Define accounting.

Accounting is an information system that measures, processes, and communicates information, primarily financial in nature, about an identifiable economic entity for the purpose of making economic decisions.

3. Recognize the many users of accounting information in society.

Accounting plays a significant role in society by providing information to managers of all institutions and to other persons with direct financial interest in those institutions, such as present or potential investors or creditors. Accounting information is also important to those with indirect financial interest such as taxing authorities, regulatory agencies, economic planners, and other groups.

4. Recognize accounting as a profession with a wide career choice.

The people who provide accounting information to users make up the accounting profession. They may be management accountants, public accountants, or government or other nonprofit accountants. Each type of accounting work is an important specialization and represents a challenging career.

5. Describe the three basic forms of business organization.

The three basic forms of business organization are sole proprietorships, partnerships, and corporations. Sole proprietorships, which are formed by one individual, and partnerships, which are formed by more than one individual, are not separate economic units from the legal standpoint. In accounting, however, they are treated separately. Corporations, whose ownership is represented by shares of stock, are separate entities for both legal and accounting purposes.

6. Relate accounting theory and practice to generally accepted accounting principles (GAAP).

Accounting theory is the underlying rationale or reasoning behind accounting practice. Acceptable accounting practice at a particular time consists of those conventions, rules, and procedures that make up generally accepted accounting principles.

7. Recognize the organizations that influence generally accepted accounting principles.

Among the organizations that influence the formulation of GAAP are the American Institute of Certified Public Accountants, the Financial Accounting Standards Board, the Securities and Exchange Commission, the Internal Revenue Service, and the Government Accounting Standards Board. Other organizations with an interest in accounting are the National Association of Accountants, the Financial Executives Institute, and the American Accounting Association.

Self-Test

Test your knowledge of the chapter by choosing the best answer for each item below.

1. Which of the following is an important reason for studying accounting?
   a. The information provided by accounting and accountants is useful in making many economic decisions.
   b. Accounting plays an important role in society.
   c. The study of accounting could lead to a challenging career.
   d. All of the above are important reasons.
2. Accounting is the same as
   a. bookkeeping.
   b. computer systems.
   c. management information systems.
   d. None of the above.

3. Which of the following groups uses accounting information for planning a company's profitability and liquidity?
    a. Management   c. Creditors
    b. Investors   d. Economic planners

4. Which of the following groups is most interested in using accounting information to determine a company's ability to pay back a loan?
    a. Management   c. Creditors
    b. Investors   d. Regulatory agencies

5. An accountant who provides services to the public for a fee is engaged in
    a. management accounting.   c. government accounting.
    b. public accounting.   d. nonprofit accounting.

6. Which of the following is not a type of management accounting?
    a. General accounting   c. Auditing
    b. Cost accounting   d. Budgeting

7. The primary service offered by a certified public accountant is
    a. general accounting.   c. tax services.
    b. auditing.   d. management advisory services.

8. Which of the following forms of organization is not treated as a separate economic unit in accounting?
    a. Sole proprietorship   c. Partnership
    b. Committee   d. Corporation

9. Generally accepted accounting principles
    a. define accounting practice at a point in time.
    b. are similar in nature to the principles of chemistry or physics.
    c. are rarely changed.
    d. are not affected by changes in the ways businesses operate.

10. The organization that has the most influence on generally accepted accounting principles is the
    a. American Institute of Certified Public Accountants.
    b. Financial Accounting Standards Board.
    c. Securities and Exchange Commission.
    d. Internal Revenue Service.

Answers to Self-Test are at the end of this chapter.

Chapter Assignments

Questions

1. Explain how decisions are made.
2. What role does accounting play in the decision system?
3. What decision makers use accounting information?
4. What is the new focus of accounting?
5. Distinguish among these terms: accounting, bookkeeping, and management information systems.
6. What objectives does management seek to achieve by using accounting information?
7. Why are investors and creditors interested in the financial statements of a company?
8. Why has society as a whole become one of the biggest users of accounting information?
9. What groups besides businesses, investors, and creditors use accounting information?
10. What are some of the fields encompassed by the accounting profession?
11. What are some activities the management accountant might participate in?
12. How is public accounting different from management accounting?

13. Describe in general terms the requirements that an individual must meet to become a CPA.

14. What does a CPA do?

15. In what important ways do sole proprietorships, partnerships, and corporations differ?

16. What is the relationship between accounting theory and practice?

17. What are generally accepted accounting principles?

18. What are the AICPA, FASB, SEC, and IRS and how do they influence accounting practice?

19. Accounting can be viewed as (1) an intellectual discipline, (2) a profession, and (3) a social force. In what sense is it each of these things?

Classroom Exercises

**Exercise 1-1
Role of
Computer,
Bookkeeper,
and Accountant
(L.O. 2)**

Bob, Betty, and Ben opened a clothing store earlier this year called The 3 Bs. They began by opening a checking account in the name of the business, renting a store, and buying some clothes to sell. They paid for the purchases and expenses out of the checking account and deposited cash in the account when they sold the clothes. At this point, they are arguing over how their business is doing and how much each of them should be paid. They also realize that they are supposed to make certain tax reports and payments, but they know very little about them. The following statements are excerpts from their conversation:

Bob: If we just had a computer, we wouldn't have had this argument.
Betty: No, what we need is a bookkeeper.
Ben: I don't know, but maybe we need an accountant.

Distinguish among a computer, a bookkeeper, and an accountant and comment on how each might help the operations of The 3 Bs.

**Exercise 1-2
Users of
Accounting
Information
(L.O. 3)**

Public companies report each year on their success or failure in making a profit. Suppose that the following item appeared in the newspaper:

New York. Commonwealth Power Company, a major electric utility, reported yesterday that its net income for the year just ended represented a 50 percent increase over the previous year. . . .

Explain why each of the following individuals or groups may be interested in seeing the accounting reports that support the above statement.

1. The management of Commonwealth Power
2. The stockholders of Commonwealth Power
3. The creditors of Commonwealth Power
4. Potential stockholders of Commonwealth Power
5. The Internal Revenue Service
6. The Securities and Exchange Commission
7. The electric workers' union
8. A consumers' group called the Public Cause
9. An economic adviser to the president

**Exercise 1-3
Accountants in
Industry
(L.O. 4)**

A U.S. senator has been quoted as saying that in recent years more top management positions in industry are being filled by accountants because their experience enables them to take an overall perspective on large, worldwide enterprises and therefore they are better able to control such businesses.[7]

7. Paraphrased from quotation in Ralph W. Estes, *Accounting and Society* (Los Angeles: Melville, 1973), p. 102.

1. What positions in industry that are typically held by accountants can you name that would justify this statement?

2. Do you believe that accountants would be able to handle top government positions?

3. In what ways might an accountant be unsuited or inadequately trained for a top position?

<table>
<tr><td>

Exercise 1-4 Role of Certified Public Accountant (L.O. 4)

</td><td>

Matt Perkins, a senior in college, was finishing his last term with a major in history when his father suffered a heart attack and died. Now Matt finds himself the sole owner of a small manufacturing company that his father founded many years ago. Because he has not made any plans for a career, he decides to try running the family business. However, he is not sure how to start. One of his friends who attends a business school suggests that he might begin by talking to a certified public accountant.

1. Why do you think his friend made this suggestion?

2. In what ways could the certified public accountant be of help?

</td></tr>
<tr><td>

Exercise 1-5 Forms of Business (L.O. 5)

</td><td>

Since Judy Hernandez began a small bridal shop in a local shopping mall two years ago, her sales have increased each year. She operates her business as a sole proprietorship. Next to her store is a women's shoe and accessory business operated by Clarence Brown. Clarence has suggested that he and Judy form a partnership and combine the two businesses into a larger, more complete business. Judy believes this is a good idea but wonders if it would be better to form a corporation instead of a partnership.

1. Distinguish among the sole proprietorship, partnership, and corporation as forms of business.

2. What advantages and disadvantages does the partnership have?

3. What advantages and disadvantages does the corporation have?

4. What form of business do you think would be better for Judy and Clarence?

</td></tr>
<tr><td>

Exercise 1-6 Contrasting Accounting Careers in Private and Public Accounting (L.O. 4)

</td><td>

Ray Phillips and Esther Bolden are both senior accounting students at the university. Ray has decided to go to work as an accounting trainee for General Motors Corporation, a worldwide automobile company. Esther has accepted a position as a junior accountant for Price Waterhouse, a worldwide accounting firm.

1. If Ray is successful at General Motors, what kinds of jobs might he hold there throughout his career?

2. If Esther is successful at Price Waterhouse, what kinds of activities might she be involved in throughout her career?

</td></tr>
</table>

Interpreting Accounting Information

<table>
<tr><td>

Published Financial Information: Public Service Electric & Gas Co. (L.O. 7)

</td><td>

The Wall Street Journal is the leading daily financial newspaper in the United States. The following excerpts from an article entitled "Public Service E & G Asks $464.5 Million Annual Rates Rise" appeared in *The Wall Street Journal* on January 10, 1983:

Newark, N.J. Public Service Electric & Gas Co. said it asked the New Jersey Board of Public Utilities to authorize increases in gas and electric rates that would add $464.5 million to annual revenue, an 11.5% jump.

The utility said that more than half of the added revenue would go to paying federal income taxes, and the state gross receipts and franchise tax.

The request asks for a 15.6% increase in electric rates, amounting to added revenue of

</td></tr>
</table>

$398 million a year, and a 4.5% increase in gas rates, which would bring added annual revenue of $67 million. . . .

Explaining its need for expanded revenue, the utility said it has suffered a decline in electricity demand as a result of the recession. Kilowatt-hour sales fell 2.7% in 1982, and gas sales dropped 2%, the utility said. . . .

Required:

1. Assume that you are a member of the New Jersey Board of Public Utilities and are faced with the above request for a rate increase. What five factors would you consider most important or relevant to your making an informed decision? Be as specific as possible.
2. What do you suppose would be the best source or sources of information about each of the factors you listed in 1?

Financial Decision Case 1-1*

(Note: This case may be done individually or in groups.)

Alpha Company or Beta Company?
(L.O. 1)

You have inherited $100,000 from a wealthy grandparent. The grandparent has, however, placed two restrictions on your receipt of the inheritance. First, you are required by the terms of the will to invest the full $100,000 in a single company for a minimum of three years. The word *invest* means that you must give the company exclusive use of your money in exchange for a future claim that must be honored by the company. The value of this claim may be more or less than $100,000 depending on how the firm performs in the next three years. Second, the will requires that your investment be in either Alpha Company or Beta Company.

Required:

1. List as many items as you can that should be considered before investing $100,000 in *any* company. Feel free to mention any item that you consider relevant to the investment decision. Once you have completed the list, try to identify the five specific items that you consider to be most important.
2. Returning to the decision to invest in either Alpha Company or Beta Company, list the possible ways to obtain relevant information about the items you identified as most important in 1. Approach this question as if all possible ways of getting information were available; that is, do not feel limited by what you know about how businesses operate or what information is presently made available. Again try to condense this list to the two or three best methods.
3. With regard to the items you viewed as most important in making an investment decision in 1 and the best ways of obtaining information about these items you listed in 2, what rules or regulations would you require concerning the quality, content, and scope of this information? In other words, assuming that you are *relying* on this information to make the decision, what do you need to know about this information? Be as specific as possible and try to list five or more items.

Answers to Self-Test

1. d	3. a	5. b	7. b	9. a
2. d	4. c	6. c	8. b	10. b

*This case was provided by Professor Thomas N. Tyson of The University of Tampa.

Learning
Objectives

Chapter
Two

Accounting as
an Information
System

1. *Discuss the concept
of accounting measure-
ment.*
2. *Recognize the impor-
tance of separate entity,
business transactions,
and the unit of measure
in accounting measure-
ment.*
3. *Demonstrate the
effects of simple trans-
actions on financial
position.*
4. *Briefly describe the
role of financial state-
ments in accounting.*
5. *Identify the four
basic financial state-
ments.*

In Chapter 1, accounting was defined as an information system that measures, processes, and communicates financial information. This chapter begins the study of the measurement and communication aspects of accounting. First, you will learn what accounting actually measures and study the effects of certain transactions on a company's financial position. Then, you are introduced to the four most important financial statements, which communicate accounting information. As a result of studying this chapter, you should be able to meet the learning objectives listed on the left.

Accounting Measurement

The accountant must answer four basic questions to make an accounting measurement:

1. What is to be measured?
2. When should the measurement occur?
3. What value should be placed on the measurement?
4. How is the measurement to be classified?

*Objective 1
Discuss the
concept of
accounting
measurement*

The first question is answered in this chapter, and the last three questions are answered in Chapter 3. All the questions deal with basic underlying assumptions and generally accepted accounting principles, and their answers establish what accounting is and what it is not. Accountants in industry, professional associations, public accounting, government, and academic circles debate the answers to these questions constantly. As explained earlier, the answers change as new knowledge and practice require, but today's accounting practice rests on a number of widely accepted concepts and conventions, which are described in this book.

What Is to Be Measured?

Objective 2
Recognize the
importance of
separate entity,
business trans-
actions, and the
unit of measure
in accounting
measurement

The world contains an unlimited number of things to measure. For example, consider a machine that makes bottle caps. How many measurements of this machine could be made? They might include size, location, weight, cost, and many others. Some attributes of this machine are relevant to accounting; some are not. Every system must define what it measures, and accounting is no exception. Basically, financial accounting is concerned with measuring business transactions of specific business entities in terms of money measures. The concepts of separate entity, business transaction, and money measure are discussed below.

The Concept of Separate Entity

For accounting purposes, a business is treated as a separate entity that is distinct not only from its creditors and customers but also from its owner or owners. It should have a completely separate set of records. Its balance sheet refers only to its own financial affairs. The business owns assets and owes creditors and owners in the amount of their claims.

For example, the Jones Florist Company should have a bank account that is separate from the account of Kay Jones, the owner. Kay Jones may own a home, a car, and other property, and she may have personal debts, but these are not the Jones Florist Company's assets or debts. Kay Jones may own another business such as a stationery shop. If so, she should have a completely separate set of records for each business.

As we saw in Chapter 1, business organizations can take three main forms: sole proprietorship, partnership, or corporation. Whichever form is used, it should be viewed for accounting purposes as a separate entity, and all its records and reports should be developed from this viewpoint.

Business Transactions as the Object of Measurement

Business transactions are economic events that affect the financial position of a business entity. Business entities may have hundreds or even thousands of transactions every day. These transactions are the raw material of accounting reports.

A transaction may involve an exchange of value (such as a purchase, sale, payment, collection, or borrowing) between two or more independent parties. A transaction may also involve a nonexchange economic event that has the same effect as an exchange transaction. Some examples of nonexchange transactions are losses from fire, flood, explosion, and theft; physical wear and tear on machinery and equipment; and day-by-day accumulation of interest.

In any case, to be recorded the transaction must relate directly to the business entity. For example, a customer buys a shovel from Ace Hardware but must buy a hoe from a competing store because Ace is out of hoes. The transaction for selling the shovel must be recorded in Ace's records. However, the purchase of a hoe from a competitor is not recorded in Ace's records because, even though it indirectly affects Ace economically, it does not directly involve an exchange of value between Ace and the customer.

Money Measure

All business transactions are recorded in terms of money; this concept is termed the **money measure.** In the United States, the basic unit of money measure is dollars. Of course, information of a nonfinancial nature may be recorded, but it is only through the recording of dollar amounts that the diverse transactions and activities of a business are measured. Money is the only factor common to all business transactions, and thus it is the only practical unit of measure that can produce financial data that are alike and can be compared.

Accounting therefore treats all dollars alike, just as we treat such standard measures as the gallon, mile, or pound in a similar way. The dollar, however, is far inferior to these standards as a unit of measure because of the instability of its purchasing power over time. When the prices of goods and services in our economy (general price level) change over time, the value of the dollar changes. Because of inflation during the last four decades, the dollar today is worth considerably less than it was in 1945. Proposals for adjusting recorded dollar amounts to reflect changes in the value of the dollar are being advocated by many accountants. But at present the assumption of stability is accepted by accountants for practical reasons and should be recognized by users as a possible limitation of financial reports.[1] The issue of the changing value of the dollar is discussed in more detail in Chapter 14.

The Effects of Transactions on Financial Position

*Objective 3
Demonstrate the effects of simple transactions on financial position*

Because business transactions are economic events that affect the financial position of a business entity, a logical question might be, How do transactions affect financial position? In the remaining parts of this chapter, we define financial position more exactly than before by using an equation, and we show how simple, but important, transactions affect it.

Financial Position and the Accounting Equation

As noted earlier, **financial position** refers to the collection of resources belonging to a company and the sources of these resources or claims on

---

1. The first major official deviation from the assumption of stability occurred in March 1976, when the Securities and Exchange Commission issued *Accounting Series Release No. 190,* which required over 1,000 large companies to disclose replacement cost information about certain assets for fiscal years ending after December 25, 1976. The FASB now requires supplemental disclosure of the effects of the changing value of the dollar and other current data by certain companies (see Chapter 14).

them at a certain point in time. Financial position is shown by a balance sheet, so called because it has two sides or parts that must always be in balance. This balance can be expressed in an equation as follows:

$$\text{assets} = \text{liabilities} + \text{owner's equity}$$

This is known as the **balance sheet equation**, or the accounting equation.

Assets

Assets are "probable future economic benefits obtained or controlled by a particular entity as a result of past transactions or events."[2] In other words, they are economic resources owned by a business that are expected to benefit future operations. Certain kinds of assets are monetary items such as receivables (money owed to the company) from customers and cash, and others are nonmonetary physical things such as inventories (goods held for sale), land, buildings, and equipment. Still other assets are nonphysical rights such as those granted by patent, trademark, or copyright.

Liabilities

Liabilities are "probable future sacrifices of economic benefits arising from present obligations of a particular entity to transfer assets or provide services to other entities in the future as a result of past transactions or events."[3] Among these are debts of the business, amounts owed to creditors for goods or services bought on credit (called *accounts payable*), borrowed money such as notes payable, salaries and wages owed to employees, and taxes owed to the government.

As debts, liabilities are a claim recognized by law. That is, the law gives to creditors the right to force the sale of a company's assets to pay debts if the company has failed to pay. Creditors have rights over owners and must be paid in full before the owners may receive anything, even if payment of the debt uses up all assets of the business.

Owner's Equity

Equity is "the residual interest in the assets of an entity that remains after deducting its liabilities."[4] In a business, the equity is called the ownership interest or **owner's equity**. The owner's equity is the resources invested in the business by the owner. It is also known as the residual equity because it is what would be left over if all the liabilities were paid. Transposing the balance sheet equation, we can state owner's equity as follows:

$$\text{assets} - \text{liabilities} = \text{owner's equity}$$

---

2. *Statement of Financial Accounting Concepts No. 3*, "Elements of Financial Statements of Business Enterprises" (Stamford, Conn.: Financial Accounting Standards Board, June 1, 1982), par. 19.
3. Ibid., par. 28.
4. Ibid., par. 43.

Suppose that Shannon Realty has assets of $42,000 and liabilities of $10,000. Then, the owner's equity must equal $32,000. If Shannon Realty repays $2,000 of the liabilities, assets will decrease to $40,000 and liabilities will decrease to $8,000, but the owner's equity will still be $32,000. So we can reason that any transaction affecting only assets and/or liabilities will not affect owner's equity. As will be shown below, owner's equity is affected by four types of transactions:

Type of Transaction	Effect on Owner's Equity
1. Owner's investments	Increase
2. Owner's withdrawals	Decrease
3. Revenues	Increase
4. Expenses	Decrease

Some Illustrations

Let us now examine the effect of some of the most common business transactions on the balance sheet equation, which is shown in the form of a balance sheet. Suppose that John Shannon is opening a real estate agency called Shannon Realty. To conduct his business, he participates in the transactions described in the following numbered paragraphs. To keep things simple, the dates that are generally part of the heading of all financial statements have not been used here.

1. Investment by Owner John begins his new business by depositing $32,000 in a bank account in the name of Shannon Realty. The first balance sheet of the new company would show the cash asset as well as the investment (capital) of the owner.

(1)

Shannon Realty
Balance Sheet

Assets		Liabilities	
Cash	$32,000	(none)	
		Owner's Equity	
		John Shannon, Capital	$32,000
		Total Liabilities and	
Total Assets	$32,000	Owner's Equity	$32,000

2. Purchase of an Asset for Cash John finds a good location and purchases a lot for $7,000 and a building for $22,000 by issuing a check to the previous owner. This transaction does not change the total assets or the owner's equity, but it does involve a shift in the composition of the assets of the company—increasing Land and Building and decreasing Cash.

(2)

Shannon Realty
Balance Sheet

Assets		Liabilities	
Cash	$ 3,000	(none)	
Land	7,000	**Owner's Equity**	
Building	22,000		
		John Shannon, Capital	$32,000
		Total Liabilities and	
Total Assets	$32,000	Owner's Equity	$32,000

3. Purchase of an Asset on Credit John was able to buy the equipment for his office building for $10,000, with a promise to pay for it at the rate of $2,000 per month for five months. This transaction increases both assets (Equipment) and liabilities (Accounts Payable, or debts of the company).

(3)

Shannon Realty
Balance Sheet

Assets		Liabilities	
Cash	$ 3,000	Accounts Payable	$10,000
Land	7,000	**Owner's Equity**	
Building	22,000		
Equipment	10,000	John Shannon, Capital	32,000
		Total Liabilities and	
Total Assets	$42,000	Owner's Equity	$42,000

4. Payment of a Liability John paid the first $2,000 owed on the equipment. This transaction reduces both assets (Cash) and liabilities (Accounts Payable).

(4)

Shannon Realty
Balance Sheet

Assets		Liabilities	
Cash	$ 1,000	Accounts Payable	$ 8,000
Land	7,000	**Owner's Equity**	
Building	22,000		
Equipment	10,000	John Shannon, Capital	32,000
		Total Liabilities and	
Total Assets	$40,000	Owner's Equity	$40,000

5. Sale of an Asset for Cash More equipment was purchased for Shannon Realty than was actually needed. Some of the unneeded equipment, which cost $2,000, was sold for $2,000 cash. This transaction affects two assets—it increases Cash and decreases Equipment—but does not change total assets.

(5)

Shannon Realty
Balance Sheet

Assets		Liabilities	
Cash	$ 3,000	Accounts Payable	$ 8,000
Land	7,000	**Owner's Equity**	
Building	22,000		
Equipment	8,000	John Shannon, Capital	32,000
		Total Liabilities and	
Total Assets	$40,000	Owner's Equity	$40,000

6. Sale of an Asset on Credit The rest of the unneeded equipment was sold to an office supply company for $1,000. The office supply company agreed to pay one-half within ten days and the other half the next month. This transaction causes only a rearrangement of assets—increasing Accounts Receivable (amounts due to the company from outsiders) and decreasing Equipment.

(6)

Shannon Realty
Balance Sheet

Assets		Liabilities	
Cash	$ 3,000	Accounts Payable	$ 8,000
Accounts Receivable	1,000		
Land	7,000	**Owner's Equity**	
Building	22,000		
Equipment	7,000	John Shannon, Capital	32,000
		Total Liabilities and	
Total Assets	$40,000	Owner's Equity	$40,000

7. Collection of Accounts Receivable Shannon Realty receives a check from the office supply company in the amount of $500. This transaction affects two assets—increasing Cash and reducing Accounts Receivable.

(7)

Shannon Realty
Balance Sheet

Assets		Liabilities	
Cash	$ 3,500	Accounts Payable	$ 8,000
Accounts Receivable	500		
Land	7,000	**Owner's Equity**	
Building	22,000		
Equipment	7,000	John Shannon, Capital	32,000
		Total Liabilities and	
Total Assets	$40,000	Owner's Equity	$40,000

8. Revenues When John sells two houses, he collects $4,000 in commissions. This transaction increases both assets (Cash) and owner's equity (John Shannon, Capital).

(8)

Shannon Realty
Balance Sheet

Assets		Liabilities	
Cash	$ 7,500	Accounts Payable	$ 8,000
Accounts Receivable	500		
Land	7,000	**Owner's Equity**	
Building	22,000		
Equipment	7,000	John Shannon, Capital	36,000
		Total Liabilities and	
Total Assets	$44,000	Owner's Equity	$44,000

9. Expenses John pays expenses of $1,500 incurred in connection with the sales in the above transaction and $500 in wages for a secretary. The payment of expenses decreases owner's equity and assets.

(9)

Shannon Realty
Balance Sheet

Assets		Liabilities	
Cash	$ 5,500	Accounts Payable	$ 8,000
Accounts Receivable	500		
Land	7,000	**Owner's Equity**	
Building	22,000		
Equipment	7,000	John Shannon, Capital	34,000
		Total Liabilities and	
Total Assets	$42,000	Owner's Equity	$42,000

10. Withdrawal by Owner John withdraws $1,000 from the bank account of Shannon Realty and deposits it in his personal account to pay his own living expenses. Withdrawals have the effect of reducing assets (Cash) and owner's equity (John Shannon, Capital).

(10)

Shannon Realty
Balance Sheet

Assets		Liabilities	
Cash	$ 4,500	Accounts Payable	$ 8,000
Accounts Receivable	500		
Land	7,000	**Owner's Equity**	
Building	22,000		
Equipment	7,000	John Shannon, Capital	33,000
		Total Liabilities and	
Total Assets	$41,000	Owner's Equity	$41,000

The balance sheet is simply a detailed presentation of the accounting equation. To emphasize this point, the ten typical transactions just illustrated are summarized in Figure 2-1, which shows how each affects the accounting equation. The assets section is made up of five kinds of

	Assets					= Liabilities +	Owner's Equity
	Cash	+ Accounts Receivable +	Land +	Building +	Equipment =	Accounts Payable +	John Shannon, Capital
1.	$32,000	$ 0	$ 0	$ 0	$ 0	$ 0	$32,000
2.	− 29,000		+ 7,000	+ 22,000			
	$ 3,000		$7,000	$22,000			$32,000
3.					+ 10,000	+ 10,000	
	$ 3,000		$7,000	$22,000	$10,000	$10,000	$32,000
4.	− 2,000					− 2,000	
	$ 1,000		$7,000	$22,000	$10,000	$ 8,000	$32,000
5.	+ 2,000				− 2,000		
	$ 3,000		$7,000	$22,000	$ 8,000	$ 8,000	$32,000
6.		+ 1,000			− 1,000		
	$ 3,000	$1,000	$7,000	$22,000	$ 7,000	$ 8,000	$32,000
7.	+ 500	− 500					
	$ 3,500	$ 500	$7,000	$22,000	$ 7,000	$ 8,000	$32,000
8.	+ 4,000						+ 4,000
	$ 7,500	$ 500	$7,000	$22,000	$ 7,000	$ 8,000	$36,000
9.	− 2,000						− 2,000
	$ 5,500	$ 500	$7,000	$22,000	$ 7,000	$ 8,000	$34,000
10.	− 1,000						− 1,000
	$ 4,500	$ 500	$7,000	$22,000	$ 7,000	$ 8,000	$33,000
		$41,000				=	$41,000

Figure 2-1 Summary of the Effects of Typical Transactions on the Balance Sheet Equation

assets. There is one kind of liability and one kind of owner's equity. Transaction 1, an investment by owner, is shown by an increase in Cash and an increase in John Shannon, Capital. Transaction 2, a purchase of assets for cash, is shown by increases in Land and Building and a decrease in Cash. After each transaction, the balance sheet equation keeps its balancing effect. Each of the remaining eight transactions is shown in a similar way.

Accounting Communication Through Financial Statements

Financial statements are a central feature of accounting because they are the primary means of communicating important accounting information

Objective 4
Briefly describe
the role of
financial state-
ments in
accounting

to users. It is helpful to think of these statements as models of the business enterprise, because they are attempts to show the business in financial terms. As is true of all models, however, financial statements are not perfect pictures of the real thing but the accountant's best effort to represent what is real. For instance, the balance sheet for Shannon Realty in the previous section showed the things owned (assets), the money owed (liabilities), and Shannon's interest (owner's equity) in the business. As mentioned before, financial statements have their limitations in communicating accounting information; but used wisely and with an awareness of these limitations, they can be very important to the wide variety of users described in Chapter 1.

The Accounting View of Business Activities

An age-old task of accounting is to measure the progress of a company in meeting its goal of making a profit. In a sense this task is easy. Suppose that the whole life of a business could be viewed at once. It would then be possible to find the difference between the owner's original investment in the business (plus any further investments during the life of the business) and the owner's investment at the end of the business (plus any withdrawals of investments during the life of the business). This difference would represent the profit or loss during the life of the business, as shown in Figure 2-2. Let us take the example of a boy selling balloons at a parade. If he starts with two dollars in the morning (original investment), invests both dollars in balloons, sells all the balloons, and ends up with four dollars that night, his short-lived business has a profit of two dollars.

Unfortunately, it is not possible to wait until a business ceases to exist before determining its financial success. All public corporations are required to publish their earnings for each year, and many companies calculate earnings quarterly or monthly. Because it is impossible to sell the business each time earnings are calculated, the accounting profession has developed ways of measuring a company's ongoing success. One way is to divide the life of a business into arbitrary but equal spans of time (such as a month or a year). Using various measurement techniques, a firm determines its financial position at the start and end of the period and the result of its profit-seeking activities during that time. Thus Figure 2-3 becomes much more realistic than Figure 2-2 because the life of the busi-

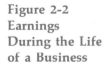

Figure 2-2
Earnings
During the Life
of a Business

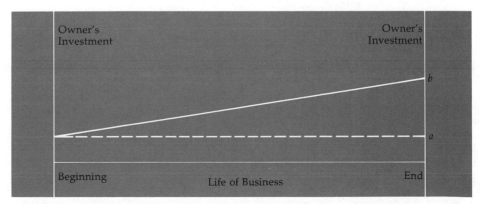

Figure 2-3
Realistic
Growth of
Owner's
Investment
During the Life
of a Business

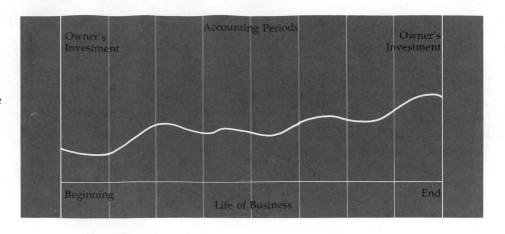

ness is divided into accounting periods. Also, as in a real business, the earnings are not steady from beginning to end.

Four major financial statements are used to communicate the required information about a business. One is the income statement, which reports income-generating activities or earnings of a business during the period. A second statement, called the statement of owner's equity, shows the changes in the owner's interest in the business. A third is the balance sheet, which you have already seen. The balance sheet shows the financial position of the business at either the beginning or the end of the accounting period. A fourth statement, called the statement of changes in financial position, is used to summarize all the changes during the year in terms of some measure of financial resources, such as cash. Figure 2-4 illustrates the relationships of the first three statements by showing how they would appear for Shannon Realty after the ten illustrative transactions. It is assumed that these transactions took place during the month of December 19xx.

Objective 5
Identify the
four basic
financial state-
ments

Note that each statement is headed in a similar way. Each identifies the company and the kind of statement for the user. The balance sheet gives the specific date to which it applies, and the income statement and statement of owner's equity give the time period to which they apply. These statements are typical ones for proprietorships. Statements for partnerships and corporations, which are similar, are discussed in Chapter 15 and later chapters.

The Income Statement

The **income statement** is a financial statement that shows the amount of income earned by a business over a period of time. Many people consider it the most important financial report because its purpose is to measure whether or not the business achieved or failed to achieve its primary objective of earning an acceptable income. In Figure 2-4, Shannon Realty had revenues in the form of commissions earned of $4,000. From this amount total expenses of $2,000 were deducted, consisting of sales expense of $1,500 and wages expense of $500.

Figure 2-4
Income
Statement,
Statement of
Owner's Equity,
and Balance
Sheet for
Shannon Realty

Shannon Realty
Income Statement
For the Month Ended December 31, 19xx

Revenues		
Commissions Earned		$4,000
Expenses		
Sales Expense	$1,500	
Wages Expense	500	
Total Expenses		2,000
Net Income		$2,000

Shannon Realty
Statement of Owner's Equity
For the Month Ended December 31, 19xx

John Shannon, Capital, December 1, 19xx		$ 0
Add: Investments by John Shannon	$32,000	
Net Income for the Month	2,000	34,000
Subtotal		$34,000
Less: Withdrawals by John Shannon		1,000
John Shannon, Capital, December 31, 19xx		$33,000

Shannon Realty
Balance Sheet
December 31, 19xx

Assets		Liabilities	
Cash	$ 4,500	Accounts Payable	$ 8,000
Accounts Receivable	500		
Land	7,000	**Owner's Equity**	
Building	22,000		
Equipment	7,000	John Shannon, Capital	33,000
		Total Liabilities and	
Total Assets	$41,000	Owner's Equity	$41,000

The Statement of Owner's Equity

The **statement of owner's equity** shows the changes in the owner's capital account during the year. In Figure 2-4, the beginning capital is zero because the company was started in this accounting period. During the month John Shannon made an investment in the business of $32,000, and the company earned an income (as shown in the income statement) of $2,000, for a total increase of $34,000. Deducted from this amount are the withdrawals for the month of $1,000, leaving an ending balance of $33,000 in Shannon's capital account.

The Balance Sheet

The purpose of the balance sheet, which has already been introduced, is to show the financial position of a business on a certain date. For this reason, it is often called the statement of financial position. The balance sheet presents a view of the business as the holder of resources or assets that are equal to the sources of or claims against those assets. The sources or claims consist of the company's liabilities and the owner's equity in the company. In Figure 2-4, Shannon Realty has several categories of assets, which total $41,000. These assets equal the total liabilities of $8,000 (accounts payable) plus the ending balance of owner's equity of $33,000 (John Shannon's capital account). Note that the capital account on the balance sheet comes from the ending balance as shown on the statement of owner's equity.

The Statement of Changes in Financial Position

During the past three decades it has become clear that the income statement has one major deficiency. It only shows the changes in financial position caused by those operations that produced an operating income or loss. Many important events, especially those relating to investing and financing activities, can take place during an accounting period and not appear on the income statement. For example, the owner may put more money into the business or take it out. Buildings, equipment or other assets may be bought or sold. New liabilities can be incurred or old ones paid off. For this reason, the statement of changes in financial position is now widely used to show all changes in financial position that take place during an accounting period.

Figure 2-5 is an example of the statement of changes in financial position for Shannon Realty. Note that the name of the company, the title of the statement, and the period covered by the statement are identified. Also note that the statement explains how Cash changed during the period. Cash increased by $4,500 (from $0 to $4,500), a change that was caused by the sources of cash ($45,000) exceeding the uses of cash ($40,500) by $4,500.

This statement is directly related to the other three statements. Notice that among the sources are net income from the income statement, investment by John Shannon from the statement of owner's equity, and two balance sheet accounts, Equipment and Accounts Payable. Among the uses are four balance sheet accounts, Land, Building, Equipment, and Accounts Receivable, and withdrawals from the statement of owner's equity. The construction and use of the statement of changes in financial position are discussed in detail in Chapter 19.

Figure 2-5
Statement of
Changes in
Financial
Position for
Shannon Realty

Shannon Realty
Statement of Changes in Financial Position
For the Month Ended December 31, 19xx

Sources of Cash

Net Income	$ 2,000	
Investments by John Shannon	32,000	
Sales of Equipment	3,000	
Increase in Accounts Payable	8,000	
Total Sources		$45,000

Uses of Cash

Purchase of Land	$ 7,000	
Purchase of Building	22,000	
Purchase of Equipment	10,000	
Increase in Accounts Receivable	500	
Withdrawals by John Shannon	1,000	
Total Uses		40,500
Increase in Cash		$ 4,500

Relationship of the Four Statements

You are not expected to understand all the fine points and terminology of these statements at this stage. They are presented to show that accounting tries to sum up in a meaningful and useful way the financial history of a business, no matter how large and complex, in four relatively simple financial statements—an amazing feat. Two of the statements—the income statement and the statement of changes in financial position—deal with the activities of the business system over time. One statement—the balance sheet—shows the state of the system at a particular point in time. Another statement—the statement of owner's equity—ties the balance sheet and income statement together over a period of time. Much of the rest of this book deals with how to develop, use, and interpret these four statements.

Chapter Review

Review of Learning Objectives

1. Discuss the concept of accounting measurement.

To make an accounting measurement, the accountant must determine what is to be measured, when the measurement should occur, what value should be placed on the measurement, and how the measurement should be classified.

2. Recognize the importance of separate entity, business transactions, and the unit of measure in accounting measurement.

Generally accepted accounting principles define the objects of accounting measurement as separate entities, business transactions, and money measures.

Relating these three concepts, financial accounting measures business transactions of separate business entities in terms of money measures.

3. Demonstrate the effects of simple transactions on financial position.

Business transactions affect financial position by decreasing or increasing assets, liabilities, and/or owner's equity in such a way that the basic balance sheet equation (assets = liabilities + owner's equity) is always in balance.

4. Briefly describe the role of financial statements in accounting.

Financial statements are the means by which accountants communicate the financial condition and activities of a business to those who have an interest in the business.

5. Identify the four basic financial statements.

The four basic financial statements are the balance sheet, the income statement, the statement of owner's equity, and the statement of changes in financial position.

Self-Test

Test your knowledge of the chapter by choosing the best answer for each item below.

1. Economic events that affect the financial position of a business are called
   a. separate entities.   c. money measures.
   b. business transactions.   d. financial actions.
2. A disadvantage of using dollars to measure business transactions is that
   a. dollars are stable measuring units.
   b. dollars are not common to all business transactions.
   c. dollars change in value over time because of inflation and deflation.
   d. dollars are not useful in measuring financial effects.
3. If a company has liabilities of $19,000 and owner's equity of $57,000, the assets of the company are
   a. $38,000.   c. $57,000.
   b. $76,000.   d. $19,000.
4. The payment of a liability will
   a. increase both assets and liabilities.
   b. increase assets and decrease liabilities.
   c. decrease assets and increase liabilities.
   d. decrease assets and decrease liabilities.
5. The purchase of an asset for cash will
   a. increase and decrease assets at the same time.
   b. increase assets and increase liabilities.
   c. increase assets and increase owner's equity.
   d. increase assets and decrease liabilities.
6. Accountants communicate financial information to users primarily through
   a. letters.   c. financial statements.
   b. memoranda.   d. financial notes.
7. The balance sheet is related to the income statement in the same way that
   a. a point in time is related to a period of time.
   b. a period of time is related to a point in time.
   c. a point in time is related to another point in time.
   d. a period of time is related to another period of time.
8. Which of the following is a proper way to date an income statement?
   a. December 31, 19xx

b. For the Year Ended December 31, 19xx
c. On the Date December 31, 19xx
d. None of the above

9. Expenses and withdrawals appear, respectively, on which of the following financial statements?
   a. Balance sheet and income statement
   b. Income statement and balance sheet
   c. Statement of owner's equity and balance sheet
   d. Income statement and statement of owner's equity

10. The ending balance of the owner's capital account appears on which pair of the following financial statements?
   a. Income statement and balance sheet
   b. Balance sheet and statement of owner's equity
   c. Income statement and statement of changes in financial position
   d. Statement of owner's equity and statement of changes in financial position

Answers to Self-Test are at the end of this chapter.

Review Problem
Effect of Transactions on the Accounting Equation

Charlene Rudek finished law school in June and immediately set up her own law practice. During the first month, she completed the following transactions:

a. Invested in the practice by placing $2,000 in a bank account established for the business.
b. Purchased a law library for $900 cash.
c. Purchased office supplies for $400 on credit.
d. Accepted $500 in cash for completing a contract.
e. Billed clients $950 for services rendered during the month.
f. Paid $200 of the amount owed for office supplies.
g. Received $250 in cash from one client previously billed for services rendered.
h. Paid for rent, utilities, secretarial services, and other expenses during the month in the amount of $1,200.

Required

Show the effect of each of these transactions on the balance sheet equation by completing a table like that in Figure 2-1.

Answer to Review Problem

		Assets			= Liabilities +	Owner's Equity
	Cash +	Accounts Receivable +	Office Supplies +	Law Library =	Accounts Payable +	Charlene Rudek, Capital
a.	$2,000	$ 0	$ 0	$ 0	$ 0	$2,000
b.	− 900			+ 900		
	$1,100			$900		$2,000
c.			+ 400		+ 400	
	$1,100		$400	$900	$400	$2,000
d.	+ 500					+ 500
	$1,600		$400	$900	$400	$2,500
e.		+ 950				+ 950
	$1,600	$950	$400	$900	$400	$3,450
f.	− 200				− 200	
	$1,400	$950	$400	$900	$200	$3,450
g.	+ 250	− 250				
	$1,650	$700	$400	$900	$200	$3,450
h.	− 1,200					− 1,200
	$ 450	$700	$400	$900	$200	$2,250
		$2,450			=	$2,450

Chapter Assignments

Questions

1. What are the four basic questions pertaining to measurement in accounting? Why are the answers to them important?

2. Why is the concept of separate entity important?

3. What is a business transaction?

4. Why does accounting use money as its unit of measure?

5. In one sentence, describe the relationship among separate entity, business transaction, and money as a unit of measure.

6. Define assets, liabilities, and owner's equity.

7. What four items affect owner's equity, and how?

8. Arnold Smith's company has assets of $22,000, and liabilities of $10,000. What is the amount of his owner's equity?

9. Give examples of the types of transactions that will (a) increase assets, (b) increase liabilities.

10. Why would the task of accountants be easier if they could wait until the end of a business's existence?

11. Why is the balance sheet sometimes called the statement of financial position?

12. Contrast the purposes of the balance sheet and those of the income statement.

13. How does the income statement differ from the statement of changes in financial position?

14. A statement for an accounting period that ends in June may have either (1) June 30, 19xx, or (2) For the Year Ended June 30, 19xx, as part of its identification. State which would be appropriate with (a) a balance sheet, and (b) an income statement.

Classroom Exercises

Exercise 2-1
The Accounting Equation
(L.O. 3)

Use the accounting equation to answer each question below, and show your calculations.

1. The assets of Rose Company are $480,000, and the owner's equity is $360,000. What is the amount of the liabilities?
2. The liabilities of Stewart Enterprises equal one-third of the total assets. The firm's owner's equity is $80,000. What is the amount of the liabilities?
3. At the beginning of the year, Warren Company's assets were $180,000, and its owner's equity was $100,000. During the year, assets increased $60,000, and liabilities decreased $10,000. What was the owner's equity at the end of the year?

Exercise 2-2
Effect of Transactions on Accounting Equation
(L.O. 3)

During the month of April, the Holton Company had the following transactions:

a. Paid salaries for April, $1,800.
b. Purchased equipment on account, $3,000.
c. Purchased supplies with cash, $100.
d. Additional investment of cash by owner, $4,000.
e. Received payment for services performed, $600.
f. Paid for part of equipment previously purchased on credit, $1,000.
g. Billed customers for services performed, $1,600.
h. Owner withdrew cash from business for personal expenses, $1,500.
i. Received payment from customers billed previously, $300.
j. Received utility bill, $70.

On a sheet of paper, list the letters **a** through **j**, with columns for Assets, Liabilities, and Owner's Equity. In the columns, indicate whether each transaction caused an increase (+), a decrease (−), or no change (NC) in assets, liabilities, and owner's equity.

Exercise 2-3
Examples of Transactions
(L.O. 3)

For each of the following categories, describe a transaction that will have the required effect on the elements of the accounting equation.

1. Increase one asset and decrease another asset.
2. Decrease an asset and decrease a liability.
3. Increase an asset and increase a liability.
4. Increase an asset and increase owner's equity.
5. Decrease an asset and decrease owner's equity.

Exercise 2-4
Balance Sheet Preparation
(L.O. 5)

Appearing in random order below are the balance sheet balances for McCray Company as of December 31, 19xx.

Accounts Payable	$ 40,000	Accounts Receivable	$50,000
Building	80,000	Cash	20,000
George McCray, Capital	160,000	Equipment	40,000
Supplies	10,000		

Sort out these balances, and prepare a balance sheet similar to the one in Figure 2-4.

Exercise 2-5
Accounting
Equation and
Determination
of Net Income
(L.O. 5)

The total assets and liabilities at the beginning and end of the year for Wagner Company are listed below.

	Assets	Liabilities	Equity
Beginning of the year	$ 70,000	$30,000	40 N
End of the year	100,000	50,000	50 N

Determine the net income for the year under each of the following alternatives:

1. The owner made no investments in the business and no withdrawals from the business during the year.
2. The owner made no investments in the business but withdrew $22,000 during the year.
3. The owner made an investment of $10,000 but made no withdrawals during the year.
4. The owner made an investment of $10,000 and withdrew $22,000 during the year.

Exercise 2-6
Balance Sheet
Preparation
(L.O. 5)

The balance sheet below for Keller Service Company contains a number of errors in placements and headings.

Keller Service Company
Balance Sheet
For the Year Ended December 31, 19xx

Cash	$ 4,000	Accounts Payable	$ 20,000
Owner's Investment	84,000	Building	70,000
Equipment	16,000	Accounts Receivable	14,000
Total Assets	$104,000	Total Liabilities	$104,000

Using the amounts provided for Keller Service Company, prepare a balance sheet in correct form similar to the one in Figure 2-4.

Interpreting Accounting Information

Published
Financial
Information:
Foote, Cone, &
Belding Com-
munications
(L.O. 5)

Foote, Cone & Belding Communications, Inc. (F,C,&B) is the fourth-largest advertising agency in the United States. Condensed balance sheets adapted from the company's annual report for 1979 and 1980 are presented on the next page.

Three students who were looking at F,C,&B's annual report were overheard to make the following comments:

Student A: What a superb year the company had in 1980! It earned a net income of $19,847,104, because total assets increased by that amount ($171,613,659 − $151,766,555).

	December 31	
	1980	1979
Assets		
Cash	$ 6,004,193	$ 12,960,929
Marketable Securities	12,607,721	11,999,108
Accounts Receivable	110,989,626	94,027,227
Other Short-Term Assets	16,832,785	13,036,475
Property and Equipment	11,446,340	9,988,233
Other Assets	13,732,994	9,754,583
Total Assets	$171,613,659	$151,766,555
Liabilities		
Accounts Payable	$ 76,472,167	$ 73,825,553
Bank Loans	5,565,969	2,696,810
Other Short-Term Liabilities	30,814,199	27,414,532
Long-Term Liabilities	6,389,605	3,595,182
Owners' Equity		
Total Owners' Equity	52,371,719	44,234,478
Total Liabilities and Owners' Equity	$171,613,659	$151,766,555

Student B: F,C,&B had a terrible year in 1980! It had net loss of $6,956,736, because cash decreased by that amount ($12,960,929 − $6,004,193).

Student C: I understand from other sources that F,C,&B had investments from owners of $1,627,607 in 1980 but that owners withdrew $4,848,098 from the company that same year. Don't you have to take these facts into consideration?

Required

1. Comment on the interpretations of Students A and B and answer student C's question.
2. Calculate the 1980 net income from the information given.

Problem Set A

Problem 2A-1
Identification of
Transactions
(L.O. 3)

Selected transactions for the Renfro Seed Company are summarized on the next page in equation form, with each of the eight transactions identified by letter.

| | Assets | | | | = Liabilities + | Owner's Equity |
	Cash +	Accounts Receivable +	Building +	Equipment =	Accounts Payable +	G. Renfro, Capital
	$ 0	$ 0	$ 0	$ 0	$ 0	$ 0
a.	+ 57,000					+ 57,000
	$57,000	0	0	0	0	$57,000
b.	− 36,000		+ 36,000			
	$21,000	0	$36,000	0	0	$57,000
c.				+ 9,000	+ 9,000	
	$21,000	0	$36,000	$9,000	$9,000	$57,000
d.		+ 1,200				+ 1,200
	$21,000	$1,200	$36,000	$9,000	$9,000	$58,200
e.	+ 2,300					+ 2,300
	$23,300	$1,200	$36,000	$9,000	$9,000	$60,500
f.	+ 600	− 600				
	$23,900	$ 600	$36,000	$9,000	$9,000	$60,500
g.	− 5,000				− 5,000	
	$18,900	$ 600	$36,000	$9,000	$4,000	$60,500
h.	− 1,700					− 1,700
	$17,200	$ 600	$36,000	$9,000	$4,000	$58,800

Required

Write an explanation of the nature of each transaction. (Assume that item **a** is the only one that involves an investment or withdrawal of capital by G. Renfro.)

**Problem 2A-2
Effect of Trans-
actions on
Accounting
Equation**
(L.O. 3)

Helen Knight, after receiving her certification as a physician, began her own practice. She completed the following transactions soon after starting the business:

a. Helen began her practice with a $10,000 cash investment, which she deposited in the bank, and a medical library, which cost $800.
b. Paid one month's rent on an office for her practice. Rent is $360 per month.
c. Purchased medical equipment for $7,000 cash.
d. Purchased $600 of medical supplies on credit.
e. Collected revenue of $30 from each of four patients.
f. Billed patient $110 upon completion of his medical treatment.
g. Paid expenses of $400.
h. Received $80 from patient billed previously.

Required

1. Arrange the assets, liabilities, and owner's equity accounts in an equation like that in Figure 2-1, using the following account titles: Cash; Accounts Receivable;

Medical Supplies; Medical Equipment; Medical Library; Accounts Payable; and Helen Knight, Capital.

2. Show by additions and subtractions, as in Figure 2-1, the effects of the transactions on the balance sheet equation. Show new totals after each transaction.

Problem 2A-3
Identification of
Transactions
(L.O. 3)

In the hypothetical situation below, successive balance sheets are prepared for Central Parking Company after each transaction.

a. Balance sheet for February 1, 19xx:

Assets		Owner's Equity	
Cash	$76,000	Capital	$76,000

b. Balance sheet for February 5, 19xx:

Assets		Liabilities	
Cash	$36,000	Accounts Payable	$ 5,000
Land	40,000	**Owner's Equity**	
Equipment	5,000		
		Capital	76,000
		Total Liabilities and	
Total Assets	$81,000	Owner's Equity	$81,000

c. Balance sheet for February 12, 19xx:

Assets		Liabilities	
Cash	$36,000	Accounts Payable	$ 8,000
Land	40,000	**Owner's Equity**	
Equipment	5,000		
		Capital	73,000
		Total Liabilities and	
Total Assets	$81,000	Owner's Equity	$81,000

d. Balance sheet for February 15, 19xx:

Assets		Liabilities	
Cash	$36,000	Accounts Payable	$ 8,000
Accounts Receivable	1,000		
Land	40,000	**Owner's Equity**	
Equipment	5,000	Capital	74,000
		Total Liabilities and	
Total Assets	$82,000	Owner's Equity	$82,000

e. Balance sheet for February 19, 19xx:

Assets		Liabilities	
Cash	$31,000	Accounts Payable	$ 3,000
Accounts Receivable	1,000		
Land	40,000	**Owner's Equity**	
Equipment	5,000	Capital	74,000
		Total Liabilities and	
Total Assets	$77,000	Owner's Equity	$77,000

Required

Write an explanation of the transaction that occurred before each new balance sheet. For example, the transaction leading to the first balance sheet could be described as follows: "On February 1, 19xx, the owner invested $76,000 cash in Central Parking Company."

Problem 2A-4
Preparation of Financial Statements
(L.O. 5)

After its first month of operation, November 19xx, the Western Riding Club had the following account balances:

Riding Lesson Revenue	$ 3,800	Building	$30,000
Salaries Expense	2,300	Locker Rental Revenue	1,500
Accounts Receivable	1,200	Utilities Expense	600
Denise Clark, Capital	50,000*	Insurance Expense	1,000
Equipment	10,000	Cash	26,600
Land	21,000	Denise Clark,	
Supplies	1,000	Investment During	
Denise Clark,		Month	16,000
Withdrawals	8,400	Accounts Payable	30,800

*Represents the initial investment by Denise Clark in the business.

Required

Using Figure 2-4 as a model, prepare an income statement, a statement of owner's equity, and a balance sheet for Western Riding Club. (Hint: The final balance of the account Denise Clark, Capital, is $59,000.)

Problem 2A-5
Effect of Transactions on Accounting Equation
(L.O. 3)

Dr. Arthur Moon, psychologist, moved from his home town to set up an office in Cincinnati. After one month, the business had the following assets: Cash, $1,900; Accounts Receivable, $680; Office Supplies, $300; Office Equipment, $1,500; and Car, $5,000. The debts were $2,600 for purchases of a car and office equipment on credit. During a short period of time, the following transactions were completed:

a. Paid one month's rent, $350.
b. Billed patient $60 for services rendered.
c. Paid $300 on office equipment previously purchased.
d. Paid for office supplies, $100.
e. Paid secretary's salary, $300.
f. Received $800 from patients.
g. Made car payment, $360.
h. Withdrew $500 for living expenses.
i. Paid telephone bill, $70.
j. Received $290 from patients previously billed.
k. Purchased additional office equipment on credit, $300.

Required

1. Arrange the assets, liabilities, and owner's equity accounts in an equation like that in Figure 2-1 using the following account titles: Cash; Accounts Receivable; Office Supplies; Office Equipment; Car; Accounts Payable; and Arthur Moon, Capital.

2. Enter the beginning balances of the assets and liabilities; then compute the balance of Arthur Moon, Capital, and enter it.

3. Show by additions and subtractions, as in Figure 2-1, the effect of the transactions on the balance sheet equation. Show new totals after each transaction.

Problem Set B

Problem 2B-1
Identification of Transactions
(L.O. 3)

Selected transactions for Randolph Company are summarized in equation form in the accompanying table, with each of the eight transactions identified by letter.

	Cash	+	Accounts Receivable	+	Building	+	Equipment	=	Accounts Payable	+	Susan Randolph, Capital
	$ 0		$ 0		$ 0		$ 0		$ 0		$ 0
a.	+ 30,000										+ 30,000
	$30,000		0		0		0		0		$30,000
b.	− 26,000				+ 26,000						
	$ 4,000		0		$26,000		0		0		$30,000
c.							+ 8,000		+ 8,000		
	$ 4,000		0		$26,000		$8,000		$8,000		$30,000
d.	+ 6,000										+ 6,000
	$10,000		0		$26,000		$8,000		$8,000		$36,000
e.			+ 5,000								+ 5,000
	$10,000		$5,000		$26,000		$8,000		$8,000		$41,000
f.	− 2,000								− 2,000		
	$ 8,000		$5,000		$26,000		$8,000		$6,000		$41,000
g.	+ 1,000		− 1,000								
	$ 9,000		$4,000		$26,000		$8,000		$6,000		$41,000
h.	− 600										− 600
	$ 8,400		$4,000		$26,000		$8,000		$6,000		$40,400

Column group headers: Assets = Liabilities + Owner's Equity

Required

Write an explanation of the nature of each transaction. (Note: Assume that item **a** is the only contribution or withdrawal of capital by the owner.)

**Problem 2B-2
Effect of Trans-
actions on
Accounting
Equation**
(L.O. 3)

Jerry Manuel graduated from law school and started a law practice in his home town. He completed the following transactions soon after starting the practice:

a. Began his practice by depositing $4,000 in a newly created bank account and investing his law library, valued at $1,500, in the law practice.
b. Purchased used office equipment for $1,200 cash.
c. Paid one month's rent of $400 on an office.
d. Purchased office supplies on credit for $300.
e. Completed his first contract, for which he was paid $150 cash.
f. Paid his secretary's salary of $300.
g. Completed a will and billed his client for $200.
h. Withdrew $600 from the practice for his first two weeks' living expenses.

Required

1. Arrange the assets, liabilities, and owner's equity accounts in an equation like that in Figure 2-1, using the following account titles: Cash; Accounts Receivable; Office Supplies; Office Equipment; Law Library; Accounts Payable; and Jerry Manuel, Capital.
2. Show by additions and subtractions, as in Figure 2-1, the effects of Manuel's transactions on the balance sheet equation. Show new totals after each transaction.

**Problem 2B-3
Identification of
Transactions**
(L.O. 3)

In the hypothetical situation below, successive balance sheets are prepared for Monarch Storage Company after each transaction.

a. Balance sheet for May 1, 19xx:

Assets		Owner's Equity	
Cash	$ 84,000	Ray Cofield, Capital	$ 84,000

b. Balance sheet for May 4, 19xx:

Assets		Liabilities	
Cash	$ 44,000	Accounts Payable	$ 20,000
Land	10,000		
Building	50,000	**Owner's Equity**	
		Ray Cofield, Capital	84,000
Total Assets	$104,000	Total Liabilities and Owner's Equity	$104,000

c. Balance sheet for May 8, 19xx:

Assets		Liabilities	
Cash	$ 20,000	Accounts Payable	$ 20,000
Supplies	4,000		
Land	10,000		
Building	50,000		
Equipment	20,000	**Owner's Equity**	
		Ray Cofield, Capital	84,000
		Total Liabilities and	
Total Assets	$104,000	Owner's Equity	$104,000

d. Balance sheet for May 12, 19xx:

Assets		Liabilities	
Cash	$10,000	Accounts Payable	$10,000
Supplies	4,000		
Land	10,000		
Building	50,000		
Equipment	20,000	**Owner's Equity**	
		Ray Cofield, Capital	84,000
		Total Liabilities and	
Total Assets	$94,000	Owner's Equity	$94,000

e. Balance sheet for May 15, 19xx:

Assets		Liabilities	
Cash	$13,600	Accounts Payable	$10,000
Accounts Receivable	400		
Supplies	4,000		
Land	10,000		
Building	50,000		
Equipment	20,000	**Owner's Equity**	
		Ray Cofield, Capital	88,000
		Total Liabilities and	
Total Assets	$98,000	Owner's Equity	$98,000

Required

Write an explanation of the transaction that occurred before each new balance sheet. For example, the transaction leading to the first balance sheet could be described as follows: "On May 1, 19xx, Ray Cofield made an investment of $84,000 cash in Monarch Storage Company."

Problem 2B-4
Preparation of Financial Statements
(L.O. 5)

After one month's operation, August 19xx, the Grandview Exercise Club had the following account balances:

Accounts Payable	$ 2,400	Dorothy Seals, Withdrawals	2,000
Accounts Receivable	1,200	Rent Expense	2,000
Cash	3,400	Exercise Equipment	4,000
Office Equipment	2,200	Exercise Room Rental Revenue	4,200
Office Supplies	600	Exercise Lesson Revenue	1,100
Office Supplies		Salaries Expense	3,400
Expense	300	Utilities and Telephone	
Dorothy Seals, Capital	12,000*	Expenses	600

*Represents investment made at beginning of month.

Required

Using Figure 2-4 as a model, prepare an income statement, a statement of owner's equity, and a balance sheet for Grandview Exercise Club. (Hint: The final balance of the account Dorothy Seals, Capital, is $9,000.)

Problem 2B-5
Effect of Transactions on Accounting Equation
(L.O. 3)

Jack Gibbs owns and operates the Gibbs Plumbing Shop. At the beginning of the month, the shop had the following assets: Cash, $3,300; Accounts Receivable, $1,900; Plumbing Supplies, $1,700; Tools, $2,550; and Truck, $5,600. The shop had debts of $1,500 for supplies and tools purchased. During a short period of time, the following transactions were completed:

a. Paid one month's rent, $400.
b. Purchased plumbing supplies with cash, $100.
c. Paid for plumbing supplies previously purchased on credit, $500.
d. Purchased tools on credit, $350.
e. Completed work for K. Bowa and collected $90 for it.
f. Purchased new tools for cash, $200.
g. Completed work for Pat Rosen on credit, $210.
h. Received payment from customer previously billed, $650.
i. Paid for oil and gas used during the month, $150.
j. Paid utility bills for the month, $180.
k. Wrote a check on the shop bank account to pay the rent for Jack Gibbs's home, $300.

Required

1. Arrange the assets, liabilities, and owner's equity accounts in an equation like that in Figure 2-1, using the following account titles: Cash; Accounts Receivable; Plumbing Supplies; Tools; Truck; Accounts Payable; and Jack Gibbs, Capital.
2. Enter the beginning balances of the assets and liabilities accounts; then compute the balance of Jack Gibbs, Capital, and enter it.
3. Show by additions and subtractions, as in Figure 2-1, the effects of the transactions on the balance sheet equation. Show new totals after each transaction.

Financial Decision Case 2-1

Murphy Lawn Services Company
(L.O. 4, 5)

Instead of hunting for a summer job after completing her junior year in college, Beth Murphy organized a lawn service company in her neighborhood. To start her business on June 1, she deposited $1,500 in a new bank account in the name of her company. The $1,500 consisted of a $1,000 loan from her father and $500 of her own money.

Using the money in this checking account, she rented lawn equipment, purchased supplies, and hired neighborhood high school students to mow and trim lawns of neighbors who had agreed to pay her for the service. At the end of each month, she mailed out bills to her customers.

On September 30, Beth was ready to dissolve her business and go back to school for the fall quarter. Because she had been so busy, she had not kept any records other than her checkbook and a list of amounts owed to her by customers. Her checkbook had a balance of $2,250, and the amount owed to her by the customers totaled $875. She expected these customers to pay her during October. She remembered that she could return unused supplies to the Lawn Care Center for a full credit of $50. When she brought back the rented lawn equipment, the Lawn Care Center would also return a deposit of $200 she had made in June. She owed the Lawn Care Center $475 for equipment rentals and supplies. In addition, she owed the students who had worked for her $100, and she still owed her father $600. Though Beth feels she did quite well, she is not sure just how successful she was.

Required

1. Prepare a balance sheet dated June 1 and one dated September 30 for Murphy Lawn Services Company.
2. Comment on the performance of Murphy Lawn Services Company by comparing the two balance sheets. Did the company have a profit or loss? (Assume that Beth used none of the company's assets for personal purposes.)
3. If Beth is to continue her business next summer, what kind of information from her record-keeping system would help make it easier to tell whether she is earning a profit or losing money?

Answers to Self-Test

1. b	3. b	5. a	7. a	9. d
2. c	4. d	6. c	8. b	10. b

Chapter
Three

The
Double-Entry
System

In the last chapter you learned the answer to the question, What is to be measured? Chapter 3 opens with a discussion of these questions: When should the measurement occur? What value should be placed on the measurement? and How is the measurement to be classified? Then, as the focus shifts from accounting concepts to actual practice, you begin working with the double-entry system and applying it to the analysis and recording of business transactions. As a result of studying this chapter, you should be able to meet the learning objectives listed on the left.

Measurement Problems

Business transactions were defined earlier as economic events that affect the financial position of a business entity. To measure a business transaction, the accountant must decide when the transaction occurred (the recognition problem), what value should be placed on the transaction (the valuation problem), and how the components of the transaction should be categorized (the classification problem).

These three problems—recognition, valuation, and classification—are at the base of almost every major issue in financial accounting today. They lie at the heart of such complex issues as accounting for pension plans, mergers of giant companies, international transactions, and the effects of inflation. In discussing the three basic problems, we follow generally accepted accounting principles and use an approach that promotes the understanding of the basic ideas of accounting. However, keep in mind that controversy does exist, and some solutions to the problems are not as cut and dried or generally agreed upon as they may appear.

The Recognition Problem

The **recognition problem** refers to the difficulty of deciding when a business transaction occurs. Often the facts of a situation are known, but there is disagreement as to when the events should be recorded. For instance, consider the problem of when to recognize or first record a simple purchase. A company orders, receives, and pays for an office desk. Which of the following actions constitutes a recordable event?

1. An employee sends a purchase requisition to the purchasing department.
2. The purchasing department sends a purchase order to the supplier.
3. The supplier ships the desk.
4. The company receives the desk.
5. The company receives the bill from the supplier.
6. The company pays the bill.

Objective 1
Explain in simple terms the generally accepted ways of solving the measurement problems of recognition, valuation, and classification

The answer to this question is important, because the amounts in the financial statements are affected by the date on which the purchase is recorded. Accounting tradition provides a guideline or generally accepted accounting principle stating that the transaction will be recognized when the title to the desk passes from supplier to purchaser and an obligation to pay results. Thus, depending on the details of the shipping agreement, the transaction is recognized at the time of either action 3 or action 4. This is the guideline that we will use generally in this book. However, in many small businesses that use simple business systems, the initial recording of the transaction occurs when the bill is received (action 5) or when the transfer of cash occurs (action 6), because these are the implied points of transfer of title.

Such problems are not always solved easily. Consider the case of an automobile manufacturer who builds a car. Value is added to the car up to the time it is finished. Should the amount of value added be recognized as the automobile is being produced or at the time it is completed? According to the above guideline, the increase in value is recorded at the time the automobile is sold. Normally, legal title passes from the automobile manufacturer to the dealer at the point of sale.

The Valuation Problem

The **valuation problem** is perhaps the most controversial issue in accounting. It has to do with the difficulty of assigning a value to a business transaction. Generally accepted accounting principles state that, in general, the appropriate valuation to assign to all business transactions, and therefore to all assets, liabilities, owner's equity, revenues, and expenses acquired by a business, is the original cost (often called historical cost). Cost is defined here as the exchange price associated with a business transaction at the point of recognition. According to this guideline, the purpose of accounting is not to account for "value," which may change after a transaction occurs, but to account for the cost or value at the time of the transaction. For example, the cost of assets is recorded when they are acquired, and their "value" is also held at that level until they are sold, expire, or are consumed. In this context, value in accounting means the cost at the time of the transaction that brought the item into or took it out of the business entity.

Suppose that a person offers a building for sale at $120,000. It may be valued for real estate taxes at $75,000, and it may be insured for $90,000. One prospective buyer may offer $100,000 for the building, and another may offer $105,000. At this point, several different, unverifiable opinions of value have been expressed. Finally, the seller and a buyer may settle on a price and complete a sale for $110,000. All these figures are values of one kind or another, but only the last figure is sufficiently reliable to be used in the records. The market value of this building may vary over the years, but it will remain on the new buyer's records at $110,000 until it is sold again. At that point, the accountant would record the new transaction at the new exchange price, and a profit or loss on the sale would be recognized.

The cost guideline is used because it meets the standard of verifiability. Cost is verifiable because it results from the actions of independent buyers and sellers who come to an agreement about price. This exchange price is an objective price that can be verified by evidence created at the time of the transaction. Both the buyer and the seller may have thought they got the better deal, but their opinions are irrelevant in recording cost. The final price of $110,000, verified by agreement of the two parties, is the price at which the transaction is recorded.

There are proposals to substitute other valuation procedures for the cost basis of accounting, just as there are proposals for adjusting figures to reflect price-level changes on the grounds of better compliance with the standard of relevance. One of the most important of these proposals is the requirement in *Statement No. 33* by the Financial Accounting Standards Board that certain large companies present, with their cost-based financial statements, supplementary financial information based both on current values and on changes in price levels. The full impact of this requirement has yet to be assessed. However, the historical or original cost is still the measure most widely accepted by accountants in the United States because it is difficult to assign values to business events not based on verifiable transactions. Some notable exceptions to this rule will be presented at appropriate points in this book.

The Classification Problem

The classification problem is that of assigning all the transactions in which a business will engage to the appropriate accounts. For example, a company's ability to borrow money may be affected by the way in which some of its debts are categorized. Or a company's income may be affected by whether a purchase of a small item such as a tool is considered an item of repair expense or an item of equipment (an asset). Proper classification depends not only on the correct analysis of the effect of each transaction on the business enterprise but also on the maintenance of a system of accounts that will reflect that effect. The rest of this chapter explains the classification of accounts and the analysis and recording of transactions.

Accounts

Objective 2
Define and use
the terms ac-
count *and*
ledger

When large amounts of data are gathered in the measurement of business transactions, a method of storage is required. Business people should be able to retrieve transaction data quickly and in the form desired. In other words, there should be a filing system to sort out all the transactions that occur in a business. Only in this way can financial statements and other reports be prepared quickly and easily. This filing system consists of accounts. An account is the basic storage unit for data in accounting. An accounting system has separate accounts for each asset, each liability, and each component of owner's equity, including revenues and expenses. Whether a company keeps records by hand or by computer, management must be able to refer to these accounts so that it can study the company's financial history and plan for the future. A very small company may need only a few dozen accounts, whereas a multinational corporation will have thousands.

Management's Use of Accounts

The accumulation of information in account form is useful to management in running a business. In the example of Shannon Realty from Chapter 2, for instance, John Shannon can keep a running balance of cash receipts and payments so that he knows how much cash is on hand at any one time. He can plan ahead to have enough funds to pay salaries and various bills when they are due. He can foresee the need to borrow money from the bank by estimating future cash payments and cash receipts. Good planning for future cash needs requires that he have a record of past receipts and expenditures as well as of his current cash balance. The Cash account gives him this information.

The Ledger

In a manual accounting system, each account is kept on a separate page or card. These pages or cards are placed together in a book or file. This book or file, which contains all the company's accounts, is called a ledger. In a computer system, which most companies have today, the accounts are maintained on magnetic tapes or disks. However, as a matter of convenience, the accountant still refers to the group of company accounts as the ledger.

To be able to find an account in the ledger easily and to identify accounts when working with the accounting records, an accountant often numbers the accounts. A list of these numbers with the corresponding account names is usually called a chart of accounts. A very simple chart of accounts is presented on the next page.

Assets		**Liabilities**	
Cash	111	Notes Payable	211
Notes Receivable	112	Accounts Payable	212
Accounts Receivable	113	Unearned Art Fees	213
Accrued Fees Receivable	114	Wages Payable	214
Art Supplies	115	Mortgage Payable	221
Office Supplies	116		
Prepaid Rent	117	**Owner's Equity**	
Prepaid Insurance	118	Joan Miller, Capital	311
Land	141	Joan Miller,	
Buildings	142	Withdrawals	312
Accumulated Depreciation,		Income Summary	313
Buildings	143		
Art Equipment	144	**Revenues and Expenses**	
Accumulated Depreciation,		Advertising Fees Earned	411
Art Equipment	145	Art Fees Earned	412
Office Equipment	146	Office Wages Expense	511
Accumulated Depreciation,		Utility Expense	512
Office Equipment	147	Telephone Expense	513
		Rent Expense	514
		Insurance Expense	515
		Art Supplies Expense	516
		Office Supplies Expense	517
		Depreciation Expense,	
		Buildings	518
		Depreciation Expense,	
		Art Equipment	519
		Depreciation Expense,	
		Office Equipment	520

You will be introduced to these accounts in the section below and over the next two-and-a-half chapters through the illustrative case of the Joan Miller Advertising Agency. At this time, notice the gaps in the sequence of numbers. These gaps allow for expansion in the number of accounts. Of course, every company develops a chart of accounts for its own needs. Seldom will two companies have exactly the same chart of accounts.

Types of Commonly Used Accounts

*Objective 3
Recognize
commonly
used assets,
liabilities,
and owner's
equity
accounts*

The specific accounts used by a company depend on the nature of the company's business. A steel company will have large investments in plant and inventory, whereas an advertising agency may have neither. Each company must design its accounts in a way that will reflect the nature of its business and the needs of its management in directing that business. There are, however, accounts that are common to most businesses. Some important ones are described in the following paragraphs. Remember that the total balances of the assets accounts equal the balances of the liabilities accounts plus the balances of the owner's equity accounts.

Assets A company must keep records of the increases and decreases in each asset that it owns. Some of the more common assets accounts are as follows:

Cash "Cash" is the title of the account used to record increases and decreases in cash. Cash consists of money or any medium of exchange that a bank will accept at face value for deposit. Included are coins, currency, checks, postal and express money orders, certificates of deposit, and money deposited in a bank or banks. The Cash account also includes cash on hand such as that in a cash register or a safe.

Notes Receivable A promissory note is a written promise to pay a definite sum of money at a fixed future date. Amounts due from others in the form of promissory notes are recorded in an account called Notes Receivable.

Accounts Receivable Companies often sell goods and services to customers on the basis of oral or implied promises to pay in the future, such as in thirty days or at the first of the month. These sales are called Credit Sales, or Sales on Account, and the promises to pay are known as Accounts Receivable. Credit sales increase Accounts Receivable, and collections from customers decrease Accounts Receivable. Of course, it is necessary to keep a record of how much each customer owes the company. How these records are kept is explained in Chapter 7.

Prepaid Expenses Companies often pay for goods and services before they receive or use them. These prepaid expenses are considered assets until they are used, at which time they become expenses. There should be a separate account for each prepaid expense. An example of a prepaid expense is Prepaid Insurance (or Unexpired Insurance). Insurance protection against fire, theft, and other hazards is usually paid in advance for a period of from one to five years. When the premiums are paid, the Prepaid Insurance account is increased. These premiums expire day by day and month by month. Therefore, at intervals, usually at the end of the accounting period, the Prepaid Insurance must be reduced by the amount of insurance that has expired. Another common type of prepaid expense is Office Supplies. Stamps, stationery, pencils, pens, paper, and other office supplies are assets when they are purchased and are recorded as an increase in Office Supplies. As the office supplies are used, the account is reduced. Other typical prepaid expenses that are assets when they are purchased and become expenses through use or the passage of time are prepaid rent, store supplies, prepaid taxes, and prepaid wages.

Land An account called Land is used to record purchases of property to be used in the ordinary operations of the business.

Buildings Purchases of structures to be used in the business are recorded in an account called Buildings. Although a building cannot be separated from the land it occupies, it is important to maintain separate accounts for the land and the building. The reason for doing so is that the building is subject to wear and tear, but the land is not. Later in the book the subject of depreciation will be introduced. Wear and tear is an important aspect of depreciation.

Equipment A company may own many different types of equipment. Usually there is a separate account for each type of equipment. For instance, changes in amounts representing the cost of desks, chairs, office machines, filing cabinets, and typewriters are recorded in an account called Office Equipment. Increases and decreases in cash registers, counters, showcases, shelves, and similar items are recorded in the Store Equipment account. When a company has a factory, it may own lathes, drill presses, and other factory equipment and would record changes in such items in an account titled Machinery and Equipment. Some companies may have use for a Trucks and Automobiles account.

Liabilities Another word for *liabilities* is *debt*. Most companies have fewer liability accounts than asset accounts. But it is just as important to keep records of what the company owes as it is to keep asset accounts. There are two types of liabilities: short-term and long-term. The distinction between them is introduced in Chapter 9. The following accounts are short-term liabilities:

Notes Payable The account called Notes Payable is the exact opposite of Notes Receivable. It is used to record increases and decreases in promissory notes owed to creditors within the next year or operating cycle.

Accounts Payable Similarly, Accounts Payable is the opposite of Accounts Receivable. It represents amounts owed to creditors on the basis of an oral or implied promise to pay. Accounts payable usually arise as the result of the purchase of merchandise, services, supplies, or equipment on credit. When Company B sells an item to Company A, which promises to pay at the beginning of the month, the amount of the transaction is an Account Payable on Company A's books and an Account Receivable on Company B's books. As with Accounts Receivable, records of amounts owed to individual creditors must be known. Chapter 7 covers the method of accomplishing this task.

Other short-term liabilities A few other liabilities and liability accounts are Wages Payable, Taxes Payable, Rent Payable, and Interest Payable. Often customers make deposits on, or pay in advance for, goods and services to be delivered in the future. Such customers' deposits are also recorded as liabilities. They are liabilities because the money must be returned to the customer if the goods or services are not delivered. These kinds of liability accounts are often called Unearned Fees, Customer Deposits, Advances from Customers, or, more commonly, Unearned Revenues.

Long-term liabilities The most common type of long-term liabilities are bonds or property mortgages. Because a wide variety of bonds and mortgages have been developed for special financing needs, it is difficult to classify them. They may or may not require the backing of certain of the company's assets for security. For example, a mortgage holder may have the right to force the sale of certain assets if the mortgage debt is not paid when due. For now, however, it will suffice to record increases and decreases in long-term debt in an account called Bonds Payable or Mortgage Payable.

Owner's Equity Accounts In the previous chapter's illustrations, several transactions affected owner's equity. The effects of all these transactions were shown by the increases or decreases in the single column representing owner's equity (see Figure 2-1). In reality, it is very important for legal and managerial reasons to separate these transactions by type. Among the most important information that management receives for business planning is a detailed breakdown of revenues and expenses. For income tax reporting, financial reporting, and other reasons, the law requires that capital contributions and withdrawals be separated from revenues and expenses. Ownership and equity accounts, especially those for partnerships and corporations, are covered in much more detail in Part IV, but for now the following accounts, whose relationships are shown in Figure 3-1, are important to the study of sole proprietorships.

Capital account When someone invests in his or her own company, the amount of the investment is recorded in a capital account. For instance, in Chapter 2 when John Shannon invested his personal resources in his firm, he recorded the amount in the owner's equity account titled John Shannon, Capital. Any additional investments by John Shannon in his firm would be recorded in this account. The capital accounts for corporations are discussed in Part IV.

Withdrawals account A person who invests in a business usually expects to earn an income and to use at least part of the assets earned from profitable operations to pay personal living expenses. Since the income for a business is determined at the end of the accounting period, the owner often finds it necessary to withdraw assets from the business for living expenses long before income has been determined. It is not legally possible for the owner of a business to pay himself or herself a salary, but it is possible for the owner to withdraw assets for personal use. As a result, it has become common practice to set up a withdrawals account to record these payments, which are made with the expectation of earning an income. For example, an account called John Shannon, Withdrawals,

Figure 3-1
Relationships
of Owner's
Equity
Accounts

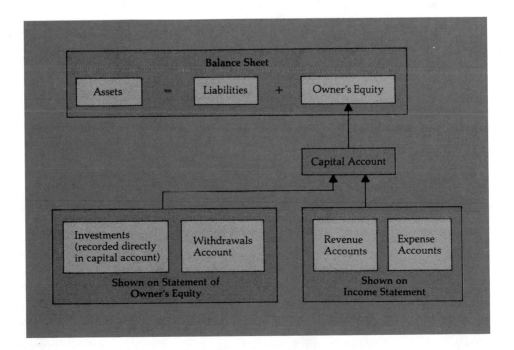

would be used to record John Shannon's withdrawals from his firm. In practice, the withdrawals account often goes by several other names. Among these other titles are Personal and Drawing. This account is not used by corporations.

Revenue and expense accounts Revenues increase owner's equity, and expenses decrease owner's equity. The greater the revenues, the more the owner's equity is increased. The greater the expenses, the more the owner's equity is decreased. Of course, when revenues are greater than expenses, the company has earned a profit or net income. When expenses are more than revenues, the company has suffered a loss or net loss. Management's major goal is to earn an income, and an important function of accounting is to give management the information that will help it meet this goal. One way of doing this is by having a ledger account for every revenue and expense item. From these accounts, management can learn exactly where all revenues come from and where all expenses go. A particular company's revenue and expense accounts will depend on its kind of business and the nature of its operations. A few of the revenue accounts used in this book are Commissions Earned, Advertising Fees Earned, and Sales. Some of the expense accounts are Wages Expense, Supplies Expense, Rent Expense, and Advertising Expense.

Titles of Accounts

The names of accounts are often confusing to beginning accounting students because some of the words are new or have special technical meanings. It is also true that the same asset, liability, or owner's equity account may be called by different names in different companies. This fact is not so strange. People too are often called different names by their friends, families, and associates.

Similarly, long-term assets may be known in various contexts as Fixed Assets, Plant and Equipment, Capital Assets, Long-Lived Assets, and so forth. Even the most acceptable names change over a period of time in accounting, and by habit some companies may use names that are out of date. In general, the account title should describe what is recorded in the account. When you encounter an account title that you do not recognize, you should examine the context of the name—that is, whether it is classified as asset, liability, owner's equity, revenue, or expense on the financial statement—and look for the kind of transaction that gave rise to the account.

The Double-Entry System:
The Basic Method of Accounting

The double-entry system, the backbone of manual accounting, evolved during the Renaissance. The first systematic presentation of double-entry bookkeeping appeared in 1494, two years after Columbus discovered America. It was described in a mathematics book written by Fra Luca Pacioli, a Franciscan monk who was a friend of Leonardo da Vinci. Goethe, the famous German poet and dramatist, referred to double-entry bookkeeping as "one of the finest discoveries of the human intellect." Werner Sombart, an eminent economist-sociologist, expressed the belief that "double-entry bookkeeping is born of the same spirit as the system of Galileo and Newton."

What is the significance of the double-entry system for accounting? The double-entry system is based on the principle of duality, which means that all events of economic importance have two aspects—effort and reward, sacrifice and benefit, sources and uses—that offset or balance each other. In the double-entry system each transaction must be recorded twice, in such a way that the total dollar amount of debits and total dollar amount of credits equal each other. Because of the way it is designed, the system as a whole is always in balance and therefore always under control. All accounting systems, no matter how sophisticated, are based on this principle of duality. The T account is a helpful place to begin the study of the double-entry system.

The T Account

In its simplest form, an account has three parts: (1) a title that describes the asset, liability, or owner's equity account; (2) a left side, which is called the debit side; and (3) a right side, which is called the credit side. This form of the account, called a T account because of its resemblance to the letter *T*, is used to analyze transactions. It appears as follows:

Title of Account

Left or Debit Side	Right or Credit Side

Thus any entry made on the left side of the account is a debit, or debit entry, and any entry made on the right side of the account is a credit, or credit entry. The terms *debit* (abbreviated Dr., from the Latin *debere*) and *credit* (abbreviated Cr., from the Latin *credere*) are simply the accountant's words for "left" and "right" (not for "increase" or "decrease"). A more complete version of the T account will be presented later in this chapter.

The Account Illustrated

In Chapter 2, Shannon Realty had several transactions that involved the receipt or payment of cash. (See Figure 2-1 for a summary of the numbered transactions given below.) These transactions can be summarized in the Cash account by recording receipts on the left or debit side of the account and payments on the right or credit side of the account as follows:

Cash

(1)	32,000	(2)	29,000
(5)	2,000	(4)	2,000
(7)	500	(9)	2,000
(8)	4,000	(10)	1,000
	38,500		34,000
Bal.	4,500		

The cash receipts have been totaled on the left as $38,500, and this total is written in small-size figures so that it will not be confused with an actual debit entry. The cash payments are totaled in a similar way on the right side. These figures are simply working totals called footings. Footings are calculated at the end of the month as an easy way to determine cash on hand. The difference in total dollars between the total debit footings and the total credit footings is called the balance or account balance. If the balance is a debit, it is written on the left side. If it is a credit, it is written on the right. Notice that Shannon Realty's Cash account has a debit balance of $4,500 ($38,500 − $34,000). This represents Shannon's cash on hand at the end of the month.

Analysis of Transactions

Objective 4
State the rules
for debit and
credit

The rules of double-entry bookkeeping are that every transaction affects at least two accounts. In other words, there must be one or more accounts debited and one or more accounts credited, and the total debits must equal the total credits.

When we look at the accounting equation

$$\text{assets} = \text{liabilities} + \text{owner's equity}$$

we can see that if a debit increases assets, then a credit must be used to increase liabilities or owner's equity. On the other hand, if a credit decreases assets, then a debit must be used to show a decrease in liabilities or owner's equity. These are the rules because assets are on the opposite side of the equation from liabilities and owner's equity. These rules can be shown as follows:

Assets		=	Liabilities		+	Owner's Equity	
Debit for Increases	Credit for Decreases		Debit for Decreases	Credit for Increases		Debit for Decreases	Credit for Increases

1. Increases in assets are debited to asset accounts. Decreases in assets are credited to asset accounts.
2. Increases in liabilities and owner's equity are credited to liability and owner's equity accounts. Decreases in liabilities and owner's equity are debited to liability and owner's equity accounts. (In applying these rules, remember that revenues increase owner's equity and expenses decrease owner's equity.)

At this point we can explain how to analyze transactions. This procedure can be used to analyze every transaction that takes place. As an example, let us suppose that Jones Company borrows $1,000 from its bank on a promissory note. The procedure is as follows:

1. Analyze the effect of the transaction on assets, liabilities, and owner's equity. In this case, both an asset (Cash) and a liability (Notes Payable) were increased.
2. Apply the correct double-entry rule. Increases in assets are recorded by debits. Increases in liabilities are recorded by credits.

Chapter Three

3. Make the entry. The increase in assets is recorded by a debit to the Cash account, and the increase in liabilities is recorded by a credit to the Notes Payable account.

Cash	Notes Payable
1,000	1,000

The debit to Cash of $1,000 equals the credit to Notes Payable of $1,000.

Another form of this entry, which will be explained later in this chapter, is as follows:

	Dr.	Cr.
Cash	1,000	
Notes Payable		1,000

Transaction Analysis Illustrated

The list below contains the transactions for the Joan Miller Advertising Agency during the month of January. We will use the transactions to illustrate the application of the principle of duality and to show how transactions are recorded in the accounts.

Objective 5
Apply the
procedure for
transaction
analysis
to simple
transactions

Jan. 1 Joan Miller invested $10,000 in her own advertising agency.

2 Rented an office, paying two months' rent in advance, $800.

3 Hired a secretary and agreed to pay $600 every two weeks. The secretary agreed to work extra hours to make up the time for the first two days of January.

4 Purchased art equipment for $4,200.

5 Purchased office equipment from Morgan Equipment for $3,000, paying $1,500 in cash and agreeing to pay the rest next month.

6 Purchased on credit art supplies for $1,800 and office supplies for $800 from Taylor Supply Company.

8 Paid $480 for a one-year insurance policy with coverage effective January 1.

9 Paid Taylor Supply Company $1,000 of the amount owed.

10 Performed a service by placing advertisements for an automobile dealer in the newspaper and collected a fee of $1,400.

12 Paid the secretary two weeks' salary, $600.

15 Accepted $1,000 as an advance fee for art work to be done for another agency.

19 Performed a service by placing several major advertisements for Ward Department Stores. The earned fees of $2,800 will be collected next month.

25 Joan Miller withdrew $1,400 from the business for personal living expenses.

26 Paid the secretary two more weeks' salary, $600.

29 Received and paid the utility bill of $100.

30 Received (but did not pay) a telephone bill, $70.

January 1: Joan Miller invested $10,000 in her own advertising agency.

Cash

Jan. 1 10,000	

Joan Miller, Capital

	Jan. 1 10,000

Transaction: Investment in business.
Analysis: Assets increased. Owner's equity increased.
Rules: Increases in assets are recorded by debits. Increases in owner's equity are recorded by credits.
Entry: Increase in assets is recorded by debit to Cash. Increase in owner's equity is recorded by credit to Joan Miller, Capital.

	Dr.	Cr.
Cash	10,000	
Joan Miller, Capital		10,000

January 2: Rented an office, paying two months' rent in advance, $800.

Cash

Jan. 1 10,000	Jan. 2 800

Prepaid Rent

Jan. 2 800	

Transaction: Expense paid in advance.
Analysis: Assets increased. Assets decreased.
Rules: Increases in assets are recorded by debits. Decreases in assets are recorded by credits.
Entry: Increase in assets is recorded by debit to Prepaid Rent. Decrease in assets is recorded by credit to Cash.

	Dr.	Cr.
Prepaid Rent	800	
Cash		800

January 3: Hired a secretary and agreed to pay $600 every two weeks.

The secretary agreed to work extra hours to make up the time for the first two days of January. *Analysis:* No entry is made because no transaction has occurred. There is no liability until the secretary actually starts to work.

January 4: Purchased art equipment for $4,200 cash.

Cash

Jan. 1 10,000	Jan. 2 800
	4 4,200

Art Equipment

Jan. 4 4,200	

Transaction: Purchase of equipment.
Analysis: Assets increased. Assets decreased.
Rules: Increases in assets are recorded by debits. Decreases in assets are recorded by credits.
Entry: Increase in assets is recorded by debit to Art Equipment. Decrease in assets is recorded by credit to Cash.

	Dr.	Cr.
Art Equipment	4,200	
Cash		4,200

January 5: Purchased office equipment from Morgan Equipment for $3,000, paying $1,500 in cash and agreeing to pay the rest next month.

Cash

Jan. 1	10,000	Jan. 2	800
		4	4,200
		5	1,500

Office Equipment

Jan. 5	3,000	

Accounts Payable

		Jan. 5	1,500

Transaction: Purchase of equipment, partial payment.

Analysis: Assets increased. Assets decreased. Liabilities increased.

Rules: Increases in assets are recorded by debits. Decreases in assets are recorded by credits. Increases in liabilities are recorded by credits.

Entry: Increase in assets is recorded by debit to Office Equipment. Decrease in assets is recorded by credit to Cash. Increase in liabilities is recorded by credit to Accounts Payable.

	Dr.	Cr.
Office Equipment	3,000	
Cash		1,500
Accounts Payable		1,500

January 6: Purchased on credit art supplies for $1,800 and office supplies for $800 from Taylor Supply Company.

Art Supplies

Jan. 6	1,800	

Office Supplies

Jan. 6	800	

Accounts Payable

		Jan. 5	1,500
		6	2,600

Transaction: Purchase of supplies on credit.

Analysis: Assets increased. Liabilities increased.

Rules: Increases in assets are recorded by debits. Increases in liabilities are recorded by credits.

Entry: Increase in assets is recorded by debits to Art Supplies and Office Supplies. Increase in liabilities is recorded by credit to Accounts Payable.

	Dr.	Cr.
Art Supplies	1,800	
Office Supplies	800	
Accounts Payable		2,600

January 8: Paid $480 for a one-year insurance policy with coverage effective January 1.

Cash

Jan. 1	10,000	Jan. 2	800
		4	4,200
		5	1,500
		8	480

Prepaid Insurance

Jan. 8	480	

Transaction: Paid for insurance coverage in advance.

Analysis: One asset increased. Another asset decreased.

Rules: Increases in assets are recorded by debits. Decreases in assets are recorded by credits.

Entry: Increase in assets is recorded by debit to Prepaid Insurance. Decrease in assets is recorded by credit to Cash.

	Dr.	Cr.
Prepaid Insurance	480	
Cash		480

January 9: Paid Taylor Supply Company $1,000 of the amount owed.

Cash

Jan. 1	10,000	Jan. 2	800
		4	4,200
		5	1,500
		8	480
		9	1,000

Accounts Payable

Jan. 9	1,000	Jan. 5	1,500
		6	2,600

Transaction: Partial payment on a liability.

Analysis: Assets decreased. Liabilities decreased.

Rules: Decreases in assets are recorded by credits. Decreases in liabilities are recorded by debits.

Entry: Decrease in liabilities is recorded by debit to Accounts Payable. Decrease in assets is recorded by credit to Cash.

	Dr.	Cr.
Accounts Payable	1,000	
Cash		1,000

January 10: Performed a service by placing advertisements for an automobile dealer in the newspaper and collected a fee of $1,400.

Cash

Jan. 1	10,000	Jan. 2	800
10	1,400	4	4,200
		5	1,500
		8	480
		9	1,000

Advertising Fees Earned

	Jan. 10	1,400

Transaction: Revenue earned and collected.

Analysis: Assets increased. Owner's equity increased.

Rules: Increases in assets are recorded by debits. Increases in owner's equity are recorded by credits.

Entry: Increase in assets is recorded by debit to Cash. Increase in owner's equity is recorded by credit to Advertising Fees Earned.

	Dr.	Cr.
Cash	1,400	
Advertising Fees Earned		1,400

January 12: Paid the secretary two weeks' salary, $600.

Cash

Jan.	1	10,000	Jan. 2		800
	10	1,400	4		4,200
			5		1,500
			8		480
			9		1,000
			12		600

Office Wages Expense

Jan. 12	600	

Transaction: Payment of wages expense.
Analysis: Assets decreased. Owner's equity decreased.
Rules: Decreases in assets are recorded by credits. Decreases in owner's equity are recorded by debits.
Entry: Decrease in owner's equity is recorded by debit to Office Wages Expense. Decrease in assets is recorded by credit to Cash.

	Dr.	Cr.
Office Wages Expense	600	
Cash		600

January 15: Accepted $1,000 as an advance fee for art work to be done for another agency.

Cash

Jan.	1	10,000	Jan.	2	800
	10	1,400		4	4,200
	15	1,000		5	1,500
				8	480
				9	1,000
				12	600

Unearned Art Fees

	Jan. 15	1,000

Transaction: Accepted payment for services to be performed.
Analysis: Assets increased. Liabilities increased.
Rules: Increases in assets are recorded by debits. Increases in liabilities are recorded by credits.
Entry: Increase in assets is recorded by debit to Cash. Increase in liabilities is recorded by credit to Unearned Art Fees.

	Dr.	Cr.
Cash	1,000	
Unearned Art Fees		1,000

January 19: Performed a service by placing several major advertisements for Ward Department Stores. The earned fees of $2,800 will be collected next month.

Accounts Receivable

Jan. 19	2,800	

Advertising Fees Earned

	Jan. 10	1,400
	19	2,800

Transaction: Revenue earned, to be received later.
Analysis: Assets increased. Owner's equity increased.
Rules: Increases in assets are recorded by debits. Increases in owner's equity are recorded by credits.
Entry: Increase in assets is recorded by debit to Accounts Receivable. Increase in owner's equity is recorded by credit to Advertising Fees Earned.

	Dr.	Cr.
Accounts Receivable	2,800	
Advertising Fees Earned		2,800

January 25: Joan Miller withdrew $1,400 from the business for personal living expenses.

Cash			
Jan. 1	10,000	Jan. 2	800
10	1,400	4	4,200
15	1,000	5	1,500
		8	480
		9	1,000
		12	600
		25	1,400

Joan Miller, Withdrawals	
Jan. 25 1,400	

Transaction: Withdrawal of assets for personal use.

Analysis: Assets decreased. Owner's equity decreased.

Rules: Decreases in assets are recorded by credits. Decreases in owner's equity are recorded by debits.

Entry: Decrease in owner's equity is recorded by debit to Joan Miller, Withdrawals. Decrease in assets is recorded by credit to Cash.

	Dr.	Cr.
Joan Miller, Withdrawals	1,400	
Cash		1,400

January 26: Paid the secretary two more weeks' salary, $600.

Cash			
Jan. 1	10,000	Jan. 2	800
10	1,400	4	4,200
15	1,000	5	1,500
		8	480
		9	1,000
		12	600
		25	1,400
		26	600

Office Wages Expense	
Jan. 12 600	
26 600	

Transaction: Payment of wages expense.

Analysis: Assets decreased. Owner's equity decreased.

Rules: Decreases in assets are recorded by credits. Decreases in owner's equity are recorded by debits.

Entry: Decrease in owner's equity is recorded by debit to Office Wages Expense. Decrease in assets is recorded by credit to Cash.

	Dr.	Cr.
Office Wages Expense	600	
Cash		600

January 29: Received and paid the utility bill of $100.

Cash			
Jan. 1	10,000	Jan. 2	800
10	1,400	4	4,200
15	1,000	5	1,500
		8	480
		9	1,000
		12	600
		25	1,400
		26	600
		29	100

Utility Expense	
Jan. 29 100	

Transaction: Payment of expenses.

Analysis: Assets decreased. Owner's equity decreased.

Rules: Decreases in assets are recorded by credits. Decreases in owner's equity are recorded by debits.

Entry: Decrease in owner's equity is recorded by debit to Utility Expense. Decrease in assets is recorded by credit to Cash.

	Dr.	Cr.
Utility Expense	100	
Cash		100

January 30: Received (but did not pay) a telephone bill, $70.

Accounts Payable

Jan. 9	1,000	Jan. 5	1,500	
		6	2,600	
		30	70	

Telephone Expense

Jan. 30	70

Transaction: Expense incurred, payment deferred.

Analysis: Liabilities increased. Owner's equity decreased.

Rules: Increases in liabilities are recorded by credits. Decreases in owner's equity are recorded by debits.

Entry: Decrease in owner's equity is recorded by debit to Telephone Expense. Increase in liabilities is recorded by credit to Accounts Payable.

	Dr.	Cr.
Telephone Expense	70	
Accounts Payable		70

Summary of Transactions

As you may have discovered from the examples, there are only a few ways in which transactions can affect the accounting equation, as follows:

Effect	Example Transactions
1. Increase both assets and liabilities	Jan. 6, 15
2. Increase both assets and owner's equity	Jan. 1, 10, 19
3. Decrease both assets and liabilities	Jan. 9
4. Decrease both assets and owner's equity	Jan. 12, 25, 26, 29
5. Increase one asset and decrease another	Jan. 2, 4, 8
6. Increase one liability or owner's equity and decrease another liability or owner's equity	Jan. 30
7. No effect	Jan. 3

The January 5 transaction is a more complex transaction; it increases one asset (Office Equipment), decreases another asset (Cash), and increases a liability (Accounts Payable). All the transactions above are presented in Figure 3-2 (next page) in their correct accounts, and their relation to the accounting equation is shown.

Recording Transactions

Objective 6
Record transactions in the general journal

So far, the analysis of transactions has been illustrated by entering the transactions directly into the T accounts. This method was used because it is a very simple and useful way of analyzing the effect of transactions. Advanced accounting students and professional accountants often use T accounts to analyze very complicated transactions. However, there are in fact three steps to be followed in the recording processes.

Assets		=	Liabilities		+	Owner's Equity	

Assets = Liabilities + Owner's Equity

Cash

Jan.	1	10,000	Jan.	2	800
	10	1,400		4	4,200
	15	1,000		5	1,500
				8	480
				9	1,000
				12	600
				25	1,400
				26	600
				29	100
		12,400			10,680
Bal.		1,720			

Accounts Payable

Jan. 9	1,000	Jan.	5	1,500
			6	2,600
			30	70
	1,000			4,170
		Bal.		3,170

Joan Miller, Capital

	Jan. 1	10,000

Accounts Receivable

Jan. 19	2,800	

Unearned Art Fees

	Jan. 15	1,000

Joan Miller, Withdrawals

Jan. 25	1,400	

Art Supplies

Jan. 6	1,800	

Office Supplies

Jan. 6	800	

Advertising Fees Earned

	Jan. 10	1,400
	19	2,800
	Bal.	4,200

Prepaid Rent

Jan. 2	800	

Office Wages Expense

Jan. 12	600	
26	600	
Bal.	1,200	

Prepaid Insurance

Jan. 8	480	

Utility Expense

Jan. 29	100	

Art Equipment

Jan. 4	4,200	

Telephone Expense

Jan. 30	70	

Office Equipment

Jan. 5	3,000	

Figure 3-2
Summary of
Illustrative
Accounts and
Transactions for
Joan Miller
Advertising
Agency

Steps in the Recording Process

1. Analyze the transactions from the source documents.
2. Enter the transactions into the journal (a procedure usually called journalizing).
3. Post the entries to the ledger (a procedure usually called posting).

The Journal

As illustrated in this chapter, transactions can be recorded directly into the accounts. When this method is used, however, it is very difficult to follow individual transactions with the debit recorded in one account and the credit in another. When a large number of transactions are involved, errors in analyzing or recording transactions are very difficult to find. The solution to this problem is to make a chronological record of all transactions by recording them in a journal. The journal is sometimes called the book of original entry, because this is where transactions are first recorded. The journal shows the transactions for each day and may contain explanatory information concerning the transactions. The debits and credits of the transactions can then be transferred to the appropriate accounts.

A separate journal entry is used to record each transaction, and the process of recording transactions is called journalizing.

The General Journal

It is common for a business to have more than one kind of journal. Several types of journals are discussed in Chapter 7. The simplest and most flexible type is the general journal, which is used in the rest of this chapter. The general journal provides for recording the following information about each transaction:

1. The date
2. The names of the accounts debited and credited
3. The dollar amounts debited or credited to each account
4. An explanation of the transaction
5. The account identification numbers, if appropriate

Two transactions for the Joan Miller Advertising Agency are recorded in Figure 3-3 (next page).

The procedures for recording transactions in the general journal can be summarized as follows:

1. Record the date by writing the year in small figures at the top of the first column, the month on the first line of the first column, and the day in the second column of the first line. For subsequent entries on the same page for the same month and year, the month and year can be omitted.

2. Write the exact names of the accounts debited and credited under the heading "Description." Write the name of the account debited next to the left margin of the first line, and indent the name of the account credited. The explanation is placed on the next line and further indented. It should be brief but sufficient to explain and identify the transaction. A transaction can have more than one debit and/or credit entry; in such a case it is called a compound entry. In a compound entry, all debit accounts involved are listed before any credit accounts.

3. Write the debit amounts in the appropriate column opposite the accounts to be debited, and write the credit amounts opposite the accounts to be credited.

Figure 3-3
The General
Journal

		General Journal	Post. Ref.	Debit	Credit
Date		Description			
19xx					
Jan.	6	Art Supplies		1,800	
		Office Supplies		800	
		Accounts Payable			2,600
		Purchase of art and office supplies on credit			
	8	Prepaid Insurance		480	
		Cash			480
		Paid one-year life insurance premium			

(Page 1, top of form)

4. At the time of recording the transactions, nothing is placed in the Post. Ref. (posting reference) column. (This column is sometimes called LP or Folio.) Later, if the company uses account numbers to identify accounts in the ledger, fill in the account numbers to provide a convenient cross-reference from general journal to ledger and to indicate that posting to the ledger has been completed. If account numbers are not used, a check (✔) is used.

5. It is customary to skip a line after each journal entry.

The Ledger Account Form

So far, the T form of account has been used as a simple and direct means of recording transactions. In practice, a somewhat more complicated form of the account is needed to record more information. The ledger account form, with four columns for dollar amounts, is illustrated in Figure 3-4 (next page).

The *account title* and *number* appear at the top of the account form. The *date* of the transaction appears in the first two columns as it does in the journal. The Item column is used only rarely, because an explanation already appears in the journal. The Post. Ref. column is used to note the journal page number where the journal entry for the transaction can be found. The dollar amount of the entry is entered in the appropriate Debit or Credit column, and a new account balance is computed in the final two columns after each entry. The advantage of this form of account over the T account is that the current balance of the account is always easily available.

Figure 3-4
Accounts
Payable in
the General
Ledger

General Ledger							
Accounts Payable						Account No. 212	
						Balance	
Date		Item	Post. Ref.	Debit	Credit	Debit	Credit
19xx Jan.	5				1,500		1,500
	6				2,600		4,100
	9			1,000			3,100
	30				70		3,170

Relationship Between the Journal and the Ledger

Objective 7
Explain the
relationship of
the journal to
the ledger

After the transactions have been entered in the journal, they must be transferred to the ledger. This process of transferring journal entry information from the journal to the ledger is called posting. Posting is usually done, not after each journal entry, but after several entries have been made—for example, at the end of each day or less frequently, depending on the number of transactions.

Posting consists of transferring each amount in the Debit column of the journal into the Debit column of the appropriate account in the ledger and copying each amount in the Credit column of the journal into the Credit column of the appropriate account in the ledger. This procedure is keyed to Figure 3-5 (next page). The steps in posting are as follows:

1. Locate in the ledger the debit account named in the journal entry.
2. Enter the date of the transaction and, in the Post. Ref. column of the ledger, the journal page number from which the entry comes.
3. Enter in the Debit column of the ledger account the amount of the debit as it appears in the journal.
4. Enter in the Post. Ref. column of the journal the account number of the account to which the amount was posted.
5. Repeat the preceding four steps for the credit side of the journal entry.

Note that Step 4 is the last step in the posting process for each debit and credit. In addition to serving as an easy reference between journal entry and ledger account, this entry in the Post. Ref. column of the journal serves as a check, indicating that all steps for the item are completed. For example, when accountants are called away from their work by telephone calls or other interruptions, they can easily find where they were before the interruption.

Figure 3-5
Posting from
the General
Journal to the
Ledger

General Journal ② Page 2

Date	Description	Post. Ref.	Debit	Credit
19xx	①	④		③
Jan. 30	Telephone Expense	513	70	
	Accounts Payable	212		70
	Received bill for			
	telephone expense			

General Ledger

Accounts Payable Account No. 212

Date	Item	Post. Ref.	Debit	Credit	Balance Debit	Balance Credit
19xx						
Jan. 5		J1		1,500		1,500
6		J1		2,600		4,100
9		J1	1,000			3,100
30		J2		70		3,170

Telephone Expense Account No. 513

Date	Item	Post. Ref.	Debit	Credit	Balance Debit	Balance Credit
19xx						
Jan. 30		J2	70		70	

The Trial Balance

The equality of debit and credit balances in the ledger can be tested periodically by preparing a **trial balance**. Figure 3-6 (next page) shows a trial balance for the Joan Miller Advertising Agency. It was prepared from the accounts in Figure 3-2. The steps to follow in preparing a trial balance are as follows:

1. Determine the balance of each account in the ledger.

Figure 3-6
Trial Balance

Joan Miller Advertising Agency
Trial Balance
January 31, 19xx

Cash	$ 1,720	
Accounts Receivable	2,800	
Art Supplies	1,800	
Office Supplies	800	
Prepaid Rent	800	
Prepaid Insurance	480	
Art Equipment	4,200	
Office Equipment	3,000	
Accounts Payable		$ 3,170
Unearned Art Fees		1,000
Joan Miller, Capital		10,000
Joan Miller, Withdrawals	1,400	
Advertising Fees Earned		4,200
Office Wages Expense	1,200	
Utility Expense	100	
Telephone Expense	70	
	$18,370	$18,370

Objective 8
Prepare a trial
balance and
recognize its
value and
limitations

2. List each account in the ledger that has a balance, with the debit balances in one column and the credit balances in another.
3. Add each column.
4. Compare the totals of each column.

In performing steps 1 and 2, recall that the account form in the ledger has two balance columns, one for debit balances and one for credit balances. The usual balance for an account is known as the normal balance. Consequently, if increases are recorded by debits, the normal balance is a debit balance; if increases are recorded by credits, the normal balance is a credit balance. The table below summarizes the normal account balances of the major account categories.

Account Category	Way of Recording Increases	Normal Balance
Asset	Debits	Debit
Liability	Credits	Credit
Owner's Equity		
Capital	Credits	Credit
Withdrawals	Debits	Debit
Revenues	Credits	Credit
Expenses	Debits	Debit

According to the table, the ledger account for Accounts Payable will typically have a credit balance and can be copied into the Trial Balance columns as a credit balance.

Once in a while, a transaction will cause an account to have a balance opposite from its normal account balance. Examples are when a customer overpays a bill or when a company overdraws its account at the bank by writing a check for more money than it has in its balance. If this happens, the abnormal balance should be copied into the Trial Balance columns.

The significance of the trial balance is that it proves whether or not the ledger is in balance. "In balance" means that equal debits and credits have been recorded for all transactions.

If the debit and credit columns of the trial balance do not equal each other, it may be the result of one or more of the following errors: (1) a debit was entered in an account as a credit, or vice versa, (2) the balance of an account was incorrectly computed, (3) an error was made in carrying the account balance to the trial balance, or (4) the trial balance was incorrectly summed.

The trial balance proof does not mean that transactions were analyzed correctly or recorded in the proper accounts. For example, there would be no way of determining from the trial balance that a debit should have been made in the Art Equipment account rather than the Office Equipment account. Further, if a transaction that should be recorded is omitted, it will not be detected by a trial balance proof because equal credits and debits will have been omitted. Also, if an error of the same amount is made both as a credit and as a debit, it will not be discovered by the trial balance. The trial balance proves only the equality of the debits and credits in the accounts.

Other than simply adding the columns wrong, the two most common mistakes in preparing a trial balance are (1) recording an account with a debit balance as a credit, or vice versa, and (2) transposing two numbers in an amount when transferring it to the trial balance (for example, transferring $23,459 as $23,549). The first of these mistakes will cause the trial balance to be out of balance by an amount divisible by 2. The second will cause the trial balance to be out of balance by a number divisible by 9. Thus if a trial balance is out of balance and the addition has been verified, determine the amount by which the trial balance is out of balance and divide it first by 2 and then by 9. If the amount is divisible by 2, look in the trial balance for an amount equal to the quotient. If such a number exists, it is likely that this amount is in the wrong column. If the amount is divisible by 9, trace each amount to the ledger account balance, checking carefully for a transposition error. If neither of these techniques identifies the error, it is necessary to recompute the balance of each account in the ledger and retrace each posting from the journal to the ledger.

Some Notes on Bookkeeping Techniques

Ruled lines appear in financial reports before each subtotal or total to indicate that the amounts above are to be added or subtracted. It is common practice to use a double line under a final total.

Dollar signs ($) are required in all financial statements including the balance sheet and income statement and in schedules such as the trial balance. On these statements, a dollar sign should be placed before the first amount in each column and before the first amount in a column following a ruled line. Dollar signs are *not* used in journals or ledgers.

On unruled paper, commas and periods are used in representing dollar amounts, but when paper with ruled columns is used in journals and ledgers, commas and periods are not needed. In this book, because most problems and illustrations are in whole dollar amounts, the cents column is usually omitted. When professional accountants deal with whole dollars, they will often use a dash in the cents column to indicate whole dollars rather than take the time to write zeros.

Chapter Review

Review of Learning Objectives

1. Explain in simple terms the generally accepted ways of solving the measurement problems of recognition, valuation, and classification.

To measure a business transaction, the accountant must determine when the transaction occurred (the recognition problem), what value should be placed on the transaction (the valuation problem), and how the components of the transaction should be categorized (the classification problem). In general, recognition occurs when title passes, and a transaction is valued at the cost or exchange price when the transaction is recognized. Classification refers to the categorizing of transactions according to a system of accounts.

2. Define and use the terms *account* and *ledger*.

An account is a device for storing data from transactions. There is one account for each asset, liability, and component of owner's equity, including revenues and expenses. The ledger is a book or file consisting of all of a company's accounts arranged according to a chart of accounts.

3. Recognize commonly used assets, liabilities, and owner's equity accounts.

Commonly used asset accounts are Cash, Notes Receivable, Accounts Receivable, Prepaid Expenses, Land, Buildings, and Equipment. Common liability accounts are Notes Payable, Accounts Payable, and Bonds or Mortgages Payable. Common owner's equity accounts are Capital, Withdrawals, Revenues, and Expenses.

4. State the rules for debit and credit.

The rules for debit and credit are (1) increases in assets are debited to asset accounts; decreases in assets are credited to asset accounts; (2) increases in liabilities and owner's equity are credited to liability and owner's equity accounts, decreases in liabilities and owner's equity are debited to liability and owner's equity accounts.

5. Apply the procedure for transaction analysis to simple transactions.

The procedures for analyzing transactions are to (1) analyze the effect of the transaction on assets, liabilities, and owner's equity; (2) apply the appropriate double-entry rule; and (3) make the entry.

6. Record transactions in the general journal.

The general journal is a chronological record of all transactions. The record of a transaction in the general journal contains the date of the transaction, the names

The Double-Entry System

of the accounts and dollar amounts debited and credited, an explanation of the journal entries, and the account numbers to which postings have been made.

7. Explain the relationship of the journal to the ledger.

After the transactions have been entered in the journal, they must be posted to the ledger. Posting is done by transferring each amount in the debit column of the journal to the debit column of the appropriate account in the ledger and transferring each amount in the credit column of the journal to the credit column of the appropriate account in the ledger.

8. Prepare a trial balance and recognize its value and limitations.

A trial balance is used to test the equality of the debit and credit balances in the ledger. It is prepared by listing each account with its balance in the appropriate debit or credit column. The two columns are added and compared to test their balance. The major limitation of the trial balance is that the equality of debit and credit balances does not mean that transactions were analyzed correctly or recorded in the proper accounts.

Self-Test

Test your knowledge of the chapter by choosing the best answer for each item below.

1. Deciding whether an expenditure for a desk is properly recorded as store equipment or office equipment is an example of
   - a. a recognition problem.
   - b. a valuation problem.
   - c. a classification problem.
   - d. a communication problem.
2. Deciding whether to record a sale when the order for services is received or when the services are performed is an example of
   - a. a recognition problem.
   - b. a valuation problem.
   - c. a classification problem.
   - d. a communication problem.
3. Recording an asset at its exchange price is an example of the accounting solution to the
   - a. recognition problem.
   - b. valuation problem.
   - c. classification problem.
   - d. communication problem.
4. The left side of an account is referred to as
   - a. the balance.
   - b. a debit.
   - c. a credit.
   - d. a footing.
5. Which of the following is a liability account?
   - a. Accounts Receivable
   - b. Withdrawals
   - c. Rent Expense
   - d. Accounts Payable
6. A purchase of office equipment on credit requires a credit to
   - a. Office Equipment.
   - b. Cash.
   - c. Accounts Payable.
   - d. Equipment Expense.
7. Payment for a two-year insurance policy requires a debit to
   - a. Prepaid Insurance.
   - b. Insurance Expense.
   - c. Cash.
   - d. Accounts Payable.
8. An agreement to spend $100 a month on advertising beginning next month requires
   - a. a debit to Advertising Expense.
   - b. a credit to Cash.
   - c. no entry.
   - d. a debit to Prepaid Advertising.
9. Transactions are initially recorded in the
   - a. trial balance.
   - b. T account.
   - c. general journal.
   - d. ledger.

10. The equality of debits and credits can be tested periodically by preparing a
  (a.) trial balance.   c. general journal.
  b. T account.   d. ledger.

Answers to Self-Test are at the end of this chapter.

Review Problem
Journal Entries, T Accounts, and Trial Balance

After graduation from veterinary school, Laura Cox entered private practice. The transactions of the business are as follows:

19xx
May 1   Laura Cox deposited $2,000 in her business bank account.
    3   Paid $300 for two months' rent in advance for an office.
    9   Purchased medical supplies for $200 in cash.
    12 Purchased $400 of equipment on credit, making a one-fourth down payment.
    15 Delivered a calf for a fee of $35.
    18 Made a partial payment of $50 on the equipment purchased on May 12.
    27 Paid a utility bill for $40.

Required

1. Record the above entries in the general journal.
2. Post the entries from the journal to the T accounts in the ledger.
3. Prepare a trial balance.

Answer to Review Problem

1. Recording journal entries

			General Journal			Page 1
Date			Description	Post. Ref.	Debit	Credit
19xx May	1		Cash		2,000	
			Laura Cox, Capital			2,000
			Laura Cox deposited $2,000 in her business bank account			
	3		Prepaid Rent		300	
			Cash			300
			Paid two months' rent in advance for an office			

(continued on next page)

Date		Description	Post. Ref.	Debit	Credit
19xx May	9	Medical Supplies		200	
		Cash			200
		Purchased medical supplies for cash			
	12	Equipment		400	
		Accounts Payable			300
		Cash			100
		Purchased equipment on credit, paying 25 percent down			
	15	Cash		35	
		Veterinary Fees Earned			35
		Collected fee for delivering a calf			
	18	Accounts Payable		50	
		Cash			50
		Made partial payment for the equipment purchased on May 12			
	27	Utility Expense		40	
		Cash			40
		Paid utility bill			

2. Posting transactions to the T accounts

Cash

5/1	2,000	5/3	300
5/15	35	5/9	200
		5/12	100
		5/18	50
		5/27	40
	2,035		**690**
Bal.	**1,345**		

Accounts Payable

5/18	50	5/12	300
		Bal.	**250**

Medical Supplies

5/9	200	

Laura Cox, Capital

		5/1	2,000

Prepaid Rent

5/3	300	

Veterinary Fees Earned

		5/15	35

Equipment

5/12	400	

Utility Expense

5/27	40	

3. Completion of trial balance

Laura Cox, Veterinarian
Trial Balance
May 31, 19xx

Cash	$1,345	
Medical Supplies	200	
Prepaid Rent	300	
Equipment	400	
Accounts Payable		$ 250
Laura Cox, Capital		2,000
Veterinary Fees Earned		35
Utility Expense	40	
	$2,285	$2,285

Chapter Assign-ments

Questions

1. What three problems underlie most accounting issues?

2. Why is recognition a problem to accountants?

3. A customer asks the owner of a store to save an item for him and swears that he will pick it up and pay for it next week. The owner agrees to hold it. Should this transaction be recorded as a sale? Explain.

4. Why is it practical for the accountant to rely on original cost for valuation purposes?

5. What is the basic limitation of using original cost in accounting measurements?

6. What is an account, and how is it related to the ledger?

7. "Debits are bad; credits are good." Comment on this statement.

8. Why is the system of recording entries called the double-entry system? What is so special about it?

9. Suppose that a system of double-entry bookkeeping were developed in which credits increased assets and debits decreased assets. How would accounting for liabilities and owner's equity be affected under that system?

10. Give the rules of debits and credits for (a) assets, (b) liabilities, and (c) owner's equity.

11. Why are the rules the same for liabilities and owner's equity?

12. What is the meaning of the statement "The Cash account has a debit balance of $500"?

13. What are the three steps in transaction analysis?

14. Tell whether each of the following accounts is an asset account, a liability account, or an owner's equity account:

a. Notes Receivable **e.** Prepaid Expense

b. Land **f.** Expense

c. Withdrawals **g.** Revenue

d. Bonds Payable

15. List the following six items in a logical sequence to illustrate the flow of events through the accounting system:

a. Analysis of transaction
b. Debits and credits posted from the journal to the ledger
c. Occurrence of business transaction
d. Preparation of financial statements
e. Entry made in a journal
f. Preparation of trial balance

16. What purposes are served by a trial balance?

17. Can errors be present even though the trial balance balances? Comment.

18. In recording entries in a journal, which is written first, the debit or the credit? How is indentation used in the general journal?

19. What is the relationship between the journal and the ledger?

20. Describe each of the following:

a. Account
b. Journal
c. Ledger
d. Book of original entry
e. Post. Ref. column
f. Journalizing
g. Posting
h. Footings
i. Compound entry

21. Does double-entry accounting refer to entering a transaction in both the journal and the ledger? Comment.

22. Is it possible or desirable to forgo the journal and enter the transaction directly into the ledger? Comment.

23. What is the normal balance of Accounts Payable? Under what conditions could an Accounts Payable account have a debit balance?

Classroom Exercises

Exercise 3-1
Transaction
Analysis
(L.O. 5)

Analyze each of the following transactions, using the form shown in the example below the list.

a. Lester Norris established Norris Barber Shop by placing $1,000 in a bank account.
b. Paid two months' rent in advance, $420.
c. Purchased supplies on credit, $60.
d. Received cash for barbering services, $50.
e. Paid for supplies purchased in c.
f. Paid utility bill, $36.

Example

a. The asset Cash was increased. Increases in assets are recorded by debits. Debit Cash $1,000.

The owner's equity Lester Norris, Capital, was increased. Increases in owner's equity are recorded by credits. Credit Lester Norris, Capital $1,000.

Exercise 3-2
Recording
Transactions in
T Accounts
(L.O. 4, 5)

Place the following T accounts on a sheet of paper: Cash; Repair Supplies; Repair Equipment; Accounts Payable; Sara deMaris, Capital; Sara deMaris, Withdrawals; Repair Fees Earned; Salary Expense; and Rent Expense. Record the following transactions directly in the T accounts using the letters to identify the transactions.

a. Sara deMaris opened the Home Repairs Service by investing $2,400 in cash and $800 in repair equipment.
b. Paid $300 for one month's rent.
c. Purchased repair supplies on credit, $400.
d. Purchased additional repair equipment, $300.
e. Paid salary of $450.

f. Paid $200 of amount purchased on credit in **c**.
g. Withdrew $600 from business for living expenses.
h. Accepted cash for repairs completed, $860.

Exercise 3-3
Trial Balance
(L.O. 8)

After recording the transactions in Exercise 3-2, prepare a trial balance for Home Repairs Service.

Exercise 3-4
Application of Recognition Point
(L.O. 1)

Clemente's Body Shop uses a large amount of supplies in its business. The following table summarizes selected transaction data for orders of supplies purchased.

Order	Date Shipped	Date Received	Amount
a	May 10	May 15	$1,400
b	16	22	800
c	23	30	1,200
d	27	June 2	1,500
e	June 1	5	1,000

Determine the total purchases of supplies for May alone under each of the following assumptions:

1. Clemente's Body Shop recognizes purchases when orders are shipped.
2. Clemente's Body Shop recognizes purchases when orders are received.

Exercise 3-5
Preparation of Trial Balance
(L.O. 8)

The following accounts of the Caldwell Service Company as of January 30, 19xx, are listed in alphabetical order. The amount of Accounts Payable is omitted.

Accounts Payable	?	Equipment	$12,000
Accounts Receivable	$ 2,000	Bill Caldwell, Capital	30,760
Building	34,000	Land	5,200
Cash	7,000	Notes Payable	20,000
		Prepaid Insurance	1,100

Prepare a trial balance with the proper heading and with the accounts listed in the correct sequence (see Figure 3-6). Compute the balance of Accounts Payable.

Exercise 3-6
Effect of Errors on Trial Balance
(L.O. 8)

Which of the following errors would cause a trial balance to have unequal totals? Explain your answers.

a. A payment to a creditor was recorded as a debit to Accounts Payable for $75 and a credit to Cash for $57.
b. A payment of $100 to a creditor for an account payable was debited to Accounts Receivable and credited to Cash.
c. A purchase of office supplies of $280 was recorded as a debit to Office Supplies for $28 and a credit to Cash for $28.
d. A purchase of equipment of $300 was recorded as a debit to Supplies for $300 and a credit to Cash for $300.

Exercise 3-7
Preparation of Ledger Account
(L.O. 7)

A T account showing the cash transactions for a month follows:

Cash

3/1	10,000	3/2	900
3/7	1,200	3/4	200
3/14	4,000	3/8	1,700
3/21	200	3/9	5,000
3/28	4,600	3/23	600

Prepare the account in ledger account form for Cash (Account 111) in a manner similar to the example in Figure 3-4.

**Exercise 3-8
Recording
Transactions in
General Journal
and Posting to
Ledger
Accounts**
(L.O. 6, 7)

On a sheet of notebook paper, draw a general journal form like the one in Figure 3-3, and label it page 10. After completing the form, record the following transactions in the journal.

Dec. 14   Purchased an item of equipment for $3,000, paying $1,000 as a cash down payment.
     28   Paid $1,000 of the amount owed on the equipment.

On a sheet of notebook paper, draw three ledger account forms like those shown in Figure 3-4. Use these account numbers: Cash, 111; Equipment, 143; and Accounts Payable, 212. After completing the forms, post the two transactions from the general journal to the ledger accounts, at the same time making proper posting references in the general journal.

**Exercise 3-9
Correcting
Errors in Trial
Balance**
(L.O. 8)

The following trial balance for Pearson Services at the end of July does not balance because of a number of errors.

**Pearson Services
Trial Balance
July 31, 19xx**

Cash	$ 1,630	
Accounts Receivable	2,830	
Supplies	60	
Prepaid Insurance	90	
Equipment	4,200	
Accounts Payable		$ 2,080
J. Pearson, Capital		5,780
J. Pearson, Withdrawals		350
Revenues		2,860
Salary Expense	1,300	
Rent Expense	300	
Advertising Expense	170	
Utility Expense	13	
	$10,593	$11,070

The accountant for Pearson has compared the amounts in the trial balance with the ledger, recomputed the account balances, and compared the postings. He found the following errors:

a. The pencil footing of the credits to cash was overstated by $200.
b. A cash payment of $210 was credited to cash for $120.
c. A debit of $60 to Accounts Receivable was not posted.
d. Supplies purchased for $30 were posted as a credit to Supplies.
e. A debit of $90 to Prepaid Insurance was overlooked and not posted.

f. The pencil footings for the Accounts Payable account were debits of $2,660 and credits of $4,400.

g. A Notes Payable account with a credit balance of $1,200 was not included in the trial balance.

h. The debit balance of J. Pearson, Withdrawals, was listed in the trial balance as a credit.

i. A $100 debit to J. Pearson, Withdrawals, was posted as a credit.

j. The Utility Expense of $130 was listed as $13 in the trial balance.

Prepare a corrected trial balance.

Interpreting Accounting Information

Published Financial Information: Zenith Radio Corporation (L.O. 3, 4, 6)

The condensed data below are adapted from the annual report of Zenith Radio Corporation, one of the world's largest manufacturers of television sets and other electronic entertainment products. All amounts are in millions of dollars.

	December 31, 1980
Accounts Payable	$ 59.1
Accounts Receivable	166.8
Buildings and Equipment	138.1
Cash	11.7
Inventories	235.8
Land	13.0
Long-Term Debt	160.0
Marketable Securities	51.6
Other Assets	9.5
Other Liabilities	145.3
Owners' Equity	291.0
Prepaid Expenses	28.9

The following quotations were also taken from the annual report:

Long-Term Obligations

"Total long-term debt increased to $160 million at December 31, 1980, from $110 million at year-end 1979. In 1980, $50 million of long-term debt due 2005, . . . , [was] sold to the public."

Capital Expenditures

"Zenith plans to use the [$50 million in proceeds] from the sales of the long-term debt, described previously, largely for investments in Buildings and Equipment related to color television assembly and picture tube manufacturing. Pending such use, at year-end 1980, the debt proceeds were invested in marketable securities."

Required

1. Using the data provided, prepare a balance sheet for Zenith at December 31, 1980.

2. What effect did the transaction described under "Long-Term Obligations" have on Zenith's balance sheet? Prepare the entry in general journal form to record the transaction.

3. From reading the information under "Capital Expenditures," you know what Zenith did with the proceeds of the sales of long-term debt in 1980 and what the company plans to do with the proceeds in 1981. Before it can carry out these plans, what transaction must occur? Prepare three entries in general journal form to record the one completed and two planned transactions. Use the account Marketable Securities to record entries related to the investments.

Problem Set A

**Problem 3A-1
Preparation of
Trial Balance**
(L.O. 8)

The Gibbons Construction Company builds foundations for buildings and parking lots. The following alphabetical list shows the account balances as of April 30, 19xx:

Accounts Payable	$ 4,400
Accounts Receivable	9,460
Cash	?
Construction Supplies	1,900
Equipment	24,500
Notes Payable	20,000
Office Trailer	2,200
Prepaid Insurance	4,600
Revenue Earned	17,400
Supplies Expense	7,200
Utility Expense	420
Sam Gibbons, Capital	40,000
Sam Gibbons, Withdrawals	7,800
Wages Expense	8,800

Required

Prepare a trial balance for the company with the proper heading. Determine the correct balance for the Cash account on April 30, 19xx.

**Problem 3A-2
Transaction
Analysis, T
Accounts, and
Trial Balance**
(L.O. 5, 8)

Christina Rogers opened a secretarial school called Modern Secretary Training.

a. As an individual, she contributed the following assets to the business:

Cash	$6,400
Typewriters	900
Office Equipment	1,200

b. Found a storefront for her business and paid the first month's rent, $260.
c. Paid $190 for advertisement announcing the opening of the school.
d. Enrolled three students in four-week secretarial program and two students in ten-day typing course.
e. Purchased supplies on credit, $330.
f. Billed enrolled students, $1,300.
g. Paid assistant one week's salary, $220.
h. Purchased a typewriter, $480, and office equipment, $380, on credit.
i. Paid for supplies purchased on credit in **e** above.
j. Repaired broken typewriter, $40.
k. Billed new students, $440.
l. Transferred $300 to personal checking account.
m. Received payment from customers previously billed, $1,080.
n. Paid utility bill, $90.
o. Paid assistant one week's salary, $220.
p. Received cash revenue from another new student, $250.

Required

1. Set up the following T accounts: Cash; Accounts Receivable; Supplies; Type-writers; Office Equipment; Accounts Payable; Christina Rogers, Capital; Christina Rogers, Withdrawals; Revenue from Business; Rent Expense; Advertising Expense; Salary Expense; Repair Expense; Utility Expense.
2. Record transactions by entering debits and credits directly in the T accounts, using the transaction letters to identify each debit and credit.
3. Prepare a trial balance using the current date.

Problem 3A-3
Transaction Analysis, General Journal, T Accounts, and Trial Balance
(L.O. 5, 6, 8)

Barry Fisher is a house painter. During the month of April, he completed the following transactions:

April 2 Began his business with equipment valued at $620 and placed $4,500 in a business checking account.
3 Purchased a used truck costing $1,100. Paid $400 cash and signed a note for the balance.
4 Purchased supplies on account, $320.
5 Completed painting two-story house and billed customer, $480.
7 Received cash for painting two rooms, $150.
8 Hired assistant to work with him, to be paid $6 an hour.
10 Purchased supplies, $160.
11 Received check from customer previously billed, $480.
12 Paid $400 on insurance policy for 18 months' coverage.
13 Billed customers, $620.
14 Paid assistant for 25 hours' work, $150.
15 Gasoline and oil for truck, $40.
18 Paid for supplies purchased on April 4.
20 Purchased new ladder (equipment) for $60 and supplies for $290 on account.
22 Received telephone bill, $60.
23 Received collection from customer previously billed, $330.
24 Transferred $300 to personal checking account.
25 Received cash for painting five-room apartment, $360.
27 Paid $200 on note signed for truck.
29 Paid assistant for 30 hours' work, $180.

Required

1. Prepare journal entries to record the above transactions in the general journal.
2. Set up the following T accounts and post all the journal entries: Cash; Accounts Receivable; Supplies; Prepaid Insurance; Equipment; Truck; Accounts Payable; Notes Payable; Barry Fisher, Capital; Barry Fisher, Withdrawals; Painting Fees Earned; Wages Expense; Telephone Expense; Truck Expense.
3. Prepare a trial balance for Barry Fisher Painting Service as of April 30, 19xx.

Problem 3A-4
Using General Journal, T Accounts, and Trial Balance
(L.O. 5, 6, 8)

The account balances for Norm's Barber Shop at the end of July are presented in the trial balance shown on the next page.
During August, Mr. Hopper completed the following transactions:

Aug. 1 Paid for supplies purchased on credit last month, $220.
2 Billed customers for services, $360.
3 Paid rent for August, $180.
5 Purchased supplies on credit, $150.

7   Received cash from customers not previously billed, $290.
8   Purchased new equipment from James Manufacturing Company on account, $1,300.
9   Received telephone bill for last month, $40.
12 Returned a portion of equipment which was defective. Purchase was made August 8, $320.
13 Received payment from customers previously billed, $190.
14 Paid telephone bill received August 9.
16 Took $110 from business for personal use.
19 Paid for supplies purchased on August 5.
20 Billed customers for services, $270.
23 Purchased equipment from a friend who is retiring, $280. Payment was made from personal checking account but equipment will be used in the business.
25 Received payment from customers previously billed, $390.
27 Paid electric bill, $30.
29 Paid $600 on note.

Norm's Barber Shop
Trial Balance
July 31, 19xx

Cash	$2,700	
Accounts Receivable	220	
Supplies	460	
Prepaid Insurance	400	
Equipment	4,400	
Accounts Payable		$ 300
Notes Payable		3,000
Norm Hopper, Capital		4,200
Norm Hopper, Withdrawals	420	
Service Revenue		1,380
Rent Expense	180	
Utility Expense	100	
	$8,880	$8,880

Required

1. Prepare journal entries to record the above transactions in the general journal.
2. Open T accounts for the accounts shown in the trial balance.
3. Enter the July 31 trial balance amounts in the T accounts. Write the abbreviation "Bal" before each amount to indicate that it is the beginning balance of the account.
4. Post the entries to the T accounts.
5. Prepare a trial balance as of August 31, 19xx.

Problem 3A-5
Relationship of General Journal, Ledger Accounts, and Trial Balance
(L.O. 6, 7, 8)

The Daycare Services Company provides baby-sitting and child-care programs. On February 1, 19xx, the company had a trial balance (account numbers) as follows:

Daycare Services Company
Trial Balance
February 1, 19xx

Cash (11)	$ 1,780	
Accounts Receivable (12)	1,600	
Equipment (21)	990	
Buses (22)	7,400	
Accounts Payable (31)		$ 1,470
Notes Payable (32)		7,000
Theresa Tetrault, Capital (41)		3,300
	$11,770	$11,770

During the month of February, the company completed the following transactions:

Feb. 2 Paid one month's rent, $140.
3 Received fees for one month's services, $400.
4 Purchased supplies on account, $85.
5 Reimbursed bus driver for gas expenses, $20.
7 Paid assistants for two weeks' services, $230.
8 Paid $170 on account.
9 Received $1,200 from customers on account.
10 Billed customers who had not yet paid for this month's services, $700.
11 Paid for supplies purchased on February 4.
13 Purchased playground equipment, $1,000.
14 Withdrew $110 for personal expenses.
17 Contributed equipment to business, $90.
19 Paid utility bills, $45.
22 Received fees for one month's services from customers previously billed, $500.
25 Paid assistants for two weeks' services, $320.
27 Purchased gas and oil for bus on account, $35.
28 Paid $290 for a one-year insurance policy.

Required

1. Enter the above transactions in the general journal (pages 17 and 18).
2. Open accounts in the ledger account form for the accounts in the trial balance plus the following accounts:

Account No.	Account Name
13	Supplies
14	Prepaid Insurance
42	Theresa Tetrault, Withdrawals
51	Service Revenue

61	Rent Expense
62	Bus Expense
63	Wages Expense
64	Utility Expense

3. Enter the February 1 account balances in the appropriate ledger account forms from the trial balance.

4. Post the entries to the ledger account. Be sure to insert the appropriate posting references in journal and ledger as you post.

5. Prepare a trial balance as of February 29, 19xx.

Problem 3A-6
Recording and
Tracing Trans-
actions from
General Journal
to Ledger
Accounts and
Trial Balance
(L.O. 6, 7, 8)

Mark Kaplan, a psychiatrist, opened an office near his home. For the first two weeks he kept his accounts informally in T accounts, but this system became confusing. He has now hired you to advise him on keeping records that are easier to understand. Dr. Kaplan's T accounts appear as follows:

Cash		11				Accounts Payable		31		
5/1 (a)	2,580	5/2 (b)	300		5/12 (h)	150	5/3 (c)	150
5/5 (d)	170	5/7 (e)	140				5/14 (j)	90
5/13 (i)	80	5/9 (f)	180					
		5/12 (h)	150					

Accounts Receivable		12				Notes Payable		32	
5/10 (g)	165	5/13 (i)	80			5/2 (b)	1,200

Supplies		13			Mark Kaplan, Capital		41	
5/3 (c)	150					5/1 (a)	2,800
5/14 (j)	90						

Prepaid Insurance		14			Treatment Revenue		51	
5/9 (f)	180					5/5 (d)	170
						5/10 (g)	165

Equipment		21			Rent Expense		61	
5/1 (a)	220				5/7 (e)	140	
5/2 (b)	1,500						

Required

1. **a.** Copy the transactions from the T accounts to the general journal (page 1), using the dates to identify each transaction in the general ledger.
   b. Post the transactions in four-column ledger account forms. Be sure to insert the appropriate posting references in journal and ledger as you post.
   c. Prepare a trial balance.

2. Explain to Dr. Kaplan the advantages of using the general journal and the four-column ledger account forms rather than entering transactions in T accounts.

Problem Set B

Problem 3B-1
Preparation of
Trial Balance
(L.O. 8)

The Esquire Theater shows first-run movies in a downtown location. The following alphabetical list shows the account balances as of October 31, 19xx:

Accounts Payable	$ 700
Accounts Receivable	2,400
Building	84,000
Cash	2,200
Land	12,000
Mortgage Payable	70,000
Office Equipment	3,600
Revenues from Ticket Sales	38,000
Salary Expense	28,000
Supplies Expense	1,800
Theater Equipment	7,400
Utilities Expense	340
Betty Ward, Capital	50,000
Betty Ward, Withdrawals	?

Required

Prepare a trial balance for the Esquire Theater with the proper heading. Indicate the correct amount for Betty Ward, Withdrawals.

Problem 3B-2
Transaction
Analysis, T
Accounts, and
Trial Balance
(L.O. 5, 8)

Charles Baxter opened a real estate agency called CB Realty Company.

a. He began his business by contributing the following assets to the business:

Cash	$11,000
Land	2,000
Building	30,000
Automobile	4,800

b. Paid $300 for advertisement announcing the opening of the agency.
c. Purchased office equipment on credit for $3,800 from Acme Furniture Company.
d. Earned and collected a commission of $2,400 from the sale of a house.
e. Purchased supplies for $1,200.
f. Paid one-half of the amount owed Acme Furniture Company.
g. Agreed to place $50 advertisement in newspaper.
h. Paid secretary $280.
i. Billed Nora Benson $3,600 for the commission on selling her house.
j. Paid utility bill, $140.
k. Received bill for advertising, $150.
l. Paid secretary $280.
m. Wrote check on CB Realty Account for personal expenses, $1,000.
n. Received partial payment from Nora Benson, $2,400.
o. Sold a house for a commission of $2,000, one-half of which was collected in cash and the other half of which is to be collected next month.
p. Purchased a three-year insurance policy, $960.

Required

1. Set up the following T accounts: Cash; Accounts Receivable; Supplies; Prepaid Insurance; Land; Building; Automobile; Office Equipment; Accounts Payable;

Charles Baxter, Capital; Charles Baxter, Withdrawals; Commission Revenue; Office Salary Expense; Advertising Expense; Utility Expense.
2. Record the transactions by entering debits and credits directly in the T accounts, using the transaction letters to identify each debit and credit.
3. Prepare a trial balance using the current date.

Problem 3B-3
Transaction Analysis, General Journal, T Accounts, and Trial Balance
(L.O. 5, 6, 8)

Jeanette Hobson, M.D., completed the following transactions in her medical practice during October 19xx.

Oct. 1 Began practice by investing $5,000.
2 Received a loan and signed a note to the bank for $20,000.
4 Purchased equipment on account, $5,600.
5 Purchased medical supplies for cash, $800.
6 Received cash from patients, $1,600.
7 Billed patients for medical services, $1,400.
8 Paid salaries:

Nurse $360
Receptionist $300

10 Purchased medical supplies on account, $500.
11 Paid two months' rent in advance, $600.
12 Paid two-year insurance policy, $560.
14 Returned for credit $80 of defective medical supplies purchased on October 10.
15 Paid cash to creditors from whom the equipment was purchased, $1,000.
16 Received cash from customers previously billed, $1,300.
20 Sold supplies to another doctor as a courtesy at cost, $100.
22 Paid salaries:

Nurse $360
Receptionist $300

23 Received bill for monthly laboratory expenses, $750.
26 Paid utilities, $200.
27 Billed patients for medical services, $1,600.
28 Received cash for services, $1,600.
29 Transferred $2,000 to Jeanette Hobson's personal account.

Required

1. Prepare journal entries to record the above transactions in the general journal.
2. Set up the following T accounts and post all the journal entries: Cash; Accounts Receivable; Medical Supplies; Prepaid Rent; Prepaid Insurance; Equipment; Accounts Payable; Notes Payable; Jeanette Hobson, Capital; Jeanette Hobson, Withdrawals; Medical Fees Earned; Nursing Salaries Expense; Office Salaries Expense; Laboratory Expense; Utility Expense.
3. Prepare a trial balance as of October 31, 19xx.

Problem 3B-4
Using General Journal, T Accounts, and Trial Balance
(L.O. 5, 6, 8)

The account balances for Inside-out Services Company on May 1, 19xx, are presented in the trial balance on page 95.
During May, Mr. Newsom completed the following transactions:

May 1 Bought supplies for $200 cash.
2 Purchased new equipment for $1,000 cash.

5   Billed customers for services, $540.
6   Collected $1,040 from customers billed last month.
8   Transferred to the company from his personal assets a special type of floor-cleaning equipment worth $460.
9   Received cash from customers for services rendered, $580.
12 Paid amount owed on account to creditors.
13 Made a $200 monthly payment on the note payable.
15 Paid wages for first half of month, $960.
16 Paid monthly rent, $280.
19 Gave a customer a $60 allowance on his account in settlement for faulty work.
22 Withdrew $1,200 from the business for personal expenses.
23 Billed customers for services rendered, $1,500.
24 Paid utility bill, $160.
25 Paid gas and oil bill for truck, $220.
27 Recorded cash collection from customers for services rendered, $480.

Inside-out Services Company
Trial Balance
May 1, 19xx

Cash	$ 2,980	
Accounts Receivable	1,560	
Supplies	940	
Prepaid Insurance	720	
Equipment	2,400	
Truck	5,400	
Accounts Payable		$ 760
Notes Payable		3,600
Jack Newsom, Capital		10,000
Jack Newsom, Withdrawals	1,260	
Service Revenue		3,480
Wages Expense	1,920	
Rent Expense	280	
Truck Expense	240	
Utility Expense	140	
	$17,840	$17,840

Required

1. Prepare the journal entries to record the above transactions in the general journal.
2. Open T accounts for the accounts shown in the trial balance.
3. Enter the May 1 trial balance amounts in the T accounts. Write the abbreviation "Bal" before each amount to indicate that it is the balance in the account from the previous month.
4. Post the entries to the T accounts.
5. Prepare a trial balance as of May 31, 19xx.

**Problem 3B-5
Relationship of
General Jour-
nal, Ledger
Accounts, and
Trial Balance**
(L.O. 6, 7, 8)

The Carlton Security Agency provides security services for apartment and office buildings in a densely populated metropolitan area on the Gulf Coast. On July 1, 19xx, the company had a trial balance (account numbers) as shown below.

Carlton Security Agency
Trial Balance
July 1, 19xx

Cash (11)	$14,400	
Accounts Receivable (12)	4,800	
Equipment (21)	13,000	
Patrol Cars (22)	24,800	
Accounts Payable (31)		$ 3,400
Andrew Parks, Capital (41)		53,600
	$57,000	$57,000

During the month of July, the company completed the following transactions:

July 1 Entered into a contract with Southern Management Company to provide services beginning July 1 to be billed monthly on the 15th of the month, $1,000 per month.

2 Paid rent for July, $400.

3 Paid $1,000 on account.

5 Purchased a new patrol car required for the Southern Management contract. The new car cost $7,200. The down payment was $1,200. A note was signed for the balance.

6 Received $4,000 from customers billed last month.

10 Purchased supplies for $200 and equipment for $750 on credit.

12 Billed customers for one month's service, $4,800.

14 Received $2,500 cash for providing security for a traveling fair.

15 Billed Southern Management for one month's service, $1,000.

16 Paid wages for one-half month, $2,200.

18 Andrew Parks took a car no longer needed in the business for his personal use. The car is recorded in the records at $1,800.

20 Paid cash operating expenses (other than wages and car expenses) of $1,120 during the month.

22 Drivers turned in gas and oil receipts of $750 and were reimbursed.

25 Andrew Parks took $1,400 for his personal expenses.

28 $2,000 was accepted in advance from Baker Realty for services to begin next month.

29 Paid wages for one-half month, $2,200.

Required

1. Enter the above transactions in the general journal (pages 10 and 11).
2. Open accounts in the ledger account form for the accounts in the trial balance plus the following accounts:

Account No.	Account Name
13	Supplies
32	Notes Payable
33	Revenue Received in Advance
42	Andrew Parks, Withdrawals
51	Revenue
61	Wages Expense
62	Car Expense
63	Rent Expense
64	Other Operating Expense

3. Enter the July 1 account balances in the appropriate ledger account forms from the trial balance.

4. Post the entries to the ledger account. Be sure to insert appropriate posting references to journal and ledger as you post.

5. Prepare a trial balance as of July 31, 19xx.

**Problem 3B-6
Recording and
Tracing Trans-
actions from
General Journal
to Ledger
Accounts and
Trial Balance**
(L.O. 6, 7, 8)

Helene Haas opened a television repair shop in her garage. She was successful and soon moved to a storefront, which she rented. She tried to keep her accounts informally in T accounts, but this system soon grew too complicated and confusing. Her T accounts appear as follows:

		Cash			11			Accounts Payable		31
8/1	(a)	3,400	8/2	(b)	200	8/12 (h)	150	8/4 (c)	150
8/9	(f)	60	8/6	(d)	500				
8/10	(g)	240	8/12	(h)	150				
8/13	(i)	30	8/15	(j)	200				

		Accounts Receivable			12			Notes Payable		32
8/7	(e)	120	8/13	(i)	30			8/6 (d)	1,000

		Repair Supplies		13			Helene Haas, Capital		41
8/2	(b)	200					8/1 (a)	4,000
8/4	(c)	150						

		Equipment			21			Repair Revenue		51
8/1	(a)	600	8/10	(g)	240			8/7 (e)	120
8/6	(d)	1,500						8/9 (f)	60

		Rent Expense		61
8/15	(j)	200		

Required

1. a. Copy the transactions from the T accounts to the general journal, using the dates to identify each transaction in the general ledger.

b. Post the transactions in four-column ledger account forms. Be sure to insert the appropriate posting references in journal and ledger as you post.

c. Prepare a trial balance.

2. What are the advantages for Helene Haas in using the system of general journal and four-column ledger account forms rather than entering transactions directly into T accounts as she had been doing?

Financial Decision Case 3-1

Gonzalez Repair Service Company
(L.O. 1, 3, 5, 8)

To start a home repair business, Luis Gonzalez engaged an attorney, who helped him start Gonzalez Repair Service Company. On March 1, Luis invested $10,000 cash in the business. When he paid the attorney's bill of $500, the attorney advised him to hire an accountant to keep his records. However, Luis was so busy that it was March 31 before he asked you to straighten out his records. Your first task will be to develop a trial balance based on a reconstruction of the March transactions. After considerable work, you come up with the information contained in the following paragraphs:

Immediately after the investment and the payment to the attorney, Mr. Gonzalez borrowed $4,000 from the bank. He later paid $140, which included interest of $40, on this loan. He also purchased a pickup truck in the name of the company, paying $1,500 down and financing the remaining $7,400. The first payment on the truck is due April 15. Luis then rented an office and paid three months' rent of $900 in advance. Cash purchases of office equipment in the amount of $700 and repair tools in the amount of $500 must be paid by April 10.

During March, Gonzalez Repair Service completed home repairs totaling $1,300, $400 of which were cash transactions. Of the credit transactions, $300 was collected during March, and only $600 remained to be paid at the end of the month. Wages of $400 were paid to employees. In the March 31 mail, the company received a $75 bill for March utility expenses and also a $50 check from a customer for repair work to be completed in April.

Required

1. Prepare a March 31 trial balance for Gonzalez Repair Service Company. To do so, you will first need to record the March transactions and then determine the balance of each T account.

2. Luis Gonzalez is not sure how to evaluate the information in your trial balance. He feels that his business is off to a better start than is indicated by the low Cash account. Explain why the Cash account is not an indicator of the earnings of the business. Also cite specific examples to show why it is difficult to determine net income by looking solely at the figures in the trial balance.

Answers to Self-Test

1. c	3. b	5. d	7. a	9. c
2. a	4. b	6. c	8. c	10. a

Chapter
Four

Business
Income and
Adjusting
Entries

In this chapter you will learn how accountants define business income. The chapter should also help you recognize the problems of assigning income to specific time periods. Then, through a realistic example, you can gain an understanding of the adjustment process necessary for measuring periodic business income. As a result of studying this chapter, you should be able to meet the learning objectives listed on the left.

Profitable operation is essential for a business to succeed or even to survive. So earning a profit is an important goal of most businesses. A major function of accounting, of course, is to measure and report the success or failure of a company in achieving this goal.

Profit has many meanings. One definition is the increase in owner's equity resulting from business operations. However, even this definition can be interpreted differently by economists, lawyers, business people, and the public. Because the word *profit* has more than one meaning, accountants prefer to use the term *net income*, which can be defined precisely from an accounting point of view. To the accountant, net income equals revenues minus expenses.

The Measurement of Business Income

Business enterprises are engaged at all times in activities aimed at earning income. As mentioned in Chapter 2, it would be fairly easy to determine the income of a company if we could wait until the business ceased to exist. However, the business environment requires a firm to report income or loss regularly for short and equal periods of time. For example, owners must receive income reports every year, and the government requires the company to pay taxes on annual income. Within the business, management often wants financial statements prepared every month, or more often, so that it can monitor performance.

Faced with these demands, the accountant measures net income in accordance with generally accepted accounting principles. Readers of financial reports who are familiar with these principles can understand how the accountant is defining net income and will be aware of its strengths and weaknesses as a measurement. The following paragraphs present the accounting definition of net income and explain the problems of implementing it.

Net Income

*Objective 1
Define net
income and its
components,
revenues and
expenses*

Net income is the net increase in owner's equity resulting from the operations of the company. Net income is measured by the difference between revenue and expenses:

$$net\ income = revenues - expenses$$

Revenues Revenues "are inflows or other enhancements of assets of an entity or settlement of its liabilities (or a combination of both) during a period from delivering or producing goods, rendering services, or other activities that constitute the entity's major or central operations."[1] In the simplest case, they equal the price of goods sold and services rendered during that time. When a business provides a service or delivers a product to a customer, it usually receives either cash or a promise to pay cash in the near future. The promise to pay is recorded in either Accounts Receivable or Notes Receivable. The revenue for a given period of time equals the total of cash and receivables from sales for that period.

As shown in Chapter 2, revenues are reflected by a rise in owner's equity. Note that liabilities are not generally affected and that there are transactions that increase cash and other assets but are not revenues. For example, borrowing money from a bank increases cash and liabilities but does not result in revenue. The collection of accounts receivable, which increases cash and decreases accounts receivable, does not result in revenue either. Remember that when a sale on credit took place, an asset called Accounts Receivable was increased, and at the same time an owner's equity revenue account was increased. So counting the collection of the receivable as revenue later would be counting the same sales event twice.

Not all increases in owner's equity arise from revenues. The investment in the company by an owner increases owner's equity, but it is not revenue.

Expenses Expenses are "outflows or other using up of assets or incurrences of liabilities (or a combination of both) during a period from deliv-

1. *Statement of Financial Accounting Concepts No. 3,* "Elements of Financial Statements of Business Enterprises" (Stamford, Conn.: Financial Accounting Standards Board, 1980), par. 63.

ering or producing goods, rendering services, or carrying out other activities that constitute the entity's ongoing major or central operations."[2] In other words, expenses are the costs of the goods and services used up in the course of gaining revenues. Often called the cost of doing business, expenses include the costs of goods sold, the costs of activities necessary to carry on the business, and the costs of attracting and serving customers. Examples are salaries, rent, advertising, telephone service, and the depreciation (allocation of the cost) of the building and office equipment.

Expenses are the opposite of revenues in that they result in a decrease in owner's equity. They also result in a decrease in assets or an increase in liabilities. Just as not all cash receipts are revenues, not all cash payments are expenses. A cash payment to reduce a liability does not result in an expense. The liability may have come from incurring an expense, such as for advertising, that is to be paid later. There may be two steps before an expenditure of cash becomes an expense. For example, prepaid expenses or plant assets (such as machinery and equipment) are recorded as assets when they are acquired. Later, as their usefulness expires in the operation of the business, their cost is transformed into expenses. In fact, expenses are sometimes called expired costs. Later in this chapter, we shall explain these terms and processes further.

Not all decreases in owner's equity arise from expenses. Withdrawals from the company by the owner decrease owner's equity, but they are not expenses.

Real and Nominal Accounts   As you saw in Chapter 2, revenues and expenses can be recorded directly as increases and decreases in owner's equity. In practice, management and others want to know the details of the increases and decreases in owner's equity caused by revenues and expenses. For this reason, separate accounts for each revenue and expense are needed. Since these accounts are temporary in nature, they are sometimes called nominal accounts. Nominal accounts show the accumulation of revenues and expenses during the accounting period. At the end of the period, their account balances are transferred to owner's equity. Thus, these nominal accounts start the next accounting period with zero balances and are ready to accumulate the specific revenues and expenses of that period. On the other hand, the balance sheet accounts, such as specific assets and liabilities, are called real accounts because their balances can extend past the end of an accounting period. The process of transferring the totals from the nominal revenue and expense accounts to the real owner's equity accounts is presented in Chapter 5.

The Accounting Period Problem

*Objective 2a
Recognize the difficulties of income measurement caused by the accounting period problem*

The accounting period problem recognizes the difficulty of assigning revenues and expenses to a short period of time such as a month or year. Not all transactions can be easily assigned to specific periods of time. Purchases of buildings and equipment, for example, have an effect that

2. Ibid., par. 65.

extends over many years of a company's life. How many years the buildings or equipment will be in use and how much of the cost should be assigned to each year must of course be an estimate. Accountants solve this problem with an assumption about **periodicity.** The assumption is that the net income for any period of time less than the life of the business must be regarded as tentative but still is a useful estimate of the net income for the period. Generally the time periods are of equal length to make comparisons easier. The time period should be noted in the financial statements.

Any twelve-month accounting period used by a company is called its **fiscal year.** Many companies use the calendar year, ending December 31, for their fiscal year. Many other companies find it convenient to choose a fiscal year that ends during a slack season rather than a peak season. In this case, the fiscal year would correspond to the natural yearly cycle of business activity for the company. Still other companies find it convenient to choose the same fiscal year as that used by many government units, which begins July 1 and ends June 30.

The Continuity Problem

Objective 2b
Recognize the
difficulties of
income measure-
ment caused by
the continuity
problem

Income measurement, as noted above, requires that certain expense transactions and revenue transactions be allocated over several accounting periods. This creates another problem for the accountant, who of course does not know how long the business will last. Many businesses last less than five years and, in any given year, thousands will go bankrupt. This dilemma is called the **continuity problem.** To prepare financial statements for an accounting period, the accountant must make an assumption about the ability of the business to continue. Specifically, the accountant assumes that unless there is evidence to the contrary, the business will continue to operate for an indefinite period. This method of dealing with the problem is sometimes called the **going concern** or continuity assumption.

For example, in measuring net income, the accountant must make assumptions regarding the life expectancy of most assets. It is a well-known fact that the value of assets often is much less if a company is not expected to continue in existence than if it is a going concern. However, we have already pointed out in Chapter 3 that the accountant, after recording assets at cost, does not record subsequent changes in their value. Assets become expenses as they are used up. The justification for all of the techniques of income measurement rests on this assumption of continuity.

If accountants have evidence that a company will not continue, of course, then their procedures must change. Sometimes accountants are asked, in bankruptcy cases, to drop the continuity assumption and prepare statements based on the assumption that the firm will go out of business and sell all its assets at liquidation values—that is, for what they will bring in cash.

Chapter Four

The Matching Problem

Objective 2c
Recognize the
difficulties of
income measure-
ment caused by
the matching
problem

Revenues and expenses may be accounted for on a cash received and cash paid basis. This is known as the **cash basis of accounting.** In certain cases, an individual or business may use the cash basis of accounting for income tax purposes. When this method is used, revenues are reported as earned in the period in which cash is received, and expenses are reported in periods in which cash is paid. Taxable income is therefore calculated as the difference between cash receipts from revenues and cash payments for expenses.

Even though the cash basis of accounting works well for some small businesses and many individuals, it does not meet the needs of most businesses. As explained above, revenues can be earned in a period other than when cash is received, and expenses can be incurred in a period other than when cash is paid. If net income is going to be measured adequately, revenues and expenses must be assigned to the appropriate accounting period. The accountant solves this problem by applying the **matching rule:**

Revenues must be assigned to the accounting period in which the goods were sold or the services performed, and expenses must be assigned to the accounting period in which they were used to produce revenue.

Though direct cause-and-effect relationships can seldom be demonstrated for certain, many costs appear to be related to particular revenue. So the accountant will recognize such expenses and related revenue in the same accounting period. Examples are the costs of goods sold and sales commissions. When there is no direct means of connecting cause and effect, the accountant tries to allocate costs in a systematic and rational way among the accounting periods that benefit from the cost. For example, a building is converted from an asset to an expense by allocating its cost over the years that benefit from its use.

Accrual Accounting

Objective 3
Define accrual
accounting and
explain two
broad ways of
accomplishing it

To apply the matching rule stated above, accountants have developed accrual accounting. Accrual accounting "attempts to record the financial effects on an enterprise of transactions and other events and circumstances . . . in the periods in which those transactions, events, and circumstances occur rather than only in the periods in which cash is received or paid by the enterprise."[3] In other words, accrual accounting consists of all the techniques developed by accountants to apply the matching rule. It is done in two general ways: (1) by recognizing revenues when earned and expenses when incurred and (2) by adjusting the accounts.

Recognizing Revenues When Earned and Expenses When Incurred The first method has already been illustrated several times in Chapter 3. For

3. *Statement of Financial Accounting Concepts No. 1,* "Objectives of Financial Reporting by Business Enterprises" (Stamford, Conn.: Financial Accounting Standards Board, 1978), par. 44.

example, when the Joan Miller Advertising Agency made sales on credit by placing the advertisements for clients (in the January 19 transaction), revenue was immediately recorded by debiting (increasing) Accounts Receivable and crediting the revenue account Advertising Fees Earned at the time of the sale. In this way, the credit sale is recognized before the collection of cash. Accounts Receivable, then, serves as a holding account until the payment is received. Also, when the Joan Miller Advertising Agency received the telephone bill on January 30, the expense was recognized both as having been incurred and as helping to produce revenue in the current month. The transaction was recorded by debiting Telephone Expense and crediting Accounts Payable. Until the bill is paid, Accounts Payable serves as a holding account. Recognition of the expense does *not* depend on payment of cash.

Adjusting the Accounts An accounting period by definition must end on a particular day. On that day, the balance sheet must contain all assets and liabilities as of the end of that day. The income statement must contain all revenues and expenses applicable to the period ending on that day. Although a business is recognized as a continuous process, there must be a cutoff point. Some transactions invariably span the cutoff point, and as a result some of the accounts need adjustment.

For example, consider the end-of-the-period trial balance for the Joan Miller Advertising Agency from Chapter 3 (also shown in Figure 4-1). On January 31, the trial balance contains prepaid rent of $800. At $400 per

Figure 4-1
Trial Balance
for the
Joan Miller
Advertising
Agency

Joan Miller Advertising Agency Trial Balance January 31, 19xx		
Cash	$ 1,720	
Accounts Receivable	2,800	
Art Supplies	1,800	
Office Supplies	800	
Prepaid Rent	800	
Prepaid Insurance	480	
Art Equipment	4,200	
Office Equipment	3,000	
Accounts Payable		$ 3,170
Unearned Art Fees		1,000
Joan Miller, Capital		10,000
Joan Miller, Withdrawals	1,400	
Advertising Fees Earned		4,200
Office Wages Expense	1,200	
Utility Expense	100	
Telephone Expense	70	
	$18,370	$18,370

Chapter Four

month, this represented rent paid in advance for the months of January and February. So at January 31, one-half of the $800, or $400, represents rent expense for January, and the remaining $400 represents the cost of asset services to be used up in February. An adjustment is needed to reflect the $400 balance of the Prepaid Rent account on the balance sheet and the $400 rent expense on the income statement. As you will see, several other accounts of the Joan Miller Advertising Agency do not reflect their proper balances. Like the Prepaid Rent account, they also need adjusting entries.

The Adjustment Process

Objective 4
State the four
principal situa-
tions that
require adjust-
ing entries

Accountants use **adjusting entries** to apply accrual accounting to transactions that span more than one accounting period. Adjusting entries are journal entries that have at least one balance sheet account entry and at least one income statement account entry. They are needed when deferrals or accruals exist. A **deferral** is the postponement of the recognition of an expense already paid or of a revenue already received. Deferrals would be needed in the following two cases:

1. There are costs recorded that must be apportioned between two or more accounting periods. Examples are the cost of a building, prepaid insurance, and supplies.
2. There are revenues recorded that must be apportioned between two or more accounting periods. An example is commissions collected in advance for services to be rendered in later periods.

An **accrual** is the recognition of an expense or revenue that has arisen but has not yet been recorded. Accruals would be required in the following two cases:

1. There are unrecorded revenues. An example is commissions earned but not yet collected or billed to customers.
2. There are unrecorded expenses. An example is the wages earned by employees in the current accounting period but after the last pay period.

Once again the Joan Miller Advertising Agency will be used to illustrate the kinds of adjusting entries that most businesses will have.

Apportioning Recorded Costs Between Two or More Accounting Periods (Deferrals)

Objective 5
Prepare typical
adjusting entries

Companies often make expenditures that benefit more than one period. These expenditures are generally debited to an asset account. At the end of the accounting period, the amount that has been used up in the period is transferred from the asset account to an expense account. Two of the more important kinds of adjustments are prepaid expenses and depreciation of plant and equipment.

Prepaid Expenses Some expenses are customarily paid in advance. These expenditures are called **prepaid expenses.** Among these items are rent, insurance, and supplies. At the end of an accounting period, a portion (or all) of these goods or services most likely will have been used up or will have expired. The part of the expenditure that has benefited current operations is treated as an expense of the period. On the other hand, the part not consumed or expired is treated as an asset that applies to the future operations of the company. If adjusting entries for prepaid expenses are not made at the end of the month, both the balance sheet and the income statement will be stated wrong. First, the assets of the company will be overstated; and second, the expenses of the company will be understated. For this reason, owner's equity on the balance sheet and net income on the income statement will both be overstated. Besides prepaid rent, the Joan Miller Advertising Agency has prepaid expenses for prepaid insurance, art supplies, and office supplies, all of which call for adjusting entries.

At the beginning of the month, the Joan Miller Advertising Agency paid two months' rent in advance. This expenditure resulted in an asset consisting of the right to occupy the office for two months. As each day in the month passed, part of the asset period expired and became a cost. By January 31, one-half had expired, and should be treated as an expense. The analysis of this economic event is shown below.

Prepaid Rent (Adjustment a)

Prepaid Rent

Jan.	2	800	Jan. 31	400

Rent Expense

Jan. 31	400	

Transaction: Expiration of one month's rent.
Analysis: Assets decreased. Owner's equity decreased.
Rules: Decreases in assets are recorded by credits. Decreases in owner's equity are recorded by debits.
Entries: Decrease in owner's equity is recorded by debit to Rent Expense. Decrease in assets is recorded by credit to Prepaid Rent.

	Dr.	Cr.
Rent Expense	400	
Prepaid Rent		400

The Prepaid Rent account now has a balance of $400, which represents one month's rent paid in advance. The Rent Expense account reflects the $400 expense for the month.

The Joan Miller Advertising Agency also purchased a one-year insurance policy, paying for it in advance. In a manner similar to prepaid rent, prepaid insurance offers protection that expires day by day. By the end of the month, one-twelfth of the protection had expired. The adjustment is analyzed and recorded as shown on the next page.

Chapter Four

Prepaid Insurance (Adjustment b)

Prepaid Insurance

Jan. 8	480	Jan. 31	40

Insurance Expense

Jan. 31	40

Transaction: Expiration of one month's insurance.

Analysis: Assets decreased. Owner's equity decreased.

Rules: Decreases in assets are recorded by credits. Decreases in owner's equity are recorded by debits.

Entries: Decrease in owner's equity is recorded by debit to Insurance Expense. Decrease in assets is recorded by credit to Prepaid Insurance.

	Dr.	Cr.
Insurance Expense	40	
Prepaid Insurance		40

The Prepaid Insurance account now has the proper balance of $440, and Insurance Expense reflects the expired cost of $40 for the month.

Early in the month, the Joan Miller Advertising Agency purchased art supplies and office supplies. As Joan Miller did art work for various clients during the month, art supplies were consumed. Her secretary also used up office supplies. There is no need to account for these supplies every day, because the financial statements are not prepared until the end of the month, and the record keeping would involve too much work.

Instead, Joan Miller makes a careful inventory of the art and office supplies at the end of the month. This inventory records the number and cost of those supplies that are still assets of the company—yet to be consumed. The inventory shows that art supplies costing $1,300 and office supplies costing $600 are still on hand. This means that of the art supplies originally purchased for $1,800, $500 worth were used up or became an expense. Of the office supplies originally costing $800, $200 worth were consumed. These transactions are analyzed and recorded as follows:

Art Supplies and Office Supplies (Adjustments c and d)

Art Supplies

Jan. 6	1,800	Jan. 31	500

Art Supplies Expense

Jan. 31	500

Office Supplies

Jan. 6	800	Jan. 31	200

Office Supplies Expense

Jan. 31	200

Transaction: Consumption of supplies.

Analysis: Assets decreased. Owner's equity decreased.

Rules: Decreases in assets are recorded by credits. Decreases in owner's equity are recorded by debits.

Entries: Decreases in owner's equity are recorded by debits to Art Supplies Expense and Office Supplies Expense. Decreases in assets are recorded by credits to Art Supplies and Office Supplies.

	Dr.	Cr.
Art Supplies Expense	500	
Art Supplies		500
Office Supplies Expense	200	
Office Supplies		200

The asset accounts of Art Supplies and Office Supplies now reflect the proper amounts of $1,300 and $600, respectively, yet to be consumed. In addition, the amounts of art and office supplies used up during the accounting period are reflected as $500 and $200, respectively.

Depreciation of Plant and Equipment When a company buys a long-lived asset such as a building, equipment, trucks, automobiles, a computer, store fixtures, or office furniture, it is basically buying or prepaying for the usefulness of that asset for as long as the asset provides a benefit to the company. Proper accounting therefore requires the allocation of the cost of the asset over its estimated useful life. The amount allocated to any one accounting period is called **depreciation** or **depreciation expense.** Depreciation is an expense just like any other cost incurred during an accounting period to obtain revenue.

It is often impossible to tell how long an asset will last or how much of the asset is used in any one period. For this reason, depreciation must be estimated. Accountants have developed a number of methods for estimating depreciation and for dealing with other complex problems concerning it. We will explain these methods in Chapter 13. Only the simplest case is presented here as an illustration.

Suppose that the Joan Miller Advertising Agency estimates that the art equipment and office equipment will last five years (sixty months) and will be worthless at the end of that time. The depreciation of art equipment and office equipment for the month is computed as $70 ($4,200 ÷ 60 months) and $50 ($3,000 ÷ 60 months), respectively. These amounts represent the cost allocated to the month, thus reducing the asset accounts and increasing the expense accounts (reducing owner's equity). These transactions can be analyzed as shown below. The use of the contra-asset account called Accumulated Depreciation is described in the next section.

Art Equipment and Office Equipment (Adjustments e and f)

Art Equipment	
Jan. 4 4,200	

Accumulated Depreciation, Art Equipment	
	Jan. 31 70

Office Equipment	
Jan. 5 3,000	

Accumulated Depreciation, Office Equipment	
	Jan. 31 50

Transaction: Recording depreciation expense. **Analysis:** Assets decreased. Owner's equity decreased.

Rules: Decreases in assets are recorded by credits. Decreases in owner's equity are recorded by debits.

Entries: Owner's equity is decreased by debits to Depreciation Expense, Art Equipment, and Depreciation Expense, Office Equipment. Assets are decreased by credits to contra-asset accounts Accumulated Depreciation, Art Equipment, and Accumulated Depreciation, Office Equipment.

Depreciation Expense, Art Equipment		Dr.	Cr.
Jan. 31 70	Depreciation Expense, Art Equipment	70	
	Accumulated Depreciation, Art Equipment		70
Depreciation Expense, Office Equipment	Depreciation Expense, Office Equipment	50	
Jan. 31 50	Accumulated Depreciation, Office Equipment		50

Accumulated Depreciation—A Contra Account Note that in the analysis of the case above, the asset accounts were not credited directly. Instead, new accounts—Accumulated Depreciation, Art Equipment, and Accumulated Depreciation, Office Equipment—were credited. These **accumulated depreciation** accounts are contra-asset accounts used to accumulate the total past depreciation on a specific long-lived asset. They are called **contra accounts** because they represent a balance that is subtracted from the balance of an associated account. In this case, the balance of Accumulated Depreciation, Art Equipment, is a deduction from the associated account Art Equipment. Likewise, Accumulated Depreciation, Office Equipment, is a deduction from Office Equipment. After these adjusting entries have been made, the plant and equipment section of the balance sheet for the Joan Miller Advertising Agency appears in Figure 4-2.

The contra account is used for two very good reasons. First, it recognizes that depreciation is an estimate. Second, the use of the contra account preserves the fact of original cost of the asset and shows how much of the asset has been allocated to expense as well as the balance left to be depreciated. As the months pass, the amount of the accumulated depreciation will grow, and so the net amount shown as an asset will be reduced. In six months, for instance, Accumulated Depreciation, Art Equipment, will have a total of $420; when this amount is subtracted from Art Equipment, a net amount of $3,780 will remain.

Other names are sometimes used for accumulated depreciation, such as "allowance for depreciation," or the wholly unacceptable term "reserve for depreciation." Accumulated depreciation is the newer, better term.

Figure 4-2
Plant and
Equipment
Section of
Balance Sheet

Joan Miller Advertising Agency
Partial Balance Sheet
January 31, 19xx

Plant and Equipment		
Art Equipment	$4,200	
Less Accumulated Depreciation	70	$4,130
Office Equipment	$3,000	
Less Accumulated Depreciation	50	2,950
Total Plant and Equipment		$7,080

Apportioning Recorded Revenues Between Two or More Accounting Periods (Deferrals)

Just as costs may be paid and recorded before they are used up, revenues may be received before they are earned. When such revenues are received in advance, the company has an obligation to deliver goods or perform services. Therefore, **unearned revenues** would be a liability account. For example, publishing companies usually receive payment for magazine subscriptions in advance. These payments must be recorded in a liability account. If the company fails to deliver the magazines for the subscription period, subscribers are entitled to their money back. As the company delivers each issue of the magazine, it earns a part of the advance payments. This earned portion must be transferred from the Unearned Subscription account to the Subscription Revenue account.

During the month, the Joan Miller Advertising Agency received $1,000 as an advance payment for art work to be done for another agency. Assume that by the end of the month, $400 of the art work was done and accepted by the other agency. This transaction is analyzed as follows:

Unearned Art Fees (Adjustment g)

Unearned Art Fees	
Jan. 31 400	Jan. 15 1,000

Art Fees Earned	
	Jan. 31 400

Transaction: Performance of services paid in advance.

Analysis: Liabilities decreased. Owner's equity increased.

Rules: Decreases in liabilities are recorded by debits. Increases in owner's equity are recorded by credits.

Entries: Decrease in liabilities is recorded by debit to Unearned Art Fees. Increase in owner's equity is recorded by credit to Art Fees Earned.

	Dr.	Cr.
Unearned Art Fees	400	
Art Fees Earned		400

The liability account Unearned Art Fees now reflects the amount of work to be performed, or $600. The revenue account Art Fees Earned reflects the amount of services performed during the month, or $400.

Unrecorded or Accrued Revenues

Unrecorded or **accrued revenues** are revenues for which the service has been performed or the goods delivered but for which no entry has been recorded in the accounts. Any revenues that have been earned but not recorded during the accounting period call for an adjusting entry that debits an asset account and credits a revenue account. For example, the interest on a note receivable is earned day by day but may not in fact be received until another accounting period. Interest Revenue should be credited and Interest Receivable debited for the interest accrued at the end of the current period.

Suppose that the Joan Miller Advertising Agency has agreed to place a series of advertisements for Marsh Tire Company and that the first appears on January 31, the last day of the month. The fee of $200 for this advertisement, which has now been earned but has not yet been recorded, should be recorded as shown below. Marsh will be billed for the series of advertisements when they are completed.

Unrecorded or Accrued Advertising Fees (Adjustment h)

Accrued Fees Receivable	
Jan. 31 200	

Advertising Fees Earned	
	Jan. 10 1,400
	19 2,800
	31 200

Transaction: Accrual of unrecorded revenue.
Analysis: Assets increased. Owner's equity increased.
Rules: Increases in assets are recorded by debits. Increases in owner's equity are recorded by credits.
Entries: Increase in assets is recorded by debit to Accrued Fees Receivable. Increase in owner's equity is recorded by credit to Advertising Fees Earned.

	Dr.	Cr.
Accrued Fees Receivable	200	
Advertising Fees Earned		200

Asset and revenue accounts now both show the proper balance: $3,000 in accrued fees receivable is owed to the company, and $4,400 in advertising fees has been earned by the company during the month.

Unrecorded or Accrued Expenses

At the end of an accounting period, there are usually expenses that have been incurred but not recorded in the accounts. These expenses require adjusting entries. One such case is borrowed money. Each day interest accumulates on the debt, and it is necessary to use an adjusting entry at the end of each accounting period to record this accumulated interest, which is an expense to the period, and the corresponding liability to pay the interest. Other comparable expenses are taxes, wages, and salaries. As the expense and the corresponding liability accumulate, they are said to accrue—hence the term accrued expenses.

Suppose that the calendar for January appears as shown in the following illustration:

January

Su	M	T	W	Th	F	Sa
	1	2	3	4	5	6
7	8	9	10	11	12	13
14	15	16	17	18	19	20
21	22	23	24	25	26	27
28	29	30	31			

By the end of business on January 31, the Joan Miller Advertising Agency's secretary will have worked three days (Monday, Tuesday, and Wednesday) beyond the last biweekly pay period, which ended on January 26. The employee has earned the salary for these days, but it is not due to be paid until the regular payday in February. The salary for these three days is rightfully an expense for January, and the liabilities should reflect the fact that the company does owe the secretary for those days. Because the secretary's salary rate is $600 every two weeks or $60 per day ($600 ÷ 10 working days), the expense is $180 ($60 × 3 days). This unrecorded or accrued expense can be analyzed as shown below.

Unrecorded or Accrued Wages (Adjustment i)

Wages Payable

	Jan. 31 180

Office Wages Expense

Jan. 12 600	
26 600	
31 180	

Transaction: Accrual of unrecorded expense.
Analysis: Liabilities increased. Owner's equity decreased.
Rules: Increases in liabilities are recorded by credits. Decreases in owner's equity are recorded by debits.
Entries: Decrease in owner's equity is recorded by debit to Office Wages Expense. Increase in liabilities is recorded by credit to Wages Payable.

	Dr.	Cr.
Office Wages Expense	180	
Wages Payable		180

The liability of $180 is now correctly reflected in the Wages Payable account. The actual expense incurred for office wages during the month is also correct at $1,380.

The Adjusted Trial Balance

*Objective 6
Prepare an
adjusted trial
balance*

In Chapter 3, a trial balance was prepared before any adjusting entries were recorded. After recording the adjusting entries in the general journal and posting them to the general ledger, it is desirable to prepare an **adjusted trial balance,** which shows all the changes in the accounts that have taken place as a result of the adjusting entries. Figure 4-3 shows the trial balance from Chapter 3, along with the adjusting entries and the resulting adjusted trial balance. If the adjusting entries have been posted correctly to the accounts, the adjusted trial balance should have equal debit and credit totals.

Using the Adjusted Trial Balance
to Prepare Financial Statements

The adjusted trial balance for the Joan Miller Advertising Agency now shows the correct balances for all the accounts. From this adjusted trial balance, the financial statements can be easily prepared. The income

Figure 4-3
Determination of the Adjusted Trial Balance

	Joan Miller Advertising Agency Preparation of Adjusted Trial Balance January 31, 19xx					
	Trial Balance		Adjustments		Adjusted Trial Balance	
Accounts	Debit	Credit	Debit	Credit	Debit	Credit
Cash	$ 1,720				$ 1,720	
Accounts Receivable	2,800				2,800	
Art Supplies	1,800			(c) $ 500	1,300	
Office Supplies	800			(d) 200	600	
Prepaid Rent	800			(a) 400	400	
Prepaid Insurance	480			(b) 40	440	
Art Equipment	4,200				4,200	
Accumulated Depreciation, Art Equipment				(e) 70		$ 70
Office Equipment	3,000				3,000	
Accumulated Depreciation, Office Equipment				(f) 50		50
Accounts Payable		$ 3,170				3,170
Unearned Art Fees		1,000	(g) $ 400			600
Joan Miller, Capital		10,000				10,000
Joan Miller, Withdrawals	1,400				1,400	
Advertising Fees Earned		4,200		(h) 200		4,400
Office Wages Expense	1,200		(i) 180		1,380	
Utility Expense	100				100	
Telephone Expense	70				70	
	$18,370	$18,370				
Rent Expense			(a) 400		400	
Insurance Expense			(b) 40		40	
Art Supplies Expense			(c) 500		500	
Office Supplies Expense			(d) 200		200	
Depreciation Expense, Art Equipment			(e) 70		70	
Depreciation Expense, Office Equipment			(f) 50		50	
Art Fees Earned				(g) 400		400
Accrued Fees Receivable			(h) 200		200	
Wages Payable				(i) 180		180
			$2,040	$2,040	$18,870	$18,870

statement can be prepared from the revenue and expense accounts, as shown in Figure 4-4 (next page). In Figure 4-5 (page 116), the balance sheet has been prepared from the balance sheet accounts, except for Joan Miller, Capital, which must come from the statement of owner's equity. Notice that the net income from the income statement is combined with withdrawals on the statement of owner's equity to give the net increase in Joan Miller's capital account of $590.

The Importance of Adjustments in Accounting

Objective 7
Relate the need
for adjusting
entries to the
usefulness of
accounting
information

One might ask, Why worry about adjustments? Doesn't everything come out all right in the end? The main reason for making adjustments is that they help accountants give accounting information that is useful to decision makers. For example, adjusting entries are necessary to measure income and financial position in a relevant and useful way. The management of a company wants to know how much it has earned during the last month, quarter, or year and what its liabilities and assets are at a certain date. This need is an important reason for making the adjusting entries. For instance, if the three days' accrued salary for Joan Miller's secretary is not recorded, the income of the agency will be overstated by $180 and the liabilities understated by $180.

Another important reason for the use of adjusting entries is that they allow financial statements to be compared from one period to the next. Management can see if the company is making progress toward earning a profit or if the company has improved its financial position. To return to our example, if the three days' accrued salary for Joan Miller's secretary is not recorded, not only will the income for January be overstated by $180, but the net income for February (the month when payment is made) will be understated by $180. This error will make the February earnings, whatever they may be, appear worse than they actually are. Look back over all the adjustments for the Joan Miller Advertising Agency for prepaid rent and insurance, art and office supplies, depreciation of office and art equipment, unearned art fees, accrued wages and expenses, and accrued advertising fees. These are all normal and usual adjustments; the combined effect of all of them on net income is significant.

Accountants also insist that adjusting procedures and entries be complete and consistent at the end of every accounting period because there is often more than one acceptable way to apply the matching rule in a given case. For example, there are several methods of determining the amount of depreciation expense for a given accounting period. Consequently, there is a need for the consistent application of accounting practice from one period to the next so that the financial statements of successive periods can be compared and understood. Accounting methods can be changed if new circumstances or other logical reasons require that they be changed. Since a change would make it hard to compare the financial statements of different periods, however, the company must explain in the

Figure 4-4
Relationship of Adjusted Trial Balance to Income Statement

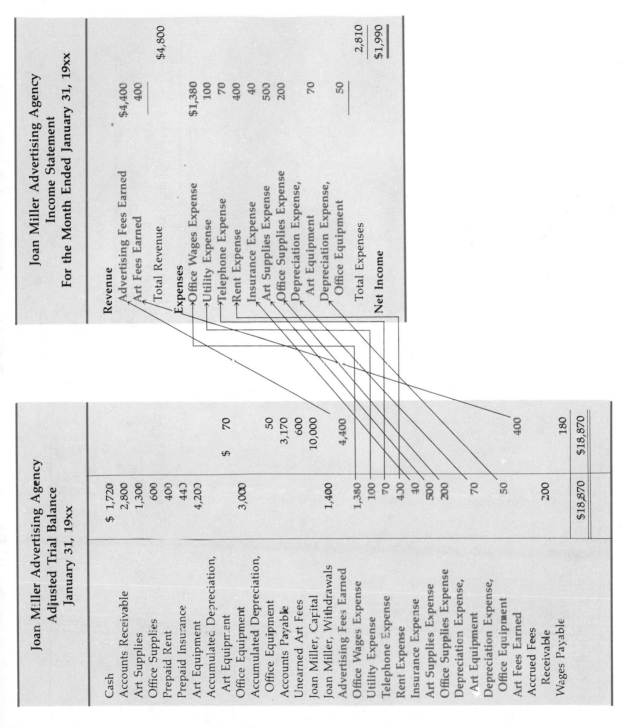

Figure 4-5
Relationship of Adjusted Trial Balance to Balance Sheet

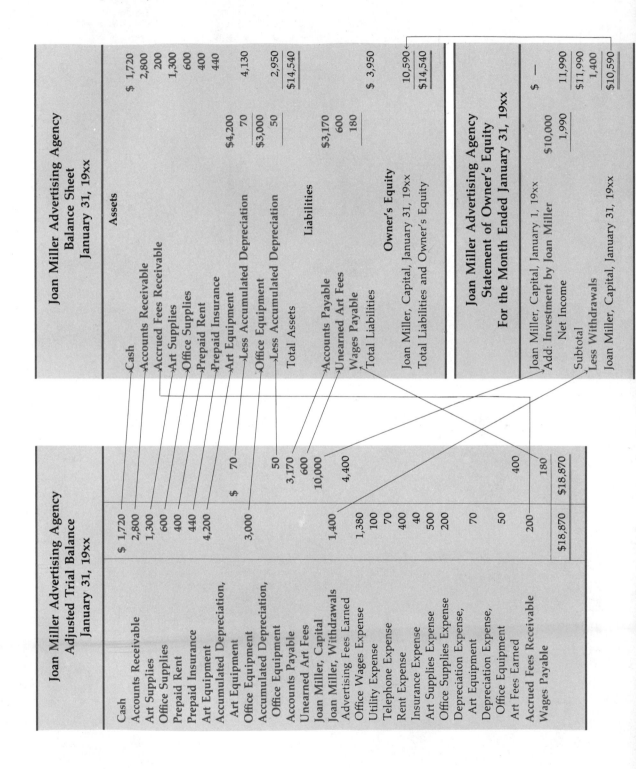

financial statements the nature and effect of the change. Without such a disclosure, the statement reader can assume that accounting methods have been consistently applied from one period to the next.

The adjustment process can also be related to the characteristic of verifiability. To the fullest extent possible, accounting practice should be based on objective, verifiable evidence. For example, transactions are recorded at cost because two independent parties have produced objective and verifiable evidence as to the value of the transactions. Accounting transactions should be supported by verifiable business documents. In making adjustments, a problem arises because estimates often must be used. Estimates, however, can be supported by objective evidence. For example, in estimating how long buildings or equipment may last, the accountant can rely on objective studies of past experience.

Correcting Errors

Objective 8
Prepare correct-
ing entries

When an error is discovered in either the journal or the ledger, it must be corrected. The method of correction will depend on the kind of error. However, the error must never be erased, because this action would seem to indicate an effort to hide something. If an error is discovered in a journal entry before it is posted to the ledger, a line drawn through the incorrect item and the correct item written above will suffice. Similarly, when a posting error involves entering an incorrect amount in the ledger, it is acceptable to draw a line through the wrong amount and write in the correct amount.

However, if a journal entry has been posted to the wrong account in the ledger, then it is necessary to prepare another journal entry to correct the error. For example, suppose that a purchase of art equipment was recorded as follows:

Feb. 20	Art Supplies	100	
	Cash		100
	To record purchase of art equipment		

It is clear that the debit should be to Art Equipment, not to Art Supplies. Therefore, the following entry is needed to correct the error:

Feb. 21	Art Equipment	100	
	Art Supplies		100
	To correct error of Feb. 20, when Art Supplies was debited in error for the purchase of art equipment		

The full explanation provides a record for those who might later question the entry. The Cash account is not involved in the correction, because it was correct originally. The effect of the correction is to reduce Art Supplies by $100 and increase Art Equipment by $100.

A Note About Journal Entries

Throughout Chapters 3 and 4, except in the above section, all journal entries have been presented with a full analysis of the transaction. This complete analysis was given to show you the thought process behind each entry. By now, you should be fully aware of the effects of transactions on the balance sheet equation and the rules of debit and credit. For this reason, journal entries will be presented in the rest of the book with explanations as shown in the section above.

Chapter Review

Review of Learning Objectives

1. Define net income and its components, revenues and expenses.

Net income is the net increase in owner's equity resulting from the profit-seeking operations of a company. Net income equals revenues minus expenses. Revenues are a measure of the asset values received from customers as a result of income-earning activity during a specific period of time. Expenses are the costs of goods and services used up in the process of obtaining revenues.

2. Recognize the difficulties of income measurement caused by (a) the accounting period problem, (b) the continuity problem, and (c) the matching problem.

The accounting period problem recognizes that net income measurements for short periods of time are necessarily tentative. The continuity problem recognizes that even though businesses face an uncertain future, accountants must assume that without evidence to the contrary, a business will continue indefinitely. The matching problem results from the difficulty of assigning revenue and expenses to a period of time and is solved by application of the matching rule.

3. Define accrual accounting and explain two broad ways of accomplishing it.

Accrual accounting consists of all the techniques developed by accountants to apply the matching rule. The two general ways of accomplishing it are (1) by recognizing revenue when earned and expenses when incurred and (2) by adjusting the accounts.

4. State the four principal situations that require adjusting entries.

Adjusting entries are required (1) when recorded costs are to be apportioned between two or more accounting periods, (2) when recorded revenues are to be apportioned between two or more accounting periods, (3) when unrecorded expenses exist, and (4) when unrecorded revenues exist.

5. Prepare typical adjusting entries.

Some of the more typical adjusting entries involve prepaid expenses such as rent, insurance, and supplies; depreciation of plant and equipment; unearned revenues; accrued expenses; and accrued revenues.

6. Prepare an adjusted trial balance.

An adjusted trial balance is a trial balance that is prepared after adjusting entries have been posted to the accounts in the ledger. Its purpose is to test the balance of the ledger after the adjusting entries are made and before financial statements are prepared.

7. Relate the need for adjusting entries to the usefulness of accounting information.

Adjusting entries are a means of implementing accrual accounting and thereby aid in producing financial statements that are comparable from period to period and relevant to the needs of users. Although adjusting entries often require estimates, the estimates are usually based on verifiable formulas or facts.

8. Prepare correcting entries.

When a correcting entry is required, it should be made in such a way as to adjust the appropriate accounts to the correct balances. A full explanation should accompany each correcting entry.

Self-Test

Test your knowledge of the chapter by choosing the best answer for each item below.

1. The net increase in owner's equity resulting from business operations is called
   a. net income.
   b. revenue.
   c. expense.
   d. asset.
2. The costs of the goods and services used up in the process of obtaining revenue are called
   a. net income.
   b. revenues.
   c. expenses.
   d. liabilities.
3. In general, the accounts in the income statement are known as
   a. real accounts.
   b. nominal accounts.
   c. unearned revenue accounts.
   d. contra-asset accounts.
4. A business may choose a fiscal year that corresponds to
   a. the calendar year.
   b. the natural business year.
   c. any twelve-month period.
   d. Any of the above.
5. Assigning revenues to the accounting period in which the goods were delivered or the services performed and expenses to the accounting period in which they were used to produce revenues is known as the
   a. accounting period problem.
   b. continuity assumption.
   c. matching rule.
   d. recognition rule.
6. Adjusting entries are essential to
   a. the matching rule.
   b. accrual accounting.
   c. a proper determination of net income.
   d. All of the above.
7. The adjustment for depreciation is an example of
   a. apportioning costs between two or more periods.
   b. apportioning revenues between two or more periods.
   c. recognizing an accrued expense.
   d. recognizing an unrecorded revenue.
8. Accumulated depreciation is an example of
   a. an expense.
   b. an unrecorded revenue.
   c. a liability.
   d. a contra account.
9. The recording of wages earned but not yet paid is an example of an adjustment that
   a. apportions revenues between two or more periods.
   b. recognizes an accrued expense.
   c. recognizes an unrecorded revenue.
   d. is none of the above.
10. Prepaid Insurance has an ending balance of $2,300. During the period, insurance in the amount of $1,200 expired. The adjusting entry would contain a debit

a. to Prepaid Insurance for $1,200.
b. to Insurance Expense for $1,200.
c. to Unexpired Insurance for $1,100.
d. to Insurance Expense for $1,100.

Answers to Self-Test are at the end of this chapter.

Review Problem
Adjusting Entries, T Accounts, and Adjusted Trial Balance

The unadjusted trial balance for Certified Answering Service appears as follows on December 31, 19xx:

Certified Answering Service
Trial Balance
December 31, 19xx

Cash	$2,160	
Accounts Receivable	1,250	
Office Supplies	180	
Prepaid Insurance	240	
Office Equipment	3,400	
Accumulated Depreciation, Office Equipment		$ 600
Accounts Payable		700
Revenue Received in Advance		460
James Neal, Capital		4,470
Answering Service Revenue		2,900
Wages Expense	1,500	
Rent Expense	400	
	$9,130	$9,130

The following information is also available:

a. Insurance that expired during December amounted to $40.
b. Office supplies on hand at the end of December totaled $75.
c. Depreciation for the month of December totaled $100.
d. Accrued wages at the end of December totaled $120.
e. Revenues earned for services performed but not yet billed on December 31 totaled $300.
f. Revenues earned for services performed that were paid in advance totaled $160.

Required

1. Prepare T accounts for the accounts in the trial balance.
2. Determine the required adjusting entries, and record them directly to the T accounts. Open any new T accounts as needed.
3. Prepare an adjusted trial balance.

Answer to Review Problem

1. T accounts set up and amounts from trial balance entered.
2. Adjusting entries recorded.

Cash		Accounts Receivable	
Bal. 2,160		Bal. 1,250	

Accrued Services Receivable		Office Supplies	
(e) 300		Bal. 180	(b) 105
		Bal. 75	

Prepaid Insurance		Office Equipment	
Bal. 240	(a) 40	Bal. 3,400	
Bal. 200			

Accumulated Depreciation, Office Equipment

		Accounts Payable	
	Bal. 600		Bal. 700
	(c) 100		
	Bal. 700		

Revenue Received in Advance		Wages Payable	
(f) 160	Bal. 460		(d) 120
	Bal. 300		

James Neal, Capital		Answering Service Revenue	
	Bal. 4,470		Bal. 2,900
			(e) 300
			(f) 160
			Bal. 3,360

Wages Expense		Rent Expense	
Bal. 1,500		Bal. 400	
(d) 120			
Bal. 1,620			

Insurance Expense		Office Supplies Expense	
(a) 40		(b) 105	

Depreciation Expense, Office Equipment

(c) 100	

3. Adjusted trial balance prepared (below).

Certified Answering Service
Adjusted Trial Balance
December 31, 19xx

Cash	$2,160	
Accounts Receivable	1,250	
Accrued Services Receivable	300	
Office Supplies	75	
Prepaid Insurance	200	
Office Equipment	3,400	
Accumulated Depreciation, Office Equipment		$ 700
Accounts Payable		700
Wages Payable		120
Revenue Received in Advance		300
James Neal, Capital		4,470
Answering Service Revenue		3,360
Wages Expense	1,620	
Rent Expense	400	
Insurance Expense	40	
Office Supplies Expense	105	
Depreciation Expense, Office Equipment	100	
	$9,650	$9,650

Chapter Assignments

Questions

1. Why does the accountant use the term *net income* instead of *profit?*
2. Define the terms *revenues* and *expenses.*
3. Why are income statement accounts called nominal accounts?
4. Why does the need for the accounting period cause problems?
5. What is the significance of the continuity assumption?
6. "The matching rule is the most significant concept in accounting." Do you agree with this statement? Explain.
7. What is the difference between the cash basis and the accrual basis of accounting?
8. In what two ways is accrual accounting accomplished?
9. Why do adjusting entries need to be made?
10. What are the four situations that require adjusting entries? Give an example of each.
11. Explain the statement, "Some assets are expenses that have not expired."
12. What is a contra account? Give an example.
13. What do plant and equipment, office supplies, and prepaid insurance have in common?
14. What is the difference between accumulated depreciation and depreciation expense?

15. Why are contra accounts used in recording depreciation?

16. How does unearned revenue arise? Give an example.

17. Where does unearned revenue appear on the balance sheet?

18. What accounting problem does a magazine publisher who sells three-year subscriptions have?

19. What is an accrued expense? Give three examples.

20. Under what circumstances might a company have unrecorded revenue? Give an example.

21. Why is the income statement usually the first statement prepared from the trial balance?

22. "Why worry about adjustments? Doesn't it all come out in the wash?" Discuss.

23. What is the difference between a correcting entry and an adjusting entry?

Classroom Exercises

Exercise 4-1
Adjusting Entries for Prepaid Insurance
(L.O. 5)

An examination of the Prepaid Insurance account shows a balance of $1,627 at the end of an accounting period before adjustments.

Prepare journal entries to record the insurance expense for the period under each of the following independent assumptions:

1. An examination of insurance policies shows unexpired insurance that cost $987 at the end of the period.

2. An examination of insurance policies shows insurance that cost $347 has expired during the period.

Exercise 4-2
Supplies Account—Missing Data
(L.O. 5)

Determine the amounts indicated by question marks in the columns below. Consider each column a separate problem.

	a	b	c	d
Supplies on hand July 1	127	224	84	?
Supplies purchased during month	26	?	87	746
Supplies consumed during month	87	486	?	916
Supplies remaining on July 31	?	218	28	494

Exercise 4-3
Adjusting Entry for Accrued Salaries
(L.O. 5)

Standco pays salaries of $35,000 each Friday.

1. Make the adjusting entry required on May 31, assuming that June 1 falls on a Thursday.

2. Make the entry to pay the salaries on June 2.

Exercise 4-4
Adjusting Entries
(L.O. 5)

Prepare year-end adjusting entries for each of the following:

a. Office Supplies had a balance of $285 on January 1. Purchases of supplies during the year amount to $415. A year end inventory reveals supplies of $75 on hand.

b. Depreciation of office equipment is estimated to be $1,450 for the year.

c. Property taxes for six months, estimated to total $750, have accrued but are unrecorded.

d. Unrecorded interest receivable on U.S. government bonds is $900.

e. The services for $300 of revenues received in advance have now been performed.

f. Services totaling $200 have been performed for which the customer has not yet been billed.

**Exercise 4-5
Relationship of
Expenses to
Cash Paid**
(L.O. 5)

The income statement for Ryan Company included the following expenses for 19xx:

Rent Expense	$ 2,400
Interest Expense	1,800
Salaries Expense	37,500

Listed below are the related balance sheet account balances at year end for last year and this year:

	Last Year	This Year
Prepaid Rent	—	$ 200
Interest Payable	$ 600	—
Salaries Payable	2,500	5,000

1. Compute cash paid for rent during the year.
2. Compute cash paid for interest during the year.
3. Compute cash paid for salaries during the year.

**Exercise 4-6
Accounting for
Revenue
Received in
Advance**
(L.O. 5, 7)

Beth Liepo, a lawyer, was paid $18,000 on September 1 to represent a client in certain real estate negotiations during the next twelve months.

Give the entries required on September 1 and at the end of the year, December 31. How would this transaction affect the balance sheet and income statement on December 31?

**Exercise 4-7
Correction of
Errors**
(L.O. 8)

A number of errors in journalizing and posting transactions are described below. Prepare the journal entries to correct the errors.

1. Rent payment of $250 for the current month was recorded as a debit to Prepaid Rent and a credit to Cash.
2. A $100 cash payment for equipment repair expense was recorded as a debit to Equipment.
3. Payment of $340 to a creditor was recorded as a debit to Accounts Payable and a credit to Cash in the amount of $430.
4. Payment of the gas and oil bill of $80 for the owner's personal car was recorded as a debit to Delivery Truck Expense and a credit to Cash.
5. A cash receipt of $100 for services yet to be performed was debited to Cash and credited to Revenue.

Interpreting Accounting Information

**Published
Financial Infor-
mation: City of
Chicago**
(L.O. 2, 3)

In 1979, Mayor Jane Byrne won the election in the city of Chicago partly on the basis of her charge that Michael Bilandic, the former mayor, had caused a budget deficit. Taking office in 1980, she hired a major international accounting firm, Peat, Marwick, Mitchell & Co., to straighten things out. The following excerpt appeared in an article from a leading Chicago business publication:

> [A riddle]
> Q: When is a budget deficit not a deficit?
> A: When it is a surplus, of course.

Chicago Mayor Jane Byrne was once again caught with egg on her face last week as she and her financial advisers tried to defend that riddle. On one hand, Comptroller Daniel J. Grim [Byrne appointee], explaining $75 million in assets the mayor [Byrne] hopes to hold in reserve in the 1981 Chicago city budget, testified in hearings that the city had actually ended 1979 with a $6 million surplus, not the much-reported deficit. He said further that the modest surplus grew to $54 million as a result of tax-enrichment supplements to the 1979 balance sheet.

On the other hand, the mayor stuck by the same guns she used last year on her predecessor: The city had ended 1979, under the Michael Bilandic Administration, not merely without a surplus, but with a deficit. The apparent discrepancy can be explained.[4]

Like most U.S. cities, Chicago operates under the modified accrual accounting basis. This is a combination of the straight cash basis and the accrual basis. The modified accrual basis differs from the accrual method in that an account receivable is recorded only when it is collected in the next accounting period. The collection of Chicago's parking tax, which is assessed on all city parking lots and garages, is an example:

The tax is assessed and collected on a quarterly basis but the city doesn't collect the amount due for the last quarter of 1980 until the first quarter of 1981. Under ideal accrual methods, the parking revenues should be recorded in the 1980 financial statement. Under a cash approach, the revenues would be recorded in the 1981 budget. What the city did before was to record the money whenever it was advantageous politically. That, combined with the infamous revolving funds, allowed the city to hide the fact it was running large deficits under [former] Mayor Bilandic. That also means that no one really knew where the city stood.[5]

The auditors are now reallocating the parking revenues to the 1981 budget but are accruing other revenues by shifting the period of collection from a year in the past. Overall, more revenues were moved into earlier fiscal years than were moved into later years, inflating those budgets. That's why the 1979 deficit is now a surplus.

The upshot is that both Mayor Byrne and Mr. Grim [the comptroller] were correct. There was a deficit in the 1979 corporate or checkbook fund, but because of corrections taking place now, a surplus exists.[6]

Required

1. Do you agree with the auditors' handling of the parking revenues? Support your answer by explaining which method of accounting you think a city should follow.
2. Comment on the statement, "Systematically applied accounting principles will allow all to know exactly where the city stands," made by the author in another part of the same article that was quoted above.

Problem Set A

Problem 4A-1 Preparation of Adjusting Entries (L.O. 5)

On June 30, the end of the current year, the following information was available to aid the Storm Company accountants in making adjusting entries.

a. Among the liabilities of the company is a mortgage payable in the amount of $200,000. On June 30, the accrued interest on this mortgage amounted to $9,000.
b. On Friday, July 2, the company will pay its regular weekly employees $15,600.
c. On June 29, the company completed negotiations and signed a contract to provide services to a new client at an annual rate of $2,000.

4. Sally Saville, "1: There Was A Deficit; 2: There Is A Surplus," *Crain's Chicago Business* (December 8–14, 1980), pp. 1 and 29.
5. Ibid.
6. Ibid.

d. The Supplies account showed a beginning balance of $1,516 and purchases during the year of $3,667. The end-of-year inventory revealed supplies on hand that cost $1,186.

e. The Prepaid Insurance account showed the following entries at June 30:

Beginning balance	$1,350
January 1	2,800
May 1	3,636

The beginning balance represents the unexpired portion of a one-year policy purchased the previous year. The January 1 entry represents a new one-year policy, and the May 1 entry represents additional coverage in the form of a three-year policy.

f. The table below contains the cost and depreciation rates for buildings and equipment, all of which were purchased before the current year:

Account	Cost	Depreciation
Buildings	$175,000	4%
Equipment	218,000	10%

g. On June 1, the company completed negotiations with another client and accepted a payment of $18,000, which represented one year's services paid in advance. The $18,000 was credited to Services Collected in Advance.

h. The company calculated that as of June 30, it had earned $2,500 on a $7,500 contract that would be completed and billed in August.

Required

Prepare adjusting entries for each item listed above.

**Problem 4A-2
Determining
Adjusting
Entries from
Changes in
Trial Balance**
(L.O. 5)

The schedule below presents the trial balance and adjusted trial balance for the Associated Consultants Company on December 31.

**Associated Consultants Company
Adjusted Trial Balance
December 31, 19xx**

	Trial Balance		Adjusted Trial Balance	
	Debit	Credit	Debit	Credit
Cash	$ 12,786		$ 12,786	
Accounts Receivable	24,840		24,840	
Accrued Fees Receivable			600	
Office Supplies	991		86	
Prepaid Rent	1,400		700	
Office Equipment	6,700		6,700	
Accumulated Depreciation, Office Equipment		$ 1,600		$ 2,200
Accounts Payable		1,820		2,020
Notes Payable		10,000		10,000
Interest Payable				600
Accrued Salaries Payable				200
Unearned Fees		2,860		1,410

	Debit	Credit	Debit	Credit
Walter Fox, Capital		29,387		29,387
Walter Fox, Withdrawals	15,000		15,000	
Fees Revenue		58,500		60,550
Salary Expense	33,000		33,200	
Utility Expense	1,750		1,950	
Rent Expense	7,700		8,400	
Office Supplies Expense			905	
Depreciation Expense, Office Equipment			600	
Interest Expense			600	
	$104,167	$104,167	$106,367	$106,367

Required

Prepare in journal form, with explanations, the eight adjusting entries that explain the changes in the account balances from the trial balance to the adjusted trial balance.

Problem 4A-3 Determining Adjusting Entries and Tracing Their Effects to Financial Statements (L.O. 5, 6)

Having graduated from college with a degree in accounting, Cynthia Jackson opened a small tax preparation service to supplement family income. At the end of its second year of operation, the Jackson Tax Service has the following trial balance:

Jackson Tax Service
Trial Balance
December 31, 19xx

	Debit	Credit
Cash	$ 742	
Accounts Receivable	986	
Prepaid Insurance	240	
Office Supplies	782	
Office Equipment	4,100	
Accumulated Depreciation, Office Equipment		$ 210
Copier	2,800	
Accumulated Depreciation, Copier		360
Accounts Payable		635
Unearned Tax Fees		219
Cynthia Jackson, Capital		5,394
Cynthia Jackson, Withdrawals	6,000	
Fees Revenue		20,400
Office Salaries Expense	8,300	
Advertising Expense	650	
Rent Expense	2,400	
Telephone Expense	218	
	$27,218	$27,218

The following information was also available:

a. Supplies on hand, December 31, 19xx, were $212.
b. Insurance still unexpired amounted to $120.
c. Estimated depreciation of office equipment was $210.
d. Estimated depreciation of copier was $360.
e. The telephone expense for December is $19. This bill has been received but not recorded.
f. The services for all unearned tax fees had been performed by the end of the year.

Required

1. Open T accounts for the accounts of the trial balance plus the following: Insurance Expense; Office Supplies Expense; Depreciation Expense, Office Equipment; Depreciation Expense, Copier. Record the balances as shown in the trial balance.
2. Determine adjusting entries, and post them directly to the T accounts.
3. Prepare an adjusted trial balance, an income statement, a statement of owner's equity, and a balance sheet.

Problem 4A-4
Determining Adjusting Entries and Tracing Their Effects to Financial Statements
(L.O. 5, 6)

At the end of its accounting period, the trial balance for Lucas Dry Cleaning appeared as follows:

Lucas Dry Cleaning
Trial Balance
September 30, 19xx

Cash	$ 1,256	
Accounts Receivable	10,280	
Prepaid Insurance	1,700	
Cleaning Supplies	3,687	
Land	9,000	
Building	75,000	
Accumulated Depreciation, Building		$ 14,200
Delivery Truck	11,500	
Accumulated Depreciation, Delivery Truck		2,600
Accounts Payable		10,200
Unearned Dry Cleaning Fees		800
Mortgage Payable		60,000
Stanley Lucas, Capital		23,642
Stanley Lucas, Withdrawals	10,000	
Dry Cleaning Revenue		57,200
Laundry Revenue		18,650
Plant Wages Expense	32,560	
Sales and Delivery Wages Expense	18,105	
Cleaning Equipment Rent Expense	3,000	
Delivery Truck Expense	2,187	
Interest Expense	5,500	
Other Expenses	3,517	
	$187,292	$187,292

The following information is also available:

a. A study of insurance policies shows that $170 is unexpired at the end of the year.
b. An inventory of cleaning supplies shows $414 on hand.
c. Estimated depreciation for the year was $4,300 on the building and $1,300 on the delivery truck.
d. Accrued interest on the mortgage payable amounted to $500.
e. On August 1, the company signed a contract with Franklin County Hospital to dry clean, for a fixed monthly charge of $200, the uniforms used by doctors in surgery. The hospital paid for four months of service in advance.
f. Unrecorded plant wages totaled $982.
g. Sales and delivery wages are paid on Friday. The weekly payroll is $350. September 30 falls on a Thursday.

Required

1. Open T accounts for each account in the trial balance plus the following: Wages Payable; Accrued Interest Payable; Insurance Expense; Cleaning Supplies Expense; Depreciation Expense, Building; Depreciation Expense, Delivery Truck. Record the balances as shown in the trial balance.
2. Determine adjusting entries, and post each directly to the T accounts.
3. Prepare an adjusted trial balance.
4. Prepare an income statement, a statement of owner's equity, and a balance sheet.

Problem 4A-5
Determining
Adjusting
Entries and
Tracing Their
Effects to
Financial
Statements
(L.O. 5, 6)

The Elite Limo Service was organized to provide limousine service between the airport and various suburban locations. At the end of its first year of operation, its trial balance appeared as follows:

Elite Limo Service
Trial Balance
June 30, 19xx

Cash (111)	$ 10,414	
Accounts Receivable (112)	12,655	
Prepaid Rent (117)	12,000	
Prepaid Insurance (118)	4,900	
Prepaid Maintenance (119)	12,000	
Spare Parts (141)	11,310	
Limousines (142)	200,000	
Notes Payable (211)		$100,000
Norman Sims, Capital (311)		78,813
Norman Sims, Withdrawals (312)	20,000	
Passenger Service Revenue (411)		426,926
Gas and Oil Expense (511)	89,300	
Salaries Expense (512)	206,360	
Advertising Expense (513)	26,800	
	$605,739	$605,739

The following information is also available:

a. To obtain space at the airport, Elite paid two years' rent in advance when it began business.

b. An examination of insurance policies reveals that $3,600 expired during the year.

c. To provide regular maintenance for the vehicles, a deposit of $12,000 was made with a local garage. Examination of maintenance invoices reveals that there are $11,277 in charges against the deposit.

d. An inventory of spare parts shows $2,110 on hand.

e. Limousines are to be depreciated at the rate of 12.5 percent a year.

f. A payment of $10,500 for one year's interest on notes payable is now due.

g. Passenger Service Revenue includes $17,815 in tickets that were purchased by employers for use by their executives and that have not been redeemed.

h. The advertising expense includes $1,250 for billboard advertising that will begin in July.

Required

1. Open ledger accounts for the accounts in the trial balance plus the following ones: Prepaid Advertising (116); Accumulated Depreciation, Limousines (143); Unearned Passenger Revenue (212); Interest Payable (213); Rent Expense (514); Insurance Expense (515); Spare Parts Expense (516); Depreciation Expense, Limousines (517); Maintenance Expense (518); Interest Expense (519). Record the balances as shown in the trial balance.

2. Record the appropriate adjusting entries in the general journal (page 14).

3. Post the adjusting entries from the general journal to the ledger accounts, showing proper references.

4. Prepare an adjusted trial balance, an income statement, a statement of owner's equity, and a balance sheet.

Problem 4A-6
Correcting
Entries and
Adjusting
Entries and
Tracing Their
Effects
(L.O. 5, 6, 7, 8)

The Metropolitan Answering Service began business three months ago. Lillian Starr, the owner, discovered that when the trial balance below was prepared, it did not balance.

Metropolitan Answering Service
Trial Balance
March 31, 19xx

Cash	$ 1,907	
Accounts Receivable	3,744	
Office Supplies	746	
Office Equipment	2,117	
Communication Equipment	2,400	
Accounts Payable		$ 1,750
Lillian Starr, Capital		5,629
Lillian Starr, Withdrawals	2,100	
Answering Service Revenue		9,405
Wages Expense	1,900	
Rent Expense	800	
Office Cleaning Expense	300	
Insurance Expense	720	
	$16,734	$16,784

Lillian engaged an accountant to examine the records and find out what errors needed to be corrected and what adjustments needed to be made to compute net income for the first three months of operation. Upon examination of the records and documents, the accountant found the following items of interest:

a. A purchase of communication equipment for $50 was posted as a debit to Accounts Payable by mistake. The Communication Equipment part of the entry was recorded correctly.

b. The balance of Office Supplies was incorrectly computed, so that there was an understatement of $70.

c. A cash receipt of $80 was posted correctly to Answering Service Revenue, but was not posted to the Cash account.

d. Another cash receipt of $96 was recorded as a debit to Cash and a credit to Answering Service Revenue in the amount of $69.

e. A $183 purchase of office equipment was debited to Office Supplies.

f. The office equipment and communication equipment are depreciated at a rate of 16 percent per year (4 percent for each three-month period).

g. An invoice for office cleaning expenses for $75 was unrecorded and due to be paid.

h. An examination of other office cleaning expenses produced an invoice for $30 that had been paid and charged to expenses but had actually been for cleaning Starr's apartment.

i. At the end of March, several customers for whom services had been provided had not been billed. These services totaled $188.

j. An examination of the Answering Service Revenue account revealed that $881 represented payments for work that had not yet been performed.

k. On March 31, salaries in the amount of $60 had accrued.

l. The Rent Expense account includes a $200 prepayment of the last month's rent of a two-year lease.

m. The Insurance Expense account represents the cost of a one-year policy purchased on January 1.

n. Office supplies on hand were inventoried at $119.

Required

1. Open T accounts for the trial balance accounts plus the following ones: Prepaid Insurance; Prepaid Rent; Accumulated Depreciation, Office Equipment; Accumulated Depreciation, Communication Equipment; Wages Payable; Unearned Answering Service Revenue; Office Supplies Expense; Depreciation Expense, Office Equipment; Depreciation Expense, Communication Equipment. Record the balances as shown in the trial balance.

2. Using data from items a through c above, prepare a trial balance that balances, and post the corrections to the T accounts.

3. Using the data from items d through n above, prepare adjusting and correcting entries, and post them directly to the T accounts.

4. Prepare an adjusted trial balance, an income statement, a statement of owner's equity, and a balance sheet.

Problem Set B

**Problem 4B-1
Preparation of
Adjusting
Entries
(L.O. 5)**

On December 31, at the end of the current year, the following information was available to aid the Marshall Company accountants in making adjusting entries.

a. The Office Supplies account showed a beginning balance of $768 and purchases during the year of $1,724. The end-of-year inventory revealed $727 worth of supplies on hand.

b. The Prepaid Insurance account showed the following debit entries at December 31:

Jan. 1 Balance	120
June 1	540
Sept. 1	420

The January 1 balance represents the unexpired portion of a one-year insurance policy purchased the previous year. The June 1 purchase represents a three-year policy, and the September 1 entry is the cost of a one-year policy.

c. Among the liabilities of the company are notes payable in the face amount of $20,000. On December 31, the accrued interest on these notes amounted to $1,000.

d. The company purchased a building on July 1 of the current year for $35,500. The company estimates the depreciation for the current year to be $710.

e. The company owns some land that it leases for a parking lot. On September 1, the tenant paid one year's rent of $2,400 in advance. The total was credited to Unearned Rent Income.

f. On December 26, the company agreed to rent a truck for $310 a month beginning January 1.

g. On Friday, January 3, the company will pay its weekly employees $760 for the regular five-day pay period, which began on Monday.

h. On December 31, the company had completed services representing $1,800 of a $6,500 contract on which the remaining services would be performed in the next fiscal year.

Required

Prepare adjusting entries for each item listed above.

Problem 4B-2
Determining Adjusting Entries from Changes in Trial Balance
(L.O. 5)

The schedule below presents the trial balance and adjusted trial balance for the Executive Investment Advisory Service on December 31.

Executive Investment Advisory Service
Adjusted Trial Balance
December 31, 19xx

	Trial Balance		Adjusted Trial Balance	
	Debit	Credit	Debit	Credit
Cash	$ 7,500		$ 7,500	
Accounts Receivable	3,750		3,750	
Office Supplies	1,210		120	
Prepaid Rent	600		200	
Office Equipment	4,200		4,200	
Accumulated Depreciation, Office Equipment		$ 700		$ 800
Accounts Payable		2,700		2,850
Notes Payable		5,000		5,000
Interest Payable				250

Unearned Fees		1,350		530
Sylvia Jarvis, Capital		10,910		10,910
Sylvia Jarvis, Withdrawals	10,000		10,000	
Fees Revenue		33,000		34,820
Salary Expense	22,000		22,000	
Utility Expense	2,400		2,550	
Rent Expense	2,000		2,400	
Office Supplies Expense			1,090	
Depreciation Expense, Office Equipment			100	
Interest Expense			250	
Accrued Fees Receivable			1,000	
	$53,660	$53,660	$55,160	$55,160

Required

Prepare in journal form, with explanations, the seven adjusting entries that explain the changes in the account balances from the trial balance to the adjusted trial balance.

Problem 4B-3
Determining Adjusting Entries and Tracing Their Effects to Financial Statements
(L.O. 5, 6)

A trial balance for Brent Real Estate at the end of its accounting year is as follows:

Brent Real Estate
Trial Balance
December 31, 19xx

Cash	$ 4,275	
Accounts Receivable	2,325	
Prepaid Insurance	585	
Office Supplies	440	
Office Equipment	5,300	
Accumulated Depreciation, Office Equipment		$ 765
Automobile	6,750	
Accumulated Depreciation, Automobile		750
Accounts Payable		1,700
Unearned Management Fees		1,500
Henry Brent, Capital		14,535
Henry Brent, Withdrawals	14,000	
Sales Commissions Earned		31,700
Office Salaries Expense	12,500	
Advertising Expense	2,525	
Rent Expense	1,650	
Telephone Expense	600	
	$50,950	$50,950

The following information was also available:

a. Supplies on hand, December 31, 19xx, were $135.
b. Insurance still unexpired amounted to $270.
c. Estimated depreciation of office equipment amounted to $375.
d. Depreciation on the automobile was estimated to be one-ninth of its cost.
e. As of December 31, the rent of $150 for December had not been paid.
f. On August 1, the company signed a contract to manage a building for a fee of $125 per month. One year's management fees were collected in advance.

Required

1. Open T accounts for the accounts of the trial balance plus the following ones: Management Fees Earned; Insurance Expense; Office Supplies Expense; Depreciation Expense, Office Equipment; Depreciation Expense, Automobile. Record the balances as shown in the trial balance.
2. Determine adjusting entries, and post them directly to the T accounts.
3. Prepare an adjusted trial balance, an income statement, a statement of owner's equity, and a balance sheet.

Problem 4B-4
Determining
Adjusting
Entries and
Tracing Their
Effects to
Financial
Statements
(L.O. 5, 6)

At the end of the current fiscal year, the trial balance for Trans-America Movers appeared as follows:

Trans-America Movers
Trial Balance
June 30, 19xx

Cash	$ 14,200	
Accounts Receivable	18,600	
Prepaid Insurance	7,900	
Packing Supplies	10,400	
Land	4,000	
Building	80,000	
Accumulated Depreciation, Building		$ 7,500
Trucks	106,000	
Accumulated Depreciation, Trucks		27,500
Accounts Payable		7,650
Unearned Storage Fees		5,400
Mortgage Payable		70,000
Harry Rose, Capital		54,740
Harry Rose, Withdrawals	18,000	
Revenue from Moving Services		209,000
Storage Fees Earned		26,400
Driver Wages Expense	94,000	
Office Salaries Expense	14,400	
Office Equipment, Rent Expense	3,000	
Gas, Oil, and Repairs Expense	23,450	
Interest Expense	4,200	
Other Expenses	10,040	
	$408,190	$408,190

The following information is also available:

a. A study of insurance policies shows that $4,250 of coverage expired during the year.

b. An inventory of packing supplies shows $2,785 worth on hand.

c. Depreciation for the year on buildings amounts to $2,500 and on trucks $21,000.

d. Accrued interest on mortgage payable amounts to $1,400.

e. Storage fees in the amount of $1,950 of the total collected in advance have been earned by the end of the period.

f. Unrecorded drivers' wages total $1,300.

g. Office salaries are paid on Friday. The weekly payroll for office salaries is $300. June 30 falls on a Tuesday.

h. An estimate of $1,200 was given on June 30 to a customer for a moving job to be done in July.

Required

1. Open T accounts for each account in the trial balance plus the following ones: Wages and Salaries Payable; Accrued Interest Payable; Insurance Expense; Packing Supplies Expense; Depreciation Expense, Building; Depreciation Expense, Trucks. Record the balances as shown in the trial balance.
2. Determine adjusting entries, and post each directly to the T accounts.
3. Prepare an adjusted trial balance.
4. Prepare an income statement, a statement of owner's equity, and a balance sheet.

Problem 4B-5
Determining Adjusting Entries and Tracing Their Effects to Financial Statements
(L.O. 5, 6)

Commuter Airways was developed to provide direct air service between Chicago's Meigs Field, a downtown commuter airport, and Milwaukee. At the end of its second year of operation, its trial balance appeared as follows:

Commuter Airways Trial Balance December 31, 19xx		
Cash (111)	$ 36,700	
Accounts Receivable (112)	17,300	
Prepaid Rent (115)	24,000	
Prepaid Insurance (116)	7,200	
Prepaid Maintenance (117)	20,000	
Spare Parts (141)	22,200	
Aircraft (142)	460,000	
Accumulated Depreciation, Aircraft (143)		$ 46,000
Notes Payable (211)		280,000
Leon Kennedy, Capital (311)		236,500
Leon Kennedy, Withdrawals (312)	26,000	
Passenger Revenue Earned (411)		138,000
Gas and Oil Expense (511)	37,500	
Salaries Expense (512)	42,000	
Advertising Expense (513)	7,600	
	$700,500	$700,500

The following information is also available:

a. To guarantee space at Meigs Field and at Milwaukee Field, the company paid two years' rent in advance on January 1, 19xx.
b. An examination of insurance policies showed $4,200 was still unexpired.
c. Normal upkeep of the aircraft is provided under a maintenance contract that calls for a $20,000 deposit. Examination of maintenance invoices shows that $13,000 of the deposit has been used.
d. An inventory of spare parts shows $7,860 on hand.
e. Aircraft are being depreciated at 10 percent a year.
f. A payment of $25,200 for one year's interest on the notes payable is now due.
g. The passenger revenue earned included $4,000 for tickets for January flights purchased in advance by passengers.
h. The advertising expense contains $2,000 for radio commercials, which were paid for last month and will run one-half in December and one-half in January.

Required

1. Open ledger accounts for the accounts in the trial balance plus the following ones: Prepaid Advertising (118); Unearned Passenger Revenue (212); Interest Payable (213); Rent Expense (514); Insurance Expense (515); Spare Parts Expense (516); Depreciation Expense, Aircraft (517); Maintenance Expense (518); Interest Expense (519). Record the balances as shown in the trial balance.
2. Record the appropriate adjusting entries in the general journal (page 28).
3. Post the adjusting entries to the ledger accounts, showing proper references.
4. Prepare an adjusted trial balance, an income statement, a statement of owner's equity, and a balance sheet.

Problem 4B-6
Correcting
Entries and
Adjusting
Entries and
Tracing Their
Effects
(L.O. 5, 6, 7, 8)

The Nu-Way Janitorial Service began business six months ago. Art Slaughter, the owner, discovered that when the trial balance was prepared, it did not balance.

Nu-Way Janitorial Service
Trial Balance
June 30, 19xx

Cash	$ 495	
Accounts Receivable	856	
Cleaning Supplies	1,336	
Cleaning Equipment	1,740	
Truck	3,600	
Accounts Payable		$ 370
Art Slaughter, Capital		7,517
Art Slaughter, Withdrawals	3,000	
Janitorial Revenue		7,420
Wages Expense	2,400	
Rent Expense	700	
Gas, Oil, and Other Truck Expense	340	
Insurance Expense	380	
	$14,847	$15,307

Art hired an accountant to straighten out the books and determine whether he had made a profit during his first six months in business. Upon examination of the records and documents, the accountant found the following items of interest:

a. The Accounts Payable balance was incorrectly computed, so that there was an overstatement of $200.

b. A $60 cash purchase of supplies was posted to the Cash account but not to the Cleaning Supplies account.

c. A receipt of $100 for janitorial services was credited to Cash by mistake.

d. Cash of $120 received from a customer was recorded as a debit to Cash and a credit to Accounts Receivable in the amount of $210.

e. A $140 purchase of cleaning supplies was debited to Cleaning Equipment.

f. The cleaning equipment and truck are depreciated at the rate of 20 percent per year (10 percent for each six months).

g. Invoices for gas and oil totaling $40 were unrecorded and are due to be paid.

h. An examination of other gas and oil invoices showed that $90 had been paid and charged to expenses but had actually been for Art's personal car.

i. During the last week of June, Art completed some work but has not yet billed customers for $350.

j. Upon examination of the Janitorial Revenue account, it was found that $460 represented a payment in advance for work to be performed next month.

k. On June 30, Art also owed his one employee $40 for two days' work. This amount would be paid on Friday, three days from this date.

l. The Rent Expense account represented a $100 payment made on January 1 toward the last month's rent of a three-year lease plus $100 rent per month for each of the past six months.

m. The insurance expense was the cost of a one-year policy purchased January 1.

n. Supplies on hand were inventoried at $76.

Required

1. Open T accounts for the trial balance accounts plus the following ones: Prepaid Insurance; Prepaid Rent; Accumulated Depreciation, Cleaning Equipment; Accumulated Depreciation, Truck; Wages Payable; Unearned Janitorial Revenue; Supplies Expense; Depreciation Expense, Cleaning Equipment; Depreciation Expense, Truck. Record the balances as shown in the trial balance.

2. Using data from Items a through c above, prepare a trial balance that balances, and post the corrections to the T accounts.

3. Using data from items d through n above, prepare adjusting and correcting entries, and post them directly to the T accounts.

4. Prepare an adjusted trial balance, an income statement, a statement of owner's equity, and a balance sheet.

Financial Decision Case 4-1

Lockyer Systems Company
(L.O. 5, 7)

Tim Lockyer began his new business, called Lockyer Systems Company, on July 1, 19xx. The company is engaged in writing computer programs with special applications for businesses that own small computers. During the first six months of operation, the business is so successful that Tim has to hire new employees on several occasions. Yet he continually has to put off creditors because he lacks the funds to pay them. He wants to apply for a bank loan, but after preparing a statement (next page) showing the totals of receipts of cash and payments of cash, he wonders whether a bank will make a loan to him on the basis of such apparently poor results. Deciding that he needs some accounting help, Tim asks you to review the statement and the company's operating results.

Lockyer Systems Company
Statement of Cash Receipts and Payments
For the Six Months Ended December 31, 19xx

Receipts from

Investment by Tim Lockyer		$15,000
Customers for Programming Services Provided		20,600
Total Cash Receipts		$35,600

Payments for

Wages	$5,800	
Insurance	2,400	
Rent	4,200	
Supplies	1,900	
Office Equipment	6,200	
Computer Rental	8,000	
Maintenance	900	
Service Van	5,000	
Oil and Gas Reimbursements	690	
Utility	540	
Telephone	300	
Total Cash Payments		$35,930
Bank Overdraft		($330)

After verifying the information in Tim's statement, you assemble the following additional facts about Lockyer Systems Company:

a. In addition to the amount received from customers, programming services totaling $9,700 had been performed but not yet paid for.
b. Employees have been paid all the wages owed to them except for $350 earned since the last payday. The next regular payday is January 3.
c. The insurance expense represents a two-year policy purchased on July 1.
d. The rent expense represents $600 per month, including the rent for January.
e. In examining the expenditures for supplies, you find invoices for $650 that have not been paid, and an inventory reveals $875 of unused supplies still on hand.
f. The office equipment is fully paid for and it is estimated it will last 5 years and be worthless at the end of that time.
g. The computer rental agreement provides for a security deposit of $2,000 plus monthly payments of $1,000.
h. The maintenance expense represents a one-year maintenance agreement, paid in advance on July 1.
i. The service van expense represents the down payment on a van purchased on December 30 for $15,000. Prior to this purchase, the company had reimbursed employees for oil and gas when using their own cars for business. A study of the documents shows that $120 in employee oil and gas receipts must still be reimbursed.

Required

1. From the information given, prepare an income statement and a balance sheet for Lockyer Systems Company.

2. What is your assessment of the company's performance? If you were a bank loan officer, would you look favorably on a loan application from Lockyer Systems Company?

Answers to Self-Test

1. a	3. b	5. c	7. a	9. b
2. c	4. d	6. d	8. d	10. b

Chapter
Five

Completing
the
Accounting
Cycle

You will see the accounting cycle completed in this chapter. First you study the uses and preparation of the work sheet, an important tool for accountants. Then, as the final step in the accounting cycle, you learn how to prepare closing entries. As a result of studying this chapter, you should be able to meet the learning objectives listed on the left.

In previous chapters, the main focus was on the measurement process in accounting. In this chapter, the emphasis is on the accounting system itself and the sequence of steps used by the accountant in completing the accounting cycle. An important part of the accounting system involves the preparation of a work sheet. So we present in detail each step in its preparation. This chapter also explains the uses of the work sheet in accomplishing the end-of-period procedures of recording the adjusting entries, preparing financial statements, and closing the accounts. The optional first step of the next accounting period, preparation of reversing entries, is also discussed.

Overview of the Accounting System

The accounting system encompasses the sequence of steps followed in the accounting process, from analyzing transactions to preparing financial statements and closing the accounts. This system is sometimes called the accounting cycle. The purpose of the system, as illustrated in Figure 5-1, is to treat the business transactions as raw material and develop the finished product of accounting—the financial statements—in a systematic way. The steps in this system are as follows:

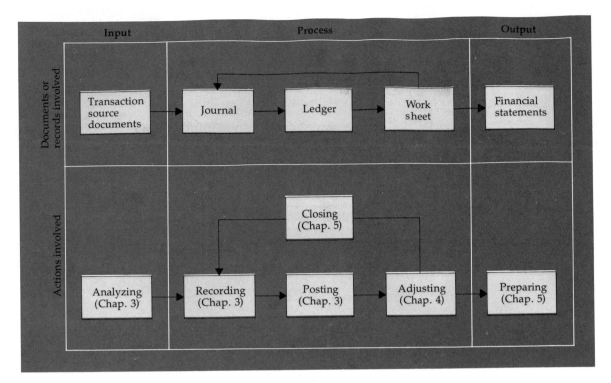

Figure 5-1
An Overview
of the
Accounting
System

1. The transactions are *analyzed* from the *source documents*.
2. The transactions are *recorded* in the *journal*.
3. The entries are *posted* to the *ledger*.
4. The accounts are *adjusted* at the end of the period with the aid of a *work sheet*.
5. *Financial statements* are *prepared* from the work sheet.
6. The accounts are *closed* to conclude the current accounting period and prepare for the beginning of the new accounting period.

Objective 1
State all the
steps in the
accounting cycle

The first four steps were introduced in Chapters 3 and 4. In this chapter, they are reviewed in conjunction with the use of the work sheet. The use of the work sheet and the final two steps are the major topics of this chapter.

The Work Sheet: A Tool of Accountants

Objective 2
Prepare a work
sheet

The flow of information affecting a business does not arbitrarily stop at the end of an accounting period. In order to prepare the financial reports, accountants must collect relevant data to determine what should and what should not go in the financial reports. For example, accountants must examine insurance policies to see how much prepaid insurance has expired, examine plant and equipment records to determine depreciation, take an inventory of supplies on hand, and calculate the amount of accrued wages. These calculations, together with the other computations, analyses, and preliminary drafts of statements, make up the accountants' working papers. Working papers are important for two reasons. First, they aid accountants in organizing their work so that they do not omit important data or steps that affect the accounting statements. Second, they provide evidence of what has been done so that accountants or auditors can retrace their steps and support the basis of the financial statements.

A special kind of working paper is the work sheet. The work sheet is used frequently as a preliminary step in the preparation of financial statements. Using a work sheet lessens the possibility of ignoring an adjustment, aids in checking the arithmetical accuracy of the accounts, and facilitates the preparation of financial statements. The work sheet is never published and is rarely seen by management. Nevertheless, it is a useful tool for the accountant.

Steps in Preparing the Work Sheet

In Chapter 4, the adjustments were entered directly in the journal and posted to the ledger, and the financial statements were prepared from the adjusted trial balance. These steps were done rather easily for the Joan Miller Advertising Agency because it is a small company. For larger companies, however, which may require many adjusting entries, a work sheet is essential. To illustrate the preparation of the work sheet, the Joan Miller Advertising Agency case will be continued.

A commonly used form of work sheet has one column for account names and/or numbers and ten more columns with appropriate headings, as shown in Figure 5-2. Note that the work sheet is identified by a heading that consists of (1) the name of the company, (2) the title "Work Sheet," and (3) the period of time covered (as on the income statement).

There are five steps in the preparation of a work sheet, as follows:

1. Enter the account balances in the Trial Balance columns.
2. Enter the adjustments in the Adjustments columns.
3. Enter the account balances as adjusted in the Adjusted Trial Balance columns.
4. Extend the account balances from the Adjusted Trial Balance columns to the Income Statement columns or the Balance Sheet columns.
5. Total the Income Statement columns and the Balance Sheet columns. Enter the net income or net loss in both pairs of columns as a balancing figure, and recompute column totals.

1. Enter the account balances in the Trial Balance columns   The titles and balances of the accounts as of January 31 are copied directly from the ledger into the Trial Balance columns, as shown in Figure 5-2. When a work sheet is prepared, a separate trial balance is not required.

2. Enter the adjustments in the Adjustments columns   The required adjustments for the Joan Miller Advertising Agency were explained in Chapter 4. The same adjustments are entered in the Adjustments col-

Joan Miller Advertising Agency
Work Sheet
For the Month Ended January 31, 19xx

Account Name	Trial Balance		Adjustments		Adjusted Trial Balance		Income Statement		Balance Sheet	
	Debit	Credit	Debit	Credit	Debit	Credit	Debit	Credit	Debit	Credit
Cash	1,720									
Accounts Receivable	2,800									
Art Supplies	1,800									
Office Supplies	800									
Prepaid Rent	800									
Prepaid Insurance	480									
Art Equipment	4,200									
Accumulated Depreciation, Art Equipment										
Office Equipment	3,000									
Accumulated Depreciation, Office Equipment										
Accounts Payable		3,170								
Unearned Art Fees		1,000								
Joan Miller, Capital		10,000								
Joan Miller, Withdrawals	1,400									
Advertising Fees Earned		4,200								
Office Wages Expense	1,200									
Utility Expense	100									
Telephone Expense	70									
	18,370	18,370								

Figure 5-2
Entering the Account Balances in the Trial Balance Columns

umns of the work sheet in Figure 5-3 (page 144). As each adjustment is entered, a letter is used to identify the debit and credit parts of the same entry. For example, the first adjustment is for recognition of rent expense, which results in a debit to Rent Expense and a credit to Prepaid Rent. This adjustment is identified by the letter *a*. In practice, this letter may be used to reference supporting computations or documentation underlying the adjusting entry.

If the adjustment calls for an account that has not already been used in the trial balance, the new account is added below the accounts listed for the trial balance. For example, Rent Expense has been added in Figure 5-3.

When all the adjustments have been made, the pair of Adjustments columns must be added. This step proves that the debits and credits of the adjustments are equal and generally reduces errors in the preparation of the work sheet.

3. **Enter the account balances as adjusted in the Adjusted Trial Balance columns** Figure 5-4 (page 145) shows the adjusted trial balance, prepared by combining the amount of each account in the original Trial Balance columns with the corresponding amounts in the Adjustments columns and entering the combined amounts on a line-by-line basis in the Adjusted Trial Balance columns.

Completing the Accounting Cycle

Joan Miller Advertising Agency
Work Sheet
For the Month Ended January 31, 19xx

Account Name	Trial Balance Debit	Trial Balance Credit	Adjustments Debit	Adjustments Credit	Adjusted Trial Balance Debit	Adjusted Trial Balance Credit	Income Statement Debit	Income Statement Credit	Balance Sheet Debit	Balance Sheet Credit
Cash	1,720									
Accounts Receivable	2,800									
Art Supplies	1,800			(c) 500						
Office Supplies	800			(d) 200						
Prepaid Rent	800			(a) 400						
Prepaid Insurance	480			(b) 40						
Art Equipment	4,200									
Accumulated Deprecia- tion, Art Equipment				(e) 70						
Office Equipment	3,000									
Accumulated Deprecia- tion, Office Equipment				(f) 50						
Accounts Payable		3,170								
Unearned Art Fees		1,000	(g) 400							
Joan Miller, Capital		10,000								
Joan Miller, Withdrawals	1,400									
Advertising Fees Earned		4,200		(h) 200						
Office Wages Expense	1,200		(i) 180							
Utility Expense	100									
Telephone Expense	70									
	18,370	18,370								
Rent Expense			(a) 400							
Insurance Expense			(b) 40							
Art Supplies Expense			(c) 500							
Office Supplies Expense			(d) 200							
Depreciation Expense, Art Equipment			(e) 70							
Depreciation Expense, Office Equipment			(f) 50							
Art Fees Earned				(g) 400						
Accrued Fees Receivable			(h) 200							
Wages Payable				(i) 180						
			2,040	2,040						

Figure 5-3
Entries in the
Adjustments
Columns

Some examples from Figure 5-4 will illustrate crossfooting. The first line shows Cash with a debit balance of $1,720. Because there are no adjustments to the Cash account, $1,720 is entered in the debit column of the Adjusted Trial Balance. The second line is Accounts Receivable, which shows a debit of $2,800 in the Trial Balance columns. Because there are no adjustments to Accounts Receivable, the $2,800 balance is carried over to the debit column of the Adjusted Trial Balance. The next line is Art Supplies, which shows a debit of $1,800 in the Trial Balance columns and a credit from adjustment c in the Adjustments columns. Subtracting $500 from $1,800 therefore results in a $1,300 debit balance in the Adjusted Trial Balance. This process is followed through all the accounts, including those added below the accounts listed for the trial balance. The

Chapter Five

Joan Miller Advertising Agency
Work Sheet
For the Month Ended January 31, 19xx

Account Name	Trial Balance Debit	Trial Balance Credit	Adjustments Debit	Adjustments Credit	Adjusted Trial Balance Debit	Adjusted Trial Balance Credit	Income Statement Debit	Income Statement Credit	Balance Sheet Debit	Balance Sheet Credit
Cash	1,720				1,720					
Accounts Receivable	2,800				2,800					
Art Supplies	1,800			(c) 500	1,300					
Office Supplies	800			(d) 200	600					
Prepaid Rent	800			(a) 400	400					
Prepaid Insurance	480			(b) 40	440					
Art Equipment	4,200				4,200					
Accumulated Deprecia-tion, Art Equipment				(e) 70		70				
Office Equipment	3,000				3,000					
Accumulated Deprecia-tion, Office Equipment				(f) 50		50				
Accounts Payable		3,170				3,170				
Unearned Art Fees		1,000	(g) 400			600				
Joan Miller, Capital		10,000				10,000				
Joan Miller, Withdrawals	1,400				1,400					
Advertising Fees Earned		4,200		(h) 200		4,400				
Office Wages Expense	1,200		(i) 180		1,380					
Utility Expense	100				100					
Telephone Expense	70				70					
	18,370	18,370								
Rent Expense			(a) 400		400					
Insurance Expense			(b) 40		40					
Art Supplies Expense			(c) 500		500					
Office Supplies Expense			(d) 200		200					
Depreciation Expense, Art Equipment			(e) 70		70					
Depreciation Expense, Office Equipment			(f) 50		50					
Art Fees Earned				(g) 400		400				
Accrued Fees Receivable			(h) 200		200					
Wages Payable				(l) 180		180				
			2,040	2,040	18,870	18,870				

Figure 5-4
Entries in the
Adjusted
Trial Balance
Columns

Adjusted Trial Balance columns are then footed, that is, totaled, to check the arithmetical accuracy of the crossfooting.

4. Extend the account balances from the Adjusted Trial Balance columns to the Income Statement columns or the Balance Sheet columns Every account in the adjusted trial balance is either a balance sheet account or an income statement account. The accounts are sorted, and each account is extended to its proper place as a debit or credit in either the Balance Sheet columns or the Income Statement columns. The result of extending the accounts is shown in Figure 5-5 (page 146). Revenue and expense accounts are moved to the Income Statement columns. Assets and liabilities as well as the capital and withdrawal accounts are then extended to the Balance Sheet columns. To avoid overlooking an account, extend the

Joan Miller Advertising Agency
Work Sheet
For the Month Ended January 31, 19xx

Account Name	Trial Balance Debit	Trial Balance Credit	Adjustments Debit	Adjustments Credit	Adjusted Trial Balance Debit	Adjusted Trial Balance Credit	Income Statement Debit	Income Statement Credit	Balance Sheet Debit	Balance Sheet Credit
Cash	1,720				1,720				1,720	
Accounts Receivable	2,800				2,800				2,800	
Art Supplies	1,800			(c) 500	1,300				1,300	
Office Supplies	800			(d) 200	600				600	
Prepaid Rent	800			(a) 400	400				400	
Prepaid Insurance	480			(b) 40	440				440	
Art Equipment	4,200				4,200				4,200	
Accumulated Depreciation, Art Equipment				(e) 70		70				70
Office Equipment	3,000				3,000				3,000	
Accumulated Depreciation, Office Equipment				(f) 50		50				50
Accounts Payable		3,170				3,170				3,170
Unearned Art Fees		1,000	(g) 400			600				600
Joan Miller, Capital		10,000				10,000				10,000
Joan Miller, Withdrawals	1,400				1,400				1,400	
Advertising Fees Earned		4,200		(h) 200		4,400		4,400		
Office Wages Expense	1,200		(i) 180		1,380		1,380			
Utility Expense	100				100		100			
Telephone Expense	70				70		70			
	18,370	18,370								
Rent Expense			(a) 400		400		400			
Insurance Expense			(b) 40		40		40			
Art Supplies Expense			(c) 500		500		500			
Office Supplies Expense			(d) 200		200		200			
Depreciation Expense, Art Equipment			(e) 70		70		70			
Depreciation Expense, Office Equipment			(f) 50		50		50			
Art Fees Earned				(g) 400		400		400		
Accrued Fees Receivable			(h) 200		200				200	
Wages Payable				(i) 180		180				180
			2,040	2,040	18,870	18,870				

Figure 5-5
Entries in the Income Statement and Balance Sheet Columns

accounts line by line, beginning with the first line (which is Cash) and not omitting any. For instance, the Cash debit balance of $1,700 is extended to the debit column of the balance sheet; the Accounts Receivable debit balance of $3,000 is extended to the same debit column, and so forth. Each amount is carried forward to only one column.

5. **Total the Income Statement columns and the Balance Sheet columns. Enter the net income or net loss in both pairs of columns as a balancing figure, and recompute column totals** This last step, as shown in Figure 5-6, is necessary to compute net income or net loss and to prove the arithmetical accuracy of the work sheet.

Net income or net loss is equal to the difference between the debit and credit columns of the income statement.

Account Name	Trial Balance Debit	Trial Balance Credit	Adjustments Debit	Adjustments Credit	Adjusted Trial Balance Debit	Adjusted Trial Balance Credit	Income Statement Debit	Income Statement Credit	Balance Sheet Debit	Balance Sheet Credit
Cash	1,720				1,720				1,720	
Accounts Receivable	2,800				2,800				2,800	
Art Supplies	1,800			(c) 500	1,300				1,300	
Office Supplies	800			(d) 200	600				600	
Prepaid Rent	800			(a) 400	400				400	
Prepaid Insurance	480			(b) 40	440				440	
Art Equipment	4,200				4,200				4,200	
Accumulated Depreciation, Art Equipment				(e) 70		70				70
Office Equipment	3,000				3,000				3,000	
Accumulated Depreciation, Office Equipment				(f) 50		50				50
Accounts Payable		3,170				3,170				3,170
Unearned Art Fees		1,000	(g) 400			600				600
Joan Miller, Capital		10,000				10,000				10,000
Joan Miller, Withdrawals	1,400				1,400				1,400	
Advertising Fees Earned		4,200		(h) 200		4,400		4,400		
Office Wages Expense	1,200		(i) 180		1,380		1,380			
Utility Expense	100				100		100			
Telephone Expense	70				70		70			
	18,370	18,370								
Rent Expense			(a) 400		400		400			
Insurance Expense			(b) 40		40		40			
Art Supplies Expense			(c) 500		500		500			
Office Supplies Expense			(d) 200		200		200			
Depreciation Expense, Art Equipment			(e) 70		70		70			
Depreciation Expense, Office Equipment			(f) 50		50		50			
Art Fees Earned				(g) 400		400		400		
Accrued Fees Receivable			(h) 200		200				200	
Wages Payable				(i) 180		180				180
			2,040	2,040	18,870	18,870	2,810	4,800	16,060	14,070
Net Income							1,990			1,990
							4,800	4,800	16,060	16,060

Figure 5-6
Entries in the Balance Sheet Columns and Totals

Revenue (Income Statement credit column total)	$4,800
Expenses (Income Statement debit column total)	2,810
Net Income	$1,990

In this case, the revenue (credit column) has exceeded the expenses (debit column). Consequently, the company has a net income of $1,990.

The $1,990 is entered in the debit side of the Income Statement columns to balance the columns, and it is entered on the credit side of the Balance Sheet columns. This is done because excess revenue (net income) increases owner's equity, and increases in owner's equity are recorded by credits.

If a net loss had occurred, the opposite rule would apply. The excess of expenses (net loss) would be placed in the credit side of the Income Statement columns as a balancing figure and extended to the debit side of the Balance Sheet columns, because a net loss causes a decrease in owner's equity, which would be shown by a debit.

As a final check, the four columns are totaled again. If the Income Statement columns and the Balance Sheet columns do not balance, there may be an account extended or sorted to the wrong column, or an error may have been made in adding the columns. Equal totals in the Balance Sheet columns, however, are not absolute proof of accuracy. If an asset has been carried to the debit column of the income statement and if a similar error involving revenues or liabilities has been made, the work sheet will still check out, but the net income figure will be wrong.

Uses of the Work Sheet

Objective 3
Identify the three principal uses of a work sheet

As mentioned earlier, the work sheet is a tool of the accountant. The work sheet has three principal uses: (1) to prepare the financial statements, (2) to record the adjusting entries, and (3) to record the closing entries, which prepare the records for the beginning of the next period.

Preparing the Financial Statements

After completion of the work sheet, it is a simple step to prepare the financial statements because the account balances have been sorted into Income Statement and Balance Sheet columns. The income statement shown in Figure 5-7 is prepared from the accounts in the Income Statement columns in Figure 5-6.

Objective 4
Prepare financial statements from a work sheet

The statement of owner's equity and the balance sheet of Joan Miller Advertising Agency are presented in Figures 5-8 and 5-9. The account balances are drawn from the Balance Sheet columns of the work sheet shown in Figure 5-6. The totals of the assets and liabilities and owner's equity in the balance sheet do not agree with the totals of the Balance Sheet columns of the work sheet because contra accounts such as Accumulated Depreciation and withdrawals are deducted from the side of the balance sheet opposite the balance of the account.

Recording the Adjusting Entries

Objective 5
Record the adjusting entries from a work sheet

It was necessary to determine the adjusting entries for Joan Miller Advertising Agency in the step just before the preparation of the adjusted trial balance on the work sheet. They are essential to the preparation of the financial statements. The adjusting entries could have been recorded in the general journal at that point. However, it is usually convenient to delay recording them until after the work sheet and the financial statements have been prepared because this task can be done at the same time as the recording of the closing entries described in the next section.

Chapter Five

Figure 5-7
Income State-
ment for the
Joan Miller
Advertising
Agency

Joan Miller Advertising Agency
Income Statement
For the Month Ended January 31, 19xx

Revenues

Advertising Fees Earned	$4,400	
Art Fees Earned	400	
Total Revenues		$4,800

Expenses

Office Wages Expense	$1,380	
Utility Expense	100	
Telephone Expense	70	
Rent Expense	400	
Insurance Expense	40	
Art Supplies Expense	500	
Office Supplies Expense	200	
Depreciation Expense, Art Equipment	70	
Depreciation Expense, Office Equipment	50	
Total Expenses		2,810
Net Income		**$1,990**

Recording the adjusting entries with appropriate explanations in the general journal, as shown in Figure 5-10 (page 151), is an easy step because they may simply be copied from the work sheet. They are then posted to the general ledger.

Recording the Closing Entries

Closing entries, which are journal entries made at the end of the accounting period, accomplish two purposes. First, at the end of an accounting period, closing entries set the stage for the next accounting period by

Figure 5-8
Statement of
Owner's Equity
for the Joan
Miller Adver-
tising Agency

Joan Miller Advertising Agency
Statement of Owner's Equity
For the Month Ended January 31, 19xx

Joan Miller, Capital, January 1, 19xx		$ —
Add: Investments by Joan Miller	$10,000	
Net Income	1,990	11,990
Subtotal		$11,990
Less Withdrawals		1,400
Joan Miller, Capital, January 31, 19xx		$10,590

Completing the Accounting Cycle

Figure 5-9
Balance Sheet
for the Joan
Miller Adver-
tising Agency

Joan Miller Advertising Agency
Balance Sheet
January 31, 19xx

Assets

Cash		$ 1,720
Accounts Receivable		2,800
Accrued Fees Receivable		200
Office Supplies		600
Art Supplies		1,300
Prepaid Rent		400
Prepaid Insurance		440
Art Equipment	$4,200	
Less Accumulated Depreciation	70	4,130
Office Equipment	$3,000	
Less Accumulated Depreciation	50	2,950
Total Assets		$14,540

Liabilities

Accounts Payable	$3,170	
Unearned Art Fees	600	
Wages Payable	180	
Total Liabilities		$ 3,950

Owner's Equity

Joan Miller, Capital, January 31		10,590
Total Liabilities and Owner's Equity		$14,540

Objective 6
Explain the pur-
poses of closing
entries

closing or clearing the expense and revenue accounts of their balances. This step must be carried out because an income statement reports the net income for a single accounting period and shows the expenses and revenues only for that period. For this reason, the expense and revenue accounts must be closed or cleared of their balances at the end of the period so that the next period may begin with a zero balance in those accounts.

The second aim of closing entries is to summarize a period's revenues and expenses. This is done by transferring the balances of revenues and expenses to the Income Summary account to record the net profit or loss in that account. The Income Summary, a new nominal account, is introduced here. This account gives us a place to summarize all revenues and expenses in a single net figure before transferring the result to the capital account.

The balance of the Income Summary equals the net income or loss in the income statement. The net income or loss is then transferred to the owner's capital account. This step is needed because, even though

Figure 5-10
Adjustments on
Work Sheet
Entered in the
General Journal

General Journal				Page 3
Date		Description	Post. Ref.	Debit	Credit

Date		Description	Post. Ref.	Debit	Credit
Jan.	31	Rent Expense	514	400	
		Prepaid Rent	117		400
		To recognize expiration of one month's rent			
	31	Insurance Expense	515	40	
		Prepaid Insurance	118		40
		To recognize expiration of one month's insurance			
	31	Art Supplies Expense	516	500	
		Art Supplies	115		500
		To recognize art supplies used during the month			
	31	Office Supplies Expense	517	200	
		Office Supplies	116		200
		To recognize office supplies used during the month			
	31	Depreciation Expense, Art Equipment	519	70	
		Accumulated Depreciation, Art Equipment	145		70
		To record depreciation of art equipment for a month			
	31	Depreciation Expense, Office Equipment	520	50	
		Accumulated Depreciation, Office Equipment	147		50
		To record depreciation of office equipment for a month			
	31	Unearned Art Fees	213	400	
		Art Fees Earned	412		400
		To recognize performance of services paid in advance			
	31	Office Wages Expense	511	180	
		Wages Payable	214		180
		To accrue unrecorded wages			
	31	Accrued Fees Receivable	114	200	
		Advertising Fees Earned	411		200
		To accrue advertising fees earned but unrecorded			

expenses and revenues are recorded in expense and revenue accounts, they actually represent decreases and increases in owner's capital. Thus closing entries must transfer the net effect of increases (revenues) and decreases (expenses) to the owner's capital account.

Closing entries are sometimes called clearing entries because one of their functions is to clear the revenue and expense accounts and leave them with zero balances.

As stated in Chapter 4, revenue and expense accounts are called nominal accounts because they are temporary. Nominal accounts begin each period at zero, accumulate a balance during the period, and return to zero by means of closing entries when the balance is transferred to owner's equity. The accountant uses these accounts to keep track of the increases and decreases in owner's equity in a way that is helpful to management and others interested in the success or progress of the company. However, nominal accounts are different from balance sheet accounts. Balance sheet, or real, accounts often begin with a balance, increase or decrease during the period, and carry the end-of-period balance into the next accounting period.

Required Closing Entries

Closing entries are needed for four important tasks:

Objective 7
Prepare the
required closing
entries

1. Transferring the revenue account balances to Income Summary
2. Transferring the expense account balances to Income Summary
3. Transferring the Income Summary balance to the capital account
4. Transferring the withdrawals account balance to the capital account

Closing the Revenue Accounts to the Income Summary

Revenue accounts have credit balances before the closing entries are posted. For this reason, an entry debiting each revenue account in the amount of its balance is needed to close the account. The credit part of the entry is made to the Income Summary account. The compound entry that closes the two revenue accounts for the Joan Miller Advertising Agency is as follows:

Jan. 31	Advertising Fees Earned	411	4,400	
	Art Fees Earned	412	400	
	Income Summary	313		4,800
	To close revenue accounts			

The effect of posting the entry is shown in Figure 5-11. Note that the dual effect of the entry is to (1) set the balances of the revenue accounts equal to zero, and (2) transfer the balances in total to the credit side of the Income Summary account. Also note that the data for closing the revenue accounts can be found in the credit side of the Income Statement columns in the work sheet illustrated in Figure 5-6.

Advertising Fees Earned						Account No. 411
		Post. Ref.	Debit	Credit	Balance Debit	Balance Credit
Date	Item	Post. Ref.	Debit	Credit	Debit	Credit
Jan. 10		J2		1,400		1,400
19		J2		2,800		4,200
31	Adj. (h)	J3		200		4,400
31		J4	4,400			—

Income Summary						Account No. 313
		Post. Ref.	Debit	Credit	Balance Debit	Balance Credit
Date	Item	Post. Ref.	Debit	Credit	Debit	Credit
Jan. 31		J4		4,800		4,800

```
                                                    4,400
                                                      400
                                                    ──────
                                                    4,800
```

Art Fees Earned						Account No. 412
		Post. Ref.	Debit	Credit	Balance Debit	Balance Credit
Date	Item	Post. Ref.	Debit	Credit	Debit	Credit
Jan. 31	Adj. (g)	J3		400		400
31		J4	400			—

Figure 5-11
Posting the
Closing Entry
of the Revenue
Accounts to the
Income
Summary

Closing the Expense Accounts to the Income Summary

Expense accounts have debit balances before the closing entries are posted. For this reason, a compound entry is needed crediting each expense account for its balance and debiting the Income Summary for the total (which can be found in the debit side of the Income Statement columns):

Jan. 31	Income Summary	313	2,810	
	Office Wages Expense	511		1,380
	Utility Expense	512		100
	Telephone Expense	513		70
	Rent Expense	514		400
	Insurance Expense	515		40
	Art Supplies Expense	516		500
	Office Supplies Expense	517		200
	Depreciation Expense, Art Equipment	519		70
	Depreciation Expense, Office Equipment	520		50
	To close the expense accounts			

The effect of posting the closing entry to the ledger accounts is shown in Figure 5-12 (next page). Note again the double effect of (1) reducing expense account balances to zero and (2) transferring the total of the account balances to the debit side of the Income Summary account. Note

Completing the Accounting Cycle

153

Office Wages Expense — Account No. 511

Date	Item	Post. Ref.	Debit	Credit	Balance Debit	Balance Credit
Jan. 12		J2	600		600	
26		J2	600		1,200	
31	Adj. (i)	J3	180		1,380	
31		J4		1,380	—	

Utility Expense — Account No. 512

Date	Item	Post. Ref.	Debit	Credit	Balance Debit	Balance Credit
Jan. 29		J2	100		100	
31		J4		100	—	

Telephone Expense — Account No. 513

Date	Item	Post. Ref.	Debit	Credit	Balance Debit	Balance Credit
Jan. 30		J2	70		70	
31		J4		70	—	

Rent Expense — Account No. 514

Date	Item	Post. Ref.	Debit	Credit	Balance Debit	Balance Credit
Jan. 31	Adj. (a)	J3	400		400	
31		J4		400	—	

Insurance Expense — Account No. 515

Date	Item	Post. Ref.	Debit	Credit	Balance Debit	Balance Credit
Jan. 31	Adj. (b)	J3	40		40	
31		J4		40	—	

Art Supplies Expense — Account No. 516

Date	Item	Post. Ref.	Debit	Credit	Balance Debit	Balance Credit
Jan. 31	Adj. (c)	J3	500		500	
31		J4		500	—	

Office Supplies Expense — Account No. 517

Date	Item	Post. Ref.	Debit	Credit	Balance Debit	Balance Credit
Jan. 31	Adj. (d)	J3	200		200	
31		J4		200	—	

Income Summary — Account No. 313

Date	Item	Post. Ref.	Debit	Credit	Balance Debit	Balance Credit
Jan. 31		J4		4,800		4,800
31		J4	2,810			1,990

1,380
100
70
400
40
500
200
50
70
2,810

Depreciation Expense, Art Equipment — Account No. 519

Date	Item	Post. Ref.	Debit	Credit	Balance Debit	Balance Credit
Jan. 31	Adj. (e)	J3	70		70	
31		J4		70	—	

Depreciation Expense, Office Equipment — Account 520

Date	Item	Post. Ref.	Debit	Credit	Balance Debit	Balance Credit
Jan. 31	Adj. (f)	J3	50		50	
31		J4		50	—	

◀ Figure 5-12
Posting the
Closing Entry
of the Expense
Accounts to the
Income
Summary

also that data for closing the expense accounts are on the debit side of the Income Statement columns of the work sheet (Figure 5-6).

Closing the Income Summary to the Capital Account

After the entries closing the revenue and expense accounts have been posted, the balance of the Income Summary account is equal to the net income or loss for the period. A net income will be indicated by a credit balance and a net loss by a debit balance. At this point, the Income Summary balance, regardless of its nature, must be closed to the capital account. For the Joan Miller Advertising Agency the entry is as follows:

Jan. 31	Income Summary	313	1,990	
	Joan Miller, Capital	311		1,990
	To close the Income			
	Summary account			

The effect of posting the closing entry is shown in Figure 5-13. Note again the double effect of (1) closing the Income Summary account balance and (2) transferring the balance, net income in this case, to Joan Miller's capital account.

Closing the Withdrawals Account to the Capital Account

The withdrawals account shows the amount by which capital is reduced during the period by withdrawals of cash or other assets of the business by the owner for personal use. For this reason, the debit balance of the withdrawals account must be closed to the capital account, as follows:

Jan. 31	Joan Miller, Capital	311	1,400	
	Joan Miller, Withdrawals	312		1,400
	To close the Withdrawals			
	account			

The effect of posting this closing entry is shown in Figure 5-14 (top of next page). The double effect of the entry is to (1) close the withdrawals account of its balance and (2) transfer the balance to the capital account.

Figure 5-13
Posting the
Closing Entry
of the Income
Summary to the
Capital Account

The Accounts After Closing

After all the steps in the closing process have been completed and the adjusting and closing entries have been posted to the accounts, the stage is

Income Summary					Account No. 313		Joan Miller, Capital					Account No. 311	
					Balance							Balance	
Date	Item	Post. Ref.	Debit	Credit	Debit	Credit	Date	Item	Post. Ref.	Debit	Credit	Debit	Credit
Jan. 31		J4		4,800		4,800	Jan. 1		J1		10,000		10,000
31		J4	2,810			1,990	31		J4		1,990		11,990
31		J4	1,990			—							

Joan Miller, Withdrawals					Account No. 312	
					Balance	
Date	Item	Post. Ref.	Debit	Credit	Debit	Credit
Jan. 25		J2	1,400		1,400	
31		J4		1,400	—	

Joan Miller, Capital					Account No. 311	
					Balance	
Date	Item	Post. Ref.	Debit	Credit	Debit	Credit
Jan. 1		J1		10,000		10,000
31		J4		1,990		11,990
31		J4	1,400			10,590

Figure 5-14
Posting the Closing Entry of the Withdrawals Account to the Capital Account

set for the next accounting period. The ledger accounts of the Joan Miller Advertising Agency as they appear at this point are shown in Figure 5-15 (below). The revenue, expense, and withdrawals accounts (nominal or temporary) have zero balances. The capital account has been increased or decreased depending on net income or loss and withdrawals. The balance sheet accounts (real accounts) have the appropriate balances, which are carried forward to the next period.

Figure 5-15
The Accounts After Closing Entries Are Posted

Cash						Account No. 111	
						Balance	
Date			Post. Ref.	Debit	Credit	Debit	Credit
Jan.	1		J1	10,000		10,000	
	2		J1		800	9,200	
	4		J1		4,200	5,000	
	5		J1		1,500	3,500	
	8		J1		480	3,020	
	9		J1		1,000	2,020	
	10		J2	1,400		3,420	
	12		J2		600	2,820	
	15		J2	1,000		3,820	
	25		J2		1,400	2,420	
	26		J2		600	1,820	
	29		J2		100	1,720	

Accounts Receivable						Account No. 113	
Jan.	19		J2	2,800		2,800	

Accrued Fees Receivable						Account No. 114	
Jan.	31	Adjustment (h)	J3	200		200	

Figure 5-15
(*continued*)

Art Supplies   Account No. 115

Date		Item	Post. Ref.	Debit	Credit	Balance Debit	Balance Credit
Jan.	6		J1	1,800		1,800	
	31	Adjustment (c)	J3		500	1,300	

Office Supplies   Account No. 116

Date		Item	Post. Ref.	Debit	Credit	Balance Debit	Balance Credit
Jan.	6		J1	800		800	
	31	Adjustment (d)	J3		200	600	

Prepaid Rent   Account No. 117

Date		Item	Post. Ref.	Debit	Credit	Balance Debit	Balance Credit
Jan.	2		J1	800		800	
	31	Adjustment (a)	J3		400	400	

Prepaid Insurance   Account No. 118

Date		Item	Post. Ref.	Debit	Credit	Balance Debit	Balance Credit
Jan.	8		J1	480		480	
	31	Adjustment (b)	J3		40	440	

Art Equipment   Account No. 144

Date		Item	Post. Ref.	Debit	Credit	Balance Debit	Balance Credit
Jan.	4		J1	4,200		4,200	

(*continued*)

Figure 5-15
(*continued*)

Accumulated Depreciation, Art Equipment — Account No. 145

Date		Item	Post. Ref.	Debit	Credit	Balance Debit	Balance Credit
Jan.	31	Adjustment (e)	J3		70		70

Office Equipment — Account No. 146

Date		Item	Post. Ref.	Debit	Credit	Balance Debit	Balance Credit
Jan.	5		J1	3,000		3,000	

Accumulated Depreciation, Office Equipment — Account No. 147

Date		Item	Post. Ref.	Debit	Credit	Balance Debit	Balance Credit
Jan.	31	Adjustment (f)	J3		50		50

Accounts Payable — Account No. 212

Date		Item	Post. Ref.	Debit	Credit	Balance Debit	Balance Credit
Jan.	5		J1		1,500		1,500
	6		J1		2,600		4,100
	9		J1	1,000			3,100
	30		J2		70		3,170

Unearned Art Fees — Account No. 213

Date		Item	Post. Ref.	Debit	Credit	Balance Debit	Balance Credit
Jan.	15		J2		1,000		1,000
	31	Adjustment (g)	J3	400			600

Figure 5-15
(continued)

Wages Payable   Account No. 214

Date		Item	Post. Ref.	Debit	Credit	Balance Debit	Balance Credit
Jan.	31	Adjustment (i)	J3		180		180

Joan Miller, Capital   Account No. 311

Date		Item	Post. Ref.	Debit	Credit	Balance Debit	Balance Credit
Jan.	1		J1		10,000		10,000
	31	Closing entry	J4		1,990		11,990
	31	Closing entry	J4	1,400			10,590

Joan Miller, Withdrawals   Account No. 312

Date		Item	Post. Ref.	Debit	Credit	Balance Debit	Balance Credit
Jan.	25		J2	1,400		1,400	
	31	Closing entry	J4		1,400	—	

Income Summary   Account No. 313

Date		Item	Post. Ref.	Debit	Credit	Balance Debit	Balance Credit
Jan.	31	Closing entry	J4		4,800		4,800
	31	Closing entry	J4	2,810			1,990
	31	Closing entry	J4	1,990			—

(continued)

Figure 5-15
(*continued*)

Advertising Fees Earned   Account No. 411

Date		Item	Post. Ref.	Debit	Credit	Balance Debit	Balance Credit
Jan.	10		J2		1,400		1,400
	19		J2		2,800		4,200
	31	Adjustment (h)	J3		200		4,400
	31	Closing entry	J4	4,400			—

Art Fees Earned   Account No. 412

Date		Item	Post. Ref.	Debit	Credit	Balance Debit	Balance Credit
Jan.	31	Adjustment (g)	J3		400		400
	31	Closing entry	J4	400			—

Office Wages Expense   Account No. 511

Date		Item	Post. Ref.	Debit	Credit	Balance Debit	Balance Credit
Jan.	12		J2	600		600	
	26		J2	600		1,200	
	31	Adjustment (i)	J3	180		1,380	
	31	Closing entry	J4		1,380	—	

Utility Expense   Account No. 512

Date		Item	Post. Ref.	Debit	Credit	Balance Debit	Balance Credit
Jan.	29		J2	100		100	
	31	Closing entry	J4		100	—	

Figure 5-15
(*continued*)

Telephone Expense   Account No. 513

Date		Item	Post. Ref.	Debit	Credit	Balance Debit	Balance Credit
Jan.	30		J2	70		70	
	31	Closing entry	J4		70	—	

Rent Expense   Account No. 514

Date		Item	Post. Ref.	Debit	Credit	Balance Debit	Balance Credit
Jan.	31	Adjustment (a)	J3	400		400	
	31	Closing entry	J4		400	—	

Insurance Expense   Account No. 515

Date		Item	Post. Ref.	Debit	Credit	Balance Debit	Balance Credit
Jan.	31	Adjustment (b)	J3	40		40	
	31	Closing entry	J4		40	—	

Art Supplies Expense   Account No. 516

Date		Item	Post. Ref.	Debit	Credit	Balance Debit	Balance Credit
Jan.	31	Adjustment (c)	J3	500		500	
	31	Closing entry	J4		500	—	

Office Supplies Expense   Account No. 517

Date		Item	Post. Ref.	Debit	Credit	Balance Debit	Balance Credit
Jan.	31	Adjustment (d)	J3	200		200	
	31	Closing entry	J4		200	—	

(*continued*)

Figure 5-15
(continued)

Depreciation Expense, Art Equipment Account No. 519

| Date | | Item | Post. Ref. | Debit | Credit | Balance | |
						Debit	Credit
Jan.	31	Adjustment (e)	J3	70		70	
	31	Closing entry	J4		70	—	

Depreciation Expense, Office Equipment Account No. 520

| Date | | Item | Post. Ref. | Debit | Credit | Balance | |
						Debit	Credit
Jan.	31	Adjustment (f)	J3	50		50	
	31	Closing entry	J4		50	—	

The Post-Closing Trial Balance

*Objective 8
Prepare the
post-closing trial
balance*

Because it is possible to make an error in posting the adjustments and closing entries to the ledger accounts, it is necessary to retest the equality of the accounts by preparing a new trial balance. This final trial balance, called a post-closing trial balance, is shown in Figure 5-16 for the Joan Miller Advertising Agency. Notice that only balance sheet accounts have balances. At this point, as explained earlier, the income statement accounts have all been closed.

Reversing Entries: Optional First Step of the Next Accounting Period

*Objective 9
Prepare revers-
ing entries as
appropriate*

At the end of each accounting period, adjusting entries are made to bring revenues and expenses into conformity with the matching rule. A reversing entry is a general journal entry made on the first day of an accounting period that is the exact reverse of an adjusting entry made in the previous period. Reversing entries are optional journal entries that are intended to simplify the bookkeeping process for transactions involving certain types of adjustments. Not all adjusting entries are reversed. For the system of recording used in this book, only adjustments for accruals (accrued revenues and accrued expenses) need to be reversed. Deferrals do not need to be reversed.

Figure 5-16
Post-Closing
Trial Balance

Joan Miller Advertising Agency Post-Closing Trial Balance January 31, 19xx		
Cash	$ 1,720	
Accounts Receivable	2,800	
Accrued Fees Receivable	200	
Art Supplies	1,300	
Office Supplies	600	
Prepaid Rent	400	
Prepaid Insurance	440	
Art Equipment	4,200	
Accumulated Depreciation, Art Equipment		$ 70
Office Equipment	3,000	
Accumulated Depreciation, Office Equipment		50
Accounts Payable		3,170
Wages Payable		180
Unearned Art Fees		600
Joan Miller, Capital		10,590
	$14,660	$14,660

To show how reversing entries can be helpful, consider the adjusting entry made in the records of Joan Miller Advertising Agency to accrue office wages expense:

Jan. 31   Office Wages Expense   180
        Wages Payable   180
            To accrue unrecorded wages

When the secretary is paid on the next regular payday, the accountant would make the following entry, using the accounting procedure that you know to this point:

Feb. 9   Wages Payable   180
        Office Wages Expense   420
        Cash   600
            To record payment of two weeks'
            wages to secretary, $180 of which
            was accrued in the previous period

Note that when the payment is made, without a prior reversing entry, the accountant must look in the records to find out how much of the $600 applied to the current accounting period and how much was accrued at the beginning of the period. This step may appear easy in this simple case, but think of the problems if the company had many employees, especially if some of them are paid on different time schedules such as weekly or monthly. A reversing entry is an accounting procedure that helps to solve this difficult problem. As noted above, a reversing entry is exactly what its name implies. It is a reversal of the adjusting entry made by debiting the credits and crediting the debits of the adjusting entry. For example, note the following sequence of transactions and their effects on the ledger account for Office Wages Expense:

Office Wages Expense — Account No. 511

1. Adjusting Entry

Jan. 31 Office Wages Expense 180
  Wages Payable 180

Date		Post. Ref.	Debit	Credit	Balance Debit	Balance Credit
Jan.	12	J2	600		600	
	26	J2	600		1,200	
	31	J3	180		1,380	

2. Closing Entry

Jan. 31 Income Summary 1,380
    Office Wages Expense 1,380

Date		Post. Ref.	Debit	Credit	Balance Debit	Balance Credit
Jan.	12	J2	600		600	
	26	J2	600		1,200	
	31	J3	180		1,380	
	31	J4		1,380	—	

3. Reversing Entry

Feb. 1 Wages Payable 180
    Office Wages Expense 180

Date		Post. Ref.	Debit	Credit	Balance Debit	Balance Credit
Jan.	12	J2	600		600	
	26	J2	600		1,200	
	31	J3	180		1,380	
	31	J4		1,380	—	
Feb.	1	J5		180		180

4. Payment Entry

Feb. 9 Office Wages Expense 600
  Cash 600

Date		Post. Ref.	Debit	Credit	Balance Debit	Balance Credit
Jan.	12	J2	600		600	
	26	J2	600		1,200	
	31	J3	180		1,380	
	31	J4		1,380	—	
Feb.	1	J5		180		180
	9	J6	600		420	

These transactions had the following effects on Office Wages Expense:

1. Adjusted Office Wages Expense to accrue $180 in the proper accounting period.
2. Closed the $1,380 in total Office Wages Expense for January to Income Summary, leaving a zero balance.
3. Set up a credit balance of $180 on February 1 in Office Wages Expense equal to the expense recognized through the adjusting entry in January (and also reduced the liability account Wages Payable to a zero balance).
4. Recorded the $600 payment of two weeks' wages, as a debit to Office Wages Expense, automatically leaving a balance of $420, which represents the correct wages expense so far for February.

Making the payment entry was simplified by the reversing entry. Reversing entries apply to any accrued expenses or revenues. In the case of the Joan Miller Advertising Agency, Office Wages Expense was the only accrued expense. However, the asset Accrued Fees Receivable was created as a result of the adjusting entry made to accrue fees earned but not yet billed. The adjusting entry for this accrued revenue would therefore require a reversing entry, as follows:

Feb. 1   Advertising Fees Earned   200
        Accrued Fees Receivable   200
           To reverse adjusting entry for
           accrued fees receivable

When the series of advertisements is finished, the company can credit the entire proceeds to Advertising Fees Earned without regard to the amount accrued in the previous period. The credit will automatically be reduced to the amount earned during February by the $200 debit in the account.

As noted above, under the system of recording used in this book, reversing entries apply only to accruals. For this reason, reversing entries do not apply to deferrals such as those that involve supplies, prepaid rent, prepaid insurance, depreciation, and unearned art fees.

Chapter Review

Review of Learning Objectives

1. State all the steps in the accounting cycle.

The steps in the accounting cycle are to (1) analyze the transactions from the source documents, (2) record the transactions in the journal, (3) post the entries to the ledger, (4) adjust the accounts at the end of the period, (5) prepare the financial statements, and (6) close the accounts.

2. Prepare a work sheet.

A work sheet is prepared by first entering the account balances in the Trial Balance columns, the adjustments in the Adjustments columns, and the adjusted account balances in the Adjusted Trial Balance columns. Then the amounts from the Adjusted Trial Balance columns are extended to the Income Statement or Balance Sheet columns as appropriate. Next, the Income Statement and Balance Sheet columns are totaled. Finally, net income or net loss is determined from the Income Statement columns and extended to the Balance Sheet columns. The statement columns should now be in balance.

3. Identify the three principal uses of a work sheet.

A work sheet is useful in (1) preparing the financial statements, (2) recording the adjusting entries, and (3) recording the closing entries.

4. Prepare financial statements from a work sheet.

The balance sheet and income statements can be prepared directly from the Balance Sheet and Income Statement columns of a completed work sheet. It is common practice to prepare a separate statement of owner's equity from the work sheet. When this is done, the balance sheet contains only the ending balance of owner's equity.

5. Prepare the adjusting entries from a work sheet.

Adjusting entries can be recorded in the general journal directly from the Adjustments columns of the work sheet.

6. Explain the purposes of closing entries.

Closing entries have two objectives. First, they close the balances from the revenue and expense accounts in preparation for the next accounting period. Second, they summarize a period's revenues and expenses in the Income Summary so that the net income or net loss for the period may be transferred as a total to owner's equity.

7. Prepare the required closing entries.

Closing entries are prepared by first transferring the revenue and expense account balances to the Income Summary. Then the balance of the Income Summary account is transferred to the capital account. Finally, the balance of the withdrawals account is transferred to the capital account.

8. Prepare the post-closing trial balance.

As a final check on the balance of the ledger, a post-closing trial balance is prepared after the closing entries have been posted to the ledger accounts.

9. Prepare reversing entries as appropriate.

Reversing entries are optional general journal entries made on the first day of a new accounting period that exactly reverse certain adjusting entries made in the prior period. They apply only to accruals and facilitate routine bookkeeping procedures.

Self-Test

Test your knowledge of the chapter by choosing the best answer for each item below.

1. Which of the following sequences of actions describes the proper sequence in the accounting cycle?
    a. Post, enter, analyze, prepare, close, adjust
    b. Analyze, enter, post, adjust, prepare, close
    c. Prepare, enter, post, adjust, analyze, close
    d. Enter, post, close, prepare, adjust, analyze
2. The work sheet is a type of
    a. ledger.
    b. journal.
    c. working paper.
    d. financial statement.
3. The normal account balances for Equipment and Accumulated Depreciation, Equipment, are
    a. debit and credit, respectively.
    b. credit and debit, respectively.
    c. debits.
    d. credits.
4. The work sheet is useful in
    a. preparing financial statements.
    b. recording adjusting entries.
    c. recording closing entries.
    d. All of the above.
5. An important purpose of closing entries is
    a. to adjust the accounts in the ledger.
    b. to set balance sheet accounts to zero in order to begin the next period.
    c. to set income statement accounts to zero in order to begin the next period.
    d. None of the above.
6. In preparing closing entries, it is helpful to refer first to
    a. the Adjustments columns of the work sheet.
    b. the Adjusted Trial Balance columns of the work sheet.
    c. the Income Statement columns of the work sheet.
    d. the general journal.
7. After all closing entries have been posted, the balance of the income summary will be
    a. a debit if a net income has been earned.

b. a debit if a net loss has been incurred.
c. a credit if a net loss has been incurred.
d. zero.

8. After closing entries have been posted, which of the following accounts would have a nonzero balance?
   a. Service Revenue Earned   Unearned Service Revenue
   b. Depreciation Expense   d. Service Wages Expense

9. The post-closing trial balance will
   a. contain only income statement accounts.
   b. contain only balance sheet accounts.
   c. contain both income statement and balance sheet accounts.
   d. be prepared before closing entries are posted to the ledger.

10. For which of the following adjustments would a reversing entry facilitate bookkeeping procedures?
    a. Adjustment for depreciation expense
    b. Adjustment to allocate prepaid insurance to the current period
    c. Adjustment made as a result of inventory of supplies
    d. Adjustment for wages earned by employees but not yet paid

Answers to Self-Test are at the end of this chapter.

Review Problem
Completion of Work Sheet, Preparation of Financial Statements, Adjusting Entries, and Closing Entries

This chapter contains an extended example of the preparation of a work sheet and the last two steps of the accounting cycle for the Joan Miller Advertising Agency. Instead of studying a demonstration problem, you should carefully review and retrace the steps through the illustrations in the chapter.

Required

1. In Figure 5-6, what is the source of the trial balance figures?
2. Trace the entries in the Adjustments column of Figure 5-6 to the journal entries in Figure 5-10.
3. Trace the journal entries in Figure 5-10 to the ledger accounts in Figure 5-15.
4. Trace the amounts in the Income Statement and Balance Sheet columns of Figure 5-6 to the income statement in Figure 5-7, the statement of owner's equity in Figure 5-8, and the balance sheet in Figure 5-9.
5. Trace the amounts in the Income Statement columns and the withdrawals account balance of Figure 5-6 to the closing entries on pages 152–155.
6. Trace the closing entries on pages 152–155 to the ledger accounts in Figure 5-15.
7. Trace the balances of the ledger accounts in Figure 5-15 to the post-closing trial balance in Figure 5-16.

Chapter Assignments

Questions

1. Arrange the following activities in proper order by placing the numbers 1 through 6 in the blanks:

_____ a. The transactions are entered in the journal.
_____ b. Financial statements are prepared.

_____ c. The transactions are analyzed from the source documents.
_____ d. A work sheet is prepared.
_____ e. Closing entries are prepared.
_____ f. The transactions are posted to the ledger.

2. Why are working papers important to the accountant?
3. Why are work sheets never published and rarely seen by management?
4. Is the work sheet a substitute for the financial statements? Discuss.
5. At the end of the accounting period, does the posting of adjusting entries to the ledger precede or follow the preparation of the work sheet?
6. What is the normal balance of the following accounts, in terms of debit and credit? Cash; Accounts Payable; Prepaid Rent; Sam Jones, Capital; Commission Revenue; Sam Jones, Withdrawals; Rent Expense; Accumulated Depreciation, Office Equipment; Office Equipment.
7. What is the probable cause of a credit balance in the Cash account?
8. Should the Adjusted Trial Balance columns of the work sheet be totaled before or after the adjusted amounts are carried to the Income Statement and Balance Sheet columns? Discuss.
9. What sequence should be followed in extending the Adjusted Trial Balance columns to the Income Statement and Balance Sheet columns? Discuss.
10. Do the totals of the Balance Sheet columns of the work sheet usually agree with the totals on the balance sheet? Explain.
11. Do the Income Statement columns and Balance Sheet columns balance after the adjusted amounts from the Adjusted Trial Balance columns are extended?
12. What is the purpose of the Income Summary account?
13. Are adjusting entries posted to the ledger accounts at the same time as the closing entries? Explain.
14. What is the difference between adjusting and closing entries?
15. What are the four basic tasks of closing entries?
16. Which of the following accounts will not have a balance after closing entries are prepared and posted? Insurance Expense; Accounts Receivable; Commission Revenue; Prepaid Insurance; Withdrawals; Supplies; Supplies Expense.
17. What is the significance of the post-closing trial balance?
18. Which of the following accounts will appear on the post-closing trial balance? Insurance Expense; Accounts Receivable; Commission Revenue; Prepaid Insurance; Withdrawals; Supplies; Supplies Expense; Capital.
19. How can reversing entries aid in the bookkeeping process?
20. To what types of adjustments do reversing entries apply? To what types do they not apply?

Classroom Exercises

**Exercise 5-1
Preparation of
Trial Balance**
(L.O. 2)

The following alphabetical list represents the accounts and balances for Walker Realty on December 31, 19xx. All accounts have normal balances.

Accounts Payable	$ 2,170
Accounts Receivable	1,750
Accumulated Depreciation, Office Equipment	450
Advertising Expense	600
Cash	2,545
Office Equipment	3,000
Prepaid Insurance	560
Rent Expense	2,400
Revenue from Commissions	19,300
Supplies	275

Wages Expense	12,000	
Walker, Capital	10,210	
Walker, Withdrawals	9,000	

Prepare a trial balance by listing the accounts on a sheet of accounting paper in the same order, with the balances in the appropriate debit or credit column.

Exercise 5-2
Preparation of
Adjusting and
Reversing
Entries from
Work Sheet
Columns
(L.O. 5, 9)

The items listed below are from the Adjustments columns of a work sheet as of December 31.

1. Prepare adjusting journal entries from the information.
2. Prepare reversing entries as appropriate.

	Adjustments	
	Debit	Credit
Prepaid Insurance		(a) 120
Office Supplies		(b) 315
Accumulated Depreciation, Office Equipment		(c) 700
Accumulated Depreciation, Store Equipment		(d) 1,100
Office Salaries Expense	(e) 120	
Store Salaries Expense	(e) 240	
Insurance Expense	(a) 120	
Office Supplies Expense	(b) 315	
Depreciation Expense, Office Equipment	(c) 700	
Depreciation Expense, Store Equipment	(d) 1,100	
Salaries Payable		(e) 360
	2,595	2,595

Exercise 5-3
Preparation of
Closing Entries
from Work
Sheet
(L.O. 7)

The following items are from the Income Statement columns of the work sheet of the Bert Oliver Repair Shop for the year ended December 31.

	Income Statement	
	Debit	Credit
Repair Revenue		24,240
Wages Expense	7,840	
Rent Expense	1,200	
Supplies Expense	4,260	
Insurance Expense	915	
Depreciation Expense, Repair Equipment	1,345	
	15,560	24,240
Net Income	8,680	
	24,240	24,240

Prepare entries to close the revenue, expense, Income Summary, and withdrawal accounts. Mr. Oliver withdrew $10,000 during the year.

Exercise 5-4
Preparing a
Statement of
Owner's Equity
(L.O. 4)

The capital, withdrawal, and Income Summary accounts for Ralph's Barber Shop for the year ended December 31, after recording of closing entries, are presented in T account form below.

Ralph Beck, Capital	
12/31 12,000	1/1 26,000
	12/31 13,000
	Bal. 27,000

Ralph Beck, Withdrawals	
4/1 4,000	12/31 12,000
7/1 4,000	
10/1 4,000	
Bal. —	

Income Summary	
12/31 39,000	12/31 52,000
12/31 13,000	
Bal. —	

Prepare a statement of owner's equity for Ralph's Barber Shop.

Exercise 5-5
Completion of
Work Sheet
(L.O. 2)

The following list of alphabetically arranged accounts and balances represents a trial balance in highly simplified form for the month ended October 31, 19xx.

Trial Balance Accounts and Balances

Accounts Payable	$ 3	Office Equipment	$ 6
Accounts Receivable	5	Prepaid Insurance	2
Accumulated Depreciation,		Service Revenue	20
Office Equipment	1	Supplies	4
Art Rosen, Capital	12	Unearned Revenue	3
Art Rosen, Withdrawals	6	Utilities Expense	2
Cash	4	Wages Expense	10

1. On accounting paper, prepare a work sheet form, entering the trial balance accounts in the same order in which they appear above. (Arrange the balances in the correct debit or credit column.)

2. Complete the work sheet using the following information:
  a. Expired insurance, $1.
  b. Of the unearned revenue, $2 has been earned by the balance sheet date.
  c. Estimated depreciation on office equipment, $1.
  d. Accrued wages, $1.
  e. Unused supplies on hand, $1.

Exercise 5-6
Deriving
Adjusting
Entries from
Trial Balance
and Income
Statement
Columns
(L.O. 5)

Presented below is a partial work sheet in which the Trial Balance and Income Statement columns have been completed. All amounts are in dollars.

Accounts	Trial Balance	Income Statement
Cash	5	
Accounts Receivable	10	
Supplies	11	
Prepaid Insurance	8	
Building	25	
Accumulated Depreciation,		
Building	8	
Accounts Payable	4	
Unearned Revenue	2	
B.T., Capital	32	

Revenue		40		42
Wages Expense	27		30	
	86	86		
Insurance Expense			4	
Supplies Expense			8	
Depreciation Expense, Building			2	
			44	42
Net Loss				2
			44	44

1. Determine the adjusting entries that have been made. Assume that no adjustments are made to Accounts Receivable or Accounts Payable.
2. Prepare a balance sheet.

Exercise 5-7
Reversing
Entries
(L.O. 9)

Selected T accounts for Sinclair Company are presented below for 19xx:

Supplies				Supplies Expense			
1/1 Bal.	430	12/31 Adjust.	640	12/31 Adjust.	640	12/31 Closing	640
19xx purchases	470						
Bal.	260			**Bal.**	—		

Accrued Fees Receivable				Fees Revenue			
12/31 Adjust.	320			19xx Closing	1,290	19xx receipts	970
Bal.	320					12/31 Adjust.	320
						Bal.	—

Selected portions of the closing entries to Income Summary are shown below:

Income Summary			
12/31 Closing	640	12/31 Closing	1,290
12/31 Closing	650		
Bal.	—		

1. In which case above is a reversing entry helpful? Why?
2. Prepare the appropriate reversing entry.
3. Prepare the entry to record receipts for fees totaling $570 in January of the next year. How much is Fees Revenue for January?

Interpreting Accounting Information

Published
Financial Infor-
mation: Sperry
& Hutchinson
(L.O. 1, 5, 7)

Sperry & Hutchinson is known as "The Green Stamp Company" because its principal business is selling S & H Green Stamps to merchants who give them to customers who, in turn, may redeem them for merchandise. When S & H sells green stamps, it incurs a liability to redeem the stamps. It makes a profit to the extent that people do not redeem the stamps. In the past, S & H has assumed that 95 percent of all stamps will be redeemed. Thus a sale of $1,000 worth of stamps would be recorded as follows:

Cash	1,000	
Liability to Redeem Stamps		950
Stamp Revenue		50

Since it may be years before some stamps are redeemed, the company keeps the liability on its balance sheet indefinitely. An article in *Forbes*, a leading business weekly magazine, commented on S & H's situation as follows:

The company [S & H] is sitting on a mountain of money held in reserve to redeem stamps already issued but not yet cashed in. How many of these stamps will ultimately be redeemed? Nobody knows for sure. But Sperry [S & H] has made some assumptions in drawing up its financial statements, and at last count it had stashed away no less than $308 million to match unredeemed stamps. That's more than last year's stamp sales. It's one-third more than the company's total [owners'] equity of $231 million. What's more, to the extent that the company has overestimated the need for that liability—setting aside cash for Green Stamps that have been thrown into the garbage—some of the cash is clearly equity in all but name.

The Liability for Redemption of Stamps became so large that in 1979 S & H began setting aside only 90 percent (instead of 95 percent) of stamp sales for redemption. The immediate effect of this change was to boost profits. The reason for this effect is, as stated in *Forbes*, "the extra 5 percent of stamps now assumed to be lost forever goes straight through as pure profit."*

Required

1. Assume that S & H has an asset account called Merchandise that represents the goods that can be redeemed. What entry would be made if $700 worth of stamps were redeemed for merchandise?
2. What does *Forbes* mean when it says that "some of the cash is clearly equity in all but name"? Is the word "cash" used properly? Show that you know what *Forbes* means by showing the adjusting entry and closing entries that would be made if S & H decided to reduce the liability for redemption of stamps.
3. Explain *Forbes's* comment that the extra 5 percent "goes straight through as pure profit."

Problem Set A

Problem 5A-1 Preparation of Financial Statements and End-of-Period Entries (L.O. 4, 5, 7, 9)

Northside Trailer Rental owns thirty small trailers that are rented by the day for local moving jobs. The Trial Balance and Adjusted Trial Balance columns of the work sheet for Northside Trailer Rental on June 30, 19xx, which is the end of the current fiscal year, appear on page 173.

Required

1. From the information given, prepare an income statement, a statement of owner's equity, and a balance sheet.
2. From the information given, record adjusting entries, closing entries, and reversing entries in the general journal.

* *Forbes*, October 12, 1981, page 73.

Chapter Five

Northside Trailer Rental
Trial Balance and Adjusted Trial Balance
For Year Ended June 30, 19xx

Account Name	Trial Balance		Adjusted Trial Balance	
	Debit	Credit	Debit	Credit
Cash	346		346	
Accounts Receivable	972		972	
Supplies	385		119	
Prepaid Insurance	720		360	
Trailers	12,000		12,000	
Accumulated Depreciation, Trailers		4,800		7,200
Accounts Payable		271		271
Rita Montoya, Capital		5,694		5,694
Rita Montoya, Withdrawals	7,200		7,200	
Trailer Rentals		45,200		45,200
Wages Expense	23,200		23,400	
Insurance Expense	360		720	
Other Expenses	10,782		10,782	
	55,965	55,965		
Supplies Expense			266	
Depreciation Expense, Trailers			2,400	
Wages Payable				200
			58,565	58,565

Problem 5A-2
Preparation of Work Sheet, Adjusting Entries, and Closing Entries
(L.O. 2, 4, 5, 7, 9)

James Laughlin began his law practice immediately after graduation from law school. To help him get started, several clients paid him retainers (payment in advance) for future services. Other clients paid when service was provided. After one year in practice, the law firm had the trial balance shown below.

James Laughlin, Attorney
Trial Balance
December 31, 19xx

Cash	$ 1,375	
Accounts Receivable	2,109	
Office Supplies	382	
Office Equipment	3,755	
Accounts Payable		$ 796
Unearned Retainers		5,000

James Laughlin, Capital		4,000
James Laughlin, Withdrawals	6,000	
Legal Fees		16,200
Rent Expense	1,800	
Utility Expense	717	
Wages Expense	9,858	
	$25,996	$25,996

Required

1. Enter the trial balance amounts in the Trial Balance columns of a work sheet, and complete the work sheet using the following information:
   a. Inventory of unused supplies, $91.
   b. Estimated depreciation on equipment, $600.
   c. Services rendered during the month but not yet billed, $650.
   d. Services rendered to clients who paid in advance that should be applied against retainers, $2,900.
   e. Salaries earned by employees but not yet paid, $60.
2. From the work sheet, prepare an income statement, a statement of owner's equity, and a balance sheet.
3. From the work sheet, prepare adjusting, closing, and reversing entries.
4. How would you evaluate the first year of James's law practice?

Problem 5A-3
Completion of Work Sheet, Preparation of Financial Statements, Adjusting, Closing, and Reversing Entries
(L.O. 2, 4, 5, 7, 9)

At the end of the current fiscal year, the trial balance of the Drexel Theater appeared as follows:

Drexel Theater
Trial Balance
September 30, 19xx

Cash	$ 9,800	
Accounts Receivable	8,472	
Prepaid Insurance	9,800	
Office Supplies	280	
Cleaning Supplies	1,795	
Land	10,000	
Building	200,000	
Accumulated Depreciation, Building		$ 18,500
Theater Furnishings	185,000	
Accumulated Depreciation, Theater Furnishings		32,500
Office Equipment	15,800	
Accumulated Depreciation, Office Equipment		7,780
Accounts Payable		22,643
Gift Books Liability		20,950
Mortgage Payable		150,000
Dave Parsons, Capital		156,324
Dave Parsons, Withdrawals	30,000	
Ticket Sales		200,000

Theater Rental		22,600
Usher Wages Expense	92,000	
Office Wages Expense	12,000	
Utilities Expense	56,350	
	$631,297	$631,297

Required

1. Enter the trial balance amounts in the Trial Balance columns of a work sheet and complete the work sheet using the following information:
   a. Expired insurance, $8,900.
   b. Inventory of unused office supplies, $88.
   c. Inventory of unused cleaning supplies, $173.
   d. Estimated depreciation on building, $5,000.
   e. Estimated depreciation on theater furnishings, $18,000.
   f. Estimated depreciation on office equipment, $1,580.
   g. The company credits all gift books sold during the year to a Gift Books Liability account. On September 30, it was estimated that $18,500 worth of the gift books had been redeemed.
   h. There are $410 worth of accrued but unpaid usher wages at the end of the year.
2. Prepare an income statement, a statement of owner's equity, and a balance sheet.
3. Prepare adjusting, closing, and reversing entries from the work sheet.

Problem 5A-4
The Complete Accounting Cycle—Two Months
(L.O. 2, 4, 5, 7, 8)

During the first month of operation, the Peterson Bicycle Repair Store completed the following transactions:

May	1	Began business by depositing $3,000 in a bank account in the name of the company.
	1	Paid the premium on a one-year insurance policy, $360.
	1	Paid one month's rent, $320.
	2	Purchased repair equipment from Ward Company for $1,900. The terms were $300 down payment and $100 per month for sixteen months. The first payment is due June 1.
	5	Purchased repair supplies from Norris Company for $195 on credit.
	14	Paid utility expense for the month of May, $77.
	15	Cash bicycle repair revenue for the first half of May, $431.
	20	Paid $100 of the amount owed to Norris Company.
	29	Owner withdrew $400 from the company for personal living expenses.
	31	Cash bicycle repair revenue for the last half of May, $566.

Required for May

1. Prepare journal entries to record the May transactions.
2. Open the following accounts: Cash (111); Prepaid Insurance (117); Repair Supplies (119); Repair Equipment (144); Accumulated Depreciation, Repair Equipment (145); Accounts Payable (212); Mike Peterson, Capital (311); Mike Peterson, Withdrawals (312); Income Summary (313); Bicycle Repair Revenue (411); Store Rent Expense (511); Utility Expense (512); Insurance Expense (513); Repair Supplies Expense (514); Depreciation Expense, Repair Equipment (515). Post the May journal entries to ledger accounts.
3. Prepare a trial balance in the Trial Balance columns of a work sheet, and complete the work sheet using the information on the next page.

a. One month's insurance has expired.
b. Inventory of unused repair supplies, $86.
c. Estimated depreciation on repair equipment, $25.

4. From the work sheet, prepare an income statement, a statement of owner's equity, and a balance sheet for May.

5. From the work sheet, prepare and post adjusting and closing entries.

6. Prepare a post-closing trial balance.

During June, Peterson Bicycle Repair Store engaged in the following transactions:

June 1 Paid the monthly rent, $320.
     1 Made the monthly payment to Ward Company, $100.
     9 Purchased additional repair supplies on credit from Norris Company, $447.
   15 Cash bicycle repair revenue for the first half of June, $525.
   18 Paid utility expense for June, $83.
   19 Paid Norris Company on account, $200.
   28 Withdrew $400 from the company for personal living expenses.
   30 Cash bicycle repair revenue for the last half of June, $436.

Required for June

7. Prepare and post journal entries to record June transactions.

8. Prepare a trial balance in the Trial Balance columns of a work sheet, and complete the work sheet based on the following information:
a. One month's insurance has expired.
b. Inventory of unused repair supplies, $191.
c. Estimated depreciation on repair equipment, $25.

9. From the work sheet, prepare the June income statement, statement of owner's equity, and balance sheet.

10. From the work sheet, prepare and post adjusting and closing entries.

11. Prepare a post-closing trial balance.

Problem 5A-5
Preparation of
Work Sheet
from Limited
Data
(L.O. 2, 4, 5)

Presented below and opposite are the income statement and trial balance for Eastmoor Bowling Lanes for the year ending December 31, 19xx:

Eastmoor Bowling Lanes
Income Statement
For the Year Ended December 31, 19xx

Revenues		$615,817
Expenses		
Wages Expense	$381,076	
Advertising Expense	15,200	
Utility Expense	42,900	
Depreciation Expense, Building	4,800	
Depreciation Expense, Equipment	11,000	
Supplies Expense	1,148	
Maintenance Expense	81,300	
Insurance Expense	1,500	

Property Tax Expense	10,000	
Miscellaneous Expense	10,200	
Total Expenses		559,124
Net Income		**$ 56,693**

Eastmoor Bowling Lanes
Trial Balance
December 31, 19xx

Cash	$ 12,741	
Accounts Receivable	7,388	
Supplies	1,304	
Unexpired Insurance	1,800	
Prepaid Advertising	900	
Land	5,000	
Building	100,000	
Accumulated Depreciation, Building		$ 19,000
Equipment	125,000	
Accumulated Depreciation, Equipment		22,000
Accounts Payable		14,317
Notes Payable		70,000
Unearned Revenues		2,300
Margaret Lord, Capital		60,813
Margaret Lord, Withdrawals	24,000	
Revenues		614,817
Wages Expense	377,114	
Advertising Expense	14,300	
Utility Expense	42,200	
Maintenance Expense	81,300	
Miscellaneous Expense	10,200	
	$803,247	$803,247

Required

1. Using the information given, fill in the Trial Balance and Income Statement columns of a work sheet.
2. Reconstruct the adjusting entries and complete the work sheet. Assume that there is no adjustment to Accounts Receivable. Then record the adjusting entries in the general journal with explanations.
3. Prepare the statement of owner's equity and the balance sheet as of December 31, 19xx.

Problem Set B

Problem 5B-1
Preparation of
Financial State-
ments and
End-of-Period
Entries
(L.O. 4, 5, 7, 9)

South Beach Marina rents one hundred slips in a large dock to owners of small boats in the area. The Trial Balance and Adjusted Trial Balance columns of the work sheet for South Beach Marina on December 31, the end of the current fiscal year, are presented below.

South Beach Marina
Trial Balance and Adjusted Trial Balance
For the Year Ended December 31, 19xx

Account Name	Trial Balance Debit	Trial Balance Credit	Adjusted Trial Balance Debit	Adjusted Trial Balance Credit
Cash	1,360		1,360	
Accounts Receivable	2,440		2,440	
Supplies	516		76	
Prepaid Insurance	742		396	
Dock	30,600		30,600	
Accumulated Depreciation, Dock		5,000		7,000
Accounts Payable		1,100		1,150
Alice Thorn, Capital		31,023		31,023
Alice Thorn, Withdrawals	12,000		12,000	
Ship Rentals		19,400		19,400
Wages Expense	7,400		7,400	
Insurance Expense	915		1,261	
Utility Expense	550		600	
	56,523	56,523		
Supplies Expense			440	
Depreciation Expense, Dock			2,000	
			58,573	58,573

Required

1. From the information given, prepare an income statement, a statement of owner's equity, and a balance sheet.
2. From the information given, record the adjusting, closing, and reversing entries in the general journal.

**Problem 5B-2
Preparation of
Work Sheet,
Adjusting,
Closing, and
Reversing
Entries**
(L.O. 2, 5, 7, 9)

Jack Morgan opened his investment advisory service on June 1, 19xx. Some customers paid for counseling services after they were rendered, and others paid in advance for one year of service. After six months of operation, Jack wanted to know how he stood. The trial balance on November 30 appears at the top of the next page.

Morgan Investment Advisory Service
Trial Balance
November 30, 19xx

Cash	$ 475	
Prepaid Rent	1,200	
Office Supplies	275	
Office Equipment	2,500	
Accounts Payable		$ 1,675
Unearned Revenue		1,215
Jack Morgan, Capital		4,000
Jack Morgan, Withdrawals	2,400	
Advisory Revenue		3,380
Telephone and Utility Expense	420	
Wages Expense	3,000	
	$10,270	$10,270

Required

1. Enter the trial balance amounts in the Trial Balance columns of a work sheet and complete the work sheet using the following information:
   a. One year's rent paid in advance when Jack began business.
   b. Inventory of unused supplies, $50.
   c. One-half year's depreciation on office equipment, $200.
   d. Service rendered that had been paid for in advance, $575.
   e. Investment advisory services rendered during the month but not yet billed, $180.
   f. Wages earned by employees but not yet paid, $125.
2. From the work sheet, prepare an income statement, a statement of owner's equity, and a balance sheet.
3. From the work sheet, prepare adjusting, closing, and reversing entries.
4. What is your evaluation of Jack's first six months in business?

**Problem 5B-3
Completion of
Work Sheet,
Preparation of
Financial Statements, Adjusting, Closing,
and Reversing
Entries**
(L.O. 2, 4, 5, 7)

The trial balance on page 180 was taken from the ledger of Colavito Moving and Storage Company on December 31, the end of the company's accounting period.

Required

1. Enter the trial balance amounts in the Trial Balance columns of a work sheet and complete the work sheet using the following information:
   a. Expired insurance, $970.

b. Inventory of unused moving supplies, $450.

c. Inventory of unused office supplies, $70.

d. Estimated depreciation, building, $4,800.

e. Estimated depreciation, trucks, $5,150.

f. Estimated depreciation, office equipment, $900.

g. The company credits the storage fees of customers who pay in advance to the Unearned Storage Fees account. Of the amount credited to this account during the year, $1,850 has been earned by December 31.

h. There are $265 worth of accrued storage fees earned but unrecorded and uncollected at the end of the accounting period.

i. There are $640 worth of accrued but unpaid truck drivers' wages at the end of the year.

2. Prepare an income statement, a statement of owner's equity, and a balance sheet.

3. Prepare adjusting, closing, and reversing entries from the work sheet.

Colavito Moving and Storage Company
Trial Balance
December 31, 19xx

Cash	$ 2,685	
Accounts Receivable	9,415	
Prepaid Insurance	1,780	
Moving Supplies	4,900	
Office Supplies	820	
Land	5,000	
Building	52,000	
Accumulated Depreciation, Building		$ 17,800
Trucks	34,600	
Accumulated Depreciation, Trucks		10,300
Office Equipment	5,300	
Accumulated Depreciation, Office Equipment		3,600
Accounts Payable		2,460
Unearned Storage Fees		2,780
Mortgage Payable		24,000
H. Colavito, Capital		42,910
H. Colavito, Withdrawals	10,000	
Moving Services Revenue		80,800
Storage Fees Earned		9,600
Truck Drivers' Wages Expense	42,600	
Office Salaries Expense	14,800	
Gas, Oil, and Truck Repairs Expense	10,350	
	$194,250	$194,250

Problem 5B-4
The Complete
Accounting
Cycle—Two
Months
(L.O. 1, 2, 4, 5, 7, 8)

On July 1, 19xx, Larry Daley opened Daley TV Repair Shop and during the month completed the following transactions for the new company:

July 1 Deposited $2,000 of his savings in a bank account in the name of the company.
  1 Paid the rent for a store for one month, $150.
  1 Paid the premium on a one-year insurance policy, $240.
  2 Purchased repair equipment from Warren Company for $2,800 on the basis of $400 down payment and $200 per month for one year. The first payment is due August 1.
  5 Purchased repair supplies from Rogers Company for $275 on credit.
  8 Purchased an advertisement in a local newspaper for $40.
  15 Cash TV repair revenue for the first half of the month, $200.
  21 Paid $150 of the amount owed to Rogers Company.
  25 Larry Daley withdrew $300 from the company bank account to pay living expenses.
  31 Cash TV repair revenue for the second half of July, $450.

Required for July

1. Prepare journal entries to record the July transactions.

2. Open the following accounts: Cash (111); Prepaid Insurance (117); Repair Supplies (119); Repair Equipment (144); Accumulated Depreciation, Repair Equipment (145); Accounts Payable (212); Larry Daley, Capital (311); Larry Daley, Withdrawals (312); Income Summary (313); TV Repair Revenue (411); Store Rent Expense (511); Advertising Expense (512); Insurance Expense (513); Repair Supplies Expense (514); Depreciation Expense, Repair Equipment (515). Post the July journal entries to ledger accounts.

3. Prepare a trial balance in the Trial Balance columns of a work sheet, and complete the work sheet using the following information:
  a. One month's insurance has expired.
  b. Remaining inventory of unused repair supplies, $105.
  c. Estimated depreciation on repair equipment, $40.

4. From the work sheet, prepare an income statement, a statement of owner's equity, and a balance sheet for July.

5. From the work sheet, prepare and post adjusting and closing entries.

6. Prepare a post-closing trial balance.

During August Larry Daley completed the following transactions for the Daley TV Repair Shop:

Aug. 1 Paid the monthly rent, $150.
  1 Made monthly payment to Warren Company, $200.
  6 Purchased additional repair supplies on credit from Rogers Company, $575.
  15 Cash TV repair revenue for the first half of the month, $575.
  20 Purchased an additional advertisement in local newspaper, $40.
  23 Paid Rogers Company on account, $400.
  25 Larry Daley withdrew $300 from the company for living expenses.
  31 Cash TV repair revenue for the last half of the month, $545.

Required for August

7. Prepare and post journal entries to record August transactions.

8. Prepare a trial balance in the Trial Balance columns of a work sheet and complete the work sheet based on the following information:
  a. One month's insurance has expired.

Completing the Accounting Cycle   **181**

b. Inventory of unused repair supplies, $275.

c. Estimated depreciation on repair equipment, $40.

9. From the work sheet, prepare the August income statement, statement of owner's equity, and balance sheet.

10. From the work sheet, prepare and post adjusting and closing entries.

11. Prepare a post-closing trial balance.

Problem 5B-5
Preparation of
Work Sheet
from Limited
Data
(L.O. 2, 4, 5)

Dick Moore started work as an accountant with the Bridgeport Golf Course on June 30, the end of the accounting period. His boss tells him that he must have an income statement and a balance sheet by 9:00 A.M. the next day in order to obtain a renewal of the bank loan. Dick takes home the general ledger and supporting data for adjusting entries. At 3:00 A.M., after completing the statements, he lights a cigarette and falls asleep. A few minutes later he awakes to find the papers on fire. He quickly puts out the fire but is horrified to discover that except for the general ledger and the income statement everything else, including the work sheet, supporting data, and balance sheet, is completely destroyed. He decides that he should be able to reconstruct the balance sheet and adjusting entries from the general ledger and the income statement, even though he had not yet recorded and posted the adjusting and closing entries. The information available is as follows:

General Ledger

Cash		Miscellaneous Expense	
Bal. 7,200		Bal. 2,300	

Prepaid Advertising		Supplies	
Bal. 1,700		Bal. 2,400	

Land		Equipment	
Bal. 248,400		Bal. 52,000	

Accumulated Depreciation, Equipment		Accounts Payable	
	Bal. 12,800		Bal. 100,000

Unearned Revenue, Locker Fees		Tom Hemming, Capital	
	Bal. 4,200		Bal. 157,050

(continued)

Chapter Five

General Ledger

Tom Hemming, Withdrawals		Revenue from Greens Fees	
Bal. 18,000			Bal. 224,500

Advertising Expense		Water and Utility Expense	
Bal. 14,750		Bal. 20,600	

Wages Expense		Maintenance Expense	
Bal. 114,000		Bal. 17,200	

Bridgeport Golf Course
Income Statement
For the Period Ended June 30, 19xx

Revenues

Revenue from Greens Fees	$224,500	
Revenue from Locker Fees	3,200	
Total Revenues		$227,700

Expenses

Wages Expense	$117,000	
Maintenance Expense	17,200	
Depreciation Expense, Equipment	4,000	
Water and Utility Expense	21,600	
Supplies Expense	2,000	
Advertising Expense	13,250	
Property Taxes Expense	7,500	
Miscellaneous Expense	2,300	
Total Expenses		184,850
Net Income		$ 42,850

Required

1. Using the information above, fill in the Trial Balance and Income Statement columns of a work sheet.
2. Reconstruct the adjusting entries and complete the work sheet. Then record the adjusting entries in the general journal with explanations.
3. Prepare the statement of owner's equity and the balance sheet for June 30, 19xx.

Financial Decision Case 5-1

Judy's Quik-Type
(L.O. 4)

Judy's Quik-Type is a very simple business. Judy provides typing services for students at the local university. Her accountant prepared the income statement on page 184 for the year ended August 31, 19x2.

In reviewing this statement, Judy is puzzled since she knows that she withdrew $8,400 in cash for personal expenses, and yet the cash balance in the company's bank account increased from $230 to $1,060 from last August 31 to this August 31. She wants to know how her net income could be less than the cash she took out of the business if there is an increase in the cash balance.

Her accountant shows her the balance sheet for August 31, 19x2, and compares it to the one for August 31, 19x1. He explains that besides the change in the cash balance, accounts receivable from customers decreased by $740, and accounts payable increased by $190 (supplies are the only items Judy buys on credit). The only other asset or liability account that changed during the year was accumulated depreciation on office equipment, which increased by $900.

Judy's Quik-Type
Income Statement
For the Year Ended August 31, 19x2

Revenues		
Typing Services		$10,600
Expenses		
Rent Expense	$1,200	
Depreciation Expense, Office Equipment	900	
Supplies Expense	480	
Other Expenses	620	
Total Expenses		3,200
Net Income		$ 7,400

Required

Explain to Judy in your own words why the accountant is answering Judy's question by pointing out year-to-year changes in the balance sheet. Then verify the increase in the cash balance by preparing a statement that lists the receipts of cash and the expenditures of cash during the year. How did you treat depreciation expense? Why?

Answers to Self-Test

1. b	3. a	5. c	7. d	9. b
2. c	4. d	6. c	8. c	10. d

Part Two

Extensions of the Basic Accounting Model

Accounting, as you have seen, is an information system that measures, processes, and communicates information, primarily financial in nature, for decision making. Part I presented the principles and practices of the basic accounting system.

In Part II, the basic accounting system is extended to more complex applications.

Chapter 6 deals with accounting for merchandising companies, which is different in certain ways from the accounting for service companies you studied earlier.

Chapter 7 addresses the goals of organizing accounting systems in order to process a large number of transactions in an efficient and time-saving way.

Chapter 8 first describes the basic principles of internal control and then applies these principles to merchandising transactions.

Chapter 9 presents the objectives and conventions underlying the use of financial statements. It also shows how classified and general-purpose external financial statements are constructed and how they are analyzed using simple ratios.

Learning
Objectives

Chapter
Six

Accounting
for
Merchandising
Operations

Up to this point, you have studied the accounting records and reports for the simplest type of business—the service company. In this chapter, you will study a more complex type of business—the merchandising company. This chapter focuses on the merchandising company's special buying and selling transactions and their effects on the income statement. As a result of studying this chapter, you should be able to meet the learning objectives listed on the left.

Service companies such as advertising agencies or law firms perform a service for a fee or commission. In determining net income, a very simple income statement is all that is needed. Net income is measured as the difference between revenues and expenses.

In contrast, many other companies attempt to earn an income by buying and selling merchandise. Merchandising companies, whether wholesale or retail, do use the same basic accounting methods as service companies, but the process of buying and selling merchandise requires some additional accounts and concepts. This process also results in a more complicated income statement than that for a service business.

Income Statement for a Merchandising Concern

Figure 6-1 highlights the three major parts of the income statement for a merchandising concern: (1) revenues from sales, (2) cost of goods sold, and (3) operating expenses. Such an income statement differs from the income statement for a service firm in that gross margin from sales must be computed before operating expenses are deducted to arrive at net income.

Revenues from sales arise from sales of goods by the merchandising company and the cost of goods sold tells how much the

Figure 6-1
The Parts of an
Income State-
ment for a
Merchandising
Concern

Fenwick Fashions Company Income Statement For the Year Ended December 31, 19xx		
Revenues from Sales		$239,325
Cost of Goods Sold		131,360
Gross Margin from Sales		$107,965
Operating Expenses		89,284
Net Income		$ 18,681

Objective 1
Identify the
components of
income state-
ments for mer-
chandising
concerns

merchant paid for the goods that were sold. The difference between revenues from sales and cost of goods sold is known as **gross margin from sales**, or simply **gross margin**. To be successful, the merchant must sell the goods for enough more than cost—that is, gross margin from sales must be great enough—to pay operating expenses and have an adequate income left over. **Operating expenses** are those expenses, other than cost of goods sold, that are incurred in running the business. In a merchandising company, operating expenses are similar to the expenses you have seen in a service company. **Net income** for merchandising companies is what is left after deducting operating expenses from gross margin. Note that Fenwick Fashions Company had a gross margin from sales of $107,965 ($239,325 − $131,360) and net income of $18,681 ($107,965 − $89,284).

All three parts of the merchandising income statement are important to a company's management. Management is interested both in the percentage of gross margin on sales and in the amount of gross margin (45 percent and $107,965, respectively, for the Fenwick Fashions Company). This information is helpful in planning business operations. For instance, management may try to increase total sales dollars by reducing the selling price. This strategy results in a reduction in the percentage of gross margin. It will work if total items sold increase enough to raise total gross margin (which raises income from operations). On the other hand, management may increase operating expenses (such as advertising expense) in an effort to increase sales dollars and the amount of gross profit. If the increase in gross margin is greater than the increase in advertising, income from operations will improve.

In this chapter, we discuss the three parts of the merchandising income statement and the transactions that give rise to the amounts in each part. Then we present two alternative methods for preparing the work sheet for a merchandising company. The chapter ends with a comprehensive illustration of the merchandising income statement.

Figure 6-2
Partial Income
Statement—
Revenues from
Sales

Fenwick Fashions Company
Partial Income Statement
For the Year Ended December 31, 19xx

Revenues from Sales		
Gross Sales		$246,350
Less: Sales Returns and Allowances	$2,750	
Sales Discounts	4,275	7,025
Net Sales		$239,325

Revenues from Sales

Objective 2
Journalize
transactions
involving reve-
nues for mer-
chandising
concerns

The first part of the merchandising income statement is revenues from sales, as presented in Figure 6-2. This section requires the computation of net sales, which consist of gross proceeds from sales of merchandise less sales returns and allowances and sales discounts. If a business is to succeed or even survive, net sales must be great enough to pay for cost of goods sold and operating expenses and to provide an adequate net income.

Management, investors, and others often consider the amount and trend of sales to be important indicators of a firm's progress. Increasing sales suggest growth, whereas decreasing sales indicate the possibility of decreased earnings and other financial problems in the future. Thus, to detect trends, comparisons are frequently made between net sales of different periods.

Gross Sales

Under accrual accounting, revenues from the sale of merchandise are considered to be earned in the accounting period in which the goods are delivered to the customer. **Gross sales** consist of total sales for cash and total sales on credit for a given accounting period. Because the customer may not pay immediately, the cash for the sale may be collected in a following period, but this does not affect the recording of sales. For this reason, there is likely to be quite a difference between revenues from sales and cash collected from those sales in a given period.

The journal entry to record a sale of merchandise for cash is as follows:

Sept. 16	Cash	1,286	
	Sales		1,286
	To record the sale of		
	merchandise for cash		

The Sales account is used only for recording sales of merchandise, whether the sale is made for cash or for credit. If the sale of merchandise is made on credit, the entry is as follows:

```
Sept. 16   Accounts Receivable          746
              Sales                            746
                    To record the sale of
                    merchandise on credit
```

Sales Returns and Allowances

If a customer receives a defective or otherwise unsatisfactory product, the seller will usually try to accommodate the customer. The business may allow the customer to return the item for a cash refund or credit on account, or it may give the customer an allowance off the sales price. A good accounting system will provide management with information about sales returns and allowances because such transactions may reveal dissatisfied customers. Each return or allowance is recorded as a debit to an account called **Sales Returns and Allowances**. An example of such a transaction follows:

```
Sept. 17   Sales Returns and Allowances     76
              Accounts Receivable (or Cash)        76
                    To record return or
                    allowance on unsatisfactory
                    merchandise
```

Sales Returns and Allowances is a contra account and is accordingly deducted from gross sales in the income statement (see Figure 6-2).

Sales Discounts

When goods are sold on credit, both parties should always have a definite understanding as to the amount and time of payment. These terms are usually printed on the sales invoice and constitute part of the sales agreement. Customary terms differ from industry to industry. In some industries, payment is expected in a short period of time such as ten days or thirty days. In these cases, the invoice may be marked "n/10" or "n/30," meaning that the amount of the invoice is due ten days or thirty days, respectively, after the invoice date. If the invoice is due ten days after the end of the month, it may be marked "n/10 eom."

In some industries it is common to give discounts for early payment, called **sales discounts**. This practice increases the seller's liquidity by reducing the amount of money tied up in accounts receivable. These terms may be stated on the invoice as 2/10, n/30 or 2/10, n/60. Terms of 2/10, n/30 mean that the debtor may take a 2 percent discount if he or she pays the invoice within ten days after the invoice date. Otherwise, the debtor may wait until thirty days after the invoice date and then must pay the full amount of the invoice without the discount.

Because it is not usually possible to know at the time of sale whether the customer will take advantage of the discount by paying within the discount period, sales discounts are recorded only at the time the customer pays. For example, assume that Fenwick Fashions Company sells merchandise to a customer on September 20 for $300 on terms of 2/10, n/60.

At the time of sale the entry would be:

Sept. 20 Accounts Receivable   300
              Sales   300
                  To record sale of
                  merchandise on credit, terms
                  2/10, n/60

The customer may take advantage of the sales discount any time on or before September 30, which is 10 days after the date of the invoice. If he or she pays on September 29, the entry in Fenwick's records is:

Sept. 29 Cash   294
              Sales Discounts   6
                  Accounts Receivable   300
                      To record payment for
                      Sept. 20 sale; discount
                      taken

At the end of the accounting period, the Sales Discounts account has accumulated all the sales discounts for the period. Because sales discounts reduce revenues from sales, they are considered a contra account and deducted from gross sales in the income statement (see Figure 6-2).

Cost of Goods Sold

Objective 3
Calculate cost
of goods sold

Cost of goods sold is an important concept. Every merchandising business has goods on hand that it holds for sale to customers. The amount of goods on hand at any one time is known as **merchandise inventory**. The total of goods available for sale during the year is the sum of two factors—merchandise inventory at the beginning of the year plus net purchases during the year.

If a company were to sell all the goods available for sale during a given accounting period or year, the cost of goods sold would then equal goods that had been available for sale. In most cases, however, the business will have goods still unsold and on hand at the end of the year. To find the actual cost of goods sold, therefore, we must subtract the merchandise inventory at the end of the year from the goods available for sale.

The partial income statement in Figure 6-3 shows the cost of goods sold section for Fenwick Fashions Company. In this case, goods costing $179,660 were available and could have been sold because Fenwick started with $52,800 in merchandise inventory at the beginning of the year and purchased $126,860 in goods during the year. At the end of the year, $48,300 in goods were left unsold and should appear as merchandise inventory on the balance sheet. When this unsold merchandise inventory is subtracted from the total available goods that could have been sold, the resulting cost of goods sold is $131,360, which should appear on the income statement.

Figure 6-3
Partial Income
Statement—Cost
of Goods Sold

Fenwick Fashions Company
Partial Income Statement
For the Year Ended December 31, 19xx

Cost of Goods Sold			
Merchandise Inventory, January 1, 19xx			$ 52,800
Purchases		$126,400	
Less: Purchases Returns and Allowances	$5,640		
Purchases Discounts	2,136	7,776	
		$118,624	
Freight In		8,236	
Net Purchases			126,860
Cost of Goods Available for Sale			$179,660
Less Merchandise Inventory, December 31, 19xx			48,300
Cost of Goods Sold			$131,360

To understand fully the concept of the cost of goods sold, it is necessary to examine merchandise inventory and net cost of purchases.

Merchandise Inventory

The inventory of a merchandising concern consists of the goods on hand and available for sale to customers. For a grocery store, inventory would be made up of meats, vegetables, canned goods, and the other items a store of this type might have for sale. For a service station, it would be gasoline, oil, and automobile parts. Merchandising concerns purchase their inventories from wholesalers, manufacturers, and other suppliers.

The merchandise inventory on hand at the beginning of the accounting period is called the **beginning inventory**. Conversely, the merchandise inventory on hand at the end of the accounting period is called the **ending inventory**. As we have seen, beginning and ending inventories are used in finding cost of goods sold on the income statement. Ending inventory appears on the balance sheet as an asset. This year's beginning inventory, you will notice, was last year's ending inventory and appeared on last year's balance sheet.

Measuring Merchandise Inventory Merchandise inventory is a key factor in determining cost of goods sold. Because merchandise inventory represents goods available for sale that are still unsold, there must be a method for determining both the quantity and the cost of these goods on hand. The two basic methods of accounting for the number of items in the merchandise inventory are the perpetual inventory method and the periodic inventory method.

A business enterprise that sells items of high unit value such as appliances or automobiles is usually able to account for the cost of each item as it is bought and sold. This system is known as the **perpetual inventory method.** Under the perpetual inventory method, records are kept of the cost of each item in inventory. As each item is sold, its cost is deducted from the Inventory account and debited to the Cost of Goods Sold account. The total cost of goods sold is determined by adding the costs of the individual items sold, and the merchandise inventory is computed by totaling the costs of goods still on hand.

However, companies that sell items of low value and high volume would find it difficult and expensive to keep track of the cost of every single item sold. Instead they rely on the **periodic inventory method.** Using this method, the company waits until the end of the accounting period to count the physical inventory that is still on hand. This actual count of the physical inventory is used along with various accounting records to determine the cost of goods sold for the entire period. A grocery store, for example, which may sell thousands of items every hour, will use the periodic inventory method. It is not practical to record the cost of every item at the time each is sold. Most drugstores, automobile parts stores, department stores, discount companies, and bookstores fall into this category. These companies count the inventory "periodically," usually at the end of the accounting period.

The periodic inventory method for determining cost of goods sold is described in this chapter. The perpetual inventory method is discussed further in Chapters 11 and 23.

The Periodic Inventory Method   Most companies rely on an actual count of goods on hand at the end of an accounting period to determine ending inventory and, indirectly, the cost of goods sold. This procedure for determining the merchandise inventory, the periodic inventory method, can be summarized as follows:

1. Make a physical count of the merchandise on hand at the end of the accounting period.
2. Multiply the quantity of each type of merchandise by its unit cost.
3. Add the resulting costs of each type of merchandise together to obtain a total. This total is the ending merchandise inventory.

The cost of the ending merchandise inventory is deducted from goods available for sale to determine cost of goods sold. The ending inventory of one period is the beginning inventory of the next period. Entries are made as part of the closing process at the end of the period—to remove the beginning inventory (the last period's ending inventory) and to enter the ending inventory of the current period. These entries are the only ones made to the Inventory account during the period. Consequently, only on the balance sheet date and after the closing entries does the Inventory account represent the actual amount on hand. As soon as purchases or sales are made, the inventory figure becomes a historical amount and remains so until the new inventory is entered at the end of the next accounting period.

Objective 4
Differentiate the
perpetual inven-
tory method
from the peri-
odic inventory
method

Taking the Physical Inventory Making a physical count of all merchandise on hand at the end of an accounting period is referred to as **taking a physical inventory**. It can be a difficult task, since it is easy to omit items or to count them twice.

Merchandise inventory includes all salable goods owned by the concern regardless of where they are located. It includes all goods on shelves, in storerooms, in warehouses, and in trucks en route between warehouses and stores. It includes goods in transit from suppliers if title to the goods has passed to the merchant. Ending inventory does not include merchandise sold to customers but not delivered or goods that cannot be sold because they are damaged or obsolete. If the damaged or obsolete goods can be sold at a reduced price, they may be included in ending inventory at the reduced value.

The actual count is usually taken after the close of business on the last day of the fiscal year. Many companies end their fiscal year in a slow season to facilitate the taking of physical inventory. Retail department stores often end their fiscal year in January or February, for example. After hours, at night or on the weekend, employees count and record all items on numbered inventory tickets or sheets. They follow established procedures to make sure that no items are missed. When the inventory tickets or sheets are completed, they are forwarded to the accounting office.

The accounting office checks to see that all numbered tickets and sheets are accounted for, and copies the information onto inventory ledgers. The appropriate unit costs are then entered and the computations made to determine ending merchandise inventory.

Net Purchases

Under the periodic inventory method, the net purchases consist of gross purchases less purchases discounts and purchases returns and allowances plus any freight charges on the purchases.

Purchases When the periodic inventory method is used, all purchases of merchandise for resale are debited to the Purchases account at the gross purchase price, as shown below.

*Objective 5
Journalize
transactions
involving pur-
chases of mer-
chandise*

Nov. 12 Purchases	1,500	
Accounts Payable		1,500
To record purchases of		
merchandise, terms 2/10, n/30		

The **Purchases** account, a nominal or temporary account, is used only for merchandise purchased for resale. Its sole purpose is to accumulate the total cost of merchandise purchased during an accounting period. Inspection of the Purchases account alone does not indicate whether the merchandise has been sold or is still on hand. Purchases of other assets such as equipment should be recorded in the appropriate asset account.

Purchases Returns and Allowances For various reasons, a company may need to return merchandise acquired for resale. The firm may not have been able to sell the merchandise and may ask to return it to the original supplier. Or the merchandise may be defective or damaged in some way and may have to be returned. In some cases, the supplier may suggest that an allowance be given as an alternative to returning the goods for full credit. In any event, **purchases returns and allowances** form a separate account and should be recorded in the journal as follows:

Nov. 14	Accounts Payable	200	
	Purchases Returns and Allowances		200
	Return of damaged merchandise		
	purchased on November 12		

Here, the purchaser receives "credit" (in the seller's accounts receivable) for the returned merchandise. Purchases Returns and Allowances is a contra account and is accordingly deducted from purchases in the income statement (see Figure 6-3). It is important that a separate account be used to record purchases returns and allowances because management needs the resulting information for decision-making purposes. It can be very costly to return merchandise for credit. There are many costs that cannot be recovered, such as ordering costs, accounting costs, sometimes freight costs, and interest on the money invested in the goods. Sometimes there are lost sales resulting from poor ordering or unusable goods. Excessive returns may call for new purchasing procedures or new suppliers.

Purchases Discounts Merchandise purchases are usually made on credit and commonly involve **purchases discounts** for early payment. It is almost always worthwhile for the company to take a discount if offered. For example, the terms 2/10, n/30 offer a 2 percent discount for paying only twenty days early (the period including the eleventh and the thirtieth days). This is an effective interest rate of 36 percent (there are 18 twenty-day periods in a year) on a yearly basis. Most companies can borrow money for less than this rate. For this reason, management wants to know the amount of discounts, which is a separate account and is recorded as follows when the payment is made:

Nov. 22	Accounts Payable	1,300	
	Purchases Discounts		26
	Cash		1,274
	Paid the invoice of Nov. 12		

Purchase Nov. 12	$1,500	
Less return	200	
Net purchase	$1,300	
Discount: 2%	26	
Cash	$1,274	

Like Purchases Returns and Allowances, Purchases Discounts is a contra account that is deducted from Purchases on the income statement. If a company is able to make only a partial payment on an invoice, most creditors will allow the company to take the discount applicable to the partial payment. The discount usually does not apply to freight, postage, or other charges that might appear on the invoice.

Good management of cash resources calls for both taking the discount and waiting as long as possible to pay. To accomplish these two objectives, some companies file invoices according to their due dates as they get them. Each day, the invoices due on that day are pulled from the file and paid. In this manner, the company uses cash as long as possible and also takes the advantageous discounts. A method commonly used to control these discounts is illustrated on pages 198–199.

Freight In In some industries, it is customary for the supplier (seller) to pay transportation costs, charging a higher price to include them. In other industries, it is customary for the purchaser to pay transportation charges on merchandise. These charges, called freight in or transportation in, should logically be included as an addition to purchases, but as in the case of purchases discounts, they should be accumulated in the Freight In account so that management can monitor this cost. The entry for the purchaser is as follows:

Nov. 12	Freight In	134	
	Cash (or Accounts Payable)		134
	Incurred freight charges on		
	merchandise purchased		

Special terms designate whether the supplier or the purchaser is to pay the freight or transportation charges. FOB shipping point means that the supplier will place the merchandise "free on board" at the point of origin, and the buyer is responsible for paying the charges from that point. In addition, the title to the merchandise passes to the buyer at that point. If you have purchased a car, you know that if the sale agreement says "FOB Detroit," you must pay the freight from that point to where you are.

On the other hand, FOB destination means that the supplier is bearing the transportation costs to the destination. In this case, title remains with the supplier until the merchandise reaches its destination. The supplier normally prepays the amount. In rare cases, the buyer may pay the charges and deduct them from the invoice.

The effects of these special shipping terms are summarized below.

Shipping Term	Where Title Passes	Who Bears Cost of Transportation
FOB shipping point	At origin	Buyer
FOB destination	At destination	Seller

In some cases, the supplier pays the freight charges but bills the buyer for them by including them as a separate item on the sales invoice. When this occurs the buyer should still record the purchases and the freight-in in separate accounts. For example, assume an invoice for purchase of merchandise inventory totaling $1,890 included the cost of merchandise of $1,600, freight charges of $290, and terms of 2/10, n/30. The entry to record this transaction would be

```
Nov. 25   Purchases                              1,600
              Freight In                             290
                 Accounts Payable                              1,890
                    Purchased merchandise for $1,600;
                    included in the invoice were
                    freight charges of $290 and terms
                    of 2/10, n/30
```

If this invoice is paid within ten days, the purchases discount will be $32 ($1,600 × 2%), because the discount would not apply to the freight charges.

It is important not to confuse freight-in costs with freight-out or delivery costs. If you, as seller, agree to pay transportation charges on goods you have sold, this expense is a cost of selling merchandise, not a cost of purchasing merchandise.

Control of Purchases Discounts

As noted in the earlier discussion of purchases discounts, it is usually worthwhile to pay invoices in time to qualify for the cash discount allowed for prompt payment. In fact, it is bad management not to take advantage of such discounts. The system of recording purchases initially at the gross purchase price, described on pages 195–197, has the disadvantage of telling management only about what discounts were taken, but not about the discounts that were not taken or, in other words, were "lost."

A procedure that will identify the discounts that are lost requires that purchases be recorded initially at the net price. Then, if the discount is not taken, a special account is debited for the amount of the lost discount. For example, suppose that a company purchases goods on November 12 for $1,500 with terms of 2/10, n/30 and that it returns $200 worth of merchandise on November 14. Suppose also that payment is not made until December 12, so the company is not eligible for the 2 percent discount. The entries to record these three transactions are as follows:

```
Nov. 12   Purchases                              1,470
                 Accounts Payable                              1,470
                    To record purchases of
                    merchandise at net price,
                    terms 2/10, n/30:
                    $1,500 − (.02 × $1,500) = $1,470

Nov. 14   Accounts Payable                        196
                 Purchases Returns and Allowances               196
                    Return of damaged merchandise
                    purchased on November 12;
                    recorded at net price:
                    $200 − (.02 × $200) = $196

Dec. 12   Accounts Payable                       1,274
              Discounts Lost                          26
                 Cash                                         1,300
```

Paid invoice of Nov. 12

Purchase Nov. 12	$1,500
Less return	200
Gross purchase	$1,300

Discount lost: .02 × $1,300 = $26

If the company pays by November 22 and uses the net method of recording purchases, it will make a payment of $1,274. Since purchases were recorded at net prices, no Purchases Discounts account would be required. However, if the company makes the payment after the discount period, as illustrated, management learns of the failure to take the discount by examining the Discounts Lost account. The amount of discounts lost is shown as an operating expense on the income statement.

Inventory Losses

Many companies have substantial losses in merchandise inventory from spoilage, shoplifting, and employee pilferage. Under the periodic inventory method, these costs are automatically included in the cost of goods sold. For example, assume that a company lost $1,250 during an accounting period because merchandise had been stolen or spoiled. Thus, when the physical inventory is taken, the missing items will not be in stock and cannot be counted. Because the ending inventory will not contain these items, the amount subtracted from goods available for sale is less than it would be if the goods were in stock. Cost of goods sold, therefore, is greater by $1,250. In a sense, cost of goods sold is inflated by the amount of merchandise that has been stolen or spoiled.

Operating Expenses

Operating expenses make up the third major part of the income statement for a merchandising concern. As noted earlier, they are expenses, other than the cost of goods sold, that are necessary to run the business. It is customary to group operating expenses into useful categories. For example, selling expenses and general and administrative expenses are common categories. Selling expenses include all expenses of storing and preparing goods for sale; displaying, advertising, and otherwise promoting sales; making the sales; and delivering the goods to the buyer if the seller bears the cost of delivery. Among the general and administrative expenses are general office expenses, those for accounting, personnel, and credit and collections, and any other expenses that apply to the overall operation of the company. Although general occupancy expenses, such as rent expense and utilities expenses, are often classified as general and administrative, they are sometimes allocated or divided between the selling and the general and administrative categories on a basis determined by management.

Handling Merchandise Inventory at the End of the Accounting Period

Objective 6
Explain the
objectives of
handling mer-
chandise inven-
tory at the end
of the account-
ing period and
how they are
achieved

Recall that under the periodic inventory system, purchases of inventory are accumulated in the Purchases account. During the accounting period, no entries are made to the Merchandise Inventory account. Its balance at the end of the period, before adjusting and closing entries, is the same as it was at the beginning of the period. Thus its balance at this point represents beginning merchandise inventory. Recall also that the cost of goods sold is determined by adding beginning merchandise inventory to net purchases and then subtracting ending merchandising inventory. The objectives of handling merchandise inventory at the end of the period are to (1) remove the beginning balance from the Merchandise Inventory account, (2) enter the ending balance in the Merchandise Inventory account, and (3) enter these two amounts in the Income Summary account in such a way as to result in the proper calculation of net income. Using the figures for Fenwick Fashions, these objectives can be accomplished if the following effects on the Merchandise Inventory and Income Summary accounts are achieved:

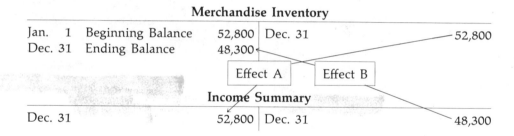

In this example, merchandise inventory was $52,800 at the beginning of the year and $48,300 at the end of the year. Effect A removes the $52,800 from Merchandise Inventory, leaving a zero balance, and transfers it to Income Summary. In Income Summary, the $52,800 is in effect added to net purchases because, like expenses, the balance of the Purchases account is debited to Income Summary by a closing entry. Effect B establishes the ending balance of Merchandise Inventory of $48,300 and enters it as a credit in the Income Summary account. The credit entry in Income Summary has the effect of deducting the ending inventory from cost of goods available for sale because both purchases and beginning inventory are entered on the debit side. In other words, beginning merchandise inventory and purchases are debits to Income Summary and ending merchandise inventory is a credit to Income Summary.

Thus the objectives stated above are accomplished if effects A and B both occur. The question then arises as to how to achieve the effects. Two acceptable methods are available. They are the adjusting entry method and the closing entry method. Each method accomplishes exactly the same result and practice varies in different regions of the country as to which method is most used. For this reason both are described here. The student should realize that both methods are simply bookkeeping techniques designed to deal with the Merchandise Inventory account under the periodic inventory system.

Using the adjusting entry method, the two entries indicated by effects A and B above are prepared at the time the other adjusting entries are made, as follows:

Adjusting Entries

Dec. 31	Income Summary	52,800	
	Merchandise Inventory		52,800
	To remove beginning balance of Merchandise Inventory and transfer it to Income Summary		
Dec. 31	Merchandise Inventory	48,300	
	Income Summary		48,300
	To establish ending balance of Merchandise Inventory and deduct it from goods available for sale in Income Summary		

The closing entry method makes the debit and the credit to Merchandise Inventory by including them among the closing entries, as follows:

Closing Entries

			Total of credits
Dec. 31	Income Summary		
	Merchandise Inventory		52,800
	Expenses and Other Income Statement Accounts with Debit Balances		Various amounts
	To close temporary expense and revenue accounts having debit balances and to remove beginning inventory		
Dec. 31	Merchandise Inventory	48,300	
	Revenues and Other Income Statement Accounts with Credit Balances	Various amounts	
	Income Summary		Total of debits
	To close temporary expense and revenue accounts having credit balances and to establish the ending merchandise inventory		

Notice that under both methods, Merchandise Inventory is credited for the beginning balance and debited for the ending balance and that the opposite entries are made to Income Summary.

Work Sheet of a Merchandising Concern

*Objective 7
Prepare a work
sheet for a
merchandising
concern under
one of two
alternative
methods*

In Chapter 5, the work sheet was presented as a useful tool in preparing adjusting entries, closing entries, and financial statements. The work sheet of a merchandising business is basically the same as that of a service business except that it has to deal with the new accounts that are needed to handle merchandising transactions. These accounts include Sales, Sales Returns and Allowances, Sales Discounts, Purchases, Purchases Returns and Allowances, Purchases Discounts, Freight In, and Merchandise Inventory. Except for Merchandise Inventory, these accounts are treated in the records and on the work sheet much as revenue and expense accounts are for a service company. In the records, they are transferred to the Income Summary account in the closing process. On the work sheet, they are extended to the Income Statement columns.

The handling of merchandise inventory, however, depends on whether the adjusting entry method or the closing entry method is to be used. The student needs to learn only one of these methods because, as already noted, they are both acceptable and they accomplish the same objectives. The student should ask the instructor which method is to be used in this course.

The Adjusting Entry Method

The work sheet for Fenwick Fashions using the adjusting entry method is presented in Figure 6-4. Each pair of columns in the work sheet and the adjusting and closing entries are discussed below.

Trial Balance Columns   The first step in preparing the work sheet is to enter the balances from the ledger accounts into the Trial Balance columns. You are already familiar with this procedure.

Adjustments Columns   Under the adjusting entry method of handling merchandise inventory, the first two adjusting entries to be entered in the work sheet were explained in the previous section. The first entry transfers beginning merchandise inventory to the Income Summary account by crediting Merchandise Inventory and debiting Income Summary for $52,800 (adjustment a). The second entry establishes the ending merchandise inventory by debiting Merchandise Inventory and crediting Income Summary for $48,300 (adjustment b). Note that the Income Summary account is listed immediately below the trial balance totals. The remaining adjustments for Fenwick Fashions are familiar to you. They involve insurance expired during the period (adjustment c), store and office supplies used (adjustments d and e), and depreciation of building and office equipment (adjustments f and g). After the adjusting entries are entered on the work sheet, the Trial Balance columns are totaled to prove the equality of the debits and credits.

Omission of Adjusted Trial Balance Columns   Note that the two columns for the adjusted trial balance do not appear on the work sheet as they did

Figure 6-4
Work Sheet
for Fenwick
Fashions Com-
pany—Adjust-
ing Entry
Method

Fenwick Fashions Company
Work Sheet
For the Year Ended December 31, 19xx

Account Name	Trial Balance Debit	Trial Balance Credit	Adjustments Debit	Adjustments Credit	Income Statement Debit	Income Statement Credit	Balance Sheet Debit	Balance Sheet Credit
Cash	29,410						29,410	
Accounts Receivable	42,400						42,400	
Merchandise Inventory	52,800		(b) 48,300	(a) 52,800			48,300	
Prepaid Insurance	17,400			(c) 5,800			11,600	
Store Supplies	2,600			(d) 1,540			1,060	
Office Supplies	1,840			(e) 1,204			636	
Land	4,500						4,500	
Building	20,260						20,260	
Accumulated Depreciation, Building		5,650		(f) 2,600				8,250
Office Equipment	8,600						8,600	
Accumulated Depreciation, Office Equipment		2,800		(g) 2,200				5,000
Accounts Payable		25,683						25,683
Joseph Fenwick, Capital		118,352						118,352
Joseph Fenwick, Withdrawals	20,000						20,000	
Sales		246,350				246,350		
Sales Returns and Allowances	2,750				2,750			
Sales Discounts	4,275				4,275			
Purchases	126,400				126,400			
Purchases Returns and Allowances		5,640				5,640		
Purchases Discounts		2,136				2,136		
Freight In	8,236				8,236			
Sales Salaries	22,500				22,500			
Freight Out Expense	5,740				5,740			
Advertising Expense	10,000				10,000			
Office Salaries	26,900				26,900			
	406,611	406,611						
Income Summary			(a) 52,800	(b) 48,300	52,800	48,300		
Insurance Expense, Selling			(c) 1,600		1,600			
Insurance Expense, General			(c) 4,200		4,200			
Selling Supplies Expense			(d) 1,540		1,540			
Office Supplies Expense			(e) 1,204		1,204			
Depreciation Expense, Building			(f) 2,600		2,600			
Depreciation Expense, Office Equipment			(g) 2,200		2,200			
			114,444	114,444	272,945	302,426	186,766	157,285
Net Income					29,481			29,481
					302,426	302,426	186,766	186,766

when the work sheet for a service company was illustrated in Chapter 5.
These columns are optional and are used when there are many adjusting
entries to record. When only a few adjusting entries are required, as is the
case for Fenwick Fashions, these columns are not necessary and may be
omitted to save time.

Income Statement and Balance Sheet Columns After the Trial Balance columns have been totaled, the adjustments entered, and the equality of the columns proved, the balances are extended to the statement columns. This process is accomplished most efficiently by beginning with the Cash account at the top of the work sheet and moving sequentially down the work sheet one account at a time. Each account balance is entered in the proper column of the income statement or balance sheet. The only exception to this rule is that both the debit (beginning merchandise inventory of $52,800) and the credit (ending merchandise inventory of $48,300) to Income Summary are extended to the same columns of the income statement. The reason for this procedure is that both the beginning and ending inventory figures are needed to prepare the cost of goods sold section of the income statement.

After all the items have been extended into the proper statement columns, the four columns are totaled. The net income or net loss is determined as the difference in the debit and credit columns of the income statement. In this case, Fenwick Fashions has earned a net income of $29,481, which is extended to the credit column of the balance sheet. The four columns are then added to prove the equality of the debits and credits for the two pairs of columns.

Objective 8
Prepare adjust-
ing and closing
entries for a
merchandising
concern

Adjusting Entries The adjusting entries are now entered from the work sheet into the general journal and posted to the ledger as they would be in a service company. The only difference is that under the adjusting entry method, the two adjustments involving Merchandise Inventory and Income Summary, already illustrated on pages 200–201, appear among the adjusting entries.

Closing Entries The closing entries for Fenwick Fashions under the adjusting entry method appear in Figure 6-5. These closing entries are very similar to those for a service company except that the new accounts for merchandising companies introduced in this chapter must also be closed to Income Summary. All income statement accounts with debit balances, including Sales Returns and Allowances, Sales Discounts, Purchases, and Freight In, are credited in the first entry. All income statement accounts with credit balances, including Sales, Purchases Returns and Allowances, and Purchases Discounts, are debited in the second entry. When copying the accounts and their balances out of the Income Statement columns of the work sheet, do not include the debit and credit to Income Summary, because these amounts are already in the Income Summary account as a result of the adjusting entries. The third and fourth entries are used to close the Income Summary account and transfer net income to the Capital account, and to close the Withdrawals account to the Capital account.

The Closing Entry Method

The work sheet for Fenwick Fashions using the closing entry method is presented in Figure 6-6. Each pair of columns in the work sheet and the adjusting and closing entries are discussed on the following pages.

Figure 6-5
Closing Entries
for a Merchan-
dising Con-
cern—Adjusting
Entry Method

Date		Description	Post. Ref.	Debit	Credit
General Journal					Page 1
Dec.	31	Income Summary		220,145	
		Sales Returns and Allowances			2,750
		Sales Discounts			4,275
		Purchases			126,400
		Freight In			8,236
		Sales Salaries Expense			22,500
		Freight Out Expense			5,740
		Advertising Expense			10,000
		Office Salaries Expense			26,900
		Insurance Expense, Selling			1,600
		Insurance Expense, General			4,200
		Selling Supplies Expense			1,540
		Office Supplies Expense			1,204
		Depreciation Expense, Building			2,600
		Depreciation Expense, Office Equipment			2,200
		To close temporary expense and revenue accounts having debit balances			
	31	Sales		246,350	
		Purchases Returns and Allowances		5,640	
		Purchases Discounts		2,136	
		Income Summary			254,126
		To close temporary expense and revenue accounts having credit balances			
	31	Income Summary		29,481	
		Joseph Fenwick, Capital			29,481
		To close the Income Summary account			
	31	Joseph Fenwick, Capital		20,000	
		Joseph Fenwick, Withdrawals			20,000
		To close the Withdrawals account			

Trial Balance Columns The first step in the preparation of the work sheet is to enter the balances from the ledger accounts into the Trial Balance columns. You are already familiar with this procedure.

Adjustments Columns Under the closing entry method of handling merchandise inventory, the adjusting entries for Fenwick Fashions are entered

Figure 6-6
Work Sheet for
Fenwick Fash-
ions Com-
pany—Closing
Entry Method

Fenwick Fashions Company
Work Sheet
For the Year Ended December 31, 19xx

Account Name	Trial Balance Debit	Trial Balance Credit	Adjustments Debit	Adjustments Credit	Income Statement Debit	Income Statement Credit	Balance Sheet Debit	Balance Sheet Credit
Cash	29,410						29,410	
Accounts Receivable	42,400						42,400	
Merchandise Inventory	52,800				52,800	48,300	48,300	
Prepaid Insurance	17,400			(a) 5,800			11,600	
Selling Supplies	2,600			(b) 1,540			1,060	
Office Supplies	1,840			(c) 1,204			636	
Land	4,500						4,500	
Building	20,260						20,260	
Accumulated Depreciation, Building		5,650		(d) 2,600				8,250
Office Equipment	8,600						8,600	
Accumulated Depreciation, Office Equipment		2,800		(e) 2,200				5,000
Accounts Payable		25,683						25,683
Joseph Fenwick, Capital		118,352						118,352
Joseph Fenwick, Withdrawals	20,000						20,000	
Sales		246,350				246,350		
Sales Returns and Allowances	2,750				2,750			
Sales Discounts	4,275				4,275			
Purchases	126,400				126,400			
Purchases Returns and Allowances		5,640				5,640		
Purchases Discounts		2,136				2,136		
Freight In	8,236				8,236			
Sales Salaries Expense	22,500				22,500			
Freight Out Expense	5,740				5,740			
Advertising Expense	10,000				10,000			
Office Salaries Expense	26,900				26,900			
	406,611	406,611						
Insurance Expense, Selling			(a) 1,600		1,600			
Insurance Expense, General			(a) 4,200		4,200			
Selling Supplies Expense			(b) 1,540		1,540			
Office Supplies Expense			(c) 1,204		1,204			
Depreciation Expense, Building			(d) 2,600		2,600			
Depreciation Expense, Office Equipment			(e) 2,200		2,200			
			13,344	13,344	272,945	302,426	186,766	157,285
Net Income					29,481			29,481
					302,426	302,426	186,766	186,766

in the adjustments columns in the same way that they were for service companies. They involve insurance expired during the period (adjustment a), store and office supplies used (adjustments b and c), and depreciation of building and office equipment (adjustments d and e). After the adjusting entries are entered on the work sheet, the Trial Balance columns are totaled to prove the equality of the debits and credits.

Omission of Adjusted Trial Balance Columns These two columns may be omitted from the work sheet. See the discussion under the adjusting entry method.

Income Statement and Balance Sheet Columns After the Trial Balance columns have been totaled, the adjustments entered, and the equality of the columns proved, the balances are extended to the statement columns. This process is accomplished most efficiently by beginning with the Cash account at the top of the work sheet and moving sequentially down the work sheet one account at a time. Each account balance is entered in the proper column of the income statement or balance sheet.

The extension that may not be obvious is in the Merchandise Inventory row. The beginning inventory balance of $52,800 (which is already in the trial balance) is first extended to the debit column of the income statement, as illustrated in Figure 6-6. This procedure has the effect of adding beginning inventory to net purchases because the Purchases account is also in the debit column of the income statement. The ending inventory balance of $48,300 (which is determined by the physical inventory and is not in the trial balance) is then inserted in the credit column of the income statement. This procedure has the effect of subtracting the ending inventory from goods available for sale. Finally, the ending merchandise inventory ($48,300) is then inserted in the debit column of the balance sheet because it will appear on the balance sheet.

After all the items have been extended into the proper statement columns, the four columns are totaled. The net income or net loss is determined as the difference in the debit and credit columns of the income statement. In this case, Fenwick Fashions has earned a net income of $29,481, which is extended to the credit column of the balance sheet. The four columns are then added to prove the equality of the debits and credits for the two pairs of columns.

Adjusting Entries The adjusting entries are now entered from the work sheet into the general journal and posted to the ledger as they would be in a service company. Under the closing entry method, there is no difference in this procedure between a service company and a merchandising company.

Closing Entries The closing entries for Fenwick Fashions under the closing entry method appear in Figure 6-7. Note that Merchandising Inventory is credited in the first entry for the amount of beginning inventory ($52,800) and debited in the second entry for the amount of the ending inventory ($48,300), as shown on page 201. Otherwise, these closing entries are very similar to those for a service company except that the new accounts for merchandising companies introduced in this chapter must also be closed to Income Summary. All income statement accounts with debit balances, for instance, Sales Returns and Allowances, Sales Discounts, Purchases, and Freight In, are credited in the first entry. All income statement accounts with credit balances, namely, Sales, Purchases Returns and Allowances, and Purchases Discounts, are debited in the second entry. The third and fourth entries are used to close the Income

Figure 6-7
Closing Entries
for a Merchan-
dising Con-
cern—Closing
Entry Method

		General Journal			Page 1
Date		Description	Post. Ref.	Debit	Credit
Dec.	31	Income Summary		272,945	
		Merchandise Inventory			52,800
		Sales Returns and Allowances			2,750
		Sales Discounts			4,275
		Purchases			126,400
		Freight In			8,236
		Sales Salaries Expense			22,500
		Freight Out Expense			5,740
		Advertising Expense			10,000
		Office Salaries Expense			26,900
		Insurance Expense, Selling			1,600
		Insurance Expense, General			4,200
		Selling Supplies Expense			1,540
		Office Supplies Expense			1,204
		Depreciation Expense, Building			2,600
		Depreciation Expense, Office Equipment			2,200
		To close temporary expense and revenue accounts having debit balances and to remove beginning inventory			
	31	Merchandise Inventory		48,300	
		Sales		246,350	
		Purchases Returns and Allowances		5,640	
		Purchases Discounts		2,136	
		Income Summary			302,426
		To close temporary expense and revenue accounts having credit balances and to establish the ending merchandise inventory			
	31	Income Summary		29,481	
		Joseph Fenwick, Capital			29,481
		To close the Income Summary account			
	31	Joseph Fenwick, Capital		20,000	
		Joseph Fenwick, Withdrawals			20,000
		To close the Withdrawals account			

Summary account and transfer net income to the Capital account and to close the Withdrawals account to the Capital account.

Income Statement Illustrated

*Objective 9
Prepare an
income state-
ment for a
merchandising
concern*

In earlier parts of this chapter, the parts of the income statement for a merchandising concern were presented and the transactions pertaining to each part were discussed. Figure 6-8 (page 210) pulls the parts together and shows the complete income statement for Fenwick Fashions Company. The statement is prepared by taking the accounts and their balances from the Income Statement columns of the work sheet. In practice, the balance sheet and statement of owner's equity would also be prepared by using the accounts and balances from the Balance Sheet columns of the work sheet. They are not presented here because they are like those of service companies except that .merchandise inventory would be listed among the assets on the balance sheet.

Chapter Review

Review of Learning Objectives

1. Identify the components of income statements for merchandising concerns.
   The merchandising company differs from the service company in that it attempts to earn a profit by buying and selling merchandise rather than by offering services. The income statement for a merchandising company has three major parts: (1) revenues from sales, (2) cost of goods sold, and (3) operating expenses. The cost of goods sold section is necessary for the computation of gross profit made on the merchandise that has been sold. Merchandisers must sell their merchandise for more than cost to pay operating expenses and have an adequate profit left over.

2. Journalize transactions involving revenues for merchandising concerns.
   Revenues from sales consist of gross sales less sales returns and allowances and sales discounts. The amount of the sales discount can be determined from the terms of the sale. Revenue transactions for merchandising firms may be summarized as follows:

Transaction	Related Accounting Entries	
	Debit	Credit
Sell merchandise to customer.	Cash (or Accounts Receivable)	Sales
Collect for merchandise sold on credit.	Cash (and Sales Discounts, if applicable)	Accounts Receivable
Permit customers to return merchandise, or grant them a reduction from original price.	Sales Returns and Allowances	Cash (or Accounts Receivable)

Figure 6-8
Income State-
ment for Fen-
wick Fashions
Company

Fenwick Fashions Company
Income Statement
For the Year Ended December 31, 19xx

Revenues from Sales
  Gross Sales $246,350

Revenues from Sales			
Gross Sales			$246,350
Less: Sales Returns and Allowances		$ 2,750	
Sales Discounts		4,275	7,025
Net Sales			$239,325
Cost of Goods Sold			
Merchandise Inventory, Jan. 1, 19xx			$ 52,800
Purchases		$126,400	
Less: Purchases Returns			
and Allowances	$ 5,640		
Purchases Discounts	2,136	7,776	
		$118,624	
Freight In		8,236	
Net Purchases			126,860
Cost of Goods Available for Sale			$179,660
Less: Merchandise Inventory,			
Dec. 31, 19xx			48,300
Cost of Goods Sold			131,360
Gross Margin from Sales			$107,965
Operating Expenses			
Selling Expenses			
Sales Salaries		$ 22,500	
Freight Out		5,740	
Advertising Expense		10,000	
Insurance Expense, Selling		1,600	
Selling Supplies Expense		1,540	
Total Selling Expenses			$ 41,380
General and Administrative Expenses			
Office Salaries Expense		$ 26,900	
Insurance Expense, General		4,200	
Office Supplies Expense		1,204	
Depreciation Expense, Building		2,600	
Depreciation Expense, Office			
Equipment		2,200	
Total General and Administrative			
Expenses			37,104
Total Operating Expenses			78,484
Net Income			$ 29,481

3. Calculate cost of goods sold.

To compute cost of goods sold, add beginning merchandise inventory to the net purchases to determine goods available for sale and then subtract ending merchandise inventory from the total.

Net Purchases are calculated by subtracting the purchases discounts and purchases returns and allowances from gross purchases and then adding any freight-in charges on the purchases. The Purchases account is used only for merchandise purchased for resale. Its sole purpose is to accumulate the total cost of merchandise purchased during an accounting period.

4. Differentiate the perpetual inventory method from the periodic inventory method.

Merchandise inventory may be determined by one of two alternative methods. (1) Under the perpetual inventory method, the balance of the inventory account is kept up to date throughout the year or as items are bought and sold. (2) Under the periodic inventory method, the company waits until the end of the accounting period to take the physical inventory. Merchandise inventory includes all salable goods owned by the concern regardless of where they are located.

5. Journalize transactions involving purchases of merchandise.

The transactions involving purchases may be summarized as follows:

Transaction	Related Accounting Entries	
	Debit	Credit
Purchase merchandise for resale.	Purchases	Cash (or Accounts Payable)
Incur transportation charges on merchandise purchased for resale.	Freight In	Cash (or Accounts Payable)
Return unsatisfactory merchandise to supplier, or obtain a reduction from original price.	Cash (or Accounts Payable)	Purchases Returns and Allowances
Pay for merchandise purchased on credit.	Accounts Payable	Cash (and Purchases Discounts, if applicable)

6. Explain the objectives of handling merchandise inventory at the end of the accounting period and how they are achieved.

At the end of the accounting period, it is necessary to (1) remove the beginning balance from the Merchandise Inventory account, (2) enter the ending balance in the Merchandise Inventory account, and (3) enter these two amounts in the Income Summary account in such a way as to result in the proper calculation of net income. These objectives are accomplished by crediting Merchandise Inventory and debiting Income Summary for the beginning balance and debiting Merchandise Inventory and crediting Income Summary for the ending balance, as shown in the following table:

Inventory Procedures at End of Period	Related Accounting Entries	
	Debit	Credit
Transfer the balance of the beginning inventory to the Income Summary account.	Income Summary	Merchandise Inventory
Take a physical inventory of goods on hand at the end of the period, and establish the balance of ending inventory.	Merchandise Inventory	Income Summary

There are two ways of accomplishing these effects. Under the adjusting entry method, the entries are included among the adjusting entries. Under the closing entry method, the entries are included among the closing entries.

7. Prepare a work sheet for a merchandising concern under one of two alternative methods.

The major difference between preparing a work sheet for a merchandising concern and preparing one for a service company are the accounts relating to merchandising transactions. The accounts necessary to compute cost of goods sold appear in the Income Statement columns. Merchandise inventory is treated differently under each of the following two methods:

Adjusting entry method: Under this method, Merchandise Inventory and Income Summary are adjusted in the Adjustments columns, the ending inventory is extended to the Balance Sheet debit column, and the two adjustments to Income Summary are extended to the Income Statement columns.

Closing entry method: Under this method, the beginning inventory from the trial balance is extended to the debit column of the income statement and the ending balance of merchandise inventory is inserted in the credit column of the income statement and the debit column of the balance sheet.

8. Prepare adjusting and closing entries for a merchandising concern.

The adjusting and closing entries for a merchandising concern are similar to those for a service business. The most unique feature is the handling of merchandise inventory, which is summarized under each of the two methods in the table below:

Method	Adjusting Entries	Closing Entries
Adjusting entry method	Dr. Income Summary Cr. Merchandise Inventory for amount of beginning inventory Dr. Merchandise Inventory Cr. Income summary for amount of ending inventory	Follow procedures for service companies
Closing entry method	Follow procedures for service companies	Include among closing entries the following:

Dr. Income Summary
Cr. Merchandise
Inventory for
amount of
beginning
inventory
Dr. Merchandise
Inventory
Cr. Income Summary
for amount of
ending inventory

9. Prepare an income statement for a merchandising concern.
The income statement of a merchandising company is constructed by displaying in each major section the individual parts of that section. The revenues from sales section will show gross sales, with contra sales accounts deducted from them to arrive at net sales. The cost of goods sold section will show the accounts that make up goods available for sale. The operating expenses section will divide the expenses into useful categories such as selling expenses and general and administrative expenses.

Review Problem
Completion of Work Sheet, Preparation of Income Statement, and Closing Entries for a Merchandising Concern

This chapter extends the basic accounting system to include the transactions necessary to handle merchandising transactions. The chapter contains a comprehensive illustration of the accounting for Fenwick Fashions Company. Instead of studying a review problem, you should carefully review and retrace the steps through the illustrations in the chapter. You need to focus only on the adjusting entry method or the closing entry method, depending on which method your school or instructor has chosen to follow.

Required

1. In Figure 6-4 (adjusting entry method) or Figure 6-6 (closing entry method), how are the merchandising accounts and merchandise inventory treated in the Adjustments columns and the Income Statement columns?
2. In Figure 6-5 (adjusting entry method) or Figure 6-7 (closing entry method), how do the closing entries relate back to the work sheet?
3. Trace the amounts in the detailed income statement in Figure 6-8 back to the Income Statement columns of the work sheet.

Chapter Assignments

Questions

1. What is the source of revenues for a merchandising concern?
2. Define gross margin from sales.
3. Kumler Nursery had a cost of goods sold during its first year of $64,000 and a gross margin equal to 40 percent of sales. What was the dollar amount of the company's sales?
4. Could Kumler Nursery (in question 3) have a net loss for the year? Explain.
5. Why is it advisable to maintain an account for sales returns and allowances when the same result could be obtained by debiting each return or allowance to the Sales account?

6. What is a sales discount? If the terms are 2/10, n/30, what is the length of the credit period? What is the length of the discount period?

7. What two related transactions are reflected in the T accounts below?

Cash				Accounts Receivable			
(b)	980			(a)	1,000	(b)	1,000

Sales				Sales Discounts			
		(a)	1,000	(b)	20		

8. How much is the cash discount on a sale of $2,250 with terms of 2/10, n/60, on which a credit memo for $250 is issued prior to payment?

9. What is the normal balance of the Sales Discounts account? Is it an asset, liability, expense, or contra revenue account?

10. During the current year, Pruitt Corporation purchased $100,000 in merchandise. Compute the cost of goods sold under each of the following conditions.

	Beginning Inventory	Ending Inventory
a.	—	100,000
b.	— 100,000	$30,000
c.	$30,000	—
d.	28,000	35,000
e.	35,000	28,000

11. Compute cost of goods sold, given the following account balances: Beginning Inventory, $30,000; Purchases, $160,000; Purchases Returns and Allowances, $4,000; Purchases Discounts, $1,600; Freight In, $3,000; Ending Inventory, $25,000.

12. In counting the ending inventory, a clerk counts a $200 item of inventory twice. What effect does this error have on the balance sheet and income statement?

13. Hornberger Hardware purchased the following items: (a) a delivery truck, (b) two dozen hammers, (c) supplies for office workers, (d) a broom for the janitor. Which item should be debited to the Purchases account?

14. What three related transactions are reflected in the T accounts below?

Cash				Accounts Payable			
		(c)	441	(b)	50	(a)	500
				(c)	450		

Purchases				Purchases Returns and Allowances			
(a)	500					(b)	50

Purchases Discounts			
		(c)	9

How would these transactions differ if the net method of recording purchases were used?

15. Is Freight In an operating expense? Explain.

16. Prices and terms are quoted from two companies and fifty units of product, as follows: Supplier A—50 at $20 per unit, FOB shipping point; Supplier B—50 at $21 per unit, FOB destination. Which supplier has quoted the best deal? Explain.

17. Does the beginning or ending inventory appear in the year-end unadjusted trial balance prepared by a company that uses the periodic inventory method?

18. Under the periodic inventory method, how is the amount of inventory at the end of the year determined?

19. What is your assessment of the following statement: "The perpetual inventory method is the best method because management always needs to know how much inventory it has"?

20. Why is the handling of merchandise inventory at the end of the accounting period of special importance to the determination of net income? What must be achieved in the accounting records in this regard for net income to be properly determined?

Classroom Exercises

Exercise 6-1
Purchases and Sales Involving Discounts
(L.O. 2, 5)

The Perez Company purchased $2,400 of merchandise, terms 2/10, n/30, from the Sandberg Company and paid for the merchandise within the discount period.

Give the entries (1) by the Perez Company to record purchase and payment, assuming purchases are recorded at gross purchase price, and (2) by the Sandberg Company to record the sale and receipt.

Exercise 6-2
Gross and Net Methods of Recording Purchases Contrasted
(L.O. 5)

Pocket Corporation purchases $7,800 of merchandise, terms 2/10, n/30, on June 10. Give the entries to record purchase and payment under each of the four assumptions below.

1. Purchases are recorded at gross amount, and payment is made June 20.
2. Purchases are recorded at gross amount, and payment is made July 10.
3. Purchases are recorded at net amount, and payment is made June 20.
4. Purchases are recorded at net amount, and payment is made July 10.

Exercise 6-3
Computation of Net Sales
(L.O. 2)

During 19xx, the Midlands Corporation had total sales on credit of $180,000. Of this amount, $120,000 was collected during the year. In addition, the corporation had cash sales of $60,000. Furthermore, customers returned merchandise for credit of $4,000, and cash discounts of $2,000 were allowed. How much would net sales be for the Midlands Corporation for 19xx?

Exercise 6-4
Parts of the Income Statement—Missing Data
(L.O. 3, 9)

Compute the dollar amount of each item indicated by a letter in the table below. Treat each horizontal row of numbers as a separate problem.

Sales	Beginning Inventory	Net Purchases	Ending Inventory	Cost of Goods Sold	Gross Margin	Expenses	Income (or Loss) from Operations
75,000	a	35,000	10,000	b	40,000	c	10,000
d	12,000	e	18,000	94,000	60,000	40,000	20,000
210,000	22,000	167,000	f	g	50,000	h	(1,000)

Exercise 6-5
Gross Margin Computation— Missing Data
(L.O. 3)

Determine the amount of gross purchases by preparing a partial income statement showing the calculation of gross margin, from the following data: Purchases Discounts, $2,500; Freight In, $11,000; Cost of Goods Sold, $175,000; Sales, $255,000;

Beginning Inventory, $15,000; Purchases Returns and Allowances, $4,000; Ending Inventory, $10,000.

Exercise 6-6
Preparation of Income Statement from Work Sheet
(L.O. 9)

Selected items from the Income Statement columns of the December 31, 19xx, work sheet for Red Cloud General Store appear below.

Account Name	Income Statement	
	Debit	Credit
Sales		284,000
Sales Returns and Allowances	11,000	
Sales Discounts	4,200	
Purchases	117,300	
Purchases Returns and Allowances		1,800
Purchases Discounts		2,200
Freight In	5,600	
Selling Expenses	48,500	
General and Administrative Expenses	37,200	

Beginning merchandise inventory was $26,000 and ending merchandise inventory is $22,000. From the information given, prepare a 19xx income statement for the company.

Exercise 6-7
Preparation of Closing Entries
(L.O. 8)

Using either the adjusting entry method or the closing entry method, prepare closing entries from the information given in Exercise 6-6, assuming that Red Cloud General Store is owned by Bart Crane and that he made withdrawals of $20,000 during the year.

Exercise 6-8
Preparation of Work Sheet
(L.O. 7)

Simplified trial balance accounts and their balances follow in alphabetical order: Accounts Payable, $3; Accounts Receivable, $5; Accumulated Depreciation, Store Equipment, $6; Cash, $10; Freight In, $2; General Expense, $15; Merchandise Inventory (Beginning), $8; Paul Burris, Capital, $67; Paul Burris, Withdrawals, $12; Prepaid Insurance, $2; Purchases, $35; Purchases Returns and Allowances, $2; Sales, $75; Sales Discounts, $3; Selling Expenses, $22; Store Equipment, $30; Store Supplies, $9.

Prepare a work sheet form on accounting paper, and copy the trial balance accounts and amounts onto it in the same order as they appear above. Complete the work sheet, using either the adjusting entry method or the closing entry method and the following information: (a) estimated depreciation on store equipment, $3; (b) ending inventory of store supplies, $2; (c) expired insurance, $1; (d) ending merchandise inventory, $7.

Interpreting Accounting Information

Published Financial Information: Sears and K mart
(L.O. 1)

Sears, Roebuck and Company and K mart Corporation, the two largest retailers in the United States, have very different approaches to retailing. Sears operates a chain of full-service department stores, whereas K mart is known as a discounter. Selected information from their annual reports for the year ended in January 1981 is presented on the next page. (All amounts are in millions.)

Sears: Net Sales, $16,865; Cost of Goods Sold, $11,447; Operating Expenses, $4,969; Ending Inventory, $2,721

K mart: Net Sales, $14,204; Cost of Goods Sold, $10,417; Operating Expenses, $3,326; Ending Inventory, $2,846

Required

1. Prepare a schedule computing gross margin and net income (ignore income taxes) for both companies as dollar amounts and as percentages of net sales. Also, compute inventory as a percentage of cost of goods sold.
2. On the basis of what you know about the different retailing approaches of these two companies, do the gross margin and net income computations prepared in 1 seem compatible with these approaches? What is it about the nature of K mart's operations that allows the company to earn less gross margin and more net income in dollar amounts and in percentages than Sears?
3. Both Sears and K mart chose a fiscal year that ends on January 31. Why do you suppose they made this choice? How realistic do you think the inventory figures are as indicators of inventory levels during the rest of the year?

Problem Set A

Note: For Problems 6A-2, 6A-4, 6A-5, 6B-2, 6B-4, and 6B-5, the instructor should indicate whether students are to use the adjusting entry method or the closing entry method.

Problem 6A-1
Merchandising
Transactions
(L.O. 2, 5)

Adriana Company, which uses the periodic inventory method, engaged in the following transactions:

Oct. 1 Sold merchandise to Chris Tolan on credit, terms 2/10, n/30, $400.
2 Purchased merchandise on credit from Dotson Company, terms 2/10, n/30, FOB shipping point, $1,800.
2 Paid Fast Freight $145 for freight charges on merchandise received.
6 Purchased store supplies on credit from Burns Supply House, terms n/20, $318.
8 Purchased merchandise on credit from RT Company, terms 2/10, n/30, FOB shipping point, $1,200.
8 Paid Fast Freight $97 for freight charges on merchandise received.
9 Purchased merchandise on credit from PHP Company, terms 2/10, n/30, FOB shipping point, $1,800, including $100 freight costs paid by PHP.
11 Received full payment from Chris Tolan for her October 1 purchase.
12 Paid Dotson Company for purchase of October 2.
13 Sold merchandise on credit to Marty Giles, terms 2/10, n/30, $600.
14 Returned for credit $300 of merchandise received on October 8.
19 Paid PHP Company for purchase of October 9.
22 Paid RT Company for purchase of October 8.
23 Received full payment from Marty Giles for his October 13 purchase.
26 Paid Burns Supply House for purchase of October 6.

Required

1. Prepare general journal entries to record the transactions, assuming purchases are recorded initially at the gross purchase price.
2. How would your entries differ if the purchases were recorded initially at net

purchase price and discounts lost were recognized? What advantages does this method have?

Problem 6A-2
Work Sheet,
Income State-
ment, Balance
Sheet, and
Closing Entries
for Merchan-
dising Com-
pany
(L.O. 7, 8, 9)

The following trial balance was taken from the ledger of Pepitone Book Store at the end of its annual accounting period:

Pepitone Book Store
Trial Balance
June 30, 19xx

Cash	$ 3,175	
Accounts Receivable	9,280	
Merchandise Inventory	29,450	
Store Supplies	1,911	
Prepaid Insurance	1,600	
Store Equipment	37,200	
Accumulated Depreciation, Store Equipment		$ 14,700
Accounts Payable		12,300
Gary Pepitone, Capital		41,994
Gary Pepitone, Withdrawals	12,000	
Sales		99,400
Sales Returns and Allowances	987	
Purchases	62,300	
Purchases Returns and Allowances		19,655
Purchases Discounts		1,356
Freight In	2,261	
Sales Salaries Expense	21,350	
Rent Expense	3,600	
Other Selling Expense	2,614	
Utilities Expense	1,677	
	$189,405	$189,405

Required

1. Enter the trial balance on a work sheet, and complete the work sheet using the following information: (a) ending merchandise inventory, $31,772; (b) ending store supplies inventory, $304; (c) unexpired insurance, $200; (d) estimated depreciation on store equipment, $4,300; (e) accrued sales salaries payable, $80; (f) accrued utilities expense, $150.
2. Prepare an income statement and a balance sheet. Sales Salaries Expense, Other Selling Expense, and Store Supplies Expense are to be considered selling expenses. The other expenses are to be considered general and administrative expenses.
3. From the work sheet, prepare closing entries.

Problem 6A-3
Journalizing
Transactions of
a Merchandis-
ing Company
(L.O. 2, 5)

Prepare general journal entries to record the following transactions, assuming that the periodic inventory method is used and that purchases are recorded at gross purchase price. Also, tell how the entries would differ if the net method of recording purchases were used.

Jan. 2 Purchased merchandise on credit from TCP Company, terms 2/10, n/30, FOB destination, $5,600.

3 Sold merchandise on credit to D. Mantle, terms 1/10, n/30, FOB shipping point, $1,000.

5 Sold merchandise for cash, $700.

6 Purchased merchandise on credit from Jackson Company, terms 2/10, n/30, FOB shipping point, $4,200.

7 Received freight bill from Midway Express for shipment received on January 6, $570.

9 Sold merchandise on credit to R. Blomberg, terms 1/10, n/30, FOB destination, $3,800.

10 Purchased merchandise from TCP Company, terms 2/10, n/30, FOB shipping point, $2,650, including freight costs of $150.

11 Received freight bill from Midway Express for sale to R. Blomberg on January 9, $291.

12 Paid TCP Company for purchase of January 2.

13 Received payment in full for D. Mantle's purchase of January 3.

14 Returned faulty merchandise worth $300 to TCP Company for credit against purchase of January 10.

16 Paid Jackson Company one-half of amount owed from purchase of January 6.

17 Sold merchandise to P. Lopez on credit, terms 2/10, n/30, FOB shipping point, $780.

19 Received payment from R. Blomberg for one-half the purchase of January 9.

20 Paid TCP Company in full for amount owed on purchase of January 10 less return on January 14.

22 Gave credit to P. Lopez for returned merchandise, $180.

26 Paid freight company for freight charges during January.

27 Received payment of amount owed by P. Lopez from purchase of January 17 less credit of January 22.

28 Paid Jackson Company for balance of January 6 purchase.

Problem 6A-4
Work Sheet, Income Statement, and Closing Entries for Merchandising Concern
(L.O. 7, 8, 9)

The year-end trial balance for McCandlish's Shoe Store appears on page 220.

Required

1. Copy the trial balance amounts into the Trial Balance columns of a work sheet, and complete the work sheet using the following information: (a) ending merchandise inventory, $29,350; (b) ending store supplies inventory, $288; (c) expired insurance, $2,400; (d) estimated depreciation on store equipment, $8,800; (e) advertising expense includes $1,470 for January clearance sale advertisements, which will begin appearing on January 2; (f) accrued store salaries, $320.

2. Prepare an income statement for the shoe store. Store Salaries Expense, Advertising Expense, and Depreciation Expense, Store Equipment, are to be considered selling expenses. The other expenses are to be considered general and administrative expenses.

3. Prepare closing entries.

Problem 6A-5
Work Sheet, Income Statement, and Closing Entries for Merchandising Concern
(L.O. 7, 8, 9)

The year-end trial balance for Barney's Camera Store appears on page 221.

Required

1. Copy the trial balance amounts into the Trial Balance columns of a work sheet, and complete the work sheet using the following information: (a) ending mer-

Accounting for Merchandising Operations

McCandlish's Shoe Store
Trial Balance
December 31, 19xx

Cash	$ 2,675	
Accounts Receivable	19,307	
Merchandise Inventory	26,500	
Store Supplies	951	
Prepaid Insurance	2,600	
Store Equipment	32,000	
Accumulated Depreciation, Store Equipment		$ 19,500
Accounts Payable		22,366
Cheri McCandlish, Capital		63,601
Cheri McCandlish, Withdrawals	15,000	
Sales		103,000
Sales Returns and Allowances	2,150	
Purchases	61,115	
Purchases Returns and Allowances		17,310
Purchases Discounts		1,300
Freight In	2,144	
Rent Expense	4,800	
Store Salaries Expense	41,600	
Advertising Expense	14,056	
Utility Expense	2,179	
	$227,077	$227,077

chandise inventory, $182,657; (b) ending inventories: selling supplies, $362; office supplies, $412; (c) estimated depreciation: store equipment, $1,800; office equipment, $1,850; (d) interest accrued on notes payable, $2,500; (e) accrued salaries: store salaries, $1,050; office salaries, $100; (f) accrued utility expense, $1,443.

2. Prepare an income statement for the camera store. Store Salaries Expense, Advertising Expense, Selling Supplies Expense, and Depreciation Expense, Store Equipment, are to be considered selling expenses. The other expenses are to be considered general and administrative expenses.

3. Prepare closing entries using (a) the adjusting entry method, and (b) the closing entry method.

Problem Set B

**Problem 6B-1
Merchandising
Transactions
(L.O. 2, 5)**

Celia Company, which uses the periodic inventory method, engaged in the following transactions:

July   1   Purchased merchandise on credit from XYZ Company, terms 2/10, n/30, FOB shipping point, $1,500.

        1   Paid Green Freight Company $75 for freight charges on merchandise received.

        3   Sold merchandise on credit to Wes Bradley, terms 2/10, n/60, $1,000.

Barney's Camera Store
Trial Balance
June 30, 19xx

Cash	$ 5,857	
Accounts Receivable	34,770	
Merchandise Inventory	176,551	
Selling Supplies	826	
Office Supplies	1,226	
Store Equipment	26,400	
Accumulated Depreciation, Store Equipment		$ 5,600
Office Equipment	9,350	
Accumulated Depreciation, Office Equipment		3,700
Accounts Payable		56,840
Notes Payable		50,000
Barney Rand, Capital		155,440
Barney Rand, Withdrawals	18,000	
Sales		396,457
Sales Returns and Allowances	11,250	
Purchases	218,350	
Purchases Returns and Allowances		26,450
Purchases Discounts		3,788
Freight In	10,078	
Store Salaries Expense	106,500	
Office Salaries Expense	26,400	
Advertising Expense	18,200	
Rent Expense	14,400	
Insurance Expense	2,800	
Utility Expense	17,317	
	$698,275	$698,275

6 Purchased merchandise on credit from Koral Company, terms 2/10, n/30, FOB shipping point, $3,200, including $200 freight costs paid by Koral.

7 Purchased merchandise on credit from ABC Company, terms 1/10, n/30, FOB shipping point, $2,000.

7 Paid Green Freight Company $85 for freight charges on merchandise received.

8 Purchased office supplies on credit from D & F Supplies, terms n/10, $800.

10 Sold merchandise on credit to Laura Terrell, terms 2/10, n/30, $800.

11 Paid XYZ Company for purchase of July 1.

12 Returned for credit $200 of damaged merchandise received from ABC Company on July 7.

13 Received check from Wes Bradley for his purchase of July 3.

16 Paid Koral Company for purchase of July 6.

19 Paid ABC Company balance of amount owed from transactions of July 7 and 12.
20 Received payment in full from Laura Terrell for sale of July 10.
23 Paid D & F Supplies for purchase of July 8.
31 Sold merchandise for cash, $500.

Required

1. Prepare general journal entries to record the transactions, assuming purchases are recorded initially at the gross purchase price.
2. How would your entries differ if the purchases were recorded initially at net purchase price and discounts lost were recognized? What advantages does this method have?

Problem 6B-2
Work Sheet,
Income State-
ment, Balance
Sheet, and
Closing Entries
for Merchan-
dising Com-
pany
(L.O. 7, 8, 9)

The year-end trial balance below was taken from the ledger of Swinehart Sporting Goods Company at the end of its annual accounting period:

Cash	$ 2,525	
Accounts Receivable	12,415	
Merchandise Inventory	35,700	
Store Supplies	1,900	
Prepaid Insurance	2,400	
Store Equipment	25,650	
Accumulated Depreciation, Store Equipment		$ 12,150
Accounts Payable		19,475
Dana Swinehart, Capital		80,675
Dana Swinehart, Withdrawals	12,000	
Sales		185,625
Sales Returns and Allowances	2,345	
Sales Discounts	1,895	
Purchases	125,200	
Purchases Returns and Allowances		1,575
Purchases Discounts		2,450
Freight In	5,200	
Sales Salaries Expense	32,300	
Rent Expense	24,000	
Other Selling Expense	16,455	
Utilities Expense	1,965	
	$301,950	$301,950

Required

1. Enter the trial balance on a work sheet, and complete the work sheet using the following information: (a) ending merchandise inventory, $42,600; (b) ending store supplies inventory, $275; (c) expired insurance, $1,200; (d) estimated depreciation on store equipment, $2,500; (e) accrued sales salaries payable, $325; (f) accrued utilities expense, $50.
2. Prepare an income statement and a balance sheet. Store Salaries Expense, Other Selling Expense, Store Supplies Expense, and Depreciation Expense, Store

Equipment, are to be considered selling expenses. The other expenses are to be considered general and administrative expenses.

3. From the work sheet, prepare closing entries using (a) the adjusting entry method, and (b) the closing entry method.

Problem 6B-3
Journalizing
Transactions of
a Merchandis-
ing Company
(L.O. 2, 5)

Prepare general journal entries to record the following transactions, assuming that the periodic inventory method is used and that purchases are recorded initially at gross purchase price. Also, tell how the entries would differ if the net method of recording purchases were used.

Aug. 1 Sold merchandise on credit to J. Jenkins, terms 2/10, n/60, FOB shipping point, $400.
      2 Purchased merchandise on credit from Spirit Manufacturing Company, terms 2/10, n/30, FOB shipping point, $3,200.
      3 Received freight bill for shipment received on August 2, $225.
      4 Sold merchandise for cash, $275.
      5 Sold merchandise on credit to R. Polster, terms 2/10, n/60, $600.
      6 Purchased merchandise from Time Corporation, terms 1/10, n/30, FOB shipping point, $1,545, including freight costs of $100.
      7 Sold merchandise on credit to B. Boren, terms 2/10, n/20, $1,100.
      8 Purchased merchandise from Spirit Manufacturing Company, terms 2/10, n/30, FOB shipping point, $4,100.
      9 Received freight bill for shipment of August 8, $365.
     10 Received check from J. Jenkins for payment in full for sale of August 1.
     11 Returned for credit merchandise of the August 6 shipment, which was the wrong size and color, $145.
     12 Paid Spirit Manufacturing Company for purchase of August 2.
     13 B. Boren returned some of merchandise sold to him on August 7 for credit, $100.
     15 Received payment from R. Polster for one-half of his purchase on August 5. A discount is allowed on partial payment.
     16 Paid Time Corporation balance due on account from transactions on August 6 and 11.
     17 In checking purchase of August 8 from Spirit Manufacturing Company, accounting department found an overcharge of $200.
     20 Paid freight company for freight charges during August.
     22 Purchased on credit cleaning supplies from Bruce Wholesale, terms n/5, $125.
     27 Received payment in full from B. Boren for transactions on August 7 and 13.
     28 Paid Spirit Manufacturing Company for purchase of August 8 less allowance of August 17.
     30 Received payment for balance of amount owed from R. Polster from transactions of August 5 and 15.

Problem 6B-4
Work Sheet,
Income State-
ment, and
Closing Entries
for Merchan-
dising Concern
(L.O. 7, 8, 9)

A year-end trial balance for Montanez Grocery appears on page 224.

Required

1. Copy the trial balance amounts into the Trial Balance columns of a work sheet, and complete the work sheet using the following information: (a) ending merchandise inventory, $56,780; (b) ending store supplies inventory, $580; (c) expired insurance, $1,800; (d) estimated depreciation on store equipment, $10,600; (e) during current year, rent paid through January of next year; amount debited to

Montanez Grocery
Trial Balance
December 31, 19xx

Cash	$ 3,560	
Accounts Receivable	4,215	
Merchandise Inventory	62,500	
Store Supplies	4,780	
Prepaid Insurance	3,600	
Store Equipment	101,200	
Accumulated Depreciation, Store Equipment		$ 27,400
Accounts Payable		35,780
José Montanez, Capital		84,225
José Montanez, Withdrawals	18,000	
Sales		656,400
Sales Returns and Allowances	5,400	
Purchases	468,250	
Purchases Returns and Allowances		8,250
Purchases Discounts		7,900
Freight In	3,200	
Rent Expense	26,000	
Store Salaries Expense	75,500	
Advertising Expense	37,770	
Utility Expense	5,980	
	$819,955	$819,955

rent expense and applicable to January of next year, $1,200; (f) accrued store salaries, $250.

2. Prepare an income statement for the grocery store. Store Salaries Expense, Advertising Expense, Store Supplies Expense, and Depreciation Expense, Store Equipment, are to be considered selling expenses. The other expenses are to be considered general and administrative expenses.

3. Prepare closing entries.

Problem 6B-5
Work Sheet,
Income State-
ment, and
Closing Entries
for Merchan-
dising Concern
(L.O. 7, 8, 9)

A year-end trial balance for Polly's Dress Shop is shown on page 225.

Required

1. Copy the trial balance into the Trial Balance columns of a work sheet, and complete the work sheet using the following information: (a) ending merchandise inventory, $26,400; (b) ending inventories: store supplies, $220; office supplies, $75; (c) expired rent, $200; (d) estimated depreciation: store equipment, $1,050; office equipment, $800; (e) interest accrued on note payable, $1,500; (f) accrued salaries: store salaries, $225; office salaries, $75.

2. Prepare an income statement for the fashion shop. Store Salaries Expense, Advertising Expense, Store Supplies Expense, and Depreciation Expense, Store Equipment, are to be considered selling expenses. The other expenses are to be considered general and administrative expenses.

Polly's Dress Shop
Trial Balance
August 31, 19xx

Cash	$ 2,100	
Accounts Receivable	32,400	
Merchandise Inventory	34,200	
Prepaid Rent	400	
Store Supplies	3,100	
Office Supplies	1,250	
Store Equipment	20,700	
Accumulated Depreciation, Store Equipment		$ 2,100
Office Equipment	4,700	
Accumulated Depreciation, Office Equipment		1,200
Accounts Payable		17,300
Notes Payable		30,000
Polly Roush, Capital		55,810
Polly Roush, Withdrawals	12,000	
Sales		142,000
Sales Returns and Allowances	2,000	
Purchases	61,400	
Purchases Returns and Allowances		1,400
Purchases Discounts		1,200
Freight In	2,300	
Store Salaries Expense	32,400	
Office Salaries Expense	12,800	
Advertising Expense	24,300	
Rent Expense	2,200	
Insurance Expense	1,200	
Utility Expense	1,560	
	$251,010	$251,010

3. Prepare closing entries using (a) the adjusting entry method, and (b) the closing entry method.

Financial Decision Case 6-1

Jefferson Jeans Company
(L.O. 3)

In 19x1, Joseph "JJ" Jefferson opened a small retail store in a suburban mall. Called Jefferson Jeans Company, the shop sold designer jeans to rather well-to-do customers. JJ worked fourteen hours a day and was in control of all aspects of the operation. All sales were made for cash or bank credit card. The business was such a success that in 19x2, JJ decided to expand by opening a second outlet in another mall. Since the new shop needed his attention, he hired a manager for the original store to work with the two sales clerks who had been helping JJ in the store.

During 19x2, the new store was successful, but the operations of the original store did not match the first year's performance. Concerned about this turn of events, JJ compared the two years' results for the original store. The figures are as follows:

	19x1	19x2
Net Sales	$350,000	$325,000
Cost of Goods Sold	225,000	225,000
Gross Margin from Sales	$125,000	$100,000
Operating Expenses	50,000	75,000
Net Income	$ 75,000	$ 25,000

In addition, JJ's analysis revealed that the cost and selling price of jeans were about the same in both years and that the level of operating expenses was roughly the same in both years except for the $25,000 salary of the new manager. Sales returns and allowances were insignificant amounts in both years.

Studying the situation further, JJ discovered the following facts about cost of goods sold:

a. Gross purchases were $271,000 in 19x1 and $200,000 in 19x2.
b. Total purchases returns and allowances and purchases discounts were $20,000 in 19x1 and $15,000 in 19x2.
c. Freight in was $27,000 in 19x1 and $19,000 in 19x2.
d. The physical inventory for 19x1 revealed $53,000 on hand at the end of 19x1 and $32,000 on hand at the end of 19x2.

Still not satisfied, JJ went through all the individual sales and purchase records for the year. Both sales and purchases were verified. However, the inventory should have been $57,000, given the unit purchases and sales during the year. After puzzling over all this information, JJ comes to you for accounting help.

Required

1. Using JJ's new information, recompute cost of goods sold for 19x1 and 19x2, and account for the difference in net income between 19x1 and 19x2.
2. Suggest at least two reasons that might have caused the difference. (Assume that the new manager's salary is proper.) How might JJ improve his management of the original store?

Chapter
Seven

Accounting
Systems and
Special-Purpose
Journals

Knowledge of accounting systems for processing information is very important today because of the many different systems in use and the rapidly changing needs of businesses. In this chapter, you first study the key ideas and principles of accounting systems design. You then learn about the major kinds of data processing, from manual systems to computer systems. Because the idea behind special-purpose journals is basic to all accounting systems, particular attention is given to the way these journals are used in manual data processing. As a result of studying this chapter, you should be able to meet the learning objectives listed on the left.

As you learned earlier, accounting systems gather data from all parts of a business, put them in useful form, and communicate the results to management. Thus accounting systems are essential to business managers. As businesses have become larger and more complicated, the role and importance of accounting systems have grown. With the development of computers, the need for a total information system with accounting as its base has become more pressing. For this reason, today's accountant must understand all phases of a company's operations as well as the latest developments in systems design and technology.

Accounting Systems Installation

The installation of an accounting system has three phases: investigation, design, and implementation. Each of these phases is necessary whether the system is a new one or an existing system that must be changed. The constant changes in a business's operations and environment call for continuous review of the current accounting system to make sure that it will always be responsive to management's need for information.

Objective 1
Describe the
phases of systems installation and the principles of systems design

The aim of a **system investigation** is to discover the needs of a new system or to judge an existing system. This phase involves studying the information needs of managers, seeking the sources of this information, and outlining the steps and processes needed that will put the data into the correct form for use. Included in this phase are a review of the organization itself and of job descriptions and a study of forms, records, reports, procedures, data processing methods, and controls presently in use. Some companies have handbooks that give all of this information in great detail. In existing systems, there is the further task of seeing that procedures are really followed. This task is done by tracing test transactions through the system and watching and talking to people as they do the work itself.

The new system or the changes in the current system are formulated in the **system design** phase and are based on the studies made during the investigation phase. For a major system, the design phase may call for accountants as well as computer experts, engineers, personnel managers, and other specialists. The design must take into account the people who run and work with the system, the documents and records used, the operational procedures, the reports to be prepared, and the equipment to be used in the system. The interaction of all these components must conform to the principles of systems design that are outlined below.

If management accepts a new system's design, the next phase, **system implementation**, follows. This phase depends on careful planning and communication to make sure that the new system is understood and accepted, properly installed, and well run. The people responsible for the operation of the new system should take an active part in the actual implementation. This involves scheduling all activities of the installation. For large systems, implementation may take months or even years. The people working with the new system must be chosen and trained. The equipment, forms, and records must be bought. The new system must be tested and then changed as suggested by the tests. After implementation, it is important to review the new system regularly as part of the system investigation.

Principles of Systems Design

In designing an accounting system, it is very important to follow four general principles: (1) the cost/benefit principle, (2) the control principle, (3) the compatibility principle, and (4) the flexibility principle.

Cost-Benefit Principle

The most important systems principle, the **cost-benefit principle**, holds that the value or benefits received from a system and its information output must be equal to or greater than its cost. Beyond certain routine tasks of an accounting system, such as payroll and tax reports, preparing financial statements, and maintaining good internal control, management may want or need other information. To be beneficial, this information must be reliable, timely, and useful to management. These benefits of additional information must be weighed against both the tangible and intangible costs of gathering it. Among the tangible costs are those for personnel, forms, and equipment. One of the intangible costs is the cost of wrong decisions stemming from lack of good information. For instance, wrong decisions may lead to loss of sales, production stoppages, or inventory losses. In some cases, companies have spent thousands of dollars on computer systems that have not offered enough benefits. On the other hand, some managers have failed to realize important benefits that could be gained from investing in more advanced systems. It is the job of the accountant as systems analyst to weigh the opposing factors of costs and benefits.

Control Principle

The control principle requires that an accounting system provide all the features of internal control needed to protect assets and make sure of the reliability of data. For example, expenditures should be approved by a responsible member of management before they are made. Chapter 8 covers the subject of internal control in detail.

Compatibility Principle

The compatibility principle holds that the design of a system must be in harmony with the organizational and human factors of a business. An organization is made up of people working in different jobs and groups. The organizational factors have to do with the organization's kind of business and how the different units of the business are formally related in meeting its objectives. For example, a company may organize its marketing efforts by region or by product. If a company is organized by region, major reports will present revenues and expenses by region. A company organized by product, on the other hand, should have a system that will report revenues and expenses first by product and then by region. The human factors of business have to do with the people within the organization and their abilities, behaviors, and personalities. The interest, support, and competence of these people are very important to systems design. In changing systems or installing new ones, the accountant must deal with the persons presently carrying out or supervising existing procedures. These people must understand, accept, and in many cases, be trained in the new procedures. The new system cannot succeed unless the system and the people in the organization are compatible.

Flexibility Principle

The flexibility principle calls for an accounting system that has enough flexibility to allow the volume of transactions to grow and organizational changes to be made in the business. Businesses do not often stay the same. They grow, offer new products, add new branch offices, sell existing divisions, or make other changes that require adjustments in the accounting system. A carefully designed system will allow a business to grow enough without making major alterations. For example, the chart of accounts should be designed to allow for adding new asset, liability, owner's equity, revenue, or expense accounts without destroying the usefulness of the accounts.

Data Processing: Three Perspectives

Data processing is the means by which the accounting system gathers data, organizes them into useful forms, and issues the resulting information to users. It can be viewed from three perspectives or points of view—functional, content, and mechanical—as shown in Figure 7-1. The functional and content points of view are closely related. The functional perspective deals with what is done, and the content perspective has to do with the data or material acted upon. The origin of the input is a bill, a report, or some other kind of document. This document, of course, is the data content. The processing function organizes the data into useful form by handling and storing them until they are needed. The output is information presented to users by means of reports. The mechanical view has to do with the devices used in carrying out data processing. In any data processing system, there must be a means of originating the data, a device

Figure 7-1
Data Processing
from Three
Perspectives

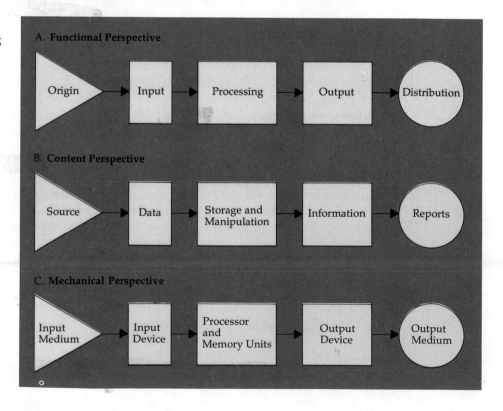

for data input, a processor and memory unit for storing and dealing with the data, a device for output of information, and a means of distributing the information.

From the mechanical point of view, the two extremes of data processing systems are manual systems and computer systems, each of which does the same job. The basic ways of handling a large amount of data using manual data processing are described in the last part of this chapter. The main features of computer systems and their use in data processing are presented in the next part.

The accountant must be able to work with many different kinds of accounting systems, and may also have a voice in choosing the right sort of data processing for a business. The first step in gaining the needed skill and knowledge is to learn how to use the special-purpose journals to process data manually. This basic knowledge can then be applied to other, more sophisticated accounting systems, such as those that take advantage of computers.

Computer Data Processing

Most data processing in business today is done by computer. The computer processes the data by passing electronic impulses through electronic circuits. Since electronic impulses travel at the speed of light, computers are able to process large amounts of data very quickly. The development of large mainframe computer systems has allowed the biggest companies to centralize their accounting operations and eliminate much of the work that used to be done by hand. The development of minicomputers and microcomputers has now made it possible for even the smallest company to keep its accounting records on a computer. Regardless of the size of a computer data processing system, it consists of four basic elements: hardware, software, personnel, and configuration.

Hardware

All of the equipment needed to operate a computer data processing system is called **hardware.** Figure 7-2 expands on the mechanical perspective of data processing presented in Figure 7-1, showing how hardware fits into that perspective. Figure 7-3 shows the hardware used in a mainframe system.

Transactions are first recorded manually on source documents of various kinds. The transactions are then transformed into a form of input that can be read by the system's input device. Each input device requires its own kind of input medium. For example, data must be on punched cards to be read by a card reader or on tape to be read by a magnetic tape unit. Increasingly, transactions are being entered directly by remote data entry terminals or stations, so that a person can communicate directly with the computer.

The **central processor** is the part of the system where the "computing" takes place. It has three components: (1) the **control unit,** which directs and coordinates all parts of the computer; (2) the **arithmetic/logic unit,**

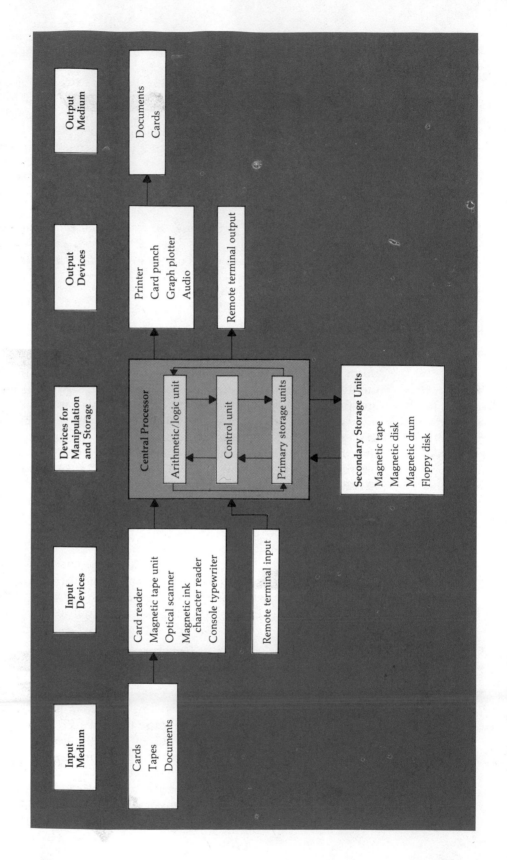

Input Medium	Input Devices	Devices for Manipulation and Storage	Output Devices	Output Medium

Cards
Tapes
Documents

Card reader
Magnetic tape unit
Optical scanner
Magnetic ink character reader
Console typewriter

Remote terminal input

Central Processor

Arithmetic/logic unit

Control unit

Primary storage units

Secondary Storage Units

Magnetic tape
Magnetic disk
Magnetic drum
Floppy disk

Printer
Card punch
Graph plotter
Audio

Remote terminal output

Documents
Cards

◀ Figure 7-2
Hardware
Components
for a Computer
Data Processing
System

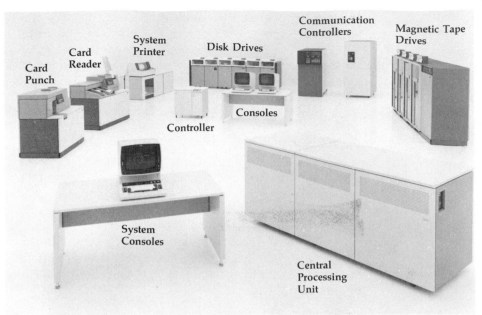

Card
Punch

Card
Reader

System
Printer

Disk Drives

Communication
Controllers

Magnetic Tape
Drives

Controller

Consoles

System
Consoles

Central
Processing
Unit

Figure 7-3
Mainframe
Computer
System

Source: Courtesy of IBM.

which does the computations and decision-making; and (3) **storage** (or memory) **units,** which store instructions and other data so that they are ready when needed. Because the central processor only deals with the data on which it is currently operating, **secondary, or auxiliary, storage** is available on which to store the many accounting records and other information. The journal and ledger are, in effect, maintained in secondary storage. The data from transactions are directed through and by the central processor to the proper places in secondary storage. The three most common types of secondary storage are magnetic tapes, magnetic disks, and magnetic drums. In microcomputer systems, floppy disks are used for secondary storage.

When the data from the transactions are needed, they are retrieved by the central processor from secondary storage and processed for whatever use is intended. The use may be to transmit the data through output devices (usually a printer) onto documents (output media) in the form of reports or financial statements.

Software

Instead of recording transactions with a pencil in a journal, posting to a ledger, and then preparing a trial balance and financial statements, the computer performs these steps internally on its hardware. To do this, the computer must be instructed to follow the proper steps. The set of instructions and steps that bring about the desired results are called **programs.** Programs are known collectively as **software.** Each step in a program is a command or instruction to the computer. Several programs would be needed to instruct the computer to record and post transactions and prepare financial statements. Think, for example, of how you would tell a person unfamiliar with accounting to take the balances from the ledger accounts and prepare a trial balance. The process would include several steps. A program is similar. It consists of many steps, and must be written in a language the computer can understand. Programs for mainframe computers are often written in such languages as FORTRAN, COBOL, or PL/1, whereas those for microcomputers are often written in BASIC or PASCAL.

Personnel

The most important personnel in a computer system are the systems analyst, the programmer, and the computer operator. The **systems analyst** designs the system on the basis of information needs. The **programmer** writes the instructions for the computer, and the **computer operator** runs the computer. The accountant works closely with the systems analyst to make sure that accounting data processing systems are designed in accordance with the principles of systems design discussed in the first part of this chapter.

Configuration

The parts of a computer data processing system can be put together in many different ways. Of course, companies use their computers for many purposes besides accounting. Overall, the company's goal is to meet all its computing needs at the lowest cost. For the accounting system, it is important to coordinate all tasks so as to provide management with the reports and statements it needs on a timely basis. There are two basic approaches to achieving this objective. The first is called **batch processing,** in which one job at a time is processed in a logical order. For example, a set of transactions for a day or a week are all processed together (as a batch). Later, a separate program will be run to update the ledger and prepare a trial balance. This is the system that is used today on most microcomputers and on many mainframe computer systems. However, more sophisticated systems use an approach called **on-line processing,** in which remote terminals are tied to the central processor, and the files are updated virtually as soon as transactions occur. For example, under this approach, recording, posting, and updating the trial balance all occur immediately as transactions are entered into the system. Regardless of the approach used, it is important for the beginning student to understand, in principle, just what the computer is accomplishing. For this reason, we turn in the next section to manual data processing.

Manual Data Processing: Journals and Procedures

The system of accounting described so far in this book, and presented in Figure 7-4, is a form of **manual data processing.** This application of the mechanical view from Figure 7-1 has been a useful way to present basic

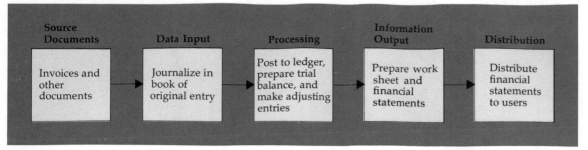

Source Documents	Data Input	Processing	Information Output	Distribution
Invoices and other documents	Journalize in book of original entry	Post to ledger, prepare trial balance, and make adjusting entries	Prepare work sheet and financial statements	Distribute financial statements to users

Figure 7-4
Steps and Devices in a Manual Accounting System

accounting theory and practice in small businesses. The recording is done manually by entering each transaction from a source document, such as an invoice, in the general journal (input device) and posting each debit and credit to the correct ledger account (processor and memory device). A work sheet (output device) is then used as an aid in preparing financial statements (output devices) to be presented to users. This system, while useful for explaining the basic ideas of accounting, is limited in practice to only the smallest of companies.

Objective 3
Explain the objectives and uses of special-purpose journals

Larger companies, faced with hundreds or thousands of transactions every week and perhaps every day, must have a more efficient and economical way of recording transactions in the journal and posting entries to the ledger. The easiest and most usual way to do this is to group the company's typical transactions into common categories and use an input device, called a special-purpose journal, for each category. Most business transactions, usually 90 to 95 percent, fall into one of four categories. Each kind of transaction may be recorded in a special-purpose journal as shown below.

Transaction	Special-Purpose Journal	Posting Abbreviation
Sales of merchandise on credit	Sales journal	S
Purchases on credit	Purchases journal	P
Receipts of cash	Cash receipts journal	CR
Disbursements of cash	Cash payments journal	CP

The general journal is used for recording transactions that do not fall into any of the special categories. For example, purchases or sales returns and adjusting and closing entries are recorded in the general journal. (When transactions are posted from the general journal to the ledger accounts, the posting abbreviation used is J.) It is important to note that use of these five journals greatly reduces the amount of detailed recording work. Also, a division of labor can be gained if each journal is assigned to a different employee. This division of labor is very important in establishing good internal control, as shown in Chapter 8.

Sales Journal

Special-purpose journals are designed to record particular kinds of transactions. Thus all transactions in a special-purpose journal result in debits

Sales Journal					Page 1
Date		Account Debited	Invoice Number	Post. Ref.	Amount
July	1	Peter Clark	721	✔	750
	5	Georgetta Jones	722	✔	500
	8	Eugene Cumberland	723	✔	335
	12	Maxwell Hertz	724	✔	1,165
	15	Peter Clark	725	✔	1,225
	25	Michael Powers	726	✔	975
					4,950
					(114/411)

Post total at end of month.

Accounts Receivable   114

Date		Post. Ref.	Debit	Credit	Balance Debit	Balance Credit
July	31	S1	4,950		4,950	

Sales   411

Date		Post. Ref.	Debit	Credit	Balance Debit	Balance Credit
July	31	S1		4,950		4,950

Figure 7-5
Sales Journal and Related Ledger Accounts

Objective 4 Construct and use the following types of special-purpose journals: sales journal, purchases journal, cash receipts journal, cash payments journal, and others as needed

and credits to the same accounts. The **sales journal,** for example, is designed to handle all credit sales, and only credit sales.

Figure 7-5 illustrates a typical sales journal. Six sales transactions involving five people are recorded in this sales journal. As each sale takes place, several copies of the sales invoice are made. The accounting department of the seller uses one copy to make the entry in the sales journal. From the invoices are copied the date, the customer's name, the invoice number, the amount of the sale, and possibly the credit terms. These data correspond to the columns of the sales journal. If the seller commonly offers different credit terms to different customers, one more column showing the terms can be used. In this case, we assume that each customer has received the same credit terms.

Note the following time-saving features of the sales journal:

1. Only one line is needed to record each transaction. Each entry consists of a debit to each customer in Accounts Receivable. The corresponding credit to Sales is understood.

2. Account names do not have to be written out, because account names occurring most frequently are used as column headings. Thus entry in a column has the effect of debiting or crediting the account.

3. No explanations are necessary, because the function of the special-purpose journal is to record one type of transaction. Only credit sales can be recorded in the sales journal. Sales for cash must be recorded in the cash receipts journal, which is described later in this chapter.

4. Only one amount—the total credit sales for the month—needs to be

Chapter Seven

posted. It is posted twice: once as a debit to Accounts Receivable and once as a credit to Sales. Instead of the six sales entries in the example, there might be hundreds of actual sales transactions in a more realistic situation. Thus one can see the saving in posting time.

Controlling Accounts and Subsidiary Ledgers   Every entry in the sales journal represents a debit to a customer's account in Accounts Receivable. In previous chapters, all such transactions have been posted to Accounts Receivable. However, this single Accounts Receivable entry does not readily tell how much each customer bought and paid for or how much each customer owes. In practice, almost all companies that sell to customers on credit keep an individual accounts receivable record for each customer. If the company has 6,000 credit customers, there are 6,000 accounts receivable. To include all these accounts in the ledger with the other assets, liabilities, and owner's equity accounts would make it very bulky. Consequently, most companies take the individual customers' accounts out of the general ledger, which contains the financial statement accounts, and place them in a separate ledger called a **subsidiary ledger.** The customers' accounts are filed alphabetically in this accounts receivable ledger.

When a company puts its individual customers' accounts in an accounts receivable ledger, there is still a need for an Accounts Receivable account in the general ledger to maintain its balance. This Accounts Receivable account in the general ledger is said to control the subsidiary ledger and is called a **controlling** or **control account.** It is a controlling account in the sense that its balance should equal the total of the individual account balances in the subsidiary ledger. This is true because in transactions involving accounts receivable, such as credit sales, there must be postings to the individual subsidiary customer accounts every day and to the controlling account in the general ledger in total each month. If an error has been made in posting, the sum of all customer account balances in the subsidiary accounts receivable ledger will not equal the balance of the Accounts Receivable controlling account in the general ledger. When these amounts do not match, the accountant knows that there is an error and can find and correct it.

The concept of controlling accounts is shown in Figure 7-6 (next page) where boxes are used for the accounts receivable ledger and the general ledger. The principle involved is that the single controlling account in the general ledger takes the place of all the individual accounts in the subsidiary ledger. The trial balance can be prepared using only the general ledger accounts.

Most companies, as you will see, use an accounts payable subsidiary ledger as well. It is also possible to use a subsidiary ledger for almost any account in the general ledger where management wants a specific account for individual items, such as Notes Receivable, Temporary Investments, and Equipment.

Summary of the Sales Journal Procedure   Observe from Figure 7-6 that the procedures for using a sales journal are as follows:

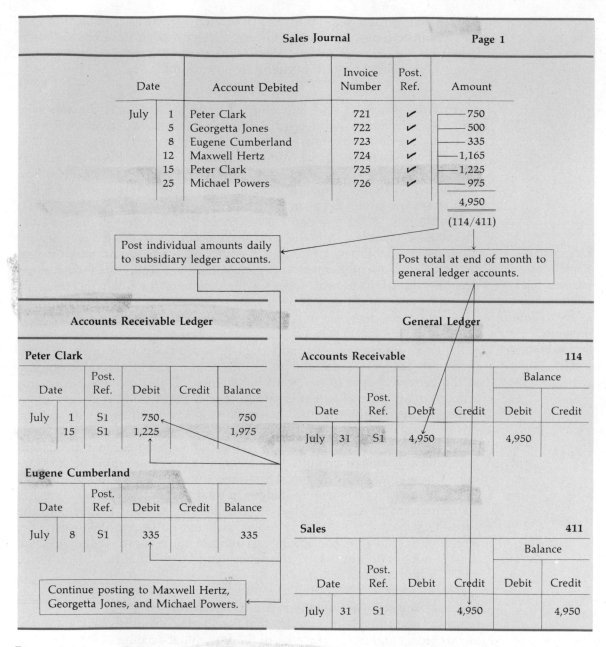

Figure 7-6
Relationship of
Sales Journal,
General Ledger,
and Accounts
Receivable
Ledger and
the Posting
Procedure

1. Enter each sales invoice in the sales journal on a single line, recording date, customer's name, invoice number, and amount.

2. At the end of each day, post each individual sale to the customer's account in the accounts receivable ledger. As each sale is posted, place a check mark in the Post. Ref. (posting reference) column to indicate that it has been posted. In the Post. Ref. column of each customer account, place an S1 (representing Sales Journal—page 1) to indicate the source of the entry.

3. At the end of the month, sum the Amount column to determine the

Figure 7-7
Schedule of
Accounts
Receivable

Mitchell's Used Car Sales
Schedule of Accounts Receivable
July 31, 19xx

Peter Clark	$1,975
Eugene Cumberland	335
Maxwell Hertz	1,165
Georgetta Jones	500
Michael Powers	975
Total Accounts Receivable	$4,950

total credit sales, and post the amount to the general ledger accounts (debit Accounts Receivable and credit Sales). Place the numbers of the accounts debited and credited beneath the total in the sales journal to indicate that this step has been completed, and place an S1 in the Post. Ref. column of each account to indicate the source of the entry.

4. Verify the accuracy of the posting by adding the account balances of the accounts receivable ledger and by matching the total with the Accounts Receivable controlling account balance in the general ledger. This step can be accomplished by listing the accounts in a schedule of accounts receivable, as shown in Figure 7-7.

Sales Taxes Other columns, such as a column for credit terms, can be added to the sales journal. The nature of the company's business will determine whether they are needed.

Many cities and states require retailers to collect a sales tax from their customers and periodically remit the total amount of the tax to the state or city. In this case, an additional column is needed in the sales journal to record the necessary credit to Sales Taxes Payable. The required entry is illustrated in Figure 7-8. The procedure for posting to the ledger is exactly the same as previously decribed except that the total of the Sales Taxes Payable column must be posted as a credit to the Sales Taxes Payable account at the end of the month.

Figure 7-8
Section of a
Sales Journal
with a Column
for Sales Taxes

Sales Journal						Page 7
				Debit	Credits	
Date	Account Debited	Invoice Number	Post. Ref.	Accounts Receivable	Sales Taxes Payable	Sales
Sept. 1	Ralph P. Hake	727		206	6	200

Most companies also make cash sales. Cash sales are usually recorded in a column of the cash receipts journal. This procedure is discussed later in the chapter.

Purchases Journal

The techniques associated with the sales journal are very similar to those of the purchases journal. The **purchases journal** is used to record all purchases on credit and may take the form of either a single-column journal or a multicolumn journal. In the single-column journal, shown in Figure 7-9, only credit purchases of merchandise for resale to customers are recorded. This kind of transaction is recorded with a debit to Purchases and a credit to Accounts Payable. When the single-column purchases journal is used, credit purchases of things other than merchandise are recorded in the general journal. Also, cash purchases are not recorded in the purchases journal but in the cash payments journal, which is explained later.

As with Accounts Receivable, the Accounts Payable account in the general ledger is used by most companies as a controlling account. So that the company will know how much it owes each supplier, it keeps a separate account for each supplier in an accounts payable subsidiary ledger. The ideas and techniques described above for the accounts receivable subsidiary ledger and general ledger account apply also to the accounts payable subsidiary ledger and general ledger account. Thus the total of the separate accounts in the accounts payable subsidiary ledger will equal the balance of the Accounts Payable controlling account in the general ledger. The reason is that the total of the individual credit purchases posted to the separate accounts each day is equal to the total credit purchases posted to the controlling account each month.

The steps for using a purchases journal, as shown in Figure 7-9, are as follows:

1. Enter each purchase invoice in the purchases journal on a single line, recording date, supplier's name, invoice date, terms if given, and amount.

2. At the end of each day, post each individual purchase to the supplier's account in the accounts payable subsidiary ledger. As each purchase is posted, place a check in the Post. Ref. column of the purchases journal to show that it has been posted. Also place a P1 (representing Purchases Journal—page 1) in the Post. Ref. column of each supplier's account to show the source of the entry.

3. At the end of the month, figure the total of the credit purchases, and post the amount in the general ledger accounts (Accounts Payable and Purchases). Place the numbers of the accounts debited and credited beneath the total in the purchases journal to show that this step has been carried out.

4. Check the accuracy of the posting by adding the balances of the accounts payable ledger accounts and matching the total with the Accounts Payable controlling account balance in the general ledger. This step may be carried out by preparing a schedule of accounts payable.

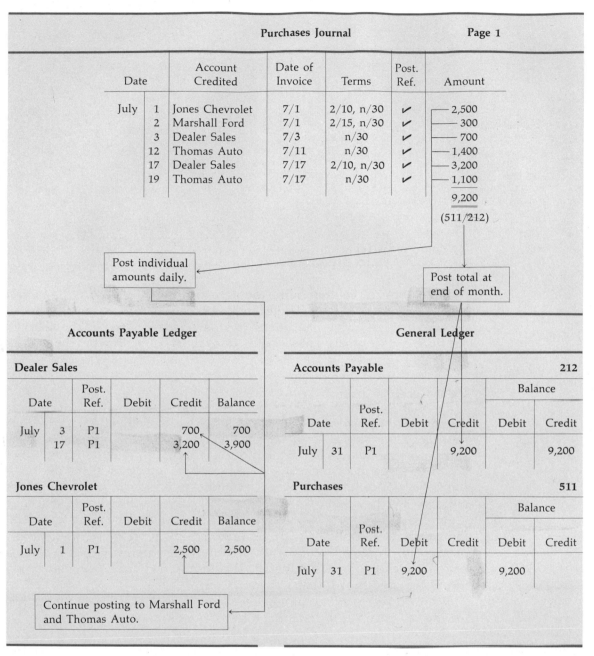

Figure 7-9
Relationship of
Single-Column
Purchases
Journal to the
General Ledger
and the Ac-
counts Payable
Ledger

The single-column purchases journal may be used to record credit purchases of things other than merchandise by adding a separate column for other debit accounts that are often used. For example, the multicolumn purchases journal in Figure 7-10 has columns for Freight In, Store Supplies, and Office Supplies. Here the total credits to Accounts Payable ($9,437) equal the total debits to Purchases, Freight In, Store Supplies, and Office Supplies ($9,200 + $50 + $145 + $42 = $9,437). As in the procedure already described, the individual transactions in the Accounts Payable column are posted daily to the accounts payable subsidiary ledger, and

			Purchases Journal						Page 1

						Credit		Debits		
Date		Account Credited	Date of Invoice	Terms	Post. Ref.	Accounts Payable	Purchases	Freight In	Store Supplies	Office Supplies
July	1	Jones Chevrolet	7/1	2/10, n/30	✓	2,500	2,500			
	2	Marshall Ford	7/1	2/15, n/30	✓	300	300			
	2	Shelby Car Delivery	7/2	n/30	✓	50		50		
	3	Dealer Sales	7/3	n/30	✓	700	700			
	12	Thomas Auto	7/11	n/30	✓	1,400	1,400			
	17	Dealer Sales	7/17	2/10, n/30	✓	3,200	3,200			
	19	Thomas Auto	7/17	n/30	✓	1,100	1,100			
	25	Osborne Supply	7/21	n/10th	✓	187			145	42
						9,437	9,200	50	145	42
						(212)	(511)	(514)	(132)	(133)

Figure 7-10
A Multicolumn
Purchases
Journal

the totals of each column in the journal are posted monthly to the correct general ledger accounts. Some credit purchases call for a debit to an account that has no special column (that is, no place to record the debit) in the purchases journal. These transactions must be recorded in the general journal.

Cash Receipts Journal

All transactions involving receipts of cash are recorded in the **cash receipts journal.** Examples of such transactions are cash from cash sales, cash from credit customers in payment of their accounts, and cash from other sources. To be most efficient, the cash receipts journal must be multicolumn. Several columns are necessary because, though all cash receipts are alike in that they require a debit to Cash, they are different in that they require a variety of credit entries. Thus you should be alert to several important differences between the cash receipts journal and the journals previously presented. Among these differences are an Other Accounts column, use of account numbers in the Post. Ref. column, and daily posting of the credits to Other Accounts.

The cash receipts journal illustrated in Figure 7-11 is based on the following selected transactions for July:

July 1 Henry Mitchell invested $20,000 in a used-car business.
5 Sold a used car for $1,200 cash.
8 Collected $500 from Georgetta Jones, less 2 percent sales discount.
13 Sold a used car for $1,400 cash.
16 Collected $750 from Peter Clark.
19 Sold a used car for $1,000 cash.
20 Sold some equipment not used in the business for $500 cash.
24 Signed a note at the bank for a loan of $5,000.
26 Sold a used car for $1,600 cash.
28 Collected $600 from Peter Clark, less 2 percent sales discount.

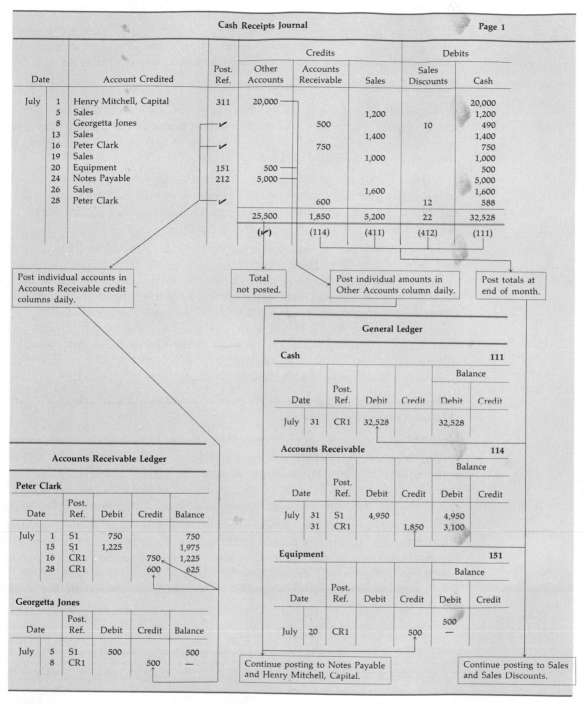

Figure 7-11
Relationship
of the Cash
Receipts
Journal to the
General Ledger
and the
Accounts
Receivable
Ledger

The cash receipts journal, as illustrated in Figure 7-11, has two debit columns and three credit columns. The two debit columns record Cash and Sales Discounts.

1. Cash Each entry must have an amount in this column because each transaction must be a receipt of cash.

2. **Sales Discounts** The company in the illustration allows a 2 percent discount for prompt payment. Therefore, it is useful to have a column for sales discounts. Note that in the transactions of July 8 and 28, the debits to Cash and Sales Discounts equal the credit to Accounts Receivable.

The credit columns are the following:

1. **Accounts Receivable** This column is used to record collections on account from customers. The customer's name is written in the space entitled Account Credited so that the payment can be entered in his or her account in the accounts receivable ledger.

2. **Sales** This column is used to record all cash sales during the month. Retail firms that normally use cash registers would make an entry at the end of each day for the total sales from each cash register for that day. The debit, of course, is in the Cash Debit column.

3. **Other Accounts** This column is sometimes called Sundry Accounts and is used for the credit portion of any entry that is neither a cash collection from Accounts Receivable nor a cash sale. The name of the account to be credited is indicated in the Account Credited column. For example, the transactions of July 1, 20, and 24 involved credits to accounts other than Accounts Receivable or Sales. If a company finds that it is consistently crediting a certain account in the Other Accounts column, it may be appropriate to add another credit column to the cash receipts journal for that particular account.

The posting of the cash receipts journal, as illustrated in Figure 7-11, can be summarized as follows:

1. Post the Accounts Receivable column daily to each individual account in the accounts receivable subsidiary ledger. A check mark in the Post. Ref. column of the cash receipts journal indicates that the amount has been posted, and a CR1 (representing Cash Receipts Journal—page 1) in the Post. Ref. column of each account indicates the source of the entry.

2. Post the credits in the Other Accounts column daily or at convenient short intervals during the month to the general ledger accounts. Write the account number in the Post. Ref. column as the individual items are posted to indicate that the posting has been done, and write CR1 in the Post. Ref. column of each account to indicate the source of the entry.

3. At the end of the month, total the columns. The sum of the debit column totals must equal the sum of the credit column totals, as follows:

Debit Column Totals		Credit Column Totals	
Cash	$32,528	Accounts Receivable	$ 1,850
Sales Discounts	22	Sales	5,200
		Other Accounts	25,500
Total Debits	$32,550	Total Credits	$32,550

This step is called crossfooting—a procedure we encountered earlier.

4. Post the column totals as follows:
   a. Cash debit column—posted as a debit to the Cash account.

b. Sales Discounts debit column—posted as a debit to the Sales Discounts account.

c. Accounts Receivable credit column—posted as a credit to the Accounts Receivable controlling account.

d. Sales credit column—posted as a credit to the Sales account.

e. The account numbers are written below each column as they are posted to indicate that this step has been completed. A CR1 is written in the Post. Ref. column of each account to indicate the source of the entry.

f. Note that the Other Accounts column total is not posted by total because each entry was posted separately. The individual accounts were posted in step 2 above. Accountants place a check mark at the bottom of the column to show that it is not posted.

Cash Payments Journal

All transactions involving payments of cash are recorded in the **cash payments journal** (also called the cash disbursements journal). Examples of such transactions are cash purchases, payments of obligations resulting from earlier purchases on credit, and other cash payments. As with the cash receipts journal, the cash payments journal must be multicolumn and is similar in design to the cash receipts journal.

The cash payments journal illustrated in Figure 7-12 (next page) is based on the following selected transactions of Mitchell's Used Car Sales for July:

July 2 Purchased merchandise (a used car) from Sondra Tidmore for cash, $400.

6 Paid for newspaper advertising in the *Daily Journal*, $200.

8 Paid one month's land and building rent to Siviglia Agency, $250.

11 Paid Jones Chevrolet for July 1 invoice (previously recorded in purchases journal in Figure 7-9), $2,500, less 2 percent purchase discount earned for payment in ten days or less.

16 Paid Charles Kuntz, a salesperson, his salary, $600.

17 Paid Marshall Ford invoice of July 2 (previously recorded in purchases journal in Figure 7-9), $300, less 2 percent discount earned for payment in fifteen days or less.

24 Paid Grabow & Company for two-year insurance policy, $480.

27 Paid Dealer Sales invoice of July 17 (previously recorded in purchases journal in Figure 7-9), $3,200, less 2 percent purchase discount earned for payment in ten days or less.

30 Purchased office equipment for $400 and service equipment for $500 from A & B Equipment Company. Issued one check for the total cost.

The cash payments journal, as illustrated in Figure 7-12, has two credit columns and two debit columns. The credit columns are as follows:

1. **Cash** Each entry must have an amount in this column because each transaction must involve a payment of cash.

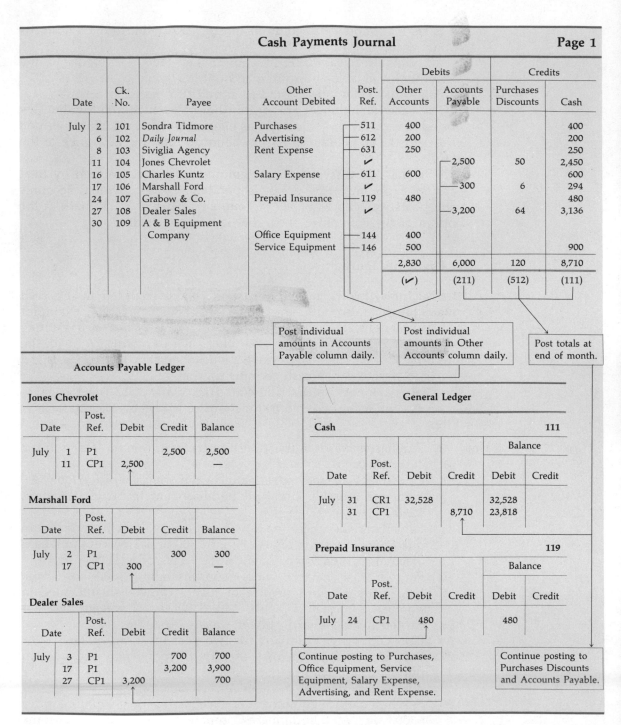

Figure 7-12
Cash Payments
Journal

2. **Purchases Discounts** When purchases discounts are taken, they are recorded in this column.

The debit columns are as follows:

1. **Accounts Payable** This column total is used to record payments to

suppliers that have extended credit to the company. The supplier's name is written in the space entitled Payee so that the payment can be entered in his or her account in the accounts payable ledger.

2. **Other Accounts** Cash can be expended for many reasons. Thus an Other Accounts or Sundry Accounts column is needed in the cash payments journal. The title of the account to be debited is written in the Other Accounts Debit column, and the amount is entered in the amount column. If a company finds that a particular account occurs often in the Other Accounts column, it may be desirable to add another debit column to the cash payments journal.

The posting of the cash payments journal, as illustrated in Figure 7-12, can be summarized as follows:

1. The Accounts Payable column should be posted daily to each individual account in the accounts payable subsidiary ledger. A check mark is placed in the Post. Ref. column to indicate that the posting is accomplished.

2. The debits in the Other Accounts debit column should be posted daily or at convenient intervals during the month to the general ledger. The account number is written in the Post. Ref. column as the individual items are posted to indicate that the posting has been completed and a CP1 (representing Cash Payments Journal—page 1) is written in the Post. Ref. column of each account.

3. At the end of the month, the columns are totaled and crossfooted. That is, the sum of the credit column totals must equal the sum of the debit column totals, as follows:

Credit Column Totals		Debit Column Totals	
Cash	$8,710	Accounts Payable	$6,000
Purchases Discounts	120	Other Accounts	2,830
Total Credits	$8,830	Total Debits	$8,830

4. The column totals for Cash, Purchases Discounts, and Accounts Payable are posted at the end of the month to their respective accounts in the general ledger. The account numbers are written below each column as they are posted to indicate that this step has been completed, and a CP1 is written in the Post. Ref. column of each account. A check mark is placed under the total of the Other Accounts column to indicate that it is not posted.

General Journal

Transactions that do not involve sales, purchases, cash receipts, or cash payments should be recorded in the general journal. Usually there are only a few such transactions. Three examples are compound entries that do not fit in a special-purpose journal, a return of merchandise, and an allowance to a supplier for credit. Adjusting and closing entries are also recorded in the general journal. Consider the following transactions:

July 24   Purchased service equipment on credit from A & B Supply for $3,500, paying $500 down and issuing a 90-day note for the balance.
25   Returned one of the used cars purchased from Dealer Sales on July 17 for credit, $700.
25   Agreed to give Maxwell Hertz a $35 allowance on his account because a tire blew out on the car he purchased.

These entries are shown in Figure 7-13.

The July 24 entry cannot be made in the cash payments journal (Figure 7-12) because the entry calls for credits to both Cash and Notes Payable but the journal allows credits only to Cash and Purchases Discounts. The entries on July 25 and 26 include a debit or a credit to a controlling account (Accounts Payable or Accounts Receivable). The name of the customer or supplier is also given here. When such a debit or credit is made to a controlling account in the general journal, the entry must be posted twice: once in the controlling account and once in the individual account in the subsidiary ledger. This procedure keeps the subsidiary ledger equal to the controlling account. Note that the July 26 transaction is posted by a debit to Sales Returns and Allowances in the general ledger (shown by the account number 413), by a credit to the Accounts Receivable controlling account in the general ledger (shown by the account number 114), and by a credit to the Maxwell Hertz account in the accounts receivable subsidiary ledger (shown by the check mark).

Figure 7-13
Transactions
Recorded in the
General Journal

General Journal					Page 1
Date		Description	Post. Ref.	Debit	Credit
July	24	Service Equipment	146	3,500	
		Cash	111		500
		Notes Payable	211		3,000
		Purchased service equipment from A & B Supply; terms: $500 down payment and 90-day note for balance			
	25	Accounts Payable—Dealer Sales	212/✔	700	
		Purchases Returns and Allowances	513		700
		Returned used car for credit; invoice date: 7/3			
	26	Sales Returns and Allowances	413	35	
		Accounts Receivable—Maxwell Hertz	114/✔		35
		Allowance given because of faulty tire			

Chapter Seven

Flexibility of Special-Purpose Journals

The functions of special-purpose journals are to reduce and simplify the work in accounting and to allow for the division of labor. These journals should be designed to fit the business in which they are used. As noted earlier, if certain accounts show up often in the Other Accounts column of a journal, it may be wise to add a column for those accounts when a new page of a special-purpose journal is prepared.

Also, if certain transactions appear over and over again in the general journal, it may be a good idea to set up a new special-purpose journal. For example, if Mitchell Used Car Sales finds that it must often give allowances to customers, it may want to set up a sales returns and allowances journal. Sometimes, a purchases returns and allowances journal may be in order. In short, special-purpose journals should be designed to take care of the kinds of transactions a company commonly encounters.

Chapter Review

Review of Learning Objectives

1. Describe the phases of systems installation and the principles of systems design.

The phases of systems installation are system investigation, system design, and system implementation. In designing an accounting system, the system designer must keep in mind the four principles of systems design: the cost-benefit principle, the control principle, the compatibility principle, and the flexibility principle.

2. Describe the basic features of computer systems and their application to data processing.

Computer data processing systems are the most advanced type of data processing systems, in which recording, posting, and other bookkeeping tasks are done with the aid of a computer. The typical computer system consists of hardware, software, procedures, and personnel. The internal processing is specified in the form of programs, which may be designed to allow batch processing (one job at a time) or on-line processing (several jobs at a time).

3. Explain the objectives and uses of special-purpose journals.

The typical manual data processing system consists of several special-purpose journals, each of which is designed to record one kind of transaction. Recording all transactions of one kind in each journal reduces and simplifies the bookkeeping work and results in the division of labor. The division of labor is important for control purposes.

4. Construct and use the following types of special-purpose journals: sales journal, purchases journal, cash receipts journal, cash payments journal, and others as needed.

A special-purpose journal is constructed by devoting a single column to a particular account (for example, debit cash in the cash receipts journal and credit cash in the cash payments journal). Other columns in such a journal depend on the kinds of transactions in which the company normally engages. The special-purpose journals also have columns for the transaction dates, explanations or subsidiary account names, and reference columns.

5. Explain the purposes and relationships of controlling accounts and subsidiary ledgers.

Subsidiary ledgers contain the individual accounts of a certain kind such as customer accounts (accounts receivable) or supplier accounts (accounts payable). The total of the balances of the subsidiary accounts will equal the total of the controlling or general ledger account because the individual items are posted daily to the subsidiary accounts and the column totals are posted monthly from the special-purpose journal.

Review Problem
Purchases Journal

Caraban Company is a retail seller of hiking and camping gear and other outdoor equipment. The company is installing a manual accounting system, and the accountant is trying to decide whether to use a single-column or a multicolumn purchases journal. Some transactions related to purchases are presented below.

Jan 5 Received a shipment of merchandise from Simons Corporation, $2,875, terms 2/10, n/30, FOB shipping point.

    10 Received a bill from Allied Freight for the freight charges on the Jan. 5 shipment, $416, terms n/30.

    15 Returned some of the merchandise received from Simons Corporation because it was not what was ordered, $315.

    20 Purchased office supplies of $117 and store supplies of $56 from Mason Company, terms n/30.

    25 Received a shipment from Thomas Manufacturing, with the bill for $1,882, including freight charges of $175, terms n/30, FOB shipping point.

Required

1. Record the transactions above, using a single-column purchases journal and a general journal.

2. Record the transactions above, using a multicolumn purchases journal and a general journal, rule and total the purchases journal, and show what postings should be made from each journal.

3. Using the principles of systems design as a basis for your answer, compare the two systems as to number of journal entries and postings and in terms of the cost/benefit, compatibility, and flexibility principles.

Answer to Review Problem

1. Transactions recorded in a single-column purchases journal and the general journal are shown below.

	Purchases Journal				Page 1
Date	Account Credited	Date of Invoice	Terms	Post. Ref.	Amount
Jan. 5	Simons Corporation	1/5	2/10, n/30		2,875

Date		Description	Post. Ref.	Debit	Credit
Jan.	10	Freight In		416	
		Accounts Payable—Allied Freight			416
		Freight charges on Simons Corp. shipment, terms n/30			
	15	Accounts Payable—Simons Corp.		315	
		Purchases Returns and Allowances			315
		Returned merchandise not ordered			
	20	Office Supplies		117	
		Store Supplies		56	
		Accounts Payable—Mason Company			173
		Purchased supplies, terms n/30			
	25	Purchases		1,707	
		Freight In		175	
		Accounts Payable—Thomas Manufacturing			1,882
		Purchased merchandise, terms n/30			

2. Transactions recorded in multicolumn purchases journal and general journal are shown below.

						Credit		Debits		
Date		Account Credited	Date of Invoice	Terms	Post. Ref.	Accounts Payable	Purchases	Freight In	Store Supplies	Office Supplies
Jan.	5	Simons Corporation	1/5	2/10, n/30		2,875	2,875			
	10	Allied Freight	1/10	n/30		416		416		
	20	Mason Company	1/20	n/30		173			56	117
	25	Thomas Manufacturing	1/25	n/30		1,882	1,707	175		
						5,346	4,582	591	56	117

Each of these accounts is posted daily to the appropriate account in the subsidiary ledger.

Each of these totals is posted monthly to the applicable general ledger account.

		General Journal			Page 1
Date		Description	Post. Ref.	Debit	Credit

Jan.	15	Accounts Payable—Simons Corporation
		    Purchases Returns and Allowances
		        Returned merchandise not
		            ordered
				→315	315 ←

> This amount is posted both to the controlling account and to the subsidiary account.

> This amount is posted to the general ledger account.

3. The first system (single-column purchases journal) requires four general journal entries plus one purchases journal entry, or sixteen separate lines, including explanations, to be written. In addition, fifteen postings to the general ledger and the accounts payable subsidiary ledger are necessary. (Also, the total of the purchases journal must be posted twice at the end of the month.) The second system (multicolumn purchases journal) calls for only one general journal entry and four purchases journal entries. Only seven lines need to be written, and only seven postings must be made (in addition, the column totals in the purchases journal must be posted at the end of the month).

In applying the cost/benefit principle, the benefits of the expanded purchases journal in terms of journalizing and posting time saved are clear from the analysis above. In addition, there are fewer chances for error when using the expanded purchases journal. So this aspect of achieving the control principle is better under the second system. It is not possible to decide which system better meets the compatibility principle because we do not know the relative proportion of transaction types. For instance, if the number of transactions like the one for January 5 outnumber all the others by ten to one, the first system may be more compatible with the needs of the company. On the other hand, if there are great numbers of transactions like those for January 10, 20, and 25, the second system may be more compatible. Finally, in terms of the flexibility principle, the multicolumn purchases journal is obviously more flexible because it can handle more kinds of transactions and may be expanded to include columns for other accounts if necessary.

Chapter Assignments

Questions

1. What are the three phases of systems installation?
2. What are the four principles of systems design? Explain the essence of each in a sentence.
3. What is the function of data processing?
4. What are three ways of viewing data processing?

5. What are the elements of a computer data processing system?

6. What is the difference between hardware and software?

7. Data are the raw material of a computer system. Trace the flow of data through the different parts of a computer system.

8. What is the purpose of a computer program?

9. What is the difference between batch processing and on-line processing?

10. How do special-purpose journals save time in entering and posting transactions?

11. Long Transit had 1,700 sales on credit during the current month.

    a. If the company uses a two-column general journal to record sales, how many times will the word *Sales* be written?

    b. How many postings to the Sales account will have to be made?

    c. If the company uses a sales journal, how many times will the word *Sales* be written?

    d. How many postings to the Sales account will have to be made?

12. What is the purpose of the Accounts Receivable controlling account? What is its relationship to the accounts receivable subsidiary ledger?

13. Why are the cash receipts journal and cash payments journal crossfooted? When is this step performed?

14. A company has the following numbers of accounts with balances: 18 asset accounts, including the Accounts Receivable account but not the individual customer accounts; 200 customer accounts; 8 liability accounts, including the Accounts Payable account but not the individual credit accounts; 100 creditor accounts; 35 owner's equity accounts, including income statement accounts. The total is 361 accounts. How many accounts in total would appear in the general ledger?

Classroom Exercises

Exercise 7-1
Matching
Transactions to
Special-Purpose
Journals
(L.O. 3)

A company uses a one-column sales journal, a one-column purchases journal, a cash receipts journal, a cash payments journal, and a general journal in recording its transactions.

    Indicate in which journal each of the following transactions would be recorded: (1) sold merchandise on credit; (2) sold merchandise for cash; (3) gave a customer credit for merchandise purchased on credit and returned; (4) paid a creditor; (5) paid office salaries; (6) customer paid for merchandise previously purchased on credit; (7) recorded adjusting and closing entries; (8) purchased merchandise on credit; (9) purchased sales department supplies on credit; (10) purchased office equipment for cash; (11) returned merchandise purchased on credit; (12) payment of taxes.

Exercise 7-2
Characteristics
of Special-Pur-
pose Journals
(L.O. 3)

Garcia Corporation uses a sales journal, a purchases journal, a cash receipts journal, a cash payments journal, and a general journal.

1. In which journal would you expect to find the fewest transactions recorded?

2. At the end of the accounting period, to which account or accounts should the total of the purchases journal be posted as a debit and/or credit?

3. At the end of the accounting period, to which account or accounts should the total of the sales journal be posted as a debit and/or credit?

4. What two subsidiary ledgers would probably be associated with the journals listed above? From which journals would postings normally be made to each of the two subsidiary ledgers?

5. In which of the journals are adjusting and closing entries made?

Exercise 7-3
Identifying the Content of a Special-Purpose Journal
(L.O. 4)

Shown below is a page from a special journal.

1. What kind of journal is this?
2. Give an explanation for each of the following transactions: (a) August 27, (b) August 28, (c) August 29, and (d) August 30.
3. Explain the following: (a) the numbers under the bottom lines, (b) the checks entered in the Post. Ref. column, (c) the numbers 215 and 515 in the Post. Ref. column, and (d) the check below the Other Accounts column.

Date		Account Credited	Post. Ref.	Credits			Debits	
				Other Accounts	Accounts Receivable	Sales	Sales Discounts	Cash
		Balance Forward		26,100	10,204	4,282	787	39,799
Aug.	27	Arch Lipman	✔		500		10	490
	28	Notes Receivable	215	1,000				
		Interest Earned	515	120				1,120
	29	Cash Sale				960		960
	30	Margaret Connelly	✔		200			200
				27,220	10,904	5,242	797	42,569
				(✔)	(214)	(510)	(511)	(111)

Exercise 7-4
Finding Errors in Special-Purpose Journals
(L.O. 4)

A company records purchases in a one-column purchases journal and records purchases returns in its general journal. During the past month an accounting clerk made each of the errors described below. Explain how each error might be discovered.

1. Correctly recorded an $86 purchase in the purchases journal but posted it to the creditor's account as a $68 purchase.
2. Made an addition error in totaling the Amount column of the purchases journal.
3. Posted a purchases return recorded in the general journal to the Purchases Returns and Allowances account and to the Accounts Payable account but did not post it to the creditor's account.
4. Made an error in determining the balance of a creditor's account.
5. Posted a purchases return to the Accounts Payable account but did not post to the Purchases Returns and Allowances account.

Exercise 7-5
Posting from a Sales Journal
(L.O. 4, 5)

Fox Corporation began business on September 1. The company maintained a sales journal, which appeared at the end of the month as shown on page 255.

1. On a sheet of paper, open general ledger accounts for Accounts Receivable (account number 112) and Sales (account number 410) and an accounts receivable subsidiary ledger with an account for each customer. Make the appropriate postings from the sales journal. State the posting references that you would place in the sales journal on page 255.
2. Prove the accounts receivable subsidiary ledger by preparing a schedule of accounts receivable.

Sales Journal					Page 1
Date		Account Debited	Invoice Number	Post. Ref.	Amount
Sept.	4	John McCoy	1001		172
	10	Elizabeth Flowers	1002		317
	15	Rita Lazado	1003		214
	17	John McCoy	1004		97
	25	Nelson Fong	1005		433
					1,233

**Exercise 7-6
Multicolumn
Purchases
Journal
(L.O. 4)**

Blum Company uses a multicolumn purchases journal similar to the one illustrated in Figure 7-10. During the month of October, Blum made the following purchases:

Oct. 1 Purchased merchandise from Emerson Company on account for $2,700, invoice dated October 1, terms 2/10, n/30.

2 Received freight bill dated Oct. 1 from Superior Freight for above merchandise, $175, terms n/30.

23 Purchased supplies from Hall, Inc., for $120; allocated one-half each to store and office; invoice dated Oct. 20, terms n/30.

27 Purchased merchandise from Jackson Company on account for $987; total included freight in of $87; invoice dated Oct. 25, terms n/30, FOB shipping point.

30 Purchased office supplies from Hall, Inc., $48, invoice dated October 30, terms n/30.

1. Draw a multicolumn purchases journal similar to the one in Figure 7-10.
2. Enter the above transactions in the purchases journal. Then foot and crossfoot the columns.

Interpreting Accounting Information

**Published
Financial
Information:
B. Dalton and
Waldenbooks
(L.O. 1)**

In the mid-1960s a new and tempting mass market was emerging. Americans were becoming better educated and more affluent. Also, the increasing number of shopping centers provided the perfect setting for a chain of national bookstores. To take advantage of this opportunity, Minneapolis-based Dayton-Hudson launched its B. Dalton Bookseller, and Los Angeles-based Carter Hawley Hale began expanding its Waldenbooks division. Today these two chains are by far the biggest book retailers in the country and are very competitive with each other. Dalton has 575 stores and plans to add 556 more by 1987. Waldenbooks has 750 outlets and is adding 80 to 90 more each year.

Forbes magazine reports that although Waldenbooks has more outlets, Dalton "looks like the leader in the fight." Each chain had roughly $250 million in sales in 1980, but Dalton sold an estimated $132 worth of books per square foot of store space to Walden's $114. *Forbes* states that "A computerized inventory system installed in 1966 is what gives Dalton its edge—and is a key to why its 10% pretax profits are well above Walden's." In the book business today, "Success depends far more on fast, high efficiency distribution than on any fundamental appreciation of literature. . . . Order a little of everything and remain secure in your capabilities to restock quickly those titles the computer says are selling fast."[1]

Required

1. Describe in your own words how you believe Dalton used the four principles of systems design in 1966 to design its computerized inventory system so that it was able to grow rapidly and to become more profitable than Waldenbooks.
2. Describe in your own words the following parts of the computerized inventory system that would allow Dalton to restock fast-selling books quickly: source documents, data input, processing, information output, and distribution.

Problem Set A

**Problem 7A-1
Identification of
Transactions**
(L.O. 4)

The manual accounting system of Bristol Company contains a general journal, purchases journal, cash receipts journal, and cash payments journal similar to those illustrated in the text.

On May 31, the Sales account in the general ledger appeared as follows:

Sales   **Account No. 411**

| Date | | Item | Post. Ref. | Debit | Credit | Balance | |
						Debit	Credit
May	31		S11		32,617		32,617
	31		CR7		21,207		53,824
	31		J17	53,824			—

On May 31, the H. Mendez account in the accounts receivable subsidiary ledger appeared as follows:

H. Mendez   **Account No. 10012**

Date		Item	Post. Ref.	Debit	Credit	Balance
May	5		S10	1,317		1,317
	9		J14		282	1,035
	15		CR6		500	535

Required

1. Write an explanation of each entry in the Sales account, including the journal from which the entry was posted.
2. Write an explanation of each entry in the H. Mendez account receivable, including the journal from which the entry was posted.

1. Jeff Blyskal, "Dalton, Walden and The Amazing Money Machine," Forbes, (January 18, 1982), p. 47.

Problem 7A-2
Cash Receipts and Cash Payments Journals
(L.O. 4)

Reston Company is a small retail business that uses a manual data processing system similar to the one illustrated in the chapter. Among its special-purpose journals are multicolumn cash receipts and cash payments journals. All cash transactions for Reston Company for the month of June are listed below.

June 1 Paid June rent to C. Herbert, $400, with check no. 782.
 2 Paid T & G Wholesale on account, $850, less a 2 percent discount, with check no. 783.
 3 Received $392, net of a 2 percent discount, on account from R. Knight.
 4 Cash sales, $1,272.
 7 Paid Cannon Freight on account, $299, with check no. 784.
 8 The owner, Paul Reston, invested an additional $5,000 in the business.
 10 Paid Ruhl Supply on account, $142, with check no. 785.
 11 Cash sales, $1,417.
 14 Paid Cannon Freight $155 with check no. 786 for a shipment of merchandise received today.
 15 Paid Travis Company on account, $784, net of a 2 percent discount, with check no. 787.
 16 Received payment on account from J. Graff, $60.
 19 Cash sales, $987.
 20 Received payment on a note receivable of $900 plus $18 interest.
 21 Purchased office supplies from Ruhl Supply, $54, with check no. 788.
 22 Paid a note payable in full to City Bank, $2,050, including $50 interest, with check no. 789.
 26 Cash sales, $1,482.
 27 Paid $250 less a 2 percent discount to T & G Wholesale, with check no. 790
 29 Paid Julie Hall, a sales clerk, $550, for her monthly salary, with check no. 791.
 30 Paul Reston withdrew $600 from the business, using check no. 792.

Required

1. Enter the above transactions in the cash receipts and cash payments journals.
2. Foot and rule the journals.

Problem 7A-3
Purchases and General Journals
(L.O. 4, 5)

Blanchard Lawn Supply Company uses a multicolumn purchases journal and general journal similar to those illustrated in the text. The company also maintains an accounts payable subsidiary ledger. The items below represent the company's credit transactions for the month of October.

Oct. 3 Purchased merchandise from Horne Fertilizer Company, $1,270.
 4 Purchased office supplies of $79 and store supplies of $117 from Bogart Supply, Inc.
 7 Purchased cleaning equipment from Target Company, $928.
 10 Purchased display equipment from Bogart Supply, Inc., $2,350.
 14 Purchased lawn mowers from E-Z Lawn Equipment Company, for resale, $4,200; the invoice included transportation charges of $175.
 15 Purchased merchandise from Horne Fertilizer Co., $1,722.
 19 Purchased a lawn mower from E-Z Lawn Equipment Company to be used in the business, $475; the invoice included transportation charges of $35.
 24 Purchased store supplies from Bogart Supply, Inc., $27.

Required

1. Enter the above transactions in the purchases journal and the general journal. Assume that all terms are n/30 and that invoice dates are the same as the transaction dates.

2. Foot and rule the purchases journal.

3. Open the following general ledger accounts: Store Supplies (116), Office Supplies (117), Lawn Equipment (142), Display Equipment (144), Cleaning Equipment (146), Accounts Payable (211), Purchases (611), and Freight In (612). Open accounts payable subsidiary ledger accounts as needed. Post from the journals to the ledger accounts.

Problem 7A-4
Comprehensive
Use of Spe-
cial-Purpose
Journals
(L.O. 4, 5)

Alamo Office Supply Company completed the following transactions:

Nov. 1 Issued check no. 2101 to Local Rentals, Inc., for November rent, $900.
2 Received merchandise from Perkins Company, $3,350, invoice dated Nov. 2, terms 2/10, n/30, FOB shipping point.
3 Received freight bill from Landon Transit for previous shipment, $276, terms n/10.
4 Sold merchandise to R. McCray, $600, terms 2/10, n/30, invoice no. 3219.
5 Received a bill from WRBB for radio commercials, $317, terms n/25th of month.
6 Received a credit memorandum from Perkins Company for merchandise returned, $250.
7 Issued check no. 2102 to Reliable Insurance for a two-year fire and casualty policy, $487.
8 Sold merchandise to C. Daniels, $840, terms 2/10, n/30, invoice no. 3220.
9 Received mechandise from Perkins Company, $1,850, invoice dated Nov. 7, terms 2/10, n/30, FOB shipping point.
10 Received freight bill from Landon Transit for previous shipment, $206, terms n/10.
11 Issued a credit memorandum to C. Daniels for merchandise returned, $40.
12 Issued check no. 2103 to Perkins Company in full payment, less discount, of Nov. 2 purchase.
13 Issued check no. 2104 to Landon Transit for balance owed.
14 Received payment in full less discount from R. McCray.
15 Cash sales for first half of month, $9,346. (To shorten these problems, cash sales are recorded only twice a month instead of daily, as they would be in actual practice.)
16 Issued check no. 2105 to Center Gas Co. for monthly heating bill, $119.
17 Issued check no. 2106 to Perkins Company for $1,000, less discount, in partial payment of amount owed.
18 Received payment from C. Daniels for one-half amount owed less discount.
19 Sold merchandise to T. Schultz, $350, terms 2/10, n/30, invoice no. 3221.
20 Received a credit memorandum from WRBB because two scheduled commercials were not played, $62.
21 Sold merchandise to C. Daniels, $159, terms 2/10, n/30, invoice no. 3222.
22 Issued check no. 2107 to State Power Co. for monthly utilities, $283.

Nov. 23 Sold merchandise to R. McCray, $496, terms 2/10, n/30, invoice no. 3223.

24 Received payment in full, less discount, from T. Schultz.

25 Issued check no. 2108 to WRBB for balance of account.

26 Received merchandise from Jayson, Inc., $2,700, invoice dated Nov. 22, terms 2/10, n/30, FOB shipping point.

27 Issued check no. 2109 to Fast Freight for transportation on previous shipment, $319.

28 Issued check no. 2110 to Perkins Company for balance of amount owed.

29 Issued check no. 2111, payable to Payroll account for monthly salaries, $4,200.

30 Cash sales for last half of month, $10,213.

Required

1. Prepare a sales journal, a one-column purchases journal, a cash receipts journal, a cash payments journal, and a general journal similar to the ones illustrated in this chapter.

2. Open the following general ledger accounts: Cash (111); Accounts Receivable (112); Prepaid Insurance (113); Accounts Payable (211); Sales (411); Sales Discounts (412); Sales Returns and Allowances (413); Purchases (511); Purchases Discounts (512); Purchases Returns and Allowances (513); Freight In (514); Salaries Expense (521); Advertising Expense (522); Rent Expense (531); and Utilities Expense (532).

3. Open the following accounts receivable subsidiary ledger accounts: C. Daniels; R. McCray; T. Schultz.

4. Open the following accounts payable subsidiary ledger accounts: Jayson, Inc.; Landon Transit; Perkins Company; WRBB.

5. Enter the transactions in the journals, and post as appropriate.

6. Foot the journals, and make end-of-month postings.

7. Prepare a trial balance of the general ledger, and prove the control balances of Accounts Receivable and Accounts Payable by preparing schedules of accounts receivable and accounts payable.

**Problem 7A-5
Comprehensive
Use of Spe-
cial-Purpose
Journals**
(L.O. 4, 5)

Jordan Book Store opened its doors for business on September 1. During September the following transactions occurred:

Sept. 1 Wendell Jordan began business by depositing $17,000 in the new company's bank account.

2 Issued check no. C001 to Campus Rentals for one month's rent, $400.

3 Received a shipment of books from Diamond Books, Inc., $7,840, invoice dated September 2, terms 5/10, n/60, FOB shipping point.

4 Received a bill for freight from Parcel Shippers for previous day's shipment, $395.

5 Received a shipment from Gateway Books, $5,650, invoice dated September 5, terms 2/10, n/30, FOB shipping point.

6 Issued check no. C002 to TOR Freight, Inc., for transportation charges on previous day's shipment, $287.

8 Issued check no. C003 to Equipment Company for store equipment, $5,200.

9 Sold books to University Center, $782, terms 5/10, n/30, invoice no. I001.

10 Returned books to Diamond Books, Inc., for credit, $380.

Sept. 11 Issued check no. C004 to WUII for radio commercials, $235.

12 Issued check no. C005 to Diamond Books, Inc., for balance of amount owed less discount.

13 Cash sales for the first two weeks, $1,814.

15 Issued check no. C006 to Gateway Books, $3,000 less discount.

16 Signed a 90-day, 10 percent note for a bank loan, $10,000, and received the $10,000 cash.

17 Sold books to Meg Taylor, $130, terms n/30, invoice no. I002.

18 Issued a credit memorandum to University Center for returned books, $62.

19 Received payment in full, less discount, from University Center.

20 Sold books to Roy Fields, $97, terms n/30, invoice no. I003.

22 Received a shipment from Victory Publishing Company, $2,302, invoice dated September 21, terms 5/10, n/60.

23 Returned additional books purchased on Sept. 3 to Diamond Books, Inc., for credit, $718.

24 Sold books to University Center, $817, terms 5/10, n/30, invoice no. I004.

25 Received a shipment from Diamond Books, Inc., $1,187, invoice dated September 22, terms 5/10, n/60, FOB shipping point.

26 Issued check no. C007 to Parcel Shippers for balance owed on account plus shipping charges of $97 on previous day's shipment.

27 Cash sales for the second two weeks, $3,744.

29 Issued check no. C008 to Payroll account for sales salaries for first four weeks of month, $700.

30 Cash sales for the last two days of month, $277.

Required

1. Prepare a sales journal, a one-column purchases journal, a cash receipts journal, a cash payments journal, and a general journal.

2. Open the following general ledger accounts: Cash (111); Accounts Receivable (112); Store Equipment (141); Accounts Payable (211); Notes Payable (212); Wendell Jordan, Capital (311); Sales (411); Sales Discounts (412); Sales Returns and Allowances (413); Purchases (511); Purchases Discounts (512); Purchases Returns and Allowances (513); Freight In (514); Sales Salaries Expense (611); Advertising Expense (612); and Rent Expense (613).

3. Open the following accounts receivable subsidiary ledger accounts: Roy Fields, University Center, and Meg Taylor.

4. Open the following accounts payable subsidiary ledger accounts: Gateway Books, Diamond Books, Inc.; Parcel Shippers; and Victory Publishing Company.

5. Enter the transactions in the journals and post as appropriate.

6. Foot the journals, and make end-of-month postings.

7. Prepare a trial balance of the general ledger, and prove the control balances of Accounts Receivable and Accounts Payable by preparing schedules of accounts receivable and accounts payable.

Problem Set B

Problem 7B-1
Identification of
Transactions
(L.O. 4)

Chandler Company uses a general journal, purchases journal, sales journal, cash receipts journal, and cash payments journal similar to those illustrated in the text.

On June 30, the J. Harper account in the accounts receivable subsidiary ledger appeared as follows:

J. Harper

Date		Item	Post. Ref.	Debit	Credit	Balance
May	31		S4	372		372
June	4		J7		27	345
	10		CR5		100	245
	15		S6	114		359

On June 30, the account of Turner Company in the accounts payable subsidiary ledger appeared as follows:

Turner Company

Date		Item	Post. Ref.	Debit	Credit	Balance
June	16		P7		982	982
	21		J9	106		876
	28		CP8	876		—

Required

1. Write an explanation of each entry affecting the J. Harper account receivable including the journal from which the entry was posted.
2. Write an explanation of each entry affecting the Turner Company account payable including the journal from which the entry was posted.

Problem 7B-2 Cash Receipts and Cash Payments Journals (L.O. 4)

The items below detail all cash transactions by Dayton Company for the month of February. The company uses multicolumn cash receipts and cash payments journals similar to those illustrated in the chapter.

Feb. 1 The owner, B. Dayton, invested $30,000 cash in the business.
2 Paid February rent to Clark Agency, $250, with check no. 101.
3 Cash sales, $800.
6 Purchased store equipment, for $2,500, from Marrs Equipment Company, with check no. 102.
7 Purchased merchandise for cash, $3,250, from Fuentes Company, with check no. 103.
8 Paid Hiller Company invoice, $900, less 2 percent, with check no. 104.
9 Paid advertising bill, $175, to *Daily News*, with check no. 105.
10 Cash sales, $1,950.
12 Received $400 on account from W. Rosenthal.
13 Purchased used truck for cash, $1,760, from K & L Auto, with check no. 106.

Feb. 19   Received $2,090 from Markum Company, in settlement of a $2,000 note plus interest.

20   Received $539 ($550 less $11 cash discount) from Jane Baldwin.

21   Paid Dayton $1,000 from business for personal use by issuing check no. 107.

23   Paid Deroco Company invoice, $1,250, less 2 percent discount, with check no. 108.

26   Paid Blue Line, Inc., for freight on merchandise received, $80, with check no. 109.

27   Cash sales, $2,400.

28   Paid L. Shoemaker for monthly salary, $700, with check no. 110.

Required

1. Enter the above transactions in the cash receipts and cash payments journals.

2. Foot and rule the journals.

**Problem 7B-3
Purchases
and General
Journals
(L.O. 4, 5)**

The items below represent the credit transactions for Hudson Supply Company during the month of March. The company uses a multicolumn purchases journal and a general journal similar to those illustrated in the text.

Mar. 2   Purchased merchandise from Thiebert Company, $600.

5   Purchased truck from GMR Company, $3,500.

8   Purchased office supplies from Supple Company, $200.

12   Purchased office table from Supple Company, $275.

14   Purchased merchandise, $700, and store supplies, $100, from Mack Company.

17   Purchased store supplies from Thiebert Company, $50, and office supplies from the Lakeside Company, $25.

20   Purchased merchandise from Mack Company, $736.

24   Purchased merchandise from Thiebert Company, $1,226; the $1,226 invoice total included shipping charges of $116.

26   Purchased office supplies from Supple Company, $75.

30   Purchased merchandise from Mack Company, $145.

Required

1. Enter the above transactions in the purchases journal and the general journal. Assume that all terms are n/30 and that invoice dates are the same as the transaction dates.

2. Foot and rule the purchases journal.

3. Open the following general ledger accounts: Store Supplies (116), Office Supplies (117), Trucks (142), Office Equipment (144), Accounts Payable (211), Purchases (611), and Freight In (612). Open accounts payable subsidiary ledger accounts as needed. Post from the journals to the ledger accounts.

**Problem 7B-4
Comprehensive
Use of Spe-
cial-Purpose
Journals
(L.O. 4, 5)**

County Auto Supply Company completed the following transactions:

July 1   Received merchandise from Potter Auto Supply, $1,250, invoice dated June 29, terms 2/10, n/30, FOB shipping point.

2   Issued check no. 116 to Morris Agency for July rent, $1,000.

3   Received merchandise from CSU Manufacturing, $2,700, invoice dated July 1, terms 2/10, n/30, FOB shipping point.

5   Issued check no. 117 to REC Electrical Company for repairs, $280.

6   Received $200 credit memorandum pertaining to July 3 shipment from

CSU Manufacturing for unsatisfactory merchandise returned to CSU Manufacturing.

July 7 Issued check no. 118 to Empire Freight for freight charges on July 1 and July 3 shipment, $92.

8 Sold merchandise to J. Parker, $500, terms 1/10, n/30, invoice no. 941.

9 Issued check no. 119 to Potter Auto Supply in full payment less discount.

10 Sold merchandise to H. Cassady for $625, terms 1/10, n/30, invoice no. 942.

11 Issued check no. 120 to CSU Manufacturing for balance of account less discount.

12 Purchased advertising on credit from the *Daily Journal*, $225, terms n/20.

14 Issued credit memorandum to H. Cassady for $25 for merchandise returned.

15 Cash sales for first half of the month, $4,835. (To shorten these problems, cash sales are recorded only twice a month instead of daily, as they would be in actual practice.)

16 Sold merchandise to D. Clark, $350, terms 1/10, n/30, invoice no. 943.

17 Received check from J. Parker for July 8 purchase less discount.

19 Received check from H. Cassady for balance of account less discount.

20 Received merchandise from Potter Auto Supply, $1,400, invoice dated July 19, terms 2/10, n/30, FOB shipping point.

21 Received freight bill from R & A Transit, $285, terms n/5.

22 Issued check no. 121 for advertising purchase of July 12.

23 Received merchandise from CSU Manufacturing, $1,800, invoice dated July 22, terms 2/10, n/30, FOB shipping point.

24 Issued check no. 122 for freight charge of July 21.

26 Sold merchandise to J. Parker, $400, terms 1/10, n/30, invoice no. 944.

27 Received credit memorandum from CSU Manufacturing for defective merchandise received July 23, $150.

28 Issued check no. 123 to Ford Equipment Company for purchase of office equipment, $175.

29 Issued check no. 124 to Potter Auto Supply for one-half of July 20 purchase less discount.

30 Received check in full from D. Clark, discount not allowed.

31 Cash sales for the last half of month, $5,780.

31 Issued check no. 125, payable to Payroll account for monthly sales salaries, $2,150.

Required

1. Prepare a sales journal, a one-column purchases journal, a cash receipts journal, a cash payments journal, and a general journal similar to the ones illustrated in this chapter.

2. Open the following general ledger accounts: Cash (111), Accounts Receivable (112), Office Equipment (141), Accounts Payable (211), Sales (411), Sales Discounts (412), Sales Returns and Allowances (413), Purchases (511), Purchases Discounts (512), Purchases Returns and Allowances (513), Freight In (514), Sales Salaries Expense (521), Advertising Expense (522), Rent Expense (531), and Repairs Expense (532).

3. Open the following accounts receivable subsidiary ledger accounts: J. Parker, H. Cassady, and D. Clark.

4. Open the following accounts payable subsidiary ledger accounts: CSU Manufacturing, *Daily Journal*, Potter Auto Supply, and R & A Transit.

5. Enter the transactions in the journals, and post as appropriate.

6. Foot the journals, and make end-of-month postings.

7. Prepare a trial balance of the general ledger, and prove the control balances of Accounts Receivable and Accounts Payable by preparing schedules of accounts receivable and accounts payable.

Problem 7B-5
Comprehensive
Use of Spe-
cial-Purpose
Journals
(L.O. 4, 5)

The following transactions were completed by Horner Sporting Goods Shop during the month of January, its first month of operation:

Jan. 2 Ron Horner deposited $10,000 in the new company's bank account.
3 Issued check no. 101 to Fox Corporation for one month's rent, $600.
4 Received merchandise from Collegiate Sports Supply, $3,500, invoice dated January 3, terms 2/10, n/60, FOB shipping point.
5 Received freight bill from Red Line Freight, $482.
6 Issued check no. 102 to Taylor Furniture for store equipment, $3,700.
7 Borrowed $4,000 from bank on a 90-day, 9 percent note.
8 Cash sales for the first week, $991.
10 Sold merchandise to local YMCA, $450, terms 2/10, n/30, invoice no. 1001.
11 Sold merchandise to Herb Williams, $150, terms n/20, invoice no. 1002.
12 Purchased advertising in *The News,* $75, terms n/15.
13 Issued check no. 103 for purchase of January 4 less discount.
14 Issued a credit memorandum for merchandise returned by Herb Williams, $15.
15 Cash sales for the second week, $1,746.
17 Received merchandise from Collegiate Sports Supply, $950, invoice dated January 16, terms 2/10, n/60, FOB shipping point.
18 Received freight bill from Red Line Freight, $131.
19 Received merchandise from Bates Company, $700, invoice dated January 17, terms 1/10, n/60, FOB destination.
20 Received payment in full, less discount, from local YMCA.
21 Received a credit memorandum from Collegiate Sports Supply for $50 of merchandise returned.
22 Cash sales for third week, $1,456.
24 Issued check no. 104 for amount owed Red Line Freight.
25 Sold merchandise to local YMCA, $342, terms 2/10, n/30, invoice no. 1003.
26 Issued check no. 105 in payment of amount owed Collegiate Sports Supply less discount.
27 Sold merchandise to Mollie Kellogg, $186, terms n/20, invoice no. 1004.
28 Issued check no. 106 for amount owed *The News.*
29 Cash sales for the fourth week, $987.
31 Issued check no. 107 to Payroll account for sales salaries for the month of January, $1,800.

Required

1. Prepare a sales journal, a one-column purchases journal, a cash receipts journal, a cash payments journal, and a general journal.

2. Open the following general ledger accounts: Cash (111); Accounts Receivable (112); Store Equipment (141); Accounts Payable (211); Notes Payable (212); Ron Horner, Capital (311); Sales (411); Sales Discounts (412); Sales Returns and Allowances (413); Purchases (511); Purchases Discounts (512); Purchases Returns and Allowances (513); Freight In (514); Sales Salaries Expense (611); Advertising Expense (612); and Rent Expense (613).

3. Open the following accounts receivable subsidiary ledger accounts: Herb Williams, Local YMCA, and Mollie Kellogg.

4. Open the following accounts payable subsidiary ledger accounts: Collegiate Sports Supply, Bates Company, Red Line Freight, and *The News.*

5. Enter the transactions in the journals, and post as appropriate.

6. Foot the journals, and make end-of-period postings.

7. Prepare a trial balance of the general ledger, and prove the control balances of Accounts Receivable and Accounts Payable by preparing schedules of accounts receivable and accounts payable.

Financial Decision Case 7-1

Buy-Rite Foods Company
(L.O. 3, 4, 5)

Buy-Rite Foods Company, owned by Taylor Haskins, is a local grocery store that accepts cash or checks in payment for food. Known for its informality, the store has been very successful and has grown with the community. Along with the growth, however, has come an increase in the number of bad checks that are written for purchases by customers. Because Taylor is concerned about the difficulty of accounting for these returned checks, he asks you to look into the problem.

In addition to a purchases journal and a cash payments journal, the company has a combination one-column sales and cash receipts journal. The combination journal has been acceptable in the past because all sales are for cash (including checks) and almost all cash receipts represent sales transactions. Thus the one column represents a debit to Cash and a credit to Sales.

The bad checks are recorded individually in the general journal by debiting Accounts Receivable and crediting Cash. When a customer pays off a bad check, another entry is made in the general journal debiting Cash and crediting Accounts Receivable. Taylor keeps the returned checks in an envelope, and when a customer comes in to pay one off, he gives the check back to the customer. No other records of the returned checks are maintained.

In studying the problem, you discover that the company is averaging ten returned checks per day totaling $500. As part of the solution, you recommend to Taylor that he establish a policy of issuing check-cashing cards to customers whose credit is approved in advance. The card must be presented when a customer offers a check in payment for groceries. You recommend further that a special journal be established for the returned checks, that a subsidiary ledger be maintained, and that the combination sales/cash receipts journal be expanded.

Required

1. Draw and label the columns for the new returned checks journal and the expanded sales/cash receipts journal. Assume that there are 300 returned checks and 280 collections per month and that the records are closed each month. How many written lines will be saved each month in recording returned checks and subsequent collections in the special journals? How many postings will be saved each month? (Ignore the effect of the subsidiary ledger.)

2. Describe the nature and use of the subsidiary ledger. What advantages do you see in having this subsidiary ledger?

3. Assuming that it takes approximately two and one-half minutes to make each entry and related postings under the old system and one minute to make each entry and related postings under the new system, what are the monthly savings if the cost is $10 an hour? What further, and possibly more significant, savings may be realized by using the suggested system?

Chapter
Eight

Internal
Control and
Merchandising
Transactions

One of the four principles of systems design identified in Chapter 7 was the concept of control. Effective control is maintained in an accounting system through a network of checks and procedures known as internal control. This chapter is an introduction to the concept of internal control and its application to certain merchandising transactions including banking transactions and voucher system transactions. As a result of studying this chapter, you should be able to meet the learning objectives listed on the left.

This chapter has five main parts. The first part presents the general principles and characteristics of internal control. In the second part, these principles are applied to certain merchandising transactions. The third and fourth parts explain the role of banking transactions and petty cash procedures in the control of cash. The fifth part describes the voucher system, a common means of controlling purchases and cash disbursements.

Internal Control: Basic Principles and Policies

Accounting for merchandising companies, as you have seen, focuses on buying and selling. These transactions involve asset accounts—cash, accounts receivable, and merchandise inventory—that are very vulnerable to theft and embezzlement. There are two reasons for this vulnerability. One is that cash and inventory are fairly easy to steal. The other is that these assets involve a large number of transactions—cash sales, receipts on account, payments for purchases, receipts and shipments of inventory, and so on. A merchandising company can have high losses of cash and inventory if it does not take steps to prevent them. The best way to do so is to set up and maintain a good system of internal control.

Internal Control Defined

Internal control is defined by the AICPA as

the plan of organization and all of the co-ordinate methods and measures adopted within a business to safeguard its assets, check the accuracy and reliability of its accounting data, promote operational efficiency, and encourage adherence to prescribed managerial policies.[1]

This is a broad definition. Clearly, a system of internal control goes beyond the matters directly related to the accounting function. In fact, there are two kinds of internal controls: internal accounting controls and internal administrative controls.

Objective 1
Define internal
accounting
control and
state its four
objectives

Internal accounting controls are used mainly to protect assets and make sure of the accuracy and reliability of the accounting records. They include systems of authorization and the separation of record-keeping duties from the duties of running a department or being the custodian of assets. They are aimed at helping to ensure that the following conditions are maintained:

a. Transactions are executed in accordance with management's general or specific authorization.
b. Transactions are recorded as necessary (1) to permit preparation of financial statements in conformity with generally accepted accounting principles . . . and (2) to maintain accountability for assets.
c. Access to assets is permitted only in accordance with management's authorization.
d. The recorded accountability for assets is compared with the existing assets at reasonable intervals and appropriate action is taken with respect to any differences.[2]

Internal administrative controls are controls that deal mainly with efficient operation and adherence to managerial policies. They are related to accounting controls in that they have to do with the decision processes leading to management's authorization of transactions. One form of internal administrative control is employee training programs that are intended to teach new employees the proper authorization methods for handling purchases, sales, and so forth. Sometimes administrative and accounting controls overlap. That is, sales and cost records broken down by departments may be used in making management decisions as well as for accounting control. In the study of internal control, any control—either administrative or accounting—that is connected with transactions involving assets or accounting records is important.

---

1. *Professional Standards* (New York: American Institute of Certified Public Accountants, June 1, 1982), Vol. I, Sec. AU 320.09.
2. Ibid., Sec. AU 320.28.

Attributes of Internal Control

Objective 2
State five attri-
butes of an
effective system
of internal
control

An effective system of internal control will have certain important attributes or qualities. These attributes are explained below.

Separation of Duties The plan of organization should describe proper separation of functional responsibilities. Authorizing transactions, running a department, handling assets, and keeping the records of assets for the department should not be the responsibility of one person. In other words, separation of duties should mean that a mistake, honest or not, cannot be made without being seen by at least one other person.

Sound Accounting System The systems of authorization and record keeping should offer good accounting control over assets, liabilities, revenues, and expenses. For records and procedures, there should be a system of routine and automatic checks and balances that should always be done exactly as prescribed. Independent checks should be made, and physical safeguards of assets should be used where possible.

Sound Personnel Policies Sound practices should be followed in managing the people who carry out the duties and functions of each department. Among these practices are good supervision, rotation of key people in different jobs, insistence that employees take earned vacations, and bonding of personnel who handle cash or inventories. Bonding means carefully checking on an employee's background and insuring the company against any theft by that person.

Reliable Personnel Personnel should be qualified to handle responsibilities, which means that employees must be well trained and well informed. It is clear that an accounting system, no matter how well designed, is only as good as the people who run it.

Regular Internal Review The system should come under regular review. Large companies often have a staff of internal auditors who regularly review their company's system of internal control to see that it is working properly and that its procedures are being followed.

Limitations of Internal Control

Objective 3
Describe the
inherent limita-
tions of internal
control

No system of internal control is without certain weaknesses. As long as people must carry out control procedures, the internal control system is open to human error. Errors may arise because of misunderstanding of instructions, mistakes of judgment, carelessness, distraction, or fatigue. The separation of duties can be defeated through collusion—that is, when employees secretly agree to deceive the company. Also, procedures designed by management may be ineffective against management errors or dishonesty. In addition, controls that may have been effective at first may become ineffective because of changes in conditions.[3]

3. Ibid., Sec. AU 320.34.

Internal Control over Merchandising Transactions

*Objective 4
Apply the
attributes of
internal control
to the control of
certain
merchandising
transactions*

Sound internal control procedures are needed in all aspects of a business, but particularly where assets are involved. Assets are especially vulnerable where they enter or leave the business. When sales are made, for example, cash or other assets enter the business, and goods or services leave the business. Procedures must be set up to prevent theft during these transactions. Likewise, purchases and payments of assets and liabilities must be controlled. The majority of these transactions can be safeguarded by adequate purchasing and payroll systems. In addition, assets on hand such as cash, investments, inventory, plant, and equipment must be protected.

In this and the following sections, internal control procedures will be applied to such merchandising transactions as sales, cash receipts, purchases, and cash payments. Internal control for other kinds of transactions will be covered at several points later in the book.

When a system of internal control is applied effectively to merchandising transactions, it can achieve some very important goals for both accounting and administrative controls. The accounting controls have two aims. They are

1. to prevent losses of cash or inventory from theft or fraud, and
2. to provide accurate records of merchandising transactions and account balances.

The administrative controls over merchandising transactions have three goals. They are

1. to keep just enough inventory on hand to sell to customers but not too much,
2. to keep enough cash on hand to pay for purchases in time to receive purchases discounts, and
3. to keep credit losses as low as possible by restricting credit sales to those customers who are likely to pay on time.

An example of an administrative control is the cash budget, which projects future cash receipts and disbursements. By maintaining adequate cash balances, the company is able to take advantage of discounts on purchases, prepare for borrowing money when necessary, and avoid the embarrassing and possibly damaging effects of not being able to pay bills when they are due. On the other hand, if the company has more cash at a particular time than it needs, this cash can be invested, earning interest, until it is needed.

An example of an accounting control is the separation of duties involving the control of cash. This separation means that theft without detection is impossible except through the collusion of two or more employees. The subdivision of duties is easier in large businesses than in small ones, where one person may have to carry out several duties. The effectiveness of internal control over cash will vary depending on the size and nature of the company. Most firms, however, should use the following procedures:

1. The functions of record keeping and the custodianship of cash should be kept separate.
2. The number of persons who have access to cash should be limited.
3. Persons who are to have responsibility for handling cash should be specifically designated.
4. Banking facilities should be used as much as possible, and the amount of cash on hand should be kept to a minimum.
5. All employees having access to cash should be bonded.
6. Cash on hand should be protected physically by the use of such devices as cash registers, cashiers' cages, and safes.
7. Surprise audits of cash on hand should be made by a person who does not handle or record cash.
8. All cash receipts should be recorded promptly.
9. All cash receipts should be deposited promptly.
10. All cash payments should be made by check.

Note that each of the above procedures helps to safeguard cash by making it more difficult for any one person to have access to cash and to steal or misuse it undetected. These procedures may be specifically related to the control of cash receipts and cash disbursements.

Control of Cash Sales Receipts

Cash receipts for sales of goods and services may be received by mail or over the counter in the form of checks or currency. Whatever the source, cash receipts should be recorded immediately upon receipt. This is generally done by making an entry in a cash receipts journal. As shown in the last chapter, this step establishes a written record of the receipt of cash and should prevent errors and make theft more difficult.

Control of Cash Receipts Received Through the Mail Cash that comes in through the mail should be handled by two or more employees. The employee who opens the mail should make a list in triplicate of the money received. This list should contain each sender's name, the purpose for which the money was sent, and the amount. One copy goes with the cash to the cashier, who deposits the money. The second copy goes to the accounting department to be recorded in the cash receipts journal. The person who opens the mail keeps the third copy of the list. Errors can be caught easily because the amount deposited by the cashier must agree with the amount received and the amount recorded in the cash receipts journal.

Control of Cash Sales Received over the Counter Two common means of controlling cash sales are through the use of cash registers and prenumbered sales tickets. Amounts from cash sales should be rung up on a cash register at the time of each sale. The cash register should be placed so that the customer can see the amount recorded. Each cash register should have a locked-in tape on which it prints the day's transactions. At the end of the day, the cashier counts the cash in the cash register and turns it in to the cashier's office. Another employee takes the tape out of the cash register and records the cash receipts for the day in the cash receipts journal. The amount of cash turned in and the amount recorded on the tape should be in agreement; if not, any differences should be accounted for. Large retail chains commonly perform this function by having each cash register tied directly into a computer. In this way each transaction is recorded as it occurs. The separation of duties involving cash receipts, cash deposits, and record keeping is thus achieved, ensuring good internal control.

In some stores, internal control is strengthened further by the use of prenumbered sales tickets and a central cash register or cashier's office, where all sales are rung up and collected by a person who does not participate in the sale. Under this procedure, the salesperson completes a prenumbered sales ticket at the time of sale, giving one copy to the customer and keeping a copy. At the end of the day, all sales tickets must be accounted for, and the sales total computed from the sales tickets should equal the total sales recorded on the cash register.

Cash Over and Short   When there are numerous transactions involving cash receipts, small mistakes are bound to occur. For example, cash registers in grocery and retail stores will often have a cash shortage or overage at the end of the day. When the shortages are consistent or large, they should, of course, be investigated. If at the end of a day a cash register shows recorded cash sales of $675 but contains only $670 in cash, the following entry would record the sales:

Cash	670	
Cash Over or Short	5	
Sales		675
To record cash sales; a cash shortage		
of $5 was found		

The Cash Over or Short account is debited with shortages and credited with overages. The use of a separate account to record cash over or short calls management's attention to irregular activity. If at the end of an accounting period a debit balance appears in Cash Over or Short, it would be reported as an expense on the income statement. A credit balance would be reported as a revenue.

Control of Purchases and Cash Disbursements

Cash disbursements are very vulnerable to fraud and embezzlement. In a recent and notable case, the treasurer of one of the nation's largest jewelry retailers was charged with having stolen over one-half million dollars by systematically overpaying federal income taxes and pocketing the refund checks as they came back to the company.

To avoid this kind of theft, cash should be paid only on the basis of specific authorization that is supported by documents establishing the validity and amount of the claim. In addition, maximum possible use should be made of the principle of separation of duties in the purchase of goods and services and the payments for them. Figure 8-1 shows how

Figure 8-1
Internal
Control for
Purchasing and
Paying for
Goods and
Services

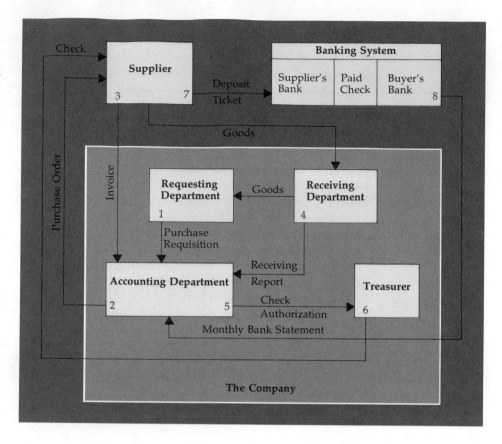

this kind of control can be achieved. In this example, four internal units (the requesting department, the accounting department, the receiving department, and the treasurer) and two external companies (the supplier and the bank) all play a role in the internal control plan. Note that business documents also play an important role in the plan. The plan is summarized in Table 8-1. Under this plan, every action is documented and subject to verification by at least one other person. For instance, the requesting department cannot work out a kickback scheme with the supplier because the receiving department independently records receipts and the accounting department verifies prices. The receiving department cannot steal goods because the receiving report must equal the invoices. For the same reason, the supplier cannot bill for more than shipped. The accounting department's work is verified by the treasurer, and the treasurer is ultimately checked by the accounting department.

Figures 8-2 through 8-6, which show typical documents used in this plan, serve as a concrete example involving the purchase of twenty boxes of typewriter ribbons. In Figure 8-2 (page 274) the credit office of Martin Maintenance fills out a **purchase requisition** for twenty boxes of typewriter ribbons. The department head approves it and forwards it to the accounting department. The people in the accounting department who carry out the purchasing activity prepare a **purchase order,** as illustrated in Figure 8-3 (page 274). The purchase order is addressed to the vendor (seller) and contains a description of the items ordered; their

Business Document	Prepared by	Sent to	Verifications and Related Procedures
Table 8-1 Internal Control Plan for Cash Disbursements			
1. Purchase requisition	Requesting department	Accounting department	Accounting verifies authorization.
2. Purchase order	Accounting department	Supplier	Supplier sends goods or services in accordance with purchase order.
3. Invoice	Supplier	Accounting department	Accounting receives invoice from supplier.
4. Receiving report	Receiving department	Accounting department	Accounting compares invoice, purchase order, and receiving report. Accounting verifies prices.
5. Check authorization (or voucher)	Accounting department	Treasurer	Accounting staples check authorization to top of invoice, purchase order, and receiving report.
6. Check	Treasurer	Supplier	Treasurer verifies all documents before preparing check.
7. Deposit ticket	Supplier	Supplier's bank	Supplier compares check with invoice. Bank deducts check from buyer's account.
8. Bank statement	Buyer's bank	Accounting department	Accounting compares amount and payee's name on returned check with check authorization.

expected price, terms, and shipping date; and other shipping instructions. Martin will not pay any bill that is not accompanied by a purchase order. Some larger companies have a separate department to perform the purchasing function.

After receiving the purchase order, the vendor, Henderson Supply Company, ships the goods (in this case delivers them) and sends an **invoice,** or bill (Figure 8-4 [page 275]) to Martin Maintenance. The invoice gives the quantity and a description of the goods delivered and the terms of payment. If all goods cannot be shipped immediately, the estimated date for shipment of the remainder is indicated.

When the goods reach the receiving department of Martin Maintenance Company, an employee of this department writes the description, quantity, and condition of the goods on the **receiving report.** The

Figure 8-2
Purchase
Requisition

PURCHASE REQUISITION

No. 7077

Martin Maintenance Company

From: Credit Office

To: Accounting Department

Please purchase the following items:

Date September 6, 19xx

Suggested Vendor: Henderson Supply Company

Quantity	Number	Description
20 boxes	X 144	Typewriter ribbons

Reason for Request	To be filled in by Accounting Department
Six months' supply for office	Date ordered 9/8/xx P.O. No. J 102
Approved BM	

Figure 8-3
Purchase Order

PURCHASE ORDER

No. J 102

Martin Maintenance Company
8428 Rocky Island Avenue
Chicago, Illinois 60643

To: Henderson Supply Company
2525 25th Street
Mesa, Illinois 61611

Ship to: Martin Maintenance Company
Above Address

Date September 8, 19xx

FOB Destination

Ship by September 12, 19xx

Terms 2/10, n/30

Please ship the following:

Quantity	✔	Number	Description	Price	Per	Amount
20 boxes		X 144	Typewriter ribbons	12.00	box	$240.00

Purchase order number must appear on all shipments and invoices.	Ordered by Marsha Owen

Figure 8-4
Invoice

INVOICE			No. 0468		

Henderson Supply Company
2525 25th Street
Mesa, Illinois 61611

Date September 12, 19xx

Your Order No. J 102

Ship to:

Same

Sold to:

Martin Maintenance Company
8428 Rocky Island Avenue
Chicago, Illinois 60643

Sales Representative: Joe Jacobs

Quantity		Description	Price	Per	Amount
Ordered	Shipped				
20	20	X 144 Typewriter Ribbons	12.00	box	$240.00

FOB Delivered	Terms: 2/10, n/30	Date Shipped: 9/12/xx	Via: Self

receiving department does not get the purchase order or invoice, so that the people in this department will not know what is to be received. In this way, because they do not know if they have received a larger quantity than ordered, they are not tempted to steal the excess.

The receiving report is sent to the accounting department, where it is compared with the purchase order and the invoice. If all is correct, the accounting department completes a **check authorization** and attaches it to the three supporting documents. The check authorization form shown in Figure 8-5 (below) has a space for each item to be checked off as it is

Figure 8-5
Check Authori-
zation

CHECK AUTHORIZATION

	NO.	CHECK
Requisition	7077	✓
Purchase Order	J 102	✓
Receiving Report	JR 065	✓
INVOICE	0468	
Price		✓
Calculations		✓
Terms		✓
Approved for Payment		

J. Joseph

Figure 8-6
Check with
Attached
Remittance
Advice

NO. 1787

9/21   19xx

PAY TO
THE ORDER OF Henderson Supply Company $ 235.20

Two hundred thirty-five and 20/100————————————————— Dollars

THE LAKE PARK NATIONAL BANK   Martin Maintenance Company
Chicago, Illinois

⑆031301532⑆ ⑈8030 647 4⑈   by *Arthur Martin*

Remittance Advice

Date	P.O. No.	DESCRIPTION	AMOUNT
9/21/xx	J 102	20 boxes typewriter ribbons Supplied Inv. No. 0468 Less 2% discount	$240.00 4.80
		Net	$235.20
		Martin Maintenance Company	

examined. Note that the accounting department has all the documentary evidence for the transaction but does not have access to the assets purchased. Nor does it write the checks for payment. For this reason, the people performing the accounting function cannot gain by falsifying the documents in an effort to conceal a fraud.

Finally, the treasurer again examines all the evidence and issues a **check** (Figure 8-6, above) for the amount of the invoice less the appropriate discount. In some systems, the accounting department fills out the check so that all the treasurer has to do is inspect and sign it. The check is then sent to the supplier, with remittance advice attached to the bottom. A supplier who is not paid the proper amount will complain, of course, thus providing a form of outside control over the payment. The supplier will deposit the check in the bank, which will return the canceled check with Martin's next monthly bank statement. If the treasurer has made the check for an incorrect amount (or altered a prefilled-in check), it will show up at this point.

There are many variations of the system just described. This example is offered as a simple system that provides adequate internal control.

Banking Transactions

Banking facilities are also an important aid to merchandising businesses (and other types of business) in controlling both cash receipts and cash disbursements. Banks are safe depositories of cash, negotiable instruments, and other valuable business documents such as stocks and bonds. The use of checks for disbursements improves control by minimizing the amount of currency on hand and by providing a permanent record of all cash payments. Furthermore, banks can serve as agents for a company in a variety of important transactions such as the collection and payment of certain kinds of debts and the exchange of foreign currencies.

Bank Account

*Objective 5
Describe a bank
account and
prepare a bank
reconciliation*

The procedure for establishing a bank account varies. In some small towns where the bank personnel are familiar with townspeople's activities, it may be very easy to open an account. In other cases, particularly in large metropolitan areas, the bank may require a financial statement and references.

The evidence used for the bank account is a **signature card.** When a person opens an account, this card must be signed by the depositor in exactly the same way that he or she expects to sign the checks. This signature card is required so that a bank teller can authenticate the depositor's signature on a check. When a corporation opens an account, the board of directors must sign an authorization giving a particular official or officials the right to sign checks. The bank receives a copy of the authorization.

Deposits

When making a deposit, the depositor fills out a **deposit ticket** (usually in duplicate), as illustrated in Figure 8-7 (next page). Space is provided for listing each check and the amounts of coin and currency deposited.

Bank Statement

Once a month the bank will send a statement to the depositor and return the canceled checks that it has paid and charged to the depositor's account. The returned checks are called "canceled" because the bank stamps, or cancels, them to show that they have been paid. The **bank statement** shows the balance at the beginning of the month, the deposits, the checks paid, other debits and credits during the month, and the balance at the end of the month. A bank statement is illustrated in Figure 8-8 (page 279).

Preparing a Bank Reconciliation

Rarely will the balance of a company's Cash account exactly equal the cash balance as shown on the bank statement when it is received. Certain transactions shown in the company's records may not be recorded by the bank, and certain bank transactions may not appear in the company's records. Therefore, a necessary step in internal control is to prove both the balance of the bank and the balance of cash in the accounting records. The term **bank reconciliation** means accounting for the differences between the balance appearing on the bank statement and the balance of cash according to the depositor's records. This process involves adjusting both balances to the adjusted cash balance.

Figure 8-7
Deposit Ticket

DEPOSIT TICKET

THE LAKE PARK NATIONAL BANK
Chicago, Illinois

Date ___10/6/xx___

Name ___Martin Maintenance Company___

Address ___8428 Rocky Island Avenue___

___Chicago, Illinois___

CASH	CURRENCY	22	00
	COIN	2	50
	CHECKS—LIST SINGLY G. Mason	30	00
	R Enterprises	39	00
	Preston Company	206	50
TOTAL		300	00
Less Cash Received		—	—
NET DEPOSIT		300	00

⑆031301532⑆ ⑈8030 647 4⑈

The most common examples of transactions shown in the company's records but not entered in the bank's records are the following:

1. **Outstanding checks**   These are checks issued and recorded by the company, but not yet presented to the bank for payment.

2. **Deposits in transit**   These are deposits mailed or taken to the bank but not received by the bank in time to be recorded before preparation of the monthly statement.

Transactions that may appear on the bank statement but have not yet been recorded by the company include the following:

1. **Service charge (SC)**   Banks cannot profitably handle small accounts without making a service charge. Many banks base the service charge on a number of factors, such as the average balance of the account during the month or the number of checks drawn.

2. **NSF (non-sufficient funds) checks**   An NSF check is a check deposited by the company that is not paid when the company's bank presents it for payment to the maker's bank. The bank charges the company's account and returns the check so that the company can try to collect the amount due. If the bank has deducted the NSF check from the

Figure 8-8
Bank Statement

Statement of Account with
THE LAKE PARK NATIONAL BANK
Chicago, Illinois

Martin Maintenance Company
8428 Rocky Island Avenue
Chicago, Illinois 60643

Checking Acct No
66–66183
Period covered
Sept. 30–Oct. 31, 19xx

Previous Balance	Checks/Debits—No.	Deposits/Credits—No.	S.C.	Current Balance
$2,645.78	$4,319.33 --15	$5,131.50 --6	$12.50	$3,471.07

CHECKS		DEPOSITS	DATE	BALANCES
			09–30–xx	2,645.78
100.00	250.00	586.00	10–01–xx	2,881.78
56.18			10–04–xx	2,825.60
425.14		1500.00	10–05–xx	3,900.46
17.12		300.00	10–06–xx	4,183.34
1,705.80	235.20		10–12–xx	2,242.34
400.00		1845.50	10–16–xx	3,687.84
29.75	69.00		10–17–xx	3,589.09
		600.00	10–21–xx	4,189.09
738.50	5.00 DM	300.00 CM	10–24–xx	3,745.59
7.50	152.00		10–25–xx	3,586.09
128.14 NSF			10–28–xx	3,457.95
12.50 SC		25.62 IN	10–31–xx	3,471.07

Explanation of Symbols:

CM —Credit Memo
DM—Debit Memo
NSF—Not Sufficient Funds
SC —Service Charge
EC —Error Correction
OD —Overdraft
IN —Interest on Average Balance

The last amount
in this column
is your balance.

Please examine; if no errors are reported within ten (10) days, the account will be considered to
be correct.

bank statement but the company has not deducted it from its book balance, an adjustment must be made in the bank reconciliation. The depositor usually reclassifies the NSF check from Cash to Accounts Receivable because the company must now collect from the person or company that wrote the check.

3. **Interest earned** It is very common for banks to pay interest on a company's average balance. These accounts are sometimes called N.O.W. accounts but can take other forms. Interest earned in this way is reported by the bank on the bank statement.

4. **Miscellaneous charges and credits** Banks also charge for other services such as collection and payment of promissory notes, stopping payment on checks, and printing checks. The bank notifies the depositor

of each deduction by including a debit memorandum with the monthly statement. A bank will sometimes serve as an agent in collecting on promissory notes for the depositor. In such a case, a credit memorandum will be included.

An error by either the bank or the depositor will, of course, require correction.

Steps in Reconciling the Bank Balance   The steps to be followed in achieving a bank reconciliation are as follows:

1. Compare the deposits listed on the bank statement with deposits shown in the accounting records. Any deposits in transit should be added to the bank balance. (Any deposits in transit from last month still not listed on the bank statement should be immediately investigated.)

2. Trace returned checks to the bank statement, making sure that all checks are issued by the company, properly charged to the company's account, and properly signed.

3. Arrange the canceled checks returned with the bank statement in numerical order, and compare them with the record of checks issued. List checks issued but not on the bank statement. (Be sure to include any checks still outstanding from last month.) Deduct outstanding checks from the bank balance.

4. Prepare a bank reconciliation similar to the one shown on page 281.

5. Deduct from the balance per books any debit memoranda issued by the bank such as NSF checks and service charges that are not yet recorded on the company's records.

6. Add to the balance per books any interest earned or credit memoranda issued by the bank such as collection of a promissory note that is not yet recorded on the company's books.

7. Make journal entries for any items on the bank statement that have not been recorded in the company's books.

Illustration of a Bank Reconciliation   The October bank statement for Martin Maintenance Company, as shown in Figure 8-8, indicates a balance on October 31 of $3,471.07. We shall assume that Martin Maintenance Company has a cash balance in its records on October 31 of $2,405.91. The purpose of a bank reconciliation is to identify the items that make up this difference and to determine the correct cash balance.

The bank reconciliation for Martin Maintenance is given in Figure 8-9. The numbered items there refer to the following:

1. A deposit in the amount of $276.00 was mailed to the bank on October 31 and was unrecorded by the bank.

2. Five checks issued in October or prior months have not yet been paid by the bank, as follows:

Figure 8-9
Bank Reconcili-
ation

Martin Maintenance Company
Bank Reconciliation
October 31, 19xx

Balance per books, October 31		$2,405.91
Add:		
④ Notes receivable collected by bank, including $20.00 of interest earned	$300.00	
⑦ Interest earned	25.62	325.62
		$2,731.53
Less:		
③ Overstatement of deposit of October 6	$ 30.00	
④ Collection fee	5.00	
⑤ NSF check of Arthur Clubb	128.14	
⑥ Service charge	12.50	175.64
Adjusted cash balance, October 31		$2,555.89
Balance per bank, October 31		$3,471.07
① Add deposit of October 31 in transit		276.00
		$3,747.07
② Less outstanding checks:		
No. 451	$150.00	
No. 576	40.68	
No. 578	500.00	
No. 579	370.00	
No. 580	130.50	1,191.18
Adjusted cash balance, October 31		$2,555.89

Note: The circled numbers refer to the items listed in the text.

Check No.	Date	Amount
451	Sept. 14	$150.00
576	Oct. 30	40.68
578	Oct. 31	500.00
579	Oct. 31	370.00
580	Oct. 31	130.50

3. The deposit for cash sales of October 6 was incorrectly recorded in Martin's records as $330.00. The bank recorded the deposit on Martin's bank statement correctly as $300.00.

4. Among the returned checks was a credit memorandum showing that the bank had collected a promissory note from A. Jacobs in the amount of $280.00 plus $20.00 in interest on the note. A debit memorandum was also enclosed for the $5.00 collection fee. No entry had been made on Martin's records.

5. Also returned with the bank statement was an NSF check for $128.14. This check had been received from a customer named Arthur Clubb. The NSF check was not reflected in Martin's accounting records.

6. A debit memorandum was enclosed for the regular monthly service charge of $12.50. This charge was not yet recorded by Martin Maintenance Company.

7. Interest earned by the company on the average balance was reported as $25.62.

Note in Figure 8-9 that, starting from their separate balances, the book and bank amounts are adjusted to the amount of $2,555.89. This adjusted balance is the amount of cash owned by the company on October 31 and thus is the amount that should appear on its October 31 balance sheet.

Adjusting the Records After Reconciliation The adjusted balance of cash differs from both the bank statement and the Martin Maintenance Company's records. The bank balance will automatically become correct when outstanding checks are presented for payment and when the deposit in transit is received and recorded by the bank. Entries are necessary, however, to adjust the company's records to the correct balance. All the items reported by the bank but not yet recorded by the company must be entered into the records by means of the following adjustments:

Oct. 31	Cash	300.00	
	Notes Receivable		280.00
	Interest Income		20.00
	Note receivable of $280.00 and interest of $20.00 collected by bank from A. Jacobs		
31	Cash	25.62	
	Interest Income		25.62
	Interest earned on average bank account balance		
31	Sales	30.00	
	Cash		30.00
	Correction of error in recording a $300.00 deposit as $330.00		
31	Accounts Receivable, Arthur Clubb	128.14	
	Cash		128.14
	NSF check of Arthur Clubb returned by bank		
31	Bank Service Charges Expense	17.50	
	Cash		17.50
	Bank service charge ($12.50) and collection fee ($5.00) for October		

Petty Cash Procedures

*Objective 6
Describe and
record the
related entries
for a simple
petty cash
system*

Under some circumstances, it is not practical to make all disbursements by check. In most businesses, for example, it is sometimes necessary to make small payments of cash for such things as a few postage stamps, incoming postage or shipping charges due, or minor purchases of supplies.

For situations when it is inconvenient to pay with a check, most companies set up a **petty cash fund**. One of the best methods to use is the **imprest system**. Under this system, a petty cash fund is established for a fixed amount and is periodically reimbursed for the exact amount necessary to bring it back to the fixed amount.

Establishing the Petty Cash Fund

Some companies have a regular cashier, secretary, or receptionist to administer the petty cash fund. To establish the petty cash fund, the company issues a check for an amount that is intended to cover two to four weeks of small expenditures. The check is cashed, and the money is placed in the petty cash box, drawer, or envelope.

The only entry required when the fund is established is one to record the issuance of the check, as follows:

Oct. 14	Petty Cash	100.00	
	Cash		100.00
	To establish petty cash fund		

Making Disbursements from the Petty Cash Fund

The custodian of the petty cash fund should prepare a **petty cash voucher** for each expenditure, as illustrated in Figure 8-10. On each petty cash voucher the custodian enters the date, amount, and purpose of the expenditure. The voucher is signed by the person receiving the payment.

The custodian should be informed that surprise audits of the fund will be made occasionally. The cash in the fund plus the sum of the petty cash vouchers should equal the fixed amount of the fund at all times.

**Figure 8-10
Petty Cash
Voucher**

PETTY CASH VOUCHER

No. X 744
Date Oct. 23, 19xx

For Postage due
Charge to Postage Expense
Amount $2.86

W.S.   *Tom Z.*
Approved by   Received by

Reimbursing the Petty Cash Fund

After a specified time or when the petty cash fund becomes low, it is replenished by a check issued to Petty Cash or to the custodian for the exact amount of the expenditures. From time to time there may be minor discrepancies in the amount of cash left in the fund at the time of reimbursement. In these cases, the amount of the discrepancy should be recorded in Cash Over or Short as a debit if short or as a credit if over.

Assume that after two weeks the petty cash fund established as described above had a cash balance of $14.27 and petty cash vouchers as follows: postage, $25.00; supplies, $30.55; freight in, $30.00. The entry to replenish, or replace, the fund is as follows:

Oct. 28	Postage Expense	25.00	
	Supplies	30.55	
	Freight In	30.00	
	Cash Over or Short	.18	
	Cash		85.73
	To replenish petty cash fund		

Note that the Petty Cash account is debited only when the fund is first established. Expense accounts will be debited each time the fund is replenished. In most cases, no further entries to the Petty Cash account are needed unless there is a desire to increase or decrease the original fixed amount of the fund.

The petty cash fund should be replenished at the end of an accounting period to bring it up to its fixed amount and to make sure that the expenses involved will be recorded in the current period's financial statements. If through an oversight the petty cash fund is not replenished at the end of the year, the expenditures must still appear on the income statement. They are shown through an entry debiting the expense accounts and crediting Petty Cash. The result is an unintentional reduction in the petty cash fund.

The Voucher System

Objective 7
Describe the components of a voucher system

A **voucher system** is any system giving documentary proof of and written authorization for business transactions. Here, a voucher system for a company's expenditures is presented. It consists of records and procedures for systematically gathering, recording, and paying a company's expenditures. It is much like the control of cash because its goal is to keep the tightest possible control over expenditures. Under this system there is strong internal control because duties and responsibilities in the following functions are separated:

1. Authorization of expenditures
2. Receipt of goods and services
3. Validation of liability by examination of invoices from suppliers for correctness of prices, extensions, shipping costs, and credit terms

4. Payment of expenditure by check, taking discounts when possible

Under the voucher system, every liability must be recorded as soon as it is incurred. A written authorization, called a **voucher,** is prepared for each expenditure, and checks are written only when an approved voucher is shown. No one person has authority both to incur expenses and to issue checks. In large companies, the duties of authorizing expenditures, verifying receipt of goods and services, checking invoices, recording liabilities, and issuing checks are divided among different people. So for both accounting and administrative control, every expenditure must be carefully and routinely reviewed and verified before payment. For each transaction, the written approval of key people leaves a trail of documentary evidence, or an **audit trail.**

Though there is more than one way to set up a voucher system, most systems would use (1) vouchers, (2) voucher checks, (3) a voucher register, and (4) a check register.

Vouchers

A voucher is a written authorization for each expenditure, and serves as the basis of an accounting entry. A separate voucher is attached to each bill as it comes in, and it is given a number. Vouchers are prenumbered in order. In the illustration of a cash disbursement system earlier in this chapter, the voucher would take the place of the check authorization form. On the face of a typical voucher (see Figure 8-11, next page), there is important information about the expenditure. The voucher must be signed by authorized individuals before payment is made. On the reverse side of the voucher is information about the accounts and amounts to be debited and credited. The voucher shown identifies the transaction by voucher number and check number and is recorded in the voucher register and check register, as described below.

Voucher Checks

Although regular checks can be used effectively with a voucher system, many businesses use a form of **voucher check** that tells the payee the reason for issuing the check. This information may be written either on the check itself or on a detachable stub.

Voucher Register

The **voucher register** is the book of original entry in which vouchers are recorded after they have been properly approved. The voucher register takes the place of the purchases journal shown in the preceding chapter. However, a major difference between the two journals is that all expenditures—that is, expenses, payroll, plant, and equipment, as well as purchases of merchandise—are recorded in the voucher register. Remember that only purchases of merchandise were recorded in the single-column purchases journal.

A voucher register appears in Figure 8-12. Note that in a voucher

Figure 8-11
Front and Back
of a Typical
Voucher Form

Thomas Appliance Company

Payee   Belmont Products   Voucher No.   704

Address   Gary, Indiana   Date Due   7/13

Date Paid   7/13

Terms   2/10, n/30   Check No.   205

Date	Invoice No.	Description	Amount
7/12	XL1066	10 cases Model 70X14	1,200 —

Approved   *M. N.*   Approved   *a. Thomas*

Controller   Treasurer

Figure 8-12
Voucher
Register

VOUCHER REGISTER

Date		Voucher No.	Payee	Payment Date	Check No.	Credit Vouchers Payable	Purchases	Freight In	Store Supplies
July	1	701	Common Utility	7/6	203	75			
	2	702	Ade Realty	7/2	201	400			
	2	703	Buy Rite Supplies	7/6	202	25			
	3	704	Belmont Products	7/13	205	1,200	1,200		
	6	705	M & M Freight			60		60	
	7	706	Petty Cash	7/7	204	50			
	8	707	Belmont Products	7/18	208	600	600		
	11	708	M & M Freight			30		30	
	11	709	Mack Truck			5,600			
	12	710	Livingstone Wholesale	7/22	209	785	750	35	
	14	711	Payroll	7/14	206	2,200			
	17	712	First National Bank	7/17	207	4,250			
	20	713	Livingstone Wholesale			525	500	25	
	21	714	Belmont Products			400	400		
	24	715	M & M Freight			18		18	
	30	716	Payroll	7/30	210	2,200			
	31	717	Petty Cash	7/31	211	47		17	
	31	718	Maintenance Company			175			
	31	719	Store Supply Company			350			350
						18,990	3,450	185	350
						(211)	(511)	(512)	(116)

Figure 8-11
(continued)

BACK OF VOUCHER

Account Debited	Acct. No.	Amount		
			Voucher No. 704	
			Payee Belmont Products	
Purchases	511	1,200.00	Address Gary, Indiana	
Freight In	512			
Rent Expense	631			
Salary Expense	611		Invoice Amount	1200.00
Utility Expense	635		Less Discount	24.00
			Net	1176.00
			Date Due	7/13
			Date Paid	7/13
Total		$1,200.00	Check No.	205

Figure 8-12
(continued)

Page 1

						Debits		
Office Supplies	Sales Salaries	Office Salaries	Maintenance, Selling	Maintenance, Office	Utilities	Other Accounts		
						Name	No.	Amount
25					75	Rent Expense	631	400
						Petty Cash	121	50
						Trucks	148	5,600
	1,400	800				Notes Payable	212	4,000
						Interest Exp.	645	250
20	1,400	800				Misc. Exp.	649	10
			100	75				
45	2,800	1,600	100	75	75			10,310
(117)	(611)	(612)	(621)	(622)	(635)			(✔)

system, instead of the Accounts Payable account column there is a new account column called Vouchers Payable. As you can see, the first entry in the voucher register records the receipt of a utility bill. It is recorded as a debit to utility expense and a credit to Vouchers Payable (not Accounts Payable). Note that the utility bill was later paid by check number 203 on July 6.

Check Register

In a voucher system, the **check register** replaces the cash payments journal in the sense that it is the journal in which the checks are listed as they are written, as shown in Figure 8-13. Study carefully the connection between the voucher register and the check register. The incurring of a liability is recorded in the voucher register; its payment is recorded in the check register.

Operation of a Voucher System

*Objective 8
State and
perform the five
steps in
operating a
voucher system*

There are five steps in the operation of a voucher system, as follows:

1. Preparing the voucher
2. Recording the voucher
3. Paying the voucher
4. Posting the voucher and check registers
5. Summarizing unpaid vouchers

Figure 8-13
Check Register

				Debit	Credits	
Check No.	Date		Payee	Voucher No.	Vouchers Payable	Purchases Discounts	Cash

Check No.	Date		Payee	Voucher No.	Vouchers Payable	Purchases Discounts	Cash
201	July	2	Ade Realty	702	400		400
202		6	Buy Rite Supplies	703	25		25
203		6	Common Utility	701	75		75
204		7	Petty Cash	706	50		50
205		13	Belmont Products	704	1,200	24	1,176
206		14	Payroll	711	2,200		2,200
207		17	First National Bank	712	4,250		4,250
208		18	Belmont Products	707	600	12	588
209		22	Livingstone Wholesale	710	785	15	770
210		30	Payroll	716	2,200		2,200
211		31	Petty Cash	717	47		47
					11,832	51	11,781
					(211)	(513)	(111)

CHECK REGISTER

1. *Preparing the Voucher* A voucher is prepared for each expenditure. All evidence such as purchase orders, invoices, receiving reports, and/or authorization statements should be attached to the voucher when it is submitted for approval.

Many companies pay their employees out of a separate bank account or Payroll account. In this case, a voucher is prepared to cover the total payroll. The check for this voucher is then deposited in the special Payroll account, and individual payroll checks are drawn on that bank account.

2. *Recording the Voucher* All approved vouchers should be recorded in the voucher register, as shown in Figure 8-12. Vouchers that do not have appropriate approvals or support documents should be investigated immediately.

3. *Paying the Voucher* After a voucher has been recorded, it is placed in an unpaid voucher file. Many companies file the vouchers by due date so that checks can be drawn each day to cover all vouchers due on that day. In this way, all discounts for prompt payment can be taken without risk of missing the discount date.

On the date the voucher is due, a check for the correct amount, accompanied by the voucher and supporting documents, is presented to the individual authorized to sign checks. The check is then entered in the check register, as shown in Figure 8-13. The date of payment and the check number are then entered in the voucher register on the same line as the corresponding voucher. This procedure aids in the preparation of a schedule of unpaid vouchers, as explained below.

A problem arises in paying a voucher when there has been a purchase return or allowance that applies to the voucher. For example, suppose a part of a shipment of merchandise is defective and is returned to the supplier for credit. At the time the merchandise is returned or the allowance is given, an entry should be made in the general journal debiting Vouchers Payable and crediting Purchases Returns and Allowances, and a notation should be made on the voucher in the voucher file. At the time of payment, only the net amount of the voucher (original amount less return or allowance and any applicable discount) should be paid and recorded in the check register. Rather than noting the change on the voucher, some companies follow the practice of cancelling the original voucher and preparing a new one for the amount to be paid.

4. *Posting the Voucher and Check Registers* Posting of the voucher and check registers is very similar to the posting of the purchases journal and of the cash payments journal, as illustrated in Chapter 7. The only exception is that the Vouchers Payable account is substituted for the Accounts Payable account.

5. *Summarizing Unpaid Vouchers* At any particular time, the sum of the vouchers in the unpaid vouchers file equals the credit balance of the Vouchers Payable account. So an accounts payable subsidiary ledger like that described in Chapter 7 is unnecessary. At the end of each accounting

Figure 8-14
Schedule of
Unpaid
Vouchers

Thomas Appliance Company
Schedule of Unpaid Vouchers
July 31, 19xx

Payee	Voucher Number	Amount
M & M Freight	705	$ 60
M & M Freight	708	30
Mack Truck	709	5,600
Livingstone Wholesale	713	525
Belmont Products	714	400
M & M Freight	715	18
Maintenance Company	718	175
Store Supply Company	719	350
Total Unpaid Vouchers		$7,158

period, the unpaid voucher file should be totaled to prove the balance of the Vouchers Payable account. Figure 8-14 (above), a schedule of unpaid vouchers, is prepared by listing all unpaid vouchers shown in Figure 8-12. A reconciliation of the voucher register (Figure 8-12) and check register (Figure 8-13) can be accomplished by simple subtraction:

Vouchers Payable credit from voucher register	$18,990
Vouchers Payable debit from check register	11,832
Vouchers payable credit balance from schedule of unpaid vouchers	$ 7,158

Sometimes the account title Vouchers Payable appears on the liability side of the balance sheet. However, it is preferred practice to use the more widely known term Accounts Payable, even when a voucher system is in use.

Chapter Review

Review of Learning Objectives

1. Define internal accounting control and state its four objectives.

Internal accounting controls are the methods and procedures employed primarily to protect assets and ensure the accuracy and reliability of the accounting records. The objectives of internal accounting control are to provide reasonable assurance that (1) transactions are executed in accordance with management's general or specific authorization, (2) transactions are recorded to permit preparation of the financial statements in accordance with generally accepted accounting principles and to maintain accountability for assets, (3) access to assets is permitted only in accordance with management's authorization, and (4) recorded accountability is compared with existing assets at reasonable intervals.

2. State five attributes of an effective system of internal control.

Five attributes of an effective system of internal control are (1) separation of duties, (2) a sound accounting system, (3) sound personnel policies, (4) reliable personnel, and (5) regular internal review.

3. Describe the inherent limitations of internal control.

To be effective, a system of internal control must rely on the people who perform the duties assigned. Thus, the effectiveness of internal control is limited by the people involved. Human errors, collusion, management interference, and failure to recognize changed conditions can all contribute to a system failure.

4. Apply the attributes of internal control to the control of certain merchandising transactions.

Internal control over sales, cash receipts, purchases, and cash disbursements is strengthened if the five attributes of effective internal control are applied. First, the functions of authorization, record keeping, and custody should be kept separate. Second, the accounting system should provide for physical protection of assets (especially cash and merchandise inventory), prompt recording and depositing of cash receipts, and payment by check only on the basis of documentary support. Third, persons who have access to cash and merchandise inventory should be specifically designated and their number limited. Fourth, personnel should be trained and bonded. Fifth, the Cash account should be reconciled monthly, and surprise audits of cash on hand should be made by an individual who does not handle or record cash.

5. Describe a bank account and prepare a bank reconciliation.

The term *bank reconciliation* means accounting for the differences between the balance appearing on the bank statement and the balance of cash according to the depositor's records. It involves adjusting both balances to arrive at the adjusted cash balance. The bank balance is adjusted for outstanding checks and deposits in transit. The depositor's book balance is adjusted for service charges, NSF checks, interest earned, and miscellaneous charges and credits.

6. Describe and record the related entries for a simple petty cash system.

A petty cash system is established by a debit to Petty Cash and a credit to Cash. It is replenished by debits to various expense accounts and a credit to Cash. Each expenditure should be supported by a petty cash voucher.

7. Describe the components of a voucher system.

A voucher system consists of written authorizations called vouchers; voucher checks; a special journal to record the vouchers, called the voucher register; and a special journal to record the voucher checks, called the check register.

8. State and perform the five steps in operating a voucher system.

The five steps in operating a voucher system are (1) preparing the voucher, (2) recording the voucher, (3) paying the voucher, (4) posting the voucher and check registers, and (5) summarizing unpaid vouchers.

Review Problem
Entries for a Voucher System and a Petty Cash Fund

Peterson Company uses a voucher system and maintains a petty cash fund. Some related transactions follow:

a. Voucher no. 1500 prepared to purchase merchandise from Robertson Company, $280.

b. Check no. 801 issued in payment of voucher no. 1500.
c. Voucher no. 1501 prepared to establish petty cash fund of $50.
d. Check no. 802 issued in payment of voucher no. 1501.
e. Voucher no. 1502 prepared to replenish the petty cash fund, which contains $5 in cash and the following receipts: supplies, $31; postage, $13.
f. Check no. 803 issued in payment of voucher no. 1502.

Required

Record each of the transactions above in general journal form, and indicate to the left of each transaction in which journal of original entry it would be recorded.

Answer to Review Problem

Voucher register	a. Purchases	280	
	Vouchers Payable		280
	Purchased merchandise, voucher no. 1500		
Check register	b. Vouchers Payable	280	
	Cash		280
	Paid voucher no. 1500 with check no. 801		
Voucher register	c. Petty Cash	50	
	Vouchers Payable		50
	Established petty cash fund, voucher no. 1501		
Check register	d. Vouchers Payable	50	
	Cash		50
	Paid voucher no. 1501 with check no. 802		
Voucher register	e. Supplies	31	
	Postage Expense	13	
	Cash Over or Short	1	
	Vouchers Payable		45
	Record petty cash expenditures and replenish fund, voucher no. 1502		
Check register	f. Vouchers Payable	45	
	Cash		45
	Issued check no. 803 to replenish petty cash fund, voucher no. 1502		

Chapter Assignments

Questions

1. Most people think of internal control as making fraud harder to commit and easier to detect. What are some other important purposes of internal control?
2. What are the attributes of an effective system of internal control?
3. Why is a separation of duties necessary to ensure sound internal control?

4. Should the bookkeeper have responsibility for determining the accounts receivable to be written off? Explain.

5. At Thrifty Variety Store, each sales clerk counts the cash in his or her cash drawer at the end of the day and then removes the cash register tape and prepares the daily cash form, noting any discrepancies. This information is checked by an employee of the cashier's office, who counts the cash, compares the total with the form, and takes the cash to the cashier's office. What is the weakness in this system of internal control?

6. How does a movie theater control cash receipts?

7. What is the difference between internal accounting controls and internal administrative controls?

8. What does a credit balance in the Cash Over or Short account indicate?

9. One of the basic principles of internal control is separation of duties. What does this principle assume about the relationships of employees in a company and the possibility of two or more of them stealing from the company?

10. Why is a bank reconciliation prepared?

11. Assume that each of the numbered items below appeared on a bank reconciliation. Which item would be (a) an addition to the balance on the bank statement? (b) a deduction from the balance on the bank statement? (c) an addition to the balance on the books? (d) a deduction from the balance on the books? Write the correct letter after each numbered item.

(1) Outstanding checks
(2) Deposits in transit
(3) Bank service charge
(4) NSF check returned with statement
(5) Note collected by bank

Which of the above items require an adjusting entry?

12. In a small business, it is sometimes impossible to obtain complete separation of duties. What are three other practices that a small business can follow to achieve the objectives of internal control over cash?

13. Explain how each of the following can contribute to internal control over cash: (a) a bank reconciliation, (b) a petty cash fund, (c) a cash register with printed receipts, (d) printed, prenumbered cash sales receipts, (e) a regular vacation for the cashier, (f) two signatures on checks, and (g) prenumbered checks.

14. At the end of the day, the combined count of cash for all cash registers in a store reveals a cash shortage of $17.20. In what account would this cash shortage be recorded? Would the account be debited or credited?

15. What is the purpose of a petty cash fund, and what is the significance of the total of the fund (the level at which the fund is established)?

16. What account or accounts are debited when a petty cash fund is established? What account or accounts are debited when a petty cash fund is replenished?

17. Should a petty cash fund be replenished as of the last day of the accounting period? Explain.

18. What is the greatest advantage of the voucher system?

19. Before a voucher for the purchase of merchandise is approved for payment, three documents should be compared to verify the amount of the liability. What are the three documents?

20. When the voucher system is used, is there an Accounts Payable controlling account and a subsidiary accounts payable ledger?

21. A company that presently uses a general journal, a sales journal, a cash receipts journal, a cash payments journal, and a purchases journal decides to adopt the voucher system. Which of the five journals would be changed or replaced? What would replace them?

22. What is the correct order for filing (a) unpaid vouchers? (b) paid vouchers?

Classroom Exercises

Exercise 8-1
Petty Cash
Entries
(L.O. 6)

The petty cash fund of Fleming Company appeared as follows on December 31, 19xx:

Cash on Hand		$ 76.97
Petty Cash vouchers		
Freight In	$ 8.47	
Postage	20.84	
Flowers for a sick employee	17.50	
Office Supplies	26.22	73.03
Total		$150.00

1. Because there is cash on hand, is there a need to replenish the petty cash fund on December 31? Explain.
2. Prepare in general journal form an entry to replenish the fund.

Exercise 8-2
Bank
Reconciliation
(L.O. 5)

Prepare a bank reconciliation from the following information: (a) balance per bank statement as of May 31, $2,944.65; (b) balance per books as of May 31, $1,786.40; (c) deposits in transit, $567.21; (d) outstanding checks, $1,727.96; (e) bank service charge, $2.50.

Exercise 8-3
Bank Reconcili-
ation—Missing
Data
(L.O. 5)

Compute the correct amounts to replace each letter in the following table:

Balance per bank statement	a	$8,200	$175	$1,200
Deposits in transit	$ 600	b	50	125
Outstanding checks	1,500	1,000	c	75
Balance per books	2,600	9,400	225	d

Exercise 8-4
Collection of
Note by Bank
(L.O. 5)

Beam Corporation received a notice with its bank statement that the bank had collected a note for $1,500.00 plus $7.50 interest from J. Booker and credited Beam Corporation's account for the total less a collection charge of $3.50.

1. Explain the effect that these items have on the bank reconciliation.
2. Prepare a general journal entry to record the information on the books of Beam Corporation.

Exercise 8-5
Voucher System
Entries
(L.O. 8)

Cobb Company uses a voucher system. The following transactions occurred recently: (a) voucher no. 700 prepared to purchase merchandise from Pink Corp., $600; (b) check no. 401 issued in payment of voucher no. 700; (c) voucher no. 701 prepared to establish petty cash fund of $100; (d) check no. 402 issued in payment of voucher no. 701; (e) voucher no. 702 prepared to replenish the petty cash fund, which contains cash of $30 and the following receipts: supplies, $27; postage, $36; and miscellaneous expense, $7; (f) check no. 403 issued in payment of voucher no. 702.

Record the transactions in general journal form. Indicate beside each transaction in which journal of original entry it would be recorded.

Exercise 8-6
Voucher System
Entries
(L.O. 8)

McCann Company uses a voucher system. Some related transactions are as follows:

Aug. 1 Voucher no. 352 prepared to purchase office equipment from Drexler Equipment Company, $640, terms n/30.
4 Voucher no. 353 prepared to purchase merchandise from Sutton Corporation, $1,200, terms 2/10, n/30, FOB shipping point.
5 Voucher no. 354 prepared to pay freight charge to Red Line Freight for August 4 shipment, $175, terms n/10.

Aug. 14 Issued check no. 846 to pay voucher no. 353.
    15 Issued check no. 847 to pay voucher no. 354.
    30 Issued check no. 848 to pay voucher no. 352.

Record each of the transactions in journal form. Beside each transaction indicate the journal of original entry in which the transaction would be recorded.

Exercise 8-7
Internal
Control
Evaluation
(L.O. 4)

Developing a convenient means of providing sales representatives with cash for their incidental expenses, such as entertaining a client at lunch, is a problem many companies face. One company has a plan whereby the sales representatives receive advances in cash from the petty cash fund. Each advance is supported by an authorization from the sales manager. The representative returns the receipt for the expenditure and any unused cash, which is replaced in the petty cash fund. The cashier of the petty cash fund is responsible for seeing that the receipt and the cash returned equal the advance. At the time that the petty cash fund is reimbursed, the amount of the representative's expenditure is debited to Direct Sales Expense.

1. What is the weak point of the procedure, and what fundamental principle of internal control has been ignored?
2. What improvement in the procedure can you suggest?

Exercise 8-8
Internal
Control
Evaluation
(L.O. 4)

An accountant and his assistants are responsible for the following procedures: (a) receipt of all cash; (b) maintenance of the general ledger; (c) maintenance of the accounts receivable ledger; (d) maintenance of the journals for recording sales, cash receipts, and purchases; and (e) preparation of monthly statements to be sent to customers. As a service to customers and employees, the company allows the accountant to cash checks of up to $50 with money from the cash receipts. The accountant may approve the cashing of such a check for current employees and customers. When the deposits are made, the checks are included in place of the cash receipts.

What weakness in internal control exists in this system?

Interpreting Accounting Information

Published
Financial
Information:
J. Walter
Thompson
(L.O. 4)

J. Walter Thompson Co. (JWT) is one of the world's largest advertising agencies, with more than $1 billion in billings per year. One of its smaller units is a television syndication unit that acquires rights to distribute television programming and sells them to local television stations, receiving in exchange advertising time that is sold to the agency's clients. Cash rarely changes hands between the unit and the television station, but the unit is supposed to recognize revenue when the television programs are exchanged for advertising time that will be used by clients at a later date.

The *Wall Street Journal* reported on February 17, 1982, that the company "had discovered 'fictitious' accounting entries that inflated revenue at the television program syndication unit." The article went on to say that "the syndication unit booked revenue of $29.3 million over a five-year period, but that $24.5 million of that amount was fictitious" and that "the accounting irregularities didn't involve an outlay of cash . . . and its (JWT's) advertising clients weren't improperly billed. . . . The fictitious sales were recorded in such a manner as to prevent the issuance of billings to advertising clients. The sole effect of these transactions was to overstate the degree to which the unit was achieving its revenue and profit objectives."

The chief financial officer of JWT indicated that "the discrepancies began to surface . . . when the company reorganized so that all accounting functions reported to the chief financial officer's central office. Previously, he said, 'we had been decentralized in accounting,' with the unit keeping its own books."

Required

1. Show an example entry to recognize revenue from the exchange of the right to televise a show for advertising time and an example entry to bill a client for using the advertising time. Using these two entries as a basis, explain how the fraud was accomplished.
2. What would motivate the head of the syndication unit to perpetrate this fraud if no cash or other assets were stolen?
3. What principles of internal control were violated that would allow this fraud to exist for five years, and how did correction of the weaknesses in internal control allow the fraud to be discovered?

Problem Set A

**Problem 8A-1
Petty Cash
Transactions**
(L.O. 6)

The Avon Theater Company established a petty cash fund in its snack bar so that payment can be made for small deliveries upon receipt. The following transactions occurred:

Oct.   1   The fund was established in the amount of $200.00 from the proceeds of a check drawn for that purpose.
      31   The petty cash fund has cash of $10.71 and the following receipts on hand: for merchandise received, $110.15; delivery charges, $32.87; laundry service, $42.00; miscellaneous expense, $4.27. A check was drawn to replenish the fund.
Nov. 30   The petty cash fund has cash of $22.50 and the following receipts on hand: merchandise, $98.42; delivery charges, $38.15; laundry service, $42.00; miscellaneous expense, $3.93. The petty cash custodian cannot account for the fact that there is an excess of $5.00 in the fund. A check is drawn to replenish the fund.

Required

In general journal form, prepare the entries necessary to record each of the above transactions.

**Problem 8A-2
Bank
Reconciliation**
(L.O. 5)

Use the following information to prepare a bank reconciliation for Mike Grove Company as of October 31, 19xx.

a. Cash on the books as of October 31 amounted to $20,827.08. Cash on the bank statement for the same date was $25,675.73.
b. A deposit of $2,610.47, representing cash receipts of October 31, did not appear on the bank statement.
c. Outstanding checks totaled $1,968.40.
d. A check for $960.00 returned with the statement was recorded incorrectly in the check register as $690.00. The check was made for a purchase of merchandise.
e. Bank service charges for October amounted to $12.50.
f. The bank collected for Mike Grove Company $6,120.00 on a note left for collection. The face value of the note was $6,000.00
g. A NSF check for $91.78 from a customer, Dave Rohr, was returned with the statement.
h. The bank mistakenly charged to the company account a check for $425.00 drawn by Mike Grove on his personal checking account.

i. The bank reported that it had credited the account with $170.00 in interest on the average balance for October.

Required

1. Prepare a bank reconciliation for Mike Grove Company as of October 31, 19xx.
2. Prepare the journal entries necessary to adjust the accounts.
3. State the amount that should appear on the balance sheet as of October 31.

Problem 8A-3
Bank
Reconciliation
(L.O. 5)

The following information comes from the records of the Bexley Company:

From the Cash Receipts Journal		Page 22

Date		Debit Cash
Feb. 1		1,416
8		14,486
15		13,214
22		10,487
28		7,802
		47,405

From the Cash Payments Journal		Page 106

Date	Check Number	Credit Cash
Jan. 26	2076	1,218
30	2077	22
Feb. 6	2078	6
7	2079	19,400
8	2080	2,620
12	2081	9,135
16	2082	14
17	2083	186
18	2084	5,662
		38,263

From the General Ledger

Cash

Date		Item	Post. Ref.	Debit	Credit	Balance Debit	Balance Credit
Jan.	31	Balance				10,570	
Feb.	28		CR22	47,405		57,975	
	28		CP106		38,263	19,712	

The bank statement for Bexley Company appears as follows:

FIRST NATIONAL BANK Statement of Bexley Company
Bexley, OH

Date		Checks and Other Debits		Deposits	Balance
Feb.	1	Balance brought forward			12,416.00
	2	510.00	32.00	1,614.00	13,488.00
	3	1,218.00	4.00		12,266.00
	5	22.00			12,244.00
	9			14,486.00	26,730.00
	10	19,400.00	1,265.00		6,065.00
	11	2,620.00			3,445.00
	12			1,654.00 CM	5,099.00
	16			13,214.00	18,313.00
	17	9,135.00	14.00		9,164.00
	18	40.00 NSF			9,124.00
	23			10,487.00	19,611.00
	24	5,662.00			13,949.00
	28	17.00 SC		101.00 IN	14,033.00

Code: CM—Credit Memo   NSF—Not Sufficient Funds
DM—Debit Memo   SC—Service Charge
IN—Interest

The NSF check was received from P. McDowell, a customer, for merchandise. The credit memorandum represents a $1,600 note collected by the bank plus interest. The February 1 deposit, recorded by Bexley as $1,416 in cash sales, was recorded correctly by the bank at $1,614. On February 1, there were only the following outstanding checks as reconciling items: No. 2056 at $510, No. 2072 at $4, No. 2073 at $35, No. 2074 at $1,265, and No. 2075 at $32.

Required

1. Prepare a bank reconciliation as of February 28, 19xx.
2. Prepare adjusting entries in general journal form.
3. What amount should appear on the balance sheet for cash as of February 28?

Problem 8A-4
Internal
Control
(L.O. 4)

Schacht Company, a large merchandising concern that stocks over 85,000 different items in inventory, has just installed a sophisticated computer system for inventory control. The computer's data storage system has random access processing and carries all pertinent data relating to individual items of inventory. The system is equipped with fifteen remote computer terminals, distributed at various locations throughout the warehouse and sales areas. Using these terminals, employees can obtain information from the computer system about the status of any inventory item. To make an inquiry, they use a keyboard, similar to a typewriter's, that forms part of the remote terminal. The answer is relayed back instantaneously on a screen, which is also part of the terminal. As inventory is received, shipped, or transferred, employees update the inventory records in the computer system by means of the remote terminals.

Required

1. What potential weakness in internal control exists in the system?
2. What suggestions do you have for improving the internal control?

Problem 8A-5
Voucher System
Transactions
(L.O. 8)

During the month of January, F and R Company had the following transactions affecting vouchers payable:

Jan. 2 Prepared voucher no. 7901, payable to Parson Realty, for January rent, $700.

2 Issued check no. 5501 for voucher no. 7901.

3 Prepared voucher no. 7902, payable to Hughes Company, for merchandise, $4,200, invoice dated January 2, terms 2/10, n/30, FOB destination.

5 Prepared voucher no. 7903, payable to Boyd Supply House, for supplies, $650, to be allocated $450 to Store Supplies and $200 to Office Supplies, terms n/10.

6 Prepared voucher no. 7904, payable to City Power and Light, for monthly utilities, $314.

6 Issued check no. 5502 for voucher no. 7904.

9 Prepared voucher no. 7905, payable to Overton Company, for merchandise, $1,700, invoice dated January 7, terms 2/10, n/30, FOB shipping point. Overton Company prepaid freight charges of $146 and added them to the invoice, for a total of $1,846.

12 Issued check no. 5503 for voucher no. 7902.

15 Issued check no. 5504 for voucher no. 7903.

16 Prepared voucher no. 7906, payable to Downing Company, for merchandise, $970, invoice dated January 14, terms 2/10, n/30, FOB shipping point.

16 Prepared voucher no. 7907, payable to Rapid Freight Company, for freight shipment from Downing Company, $118, terms n/10th of next month.

17 Issued check no. 5505 for voucher no. 7905.

18 Returned $220 in defective merchandise to Downing Company for credit.

22 Prepared voucher no. 7908, payable to Boyd Supply House, for supplies, $375, to be allocated $200 to Store Supplies and $175 to Office Supplies, terms n/10.

23 Prepared voucher no. 7909, payable to American National Bank, for 90-day note, which is due, $5,000 plus $150 interest.

23 Issued check no. 5506 for voucher no. 7909.

24 Issued check no. 5507 for voucher no. 7906.

26 Prepared voucher no. 7910, payable to Overton Company, for merchandise, $2,100, invoice dated January 24, terms 2/10, n/30, FOB shipping point. Overton Company prepaid freight charges of $206 and added them to the invoice, for a total of $2,306.

27 Prepared voucher no. 7911, payable to Telephone Company, $37. Payments for telephone are considered a utility expense.

27 Issued check no. 5508 for voucher no. 7911.

30 Prepared voucher no. 7912, payable to Payroll account, for monthly payroll, $17,200, to be allocated $13,300 to Sales Salaries and $3,900 to Office Salaries.

30 Issued check no. 5509 for voucher no. 7912.

31 Prepared voucher no. 7913, payable to Maintenance Company, $360, to be allocated two-thirds to Selling Maintenance and one-third to Office Maintenance.

Required

1. Prepare a voucher register and a check register similar to those illustrated in this chapter, and prepare a general journal. Record the transactions.

2. Prepare a Vouchers Payable account (number 211), and post the appropriate portions of the journal and register entries. Assume that the December 31 balance of Vouchers Payable was zero.

3. Prove the balance of the Vouchers Payable account by preparing a schedule of unpaid vouchers.

**Problem 8A-6
Voucher System
Transactions**
(L.O. 8)

Elie Afshar began a business, Afshar Fashions, on May 1 and completed the following transactions involving vouchers payable during the month:

May 1 Prepared voucher no. 001, payable to Thomas Realty, for one month's rent, $300.

1 Issued check no. 1001 for voucher no. 001.

2 Prepared voucher no. 002, payable to Kuhn Office Outfitters, for office equipment, $1,100.

2 Issued check no. 1002, for voucher no. 002.

3 Prepared vouchers no. 003, 004, and 005, payable to Acme Company, for store fixtures, $1,000 down and $1,000 per month for two months.

4 Issued check no. 1003 for voucher no. 003.

5 Prepared voucher no. 006, payable to Chicago Textile Company, for merchandise, $4,200, invoice dated May 2, terms 2/10, n/30, FOB shipping point. Chicago Textile paid the freight of $342 and added it to the bill for a total of $4,542.

6 Prepared voucher no. 007, payable to Brand Fashions, for merchandise, $2,700, invoice dated May 4, terms 2/10, n/30, FOB shipping point.

6 Prepared voucher no. 008, payable to Fast Motor Freight, for shipping charges on today's shipment, $227, terms n/10.

7 Prepared voucher no. 009, payable to Office Supply Company, for supplies, $150 for store supplies and $100 for office supplies, terms n/10.

8 Prepared voucher no. 010, payable to All-Nite Maintenance, $200, to be allocated three-fourths to selling and one-fourth to office.

8 Issued check no. 1004 for voucher no. 010.

9 Prepared voucher no. 011, payable to Petty Cash, Cashier, to establish a petty cash fund, $50.

May 9 Issued check no. 1005 to pay voucher no. 011.
   11 Returned defective merchandise to Brand Fashions for credit, $250.
   12 Issued check no. 1006 for voucher no. 006.
   14 Issued check no. 1007 for voucher no. 007.
   15 Prepared voucher no. 012, payable to Payroll account, for one-half month's salaries, $1,200, to be allocated two-thirds to selling and one-third to office.
   15 Issued check no. 1008 for voucher no. 012.
   16 Issued check no. 1009 for voucher no. 008.
   17 Issued check no. 1010 for voucher no. 009.
   20 Prepared voucher no. 013, payable to *Weekly Bulletin*, for advertising, $189, terms n/10th of next month.
   22 Prepared voucher no. 014, payable to Chicago Textile Company, for merchandise, $2,600, invoice dated May 20, terms 2/10, n/30, FOB shipping point. Chicago Textile paid the freight of $176 and added it to the bill for a total of $2,776.
   23 Prepared voucher no. 015, payable to Elie Afshar, for personal living expenses, $600.
   23 Issued check no. 1011 for voucher no. 015.
   24 Prepared voucher no. 016, payable to Town and Country Utilities for monthly utility bill, $134.
   25 Prepared voucher no. 017, payable to Brand Fashions, for merchandise, $1,800, invoice dated May 23, terms 2/10, n/30, FOB shipping point.
   25 Prepared voucher no. 018, payable to Fast Motor Freight, for shipping charges on today's shipment, $181, terms n/10.
   27 Prepared voucher no. 019, payable to Office Supply Company, for supplies, $92 for store supplies and $67 for office supplies, terms n/10.
   30 Issued check no. 1012 for voucher no. 014.
   31 Prepared voucher no. 020, payable to Payroll account, for one-half month's salaries, $1,800, to be allocated two-thirds to selling and one-third to office.
   31 Issued check no. 1013 for voucher no. 020.
   31 Prepared voucher no. 021, payable to Petty Cash Cashier. The petty cash fund has $4 in cash plus receipts for the following: office supplies, $13; postage, $26; newspaper subscription, $5.
   31 Issued check no. 1014 for voucher no. 021.

Required

1. Prepare a voucher register and a check register, similar to those illustrated in this chapter, and prepare a general journal. Record the transactions.
2. Prepare a Vouchers Payable account (number 211), and post those portions of the journal and register entries that affect this account.
3. Prove the balance of the Vouchers Payable account by preparing a schedule of unpaid vouchers.

Problem Set B

**Problem 8B-1
Petty Cash
Transactions**
(L.O. 6)

A small company maintains a petty cash fund in its office for small expenditures. The following transactions occurred:

a. The fund was established in the amount of $40.00 on February 1 from the proceeds of check no. 1402, issued for the purpose.

b. On February 28, the petty cash fund had cash of $1.73 and the following receipts on hand: postage, $17.50; supplies, $12.47; delivery service, $6.20; and a rubber stamp, $2.10. Check no. 1473 was drawn to replenish the fund.

c. On March 31, the petty cash fund had cash of $2.53 and the following receipts on hand: postage, $15.60; supplies, $16.42; and delivery service, $3.20. The petty cash custodian could not account for the shortage of $2.25. Check no. 1542 was written to replenish the fund.

Required

Prepare in general journal form the entries necessary to record each of the above transactions.

Problem 8B-2
Bank
Reconciliation
(L.O. 5)

Use the following information to prepare a bank reconciliation for Cole Company as of November 30, 19xx:

a. Cash on the books as of November 30 amounted to $27,246.26. Cash on the bank statement for the same date was $34,256.71.

b. A deposit of $3,562.46, representing cash receipts of November 30, did not appear on the bank statement.

c. Outstanding checks totaled $1,823.41.

d. A check for $605.00 returned with the statement was recorded in the cash payments journal as $506.00. The check was made in payment for advertising.

e. Bank service charges for November amounted to $6.50.

f. The bank collected for Cole Company $9,100.00 on a note left for collection. The face value of the note was $9,000.00

g. An NSF check for $285.00 from a customer, Charles Law, was returned with the statement.

h. The bank mistakenly deducted a check for $200.00 drawn by Trout Corporation.

i. The bank reported a credit to the account of $240.00 for interest earned on the average balance.

Required

1. Prepare a bank reconciliation for Cole Company as of November 30, 19xx.
2. Prepare the journal entries necessary to adjust the accounts.
3. State the amount of cash that should appear on the balance sheet as of November 30.

Problem 8B-3
Bank
Reconciliation
(L.O. 5)

The following information comes from the records of Harper Company:

From the Cash Receipts Journal		Page 7
Date	Debit Cash	
Sept. 1	914	
7	1,012	
14	3,240	
21	2,646	
30	1,942	
	9,754	

Date	Check Number	Credit Cash
Aug. 28	913	14
Sept. 2	914	283
3	915	416
4	916	27
5	918	5
10	919	5,746
11	920	709
20	921	1,246
21	922	76
		8,522

From the General Ledger

Cash   Account No. 111

Date		Item	Post. Ref.	Debit	Credit	Balance Debit	Balance Credit
Aug.	31	Balance				2,465	
Sept.	30		CR7	9,754		12,219	
	30		CP10		8,522	3,697	

The bank statement for Harper Company appears as follows:

LAKE NATIONAL BANK			Statement of Harper Company Main and 2nd Streets	
Date	Checks and Other Debits		Deposits	Balance
Sept. 1	Balance brought forward			3,785.00
2	100.00	500.00	914.00	4,099.00
4	460.00	14.00		3,625.00
6	416.00			3,209.00
8	27.00		1,012.00	4,194.00
12	5.00	15.00 NSF		4,174.00
14	907.00			3,267.00
15			3,240.00	6,507.00
22			2,646.00	9,153.00
24	5,746.00			3,407.00
26	76.00		408.00 CM	3,739.00
30	4.00 SC		42.00 IN	3,777.00

Code: CM—Credit Memo   NSF—Not Sufficient Funds
DM—Debit Memo   SC—Service Charge
IN—Interest

The NSF check was received from S. Brown, a customer, for merchandise. The credit memorandum represents a $400 note collected by the bank plus interest. Check number 920 for a purchase of merchandise was incorrectly recorded in the cash payments journal as $709 instead of as the correct amount of $907. On September 1, there were only the following outstanding checks as reconciling items: number 892 at $100, number 899 at $500, number 911 at $260, and number 912 at $460.

Required

1. Prepare a bank reconciliation as of September 30, 19xx.
2. Prepare adjusting entries in general journal form.
3. What amount should appear on the balance sheet for cash as of September 30?

**Problem 8B-4
Internal
Control**
(L.O. 4)

Wingate Company, a small concern, is attempting to organize its accounting department to achieve maximum internal control, subject to the constraint of limited resources. There are three employees (1, 2, and 3) in the accounting department, each of whom has had accounting courses and some accounting experience. The accounting department must accomplish the following functions: (a) maintain the general ledger, (b) maintain the accounts payable ledger, (c) maintain the accounts receivable ledger, (d) prepare checks for signature, (e) maintain the cash payments journal, (f) issue credits on returns and allowances, (g) reconcile the bank account, and (h) handle and deposit cash receipts.

Required

1. Assuming that each employee will do only the jobs assigned, assign the functions to the three employees in a way that will ensure the highest degree of internal control possible.
2. Identify four possible unsatisfactory combinations of functions.

Problem 8B-5
Voucher System
Transactions
(L.O. 8)

During the month of October, Stieg Company had the following transactions affecting vouchers payable:

Oct. 1 Prepared voucher no. 471, payable to Bozman Company, for merchandise, $900, invoice dated September 30, terms 2/10, n/30, FOB destination.

3 Prepared voucher no. 472, payable to Palmer Corporation, for merchandise, $2,700, invoice dated October 1, terms 2/10, n/30, FOB shipping point.

5 Prepared voucher no. 473, payable to Delancy Agency, for one month's rent, $900.

5 Issued check no. 2612 for voucher no. 473.

6 Prepared voucher no. 474, payable to Sloan Corporation, for merchandise, $500, invoice dated October 5, terms 2/10, n/30, FOB shipping point. Sloan Corporation prepaid freight charges of $76 and added them to the invoice, making a total of $576.

8 Prepared voucher no. 475, payable to the *Daily Journal* for advertising, $375.

8 Issued check no. 2613 for voucher no. 475.

10 Issued check no. 2614 for voucher no. 471.

11 Received a credit memorandum from Palmer Corporation for merchandise returned, $300.

11 Issued check no. 2615 for voucher no. 472.

12 Prepared voucher no. 476, payable to First National Bank, for repayment of note, $1,000 plus $30 interest.

12 Issued check no. 2616 for voucher no. 476.

13 Issued check no. 2617 for voucher no. 474.

16 Prepared vouchers no. 477, 478, and 479, payable to Modern Truck Company, for the down payment and subsequent payments on a new truck, terms $1,000 down, $1,500 in 60 days, $1,500 in 120 days.

16 Issued check no. 2618 for voucher no. 477.

21 Prepared voucher no. 480, payable to Palmer Corporation, for merchandise, $1,200, invoice dated October 17, terms 2/10, n/30, FOB shipping point.

22 Prepared voucher no. 481, payable to Sloan Corporation, for merchandise, $1,000, invoice dated October 22, terms 2/10, n/30, FOB shipping point. Sloan Corporation prepaid freight charges of $46 and added them to the invoice, for a total of $1,046.

25 Prepared voucher no. 482, payable to Speedy Freight, for freight in on merchandise received from Palmer Corporation during month, $360, terms n/10th of next month.

27 Issued check no. 2619 for voucher no. 480.

30 Prepared voucher no. 483, payable to Payroll account, for monthly payroll of $7,700 (to be divided between sales salaries of $5,700 and office salaries of $2,000).

30 Issued check no. 2620 for voucher no. 483.

31 Prepared voucher no. 484, payable to Mesa Power and Light, for monthly utility expenses, $287.

Required

1. Prepare a voucher register and a check register similar to those illustrated in this chapter, and prepare a general journal. Record the transactions.
2. Prepare a Vouchers Payable account (number 211), and post the appropriate

Internal Control and Merchandising Transactions

portions of the journal and register entries. Assume that the September 30 balance of Vouchers Payable was zero.

3. Prove the balance of the Vouchers Payable account by preparing a schedule of unpaid vouchers.

Problem 8B-6
Voucher System
Transactions
(L.O. 8)

During the month of July, Golden Records had the following transactions affecting vouchers payable:

July 1   Prepared voucher no. 531, payable to Petty Cash Cashier, to establish a petty cash fund, $100.

    1   Issued check no. 1201 for voucher no. 531.

    2   Prepared voucher no. 532, payable to Drake Records, for a shipment of merchandise, $350, invoice dated July 1, terms 2/10, n/60, FOB shipping point. Drake prepaid freight of $20 and added it to the invoice, for a total of $370.

    3   Prepared voucher no. 533, payable to Gibbs Realty, for July's rent, $500.

    3   Issued check no. 1202 for voucher no. 533.

    5   Prepared voucher no. 534, payable to Weiss Records, for merchandise, $500, invoice dated July 3, terms 2/10, n/60, FOB shipping point.

    6   Prepared voucher no. 535, payable to Parcel Express, for freight in on July 5 shipment, $32, terms n/10.

    7   Prepared voucher no. 536, payable to Valley Hardware, for office equipment, $200, terms n/30.

    8   Received credit memorandum from Weiss Records for damaged records returned, $50.

    9   Prepared voucher no. 537, payable to Weiss Records, for merchandise, $650, invoice dated July 8, terms 2/10, n/60, FOB shipping point.

  10   Prepared voucher no. 538, payable to Parcel Express, for freight in on July 9, $47, terms n/10.

  11   Issued check no. 1203 for voucher no. 532.

  12   Prepared voucher no. 539, payable to Roy Golden, for his personal expenses, $500.

  12   Issued check no. 1204 for voucher no. 539.

  13   Issued check no. 1205 for voucher no. 534.

  15   Issued check no. 1206 for voucher no. 535.

  17   Prepared vouchers no. 540, 541, 542, and 543, payable to City Furniture, for office furniture having an invoice price of $1,200, terms one-fourth down and one-fourth each month for three months.

  17   Issued check no. 1207 for voucher no. 540.

  18   Issued check no. 1208 for voucher no. 537.

  19   Issued check no. 1209 for voucher no. 538.

  20   Prepared voucher no. 544, payable to Hill Supply, $135 ($95 to be charged to Store Supplies and $40 to Office Supplies), terms n/10th of next month.

  22   Prepared voucher no. 545, payable to Drake Wholesale Records, for merchandise, $165, invoice dated July 19, terms 2/10, n/30, FOB shipping point. Freight prepaid by shipper and included in invoice total, $15.

  23   Prepared voucher no. 546, payable to River National Bank, in payment of a $2,000 note plus interest, $50, total $2,050.

  23   Issued check no. 1210 for voucher no. 546.

  24   Prepared voucher no. 547, payable to AACE Insurance Company, for a one-year policy, $240.

  24   Issued check no. 1211 for voucher no. 547.

26 Prepared voucher no. 548, payable to Weiss Records, for merchandise, $300, invoice dated July 25, terms 2/10, n/60, FOB shipping point.

27 Prepared voucher no. 549, payable to Parcel Express, for freight in on shipment of July 26, $19.

28 Prepared voucher no. 550, payable to Payroll account, for monthly salaries, $3,950 (to be divided as follows: sales salaries, $2,200, and office salaries, $1,750).

28 Issued check no. 1212 for voucher no. 550.

29 Issued check no. 1213 for voucher no. 545.

31 Prepared voucher no. 551 to reimburse petty cash fund. A count of the fund revealed cash on hand, $15, and the following receipts: postage, $22; office supplies, $17; collect telegram, $3; flowers for sick employee, $10; delivery service, $27.

31 Issued check no. 1214 for voucher no. 551.

Required

1. Prepare a voucher register, a check register, and a general journal similar to those illustrated in this chapter, and record the transactions.

2. Prepare a Vouchers Payable account (number 211), and post those portions of the journal and register entries that affect this account. Assume the Vouchers Payable account had a zero balance on June 30.

3. Prove the balance of the Vouchers Payable account by preparing a schedule of unpaid vouchers.

Financial Decision Case 8-1

Gabhart's
(L.O. 4)

Gabhart's is a retail department store with several departments. Its internal control procedures for cash sales and purchases are described below.

Cash sales Every cash sale is rung up by the sales clerk assigned to a particular department on the cash register for that department. The cash register produces a sales slip to be given to the customer with the merchandise. A carbon copy of the sales ticket is made on a continuous tape locked inside the machine. At the end of each day, a "total" key is pressed, and the machine prints the total sales for the day on the continuous tape. Then the sales clerk unlocks the machine, takes off the total sales figure, makes the entry in the accounting records for the day's cash sales, counts the cash in the drawer, retains the basic $50 change fund, and gives the cash received to the cashier. The sales clerk then files the cash register tape and is ready for the next day's business.

Purchases All goods are ordered by the purchasing agent upon the request of the various department heads. When the goods are received, the receiving clerk prepares a receiving report in triplicate. One copy is sent to the purchasing agent, one copy is forwarded to the department head, and one copy is kept by the receiving clerk. Invoices are forwarded immediately to the accounting department to ensure payment before the discount period elapses. After payment, the invoice is forwarded to the purchasing agent for comparison with the purchase order and the receiving report and is then returned to the accounting office for filing.

Required

For each of the above situations, identify at least one major internal control weakness and tell what you would suggest to improve the system.

Learning Objectives

Chapter Nine

General-Purpose External Financial Statements

1. *State the objectives of financial reporting.*

2. *State the qualitative characteristics of accounting information and describe their interrelationships.*

3. *Define and describe the use of the conventions of comparability and consistency, materiality, conservatism, full disclosure, and cost-benefit.*

4. *Identify and describe the basic components of a classified balance sheet.*

5. *Define comprehensive income and distinguish between the multistep and single-step types of classified income statements.*

6. *Relate a chart of accounts to classified financial statements.*

7. *Use classified financial statements for the simple evaluation of liquidity and profitability.*

8. *Identify the major components of a corporate annual report.*

Financial reporting has both internal and external aspects. Internal management has an interest in the resources, debts, and earnings of the business and in changes in these items. Management is also responsible for informing those outside the business about the financial position and performance of the company. Financial statements are the most important means of communicating accounting information to external users. To add to their reliability, these financial statements are often audited by independent accountants. This chapter looks at the objectives, form, and evaluation of financial statements in external reporting. After studying this chapter, you should be able to meet the learning objectives listed on the left.

To be useful to those outside a company who have a financial interest in it, financial statements must meet certain standards. This chapter begins by describing the objectives of financial information. It then discusses some of the qualities that accounting information ought to have and some of the conventions that are helpful in interpreting it.

One way of making financial statements more useful is to break down the information into special categories. After the balance sheet and income statement are divided into useful categories, this chapter explains how to use the categories in the financial statements to analyze a business. Finally, the financial statements of a major U.S. corporation are used to give you a realistic picture of the company's activities.

Objectives of Financial Information[1]

The United States has a highly developed exchange economy. In such an economy, most goods and services are exchanged for money or claims to money instead of being used or bartered by their producers. Most business is carried on through investor-owned companies called corporations, including many large ones that buy, sell, and get financing in U.S. and world markets.

1. The discussion in this section is based on *Statement of Financial Accounting Concepts No. 1,* "Objectives of Financial Reporting by Business Enterprises" (Stamford, Conn.: Financial Accounting Standards Board, 1978), pars. 6–16 and 28–40.

Objective 1
State the
objectives
of financial
reporting

By issuing stocks and bonds that are traded in the market, businesses can raise capital for production and marketing activities through financial institutions, small groups, and the public at large. Investors are interested mainly in returns from dividends and in the market prices of their investments, rather than in managing a company's business. Creditors want to know if a business can repay a loan according to the loan terms. For this reason, investors and creditors both need to know if a company can generate favorable cash flows. Financial statements are important to both groups in making this judgment. They offer valuable information that helps investors and creditors judge a company's ability to pay dividends and pay back debts with interest. So they can help the market put scarce resources to work in companies that can use them most efficiently.

The needs of users and the general business environment described above are the basis for the Financial Accounting Standards Board's three objectives of financial reporting:

1. To furnish information useful in making investment and credit decisions Financial reporting should offer information that is useful to present and potential investors and creditors as well as to others in making rational investment and credit decisions. The reports should be in a form that makes sense to those who have some understanding of business and are willing to study the information carefully.

2. To provide information useful in assessing cash flow prospects Financial reporting should supply information to help present and potential investors and creditors and others judge the amounts, timing, and risk of expected cash receipts from dividends or interest and the proceeds from the sale, redemption, or maturity of stocks or loans.

3. To provide information about business resources, claims to those resources, and changes in them Financial reporting should give information about the business resources of a company, the obligations of the business to transfer resources to other units and to owner's equity, and the effects of transactions that change its resources and claims to those resources.

General-purpose external financial statements are the most important way of periodically presenting the information that has been gathered and processed in the accounting system to investors, creditors, and other interested parties outside the business. For this reason, these statements—the balance sheet, the income statement, the statement of owner's equity, and the statement of changes in financial position—are the most important output of the accounting system. These financial statements are called "general purpose" because of their potential use for a wide audience. They are "external" because their users are outside the business. As there may be some differences between managers, who must prepare the statements, and the investors or creditors, who invest in or lend money to the businesses, these statements are often audited by accountants outside the company to increase confidence in their reliability.

Qualitative Characteristics
of Accounting Information[2]

It is easy for a student in the first accounting course to get the idea that accounting is 100 percent accurate. This idea is reinforced by the fact that all the problems in this book and other introductory books can be solved. The numbers all add up, what is supposed to equal something else does, and so forth. Accounting seems very much like mathematics in its perfection. In this course, the basics of accounting are presented in a simple form at first to promote better understanding. In practice, however, accounting information is neither simple nor perfect and rarely satisfies all criteria. The FASB emphasizes this fact in the following statement:

The information provided by financial reporting often results from approximate, rather than exact, measures. The measures commonly involve numerous estimates, classifications, summarizations, judgments and allocations. The outcome of economic activity in a dynamic economy is uncertain and results from combinations of many factors. Thus, despite the aura of precision that may seem to surround financial reporting in general and financial statements in particular, with few exceptions the measures are approximations, which may be based on rules and conventions, rather than exact amounts.[3]

Understandability

The goal of accounting information—to provide the basic data that different users need to make informed decisions—is an ideal. The gap between the ideal and the actual provides much of the interest and controversy in accounting. It is also a major reason why the burden for interpreting and using the information properly falls partly on the decision maker. The decision maker not only must judge what information to use and how to use it but also must understand it. The **understandability** of the information, however, depends on both the decision maker and the accountant. The accountant presents information that is believed to be generally useful, but the decision maker must interpret the information and use it in making the decision. To aid in understanding this process of interpretation, the FASB has described the qualitative characteristics of accounting information. **Qualitative characteristics** are the standards for judging the information that accountants give to decision makers. They are shown in Figure 9-1.

The Usefulness of Accounting Information

If accounting information is to be useful, it must have two major qualitative characteristics, relevance and reliability.

---

2. The discussion in this section is based on *Statement of Financial Accounting Concepts No. 2,* "Qualitative Characteristics of Accounting Information" (Stamford, Conn.: Financial Accounting Standards Board, 1980).
3. *Statement of Financial Accounting Concepts No. 1,* par. 20.

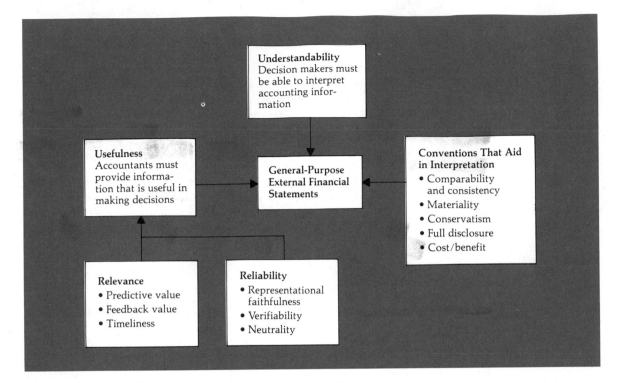

Figure 9-1
The Qualitative
Characteristics
of Accounting
Information

Relevance Relevance means that the information is able to make a difference to the outcome of a decision. Information can influence a decision if it has predictive value and feedback value and if it is timely. **Predictive value** means that the information is useful to the decision maker in making a prediction, not that it is itself a prediction. To have **feedback value**, the information must tell something about the accuracy of earlier expectations. **Timeliness** means having the accounting information arrive in time for the user to make a decision. If the information is not ready when needed, it has no value for future action and is not relevant.

Objective 2
State the
qualitative
characteristics
of accounting
information
and describe
their inter-
relationships

Reliability To be useful, information must be reliable as well as relevant. **Reliability** is related to representational faithfulness, verifiability, and neutrality. **Representational faithfulness** has to do with how well the information agrees with what it is meant to represent. Accounting information is supposed to give a clear picture of the economic resources and obligations of a business and the events affecting those resources and obligations. **Verifiability** deals with the credibility of accounting information and means that the information can be confirmed or duplicated by independent parties using the same ways of measuring. **Neutrality** means that in carrying out generally accepted accounting principles, the main concern should be the relevance and reliability of the accounting information, not the effect that carrying out the principles may have on a particular interest. Neutrality does not mean that accounting information should be without purpose. It simply means that business activity must be reported as faithfully as possible, without coloring the picture that is being presented in order to influence anyone in a certain direction.

Conventions to Aid Interpretation
of Financial Information

*Objective 3
Define and
describe the use
of the conven-
tions of compa-
rability and
consistency,
materiality,
conservatism,
full disclosure,
and cost-benefit.*

To a large extent, financial statements are based on estimates and on rather arbitrary rules of recognition and allocation. In this book we point out a number of flaws that financial statements may have. One is failing to recognize the changing value of the dollar. Another is treating intangibles, like research and development costs, as assets only if purchased outside the company, but not if developed within the company. These problems do not mean that financial statements are useless; they are, of course, essential. However, the people who use them must know how to interpret them. To help users in this interpretation, accountants depend on five conventions: (1) comparability and consistency, (2) materiality, (3) conservatism, (4) full disclosure, and (5) cost/benefit.

Comparability and Consistency

Adding to the usefulness of accounting information is the characteristic of comparability. Information about a company is more useful if it can be compared with similar facts about the same company over several time periods or about another company for the same time period. **Comparability** means that the information is presented in such a way that the decision maker can recognize similarities, differences, and trends. Consistent use of accounting measures and procedures is important in achieving comparability. The **consistency** convention requires that a particular accounting procedure, once adopted, will not be changed from one period to another unless the user is informed of the change. Thus, without a statement to the contrary, users of financial statements may assume that there have been no arbitrary changes in methods that may affect interpretation of the statements.

If management decides that a certain procedure is not appropriate and should be changed, generally accepted accounting principles require that the fact of the change and its dollar effect be described in the independent accountant's report:

The nature of and justification for a change in accounting principle and its effect on income should be disclosed in the financial statements of the period in which the change is made. The justification for the change should explain clearly why the newly adopted accounting principle is preferable.[4]

For example, during the current year, a company might report that it had changed its method of accounting for inventories because management felt the new method reflected actual cost flows more realistically.

---

4. Accounting Principles Board, *Opinion No. 20,* "Accounting Changes" (New York: American Institute of Certified Public Accountants, 1971), par. 17.

Materiality

The term **materiality** refers to the relative importance of an item or event. If an item or event is material, it is likely to be relevant to the user of the financial statements. The accountant is often faced with many small items or events that make little difference to users no matter how they are handled. For example, in Chapter 13 it is suggested that it is more practical to account for small tools on an inventory basis than to depreciate them. Also, small capital expenditures of less than $25 or $50 may be charged as expense rather than recorded as equipment and depreciated.

In general, an item is material if there is a reasonable expectation that knowing about it would influence the decisions of users of financial statements. The materiality of an item depends on the nature of the item as well as the amount of the item. For example, in a multimillion-dollar company, a mistake in recording an item of $5,000 may not be important, but discovering a $5,000 bribe or theft may be very significant. Also, a great many small errors together may result in a material amount. Accountants must judge the materiality of many things, and the users of financial statements must depend on their judgment.

Conservatism

Accountants try to base their decisions on logic and evidence that will lead to the fairest report of what really happened. In judging and estimating, however, accountants are often faced with uncertainties or doubts. In these cases, they look to the convention of **conservatism.** This convention means that when accountants face major uncertainties as to which accounting procedure to use, they are generally careful to choose the one that will be least likely to overstate assets and income.

One of the most common applications of the conservatism convention is the use of the lower-of-cost-or-market method in accounting for short-term investments, described in Chapter 10, and for inventories, presented in Chapter 11. Under this method, if the market value is greater than cost, the more conservative cost figure is used. If the market value is less than cost, then the more conservative market value is used.

Conservatism can be a useful tool in doubtful cases, but the abuse of this convention will certainly lead to incorrect and misleading financial statements. Suppose that someone incorrectly applied the conservatism convention by charging a long-term asset to expense in the period of purchase. In this case, income and assets for the current period would be understated, and income of future periods would be overstated. For this reason, accountants depend on the conservatism convention only as a last resort.

Full Disclosure

The convention of **full disclosure** requires that financial statements and their footnotes present all information relevant to the user's understanding of the case. In other words, accounting information should offer any explanation that is needed to keep it from being misleading. For instance, as noted in the section on consistency above, a change from one accounting procedure to another should be reported. In general, the form of the financial statements, as described later in this chapter, may affect their usefulness in making certain decisions. Also, certain items are considered essential to financial statement readers, such as the amount of depreciation expense and income tax expense on the income statement and the amount of the accumulated depreciation accounts on the balance sheet.

Other examples of disclosures required by the Financial Accounting Standards Board and other official bodies are the accounting procedures used in preparing the statements, important changes in accounting estimates, important events taking place after the date of the statements, and assets and income of the major divisions of a company. However, there is a point where the statements become so cluttered that they impede rather than aid understanding. Beyond required disclosures, the application of the full-disclosure convention is based not on definite standards, but on the judgment of management and the accountants who prepare the statements.

The principle of full disclosure has also been influenced by users of accounting information in recent years. To protect the investor independent auditors, the stock exchanges, and the SEC have all made many more demands for disclosure by publicly owned companies. The SEC has been pushing especially hard for the enforcement of full disclosure. So today more and better information about corporations is available to the public than ever before.

Cost-Benefit

The cost-benefit convention underlies all the qualitative characteristics and conventions. It holds that the benefits to be gained from providing new accounting information should be greater than the costs of providing it. Of course, certain minimum levels of relevance and reliability must be reached for accounting information to be useful. Beyond these minimum levels, however, it is up to the FASB and the SEC, which require the information, and the accountant, who provides the information, to judge the costs and benefits in each case. Most of the costs of providing information fall at first on the preparers, though the benefits are reaped by both preparers and users. Finally, both the costs and the benefits are passed on to society in the form of prices and social benefits from more efficient allocation of resources. The costs and benefits of a particular requirement for an accounting disclosure are both direct and indirect, immediate and deferred. For example, it is hard to judge the final costs and benefits of a far-reaching and costly regulation. The FASB, for instance, requires that certain large companies make a supplemental disclosure of the effects of changes in price levels and current costs on their financial statements (presented in Chapter 14). Cost-benefit is a question faced by all regulators, including the FASB and the SEC. Even though there are no definitive ways of measuring costs and benefits, much of the accountant's work deals with these concepts.

Classified Balance Sheet

*Objective 4
Identify and
describe the
basic compo-
nents of a
classified
balance sheet*

So far in this book, balance sheets have listed the balances of accounts that fell in the categories of assets, liabilities, and owner's equity. Because even a fairly small company may have hundreds of accounts, simply listing these accounts by broad categories is not very helpful to a statement user. Setting up subcategories within the major categories will often make the financial statements much more useful. Investors and creditors often study and evaluate the relationships among the subcategories. When general-purpose external financial statements are divided into useful subcategories, they are called **classified financial statements.**

The balance sheet presents the financial position of a company at a particular time. The classified balance sheet shown in Figure 9-2 (next page) has subdivisions that are typical of most companies in the United States. The subdivisions under owner's equity, of course, depend on the form of business.

Assets

The assets of a company are often divided into four categories: (1) current assets; (2) investments; (3) property, plant, and equipment; and (4) intangible assets. Some companies use a fifth category called other assets if there are miscellaneous assets that do not fall into any of the other groups. These categories are listed in the order of their presumed liquidity (the ease with which an asset can be converted into cash). For example, current assets are said to be more liquid than property, plant, and equipment.

Current Assets The Accounting Principles Board has defined **current assets** in the following way:

Current assets are defined as . . . cash or other assets that are reasonably expected to be realized in cash or sold during a normal operating cycle of a business or within one year if the operating cycle is shorter than one year.[5]

The normal operating cycle of a company is the average time that is needed to go from cash to cash. Cash is used to buy merchandise inventory, which is sold for cash or for a promise of cash (a receivable) if the sale is made on account (for credit). If the sales are on account, the resulting receivables must be collected before the cycle is completed.

The normal operating cycle for most companies is less than one year, but there are exceptions. Tobacco companies, for example, must cure the tobacco for two or three years before their inventory can be sold. The tobacco inventory is still considered a current asset because it will be sold within the normal operating cycle. Another example is a company that sells on the installment basis. The collection payments for a television set or stove may be as long as twenty-four or thirty-six months, but these receivables are still considered current assets.

5. Accounting Principles Board, *Statement of the Accounting Principles Board, No. 4* (New York: American Institute of Certified Public Accountants, 1970), par. 198.

Figure 9-2
Classified
Balance Sheet
for Shafer Auto
Parts Company

Shafer Auto Parts Company
Balance Sheet
December 31, 19xx

Assets

Current Assets

Cash	$10,360	
Short-Term Investments	2,000	
Notes Receivable	8,000	
Accounts Receivable	35,300	
Merchandise Inventory	60,400	
Prepaid Insurance	6,600	
Store Supplies	1,060	
Office Supplies	636	
Total Current Assets		$124,356

Investments

Land Held for Future Use		5,000

Property, Plant, and Equipment

Land		$ 4,500	
Building	$20,650		
Less Accumulated Depreciation	8,640	12,010	
Delivery Equipment	$18,400		
Less Accumulated Depreciation	9,450	8,950	
Office Equipment	$ 8,600		
Less Accumulated Depreciation	5,000	3,600	
Total Property, Plant, and Equipment			29,060

Intangible Assets

Trademark		500
Total Assets		$158,916

Liabilities

Current Liabilities

Notes Payable	$15,000	
Accounts Payable	25,683	
Salaries Payable	2,000	
Total Current Liabilities		$42,683

Long-Term Liabilities

Mortgage Payable		17,800
Total Liabilities		$ 60,483

Owner's Equity

Fred Shafer, Capital	98,433
Total Liabilities and Owner's Equity	$158,916

Cash is obviously a current asset. Temporary investments, accounts and notes receivable, and inventory are also current assets because they are expected to be converted to cash within the next year or during the normal operating cycle of most firms. They are listed in the order of the ease of their conversion into cash. Accounting for these short-term assets is presented in Chapter 10.

Prepaid expenses, such as rent and insurance paid for in advance, and inventories of various supplies bought for use rather than for sale should also be classified as current assets. These kinds of property are current in the sense that, if they had not been bought earlier, a current outlay of cash would be needed to obtain them. They are an exception to the current asset definition presented earlier.[6]

In deciding whether or not an asset is current or noncurrent, the idea of "reasonable expectation" is important. For example, short-term investments represent an account used for temporary investments of idle cash or cash not immediately required for operating purposes. As a need for cash arises, these securities will be sold to meet this need. Investments in securities that management does not expect to sell within the next year and that do not involve the temporary use of idle cash should be shown in the investments category of a classified balance sheet.

Investments The investments category includes assets, generally of a long-term nature, that are not used in the normal operation of a business and that management does not plan to convert to cash within the next year. Items in this category are securities held for long-term investment, land held for future use, plant or equipment not used in the business, and special funds such as a fund to be used to pay off a debt or buy a building. Also in this category are large permanent investments in another company for the purpose of controlling that company. These topics are covered in Chapter 20.

Property, Plant, and Equipment The property, plant, and equipment category includes long-term assets that are used in the continuing operation of the business. They represent a place to operate (land and buildings) and equipment to produce, sell, deliver, and service its goods. For this reason, they are often called operating assets or sometimes fixed assets, tangible assets, or long-lived assets. We have seen earlier in the book that, through depreciation, the cost of these assets (except land) is spread over the periods they benefit. Past depreciation is recorded by the accumulated depreciation accounts. The exact order in which property, plant, and equipment are listed is not the same everywhere in practice. Assets not used in the regular course of business should be listed in the investments category, as noted above. Chapters 13 and 14 are devoted largely to property, plant, and equipment.

Intangible Assets Intangible assets are long-term assets that have no physical substance but have a value based on rights or privileges that

6. *Accounting Research and Terminology Bulletin,* Final Edition (New York: American Institute of Certified Public Accountants, 1961), p. 20.

belong to the owner. Examples are patents, copyrights, goodwill, franchises, and trademarks. These assets are recorded at cost, which is spread over the expected life of the right or privilege. These assets are explained further in Chapter 14.

Liabilities

Liabilities are divided into two categories: current liabilities and long-term liabilities.

Current Liabilities   The category called **current liabilities** is made up of obligations due within the normal operating cycle of the business or within a year, whichever is longer. They are generally paid from current assets or by incurring new short-term liabilities. Under this heading are notes payable, accounts payable, wages payable, taxes payable, and customer advances (unearned revenues). Current liabilities are presented in more detail in Chapter 12.

Long-Term Liabilities   Debts of a business that fall due more than one year ahead or beyond the normal operating cycle, or that are to be paid out of noncurrent assets are **long-term liabilities**. Mortgages payable, long-term notes, bonds payable, employee pension obligations, and long-term lease liabilities generally fall in this category.

Owner's Equity

The terms *owner's equity, proprietorship, capital,* and *net worth* are used interchangeably. They all stand for the owner's interest in the company. The first three terms are felt to be better usage than *net worth* because most assets are recorded at original cost rather than at current value. For this reason, the ownership section will not represent "worth." It is really a claim against the assets.

The accounting treatment of assets and liabilities is not generally affected by the form of business organization. However, the owner's equity section of the balance sheet will be different depending on whether the business is a sole proprietorship, a partnership, or a corporation.

Sole Proprietorship   You are familiar with the owner's equity section of a sole proprietorship as shown in the balance sheet for Shafer Auto Parts Company (Figure 9-2, page 316).

Partnership   The owners' equity section of the balance sheet for a partnership is called partners' equity and is much like that of the sole proprietorship. It might appear as follows:

	Partners' Equity	
A. J. Martin, Capital	$21,666	
R. C. Moore, Capital	35,724	
Total Partners' Equity		$57,390

Corporation Corporations are by law separate and legal entities. The owners are the stockholders. The owners' equity section of a balance sheet for a corporation is called stockholders' equity and has two parts: contributed or paid-in capital and earned capital or retained earnings. This might appear as follows:

Stockholders' Equity

Contributed Capital		
Common Stock—$10 par value, 5,000 shares authorized, issued, and outstanding	$50,000	
Paid-in Capital in Excess of Par Value	10,000	
Total Contributed Capital		$60,000
Retained Earnings		37,500
Total Stockholders' Equity		$97,500

As you will remember, owner's equity accounts show the sources of and claims on assets. Of course, these claims are not on any particular asset but rather on the assets as a whole. It follows, then, that contributed and earned capital accounts of a corporation measure stockholders' claims on property and also measure the sources of the property. Contributed or paid-in capital accounts reveal the amounts of assets invested by stockholders themselves. Generally, contributed capital is shown on corporate balance sheets by two amounts: (1) the face or par value of issued stock, and (2) amounts paid in or contributed in excess of the face or par value per share. In the above illustration, stockholders invested amounts equal to par value of the outstanding stock (5,000 × $10) plus $10,000 more.

The **Retained Earnings** account is sometimes called Earned Capital because it represents the stockholders' claim to the assets earned during profitable operations and plowed back into, or reinvested in, corporate operations. Distributions of assets to shareholders, called dividends, reduce the Retained Earnings account balance just as withdrawals of assets by the owner of a business lower his or her capital account balance. Thus the Retained Earnings account balance, in its simplest form, represents the earnings of the corporation less dividends paid to stockholders over the life of the business.

Forms of the Income Statement

Objective 5
Define comprehensive income and distinguish between the multistep and single-step types of classified income statements

The income statement measures comprehensive income. Comprehensive income is defined by the Financial Accounting Standards Board as "the change in equity (net assets) of an entity during a period from transactions and other events and circumstances from nonowner sources. It includes all changes in equity during a period except those resulting from investments by owners and distributions to withdrawals by owners."[7] It repre-

7. *Statement of Financial Accounting Concepts No. 3*, "Elements of Financial Statements of Business Enterprises" (Stamford, Conn.: Financial Accounting Standards Board, 1980), par. 56.

sents revenues earned, expenses incurred, and gains and losses (if any) recognized during the accounting period.

For internal management, a detailed income statement such as the one you learned about in Chapter 6 and the one for Shafer Auto Parts Company in Figure 9-3 is helpful in analyzing the company's performance. In the Shafer statement, gross margin from sales less operating expenses is called income from operations, and a new section, other revenues and expenses, is added to the statement to include nonoperating revenues and expenses. This latter section includes revenues from investments (such as dividends and interest from stocks and bonds and savings accounts) and interest earned on credit or notes extended to customers. It also includes interest expense and other expenses that result from borrowing money or from credit being extended to the company. If the company has other revenues and expenses unrelated to normal business operations, they too are classified in this part of the income statement. Income taxes expense and earnings per share information do not appear on the income statement for Shafer Auto Parts Company because they apply to corporation accounting.

For external reporting purposes, the income statement is usually presented in condensed form. Condensed financial statements present only the major categories of the financial statement. There are two common forms of the condensed income statement, the multistep form and the single-step form. The multistep form, illustrated in Figure 9-4 (page 322), derives net income in the same step-by-step fashion as the detailed income statement for Shafer Auto Parts Company in Figure 9-3 except that only the totals of significant categories are given. Usually some breakdown is shown for operating expenses such as the totals for selling expenses and for general and administrative expenses. Other revenues and expenses are also usually broken down. The single-step form, illustrated in Figure 9-5 (page 322), derives net income in a single step by putting the major categories of revenues in the first part of the statement and the major categories of costs and expenses in the second part. Each of these forms has its advantages. The multistep form shows the components used in deriving net income, while the single-step form has the advantage of simplicity. About an equal number of large U.S. companies use each form in their public reports.

Other Financial Statements

Two other statements that are necessary to an understanding of a company's financial operations are the statement of owner's equity and the statement of changes in financial position.

The statement of owner's equity for Shafer Auto Parts Company is shown in Figure 9-6 (page 323). The statement of retained earnings for a corporation is very similar. In place of the beginning and ending balances of capital are the beginning and ending balances of retained earnings. Instead of withdrawals there are dividends paid to stockholders. Net income is added in a similar way in the statement of retained earnings.

Figure 9-3
Income
Statement for
Shafer Auto
Parts Company

Shafer Auto Parts Company
Income Statement
For the Year Ended December 31, 19xx

Revenues from Sales			
Gross Sales		$299,156	
Less: Sales Returns and Allowances	$ 6,300		
Sales Discounts	3,200	9,500	
Net Sales			$289,656
Cost of Goods Sold			
Merchandise Inventory, January 1, 19xx		$ 64,800	
Purchases	$168,624		
Freight In	8,236	176,860	
Goods Available for Sale		$241,660	
Merchandise Inventory, December 31, 19xx		60,400	
Cost of Goods Sold			181,260
Gross Margin from Sales			$108,396
Operating Expenses			
Selling Expenses			
Sales Salaries Expense	$ 22,500		
Rent Expense, Store Fixtures	5,600		
Freight Out Expense	5,740		
Advertising Expense	10,000		
Insurance Expense, Selling	1,600		
Store Supplies Expense	1,540		
Depreciation Expense, Building	2,600		
Depreciation Expense, Delivery Equipment	5,200		
Total Selling Expenses		$ 54,780	
General and Administrative Expenses			
Office Salaries Expense	$ 26,900		
Insurance Expense, General	4,200		
Office Supplies Expense	1,204		
Depreciation Expense, Office Equipment	2,200		
Total General and Administrative Expenses		34,504	
Total Operating Expenses			89,284
Income from Operations			$ 19,112
Other Revenues and Expenses			
Interest Earned		$ 1,400	
Less Interest Expense		2,631	
Excess Expenses over Revenues			1,231
Net Income			$ 17,881

Figure 9-4
Condensed
Multistep
Income
Statement for
Shafer Auto
Parts Company

Shafer Auto Parts Company
Income Statement
For the Year Ended December 31, 19xx

Revenues from Sales		$289,656
Cost of Goods Sold		181,260
Gross Margin from Sales		$108,396
Operating Expenses		
Selling Expenses	$54,780	
General and Administrative Expenses	34,504	
Total Operating Expenses		89,284
Income from Operations		$ 19,112
Other Revenues and Expenses		
Interest Earned	$ 1,400	
Less Interest Expense	2,631	
Excess Expenses over Revenues		(1,231)
Net Income		$ 17,881

Later in this chapter, the statement related to the owners' equity of a major corporation is presented. Chapters 16 and 17 deal with the special problems of the equity section of the balance sheet for corporations.

A simple form of the statement of changes in financial position was shown in Chapter 2. A more complicated one appears in Figure 9-10 near

Figure 9-5
Condensed
Single-Step
Income
Statement for
Shafer Auto
Parts Company

Shafer Auto Parts Company
Income Statement
For the Year Ended December 31, 19xx

Revenues		
Net Sales	$289,656	
Interest Income	1,400	
Total Revenues		$291,056
Costs and Expenses		
Cost of Goods Sold	$181,260	
Selling Expenses	54,780	
General and Administrative Expenses	34,504	
Interest Expense	2,631	
Total Costs and Expenses		273,175
Net Income		$ 17,881

Chapter Nine

Figure 9-6
Statement of
Owner's Equity
for Shafer Auto
Parts Company

Shafer Auto Parts Company
Statement of Owner's Equity
For the Year Ended December 31, 19xx

Fred Shafer, Capital, January 1, 19xx	$100,552
Net Income for the year	17,881
	$118,433
Less Withdrawals	20,000
Fred Shafer, Capital, December 31, 19xx	$ 98,433

the end of this chapter. This important statement is explained in detail in Chapter 19.

Chart of Accounts

*Objective 6
Relate a chart
of accounts
to classified
financial
statements*

Classified financial statements are prepared, of course, from the ledger accounts. For this reason, the ledger accounts are arranged in the same order as in the financial statements. Also, because it is necessary to find accounts quickly for posting and for management purposes, most companies have a systematic numbering scheme for identifying the accounts in the ledger, called the **chart of accounts**. The account number tells both the location of the account and its financial statement classification. Each company develops a chart of accounts that is most appropriate for its operations, and it would be only by chance that two companies would have the same numbering plan. A common three-digit numbering system that would be appropriate for a merchandising firm will be used in our example.

The first digit refers to the major financial statement classification. An account number beginning with the digit 1 is an asset, an account number beginning with the digit 2 is a liability, and so forth. In our chart, 111 to 199 are assigned to asset accounts, 211 to 299 to liability accounts, 311 to 399 to owner's equity accounts, 411 to 499 to sales or revenue accounts, 511 to 599 to cost of goods sold accounts, 611 to 699 to operating expense accounts, and 711 to 799 to other revenue and expense accounts.

The second digit refers to the subclassification of each major statement category. In our chart, under the asset accounts (111–199), subdivisions 111 to 129 are current assets accounts (second digits of 1 and 2), 131 to 139 are investment accounts (second digit of 3), 141 to 159 are property, plant, and equipment asset accounts (second digits of 4 and 5), and 161 to 179 are intangible asset accounts (second digits of 6 and 7).

The third digit refers to the specific account. Using this numbering scheme, the chart of accounts for Shafer Auto Parts Company would appear as in Table 9-1 (next page).

Cash	111	Sales	411
Short-Term Investments	112	Sales Returns and Allowances	412
Notes Receivable	113	Sales Discounts	413
Accounts Receivable	114	Purchases	511
Merchandise Inventory	116	Purchases Returns and	
Prepaid Insurance	117	Allowances	512
Store Supplies	118	Purchases Discounts	513
Office Supplies	119	Freight In	514
Investments	131	Sales Salaries Expense	611
Land	141	Rent Expense, Store Fixtures	612
Building	142	Freight Out Expense	613
Accumulated Depreciation,		Advertising Expense	614
Building	143	Insurance Expense, Selling	615
Delivery Equipment	144	Store Supplies Expense	616
Accumulated Depreciation,		Depreciation Expense,	
Delivery Equipment	145	Building	617
Office Equipment	146	Depreciation Expense, Delivery	
Accumulated Depreciation,		Equipment	618
Office Equipment	147	Office Salaries Expense	631
Trademark	161	Insurance Expense, General	632
Notes Payable	211	Office Supplies Expense	633
Accounts Payable	212	Depreciation Expense, Office	
Salaries Payable	213	Equipment	634
Mortgage Payable	221	Interest Income	711
Fred Shafer, Capital	311	Interest Expense	721
Fred Shafer, Withdrawals	312		

Using Classified Financial Statements

Objective 7
Use classified
financial
statements for
the simple
evaluation of
liquidity and
profitability

A major reason for classifying financial statements is to aid in the evaluation of a business. Though the analysis and interpretation of financial statements is the subject of Chapter 21, it is helpful at this point to explain briefly how classified financial statements can be used to show meaningful relationships. Earlier in this chapter you learned that the objectives of financial reporting, according to the Financial Accounting Standards Board, are to provide information that is useful in making investment and credit decisions, in judging cash flow prospects, and in understanding business resources and obligations and changes in them. These objectives are related to two of the more important goals of management (explained in Chapter 1)—those of (1) maintaining adequate liquidity and (2) achieving satisfactory profitability—because the decisions made by investors and creditors are based largely on their assessment of the company's potential liquidity and profitability. The following analysis focuses on these two important goals.

Evaluation of Liquidity

Liquidity means having enough money on hand to (1) pay a company's bills when they are due and (2) take care of unexpected needs for cash. Two measures of liquidity often used are working capital and the current ratio.

Working Capital The first measure, **working capital**, is the amount by which total current assets exceed total current liabilities. This is an important measure of liquidity, because current liabilities are debts to be paid within one year and current assets are assets to be realized in cash within one year. By definition, current liabilities will be paid out of current assets. So the excess of current assets over current liabilities is, in fact, the money on hand to continue business operations. It is the money or working capital that can be used to buy inventory, get credit, and finance expanded sales. Lack of working capital can lead to the failure of a company. For Shafer Auto Parts Company, the working capital is figured as follows:

Current Assets	$124,356
Less Current Liabilities	42,683
Working Capital	$ 81,673

As shown earlier, changes in working capital from one period to the next are examined with great care in the statement of changes in financial position.

Current Ratio The second measure of liquidity, called the current ratio, is closely related to working capital and is believed by many bankers and other kinds of creditors to be a good indicator of a company's ability to pay its bills and to repay outstanding loans. The **current ratio** is the ratio of current assets to current liabilities. For Shafer Auto Parts Company, it would be computed as follows:

$$\text{current ratio} = \frac{\text{current assets}}{\text{current liabilities}} = \frac{\$124,356}{\$42,683} = 2.9$$

Judging the current ratio of a company intelligently means comparing this year's ratio with those of earlier years and with similar measures in successful companies in the same industry. A very low current ratio can, of course, be unfavorable, but a very high one can be too. The latter may indicate that the company is not using its assets effectively.

Evaluation of Profitability

Equally important as paying one's bills on time is the goal of **profitability**—the ability to earn a satisfactory level of earnings. As a goal, profitability competes with liquidity for managerial attention because liquid assets, while important, are not the best profit-producing resources. Cash, for example, means purchasing power, but a satisfactory profit will result only if purchasing power is used to buy profit-producing (and less liquid) assets such as inventory and long-term assets.

Among the common measures that have to do with a company's ability to make a profit are (1) profit margin, (2) return on assets, (3) debt to equity, and (4) return on equity. To evaluate a company meaningfully, one must relate a company's profit performance to its past and its prospects as well as to the norms (averages) of other companies competing in the same industry.

Profit Margin The **profit margin** shows the percentage of each sales dollar that results in net income. It is figured by dividing net income by sales. For Shafer Auto Parts Company, it is as follows:

$$\text{profit margin} = \frac{\text{net income}}{\text{sales}} = \frac{\$17,881}{\$289,656} = .062 \ (6.2\%)$$

On each dollar of sales, Shafer Auto Parts Company made 6.2¢. A difference of 1 or 2 percent in a company's profit margin may mean the difference between a fair year and a very profitable one.

Return on Assets The profit margin does not take into consideration the assets necessary to produce the income. The **return on assets** ratio overcomes this deficiency by relating net income to average total assets. This ratio shows the relationship between an income statement measure and a balance sheet measure. Average total assets is computed by adding total assets at the beginning of the year to total assets at the end of the year and dividing by 2. Assuming total assets for Shafer Auto Parts Company were $148,620 at the beginning of the year, the return on assets ratio is figured as follows:

$$\text{return on assets} = \frac{\text{net income}}{\text{average total assets}}$$

$$= \frac{\$17,881}{(\$148,620 + \$158,916)\frac{1}{2}}$$

$$= \frac{\$17,881}{\$153,768} = .116 \ (\text{or } 11.6\%)$$

This measure shows how efficiently a company is using all its assets. It also indicates the income-generating strength of a company's resources. So for each dollar invested, Shafer Auto Parts Company's assets generated 11.6¢ of income.

Debt to Equity Another useful measure is the **debt to equity** ratio, which shows the proportion of the company financed by creditors in comparison to that financed by the owner. This ratio is computed by dividing total liabilities by owner's equity. A debt to equity ratio of 1.0 means that total liabilities equal owner's equity and that one-half of the company's assets are financed by creditors. A ratio of .5 would mean that one-third of the assets were financed by creditors. A company with a high debt to equity ratio is more vulnerable in poor economic times because it must continue to pay creditors what is owed them. Owner's investments, on the other

Chapter Nine

hand, do not have to be repaid and withdrawals can be deferred if the company is suffering because of a poor economy. The debt to equity ratio for Shafer Auto Parts Company is computed as follows:

$$\text{debt to equity} = \frac{\text{total liabilities}}{\text{owner's equity}} = \frac{\$60,483}{\$98,433} = .614 \text{ (or 61.4\%)}$$

Because its ratio of debt to equity is 61.4 percent, about 40 percent of Shafer Auto Parts Company is financed by creditors and roughly 60 percent is financed by Fred Shafer's capital.

The debt to equity ratio does not fit neatly into either the liquidity or profitability category. It is clearly very important to liquidity analysis because it relates to debt and its repayment. However, it is relevant to profitability for two reasons. First, creditors are interested in the proportion of the business that is debt financed because the more debt a company has, the more profit it must earn to protect the payment of interest to the creditors. Second, owners are interested in the proportion of the business that is debt financed because the amount of interest that must be paid affects the amount of profit that is left to provide a return on owner's investment.[8] The debt to equity ratio also shows how much expansion might be possible by borrowing additional long-term funds.

Return on Equity   Of course, Fred Shafer is interested in how much he as the owner earned on his investment in the business. His **return on equity** is measured by the ratio of net income to average owner's equity. The beginning and ending owner's equity needed to compute average owner's equity are found on the statement of owner's equity (Figure 9-6, page 323). The return on equity for the company is computed as follows:

$$\text{return on equity} = \frac{\text{net income}}{\text{average owner's equity}}$$

$$= \frac{\$17,881}{(\$100,552 + \$98,433)\frac{1}{2}}$$

$$= \frac{\$17,881}{\$99,492.50} = .180 \text{ (or 18.0\%)}$$

So in 19xx Shafer Auto Parts Company has earned 18¢ for every dollar invested by the owner, Fred Shafer.

The Annual Report of a Major Corporation

So far, very simple financial statements have been presented. Statements for major corporations, however, are quite complicated and have many other features. Figures 9-7 to 9-11 present the financial statements of a well-known firm, General Mills, Inc. These statements are a part of the

8. For a more detailed discussion of this topic, see *Statement of Financial Accounting Standards No. 34*, "Capitalization of Interest Costs" (Stamford, Conn.: Financial Accounting Standards Board, 1979).

company's **annual report**, which each year is printed and sent to stockholders as part of management's responsibility to report to the owners of the company. These statements and other data are also filed annually with the Securities and Exchange Commission.

The published annual report usually includes a number of features besides the financial statements. Among them are the letter to the stockholders from the president and chairman of the board, descriptions and pictures of the products and operations, lists of the principal officers of the corporation, and other items of interest. For example, it is possible to learn from General Mills' annual report that besides owning such well-known cereal brands as Cheerios and Wheaties, General Mills runs over 400 restaurants including the Red Lobster Inns, a large toy business including Parker Games (Monopoly), fashion and accessories businesses, and several specialty retailing businesses.

Objective 8
Identify the
major compo-
nents of a
corporate
annual report

Here, the focus is on the financial statements and their important features. Each feature of the financial statements explained is keyed to a numbered text paragraph. As beginning accounting students, you are not expected to understand everything in the report, but you should be able to relate these statements to the simpler ones presented earlier, for Shafer Auto Parts Company.

Consolidated Statements of Income (Figure 9-7)

1. The word **consolidated** used in the title of each statement means that General Mills owns other companies that are combined with it for financial reporting purposes.

2. The consolidated statements of income contain data for the years

Figure 9-7
Income
Statement for
General Mills,
Inc.

Consolidated Statements of Income ①

		Fiscal Year Ended ②	
(Amounts in Millions, Except Per Share Data)	May 30, 1982 (52 Weeks)	May 31, 1981 (53 Weeks)	May 25, 1980 (52 Weeks)
③ **Sales**	$5,312.1	$4,852.4	$4,170.3
Costs and Expenses:			
Cost of sales, exclusive of items below	3,081.6	2,936.9	2,578.5
Selling, general and administrative expenses	1,635.5	1,384.0	1,145.5
Depreciation and amortization expenses	113.2	99.5	81.1
Interest expense	75.1	57.6	48.6
Total Costs and Expenses	4,905.4	4,478.0	3,853.7
Earnings before Income Taxes	406.7	374.4	316.6
④ **Income Taxes**	(181.2)	(177.8)	(146.6)
Net Earnings	$ 225.5	$ 196.6	$ 170.0
⑤ **Earnings per Common Share and Common Share Equivalent**	$ 4.46	$ 3.90	$ 3.37
Average Number of Common Shares and Common Share Equivalents	50.6	50.4	50.5

Reprinted courtesy of General Mills, Inc. The footnotes to the financial statement, which are an integral part of the report, are not included.

Chapter Nine

ended in 1982, 1981, and 1980, shown in the columns at the right, to aid in the evaluation of the company over the years. Financial statements presented in this fashion are called **comparative financial statements.** This form of reporting is in accordance with generally accepted accounting principles. For General Mills, the fiscal year ends on the last Sunday in May.

3. General Mills uses the single-step form of the income statement and so includes all costs and expenses as a deduction from sales to arrive at Earnings before Income Taxes. The Sales figure represents net sales.

4. Income taxes, also referred to as **provision for income taxes,** or **income tax expense,** are the expense for federal and state income tax on General Mills' corporate income. Federal and state income tax laws do not treat sole proprietorships and partnerships as taxable units. The individuals involved are the tax-paying units, and they pay income tax on their share of the business income. Corporations, however, must report and pay income tax on earnings. For this reason, income tax expense is always shown as a separate item on the income statement of the corporation. The amount of the federal income tax is based on taxable net income as defined by the Internal Revenue Code, which may or may not agree with the income as determined by generally accepted accounting principles. Income taxes for corporations are substantial, often approaching 50 percent of income before taxes, and thus have a significant effect on business decisions. Most other taxes, such as property taxes and employment taxes, are shown among the operating expenses. Corporate income taxes are discussed in more detail in Chapter 17.

5. **Earnings per common share,** often called **net income per share** of common stock, is also unique to corporation reporting. Ownership in corporations is represented by shares of stock, and the net income per share is reported immediately below net income on the income statement. It is computed by dividing the net income by the average number of common shares and common share equivalents outstanding during the period. For example, if a company has a net income of $286,000 and has 100,000 shares of common shares and common share equivalents outstanding during the period, the earnings per share are $2.86. Investors have found the figure useful as a shorthand way of assessing a company's profit-earning success and also in evaluating the earnings in relation to the market price of the stock. General Mills reports both earnings per share and the average number of common shares outstanding. *Common share equivalents* are securities such as convertible debt and certain stocks or stock options that could result in more common shares being issued at the choice of the holders of the securities. Generally accepted accounting principles require that these shares be included in the number of shares used to compute earnings per share. Earnings per share are discussed in more detail in Chapter 17.

Consolidated Statements of Retained Earnings (Figure 9-8)

The consolidated statement of retained earnings for General Mills corresponds to the statement of owner's equity for a sole proprietorship. For

Figure 9-8
Statement of
Retained
Earnings for
General Mills,
Inc.

**Consolidated Statements
of Retained Earnings**

(Amounts in Millions, Except Per Share Data)	Fiscal Year Ended		
	May 30, 1982 (52 Weeks)	May 31, 1981 (53 Weeks)	May 25, 1980 (52 Weeks)
Retained Earnings at Beginning of Year, restated for vacation accrual	$ 942.0	$ 817.7	$ 712.1
Add net earnings	225.5	196.6	170.0
Deduct dividends on common stock of $1.64 per share in 1982, $1.44 per share in 1981, and $1.28 per share in 1980	(82.3)	(72.3)	(64.4)
Retained Earnings at End of Year	$1,085.2	$ 942.0	$ 817.7

Reprinted courtesy of General Mills, Inc. The footnotes to the financial statement, which are an integral part of the report, are not included.

General Mills it is a very simple statement. The only items affecting retained earnings were the addition of net earnings and the deduction of dividends. You may want to compare the net income amounts in this statement with those in the statement of income (Figure 9-7).

Consolidated Balance Sheets (Figure 9-9)

1. General Mills also presents consolidated balance sheets in comparative form. In contrast to the statements of income, retained earnings, and changes in financial position, only two years of comparative data are required for the balance sheet.

2. General Mills has a typical set of current assets.

3. General Mills has a large investment in land, buildings, and equipment. Note the contrast in handling the contra account Accumulated Depreciation and the contra account Allowance for Doubtful Accounts in the current asset section.

4. In place of an investment category and an intangible asset category, General Mills has a catchall group of Other Assets. The goodwill and other intangible assets arose mainly when other businesses were purchased.

5. The current liabilities section contains, among other typical current liabilities, the amount of long-term debt that must be paid within one year.

6. Another liability in General Mills' balance sheet is Long-Term Debt (excluding the current portion). Also included is Deferred Federal Income Taxes, an account that is sometimes hard for beginning students to understand. In general, deferred income taxes are income tax expenses that will not have to be paid until sometime in the future. The subject of deferred income taxes is covered in Chapter 18.

7. There are three items in the stockholders' equity section. As explained earlier in this chapter, common stock represents investments paid to the company by the stockholders, and retained earnings is the total of earn-

Figure 9-9
Balance Sheet
for General
Mills, Inc.

Consolidated Balance ①
Sheets

Assets

(In Millions)	May 30, 1982	May 31, 1981
Current Assets:		
Cash and short-term investments	$ 33.4	$ 39.1
② Receivables, less allowance for doubtful accounts of $16.0 in 1982 and $12.6 in 1981	408.6	391.4
Inventories	660.6	611.4
Investment in tax leases	124.9	—
Prepaid expenses	31.5	34.0
Total Current Assets	1,259.0	1,075.9
Land, Buildings and Equipment, at cost:		
Land	105.4	82.8
③ Buildings	560.5	494.1
Equipment	762.2	677.2
Construction in progress	124.0	114.5
	1,552.1	1,368.6
Less accumulated depreciation	(498.0)	(448.0)
Net Land, Buildings and Equipment	1,054.1	920.6
Other Assets:		
④ Goodwill and other intangible assets	198.0	201.5
Investments and miscellaneous assets	190.6	103.3
Total Other Assets	388.6	304.8
Total Assets	$2,701.7	$2,301.3

Liabilities and Stockholders' Equity

Current Liabilities:		
Accounts payable	$ 333.1	$ 322.8
Current portion of long-term debt	20.0	17.7
⑤ Notes payable	409.2	155.5
Accrued taxes	68.9	84.7
Accrued payroll	96.7	84.4
Other current liabilities	120.4	91.0
Total Current Liabilities	1,048.3	756.1
⑥ Long-Term Debt	331.9	348.6
Deferred Income Taxes	46.0	38.2
Other Liabilities and Deferred Credits	43.3	26.4
Total Liabilities	1,469.5	1,169.3
Stockholders' Equity:		
Common stock	206.6	196.6
⑦ Retained earnings	1,085.2	942.0
Less common stock in treasury, at cost	(19.5)	(6.6)
Cumulative foreign currency adjustment	(40.1)	—
Total Stockholders' Equity	1,232.2	1,132.0
Total Liabilities and Stockholders' Equity	$2,701.7	$2,301.3

Reprinted courtesy of General Mills, Inc. The footnotes to the financial statement, which are an integral part of the report, are not included.

ings accumulated over the life of the business less dividends declared. You are familiar with Common Stock and Retained Earnings. Common Stock in the Treasury is a contra owners' equity account that represents the cost of previously issued shares that have been bought back by the company.

8. At the bottom of each page of financial statements, the company reminds the reader that the notes accompanying the financial statements are an integral part of the statements and must be consulted in interpreting the financial statements.

Consolidated Statements of Changes in Financial Position (Figure 9-10)

1. The consolidated statements of changes in financial position for General Mills are complex, and their construction is the subject of Chapter 19. However, it is worthwhile for you to look at the major sections of the report at this point to see what you can learn from it about General Mills. The statement provides an overview of General Mills' major financing and investing activities during the year. It does this by explaining the net increase or decrease in cash and short-term investments during the year.

2. The first major section of the statement is the funds provided from operations, and it is divided into two parts. The first part shows that working capital (current assets minus current liabilities) was increased as a result of the company's profitable operations by $367.3 million in 1982. The second part shows the changes in the various components of working capital. The result is that the cash provided (increased) by the company's operations was $280.2 million.

3. The next section of the statement summarizes General Mills' investment activities. Note that in 1982 General Mills used a net amount of $293.7 million for investment activities, primarily for the purchase of land, buildings, and equipment and the purchase of other businesses.

4. In 1982, General Mills used a total of $82.3 million to pay dividends to its stockholders.

5. The next major section of this statement summarizes General Mills' financing activities. Note that General Mills received funds by issuing long-term debt, common stock, and notes payable. It used cash to reduce its long-term debt, to buy its own stock (treasury stock), and to invest in tax leases.

6. The results of all these investing and financing activities are summarized at the bottom of the statement. Note that the net effect of these activities on cash and short-term investments for 1982 is a small decrease of $5.7 million. One might conclude by looking just at this figure that not much happened at General Mills during the year, but by examining the components of the statement of changes in financial position, one can see that very much was happening. You will learn in Chapter 19 that there are other ways to set up a statement of changes in financial position.

Figure 9-10
Statement of
Changes in
Financial
Position for
General Mills,
Inc.

(In Millions)	Fiscal Year Ended		
	May 30, 1982 (52 Weeks)	May 31, 1981 (53 Weeks)	May 25, 1980 (52 Weeks)
Funds Provided from (Used for) Operations:			
Net earnings	$225.5	$196.6	$170.0
Depreciation and amortization	113.2	99.5	81.1
Deferred income taxes	12.2	16.7	2.6
Provision for losses on dispositions	33.8	—	—
Other	(17.4)	5.0	9.0
Working capital provided from operations	367.3	317.8	262.7
Changes in working capital affecting operations:			
(Increase) in receivables	(42.8)	(10.3)	(60.8)
(Increase) in inventories	(77.0)	(38.5)	(41.3)
(Increase) in prepaid expenses	(1.9)	(2.9)	(5.4)
Increase (decrease) in accrued taxes	(14.2)	(2.0)	22.2
Increase in accounts payable and other current liabilities	48.8	79.1	15.9
Cash Provided from Operations	280.2	343.2	193.3
Funds Provided from (Used for) Investment Activities:			
Purchase of land, buildings and equipment	(287.3)	(246.6)	(196.5)
Purchase price of businesses acquired, net of cash received	(9.3)	(81.0)	(3.1)
Cash provided from disposal of land, buildings and equipment	12.5	11.5	11.2
Proceeds from completed dispositions	24.8	11.9	—
Decrease in net non-cash assets caused by changes in foreign currency rates	37.7		
(Decrease) in stockholders' equity due to changes in foreign currency rates	(40.1)	—	—
Other	(32.0)	(4.7)	(26.0)
Net Cash Used for Investment Activities	(293.7)	(308.9)	(214.4)
Funds Used for Dividends	(82.3)	(72.3)	(64.4)
Funds Provided from (Used for) Financing Activities:			
Issuance of long-term debt	69.1	37.0	24.7
Common stock issued	19.6	23.0	2.7
Increase in notes payable	263.1	64.6	39.2
Reduction of long-term debt	(62.7)	(64.0)	(35.2)
Purchase of treasury stock	(22.5)	(22.6)	(3.8)
Investment in tax leases	(236.5)	—	—
Income tax cash flows from tax leases	60.0	—	—
Net Cash Provided from Financing Activities	90.1	38.0	27.6
Net (Decrease) in Cash and Short-Term Investments	(5.7)	—	(57.9)
Cash and Short-Term Investments at Beginning of Year	39.1	39.1	97.0
Cash and Short-Term Investments at End of Year	$ 33.4	$ 39.1	$ 39.1

② ③ ④ ⑤ ⑥

Reprinted courtesy of General Mills, Inc. The footnotes to the financial statement, which are an integral part of the report, are not included.

Notes to Consolidated Financial Statements

To meet the requirement of full disclosure, the company must add **notes to the financial statements** to help the user interpret some of the more complex items in the published financial statements. In fact, the need for explanation and further details has become so great in recent years that the notes often take up more space than the statements themselves. In the

General Mills annual report, the statements take four pages and the notes take ten pages! The notes to the financial statements can be put into three broad groups: summary of significant accounting policies, explanatory notes, and supplementary information notes.

Summary of Significant Accounting Policies In its *Opinion No. 22,* the Accounting Principles Board requires that the financial statements include a **summary of significant accounting policies.** In most cases, this summary is presented in the first note to the financial statements or as a separate part just before the notes. In this part, the company tells which generally accepted accounting principles it has followed in preparing the statements. In the General Mills report the company states the principles followed for land, buildings, and equipment:

Buildings and equipment are depreciated over estimated useful lives ranging from 3 to 50 years primarily using the straight line method. Accelerated depreciation methods are generally used for income tax purposes.

Other important accounting policies listed by General Mills deal with principles of consolidation, capitalization of construction interest, inventories, amortization of intangibles, research and development, income taxes, and earnings per share.

Explanatory Notes Other notes to the financial statements explain some of the items in the financial statements. General Mills showed the details of its Notes Payable account in the following table (dollars in millions):

	May 30, 1982	May 31, 1981
Banks	$ 85.0	$ 71.6
U.S. commercial paper	321.3	83.6
Miscellaneous	2.9	.3
Total	$409.2	$155.5

Other notes had to do with acquisitions, inventories, long-term debt, changes in capital stock, stock options, employee retirement plans, profit-sharing plans, income taxes, leases, the sale of a division, and legal suits and claims.

Supplementary Information Notes In recent years, the FASB and SEC have ruled that certain supplemental information be presented along with financial statements. An example is the quarterly report that most companies make to their stockholders and to the Securities and Exchange Commission. These quarterly reports, which are called **interim financial statements,** are in most cases reviewed but not audited by the company's independent CPA firm. General Mills presented unaudited interim figures from its 1982 quarterly statements, which are shown in the table on the next page (dollars in millions, except per share and market price amounts).

Interim data were presented for 1981 as well. In *Statement No. 14,* the FASB also requires that when the company engages in more than one principal line of business and/or region of the world, it report its opera-

	Three Months Ended			
	August	November	February	May
Fiscal 1982				
Sales	$1,345.1	$1,494.6	$1,233.8	$1,238.6
Gross profit	560.9	640.4	510.7	518.5
Net earnings	68.0	80.4	42.4	34.7
Net earnings per share	1.34	1.60	.84	.68
Dividends per share	.41	.41	.41	.41
Market price of common stock:				
High	$39\frac{1}{2}$	$38\frac{1}{2}$	$38\frac{3}{8}$	$42\frac{1}{8}$
Low	$32\frac{5}{8}$	$32\frac{7}{8}$	$32\frac{7}{8}$	$36\frac{3}{8}$

tions for each of these major segments. General Mills reported segment information for five principal lines of business and for four parts of the world. Finally, in *Statement No. 33*, the FASB requires that large companies report the effects of inflation on their operations over the last five years. In the case of General Mills, this complex note took two pages.

Five- or Ten-Year Financial Summary

Most companies present a five- or ten-year summary of key financial results and ratios in order that the investor or creditor may see the long-run progress of the company. General Mills offers this information.

Report of Management Responsibilities

A statement of management's responsibility for the financial statements and the system of internal control may accompany the financial statements. A part of the statement by General Mills' management is as follows:

The management of General Mills, Inc., includes corporate executives, operating managers, controllers and other personnel working full-time on company business. Such management is responsible for the fairness and accuracy of the financial statements of the company. The statements have been prepared in accordance with generally accepted accounting principles consistently applied, using management's best estimates and judgments, where appropriate. The financial information elsewhere in this report is consistent with the statements.

Management's Discussion and Analysis of Earnings

An analysis of the statement of earnings by management is also usually presented. In this section, management explains the difference from one year to the next. The management of General Mills describes the results of operations in the following way:

General Mills' sales were $5.3 billion in fiscal 1982, an increase of 9.5 percent over 1981. Approximately one-half of this gain resulted from unit volume increases. Sales growth in 1981 and 1980 was 16.4 percent and 15.3 percent, respectively, adjusting for operations disposed of in fiscal 1979. This year's growth rate reflected the lower rate of inflation coupled with the difficult economic climate. Toy Group sales in fiscal 1982 were down due to foreign exchange translation and a decline in the sale of hand-held electronic games.

Net earnings increased 14.7 percent in 1982. In the prior two years, net earnings grew 15.6 percent each year. Four of the company's five business areas— Consumer Foods, Fashion, Toys and Restaurants—set new earnings records, while Specialty Retailing, the smallest group, showed a decline in operating profits.

Report of Certified Public Accountants (Figure 9-11)

1. The **accountants' report** (or auditors' report) deals with the credibility of the financial statements. This report by independent public accountants gives the accountants' opinion about how fairly these statements have been presented. Using financial statements prepared by managers without an independent audit would be like having a judge hear a case in which he or she was personally involved or having a member of a team taking part in a football game act as a referee. Management, through its internal accounting system, is logically responsible for record keeping because it needs similar information for its own use in operating the business. The certified public accountant, acting independently, adds the necessary credibility to management's figures for interested third parties. Note that the certified public accountant reports to the board of directors and the stockholders rather than to management.

Figure 9-11
Accountants'
Report for
General Mills,
Inc.

Accountants' Report

The Stockholders and the Board of Directors of General Mills, Inc.:

We have examined the consolidated balance sheets of General Mills, Inc. and subsidiaries as of May 30, 1982 and May 31, 1981 and the related consolidated statements of income, retained earnings and changes in financial position for each of the years in the three-year period ended May 30, 1982. Our examinations were made in accordance with generally accepted auditing standards and, accordingly, included such tests of the accounting records and such other auditing procedures as we considered necessary in the circumstances.

In our opinion, the aforementioned consolidated financial statements present fairly the financial position of General Mills, Inc. and subsidiaries at May 30, 1982 and May 31, 1981 and the results of their operations and the changes in their financial position for each of the years in the three-year period ended May 30, 1982, in conformity with generally accepted accounting principles consistently applied during the period except for the change in 1982, with which we concur, in the method of accounting for foreign currency translation as described in note 2 to the consolidated financial statements.

Peat, Marwick, Mitchell & Co.

Minneapolis, Minnesota
July 23, 1982

Reprinted courtesy of General Mills, Inc. The footnotes to the financial statement, which are an integral part of the report, are not included.

In form and language, most auditors' reports are like the one shown in Figure 9-11. Usually such a report is short, but its language is very important. The report is divided into two parts: scope and opinion.

2. The **scope section** tells that the auditor has examined the consolidated balance sheet and the other financial statements for General Mills. It states that the examination was made in accordance with generally accepted auditing standards. These standards call for an acceptable level of quality in ten areas established by the American Institute of Certified Public Accountants. The CPAs also use any tests and other auditing procedures they think are needed to satisfy themselves about what is presented in the statements.

3. The **opinion section** states the results of the auditor's examination. The use of the word *opinion* is very important because the auditor does not certify or guarantee that the statements are absolutely correct. To do so would go beyond the truth, because many items, such as depreciation, are based on estimates. Instead, the auditor simply gives an opinion as to whether, overall, the financial statements "present fairly" the financial position and results of operations of the company. This means that the statements are prepared in accordance with generally accepted accounting principles. If in the auditor's opinion they are not, the auditor must explain why and to what extent they do not meet the standards.

Chapter Review

Review of Learning Objectives

1. State the objectives of financial reporting.

The objectives of financial reporting are that financial statements should provide (1) information useful in making investment and credit decisions, (2) information useful in assessing cash flow prospects, and (3) information about enterprise resources, claims to those resources, and changes in them.

2. State the qualitative characteristics of accounting information, and describe their interrelationships.

Understandability depends on the knowledge of the user and the ability of the accountant to provide useful information. Usefulness is a function of two primary characteristics, relevance and reliability. Relevance depends on the information's predictive value, feedback value, and timeliness. Reliability depends on the information's representational faithfulness and verifiability, both of which are related to neutrality.

3. Define and describe the use of the conventions of comparability and consistency, materiality, conservatism, full disclosure, and cost-benefit.

Because accountants' measurements are not exact, certain conventions have come to be applied in current practice to aid the reader in interpreting the financial statements. One of these conventions is consistency, which requires the use of the same accounting procedures from period to period. Second is materiality, which involves the relative importance of an item. Third is conservatism, which entails the use of the procedure that will be least likely to overstate assets and income. Fourth is full disclosure, which means including all relevant information in the financial statements. Fifth is cost-benefit, which suggests that after providing a minimum level of information, additional information should be provided only if the benefits derived from the information exceed the costs of providing it.

4. Identify and describe the basic components of a classified balance sheet.
The classified balance sheet is subdivided as follows:

Assets	Liabilities
Current Assets	Current Liabilities
Investments	Long-Term Liabilities
Property, Plant, and Equipment	**Owner's Equity**
Intangible Assets	(category depends on
	form of business)

A current asset is an asset that can reasonably be expected to be realized in cash during the next year or normal operating cycle. In general, assets are listed in the order of the ease of their conversion into cash. A current liability is a liability that can reasonably be expected to be paid during the next year or normal operating cycle. The owners' (stockholders') equity section for a corporation differs from that of a proprietorship in that it has subdivisions of contributed capital and retained earnings.

5. Define comprehensive income and distinguish between the multistep and single-step types of classified income statements.
Comprehensive income is, according to the FASB's definition, "the change in equity [net assets] of an entity during a period from transactions and other events and circumstances from nonowner sources." Condensed income statements for external reporting may be in multistep or single-step form. The multistep form arrives at net income through a series of steps, whereas the single-step form arrives at net income in a single step. There is usually a separate section in the multistep form for other revenues and expenses.

6. Relate a chart of accounts to classified financial statements.
The chart of accounts is a systematic numbering scheme for identifying accounts in the ledger. Each account has a unique number. The initial digits of the account number usually identify the major sections of classified financial statements.

7. Use classified financial statements for the simple evaluation of liquidity and profitability.
One major use of classified financial statements is to evaluate the company's liquidity and profitability. Two simple measures of liquidity are working capital and the current ratio. Four simple measures pertaining to profitability are profit margin, return on assets, debt to equity, and return on equity.

8. Identify the major components of a corporate annual report.
A corporation's annual report is the mechanism by which management reports to the stockholders the company's financial results for the year. The annual report has the following principal components: the four basic financial statements, notes to the financial statements, ten-year financial summary, report of management responsibilities, management's discussion and analysis of earnings, and the report of the certified public accountant.

Review Problem
Analyzing Liquidity and Profitability Using Ratios

Flavin Shirt Company has faced increased competition from imported shirts in recent years. Presented below is summary information for the past two years:

	19x2	19x1
Current Assets	$ 200,000	$ 170,000
Total Assets	880,000	710,000

Current Liabilities	90,000	50,000
Long-Term Liabilities	150,000	50,000
Owner's Equity	640,000	610,000
Sales	1,200,000	1,050,000
Net Income	60,000	80,000

Total assets and owner's equity at the beginning of 19x1 were $690,000 and $590,000, respectively.

Required

Use liquidity and profitability analyses to document the declining financial position of Flavin Shirt Company.

Answer to Review Problem

Liquidity analysis:

	Current Assets	Current Liabilities	Working Capital	Current Ratio
19x1	$170,000	$50,000	$120,000	3.40
19x2	200,000	90,000	110,000	2.22
Decrease in working capital			$ 10,000	
Decrease in current ratio				1.18

Both working capital and the current ratio declined because, although current assets increased by $30,000 ($200,000 − $170,000), current liabilities increased by the greater amount of $40,000 ($90,000 − $50,000) from 19x1 to 19x2.

Profitability analysis:

	Sales			Average Total Assets		Average Owner's Equity	
	Net Income	Sales	Profit Margin	Amount	Return on Assets	Amount	Return on Equity
19x1	$80,000	$1,050,000	7.6%	$700,000[1]	11.4%	$600,000[3]	13.3%
19x2	60,000	1,200,000	5.0%	795,000[2]	7.5%	625,000[4]	9.6%
Increase (Decrease)	$(20,000)	$ 150,000	(2.6%)	$ 95,000	(3.9%)	$ 25,000	(3.7%)

[1]($690,000 + $710,000) ÷ 2   [3]($590,000 + $610,000) ÷ 2
[2]($710,000 + $880,000) ÷ 2   [4]($610,000 + $640,000) ÷ 2

Net income decreased by $20,000 in spite of an increase in sales of $150,000 and an increase in average total assets of $95,000. The results were decreases in profit margin from 7.6 percent to 5.0 percent and in return on assets from 11.4 percent to 7.5 percent. The decrease in return on equity from 13.3 percent to 9.6 percent was not as much as the decrease in return on assets because the growth in total assets was financed by debt instead of owner's equity, as shown by the capital structure analysis below:

	Total Liabilities	Owner's Equity	Debt to Equity Ratio
19x1	$100,000	$600,000	16.7%
19x2	240,000	625,000	38.4%
Increase	$140,000	$ 25,000	21.7%

Total liabilities increased by $140,000 while owner's equity remained almost unchanged. As a result, the amount of the business financed by debt in relation to owner's equity increased from 16.7 percent to 40.0 percent.

Chapter Assignments

Questions

1. What are the three objectives of financial reporting?
2. What are the qualitative characteristics of accounting information, what is their significance, and how are they interrelated?
3. What are the accounting conventions, and how does each aid in the interpretation of financial information?
4. What is the purpose of classified financial statements?
5. What are four common categories of assets?
6. What criteria must an asset meet to be classified as current? Under what condition will an asset be considered current even though it will not be realized as cash within a year? What are two examples of assets that fall into this category?
7. In what order should current assets be listed?
8. How does one distinguish a short-term investment in the current asset section from a security in the investments section of the balance sheet?
9. What is an intangible asset? Give at least three examples.
10. Name the two major categories of liabilities.
11. What are the primary differences between the owners' equity section of a sole proprietorship or partnership and the corresponding section for a corporation?
12. Explain the difference between contributed capital and retained earnings.
13. Explain how the multistep form of the income statement differs from the single-step form. What are the relative merits of each?
14. Why are other revenues and expenses separated from operating revenues and expenses on the multistep income statement?
15. Why is there a need for a chart of accounts?
16. Define liquidity, and name two measures of liquidity.
17. How is the current ratio computed?

18. Which is the more important goal—liquidity or profitability?

19. Name four measures of profitability.

20. Evaluate this statement: "Return on assets is a better measure of profitability than profit margin."

21. What are some of the differences between the income statement for a sole proprietorship and that for a corporation?

22. Explain earnings per share and how this figure appears on the income statement.

23. What is the purpose of the accountant's report?

24. Why are notes to financial statements necessary?

Classroom Exercises

Exercise 9-1
Classification of Accounts—Balance Sheet
(L.O. 4)

The lettered items below represent a classification scheme for a balance sheet, and the numbered items are account titles. In the blank next to each account, write the letter indicating in which category it belongs.

a. Current assets
b. Investments
c. Property, plant, and equipment
d. Intangible assets

e. Current liabilities
f. Long-term liabilities
g. Owner's equity
h. Not on balance sheet

d 1. Patent
b 2. Building Held for Sale
a 3. Prepaid Rent
e 4. Wages Payable
f 5. Note Payable in Five Years
c 6. Building Used in Operations
b 7. Fund Held to Pay Off Long-Term Debt

a 8. Inventory
a 9. Prepaid Insurance
h 10. Depreciation Expense
a 11. Accounts Receivable
h 12. Interest Expense
e 13. Revenue Received in Advance
a 14. Short-Term Investments
c 15. Accumulated Depreciation — CR bal
g 16. T. Parker, Capital

Exercise 9-2
Classification of Accounts—Income Statement
(L.O. 5)

Using the classification scheme below for a multistep income statement, write in the blank the letter of the category in which each of the numbered accounts belongs.

a. Revenue
b. Cost of goods sold
c. Selling expense

d. General and administrative expense
e. Other revenue or expense
f. Not on income statement

b 1. Purchases
a 2. Sales Discounts
b 3. Beginning Merchandise Inventory
e 4. Dividend Income
c 5. Advertising Expense
d 6. Office Salaries Expense
c 7. Freight Out Expense
f 8. Unexpired Insurance
cd 9. Utility Expense

c 10. Sales Salaries
cd 11. Rent Expense
b 12. Purchases Returns
b 13. Freight In
c 14. Depreciation Expense, Delivery Equipment
f 15. Taxes Payable
e 16. Interest Expense

Exercise 9-3
Preparation of Income Statements
(L.O. 5)

The following data pertain to a sole proprietorship: Sales, $680,000; Cost of Goods Sold, $370,000; Selling Expense, $160,000; General and Administrative Expense, $100,000; Interest Expense, $4,000; Interest Revenue, $3,000.

1. Prepare a condensed single-step income statement.
2. Prepare a condensed multistep income statement.

**Exercise 9-4
Classified
Balance Sheet
Preparation
(L.O. 4)**

The following data pertain to a corporation: Cash, $3,500; Investment in Six-Month Government Securities, $14,600; Accounts Receivable, $38,000; Inventory, $40,000; Prepaid Rent, $1,200; Investment in Corporate Securities (long-term), $20,000; Land, $8,000; Building, $70,000; Accumulated Depreciation, Building, $14,000; Equipment, $152,000; Accumulated Depreciation, Equipment, $17,000; Copyright, $6,200; Accounts Payable, $32,000; Revenue Received in Advance, $2,800; Bonds Payable, $60,000; Common Stock—$10 par, 10,000 shares issued and outstanding, $100,000; Contributed Capital in Excess of Par Value, $50,000; Retained Earnings, $77,700.

Prepare a classified balance sheet.

**Exercise 9-5
Computation of
Ratios
(L.O. 7)**

On exam

The simplified balance sheet and income statement for a sole proprietorship appear as follows:

**Balance Sheet
December 31**

Assets		Liabilities	
Current Assets	$ 90,000	Current Liabilities	$ 30,000
Investments	10,000	Long-Term Liabilities	50,000
Property, Plant, and		Total Liabilities	$ 80,000
Equipment	283,000	**Owner's Equity**	
Intangible Assets	17,000	D. Alvis, Capital	320,000
		Total Liabilities and	
Total Assets	$400,000	Owner's Equity	$400,000

**Income Statement
For the Year Ended December 31, 19xx**

Revenue from Sales (net)	$800,000
Cost of Goods Sold	480,000
Gross Margin from Sales	$320,000
Operating Expenses	280,000
Net Income	$ 40,000

Total assets and owner's equity at the beginning of 19xx were $360,000 and $280,000, respectively.

1. Compute the following liquidity measures: (a) working capital and (b) current ratio.

2. Compute the following profitability measures: (a) profit margin, (b) return on assets, (c) debt to equity, and (d) return on equity.

Each of the statements below violates a convention in accounting. In each case, state which of the following concepts or conventions is violated: consistency, materiality, conservatism, full disclosure, or cost/benefit.

1. A company changes from one method of accounting for depreciation to another method.

2. The same company does not indicate in the financial statements that the method of depreciation was changed, nor does it specify the effect of the change on net income.

3. A series of reports that are time-consuming and expensive to prepare are presented to the board of directors each month even though the reports are never used.

4. A new office building next to the factory is debited to the Factory account because it represents a fairly small dollar amount in relation to the factory.

5. The asset account for a pickup truck still used in the business is written down to salvage value even though the carrying value under conventional depreciation methods is higher.

Interpreting Accounting Information

The questions in this exercise pertain to the financial statements of General Mills, Inc., in Figures 9-7 to 9-11 and are designed to help you read published financial statements. (Note that 1982 refers to the year ended May 30, 1982, and 1981 refers to the year ended May 31, 1981.)

Required

1. Consolidated balance sheet: (a) Did the amount of working capital increase or decrease from 1981 to 1982? By how much? (b) Did the current ratio improve from 1981 to 1982? (c) Does the company have long-term investments or intangible assets? (d) Why does the phrase "long-term debt" appear in both the current liability section and the other liability section? (e) Did the capital structure of General Mills change from 1981 to 1982? (f) How much is the contributed capital for 1982? How does it compare with retained earnings?

2. Consolidated income statement: (a) Does General Mills use a multistep or single-step form of income statement? (b) Is it a comparative statement? (c) Did net income increase from 1981 to 1982? (d) How significant are income taxes for General Mills? (e) Did net income per share increase from 1981 to 1982? (f) Did the profit margin increase from 1981 to 1982? (g) Did the return on assets increase from 1981 to 1982? (h) Did the return on equity increase from 1981 to 1982? On May 25, 1980, General Mills reported total assets of $2,012,400,000 and total stockholders' equity of $1,020,700,000.

3. Consolidated statement of retained earnings: (a) What figure came from the income statement? (b) Why are dividends listed in this statement? (c) What figures from this statement also appear in the balance sheet?

4. Statement of changes in financial position: (a) Why did the increases in Accounts Receivable and Accounts Payable have opposite effects on cash provided from operations? (b) What was the most important investment activity in 1982? (c) What was the most important financing activity in 1982? (d) How did these activities compare with those in prior years? (e) Why are Dividends on this statement, and on what other statement does this account appear? (f) How did the change in Cash and Short-Term Investments in 1982 compare to that in other years?

5. Report of the certified public accountants: (a) What was the name of General Mills' independent auditor? (b) Did the accountants think that the financial statements presented fairly the financial situation of the company? (c) Did the company comply with generally accepted accounting principles? (d) Were the accounting principles applied consistently among the years presented?

Problem Set A

**Problem 9A-1
Accounting
Conventions**
(L.O. 3)

In each case below, accounting conventions may have been violated.

1. Sampson Company closed its books on December 31, 19x8, before preparing its annual report. On December 30, 19x8, a fire had destroyed one of the company's two factories. Although the company had fire insurance and would not suffer a loss on the building, a significant decrease in sales in 19x9 was expected because of the fire. The fire damage was not reported in the 19x8 financial statements because the operations for that year were not affected by the fire.

2. Grady Drug Company spends a substantial portion of its profits on research and development. The company has been reporting its $2,500,000 expenditure for research and development as a lump sum, but management recently decided to begin classifying the expenditures by project even though the record-keeping costs will increase.

3. During the current year, Ruiz Company changed from one generally accepted method of accounting for inventories to another method.

4. Bailey Manufacturing Company uses the cost method for computing the balance sheet amount of inventory unless the market value of the inventory is less than the cost, in which case the market value is used. At the end of the current year, the market value is $77,000 and the cost is $80,000. Bailey uses the $77,000 figure to compute net income because management feels that the more cautious approach is to use the market figure.

5. Jensen Company has annual sales of $5,000,000. It follows the practice of charging any items costing less than $100 to expense in the year purchased. During the current year, it purchased several chairs at different times for the executive conference rooms at $97 each, including freight. Although the chairs were expected to last for at least ten years, the chairs were charged to expense in accordance with company policy.

Required

In each case, state the convention, if any, that has been violated, and explain briefly the nature of the violation. If you believe that the treatment is in accord with the convention and generally accepted accounting principles, explain why.

**Problem 9A-2
Forms of the
Income
Statement**
(L.O. 5)

Income Statement accounts from the June 30, 19xx, year-end adjusted trial balance of Sher Hardware Company appear on the next page. Beginning merchandise inventory was $172,500 and ending merchandise inventory is $156,750. The company is a sole proprietorship.

Required

From the information provided, prepare the following:

1. A detailed income statement

Account Name	Debit	Credit
Sales		527,770
Sales Discounts	4,110	
Sales Returns and Allowances	9,782	
Purchases	209,060	
Purchases Discounts		1,877
Purchases Returns and Allowances		4,282
Freight In	11,221	
Sales Salaries Expense	102,030	
Sales Supplies Expense	1,642	
Rent Expense, Selling Space	18,000	
Utilities Expense, Selling Space	11,256	
Advertising Expense	21,986	
Depreciation Expense, Selling Fixtures	6,778	
Office Salaries Expense	47,912	
Office Supplies Expense	782	
Rent Expense, Office Space	4,000	
Depreciation Expense, Office Equipment	3,251	
Utilities Expense, Office Space	3,114	
Postage Expense	626	
Insurance Expense	2,700	
Miscellaneous Expense	481	
Interest Expense	3,600	
Interest Income		800

2. A condensed income statement in multistep form
3. A condensed income statement in single-step form

Problem 9A-3
Classified
Balance Sheet
(L.O. 4)

Accounts from the June 30, 19xx, post-closing trial balance of Sher Hardware Company appear on the next page.

Required

From the information provided, prepare a classified balance sheet.

Problem 9A-4
Ratio Analysis—
Liquidity and
Profitability
(L.O. 7)

A summary of data taken from the income statements and balance sheets for Corrales Construction Supply for the past two years appears below.

	19x2	19x1
Current Assets	$ 135,000	$ 120,000
Total Assets	1,060,000	780,000
Current Liabilities	90,000	60,000
Long-Term Liabilities	300,000	200,000
Owner's Equity	670,000	520,000
Sales	2,200,000	1,740,000
Net Income	200,000	174,000

Total assets and owner's equity at the beginning of 19x1 were $680,000 and $420,000, respectively.

Account Name	Debit	Credit
Cash	3,700	
Short-Term Investments	11,350	
Notes Receivable	40,500	
Accounts Receivable	76,570	
Merchandise Inventory	156,750	
Prepaid Rent	2,000	
Prepaid Insurance	1,200	
Sales Supplies	426	
Office Supplies	97	
Land, Held for Future Expansion	11,500	
Fixtures	72,400	
Accumulated Depreciation, Fixtures		21,000
Office Equipment	24,100	
Accumulated Depreciation, Office Equipment		10,250
Trademark	4,000	
Accounts Payable		91,245
Salaries Payable		787
Interest Payable		600
Notes Payable (due in three years)		36,000
Henry Sher, Capital		244,711

Required

1. Compute the following measures of liquidity for 19x1 and 19x2: (a) working capital and (b) current ratio. Comment on the differences between the years.
2. Compute the following measures of profitability for 19x1 and 19x2: (a) profit margin, (b) return on assets, (c) debt to equity, and (d) return on equity. Comment on the change in performance from 19x1 to 19x2.

Problem 9A-5
Multistep
Income
Statement
(L.O. 5)

During her first year of operation, Judy, who owns Judy's Candy Shop, has kept accurate records of all revenues and expenses. At the end of the year, she prepared the income statement shown on the next page. Although the net income appears to be low in relation to sales, Judy finds the statement difficult to interpret. The shop's beginning inventory was $6,000, and the ending inventory was $5,500.

Required

1. To aid Judy in evaluating her company, prepare a condensed multistep income statement for her candy shop. Show the calculations of the components. Assume that salaries, supplies, and miscellaneous expenses should be divided in the ratio of $\frac{2}{3}$ sales expense and $\frac{1}{3}$ general expense and that rent, insurance, property taxes, depreciation, and utility expenses are allocated $\frac{3}{4}$ to sales expense and $\frac{1}{4}$ to general expense.
2. What incorrect classifications did Judy make?
3. What did you learn about Judy's Candy Shop by using the multistep form of income statement?

Judy's Candy Shop
Income Statement
December 31, 19xx

Revenues

Sales	$177,300	
Purchases Discounts	2,700	
Purchases Returns and Allowances	6,420	
Interest on Government Bonds	2,000	
Rent Income	4,000	
Total Revenues		$192,420

Expenses

Salaries Expense	$ 57,000	
Rent Expense	4,000	
Supplies Expense	1,500	
Interest Expense	2,900	
Insurance Expense	1,800	
Property Taxes Expense	2,400	
Miscellaneous Expense	900	
Sales Discounts	1,200	
Sales Returns and Allowances	945	
Owner's Withdrawals	8,000	
Purchases	89,051	
Depreciation Expense	3,200	
Utility Expense	2,400	
Total Expenses		175,296
Net Income		$ 17,124

Problem 9A-6
Classified
Financial
Statement
Preparation and
Evaluation
(L.O. 4, 5, 7)

The following accounts (in alphabetical order) and amounts were taken or calculated from the December 31, 19xx, year-end adjusted trial balance of Sunshine Lawn Equipment Center: Accounts Payable, $33,600; Accounts Receivable, $87,400; Accumulated Depreciation, Building, $26,200; Accumulated Depreciation, Equipment, $17,400; Building, $110,000; Cash, $6,250; Cost of Goods Sold, $246,000; Depreciation Expense, Building, $4,500; Depreciation Expense, Equipment, $6,100; Dividend Income, $50; Equipment, $75,600; Investment in General Motors—100 shares (short-term), $6,500; Interest Expense, $12,200; Inventory, $56,150; Land Held for Future Use, $20,000; Land Used in Operations, $29,000; Mortgage Payable, $90,000; Notes Payable (short-term), $25,000; Notes Receivable, $12,000; Operating Expenses Excluding Depreciation, $151,350; Sales (Net), $426,000; Tona Avila, Capital, $235,450; Tona Avila, Withdrawals, $23,900; Trademark, $6,750. Total assets at the beginning of the year were $373,950.

Required

1. From the information above, prepare (a) an income statement in condensed multistep form, (b) a statement of owner's equity, and (c) a classified balance sheet.

2. Calculate the following measures of liquidity: (a) working capital and (b) current ratio.

3. Calculate the following measures of profitability: (a) profit margin, (b) return on assets, (c) debt to equity, and (d) return on equity.

Problem 9A-7
Classified
Financial
Statement
Preparation and
Evaluation
(L.O. 4, 5, 7)

At the end of 19xx, the financial information below was available for Carlton Corporation, a company that distributes plastic products.

Income Statement Information

Cost of Goods Sold	$ 816,400
Dividend Income	22,600
General Expenses	122,860
Income Tax Expense	32,000
Interest Expense	5,900
Interest Income	6,450
Net Sales	1,486,000
Selling Expenses	472,200

Balance Sheet Information

Accounts Payable	$162,300	Investment in Plasco	
Accounts Receivable	183,430	Corporation (long-	
Accumulated Depreciation,		term)	$218,600
Delivery Equipment	27,910	Investment in U.S.	
Accumulated Depreciation,		Government Securities	
Fixtures	32,960	(short-term)	50,000
Accumulated Depreciation,		Notes Payable	
Office Equipment	11,260	(long-term)	80,000
Cash	23,520	Notes Payable	
Common Stock—$10 par		(short-term)	20,000
value, 20,000 shares		Notes Receivable	
issued and outstanding	200,000	(long-term)	30,000
Contributed Capital in		Notes Receivable	
Excess of Par Value	350,000	(short-term)	50,000
Delivery Equipment	126,200	Office Equipment	35,625
Fixtures	97,500	Prepaid Expenses	14,700
Franchise	42,000	Retained Earnings	296,245
Inventory	321,390	Revenue Received in	
		Advance	12,290

Total assets and total stockholders' equity at the beginning of 19xx were $1,039,165 and $780,555, respectively.

Required

1. From the information above, prepare the following: (a) an income statement in condensed single-step form (beneath the income statement show earnings per share) and (b) a classified balance sheet.

2. From the two statements you have prepared, compute the following measures: (a) for liquidity—working capital and current ratio and (b) for profitability—profit margin, return on assets, debt to equity, and return on equity.

Problem Set B

In each case below, an accounting convention may have been violated.

1. Mattis Corporation has in the past recorded operating expenses in general accounts for each classification, such as Salaries Expense, Depreciation Expense, and Utility Expense. Management has determined that in spite of the additional record-keeping costs, the company's income statement should break down each operating expense into its selling expense and administrative expense components.

2. Carter, the auditor of King Corporation, discovered that an official of the company may have authorized the payment of a $1,000 bribe to a local official. Management argued that, because the item was so small in relation to the size of the company ($1,000,000 in sales), the illegal payment should not be disclosed.

3. Elizabeth's Stereo Center built a small addition to the main building to house a new discount record division. Because of uncertainty about whether the record division would succeed or not, a conservative approach was taken by recording the addition as expense.

4. Since its origin ten years ago, R-B Electronics has used the same generally accepted inventory method. Because there has been no change in the inventory method, the company does not declare in its financial statements what inventory method it uses.

5. After careful study, Jumer Company, which has offices in forty states, has determined that, in the future, the depreciation of its office furniture should be changed. The new method is adopted for the current year, and the change is noted in the financial statements.

Required

In each case, state the convention, if any, that has been violated, and explain briefly the nature of the violation. If you believe that the treatment is in accord with the convention and generally accepted accounting principles, explain why.

Income Statement accounts from the December 31, 19xx, year-end adjusted trial balance of Dipple Furniture Company appear on the next page. Beginning merchandise inventory was $42,300 and ending merchandise inventory is $37,600. The company is a sole proprietorship.

Required

From the information provided, prepare the following:

1. A detailed income statement
2. A condensed income statement in multistep form
3. A condensed income statement in single-step form

Problem 9B-2
(continued)

Account Name	Debit	Credit
Sales		224,600
Sales Discounts	2,600	
Sales Returns and Allowances	9,400	
Purchases	111,100	
Purchases Discounts		1,900
Purchases Returns and Allowances		4,060
Freight In	8,700	
Sales Salaries Expense	31,080	
Sales Supplies Expense	820	
Rent Expense, Selling Space	3,600	
Utilities Expense, Selling Space	1,480	
Advertising Expense	8,400	
Depreciation Expense, Delivery Equipment	2,200	
Office Salaries Expense	14,620	
Office Supplies Expense	4,380	
Rent Expense, Office Space	1,200	
Utilities Expense, Office Space	500	
Postage Expense	1,160	
Insurance Expense	1,340	
Miscellaneous Expense	720	
General Management Salaries Expense	21,000	
Interest Expense	2,800	
Interest Income		210

**Problem 9B-3
Classified
Balance Sheet**
(L.O. 4)

Accounts from the December 31, 19xx, after-closing trial balance of Dipple Furniture Company appear on the next page.

Required

From the information provided, prepare a classified balance sheet.

Chapter Nine

Problem 9B-3
(continued)

Account Name	Debit	Credit
Cash	7,200	
Short-Term Investments	7,800	
Notes Receivable	2,000	
Accounts Receivable	69,000	
Merchandise Inventory	37,600	
Prepaid Rent	400	
Unexpired Insurance	1,200	
Sales Supplies	320	
Office Supplies	110	
Deposit for Future Advertising	920	
Building, Not in Use	12,400	
Land	5,600	
Delivery Equipment	10,300	
Accumulated Depreciation, Delivery Equipment		6,200
Franchise Fee	1,000	
Accounts Payable		26,860
Salaries Payable		1,300
Interest Payable		210
Long-Term Notes Payable		20,000
Ernest Dipple, Capital		101,280

**Problem 9B-4
Ratio Analysis—
Liquidity and
Profitability**
(L.O. 7)

Rose Products Company has been disappointed with its operating results for the past two years. As accountant for the company, you have the following information available (see top of page 352).

	19x2	19x1
Current Assets	$ 40,000	$ 30,000
Total Assets	140,000	100,000
Current Liabilities	20,000	10,000
Long-Term Liabilities	20,000	—
Owner's Equity	100,000	90,000
Sales	252,000	200,000
Net Income	12,000	10,000

Total assets and total owner's equity at the beginning of 19x1 were $90,000 and $80,000, respectively.

Required

1. Compute the following measures of liquidity for 19x1 and 19x2: (a) working capital and (b) current ratio. Comment on the differences between the years.
2. Compute the following measures of profitability for 19x1 and 19x2: (a) profit margin, (b) return on assets, (c) debt to equity, and (d) return on equity. Comment on the change in performance from 19x1 to 19x2.

Problem 9B-5
Multistep
Income
Statement
(L.O. 5)

Margo's Card Shop has been in business for one year. During this time, Margo has kept track of all her revenues and expenses. She feels that her sales have been good, but her profit is not as high as she would like. As a friend, you have agreed to look at her income statement. Margo gives you the statement shown on the next page.

Required

1. Prepare a condensed multistep income statement in good form for Margo's Card Shop, taking into account beginning merchandise inventory of $11,200 and ending merchandise inventory of $12,400. Show the calculations of the components.
2. What incorrect classifications did Margo make?
3. Comment on the usefulness of the multistep form over the single-step form of income statement as applied to Margo's Card Shop. (Hint: What have you learned about Margo's operations from the multistep form?)

Problem 9B-6
Classified
Financial
Statement
Preparation and
Evaluation
(L.O. 4, 5, 7)

The following accounts (in alphabetical order) and amounts were taken or calculated from the year-end adjusted trial balance of Stern's Slacks Company on June 30, 19xx: Accounts Payable, $16,000; Accounts Receivable, $12,360; Accumulated Depreciation, Building, $15,600; Accumulated Depreciation, Equipment, $7,900; Building, $59,000; Cash, $1,340; Cost of Goods Sold, $106,050; Depreciation Expense, Building, $3,000; Depreciation Expense, Equipment, $3,950; Equipment, $29,500; Interest Expense, $4,170; Interest Income, $220; Inventory, $22,440; Robert Stern, Capital, $60,190; Land Held for Future Use, $31,100; Land Used in Operations, $11,000; Mortgage Payable, $50,000; Notes Payable (short-term), $6,000; Notes Receivable, $1,400; Operating Expense Excluding Depreciation, $79,250; Revenue Received in Advance, $350; Sales (Net), $213,300; Investment in Xerox Corporation—100 shares (short-term), $5,000. Total assets at the beginning of the fiscal year were $130,360.

Required

1. From the information above, prepare (a) an income statement in condensed multistep form, (b) a statement of owner's equity, and (c) a classified balance sheet.

Margo's Card Shop
Income Statement
December 31, 19xx

Revenues

Sales for the Year	$117,300	
Interest on Savings Account	840	
Rent on Building Not Used in Business	3,300	
Purchases Discounts	1,000	
Total Revenues		$122,440

Expenses

Salaries, Sales Staff	$ 19,300	
Salaries, Administrative	17,070	
Rent, Fixtures: $\frac{2}{3}$ Sales, $\frac{1}{3}$ Administration	4,800	
Supplies Expense: $\frac{3}{4}$ Sales, $\frac{1}{4}$ Administration	840	
Interest on Debt	2,940	
Insurance: $\frac{1}{2}$ Sales, $\frac{1}{2}$ Administration	2,120	
Property Taxes: $\frac{2}{3}$ Sales, $\frac{1}{3}$ Administration	2,430	
Miscellaneous Expenses: $\frac{1}{2}$ Sales, $\frac{1}{2}$ Administration	1,480	
Sales Discounts	940	
Advertising	10,060	
Withdrawals by Owner	6,000	
Purchases	42,460	
Depreciation Expense: $\frac{2}{3}$ Sales, $\frac{1}{3}$ Administration	4,500	
Utility Expense: $\frac{2}{3}$ Sales, $\frac{1}{3}$ Administration	3,990	
Total Expenses		118,930
Net Income		$ 3,510

2. Calculate the following measures of liquidity: (a) working capital and (b) current ratio.

3. Calculate the following measures of profitability: (a) profit margin, (b) return on assets, (c) debt to equity, and (d) return on equity.

Problem 9B-7
Classified
Financial
Statement
Preparation and
Evaluation
(L.O. 4, 5, 7)

Diamond Corporation sells outdoor sports equipment. At the end of the year 19xx, the following financial information was available from the income statement: Administrative Expenses, $39,400; Cost of Goods Sold, $175,210; Federal Income Tax Expense, $6,335; Interest Expense, $11,320; Interest Income, $1,400; Net Sales, $347,465; Selling Expenses, $110,100.

The following information was available from the balance sheet: Accounts Payable, $16,300; Accounts Receivable, $52,400; Accumulated Depreciation,

Delivery Equipment, $8,550; Accumulated Depreciation, Store Fixtures, $21,110; Cash, $12,400; Common Stock—$1 par value, 5,000 shares issued and outstanding, $5,000; Contributed Capital in Excess of Par Value, $45,000; Delivery Equipment, $42,900; Inventory, $68,270; Investment in M Corporation (long-term), $28,000; Investment in U.S. Government Securities (short-term), $19,800; Notes Payable (long-term), $50,000; Notes Payable (short-term), $25,000; Retained Earnings, $126,500; Short-Term Prepaid Expenses, $2,880; Store Fixtures, $70,810.

Total assets and total stockholders' equity at the beginning of 19xx were $262,200 and $170,000, respectively.

Required

1. From the information above, prepare the following: (a) an income statement in single-step form (beneath the income statement, show earnings per share) and (b) a classified balance sheet.
2. From the two statements you have prepared, compute the following measures: (a) for liquidity—working capital and current ratio and (b) for profitability—profit margin, return on assets, debt to equity, and return on equity.

Financial Decision Case 9-1

First National Bank
(L.O. 7)

Steve Sullivan was recently promoted to loan officer at the First National Bank. He has authority to issue loans up to $50,000 without approval from a higher bank official. This week two small companies, Handy Harvey and Shiela's Fashions, have each submitted a proposal for a six-month $50,000 loan. In order to prepare a financial analysis of the two companies, Steve has obtained the information summarized below.

Handy Harvey, Inc., is a local lumber and home improvement company. Because sales have increased so much during the past two years, Handy Harvey has had to raise additional working capital, especially as represented by receivables and inventory. The $50,000 loan is needed to assure the company of enough working capital for the next year. Handy Harvey began the year with total assets of $740,000 and stockholders' equity of $260,000, and during the past year the company had a net income of $40,000 on sales of $760,000. The company's current unclassified balance sheet appears as follows:

Assets		Liabilities and Stockholders' Equity	
Cash	$ 30,000	Accounts Payable	$200,000
Accounts Receivable (net)	150,000	Note Payable (short-term)	100,000
Inventory	250,000	Mortgage Payable	200,000
Land	50,000	Common Stock	250,000
Buildings (net)	250,000	Retained Earnings	50,000
Equipment (net)	70,000	Total Liabilities and	
Total Assets	$800,000	Stockholders' Equity	$800,000

Shiela's Fashions, Inc., has for three years been a successful clothing store for young professional women. The leased store is located in the downtown financial district. Shiela's loan proposal asks for $50,000 to pay for stocking a new line of professional suits for working women during the coming season. At the beginning of the year, the company had total assets of $200,000 and total stockholders' equity of $114,000. Over the past year, the company earned a net income of

$36,000 on sales of $480,000. The firm's unclassified balance sheet at the current date appears as follows:

Assets		Liabilities and Stockholders' Equity	
Cash	$ 10,000	Accounts Payable	$ 80,000
Accounts Receivable (net)	50,000	Accrued Liabilities	10,000
Inventory	135,000	Common Stock	50,000
Prepaid Expenses	5,000	Retained Earnings	100,000
Equipment (net)	40,000	Total Liabilities and	
Total Assets	$240,000	Stockholders' Equity	$240,000

Required

1. Prepare a financial analysis of both companies' liquidity before and after receiving the proposed loan. Also, compute profitability ratios before and after as appropriate. Write a brief summary of the effect of the proposed loan on each company's financial position.

2. To which company do you suppose Steve would be most willing to make a $50,000 loan? What are the positive and negative factors related to each company's ability to pay back the loan in the next year? What other information of a financial or nonfinancial nature would be helpful before making a final decision?

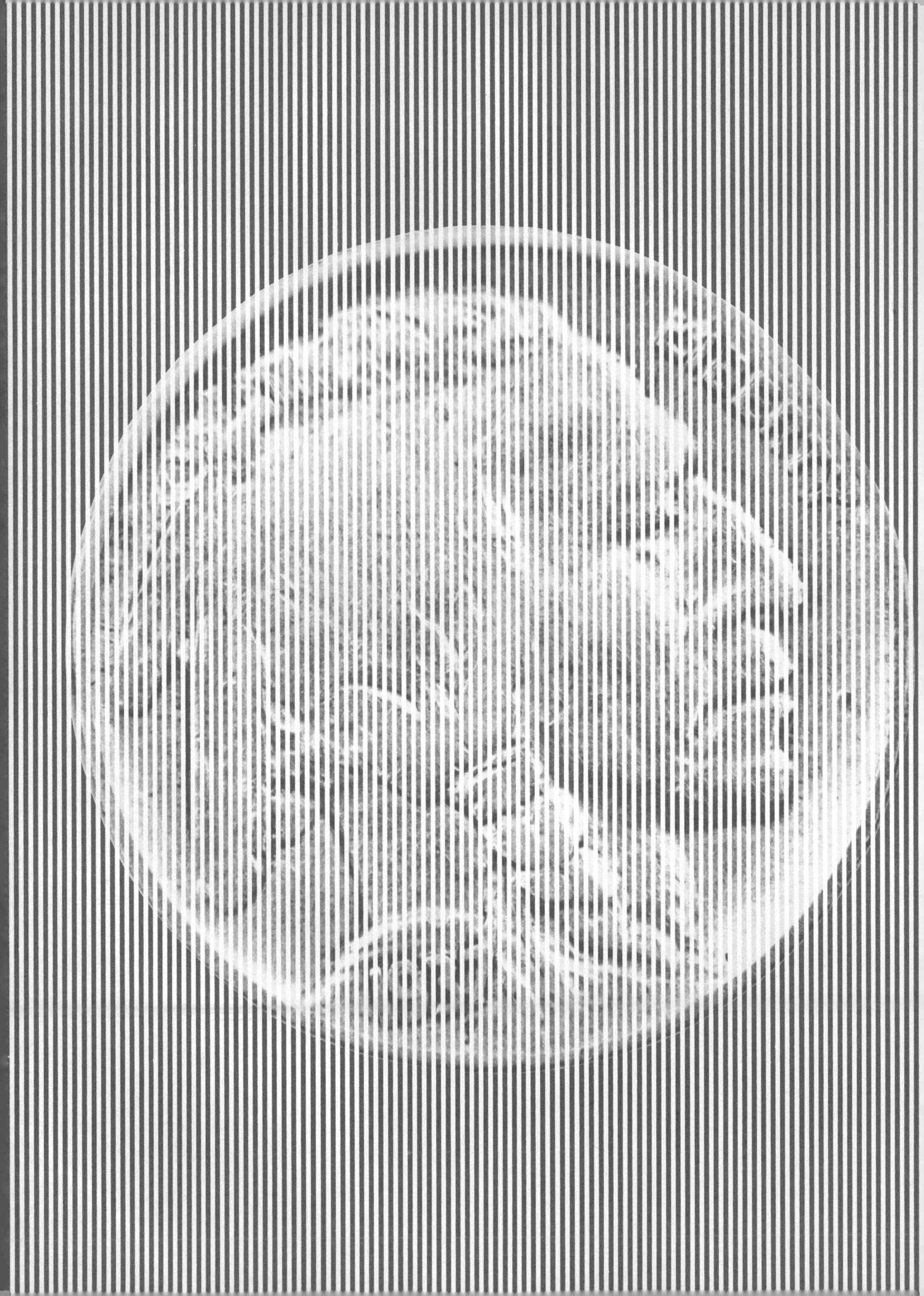

Part Three

Measuring and Reporting Assets and Current Liabilities

In Parts I and II, the basic accounting model was first presented and then extended to more complex applications.

Part III considers each of the major types of assets as well as the category of current liabilities and payroll accounting, with particular emphasis on the effect of their measurement on net income and their presentation in the financial statements. It also provides an overview of revenue and expense issues and discusses the effects of inflation on accounting.

Chapter 10 focuses on the major types of short-term liquid assets: cash and short-term investments, accounts receivable, and notes receivable.

Chapter 11 presents the accounting concepts and techniques associated with inventories.

Chapter 12 deals with current liabilities and payroll accounting.

Chapter 13 discusses property, plant, and equipment, and natural resources, including the concepts and techniques of depreciation and depletion.

Chapter 14 discusses in more detail the application of the matching rule to revenue recognition and to allocation of expired costs. In addition, accounting for price level changes and current values is described and related to the requirements of FASB Statement No. 33.

Learning Objectives

Chapter Ten

Short-Term Liquid Assets

In this chapter, you study the measurement and reporting issues associated with short-term liquid assets. **Short-term liquid assets** are assets that arise from cash transactions and the extension of credit. They include cash, short-term investments, accounts receivable, and notes receivable. They are useful because they are quickly available for paying current obligations. Of course, assets used in the productive functions of the business are less liquid. Among these productive assets are inventories; property, plant, and equipment; natural resources; and intangibles. After studying this chapter, you should be able to meet the learning objectives listed on the left.

Accounting for Cash and Short-Term Investments

Of all the short-term liquid assets, cash is the most liquid and the most readily available to pay debts. In Chapter 8, we discussed the control of cash receipts and payments, but we did not deal with the content of the Cash account on the balance sheet. Cash is generally considered to consist of coin and currency on hand, checks and money orders received from customers, and deposits in bank checking accounts. Certificates of deposit and time deposits such as savings accounts are also considered cash because of their ready availability. The cash account may also include an amount that is not entirely free to be spent called a **compensating balance.** A compensating balance is a minimum amount that a bank requires a company to keep in its bank account as part of a credit-granting arrangement. This arrangement does, in fact,

Objective 1
Describe
accounting for
cash and short-
term invest-
ments

restrict cash and may reduce a company's liquidity. Therefore, the SEC requires companies to disclose in a note to the financial statements the amount of any compensating balance.

Sometimes during the year, a company may find that it has more cash on hand than it needs to pay current obligations. Because it is not wise to allow this cash to lie idle, especially in periods of high interest rates, the company may invest the excess cash in government securities or other marketable securities. Such investments are considered current assets because the intent is to hold the investments only until needed to pay current obligations.

On the balance sheet, these investments are called **short-term invest-ments** or **marketable securities.** Though the term *marketable securities* is used widely, it is preferable to call them short-term investments because long-term investments may also contain securities that are just as market-able as the short-term investments. The difference is that management plans to hold the long-term investments for an indefinite period of time longer than one year.

Some companies are so successful that they accumulate large amounts of cash from earnings, which they put into short-term investments. For example, in a recent year General Motors Corporation's balance sheet contained the following information:

Current Assets

Cash	$ 297,100,000
Marketable Securities	2,739,300,000

Short-term investments are at first recorded at cost. Suppose that on March 1, ST Company purchased U.S. Treasury bills, which are short-term debt of the U.S. government, for $97,000 and that the bills will mature in 90 days at $100,000. The following entry would be made by ST:

Mar. 1	Short-Term Investments	97,000	
	Cash		97,000
	Purchase of U.S. Treasury bills that mature in 90 days at $100,000		

Income on short-term investments is recorded as received. For example, dividends and interest on stocks and bonds held as short-term investments would be recorded as Dividend Income or Interest Income at the time it is received. In the case of the investment by ST Company, the interest is received when the bills are paid at maturity, as shown in the entry below:

May 30	Cash	100,000	
	Interest Income		3,000
	Short-Term Investments		97,000
	Receipt of cash on U.S. Treasury Bills and recognition of related income		

When short-term investments are sold, a gain or loss usually results.

Suppose that ST Company sells 5,000 shares of an investment in Mobil Corporation on December 5. It bought the shares for $35 per share, including broker's commissions. When it sells them at $25 per share net of (not including) broker's commissions, the following entry results:

Dec. 5	Cash	125,000	
	Loss on Sale of Investments	50,000	
	Short-Term Investments		175,000
	Sale of 5,000 shares of Mobil		
	Corporation at $25 net of		
	commissions		

In *Statement of Financial Accounting Standards No. 12*, the Financial Accounting Standards Board requires that investments in debt securities such as U.S. Treasury bills or corporate debt be listed at cost, unless there is reason to believe the value of the security is permanently impaired. However, the board requires that investments in equity securities such as capital stock be reported at the lower of historical cost or the market value determined at the balance sheet date.[1] For example, assume that at its year end of December 31, ST Company still owns 10,000 shares of Mobil Corporation that it purchased for $35 per share and that are now worth $25 per share. The balance sheet presentation of this information is as follows:

Current Assets

Short-Term Investments (at lower of cost or
  market; cost equals $350,000) $250,000

Note that this method is inconsistent with the concept of historical cost and with the consistency convention. First, under historical cost the cost value would be presented on the balance sheet until the asset is sold. Second, if decreases in the market value below historical cost are to be recognized, then the consistency convention would seem to require that increases in the market value also be recognized. Neither principle is followed in the case of short-term investments. Accountants justify these inconsistencies on the basis of the conservatism convention. That is, they recognize the potential loss immediately but put off recognition of any potential gain until it is actually realized. The accounting entries related to the lower-of-cost-or-market method are the same for short- and long-term investments, but we will put off illustrating them until the discussion of long-term investments in Chapter 20.

Accounting for Accounts Receivable

The other two major types of short-term liquid assets are accounts receivable and notes receivable. Both result from credit sales to custom-

1. *Statement of Financial Accounting Standards No. 12,* "Accounting for Certain Marketable Securities" (Stamford, Conn.: Financial Accounting Standards Board, 1975).

ers. Because credit is available to individuals, many people can buy valuable things such as automobiles, refrigerators, and other appliances that they could not have afforded without credit. Retail companies such as Sears, Roebuck and Company have made credit available to nearly every responsible person in the United States. We live in a credit card society, where every field of retail trade has expanded by allowing customers the right to make payments a month or more after the date of sale. What is not so apparent is that credit at the wholesale and manufacturing levels has expanded even more than that at the retail level. The purpose of the rest of this chapter is to show the accounting for accounts and notes receivable, which play a key role in this credit expansion.

Accounts receivable are short-term liquid assets that arise from sales on credit to customers at either the wholesale or the retail level. This type of credit is often called **trade credit.**

Credit Policies and Uncollectible Accounts

Companies that make sales on credit naturally do not want to sell to customers who will not pay. Therefore, most companies that sell on credit at either the retail or the wholesale level develop certain control procedures to increase the likelihood of selling only to customers who will pay when they are supposed to. As a result of these procedures, a company generally sets up a credit department. This department's responsibilities include the examination of each person or company that applies for credit and the approval or disapproval of the sale to that customer on credit. Typically, the credit department will ask for information on the customer's financial resources and debts. In addition, it may check personal references and established credit bureaus, which may have information about the customer. On the basis of this information, the credit department will decide whether to sell on credit to that customer. It may recommend the amount of payment, limit the amount of credit, or ask the customer to put up certain assets as security for the credit.

Regardless of how thorough and efficient its credit control system is, the company will always have some customers who will not pay. The accounts owed by such customers are called **uncollectible accounts,** or bad debts, and are a loss or an expense of selling on credit. One might ask, why does a company sell on credit if it expects that some of its accounts will not be paid? The answer is that by extending credit, the company expects to sell much more than it would if it did not sell on credit and, as a result, to make more profit overall. When a customer does not pay his or her account, it reflects the company's poor judgment in making the sale in the first place. But some uncollectible accounts are expected and are the natural result of management's wish to make a profit on total sales. Management may be so conservative in granting credit that it has no credit sales, or it may have very small losses on credit sales. In such cases, it may be losing profitable business from perfectly good customers it has rejected.

Matching Losses on Uncollectible Accounts with Sales

*Objective 2
Explain why
estimated losses
from uncol-
lectible accounts
are important to
income determi-
nation*

A balance must be reached between an acceptable level of credit losses and the potential profit on total credit sales. The loss occurs on an individual uncollectible account at the moment credit is granted and a sale is made to the customer. In accounting for these uncollectible accounts, the basic rule of accounting is the matching rule, as it has been in dealing with other issues in this book. Expenses should be matched against the sales they help to produce. If bad debt losses are incurred in the process of building sales income, they should be charged against the sales income they helped to create. Of course, a company does not know at the time of a credit sale that the debt will not be collected. In fact, it may take a year or more to exhaust every possible means of collection. Even though the loss may not be specifically identified until a later accounting period, it is still an expense of the accounting period in which the sale was made. Therefore, losses from the uncollectible accounts must be estimated for the accounting period, and this estimate becomes the expense for the year.

For example, let us assume that Cottage Sales Company made most of its sales on credit during its first year of operation. At the end of the year, accounts receivable amounted to $100,000. On this date, management reviewed the status of the accounts receivable, particularly noting accounts past due. Approximately $6,000 of the $100,000 of accounts reviewed were estimated to be uncollectible. Thus the uncollectible accounts expense for the first year of operation amounted to $6,000. The following adjusting entry would be made on December 31 of that year:

Dec. 31	Uncollectible Accounts Expense	6,000
	Allowance for Uncollectible	
	Accounts	6,000
	To record the estimated	
	uncollectible accounts expense	
	for the year 19xx	

The uncollectible accounts expense created by the debit part of the entry is closed to the Income Summary account in the same manner as the other expense accounts. The **allowance for uncollectible accounts** that was credited in the above journal entry will appear in the balance sheet as a deduction from the face value of accounts receivable. It serves to reduce the accounts receivable to the amount that is expected to be collectible, as shown in Figure 10-1.

Allowance for Uncollectible Accounts

The allowance method of accounting for uncollectible accounts argues that losses from an uncollectible account occur at the moment the sale is made to the customer who will not pay. Because the company does not know until after the sale that the customer will not pay, the amount of the loss must be estimated if it is to be matched against the sales or revenue for the period. It is not possible, of course, to credit the account of any particular customer to reflect the overall estimate of the year's credit

Figure 10-1
Partial Balance
Sheet Showing
Allowance for
Uncollectible
Accounts

Cottage Sales Company
Partial Balance Sheet
December 31, 19xx

Current Assets		
Cash		$ 10,000
Short-term Investments		15,000
Accounts Receivable	$100,000	
Less Allowance for Uncollectible Accounts	6,000	94,000
Inventory		56,000
Total Current Assets		$175,000

losses. Also, it is not possible to credit the Accounts Receivable controlling account in the general ledger because doing so would cause the controlling account to be out of balance with the many customers' accounts in the subsidiary ledger. Therefore, as described above, a separate account called Allowance for Uncollectible Accounts is used to carry the amount of estimated uncollectible accounts. In Figure 10-1, the allowance for uncollectible accounts is deducted from the gross accounts receivable in the current assets section of the balance sheet. It is called a contra account, like the Accumulated Depreciation account illustrated earlier in this book.[2]

As shown above, the initial balance of the Allowance for Uncollectible Accounts account is established by an adjusting entry made at the end of the year. As accounts are recognized as uncollectible during the following accounting periods, they are written off by a debit to the Allowance account and a credit to the Accounts Receivable account. In other words, the balance of the Allowance account is reduced as people or companies who owe the company do not pay. For this reason, the credit balance of the Allowance account at any one time represents the remaining estimated credit sales from earlier accounting periods that have not yet been identified as being uncollectible. This credit balance is offset against the total accounts receivable on the balance sheet to present the amount of accounts receivable expected to be collected.

The Allowance for Uncollectible Accounts will often have other titles such as Allowance for Doubtful Accounts or Allowance for Bad Debts. Once in a while, the older phrase Reserve for Bad Debts will be seen, but in modern practice it should not be used. Bad Debts Expense is often used as another title for Uncollectible Accounts Expense.

2. Note that although the purpose of the allowance for uncollectible accounts is to reduce the gross accounts receivable to the estimated amount collectible (estimated value), the purpose of the Accumulated Depreciation account is not to reduce the gross plant and equipment accounts to realizable value. The purpose of the Accumulated Depreciation account is to show how much of the cost of the plant and equipment has been allocated as an expense to previous accounting periods.

Estimating Uncollectible Accounts Expense

Because it is impossible to know which accounts will be uncollectible at the time financial statements are prepared at the end of the accounting period, it is necessary to give an estimate of the expense for the year that is large enough to cover the expected losses. Of course, estimates can vary widely. If one takes an optimistic view and projects a small loss from uncollectible accounts, the resulting net accounts receivable will be larger than if one takes a pessimistic view. Also, the net income will be larger under the optimistic view because the estimated expense will be smaller. The company's accountant makes an estimate based on past experience, modified by current economic conditions. For example, losses from uncollectible accounts are normally expected to be greater in periods of recession than in periods of economic growth. But the final decision as to how much is enough is made by management. This decision will depend on objective information such as the accountant's analyses and on certain qualitative factors such as how investors, bankers, creditors, and others may view the performance of the company. Regardless of the qualitative considerations, the estimated losses from uncollectible accounts should be realistic.

The accountant has two common methods available for estimating uncollectible accounts expense for an accounting period: the percentage of net sales method and the accounts receivable aging method.

Percentage of Net Sales Method   The **percentage of net sales method** asks the question, How much of this year's net sales will not be collected? The answer determines the amount of uncollectible accounts expense for the year.

*Objective 3
Apply the
percentage of
net sales
method and the
accounts
receivable aging
method to
accounting for
uncollectible
accounts*

For example, assume that the following balances represent the ending figures for Hassel Company for the year 19x9:

	Dr.	Cr.
Sales		$645,000
Sales Returns and Allowances	$40,000	
Sales Discounts	5,000	
Allowance for Uncollectible Accounts		3,600

Assume that actual losses from uncollectible accounts for the past three years have been as follows:

Year	Net Sales	Losses from Uncollectible Accounts	Percentage
19x6	$ 520,000	$10,200	
19x7	595,000	13,900	
19x8	585,000	9,900	
Total	$1,700,000	$34,000	2%

Management believes that uncollectible accounts will continue to be about 2 percent of net sales. The uncollectible accounts expense for the year 19x9 is therefore estimated to be:

$$.02 \times (\$645,000 - \$40,000 - \$5,000) = .02 \times \$600,000 = \$12,000$$

Objective 4
Journalize
entries
involving the
allowance
method of
accounting for
uncollectible
accounts

The entry to record this estimate is:

Dec. 31	Uncollectible Accounts Expense	12,000	
	Allowance for Uncollectible		
	Accounts		12,000
	To record uncollectible		
	accounts expense at 2 percent		
	of $600,000 net sales		

The Allowance for Uncollectible Accounts now has a balance of $15,600. This figure consists of the $12,000 estimated uncollectible accounts receivable from 19x9 sales and the $3,600 estimated uncollectible accounts receivable from previous years. They have not yet been matched with specific uncollectible and written-off accounts receivable resulting from sales in those years.

Accounts Receivable Aging Method The accounts receivable aging method asks the question, How much of the year-end balance of accounts receivable will not be collected? The answer determines the amount that the allowance for uncollectible accounts is supposed to be at the end of the year. The difference between this amount and the actual balance of the Allowance account is the expense for the year. In theory, this method should produce the same result as the percentage of net sales method, but in practice it rarely does. The aging of accounts receivable is the process of listing each customer in accounts receivable according to the due date of the account. If a customer is past due on the account, there is a possibility that the account will not or cannot be paid. The further past due an account is, the greater the danger that the customer will not pay. The aging of accounts receivable is useful to management in evaluating its credit and collection policies and alerting it to possible problems of collection. The aging of accounts receivable for Myer Company is shown in Figure 10-2 (next page). Each account receivable is classified as being not yet due, or 1–30 days, 31–60 days, 61–90 days, or over 90 days past due. The percentage of total accounts receivable represented by each of these categories is calculated so that management may compare the analysis with previous periods.

The aging of accounts receivable method is useful to the accountant in determining the proper balance of the Allowance for Uncollectible Accounts. The accountant knows from experience that the further past due an account is, the less likely it is to be collected. In Figure 10-3 (page 367), estimates based on past experience show that only 1 percent of the accounts not yet due and 2 percent of the 1–30 days past due accounts will not be collected. Past experience also indicates that of the 31–60 days, 61–90 days, and over 90 days accounts, 10 percent, 30 percent, and 50 percent, respectively, will not be collected. In total, it is estimated that $2,459 of the $44,400 in accounts receivable will not be collected.

Let us assume that the current credit balance of the Allowance for Uncollectible Accounts for Myer Company is $800. Thus the estimated

Myer Company
Analysis of Accounts Receivable by Age
December 31, 19xx

Customer	Total	Not Yet Due	1–30 Days Past Due	31–60 Days Past Due	61–90 Days Past Due	Over 90 Days Past Due
A. Arnold	$ 150		$ 150			
M. Benoit	400			$ 400		
J. Connolly	1,000	$ 900	100			
R. DiCarlo	250				$ 250	
Others	42,600	21,000	14,000	3,800	2,200	$1,600
Totals	$44,400	$21,900	$14,250	$4,200	$2,450	$1,600
Percentage	100.0	49.3	32.1	9.5	5.5	3.6

Figure 10-2
Analysis of
Accounts
Receivable
by Age

uncollectible accounts expense for the year is $1,659, which is calculated as follows:

Estimated Uncollectible Accounts	$2,459
Credit Balance—Allowance for Uncollectible Accounts	800[3]
Uncollectible Accounts Expense	$1,659

The uncollectible accounts expense is recorded as follows:

Dec. 31 Uncollectible Accounts Expense	1,659	
Allowance for Uncollectible Accounts		1,659
To increase the allowance for uncollectible accounts to the level of expected losses		

Comparison of the Two Methods Both methods try to comply with the matching rule, but they do so in different ways. The percentage of net sales method represents an income statement viewpoint. It is based on the proposition that of each dollar of sales a certain proportion will not be collected, and this proportion is the expense for the year. Because this method matches expenses against revenues, it is in accordance with the matching rule. However, this way of determining expense is independent of the current balance of the Allowance for Uncollectible Accounts. The estimated proportion of net sales not expected to be collected is added to the current balance of the Allowance account.

3. If the Allowance for Uncollectible Accounts had had a debit balance, the amount of the debit balance would have to be added to the estimated uncollectible accounts to obtain the uncollectible accounts expense.

Figure 10-3
Calculation of
Estimated
Uncollectible
Accounts

Myer Company
Estimated Uncollectible Accounts
December 31, 19xx

	Amount	Percentage Considered Uncollectible	Allowance for Uncollectible Accounts
Not yet due	$21,900	1	$ 219
1–30 days	14,250	2	285
31–60 days	4,200	10	420
61–90 days	2,450	30	735
Over 90 days	1,600	50	800
	$44,400		$2,459

The aging of accounts receivable represents a balance sheet viewpoint and is a more direct valuation method. It is based on the proposition that of each dollar of accounts receivable outstanding, a certain proportion will not be collected, and this proportion should be the balance of the Allowance account at the end of the year. This method also agrees with the matching rule because the expense is the difference between what the account is and what it should be. This difference is assumed to be applicable to the current year.

Writing Off an Uncollectible Account

The Allowance for Uncollectible Accounts exists because it is not known in the accounting period which sale or account will not be collected. When it becomes clear that a specific account will not be collected, the amount should be written off to the Allowance for Uncollectible Accounts. Remember that it was already accounted for as an expense when the allowance was established. For example, assume that R. Deering, who owes the Murray Company $250, is declared bankrupt by a federal court. The entry to write off this account is as follows:

Jan. 15 Allowance for Uncollectible
     Accounts   250
       Accounts Receivable, R. Deering   250
         To write off receivable from
         R. Deering as uncollectible;
         Deering declared bankruptcy on
         January 15

Note that the write-off does not affect the estimated net amount of accounts receivable because there is no expense involved and because the related allowance for uncollectible accounts has already been deducted from the receivables. The write-off simply reduces R. Deering's account to zero and reduces the Allowance for Uncollectible Accounts by a similar amount, as the following table shows:

	Before Write-off	After Write-off
Accounts Receivable	$44,400	$44,150
Less Allowance for Uncollectible Accounts	2,459	2,209
Estimated net value of Accounts Receivable	$41,941	$41,941

Why Accounts Written Off Will Differ from Estimates The total of accounts receivable written off in any given year will rarely equal the estimated amount credited to the Allowance for Uncollectible Accounts. The Allowance account will show a credit balance when the accounts written off are less than the estimated uncollectible accounts. If the company underestimates the amount of uncollectible receivables, the accounts receivable written off will be greater than the amount of the Allowance account, which will create a debit balance in the Allowance account. The adjusting entry that is made to record the estimated uncollectible accounts expense for the current year will eliminate the debit balance at the end of the accounting period.

If the percentage of net sales method is used, the new balance of the Allowance account after the adjusting entry will equal the percentage of sales estimated to be uncollectible minus the debit balance. If the accounts receivable aging method is used, the amount of the adjustment must equal the estimated uncollectible accounts plus the debit balance in the Allowance for Uncollectible Accounts. Of course, if the estimates are consistently wrong, management should reexamine the company's estimation rates.

Recovery of Accounts Receivable Written Off Sometimes a customer whose account has been written off as uncollectible will later be able to pay the amount in full or in part. When this happens, it is necessary to make two journal entries: one to reverse the earlier write-off, which was incorrect in the first place; and another to show the collection of the account.

For example, assume that on September 1, R. Deering, after his bankruptcy on January 15 (see previous page), notified the company that he would be able to pay $100 of his account and sent a check for $50. The entries to record this transaction are as follows:

Sept. 1	Accounts Receivable, R. Deering	100	
	Allowance for Uncollectible Accounts		100
	To reinstate the portion of the account of R. Deering now considered collectible, which had been written off January 15		

Sept. 1	Cash	50	
	Accounts Receivable, R. Deering		50
	To record collection from R. Deering		

The collectible portion of R. Deering's account must be restored to his account and credited to the Allowance for Uncollectible Accounts for two reasons. First, as it turned out, it was an error of judgment to write off the full $250 on January 15. Only $150 was actually uncollectible. Second, the Accounts Receivable subsidiary account for R. Deering should reflect his ability to pay part of the money he owed in spite of his bankruptcy. This action will give a clear picture of his credit record for future credit action.

Direct Charge-off Method

Some companies record uncollectible accounts by debiting expenses directly when bad debts are discovered instead of using the Allowance for Uncollectible Accounts and adjusting entries to estimate the amount of uncollectible expense in an accounting period. The **direct charge-off method** is not in accordance with good accounting theory because it makes no attempt to match revenues and expenses. Uncollectible accounts are charged to expenses in the accounting period in which they are discovered rather than in the period of the sale. On the balance sheet the accounts receivable are shown at gross value, not realizable value, because there is no Allowance for Uncollectible Accounts. Both the direct charge-off method and the allowance method of estimating uncollectible accounts expense are acceptable for use in computing taxable income under federal income tax regulations. Only the allowance method is used in this book because it is better from the standpoint of accounting theory.

Credit Balances in Accounts Receivable

Objective 5
Recognize types
of receivables
not classified as
accounts
receivable and
specify their
balance sheet
presentation

Sometimes customers overpay their accounts because of mistakes or in anticipation of future purchases. When customer accounts show credit balances in the accounts receivable ledger, the balance of the Accounts Receivable controlling account should not appear on the balance sheet as the amount of the accounts receivable. The total of the customers' accounts with credit balances should be shown as a current liability because the company is liable to these customers for their overpayments. For example, assume that the balances in the Accounts Receivable controlling account are as follows:

165 accounts with debit balances	$182,400
10 accounts with credit balances	4,200
Net balance of 175 customer accounts	$178,200

Because the customer accounts with credit balances are liabilities, the balance sheet presentation should be as follows:

Current Assets		Current Liabilities	
Accounts Receivable	$182,400	Credit Balances in Customer Accounts	$4,200

Sales to and Purchases from the Same Firm

Where a firm has made both sales to and purchases from the same company, two separate accounts should be maintained, and they should not be offset against each other. The receivable account should be part of the accounts receivable subsidiary ledger. It should be shown on the balance sheet as accounts receivable. The payable account should be part of the accounts payable subsidiary ledger. It should be shown as accounts payable on the balance sheet.

Installment Accounts Receivable

Installment sales make up a significant portion of the accounts receivable of many retail companies. Department stores, appliance stores, and retail chains all sell goods that are paid for in a series of time payments. Companies such as J. C. Penney and Sears have millions of dollars in these **installment accounts receivable.** Although the payment period may be twenty-four months or more, installment accounts receivable are classified as current assets if such credit policies are customary in the industry. There are special accounting rules that apply to installment sales. Because these rules can be very complicated, the study of such practices is usually deferred until a more advanced accounting course.

Credit Card Sales

Many retailers allow customers to charge their purchases to a third-party company that the customer will pay later. These transactions are normally handled with credit cards. The five most widely used national credit cards are American Express, Carte Blanche, Diners Club, Master Card, and VISA. The customer establishes credit with the lender and receives a plastic card to use in making charge purchases. If the seller accepts the card, an invoice is made at the time of the sale that is imprinted by the charge card and signed by the customer. The seller then sends the invoice to the lender and receives cash. Because the seller does not have to establish the customer's credit, collect from the customer, or tie money up in accounts receivable, the seller receives an economic benefit that is provided by the lender. For this reason, the credit card company does not pay 100 percent of the total amount of the credit card sales invoices. The lender takes a discount of 2 to 5 percent on the credit card sales invoices.

One of two procedures is used in accounting for credit card sales, depending on whether the merchant must wait for collection from the credit card company or may deposit the sales invoices in a checking account immediately. The following example illustrates the procedure used in the first case. Assume that, at the end of the day, a restaurant has

American Express invoices totaling $1,000. These sales are recorded as follows:

Accounts Receivable, American Express	1,000	
Sales		1,000
Sales made for which American Express cards were accepted		

The seller now mails the American Express invoices to American Express and later receives payment for them at 95 percent of their face value. When cash is received, the entry is as follows:

Cash	950	
Credit Card Discount Expense	50	
Accounts Receivable, American Express		1,000
Receipt of payment from American Express for invoices at 95 percent of face value		

The second case is typical of sales made through bank credit cards such as VISA and MasterCard. For example, assume that the restaurant made sales of $1,000 on VISA credit cards and that VISA takes a 5 percent discount on the sales. Assume also that the sales invoices may be deposited in a special VISA bank account in the name of the company in much the same way that checks from cash sales may be deposited. These sales may be recorded as follows:

Cash	950	
Credit Card Discount Expense	50	
Sales		1,000
Sales for which VISA cards were accepted		

Other Accounts Receivable

The title Accounts Receivable on the balance sheet should be reserved for sales made to regular customers in the ordinary course of business. If loans or sales that do not fall in this category are made to employees, officers of a corporation, or owners, they should be shown separately on the balance sheet with an asset title such as Receivables from Employees and Officers.

Accounting for Notes Receivable

Objective 6
Define and
describe a
promissory note

A promissory note is an unconditional promise to pay a definite sum of money on demand or at a future date. The person who signs the note and thereby promises to pay is called the maker of the note. The person to whom payment is to be made is called the payee. When the note is due in less than a year, the payee should record it as a note receivable in the current asset section of the balance sheet, and the maker should record it as a note payable in the current liability section of the balance sheet.

In this chapter, we are concerned primarily with notes received from customers. The nature of the business generally determines how frequently promissory notes are received from customers. In companies that sell on an installment basis, installment contracts instead of promissory notes are generally used. Firms selling durable goods of high value, such as farm machinery and automobiles, will often take promissory notes in payment. One advantage of promissory notes in these situations is that the notes can be resold to banks as a financing method. Almost all companies will occasionally receive a note, and many companies obtain notes receivable in settlement of past-due accounts.

Computations Associated with Promissory Notes

In accounting for promissory notes, several terms are important. These terms are (1) maturity date, (2) duration of note, (3) interest and interest rate, (4) maturity value, (5) discount, and (6) proceeds from discounting.

Objective 7
Make calculations involving promissory notes

Maturity Date The **maturity date** is the date on which the note must be paid. It must either be stated on the promissory note or be determinable from the facts stated on the note. Among the most common statements of maturity date are the following:

1. A specific date, such as "November 14, 19xx"
2. A specific number of months after the date of the note, for example, "3 months after date"
3. A specific number of days after the date of the note, for example, "60 days after date"

There is no problem in determining the maturity date when it is stated. When the number of months from date of note is the maturity date, one simply uses the same day of the month as the note in the appropriate month in the future. For example, a note dated January 20 that is due two months from that date would be due on March 20.

When the computation of maturity date is based on a specific number of days, the maturity date must be determined on the basis of the passage of the exact number of days. In computing the maturity, it is important to exclude the date of the note and to include the maturity day. For example, a note dated May 20, and due in 90 days, would be due on August 18, computed as follows:

Days remaining in May (31 − 20)	11
Days in June	30
Days in July	31
Days in August	18
Total days	90

Duration of Note Determining the **duration of note,** or its length of time in days, is the opposite problem from determining the maturity date. This calculation is important because interest must be calculated on the basis of the exact number of days. There is no problem when the maturity date is based on the number of days from date of note. However, if the maturity date is a specified date or a specified number of months from date, the exact number of days must be determined. Assume that the length of time of a note is from May 10 to August 10. The length of time is 92 days, determined as follows:

Days remaining in May (31 − 10)	21
Days in June	30
Days in July	31
Days in August	10
Total days	92

Interest and Interest Rate The interest is the cost of borrowing money or the reward for loaning money, depending on whether one is the borrower or the lender. The amount of interest is based on three factors: the principal (the amount of money borrowed or loaned), the rate of interest, and the loan's length of time. The formula used in computing interest is as follows:

$$\text{principal} \times \text{rate of interest} \times \text{time} = \text{interest}$$

Interest rates are usually stated on an annual basis. For example, the interest on a $1,000, one-year, 8 percent note is computed as follows: $1,000 \times 8/100 \times 1 = \$80$.

If the term of the note were three months instead of a year, the interest charge would be $20, computed as follows: $1,000 \times 8/100 \times 3/12 = \$20$.

When the terms of a note are expressed in days, the exact number of days must be used in computing the interest. To keep the computation simple, let us compute interest on the basis of 360[4] days per year. Therefore, if the term of the above note were 45 days, the interest would be $10, computed as follows: $1,000 \times 8/100 \times 45/360 = \$10$.

Accountants, using a 360-day year and a 12 percent rate of interest, frequently employ a short-cut method of determining the interest known as the 12 percent method. If the interest rate is 12 percent a year, the interest for 30 days on any amount of money may be determined simply by moving the decimal point two places to the left ($12/100 \times 30/360 = 1/100 = .01$ or 1%). For example, the interest at 12 percent for 30 days on $2,462 is $24.62, and the interest at 12 percent for 30 days on $1,946.25 is $19.46.[5]

The 30-day, 12 percent method can be used for time periods other than 30 days by stating the time period as a fraction of 30 days. For instance, the following examples show the calculation of interest on a 12 percent, $2,000 note, on which interest for 30 days would be $20:

---

4. Interest is computed in practice on the basis of 365 days in a year. In this book, use 360 days in a year to keep computations simple.

5. Proof: $\$2,462 \times 12/100 \times 30/360 = \$2,462 \times 1/100 = \$24.62$; $\$1,946.25 \times 12/100 \times 30/360 = \$1,946.25 \times 1/100 = \$19.46$.

15 days: 15/30 or 1/2 times the interest for 30 days =
        1/2 × \$20 = \$10.
45 days: 45/30 or 3/2 times the interest for 30 days =
        3/2 × \$20 = \$30.
60 days: 6/3 or 2 times the interest for 30 days =
        2 × \$20 = \$40.

The 30-day, 12 percent method can also be used to compute the interest when the rate is other than 12 percent by stating the rate as a fraction of 12 percent. Study the following example of the calculation of interest on a 30-day, \$6,000 note, on which the interest for 30 days would be \$60:

 9 percent rate: 3/4 times the interest at 12% = 3/4 × \$60 = \$45.
18 percent rate: 18/12 times the interest at 12% = 3/2 × \$60 = \$90.

Maturity Value   It is necessary to determine the **maturity value** of a note or the total proceeds of the note at maturity date. Maturity value is the face value of the note plus interest. The maturity value of a 90-day, 8 percent, \$1,000 note is computed as follows:

maturity value = principal + interest
             = \$1,000 + (\$1,000 × 8/100 × 90/360)
             = \$1,000 + \$20
             = \$1,020

Occasionally, one will encounter a noninterest-bearing note, in which case the maturity value is the face value or principal amount.

Discount   To **discount** a note means to take out the interest in advance. The **discount** is the amount of interest deducted. It is very common for banks to use this method when loaning money on promissory notes. The amount of the discount is computed as follows:

discount = maturity value × rate × time

For example, assume that a noninterest-bearing \$1,000 note due in 90 days is discounted at a 10 percent rate of interest:

discount = \$1,000 × 10/100 × 90/360 = \$25

Proceeds from Discounting   When someone borrows money on an interest-bearing note, the amount he or she receives or borrows is the face value or principal. When a note receivable is discounted, the amount the borrower receives is called the **proceeds from discounting** and must be computed as follows:

proceeds = maturity value − discount

Thus, in the preceding example, the proceeds would be computed as follows:

proceeds = \$1,000 − (\$1,000 × 10/100 × 90/360)
        = \$1,000 − \$25
        = \$975

This calculation is very simple when a noninterest-bearing note is involved, as illustrated here. However, the calculation is more complicated when an interest-bearing note is involved, as in the case when an interest-bearing note from a customer is discounted to the bank. In this situation, the maturity value must first be computed under the formula described for computing maturity value. Then the discount must be computed on the basis of the maturity value and, finally, the proceeds are determined by deducting the discount from the maturity value. For example, the proceeds of a $2,000, 8 percent, 90-day note, discounted on the date it is drawn at the bank at 10 percent, would be $1,989, determined as follows:

$$\text{maturity value} = \text{principal} + \text{interest}$$
$$= \$2,000 + (\$2,000 \times 8/100 \times 90/360)$$
$$= \$2,000 + \$40$$
$$= \$2,040$$

$$\text{discount} = \text{maturity value} \times \text{rate} \times \text{time}$$
$$= \$2,040 \times 10/100 \times 90/360$$
$$= \$51$$

$$\text{proceeds} = \text{maturity value} - \text{discount}$$
$$= \$2,040 - \$51$$
$$= \$1,989$$

In this example, the note was discounted to the bank on the same day it was written. Usually some days will go by between the date the note is written and the date it is discounted. In such a case, the number of days used in computing the proceeds should be the days remaining until the maturity date of the note, because that is the length of time for which the bank is lending the money to the company holding the note. For example, assume the same facts as above except that the company holding the note waits 30 days to discount the note to the bank. In other words, at the date of discounting, there are 60 (90 − 30) days remaining until the maturity date. The proceeds are determined as follows:

$$\text{maturity value} = \text{principal} + \text{interest}$$
$$= \$2,040 \text{ (from above)}$$

$$\text{discount} = \text{maturity value} \times \text{rate} \times \text{time}$$
$$= \$2,040 \times 10/100 \times 60/360$$
$$= \$34$$

$$\text{proceeds} = \text{maturity value} - \text{discount}$$
$$= \$2,040 - \$34$$
$$= \$2,006$$

The difference in discount of $17 ($51 − $34) between the two cases is equal to the discount on the 30 days lapsed between writing and discounting the note ($2,040 × 10/100 × 30/360 = $17).

Illustrative Accounting Entries

Objective 8
Journalize
entries
involving notes
receivable

The accounting entries for promissory notes receivable fall into five groups: (1) receipt of a note, (2) collection of a note, (3) recording a dishonored note, (4) discounting a note, and (5) recording adjusting entries.

Receipt of a Note Assume that a 12 percent, 30-day note is received from a customer, J. Halsted, in settlement of an existing account receivable of $4,000. The entry for this transaction is as follows:

June 1	Notes Receivable	4,000	
	Accounts Receivable, J. Halsted		4,000
	Received 12 percent, 30-day		
	note in payment of account		

Collection of a Note When the note plus interest is collected 30 days later, the entry is as follows:

July 1	Cash	4,040	
	Notes Receivable		4,000
	Interest Income		40
	Collected 12 percent, 30-day		
	note from J. Halsted		

Recording a Dishonored Note When the maker of a note does not pay the note at maturity, the note is said to be dishonored. In the case of a dishonored note, an entry should be made by the holder or payee to transfer the amount due from the Notes Receivable account to an account receivable from the debtor. If it is assumed that J. Halsted did not pay his note on July 1 but dishonored it, the following entry would be made:

July 1	Accounts Receivable, J. Halsted	4,040	
	Notes Receivable		4,000
	Interest Income		40
	To record 12 percent, 30-day note		
	dishonored by J. Halsted		

The interest earned is recorded because although J. Halsted did not pay the note, he is still obligated to pay both the principal amount and the interest.

Two things are accomplished by transferring dishonored notes receivable into an accounts receivable account. First, it leaves the Notes Receivable account with only notes that have not matured and are presumably negotiable and collectible. Second, it establishes a record in the borrower's account receivable that he or she has dishonored a note receivable. This information may be helpful in deciding whether to extend more credit to this customer in the future.

Discounting a Note Many companies raise money for operations by selling notes receivable from customers to banks or finance companies for cash rather than holding them until maturity. This type of financing is usually called discounting because the bank deducts the interest from the maturity value of the note to determine the proceeds. The holder of the note (usually the payee) signs his or her name on the back of the note (as in endorsing a check) and delivers the note to the bank. The bank expects to collect the maturity value of the note (principal plus interest) on the maturity date. If the maker fails to pay, the endorser is liable to the bank for payment.

For example, assume that we take a $1,000, 12 percent, 90-day note to the bank 60 days before maturity and that we discount it at 15 percent for cash. The cash to be received (proceeds from discounting) is calculated as the maturity value less the discount, and this transaction can be recorded as follows:

Cash	1,004.25	
Notes Receivable		1,000.00
Interest Income		4.25

To record discounting of a 12 percent, 90-day note with 60 days left at 15 percent

Maturity value:

$$\$1,000 + (\$1,000 \times 12/100 \times 90/360) = \$1,030.00$$

Less discount:

$$\$1,030 \times 15/100 \times 60/360 = \underline{25.75}$$

Proceeds from discounted note receivable $\underline{\underline{\$1,004.25}}$

Before discussing the transaction, there are two things to note about the calculations. First, if the proceeds had been less than the note receivable, the difference would have been recorded as a debit to Interest Expense. For example, if the proceeds had been $995.75 instead of $1,004.25, Interest Expense would have been debited for $4.25, and there would have been no entry to Interest Income. Second, neither the length of the discounting period nor the discount rate is the same as the term or the rate of interest of the note. This situation is typical.

Regarding the journal entry, notice that the account Notes Receivable is credited. Although this entry removes the note from the records, remember that if the maker cannot or will not pay the bank, the endorser is liable to the bank for the note. In accounting terminology, the endorser is said to be contingently liable to the bank. A **contingent liability** is a potential liability that can develop into a real liability if a possible subsequent event occurs. In this case, the subsequent event would be the nonpayment of the note by the maker.

Before the maturity date of the discounted note, the bank will notify the maker that it is holding the note and that payment should be made directly to the bank. If the maker pays the bank as agreed, then no entry is required in the records of the endorser. If the maker does not pay the note and interest on the due date, the note is said to be dishonored. To hold the endorser liable for the note, the bank must notify the endorser that the note is dishonored. The bank will normally notify the endorser by protesting the note. The bank does this by preparing and mailing a notice of protest to the endorser. The **notice of protest** is a sworn statement that the note was presented to the maker for payment and the maker refused to pay. The bank typically charges a **protest fee** for protesting the note, which must be paid when the endorser pays the bank the amount due on the dishonored note.

If the note discounted in the example above is dishonored by the maker on the maturity date, the following entry should be made by the endorser when paying the obligation:

Accounts Receivable, Name of Maker	1,040	
Cash		1,040
To record payment of principal and		
interest on discounted note (maturity		
value of $1,030), plus a protest fee		
of $10 to bank; the note was		
dishonored by the maker		

Recording Adjusting Entries A promissory note received in one period may not be due until a following accounting period. Because the interest on the note accrues by a small amount each day of the duration of the note, it is necessary, according to the matching rule, to apportion the interest earned to the period in which it belongs. For example, assume that on August 31 a 60-day, 8 percent, $2,000 note was received and that the company prepares financial statements monthly. The following adjusting entry on September 30 is necessary to show how the interest earned for September has accrued:

Sept. 30 Accrued Interest Receivable	13.33	
Interest Income		13.33
To accrue 30 days' interest		
earned on note receivable		
$2,000 \times 8/100 \times 30/360 = \$13.33		

The account Accrued Interest Receivable is a current asset on the balance sheet. Upon payment of the note plus interest on October 30, the following entry is made:[6]

Oct. 30 Cash	2,026.67	
Note Receivable		2,000.00
Accrued Interest Receivable		13.33
Interest Income		13.34
To record payment of note		
receivable plus interest		

6. Some firms may follow the practice of reversing the September 30 adjusting entry. Here we assume that a reversing entry is not made.

As can be clearly seen from the above transactions, both September and October receive the benefit of one-half the interest earned.

Chapter Review

Review of Learning Objectives

1. Describe accounting for cash and short-term investments.

Cash consists of coin and currency on hand, checks and money orders received from customers, deposits in bank accounts, certificates of deposit, and time deposits. Short-term investments, sometimes called marketable securities, are first recorded at cost. Afterwards, investments in debt securities are carried at cost unless there is a permanent drop in the market value. Investments in equity securities are reported at the lower of cost or market.

2. Explain why estimated losses from uncollectible accounts are important to income determination.

Because credit is offered to increase sales, it is reasonable that bad debts associated with the sales should be charged as expenses in the period in which the sale is made. However, because there is a time lag between the time a sale is made on credit and the time the account is judged to be uncollectible, the accountant must estimate the amount of bad debts in any given period.

3. Apply the percentage of net sales method and the accounts receivable aging method to accounting for uncollectible accounts.

Uncollectible accounts expense is estimated by either the percentage of net sales method or the accounts receivable aging method. When the first method is used, bad debts are judged to be a certain percentage of sales during the period. When the second method is used, certain percentages are applied to groups of the accounts receivable that have been arranged by due dates.

4. Journalize entries involving the allowance method of accounting for uncollectible accounts.

When the estimate of uncollectible accounts is made, an Allowance for Uncollectible Accounts is set up as a contra account to Accounts Receivable by a debit to expense and a credit to the Allowance account. When an individual account is determined to be uncollectible, it is removed from Accounts Receivable by debiting the Allowance account and crediting Accounts Receivable. If this account should later be collected, the earlier entry should be reversed and the collection recorded in the normal way.

5. Recognize types of receivables not classified as accounts receivable and specify their balance sheet presentation.

Accounts of customers with credit balances should not be classified as negative accounts receivable but as current liabilities on the balance sheet. Installment accounts receivable are classified as current assets if such credit policies are followed in the industry. Receivables from credit card companies should be classified as current assets. Receivables from employees, officers, stockholders, and others not made in the normal course of business should not be listed among accounts receivable. They may be either short- or long-term assets depending on when collection is expected to take place.

6. Define and describe a promissory note.

A promissory note is an unconditional promise to pay a definite sum of money on demand or at a future date. Companies selling durable goods of high value such as farm machinery and automobiles will often take promissory notes, which can be sold to banks as a financing method.

7. Make calculations involving promissory notes.

In accounting for promissory notes, it is important to know how to calculate the following: maturity date, duration of note, interest, maturity value, discount, and proceeds from discounting. Discounting is the act of taking out the interest in advance when making a loan on a note.

8. Journalize entries involving notes receivable.

The accounting entries for promissory notes receivable fall into five groups: receipt of a note, collection of a note, recording a dishonored note, discounting a note, and recording adjusting entries.

Review Problem
Entries for Uncollectible Accounts Expense and Notes Receivable Transactions

The Farm Implement Company sells merchandise on credit and also accepts notes for payment, which are discounted to the bank. During the past year ended June 30, the company had net credit sales of $1,200,000 and at the end of the year had total accounts receivable of $400,000 and a debit balance in the Allowance for Uncollectible Accounts of $2,100. In the past, approximately 1.5 percent of net sales have proved to be uncollectible. Also, an aging analysis of accounts receivable reveals that $17,000 in accounts receivable appears to be uncollectible.

The Farm Implement Company sold a tractor to R. C. Sims. Payment was received in the form of a $15,000, 9 percent, 90-day note dated March 16. On March 31, the note was discounted to the bank at 10 percent. On June 14, the bank notified the company that Sims had dishonored the note. The company paid the bank the maturity value of the note plus a fee of $15. On June 29, the company received payment in full from Sims.

Required

1. Prepare journal entries to record uncollectible accounts expense using (a) the percentage of net sales method and (b) the accounts receivable aging method.
2. Prepare journal entries relating to the note received from R. C. Sims.

Answer to Review Problem

1. Journal entries for uncollectible accounts prepared:
   a. Percentage of net sales method:

June 30	Uncollectible Accounts Expense	18,000	
	Allowance for Uncollectible Accounts		18,000
	To record estimated uncollectible accounts expense at 1.5 percent of $1,200,000		

   b. Accounts receivable aging method:

June 30	Uncollectible Accounts Expense	19,100	
	Allowance for Uncollectible Accounts		19,100
	To record estimated uncollectible accounts expense. The debit		

balance in the Allowance account
must be added to the estimated
uncollectible accounts
$2,100 + $17,000 = $19,100

2. Journal entries related to note prepared:

March 16	Notes Receivable	15,000.00	
	Sales		15,000.00
	Tractor sold to R. C. Sims; terms of note: 9%, 90 days		
31	Cash	15,017.97	
	Interest Income		17.97
	Notes Receivable		15,000.00
	To record note discounted at bank at 10 percent		

Maturity value: $15,000 + ($15,000 \times 9/100 \times 90/360)$ = $15,337.50

Less discount ($15,337.50 \times 10/100 \times 75/360)$ = 319.53

Proceeds from discounted note receivable $15,017.97

June 14	Accounts Receivable, R. C. Sims	15,352.50	
	Cash		15,352.50
	To record payment of principal and interest on discounted note (maturity value $15,337.50), plus a $15 fee to bank; the note was dishonored by Sims		
29	Cash	15,352.50	
	Accounts Receivable, R. C. Sims		15,352.50
	Received payment in full from R. C. Sims $15,337.50 + $15.00		

Chapter Assignments

Questions

1. What items are included in the cash account? Is a compensating balance part of the cash account?

2. Why does a business need short-term liquid assets? Why is it acceptable to account for certain short-term investments by the lower-of-cost-or-market method?

3. Why does a company sell on credit if it expects that some of the accounts will not be paid? What role does a credit department play in selling on credit?

4. According to the accountant, at what point in the cycle of selling and collecting does the bad debt loss occur?

5. If management estimates that $5,000 of the year's sales will not be collected, what entry should be made at year end?

6. After adjusting and closing entries at the end of the year, suppose that the Accounts Receivable balance is $176,000, and the Allowance for Uncollectible Accounts balance is $14,500. (a) What is the collectible value of Accounts Receivable? (b) If the $450 account of a bankrupt customer is written off in the first

month of the new year, what will be the resulting collectible value of Accounts Receivable?

7. What is the effect on net income of an optimistic versus a pessimistic view by management of estimated uncollectible accounts?

8. In what ways is the Allowance for Uncollectible Accounts similar to Accumulated Depreciation? In what ways is it different?

9. What procedure for estimating uncollectible accounts also gives management a view of the status of collections and the overall quality of accounts receivable?

10. What is the underlying reasoning behind the percentage of net sales and the accounts receivable aging methods of estimating uncollectible accounts?

11. Are the following terms different in any way: allowance for bad debts, allowance for doubtful accounts, allowance for uncollectible accounts?

12. Why should the entry for an account that has been written off as uncollectible be reinstated if the amount owed is subsequently collected?

13. What accounting rule is violated by the direct charge-off method of recognizing uncollectible accounts? Why?

14. Which of the lettered items below should be in Accounts Receivable? For those that do not belong in Accounts Receivable, tell where they do belong on the balance sheet: (a) installment accounts receivable from regular customers, due monthly for three years; (b) debit balances in customers' accounts; (c) receivables from employees; (d) credit balances in customers' accounts; (e) receivables from officers of the company; (f) accounts payable to a company that are less than accounts receivable from the same company.

15. What is a promissory note? Who is the maker? Who is the payee?

16. What are the due dates of the following notes: (a) a 3-month note dated August 16, (b) a 90-day note dated August 16, (c) a 60-day note dated March 25?

17. What is the difference between a cash discount and a discount on a note?

18. What is the difference between the interest on a note and the discount on a note?

19. A bank is offering Diane Wedge two alternatives for borrowing $2,000. The first alternative is a $2,000, 12 percent, 30-day note. The second alternative is a $2,000, 30-day, noninterest-bearing note discounted at 12 percent. (a) What entries are required by the bank to record the two loans? (b) What entries are needed by the bank to record the collection of the two loans? (c) Which alternative favors the bank, and why?

Classroom Exercises

**Exercise 10-1
Accounting for
Short-Term
Investments
(L.O. 1)**

During certain periods of its fiscal year, AHA Associates Company invests its excess cash balances until they are needed at other times in the year. On December 16, the company invested $194,000 in 90-day U.S. Treasury bills that had a maturity value of $200,000. The bills matured on March 16 and the company received $200,000 in cash. On April 15, AHA Associates purchased 5,000 shares of International Paper common stock at $35 per share and 10,000 shares of Commonwealth Edison common stock at $20 per share. On May 15, it received quarterly dividends of 92.25 cents per share from Commonwealth Edison and 60 cents per share from International Paper. On June 15, the company sold all the shares of International Paper for $38 per share. On June 30, the value of the Commonwealth Edison stock was $18 per share.

Prepare journal entries to record the transactions on December 16, March 16, April 15, May 15, and June 15. Also, show the balance sheet presentations of short-term investments on June 30.

**Exercise 10-2
Adjusting
Entries—
Accounts
Receivable
Aging Method**
(L.O. 3, 4)

The general ledger controlling account for accounts receivable of Tomye Company shows a debit balance of $90,000 at the end of the year. An aging method analysis of the individual accounts indicates estimated uncollectible accounts to be $4,200.

Give the general journal entry to record the uncollectible accounts expense under each of the following assumptions: (1) The Allowance for Uncollectible Accounts has a credit balance of $300. (2) The Allowance for Uncollectible Accounts has a debit balance of $300.

**Exercise 10-3
Adjusting
Entry—Percent-
age of Net
Sales Method**
(L.O. 4)

At the end of the year, Simons Enterprises estimates the uncollectible accounts expense to be .5 percent of net sales of $9,200,000. The current credit balance of the Allowance for Uncollectible Accounts is $15,600.

Prepare the general journal entry to record the uncollectible accounts expense.

**Exercise 10-4
Accounts
Receivable
Transactions**
(L.O. 4)

Assuming that the allowance method is being used, prepare journal entries to record the following transactions:

May 17, 19x8   Sold merchandise to Jerry Bennett for $1,200, terms n/10.
Sept. 20, 19x8   Received $400 from Jerry Bennett on account.
June 25, 19x9   Wrote off as uncollectible the balance of the Jerry Bennett account when he was declared bankrupt.
July 27, 19x9   Unexpectedly received a check for $200 from Jerry Bennett.

**Exercise 10-5
Interest Com-
putations—12
Percent Method**
(L.O. 7)

Using the 30-day, 12 percent method, determine the interest on the following notes: (a) $10,360 at 12 percent for 60 days; (b) $6,000 at 12 percent for 90 days; (c) $10,000 at 12 percent for 30 days; (d) $8,000 at 9 percent for 60 days; (e) $12,000 at 15 percent for 120 days; (f) $4,500 at 12 percent for 30 days.

**Exercise 10-6
Discounting
Notes**
(L.O. 7)

In an effort to raise cash, Hewitt Company discounted two notes at the bank on September 15. The bank charged a discount rate of 12 percent applied to the maturity value.

Compute the proceeds from discounting of each of the following notes:

Date of Note	Amount	Interest Rate	Life of Note
a. Aug. 1	$ 4,500	9%	120 days
b. July 20	$22,000	10%	90 days

**Exercise 10-7
Notes Receiva-
ble Transac-
tions**
(L.O. 8)

Prepare general journal entries to record the following transactions:

Jan. 16   Sold merchandise to Eastern Corporation on account for $28,000, terms n/30.
Feb. 15   Accepted a $28,000, 12 percent, 60-day note from Eastern Corporation granting an extension on the previous sales.
Mar. 17   Discounted Eastern Corporation note at bank at 10 percent.
Apr. 16   Received notice that Eastern dishonored the note. Paid the bank the maturity value of the note plus a protest fee of $15.
May 15   Received payment in full from Eastern Corporation.

**Exercise 10-8
Credit Card
Sales Transac-
tions**
(L.O. 5)

Prepare journal entries to record the following transactions for Nancy's Specialty Shop:

Dec. 4   A tabulation of invoices at the end of the day showed $300 in American Express invoices and $400 in Diners Club invoices. American Express takes a discount of 4 percent, and Diners Club takes a 5 percent discount.
8   Received payment from American Express at 96 percent of face value and from Diners Club at 95 percent of face value.

Dec. 9 A tabulation of invoices at the end of the day showed $200 in VISA invoices, which are deposited in a special bank account at full value less 5 percent discount.

Exercise 10-9 Adjusting Entries—Interest Expense
(L.O. 8)

Prepare journal entries to record the following:

Dec. 1 Received a 90-day, 12 percent note for $2,000 from a customer for a sale of merchandise, terms n/30.

     31 Made end-of-year adjustment for accrued interest earned.

Mar. 1 Received payment in full for note and interest.

Interpreting Accounting Information

Published Financial Information: Chrysler Corporation
(L.O. 2)

The automobile industry, especially Chrysler Corporation, has had difficult financial problems in recent years. Chrysler incurred operating losses of over $1 billion in both 1979 and 1980. It has received U.S. Government loan guarantees of $1 billion and more. Chrysler's short-term liquid assets for 1979 and 1980 were presented in its annual report as follows (in millions of dollars):

	1980	1979
Cash	$101.1	$ 188.2
Time Deposits	2.6	120.8
Marketable Securities—at lower of cost or market	193.6	165.3
Accounts Receivable (less allowance for doubtful accounts: 1980—$40.3 million; 1979—$34.9 million)	476.2	610.3
Total Short-Term Liquid Assets	$773.5	$1,084.6

The company also reported current liabilities of $3,231.6 million in 1979 and $3,029.3 million in 1980. Sales totaled $12,001.9 million in 1979 and $9,225.3 million in 1980. In management's discussion and analysis of financial conditions and results of operations, it was noted that "Chrysler had to defer paying its major suppliers until it received the proceeds from the additional $400 million of federally guaranteed debt. Chrysler's liquidity and its long-term viability are predicated on a return to sustained profitable operations."

Required

1. Compute Chrysler's ratio of short-term liquid assets to current liabilities for 1979 and 1980. Did Chrysler's short-term liquidity position improve or deteriorate from 1979 to 1980? What apparent effect did the 1980 $400 million federally guaranteed loan have on the balance sheet and on the liquidity position?

2. It is important to Chrysler's survival that its customers pay their debts, and pay them on time. Compute for both years the ratio of the allowance for doubtful accounts to *gross* accounts receivable and the ratio of *net* accounts receivable to sales. What can you conclude from these computations about Chrysler's ability to collect from its customers?

Problem Set A

Problem 10A-1 Percentage of Net Sales Method
(L.O. 3, 4)

At the beginning of the current year, Foster Company had accounts receivable of $321,000 and a credit balance in the Allowance for Uncollectible Accounts of

$19,100. During the year, the company's records included the following selected activities: sales on account, $1,170,500; sales returns and allowances, $65,500; collections from customers, $1,151,000; accounts written off as worthless, $18,500; written-off accounts unexpectedly collected, $1,500. The company's experience with credit sales has shown that 2 percent of net sales will probably not be collected.

Required

1. Give the summary general journal entries required to record each of the five items listed above.
2. Give the general journal entry required to record the estimated uncollectible accounts expense for the year.
3. Open ledger accounts for the Accounts Receivable controlling account (112) and the Allowance for Uncollectible Accounts (113), enter the beginning balances in these accounts, and post the appropriate parts of the transactions in 1 and 2 to these accounts.

Problem 10A-2
Accounts
Receivable
Aging Method
(L.O. 3, 4)

At the beginning of the current year, Vander Molen Department Store, a company that uses the accounts receivable aging method to estimate uncollectible accounts, had balances in its Accounts Receivable controlling account and Allowance for Uncollectible Accounts of $454,000 and $42,000, respectively. During the year, the company had sales on account of $3,954,000, sales returns and allowances of $74,000, worthless accounts written off of $49,000, and collections from customers of $3,570,000.

As part of the end-of-year (January 31) procedures, an aging analysis of accounts receivable is prepared. The analysis is partially complete. The totals carried over to the top of page 5 of the analysis appear below.

Customer Account	Total	Not Yet Due	1–30 Days Past Due	31–60 Days Past Due	61–90 Days Past Due	Over 90 Days Past Due
Balance forward	$664,700	$354,560	$144,600	$85,400	$46,400	$33,740

The following accounts remain to be classified in order to finish the analysis:

Account	Amount	Due Date
S. Ursey	$ 9,354	January 15
T. Vasser	1,832	February 15 (next fiscal year)
A. Wertz	6,414	December 20
B. Wilson	294	October 1
J. Yancey	5,400	January 4
T. Zempel	7,834	November 15
D. Ziegler	19,172	March 1 (next fiscal year)
	$50,300	

From past experience, the company has found that the following rates for estimating uncollectible accounts produce an adequate balance for the Allowance for Uncollectible Accounts:

Time Past Due	Percentage Considered Uncollectible
Not yet due	2
1–30 days	5

31–60 days	15
61–90 days	25
Over 90 days	50

Required

1. Complete the aging analysis of accounts receivable.
2. Using the beginning balance and other data in the first paragraph, compute the end-of-year balance (before adjustments) for the Accounts Receivable Controlling account and the Allowance for Uncollectible Accounts.
3. Prepare an analysis computing the estimated uncollectible accounts.
4. Prepare a general journal entry to record the estimated uncollectible accounts expense for the year. (Round your adjustment to the nearest dollar.)

Problem 10A-3
Notes Receivable Transactions
(L.O. 7, 8)

Caffoe Manufacturing Company sells frames to various companies. To improve its liquidity, Caffoe follows the practice of discounting any promissory note it receives. The company engaged in the following transactions involving promissory notes:

Jan. 20   Sold frames to Justin Company for $30,000, terms n/10.
     30   Accepted a 90-day, 12 percent promissory note in settlement of the account of Justin.
Feb. 4   Discounted the note from Justin at the bank at 15 percent.
Apr. 30   Because no notice that the note had been dishonored was received, it was assumed that Justin paid the bank.
May 2   Sold merchandise to Redi Company for $20,000, terms n/10.
     12   Received $4,000 cash and a 60-day, 11 percent note for $16,000 in settlement of the Redi account.
     22   Discounted the note from Redi to the bank at 15 percent.
July 11   Received notice that Redi had dishonored the note. Paid the bank the maturity value of the note plus a protest fee of $10.
Aug. 1   Wrote off the Redi account as uncollectible following news that the company had been declared bankrupt.
     24   Received a 120-day, 12 percent note for $30,000 from Multi-Jump Company in settlement of an account receivable.
     28   Discounted the note from Multi-Jump at the bank at 11 percent.
Dec. 22   Received notice that Multi-Jump had dishonored the note. Paid the bank the maturity value of the note plus a protest fee of $10.
     31   Received payment in full from Multi-Jump including 15 percent interest for the 9 days since the note was dishonored.

Required

Prepare general journal entries to record the above transactions.

Problem 10A-4
Notes Receivable Transactions
(L.O. 7, 8)

It is the policy of Hartsock Electronics Company to accept notes in payment for large sales. The transactions involving notes for the months of June and October are presented below.

June 4   Accepted a $12,000, 120-day, 10 percent note from Wu Company in payment for merchandise.
     6   Accepted a $16,200, 120-day, 12 percent note from Phillips Equipment in payment for a purchase of merchandise.
     11   Discounted the Wu Company note at the bank at 12 percent.
     21   Discounted the Phillips Equipment note at the bank at 14 percent.

26 Accepted a $20,100, 120-day, 9 percent note from Levey Company in payment for a purchase of merchandise.

28 Accepted a $28,200, 120-day, 10 percent note from Villas Company in payment for a purchase of merchandise.

Oct. 2 Received no notice of dishonor by Wu Company and assumed that the company had paid its obligation to the bank.

4 Received notice from the bank that Phillips Equipment had dishonored its note. Paid the bank the maturity value plus a protest fee of $10.

18 Delivered the Villas Company note to the bank for collection.

24 Levey Company dishonored its note.

26 Received notice that Villas Company paid its note plus interest in full to the bank. The bank credited the amount to Hartsock's account and charged a $12 collection fee.

29 Received payment from Phillips Equipment for the total amount owed, including maturity value, protest fee, and interest at 9 percent for the 25 days past maturity.

31 Read in the *Wall Street Journal* that Levey Company was filing for bankruptcy. Wrote the Levey account off as uncollectible. (Hartsock uses the allowance method.)

Required

Prepare general journal entries to record the above transactions.

Problem 10A-5
Short-Term
Financing by
Discounting
Customers'
Notes
(L.O. 7, 8)

The management of Toppe Toy Company believes that the company will be at a competitive advantage if terms of 120 days can be offered to toy distributors. These terms enable the distributors to buy toys in September for the Christmas season and collect for them from the retailers before payment must be made in January. The cash flow of the company is not adequate to allow such generous terms. However, the controller of the company has worked out a plan with the bank to finance the receivables from the sales. The plan calls for the company to receive a 120-day, 12 percent note for each sale to each distributor. Each note will be discounted at the bank at the rate of 15 percent.

During September, Toppe Toy made the following sales under the plan:

Company	Amount of Note	Date of Note	Discount Date
Jay Co.	$438,400	Sept. 4	Sept. 6
Toy Shoppe	295,000	Sept. 10	Sept. 18
F & G Co.	364,600	Sept. 21	Sept. 24

During January, Jay and F & G paid on the due date. Toy Shoppe dishonored the note. The note was then paid, along with a protest fee of $15, by Toppe Toy. Toppe Toy collected in full from Toy Shoppe on January 31. No interest from the maturity date was collected.

Required

1. Prepare general journal entries to record September transactions on Toppe Toy Company records.

2. What was the total cash generated during September from the discounting of notes receivable?

3. Prepare general journal entries to record January transactions on Toppe Toy records.

4. What is your evaluation of the plan? What offsetting factors occur in later months such as January?

Problem Set B

**Problem 10B-1
Percentage of
Net Sales
Method
(L.O. 3, 4)**

On December 31 of last year, the balance sheet of Griffin Company had accounts receivable of $157,000 and a credit balance in the Allowance for Uncollectible Accounts of $9,700. During the current year, the company's records included the following selected activities: sales on account, $607,500; sales returns and allowances, $37,500; collections from customers, $575,000; accounts written off as worthless, $8,000; written-off accounts unexpectedly collected, $1,000. In the past, the company had found that 1.5 percent of net sales would not be collected.

Required

1. Give the summary general journal entries to record each of the five items listed above.
2. Give the general journal entry to record the estimated uncollectible accounts expense for the year.
3. Open ledger accounts for the Accounts Receivable controlling account (112) and the Allowance for Uncollectible Accounts (113), enter the beginning balances in these accounts, and post the appropriate parts of the transactions in **1** and **2** to these accounts.

**Problem 10B-2
Accounts
Receivable
Aging Method
(L.O. 3, 4)**

Kerr Company uses the accounts receivable aging method to estimate uncollectible accounts. The Accounts Receivable controlling account and the Allowance for Uncollectible Accounts had balances of $344,000 and $24,000, respectively, at the beginning of the year. During the year, the company had sales on account of $1,892,000, sales returns and allowances of $16,800, worthless accounts written off of $28,300, and collections from customers of $1,802,920.

At the end of the year (December 31), a junior accountant for the company was preparing an aging analysis of accounts receivable. At the top of page 6 of his report, his totals appeared as follows:

Customer Account	Total	Not Yet Due	1–30 Days Past Due	31–60 Days Past Due	61–90 Days Past Due	Over 90 Days Past Due
Balance forward	$352,500	$194,600	$92,900	$35,720	$16,480	$12,800

He had the following accounts remaining to finish the analysis:

Account	Amount	Due Date
J. Upton	$ 3,480	Jan. 14 (next year)
A. Vermil	2,360	Dec. 24
R. Vickrey	7,820	Sept. 28
J. Wilkerson	8,400	Aug. 16
B. Youngblood	1,500	Dec. 14
N. Youst	10,740	Jan. 23 (next year)
T. Zimmer	1,180	Nov. 5
	$35,480	

The company has found from past experience that the following rates of estimated uncollectible accounts produce an adequate balance for the Allowance for Uncollectible Accounts:

Time Past Due	Percentage Considered Uncollectible
Not yet due	2
1–30 days	4
31–60 days	20
61–90 days	30
Over 90 days	50

Required

1. Complete the aging analysis of accounts receivable.
2. Using the beginning balance and the other data in the first paragraph, compute the end-of-year balance (before adjustments) for the Accounts Receivable Controlling account and the Allowance for Uncollectible Accounts.
3. Prepare an analysis computing the estimated uncollectible accounts.
4. Prepare a general journal entry to record the estimated uncollectible accounts expense for the year. (Round adjustment to the nearest dollar.)

Problem 10B-3
Notes Receivable Transactions
(L.O. 8)

Ross Manufacturing Company engaged in the following transactions involving promissory notes:

Jan. 14	Sold merchandise to James Sales Company for $7,100, terms n/30.
Feb. 13	Received $2,100 in cash from James Sales and received a 90-day, 8 percent promissory note for the balance of the account.
23	Discounted the note at the bank at 10 percent.
May 14	Because no notice that the note had been dishonored was received, it was assumed that James Sales paid the bank.
15	Received a 60-day, 12 percent note from Gay Sales Company in payment of a past-due account, $3,000.
30	Discounted the note at the bank at 15 percent.
July 14	Received notice that Gay Sales dishonored the note. Paid the bank the maturity value of the note plus a protest fee of $5.
20	Received a check from Gay Sales for payment of the maturity value of the note, the $5 protest fee, and interest at 12 percent for the six days beyond maturity.
25	Sold merchandise to Mussel Sales Company for $9,000, with payment of $1,500 cash down and the remainder on account.
31	Received a $7,500, 45-day, 10 percent promissory note from Mussel Sales for the outstanding account.
Aug. 5	Discounted the note at the bank at 14 percent.
Sept. 14	Received notice that Mussel Sales dishonored the note. Paid the bank the maturity value of the note plus a protest fee of $6.
25	Wrote off the Mussel Sales Company account as uncollectible following news that the company had been declared bankrupt.

Required

Prepare general journal entries to record the above transactions.

Problem 10B-4
Notes Receivable Transactions
(L.O. 8)

Merriman Hardware Store engaged in the following transactions:

Jan. 2	Accepted a $10,800, 90-day, 14 percent note from Joan Revel as an extension on her past-due account.
5	Accepted a $1,800, 90-day, 12 percent note from Kevin Harris in payment of a past-due account receivable.

Jan. 10 Accepted a $3,600, 90-day, 10 percent note from Ray Muhmed as an extension of a past-due account.
  12 Discounted the Joan Revel note at the bank at 10 percent.
  25 Discounted the Ray Muhmed note at the bank at 12 percent.
  30 Accepted a $5,200, 90-day, 12 percent note from Robert Simons in lieu of immediate payment of a past-due account.
Apr. 2 Received notice that Joan Revel had dishonored her note. Paid the bank the maturity value plus a protest fee of $6.
  5 Kevin Harris dishonored his note.
  10 Received no notice of dishonor by Ray Muhmed and assumed he paid his obligation to the bank.
  22 Received payment from Joan Revel for the total amount owed including maturity value, protest fee, and interest at 10 percent for the twenty days past maturity.
  25 Wrote off the Kevin Harris account as uncollectible because he could not be located.
  26 Delivered the Robert Simons note to bank for collection.
  30 Received notice that Robert Simons paid his note plus interest in full to the bank. The bank credited the amount to Merriman's account and charged a $5 collection fee.

Required

Prepare general journal entries to record the above transactions.

Problem 10B-5
Short-Term Financing by Discounting Customers' Notes
(L.O. 7, 8)

The Lacking Company is faced with a severe cash shortage because of slowing sales and past-due accounts. The financial vice president has studied the situation and has found a number of very large past-due accounts. He makes the following recommendations: (a) that the company seek promissory notes from past-due accounts to encourage the customers to pay on time and to earn interest on the money invested in these accounts, and (b) that the company generate cash by discounting the notes at the bank at the going rate of interest. During the first month of this program, the company was successful, as indicated by the following table:

Company	Amount of Note	Length of Note	Date of Note	Interest Rate	Discount Date	Discount Rate
Eve Manufacturing Company	$ 65,000	60 days	Apr. 5	15%	Apr. 7	15%
Johnson Company	100,000	60 days	Apr. 10	12%	Apr. 13	15%
Dean Corporation	40,000	60 days	Apr. 15	14%	Apr. 20	15%

Eve Manufacturing and Johnson Company paid their notes on the due dates. Dean Corporation dishonored its note on the due date.

Required

1. Prepare appropriate general journal entries for April.
2. What was the total cash generated during April by the vice president's plan?
3. Prepare appropriate general journal entries for June.
4. What is your evaluation of the plan? What offsetting factors occur in later months such as June?

Financial Decision Case 10-1

Elliot Electron-ics, Inc.
(L.O. 1, 2)

Two years ago Mark and Prudence Elliot began Elliot Electronics on a shoestring budget. Hard work and personal attention have brought success to their business, which sells television sets, video-tape machines, and other electronic entertainment devices. However, because of insufficient funds to finance credit sales, they have accepted only cash and bank credit cards. They are now considering a new policy of offering installment sales on terms of 25 percent down and 25 percent per month for three months, as well as continuing to accept cash and bank credit cards. They feel that this policy will boost sales greatly during the coming fall season. But to follow through on the new policy they will need a bank loan. To apply for the loan, they must make financial projections showing the effects of the new policy.

The Elliots project sales for the last third of the year as follows:

September	October	November	December
$30,000	$50,000	$80,000	$100,000

They also expect 20 percent of sales to be for cash, 30 percent to be by credit card on which a 5 percent fee is paid, and 50 percent to be on installment sales.

The Elliots have a financial agreement with their suppliers that requires them to buy and pay for their inventory in the month that they sell the items. This arrangement is called buying on consignment. Part of the Elliots' success has stemmed from their policy of selling at a discount price. They set the price at one-third above cost. (In other words, cost equals 75 percent of selling price.) This price is lower than that charged by most retail stores, and they intend to continue this policy. The Elliots feel that other costs associated with the new policy will increase cash outlays for operating expenses to $7,000 per month.

Required

1. Prepare a schedule that will show the impact of the new credit policy on cash receipts and payments for each of the four months. How much money in total will the Elliots need to borrow by December 31 to finance the new credit policy?
2. What will the level of accounts receivable be on December 31 if the Elliots' projections are met? What factors have they ignored? How would you change their projections to make them more realistic? What technique would you apply to accounts receivable at the end of each month to determine if the assumptions about collectibility are being met?

This chapter begins by describing nonmonetary assets and their relationship to the matching rule. The rest of the chapter deals with inventory measurement, emphasizing its importance to income determination and explaining several different ways of determining, valuing, and estimating inventories. After studying this chapter, you should be able to meet the learning objectives listed at the left.

Nonmonetary Assets and the Matching Rule

On the one hand, **monetary assets** consist of cash and other assets representing the right to receive a specific amount of cash. **Nonmonetary assets,** on the other hand, are unexpired costs that will become expenses in future accounting periods. These assets are recorded at historical cost and are allocated to expense in accordance with the matching rule. It is not likely that the amount at which they are shown on the balance sheet would represent the amount of cash that could be gained from their sale because the allocation process is not an attempt to reflect the changing prices of the assets since their purchase.

Nonmonetary assets are of two kinds: short-term and long-term. **Short-term nonmonetary assets** come under the heading of current assets. Among these assets are prepaid rent, prepaid insurance, and other prepaid expenses. Inventories, too, are usually considered short-term nonmonetary assets.

Long-term nonmonetary assets must be allocated as expenses to two or more future years because they will have a positive effect on revenues during those years. In other words, they are unexpired costs that will expire over more than one future year. In most cases, long-term nonmonetary assets fall into the following three groups: (1) property, plant, and equipment; (2) natural resources; and (3) intangibles.

The most important accounting problem that arises in connection with all nonmonetary assets is the application of the matching rule. Nonmonetary assets are recorded at first as assets or unexpired costs. According to the matching rule, they must be recorded as expenses in the accounting period that they benefit. We have seen, for example, that a three-year insurance policy is recorded as a debit to Prepaid Insurance and a credit to Cash or Accounts Payable. As time passes, it is necessary to use adjusting entries to charge the expired part of the policy to expense by debiting Insurance Expense and crediting Prepaid Insurance. To measure income properly, two important questions must be answered about each nonmonetary asset: (1) How much of the asset is used up or has expired during the current accounting period and should be transferred to expense? (2) How much of the asset is still unused or unexpired and should remain on the balance sheet as an asset?

Objective 1
Define nonmonetary assets and state their relationship to the matching rule

Determining the amount of the expense will automatically establish the amount of the asset. In the case of insurance and other prepaid expenses, these calculations are fairly simple. However, the theoretical and practical problems associated with these measurements for inventories and long-term nonmonetary assets are among the most complex in accounting and have created much debate within and outside the accounting profession. For this reason, the rest of this chapter will deal with the application of the matching rule to inventories. Chapter 13 covers property, plant, and equipment, as well as natural resources, and part of Chapter 14 covers intangibles.

Inventories and Income Determination

The major source of revenue for retail or wholesale businesses is the sale of merchandise. In terms of dollars invested, the inventory of goods held for sale is one of the largest assets for a merchandising business. Because merchandise is continuously bought and sold, the cost of goods sold is the largest deduction from sales. In fact, it is often larger than all other expenses together.

Objective 2
Define merchandise inventory and show how the inventory measurement affects income determination

Merchandise inventory consists of all goods that are owned and held for sale in the regular course of business, including goods in transit if shipped FOB shipping point. Because it will normally be converted into cash within a year's time, merchandise inventory is considered a current asset. It is shown on the balance sheet just below Accounts Receivable because it is one step further removed from Cash.

In a manufacturing company, inventories are of three major kinds: materials, partly completed products (often called work in process), and finished goods. The discussion in this chapter applies to manufacturing as well as to merchandising inventories. However, accounting for manufacturing operations will be covered in Part VI.

Objective of Inventory Measurement

The American Institute of Certified Public Accountants states, "A major objective of accounting for inventories is the proper determination of income through the process of matching appropriate costs against revenues."[1] Note that the objective is to determine the best measure of income, not the most realistic inventory value. As you will see, the two objectives are sometimes incompatible, in which case the objective of income determination takes precedence over a realistic inventory figure for the balance sheet.

Review of Gross Margin and Cost of Goods Sold Computations

Because the computations of gross margin and cost of goods sold were presented much earlier in the text, a review might help to show how the cost assigned to inventory and these computations are related. The gross margin on sales earned during an accounting period is computed by deducting cost of goods sold from the net sales of the period. Cost of goods sold is measured by deducting ending inventory from cost of goods available for sale.

It is clear that the higher the cost of ending inventory, the lower the cost of goods sold will be and the higher the resulting gross margin. Conversely, the lower the value assigned to ending inventory, the higher the cost of goods sold will be and the lower the gross margin. *In effect, the value assigned to the ending inventory determines what portion of the cost of goods originally available for sale will be deducted from net sales as cost of goods sold and what portion will be carried to the next period as beginning inventory.* Remember that the amount of goods available for sale includes the beginning inventory (unexpired costs passed from the last period to this period) plus net purchases during this period. The effects on income of errors in the cost of ending inventory are demonstrated in the next section.

Effects of Errors in Inventory Measurement

As seen above, the basic problem of separating goods available for sale into the two components, goods sold and goods not sold, is that of assigning a cost to the goods not sold or to the ending inventory. However, the determination of an ending inventory cost in effect decides the cost of goods sold. The reason is that whatever portion of the cost of goods available for sale is assigned to the ending inventory, the remainder is cost of goods sold.

For this reason, an error made in determining the inventory figure at the end of the period will cause an equal error in gross margin and net income in the income statement. The amount of assets and owner's equity in the balance sheet also will be misstated by the same amount. The consequences of overstatement and understatement of inventory are illustrated

1. American Institute of Certified Public Accountants, *Accounting Research Bulletins*, No. 43, Ch. 4 (New York: AICPA, 1968).

Chapter Eleven

in the three simplified examples given below. In each case, beginning inventory, purchases, and cost of goods available for sale are correctly stated. In the first example, ending inventory has been stated correctly. In the second example, inventory is overstated by $6,000, and in the third example, inventory is understated by $6,000.

Example 1. Ending Inventory Correctly Stated at $10,000

Income Statement for the Year		Cost of Goods Sold for the Year	
Net Sales	$100,000	Beginning Inventory	$12,000
Cost of Goods Sold	60,000 ←	Net Purchases	58,000
Gross Margin	$40,000	Cost of Goods Available for Sale	$70,000
Expenses	30,000	Ending Inventory	10,000
Net Income	$10,000	→ Cost of Goods Sold	$60,000

Example 2. Ending Inventory Overstated by $6,000

Income Statement for the Year		Cost of Goods Sold for the Year	
Net Sales	$100,000	Beginning Inventory	$12,000
Cost of Goods Sold	54,000 ←	Net Purchases	58,000
Gross Margin	$46,000	Cost of Goods Available for Sale	$70,000
Expenses	30,000	Ending Inventory	16,000
Net Income	$16,000	→ Cost of Goods Sold	$54,000

Example 3. Ending Inventory Understated by $6,000

Income Statement for the Year		Cost of Goods Sold for the Year	
Net Sales	$100,000	Beginning Inventory	$12,000
Cost of Goods Sold	66,000 ←	Net Purchases	58,000
Gross Margin	$34,000	Cost of Goods Available for Sale	$70,000
Expenses	30,000	Ending Inventory	4,000
Net Income	$4,000	→ Cost of Goods Sold	$66,000

In these examples, the total cost of goods available for sale amounted to $70,000 in each case. The difference in net income resulted from how this $70,000 was divided among ending inventory and cost of goods sold.

Because the ending inventory in one period becomes the beginning inventory in the following period, it is important to recognize that an error in inventory valuation affects not only the current period but also the income statement for the following period. Using the same figures as examples 1 and 2 above, the income statements for two successive years in Figure 11-1 illustrate this carry-over effect.

Note that over a period of two years the errors will be offset or counter-balanced with regard to net income. In Figure 11-1, for example, the overstatement of ending inventory in 19x1 caused a $6,000 overstatement of beginning inventory in the following year, resulting in an understatement of income by the same amount. This offsetting effect is shown as follows:

	With Inventory Correctly Stated	With Inventory at Dec. 31, 19x1, Overstated	
		Reported Net Income Will Be	Reported Net Income Will Be Overstated (Understated)
Net Income for 19x1	$10,000	$16,000	$6,000
Net Income for 19x2	15,000	9,000	(6,000)
Total Net Income for Two Years	$25,000	$25,000	—

Because the total income for the two years is the same, there may be a tendency to think that one does not need to worry about inventory errors. This idea is not correct because many management decisions as well as creditor and investor decisions are made on an annual basis and depend on the accountant's description of net income. The accountant has an obligation to make the net income figure as useful as possible.

The effects of errors in inventory on net income can be summarized as follows:

1. When the *ending* inventory is understated, the net income for the period will be understated.
2. When the *ending* inventory is overstated, the net income for the period will be overstated.
3. When the *beginning* inventory is understated, the net income for the period will be overstated.
4. When the *beginning* inventory is overstated, the net income for the period will be understated.

If we assume no income tax effects, a change or error in inventory of one amount results in a change or error in net income of the same amount. Thus the measurement of inventory is an important problem and is the subject of the remainder of this chapter.

Figure 11-1
Effect of Error in Ending Inventory on Current and Succeeding
Year

Effect of Error in Inventory
Income Statement
For the Year Ended December 31, 19x1

	Correct Statement of Ending Inventory		Overstatement of Ending Inventory	
Sales		$100,000		$100,000
Cost of Goods Sold				
Beginning Inventory, Dec. 31, 19x0	$12,000		$12,000	
Purchases	58,000		58,000	
Cost of Goods Available for Sale	$70,000		$70,000	
Less Ending Inventory, Dec. 31, 19x1	10,000		16,000	
Cost of Goods Sold		60,000		54,000
Gross Margin on Sales		$ 40,000		$ 46,000
Operating Expenses		30,000		30,000
Net Income		$ 10,000		$ 16,000

Effect on Succeeding Year
Income Statement
For the Year Ended December 31, 19x2

	Correct Statement of Beginning Inventory		Overstatement of Beginning Inventory	
Sales		$130,000		$130,000
Cost of Goods Sold				
Beginning Inventory, Dec. 31, 19x1	$10,000		$16,000	
Purchases	68,000		68,000	
Cost of Goods Available for Sale	$78,000		$84,000	
Less Ending Inventory, Dec. 31, 19x2	13,000		13,000	
Cost of Goods Sold		65,000		71,000
Gross Margin on Sales		$ 65,000		$ 59,000
Operating Expenses		50,000		50,000
Net Income		$ 15,000		$ 9,000

Inventory Measurement

The cost assigned to ending inventory depends on two measurements: quantity and price. At least once each year, a business must take an actual physical count of all items of merchandise held for sale. This process is called taking a physical inventory, or simply taking inventory, as described in Chapter 6. Although some companies take inventory at various times during the year, many companies take inventory only at the end of each year. Taking the inventory consists of (1) counting the items on hand, (2) pricing each item, and (3) extending (multiplying) to determine the total.

Merchandise in Transit

Because merchandise inventory includes items owned by the company and held for sale, purchased merchandise in transit should be included in the inventory count if title to the goods has passed. In Chapter 6, we pointed out that the terms of the shipping agreement must be examined to determine if title has passed. If goods were shipped FOB shipping point, then title was passed when the goods were given to the common carrier, and they should be counted in the purchaser's inventory even though they may not have been received by the date of the inventory. If the shipping terms were FOB destination, however, then the goods do not belong to the purchaser until they are actually delivered and thus should not be counted in the inventory if they have not been received.

Sold Merchandise on Hand

At the time a physical inventory is taken, a business will undoubtedly have some orders for goods on hand, and some of these goods may be segregated for delivery. If the sale is completed and the goods in question now belong to the buyer and await delivery, title is assumed to have passed to the buyer, and the goods should not be counted in inventory. Of course, the sale must also have been recorded as revenue.

Pricing the Inventory at Cost

The pricing of inventory is one of the most interesting and most widely debated problems in accounting. As demonstrated above, the value placed on ending inventory can have a dramatic effect on net income for each of two consecutive years. For this reason, the ability of companies to raise money by borrowing and by selling more capital stock as well as the amount of dividends they can pay are affected by the value of the inventory. Also, because federal income taxes are based on income, the valuation of inventory may have a considerable effect on the amount of income taxes to be paid. Federal income tax authorities have therefore been interested in the effects of various inventory valuation procedures and have specific regulations about the acceptability of different methods. So the accountant is sometimes faced with the problem of balancing the goals of proper income determination with those of minimizing income taxes payable.

There are a number of acceptable methods of valuing inventories in the accounts and on the financial statements. Most are based either on cost or on the lower of cost or market. Both methods are acceptable for income tax purposes. We will first explain variations of the cost basis of inventory valuation and then turn to the lower-of-cost-or-market method.

Cost Defined

According to the AICPA, "The primary basis of accounting for inventory is cost, which has been defined generally as the price paid or consideration given to acquire an asset. As applied to inventories, cost means in principle the sum of the applicable expenditures and charges directly or indirectly incurred in bringing an article to its existing condition and location."[2]

This definition of inventory cost has generally been interpreted in practice to include the following costs: (1) invoice price less cash discounts; (2) freight or transportation in, including insurance in transit; and (3) applicable taxes and tariffs.

Other costs, such as those for purchasing, receiving, and storage, should in principle also be included in inventory cost. In practice, however, it is so hard to allocate these costs to specific inventory items that they are in most cases considered an expense of the accounting period instead of an inventory cost.

Methods of Pricing Inventory at Cost

The prices of most kinds of merchandise vary during the year, and identical lots of merchandise may have been purchased at different prices. Also, when identical items are bought and sold, it is often impossible to tell which items have been sold and which are still in inventory. For this reason, it is necessary to make an assumption about the order in which items have been sold. Because the assumed order of sale may or may not be the same as the actual order of sale, the assumption is really an assumption about the flow of costs rather than the flow of physical inventory.

Thus the term goods flow refers to the actual physical movement of goods in the operations of the company, and the term cost flow refers to the association of costs with their *assumed* flow within the operations of the company. The assumed cost flow may or may not be the same as the actual goods flow. Though this statement may seem strange at first, there is nothing wrong with it. Several assumed cost flows are acceptable under generally accepted accounting principles. In fact, it is sometimes preferable to use an assumed cost flow that bears no relationship to goods flow because it gives a better estimate of income, which, as stated earlier, is the major goal of inventory valuation.

2. Ibid.

Accountants usually price inventory by using one of the following generally accepted methods, each based on a different assumption of cost flow: (1) specific identification method; (2) average-cost method; (3) first-in, first-out method (FIFO); and (4) last-in, first-out method (LIFO).

Under the **specific identification method,** the actual cost of a particular item is assigned to that item. But because specific identification is not practical in most cases, accountants usually price inventory by using one of the other three generally accepted methods. The **average-cost method** assumes that each item carries an equal cost, which is figured by dividing the total cost of the goods available for sale by the number of units available for sale to arrive at an average unit cost. Under the **first-in, first-out (FIFO) method,** it is assumed that the costs of the first items purchased are assigned to the first items sold and the costs of the last items purchased are assigned to the items remaining in inventory. Under the **last-in, first-out (LIFO) method,** it is assumed that the costs of the last items purchased are assigned to the first items sold. As a result, the cost of the inventory on hand is composed of the costs of items from the oldest purchases. The inventory cost methods used by six hundred large companies are shown in Figure 11-2.

To illustrate the four methods, the following data for the month of June will be used:

Inventory Data, June 30

June	1	Inventory	50 units at $1.00	$ 50
	6	Purchased	50 units at $1.10	55
	13	Purchased	150 units at $1.20	180
	20	Purchased	100 units at $1.30	130
	25	Purchased	150 units at $1.40	210
Totals			500 units	$625
Sales			280 units	
On hand June 30			220 units	

Figure 11-2
Inventory Cost
Methods Used
by 600 Large
Companies

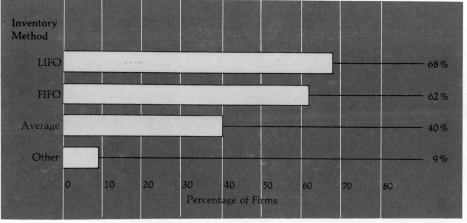

Total percentage exceeds 100 because some companies used different methods for different types of inventory.
Source: American Institute of Certified Public Accountants, *Accounting Trends and Techniques* (New York: AICPA, 1982).

Chapter Eleven

Note that the total available for sale is 500 units, at a total cost of $625. Stated simply, the problem of inventory pricing is to divide the $625 between the 280 units sold and the 220 units on hand.

Specific Identification Method If the units in the ending inventory can be identified as coming from specific purchases, they may be priced at the specific prices of these purchases. For instance, assume that the June 30 inventory consisted of 50 units from the inventory on hand June 1, 100 units of the purchase of June 13, and 70 units of the purchase of June 25. The cost to be assigned to the inventory under the specific identification method would be $268, determined as follows:

*Objective 3a
Calculate the
pricing of inven-
tory, using the
cost basis
according to the
specific identifi-
cation method*

Inventory, June 30—Specific Identification Method

50 units at $1.00	$ 50
100 units at $1.20	120
70 units at $1.40	98
220 units at a value of	$268

The cost of goods sold during June under the specific identification method is determined as follows:

Cost of Goods Available for Sale	$625
Less June 30 Inventory	268
Cost of Goods Sold	$357

The specific identification method might be used in the purchase and sale of high-priced articles such as automobiles, heavy equipment, and jewelry. However, although this method may appear to have a certain logic to it, it is not actually used much because it has two definite disadvantages. First, it is very difficult and impractical in most cases to keep track of the purchase and sale of individual items. Second, when a company deals in items of an identical nature, deciding which items are sold becomes arbitrary; thus the company can raise or lower income by choosing to sell the high- or low-cost items.

Average-Cost Method Under the average cost method, it is assumed that the cost of inventory is the average cost of goods on hand at the beginning of the period plus all goods purchased during the period. Average cost is computed by dividing the total cost of goods available for sale by the total units available for sale. This gives a weighted-average unit cost, that is applied to the units in the ending inventory. The ending inventory in the illustration when the average-cost method is used would be $1.25 per unit, or a total of $275, determined as follows:

*Objective 3b
Calculate the
pricing of
inventory, using
the cost basis
according to the
average-cost
method*

Inventory, June 30—Average-Cost Method

June	1	Inventory	50 at $1.00	$ 50
	6	Purchased	50 at $1.10	55
	13	Purchased	150 at $1.20	180
	20	Purchased	100 at $1.30	130
	25	Purchased	150 at $1.40	210
Totals			500 units	$625

Average unit cost: $625 ÷ 500 = $1.25
Ending inventory: 220 units @ $1.25 = $275

The cost of goods sold during June under the average-cost method would be as follows:

Cost of Goods Available for Sale	$625
Less June 30 Inventory	275
Cost of Goods Sold	$350

The cost figure obtained for the ending inventory under the average-cost method is influenced by all the prices paid during the year and thus tends to level out the effects that cost increases and decreases during the year have on income. Some criticize the average-cost method because they feel that more recent costs should receive more attention and are more relevant for income measurement and decision making.

First-In, First-Out (FIFO) Method The first-in, first-out method, usually called FIFO, is based on the assumption that the costs of the first items acquired should be assigned to the first items sold. The costs of the goods on hand at the end of a period are assumed to be from the most recent purchases and the costs assigned to goods that have been sold are assumed to be from the earliest purchases. The FIFO method of determining inventory cost may be adopted by any business, regardless of the actual physical flow of goods, because the assumption is made regarding the flow of costs and not the flow of goods.

Objective 3c Calculate the pricing of inventory, using the cost basis according to the first-in, first-out (FIFO) method

For example, in our illustration, the June 30 inventory would be $301 when the FIFO method is used. It is computed as follows:

Inventory, June 30—First-In, First-Out Method

150 units at $1.40 from the purchase of June 25	$210
70 units at $1.30 from the purchase of June 20	91
220 units at a value of	$301

The cost of goods sold during June under the FIFO method would be $324, determined as follows:

Cost of Goods Available for Sale	$625
Less June 30 Inventory	301
Cost of Goods Sold	$324

The effect of the FIFO method is to value the ending inventory at the most recent prices and include earlier prices in cost of goods sold. During periods of consistently rising prices, the FIFO method yields the highest possible amount of net income. One reason for this result is that businesses tend to increase selling prices as prices rise, regardless of the fact that inventories may have been purchased before the price rise. The reverse effect occurs in periods of price decreases. For these reasons a major criticism of FIFO is that it stresses the effects of the business cycle on business income.

Objective 3d
Calculate the
pricing of
inventory, using
the cost basis
according to the
last-in, first-out
(LIFO) method

Last-In, First-Out (LIFO) Method The LIFO method of costing inventories is based on the assumption that the costs of the last items purchased should be assigned to the first to be used or sold and that the cost of the ending inventory consists of the cost of merchandise purchased earlier.

Under this method, the June 30 inventory would be $249, computed as follows:

Inventory, June 30—Last-In, First-Out Method

50 units at $1.00 from June 1 inventory	$ 50
50 units at $1.10 from purchase of June 6	55
120 units at $1.20 from purchase of June 13	144
220 units at a value of	$249

The cost of goods sold during June under the LIFO method would be $376, computed as follows:

Cost of Goods Available for Sale	$625
Less June 30 Inventory	249
Cost of Goods Sold	$376

The effect of LIFO is to value inventory at earlier prices and to include in cost of goods sold the most recent purchases of goods. This assumption, of course, does not agree with the actual physical movement of goods in most businesses.

However, there is a strong logical argument to support this method, based on the fact that a certain size inventory is necessary in a going concern. When inventory is sold, it must be replaced with more goods. The supporters of LIFO reason that the fairest determination of income occurs if the current costs of merchandise are matched against current sales prices, regardless of which physical units of merchandise are sold. When prices are moving either upward or downward, LIFO will mean that the cost of goods sold will show costs closer to the price level at the time the sales of goods are made. As a result, the LIFO method tends to show a smaller net income during inflationary times and a larger net income during deflationary times than other methods of inventory valuation. Thus the peaks and valleys of the business cycle tend to be smoothed out. The important factor here is that in inventory valuation the flow of costs and hence income determination is more important than the physical movement of goods and balance sheet valuation.

An argument may also be made against the LIFO method. Because the inventory valuation on the balance sheet reflects earlier prices, this value is often unrealistic with respect to the current value of the inventory. Thus such balance sheet measures as working capital and current ratio may have limited usefulness.

Comparison of the Alternative Methods of Pricing Inventory

The specific identification, average-cost, FIFO, and LIFO methods of pricing inventory have now been illustrated. The specific identification

Objective 4
Recognize the
effects of each
method on
income determi-
nation in peri-
ods of changing
prices

method is based on actual costs, whereas the other three methods are based on assumptions regarding the flow of costs. Let us now compare the effects of the four methods on net income using the same data as before and assuming sales during June of $500.

	Specific Identification Method	Average-Cost Method	First-In, First-Out Method	Last-In, First-Out Method
Sales	$500	$500	$500	$500
Cost of Goods Sold				
Beginning Inventory	$ 50	$ 50	$ 50	$ 50
Purchases	575	575	575	575
Cost of Goods Available for Sale	$625	$625	$625	$625
Less Ending Inventory	268	275	301	249
Cost of Goods Sold	$357	$350	$324	$376
Gross Margin on Sales	$143	$150	$176	$124

Keeping in mind that in the illustration June was a period of rising prices, we can see that LIFO, which charges the most recent and in this case the highest prices to cost of goods sold, resulted in the lowest net income. Conversely, FIFO, which charges the earliest and in this case the lowest prices to cost of goods sold, produced the highest net income. The net income under the average-cost method is somewhere between those computed under LIFO and FIFO. Thus it is clear that this method has a leveling effect.

During a period of declining prices, the reverse effects would occur. The LIFO method would produce a higher net income than the FIFO method. It is apparent that the method of inventory valuation takes on the greatest importance during prolonged periods of price changes in one direction, either up or down.

Effect on the Financial Statements Each of the four methods of inventory pricing presented above is acceptable for use in published financial statements. Each has its advantages and disadvantages, and none can be considered as best or perfect. The factors that should be considered in choosing an inventory method are the effects of each method on the balance sheet, the income statement, income taxes, and management decisions.

A basic problem in determining the best inventory measure for a particular company is that inventory appears on both the balance sheet and the income statement. As we have seen, the LIFO method is best suited for the income statement because it best matches revenues and cost of goods sold. But it is not the best measure of the current balance sheet value of inventory, particularly when there has been a prolonged period of price rises or decreases. The FIFO method, on the other hand, is best suited to the balance sheet because the ending inventory is closest to current values and thus gives a more realistic view of the current financial assets of a business. Readers of financial statements must be alert to inventory methods and be able to assess their effects.

Effect on Income Taxes When prices are changing rapidly, management must base its sales policies on current replacement costs of the goods being sold. The LIFO method most nearly represents the measurement of net income based on these current costs. In addition, as seen in the illustration above, in periods of rising prices LIFO shows a smaller profit. Thus, many businesses use LIFO to reduce the amount of income taxes to be paid.

Many accountants believe that the use of FIFO or average-cost methods in periods of rising prices causes businesses to report fictitious profit, resulting in the payment of excess income taxes. The profit is fictitious because the company must now buy inventory at new higher prices, but some of the funds that should have been used for purchase of replacement inventory went to pay income taxes. During the rapid inflation of 1979 to 1982, billions of dollars reported as profits and paid in income taxes were believed to be the result of poor matching of current costs and revenues under the FIFO and average-cost methods. Consequently, many companies have since switched to the LIFO inventory method.

Valuing the Inventory at the Lower of Cost or Market (LCM)

*Objective 5
Apply the
lower-of-cost-or-
market (LCM)
rule to inven-
tory valuation*

Although cost is usually the most appropriate basis for valuation of inventory, there are times when inventory may properly be valued at less than its cost. If by reason of physical deterioration, obsolescence, or decline in price level the market value of the inventory falls below the cost, a loss has occurred. This loss may be recognized by writing the inventory down to market. The term **market** is used here to mean current replacement cost. For a merchandising company, market is the amount that the company would pay at the present time for the same goods, purchased from the usual suppliers and in the usual quantities. It may help in applying the **lower-of-cost-or-market (LCM) rule** by thinking of it as the "lower-of-cost-or-replacement-cost" rule.

Methods of Applying LCM

There are three basic methods of valuing inventories at the lower of cost or market, as follows: (1) the item-by-item method, (2) the major category method, and (3) the total inventory method.

For example, a stereo shop could determine lower of cost or market for each kind of speaker, receiver, and turntable (item by item); for all speakers, all receivers, and all turntables (major categories); or for all speakers, receivers, and turntables together (total inventory).

Item-by-Item Method   When the item-by-item method is used, cost and market are compared for each item in the inventory. The individual items are then valued at their lower price.

Lower of Cost or Market with Item-by-Item Method

| | | Per Unit | | Lower of |
	Quantity	Cost	Market	Cost or Market
Category I				
Item a	200	$1.50	$1.70	$ 300
Item b	100	2.00	1.80	180
Item c	100	2.50	2.60	250
Category II				
Item d	300	5.00	4.50	1,350
Item e	200	4.00	4.10	800
Inventory at the lower of cost or market				$2,880

Major Category Method   Under the major category method, the total cost and total market for each category of items are compared. Each category is then valued at its lower price.

Lower of Cost or Market with Major Category Method

| | | Per Unit | | Total | | Lower of |
	Quantity	Cost	Market	Cost	Market	Cost or Market
Category I						
Item a	200	$1.50	$1.70	$ 300	$ 340	
Item b	100	2.00	1.80	200	180	
Item c	100	2.50	2.60	250	260	
Totals				$ 750	$ 780	$ 750
Category II						
Item d	300	5.00	4.50	$1,500	$1,350	
Item e	200	4.00	4.10	800	820	
Totals				$2,300	$2,170	2,170
Inventory at the lower of cost or market						$2,920

Total Inventory Method   Under the total inventory method, the entire inventory is valued at both cost and market, and the lower price is used to value inventory. Since this method is not acceptable for federal income tax purposes, it is not illustrated here.

A Note on Inventory Valuation and Federal Income Taxes

The Internal Revenue Service has developed several rules for the valuation of inventories for federal income tax purposes. A company has a wide choice of methods, including cost or lower of cost or market and FIFO or LIFO. But once a method is chosen, it must be used consistently from one year to the next. The IRS must approve any changes in inventory valuation method for income tax purposes. This requirement, of course, is also in agreement with the rule of consistency in accounting in that changes in inventory method would cause income to fluctuate too much and would make income statements hard to interpret from year to year. A company can change its inventory method if there is a good reason for doing so. The nature and effect of the change must be shown in its financial statements.

If a company uses the LIFO method in reporting income for tax purposes, the IRS requires that the LIFO method also be used in the accounting records. New regulations may relax this requirement. Also, the IRS will not allow the use of the lower-of-cost-or-market rule if the method of determining cost is the LIFO method. In this case, only the LIFO cost can be used. As noted, another regulation bars the use of the total inventory method for determining lower of cost or market.

Valuing the Inventory by Estimation

It is sometimes necessary or desirable to estimate the value of ending inventory. The methods most commonly used for this purpose are the retail method and the gross profit method.

Retail Method of Inventory Estimation

*Objective 6a
Estimate the
cost of ending
inventory by
using the retail
inventory
method*

The retail method, as its name implies, is used in retail merchandising businesses. There are two principal reasons for the use of the retail method. First, management usually requires that financial statements be prepared at least once a month and, as it is time-consuming and expensive to take physical inventory each month, the retail method must be used to estimate the value of inventory. Second, because items in a retail store normally have a price tag, it is common to take the physical inventory at retail from these price tags and reduce the total value to cost through use of the retail method.

When the retail method is used to estimate an end-of-period inventory, the records must show the amount of inventory at the beginning of the period at cost and at retail. The term *at retail* means the amount of the inventory at the marked selling prices of the inventory items. The records must also show the amount of goods purchased during the period both at cost and at retail. The net sales at retail are, of course, the balance of the

Sales account less returns and discounts. A simple example of the retail method is shown below.

The Retail Method of Inventory Valuation

	Cost	Retail
Beginning Inventory	$ 40,000	$ 55,000
Net Purchases for the Period	107,000	145,000
Freight In	3,000	
Merchandise Available for Sale	$150,000	$200,000
Ratio of cost to retail price: $\frac{\$150,000}{\$200,000} = 75\%$		
Net Sales During the Period		160,000
Ending Inventory at Retail		$ 40,000
Ratio of cost to retail		75%
Estimated Cost of Ending Inventory		$ 30,000

Merchandise available for sale is determined both at cost and at retail by listing beginning inventory and net purchases for the period at cost and at the expected selling price of the goods, adding freight in to the cost column, and totaling. The ratio of these two amounts (cost to retail price) provides an estimate of the cost of each dollar of retail sales value. The ending inventory at retail is then determined by deducting sales for the period from the retail price of the goods that were available for sale during the period. The inventory at retail is now converted to cost on the basis of estimated gross margin. Estimated gross margin is determined by finding the ratio of the cost of merchandise available for sale to the retail (selling) price of the merchandise available for sale. The retail method can be harder to apply in practice because of certain complications such as changes in the retail price that take place during the year.

Gross Profit Method of Inventory Estimation

Objective 6b
Estimate the
cost of ending
inventory by
using the gross
profit method

The gross profit method assumes that the ratio of gross margin for a business remains relatively stable from year to year. It is used in place of the retail method when records of the retail prices of beginning inventory and purchases are not kept. It is also useful in estimating the amount of inventory lost or destroyed by theft, fire, or other hazards. Insurance companies often use this method to verify loss claims.

The gross profit method is very simple to use. First, figure the cost of goods available for sale in the usual way (add purchases to beginning inventory). Second, estimate the cost of goods sold by deducting the estimated gross margin from sales. Third, deduct the estimated cost of goods sold from the goods available for sale. This method is illustrated at the top of the next page.

The Gross Profit Method of Inventory Valuation

1. Beginning Inventory at Cost		$ 50,000
Purchases at Cost		290,000
Cost of Goods Available for Sale		$340,000
2. Less Estimated Cost of Goods Sold		
Sales at Selling Price	$400,000	
Less Estimated Gross Margin of 30%	120,000	
Cost of Goods Sold		280,000
3. Estimated Cost of Ending Inventory		$ 60,000

Periodic and Perpetual Inventory Systems

Objective 7
Distinguish
between perpet-
ual and periodic
inventory
systems

The system of inventories used so far in this book has been based on periodic physical inventories and is known as the **periodic inventory method.** Under this system, the cost of goods sold is figured by adding the net cost of purchases to beginning inventory and subtracting the ending inventory. A physical inventory must be taken or estimated by the retail method or gross profit method to determine inventory at any point in time and must also be taken at the end of the period to figure the cost of goods sold.

Periodic inventory systems are used in many retail and wholesale businesses. However, companies that sell goods having a high unit cost and companies that want to have more control over their inventories may use the **perpetual inventory method.** Under this method, the dollar price per unit and the number of individual items sold or purchased are recorded continuously. So the cost of goods sold during a period and the inventory may be found from the accounting records without taking a physical inventory. Today, because computers can keep records of many inventory items fairly cheaply, the perpetual inventory method is used more often than in the past.

The perpetual inventory system does not separate the Purchases account from the Merchandise Inventory account. Instead, one Merchandise Inventory account that is a controlling account for a subsidiary file of inventory accounts is maintained. This mechanism is very much like that of the Accounts Receivable controlling account and its subsidiary ledger. In the inventory subsidiary file, each item has a card on which purchases and sales are entered as they take place. In this way, the inventory of each item is always kept up to date. A sample perpetual inventory card is shown in Figure 11-3. At any time, this card will show the number of pencil sharpeners on hand, and the total of all the cards is the merchandise inventory.

On June 1, there is a balance of 60 pencil sharpeners that cost $5 each. A sale on June 4 reduces the balance by 10 pencil sharpeners. On June 10, 100 pencil sharpeners are purchased at $6 each. Now the inventory con-

	Item: Pencil Sharpener, Model D-222								
	Received			Sold			Balance		
Date	Units	Cost	Total	Units	Cost	Total	Units	Cost	Balance
June 1							60	5.00	300.00
4				10	5.00	50.00	50	5.00	250.00
10	100	6.00	600.00				50 100	5.00 6.00	850.00
20				30	5.00	150.00	20 100	5.00 6.00	700.00

Figure 11-3
Perpetual
Inventory Rec-
ord Card, FIFO

sists of 50 pencil sharpeners purchased at $5 each and 100 pencil sharpeners purchased at $6 each. The method of inventory valuation in Figure 11-3 is first-in, first-out, as can be determined by looking at the June 20 sale. The entire sale of 30 pencil sharpeners is taken from the 50 sharpeners still left from the beginning inventory. If the LIFO method were used, the sale would be deducted from the latest purchase of 100 pencil sharpeners at $6 each. Under LIFO the resulting balance would be $670 [(50 × $5) + (70 × $6)].

Handling Inventory Systems in the Accounts

Under the periodic inventory method, a Purchases account is used to record merchandise when it is purchased. The Inventory account stays at its beginning level until it is adjusted. This adjustment usually takes place when closing entries are made at the end of the accounting period, as illustrated in Chapter 6.

Under the perpetual inventory method, the Merchandise Inventory account is continuously adjusted by entering purchases and sales as they occur and thus is always up to date. This method is summarized as follows (using examples from Figure 11-3):

1. Recording purchases under the perpetual inventory method:

June 10   Merchandise Inventory   600
               Accounts Payable   600
                    To record purchases of inventory

2. Recording sales under the perpetual inventory method:

June 20   Accounts Receivable   300
               Sales   300
                    To record sales

June 20	Cost of Goods Sold	150	
	Merchandise Inventory		150
	To record cost of merchandise		
	sold		

Note first that the Purchases account is not used, and second that when a sale is made, the cost of the merchandise for that sale is taken out of the Merchandise Inventory account and debited to the Cost of Goods Sold account. The Cost of Goods Sold account will contain a running total of the cost of goods sold for the year. Therefore, at the end of the year, neither adjustments to Merchandise Inventory nor corresponding debits and credits to Income Summary are needed because the Merchandise Inventory account has been continually updated during the year, and thus there is no need to establish the ending inventory in the records. The only closing entry required is to close Cost of Goods Sold to Income Summary.

Need for Physical Inventories Under the Perpetual Inventory System

The use of the perpetual inventory system does not eliminate the need for a physical inventory at the end of the accounting year. The perpetual inventory records show what should be on hand, not necessarily what is on hand. There may be losses due to spoilage, pilferage, theft, or other causes. If a loss has occurred, it is reflected in the accounts by a debit to Cost of Goods Sold and a credit to Merchandise Inventory. The individual inventory cards, which may also be the subsidiary ledger, must also be adjusted.

Chapter Review

Review of Learning Objectives

1. Define nonmonetary assets and state their relationship to the matching rule.

Nonmonetary assets are unexpired costs that will become expenses in future accounting periods. Typical nonmonetary assets are inventory; prepaid expenses; property, plant, and equipment; natural resources, and intangible assets. To apply the matching rule to nonmonetary assets, one must determine how much of the asset is used up or expired during the current accounting period and how much of the asset is still unused or unexpired. The former amount is an expense of the period; the latter is an asset.

2. Define merchandise inventory and show how inventory measurement affects income determination.

Merchandise inventory consists of all goods owned and held for sale in the regular course of business. The objective of accounting for inventories is the proper determination of income. If the value of ending inventory is understated or overstated, a corresponding error—dollar for dollar—will be made in net income. Furthermore, because the ending inventory of one period is the beginning inventory of the next, the misstatement affects two accounting periods, although the effects are opposite.

3. Calculate the pricing of inventory, using the cost basis according to the specific identification method, the average-cost method, the first-in, first-out (FIFO) method, and the last-in, first-out (LIFO) method.

The value assigned to the ending inventory is the result of two measurements:

quantity and price. Quantity is determined by taking a physical inventory. The pricing of inventory is usually based on the assumed cost flow of the goods as they are bought and sold. One of four assumptions is usually made regarding cost flow. These assumptions are represented by four inventory methods. Inventory pricing could be determined by the specific identification method, which associates the actual cost with each item of inventory but is rarely used. The average-cost method assumes that the cost of inventory is the average cost of goods available for sale during the period. The first-in, first-out (FIFO) method assumes that the costs of the first items acquired should be assigned to the first items sold. The last-in, first-out (LIFO) method assumes that the costs of the last items acquired should be assigned to the first items sold. The method chosen may or may not be equivalent to the actual flow of physical goods.

4. Recognize the effects of each method on income determination in periods of changing prices.

During periods of rising prices, the LIFO method will show the lowest net income; FIFO, the highest; and average cost, in between. The opposite effects occur in periods of falling prices. No generalization can be made regarding the specific identification method.

5. Apply the lower-of-cost-or-market (LCM) rule to inventory valuation.

The lower-of-cost-or-market rule can be applied to the above methods of determining inventory at cost. This rule states that if the replacement cost (market) of the inventory is lower than what the inventory cost, the lower figure should be used. The Internal Revenue Service requires that if LIFO is used for tax purposes, it must also be used for book purposes, and that the lower-of-cost-or-market rule cannot be applied to the LIFO method.

6. Estimate the cost of ending inventory using the retail inventory method and the gross profit method.

Two methods of estimating the value of inventory are the retail inventory method and the gross profit method. Under the retail inventory method, inventory is determined at retail prices and is reduced to estimated cost by applying a ratio of cost to retail price. Under the gross profit method, cost of goods sold is estimated by reducing sales by estimated gross margin. The estimated cost of goods sold is then deducted from cost of goods available for sale to estimate the inventory.

7. Distinguish between perpetual and periodic inventory systems.

Under the periodic inventory system, the one used earlier in this book, inventory is determined by a physical count at the end of the accounting period. Under the perpetual inventory system, the inventory control account is constantly updated as sales and purchases are made during the accounting period.

Review Problem
Periodic and Perpetual Inventory Methods

The table on the next page summarizes the beginning inventory, purchases, and sales of Psi Company's single product during January.

Required

1. Assuming that the company uses the periodic inventory method, compute the cost that should be assigned to ending inventory using (a) a FIFO basis and (b) a LIFO basis.

Date	Inventory			Purchases			Sales Units
	Units	Cost	Total	Units	Cost	Total	
Jan. 1	1,400	$19	$26,600				
4							300
8				600	$20	$12,000	
10							1,300
12				900	21	18,900	
15							150
18				500	22	11,000	
24				800	23	18,400	
31							1,350
Totals	1,400		$26,600	2,800		$60,300	3,100

2. Assuming that the company uses the perpetual inventory method, compute the cost that should be assigned to ending inventory using (a) a FIFO basis and (b) a LIFO basis. (Hint: It is helpful to use a form similar to the perpetual inventory card in Figure 11-3.)

Answer to Review Problem

	Units	Dollars
Beginning Inventory	1,400	$26,600
Purchases	2,800	60,300
Available for Sale	4,200	$86,900
Sales	3,100	
Ending Inventory	1,100	

1. Periodic inventory method
   a. FIFO basis
   Ending inventory consists of
   Jan. 24 purchases (800 × $23) $18,400
   Jan. 18 purchases (300 × $22)   6,600 $25,000

   b. LIFO basis
   Ending inventory consists of
   Beginning inventory (1,100 × $19) $20,900

2. Perpetual inventory method
   a. FIFO basis

	Received			Sold			Balance		
Date	Units	Cost	Total	Units	Cost	Total	Units	Cost	Total
Jan. 1							1,400	$19	$26,600
4				300	$19	$ 5,700	1,100	19	20,900
8	600	$20	$12,000				1,100	19	
							600	20	32,900
10				1,100	19				
				200	20	24,900	400	20	8,000
12	900	21	18,900				400	20	
							900	21	26,900
15				150	20	3,000	250	20	
							900	21	23,900
18	500	22	11,000				250	20	
							900	21	
							500	22	34,900
24	800	23	18,400				250	20	
							900	21	
							500	22	
							800	23	53,300
31				250	20				
				900	21				
				200	22	28,300	300	22	
							800	23	25,000

b. LIFO basis

	Received			Sold			Balance		
Date	Units	Cost	Total	Units	Cost	Total	Units	Cost	Total
Jan. 1							1,400	$19	$26,600
4				300	$19	$ 5,700	1,100	19	20,900
8	600	$20	$12,000				1,100	19	
							600	20	32,900
10				600	20				
				700	19	25,300	400	19	7,600
12	900	21	18,900				400	19	
							900	21	26,500
15				150	21	3,150	400	19	
							750	21	23,350
18	500	22	11,000				400	19	
							750	21	
							500	22	34,350

24	800	23	18,400				400	19	
							750	21	
							500	22	
							800	23	52,750
31				800	23				
				500	22				
				50	21	30,450	400	19	
							700	21	22,300

Chapter Assignments

Questions

1. Why is inventory called a nonmonetary asset, and what measurements of nonmonetary assets must be taken to make a proper income determination? What is the relationship of nonmonetary assets to the matching rule?

2. What is merchandise inventory, and what is the primary objective of inventory measurement?

3. If the merchandise inventory is mistakenly overstated at the end of 19x8, what is the effect on (a) 19x8 net income, (b) 19x8 year-end balance sheet value, (c) 19x9 net income, (d) 19x9 year-end balance sheet value?

4. Fargo Sales Company is very busy at the end of its fiscal year on June 30. There is an order for 130 units of product in the warehouse. Although the shipping department tries, it cannot ship the product by June 30, and title has not yet passed. Should the 130 units be included in the year-end count of inventory?

5. What does the term *taking a physical inventory* mean?

6. What items are included in the cost of inventory?

7. In periods of steadily rising prices, which of the three inventory methods—average-cost, FIFO, or LIFO—will give the (a) highest inventory cost, (b) lowest inventory cost, (c) highest net income, and (d) lowest net income?

8. May a company change its inventory costing method from year to year? Explain.

9. Do FIFO and LIFO result in different quantities of ending inventory?

10. Under which method of cost flow are (a) the earliest costs assigned to inventory, (b) the latest costs assigned to inventory, (c) the average costs assigned to inventory?

11. What are the relative advantages and disadvantages of FIFO and LIFO from management's point of view?

12. In the phrase "lower of cost or market," what is meant by "market"?

13. What methods can be used to determine lower of cost or market?

14. What effects do income taxes have on inventory valuation?

15. What are some reasons why management may want to use the gross profit method of determining inventory?

16. Does using the retail inventory method mean that inventories are measured at retail value on the balance sheet? Explain.

17. Which of the following companies would find a perpetual inventory system practical: a drug store, a grocery store, a restaurant, an automobile dealer, a wholesale auto parts dealer? Why?

18. Which is more expensive to maintain: a perpetual inventory system or a periodic inventory system? Why?

19. What differences occur in recording sales, purchases, and closing entries under the perpetual and periodic inventory systems?

20. Which of the following inventory systems do not require a physical inventory: (a) perpetual, (b) periodic, (c) retail, (d) gross profit?

Classroom Exercises

Exercise 11-1
Inventory Cost Methods
(L.O. 3)

Lynn's Farm Store had the following purchases and sales of fertilizer during the year:

Jan. 1	Beginning inventory	200 cases at $24 =	$ 4,800
Feb. 25	Purchased	100 cases at $26 =	2,600
June 15	Purchased	400 cases at $28 =	11,200
Aug. 15	Purchased	100 cases at $26 =	2,600
Oct. 15	Purchased	300 cases at $28 =	8,400
Dec. 15	Purchased	200 cases at $30 =	6,000
	Totals	1,300 cases	$35,600
	Total sales	1,000 cases	
	Dec. 31 Ending inventory	300 cases	

Assume that all of the June 15 purchase and 200 cases each from the January 1 beginning inventory, the October 15 purchase, and the December 15 purchase were sold.

Determine the costs that should be assigned to cost of goods sold and ending inventory under each of the following assumptions: (1) Costs are assigned by the specific identification method. (2) Costs are assigned on an average-cost basis. (3) Costs are assigned on a FIFO basis. (4) Costs are assigned on a LIFO basis. What conclusions can you draw from your answers?

Exercise 11-2
Effects of Inventory Errors
(L.O. 2)

Condensed income statements for E. T. Company for two years are shown below.

	19x2	19x1
Sales	$44,000	$37,000
Cost of Goods Sold	26,000	19,000
Gross Margin on Sales	$18,000	$18,000
Operating Expenses	9,000	9,000
Net Income	$ 9,000	$ 9,000

After the end of 19x2, it was discovered that an error had been made in 19x1 that resulted in an understatement of the ending inventory of 19x1 by $4,000.

Compute the corrected net income for 19x1 and 19x2. What effect will the error have on net income and owner's equity for 19x3?

Exercise 11-3
Inventory Cost Methods
(L.O. 3)

During its first year of operation, Mackey Company purchased 5,500 units of a product at $20 per unit. During the second year, it purchased 6,000 units of the same product at $24 per unit. During the third year, it purchased 5,000 units at $30 per unit. Mackey Company managed to have an ending inventory each year of 1,000 units. The company sells goods at a 100 percent markup over cost.

Prepare cost of goods sold statements that compare the value of ending inventory and the cost of goods sold for each of the three years using (1) the FIFO method and (2) the LIFO method. What conclusions can you draw from the resulting data about the relationships between changes in unit price and changes in the value of ending inventory?

Exercise 11-4
Retail Method
(L.O. 6)

Julie's Dress Shop had net retail sales of $220,000 during the current year. The following additional information was obtained from the accounting records:

	At Cost	At Retail
Beginning Inventory	$ 30,000	$ 45,000
Net Purchases	140,000	220,000
Freight In	7,550	

1. Estimate the company's ending inventory at cost using the retail method.
2. Assume that a physical inventory taken at year end revealed an inventory on hand of $38,000 at retail value. What is the estimated amount of inventory shrinkage (loss due to theft, damage, and so forth) at cost?
3. Prepare the journal entry to record the inventory shrinkage.

**Exercise 11-5
Gross Profit
Method**
(L.O. 6)

Carl Womack was at home watching television when he received a call from the fire department. His business was a total loss from fire. The insurance company asked him to prove his inventory loss. For the year, until the date of the fire, Carl's company had sales of $450,000 and purchases of $280,000. Freight in amounted to $13,700, and the beginning inventory was $45,000. It was Carl's custom to price goods in such a way as to have a gross margin of 40 percent on sales.

Compute Carl's estimated inventory loss.

**Exercise 11-6
Lower-of-Cost-
or-Market
Method**
(L.O. 5)

Todd Company values its inventory, shown below, at the lower of cost or market. Compute Todd's inventory value using (1) the item-by-item method and (2) the major category method.

		Per Unit	
	Quantity	Cost	Market
Category 1			
Item aa	100	$1.00	$ .90
Item bb	120	2.00	2.20
Item cc	200	4.00	3.75
Category 2			
Item dd	600	6.00	6.50
Item ee	800	9.00	9.10

Interpreting Accounting Information

**Published
Financial Infor-
mation:
Iowa Beef
Processors**
(L.O. 4)

Iowa Beef Processors, Inc., helped to revolutionize the beef-packing industry when in 1960 it began building processing plants in the plains states where the cattle were located rather than in the big cities. By saving on both labor and transportation costs, it was able to undercut the prices of the more traditional companies and still make a profit. A portion of the company's 1979 and 1980 income statements appears as follows:

Inventories

	1980	1979
Net sales	$4,639,454,000	$4,216,370,000
Cost of products sold	4,506,150,000	4,105,533,000
Gross margin	$ 133,304,000	$ 110,837,000
Selling, general and administrative expenses	42,924,000	34,326,000
Income from operations	$ 90,380,000	$ 76,511,000
Interest income (expense)	3,724,000	(2,038,000)
Earnings before income taxes	$ 94,104,000	$ 74,473,000
Income taxes	40,940,000	31,726,000
Net income	$ 53,164,000	$ 42,747,000

In the summary of significant accounting policies, Iowa Beef Processors indicates that product inventories are maintained on a last-in, first-out (LIFO) basis. In another note to the financial statements titled "Inventories," it is reported that inventories on a LIFO cost basis were $68,683,000 at the end of 1979 and $83,993,000 at the end of 1980. The note also contains the following statement: "Inventories when valued at first-in, first-out exceeded LIFO cost by $32,461,000 at [the end of] 1980 and $26,598,000 at [the end of] 1979."

Required

1. Prepare a schedule that compares income from operations for 1980 on a LIFO basis with that on a FIFO basis in dollar amounts and as percentages. Also determine the apparent effect on net earnings in 1980 of using FIFO rather than LIFO, assuming that the ratio of income taxes to earnings before income taxes is the appropriate tax rate to use. Compute the profit margin under both alternatives.
2. For what reasons do you suppose the management of Iowa Beef Processors chooses to use the LIFO inventory method? On what economic conditions, if any, do these reasons depend? Why might a company choose the FIFO method?

Problem Set A

**Problem 11A-1
Inventory Cost
Methods
(L.O. 3)**

Zack Company merchandises a single product called Zack-12. The following data represent beginning inventory and purchases of product Zack-12 during the past year: January 1 inventory, 34,000 units at $6.00; February purchases, 40,000 units at $6.50; March purchases, 80,000 units at $6.20; May purchases, 60,000 units at $6.30; July purchases, 100,000 units at $6.40; September purchases, 80,000 units at $6.30; November purchases, 30,000 units at $6.60. Sales of product Zack-12 totaled 384,000 units at $10 per unit. Selling and administrative expenses totaled $1,184,000 for the year, and Zack Company uses a periodic inventory method.

Required

1. Prepare a schedule to compute the cost of goods available for sale.
2. Prepare an income statement under each of the following assumptions: (a) Costs are assigned to inventory on an average-cost basis. (b) Costs are assigned to inventory on a FIFO basis. (c) Costs are assigned to inventory on a LIFO basis.

**Problem 11A-2
Lower-of-Cost-
or-Market
Method
(L.O. 5)**

After taking the physical inventory, the accountant for Roycee Company prepared the inventory schedule shown at the top of the next page.

	Quantity	Per Unit Cost	Per Unit Market
Product line 1			
Item 11	340	$10	$10
Item 12	540	8	10
Item 13	420	16	14
Product line 2			
Item 21	220	30	34
Item 22	800	42	40
Item 23	140	36	40
Product line 3			
Item 31	740	52	40
Item 32	620	60	56
Item 33	240	68	78

Required

Determine the value of the inventory at lower of cost or market using (1) the item-by-item method and (2) the major category method.

Problem 11A-3 Perpetual Inventory System (L.O. 7)

The beginning inventory of Product Z54 and data on purchases and sales for a two-month period are presented below.

Apr. 1	Inventory	25 units at $100
10	Purchase	50 units at $110
17	Sale	30 units
25	Sale	15 units
May 2	Purchase	50 units at $108
8	Sale	20 units
14	Purchase	25 units at $112
18	Sale	20 units
22	Purchase	25 units at $115
26	Sale	15 units
31	Sale	35 units

Required

1. Assume that the company maintains a perpetual inventory system on a FIFO basis and uses perpetual inventory cards similar to the one illustrated in Figure 11-3. Follow the example in the text and record the transactions on such a card using two or more lines to show units on hand at each price or units sold when units costing different amounts are on hand or sold.
2. Assume that the company keeps its records on a LIFO basis, and record the transactions on a second record card.
3. Assume that the May 31 sale was made to Redfern Corporation on credit for $7,000. Prepare a general journal entry to record the sale and cost of goods sold on a LIFO basis.
4. Assume the company takes a periodic inventory on May 31. The value of the inventory was $4,300. Record an inventory loss if necessary. Assume the FIFO basis of evaluating inventory.

Problem 11A-4
Periodic Inventory System
(L.O. 7)

Assume the same data as presented in Problem 11A-3, except that the company uses a periodic inventory system. The company closes its books at the end of each month.

Required

1. Compute the value of the ending inventory on April 30 and May 31 on a FIFO basis.
2. Compute the value of the ending inventory on April 30 and May 31 on a LIFO basis.
3. Prepare a general journal entry to record the sale on May 31 to Redfern Corporation on credit for $7,000.

Problem 11A-5
Retail Inventory Method
(L.O. 6)

Maier Company operates a large discount store that uses the retail inventory method to estimate the cost of ending inventory. Management suspects that in recent weeks there have been unusually heavy losses from shoplifting or employee pilferage. To estimate the amount of the loss, the company has taken a physical inventory and will compare the results with the estimated cost of inventory. Data from the accounting records and from a year-end physical inventory are as follows:

	At Cost	At Retail
October 1 Beginning Inventory	$100,908	$143,200
Purchases	143,416	211,600
Purchases Returns and Allowances	4,086	6,400
Freight In	1,900	
Sales		218,365
Sales Returns and Allowances		1,865
October 31 Physical Inventory		123,500

Required

Prepare a schedule to do the following: (1) estimate the dollar amount of the store's year-end inventory using the retail method, (2) use the store's cost ratio to reduce the retail value of the physical inventory to cost, and (3) calculate the estimated amount of inventory shortage at cost and at retail.

Problem 11A-6
Gross Profit Method
(L.O. 6)

Mueller Brothers is a large retail furniture company that operates in two adjacent warehouses. One warehouse serves as a showroom, and the other is used for storage of merchandise. On the night of April 22, a fire broke out in the storage warehouse and totally destroyed the merchandise stored there. Fortunately, the fire did not reach the showroom; so all the merchandise on display was saved. Although the company maintained a perpetual inventory system, its records were rather haphazard, and the last reliable physical inventory was taken on December 31. In addition, there was no control of the flow of the goods between the showroom and the warehouse. Thus it was impossible to tell what goods should be in either place. As a result, the insurance company required an independent estimate of the amount of loss. The insurance company examiners were satisfied with the following information:

1. Merchandise inventory on December 31	$1,438,250
2. Purchases, January 1 to April 22	2,386,135
3. Purchases returns, January 1 to April 22	10,705
4. Freight in, January 1 to April 22	53,100
5. Sales, January 1 to April 22	3,959,050

6. Sales returns, January 1 to April 22	29,800
7. Merchandise inventory in showroom on April 22	393,740
8. Average gross profit margin, 42 percent	

Required

Prepare a schedule showing the amount of inventory that should have been on hand on April 22, and estimate the amount of the loss.

Problem Set B

**Problem 11B-1
Inventory Cost
Methods
(L.O. 3)**

During 19xx, Floor Mart sold 1,700 units of product FIX at $120 per unit. Its beginning inventory and purchases during the year were as follows: January 1 inventory, 150 units at $50; February purchases, 200 units at $55; April purchases, 300 units at $60; June purchases, 750 units at $55; August purchases, 350 units at $60; October purchases, 150 units at $62; December purchases, 100 units at $65. The company's selling and administrative expenses totaled $80,000, and it uses a periodic inventory method.

Required

1. Prepare a schedule to compute the cost of goods available for sale.
2. Prepare an income statement under each of the following assumptions: (a) Costs are assigned to inventory on an average-cost basis. (b) Costs are assigned to inventory on a FIFO basis. (c) Costs are assigned to inventory on a LIFO basis.

**Problem 11B-2
Lower-of-Cost-
or-Market
Method
(L.O. 5)**

The physical inventory for Felix Company appears below.

		Per Unit	
	Quantity	Cost	Market
Category A			
Item A1	140	$50.00	$ 46.00
Item A2	80	94.00	102.00
Item A3	180	62.00	60.00
Category B			
Item B1	125	8.50	9.20
Item B2	150	7.75	8.00
Item B3	60	6.00	5.50
Category C			
Item C1	425	1.75	1.85
Item C2	455	2.00	1.90
Item C3	125	5.50	4.50

Required

Determine the value of the inventory at lower of cost or market using (1) the item-by-item method and (2) the major category method.

**Problem 11B-3
Perpetual In-
ventory System
(L.O. 7)**

The beginning inventory of Product 2A and data on purchases and sales for a two-month period are presented at the top of the next page.

June	1	Inventory	40 units at $40
	15	Purchase	120 units at $44
	18	Sale	80 units
	25	Sale	30 units
July	3	Purchase	60 units at $42
	10	Sale	40 units
	16	Purchase	120 units at $45
	19	Sale	100 units
	21	Purchase	40 units at $47
	24	Sale	30 units
	31	Sale	40 units

Required

1. Assume that the company maintains a perpetual inventory system on a FIFO basis and uses perpetual inventory cards similar to the one illustrated in Figure 11-3. Follow the example in the text and record the transactions on such a card using two or more lines to show units on hand at each price or units sold when units costing different amounts are on hand or sold.

2. Assume that the company keeps its records on a LIFO basis, and record the transactions on a second record card.

3. Assume that the July 31 sale was made to Ron Rutledge on credit for $4,000. Prepare a general journal entry to record the sale and cost of goods sold on a FIFO basis.

4. Assume the LIFO method of valuing inventory. The company took a physical inventory on July 31. The inventory was $2,000. Record any inventory loss as necessary.

**Problem 11B-4
Periodic Inventory System**
(L.O. 7)

Assume the same data as presented in Problem 11B-3 except that the company uses a periodic inventory system. The company closes its books at the end of each month.

Required

1. Compute the value of the ending inventory on June 30 and July 31 on a FIFO basis.

2. Compute the value of the ending inventory on June 30 and July 31 on a LIFO basis.

3. Prepare a general journal entry to record the sale on July 31 to Ron Rutledge on credit for $4,000.

**Problem 11B-5
Retail Inventory Method**
(L.O. 6)

Comtec uses the retail inventory method to estimate the cost of ending inventory. To test its controls against shoplifting and employee pilferage, the company makes a practice of taking a physical inventory at retail to compare with the estimate. Data from the accounting records and from a year-end physical inventory are as follows:

	At Cost	At Retail
July 1 Beginning Inventory	$ 30,428	$ 55,482.00
Purchases	110,836	213,391.50
Purchases Returns and Allowances	1,906	5,218.50
Freight In	4,280	
Sales		204,414.00
Sales Returns and Allowances		5,229.00
July 30 Physical Inventory		33,306.00

Required

Prepare a schedule to do the following: (1) Estimate the dollar amount of the store's year-end inventory using the retail method. (2) Use the store's cost ratio to reduce the retail value of the physical inventory to cost. (3) Calculate the estimated amount of inventory shortage at cost and at retail.

Problem 11B-6
Gross Profit
Method
(L.O. 6)

Worldwide Distributors is a wholesale computer dealer that sells mainly to commercial companies. The company maintains an office in the front of a large warehouse where it keeps its inventory. On the night of November 11, the night watchman was overpowered by armed robbers who backed a large truck up to the warehouse and stole several hundred microcomputers. Because the company does not maintain perpetual inventory records, the accountant for the company must estimate the amount of the loss.

By noon, the accountant was able to collect the following information: (a) merchandise inventory on October 1, $351,900; (b) purchases, October 1 through November 11, $918,810; (c) purchases returns, October 1 through November 11, $6,660; (d) freight in for the period, $64,380; (e) sales, October 1 through November 11, $1,461,624; (f) sales returns, October 1 through November 11, $29,364; (g) merchandise inventory still on hand (not stolen), November 11, at cost, $156,900; (h) average gross margin, $33\frac{1}{3}$ percent.

Required

Prepare a schedule showing the amount of inventory that should have been in the warehouse on November 11, and estimate the amount of the loss.

Financial Decision Case 11-1

RTS Company
(L.O. 4)

Refrigerated Truck Sales Company (RTS Company) buys large refrigerated trucks from the manufacturer and sells them to companies and independent truckers who haul perishable goods such as frozen beef for long distances. RTS has been successful in this specialized niche of the industry because it provides a unique product and specialized service to these truckers. Because of the high cost of these trucks and the high cost of financing inventory, RTS tries to maintain as small an inventory as possible. In fact, at the beginning of March the company had no inventory or liabilities, as shown by the following balance sheet:

RTS Company
Balance Sheet
March 1, 19xx

Assets		Owner's Equity	
Cash	$500,000	Robert Trinker, Capital	$500,000
		Total Owner's	
Total Assets	$500,000	Equity	$500,000

On March 5, RTS takes delivery of a truck at a price of $150,000. On March 15 after a rise in price, an identical truck is delivered to the company at a price of $160,000. On March 25, the company sells one of the trucks for $195,000. During March, expenses totaled $15,000. All transactions were paid in cash.

Required

1. Prepare income statements and balance sheets for RTS at March 31 using (a) the FIFO method of inventory valuation and (b) the LIFO method of inventory valuation. Explain the effects that each method has on the financial statements.
2. Assume that Robert Trinker, owner of RTS Company, follows the policy of withdrawing cash each period that is exactly equal to net income. What effect does this action have on each balance sheet prepared in **1**, and how do they compare with the balance sheet at the beginning of the month? Which inventory method, if either, do you feel is more realistic in representing RTS's income?
3. Assume that RTS receives notice of another price increase of $10,000 on refrigerated trucks, to take effect on April 1. How does this information relate to the withdrawal policy of the owner, and how will it affect next month's operations?

Learning Objectives

Chapter Twelve

Current Liabilities and Payroll Accounting

1. Define liability and explain how the problems of recognition, valuation, and classification apply to liabilities.

2. Identify, compute, and record definitely determinable and estimated current liabilities.

3. Define a contingent liability.

4. Identify and compute the liabilities associated with payroll accounting.

5. Record transactions associated with payroll accounting.

6. Apply internal control to the payroll system.

This chapter gives you a general view of current liabilities and introduces you to payroll accounting. As a result of studying this chapter, you should be able to meet the learning objectives listed on the left.

As one of the three major parts of the balance sheet, liabilities are, in general, a company's obligations to nonowners. The two major kinds of liabilities are current and long-term liabilities. This chapter deals with the nature and measurement of current liabilities. The subject of long-term liabilities is covered in Chapter 18. Because a number of current liabilities arise through the payroll process, the fundamentals of payroll accounting are also presented in this chapter.

Nature and Measurement of Liabilities

Liabilities are the result of a company's past transactions and are legal obligations for the future payment of assets or the future performance of services. Note that they are, in fact, more than monetary obligations. For example, revenues received in advance are for services that must be provided to customers. In most cases, the amount and due date are definite or else subject to reasonable estimation. The problems of recognition, valuation, and classification apply equally to liabilities and assets.

Recognition of Liabilities

Objective 1
Define liability
and explain
how the
problems of
recognition,
valuation, and
classification
apply to liabil-
ities

Timing is important in the recognition of liabilities. Very often failure to record a liability in an accounting period goes along with failure to record an expense. Thus it leads to an understatement of expense and an over-statement of income. Liabilities are recorded when an obligation occurs. This rule is harder to apply than it appears on the surface. When there is a transaction that obligates the company to make future payments, a lia-bility arises and is recognized, as when goods are bought on credit. However, current liabilities often are not represented by a direct transac-tion. One of the major reasons for adjusting entries at the end of an accounting period is to recognize unrecorded liabilities. Among these accrued liabilities are salaries payable and interest payable. Other liabili-ties that can only be estimated, such as taxes payable, must also be recog-nized by adjusting entries.

On the other hand, a company may sometimes enter into an agreement for future transactions. For instance, a company may agree to pay an executive $50,000 a year for three years, or a public utility may agree to buy an unspecified quantity of coal at a certain price over the next five years. These contracts, though they are definite commitments, are not liabilities because they are for future—not past—transactions. As there is no current obligation, no liability is recognized.

Valuation of Liabilities

Liabilities are generally valued at the amount of money needed to pay the debt or at the fair market value of goods or services to be delivered. For most liabilities the amount is definitely known, but for some it must be estimated. For example, an automobile dealer who sells a car with a one-year warranty must provide parts and services during the year. The obligation is definite, but the amount must be estimated.

Classification of Liabilities

Current liabilities are debts and obligations that are expected to be satis-fied in one year or within the current operating cycle, whichever is longer. In most cases, they are paid out of current assets or by taking on another short-term liability. The classification of current liabilities directly matches the classification of current assets. In Chapter 9, we noted that two important measures of liquidity are working capital (current assets less current liabilities) and the current ratio (current assets divided by current liabilities). Liabilities that will not be due during the next year or during the normal operating cycle are listed as long-term liabilities.

Common Categories of Current Liabilities

Current liabilities fall into two major groups: (1) definitely determinable liabilities and (2) estimated liabilities. Discussions on each follow.

Definitely Determinable Liabilities

Objective 2
Identify,
compute, and
record definitely
determinable
and estimated
current liabil-
ities

Current liabilities that are set by contract or by statute and so can be measured exactly are called **definitely determinable liabilities.** The accounting problems connected with these liabilities are to determine the existence and amount of the liability and to see that the liability is recorded properly. Among the definitely determinable liabilities are trade accounts payable, notes payable, dividends payable, sales and excise taxes payable, current portions of long-term debt, accrued liabilities, payroll liabilities, and deferred revenues.

Trade Accounts Payable Trade accounts payable are short-term obligations to suppliers for goods and services. The amount in the Trade Accounts Payable account is generally supported by an accounts payable subsidiary ledger. Under the voucher system, this account is called Vouchers Payable. Accounting for trade accounts payable has been treated at length earlier in the book.

Notes Payable Short-term notes payable, which also arise out of the ordinary course of business, are obligations represented by promissory notes. The two major sources of notes payable are bank loans and payments to suppliers for goods and services. As with notes receivable, presented in Chapter 10, the interest on notes may be stated separately on the face of the note (Case 1 in Figure 12-1), or it may be deducted in advance by discounting (Case 2). For example, in Case 1, Caron Corporation borrows $5,000 from the bank on a 60-day, short-term promissory note at 12 percent interest. In Case 2, Caron Corporation borrows funds on a 60-day,

Figure 12-1
Two Promissory
Notes: One with
Interest Stated
Separately; One
with Interest
in Face Amount

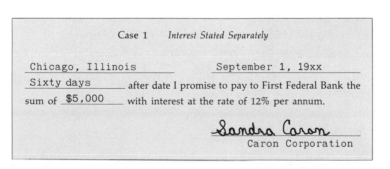

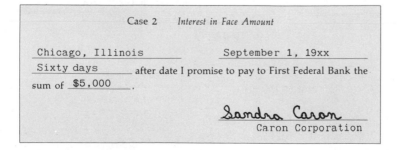

short-term, 12 percent promissory note with interest included in the face amount. The entries to record the note in each case are as follows:

Case 1

Aug. 31	Cash	5,000	
	Notes Payable		5,000
	To record 60-day, 12% promissory note with interest stated separately		

Case 2

Aug. 31	Cash	4,900	
	Discount on Notes Payable	100	
	Notes Payable		5,000
	To record 60-day, 12% promissory note with interest included in face amount		

$$\text{Discount} = \$5,000 \times \frac{60}{360} \times .12 = \$100$$

Note that in Case 1 the money borrowed equaled the face value of the note, whereas in Case 2 the money borrowed ($4,900) was less than the face value ($5,000) of the note. The amount of the discount equals the amount of the interest for sixty days. To show the correct amount of the liability on the balance sheet, the Discount on Notes Payable is deducted from the Notes Payable as a contra-liability account, as follows:

Partial Balance Sheet

Current Liabilities		
Notes Payable	$5,000	
Less Discount on Notes Payable	100	$4,900

On October 30, when the note is paid, each alternative is recorded as follows:

Case 1

Oct. 30	Notes Payable	5,000	
	Interest Expense	100	
	Cash		5,100
	Payment of note with interest stated separately		

Case 2

Oct. 30	Notes Payable	5,000	
	Cash		5,000
	Payment of note with interest included in face value		

```
30   Interest Expense                              100
        Discount on Notes Payable                         100
           To record interest expense on
        matured note
```

Dividends Payable   Dividends are a distribution of earnings by a corporation. The payment of dividends is solely the decision of the corporation's board of directors. So a liability does not exist until the board declares the dividends. There is usually a short time between the date of declaration and the date of payment of dividends. During that short time, the dividends declared are current liabilities of the corporation. Accounting for dividends is treated extensively in Chapter 17.

Sales and Excise Taxes Payable   Most states and many cities levy a sales tax on retail transactions. On some products, such as automobile tires, there are federal excise taxes. The merchant who sells goods subject to these taxes must collect the taxes and remit, or pay, them periodically to the appropriate government agency. The amount of tax collected represents a current liability until it is remitted to the government. For example, assume that a merchant makes a $100 sale that is subject to a 5 percent sales tax and a 10 percent excise tax. Assuming that the sale took place on June 1, the correct entry to record the sale is as follows:

```
June 1   Cash                                     115
            Sales                                         100
            Sales Tax Payable                               5
            Excise Tax Payable                             10
               To record sale of merchandise and
            collection of sales and excise taxes
```

The sale is properly recorded at $100, and the tax collections are recorded as liabilities to be remitted at the proper time.

Current Portions of Long-Term Debt   If a portion of long-term debt is due within the coming year and is to be paid out of current assets, then the current portion of long-term debt is properly classified as a current liability. For example, suppose that a $500,000 debt is to be paid in installments of $100,000 per year for the next five years. The $100,000 installment due in the current year should be classified as a current liability. The remaining $400,000 should be classified as a long-term liability.

Accrued Liabilities   A principal reason for adjusting entries at the end of an accounting period is to recognize and record liabilities that are not already recorded in the accounting records. This practice applies to any type of liability. For example, in previous chapters, adjustments relating to accrued salaries payable were made. As you will see, accrued liabilities can also apply to estimated liabilities. Here the focus is on interest payable, a definitely determinable liability. If a note is interest bearing, there is a daily increase in the interest obligation. At the end of the accounting period, an adjusting entry should be made in accordance with the match-

Figure 12-2
Growth in
Liability of
Interest-bearing
Note, with
Interest
Expense
Allocated to
Two
Accounting
Periods

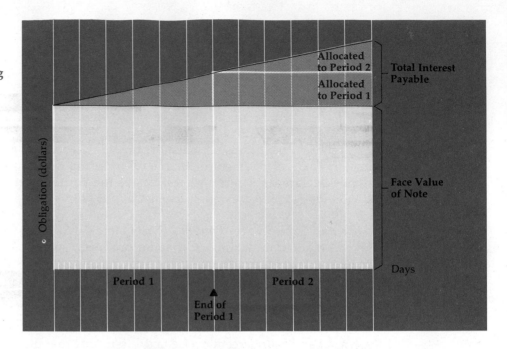

ing rule to record the interest obligation up to that point in time. Figure 12-2 illustrates the increase in this obligation and the allocation of the resulting expense to each accounting period. Let us again use the example of the two notes presented earlier in this chapter. If we assume that the accounting period ends on September 30, or thirty days after the issuance of the sixty-day notes, the adjusting entries for each case would be as follows:

Case 1

Sept. 30	Interest Expense	50	
	Interest Payable		50
	To record interest expense for 30 days on note with interest stated separately		

Case 2

Sept. 30	Interest Expense	50	
	Discount on Notes Payable		50
	To record interest expense for 30 days on note with interest included in face amount		

In Case 2, current liabilities are increased by the credit to Discount on Notes Payable because this credit has the effect of increasing the net amount of Notes Payable from $4,900 on August 31 to $4,950 on September 30. On the latter date, the notes payable would appear on the balance sheet as follows:

Partial Balance Sheet

Current Liabilities
Notes Payable $5,000
Less Discount on Notes Payable   50 $4,950

Payroll Liabilities A number of current liabilities are associated with payroll accounting. These liabilities are discussed in a major section at the end of this chapter.

Unearned or Deferred Revenues **Unearned** or **deferred revenues** represent obligations for goods or services that the company must deliver in return for an advance payment from a customer. For example, most magazines accept payments for subscriptions in advance. The publisher then has a liability that expires when the magazine is delivered. Many businesses such as repair companies, construction companies, and special-order firms ask for a deposit or advance from a customer before they will begin work. These advances are also current liabilities until the goods or services are delivered.

Estimated Liabilities

Estimated liabilities are a company's definite obligations for which the exact amount cannot be known until a later date. In these cases, because there is no doubt as to the existence of the legal obligation, the primary accounting problem is to estimate and record the amount of the liability. Examples of estimated liabilities are income taxes, property taxes, product warranties, and vacation pay.

Income Tax The income of a corporation is taxed by the federal government, most state governments, and some cities and towns. The amount of income tax liability depends on the results of operations. Often it is not certain until after the end of the year. In cases of disputes between the corporation and the taxing authority, it may be years before the final tax is established. However, because income taxes are an expense in the year in which income is earned, an adjusting entry is necessary to record the estimated tax liability. An example of this entry follows:

Dec. 31   Federal Income Tax Expense   53,000
          Federal Income Tax Payable   53,000
            To record estimated federal income tax

Remember that the income of sole proprietorships and partnerships is not subject to income taxes. Their owners must report their share of the firm's income on their individual tax returns.

Property Taxes Payable Property taxes are taxes levied on real property such as land and buildings and on personal property such as inventory and equipment. Property taxes are a main source of revenue for local governments. Usually they are assessed annually against the property involved. Because the fiscal years of local governments and their assessment dates rarely correspond to those of the firm, it is often necessary to estimate the amount of property taxes that applies to each month of the year. Assume, for instance, that a local government has a fiscal year of July 1 to June 30, that its assessment date is November 1 for the fiscal year beginning the previous July 1, and that its payment date is December 15. Assume also that on July 1, Janis Corporation estimates that its property tax assessment will be $24,000 for the coming year. The adjusting entry to be made on July 31, which would be repeated on August 31, September 30, and October 31, would be as follows:

July 31	Property Tax Expense	2,000	
	Estimated Property Tax Payable		2,000
	To record estimated property tax expense for the month $24,000 \div 12$ months = $2,000		

On November 1, the firm receives a property tax bill for $24,720. The estimate made in July was too low. The monthly charge should have been $2,060 per month. Because the difference between the actual and the estimate is small, the company decides to absorb in November the amount undercharged in the previous four months. Therefore, the property tax expense for November is $2,300 [$2,060 + 4($60)] and is recorded as follows:

Nov. 30	Property Tax Expense	2,300	
	Estimated Property Tax Payable		2,300
	To record estimated property tax		

The Estimated Property Tax Payable account now has a balance of $10,300. The entry to record payment on December 15 would be as follows:

Dec. 15	Estimated Property Tax Payable	10,300	
	Prepaid Property Taxes	14,420	
	Cash		24,720
	To record payment of property taxes		

Beginning December 31 and each month afterward until June 30, property tax expense is recorded by a debit to Property Tax Expense and a credit to Prepaid Property Taxes in the amount of $2,060. The total of these seven entries will reduce the Prepaid Property Taxes account to zero on June 30.

Product Warranty Liability When a firm places a warranty or guarantee on its product at the time of sale, a liability exists for the length of the warranty. The cost of the warranty is properly debited to an expense account in the period of sale because it is a feature of the product or service sold and thus was one of the reasons the customer made the purchase. On the basis of experience, it should be possible to estimate the amount the warranty will cost in the future. Some products or services will require little warranty service; others may require much. Thus there will be an average cost per product or service. For example, assume that a muffler company guarantees that it will replace any muffler free of charge if it fails any time as long as you own your car. The company makes only a small service charge for replacing the muffler. This guarantee is an important selling feature for the firm's mufflers. In the past, 4 percent of the mufflers sold have been returned for replacement under the guarantee. The average cost of a muffler is $25. Assume that during July, 350 mufflers were sold. This accrued liability would be recorded as an adjustment at the end of July as follows:

July 31	Product Warranty Expense	350	
	Estimated Product Warranty Liability		350
	To record estimated product warranty expense, calculated as follows:		

Number of units sold	350
Rate of replacements under warranty	$\times$ .04
Estimated units to be replaced	14
Estimated cost per unit	$\times$ $25
Estimated liability for product warranty	$350

When a muffler is returned for replacement under the product warranty in a subsequent accounting period, the cost of the muffler is charged against the estimated product warranty liability account. For example, assume that a customer returns on December 5 with a defective muffler and pays a $10 service charge to have the muffler replaced. Assume that this particular muffler cost $20. The entry is as follows:

Dec. 5	Cash	10	
	Estimated Product Warranty Liability	20	
	Service Revenue		10
	Merchandise Inventory		20
	To record replacement of muffler under warranty		

Vacation Pay Liability In most companies, employees earn the right to paid vacation days or weeks as they work during the year. For example, an employee may earn two weeks of paid vacation for each fifty weeks of work. Therefore, she or he is paid fifty-two weeks' salary for fifty weeks' work. Theoretically, the cost of the two weeks' vacation should be allocated as expense over the whole year. So vacation pay represents 4 percent (two weeks' vacation divided by fifty weeks) of a worker's pay. Every week worked earns the employee a small fraction (4 percent) of his or her vacation pay. Not all employees in every company will collect vacation pay because of turnover and rules regarding term of employment.

Suppose that a company with the above policy has a weekly payroll of $20,000 and that experience has shown that 75 percent of employees will ultimately collect vacation pay. The computation of vacation pay expense is as follows: $20,000 × 4 percent × 75 percent = $600.

The entry to record vacation pay expense for the week ended April 20 is as follows:

Apr. 20	Vacation Pay Expense	600	
	Estimated Liability for Vacation Pay		600
	To record estimated vacation pay expense		

At the time that a person receives his or her vacation pay, an entry is made debiting Estimated Liability for Vacation Pay and crediting Cash or Wages Payable. For example, assume that an employee is paid $550 during a two-week vacation ending August 31; the entry is as follows:

Aug. 31	Estimated Liability for Vacation Pay	550	
	Cash (or Wages Payable)		550
	To record wages of employee on		
	vacation		

Contingent Liabilities

*Objective 3
Define a
contingent
liability*

A **contingent liability** is not an existing liability. Rather, it is a potential liability because it depends on a future event arising out of a past transaction. For instance, a construction company that built a bridge may have been sued by the state for using poor materials. The past transaction is the building of the bridge under contract. The future event whose outcome is not known is the suit against the company. Two conditions have been established by the FASB for determining when a contingency should be entered in the accounting records. They are that the liability must be probable and that it must be reasonably estimated.[1] Estimated liabilities such as the estimated income taxes liability, warranty liability, and vacation pay liability that were described earlier in this chapter meet these conditions. So they are accrued in the accounting records. Potential liabilities that do not meet both conditions are reported in the notes to the financial statements. The following example comes from a recent annual report of Exxon Corporation:

The corporation, together with a number of other petroleum companies, is named as a respondent in an antitrust proceeding commenced by the Federal Trade Commission (FTC) in 1973 in which violations of Section 5 of the Federal Trade Commission Act are alleged. The FTC staff counsel have indicated that they may seek partial refining divestiture among other forms of injunctive relief. Several states have commenced separate lawsuits which allege similar violations of federal and state monopoly and restraint of trade statutes and seek somewhat similar relief together with money damages.

The allegations of unlawful practices in these actions have been denied, and the actions will be vigorously defended by the corporation. The corporation firmly

1. *Statement of Financial Accounting Standards No. 5,* "Accounting for Contingencies" (Stamford, Conn.: Financial Accounting Standards Board, 1975).

believes the actions can be successfully defended; in view of the broad relief sought, however, an adverse decision could have a significant effect upon the scope and nature of the corporation's operations. Final judicial determination is expected to take a number of years.

Contingent liabilities arise not only from lawsuits but also sometimes from income tax disputes, failure to follow government regulations, discounted notes receivable, and guarantees of the debt of other companies.

Introduction to Payroll Accounting

Objective 4
Identify and
compute the
liabilities
associated with
payroll
accounting

A major expense of most companies is the cost of labor and related payroll taxes. In some industries such as banking and airlines, payroll costs represent more than half of the operating costs.

Payroll accounting is important not only because of the amounts of money involved but also because the employer must conform to many complex laws governing taxes on payrolls. The employer has many reporting requirements and liabilities for amounts of money withheld from employees' salaries and for taxes on the payroll.

Also, the payroll accounting system is subject to complaints and to possible fraud. Every employee must be paid on time and receive a detailed explanation of the amount of his or her pay. The payroll system calls for strong internal control and efficient processing and distribution of checks, as well as accurate reporting to the government agencies.

This section will focus first on the liabilities and records connected with payroll accounting and then on the control requirements of payroll accounting. The three general kinds of liabilities associated with payroll accounting are (1) liabilities for employee compensation, (2) liabilities for employee payroll withholdings, and (3) liabilities for employer payroll taxes.

It is important to distinguish between employees and independent contractors. Payroll accounting applies to employees of the company. Employees are paid a wage or salary by the company and are under its direct supervision and control. Independent contractors, on the other hand, are not employees of the company. So they are not accounted for under the payroll system. They offer services to the firm for a fee but are not under its direct control or supervision. Some examples of independent contractors are certified public accountants, advertising agencies, lawyers, and computer service companies.

Liabilities for Employee Compensation

The employer is liable to employees for wages and salaries. The term **wages** refers to payment for the services of employees at an hourly rate or on a piecework basis. The term **salaries** refers to the compensation for employees who are paid at a monthly or yearly rate. Generally, these employees are administrators or managers.

Besides setting minimum wage levels, the federal Fair Labor Standards

Act (also called the Wages and Hours Law) regulates overtime pay. Employers who take part in interstate commerce must pay overtime for hours worked beyond forty hours a week or more than eight hours a day. This overtime pay must be at least one and one-half times the regular rate. Work on Saturdays, Sundays, or holidays may also call for overtime pay under separate wage agreements. Overtime pay under union or other employment contracts may exceed these minimums.

For example, suppose that the employment contract of Robert Jones calls for a regular wage of $5 an hour, one and one-half times the regular rate for work over eight hours in any weekday, and twice the regular rate for work on Saturdays, Sundays, or holidays. He works the following days and hours during the week of January 18, 19xx:

Day	Total Hours Worked	Regular Time	Overtime
Monday	10	8	2
Tuesday	8	8	0
Wednesday	8	8	0
Thursday	9	8	1
Friday	10	8	2
Saturday	2	0	2
	47	40	7

Jones's wages would be figured as follows:

Regular time	40 hours × $5	$200.00
Overtime, weekdays	5 hours × $5 × 1.5	37.50
Overtime, weekend	2 hours × $5 × 2	20.00
Total wages		$257.50

Liabilities for Employee Payroll Withholdings

The amount paid to employees is generally less than the wages they have earned because the employer is required by law to withhold certain amounts from the employees' wages and send them directly to government agencies to pay taxes owed by the employees. Also, certain withholdings are made for the employees' benefit and often at their request. In the first group are FICA taxes, federal income taxes, and state income taxes. In the second group are pension payments, medical insurance premiums, life insurance premiums, union dues, and charitable contributions. No matter what the reason is for the withholding from the employees' wages, the employer is liable for payment to the proper agency, fund, or organization.

FICA Tax With the passage of the U.S. social security program in the 1930s, the federal government began to take more responsibility for the well-being of its citizens. The social security program offers retirement and disability benefits, survivor's benefits, and hospitalization and other medical benefits. One of the major extensions of the program provides hospitalization and medical insurance for persons over sixty-five.

The social security program is financed by taxes on employees, employers, and the self-employed. About 90 percent of the people working in the United States fall under the provisions of this program.

The Federal Insurance Contributions Act (FICA) set up the tax to pay for this program. The tax is paid by *both* employee and employer and is now based on the following schedule up to 1986.

	1984	1985	1986
FICA tax rate	7.0%	7.05%	7.15%
Maximum wage taxed under present law	$36,000.00	$38,100.00	$40,200.00
Present maximum tax	$ 2,520.00	$ 2,686.05	$ 2,874.30

Although this is the current schedule, it is subject to frequent amendments by Congress. In this text, we will use the figures given above.

The FICA tax applies to the pay of each employee up to a certain level. In 1984, it applies to the level of $36,000. There is no tax on individual earnings above this amount. So the largest possible FICA tax for each employee is $2,520 ($36,000 × .07). The employee and the employer must each pay this amount. The employer deducts this tax from the employee's wages and sends the amount, along with other employees' withholdings of FICA taxes, to the government along with the employer's FICA taxes as well. Because of inflation and rising benefits under the social security system, these provisions are under constant study by Congress. They are subject to change and should be verified each year.

As an example of the FICA tax, suppose that Robert Jones will earn less than $36,000 this year, and that the FICA withholding for taxes on his paycheck this week is $18.03 ($257.50 × .07). The employer must pay an equal tax of $18.03.

Federal Income Tax The largest deduction from many employees' earnings is their estimated liability for federal income taxes. The system of tax collection for federal income taxes is to "pay as you go." The employer is required to withhold the amount of the taxes from employees' paychecks and turn it over to the Internal Revenue Service.

The amount to be withheld depends on the amount of each employee's earnings and on the number of the employee's exemptions. All employees are required by law to indicate their exemptions by filing a Form W-4 (Employee's Withholding Exemption Certificate). Each employee is entitled to one exemption for himself or herself and one for each dependent. Additional exemptions are possible if the individual is blind or over sixty-five years of age. In our example, Robert Jones has four exemptions—one for himself, one for his wife, and one for each of two children.

The Internal Revenue Service provides employers with tables to aid them in computing the amount of withholdings. For example, Figure 12-3 is a withholding table for married employees who are paid weekly. The withholding from Robert Jones's $257.50 weekly earnings is $15.80.

		Weekly Payroll Period—Employee Married										
And the wages are—		And the number of withholding allowances claimed is—										
At least	But less than	0	1	2	3	4	5	6	7	8	9	10 or more
		The amount of income tax to be withheld shall be—										
$200	$210	$20.10	$16.80	$14.40	$12.10	$ 9.80	$ 7.50	$ 5.20	$ 2.90	$ .60	$ 0	$0
210	220	21.80	18.50	15.60	13.30	11.00	8.70	6.40	4.10	1.80	0	0
220	230	23.50	20.20	16.90	14.50	12.20	9.90	7.60	5.30	3.00	.70	0
230	240	25.20	21.90	18.60	15.70	13.40	11.10	8.80	6.50	4.20	1.90	0
240	250	26.90	23.60	20.30	17.10	14.60	12.30	10.00	7.70	5.40	3.10	.80
250	260	28.60	25.30	22.00	18.80	15.80	13.50	11.20	8.90	6.60	4.30	2.00
260	270	30.30	27.00	23.70	20.50	17.20	14.70	12.40	10.10	7.80	5.50	3.20
270	280	32.00	28.70	25.40	22.20	18.90	15.90	13.60	11.30	9.00	6.70	4.40
280	290	33.70	30.40	27.10	23.90	20.60	17.30	14.80	12.50	10.20	7.90	5.60
290	300	35.40	32.10	28.80	25.60	22.30	19.00	16.00	13.70	11.40	9.10	6.80
300	310	37.10	33.80	30.50	27.30	24.00	20.70	17.50	14.90	12.60	10.30	8.00

**Figure 12-3
Wage-Bracket
Table**

State Income Tax Most states have income taxes, and in most cases the procedures for withholding are similar to those for federal income taxes.

Other Withholdings Some of the other withholdings, such as for a retirement or pension plan, are required of each employee. Others, such as withholdings for insurance premiums or savings plans, may be requested by the employee. The payroll system must allow for treating each employee separately with regard to withholdings and the records of these withholdings. The employer is liable to account for all withholdings and to make proper remittances.

Computation of an Employee's Take-Home Pay: An Illustration

*Objective 5
Record transactions associated with payroll accounting*

To continue with the example of Robert Jones, let us now compute his take-home pay. We know that his total earnings for the week of January 18 are $257.50, that his FICA tax rate at 7.0 percent is $18.03 (he has not earned over $36,000), and that his federal income tax withholding is $15.80. Assume also that his union dues are $2.00, his medical insurance premiums are $7.60, his life insurance premium is $6.00, he places $15.00 per week in savings bonds, and he contributes $1.00 per week to United Charities. His net (take-home) pay is computed as follows:

Gross earnings		$257.50
Deductions		
FICA tax	$18.03	
Federal income tax withheld	15.80	
Union dues	2.00	

Chapter Twelve

Medical insurance	7.60
Life insurance	6.00
Savings bonds	15.00
United Charities contribution	1.00
Total withheld	65.43
Net (take-home) pay	$192.07

Employee Earnings Record Each employer must keep a record of earnings and withholdings for each employee. Many companies today use computers to maintain these records, but small companies use manual records. The manual form of **employee earnings record** used for Robert Jones is shown in Figure 12-4 (next page). This form is designed to help the employer meet legal reporting requirements. Each deduction must be shown to have been paid to the proper agency and the employee must receive a report of the deductions made each year. Most columns are self-explanatory. Note, however, the column on the far right, where cumulative earnings (earnings to date) are recorded. This record helps the employer comply with the rule of applying FICA taxes only up to the maximum wage level. At the end of the year, the employer reports to the employee on Form W-2, the Wage and Tax Statement, the totals of earnings and deductions for the year so that the employee can complete his or her individual tax return. The employer sends a copy of the W-2 to the Internal Revenue Service. Thus the IRS can check on whether the employee has reported all income earned from that employer.

Payroll Register The **payroll register** is a detailed listing of the firm's total payroll that is prepared each payday. A payroll register is presented in Figure 12-5 (next page). Note that the name, hours, earnings, deductions, and net pay of each employee are listed. Compare the January 18 entry in the employee earnings record (Figure 12-4) of Robert Jones with the entry for Robert Jones in the payroll register. Except for the first column, which lists the employee names, and the last column, which shows the wage or salary as either sales or office expense, the columns are the same. The columns help employers to record the payroll in the accounting records and to meet legal reporting requirements as noted above. The last two columns are needed to divide the expenses on the income statement into selling and administrative categories.

Recording the Payroll The journal entry for recording the payroll is based on the total of the columns from the payroll register. The journal entry to record the payroll of January 18 is as follows:

Jan. 18	Sales Salaries Expense	1,061.50	
	Office Salaries Expense	520.00	
	FICA Tax Payable		110.71
	Employees' Federal Income Tax Payable		151.80
	Union Dues Payable		6.00
	Medical Insurance Premiums Payable		48.80
	Life Insurance Premiums Payable		20.00

Figure 12-4
Employee Earnings Record

Employee Earnings Record

Employee's Name: Robert Jones
Address: 777 20th Street
Marshall, Michigan 52603
Date of Birth: September 20, 1952
Position: Sales Assistant

Social Security Number: 444-66-9999
Sex: Male
Single ___ Married X
Exemptions (W-4): 4
Date of Employment: July 15, 1978

Employee No.: 705
Weekly Pay Rate: $200
Hourly Rate: $5
Date Employment Ended: ___

1984		Earnings			Deductions							Payment		Cumulative Gross Earnings
Period Ended	Total Hours	Regular	Overtime	Gross	FICA Tax	Federal Income Tax	Union Dues	Medical Insurance	Life Insurance	Savings Bonds	Other: A—United Charities	Net Earnings	Check No.	
Jan. 6	40	200.00	0	200.00	14.00	9.80	2.00	7.60	6.00	15.00	A 1.00	144.60	717	200.00
13	44	200.00	30.00	230.00	16.10	13.40	2.00	7.60	6.00	15.00	A 1.00	168.90	822	430.00
20	47	200.00	57.50	257.50	18.03	15.80	2.00	7.60	6.00	15.00	A 1.00	192.07	926	687.50

Figure 12-5
Payroll Register

Payroll Register   Pay Period: Week ended January 18

Employee	Total Hours	Earnings			Deductions							Payment		Distribution	
		Regular	Overtime	Gross	FICA Tax	Federal Income Tax	Union Dues	Medical Insurance	Life Insurance	Savings Bonds	Other: A—United Charities	Net Earnings	Check No.	Sales Salaries Expense	Office Salaries Expense
Linda Duval	40	160.00		160.00	11.20	12.00		5.80				131.00	923		160.00
John Franks	44	160.00	24.00	184.00	12.88	14.40	2.00	7.60			A 10.00	137.12	924	184.00	
Samuel Goetz	40	400.00		400.00	28.00	51.70		10.40	14.00		A 3.00	292.90	925	400.00	
Robert Jones	47	200.00	57.50	257.50	18.03	15.80	2.00	7.60	6.00	15.00	A 1.00	192.07	926	257.50	
Billie Matthews	40	160.00		160.00	11.20	14.30		5.80				128.70	927		160.00
Rosaire O'Brian	42	200.00	20.00	220.00	15.40	23.50	2.00	5.80				173.30	928	220.00	
James Van Dyke	40	200.00		200.00	14.00	20.10		5.80				160.10	929		200.00
		1,480.00	101.50	1,581.50	110.71	151.80	6.00	48.80	20.00	15.00	14.00	1,215.19		1,061.50	520.00

Savings Bonds Payable	15.00
United Charities Payable	14.00
Salaries Payable	1,215.19

To record weekly payroll

Note that each account debited or credited is a total from the payroll register. If the payroll register is considered a special-purpose journal like those in Chapter 7, the column can be entered directly in the ledger accounts with the correct account numbers shown at the bottom of each column.

Liabilities for Employer Payroll Taxes

The payroll taxes discussed so far were deducted from the employee's gross earnings, to be paid by the employer. There are three major taxes on salaries that the employer must also pay: the FICA tax, the federal unemployment insurance tax, and state unemployment compensation tax. These taxes are considered operating expenses.

FICA Tax The employer must pay FICA tax equal to that paid by the employees. That is, from the payroll register in Figure 12-5, the employer would have to pay an FICA tax of $110.71, equal to that paid by the employees.

Federal Unemployment Insurance Tax The Federal Unemployment Tax Act (FUTA) is another part of the U.S. social security system. It is intended to pay for operating programs to help unemployed workers. In this way, it is different from FICA taxes and state unemployment taxes. The dollars paid through FUTA provide for unemployment compensation. Unlike the FICA tax, which is levied on both employees and employers, the FUTA is assessed only against employers.

Although the amount of tax can vary, it amounted recently to 3.5 percent of the first $7,000 earned by each employee. The employer, however, is allowed a credit against this federal tax for unemployment taxes paid to the state. The maximum credit is 2.7 percent of the first $7,000 of each employee's earnings. Most states set their rate at this maximum. Therefore, the FUTA paid is 0.8 percent (3.5 percent − 2.7 percent) of the taxable wages.

State Unemployment Insurance Tax All state unemployment plans provide for unemployment compensation to be paid to eligible unemployed workers. This compensation is paid out of the fund provided by the 2.7 percent of the first $7,000 earned by each employee. In some states, employers with favorable employment records may be entitled to pay less than the 2.7 percent.

Recording Payroll Taxes According to Figure 12-5, the gross payroll for the week ended January 18 was $1,581.50. Because it was the first month of the year, all employees had accumulated less than the $36,000 and $7,000 maximum taxable salaries. Therefore, the FICA tax was $110.71

(equal to tax on employees); the FUTA was $12.65 (.008 $\times$ $1,581.50); and the state unemployment tax was $42.70 (.027 $\times$ $1,581.50). The entry to record this expense and related liability in the general journal is as follows:

Jan. 18	Payroll Tax Expense	166.06	
	FICA Tax Payable		110.71
	Federal Unemployment Tax Payable		12.65
	State Unemployment Tax Payable		42.70
	To record weekly payroll taxes expense		

Payment of Payroll and Payroll Taxes

After the weekly payroll is recorded, as illustrated earlier, a liability of $1,215.19 exists for salaries payable. How this liability will be paid depends on the system used by the company. Many companies use a special payroll account against which payroll checks are drawn. Under this system, a check must first be drawn on the regular checking account for net earnings and deposited in the special payroll account before the payroll checks are issued to the employees. If a voucher system is combined with a special payroll account, a voucher for the total salaries payable ($1,215.19) is prepared and recorded in the voucher register as a debit to Payroll Bank Account and a credit to Vouchers Payable.

The combined FICA taxes (both employees' and employer's share) and the federal income taxes must be paid to the Internal Revenue Service at least quarterly. Monthly payments are necessary if more than a certain amount of money is involved. The federal unemployment insurance taxes are paid yearly if the amount is less than $100. If it is more than $100, quarterly payments are necessary. The payment dates among the states vary. Other payroll deductions must be paid according to the particular contracts or agreements involved.

Internal Control for Payroll

Objective 6
Apply internal control to the payroll system

Because a great deal of money passes through the payroll system of most companies, it is important to have good internal control over the system. Consider the following possible payroll frauds: An employee who does not exist may be entered on the payroll, and the check may be collected by someone else. Or time cards for employees who no longer work at the company may be turned in. Or an employee may not work all the hours reported.

To avoid these and other payroll frauds, the principles of internal control stated in Chapter 8 should be applied to the payroll system. For example, there should be a separation of duties for the major payroll functions. In brief, these functions may be described as follows:

1. **The personnel function.** All employees hired should have a central employment record that includes, among other things, their wage rate and termination date (if they leave the company).

2. **The timekeeping function.** Employees paid by the hour should be required to punch a time clock as they arrive or leave. Salaried employees should prepare time sheets, which are approved by their supervisors.

3. **The accounting function.** A payroll department should prepare checks based on data from the timekeeping function about time worked and from the personnel function on the pay rate and payroll deductions.

4. **The distribution function.** The paychecks from the accounting function should be distributed by an office separate from any of the above functions. Employees should be required to present proper identification and sign their names in order to receive their checks.

Chapter Review

Review of Learning Objectives

1. Define liability and explain how the problems of recognition, valuation, and classification apply to liabilities.

Liabilities represent present legal obligations of the firm for future payment of assets or the future performance of services. They result from past transactions and should be recognized when there is a transaction that obligates the company to make future payments. Liabilities are valued at the amount of money necessary to satisfy the obligation or the fair market value of goods or services that must be delivered. Liabilities are classified as current or long-term.

2. Identify, compute, and record definitely determinable and estimated current liabilities.

Two principal categories of current liabilities are definitely determinable liabilities and estimated liabilities. Although definitely determinable liabilities such as accounts payable, notes payable, dividends payable, accrued liabilities, and the current portion of long-term debt can be measured exactly, the accountant must still be careful not to overlook existing liabilities in these categories. Estimated liabilities such as liabilities for income taxes, property taxes, product warranties, and others definitely exist, but the amounts must be estimated and recorded properly.

3. Define a contingent liability.

A contingent liability is a potential liability arising from a past transaction and dependent on a future event. Examples are lawsuits, income tax disputes, discounted notes receivable, guarantees of debt, and the potential cost of changes in government regulations.

4. Identify and compute the liabilities associated with payroll accounting.

Labor costs are a large segment of the total cost of most businesses. In addition, three important categories of liabilities are associated with the payroll. The employer is liable for the compensation to the employee, for withholdings from the employee's gross pay, and for the employer portion of payroll taxes. The most common payroll withholdings are the FICA tax, federal and state income taxes, and employee-requested withholdings. The principal employer-paid taxes are FICA (an amount equal to that of the employee) and federal and state unemployment compensation taxes.

5. Record transactions associated with payroll accounting.

The salary and deductions for each employee are recorded each pay period in the payroll register. From the payroll register the details of each employee's earnings are transferred to the employee's earnings record. The column totals of the payroll register are used to prepare a general journal entry that records the payroll and accompanying liabilities. One further general journal entry is needed to record the employer's share of the FICA taxes and the federal and state unemployment taxes.

6. Apply internal control to the payroll system.

Because of the large amount of money involved and the possibility of fraud, good internal control is important for payroll systems. There should be a separation of duties for the following main payroll functions: the personnel function, the timekeeping function, the accounting function, and the distribution function.

Review Problem
Notes Payable Transactions and End-of-Period Entries

McLaughlin, Inc., whose fiscal year ends June 30, completed the following transactions involving notes payable:

May 11   Purchased a small crane by issuing a 60-day, 12 percent note for $54,000. The face of the note does not include interest.

     16   Obtained a $40,000 loan from the bank to finance a temporary increase in receivables by signing a 90-day, 10 percent note. The face value includes interest.

June 30   Made end-of-year adjusting entry to accrue interest expense.

     30   Made end-of-year closing entry pertaining to interest expense.

July 1   Made appropriate reversing entry.

     10   Paid the note plus interest on the crane purchase.

Aug. 14   Paid off the note to the bank.

Required

1. Prepare general journal entries for the above transactions.
2. Open general ledger accounts for Notes Payable (212), Discount on Notes Payable (213), Interest Payable (214), and Interest Expense (721). Post the relevant portions of the entries to these general ledger accounts.

Answer to Review Problem

1. Journal entries prepared (facing page).
2. Accounts opened and amounts posted (page 446).

Chapter Assignments

Questions

1. What are liabilities?
2. Why is the timing of liability recognition an important consideration in accounting?
3. At the end of the accounting period, Janson Company had a legal obligation to accept delivery and pay for a truckload of hospital supplies the following week. Is this legal obligation a liability?
4. Ned Johnson, a star college basketball player, received a contract from the Midwest Blazers to play professional basketball. The contract calls for a salary of $300,000 a year for four years, dependent on his making the team in each of those years. Should this contract be considered a liability and recorded on the books of the basketball team?
5. What is the rule for determining a current liability?

Date		Description	Post. Ref.	Debit	Credit
19xx					
May	11	Equipment		54,000	
		Notes Payable	212		54,000
		Purchase of crane with			
		60-day, 12 percent note			
	16	Cash		39,000	
		Discount on Notes Payable	213	1,000	
		Notes Payable	212		40,000
		Loan from bank obtained by			
		signing 90-day, 10 percent note;			
		discount			
		$40,000 \times .1 \times 90/360 = \$1,000$			
June	30	Interest Expense	721	1,400	
		Discount on Notes Payable	213		500
		Interest Payable	214		900
		To accrue interest expense			
		$\$1,000 \times 45/90 = \$500$			
		$\$54,000 \times .12 \times 50/360 = \$900$			
	30	Income Summary		1,400	
		Interest Expense	721		1,400
		To close interest expense			
July	1	Discount on Notes Payable	213	500	
		Interest Payable	214	900	
		Interest Expense	721		1,400
		To reverse interest expense			
		adjustment			
	10	Notes Payable	212	54,000	
		Interest Expense	721	1,080	
		Cash			55,080
		Payment of note on equipment			
		$\$54,000 \times .12 \times 60/360 = \$1,080$			
Aug.	14	Notes Payable	212	40,000	
		Cash			40,000
		Payment of bank loan			
	14	Interest Expense	721	1,000	
		Discount on Notes Payable	213		1,000
		To record interest expense on			
		notes payable			

Notes Payable   Account No. 212

Date		Item	Post. Ref.	Debit	Credit	Balance Debit	Balance Credit
May	11		J26		54,000		54,000
	16		J26		40,000		94,000
July	10		J26	54,000			40,000
Aug.	14		J26	40,000			—

Discount on Notes Payable   Account No. 213

Date		Item	Post. Ref.	Debit	Credit	Balance Debit	Balance Credit
May	16		J26	1,000		1,000	
June	30		J26		500	500	
July	1		J26	500		1,000	
Aug.	14		J26		1,000	—	

Interest Payable   Account No. 214

Date		Item	Post. Ref.	Debit	Credit	Balance Debit	Balance Credit
June	30		J26		900		900
July	1		J26	900			—

Interest Expense   Account No. 721

Date		Item	Post. Ref.	Debit	Credit	Balance Debit	Balance Credit
June	30		J26	1,400		1,400	
	30		J26		1,400	—	
July	1		J26		1,400		1,400
	10		J26	1,080			320
Aug.	14		J26	1,000		680	

6. Where should the Discount on Notes Payable account appear on the balance sheet?

7. When can a portion of long-term debt be classified as a current liability?

8. Why are deferred revenues classified as liabilities?

9. What is definite about an estimated liability?

10. Why are income taxes payable considered to be estimated liabilities?

11. When does a company incur a liability for a product warranty?

12. What is a contingent liability, and how does it differ from an estimated liability?

13. What are some examples of contingent liabilities, and why is each a contingent liability?

14. Why is payroll accounting important?

15. How does an employee differ from an independent contractor?

16. What are three types of employer-related payroll liabilities?

17. Who pays the FICA tax?

18. What role does the W-4 form play in determining the withholding for estimated federal income taxes?

19. What withholdings might an employee voluntarily request?

20. Why is an employee earnings record necessary, and how does it relate to the W-2 form?

21. How can the payroll register be used as a special-purpose journal?

22. What payroll functions should be separated for good internal control?

Classroom Exercises

**Exercise 12-1
Interest Expense—
Interest Not Included in Face of Note**
(L.O. 2)

On the last day of October, McMan Company borrows $20,000 from a bank on a note for sixty days at 12 percent interest.

Assume that interest is not included in the face amount. Prepare the following general journal entries: (1) October 31, recording of note; (2) November 30, accrual of interest expense; (3) November 30, closing entry; (4) December 1, reversing entry; (5) December 30, payment of note plus interest.

**Exercise 12-2
Interest Expense—
Interest Included in Face of Note**
(L.O. 2)

Assume the same facts as in Exercise 12-1, except that interest is included in the face amount of the note and the note is discounted at the bank on October 31. Prepare the following general journal entries: (1) October 31, recording of note; (2) November 30, accrual of interest expense; (3) November 30, closing entry; (4) December 1, reversing entry; (5) December 30, payment of note and recording of interest expense.

**Exercise 12-3
Excise and Sales Taxes**
(L.O. 2)

Duval Speed Call billed its customers for the month of May for a total of $1,140,000, including 9 percent federal excise tax and 5 percent state sales tax.

1. Determine the proper amount of revenue to report for the month.
2. Prepare a general journal entry to record the revenue and related liabilities for the month.

**Exercise 12-4
Vacation Pay Liability**
(L.O. 4, 5)

Wrangler Corporation currently allows each employee three weeks' paid vacation after working at the company for one year. On the basis of studies of employee turnover and previous experience, management estimates that 70 percent of the employees will qualify for vacation pay this year.

1. Assume that the August payroll for Wrangler is $400,000. Figure the estimated employee benefit for the month.
2. Prepare a general journal entry to record the employee benefit for August.

Current Liabilities and Payroll Accounting

Exercise 12-5
Payroll Trans-
actions
(L.O. 4, 5)

Ben Wilson earns a salary of $40,000 during the year. FICA taxes are 7.0 percent up to $36,000. Federal unemployment insurance taxes are 3.5 percent of the first $7,000; however, a credit is allowed equal to the state unemployment insurance taxes of 2.7 percent on the $7,000. During the year, $10,200 was withheld for federal income taxes.

1. Prepare a general journal entry summarizing the payment of $40,000 to Wilson during the year.
2. Prepare a general journal entry summarizing the employer payroll taxes on Wilson's salary for the year.
3. Determine the total cost of employing Wilson for the year.

Exercise 12-6
Net Pay Calcu-
lation and
Payroll Entries
(L.O. 4, 5)

Judy Laney is an employee whose overtime pay is regulated by the Fair Labor Standards Act. Her hourly rate is $7.00, and during the week ended July 11, she worked forty-two hours. Judy claims two exemptions, including one for herself, on her W-4 form. So far this year she has earned $8,650. Each week $12 is deducted from her paycheck for medical insurance.

1. Compute the following items related to the pay for Judy Laney for the week of July 11: (a) gross pay, (b) FICA taxes (assume a rate of 7.0 percent), (c) federal income tax withholding (use Figure 12-3), and (d) net pay.
2. Prepare a general journal entry to record the wages expense and related liabilities for Judy Laney for the week ended July 11.

Exercise 12-7
Product
Warranty
Liability
(L.O. 2)

Atonic manufactures and sells electronic games. Each game costs $60 and sells for $100. In addition, each game carries a warranty that provides for free replacement if it fails for any reason during the two years following the sale. In the past, 6 percent of the games sold had to be replaced under the warranty. During October, Atonic sold 24,000 games and 1,300 games were replaced under the warranty.

1. Prepare a general journal entry to record the estimated liability for product warranties during the month.
2. Prepare a general journal entry to record the games replaced under warranty during the month.

Exercise 12-8
Property Tax
Liability
(L.O. 2)

Capstone Company accrues estimated liabilities for property taxes. The company's fiscal year ends December 31. The estimated property taxes for the year are $12,000. The bill for property taxes is usually received on March 1 and is due on May 1.

Prepare general journal entries for the following: January 31, accrual of property tax expense; February 28, accrual of property tax expense; March 31, accrual of property tax expense, assuming that the actual bill is $12,300; April 30, accrual of property tax expense; May 1, payment of property taxes; May 31, accrual of property tax expense.

Chapter Twelve

Interpreting Accounting Information

Published Financial Information: Daniel Industries (L.O. 1)

Selected parts of the financial statements of Daniel Industries are shown below.

	1982	1981
	(in thousands)	
Current Assets		
Cash	$ 2,654	$ 1,896
Short-Term Investments	2,245	12,797
Accounts Receivable	45,120	23,365
Other Receivables	782	977
Prepaid Expenses	5,387	11,632
Inventories	39,901	35,684
Other	306	351
Total Current Assets	$96,395	$86,702
Current Liabilities		
Notes Payable	$ 3,151	$ 1,933
Accounts Payable	20,643	11,646
Salaries Payable	2,850	2,185
Accrued Contributions	2,683	2,478
Other Accrued Expenses	5,298	4,355
Taxes Payable	4,813	1,208
Deferred Taxes	1,738	2,215
Billings in Excess of Costs	246	—
Total Current Liabilities	$41,422	$26,020
Revenues		
Sales, Less Returns and Allowances	$185,340	$162,020
Other	1,289	916
	$186,629	$162,936
Cost of Goods Sold	$111,147	$103,619

There has been a significant increase (59 percent) in total current liabilities between the two years. A closer look at current assets, sales, and cost of goods sold does not reveal as large an increase in percentage terms.

Required

1. What specific items have contributed most to the large increase in current liabilities?
2. Identify several possible reasons for the significant increase in current liabilities between years? You should recognize that there are relationships between current liabilities and other items on the financial statements.
3. Does Daniel Industries have sufficient current assets to pay its current liabilities? Would your answer be the same if the payments were to be made immediately? Why?

Problem Set A

**Problem 12A-1
Payroll Entries
(L.O. 4, 5)**

At the end of October, the payroll register for McTalley Corporation contained the following totals: sales salaries, $54,540; office salaries, $29,360; administrative salaries, $34,480; FICA taxes withheld, $7,872; federal income taxes withheld, $29,828; state income taxes withheld, $4,792; medical insurance deductions, $4,230; life insurance deductions, $3,724; union dues deductions, $432; salaries subject to unemployment taxes, $17,880.

Required

Prepare general journal entries to record the following: (1) accrual of the monthly payroll, (2) payment of the net payroll, (3) accrual of employer's payroll taxes (assuming an FICA tax equal to the amount for employees, a federal unemployment insurance tax of 0.8 percent, and a state unemployment tax of 2.7 percent), (4) payment of all liabilities related to the payroll (assuming that all are settled at the same time).

**Problem 12A-2
Product
Warranty
Liability
(L.O. 2)**

Greenfeld Tire Company guarantees the tires it sells until they wear out. If a tire fails, the customer is charged a percentage of the retail price based on the percentage of the tire that is worn, plus a service charge for putting the tire on the car. In the past, management found that only 2 percent of the tires sold required replacement under warranty, and of those replaced an average of 20 percent of the cost is collected under the percentage pricing system. The average tire costs the company $70. At the beginning of July, the account for estimated liability for product warranties had a credit balance of $45,492. During July, 250 tires were returned under the warranty. The cost of the replacement tires was $9,250, of which $2,250 was recovered under the percentage-worn formula. Service revenue amounted to $1,062. During the month, the company sold 7,050 tires.

Required

1. Prepare general journal entries to record each of the following: (a) the warranty work completed during the month including related revenue; (b) the estimated liability for product warranties for tires sold during the month.
2. Compute the balance of the estimated product warranty liabilities at the end of the month.

**Problem 12A-3
Notes Payable
Transactions
and End-of-
Period Entries
(L.O. 2)**

Young Company, whose fiscal year ends September 30, completed the following transactions involving notes payable:

Aug. 16   Purchased a new special-purpose truck by issuing a 90-day, 11 percent note for $28,000. The note is to be paid in full plus interest.
Sept. 10   Borrowed $15,000 from the bank to finance a temporary increase in inventory by signing a 60-day, 10 percent note. The face value includes interest.
     30   Made end-of-year adjusting entry to accrue interest expense.
     30   Made end-of-year closing entry pertaining to interest expense.
Oct.   1   Made appropriate reversing entry.
Nov.   9   Paid off the note to the bank.
     14   Paid off the note plus interest in the truck purchase.

Required

1. Prepare general journal entries for the above transactions.
2. Open general ledger accounts for Notes Payable (212), Discount on Notes Payable (213), Interest Payable (214), and Interest Expense (721). Post the relevant portions of the entries to these general ledger accounts.

**Problem 12A-4
Property Tax
and Vacation
Pay Liabilities**
(L.O. 2, 4, 5)

It is the policy of Tronics Corporation to accrue estimated liabilities for property taxes and for vacation pay. The company's fiscal year ends February 28. It is now March, the first month of the new fiscal year, and data are being gathered for the computation of estimated liabilities. The property taxes for the previous year were $66,000 and are expected to increase by 6 percent in the current year. The bill for property taxes is usually received near May 1, to be paid July 1. In addition, the company allows employees two weeks' paid vacation each year. In the past, 80 percent of the employees qualified for this benefit.

Required

1. Compute the proper monthly charge to property taxes expense, and prepare general journal entries for the following:

Mar. 31 Accrual of property tax expense
Apr. 30 Accrual of property tax expense
May 31 Accrual of property tax expense, assuming the actual tax bill is $69,720
June 30 Accrual of property tax expense
July 1 Payment of property tax
    31 Accrual of property tax expense

2. Assume that for March the total payroll was $178,000 and that $3,944 was paid to employees who were on paid vacations. (a) Compute the vacation pay expense for March. (b) Prepare a general journal entry to record the accrual of vacation pay expense for March. (c) Prepare a general journal entry to record the wages of employees on vacation in March (ignore payroll deductions and taxes).

**Problem 12A-5
FICA and
Unemployment
Taxes**
(L.O. 4)

During the current year, Quick Training Company had twelve employees whose cumulative earnings for the year were as follows:

Employee	Cumulative Earnings	Employee	Cumulative Earnings
Axmear, J.	$14,850	Lu, C.	$ 6,900
Bado, R.	2,936	Nelson, K.	10,211
Damte, N.	3,239	Trezzo, J.	3,140
Edens, T.	9,470	Voss, B.	13,650
Huden, P.	38,200	Votaw, A.	9,871
Lupe, D.	15,900	Walker, H.	8,392

FICA taxes in effect at this time are 7.0 percent for both employee and employer on the first $36,000 earned by each employee during the year. The company is subject to a 2.7 percent state unemployment insurance tax and, after credits, an 0.8 percent federal unemployment insurance tax. Currently, both federal and state unemployment taxes apply to the first $7,000 earned by each employee.

Required

1. Prepare and complete a schedule with the following columns: Employee Name; Cumulative Earnings; Earnings Subject to FICA Tax; Earnings Subject to Unemployment Tax. Total the columns.
2. Compute the total FICA taxes and the federal and state unemployment taxes.

**Problem 12A-6
Payroll Register
and Related
Entries**
(L.O. 4, 5)

Dietz Digital Company has eight employees, two of whom are administrators and are paid a monthly salary. The other six employees are sales personnel who are paid a set rate for regular hours plus two times their hourly rate for overtime hours. Hourly employees are paid once a week. The employees and employer are subject to 7.0 percent FICA taxes on the first $36,000 earned by each employee. The unemployment insurance tax rates are 2.7 percent for the state and 0.8 percent for the federal government. The unemployment insurance tax applies to the first $7,000 earned by each employee and is levied only on the employer.

Each employee qualifies for a supplemental benefit plan that includes medical insurance, life insurance, and additional retirement funds. Under this plan, each employee contributes 6 percent of his or her gross income as a payroll withholding, and the company matches this amount.

The data for the last payday of October are as follows:

| Employee | Hours | | Pay Rate | Cumulative Gross Pay Excluding Current Pay Period | Federal Income Tax to Be Withheld |
	Regular	Overtime			
Austin, L.	40	4	$ 8.00	$14,350.00	$ 40.50
Cox, C.	40		7.75	11,275.00	20.75
Glasskins, I.	Salary		2,000.00	18,000.00	412.50
Lzak, L.	40	10	9.00	5,100.00	35.60
Recknor, P.	40	6	8.50	1,962.00	60.50
Sloan, S.	40		8.00	7,219.00	23.00
Tokocy, Q.	Salary		1,700.00	15,300.00	241.00
Yee, B.	40	1	6.00	8,292.00	30.00

Required

1. Prepare a payroll register for the pay period ended October 31. The payroll register should have the following columns:

Employee
Total Hours
Earnings
  Regular
  Overtime
  Gross
  Cumulative

Deductions
  FICA Tax
  Federal Income Tax
  Supplemental Benefits Plan
Payment
Distribution
  Sales Expense
  Administrative Expense

2. Prepare a general journal entry to record the payroll and related liabilities for deductions for the period ended October 31.

3. Prepare general journal entries to record the expenses and related liabilities for the employer's payroll taxes and contribution to the supplemental benefit plan.

Problem Set B

**Problem 12B-1
Payroll Entries
(L.O. 4, 5)**

The following payroll totals for the month of April were taken from the payroll register of Mudoch Corporation: sales salaries, $26,400; office salaries, $12,900; general salaries, $14,220; FICA taxes withheld, $3,560; income taxes withheld, $8,760; medical insurance deductions, $1,960; life insurance deductions, $940; salaries subject to unemployment taxes, $36,900.

Required

Prepare general journal entries to record the following: (1) accrual of the monthly payroll, (2) payment of the net payroll, (3) accrual of employer's payroll taxes (assuming an FICA tax equal to the amount for employees, a federal unemployment insurance tax of 0.8 percent, and a state unemployment tax of 2.7 percent), and (4) payment of all liabilities related to the payroll (assuming that all are settled at the same time).

**Problem 12B-2
Product
Warranty
Liability
(L.O. 2)**

Navarro Company is engaged in the retail sale of washing machines. Each machine has a twenty-four-month warranty on parts. If a repair under warranty is required, a charge for the labor is made. Management has found that 20 percent of the machines sold require some warranty work before the twenty-four months pass. Furthermore, the average cost of replacement parts has been $60 per repair. At the beginning of February, the account for the estimated liability for product warranties had a credit balance of $10,680. During February, 60 machines were returned under the warranty. The cost of the parts used in repairing the machines was $1,712, and $1,836 was collected as service revenue for the labor involved. Also, during the month, 220 new machines were sold.

Required

1. Prepare general journal entries to record each of the following: (a) the warranty work completed during the month, including related revenue; (b) the estimated liability for product warranties for machines sold during the month.
2. Compute the balance of the estimated product warranty liabilities at the end of the month.

**Problem 12B-3
Notes Payable
Transactions
and End-of-
Period Entries
(L.O. 2)**

Segura Corporation, whose fiscal year ends April 30, completed the following transactions involving notes payable:

Mar. 11   Signed a 90-day, 10 percent, $60,000 note payable to Banc West for a working capital loan. The face value included interest.
21   Obtained a 60-day extension on a $36,000 trade account payable owed to a supplier by signing a 60-day, $36,000 note. Interest is in addition to the face value at the rate of 12 percent.
Apr. 30   Made end-of-year adjusting entry to accrue interest expense.
30   Made end-of-year closing entry pertaining to interest expense.
May 1   Made appropriate reversing entry.
20   Paid off the note plus interest due the supplier.
June 9   Paid amount due bank on 90-day note.

Required

1. Prepare general journal entries for the above transactions.
2. Open general ledger accounts for Notes Payable (212), Discount on Notes Payable (213), Interest Payable (214), and Interest Expense (721). Post the relevant portions of the entries to these general ledger accounts.

Problem 12B-4
Property Tax
and Vacation
Pay Liabilities
(L.O. 2, 4, 5)

Lomax Corporation prepares monthly financial statements and ends its fiscal year on June 30. In July, your first month as accountant for the company, you find that the company has not previously accrued estimated liabilities. In the past, the company, which has a large property tax bill, has charged property taxes to the month in which the bill is paid. The tax bill for last year was $33,000, and it is estimated that the tax will increase by 10 percent in the coming year. The tax bill is usually received on September 1, to be paid November 1. You also discover that the company allows employees who have worked for the company for one year to take two weeks' paid vacation each year. The cost of these vacations had been charged to expense in the month of payment. Approximately 80 percent of the employees qualify for this benefit.

You suggest to management that proper accounting treatment for these expenses is to spread their cost over the entire year. Management agrees and asks you to make the proper adjustments.

Required

1. Figure the proper monthly charge to property taxes expense, and prepare general journal entries for the following:

July 31   Accrual of property tax expense
Aug. 31   Accrual of property tax expense
Sept. 30 Accrual of property tax expense, assuming the actual tax bill is $36,660.
Oct. 31   Accrual of property tax expense
Nov. 1   Payment of property tax
Nov. 30   Accrual of property tax expense

2. Assume that for July, the total payroll is $212,000, which includes $7,400 paid to employees who were on vacation. (a) Compute the vacation pay expense for July. All employees qualify for a two-week vacation. (b) Prepare a general journal entry to record the accrual of vacation pay expense for July. (c) Prepare a general journal entry to record the wages of employees on vacation in July (ignore payroll deductions and taxes).

Problem 12B-5
FICA and
Unemployment
Taxes
(L.O. 4)

Mullenberg Company is subject to a 2.7 percent state unemployment insurance tax and an 0.8 percent federal unemployment insurance tax after credits. Currently, both federal and state unemployment taxes apply to the first $7,000 earned by each employee. FICA taxes in effect at this time are 7.0 percent for both employee and employer on the first $36,000 earned by each employee during this year.

During the current year, the cumulative earnings for each employee of the company are as follows:

Employee	Cumulative Earnings	Employee	Cumulative Earnings
Barbee, H.	$14,620	Norred, J.	$ 8,660
Boney, M.	4,260	Orta, J.	4,420
Clipp, C.	16,820	Perry, B.	21,650
Drewes, R.	15,130	Rice, M.	16,100
Inga, L.	36,250	Stoker, E.	13,645
Moore, D.	5,120	Ubben, T.	5,176

Required

1. Prepare and complete a schedule with the following columns: Employee Name, Cumulative Earnings, Earnings Subject to FICA Taxes, Earnings Subject to Unemployment Taxes. Total the columns.
2. Compute the FICA taxes and the federal and state unemployment taxes.

**Problem 12B-6
Payroll Register
and Related
Entries
(L.O. 4, 5)**

Blue Diamond Pools has seven employees. The salaried employees are paid on the last biweekly payday of each month. Employees paid hourly receive a set rate for regular hours plus one and one-half times their hourly rate for overtime hours. They are paid every two weeks. The employees and company are subject to 7.0 percent FICA taxes on the first $36,000 earned by each employee. The unemployment insurance tax rates are 2.7 percent for the state and 0.8 percent for the federal government. The unemployment insurance tax applies to the first $7,000 earned by each employee and is levied only on the employer.

The company maintains a supplemental benefit plan that includes medical insurance, life insurance, and additional retirement funds for employees. Under the plan, each employee contributes 5 percent of his or her gross income as a payroll withholding, and the company matches this amount.

Data for the November 30 payroll, the last payday of November, follow:

Employee	Hours Regular	Overtime	Pay Rate	Cumulative Gross Pay Excluding Current Pay Period	Federal Income Tax to Be Withheld
*Adkins, E.	80	10	$ 6.00	$ 3,650.00	$ 53.60
*Bishop, D.	Salary		1,400.00	14,000.00	265.00
Castillo, M.	80	6	6.50	3,810.00	74.00
Flood, B.	80		5.00	8,250.00	32.25
Hudson, P.	Salary		1,000.00	10,000.00	147.20
Marco, T.	80	12	10.00	8,220.00	71.00
*Rizo, U.	Salary		1,500.00	15,000.00	210.00

*Denotes administrative; the rest are sales.

Required

1. Prepare a payroll register for the pay period ended November 30. The payroll register should have the following columns:

Employee
Total Hours
Earnings
   Regular
   Overtime
   Gross
   Cumulative

Deductions
   FICA Tax
   Federal Income Tax
   Supplemental Benefits Plan
Payment
Distribution
   Sales Expense
   Administrative Expense

2. Prepare a general journal entry to record the payroll and related liabilities for deductions for the period ended November 30.
3. Prepare general journal entries to record the expenses and related liabilities for the employer's payroll taxes and contribution to the supplemental benefit plan.

Financial Decision Case 12-1

Highland Television Repair
(L.O. 1, 2, 4)

Jerry Highland opened a small television repair shop on January 2, 19xx. He also sold a small line of television sets. Jerry's wife, Jane, was the sole salesperson for the television sets, and Jerry was the only person doing repairs. Jerry had worked for another television repair store for twenty years where he was the supervisor for six repairmen. The new business was such a success that he hired two assistants on March 1, 19xx. In October Jerry received a letter from the Internal Revenue Service informing him that he had failed to file any tax reports for his business since its inception and probably owed a considerable amount of taxes. Since Jerry has limited experience in maintaining business records, he has brought the letter and all his business records to you for help. The records include a checkbook, cancelled checks, deposit slips, invoices from his suppliers, notice of annual property taxes of $4,260 due to the city November 1, 19xx, and a promissory note to his father-in-law for $5,000. He wants you to determine what his business owes to the government and other parties.

You analyze all his records and determine the following:

Supplies Invoices	$ 2,650
Sales	70,650
Workers' Salaries	16,800
Repair Revenues	120,600

You learn that the shop workers are each paid $300 per week. Each is married and claims four income tax exemptions. The current FICA tax is 7 percent. The FUTA tax is 2.7 percent to the state and 0.8 percent to the federal government. Also, the state levies a sales tax of 5 percent on all retail sales of merchandise. Jerry has not filed a sales tax report to the state.

Required

1. Given these limited facts, determine Highland Television Repair's liabilities as of October 31, 19xx. (For employee income tax withholding, use Figure 12-3. Compute payroll-related liabilities on the two assistants only.)
2. What additional information would you want from Jerry to satisfy yourself that all liabilities have been identified?

Learning
Objectives

Chapter
Thirteen

Property,
Plant, and
Equipment

In this chapter, you will learn the accounting treatment of long-term nonmonetary assets. The focus will be on the major categories of plant assets and natural resources, accounting for their acquisition cost, their use over time through depreciation or depletion, and their disposal. After studying this chapter, you should be able to meet the learning objectives listed on the left.

Long-Term Nonmonetary Assets

Let us take a closer look at long-term nonmonetary assets, which were defined briefly in Chapter 11. Long-term nonmonetary assets (or simply long-term assets) are assets that (1) have a useful life of more than one year, (2) are acquired for use in the operation of the business, and (3) are not intended for resale to customers. These assets are usually classified on the balance sheet as property, plant, and equipment, or some combination of these categories. For many years, it was common to refer to long-term assets as fixed assets, but this term is no longer in wide use because the word *fixed* implies that they last forever.

Although there is no strict minimum length of time for an asset to be classified as long-term, the most common criterion is that the asset must be capable of repeated use for a period of at least a year. Included in this category is equipment that is used only in peak or emergency periods such as a generator.

Assets not used in the normal course of business should not be included in this category. Thus land held for speculative reasons or buildings that are no longer used in the ordinary business operations should not be included in the property, plant, and equipment category. Instead, they should be classified as long-term investments.

Finally, if an item is held for resale to customers, it should be classified as inventory—not plant and equipment—no matter how durable it is. For example, a printing press held for sale by a printing press manufacturer would be considered inventory, whereas the same printing press would be plant and equipment for a printing company that buys the press to use in its operations.

Life of Long-Term Nonmonetary Assets

*Objective 1
Describe the
nature, types,
and problems of
long-term
nonmonetary
assets*

The primary accounting problem in dealing with short-term nonmonetary assets was to determine how much of the asset benefited the current period and how much should be carried forward as an asset to benefit future periods. This problem was common to inventory and prepaid expenses. Note that exactly the same problem applies to long-term assets because they are long-term unexpired costs.

It is helpful to think of a long-term nonmonetary asset as a bundle of services that are to be used in the operation of the business over a period of years. A delivery truck may provide 100,000 miles of service over its life. A piece of equipment may have the potential to produce 500,000 parts. A building may provide shelter for fifty years. As each of these assets is purchased, the company is paying in advance (prepaying) for 100,000 miles, 500,000 parts, or fifty years of service. In essence, each of these assets is a type of long-term prepaid expense. The accounting problem is to spread the cost of these services over the useful life of the asset. As the services benefit the company over the years, the cost becomes an expense rather than an asset. The expense is called depreciation expense in the case of plant, buildings, and equipment; depletion expense in the case of natural resources; and amortization expense in the case of intangible assets.

Types of Long-Term Nonmonetary Assets

Long-term nonmonetary assets are customarily divided into the following categories:

Asset	Expense
Tangible Assets	
Land	None
Plant, buildings, and equipment (plant assets)	Depreciation
Natural resources	Depletion
Intangible Assets	Amortization

Tangible assets have physical substance. Land is a tangible asset, and because it has an unlimited life it is the only asset not subject to depreciation or other expense. Plant, buildings, and equipment (referred to hereafter as plant assets) are subject to depreciation. Depreciation refers to periodic allocation of the cost of a tangible long-lived asset over its useful life. The term applies to manmade assets only. Note that accounting for depreciation is an allocation process, not a valuation process. This point is discussed in more detail later.

Natural resources differ from land in that they are purchased for the substances that can be taken from them and used up rather than for the value of their location. Among natural resources are the ore from mines, the oil and gas from oil and gas fields, and lumber from the forest. Natural resources are subject to depletion rather than to depreciation. The term depletion refers to the exhaustion of a natural resource through mining, cutting, pumping, or otherwise using up the resource, and to the way in which the cost is allocated.

Intangible assets are long-term assets that do not have physical substance and in most cases have to do with legal rights or advantages held. Among them are patents, copyrights, trademarks, franchises, organization costs, leaseholds, leasehold improvements, and goodwill. The allocation of intangible assets to the periods that they benefit is called **amortization.** Even though the current assets accounts receivable and prepaid expenses do not have physical substance, they are not intangible assets because they are not long-term.

Problems of Accounting for Long-Term Nonmonetary Assets

As with inventories and prepaid expenses, there are two important accounting problems connected with long-term nonmonetary assets. The first one is figuring how much of the total cost should be allocated to expense in the current accounting period. The second one is figuring how much should remain on the balance sheet as an asset to benefit future periods. To solve these problems, four important questions (shown in Figure 13-1) must be answered:

1. How is the cost of the long-term assets determined?
2. How should the expired portion of the cost of the long-term assets be allocated against revenues over time?
3. How should later expenditures such as repairs, maintenance, and additions be treated?
4. How should disposal of long-term assets be recorded?

Figure 13-1
Problems of Accounting for Long-Term Assets

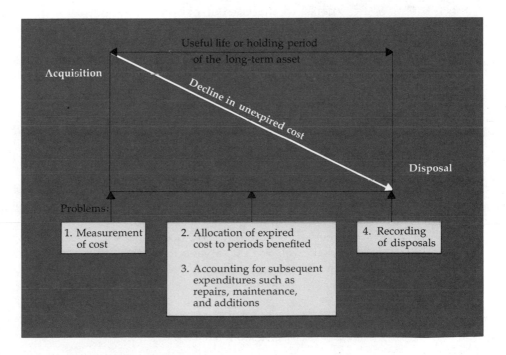

The rest of this chapter deals with the answers to questions 1, 2, and 4 for plant assets. The discussion of question 3 is postponed until Chapter 14 because expenditures for repairs, maintenance, and additions complicate the basic accounting treatment of long-term assets presented in this chapter. Specific discussion of intangibles is also in Chapter 14.

Acquisition Cost of Property, Plant, and Equipment

Objective 2
Account for the cost of long-term nonmonetary assets

The acquisition cost of property, plant, and equipment includes all expenditures reasonable and necessary to get them in place and ready for use. For example, the cost of installing and testing a machine is a legitimate cost of the machine. However, if the machine is damaged during installation, the cost of repairing the machine is not a cost of the machine.

Cost is easiest to determine when a transaction is made for cash. In this case, the cost of the asset is equal to the cash paid for the asset plus expenditures for freight, insurance while in transit, installation, and other necessary related costs. If a debt is incurred in the purchase of the asset, the interest charges are not a cost of the asset but are a cost of borrowing the money to buy the asset. They are therefore an expense for the period. An exception to this principle is that interest costs during the construction of an asset are properly included as a cost of the asset.[1]

Expenditures such as freight, insurance while in transit, and installation are included in the cost of the asset because these expenditures are necessary for the asset to function. In accordance with the matching rule, therefore, they are allocated to the useful life of the asset rather than charged as an expense in the current period.

Some of the problems of determining the cost of a long-lived asset are demonstrated in the illustrations for land, buildings, equipment, land improvements, and group purchases presented in the next few sections.

Land

In buying land, there are often expenditures in addition to the price of the land that should be debited to the Land account. Some examples are commissions to real estate agents; lawyers' fees; accrued taxes paid by the purchaser; cost of draining, clearing, and grading; and assessments for local improvements such as streets and sewage systems.

Let us assume that a company buys land for a new retail operation. It pays a net purchase price of $170,000, pays brokerage fees of $6,000 and legal fees of $2,000, pays $10,000 to have an old building on the site torn down, receives $4,000 salvage from the old building, and pays $1,000 to have the site graded. The cost of the land will be $185,000, determined as follows:

---

1. "Capitalization of Interest Costs," *Statement of Financial Accounting Standards No. 34* (Stamford, Conn.: Financial Accounting Standards Board, 1979), par. 9-11.

Net purchase price		$170,000
Brokerage fees		6,000
Legal fees		2,000
Tearing down old building	$10,000	
Less salvage	4,000	6,000
Grading		1,000
		$185,000

Sometimes land and buildings will be purchased for a lump sum. Because land is a nondepreciable asset and has an unlimited life, separate ledger accounts must be kept for land and buildings. For this reason, the lump-sum purchase price must be apportioned between the land and the building. This is usually done by appraising the value of the land and building and dividing the purchase price accordingly (see the example at the top of the next page).

Building

When an existing building is purchased, its cost includes the purchase price plus all repair and other expenditures required to put it in usable condition. When a business constructs its own building, the cost includes all reasonable and necessary expenditures, such as those for materials, labor, part of the overhead and other indirect costs, the architects' fees, insurance during construction, interest on construction loans, the lawyers' fees, and building permits. If outside contractors are used in the construction, the net contract price plus other expenditures necessary to put the building in usable condition are included.

Equipment

The cost of equipment includes all expenditures connected with purchasing the equipment and preparing it for use. These expenditures include invoice price less cash discounts; freight or transportation, including insurance; excise taxes and tariffs; buying expenses; installation costs; and test runs to ready the equipment for operation.

Land Improvements

Improvements to real estate such as driveways, parking lots, and fences have a limited life and so are subject to depreciation. They should be recorded in an account called Land Improvements rather than in the Land account.

Group Purchases

When a combination or group of long-term assets are purchased for a lump-sum payment, the total purchase price must be apportioned among the assets acquired. For example, assume that a building and the land on which it is situated are purchased for a lump-sum payment of $85,000.

The apportionment can be made by determining the price of each if purchased separately and applying the appropriate percentages to the lump-sum price. Assume that appraisals yield estimates of $10,000 for the land and $90,000 for the building if purchased separately. In that case, 10 percent, or $8,500, of the lump-sum price would be allocated to the land and 90 percent, or $76,500, would be allocated to the building, as shown below.

	Appraisal	Percentage	Apportionment
Land	$ 10,000	10	$ 8,500
Building	90,000	90	76,500
Totals	$100,000	100	$85,000

Accounting for Depreciation

Depreciation accounting is described by the AICPA as follows:

Objective 3
Define depreci-
ation, show how
to record it, and
state the factors
that affect its
computation

The cost of a productive facility is one of the costs of the services it renders during its useful economic life. Generally accepted accounting principles require that this cost be spread over the expected useful life of the facility in such a way as to allocate it as equitably as possible to the periods during which services are obtained from the use of the facility. This procedure is known as depreciation accounting, a system of accounting which aims to distribute the cost or other basic value of tangible capital assets, less salvage (if any), over the estimated useful life of the unit . . . in a systematic and rational manner. It is a process of allocation, not of valuation.[2]

This description contains several important points. First, all tangible assets except land—that is, plant and equipment assets—eventually wear out or become obsolete. Thus the cost of these assets must be distributed as expenses over the years that they benefit.

Second, the term *depreciation*, as used in accounting, does not mean the physical deterioration of an asset or the decrease in market value of an asset over time. Depreciation means the allocation of the cost of a plant asset to the periods that benefit from the services of the asset. The term is used to describe the gradual conversion of the cost of the asset into an expense.

Third, depreciation is not a process of valuation. Accounting records are kept in accordance with the cost principle and thus are not meant to be indicators of changing price levels. It is possible that, through an advantageous buy and specific market conditions, the market value of a building may rise. Nevertheless, depreciation must continue to be recorded because it is the result of an allocation, not a valuation, process. Eventually the building will wear out or become obsolete regardless of interim fluctuations in market value.

2. *Financial Accounting Standards: Original Pronouncements as of July 1, 1977* (Stamford, Conn.: Financial Accounting Standards Board, 1977), ARB No. 43, Chap. 9, Sec. C, par. 5.

Causes of Limited Useful Life

There are two major causes of the limited useful life of a depreciable asset: physical deterioration and obsolescence.

Physical Deterioration The physical deterioration of tangible assets results from use and from exposure to the elements, such as wind and sun. Periodic repairs and a sound maintenance policy may keep buildings and equipment in good running order or "as good as new" and extract the maximum useful life from them, but every machine or building at some point must be discarded. The need for depreciation is not eliminated by repairs.

Obsolescence The process of becoming out of date is called **obsolescence**. With fast-changing technology as well as fast-changing demands, machinery and even buildings often become obsolete before they wear out. Most companies consider about five years to be the useful life of a computer because they know that, although it will continue to work, it will be displaced by newer models that are technically better. In some cases, a machine may become inadequate because it cannot handle an expanded volume of activity. Some buildings used in retail businesses become obsolete because of shifts in population. Accountants do not distinguish between physical deterioration and obsolescence because they are interested in the length of the useful life of the asset regardless of what limits that useful life.

Recording Depreciation in the Accounts

When a depreciable asset is purchased, it is debited to an asset account. Depreciation is recorded by debiting Depreciation Expense and crediting Accumulated Depreciation. Accumulated Depreciation is a contra-asset account, and its balance is deducted from the asset account on the balance sheet in much the same way as the Allowance for Uncollectible Accounts is deducted from Accounts Receivable. Furthermore, it is a permanent account that lasts throughout the life of the asset.

For example, assume that a piece of office equipment was purchased on January 1 at a cost of $2,000. During the year, the depreciation was determined to be $400. The entries would be as follows:

Jan. 1	Office Equipment	2,000	
	Cash		2,000
	Purchase of office equipment		
Dec. 31	Depreciation Expense, Office Equipment	400	
	Accumulated Depreciation, Office Equipment		400
	To record depreciation for year		

The income statement would show Depreciation Expense, Office

Equipment; the balance sheet would record Accumulated Depreciation, Office Equipment, as follows:

| Office Equipment | $2,000 | |
| Less Accumulated Depreciation | 400 | $1,600 |

The unexpired part of the cost of an asset ($1,600 in the illustration) is generally called its book value or **carrying value.** The second term is used in this book when referring to long-term nonmonetary assets.

A separate Depreciation Expense account and a separate Accumulated Depreciation account are generally kept for each group of depreciable assets, such as building, store equipment, office equipment, and delivery equipment. This is done so that costs can be properly allocated among different business functions, such as manufacturing, selling, and general expenses.

Factors That Affect the Computation of Depreciation

The computation of depreciation for an accounting period is affected by (1) cost, (2) residual value, (3) depreciable cost, and (4) estimated useful life.

Cost As explained above, cost is the net purchase price plus all reasonable and necessary expenditures to get the asset in place and ready for use.

Residual Value The **residual value** of an asset is its estimated net scrap, salvage, or trade-in value as of the estimated date of disposal. Other terms often used are **salvage value** or **disposal value.**

Depreciable Cost The **depreciable cost** of an asset is its cost less its residual value. For example, a truck that costs $12,000 and has a residual value of $3,000 would have a depreciable cost of $9,000.

Estimated Useful Life The **estimated useful life** of an asset is the total number of service units expected from the asset. Service units may be measured in terms of years the asset is expected to be used, units expected to be produced, miles expected to be driven, or similar measures. In figuring the estimated useful life of an asset, the accountant should consider all relevant information including (1) past experience with similar assets, (2) the asset's present condition, (3) the company's repair and maintenance policy, (4) current technological and industry trends, and (5) local conditions such as weather.

Methods of Computing Depreciation

Many methods are used to allocate the cost of a plant asset to accounting periods through depreciation. Each of them is proper for certain circum-

Objective 4
Compute
periodic depreci-
ation under
each of four
methods

stances. The most common methods are (1) the straight-line method, (2) the production method, and (3) two accelerated methods known as the sum-of-the-years'-digits method and the declining-balance method.

The **straight-line method** is based on the assumption that depreciation depends only on the passage of time. The **production method,** on the other hand, is based on the assumption that depreciation depends only on how much an asset is used. Thus the straight-line method allocates the cost of an asset evenly over its useful life regardless of use, but the production method ignores the passage of time and bases depreciation on use.

Accelerated methods result in relatively large amounts of depreciation in the early years and smaller amounts in later years. These methods, which are based on the passage of time, assume that many kinds of plant assets are most efficient when new, so they provide more and better service in the early years of useful life. It is consistent with the matching rule to allocate more depreciation to the early years than to later years if the benefits or services received in the early years are greater.

The accelerated methods also recognize that changing technologies make some equipment lose service value rapidly. Thus it is realistic to allocate more to depreciation in current years than in future years. New inventions and products result in obsolescence of equipment bought earlier, making it necessary to replace equipment sooner than if our technology changed more slowly.

Another argument in favor of accelerated methods is that repair expense is likely to be greater in future years than in current years. Thus, the total of repair and depreciation expense remains fairly constant over a period of years. This result naturally assumes that the services received from the asset are roughly equal from year to year.

The depreciation methods used by six hundred large companies are illustrated in Figure 13-2.

Figure 13-2
Depreciation
Methods Used
by 600 Large
Companies

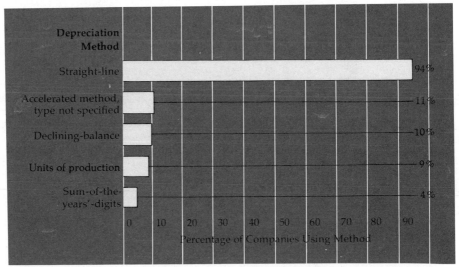

Total percentage exceeds 100 because some companies used different methods for different types of depreciable assets.
Source: American Institute of Certified Public Accountants, *Accounting Trends and Techniques* (New York, AICPA, 1982).

Property, Plant, and Equipment

Straight-Line Method

Objective 4a
Compute
periodic depreci-
ation under the
straight-line
method

When the straight-line method is used to allocate depreciation, the depreciable cost of the asset is spread evenly over the life of the asset. The depreciation expense for each period is figured by dividing the depreciable cost (cost of the depreciating asset less its residual value) by the number of accounting periods in the estimated useful life. Suppose, for example, that a delivery truck costs $10,000 and has an estimated residual value of $1,000 at the end of its estimated useful life of five years. In this case, the annual depreciation would be $1,800 under the straight-line method. This calculation is as follows:

$$\frac{\text{cost} - \text{residual value}}{\text{useful life}} = \frac{\$10,000 - \$1,000}{5} = \$1,800$$

The depreciation for the five years would be as follows:

Depreciation Schedule, Straight-Line Method

	Cost	Yearly Depreciation	Accumulated Depreciation	Carrying Value
Date of purchase	$10,000	—	—	$10,000
End of first year	10,000	$1,800	$1,800	8,200
End of second year	10,000	1,800	3,600	6,400
End of third year	10,000	1,800	5,400	4,600
End of fourth year	10,000	1,800	7,200	2,800
End of fifth year	10,000	1,800	9,000	1,000

There are three important points to note from the schedule for the straight-line depreciation method. First, the depreciation is the same each year. Second, the accumulated depreciation increases uniformly. Third, the carrying value decreases uniformly until it reaches the estimated residual value.

Production Method

Objective 4b
Compute
periodic depreci-
ation under the
production
method

The production method of depreciation on assets is based on the assumption that depreciation is solely the result of use and that the passage of time plays no role in the depreciation process. If we assume that the delivery truck from the example above has an estimated useful life of 90,000 miles, the depreciation cost per mile would be determined as follows:

$$\frac{\text{cost} - \text{residual value}}{\text{estimated units of useful life}} = \frac{\$10,000 - \$1,000}{90,000 \text{ miles}} = \$.10 \text{ per mile}$$

If we assume that the mileage use of the truck was 20,000 miles for the first year, 30,000 miles for the second, 10,000 miles for the third, 20,000 miles for the fourth, and 10,000 miles for the fifth, the depreciation schedule for the delivery truck would appear as follows:

Depreciation Schedule, Production Method

	Cost	Miles	Yearly Deprecia-tion	Accumulated Deprecia-tion	Carrying Value
Date of purchase	$10,000	—	—	—	$10,000
End of first year	10,000	20,000	$2,000	$2,000	8,000
End of second year	10,000	30,000	3,000	5,000	5,000
End of third year	10,000	10,000	1,000	6,000	4,000
End of fourth year	10,000	20,000	2,000	8,000	2,000
End of fifth year	10,000	10,000	1,000	9,000	1,000

Note the direct relation between the amount of depreciation each year and the units of output or use. Also, the accumulated depreciation increases each year in direct relation to units of output or use. Finally, the carrying value decreases each year in direct relation to units of output or use until it reaches the actual residual value.

Under the production method, the unit of output or use that is used to measure estimated useful life for each asset should be appropriate for that asset. For example, the number of items produced may be appropriate for one machine, whereas the number of hours of use may be a better indicator of depreciation for another. This method should only be used when the output of an asset over its useful life can be estimated with reasonable accuracy.

Sum-of-the-Years'-Digits Method

Objective 4c(1)
Compute periodic depreci-ation under the sum-of-the-years'-digits method

As noted earlier, the accelerated methods of computing depreciation assume that an asset depreciates more in its early years than in its later years. Therefore, these methods result in more depreciation being charged to early years and a constantly decreasing amount being charged to later years.

Under the **sum-of-the-years'-digits method,** the years in the service life of an asset are added. Their sum becomes the denominator of a series of fractions, which are applied against the depreciable cost of the asset in allocating the total depreciation over the estimated useful life. The numerators of the fractions are the individual years in the estimated useful life of the asset in their reverse order.

For the delivery truck used in the illustrations above, the estimated useful life is five years. The sum of the years' digits is as follows:[3]

$$1 + 2 + 3 + 4 + 5 = 15$$

3. The denominator used in the sum-of-the-years'-digits method can be computed quickly from the following formula:

$$S = \frac{N(N + 1)}{2}$$

where S equals the sum of the digits and N equals the number of years in the estimated useful life. For example, for an asset with an estimated useful life of ten years, the sum of the digits equals 55, calculated as follows:

$$S = \frac{10(10 + 1)}{2} = \frac{110}{2} = 55$$

The annual depreciation is then determined by multiplying each of the following fractions by the depreciable cost of $9,000 ($10,000 − $1,000): $5/15$, $4/15$, $3/15$, $2/15$, $1/15$. The depreciation schedule for the sum-of-the-years'-digits method is as follows:

Depreciation Schedule, Sum-of-the-Years'-Digits Method

	Cost	Yearly Depreciation		Accumulated Depreciation	Carrying Value
Date of purchase	$10,000	—		—	$10,000
End of first year	10,000	($5/15$ × $9,000)	$3,000	$3,000	7,000
End of second year	10,000	($4/15$ × $9,000)	2,400	5,400	4,600
End of third year	10,000	($3/15$ × $9,000)	1,800	7,200	2,800
End of fourth year	10,000	($2/15$ × $9,000)	1,200	8,400	1,600
End of fifth year	10,000	($1/15$ × $9,000)	600	9,000	1,000

From the schedule, note that the depreciation is greatest in the first year and declines each year after that. Also, the accumulated depreciation increases by a smaller amount each year. Finally, the carrying value decreases each year by the amount of depreciation until it reaches the residual value.

Declining-Balance Method

Objective 4c(2) Compute periodic depreciation under the declining-balance method

The **declining-balance method** is based on the same assumption as the sum-of-the-years'-digits method. Both methods result in higher depreciation charges during the early years of a plant asset's life. Though any fixed rate might be used under the method, the most common rate is a percentage equal to twice the straight-line percentage. When twice the straight-line rate is used, the method is usually called the **double-declining-balance method.**

In our earlier example, the delivery truck had an estimated useful life of five years. Consequently, under the straight-line method, the percentage depreciation for each year was 20 percent (100 percent ÷ 5 years). Under the double-declining-balance method, the fixed-percentage rate is therefore 40 percent (2 × 20 percent). This fixed rate of 40 percent is applied to the *remaining carrying value* at the end of each year. Estimated residual value is *not* taken into account in figuring depreciation except in the last year, when depreciation is limited to the amount necessary to bring the carrying value down to the estimated residual value. The depreciation schedule for this method is shown below.

Depreciation Schedule, Double-Declining-Balance Method

	Cost	Yearly Depreciation		Accumulated Depreciation	Carrying Value
Date of purchase	$10,000	—		—	$10,000
End of first year	10,000	(40% × $10,000)	$4,000	$4,000	6,000

End of second year	10,000	(40% × $6,000)	2,400	6,400	3,600
End of third year	10,000	(40% × $3,600)	1,440	7,840	2,160
End of fourth year	10,000	(40% × $2,160)	864	8,704	1,296
End of fifth year	10,000		296*	9,000	1,000

*Depreciation limited to amount necessary to reduce carrying value to residual value.

Note that the fixed rate is always applied to the carrying value of the previous year. Next, the depreciation is greatest in the first year and declines each year after that. Finally, the depreciation in the last year is limited to the amount necessary to reduce carrying value to residual value.

Comparing the Four Methods

A visual comparison may help give you a better understanding of the four methods used to compute depreciation that are described above. Figure 13-3 (below) compares periodic depreciation, accumulated depreciation, and carrying value under the four methods. In the graph that shows yearly depreciation, straight-line depreciation is uniform over the five-year period at $1,800. However, both accelerated depreciation methods (sum-of-the-years'-digits and declining-balance) begin at amounts greater than straight-line ($3,000 and $4,000, respectively), and decrease each year

Figure 13-3
Graphical
Comparison of
the Four
Methods of
Determining
Depreciation

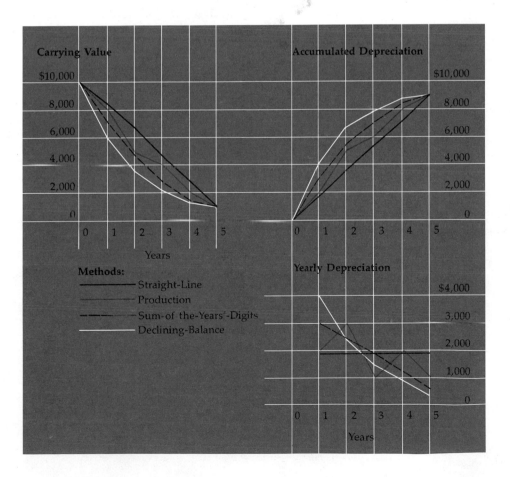

to amounts less than straight-line ($600 and $296, respectively). The production method does not produce a regular pattern of depreciation because of the random fluctuation of the depreciation base from year to year. These yearly depreciation patterns are reflected in the carrying value and accumulated depreciation graphs. For instance, the carrying value for the straight-line method is always greater than that for the accelerated methods, and the accumulated depreciation for the straight-line method is always less than that for the accelerated methods. However, in the latter two graphs, each method starts in the same place (cost of $10,000 or 0) and ends at the same place (residual value of $1,000, or cost less residual value of $9,000). It is the patterns during the life of the asset that are different.

Special Problems of Depreciating Plant Assets

Objective 5
Apply depreci-
ation methods
to problems of
partial years,
revised rates,
items of small
unit value, and
groups of
similar items

The illustrations used so far in this chapter have been simplified to explain the concepts and methods of depreciation. In real business practice, there is often a need to (1) calculate depreciation for partial years, (2) revise the depreciation rates on the basis of new estimates of the useful life or residual value, (3) develop more practical ways of depreciating items of small unit value, and (4) group items that are alike together in order to calculate depreciation. The sections below discuss these four cases.

Depreciation for Partial Years

So far, the illustrations of the depreciation methods have assumed that the plant assets were purchased and discarded at the beginning or end of the accounting period. However, business people do not often buy assets exactly at the beginning or end of the accounting period. In most cases, they buy the assets when they are needed and sell or discard them when they are no longer useful or needed. The time of the year is normally not a factor in the decision. Consequently, it is often necessary to calculate depreciation for partial years.

For example, assume that a piece of equipment is purchased for $3,500 and that it has an estimated service life of six years, with an estimated residual value of $500 after that length of time. Assume also that it is purchased on September 5 and that the yearly accounting period ends on December 31. Depreciation must be recorded for four months, or four-twelfths of the year. This factor is applied to the calculated depreciation for the entire year. The four months' depreciation under the straight-line method is calculated as follows:

$$\frac{\$3,500 - \$500}{6 \text{ years}} \times {}^{4}/_{12} = \$166.67$$

For other depreciation methods, most companies will compute the first year's depreciation and multiply by the partial year factor. For example, if the company used the double-declining-balance method on the above equipment, the depreciation would be computed as follows:

$$\$3,500 \times .33 \times \tfrac{4}{12} = \$385$$

Typically, the depreciation calculation is rounded off to the nearest whole month. In this case, depreciation was recorded from the beginning of September even though the purchase was made on September 5. If the equipment had been purchased on September 16 or thereafter, depreciation would be charged beginning October 1, as if the equipment were purchased on that date. Some companies round off all partial years to the nearest one-half year for ease of calculation.

When a plant asset is disposed of, the depreciation on this asset must be brought up to the date of disposal. For example, if the asset is not disposed of at the beginning or end of the year, depreciation must be recorded for a partial year, reflecting the time to the date of disposal. The accounting treatment of disposals is covered later in this chapter.

Revision of Depreciation Rates

Because depreciation rates are based on an estimate of the useful life of an asset, the periodic depreciation charge is seldom precisely accurate. Sometimes it is very inadequate or excessive. This situation may result from an underestimate or overestimate of the asset's useful life or perhaps from a wrong estimate of the residual value. What action should be taken when it is found, after using a piece of equipment for several years, that the equipment will not last as long as—or will last longer than—originally thought? Sometimes it is necessary to revise the estimate of the useful life, so that the periodic depreciation expense increases or decreases. In such a case, the method for correcting the depreciation program is to spread the undepreciated cost of the asset over the years of remaining useful life.

Under this method, the annual depreciation expense is increased or decreased so that the remaining depreciation of the asset will reduce its carrying value to residual value at the end of the remaining useful life. To illustrate, assume that a delivery truck was purchased for a price of $7,000, with a residual value of $1,000. At the time of the purchase, it was thought that the truck would last six years, and it was depreciated accordingly on the straight-line basis. However, after two years of intensive use, it is determined that the delivery truck will last only two more years and will continue to carry an estimated residual value of $1,000 at the end of the two years. In other words, at the end of the second year, the estimated useful life has been reduced from six years to four years. At that time, the asset account and its related accumulated depreciation account would appear as follows:

Delivery Truck		Accumulated Depreciation, Delivery Truck	
Cost 7,000		Depreciation, year 1	1,000
		Depreciation, year 2	1,000

The remaining depreciable cost is computed as follows:

$$\underbrace{\$7{,}000}_{\text{cost}} \;-\; \underbrace{\$1{,}000}_{\text{minus residual value}} \;-\; \underbrace{\$2{,}000}_{\text{minus depreciation already taken}} \;=\; \$4{,}000$$

The new annual periodic depreciation charge is computed by dividing the remaining depreciable cost of \$4,000 by the remaining useful life of two years. Therefore, the new periodic depreciation charge is \$2,000. The annual adjusting entry for depreciation for the next two years would be as follows:

| Dec. 31 | Depreciation Expense, Delivery Truck | 2,000 | |
| | Accumulated Depreciation, Delivery Truck | | 2,000 |

This method of revising a depreciation program is used widely in industry and is acceptable for figuring taxable income. It is also supported by the Accounting Principles Board of the AICPA in Accounting Principles Board *Opinion No. 9* and *Opinion No. 20.*

Accounting for Assets of Low Unit Cost

Some classes of plant assets are made up of many individual items of low unit cost. In this category are included small tools such as hammers, wrenches, and drills, as well as dies, molds, patterns, and spare parts. Because of their large numbers, hard usage, breakage, and pilferage, assets such as these are relatively short-lived and require constant replacement. It is impractical to use the ordinary depreciation methods for such assets, and it is often costly to keep records of individual items.

There are two basic methods for accounting for plant assets of low unit cost. The first method is simply to charge the items as expenses when they are purchased. This method assumes that the annual loss on these items from use, depreciation, breakage, and other causes will approximately equal the amount of these items purchased during the year.

The second method used for plant assets of low unit cost is to account for them on an inventory basis. This method is best used when the amounts of items purchased vary greatly from year to year. The inventory basis of accounting for items of small unit value is very similar to the method of accounting for supplies, which you already know. Let us assume that a company account for spare parts on hand at the beginning of the accounting period is represented by a debit balance in the asset account Spare Parts. As spare parts are purchased during the accounting period, their cost is debited to this account. At the end of the period, a physical inventory of usable spare parts on hand in the factory is taken. This inventory amount is subtracted from the end-of-period balance in the Spare Parts account to determine the cost of spare parts lost, broken, and used during this period. This cost, assumed in this case to be \$700, is then charged to an expense account as a work sheet adjustment with an adjusting entry as follows:

Dec. 31   Spare Parts Expense   700
               Spare Parts   700
                    To record cost of spare parts
                    used or lost

Group Depreciation

To say that the estimated useful life of an asset, such as a piece of equipment, is six years means that the average piece of equipment will last six years. In reality, some equipment may last only two or three years, and other equipment may last eight or nine years, or longer. For this reason and also for reasons of convenience, large companies will group items of similar plant assets together for purposes of calculating depreciation. This method is called **group depreciation**.

For example, a large milk company in a metropolitan area may have several hundred delivery trucks, all of a similar nature and with similar estimated useful lives. Rather than compute depreciation on each individual truck, the company accumulates the original cost of all the trucks in one summary account. Depreciation is then computed, not item by item, but for the group in total. The group rate is based on the average estimated life of the whole group. If the total cost of the delivery trucks was $2,700,000, the estimated residual value was $300,000, and the average estimated useful life was six years, then under the straight-line method the annual depreciation charge would be $400,000. The declining-balance method may also be used in computing group depreciation.

Group depreciation is used widely in all fields of industry and business, including the utility and telephone industries, which use group depreciation for such assets as power lines, utility poles, and transformers.

Income Taxes and Plant Assets

The most significant change for business in the Economic Recovery Tax Act of 1981 is the new **accelerated cost recovery system (ACRS)**. For years economists, business managers, and government leaders have called for increasing capital cost recovery in the tax system as a means of stimulating economic growth. Congress has now dramatically changed the rules for tax depreciation by installing ACRS, which is simpler than the old system. ACRS is a completely new and mandatory cost recovery system that for tax purposes discards the concepts of estimated useful life and salvage value and instead requires that a cost recovery allowance be computed on the unadjusted cost of the property being recovered. Recovery property is generally defined by the new law as tangible property subject to accumulated depreciation and placed in service after December 31, 1980.

In effect, this new law means that a company may write off or deduct on its tax return a certain percentage of an asset's cost. The amount that can be written off depends on the category in which the asset falls. Categories of three, five, ten, and fifteen years have been established. For example, property whose midpoint of useful life is under four years may be written off over three years at the rate of 25 percent the first year, 38 percent the second, and 37 percent the third. Automobiles, light-duty trucks, and special tools are typical assets that fall in this category. Most depreciable real estate falls in the fifteen-year category. Tables provide the amount that is to be written off for each category in each year. Since most cars and trucks last more than three years and most real estate lasts longer than fifteen years, the amount of depreciation on a company's income statement and the amount of cost recovery on the income tax return will usually differ by material amounts. Accounting for the effects of these differences is treated in Chapter 11.

Disposal of Depreciable Assets

Objective 6
Account for
disposal of
depreciable
assets

When items of plant assets are no longer useful in a business because they are worn out or obsolete, they may be discarded, sold, or traded in on the purchase of new plant and equipment. Regardless of the method of disposal, it is necessary to bring the depreciation up to the date of disposal and to remove both the cost and the accumulated depreciation of the asset from the accounts. This step is accomplished by debiting the Accumulated Depreciation account for the total depreciation to the date of disposal and crediting the asset account for the cost of the asset. A Gain or Loss on Disposal may result, depending on the facts of the situation.

If an asset lasts longer than its estimated life, as often occurs, and as a result is fully depreciated, it should not continue to be depreciated. In addition, the asset should not be written off until it is actually disposed of. The purpose of depreciation is to spread the depreciable cost of the asset over the future life of the asset. Thus the total accumulated depreciation should never exceed the total depreciable cost. If the asset is still used in the business, this fact should be supported by its cost and accumulated depreciation remaining in the ledger accounts. Proper records will thus be available for maintaining control over plant assets. If the asset is no longer used in the business, the cost and accumulated depreciation should be written off.

Assumptions for the Comprehensive Illustration

For accounting purposes, a plant asset may be disposed of in three ways: (1) discarded, (2) sold for cash, or (3) exchanged for another asset. To illustrate how each of these cases is recorded, assume the following facts. MGC Corporation purchased a machine on January 1, 19x0, for $6,500 and depreciated it on a straight-line basis over an estimated useful life of ten years. The residual value at the end of ten years was estimated to be $500. On January 1, 19x7, the balances of the relevant accounts in the plant ledger appeared as follows:

Machinery	Accumulated Depreciation, Machinery
6,500	4,200

On September 30, management disposed of the asset. The next few sections illustrate the accounting treatment to record depreciation for the fractional year and under the following assumptions:

1. Discarded the machinery.

2. Sold the machinery for cash at (a) carrying value—$1,850, (b) less than carrying value—$1,000, or (c) more than carrying value—$2,000.

3. Exchanged the machinery for similar new machinery, with (a) loss recognized on the exchange (Accounting Principles Board Rule), (b) gain not recognized on the exchange (Accounting Principles Board Rule), or (c) gain or loss not recognized on the exchange (income tax rules).

Depreciation for Fractional Period Prior to Disposal

When items of plant assets are discarded or disposed of in some other way, it is necessary to record depreciation expense up to the date of disposal. This step is required because the asset was used until that date and under the matching rule the accounting period should receive the proper allocation of depreciation expense.

The depreciation expense for the fractional period before disposal is calculated in exactly the same way as it is calculated for the fractional period after purchase.

In the comprehensive illustration given above, MGC Corporation disposes of the machinery on September 30. The entry to record the depreciation for the first nine months of 19x7 is as follows:

Sept. 30	Depreciation Expense, Machinery	450	
	Accumulated Depreciation, Machinery		450
	To record depreciation for nine months prior to disposal of machinery:		

$$\frac{\$6{,}500 - \$500}{10} \times \frac{9}{12} = \$450$$

The relevant accounts in the plant ledger accounts appear as follows after the entry is posted:

Machinery	Accumulated Depreciation, Machinery
6,500	4,650

Recording Discarded Plant Assets

Even though it is depreciated over its estimated life, a plant asset rarely lasts exactly as long as its estimated life. If it lasts longer than its estimated life, it is no longer depreciated. When it is discarded, the original cost equals accumulated depreciation plus residual value, as described in the first part of this discussion.

In the comprehensive illustration, however, the discarded equipment is not totally depreciated at the time of the disposal. When this situation occurs, a loss equal to the carrying value should be recorded upon the disposal, as follows:

Sept. 30	Accumulated Depreciation, Machinery	4,650	
	Loss on Disposal of Machinery	1,850	
	Machinery		6,500
	Disposal of machine no longer used in the business		

Recording Plant Assets Sold for Cash

The entries to record an asset sold for cash are similar to the one illustrated above except that the receipt of cash should also be recorded. The following entries show how to record the sale of machinery under the three assumptions about the selling price:

Sept. 30	Cash	1,850	
	Accumulated Depreciation, Machinery	4,650	
	Machinery		6,500
	Sale of machinery at carrying value, no gain or loss		
Sept. 30	Cash	1,000	
	Accumulated Depreciation, Machinery	4,650	
	Loss on Sale of Machinery	850	
	Machinery		6,500
	Sale of machinery at less than carrying value, loss of $850 recorded		
Sept. 30	Cash	2,000	
	Accumulated Depreciation, Machinery	4,650	
	Machinery		6,500
	Gain on Sale of Machinery		150
	Sale of machinery at more than carrying value, gain of $150 recorded		

Recording Exchanges of Similar Plant Assets

Of course, business concerns sometimes dispose of plant assets by trading them in on the purchase of similar new plant assets. In such cases, the purchase price is reduced by the amount of a trade-in allowance given for the old plant asset exchanged. If the trade-in allowance is less than the carrying value of the old plant asset, a loss occurs. Conversely, if the trade-in allowance is greater than the carrying value of the old plant asset, a gain occurs. The Accounting Principles Board has ruled that such losses and gains should be handled differently in the accounting records. *Opinion No. 29* states that in exchanges of similar assets, (a) losses should be recognized, and (b) gains should not be recognized.[4]

Loss Recognized on the Exchange To illustrate the first case, let us assume that the firm in our comprehensive example exchanges the machinery for newer, more modern machinery on the following terms:

Price of new machinery	$12,000
Trade-in allowance for old machinery	1,000
Cash payment required	$11,000

In this case, the trade-in allowance ($1,000) is less than the carrying value ($1,850) of the old machinery. Thus there is a loss on the exchange of $850 ($1,850 − $1,000). The following journal entry records this transaction under the assumption that the loss is to be recognized:

Sept. 30	Machinery (new)	12,000	
	Accumulated Depreciation, Machinery	4,650	
	Loss on Exchange of Machinery	850	
	Machinery (old)		6,500
	Cash		11,000
	Exchange of machinery—		
	cost of old machinery and its		
	accumulated depreciation		
	removed from the books		
	and new machinery		
	recorded at list price, loss		
	recognized		

Gain Not Recognized on the Exchange When an exchange of similar assets involving both a trade-in and a cash payment results in a gain, the Accounting Principles Board states that the new asset must be recorded as the sum of the cash paid plus the carrying value of the old asset. In this way, the gain is not recognized in the records. To illustrate this point, we will continue the comprehensive example by assuming the following terms of the exchange:

4. Accounting Principles Board, *Opinion No. 29,* "Accounting for Nonmonetary Transactions" (New York: American Institute of Certified Public Accountants, 1973), par. 22.

Price of new machinery	$12,000
Trade-in allowance for old machinery	3,000
Cash payment required	$ 9,000

Here, the trade-in allowance ($3,000) exceeds the carrying value ($1,850) of the old machinery by $1,150. Thus there is a gain on the exchange if we assume that the price of the new machinery is not a figure that has been inflated for the purpose of allowing an excessive trade-in value. In other words, there is a gain if the trade-in allowance represents the fair market value of the old machinery. Because the gain is not to be recognized in the accounting records, the cost basis of the new machinery must indicate the effect of the unrecorded gain. This cost basis is computed by adding the cash payment to the carrying value of the old asset:

Carrying value of old machinery	$ 1,850
Cash paid	9,000
Cost basis of new machinery	$10,850

The entry to record the transaction is as follows:

Sept. 30	Machinery (new)	10,850	
	Accumulated Depreciation, Machinery	4,650	
	Machinery (old)		6,500
	Cash		9,000
	Exchange of machinery—cost of old machinery and its accumulated depreciation removed from books; machinery recorded at amount to equal carrying value of old machinery plus cash paid, no gain recognized		

The nonrecognition of the gain on the exchange is, in effect, a postponement of the gain. For example, in the illustration above, when the new machinery is eventually discarded or sold, its cost basis will be $10,850 instead of its original price of $12,000. Therefore, any future gain will be increased by $1,150 or future loss reduced by $1,150. If the machinery is not sold, the "unrecognized" gain is reflected in less depreciation each year than if the gain had been recognized. The Accounting Principles Board justifies this position by stating that revenue (that is, the gain) should not be recognized merely because one productive asset is substituted for another but should be recognized in the form of increased net income resulting from the smaller depreciation charges each year over the productive life of the asset.

Gain or Loss Not Recognized on the Exchange (Income Tax Rules) Accounting for exchanges of similar plant assets is further complicated by the fact that the income tax rules agree with the Accounting Principles Board in the nonrecognition of gains but disagree in the treatment of losses. Whereas the Accounting Principles Board requires the recognition of losses on exchanges, the income tax rules state that losses should not be recognized. In other words, for tax purposes the cost basis of an asset acquired in exchange for a similar asset is the total of the cash payment plus the carrying value of the old asset. This rule applies regardless of whether there is a gain or loss on the exchange. Thus in the previous example where a loss was recognized, the new asset was recorded at the purchase price of $12,000 and a loss of $850 was recorded. Under the income tax method, the new asset would be recorded at $12,850 ($11,000 cash payment + $1,850 carrying value), and no loss would be recognized. So when a company exchanges similar assets at a loss, two sets of plant asset records must be kept. One would record depreciation for accounting records on a cost basis of $12,000, and the other would record depreciation for income tax records on a cost basis of $12,850.

Control of Plant Assets

*Objective 7
Record property, plant, and equipment transactions in the plant asset records*

Most businesses divide their plant assets into functional groups and have separate asset and accumulated depreciation control accounts for each group. For example, a company will usually have separate controlling accounts for Store Equipment, Office Equipment, and Delivery Truck, with an Accumulated Depreciation controlling account for each of these groups. All transactions affecting any one of the functional groups are recorded in the asset and the Accumulated Depreciation controlling accounts of that group. The purchase, depreciation, exchange, or sale of all delivery equipment will therefore be recorded in one Delivery Equipment account and its related Accumulated Depreciation account. Most businesses must have a subsidiary ledger with a detailed record for each asset, just as they do for each account receivable and account payable, but it is possible that a very small business may be able to function without it. Today's complicated income tax rules require most businesses to give evidence of depreciation and gains and losses from sales of assets by means of such detailed records. Normally a subsidiary ledger is the source of these records.

There are many ways to devise these records. One way is illustrated in Figure 13-4 (next page). In this simple example, the company has only two delivery trucks. The information on the subsidiary records is self-evident. But note that when the two subsidiary records for plant assets 1 and 2 are combined, they equal the balance in the general ledger accounts for both delivery trucks and accumulated depreciation on the delivery trucks. This method of using subsidiary ledgers for plant assets is very much like the one you have already learned in accounting for accounts receivable and accounts payable. Subsidiary ledgers for plant assets are useful to the accounting department in (1) determining the periodic depreciation expense, (2) recording disposal of individual items, (3) preparing tax returns, and (4) preparing insurance claims in the event of insured losses. Forms may be expanded to provide spaces for gathering data on

Figure 13-4
Illustration of
Plant Asset
Subsidiary
Records and
Controlling
Accounts

Controlling Accounts in General Ledger

Delivery Truck   Account No. 132

Date		Item	Post. Ref.	Debit	Credit	Balance Debit	Balance Credit
19x5 Jan.	1	Delivery Truck T4862	J1	5,400		5,400	
19x6 Jan.	1	Delivery Truck ST74289	J20	6,200		11,600	

Accumulated Depreciation   Account No. 133

Date		Item	Post. Ref.	Debit	Credit	Balance Debit	Balance Credit
19x5 Dec.	31	Delivery Truck T4862	J19		800		800
19x6 Dec.	31	Delivery Truck T4862	J40		800		1,600
	31	Delivery Truck ST74289	J40		900		2,500

Subsidiary Plant Asset and Depreciation Record   Plant Asset No. 1

Item: Delivery Truck   Serial No.: T4862
General Ledger Account: Delivery Truck   Purchased from:
                                                 GMR Corporation
Where Located: Warehouse
Person Responsible for Asset: Delivery foreman
Estimated Life: 6 years   Estimated Residual Value: $600.00
Depreciation Method: SL   Depreciation per Year: $800.00
                                            Mo.: $66.67

Date	Explanation	Post. Ref.	Asset Record Dr.	Asset Record Cr.	Asset Record Bal.	Depreciation Dr.	Depreciation Cr.	Depreciation Bal.
Jan. 1, 19x5		J1	5,400		5,400			
Dec. 31, 19x5		J19					800	800
Dec. 31, 19x6		J40					800	1,600

Figure 13-4
(*continued*)

Subsidiary Plant Asset and Depreciation Record		Plant Asset No. 2

Item: Delivery Truck   Serial No.: ST74289
General Ledger Account: Delivery Truck   Purchased from:
                                              AMG Corporation

Where Located: Warehouse
Person Responsible for Asset: Warehouse foreman
Estimated Life: 6 years   Estimated Residual Value: $800
Depreciation Method: SL   Depreciation per Year: $900
                                          Mo.: $75

Date	Explanation	Post. Ref.	Asset Record			Depreciation		
			Dr.	Cr.	Bal.	Dr.	Cr.	Bal.
Jan. 1, 19x6		J20	6,200		6,200			
Dec. 31, 19x6		J40					900	900

the operating efficiency of the assets. Such information as the frequency of breakdowns, the length of time out of service, and the cost of repairs is useful in evaluating equipment.

Plant assets, of course, represent a significant investment on the part of a company. Most companies identify each plant asset with a number when it is purchased. Periodically, an inspection and inventory of plant assets should be made and compared with the information on the subsidiary records. Such an inventory should disclose changes in use of the plant assets, unusual wear and tear, and loss from theft, damage, or negligence.

Accounting for Natural Resources

Objective 8
Identify the
accounting
issues associated
with natural
resources and
compute
depletion

Natural resources are also known as wasting assets. Examples of natural resources are standing timber, oil and gas fields, and mineral deposits. The distinguishing characteristic of these wasting assets is that they are converted into inventory by cutting, pumping, or mining. For example, an oil field is a reservoir of unpumped oil, and a coal mine is a deposit of unmined coal.

Natural resources are shown on the balance sheet as long-term assets with descriptive titles such as Timber Lands, Oil and Gas Reserves, and Mineral Deposits. When the timber is cut, the oil is pumped, or the coal is mined, it becomes an inventory of the product to be sold.

Natural resources are recorded at acquisition cost, which may also include some costs of development. As the resource is converted through the process of cutting, pumping, or mining, the asset account must be proportionally reduced. The carrying value of oil reserves on the balance

Property, Plant, and Equipment

481

sheet, for example, is reduced by a small amount for each barrel of oil pumped. As a result, the original cost of the oil reserves is gradually reduced, and depletion is recognized by the amount of the decrease.

Depletion

The term depletion is used to describe not only the exhaustion of a natural resource but also the proportional allocation of the cost of a natural resource to the units removed. The costs are allocated in a way that is much like the production method used for depreciation. When a natural resource is purchased or developed, there must be an estimate of the total units that will be available, such as barrels of oil, tons of coal, or board-feet of lumber. The depletion cost per unit is determined by dividing the cost (less residual value, if any) of the natural resource by the estimated number of units available. The amount of the depletion cost for each accounting period is then computed by multiplying the depletion cost per unit by the number of units pumped, mined, or cut. For example, for a mine having an estimated 1,500,000 tons of coal, a cost of $1,800,000, and an estimated residual value of $300,000, the depletion charge per ton of coal is $1. Also, if 115,000 tons of coal are mined and sold during the first year, the depletion charge for the year is $115,000. It is recorded as follows:

Dec. 31	Depletion Expense, Coal Mine	115,000	
	Accumulated Depletion, Coal Mine		115,000
	To record depletion of coal mine: 115,000 tons mined at $1 per ton		

On the balance sheet, the mine would be presented as follows:

Coal Mine	$1,800,000	
Less Accumulated Depletion	115,000	$1,685,000

A natural resource that is extracted in one year may not be sold until a later year. It is important to note that it is recorded as depletion *expense* in the year it is sold. The part not sold is considered inventory in the current asset section of the balance sheet. For example, if only 100,000 tons of coal in the illustration above were actually sold during the accounting period, $15,000 would be credited to Depletion Expense and $15,000 would be debited to Coal Inventory. The $100,000 remaining in Depletion Expense would be shown on the income statement and the $15,000 in Coal Inventory on the balance sheet.

Depreciation of Closely Related Plant Assets

Natural resources often require special on-site buildings and equipment, such as conveyors, roads, tracks, and drilling and pumping devices, that are necessary to extract the resource. If the useful life of these assets is longer than the estimated time it will take to deplete the resource, a special problem arises. Because these long-term assets are often abandoned and have no useful purpose beyond the time when the resources are extracted, they should be depreciated on the same basis as the depletion is computed. For example, if machinery with a useful life of ten years is installed on an oil field that is expected to be depleted in eight years, the machinery should be depreciated over the eight-year period using the production method. In other words, each year's depreciation charge should be proportional to the depletion charge. If one-sixth of the oil field's total reserves is pumped in one year, then the depreciation should be one-sixth of the machinery's cost minus the scrap value. If the useful life of a long-term asset is less than the expected life of the depleting asset, the shorter life should be used to compute depreciation. In this case or when an asset is not to be abandoned when the reserves are fully depleted, other depreciation methods such as straight-line or accelerated methods are appropriate.

Development and Exploration Costs in the Oil and Gas Industry

Accounting for the costs of exploration and development of oil and gas resources has been a source of continuing controversy. Until recently, oil and gas companies were free to account for these costs under either of two methods. Under **successful efforts accounting,** successful exploration— for example, the cost of a producing oil well—is a cost of the resource. This cost should be capitalized and depleted over the estimated life of the resource. On the other hand, an unsuccessful exploration—such as the cost of a dry well—is written off immediately as a loss. Because of these immediate write-offs, successful efforts accounting is generally considered the more conservative method and is used by most large oil companies.

Exploration-minded independent oil companies, on the other hand, argue that the cost of the dry wells is a part of the overall cost of the systematic development of the oil field and thus a part of the cost of producing wells. Under this **full-costing** method, all costs including the cost of dry wells are recorded as assets and depleted over the estimated life of the producing resources. This method tends to improve the earnings performance in the early years of companies that use it.

The controversy was apparently resolved when the Financial Accounting Standards Board endorsed successful efforts accounting and prohibited full-cost accounting.[5] However, the controversy began again when the Securities and Exchange Commission—rejecting both of these methods—proposed a radically new method, called **reserve recognition accounting.**[6] Its basic tenet is that the discovery of oil and gas is the most significant event in exploration, development, and production activities. This being the case, the current value of new proved reserves discovered every year should be recognized immediately, on both the balance sheet

5. *Statement of Financial Accounting Standards No. 19,* "Financial Accounting and Reporting by Oil and Gas Producing Companies" (Stamford, Conn.: Financial Accounting Standards Board, 1978).
6. Securities and Exchange Commission, *Accounting Series Release No. 253* (Washington: Securities and Exchange Commission, August 1978).

and the income statement. This is a simple concept, but it is a radical departure from the successful efforts and full-costing methods, which are both historical cost methods.

Under reserve recognition accounting (RRA), revenue on the income statement is redefined as the difference between the value of a company's reserves at the beginning of a year and their value at year end. Reported income would soar, compared with that calculated on the usual historical-cost basis. For example, in 1979 Gulf Oil, using the RRA basis, reported earnings from oil and gas production of $12.7 billion, compared with $2.4 billion on the traditional basis. The benefit of RRA to investors is to force a company to tell how much oil and gas it thinks it has and what prices it could get. However, critics point out that reserves are costly to estimate and that the estimates are highly unreliable. In addition to these objections, the FASB, through *Statement No. 33* and later pronouncements, is addressing the problem of providing more information about current value. For these reasons, the SEC retreated in 1981 from its requirement for RRA. Though it is deferring to the FASB on the question of oil and gas accounting for the time being, the debate is far from settled.

Chapter Review

Review of Learning Objectives

1. Describe the nature, types, and problems of long-term nonmonetary assets.

Long-term nonmonetary assets are unexpired costs that are used in the operation of the business, are not intended for resale, and have a useful life of more than one year. Long-term assets are either tangible or intangible. In the former category are land, plant assets, and natural resources. In the latter are trademarks, patents, franchises, goodwill, and other rights. The problems associated with accounting for long-term nonmonetary assets are the determination of cost, the allocation of expired cost, and the handling of repairs, maintenance, additions, and disposals.

2. Account for the cost of long-term nonmonetary assets.

The acquisition cost of a long-term asset includes all expenditures reasonable and necessary to get it in place and ready for use.

3. Define depreciation, show how to record it, and state the factors that affect its computation.

Depreciation is the periodic allocation of the cost of a plant asset over its estimated useful life. It is recorded by debiting Depreciation Expense and crediting a related contra-asset account called Accumulated Depreciation. Factors that affect its computation are its cost, residual value, depreciable cost, and estimated useful life.

4. Compute periodic depreciation under the (a) straight-line method, (b) production method, and (c) accelerated methods, including (1) sum-of-the-years'-digits method and (2) declining-balance method.

Depreciation is commonly computed by the straight-line method, the production method, or one of the accelerated methods. The two most widely used accelerated methods are the sum-of-the-years'-digits method and the declining-balance method. The straight-line method is related directly to the passage of time, whereas the production method is related directly to use. Accelerated methods, which result in relatively large amounts of depreciation in the early years and reduced amounts in later years, are based on the assumption that plant assets provide greater economic benefit in their early years than in later years.

5. Apply depreciation methods to problems of partial years, revised rates, items of small unit value, and groups of similar items.

In the application of depreciation methods, it may be necessary to calculate depreciation for partial years and to revise depreciation rates. In addition, it may be practical to apply these methods to groups of similar assets and to apply an inventory method to items of small unit value.

6. Account for disposal of depreciable assets.

In the disposal of long-term assets, it is necessary to bring the depreciation up to the date of disposal and to remove the carrying value from the accounts by removing the cost from the asset account and the depreciation to date from the accumulated depreciation account. If a long-term asset is sold at a price different from carrying value, there is a gain or loss that should be recorded and reported in the income statement. In recording exchanges of similar plant assets, a gain or loss may also arise. According to the Accounting Principles Board, losses, but not gains, should be recognized at the time of the exchange. When a gain is not recognized, the new asset is recorded at the carrying value of the old asset plus any cash paid. For income tax purposes, neither gains nor losses are recognized.

7. Record property, plant, and equipment transactions in the plant asset records.

The use of controlling accounts and subsidiary plant ledgers detailing acquisitions, subsequent transactions, depreciation, and disposals is usually necessary to provide adequate control over long-term assets.

8. Identify the accounting issues associated with natural resources and compute depletion.

Natural resources are wasting assets, which are converted to inventory by cutting, pumping, mining, or other forms of extraction. Natural resources are recorded at cost as long-term assets. They are allocated as expenses through depletion charges when the resources are depleted. The depletion charge is based on the ratio of the resource extracted to the total estimated resource. A major unresolved issue related to this subject is accounting for oil and gas reserves.

Review Problem
Depreciation Methods and Recording Disposal

Norton Construction Company purchased a cement mixer for $14,500. The mixer is expected to have a useful life of five years and a residual value of $1,000 at the end of that time. According to estimates by company engineers, the mixer has an estimated service life of 7,500 hours.

Required

1. Compute the depreciation expense for the *second* year of operation using the following methods:
  a. Straight-line
  b. Production, assuming 2,625 hours of use in the second year
  c. Sum-of-the-years'-digits
  d. Declining-balance (double straight-line rate)

2. Prepare journal entries to record the disposal of the mixer at the end of the second year, assuming that the straight-line method was used and that
  a. it was sold for $10,000 cash.
  b. it was sold for $8,000 cash.

c. it was traded in on a similar mixer having a list price of $16,500, a trade-in allowance of $8,000 was given, and the balance was paid in cash (follow the Accounting Principles Board rule).

d. same as **c** except that the income tax method was used and thus no gain or loss is recognized.

Answer to Review Problem

1. Depreciation expense for second year:

a. Straight-line method

$$(\$14,500 - \$1,000) \div 5 = \$2,700$$

b. Production method

$$(\$14,500 - \$1,000) \times \frac{2,625}{7,500} = \$4,725$$

c. Sum-of-the-years'-digits

$$(\$14,500 - \$1,000) \times \frac{4}{15} = \$3,600$$

d. Declining-balance (double straight-line rate)

First year—$14,500 × .4 = $5,800
Second year—($14,500 − $5,800) × .4 = $3,480

2. Entries for disposal of mixer (under the straight-line method, the accumulated depreciation is $5,400 at the end of the second year):

a. Cash	10,000	
Accumulated Depreciation, Mixer	5,400	
Gain on Sale of Mixer		900
Mixer		14,500
Sale of mixer at a gain		
b. Cash	8,000	
Accumulated Depreciation, Mixer	5,400	
Loss on Sale of Mixer	1,100	
Mixer		14,500
Sale of mixer at a loss		
c. Mixer	16,500	
Accumulated Depreciation, Mixer	5,400	
Loss in Exchange of Mixer	1,100	
Mixer		14,500
Cash		8,500
Exchange of mixer; loss recognized		
d. Mixer	17,600	
Accumulated Depreciation, Mixer	5,400	
Mixer		14,500
Cash		8,500
Exchange of mixer; no loss recognized under income tax method		

Chapter Assignments

Questions

1. What are the characteristics of long-term nonmonetary assets?

2. Which of the following items would be classified as plant assets on the balance sheet: (a) a truck held for sale by a truck dealer, (b) an office building that was once the company headquarters but is now to be sold, (c) a typewriter used by a secretary of the company, (d) a machine that is used in the manufacturing operations but is now fully depreciated, (e) pollution-control equipment that does not reduce the cost or improve the efficiency of the factory, (f) a parking lot for company employees?

3. Why is it useful to think of plant assets as a bundle of services?

4. Why is land different from other long-term nonmonetary assets?

5. What in general is included in the cost of a long-term nonmonetary asset?

6. Which of the following expenditures incurred in connection with the purchase of a computer system would be charged to the asset account: (a) purchase price of the equipment, (b) interest on debt incurred to purchase the equipment, (c) freight charges, (d) installation charges, (e) cost of special communications outlets at the computer site, (f) cost of repairing door that was damaged during installation, (g) cost of adjustments to the system during first month of operation?

7. Hale's Grocery obtained bids on the construction of a dock for receiving goods at the back of its store. The lowest bid was $22,000. The company, however, decided to build the dock itself and was able to do it for $20,000, which it borrowed. The activity was recorded as a debit to Buildings for $22,000 and credits to Notes Payable for $20,000 and Gain on Construction for $2,000. Do you agree with the entry?

8. What do accountants mean by the term *depreciation,* and what is its relationship to depletion and amortization?

9. A firm buys a piece of technical equipment that is expected to last twelve years. Why might the equipment have to be depreciated over a shorter period of time?

10. A company purchased a building five years ago. The market value of the building is now greater than it was when the building was purchased. Should the company stop depreciating the building?

11. Evaluate the following statement: "A parking lot should not be depreciated because adequate repairs will make it last forever."

12. Is the purpose of depreciation to determine the value of equipment? Explain.

13. Contrast the assumptions underlying the straight-line depreciation method with the assumptions underlying the production depreciation method.

14. What is the principal argument supporting accelerated depreciation methods?

15. What does the balance of the Accumulated Depreciation account represent? Does it represent funds available to purchase new plant assets?

16. If a plant asset is sold during the year, why should depreciation be computed for the partial year prior to the date of the sale?

17. What basic procedure should be followed in revising a depreciation rate?

18. Explain why and how plant assets of small unit value can be accounted for on a basis similar to handling supplies inventory.

19. On what basis can depreciation be taken on a group of assets rather than on individual items?

20. If a plant asset is discarded before the end of its useful life, how is the amount of loss measured?

21. When similar assets are exchanged, at what amount is the new asset recorded for federal income tax purposes?

22. When an exchange of similar assets occurs in which there is an unrecorded loss for federal income tax purposes, is the taxpayer ever able to deduct or receive credit for the loss?

23. What records are usually necessary for good control over plant assets?

24. Old Stake Mining Company computes the depletion rate to be $2 per ton. During 19xx, the company mined 400,000 tons of ore and sold 370,000 tons.

What amount should be deducted from revenues for depletion expense during the year?

25. Under what circumstances can a mining company depreciate its plant assets over a period of time that is less than their useful lives?

Classroom Exercises

**Exercise 13-1
Determining
Cost of
Long-Term
Assets
(L.O. 2)**

Standford Manufacturing purchased land next to its factory to be used as a parking lot. Expenditures incurred by the company were as follows: purchase price, $75,000; broker's fees, $4,000; title search and other fees, $350; demolition of a shack on the property, $1,000; grading, $750; parking lots, $10,000; lighting, $8,000; signs, $600.

Determine the amount that should be debited to the Land account.

**Exercise 13-2
Depreciation
Methods
(L.O. 4)**

Davis Oil purchased a drilling-equipment truck for $18,200. The company expected the truck to last five years or 200,000 miles, with an estimated residual value of $3,200 at the end of that time. During the second year the truck was driven 40,000 miles.

Compute the depreciation for the second year under each of the following methods: (1) straight-line, (2) production, (3) sum-of-the-years'-digits, and (4) declining-balance at a rate double the straight-line rate.

**Exercise 13-3
Declining-
Balance Method
(L.O. 4)**

Conley Company purchased a word processor for $2,240. It has an estimated useful life of four years and an estimated residual value of $240.

Compute the depreciation charge for each of the four years using the declining-balance method at a rate double the straight-line rate.

**Exercise 13-4
Straight-Line
Method—Partial
Years
(L.O. 4, 5)**

McCoy Corporation purchased three machines during the year as follows:

February 10	Machine 1	$12,000
July 26	Machine 2	2,400
October 11	Machine 3	14,400

The machines are assumed to last six years and have no estimated residual value. The company's fiscal year corresponds to the calendar year.

Using the straight-line method, compute the depreciation charge for each machine for the year.

**Exercise 13-5
Revision of
Depreciation
Rates
(L.O. 4, 5)**

Greenhill Hospital purchased a special x-ray machine for its operating room. The machine, which cost $147,360, was expected to last ten years, with an estimated residual value of $11,360. After two years of operation (and depreciation charges using the straight-line rate), it became evident that the x-ray machine would last a total of only seven years. At that time, the estimated residual value would remain the same.

Determine the new depreciation charge for the third year on the basis of the new estimated useful life.

**Exercise 13-6
Accounting for
Items of Small
Unit Value
(L.O. 5)**

Cool Air Conditioner Service Company maintains a large supply of small tools for servicing air conditioners. The company uses the inventory basis for accounting for the tools and assumes that depreciation expense is approximately equal to the cost of tools lost and discarded during the year. At the beginning of the year, the company had an inventory of small tools on hand in the amount of $6,150. During the year, small tools were purchased in the amount of $2,800. At the end of the year (December 31), a physical inventory revealed small tools in the amount of $5,575 on hand.

Prepare a general journal entry to record small tools expense for the year.

Exercise 13-7
Disposal of
Plant Assets
(L.O. 6)

A piece of equipment that cost $16,200 and on which $9,000 of accumulated depreciation had been recorded was disposed of on January 2, the first day of business of the current year.

Give general journal entries to record the disposal under each of the following assumptions: (1) It was discarded as having no value. (2) It was sold for $3,000 cash. (3) It was sold for $9,000 cash. (4) The equipment was traded in on similar equipment having a list price of $24,000. A $7,800 trade-in was allowed, and the balance was paid in cash. Follow the Accounting Principles Board rules. (5) The equipment was traded in on similar equipment having a list price of $24,000. A $3,600 trade-in was allowed, and the balance was paid in cash. Follow the Accounting Principles Board rules. (6) Same as (5) except that the income tax method was used.

Exercise 13-8
Disposal of
Plant Assets
(L.O. 6)

A commercial vacuum cleaner costing $2,450, with accumulated depreciation of $1,800, was traded in on a new model that had a list price of $3,050. A trade-in allowance of $500 was given.

1. Compute the carrying value of the old vacuum cleaner.
2. Determine the amount of cash required to purchase the new vacuum cleaner.
3. Compute the amount of loss on the exchange.
4. Determine the cost basis of the new vacuum cleaner for federal income tax purposes.
5. Compute the yearly depreciation on the new vacuum cleaner for both accounting records and income tax purposes, assuming a useful life of five years, a residual value of $800, and straight-line depreciation.

Exercise 13-9
Natural
Resource
Depletion and
Depreciation of
Related Plant
Assets
(L.O. 4, 8)

Vulcan Mining Corporation purchased land containing an estimated 12 million tons of ore for a cost of $4,400,000. The land without the ore is estimated to be worth $800,000. The company expects that all the usable ore can be mined in ten years. Buildings costing $400,000, with an estimated useful life of thirty years, were erected on the site. Equipment costing $480,000, with an estimated useful life of ten years, was installed. Because of the remote location, neither the buildings nor the equipment has an estimated residual value. During its first year of operation, the company mined and sold 1 million tons of ore.

1. Compute the depletion charge per ton.
2. Compute the depletion expense that should be charged against revenue for the year.
3. Determine the annual depreciation expense for the buildings, making it proportional to the depletion charge.
4. Determine the annual depreciation expense for the equipment, using the straight-line method and making the expense proportional to the depletion charge.

Interpreting Accounting Information

Published
Financial
Information:
International
Paper Company
(L.O. 8)

The balance sheet of International Paper Company, the world's largest manufacturer of paper and packaging, presents long-term assets as follows (in millions):

	1980	1979
Plants, Properties, and Equipment, Net	$2,563.4	$2,005.1
Timberlands, Net	792.0	806.9

International Paper's income statement contains the following costs and expenses:

	1980	1979
Depreciation	$211.9	$196.8
Cost of Timber Harvested	52.2	53.5

In the summary of significant accounting policies, accounting for timberlands by International Paper is explained as follows:

Timberlands, including capitalized timber harvesting rights, are stated at cost, less accumulated cost of timber harvested. The Company capitalizes those timber cutting contracts where the gross price to be paid is fixed. The portion of the cost of timberlands attributed to standing timber is charged against income as timber is cut, at rates determined annually, based on the relationship of unamortized timber costs to the estimated volume of recoverable timber. The costs of roads and land improvements are capitalized and amortized over their economic lives.

Elsewhere in the annual report, it is reported that with 7 million acres of timberlands, International Paper is the largest industrial owner of timberlands in North America.

Required

1. Why is it logical for International Paper to report the amount of plants, properties, and equipment separately from timberlands? Are not timberlands property?
2. In your own words, tell how International Paper computed the cost of timber harvested, and describe the journal entry to record it. Assuming that during 1980 the company sold timberland originally recorded at $16.0 million, how much timberland did the company buy or contract for in 1980?
3. International Paper uses the production method to depreciate its pulp and paper mills and the straight-line method to depreciate other assets. In what underlying way is cost of timber harvested like depreciation, and to which depreciation method is the determination of costs of timber harvested most similar?
4. Management states that "The company's timberland is carried on the balance sheet at an historic cost well below market value" and that the company replants much of its land after the timber has been harvested. What effect does this information have on your interpretation of the reported costs of timber harvested?

Problem Set A

**Problem 13A-1
Comparison of
Depreciation
Methods**
(L.O. 4)

Collins Construction Company purchased a new crane for $334,500. The crane has an estimated residual value of $30,000 and an estimated useful life of six years.

Required

1. Compute the annual depreciation for each of the six years by completing the table on the next page (round to nearest dollar where necessary).
2. Prepare a pair of graphs similar to the two on the next page, and graph each column from 1.
3. What conclusions can you draw from the graphs in 2?

End of Year	Straight-Line		Sum-of-the-Years'-Digits		Declining-Balance (double straight-line rate)	
	Depreciation	Carrying Value	Depreciation	Carrying Value	Depreciation	Carrying Value
Date of Purchase						
1						
2						
3						
4						
5						
6						

Problem 13A-2 Determining Cost of Plant Assets (L.O. 2, 4)

DODA Corporation began operation on January 1 of the current year. At the end of the year, the company's auditor discovered that all expenditures involving long-term assets were debited to an account called Fixed Assets. An analysis of the account, which has a balance at the end of the year of $2,669,802, disclosed that it contained the following items:

Cost of land	$352,400
Surveying costs	3,300
Transfer and other fees	750
Broker's fees	21,144
Attorney's fees associated with land acquisition	7,048
Cost of removing unusable timber from land	50,400

Cost of grading land	4,200
Cost of digging building foundation	34,600
Architect's fee for building and land improvements (80 percent building)	64,800
Cost of building	655,000
Cost of sidewalks	11,400
Cost of parking lots	54,400
Cost of lighting for grounds	80,300
Cost of landscaping	11,800
Cost of machinery	1,034,000
Shipping cost on machinery	55,300
Cost of installing machinery	176,200
Cost of testing machinery	22,100
Cost of changes in building due to safety regulations required because of machinery	12,540
Cost of repairing building that was damaged in the installation of machinery	8,900
Cost of medical bill for injury received by employee while installing machinery	2,400
Cost of water damage to building during heavy rains prior to opening the plant for operation	6,820
Account balance	$2,669,802

The timber that was cleared from the land was sold to a firewood dealer for $4,000. This amount was credited to Miscellaneous Income. During the construction period, two supervisors devoted their full time to the construction project. These people earn $60,000 and $48,000, respectively. They spent two months on the purchase and preparation of the land, six months on the construction of the building (approximately one-sixth of which was devoted to improvements on the grounds), and two months on installation of machinery. The plant began operation on November 1, and the supervisors returned to their regular duties. Their salaries were debited to Factory Salary Expense.

Required

1. Prepare a schedule with the following column headings: Land, Land Improvements, Buildings, Machinery, and Losses. List the items appropriate to these accounts and sort them out into their proper accounts. Negative amounts should be shown in parentheses. Total the columns.
2. Prepare an entry to adjust the accounts based on all the information given, assuming the company's accounts have not been closed at the end of the year.
3. Assume that the plant was in operation for two months during the year. Prepare an adjusting entry to record depreciation expense, assuming that the land improvements are depreciated over twenty years with no residual value, that the buildings are depreciated over thirty years with no estimated residual value, and that the machinery is depreciated over twelve years with the estimated residual value equal to 10 percent of cost. The company uses the straight-line method.

Problem 13A-3
Depreciation
Methods and
Partial Years
(L.O. 4, 5)

Vines Corporation operates four types of equipment. Because of their varied functions, company accounting policy requires the application of four different depreciation methods to the equipment. Data on this equipment are summarized below.

Chapter Thirteen

50,000 *50,000 − 5,000 = 5625*
8
100

17,5

Equip-ment	Date Purchased	Cost	Instal-lation Cost	Estimated Residual Value	Estimated Life	Depreciation Method
1	1/12/x1	$48,200	$1,800	$ 5,000	8 years	Double-declining-balance
2	1/7/x1	76,675	2,750	7,500	6 years	Sum-of-the-years'-digits
3	7/9/x1	55,800	5,200	6,000	10 years	Straight-line
4	10/2/x1	96,900	2,700	11,200	20,000 hours	Production

Required

Assuming that the fiscal year ends December 31, compute the depreciation charges for 19x1, 19x2, and 19x3 by filling in a table with the headings shown below.

		Depreciation		
Equipment No.	Computations	19x1	19x2	19x3

Assume that production for Equipment 4 was 1,600 hours in 19x1, 3,500 hours in 19x2, and 2,700 hours in 19x3. Show your computations.

**Problem 13A-4
Plant Asset
Transactions,
Revised
Depreciation,
and Spare Parts**
(L.O. 2, 5)

Tami Culp entered the jewelry refinishing business in early 19x1. She was able to purchase refinishing equipment for $57,125. It cost her $5,200 to have the equipment moved to her building and $1,890 to have it installed. It cost another $1,065 to adjust the equipment. She estimated that the equipment would have a useful life of ten years and a residual value of $5,000. Small tools were purchased at a cost of $490, and regular maintenance of the equipment came to $1,305. At the end of the year, an inventory revealed that $120 in small tools were still on hand.

During 19x2, small tools of $725 were purchased, and the physical inventory disclosed $230 on hand at the end of the year. Regular maintenance costs increased to $2,070 during the year. Soon it became apparent that the equipment would last a total of only six years instead of the originally estimated ten years and the estimated residual value at the end of six years would be only $2,500.

Required

1. Prepare general journal entries for 19x1 to record the purchase of equipment, costs associated with the purchase, the transactions involving small tools, the upkeep costs, the year-end depreciation charge, and the small tools expense. The company uses the inventory method of recording small tools expense and the straight-line method for computing depreciation expense.
2. Prepare general journal entries for 19x2 for small tools, maintenance, and depreciation expense. The depreciation expense should be based on the new estimates regarding the equipment.

**Problem 13A-5
Plant Asset
Transactions
and Record
Cards**
(L.O. 2, 4, 6, 7)

Ms. Wares Bread Company completed the following transactions involving its delivery trucks, which are under the control of the delivery supervisor:

19x1
Mar. 1 Purchased a delivery truck on credit from Early Chevrolet, serial number N746879, for $17,250. The truck has an estimated useful life of five years and an estimated residual value of $2,250. The delivery truck is assigned Plant Asset No. Y9-01.

July   2   Purchased a delivery truck on credit from Jason Dodge, serial number RG20017780, for $15,750. The truck has an estimated useful life of five years and an estimated residual value of $2,000. The delivery truck is assigned Plant Asset No. Y9-02.

Dec. 31   Recorded 19x1 depreciation on delivery equipment using the straight-line method.

19x2

Oct.   1   Purchased a delivery truck on credit from Delaney Ford, serial number P276431, for $11,125. The truck has an estimated useful life of five years and an estimated residual value of $1,875. The delivery truck is assigned Plant Asset No. Y10-01.

Dec. 31   Recorded 19x2 depreciation on delivery equipment using the straight-line method.

19x3

Jan.   3   Sold Plant Asset No. Y9-01 for $9,125.

Dec. 31   Recorded 19x3 depreciation on delivery equipment using the straight-line method.

Required

1. Prepare general journal entries to record transactions in 19x1, 19x2, and 19x3.
2. Open ledger accounts for Delivery Equipment (143) and Accumulated Depreciation, Delivery Equipment (144), and prepare three plant asset record cards. Post to the general ledger accounts and plant asset cards, recording all available information.
3. Prepare a schedule for the end of 19x3 listing the cost and accumulated depreciation to date for each item of delivery equipment, and compare with the balances of the delivery equipment and related accumulated depreciation accounts.

Problem 13A-6
Comprehensive
Problem: Initial
Recording,
Depreciation
Methods, and
Disposals
(L.O. 2, 4, 6)

Trenholm Moving Company began operations on January 2, 19x1, when Lucas Trenholm purchased a new van. During its five years of operation, the company owned a total of four vans. The transactions related to these vans are presented below.

Van	Acquisition Date	Cost	Estimated Residual Value	Estimated Life	Depreciation Method	Facts Regarding Disposal
1	1/2/x1	$9,000	$1,000	4 years	Double-declining-balance	Exchange on 1/3/x3 for Van 3; $1,750 trade-in allowed
2	5/11/x2	10,400	2,750	100,000 miles	Production	Exchange on 5/1/x4 for Van 4; $5,000 trade-in allowed
3	1/3/x3	9,950	2,350	4 years	Sum-of-the-years'-digits	Sold on 12/31/x5, for $3,000 cash
4	5/1/x4	11,088	2,350	4 years	Straight-line	Sold on 11/1/x5 for $6,000 cash

Van 2 was driven 25,000 miles in 19x2, 30,000 miles in 19x3, and 20,000 miles in 19x4. The company's fiscal year ends December 31, and the company follows the practice of recognizing losses but not gains on exchanges at the time of the exchange.

Required

Prepare in chronological order all general journal entries for the years 19x1 to 19x5 that are necessary to record the acquisition of each van (assume that each purchase is made for cash), the end-of-year adjustment for depreciation expense for each year, and the disposal of each van.

Problem 13A-7
Comprehensive
Natural
Resource
Entries
(L.O. 2, 4, 8)

Billy Bob Daniels is a gravel man from Oklahoma. On January 3, 19x2, Billy Bob purchased a piece of property with gravel deposits for $6,310,000. He estimated that the gravel deposits contained 4,700,000 cubic yards of gravel. The gravel is used for making roads. After the gravel is gone, the land, which is in the desert, will be worth only about $200,000.

The equipment required to extract the gravel cost $1,452,000. In addition, Billy Bob had to build a small frame building to house the mine office and a small dining hall for the workers. The building cost $152,000 and would have no residual value after its estimated useful life of ten years. It cannot be moved from the mine site. The equipment has an estimated useful life of six years (with no residual value).

Trucks for the project cost $308,000 (estimated life, six years; residual value, $20,000). The trucks, of course, can be used at a different site.

Billy Bob estimated that in five years all the gravel would be mined and the mine would be shut down. During 19x2, 1,175,000 cubic yards of gravel were mined. The average selling price during the year was $2.66 per cubic yard, and at the end of the year 125,000 cubic yards remained unsold. Operating expenses were $852,000 for labor and $232,000 for other expenses.

Required

1. Prepare general journal entries to record the purchase of the property and all the buildings and equipment associated with the mine.
2. Prepare adjusting entries to record depletion and depreciation for the first year of operation (19x2). Assume that the depreciation rate is equal to the percentage of the total gravel mined during the year unless the asset is movable. For movable assets, use the straight-line method.
3. Prepare an income statement for 19x2 for the Daniels Gravel Company.

Problem Set B

Problem 13B-1
Comparison of
Depreciation
Methods
(L.O. 4)

Robert Rice Company acquired new fixtures for its retail store for $148,000, with an estimated residual value of $11,200 and an estimated useful life of eight years.

Required

1. Compute the annual depreciation for each of the eight years by completing the table on the next page (round to nearest dollar where necessary).
2. Prepare a pair of graphs similar to the two on the next page, and graph each column from 1.
3. What conclusions can you draw from the graphs in 2?

Problem 13B-2
Determining
Cost of Plant
Assets
(L.O. 2, 4)

Nichols Manufacturing Company began operations on January 1, 19xx. The bookkeeper for this company was inexperienced and debited one account called Land, Buildings, and Equipment for all expenditures involving long-term assets. The account had a balance at the end of the year of $299,135, made up of the following items:

End of Year	Straight-Line		Sum-of-the-Years'-Digits		Declining-Balance (double straight-line rate)	
	Depreciation	Carrying Value	Depreciation	Carrying Value	Depreciation	Carrying Value
Date of Purchase						
1						
2						
3						
4						
5						
6						
7						
8						

Problem 13B-1
(*continued*)

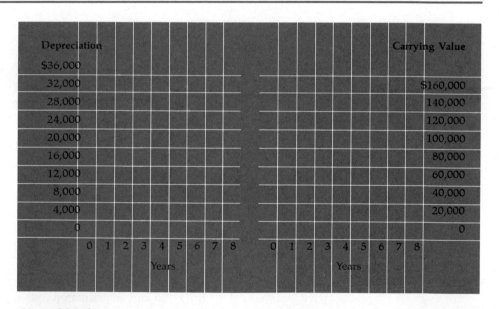

Problem 13B-2
(*continued*)

Cost of land	$33,500
Broker's fees for land purchase	2,350
Attorney's fees for land purchase	600
Other fees connected with land purchase	325
Cost of draining a small pond from land	1,625
Cost of building up land to prevent further flooding	6,320
Cost of digging basement and foundation for building	3,740
Architect's fee for designing building	13,925
Cost of new building (payment made with $20,000 cash plus U.S. Treasury notes having a face value and book value [cost] of $100,000 and a market value of $99,000 at time of purchase)	120,000
Cost of sidewalks	3,950

Cost of parking lots	7,800
Cost of parking lot lights	3,900
Cost of landscaping	1,900
Cost of machinery	89,200
Cost of delivering machinery	900
Cost of repairing parking lot after equipment delivery	250
Cost of installing machinery	6,200
Payment of lawsuit settlement to injured employee	2,500
Cost of repairing windows broken by vandals before building was in use	150
Account balance	$299,135

When the land was purchased, it contained several piles of scrap metal, which were sold for $925. This amount was credited to Miscellaneous Income. During construction, the company assigned the factory superintendent and two supervisors to the construction project. These people earn $18,000, $12,000, and $12,000, respectively, per year. They spent six months overseeing the construction of the building, three months supervising the installation of machinery, and three months in their regular factory duties. Their salaries were debited to Factory Payroll Expense.

Required

1. Prepare a schedule with the following headings: Land, Land Improvements, Buildings, Machinery, and Losses. List the items appropriate to these accounts and sort them out into their proper accounts. Negative amounts should be shown in parentheses. Total the columns.
2. Prepare an entry to adjust the accounts based on all the information given, assuming the company's accounts have not been closed at the end of the year.
3. Assume that the factory was in operation for three months during the year. Prepare an adjusting entry to record depreciation expense, assuming that the land improvements are depreciated over fifteen years with no residual value, the buildings are depreciated over twenty-five years with no estimated residual value, and the machinery is depreciated over ten years with the estimated residual value equal to 10 percent of cost. The company uses the straight-line method of depreciation.

**Problem 13B-3
Depreciation
Methods and
Partial Years**
(L.O. 4, 5)

During 19x1, Able Company purchased four machines that performed very different operations. Because of their varied functions, the company accountant felt that four different depreciation methods were appropriate. Data on these machines are summarized as follows:

Machine	Date Purchased	Cost	Installation Cost	Estimated Residual Value	Estimated Life	Depreciation Method
1	1/1/x1	$6,400	$ 600	$950	10 years	Declining-balance
2	1/1/x1	8,100	200	880	7 years	Sum-of-the-years'-digits
3	4/4/x1	3,700	450	650	5 years	Straight-line
4	8/25/x1	8,500	1,000	500	180,000 units	Production

Assuming that the fiscal year ended December 31, compute the depreciation charges for 19x1, 19x2, and 19x3 by filling in a table with the following column heads:

Equipment No.	Computations	Depreciation		
		19x1	19x2	19x3

Assume that double the straight-line rate is used for the declining-balance method and that production for machine 4 was 24,000 units in 19x1, 46,500 units in 19x2, and 37,800 units in 19x3. Show your computations.

**Problem 13B-4
Plant Asset
Transactions,
Revised
Depreciation,
and Spare Parts**
(L.O. 2, 5)

James Stein's lifelong dream was to operate a small printing shop. At the beginning of 19x1, he purchased used printing equipment for $96,400 and had it moved for $5,400 to a building he owned. It cost him $3,400 to have the equipment installed and $1,000 to have it cleaned. He paid an experienced repairman $6,000 to get the equipment running and adjusted. He felt that a reasonable useful life for the equipment was three years, with an estimated residual value of $12,000. Because his printing press was old, he purchased $4,200 of spare parts so that it could be fixed at a moment's notice. During the year, he purchased additional spare parts totaling $1,200 and spent $1,800 on regular oiling and upkeep of the equipment. At the end of the year, an inventory disclosed $3,300 of spare parts on hand.

During 19x2, it became clear that with regular maintenance the equipment would last five years rather than the three years previously estimated. At the end of five years, the estimated residual value would be $17,200. In 19x2, spare parts of $2,300 were purchased, and the physical inventory revealed $3,080 worth on hand at the end of the year. Regular maintenance costs were $3,570.

Required

1. Prepare general journal entries for 19x1 to record the purchase of equipment, costs associated with the purchase, the transactions involving spare parts, the upkeep costs, the year-end depreciation charge, and the spare parts expense. The company uses the inventory method for recording spare parts expense and the straight-line method for computing depreciation expense.
2. Prepare general journal entries for 19x2 for spare parts, maintenance, and depreciation expense. The depreciation expense should be based on the new estimates regarding the equipment.

**Problem 13B-5
Plant Asset
Transactions
and Record
Cards**
(L.O. 2, 4, 6, 7)

Asay Corporation completed the following transactions for equipment under the control of the office manager:

19x1
Jan. 2 Purchased on credit from ITD a word processor, serial number A241 for $2,360. The machine has an estimated useful life of five years and an estimated residual value of $160. The word processor is assigned Asset No. 78-01.
June 27 Purchased on credit from Yates Company a second word processor, serial number BC21, for $3,400. The machine has an estimated useful life of eight years and an estimated residual value of $200. The word processor is assigned Asset No. 78-02.
Dec. 31 Recorded the 19x1 depreciation on the word processors using the straight-line method.

19x2

Mar. 24 Purchased on credit from ITD a word processor, serial number A5203, for $3,040. The machine has an estimated useful life of five years and an estimated residual value of $240. The word processor is assigned Asset No. 79-01.

Dec. 31 Recorded the 19x2 depreciation on the word processors using the straight-line method.

19x3

Jan. 2 Sold Asset No. 78-01 for $800.

Dec. 31 Recorded the 19x3 depreciation on the word processors using the straight-line method.

Required

1. Prepare general journal entries to record the transactions in 19x1, 19x2, and 19x3.

2. Open ledger accounts for Word Processors (141) and Accumulated Depreciation, Word Processors (142), and prepare three plant asset record cards. Post to the general ledger accounts and plant asset record cards, recording all available information.

3. Prepare a schedule listing the cost and accumulated depreciation to date for each word processor, and compare with the balances of the Word Processors and related depreciation accounts.

Problem 13B-6
Comprehensive
Problem: Initial
Recording,
Depreciation
Methods, and
Disposals
(L.O. 2, 4, 6)

Connell Manufacturing Company makes metal parts using a special type of machine tool. The company began operating on January 1, 19x1. Transactions involving four of these machines are presented below.

Machine Tool	Acquisition Date	Cost	Estimated Residual Value	Estimated Life	Depreciation Method	Facts Regarding Disposal
1	1/2/x1	$9,450	$1,200	7 years	Sum-of-the-years'-digits	Exchanged on 1/3/x3 for Machine Tool 3; $4,900 trade-in allowed
2	4/4/x2	9,950	1,450	5 years	Straight-line	Sold on 10/1/x5 for $1,500 cash
3	1/3/x3	12,200	1,750	20,000 units	Production	Exchanged on 12/28/x4 for Machine Tool 4; $5,000 trade-in allowed
4	12/28/x4	12,100	2,000	5 years	Declining-balance (double S-L rate)	Sold on 12/31/x6 for $4,000 cash

The company's fiscal year ends December 31. Production on Machine Tool 3 was 6,000 units in 19x3 and 8,000 units in 19x4. The company follows the rules prescribed by the Accounting Principles Board in recording exchanges.

Required

Prepare in chronological order all general journal entries for the years 19x1 to 19x6 that are necessary to record the acquisition of each machine tool (assume that each purchase is made for cash), the end-of-year adjustment for depreciation expense for each year, and the disposal of each machine tool.

Problem 13B-7
Comprehensive
Natural
Resource
Entries
(L.O. 2, 4, 8)

Jasper Coal Company purchased property with coal deposits in January 19x1 for $21,400,000. Company geologists estimated that 3,300,000 tons of coal could be extracted from the property and that, when the mining company left, the land would have a residual value of $1,600,000, net of the costs of restoring the property to pasture land.

At the mining site, the company invested in equipment that cost $5,200,000 and would have a residual value of $1,000,000 after eight years, and in shelters and other storage buildings that cost $1,440,000 and would last twenty years with no residual value. Power lines to the site cost $1,120,000 and would last twelve years.

The geologists estimated that the coal could be removed from the site in six years. When finished with the site, the company would move the equipment to a new mine but would scrap the buildings and power lines. The cost of removing the last two items would approximately equal anything that could be salvaged.

During 19x1, 924,000 tons of coal were mined, of which 870,000 tons were sold at an average price of $12.20 per ton. Operating expenses during the year were $1,120,000 for labor and $492,000 for other expenses including hauling.

Required

1. Prepare general journal entries to record the purchase of the property and the buildings, equipment, and power lines associated with the mine.
2. Prepare adjusting entries to record depletion and depreciation for the first year (19x1) of operation. Assume that the depreciation rate is equal to the percentage of the total coal mined during the year unless the asset is to be moved. For movable assets, use the straight-line method.
3. Prepare an income statement for 19x1.

Financial Decision Case 13-1

The Primary Computer Company manufactures computers for sale or rent. On January 2, 19x1, the company completed the manufacture of a computer for a total cost of $165,000. A customer leased the computer on the same day for a five-year period at a monthly rental of $4,000. Although the computer will last longer than five years, it is likely that it will be technologically obsolete by the end of the five-year period because of the rapid change in the manufacture of computers. However, it is possible that it will not be obsolete. Primary's management estimates that if the computer is obsolete, it can be sold for $15,000 at the end of the lease, and if it is not obsolete, it can be sold for $30,000 because it would probably last for another two years.

On the basis of its experience in leasing many computers, management estimates that the expenses associated with the lease of this computer will be as follows:

	Insurance and Property Taxes	Repairs and Maintenance
19x1	$6,000	$2,500
19x2	5,400	4,000
19x3	4,800	5,500
19x4	4,200	7,000
19x5	3,600	8,500

Required

1. What estimated useful life and estimated residual value do you recommend that Primary use for the computer? Explain.

2. Prepare two schedules that show for each year the lease revenue, expenses, and income before income taxes. Also, show on each schedule for each year the carrying value of the computer at the end of the year, and compute the ratio of income before income taxes to carrying value (return on assets). The first schedule should compute depreciation by using the straight-line method and the second method should use the sum-of-the-years'-digits method.

3. Compare the two schedules in **2**, and discuss the results. Which of the methods do you feel produces the most realistic pattern of income before taxes, and why?

4. If you were asked to determine the amount of cash generated each year from this lease (cash received minus cash disbursed), what effect, if any, would the method of depreciation have on your computations?

Learning Objectives

Chapter Fourteen

Revenue and Expense Issues and Inflation Accounting

1. *Apply the matching rule to revenue recognition.*

2. *Apply the matching rule to the allocation of expired costs as it relates to capital expenditures and revenue expenditures.*

3. *Apply the matching rule to the accounting problems associated with intangible assets, including research and development costs and goodwill.*

4. *Demonstrate the effects of arbitrary allocation procedures on reported net income.*

5. *Identify the two principal types of price changes.*

6. *Using constant dollar accounting, compute purchasing power gains and losses, and restate a balance sheet for changes in the general price level.*

7. *Describe the FASB's approach to accounting for changing prices.*

This chapter addresses two topics that affect the interpretation of financial statements. The first is a further examination of the matching rule, including its application to intangible assets. The second is inflation and how it affects the concepts of historical cost and the stable monetary unit. As a result of studying this chapter, you should be able to meet the learning objectives listed on the left.

As emphasized throughout this book, an important goal of accounting is to determine periodic net income in accordance with the matching rule. Applying the matching rule involves (1) recognizing the revenue earned in a period and (2) allocating the expired costs to the period. The result of these measurements is a matching of revenues and expenses, and the difference between them is the net income or net loss for the period.

Applying the Matching Rule to Revenue Recognition

Revenue is measured by the amount charged for goods sold and services rendered to customers. An important accounting problem associated with revenue is getting an accurate cutoff at the end of the accounting period—in other words, deciding what revenue should be counted in one accounting period and what revenue should be counted in the next. To determine the point at which revenue should be recognized, two approaches are commonly used: the point of sale basis and the cash basis.

Point of Sale Basis

From the ordering of merchandise to delivery and collection of cash, a single sale may spread over several weeks or months. So far in this book, we have recognized revenue at the point when the title passes to the buyer, which is usually the date of delivery. This is the most commonly used point of recognition in business and is called the **point of sale basis.**

When the sale involves the performance of services, no title transfer exists to mark the recognition point. Theoretically, revenue is earned as the services are being performed. Until the service is performed and the customer accepts the service as satisfactory, however, no claim to the revenue exists. Therefore, even though the price and terms of the service may be agreed upon in advance, revenue is not usually recognized until the work is completed.

*Objective 1
Apply the
matching rule
to revenue
recognition*

Cash Basis

In some circumstances, revenue recognition is postponed until cash is received. On the cash basis, revenue is considered to be earned when the cash is collected, regardless of when the sale is made. This method is theoretically justifiable only when there is considerable doubt as to the ultimate collection on a sale. As a practical matter, many people who provide services, such as doctors, lawyers, and accountants, use the cash basis because it is simple and eliminates the need to estimate uncollectible accounts. The federal income tax regulations allow individuals who perform services to use the cash basis for reporting their federal income tax liability. This regulation undoubtedly contributes to use of the cash basis by individuals.

Applying the Matching Rule to Allocation of Expired Costs

*Objective 2
Apply the
matching rule to
the allocation
of expired costs
as it relates to
capital expendi-
tures and
revenue expendi-
tures*

The second major measurement related to the application of the matching rule is the allocation of expired costs to the accounting period. In earlier chapters, allocations have been made according to simple rules and procedures to demonstrate the basic procedures of accounting. However, these straightforward practices are not as cut and dried as they appear on the surface, as was also true in the case of revenue recognition. Here we discuss the difficulty of distinguishing between expenditures for assets and expenditures for expenses as well as the arbitrariness of many accounting allocations.

Capital Expenditures and Revenue Expenditures

The term expenditure refers to a payment or incurrence of an obligation to make a future payment for an asset, such as a truck, or a service rendered, such as a repair. When the payment or debt is for an asset or a service, it is correctly called an expenditure. A capital expenditure is an expenditure for the purchase or expansion of plant assets and is recorded in the asset accounts. An expenditure for repairs, maintenance, fuel, or other things needed to maintain and operate plant and equipment is called a revenue expenditure because it is an immediate charge as an expense against revenue. These are recorded by debits to expense accounts. Revenue expenditures are charged to expense because the benefits from the expenditures will be used up in the current period. For this reason, they will be deducted from the revenues of the current period in determining the net income. In summary, any expenditure that will benefit several accounting periods is considered a capital expenditure. Any expenditure that will benefit only the current accounting period is called a revenue expenditure.

It is important to note this careful distinction between capital and revenue expenditures. In accordance with the matching rule, expenditures of any type should be charged to the period that they benefit. For example, if a purchase of an automobile had been mistakenly charged as a revenue expenditure, the expense for the current period would be overstated on the income statement. As a result, current net income would be understated, and in future periods net income would be overstated. If, on the other hand, a revenue expenditure such as the painting of a building were charged to an asset account, the expense of the current period would be understated. Current net income would be overstated by the same amount, and net income of future periods would be understated.

Because it is important to distinguish between capital and revenue expenditures, many companies follow policies that state what constitutes a revenue or a capital expenditure. For example, they may set a minimum dollar amount such as $50 or $100 for a capital expenditure. They may feel that small expenditures are not worth the time and expense of accounting for them. Even though a wastepaper basket, for instance, will last longer than one year, the costs of accounting for it as a depreciable asset may be greater than its total original cost.

Among the more usual kinds of capital expenditures are the following:

1. **Acquisition of plant and equipment including freight, sales tax, and installation charges**   When secondhand property is purchased, the cost of any repairs made to put the property in good operating condition before placing it in use is also considered a capital expenditure and is charged to the asset account.

2. **Additions**   Additions are enlargements to the physical layout of a plant asset. If a new wing is added to a building, the benefits from the expenditure will be received over several years, and the amount paid for it should be debited to the asset account.

3. **Betterments**   Betterments are improvements to plant assets that do not add to the physical layout of the asset. Installation of an air-conditioning system is an example of an expenditure for a betterment or improvement that will offer benefits over a period of years and so should be charged to the asset account.

4. **Acquisition of intangible assets**   See the discussion on pages 505–506.

Among the more usual kinds of revenue expenditures relating to plant equipment are the repairs, maintenance, lubrication, cleaning, and inspection necessary to keep an asset in good working condition.

Repairs fall into two categories: ordinary repairs and extraordinary repairs. **Ordinary repairs** are expenditures that are necessary to maintain an asset in good operating condition. Trucks must have tune-ups, tires and batteries must be replaced regularly, and other ordinary repairs must be made. Offices and halls must be painted regularly and have broken tiles or woodwork replaced. Ordinary repairs consist of any expenditures needed to maintain a plant asset in its normal state of operation. Such repairs are a current expense.

Extraordinary repairs are repairs of a more significant nature—they affect the estimated residual value or estimated useful life of an asset. For example, a boiler for heating a building may receive a complete overhaul, at a cost of several thousand dollars, which will extend the useful life of the boiler five years.

Typically, extraordinary repairs are recorded by debiting the Accumulated Depreciation account, under the assumption that some of the depreciation previously recorded has now been eliminated. The effect of this reduction in the Accumulated Depreciation account is to increase the book or carrying value of the asset by the cost of the extraordinary repair. Consequently, the new carrying value of the asset should be depreciated over the new estimated useful life. Let us assume that a machine costing $10,000 had no estimated residual value and an original estimated useful life of ten years. After eight years, the accumulated depreciation (straight-line method assumed) would be $8,000, and the carrying value would be $2,000 ($10,000 − $8,000). Assume that, at this point, the machine was given a major overhaul costing $1,500. This expenditure extends the useful life three years beyond the original ten years. The entry for extraordinary repair would be as follows:

Mar. 14	Accumulated Depreciation, Machinery	1,500	
	Cash		1,500
	To record extraordinary repair		
	to machinery		

The annual periodic depreciation for each of the five years remaining in the machine's useful life would be calculated as follows:

Carrying value before extraordinary repairs	$2,000
Extraordinary repairs	1,500
Total	$3,500

$$\text{Annual periodic depreciation} = \frac{\$3,500}{5 \text{ years}} = \$700$$

If the machine remains in use for the five years expected after the major overhaul, the annual periodic depreciation charges of $700 will exactly write off the new carrying value, including the cost of extraordinary repairs.

Intangible Assets

The purchase of an intangible asset is a special kind of capital expenditure. An intangible asset is long-term, but it has no physical substance.

Objective 3
Apply the
matching rule
to the
accounting
problems
associated with
intangible assets,
including
research and
development
costs and
goodwill

Its value comes from the long-term rights or advantages that it offers to the owner. Among the most common examples are patents, copyrights, leaseholds, leasehold improvements, trademarks and brand names, franchises, licenses, formulas, processes, and goodwill. Some current assets such as accounts receivable and certain prepaid expenses have no physical nature, but they are not called intangible assets because they are short-term. Intangible assets are both long-term and nonphysical.

Intangible assets are accounted for at acquisition cost, that is, the amount paid for them. Some intangible assets such as goodwill or trademarks may have been acquired at little or no cost. Even though they may have great value and are needed for profitable operations, they should not appear on the balance sheet unless they have been bought.

The accounting problems connected with intangible assets are the same as those connected with other long-lived assets. The Accounting Principles Board, in its *Opinion No. 17*, lists them as follows:

1. Determining an initial carrying amount
2. Accounting for that amount after acquisition under normal business conditions—that is, through periodic write-off or amortization—in a manner similar to depreciation
3. Accounting for that amount if the value declines substantially and permanently[1]

Besides these three problems, an intangible asset has no physical qualities and so in some cases may be impossible to identify. For these reasons, its value and its useful life may be quite hard to estimate.

The Accounting Principles Board has decided that a company should record as assets the costs of intangible assets acquired from others. However, the company should record as expenses the costs of developing intangible assets. Also, intangible assets that have a determinable life, such as patents, copyrights, and leaseholds, should be written off through periodic amortization over that useful life in much the same way as plant assets are depreciated. Even though some intangible assets, such as goodwill and trademarks, have no measurable limit on their lives, they should also be amortized over a reasonable length of time (but not more than forty years) because few things last forever. Accounting for the different kinds of intangible assets is outlined in Table 14-1.

Research and Development Costs Most successful companies carry out activities, possibly within a separate department, involving research and development. Among these activities are development of new products, testing of existing and proposed products, and pure research. In the past, some companies would record as an asset those costs of research and development that could be directly traced to the development of certain patents, formulas, or other rights. Other costs, such as those for testing and pure research, were treated as expenses of the accounting period and deducted from income.

The Financial Accounting Standards Board has stated that all research

---

1. Adapted from Accounting Principles Board, *Opinion No. 17*, "Intangible Assets" (New York: American Institute of Certified Public Accountants, 1970), par. 2.

Chapter Fourteen

	Type	Description	Special Accounting Problems
Table 14-1 Accounting for Intangible Assets	Patent	An exclusive right granted by the federal government for a period of 17 years to make a particular product or use a specific process.	The cost of successfully defending a patent in a patent infringement suit is added to the acquisition cost of the patent. Amortize over the useful life, which may be less than the legal life of 17 years.
	Copyright	An exclusive right granted by the federal government to the possessor to publish and sell literary, musical, and other artistic materials for a period of the author's life plus 50 years. Includes computer programs.	Record at acquisition cost, and amortize over the useful life, which is often much shorter than the legal life. For example, the cost of paperback rights to a popular novel would typically be amortized over a useful life of two to four years.
	Leasehold	A payment to secure the right to a lease. For example, Company A, which has a 10-year lease to a prime location but does not want to operate in that location, sells the right to Company B. Company B has purchased a leasehold.	Debit Leasehold for the amount of the payment, and amortize it over the remaining life of the lease. Payments to the lessor during the life of the lease should be debited to Lease Expense.
	Leasehold improvements	Improvements to leased property that become the property of the lessor (the person who owns the property) at the end of the lease.	Debit Leasehold Improvements for the cost of improvements, and amortize the cost of the improvements over the remaining life of the lease.
	Trademark, brand name	A registered symbol or name giving the holder the right to use it to identify a product or service.	Debit the trademark or brand name for the acquisition cost, and amortize it over a reasonable life, not over 40 years.
	Franchise, License, Formula, Process	A right to an exclusive territory or to exclusive use of a formula, technique, or design.	Debit the franchise, license, formula, or process for the acquisition cost, and amortize it over a reasonable life, not to exceed 40 years.
	Goodwill	The excess of the cost of a group of assets (usually a business) over the market value of the assets individually.	Debit Goodwill for the acquisition cost, and amortize it over a reasonable life, not to exceed 40 years.

and development costs should be treated as revenue expenditures and charged to expense in the period when incurred.[2] The board argues that it is too hard to trace specific costs to specific profitable developments. Also, the costs of doing research and development are continuous, and necessary for the success of a business and so should be treated as current expenses. To support this conclusion, the board cites studies showing that 30 to 90 percent of all new products fail and that three-fourths of new product expenses go to unsuccessful products.

Goodwill The term goodwill is widely used by business people, lawyers, and the public to mean different things. In most cases one thinks of goodwill as meaning the good reputation of a company. In fact, goodwill applies to all the good qualities that might cause a company to earn more in future years than is normal in its own industry. Among these factors are not only customer satisfaction but also superior management, manufacturing efficiency, advantages of holding a monopoly, good location, and good employee relations.

The following example shows what is meant by above-average earnings.

	Company A	Average of Similar Companies in Same Industry
Net assets other than goodwill	$10,000,000	$10,000,000
Normal rate of return	10%	10%
Normal net income	$ 1,000,000	$ 1,000,000
Actual net income (five-year average)	1,200,000	1,000,000
Earnings above average	$ 200,000	—

There is evidence of goodwill when a purchaser pays more for a business than the fair market value of the assets if purchased separately. Because the purchaser has paid more than the fair market value of the physical assets, there must be intangible assets. If the company being purchased does not have patents, copyrights, trademarks, or other intangible assets of value, one must conclude that the excess payment is for goodwill. The payment above and beyond the fair market value of the tangible assets and other specific intangible assets is properly recorded in the Goodwill account.

In *Opinion No. 17*, the Accounting Principles Board states that the benefits arising from purchased goodwill will in time disappear. It is hard for a company to keep having above-average earnings unless new factors of goodwill replace the old ones. For this reason, goodwill should be amortized or written off by systematic charges to income over a reasona-

2. *Statement of Financial Accounting Standards No. 2,* "Accounting for Research and Development Costs" (Stamford, Conn.: Financial Accounting Standards Board, 1974), par. 12.

ble number of future time periods. The time period should in no case be more than forty years.[3]

Goodwill, as stated above, should not be recorded unless it is purchased. There are several methods available to the accountant for placing a cost value on goodwill when a business is purchased. Three common methods are as follows:

1. The value of goodwill may be arbitrarily set by the buyer and seller. For example, in the sale of a successful business for $260,000, if the buyer and seller agree that net assets other than goodwill are valued at $220,000, goodwill should be recorded at $40,000.

2. Goodwill may be arbitrarily valued at some multiple of the expected earnings in excess of the average. For example, if for the next four years a company expected to earn $10,000 more a year than a similar company in the same industry, goodwill would be valued at $40,000 ($10,000 × 4 years).

3. Goodwill may be measured by capitalizing expected earnings in excess of the average at a rate that is normal in the industry. Expected earnings are capitalized by dividing them by the average rate of return. For example, if (a) a company is expected to earn $6,000 a year more than the average similar company in the industry and (b) the average rate of return in the industry is 12 percent, the goodwill is valued at $50,000 ($6,000 ÷ .12). This is the most theoretically correct way of computing goodwill because it, in effect, answers the question, How many dollars would the company need to invest in assets to earn the $6,000 (12 percent × $50,000) of above-normal earnings that come from goodwill? Note that the higher the average rate of return, the lower the amount of goodwill will be.

Arbitrary Allocation Procedures

Objective 4
Demonstrate the
effects of
arbitrary
allocation
procedures on
reported net
income

At various points in earlier chapters, various acceptable alternative methods were used in the application of the matching rule. These methods are based on allocation procedures, which in turn are based on certain assumptions. Here are some of these procedures:

1. For estimating uncollectible accounts expense: percentage-of-net-sales method and accounts receivable aging method
2. For pricing the ending inventory: average cost method, first-in, first-out (FIFO), and last-in, first-out (LIFO)
3. For estimating depreciation expense: straight-line method, production method, sum-of-the-years'-digits method, and declining-balance method
4. For estimating depletion expense: production (extraction) method
5. For estimating amortization of intangibles: straight-line method

All of these procedures attempt to allocate the costs of assets to the periods in which those costs contribute to the production of revenue. They are based on a determination of the benefits to the current period

3. Accounting Principles Board, *Opinion No. 17*, par. 29.

(expenses) versus the benefits to future periods (assets). They are estimates and cannot be proved conclusively. They are also rather arbitrary because in practice it is hard to justify one method of estimation over another. For this reason, it is important for the accountant as well as the financial statement user to understand the possible effects of different accounting procedures on net income and financial position. For example, suppose that two companies have similar operations but that one uses FIFO for inventory pricing and the straight-line method for figuring depreciation and the other uses LIFO for inventory pricing and the sum-of-the-years'-digits (SYD) method for figuring depreciation. The income statements of the two companies might appear as follows:

	FIFO and Straight-Line Company	LIFO and SYD Company
Sales	$500,000	$500,000
Goods Available for Sale	$300,000	$300,000
Less Ending Inventory	60,000	50,000
Cost of Goods Sold	$240,000	$250,000
Gross Margin	$260,000	$250,000
Less:		
Depreciation Expense	$ 40,000	$ 70,000
Other Expenses	170,000	170,000
Total Operating Expenses	$210,000	$240,000
Net Income	$ 50,000	$ 10,000

In practice, of course, differences in net income stem from many factors. However, the above case is representative of the important differences that can be caused by using different procedures for allocating costs to accounting periods.

The existence of these alternatives could cause problems in the interpretation of financial statements were it not for the conventions of full disclosure and consistency, described earlier in the book (Chapter 9). Full disclosure requires that management explain the significant accounting policies used in preparing the financial statements in a note to the statements. Consistency requires that the same accounting procedure be followed from year to year. If a change in procedure is made, the nature of the change and its monetary effect must be explained in a note.

The Nature of Inflation

In the application of the matching rule, accountants attempt to provide a basis for evaluating a company over a period of time. However, the steady and sometimes very high inflation that has been occurring in this country and others for more than a generation is distorting financial statements prepared under traditional accounting methods. One of the most difficult challenges to the accounting profession is to find better ways of dealing with this chronic problem. It is an especially difficult problem because, to deal effectively with inflation, accountants must re-examine several basic ideas of accounting theory. The most important of these ideas are the concept of historical cost and the assumption of a stable measuring unit. To understand how these principles are affected, it is first necessary to examine the nature of inflation.

Objective 5
Identify the two
principal types
of price changes

In a dynamic society, the price of an electronic calculator may drop 50 percent while at the same time the price of an automobile increases by 20 percent. Each of these price changes relates to inflation, but to the layperson the relationship may be confusing. Part of the confusion arises from the fact that two types of price changes are involved. First, there are changes in **specific price levels**—the price changes of specific items or services, such as the calculator or automobile mentioned above. Second, there are changes in **general price levels**—the price changes of a group, or basket, of goods and services. Changes in specific price levels, which may vary widely, contribute to the overall price change as reflected in the general price level. **Inflation,** in the technical sense, refers to upward change in the general price level.

When the general price level increases, it takes more dollars to buy the same basket of goods than it did before. As a result, the dollar's **purchasing power**—its ability at a point in time to purchase goods or services—has gone down. In the opposite case of **deflation,** when a decrease occurs in the general price level, the purchasing power of the dollar increases because it takes fewer dollars to purchase the same goods and services than it did before. In other words, as the general price level changes, the amount of real goods and services that a single dollar can purchase also changes. Therefore, in terms of real goods and services, the dollar is an unstable measuring unit. One might compare this situation to the difficulty of expressing the distance between two cities if the number of feet in a mile were continually changing. In periods when there is little change in the general price level, the unstable dollar does not have much effect on financial statements. In periods of great change, however, the dollars in the financial statements soon become unrealistic measures of the items they are supposed to represent.

Price Indexes

To show how specific price changes contribute to general price changes, it is helpful to know how a price index is constructed. A **price index** is a series of numbers, one for each period, representing an average price of a group of goods and services, relative to the average price of the same group of goods and services at a beginning date. Consider the figures in Table 14-2. In this example, a price index for a typical basket of groceries is computed. During the year, the specific price changes of individual items ranged from a decrease of 33.6 percent in the price of sugar to an increase of 102.6 percent in the price of lettuce. Overall, the price index of the basket increased from 100 at the beginning point to 107 at the end of the first year, or 7 percent. One must be careful in interpreting the change in an index number from one year to the next, however. For example,

Table 14-2
Construction
of a Price
Index

Item	January 1	December 31	Percentage Change in Market Price of Individual Items
Hamburger (pound)	$1.19	$1.39	+16.8
Bread (pound loaf)	.49	.59	+20.4
Milk (gallon)	1.83	1.75	−4.4
Lettuce (head)	.39	.79	+102.6
Sugar (5 pounds)	1.19	.79	−33.6
Soap (bar)	.45	.57	+26.7
Tissue (box)	.46	.54	+17.4
	$6.00	$6.42	
Price index (January = 100)	100	107 ($6.42 ÷ $6.00)	

assume that the price index in Table 14-2 increased to 114 by the end of the next year. It would be incorrect to say that prices increased by 7 percent, because on the basis of last year's starting point of 107 the actual percentage change is less. The percentage change from the first year to the second year is 6.54 percent, calculated as follows:

$$\frac{\text{change in index}}{\text{previous year's index}} = \frac{114 - 107}{107} = \frac{7}{107} = 6.54 \text{ percent}$$

General Price Indexes

Agencies of the U.S. government publish several general price indexes. The most widely known general price index is the Consumer Price Index for All Urban Consumers (CPI-U), published by the Bureau of Labor Statistics of the Department of Labor in *Monthly Labor Review*. The Financial Accounting Standards Board uses this index when adjusting financial statements for changes in the general price level because it is readily available, is issued on a monthly basis, and is not revised after its initial publication. Also, it tends to produce a result comparable to other general price indexes.[4]

A partial listing from the CPI-U is reproduced in Table 14-3, with 1967 as a base year. Note that the purchasing power of the dollar as measured by this index was about one-third in 1980 what it was in 1960—that is, the index more than doubled (88.7 to 246.8). This statistic means that it took almost three times as many dollars to buy the same good or service in 1980 as it did in 1960. For example, assume that it cost $100,000 to buy a building in 1960. A payment of $278,241 would be required in 1980 to

4. *Statement of Financial Accounting Standards No. 33,* "Financial Reporting and Changing Prices" (Stamford, Conn.: Financial Accounting Standards Board, 1979), par. 39.

Table 14-3 Consumer Price Index for Urban Consumers	Year	Index (1967 = 100)	Year	Index (1967 = 100)
	1960	88.7	1978	195.4
	1967	100	1979	217.4
	1970	116.3	1980	246.8
	1975	161.2	1981	272.5
	1976	170.5	1982	289.6
	1977	181.5		

equal the payment of $100,000 in 1960. This computation is made as follows:

$$\frac{\text{index of year to which dollars are being converted}}{\text{index of year from which dollars are being converted}} \times \text{dollar amount} = \text{restated amount}$$

$$\frac{1980 \text{ index}}{1960 \text{ index}} \times \text{cost of building} = \text{restated cost of building}$$

$$\frac{246.8}{88.7} \times \$100,000 = \$278,241 \text{ (rounded to nearest dollar)}$$

Reporting the Effects of Price Changes

There are two principal methods of accounting for the effects of changing prices on financial statements. One is to restate historical cost financial statements for changes in the general price level (constant dollar accounting). The other is to develop financial statements based on changes in specific price levels (current value accounting). These approaches are described below, along with the pros and cons of each.

Constant Dollar Accounting

Objective 6
Using constant dollar accounting, compute purchasing power gains and losses, and restate a balance sheet for changes in the general price level

Constant dollar accounting involves the restatement of historical cost statements for general price level changes. Its objective is to state all amounts in dollars of uniform general purchasing power. As a result, the financial statements are based on a uniform, or constant, monetary measuring unit as of the balance sheet date. The general approach is to convert the number of dollars received or spent at various price levels (corresponding to various balance sheet dates) to an equivalent number of dollars at the price level on the latest balance sheet date.

For instance, according to Table 14-3, a building costing $100,000 in 1960 would be restated as follows at various dates:

Date	1960 Cost	Index	Conversion Factor	Restate Cost
1960	$100,000	88.7		$100,000
1970	$100,000	116.3	$\frac{116.3}{88.7}$	$131,116
1980	$100,000	246.8	$\frac{246.8}{88.7}$	$278,241

When more than one asset is involved, the denominator of the conversion factor for each asset is the index of the year in which the asset was purchased. For example, assume that the business mentioned in the example above had another building that cost $200,000 in 1975, in addition to the one that cost $100,000 in 1960. The costs of these two buildings can be restated in terms of common 1982 dollars as follows:

Item	Historical Cost	Conversions (from Table 14-3)	Restatement in Terms of 1982 Dollars
1960 building	$100,000	$\frac{289.6}{88.7}$	$326,494
1975 building	200,000	$\frac{289.6}{161.2}$	359,305
Totals	$300,000		$685,799

Note two important things about this restatement. First, restatement for general price changes is *not* a departure from historical cost, but it is a departure from the accountant's assumption of a stable measuring unit. In this case, the $685,799 is based on an adjustment of historical cost figures of $300,000 to a common or constant 1982 measuring unit. Second, the $685,799 is *not* meant to be a contemporary or market value of the buildings. During the years in question (1960–1982), the specific price level changes and market prices for buildings of the kind used by this company may have differed radically from the general price levels. In summary, general price level restatement, or constant dollar accounting, focuses on changes in the purchasing power of the monetary unit, not on changes in the value of the asset.

It is also important to distinguish monetary from nonmonetary items because changes in the general price level affect them differently. Since monetary items, such as cash, receivables, and liabilities, represent ownership of cash or claims to receive it, or obligations to pay cash, they are stated in terms of current dollars at all times. **Purchasing power gains and losses** occur as a result of holding these items during periods of inflation or deflation because the amounts that must be paid or received are fixed in dollar amounts regardless of any inflation or deflation that might occur. For instance, one who holds cash in a period of inflation will find that the cash purchases fewer goods and services as time passes. Debtors, on the other hand, will be able to retire debts with dollars that are worth less and less in terms of goods and services. On the other side of the transaction, creditors will receive dollars that are worth less. Simply stated, in times of inflation, owning monetary assets causes a loss in purchasing power, and owing liabilities causes a gain in purchasing power. These results are reversed during times of deflation.

In contrast, holding nonmonetary items, including inventories, investments, plant assets, intangibles, and owners' equity during inflationary or deflationary periods does *not* result in purchasing power gains and losses. Because these items are not tied physically or contractually to a certain dollar amount, they reflect the particular price level in effect when a transaction involving them takes place. In summary, the business does not gain or lose as a result of inflation or deflation from holding or completing transactions involving nonmonetary items.

Purchasing Power Gains and Losses   Consider the following data for Town Theater, a simple company with only two monetary items.

	Dec. 31, 19x1	Dec. 31, 19x2	For the Year 19x2
Monetary items			
Cash	$10,000	$20,000	
Notes payable	10,000	10,000	
Ticket receipts			$300,000
Payments for expenses			290,000
General price index	120	144	132 (average)

The purchasing power gain or loss for Town Theater can be calculated in three steps, as shown in Figure 14-1 (next page). First, the purchasing power loss from holding monetary assets (cash) is calculated by restating the beginning cash balances. The December 31, 19x1, price index was 120 and the December 31, 19x2, price index was 144. Therefore, the cash balance is restated in December 31, 19x2, dollars as follows: $10,000 \times 144/120 = $12,000$. Next, each increase or decrease in cash is adjusted using the price index existing at the time of the change. Since it is assumed that cash receipts and payments are uniform over time, the average price level (132) for the year 19x2 is used for the denominator in the conversion factor. Thus ticket receipts and payments for expenses are restated as shown in Figure 14-1. The ending balance restated is then calculated by adding the restated figures. Because the ending cash balance is in current dollars and does not need restatement, it is deducted from the restated balance to obtain the purchasing power loss from holding monetary assets ($22,909 − $20,000 = $2,909).

The second step is to calculate the purchasing power gain from owing the note payable of $10,000 for the full year. The beginning balance is adjusted for the change in price level ($10,000 \times 144/120 = $12,000$). From this amount the actual ending balance of $10,000 is deducted to obtain the purchasing power gain of $2,000 from owing the monetary liability.

The third step is to calculate the net purchasing power gain or loss by determining the difference of the figures in the first two steps. In this case, Town Theater had a net purchasing power loss of $909.

Balance Sheet Restatement   To continue the case of the Town Theater, assume that the nonmonetary balance sheet items on December 31, 19x2, are as follows:

Assets
    Theater $300,000
    Accumulated Depreciation   90,000 $210,000
Stockholders' Equity
    Common Stock $150,000
    Retained Earnings   70,000 $220,000

Assume also that the theater was purchased and the capital stock was issued at the same time, when the general price index was 108.

The restated balance sheet is presented in Figure 14-2. It is not necessary to restate monetary items (cash and notes payable) because they have a fixed monetary amount on the balance sheet date. The nonmonetary items are restated by multiplying the dollar amount by the ratio of the current general price index (144) to the general price index when the transaction took place (108). The retained earnings balance is determined

Figure 14-1
Calculation of
Purchasing
Power Gain or
Loss

		Town Theater Calculation of Purchasing Power Gain or Loss For the Year Ended December 31, 19x2		
	Recorded Amount	Conversion Factor	Restated Amount	Gain or (Loss)
Cash				
Beginning balance	$ 10,000	144/120	$ 12,000	
Ticket receipts	300,000	144/132	327,273	
Payments for expenses	(290,000)	144/132	(316,364)	
Ending balance, restated	—		$ 22,909	
Ending balance, actual	$ 20,000		(20,000)	
Purchasing power loss				($2,909)
Notes payable				
Beginning balance	$ 10,000	144/120	$12,000	
Ending balance, actual	$ 10,000		(10,000)	
Purchasing power gain				2,000
Net purchasing power loss				($ 909)

Figure 14-2
Restatement of
Balance Sheet

Town Theater
Restatement of Balance Sheet
December 31, 19x2

	Recorded Amount	Conversion Factor	Restated Amount
Cash	$ 20,000	No restatement	$ 20,000
Theater	300,000	144/108	400,000
Accumulated Depreciation	(90,000)	144/108	(120,000)
	$230,000		$300,000
Note Payable	$ 10,000	No restatement	$ 10,000
Common Stock	150,000	144/108	200,000
Retained Earnings	70,000	(See text)	90,000
	$230,000		$300,000

by putting in the amount necessary to make the balance sheet balance, as follows:

Total assets adjusted		$300,000
Less: Note Payable	$ 10,000	
Common Stock	200,000	210,000
Retained Earnings		$ 90,000

This retained earnings balance results from balance sheet and income statement effects as well as the purchasing power loss of $909 calculated in the section above. The details of these effects will be studied in more advanced courses.

Arguments for and Against Restatement The restatement of financial statements for changes in the general price level is very controversial. Those who favor restated financial statements argue, first, that the yearly rate of inflation in the United States is often so high that the assumption of a stable measuring unit no longer holds and unadjusted financial statements are very unrealistic. A second argument is that the restatement procedure is based on the traditional historical cost financial statements and so is as objective, verifiable, and auditable as the traditional statement. Third, amounts that are adjusted for price level, including purchasing power gains and losses, are helpful to users.

Critics of statements adjusted for price level argue, first of all, that two sets of financial statements would not be understood by most users. Second, they claim that the measures of general price level are too broad to make purchasing power gains and losses meaningful when applied to an individual company. A third argument is that changes in the general price level may not agree with real value changes. Finally, these critics say that financial analysts and bankers do not consider the information provided by such statements useful.

Current Value Accounting

In restating financial statements for changes in general purchasing power in the last section, we relaxed the stable measuring unit assumption but did not abandon historical cost measurement. The 1975 building cost that was adjusted from $200,000 to $359,799 because of a change in the general price level from 161.2 to 289.6 may have a current market value of $50,000 or $300,000. The restated figure is not a measure of current value. One of the strongest arguments against restatement is that the resulting financial statements do not reflect specific price changes that have affected a particular company. A lumber company, whose assets consist mostly of lumber inventory, may be much more concerned with changes in the price of lumber than with changes in the general price level. Such a lumber company would have faced the followed indexes in 1979 and 1980.[5]

Year	Consumer Price Index— Urban (1967 = 100)	Lumber Index (1967 = 100)
1979	217.4	300
1980	246.8	286

If this company had on the average $1,000,000, or three-fourths of its nonmonetary assets, invested in inventory in 1979 and 1980, one could make the following restatements:

Index	Restatement Computation	Restated Amount	Change
General	246.8/217.4 × $1,000,000	$1,135,235	$135,235
Specific	286/300 × $1,000,000	953,333	(46,667)
Total effect			$181,902

It would be hard to convince the manager of this lumber company that the lumber inventory should show an increase of $135,235 on the financial statements, when in fact its value in the market dropped by $46,667.

A method of accounting that would recognize the effects of such specific price changes in the financial statements is called **current value accounting.** Current value accounting represents a movement away from historical cost accounting. Its advocates call for a three-step changeover to current value statements, as follows:

Step 1. Footnote disclosures of the current value of inventories, cost of goods sold, plant assets, and depreciation

Step 2. Statements expressed in current values as supplements to historical cost statements

Step 3. Presentation only of current value statements

5. Source: *Statistical Abstract of the United States, 1983.*

A major problem with current value statements is agreement on how to measure current value. There are two main schools of thought. One school favors the use of **net realizable value.** Net realizable value is an exit value in that it represents what the company could sell its assets for. It is recommended because it is a measure of the company's ability to adapt to the marketplace. The other school of thought recommends **replacement cost.** Replacement cost is an entry value because it represents the cost of buying (or replacing), in the normal course of business, new assets of about equal operating or productive capacity. This method is favored because it is more closely related to the idea of maintaining a company's productive capacity as a going concern. This discussion, which must be brief, will center on replacement cost accounting because of the attention drawn to it by the SEC's requirement in 1976 for the reporting of replacement costs[6] and its later repeal of the rule when the FASB issued *Statement No. 33.*

Arguments for Replacement Cost Disclosure A major argument for replacement cost disclosure is that it is more realistic than historical cost statements. Specific price changes are a fact of life. If they are reflected in the financial statements, they make the information there more useful. A second major argument for replacement cost is that the economy as a whole is hindered by the unrealistic depreciation rates under historical costing. Because the role of plant assets in most cases would rise sharply if replacement costs were used, depreciation would also increase sharply. So these higher costs are more in line with replacing current productive capacity and offer more realistic earnings figures on which to base such things as investment and dividend policies.

Arguments Against Replacement Cost Disclosure On the other side of the question, critics emphasize that there are no accepted ways of measuring replacement costs, and replacement costs are not based on objective, verifiable transactions that can be audited. For this reason, they say, the resulting information is less helpful to users.

Critics also say that through wise use of current accounting techniques, income measures close to those obtained under replacement cost accounting can be found in historical cost statements. For example, by using LIFO inventory, a company in effect charges the most current inventory purchases against income. This method produces a gross margin close to that which would have been obtained by using replacement costs for inventory. Also, by using accelerated depreciation methods, a faster write-off of plant assets is gained in the early years, which may help offset rises in replacement costs.

The FASB Position

Over the years, the Financial Accounting Standards Board has changed its stand on the question of constant-dollar versus current value accounting.

6. *Accounting Series Release No. 190* (Washington: Securities and Exchange Commission, 1976).

Objective 7
Describe the
FASB's
approach to
accounting for
changing prices

In 1974, it followed an earlier Accounting Principles Board recommendation that all companies put in their annual reports supplemental financial statements expressed in units of general purchasing power.[7] This proposal was not acted upon, partly because it was upstaged by the 1976 SEC release on replacement cost disclosure. By 1979, the FASB had taken a different stand and issued another statement, calling for certain large publicly held companies (those with inventories and property, plant, and equipment of more than $125 million or total assets of more than $1 billion) to report supplemental information on both a constant dollar basis and a current value basis.[8] The current value basis used by the FASB is the lower of current cost or net realizable value at the balance sheet date.

Figure 14-3
Disclosure for
Current Year
from Annual
Report of
Westinghouse
Electric Corporation

7. *Proposed Statement of Financial Accounting Standards, Exposure Draft,* "Financial Reporting in Units of General Purchasing Power" (Stamford, Conn.: Financial Accounting Standards Board, 1974); also see Accounting Principles Board, *Statement No. 3,* "Financial Statements Restated for General Price Level Changes" (New York: American Institute of Certified Public Accountants, 1969).
8. *Statement of Financial Accounting Standards No. 33.*

Supplementary 1982 Statement of Income from Continuing Operations Adjusted for Changing Prices (*unaudited*) (*in millions*)

	As reported in the Primary Statements	Adjusted for General Price Changes (Constant Dollar)	Adjusted for Specific Price Changes (Current Cost)
Sales and operating revenues	$9,745.4	$9,745.4	$9,745.4
Cost of sales	7,215.6	7,341.6	7,311.5
Distribution, administration and general expenses	1,684.0	1,684.0	1,684.0
Depreciation and amortization	322.0	417.0	435.0
Interest expense	185.8	185.8	185.8
Other income and minority interest	205.9	205.9	205.9
Income taxes	94.6	94.6	94.6
Net income	$ 449.3	$ 228.3	$ 240.4
Comparison of Price Changes— Inventories and Plant and Equipment Held During the Year* Effect of general price changes measured by the consumer price index			$ 171.3
Effect of specific price changes (current cost)			$ 223.9
Amount by which specific price increases exceed general price increases			$ 52.6

*At December 31, 1982 current cost of inventory was $1,916 million and current cost of plant and equipment, net of accumulated depreciation was $4,086 million.

Chapter Fourteen

Figure 14-4
Disclosure for
Most Recent
Five Years from
Annual Report
of Westing-
house Electric
Corporation

By current cost, the FASB means the lowest current buying price or production cost of an asset of the same age and in the same condition as the asset owned. So the FASB's view of current value brought together the two ideas of net realizable value and replacement cost.

Specifically, the FASB requires supplemental disclosure for the current year, like that shown in Figure 14-3 for Westinghouse (see previous page). Also, the FASB requires supplemental disclosure for the most recent five years, like the information shown in Figure 14-4 (see below).

Comparison of Selected Supplementary Financial Data Adjusted for Effects of Changing Prices (unaudited)* (in millions except per share amounts)

		1982	1981	1980	1979	1978
Sales and operating revenues	Reported	$9,745.4	$9,367.5	$8,514.3	$7,443.1	$ 6,779.8
	Constant dollars	9,745.4	9,941.8	9,973.6	9,897.9	10,030.9
Net income	Reported	$ 449.3	$ 438.0	$ 402.9	$ 331.1	$ 311.3
	Constant dollars	228.3	276.3	259.3	260.8	
	Current cost	240.4	283.2	277.3	257.9	
Per common share	Reported	$ 5.16	$ 5.10	$ 4.71	$ 3.85	$ 3.59
	Constant dollars	2.62	3.22	3.04	3.04	
	Current cost	2.76	3.30	3.25	2.99	
Purchasing power gain (loss) on net monetary items		$ 15.5	$ (39.5)	$ (132.8)	$ (167.6)	
Amount by which specific price increases exceed general price increases		$ 52.6	$ (88.5)	$ (112.1)	$ (31.7)	
Dividends per common share	Reported	$ 1.80	$ 1.80	$ 1.40	$ .972	$ .972
	Constant dollars	1.80	1.91	1.64	1.29	1.44
Market price per common share at year-end	Reported	$38\frac{7}{8}$	$25\frac{1}{2}$	$29\frac{5}{8}$	$20\frac{1}{8}$	$16\frac{5}{8}$
	Constant dollars	$38\frac{3}{8}$	$26\frac{1}{8}$	$33\frac{1}{8}$	$25\frac{1}{4}$	$23\frac{3}{4}$
Net assets at year-end	Reported	$3,175.0	$2,820.7	$2,529.9	$2,250.0	$ 2,423.0
	Constant dollars	4,945.6	4,672.2	4,651.5	4,514.7	
	Current cost	5,250.0	4,922.9	2,950.4	4,866.8	
Average consumer price index	(1967 = 100)	289.1	272.4	246.8	217.4	195.4

*Amounts shown for constant dollars and current cost are stated in average 1982 dollars based on the average consumer price index.

There are several important points to make about these disclosures. First, they are supplementary to the historical cost financial statements. The FASB believes that most people will still use historical cost financial statements and that there are four good reasons for keeping them as the major financial statements, as follows: (1) Historical cost financial statements depend on real transactions, which determine the change in owners' equity in the long run. (2) Because historical costs are generally the result of a completed agreement, they provide a basis for reliably measuring the results of transactions and so can be independently verified. (3) Users' understanding of the effect of changing prices may be improved if they are able to compare the measurements in the major financial statements with measurements showing changing prices. (4) Users understand the present financial statements.

The second point is that even though historical cost statements are important, the FASB believes that the supplemental reporting of the effects of changing prices is needed because this information will aid in the assessment of (1) future cash flows, (2) business performance, (3) the loss of operating capacity, and (4) the loss of purchasing power.

Third, the FASB recognizes that many problems remain to be solved in measuring the effect of changing prices. It plans to review the effects of *Statement No. 33* on an ongoing basis and to begin a full review of the statement after a period of no more than five years.

Chapter Review

Review of Learning Objectives

1. Apply the matching rule to revenue recognition.

Two bases are used in practice to apply the matching rule to revenue recognition. The point of sale basis is the most common basis and is the one used generally in earlier chapters. The cash basis is often used by individuals and recognizes revenue only when cash is received.

2. Apply the matching rule to the allocation of expired costs as it relates to capital expenditures and revenue expenditures.

It is important to distinguish between capital expenditures, which are recorded as assets, and revenue expenditures, which are charged immediately against income, because the error of classifying one as the other will have an important effect on net income. Expenditures for plant assets, additions, betterments, and intangible assets are capital expenditures. Extraordinary repairs are also treated as capital expenditures, whereas ordinary repairs are revenue expenditures.

3. Apply the matching rule to the accounting problems associated with intangible assets, including research and development costs and goodwill.

Purchases of intangible assets should be treated as capital expenditures and recorded at acquisition cost, which in turn should be amortized over the useful life of the assets (but not more than forty years). The FASB requires that research and development costs be treated as revenue expenditures and charged as expense in the period of the expenditure. Goodwill is the excess of cost over the market value in the purchase of a business and is usually related to the superior earning potential of the assets. It should be recorded only if purchased and should be amortized over a period not to exceed forty years.

4. Demonstrate the effects of arbitrary allocation procedures on reported net income.

In interpreting financial statements, the accounting procedures chosen by management to apply the matching rule can significantly affect reported net income. Examples of such choices are in methods of accounting for uncollectible accounts, inventories, depreciation, depletion, and amortization.

5. Identify the two principal types of price changes.

The two principal types of price changes that affect financial statements are specific price changes in the price of an individual item or service, and general price changes in the price of a group of goods or services. General price changes result in purchasing power gains or losses.

6. Using constant dollar accounting, compute purchasing power gains and losses, and restate a balance sheet for changes in the general price level.

Holding monetary items during periods of inflation or deflation results in purchasing power gains or losses because monetary items are fixed in terms of current dollars at all times and cannot fluctuate to compensate for the changes in general price level. In contrast, holding nonmonetary items during similar periods does not result in purchasing power gains or losses. Under constant dollar accounting, historical cost statements are restated for general price level changes. Under this method, purchasing power gains or losses are calculated by multiplying the dollar amount by the current price level divided by the price level when the item originated. A balance sheet is restated by adjusting the nonmonetary items for the change in price level since the item's origin. Retained earnings are computed as a balancing figure.

7. Describe the FASB's approach to accounting for changing prices.

Although the FASB believes that historical cost financial statements should be the primary financial statements, it requires that certain large companies provide supplemental information, both for the current year and for a five-year period, on both a constant dollar basis and a current value basis. Current value accounting, which recognizes the effects of specific price level changes in the financial statements, is defined by the FASB to be the lower of current cost or net realizable value. The FASB is encouraging a period of experimentation in reporting the effects of changing prices.

Review Problem
Comprehensive Capital and Revenue Expenditure Entries

The Haywood Haberdashery, Inc., operates several stores featuring men's fashions. The transactions below describe the capital and revenue expenditures that relate to one of the company's stores. All expenditures are made with cash.

The building was purchased on January 1, 1967, for $117,000. At that time the building was repaired and renovated for use as a clothing store at a cost of $63,000. It was estimated that the building would have a useful life of forty years and a residual value after that time of $20,000.

On April 15, 1971, the front windows were replaced because they were cracked, and the roof was repaired because it was leaking. The repairs cost a total of $9,800.

On January 10, 1972, a new addition to the building was completed at a cost of $115,000. The addition did not add to the estimated useful life of the building but did increase the residual value by $10,000.

On August, 3, 1975, the building was painted at a cost of $17,500.

On January 7, 1977, a complete overhaul of the heating and cooling system was completed at a cost of $20,000. It was estimated that this work would add ten years to the useful life of the building but would not increase its residual value.

Because of a decline in business, the building was sold on January 1, 1982, for $260,000 in cash.

Required

1. Prepare general journal entries for the following dates: (a) January 1, 1967; (b) April 15, 1971; (c) January 10, 1972; (d) August 3, 1975; (e) January 7, 1977; and (f) January 1, 1982.

2. Open ledger accounts for Building (141) and for Accumulated Depreciation, Building (142) and post the relevant portions of the entries in **1**.

3. Compute depreciation expense for each year until the date of sale, assuming that the straight-line method is used and that the company's fiscal year ends on December 31. Enter the amounts in the account for Accumulated Depreciation, Building.

4. Prepare a general journal entry to record the sale of the building on January 1, 1982. Post the relevant portions of the entry to the two accounts opened in **2**.

Answer to Review Problem

1 and 4. Journal entries prepared:

General Journal **Page**

Date		Description	Post. Ref.	Debit	Credit
1967					
Jan.	1	Building	141	180,000	
		Cash			180,000
		Purchase of building:			
		Cost $117,000			
		Repair and renovation 63,000			
		Total cost $180,000			
1971					
Apr.	15	Repair Expense		9,800	
		Cash			9,800
		Replacement of windows and repair of roof			
1972					
Jan.	10	Building	141	115,000	
		Cash			115,000
		Addition to building			
1975					
Aug.	3	Repair Expense		17,500	
		Cash			17,500
		Painting of building			

1977						
Jan.	7	Accumulated Depreciation, Building	142	20,000		
		Cash			20,000	
		Overhaul of heating and cooling system				
1982						
Jan.	1	Cash		260,000		
		Accumulated Depreciation, Building	142	63,750		
		Building	141		295,000	
		Gain on Sale of Building			28,750	
		Sale of building				

2. Ledger accounts opened and posted:

Building   Account No. 141

Date		Item	Post. Ref.	Debit	Credit	Balance Debit	Balance Credit
1967							
Jan.	1		J	180,000		180,000	
1972							
Jan.	10		J	115,000		295,000	
1982							
Jan.	1		J		295,000		

Accumulated Depreciation, Building   Account No. 142

Date		Item	Post. Ref.	Debit	Credit	Balance Debit	Balance Credit
1967			J		4,000		4,000
1968			J		4,000		8,000
1969			J		4,000		12,000
1970			J		4,000		16,000
1971			J		4,000		20,000
1972			J		7,000		27,000
1973			J		7,000		34,000
1974			J		7,000		41,000
1975			J		7,000		48,000
1976			J		7,000		55,000
1977							
Jan.	7		J	20,000			35,000
Dec.	31		J		5,750		40,750
1978			J		5,750		46,500
1979			J		5,750		52,250
1980			J		5,750		58,000
1981			J		5,750		63,750
1982							
Jan.	1		J	63,750			—

3. Depreciation expense computed:

January 1, 1967, to December 31, 1971—five years

$$(\$180{,}000 - \$20{,}000) \div 40 \text{ years} = \$4{,}000 \text{ per year}$$

January 1, 1972, to December 31, 1976—five years

$$(\$295{,}000 - \$30{,}000 - \$20{,}000) \div 35 \text{ years} = \$7{,}000 \text{ per year}$$

January 1, 1977, to December 31, 1981—five years
Book value before extraordinary repair:

Building account	$295,000	
Accumulated Depreciation	55,000	$240,000
Extraordinary Repair		20,000
New carrying value		$260,000
Less residual value		30,000
Depreciable cost		$230,000
Divide by years remaining in useful life:		
Years remaining before extraordinary item	30	
Years added by extraordinary item	10	40
Depreciation per year		$ 5,750

Chapter Assignments

Questions

1. What are the two principal aspects of applying the matching rule?

2. From the standpoint of matching, why is the point of sale basis of revenue recognition considered better than the cash basis?

3. What is the distinction between revenue expenditures and capital expenditures, and why is this distinction important?

4. What will be the effect on future years' income of charging an addition to a building as repair expense?

5. In what ways do an addition, a betterment, and an extraordinary repair differ?

6. How does an extraordinary repair differ from an ordinary repair? What is the accounting treatment for each?

7. What is the basis of the following statement? "Accounting for net income is a useless measurement because it is based on so many arbitrary estimates."

8. Because accounts receivable have no physical substance, can they be classified as intangible assets?

9. Under what circumstances can a company have intangible assets that do not appear on the balance sheet?

10. When the Accounting Principles Board indicates that accounting for intangible assets involves the same problem as accounting for tangible assets, what problem is it referring to?

11. How does the Financial Accounting Standards Board recommend that research and development costs be treated?

12. Under what conditions should goodwill be recorded? Should it remain in the records permanently once it is recorded?

13. Why has the assumption of a stable monetary unit been questioned in recent years?

14. Distinguish specific price changes from general price changes.

15. "We love debt," says G. James Williams, vice president—finance (of Dow Chemical). "The $3 billion we have in long-term debt is one of the greatest assets of Dow Chemical Company." For forty years, Williams explained, the company has regarded inflation as a fact of American life, from which springs this corollary: borrow now to repay in cheaper dollars. (Quoted from *Barron's*, October 9, 1978, p. 4.) Why does Dow Chemical feel that it is an asset to be a debtor?

16. How does current value accounting differ from constant dollar accounting?

17. What are the FASB requirements for the disclosure of the effects of changing prices?

Classroom Exercises

Exercise 14-1
Balance Sheet Restatement for General Price Changes
(L.O. 6)

The Vinson Company's balance sheet appears as follows:

Vinson Company
Balance Sheet
December 31, 19xx

Cash	$ 50,000	Note Payable	$100,000
Building	210,000	Common Stock	250,000
Accumulated Depreciation	(15,000)	Retained Earnings	105,000
Equipment	300,000		
Accumulated Depreciation	(90,000)	Total Liabilities and	
Total Assets	$455,000	Stockholders' Equity	$455,000

The following general price level indexes are applicable:

Beginning of year	160	At the time of	
End of year	200	Building purchase	120
Average for year	180	Equipment purchase	150
		Capital stock issue	100

Restate the balance sheet for changes in the general price level.

Exercise 14-2
Amortization of Copyrights and Trademarks
(L.O. 3)

1. Kendall Publishing Company purchased the copyright to a basic computer textbook for $10,000. The usual life of a textbook is about four years. However, the copyright will remain in effect for another fifty years.

   Calculate the annual amortization of the copyright.

2. Moser Company purchased a trademark from a well-known supermarket for $80,000. The management of the company argued that the trademark value

would last forever and might even increase and so no amortization should be charged.

Calculate the minimum amount of annual amortization that should be charged, according to guidelines of the appropriate Accounting Principles Board opinion.

**Exercise 14-3
Computation of
Goodwill**
(L.O. 3)

Weston Corporation has assets of $380,000 and liabilities of $100,000. In Weston Corporation's industry, the typical return is 10 percent of *net* assets. Over the last five years, Weston Corporation has earned $35,000 per year, with net assets similar to those throughout the industry. Parks Corporation has offered to buy out Weston Corporation for a cash payment equal to net assets plus five times the excess earnings over industry average.

1. Determine the net assets for Weston Corporation.
2. Determine by how much Weston Corporation's earnings exceed the industry average.
3. Calculate how much Parks Corporation is offering for Weston Corporation.
4. Compute the value of goodwill.

**Exercise 14-4
Extraordinary
Repairs**
(L.O. 2)

Ritchey Manufacturing Company has an incinerator that originally cost $74,800 and now has accumulated depreciation of $58,300. The incinerator just completed its fifteenth year of service in an estimated useful life of twenty years. At the beginning of the sixteenth year, the company spent $19,300 repairing and modernizing the incinerator to comply with pollution control standards. Therefore, instead of five years, the incinerator is now expected to last ten more years. It will not, however, have more capacity than it did in the past or a residual value at the end of its useful life.

1. Prepare the entry to record the cost of the repairs.
2. Compute the book value of the incinerator after the entry.
3. Prepare the entry to record the depreciation (assuming straight-line method) for the current year.

**Exercise 14-5
Effect of
Alternative
Accounting
Methods**
(L.O. 4)

At the end of its first year of operations, a company could calculate its ending merchandise inventory, according to three different methods, as follows: FIFO, $62,500; weighted average, $60,000; LIFO, $58,000. If the weighted-average method is used, the net income for the year would be $28,000.

1. Determine the net income if the FIFO method is used.
2. Determine the net income if the LIFO method is used.
3. Which method is most conservative?
4. Will the consistency convention be violated if the LIFO method is chosen?
5. Does the full-disclosure convention require disclosure of the inventory method selected by management in the financial statements?

**Exercise 14-6
Calculation of
Purchasing
Power Gains
and Losses**
(L.O. 6)

Companies J and K both began operation on January 1 with $50,000 in cash. Company J raised the cash by issuing capital stock, and Company K by issuing a two-year note payable. During the year, both companies had cash receipts of $550,000 and cash payments of $440,000. Also, during the year, the general price level began at 150, ended at 180, and averaged 165.

Calculate the purchasing power gain or loss for each company.

Interpreting Accounting Information

Published Financial Information: Westinghouse Electric
(L.O. 6)

Westinghouse Electric Corporation is one of the world's largest electrical products companies. Figures 14-3 and 14-4 present a supplementary statement of income and other selected financial data adjusted for changing prices for the company. Referring to these figures, make calculations where appropriate and answer the following questions:

1. In Figure 14-3, why are reported sales the same as sales adjusted for general price changes and for specific price changes?

2. In Figure 14-3, reported income from operations in 1982 of $449.3 million adjusted for general price changes is $228.3 million and for specific price changes is $240.4 million. Account for these differences by indicating which income statement items led to the differences and by how much. Explain the circumstances that would cause the items identified to have such an impact on reported income from operations.

3. In Figure 14-4, why are reported sales and operating revenues in the years 1978–1981 less than the amount in constant dollars? Demonstrate how the constant dollar amounts were calculated for 1980 and 1981.

4. In Figure 14-4, compute the ratio of reported dividends per common share to reported income per common share (payout ratio) for 1981 and for 1982. Compute the same ratio, using constant dollars for each year. What issues do these calculations raise with regard to the dividend policy of the company?

Problem Set A

Problem 14A-1 Effect of Alternative Accounting Methods
(L.O. 4)

Hilliard Company began operations by purchasing $200,000 in equipment that has an estimated useful life of nine years and an estimated residual value of $20,000.

During the year, the company purchased inventory as follows:

January	2,000 units at $25	$ 50,000
March	4,000 units at $24	96,000
May	1,000 units at $27	27,000
July	5,000 units at $27	135,000
September	6,000 units at $28	168,000
November	2,000 units at $29	58,000
December	3,000 units at $28	84,000
Totals	23,000 units	$618,000

The company sold 19,000 units for a total of $840,000 and incurred salary expenses of $170,000 and expenses other than depreciation of $120,000.

Hilliard's management is anxious to present its income statement most fairly in its first year of operation and realizes that there are alternative accounting methods available for accounting for inventory and equipment. Management wants to determine the effect of various alternatives on this year's income. Two sets of alternatives are proposed.

Required

1. Prepare two income statements for Hilliard Company: one using the FIFO basis for inventory and the straight-line method for depreciation; the other using the LIFO basis for inventory and the sum-of-the-years'-digits method for depreciation.

2. Prepare a schedule accounting for the difference in the two net income figures in **1**.

**Problem 14A-2
Amortization of
Exclusive
License**
(L.O. 3)

On January 1, Entertainment Toys, Inc. (ETI), purchased the exclusive license to make dolls based on the characters in a new hit series on television called "Tricks 'n' Treats." The exclusive license cost $1,500,000, and there was no termination date on the rights.

Immediately after signing the contract, the company sued a rival firm that claimed it had already received the exclusive license to the series characters. ETI successfully defended its rights at a cost of $250,000. During the first year and the next, ETI marketed toys based on the series. Because a successful television series lasts about five years, the company felt it could market the toys for three more years. However, before the third year of the series could get underway, a controversy arose between the two stars of the series and the producer. As a result, the stars refused to do the third year and the show was canceled, rendering exclusive rights worthless.

Required

Prepare journal entries to record the following: (a) purchase of the exclusive license; (b) successful defense of the license; (c) amortization expense, if any, for the first year; (d) news of the series cancellation.

**Problem 14A-3
Amortization of
Leasehold and
Leasehold
Improvements**
(L.O. 3)

Teresa Schoenfeld purchased a six-year sublease on a building from the estate of the former tenant, who had died suddenly. It was a good location for her business, and the annual rent of $2,400, which had been established ten years ago, was low for such a good location. The cost of the sublease was $6,300.

To use the building, Teresa had to make certain alterations. First she moved some panels at a cost of $1,700 and installed others for $6,100. Then she added carpet, lighting fixtures, and a sign at costs of $2,900, $3,100, and $1,200, respectively. All items except the carpet would last for at least twelve years. The expected life of the carpet was six years. None of the improvements would have a residual value at the end of those times.

Required

Prepare general journal entries to record the following: (a) the payment for the sublease; (b) the payments for the alterations, panels, carpet, lighting fixtures, and sign; (c) the lease payment for the first year; (d) the expense, if any, associated with the sublease; (e) the expense, if any, associated with the alterations, panels, carpet, lighting fixtures, and sign.

**Problem 14A-4
Calculation of
Purchasing
Power Gain or
Loss and
Balance Sheet
Restatement**
(L.O. 6)

Eastmoor Skating, Inc., began on January 1, 19x1, by issuing common stock and purchasing a skating rink. Its balance sheet on December 31, 19x2, follows:

Assets

Cash	$ 30,000
Skating Rink	260,000
Accumulated Depreciation	(39,000)
Total Assets	$251,000

Liabilities and Stockholders' Equity

Note Payable	$ 10,000
Common Stock	273,000
Retained Earnings	(32,000)
Total Liabilities and Stockholders' Equity	$251,000

The company operates strictly on a cash basis. On January 2, 19x2, the company had a cash balance of $17,000, including the proceeds from the note payable it issued on that date. During the year, its cash receipts were $162,500, and its payments for expenses were $149,500. The general price level on different dates varied as follows:

January 1, 19x1	100
January 1, 19x2	120
December 31, 19x2	138
Average for 19x2	130

Required

1. Compute the purchasing power gain or loss for Eastmoor Skating, Inc., during 19x2.
2. Prepare a restated balance sheet at December 31, 19x2.

**Problem 14A-5
Comprehensive
Capital and
Revenue
Expenditure
Entries**
(L.O. 2)

Leonard's, Inc., operates a chain of self-service gasoline stations in several southern states. The transactions below describe the capital and revenue expenditures for one station.

Construction on the station was completed on July 1, 1970, at a cost of $275,000. It was estimated that the station would have a useful life of thirty-five years and a residual value of $30,000.

On September 15, 1974, scheduled painting and minor repairs affecting the appearance of the station were completed at a cost of $3,950.

On July 9, 1978, a new gasoline tank was added at a cost of $80,000. The tank did not add to the useful life of the station, but it did add $7,000 to its estimated residual value.

On October 22, 1979, the driveway of the station was resurfaced at a cost of $1,900.

The cost of major repairs and renovation, which were completed on July 3, 1980, was $55,000. It was estimated that this work would extend the life of the station by five years and would not increase the residual value.

A change in the routing of a major highway led to the sale of the station on January 2, 1983, for $200,000. The company received $20,000 in cash and a note for the balance of the $200,000.

Required

1. Prepare general journal entries for the following dates: (a) July 1, 1970; (b) September 15, 1974; (c) July 9, 1978; (d) October 22, 1979; and (e) July 3, 1980.
2. Open ledger accounts for Station (143) and for Accumulated Depreciation, Station (144), and post the relevant portions of the entries in 1.
3. Compute depreciation expense for each year and partial year until the date of sale, assuming that the straight-line method is used and that the company's fiscal year ends on June 30. Enter the amounts in the account for Accumulated Depreciation, Station.
4. Prepare a general journal entry to record the sale of the station on January 2, 1983. Post the relevant portions of the entry to the two accounts opened in 2.

**Problem 14A-6
Purchase of
Business with
Goodwill**
(L.O. 3)

Ed Camp, the owner of Camp Corporation, has reached an agreement for the purchase of the Wright Company from Tony Wright.

Information from the balance sheet of the Wright Company follows:

Cash		$ 112,400
Other Current Assets		286,600
Plant Assets		
Land		82,000
Buildings	$597,000	
Less Accumulated Depreciation	216,000	381,000
Equipment	$786,000	
Less Accumulated Depreciation	329,000	457,000
Patent		35,000
Total Assets		$1,354,000
Current Liabilities		$ 99,000
Long-Term Mortgage		360,000
Tony Wright, Capital		895,000
Total Liabilities and Owner's Equity		$1,354,000

The terms of the agreement were as follows:

a. Camp Corporation would purchase the assets, other than cash, and an unused building and assume the liabilities of Wright Company, by issuing long-term bonds for the amount of the purchase. The cost of the building was $132,000, and it had $37,000 of accumulated depreciation.

b. Wright Company would adjust its books to reflect a reduction of $20,000 for obsolete inventory, an increase in the patent account of $15,000, and an increase in current liabilities of $27,000 to acknowledge unrecorded debt.

c. In addition to the amount in **a**, Camp would pay Wright for goodwill in the amount of five times the amount by which Wright's earnings exceeded the industry average. During the past five years, Wright earned an average of $106,000. The industry average was 9 percent of net assets.

Required

1. Prepare a general journal entry to adjust Wright's books in accordance with the agreement.
2. Compute the net assets exclusive of the building not used in the business.
3. Compute the amount of goodwill to be paid, based on your answer in **2**.
4. Prepare a general journal entry in Camp's records to show the purchase of Wright.

Problem Set B

Problem 14B-1
Effect of Alternative Accounting Methods
(L.O. 4)

Mendez Company began operations this year. At the beginning of the year, the company purchased plant assets of $165,000, with an estimated useful life of ten years and no salvage value.

During the year, the company had sales of $300,000, salary expense of $50,000, and other expenses of $20,000, excluding depreciation. In addition, the company purchased inventory as follows:

January 15	400 units at $100	$ 40,000
March 20	200 units at $102	20,400
June 15	800 units at $104	83,200
September 18	600 units at $103	61,800
December 9	300 units at $105	31,500
Totals	2,300 units	$236,900

At the end of the year, a physical inventory disclosed 500 units still on hand. The managers of Mendez Company know that they have a choice of accounting methods but are not sure what the effect of the methods will be on net income. They have heard of FIFO and LIFO for inventory methods and straight-line and sum-of-the-years'-digits for depreciation methods.

Required

1. Prepare two income statements for Mendez Company: one using the FIFO basis and the straight-line method; the other using the LIFO basis and the sum-of-the-years'-digits method.
2. Prepare a schedule accounting for the difference in the two net income figures in 1.

Problem 14B-2
Amortization of
Patent
(L.O. 3)

Midwest Ecology, Inc., purchased a patent for $117,000 on April 1, 19x6, for a new device to remove harmful particles from smoke. If successful, the device would greatly cut the cost of cleaning the smoke from industrial plants.

The company immediately began patent infringement suits against four other companies. Midwest Ecology won these suits and now has the exclusive right to manufacture the device. The costs of defending the patent were $83,000, all incurred during 19x6. The company manufactured and sold the device during 19x6, 19x7, and 19x8. Although the patent was good for fifteen years beyond the purchase date, the company's management felt eight years to be a reasonable estimated life, given the fast-changing technology in the field.

It became clear in January 19x9 that the device could not be modified to meet the stricter pollution control standards of the Environmental Protection Agency. Thus, existing orders for the device were canceled.

Required

Prepare general journal entries to record the following: (a) the purchase of the patent, (b) the successful defense of the patent, (c) the amortization expense on December 31, 19x6, and (d) the news of January 19x9.

Problem 14B-3
Amortization of
Leasehold and
Leasehold
Improvements
(L.O. 3)

Daryl Wallace obtained an eight-year sublease on a two-story building to open an art gallery. To get the sublease, he had to pay $5,600 to the current tenant, who had eight years to go on his lease. Daryl was willing to pay for the leasehold because of the excellent location of the proposed gallery and the current low rent of only $3,600 per year for the building.

In addition, Daryl had to make certain improvements in the building to convert it to a gallery. These included fixtures and lighting, $2,100; carpet, $3,200; a small elevator between floors, $7,800; and an art vault, $5,900. He estimated that the carpeting would last eight years and that the other improvements would last twenty years, with no estimated residual value.

Required

Prepare general journal entries to record (a) the payment for the sublease; (b) the payments for the fixtures and lighting, carpet, elevator, and vault, none of which can be removed at the end of the lease; (c) the lease payment for the first year; (d) the expense, if any, associated with the sublease; and (e) the expense, if any, associated with the fixtures and lighting, carpet, elevator, and vault.

Problem 14B-4
Purchasing
Power Gain or
Loss and
Balance Sheet
Restatement
(L.O. 6)

The Urban Parking Company operates a single parking lot. All receipts are in cash, and expenses are paid in cash. During 19x2, the company had revenues of $341,000 and expenses of $242,000. At the end of 19x2, the company's balance sheet appeared as follows:

Urban Parking Company
Balance Sheet
December 31, 19x2

Assets

Cash	$150,000
Land	20,000
Parking Building	300,000
Accumulated Depreciation	(60,000)
Total Assets	$410,000

Liabilities and Stockholders' Equity

Note Payable	$250,000
Common Stock	70,000
Retained Earnings	90,000
Total Liabilities and Stockholders' Equity	$410,000

The company was founded on January 1, 19x1, when the land and parking building were purchased and the capital stock was issued. The note has been outstanding during all of 19x2, and the cash balance at the beginning of 19x2 was $51,000. The general price level during the past two years varied as follows:

January 1, 19x1	200
January 1, 19x2	210
December 31, 19x2	231
Average for 19x2	220

Required

1. Compute the purchasing power gain or loss for Urban Parking Company for 19x2.
2. Prepare a restated balance sheet at December 31, 19x2.

Problem 14B-5
Comprehensive
Capital and
Revenue
Expenditure
Entries
(L.O. 2)

Hooper Foods runs a chain of small grocery stores. On January 1, 1971, the company purchased a building on Main Street in a small town outside Atlanta for $224,000. At the time of purchase, it cost $112,000 to repair the building and convert it into a grocery store. The building had an estimated useful life of thirty years and an estimated residual value of $30,000.

On August 13, 1975, the roof of the building was repaired at a cost of $2,150.

The store prospered, and on January 10, 1976, a new addition to the building was constructed at a cost of $75,000. The addition increased the estimated residual value of the building by $10,000.

On April 25, 1979, the building was repainted at a cost of $12,650.

Because of structural damage, major repairs costing $45,000 were completed on January 6, 1981. Management felt these repairs would extend the useful life of the building five years but would not increase the residual value.

On January 1, 1982, new managers took over Hooper Foods and on July 1, 1983, sold the building on Main Street for $240,000. They received $20,000 cash, land valued at $40,000, and a mortgage for the remainder.

Required

1. Prepare general journal entries for the following dates: (a) January 1, 1971; (b) August 13, 1975; (c) January 10, 1976; (d) April 25, 1979; and (e) January 6, 1981.
2. Open ledger accounts for Buildings (143) and for Accumulated Depreciation, Buildings (144), and post the relevant portions of the entries in 1.
3. Compute depreciation expense for each year and partial year until the date of sale, assuming that the straight-line method is used and the company's fiscal year is the same as the calendar year. Post the amounts in the account for Accumulated Depreciation, Buildings.
4. Prepare a general journal entry to record the sale of the building on July 1, 1983. Post the relevant portions of the entry to the two accounts opened in 2.

**Problem 14B-6
Purchase of
Business with
Goodwill
Resulting
(L.O. 3)**

Alex Burrell has been looking for a good business to purchase. He found one in Piercy Enterprises, which has earned an average of $44,000 a year for the last five years.

Burrell proposed that he purchase all the assets, except for cash, of Piercy Enterprises and assume the liabilities of Piercy. He will pay $150,000 cash and give a one-year note for the balance. He is willing to pay for goodwill equal to four times those earnings that exceed the industry average earnings of 10 percent of net tangible assets, excluding cash.

Information from the current balance sheet for Piercy Enterprises follows:

Cash		$ 22,000
Other Current Assets		164,000
Plant Assets		
Land		5,000
Buildings	$124,000	
Less Accumulated Depreciation	42,000	82,000
Equipment	$289,000	
Less Accumulated Depreciation	106,000	183,000
Trademark		22,000
Franchise		17,000
Total Assets		$495,000
Current Liabilities		$ 46,000
Long-Term Note Payable		100,000
Scott Piercy, Capital		349,000
Total Liabilities and Owner's Equity		$495,000

Alex Burrell and Scott Piercy agree to adjust the Piercy Enterprises books in two ways. First of all, the land, which had been purchased many years before by the Piercy family, was not realistically valued and should have a value of $25,000. Second, the trademark and franchise that had been on the books for many years without being amortized should not be considered to have any value.

Required

1. Prepare a general journal entry to adjust the Piercy Enterprises books in accordance with the agreement.

2. Compute the net tangible assets exclusive of cash.

3. Compute the amount of goodwill to be paid.

4. Prepare a general journal entry in Burrell's records to show the purchase of Piercy Enterprises.

Financial Decision Case 14-1

Tedtronics Company
(L.O. 4)

Ted Lazzerini is the owner of Tedtronics Company, a successful producer of word-processing equipment. At the beginning of 19xx, Ted retired from active management in the company and hired new management to run the business. As an incentive to the new management, Ted developed an executive compensation plan, which provides cash bonuses to key executives for the years in which the company's net income exceeds $2,000,000 plus a $200,000 increase for each future year. Thus for management to receive the bonuses, the company must earn net income of $2,000,000 the first year, $2,200,000 the second, $2,400,000 the third, and so forth.

Net income for the first three years of operation under the new management was as follows:

	19x3	19x2	19x1
Net income	$2,500,000	$2,500,000	$2,500,000

During this time management earned bonuses totaling more than $1,000,000 under the compensation plan. Ted, who had taken no active part in the business, began to worry about the unchanging level of earnings and decided to study the company's financial reports more carefully. The notes to the financial statements revealed the following information:

a. Management changed from using the LIFO inventory method to the FIFO method in 19x1. The effect of this change was to decrease the cost of goods sold by $200,000 in 19x1, $300,000 in 19x2, and $400,000 in 19x3.

b. In 19x2, management changed from using the double-declining-balance accelerated depreciation method to using the straight-line method. The effect of this change was to decrease depreciation by $400,000 in 19x2 and by $500,000 in 19x3.

c. In 19x3, management increased the estimated useful life of intangible assets from five to ten years. The effect of this change was to decrease amortization expense by $100,000 in 19x3.

Required

1. Compute net income for each year according to the accounting methods in use at the beginning of 19x1.

2. Have the executives earned their bonuses? What serious effect has the compensation package apparently had on the net assets of Tedtronics? How could Ted have protected himself from what has happened?

Part Four

Accounting for Partnerships and Corporations

In the earlier parts of this book, except for the demonstration using financial statements from General Mills Corporation (Chapter 9), the sole proprietorship has been the major form of business organization discussed.

In Part IV, introductory accounting concepts and practices of partnerships and corporations are presented.

Chapter 15 deals with the formation and liquidation of partnerships, as well as with how income and losses are distributed among partners.

Chapter 16 introduces accounting for the corporate form of business, including the issuance of capital stock and other transactions.

Chapter 17 focuses on accounting for retained earnings, a number of other transactions that affect the stockholders' equity of a corporation, and the parts that make up the corporate income statement.

Chapter 18 introduces the long-term liabilities of corporations, with special attention to accounting for bond liabilities.

Learning
Objectives

Chapter
Fifteen

Accounting
for
Partnerships

1. *Identify the major characteristics of a partnership.*

2. *Identify the advantages and disadvantages of the partnership form of business.*

3. *Record investments of cash and of other assets by the partners in forming a partnership.*

4. *Compute the income or losses that partners share, based on a stated ratio, the capital investment ratio, and salaries and interest to partners.*

5. *Record a person's admission to or withdrawal from a partnership.*

6. *Compute the distribution of assets to partners when they liquidate their partnership.*

In the first half of this book, we used the sole proprietorship to illustrate the basic principles and practices of accounting. This chapter will focus on accounting for the partnership form of business organization. As a result of studying this chapter, you should be able to meet the learning objectives listed on the left.

The Uniform Partnership Act, which has been adopted by most of the states, defines a **partnership** as "an association of two or more persons to carry on as co-owners of a business for profit." Generally, partnerships are formed when owners of small businesses wish to combine capital or managerial talents for some common business purpose.

Partnership Characteristics

Partnerships differ in many ways from other forms of business. The next few paragraphs describe some of the important characteristics of a partnership.

Voluntary Association

A partnership is a voluntary association of individuals rather than a legal entity in itself. Therefore, a partner is responsible under the law for his or her partner's business actions within the scope of the partnership. A partner also has unlimited liability for the debts of the partnership. Because of these potential liabilities, an individual must be allowed to choose the people who will join the partnership. A person should select as partners individuals who share his or her business objectives.

Partnership Agreement

A partnership is easy to form. Two or more competent people simply agree to be partners in some common business purpose. This agreement is known as the partnership agreement and does not have to be in writing. However, good business practice calls for a written document that clearly states the details of the partnership. The contract should include the name, location, and purpose of the business; the partners and their respective duties; the investments of each partner; the methods for distributing profits and losses; the admission or withdrawal of partners; the withdrawals of assets allowed each partner; and procedures for dissolving, or ending, the business.

Limited Life

Because a partnership is formed by a contract between partners, it has limited life: anything that ends the contract dissolves the partnership. A partnership is dissolved when (1) a partner withdraws, (2) a partner goes bankrupt, (3) a partner is incapacitated (as when a partner becomes ill), (4) a partner dies, (5) a new partner is admitted, (6) a partner retires, or (7) the partnership ends according to the partnership agreement (as when a major project is completed).

Mutual Agency

Each partner is an agent of the partnership within the scope of the business. Because of this mutual agency feature, any partner can bind the partnership to a business agreement as long as he or she acts within the scope of normal operations of the business. For example, a partner in a used-car business can bind the partnership through the purchase or sale of used cars. However, this partner cannot bind the partnership to a contract for buying men's clothing or any other goods unrelated to the used-car business. Because of this mutual agency characteristic, it is very important for an individual to choose business partners who have integrity and business objectives similar to his or her own.

Unlimited Liability

Each partner is personally liable for all the debts of the partnership. If a partnership is in poor financial condition and cannot pay its debts, the creditors must first satisfy their claims from the assets of the partnership. When the assets of the business are not enough to pay all debts, the creditors may seek payment from the personal assets of each partner. If a partner's personal assets are used up before the debts are paid, the creditors may claim additional assets from the remaining partners who are able to pay the debts. Each partner could conceivably be required by law to pay all the debts of the partnership; therefore, all the partners have unlimited liability for their company's debt.

Co-ownership of Partnership Property

When individuals invest property in a partnership, they give up the right to their separate use of the property. The property becomes an asset of the partnership and is owned jointly by all the partners.

Participation in Partnership Income

Each partner has the right to share in the company's profits and the responsibility to share in its losses. The partnership agreement should state the method of distributing profits and losses to each partner. If the agreement describes how profits are to be shared but does not mention losses, the losses are distributed in the same way as profits. If the partners fail to describe the method of profit and loss distribution in the partnership agreement, the law states that profits and losses be shared equally.

Summary of the Advantages and Disadvantages of Partnerships

*Objective 2
Identify the
advantages and
disadvantages
of the partner-
ship form of
business*

Partnerships have both advantages and disadvantages. Several of the advantages are that the partnership is easy to form and to dissolve; it is able to pool capital resources and individual talents; it has no corporate tax burden (because the partnership is not a legal entity, it does not have to pay an income tax but must file an informational return); and it gives freedom and flexibility to its partners' actions. Several of the disadvantages of a partnership are that its life is limited; one partner can bind the partnership to a contract (mutual agency); the partners have unlimited personal liability; and it is hard in a partnership to raise large amounts of capital and to transfer ownership interest.

Accounting for Partners' Equity

Accounting for a partnership is very similar to accounting for a sole proprietorship. A major difference is that the owners' equity of a partnership is called **partners' equity.** In accounting for partners' equity, it is necessary to maintain separate capital and withdrawal accounts for each partner and to divide the profits and losses of the company among the partners. The differences in the capital accounts of a sole proprietorship and a partnership are illustrated below.

Sole Proprietorship	Partnership	

Blake, Capital		Desmond, Capital		Frank, Capital	
	50,000		30,000		40,000

Blake, Withdrawals		Desmond, Withdrawals		Frank, Withdrawals	
12,000		5,000		6,000	

In the partners' equity section of the balance sheet, the balance of each partner's capital account is listed separately, as shown in the partial balance sheet below.

Liabilities and Partners' Equity

Total Liabilities		$28,000
Partners' Equity		
Desmond, Capital	$25,000	
Frank, Capital	34,000	
Total Partners' Equity		59,000
Total Liabilities and Partners' Equity		$87,000

Objective 3
Record invest-
ments of cash
and of other
assets by the
partners in
forming a part-
nership

Each partner invests cash, other assets, or a combination of both in the partnership according to the agreement. When other assets are invested, the partners must agree on their value. The value of noncash assets should be their fair market value on the date they are transferred to the partnership. The assets invested by a partner are debited to the proper account, and the total amount is credited to the partner's capital account.

To illustrate the recording of partners' investments, we shall assume that Jerry Adcock and Rose Villa agree to combine their capital and equipment in a partnership for the purpose of operating a jewelry store. Adcock will invest $28,000 cash and $37,000 of furniture and displays, and Villa $40,000 cash and $20,000 of equipment, according to the partnership agreement. The general journal entries that record the initial investments of Adcock and Villa are as follows:

July 1	Cash	28,000	
	Furniture and Displays	37,000	
	Jerry Adcock, Capital		65,000
	To record the initial investment		
	of Jerry Adcock in Adcock and		
	Villa		
July 1	Cash	40,000	
	Equipment	20,000	
	Rose Villa, Capital		60,000
	To record the initial investment		
	of Rose Villa in Adcock and		
	Villa		

The values assigned to the assets in the above illustration would have had to be included in the partnership agreement. These values may differ from those carried on the partners' personal books. For example, the equipment that Rose Villa contributed may have had a value of only $12,000 on her books. However, after she purchased the equipment, its market value increased considerably. Regardless of book value, Villa's investment should be recognized at the fair market value of the equipment at the time of transfer, because that value represents the amount of money that Villa has put into the partnership.

Further investments are recorded in the same way. Also, the partnership may assume liabilities that are related to investments. For example, assume that after three months Rose Villa invests additional equipment with a fair market value of $45,000 in the partnership. Related to the equipment is a note payable for $37,000, which the partnership assumes. The entry that records the transaction is as follows:

Oct. 1	Equipment	45,000	
	Notes Payable		37,000
	Rose Villa, Capital		8,000
	To record additional investment by Rose Villa in Adcock and Villa		

Distribution of Partnership Income and Losses

Objective 4
Compute the
income or losses
that partners
share, based on
a stated ratio,
the capital
investment
ratio, and sala-
ries and interest
to partners

A partnership's income and losses can be distributed according to any method that the partners specify in the partnership agreement. The agreement should be specific and clear to avoid disputes among the partners over later distributions of income and losses. However, if the partnership agreement does not mention the distribution of income and losses, the law requires that they be shared equally by all partners. Also, if the partnership agreement mentions only the distribution of income, the law requires that losses be distributed in the same ratio as income.

The income of a partnership normally has three components: (1) return to the partners for the use of their capital, (2) compensation for services that the partners have rendered, and (3) further economic income for the business risks the partners have taken. The breakdown of total income into its three components helps to clarify how much each partner has contributed to the firm.

If all partners are spending the same amount of time, are contributing equal capital, and have similar managerial talents, then an equal sharing of income and losses would be fair. However, if one partner works full time in the firm whereas another partner devotes only one-fourth of his or her time, then the distribution of income or losses should reflect this difference. This arrangement would apply to any situation in which the partners contribute unequally to the business.

Several ways for partners to share income are (1) by stated ratio, (2) by capital investment ratio, and (3) by salaries to the partners and interest on partners' capital, with the remaining income shared according to a stated ratio.

Stated Ratio

One method of distributing income and losses is to give each partner a stated ratio of the total. If each partner is making an equal contribution to the firm, each may assume the same share of the income and losses. The equal contribution of the partners may take many forms. For example, each partner may have made an equal investment in the firm. On the other hand, one partner may be devoting more time and talent to the firm, whereas the second partner may make a larger capital investment. Also, if the partners contribute unequally to the firm, unequal stated ratios can be appropriate, such as 60 percent, 30 percent, and 10 percent for a partnership of three persons.

To illustrate this method, we shall assume that Adcock and Villa had a net income last year of $30,000. The partnership agreement states that the percentages of income and losses distributed to Adcock and Villa will be 60 and 40, respectively. The computation of each partner's share of the income and the journal entry to show the distribution are as follows:

Adcock ($30,000 × 60%)	$18,000
Villa ($30,000 × 40%)	12,000
Net income	$30,000

June 30	Income Summary	30,000	
	Jerry Adcock, Capital		18,000
	Rose Villa, Capital		12,000
	To distribute the income for the year to the partners' capital accounts		

Capital Investment Ratio

If the invested capital produces the most income for the partnership business, then income and losses may be distributed according to capital investment. One way of distributing income and losses in this case is to use the ratio of capital balances of each partner at the beginning of the year. Another way is to use the average capital balance of each partner during the year.

To show how the first method works, we will assume the following balances for the capital accounts of Adcock and Villa for their first year of operation, which was July 1, 19x1, through June 30, 19x2. Income for the year was $140,000.

Jerry Adcock, Capital		Jerry Adcock, Withdrawals	
	7/1 65,000	1/1 10,000	

Rose Villa, Capital		Rose Villa, Withdrawals	
	7/1 60,000	11/1 10,000	
	2/1 8,000		

Beginning capital balances for Adcock and Villa were as follows:

	Capital	Capital Ratio
Jerry Adcock	$ 65,000	65/125
Rose Villa	60,000	60/125
Total capital	$125,000	

The income that each partner will receive when distribution is based on beginning capital investment ratios is figured by multiplying the total income by each partner's capital ratio.

Jerry Adcock $140,000 × 65/125 = $ 72,800
Rose Villa $140,000 × 60/125 =   67,200
                                            $140,000

The entry showing distribution of income is as follows:

June 30	Income Summary	140,000	
	Jerry Adcock, Capital		72,800
	Rose Villa, Capital		67,200
	To distribute the income for the year to the partners' capital accounts		

If Adcock and Villa use their beginning capital investments to determine the ratio for distributing income, they do not consider any withdrawals or further investments made during the year. However, such investments and withdrawals usually change the partners' capital ratio. Therefore, the partnership agreement should state which capital balances will determine the ratio for distributing income and losses.

If partners believe their capital balances will change very much during the year, they may select their average capital balances as a fairer means of distributing income and losses. To illustrate this method, we will assume that, during the first year, Jerry Adcock withdrew $10,000 on January 1, 19x2, and Rose Villa withdrew $10,000 on November 1, 19x1, and invested the additional $8,000 on February 1, 19x2. The income for the year's operation was $140,000. The calculations for the average capital balances and the distribution of income are as follows:

Average Capital Balances

Partner	Date	Capital Balance	×	Months Unchanged	=	Total	Average Capital
Adcock	7/x1–12/x1	$65,000	×	6	=	$390,000	
	1/x2–6/x2	55,000	×	6	=	330,000	
				12		$720,000 ÷ 12	= $ 60,000
Villa	7/x1–10/x1	$60,000	×	4	=	$240,000	
	11/x1–1/x2	50,000	×	3	=	150,000	
	2/x2–6/x2	58,000	×	5	=	290,000	
				12		$680,000 ÷ 12	= 56,667
						Total average capital	$116,667

Average Capital Balance Ratios

$$\text{Adcock} = \frac{\text{Adcock's average capital balance}}{\text{total average capital}} = \frac{\$60,000}{\$116,667} = 51.4\%$$

$$\text{Villa} = \frac{\text{Villa's average capital balance}}{\text{total average capital}} = \frac{\$56,667}{\$116,667} = 48.6\%$$

Distribution of Income

Partner	Income × Ratio	=	Share of Income
Adcock	$140,000 × 51.4%	=	$ 71,960
Villa	$140,000 × 48.6%	=	68,040
	Total income		$140,000

Note that this calculation calls for determining (1) average capital balances, (2) average capital balance ratios, and (3) each partner's share of income or loss. To figure a partner's average capital balance, it is necessary to examine the changes that have taken place during the year in the partner's capital balance. These changes result from further investments and withdrawals. The partner's beginning capital is multiplied by the number of months the balance remains unchanged. After the balance changes, the new balance is multiplied by the number of months it remains unchanged. This process continues until the end of the year. The totals of these computations are added together, then divided by twelve, to determine the average capital balances. Once the average capital balances are determined, the method of figuring capital balance ratios for sharing income and losses is the same as that used for beginning capital balances.

The entry showing how the earnings for the year are distributed to the partners' capital accounts is as follows:

June 30	Income Summary	140,000	
	Jerry Adcock, Capital		71,960
	Rose Villa, Capital		68,040
	To distribute the income for the year to the partners' capital accounts		

Salaries, Interest, and Stated Ratio

Partners generally do not contribute equally to a firm. To make up for these unequal contributions, some partnership agreements will allow for partners' salaries, interest on partners' capital balances, or a combination of both in the distribution of income. Salaries and interest of this kind are not deducted as expenses before the partnership income is determined. They represent a method of arriving at an equitable distribution of the income or loss.

To illustrate an allowance for partners' salaries, we shall assume that Adcock and Villa agree to the following salaries: $8,000 for Adcock and $7,000 for Villa. Any remaining income will be divided equally. Each salary is charged to the appropriate partner's withdrawal account. If we assume the same $140,000 income for the first year, the calculations and journal entry for Adcock and Villa are shown on the next page.

	Income of Partners		Income Distributed
	Adcock	Villa	
Total Income for Distribution			$140,000
Distribution of Salaries			
Adcock	$ 8,000		
Villa		$ 7,000	15,000
Remaining Income After Salaries			$125,000
Equal Distribution of Remaining Income			
Adcock	62,500		
Villa		62,500	125,000
Remaining Income			—
Income of Partners	$70,500	$69,500	

June 30	Income Summary	140,000	
	Jerry Adcock, Capital		70,500
	Rose Villa, Capital		69,500
	To distribute the income for the year to the partners' capital accounts		

Salaries allow for differences in the services that partners provide to the business. However, they do not consider differences in invested capital. To allow for capital differences, each partner may receive, in addition to salary, a stated interest on his or her invested capital. To illustrate, we will assume that Adcock and Villa agree to receive 10 percent interest on their beginning capital balances as well as annual salaries of $8,000 for Adcock and $7,000 for Villa. They will share any remaining income equally. The calculations for Adcock and Villa, if we assume income of $140,000, are at the top of the next page. The journal entry is

June 30	Income Summary	140,000	
	Jerry Adcock, Capital		70,750
	Rose Villa, Capital		69,250
	To distribute the income for the year to the partners' capital accounts		

If the partnership agreement allows for paying salaries or interest or both, these amounts must be allocated to the partners even if the profits are not enough to cover the salaries and interest. Such a situation would result in the partners' sharing a negative amount after salaries and interest are paid. If the company has a loss, these allocations must still occur. The negative amount after allocation of salaries and interest must be distributed according to the stated ratio in the partnership agreement. If the

| | Income of Partners | | Income Distributed |
	Adcock	Villa	
Total Income for Distribution			$140,000
Distribution of Salaries			
Adcock	$ 8,000		
Villa		$ 7,000	15,000
Remaining Income After Salaries			$125,000
Distribution of Interest			
Adcock ($65,000 × 10%)	6,500		
Villa ($60,000 × 10%)		6,000	12,500
Remaining Income After Salaries and Interest			$112,500
Equal Distribution of Remaining Income			
Adcock	56,250		
Villa		56,250	112,500
Remaining Income			—
Income of Partners	$70,750	$69,250	

agreement does not mention a ratio, the negative amount is distributed equally. To illustrate this situation, we will assume that the partnership of Adcock and Villa agrees to the following conditions for the distribution of income and losses:

	Salaries	**Interest**	**Beginning Capital Balance**
Adcock	$70,000	10 percent of beginning	$65,000
Villa	60,000	capital balances	60,000

The income for the first year of operation was $140,000. The computation for the distribution of the income and loss is shown at the top of the next page. The journal entry is

June 30	Income Summary	140,000	
	Jerry Adcock, Capital		75,250
	Rose Villa, Capital		64,750
	To distribute the income for the year to the partners' capital accounts		

On the income statement for the partnership, the distribution of income or losses is shown below the net income figure. The partial income statement on the next page illustrates this point using the last example.

	Income of Partners		Income Distributed
	Adcock	Villa	
Total Income for Distribution			$140,000
Distribution of Salaries			
Adcock	$70,000		
Villa		$60,000	130,000
Remaining Income After Salaries			$ 10,000
Distribution of Interest			
Adcock ($65,000 × 10%)	6,500		
Villa ($60,000 × 10%)		6,000	12,500
Negative Amount After Distribution of Salaries and Interest			($2,500)
Adcock*	($1,250)		
Villa*		($1,250)	2,500
Remaining Income			—
Income of Partners	$75,250	$64,750	

*Notice that the negative amount was distributed equally because the agreement did not indicate how income and losses would be distributed after salaries and interest were paid.

Adcock and Villa
Partial Income Statement
For the Year Ended June 30, 19xx

Net Income		$140,000
Distribution to the partners		
Adcock		
Salary distribution	$70,000	
Interest on beginning capital balance	6,500	
Total	$76,500	
One-half of remaining negative amount	(1,250)	
Share of net income		$ 75,250
Villa		
Salary distribution	$60,000	
Interest on beginning capital balance	6,000	
Total	$66,000	
One-half of remaining negative amount	(1,250)	
Share of net income		64,750
Net Income Distributed		$140,000

Dissolution of a Partnership

*Objective 5
Record a person's admission to or withdrawal from a partnership*

Dissolution of a partnership occurs when there is a change in the original association of the partners. When a partnership is dissolved, the partners lose their authority to continue the business as a going concern. This does not mean that the business operation is necessarily ended or interrupted. The remaining partners can act for the partnership in finishing the affairs of the business or in forming a new partnership. The dissolution of a partnership through admission of a new partner, withdrawal of a partner, or death of a partner will be discussed next.

Admission of a New Partner

Admission of a new partner will dissolve the old partnership because a new association has been formed. However, the firm cannot admit a new partner without the consent of all the old partners. When a new partner is admitted, a new partnership agreement should describe the new arrangement in detail.

An individual may be admitted into a firm in one of two ways: (1) by purchasing an interest in the partnership from one or more of the original partners, or (2) by investing assets in the partnership.

In the first case, when an individual is admitted to a firm by purchasing an interest from an old partner, each partner must agree to the change. The interest purchased must be transferred from the capital account of the selling partner to the capital account of the new partner.

For example, assume that Jerry Adcock of Adcock and Villa decides to sell his $70,000 interest in the business to Richard Davis for $100,000 on August 31, 19x3. Rose Villa agrees to the sale. The entry that records the sale would be:

Aug. 31	Jerry Adcock, Capital	70,000	
	Richard Davis, Capital		70,000
	To record the transfer of Jerry		
	Adcock's equity to Richard Davis		

Note that the entry above records the book value of the equity and not the amount paid by Davis. The amount that Davis paid is a personal matter between him and Adcock. Because the amount paid did not affect the assets or liabilities of the firm, it should not be entered into the records.

For another example of a purchase, assume that Richard Davis purchases one-half of Jerry Adcock's $70,000 and one-half of Rose Villa's $80,000 interest in the partnership by paying a total of $100,000 to the two partners on August 31, 19x3. The entry that records this transaction follows:

Aug. 31	Jerry Adcock, Capital	35,000	
	Rose Villa, Capital	40,000	
	Richard Davis, Capital		75,000
	To record the transfer of one-		
	half of Jerry Adcock's and Rose		
	Villa's equity to Richard Davis		

In the second case, when a new partner is admitted by an investment in the partnership, both the assets and the owners' equity of the firm are increased. This is so because, in contrast to the case of buying a partner out, the assets that the new partner invests become partnership assets, and this increase in assets creates a corresponding increase in owners' equity. For example, assume that Richard Davis wished to invest $75,000 for a one-third interest in the partnership of Adcock and Villa. The capital accounts of Adcock and Villa are $70,000 and $80,000, respectively. The assets of the firm are correctly valued. Thus the partners agree to admit Davis to a one-third interest in the firm for a $75,000 investment. Davis's $75,000 investment will equal a one-third interest in the firm after the investment is added to the previously existing capital, as shown below.

Adcock, Capital	$ 70,000
Villa, Capital	80,000
Davis's investment	75,000
Total capital after Davis's investment	$225,000

$$\text{One-third interest} = \frac{\$225,000}{3} = \qquad \$ 75,000$$

The entry to record this investment is:

Oct. 1 Cash	75,000	
Richard Davis, Capital		75,000
To record the admission of		
Richard Davis to a one-third		
interest in the company		

Sometimes a partnership is so profitable or otherwise advantageous that a new investor will be willing to pay more than the actual dollar interest that he or she receives in the partnership. An individual may have to pay $100,000 for an $80,000 interest in a partnership. The $20,000 excess of the payment over the interest purchased is considered a **bonus** to the original partners. The bonus should be distributed to the original partners according to their agreement concerning distribution of income and losses.

As an illustration of the bonus method, assume that the Adcock and Villa Company has operated for several years and that the partners' capital balances and the new ratio for distribution of income and loss are as shown below.

Partners	Capital Balances	Stated Ratio
Adcock	$160,000	55%
Villa	140,000	45%
	$300,000	100%

Richard Davis wishes to join the firm, and he offers to invest $100,000 for a one-fifth interest in the business and income. The original partners agree to the offer. The computation of the bonus to the original partners is as follows:

Partners' equity in the original partnership		$300,000
Cash investment by Richard Davis		100,000
Partners' equity in the new partnership		$400,000
Partners' equity assigned to Richard Davis ($400,000 × 1/5)		$ 80,000
Bonus to the original partners		
Investment by Richard Davis	$100,000	
Less equity assigned to Richard Davis	80,000	$ 20,000
Distribution of bonus to original partners		
Jerry Adcock ($20,000 × 55%)	$ 11,000	
Rose Villa ($20,000 × 45%)	9,000	$ 20,000

The journal entry that records the admission of Davis to the partnership is as follows:

Dec. 1	Cash	100,000	
	Jerry Adcock, Capital		11,000
	Rose Villa, Capital		9,000
	Richard Davis, Capital		80,000
	To record the sale of one-fifth interest in the firm to Richard Davis and the bonus he paid to the original partners		

In addition, there are several reasons why a partnership might seek a new partner. For example, a firm in financial trouble might seek additional cash from a new partner. Or the original partners, wishing to expand the firm's markets, might require more capital than they can provide. Also, the partners might know a person who would add a unique talent to the firm. Under these conditions, a new partner may be admitted to the partnership with the understanding that part of the original partners' capital will be transferred to the new partner's capital as a bonus.

For example, assume that Adcock and Villa have invited Richard Davis to join the firm. Davis is to invest $60,000 for a one-fourth interest in the company's capital and income. The capital balances of Adcock and Villa are $160,000 and $140,000, respectively. If Davis is to receive a one-fourth interest in the firm, the interest of the original partners represents a three-fourths interest in the business. The computation of the bonus to Davis follows.

Total equity in partnership	
Adcock, Capital	$160,000
Villa, Capital	140,000
Investment by Richard Davis	60,000
Partners' equity in the new partnership	$360,000
Partners' equity assigned to Richard Davis ($360,000 × 1/4)	$ 90,000

Bonus
    One-fourth interest, Richard Davis $90,000
    Cash investment by Richard Davis   60,000 $ 30,000

Distribution from original partners
    Jerry Adcock ($30,000 × 55%) $16,500
    Rose Villa ($30,000 × 45%)   13,500 $ 30,000

The journal entry that records the admission of Davis to the partnership is as follows:

Sept. 1	Cash	60,000	
	Jerry Adcock, Capital	16,500	
	Rose Villa, Capital	13,500	
	Richard Davis, Capital		90,000
	To record the investment of Richard Davis of cash and a bonus		

Withdrawal of a Partner

A partner has the right to withdraw from a partnership whenever he or she chooses. To avoid any disputes when a partner does decide to withdraw or retire from the firm, the partnership agreement should describe the appropriate actions to be taken. The agreement may specify (1) whether or not an audit will be performed by CPAs, (2) how the assets will be reappraised, (3) how a bonus is to be determined, and (4) by what method the withdrawing partner will be paid.

There are several ways in which a partner may withdraw from a partnership. For example, a partner may (1) sell his or her interest to an outsider with the consent of the remaining partners, (2) sell his or her interest to another partner with the consent of the remaining partners, (3) withdraw assets that are equal to his or her capital balance, (4) withdraw assets that are greater than his or her capital balance (in this case the withdrawing partner must receive a bonus), or (5) withdraw assets that are less than his or her capital balance (in this case the remaining partners must receive a bonus). These alternatives are illustrated in Figure 15-1.

When a partner sells his or her interest to an outsider or to another partner with the consent of the other partners, the transaction is personal and does not change the partnership assets or the owners' equity. For example, we will assume that the capital balances of Adcock, Villa, and Davis are $140,000, $100,000, and $60,000, respectively, for a total of $300,000.

Villa is withdrawing from the partnership and is reviewing two offers for her interest. The offers are to (1) sell her interest to Judy Jones for $120,000 or (2) sell her interest to Davis for $110,000. The remaining partners have agreed to either potential transaction. Because Jones and Davis will pay for Villa's interest from their personal assets, the partnership accounting records will show only the transfer of Villa's interest to

Figure 15-1
Alternative
Ways for a
Partner to
Withdraw

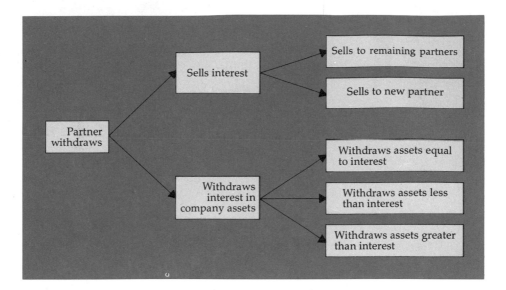

Jones or Davis. The entries that record these possible transfers are as follows:

1. If Villa's interest is purchased by Jones:

Rose Villa, Capital	100,000	
Judy Jones, Capital		100,000
To record sale of Villa's partner-		
ship interest to Jones		

2. If Villa's interest is purchased by Davis:

Rose Villa, Capital	100,000	
Richard Davis, Capital		100,000
To record sale of Villa's partner-		
ship interest to Davis		

A partnership agreement may state that a withdrawing partner is allowed to remove assets from the firm equal to his or her capital balance. Assume that Richard Davis decides to withdraw from Adcock, Villa, Davis & Company. Davis's capital balance is $60,000, and the partnership agreement states that he may withdraw cash from the firm equal to his capital balance. If there is not enough cash, he is to accept a promissory note from the new partnership for the balance. The remaining partners of the firm request that Davis take only $50,000 in cash because of a cash shortage at the time of his withdrawal. He agrees to this condition. The journal entry that records Davis's withdrawal is as follows:

Jan. 21	Richard Davis, Capital	60,000	
	Cash		50,000
	Notes Payable, Richard Davis		10,000
	To record the withdrawal of		
	Richard Davis from the		
	partnership		

Partners can make an alternative arrangement if the partnership agreement states that the assets of the business must be reappraised and any gain or loss distributed to the partners and that the withdrawing partner must remove assets equal to his or her new capital balance. To illustrate this condition, we will assume that the partnership agreement of Adcock, Villa, Davis & Company calls for an audit and that the assets must be revalued before a partner can withdraw. After the assets are revalued, the withdrawing partner is allowed to remove cash, or cash plus a promissory note, equal to his or her capital balance. Davis, whose current capital balance is $60,000, decides to withdraw from the firm. According to the partnership agreement, an audit and revaluation of the assets are to be carried out. The current balances of the Equipment account and the Accumulated Depreciation account are $26,000 and $9,000, respectively. The results of the audit show that the inventory was undervalued by $10,000 and that Equipment should be valued at $30,000 and Accumulated Depreciation at $10,000.

The increase in inventory would have to be recorded and the increase shared by the partners according to their stated ratio. Also, the Equipment account would be increased by $4,000 and Accumulated Depreciation on the equipment by $1,000, or a net increase of $3,000, which would also be shared by the partners in their stated ratio. Adcock's, Villa's, and Davis's percentage of profits and losses are 40, 40, and 20, respectively. If Davis withdraws $50,000 cash plus a note, the entries that record the revaluation of the assets and Davis's withdrawal are as follows:

Mar. 1	Merchandise Inventory	10,000	
	Jerry Adcock, Capital		4,000
	Rose Villa, Capital		4,000
	Richard Davis, Capital		2,000
	To record the revaluation of inventory and to distribute the gain to the partners in their stated ratios		
1	Equipment	4,000	
	Accumulated Depreciation, Equipment		1,000
	Jerry Adcock, Capital		1,200
	Rose Villa, Capital		1,200
	Richard Davis, Capital		600
	To record the revaluation of the equipment and to distribute the gain to the partners in their stated ratios		
1	Richard Davis, Capital	62,600	
	Cash		50,000
	Notes Payable, Richard Davis		12,600
	To record the withdrawal of Richard Davis from the partnership		

Note that any gain or loss on revaluation of the firm's assets is distributed to the partners' capital accounts according to their stated ratio.

A partner may withdraw from a firm and remove assets that are greater than the book value of his or her capital balance. However, the partnership agreement need not require an audit and revaluation of the assets before the partner withdraws. If the firm has been successful, the business will normally be worth more than its book value. A withdrawing partner who recognizes this fact will request more than his or her capital balance upon withdrawal. A withdrawing partner might also receive assets greater than his or her capital if the other partners have asked him or her to withdraw. Rather than revalue the assets and incur the costs of an audit, the remaining partners may agree to give the withdrawing partner a bonus.

When a partner withdraws assets greater than his or her capital balance, the excess may be treated as a bonus. The remaining partners then absorb the bonus according to their stated ratio.

To illustrate, we will assume that the partnership agreement of Adcock, Villa, Davis & Company states that when a partner withdraws at the request of the remaining partners, the withdrawing partner will receive a bonus. Because Adcock and Villa are having difficulty with Davis, they ask him to withdraw from the firm. Adcock and Villa are willing to allow Davis to withdraw $70,000 in cash from the company for his $60,000 interest in the business. Davis agrees to this arrangement and withdraws from the firm. The stated ratios of Adcock, Villa, and Davis are 40, 40, and 20, respectively. The entry that records the withdrawal of Davis follows:

Nov. 16	Richard Davis, Capital	60,000	
	Jerry Adcock, Capital	5,000	
	Rose Villa, Capital	5,000	
	Cash		70,000
	To record the withdrawal of Richard Davis from the partnership		

Sometimes a partner may wish to withdraw from a firm quickly, or at a time when the assets of the firm are overvalued. In such cases, the withdrawing partner may take out assets that represent less than his or her capital balance. A partner who withdraws under these conditions leaves a part of his or her capital in the business. The remaining partners will divide the remaining equity according to their stated ratios. This distribution is considered a bonus to the remaining partners.

To illustrate, we will assume that Richard Davis of Adcock, Villa, Davis & Company plans to withdraw from the firm. Because he is very eager to leave the partnership, he plans to withdraw assets that represent less than his capital balance. Davis, whose current capital balance is $60,000, and the remaining partners agree that he should withdraw $40,000 when he leaves the firm. Adcock's, Villa's, and Davis's current stated ratios are 40, 40, and 20, respectively. The computation of the bonus and the entry that records Davis's withdrawal are as follows:

Bonus to remaining partners	
Davis, Capital	$60,000
Less assets to be withdrawn	40,000
Bonus to remaining partners	$20,000

Distribution of bonus to remaining partners	
Adcock ($20,000 × 4/8)	$10,000
Villa ($20,000 × 4/8)	10,000
Total	$20,000

Feb. 16	Richard Davis, Capital	60,000	
	Cash		40,000
	Jerry Adcock, Capital		10,000
	Rose Villa, Capital		10,000
	To record the withdrawal of Davis		

Death of a Partner

When a partner dies, the partnership is dissolved because the original association has changed. The partnership agreement should state the action to be taken upon the death of a partner. Normally the books will be closed and financial statements will be prepared. These actions are necessary to determine the capital balance of each of the partners at the date of the death. The agreement may also indicate whether or not an audit should be conducted, assets appraised, and a bonus recorded, as well as the procedures for settling with the heirs of the deceased partner. The conditions for settling with the heirs may be that the remaining partners purchase the deceased's equity, sell it to outsiders, or deliver certain business assets to the estate. If the firm intends to continue, a new partnership must be formed.

Liquidation of a Partnership

*Objective 6
Compute the
distribution of
assets to part-
ners when they
liquidate their
partnership*

Liquidation of a partnership is the process of ending a business, which entails selling enough assets to pay the liabilities and distributing any remaining assets among the partners. Unlike the case of dissolution, if a partnership is liquidated, the business will not continue.

The partnership agreement should indicate the procedures to be followed in the case of liquidation. Normally, the books should be adjusted and closed, with the income or loss being distributed to the partners. As the assets of the business are sold, any gain or loss should be distributed among the partners according to the established stated ratio. As cash becomes available, it must be applied first to outside creditors, then to partners' loans, and finally to the partners' capital balances.

The process of liquidation may have a variety of financial results. However, we will describe only the following three: (1) assets sold for a gain, (2) assets sold for a loss but absorbed by capital balances, and (3) assets sold for a loss when a partner's capital balance is insufficient to absorb the loss. For each alternative we will assume that the books have been closed for Adcock, Villa, Davis & Company and that the following balance sheet exists prior to liquidation:

Adcock, Villa, Davis & Company
Balance Sheet
February 2, 19xx

Assets		Liabilities and Partners' Equity	
Cash	$ 60,000	Accounts Payable	$120,000
Accounts Receivable	40,000	Adcock, Capital	85,000
Merchandise Inventory	100,000	Villa, Capital	95,000
Plant Assets (net)	200,000	Davis, Capital	100,000
Total Assets	$400,000	Total Liabilities and Partners' Equity	$400,000

The stated ratios of Adcock, Villa, and Davis will be 30, 30, and 40, respectively.

Gain on Sale of Assets

Let us assume that the following transactions occurred in the liquidation of Adcock, Villa, Davis & Company. The accounts receivable were collected for $35,000, and the inventory and plant assets were sold for $110,000 and $200,000, respectively. After the accounts payable were paid off, the partners shared the remaining cash. These transactions are summarized in the statement of liquidation in Figure 15-2 (next page). The journal entries that record the transactions are shown here and on the next two pages.

	Journal Entries		Explanation on Statement of Liquidation	
Feb. 13	Cash	35,000		1
	Gain or Loss from Realization	5,000		
	Accounts Receivable		40,000	
	To record collection of accounts receivable			
14	Cash	110,000		2
	Merchandise Inventory		100,000	
	Gain or Loss from Realization		10,000	
	To record the sale of inventory			

Adcock, Villa, Davis & Company
Statement of Liquidation
February 2–20, 19xx

	Explanation	Cash	Other Assets	Accounts Payable	Adcock, Capital (30%)	Villa, Capital (30%)	Davis, Capital (40%)	Gain (or Loss) from Realization
	Balance 2/2	$ 60,000	$340,000	$120,000	$ 85,000	$ 95,000	$100,000	
1.	Collection of Accounts Receivable	35,000	(40,000)					($5,000)
		$ 95,000	$300,000	$120,000	$ 85,000	$ 95,000	$100,000	($ 5,000)
2.	Sale of Inventory	110,000	(100,000)					10,000
		$205,000	$200,000	$120,000	$ 85,000	$ 95,000	$100,000	$ 5,000
3.	Sale of Plant Assets	200,000	(200,000)					
		$405,000	—	$120,000	$ 85,000	$ 95,000	$100,000	$ 5,000
4.	Payment of Liabilities	(120,000)		(120,000)				
		$285,000		—	$ 85,000	$ 95,000	$100,000	$ 5,000
5.	Distribution of Gain or Loss from Realization				1,500	1,500	2,000	(5,000)
		$285,000			$ 86,500	$ 96,500	$102,000	—
6.	Distribution to Partners	(285,000)			(86,500)	(96,500)	(102,000)	
		—			—	—	—	

Figure 15-2 Statement of Liquidation Showing Gain on Sale of Assets

Feb. 16	Cash	200,000		3
	Plant Assets		200,000	
	To record the sale of plant assets			
16	Accounts Payable	120,000		4
	Cash		120,000	
	To record the payment of accounts payable			
20	Gain or Loss from Realization	5,000		5
	Jerry Adcock, Capital		1,500	
	Rose Villa, Capital		1,500	
	Richard Davis, Capital		2,000	
	To record the distribution of the gain on assets ($10,000 gain minus $5,000 loss) to the partners			

20	Jerry Adcock, Capital	86,500	
	Rose Villa, Capital	96,500	
	Richard Davis, Capital	102,000	
	Cash		285,000

To record the distribution of
cash to the partners

Note that cash distributed to the partners is the balance in their respective capital accounts. Cash is *not* distributed according to the partners' stated ratio.

Loss on Sale of Assets

We will discuss two cases in which there are losses on the sale of the company's assets. In the first case, the losses are small enough to be absorbed by the partners' capital balances. In the second case, one partner's share of the losses is too large for his or her capital balance to absorb.

When a firm's assets are sold at a loss, the partners will share the loss on liquidation according to their stated ratio. As an example of this situation, assume that during the liquidation of Adcock, Villa, Davis & Company, the total cash received from the collection of accounts receivable and the sale of inventory and plant assets was $140,000. The statement of liquidation appears in Figure 15-3 (next page), and the journal entries for the transaction are shown below and on the next page.

Journal Entries			**Explanation on Statement of Liquidation** ⟶	
Feb. 15	Cash	140,000		1
	Gain or Loss from Realization	200,000		
	Accounts Receivable		40,000	
	Merchandise Inventory		100,000	
	Plant Assets		200,000	
	To record the collection of accounts receivable and the sale of the other assets			
16	Accounts Payable	120,000		2
	Cash		120,000	
	To record the payment of accounts payable			
20	Jerry Adcock, Capital	60,000		3
	Rose Villa, Capital	60,000		
	Richard Davis, Capital	80,000		
	Gain or Loss from Realization		200,000	
	To record the distribution of the loss on assets to the partners			

Adcock, Villa, Davis & Company
Statement of Liquidation
February 2–20, 19xx

Explanation	Cash	Other Assets	Accounts Payable	Adcock, Capital (30%)	Villa, Capital (30%)	Davis, Capital (40%)	Gain (or Loss) from Realization
Balance 2/2	$ 60,000	$340,000	$120,000	$ 85,000	$ 95,000	$100,000	
1. Collection of Accounts Receivable and Sale of Inventory and Plant Assets	140,000	(340,000)					($200,000)
	$200,000	—	$120,000	$ 85,000	$ 95,000	$100,000	($200,000)
2. Payment of Liabilities	(120,000)		(120,000)				
	$ 80,000		—	$ 85,000	$ 95,000	$100,000	($200,000)
3. Distribution of Gain or Loss from Realization				(60,000)	(60,000)	(80,000)	200,000
	$80,000			$ 25,000	$ 35,000	$ 20,000	—
4. Distribution to Partners	(80,000)			(25,000)	(35,000)	(20,000)	
	—			—	—	—	

**Figure 15-3
Statement of
Liquidation
Showing Loss
on Sale of
Assets**

Feb. 20	Jerry Adcock, Capital		25,000		4
	Rose Villa, Capital		35,000		
	Richard Davis, Capital		20,000		
	Cash			80,000	
	To record the distribution of cash to the partners				

In some liquidation cases, a partner's share of the losses is greater than his or her capital balance. In this situation, the partner must make up the deficit in his or her capital account from personal assets. For example, assume that after the sale of assets and the payment of liabilities the following conditions exist during the liquidation of Adcock, Villa, Davis & Company:

Assets		
Cash		$30,000
Partners' Equity		
Adcock, Capital	$25,000	
Villa, Capital	20,000	
Davis, Capital	(15,000)	$30,000

Richard Davis must pay $15,000 into the partnership from personal funds to cover his deficit. If we assume that he paid cash to the partnership, the following entry would record his cash contribution:

Feb. 20	Cash	15,000	
	Richard Davis, Capital		15,000
	To record the additional		
	investment of Richard Davis		
	to cover his liquidation losses		

After Davis's payment of $15,000, there is sufficient cash to pay Adcock and Villa their capital balances and thus to complete the liquidation. This transaction is recorded as follows:

Feb. 20	Jerry Adcock, Capital	25,000	
	Rose Villa, Capital	20,000	
	Cash		45,000
	To record the distribution of		
	cash to the partners		

During liquidation, a partner might not have any additional cash to cover his or her obligations to the partnership. When this situation occurs, the remaining partners must share the loss according to their established stated ratio. This procedure is necessary because all partners have unlimited liability, which is characteristic of a partnership. Assume that Richard Davis cannot pay the $15,000 deficit in his capital account. Adcock and Villa must share the deficit according to the stated ratio. Their percentages are 30 and 30, respectively. Therefore, they will each pay 50 percent of the losses that Davis cannot pay. The new stated ratio for Adcock and Villa is computed as follows:

	Old Ratios	New Ratios	
Adcock	30%	30/60 =	50%
Villa	30%	30/60 =	50%
	60%		100%

The journal entries that record these transactions are as follows:

Feb. 20	Jerry Adcock, Capital	7,500	
	Rose Villa, Capital	7,500	
	Richard Davis, Capital		15,000
	To record the transfer of Davis's		
	deficit to Adcock and Villa		

Feb. 20	Jerry Adcock, Capital	17,500	
	Rose Villa, Capital	12,500	
	Cash		30,000
	To record the cash distribution		
	to the partners		

Richard Davis's inability to meet his obligations at the time of liquidation does not relieve him of his liabilities to Adcock and Villa. If he is able to pay his liabilities sometime in the future, Adcock and Villa may collect the amounts of Davis's deficit that they absorbed.

Chapter Review

Review of Learning Objectives

1. Identify the major characteristics of a partnership.

The partnership form of business organization has several major characteristics that distinguish it from other forms of business. A partnership is a voluntary association of two or more persons who combine their talents and resources for the purpose of making a profit. This joint effort should be supported by a partnership agreement, which specifies the details of operation for the partnership. A partnership is easily dissolved by the admission, withdrawal, or death of a partner, and therefore has a limited life. In addition, each partner acts as an agent of the partnership within the scope of normal operations of the business and is personally liable for the partnership's debts.

2. Identify the advantages and disadvantages of the partnership form of business.

The advantages are ease of formation and dissolution, the opportunity to pool several individuals' talents and resources, the freedom of action each partner enjoys, and no tax burden. The disadvantages are the limited life of the partnership, the unlimited personal liability of the partners, the difficulty of transferring partners' interest and of raising large amounts of capital, and the risk inherent in each partner's being able to bind the partnership to a contract.

3. Record investments of cash and of other assets by the partners in forming a partnership.

Normally a partnership is formed when the partners contribute cash, other assets, or a combination of both to the business in accordance with the partnership agreement. The recording of initial investments entails a debit to the Cash or other asset account and a credit to the investing partner's capital account. The recorded amount of the other assets should be their fair value on the date of transfer to the partnership. In addition, a partnership may assume the investing partner's liabilities. When this occurs, the partner's capital account is credited with the difference between the assets invested and the liabilities assumed.

4. Compute the income or losses that partners share, based on a stated ratio, the capital investment ratio, and salaries and interest to partners.

The partners should share income and losses in accordance with the partnership agreement. If the agreement says nothing about the distribution of income and loss, the partners will share them equally. Some common methods used for distributing income and losses to partners include the use of stated ratios or capital investment ratios, and the payment of salaries and interest on capital investments. Each method tries to measure the contributions of each partner to the operations of the business. A stated ratio is usually based on the partners' relative contribution of effort to the partnership. If the capital investment ratio is used, the income (or losses) is divided strictly on the amount of capital provided to the partnership by each partner. The use of salaries and interest on capital investment takes into account both efforts (salary) and capital investment (interest) in dividing income (or losses) among the partners.

5. Record a person's admission to or withdrawal from a partnership.

An individual is admitted to a partnership by purchasing a partner's interest or by contributing additional assets. When an interest is purchased, the old partner's capital is transferred to the new partner. When the new partner contributes assets to the partnership, it may be necessary to recognize a bonus to be shared or borne by the old partners.

When a partner withdraws from a partnership, the partner either sells his or her interest in the business or withdraws company assets. When assets are withdrawn, the amount can be equal to, greater than, or less than the partner's capital interest. When assets that have a value greater than or less than the partner's interest are withdrawn, a bonus is recognized and distributed among the appropriate partners.

6. Compute the distribution of assets to partners when they liquidate their partnership.
Liquidation of a partnership entails selling the assets necessary to pay the company's liabilities, then distributing any remaining assets to the partners. Any gain or loss in the sale of the assets is shared by the partners according to their stated ratio. When a partner has a deficit balance in a capital account, that partner must contribute personal assets equal to the deficit. When a partner does not have personal assets to cover a capital deficit, the deficit must be absorbed by the solvent partners according to their stated ratio.

Review Problem
Distribution of Income and Admission of Partner

Jack Holder and Dan Williams reached an agreement in 19x7 to pool their resources for the purpose of forming a partnership to manufacture and sell university T-shirts. In forming the partnership, Holder and Williams contributed $100,000 and $150,000, respectively. They drafted a partnership agreement stating that Holder was to receive an annual salary of $6,000 and Williams was to receive 3 percent interest annually on his original investment in the business. Income and losses after salary and interest were to be shared by Holder and Williams in a 2:3 ratio.

Required

1. Compute the income or loss that Holder and Williams share, and prepare the required journal entries, assuming the following income and loss before salary and interest: 19x7—$27,000 income; 19x8—$2,000 loss.
2. Assume that Jean Ratcliffe offers Holder and Williams $60,000 for a 15 percent interest in the partnership on January 1, 19x9. Holder and Williams agree to Ratcliffe's offer because they need her resources to expand the business. The capital balances of Holder and Williams are $113,600 and $161,400, respectively, on January 1, 19x9. Record the admission of Ratcliffe to the partnership, assuming that her investment is to represent a 15 percent interest in the total partners' capital and that a bonus is to be given to Holder and Williams in the ratio of 2:3.

Answer to Review Problem

1. Income distribution to partners computed:

	Income of Partner		Income Distributed
	Holder	Williams	
19x7			
Total Income for Distribution			$27,000
Distribution of Salary			
Holder	$ 6,000		6,000
Remaining Income After Salary			$21,000
Distribution of Interest			
Williams ($150,000 × 3%)		4,500	4,500
Remaining Income After Salary and Interest			$16,500
Distribution of Remaining Income			
Holder ($16,500 × 2/5)	6,600		
Williams ($16,500 × 3/5)		9,900	16,500
Remaining Income			—
Income of Partners	$12,600	$14,400	
19x8			
Total Income for Distribution			($2,000)
Distribution of Salary			
Holder	$ 6,000		6,000
Remaining Loss After Salary			($8,000)
Distribution of Interest			
Williams ($150,000 × 3%)		$ 4,500	4,500
Negative Amount After Distribution of Salary and Interest			($12,500)
Distribution of Remaining Loss in Profit/Loss Ratio			
Holder ($12,500 × 2/5)	(5,000)		
Williams ($12,500 × 3/5)		(7,500)	(12,500)
Remaining Income			—
Income of Partners	$ 1,000	($3,000)	

Journal entry—19x7

Income Summary	27,000	
Jack Holder, Capital		12,600
Dan Williams, Capital		14,400
To record the distribution (based on salary, interest, and stated ratio) of $27,000 profit for 19x7		

Journal entry—19x8

Dan Williams, Capital	3,000	
Income Summary		2,000
Jack Holder, Capital		1,000
To record the distribution (based on salary, interest, and stated ratio) of $2,000 loss for 19x8		

2. Admission of new partner recorded:

19x9			
Jan. 1	Cash	60,000	
	Jack Holder, Capital		3,900
	Dan Williams, Capital		5,850
	Jean Ratcliffe, Capital		50,250

To record the $60,000 cash investment by Jean Ratcliffe for a 15 percent interest in the partnership, a bonus being allocated to original partners

Computation

Ratcliffe, Capital = (original partners' capital + investment) × 15 percent
= ($113,600 + $161,400 + $60,000) × 15% = $50,250
Bonus = investment − Ratcliffe, Capital
= $60,000 − $50,250 = $9,750

Distribution of bonus:
Holder = $9,750 × 2/5 = $3,900
Williams = $9,750 × 3/5 = $5,850

Total bonus $9,750

Chapter Assignments

Questions

1. Briefly define a partnership, and list several major characteristics of the partnership form of business.

2. What is the meaning of unlimited liability when applied to a partnership?

3. Abe and Bill are partners in a drilling operation. Abe purchased a drilling rig to be used in the partnership's operations. Is this purchase binding on Bill even though he was not involved in it?

4. The partnership agreement for Karla and Jean's partnership does not disclose how they will share income and losses. How would the income and losses be shared in this partnership?

5. What are several major advantages of a partnership? What are some possible disadvantages?

6. Edward contributes $10,000 in cash and a building with a book value of $40,000 and fair market value of $50,000 to the Edward and Francis partnership. What is the balance of Edward's capital account in the partnership if the building is recorded at its fair market value?

7. Gayle and Henry share income and losses in their partnership in a 3:2 ratio. The firm's net income for the current year is $80,000. How would the distribution of income be recorded in the journal?

8. Irene purchases Jane's interest in the Jane and Kane partnership for $62,000. Jane has a $57,000 capital interest in the partnership. How would this transaction be recorded in the partnership books?

9. Larry and Madison each own a $50,000 interest in a partnership. They agree to admit Nancy as a partner by selling her a one-third interest for $80,000. How large a bonus will be distributed to Larry and Madison?

10. Opel and Paul share income in their partnership in a 2:4 ratio. Opel and Paul receive salaries of $6,000 and $10,000, respectively. How would they share a net income before salaries of $22,000?

11. In the liquidation of a partnership, Robert's capital account showed a $5,000 deficit balance after all the creditors were paid. What obligation does Robert have to the partnership?

12. Describe how a dissolution of a partnership may differ from a liquidation of a partnership.

13. Tom Howard and Sharon Thomas are forming a partnership. What are some of the factors they should consider in deciding how income might be divided?

Classroom Exercises

Exercise 15-1
Partnership
Formation
(L.O. 3)

Charles Rossi and Phil Stem are electricians who wish to form a partnership and open a business. They have their attorney prepare their partnership agreement, which indicates that assets invested in the partnership will be recorded at their fair market value. The assets contributed by each partner and their fair market value are as follows:

Assets	Charles Rossi	Phil Stem	Total
Cash	$40,000	$30,000	$70,000
Accounts Receivable	52,000	20,000	72,000
Allowance for Uncollectible			
Accounts	(4,000)	(3,000)	(7,000)
Supplies	1,000	500	1,500
Equipment	20,000	10,000	30,000
Accounts Payable	(32,000)	(9,000)	(41,000)

Prepare the journal entry necessary to record the original investments of Rossi and Stem in the partnership.

Exercise 15-2
Distribution of
Income and
Losses
(L.O. 4)

Jack O'Grady and Mary Foster agreed to form a partnership. O'Grady contributed $50,000 in cash, and Foster contributed assets with a fair market value of $100,000. The partnership was very successful in its initial year and reported income of $30,000.

Determine how the partners would share the first year's income, and prepare the journal entry to distribute the income to the partners under each of the following conditions: (1) O'Grady and Foster failed to include stated ratios in the partnership agreement. (2) O'Grady and Foster agreed to share the income and losses in a 3:2 ratio. (3) O'Grady and Foster agreed to share the income and losses in the ratio of original investments. (4) O'Grady and Foster agreed to share the income and losses by allowing 10 percent interest on original investments and sharing any remainder equally.

Exercise 15-3
Distribution of
Income—Salary
and Interest
(L.O. 4)

Assume that the partnership agreement of O'Grady and Foster in Exercise 15-2 states that O'Grady and Foster are to receive salaries of $5,000 and $6,000, respectively; that O'Grady is to receive 6 percent interest on his capital balance at the beginning of the year; and that the remainder of income and losses are to be shared equally.

Prepare the journal entries for distributing the income under the following conditions: (1) Income totaled $30,000 before deductions for salaries and interest. (2) Income totaled $12,000 before deductions for salaries and interest.

Exercise 15-4
Admission of
New Partner—
Bonus to Old
Partners
(L.O. 5)

Larry, Steve, and Todd have equities in a partnership of $40,000, $40,000, and $60,000, respectively, and share income and losses in a ratio of 1:1:3. The partners have agreed to admit Devin to the partnership.

Prepare journal entries to record the admission of Devin to the partnership under the following assumptions: (1) Devin invests $60,000 for a one-fifth interest in the partnership, and a bonus is recorded for the original partners. (2) Devin invests $60,000 for a 40 percent interest in the partnership, and a bonus is recorded for Devin.

Exercise 15-5
Partnership
Liquidation
(L.O. 6)

Assume the following assets, liabilities, and owners' equity of the Redd and McPhee partnership on December 31, 19xx:

Assets = Liabilities + Redd, Capital + McPhee, Capital
$40,000 = $2,500 + $22,500 + $15,000

When the partners agree to liquidate the business, the assets are sold for $30,000 and the liabilities are paid. Redd and McPhee share income and losses in a ratio of 3:1.

1. What is the final cash distribution to the partners after liquidation?
2. Prepare journal entries for the sale of assets, payment of liabilities, distribution of loss from realization, and final distribution of cash to Redd and McPhee.

Exercise 15-6
Withdrawal of
Partner
(L.O. 5)

Kenneth, Tobey, and Miles are partners who share income and losses in the ratio of 3:2:1. Miles's capital account has a $40,000 balance. Kenneth and Tobey have agreed to let Miles take $50,000 of the company's cash when he retires.
   What journal entry must be made on the partnership's books when Miles retires, assuming that a bonus to Miles is recognized and absorbed by the remaining partners?

Interpreting Accounting Information

Meriweather
Clinic
(L.O. 2, 4)

The Meriweather Clinic is owned and operated by ten local doctors. The balance sheet for 19xx is shown below.

Meriweather Clinic
Balance Sheet
December 31, 19xx

Assets

Current Assets		
Cash	$ 50,000	
Short-Term Investments	12,000	
Accounts Receivable	26,000	
Unbilled Services	10,000	
Other	5,000	
Total Current Assets		$103,000
Property, Plant, and Equipment		
Buildings	$ 85,000	
Furniture and Equipment	35,000	
	$120,000	
Less Accumulated Depreciation	45,000	
Total Property, Plant, and Equipment		75,000
Total Assets		$178,000

Liabilities and Partners' Equity

Current Liabilities			
Notes Payable	$ 15,700		
Current Portion of Long-Term Debt	20,000		
Accounts Payable	5,600		
Salaries Payable	4,500		
Other	2,000		
Total Current Liabilities		$ 47,800	
Long-Term Debt		75,000	
Total Liabilities			$122,800
Partners' Equity		$ 55,200	
Total Liabilities and Partners' Equity			$178,000

Recently, several patients have sued the clinic for malpractice for a total of $1,000,000. There is no mention of these suits in the partnership's financial statements.

Required

1. How should information on these lawsuits be disclosed in the December 31, 19xx, financial statements of the partnership?
2. Assume that the clinic settles out of court for a payment by the clinic of $70,000 from Cash and Short-term Investments. What will be the effect of this payment on the clinic's December 31, 19xx, financial statements? Discuss the effect of the settlement on the doctors' personal financial returns.

Problem Set A

**Problem 15A-1
Partnership
Formation and
Distribution of
Income
(L.O. 3, 4)**

On January 1, 19x1, Nancy James and Leilani Widner agreed to form a partnership to establish a children's clothing store in their neighborhood. James and Widner invested cash of $120,000 and $80,000, respectively, in the partnership. The business had normal first-year problems, but during the second year the operation was very successful. For 19x1 they reported a $40,000 loss, and for 19x2 a $120,000 income.

Required

1. Prepare the journal entry to record both partners' investments.
2. Determine James's and Widner's share of the income or loss for each year, assuming each of the following methods of sharing income and losses: (a) The partners agreed to share income and losses equally. (b) The partners agreed to share income and losses in the ratio of 7:3 for James and Widner, respectively. (c) The partners agreed to share income according to their original capital investments ratio, but the agreement did not mention losses. (d) The partners agreed to share income and losses in the ratio of their capital investments at the beginning of the year. (e) The partners agreed to share income and losses by allowing interest of 10 percent on original investments and dividing the remainder equally. (f) The partners agreed to share income and losses by allowing interest of 10 percent on original investments, paying salaries of $30,000 to James and $20,000 to Widner, and dividing the remainder equally.

Problem 15A-2
Distribution
of Income—
Salaries and
Interest
(L.O. 4)

Kevin, Roy, and Don are partners in the You-Do-It Photo Company. The partnership agreement states that Kevin is to receive 6 percent interest on his capital investment at the beginning of the year, Roy is to receive a salary of $20,000 a year, and Don will be paid interest of 5 percent on his average capital balance during the year. Kevin, Roy, and Don will share any income or loss after salaries and interest in a 5:3:2 ratio. Kevin's capital investment at the beginning of the year was $120,000, and Don's average capital balance for the year was $140,000.

Required

Determine each partner's share of income and losses under each of the following assumptions: (1) The income was $234,200. (2) The income was $28,200. (3) The loss was $18,600.

Problem 15A-3
Admission of a
Partner
(L.O. 5)

DeHaan, Johnson, and Baskin are partners in the Cookie Machine. The balances in the capital accounts of DeHaan, Johnson, and Baskin as of September 30, 19xx, are $10,000, $15,000, and $25,000, respectively. The partners share income and losses in a ratio of 2:3:5.

Required

Prepare journal entries for each of the following conditions: (1) Stuart pays Baskin $25,000 for four-fifths of Baskin's interest. (2) Stuart is to be admitted to the partnership with a one-third interest for a $25,000 cash investment. (3) Stuart is to be admitted to the partnership with a one-third interest for a $40,000 cash investment. A bonus is to be distributed to the original partners when Stuart is admitted. (4) Stuart is to be admitted to the partnership with a one-third interest for a $20,500 cash investment. A bonus is to be given to Stuart upon admission.

Problem 15A-4
Partnership
Liquidation
(L.O. 6)

Tomi and Dutton are partners in a video game parlor. Business has declined recently because alternative kinds of entertainment have become available in the community. Thus Tomi and Dutton agree to liquidate their business, in which they have shared income in a 3:2 ratio. The balance sheet prior to liquidation is as follows:

Cash	$ 20,000	Accounts Payable	$ 30,000
Building	200,000	Long-Term Debt	40,000
Equipment	50,000	Tomi, Capital	120,000
		Dutton, Capital	80,000
Total	$270,000	Total	$270,000

On January 21, 19xx, the building and equipment are sold for $150,000 and $40,000, respectively, and the partnership is liquidated.

Required

Prepare journal entries to record the following components of liquidation:

1. Sale of the building
2. Sale of the equipment
3. Payment of all liabilities
4. Distribution of any gain or loss on liquidation to the partners
5. Distribution of the remaining cash to the partners

**Problem 15A-5
Partnership
Liquidation**
(L.O. 6)

The balance sheet of the RED Partnership as of September 30, 19xx, is shown below.

<table>
<tr><th colspan="5">RED Partnership
Balance Sheet
September 30, 19xx</th></tr>
<tr><th colspan="2">Assets</th><th colspan="2">Liabilities and Partners' Equity</th></tr>
<tr><td>Cash</td><td>$ 1,000</td><td>Accounts Payable</td><td>$ 80,000</td></tr>
<tr><td>Accounts Receivable</td><td>20,000</td><td>Ronnie, Capital</td><td>12,000</td></tr>
<tr><td>Inventory</td><td>44,000</td><td>Edward, Capital</td><td>30,000</td></tr>
<tr><td>Equipment (net)</td><td>77,000</td><td>Darrel, Capital</td><td>20,000</td></tr>
<tr><td></td><td></td><td>Total Liabilities and</td><td></td></tr>
<tr><td>Total Assets</td><td>$142,000</td><td>Partners' Equity</td><td>$142,000</td></tr>
</table>

Ronnie, Edward, and Darrel share income and losses in the ratio of 5:3:2. Because of economic conditions in their industry, the partners have agreed to liquidate the business.

Required

1. Prepare journal entries to liquidate the partnership and distribute any remaining cash. Assume that Ronnie cannot contribute any additional personal assets to the company during liquidation and that the following transactions occurred during liquidation: (a) Accounts receivable were sold for 60 percent of their book value. (b) Inventory was sold for $46,000. (c) Equipment was sold for $50,000. (d) Accounts payable were paid in full. (e) Gain or loss from realization was distributed to the partners' capital accounts. (f) Ronnie's deficit was transferred to the remaining partners in their new profit and loss ratio. (g) The remaining cash was distributed to the partners.
2. Prepare a statement of liquidation.

**Problem 15A-6
Comprehensive
Partnership
Transactions**
(L.O. 3, 4, 5, 6)

Tina Stein and Gay Caffoe formed a partnership on January 1, 19x1, to operate a modeling agency. To begin the partnership, Tina transferred cash totaling $58,000 and office equipment valued at $42,000 to the partnership. Gay transferred cash of $28,000, land valued at $18,000, and a building valued at $150,000. In addition, the partnership assumed the mortgage of $116,000 on the building.

During the first year, the partnership was unsuccessful and on December 31 reported a loss of $8,000. In the partnership agreement, the women had specified the distribution of income and losses by allowing interest of 10 percent on beginning capital, salaries of $10,000 to Tina and $24,000 to Gay, and the remaining amount to be divided in the ratio of 3:2.

On January 1, 19x2, the partners brought Carol Austin, who was experienced in the modeling business, into the partnership. Carol invested $28,000 in the partnership for a 20 percent interest. The bonus to Carol was transferred from the original partners' accounts in the ratio of 3:2.

During 19x2, the partnership earned an income of $54,000. The new partnership agreement required that income and losses be divided by providing interest of 10 percent on beginning capital balances and salaries of $10,000, $24,000, and

$30,000 for Tina, Gay, and Carol, respectively. Remaining amounts were to be divided equally.

Because of disagreements among the partners and the lack of sufficient income, the partners decided to liquidate the partnership on January 1, 19x3. On that date, the assets and liabilities of the partnership were as follows: Cash, $122,000; Accounts Receivable, $76,000; Land, $18,000; Building (net), $140,000; Office Equipment (net), $54,000; Accounts Payable, $54,000; Mortgage Payable, $102,000.

The office equipment was sold for $36,000, and the accounts receivable were valued at $64,000. The resulting losses were distributed equally to the partners' capital accounts, and the accounts payable were paid. Tina agreed to accept the accounts receivable plus cash in payment for her partnership interest. Gay accepted the land, building, and mortgage payable at book value plus cash for her share in the liquidation. Carol was paid in cash.

Required

Prepare general journal entries to record all the above facts. Support your computations with schedules, and prepare a statement of liquidation in connection with the January 1, 19x3, entries.

Problem Set B

Problem 15B-1
Partnership
Formation and
Distribution of
Income
(L.O. 3, 4)

Bill Ewing and David Meenan agreed in January 19x1 to form a partnership to produce and sell soccer equipment. Ewing contributed $12,000 in cash to the new business, and Meenan contributed equipment and supplies with agreed values of $3,000 and $5,000, respectively. The partnership had income of $21,000 during 19x1 but was less successful during 19x2, when income was only $10,000.

Required

1. Prepare the journal entry to record the investments of both partners.
2. Determine the share of income for each partner in 19x1 and 19x2 under each of the following conditions: (a) The partners agreed to share income equally. (b) The partners failed to agree on an income-sharing arrangement. (c) The partners agreed to share income according to their original capital investment ratio. (d) The partners agreed to share income by allowing interest of 9 percent on original investment and dividing the remainder equally. (e) The partners agreed to share income by allowing salaries of $9,000 for Bill and $6,000 for David and dividing the remainder equally. (f) The partners agreed to share income by allowing interest of 9 percent on original investment, paying salaries of $9,000 to Bill and $6,000 to David, and dividing the remainder equally.

Problem 15B-2
Distribution
of Income—
Salaries and
Interest
(L.O. 4)

Neil and Luann are partners in an ice-cream shop. They have agreed that Neil will operate the shop and receive a salary of $24,000 per year. Luann is to receive 4 percent interest on her original capital investment of $160,000. The remaining income and losses are to be shared by Neil and Luann in a 2:1 ratio.

Required

Determine each partner's share of income and losses under each of the following conditions. In each case, the income or loss is stated before distribution of salary and interest. (1) The income was $48,400. (2) The income was $28,000. (3) The loss was $5,600.

Problem 15B-3
Admission of a
Partner
(L.O. 5)

Van, Calvin, and Gayle are partners in the Carpet Clean Company. Their capital balances as of August 31, 19xx, are as follows:

Van, Capital	Calvin, Capital	Gayle, Capital
25,000	30,000	20,000

The partners have agreed to admit Wayne to the partnership.

Required

Prepare the journal entries to record Wayne's admission to the partnership under each of the following conditions: (1) Wayne pays Gayle $22,500 for one-half of her interest. (2) Wayne invests $22,500 cash in the partnership. (3) Wayne invests $25,000 cash in the partnership for a 20 percent interest in the business. A bonus is to be recorded for the original partners on the basis of their capital investment balances. (4) Wayne invests $25,000 cash in the firm for a 30 percent interest in the business. The old partners give Wayne a bonus according to the ratio of their capital investment balances on August 31, 19xx.

Problem 15B-4
Partnership
Liquidation
(L.O. 6)

Temple, Thompson, and Bevers are partners who share income and losses in the ratio of 4:3:3, respectively. The partners have agreed to liquidate the partnership. The partnership balance sheet prior to liquidation is as follows:

Cash	$ 20,000	Accounts Payable	$ 30,000
Other Assets	170,000	Temple, Capital	60,000
		Thompson, Capital	60,000
		Bevers, Capital	40,000
Totals	$190,000		$190,000

On December 15, 19xx, the other assets are sold for $130,000, and the partnership is liquidated.

Required

Prepare the following journal entries: (1) sale of the other assets, (2) payment of the accounts payable, (3) distribution to the partners of gain or loss on liquidation, and (4) distribution to the partners of the remaining cash.

Problem 15B-5
Partnership
Liquidation
(L.O. 6)

Stephanie, Susan, and Sharon decided to pool their resources and form a partnership on Jaunary 1, 19x1, to produce and sell ceramics. The original investments for Stephanie, Susan, and Sharon were $10,000, $12,000, and equipment with a fair market value of $8,000, respectively.

After operating for three years, the partners have decided to liquidate the business as of January 1, 19x4. At that time, the stated income sharing ratios to the nearest percent are 34:39:27, respectively, for Stephanie, Susan, and Sharon. The following accounts and balances appear in the company's general ledger as of December 31, 19x3: Cash, $32,000; Accounts Receivable, $30,000; Inventory, $50,000; Equipment, $32,000; Accounts Payable, $10,000; Stephanie, Capital, $45,600; Susan, Capital, $52,000; Sharon, Capital, $36,400.

Required

1. Journalize the following liquidation transactions: (a) Accounts receivable are sold for $20,000. (b) Inventory is sold for $70,000. (c) With the partners' permission, Sharon withdraws the equipment from the business. The partners agree that the withdrawal should be recorded at book value. (d) The accounts payable are paid in full. (e) The gain or loss from realization is distributed to the partners' capital accounts. (f) The final cash is distributed to the partners.
2. Prepare a statement of liquidation.

Problem 15B-6
Comprehensive
Partnership
Transactions
(L.O. 3, 4, 5, 6)

The events below pertain to a partnership formed by Jerry Mendoza and Frank Bennett to operate a floor cleaning company.

19x1

Feb. 14   The partnership was formed. Mendoza transferred to the partnership $40,000 cash, land worth $40,000, a building worth $240,000, and a mortgage on the building of $120,000. Bennett transferred to the partnership $20,000 cash and equipment worth $80,000.

Dec. 31   During 19x1, the partnership made an income of only $42,000. The partnership agreement specified that income and losses were to be divided by allowing 8 percent interest on beginning capital investment, paying salaries of $20,000 to Mendoza and $30,000 to Bennett, and dividing any remainder equally.

19x2

Jan. 1   To improve the prospects for the company, the partners decided to take in a new partner, Diane Wong, who had experience in the floor cleaning business. Diane invested $78,000 for a 25 percent interest in the business. A bonus was transferred in equal amounts from the previous partners' capital accounts to Diane's capital account.

Dec. 31   During 19x2, the company earned an income of $43,600. The new partnership agreement specified that income and losses would be divided by allowing 8 percent interest on beginning capital balances after Diane's admission, paying salaries of $30,000 to Bennett and $40,000 to Diane (no salary to Mendoza), and dividing the remainder equally.

19x3

Jan. 1   Because it appeared that the business could not support the three partners, the partners decided to liquidate the partnership. The asset and liability accounts of the partnership were as follows: Cash, $203,600; Accounts Receivable, $34,000; Land, $40,000; Building (net), $224,000; Equipment (net), $118,000; Accounts Payable, $44,000; Mortgage Payable, $112,000. The equipment was sold for $100,000, and the resulting loss was distributed equally to the partners' accounts. The accounts payable were paid. A statement of liquidation was prepared, and the remaining assets and liabilities were distributed. Mendoza agreed to accept cash plus the land and buildings at book value and the mortgage payable as payment for his share. Bennett accepted cash and the accounts receivable for his share. Wong was paid in cash.

Required

Prepare general journal entries to record all the above facts. Support your computations with schedules, and prepare a statement of liquidation in connection with the January 1, 19x3, entries.

Financial Decision Case 15-1

L & T Oyster Bar
(L.O. 4, 5)

The L & T Oyster Bar is owned by James Land and Larry Teague. The business has been very successful since its inception five years ago. James and Larry work ten to eleven hours a day at the business. They have decided to expand by opening up another bar in the north part of town. James has approached you about becoming a partner in their business. They are interested in you because of your past experience in operating a small oyster bar. In addition, they will need additional funds to expand their business.

Projected income after the expansion but before partner salaries for the next five years is

19x1	19x2	19x3	19x4	19x5
$100,000	$120,000	$130,000	$140,000	$150,000

Currently, James and Larry each draw $25,000 salary and share remaining profits equally. They are willing to give you an equal share of the business for $142,000. You will receive $25,000 salary and $\frac{1}{3}$ of the remaining profits. You would work the same hours as James and Larry. Your expected salary for the next five years where you currently work is expected to be:

19x1	19x2	19x3	19x4	19x5
$34,000	$38,000	$42,000	$45,000	$50,000

Financial information for the L & T Oyster Bar is shown as follows:

Current assets	$ 45,000
Fixed assets	365,000
Current liabilities	50,000
Long-term liabilities	100,000
Land, capital	140,000
Teague, capital	120,000

Required

1. Compute your capital balance if you decide to join James and Larry in the partnership.
2. Analyze your expected income for the next five years. Should you invest in the L & T Oyster Bar?
3. Assume that you do not consider James and Larry's offer to be very attractive. Develop a counter offer that you would be willing to accept to join the partnership (be realistic in your proposed arrangement).

Learning Objectives

Chapter Sixteen

Corporations: Organization and Contributed Capital

1. *Define a corporation and describe its basic organization and key personnel.*

2. *State the advantages and disadvantages of the corporate form of business.*

3. *Account for organization costs.*

4. *Identify the components of stockholders' equity.*

5. *Calculate the division of dividends between common and preferred stockholders.*

6. *Account for the issuance of common and preferred stock for cash and other assets.*

7. *Account for stock subscriptions.*

8. *Account for the retirement of stock and donations of stock and other assets.*

9. *Calculate book value per share, and distinguish it from market value.*

There are fewer corporations than sole proprietorships or partnerships in the United States. However, the corporate form of business dominates the economy in total dollars of assets and output of goods and services. The major reason for this dominance is that it is easier for a corporation to gather a large amount of capital. Also, the corporate form of business is well suited to today's trends toward large organizations, international trade, and professional management.

This chapter begins by outlining some of the important characteristics of the corporate form of business. Then it explains accounting for organization costs and describes the components of stockholders' equity. The rest of the chapter focuses on accounting for the issuance of stock and other stock transactions and on calculating the book value per share of stock. As a result of studying this chapter, you should be able to meet the learning objectives listed on the left.

The Corporation and Its Organization

A **corporation** is defined as "a body of persons granted a charter legally recognizing them as a separate entity having its own rights, privileges, and liabilities distinct from those of its members."[1] In other words, the corporation is a legal entity separate from its owners. For this reason, corporate accounting is different in some ways from that for proprietorships and partnerships.

Formation of a Corporation

To form a corporation in most states an application is filed with the proper state official. The application contains the **articles of incorporation**. If approved by the state, these articles become

1. © 1973 Houghton Mifflin Company. Reprinted by permission from *The American Heritage Dictionary of the English Language*.

Objective 1
Define a corpo-
ration and
describe its
basic organi-
zation and key
personnel

a contract between the state and the incorporators, called the company charter. After the charter is approved, the company is authorized to do business. First, the incorporators hold a meeting to elect a board of directors and pass a set of bylaws to guide the operations of the corporation. Then, the board of directors holds a meeting to elect officers of the corporation. Finally, when beginning capital is raised through the issuance of shares of stock, the corporation is ready to begin operating.

Organization of a Corporation

The authority to manage the corporation is given by the stockholders to the board of directors and by the board of directors to the corporate officers (see Figure 16-1). That is, the stockholders elect the board of directors, which sets company policies and chooses the corporate officers. The officers in turn carry out the corporate policies by managing the business.

Stockholders   A unit of ownership in a corporation is called a share of stock. The articles of incorporation state the maximum or authorized number of shares of a stock that the corporation will be allowed to issue. The number of shares held by stockholders is the outstanding capital stock, and it may be less than the number of authorized shares. To invest in a corporation, a stockholder transfers cash or other resources to the corporation. In return, the stockholder receives shares of stock representing a proportionate share of ownership in the corporation. Afterward, the stockholder may transfer the shares at will. Corporations may have more than one kind of capital stock, but the first part of this chapter will refer only to common stock.

Individual stockholders do not normally take part in the day-to-day management of a corporation. However, a stockholder may serve as a member of the board if elected or as an officer of the company if appointed. But, in general, stockholders participate in management only through electing the board of directors and voting on particular issues at stockholders' meetings.

Stockholders will normally meet once a year to elect directors and carry on other business as provided for in the company's bylaws. Business transacted at these meetings may include the election of auditors, review of proposed mergers and acquisitions, changes in the charter, stock option plans, and issuance of additional stock and of long-term debt. Each stockholder has one vote for each share of voting stock held. Today, ownership of large corporations is spread over the entire country. As a result, only a few stockholders may be able to attend the annual stockholders' meeting.

Figure 16-1
The Corporate
Form of Busi-
ness

Stockholders	Board of Directors	Management
invest in shares of capital stock and elect board of directors	determine corporate policy, declare dividends, and appoint management	executes policy and carries out day-to-day operations

A stockholder who cannot attend the meeting may vote by proxy. The proxy is a legal document, signed by the stockholder, giving another party the right to vote his or her shares. Normally, this right is given to the current management of the corporation.

Board of Directors As noted, the stockholders elect the board of directors, which in turn decides on the major business policies of the corporation. Among the duties of the board are authorizing contracts, deciding on executive salaries, and arranging major loans with banks. The declaration of dividends is also an important function of the board of directors. Only the board has the authority to declare dividends. Dividends are distributions of resources, generally in the form of cash, to the stockholders. They are one way of rewarding stockholders for their investment in the corporation when it has been successful in earning a profit. (The other way is a rise in the market value of the stock.) There is usually a delay of two or three weeks between the time when the board declares a dividend and the date of the actual payment.

The make-up of the board of directors will be different from company to company. In most cases, though, it will contain several officers of the corporation and several outsiders. Today, it is common to form an **audit committee** with several outside directors to make sure that the board will be objective in judging management's performance. One of the audit committee's tasks is to hire the company's independent auditors and review their work.

Management The board of directors appoints the managers of a corporation to carry out the company's policies and to run the day-to-day operations. The management consists of the operating officers, who are generally the president, vice-presidents, controller, treasurer, and secretary. Besides being responsible for running the business, management has the duty to report the financial results of its administration to the board of directors and to the stockholders. Though management may and generally does report more often, it must report at least once a year. For large public corporations, these annual reports are available to the public. Parts of many of them have been used in this book.

Advantages of a Corporation

Objective 2
State the
advantages and
disadvantages
of the corporate
form of
business

The corporate form of a business organization has several advantages over the sole proprietorship and the partnership. Among these advantages are separate legal entity, limited liability, ease of capital generation, ease of transfer of ownership, lack of mutual agency, continuous existence, centralized authority and responsibility, and professional management.

Separate Legal Entity A corporation is a separate legal entity and has most of the rights of a person except those of voting and marrying. So it may buy, sell, or own property, sue and be sued, enter into contracts with all parties, and hire and fire employees.

Limited Liability   Because a corporation is a separate legal entity, it is responsible for its own actions and liabilities. For this reason, a corporation's creditors generally cannot look beyond the assets of the company to satisfy their claims. In other words, the creditors can satisfy their claims only against the assets of the corporation, and not against the personal property of the owners of the company. Because owners of a corporation are not responsible for the debts of the company, their liability is limited to the amount of their investment. The personal property of sole proprietors and partners, however, may be available to creditors.

Ease of Capital Generation   It is fairly easy for a corporation to raise money because many people can take part in the ownership of the business by investing small amounts of money. So a single corporation may be owned by many people.

Ease of Transfer of Ownership   The ownership of a corporation is represented by a transferable unit called a share of stock. The owner of the share of stock, or the stockholder, can buy and sell shares of stock without affecting the activities of the corporation or needing the approval of other owners.

Lack of Mutual Agency   There is no mutual agency with the corporate form of business. If a stockholder, acting as an owner, tries to enter into a contract for the corporation, the corporation will not be bound by the contract. But a partnership, where there is mutual agency, can be bound by a partner's actions.

Continuous Existence   Another advantage of the corporation being a legal entity separate from its owners is that an owner's death, incapacity, or withdrawal does not affect the life of the corporation. The life of a corporation is set by its charter and regulated by state laws.

Centralized Authority and Responsibility   The responsibility and authority for running the corporation are given to the president of the organization. This power is not divided among the many owners of the business. The president may delegate authority for certain segments of the business to others, but he or she has the final responsibility for the business. If the owners are dissatisfied with the performance of the president, they can replace him or her.

Professional Management   A corporation is owned by many people who probably do not have the time or training to make timely operating decisions for the business. So, in most cases, management and ownership are separated. This arrangement allows the corporation to hire the best talent available for managing the business.

Disadvantages of a Corporation

The corporate form of business of course has its disadvantages. Among the more important ones are government regulation, taxation, limited liability, and separate ownership and control.

Government Regulation When corporations are created, they must meet the requirements of state laws. For this reason, they are said to be "creatures of the state" and are subject to greater control and regulation by the state than other forms of business. Corporations must file many reports with the states in which they are chartered. Also, corporations that are publicly held must file reports with the Securities and Exchange Commission and with the stock exchanges. Meeting these requirements becomes very costly.

Taxation A major disadvantage of a corporation is double taxation. Because the corporation is a separate legal entity, its earnings are subject to federal and state income taxes. These taxes may approach 50 percent of the corporate earnings. If the corporation's after-tax earnings are then paid out to its stockholders as dividends, these earnings are again taxed as income to the stockholders who receive them. Taxation is different for the sole proprietorship and the partnership. Their earnings are taxed only as personal income to the owners.

Limited Liability Earlier, limited liability was listed as an advantage of a corporation. This same feature, however, may limit the ability of a small corporation to borrow money. Credit of a small corporation is reduced because the stockholders have limited liability and the creditors will have claims only to the assets of the corporation. In such cases, the creditors will limit their loans to the level secured by the assets of the corporation or ask the stockholders to personally guarantee the loans.

Separation of Ownership and Control Just as limited liability may be a drawback, so may the separation of ownership and control. Sometimes management makes decisions that are not good for the corporation as a whole. Also, poor communication can make it hard for stockholders to exercise control over the corporation or even to recognize that management's decisions are harmful.

Organization Costs

Objective 3
Account for
organization
costs

The costs of forming a corporation are called organization costs. These costs include such items as state incorporation fees, attorneys' fees for drawing up the articles of incorporation, and promoters' fees. Also included are the cost of printing stock, accountants' fees for services rendered in registering the firm's initial stock, and other expenditures necessary for forming the corporation.

The benefits to be received from these costs should actually run through the entire life of the organization. For this reason, the costs should be capitalized as intangible assets and amortized over the years. However, the life of a corporation is normally unknown, so accountants amortize these costs over the early years of a corporation's life. Also, the income tax regulations allow organization costs to be amortized over five years or more. Therefore most companies amortize these costs over a five-year period. Organization costs normally appear as Other Assets or Intangible Assets on the balance sheet.

To illustrate accounting practice for organization costs, we will assume that a corporation pays a lawyer $5,000 for services rendered in preparing the application for a charter with the state. The entry to record this cost would be as follows:

```
19x0
July 1   Organization Costs                          5,000
            Cash                                               5,000
               To record $5,000 lawyer's fee for
               services rendered in corporate
               organization
```

If the corporation amortizes the organization costs over a five-year period, the entry to record the amortization at the end of the fiscal year on June 30, 19x1, would be:

```
19x1
June 30   Amortization of Expense, Organization Costs   1,000
             Organization Costs                                  1,000
                To record one year's amortiza-
                tion costs:
                $5,000 ÷ 5 years = $1,000
```

The Components of Stockholders' Equity

*Objective 4
Identify the
components of
stockholders'
equity*

The major difference in accounting for corporations and accounting for sole proprietorships or partnerships involves the owners' equity. The assets and liabilities of a corporation are handled in the same way as they are for other forms of business. In a corporation's balance sheet, the owners' claims to the business are called **stockholders' equity**, as follows:

Stockholders' Equity

Contributed Capital		
Preferred Stock—$50 par value, 1,000 shares		
authorized and issued		$ 50,000
Common Stock—$5 par value, 30,000 shares		
authorized, 20,000 shares issued	$100,000	
Paid-in Capital in Excess of Par Value, Common	50,000	150,000
Total Contributed Capital		$200,000
Retained Earnings		60,000
Total Stockholders' Equity		$260,000

This equity section is different from the balance sheet presentation of a proprietorship and partnership in that it is divided into two parts: (1) contributed capital and (2) retained earnings. The **contributed capital** represents the investments made by the stockholders in the corporation. The retained earnings are the earnings of the business that are not distributed to the stockholders but are reinvested in the business.

The contributed capital part of stockholders' equity gives a great deal of information about the stock of a corporation. For example, the kinds of stock, their par value, and the number of shares authorized and issued are reported in this part of stockholders' equity. This information in the contributed capital part of stockholders' equity is the subject of the rest of this chapter. Retained earnings will be explained in Chapter 17.

Capital Stock

A unit of ownership in a corporation is called a share of stock. A stock certificate will be issued to the owner. It shows the number of shares of the corporation's stock owned by the stockholder. Stockholders can transfer their ownership at will, but they must sign their stock certificate and send it to the corporation's secretary. In large corporations listed on the organized stock exchanges, it is hard to maintain stockholders' records. Such companies may have millions of shares of stock, several thousand of which may change ownership every day. Therefore, these corporations often appoint independent registrars and transfer agents to aid in performing the secretary's duties. The registrars and the transfer agents are usually banks and trust companies. They are responsible for transferring the corporation's stock, maintaining stockholders' records, preparing a list of stockholders for stockholders' meetings, and paying the dividends. To help with the initial issue of capital stock, corporations often engage an underwriter. The underwriter is an intermediary, or contact, between the corporation and the investing public. For a fee—usually the difference between the price the public pays for the stock and the price the corporation receives—the underwriter guarantees the sale of the stock.

Authorization of Stock

When a corporation applies for a charter, the articles of incorporation indicate the maximum number of shares of stock a corporation will be allowed to issue. This number represents authorized stock. Most corporations get an authorization to issue more shares of stock than are necessary at the time of organization. This action enables the corporation to issue stock in the future to raise additional capital. For example, if a corporation is planning to expand later, a possible source of capital would be the unissued shares of stock that were authorized in its charter. If all authorized stock is issued immediately, the corporation must change its charter by applying to the state to increase the number of shares of authorized stock. The charter also shows the par value of the stock that has been authorized. The par value is the amount to be printed on each share of stock. It must be recorded in the capital stock accounts. When the corporation is formed, a memorandum entry may be made in the general journal giving the number and description of authorized shares.

Issued and Outstanding Stock

The **issued stock** of a corporation is the shares sold or otherwise transferred to the stockholders. For example, a corporation may have been authorized to issue 500,000 shares of stock but chose to issue only 300,000 shares when the company was organized. The 300,000 shares represent the issued stock. The holders of those shares own 100 percent of the corporation. The remaining 200,000 shares of stock are unissued shares. No rights or privileges are associated with them until they are issued. A share of stock may be an issued stock but may not be an **outstanding stock** because it has been repurchased by the corporation or given back to the company by a shareholder. In such cases, a company can have more shares issued than are currently outstanding or held by the stockholders. The reasons for holding this stock, called treasury stock, are explained in Chapter 17 under the heading of treasury stock.

Common Stock

A corporation may issue two basic types of stock: common stock and preferred stock. If only one kind of stock is issued, it is called **common stock,** and the stockholders have the rights that were listed earlier. The common stock is the **residual equity** of a company. This term means that all other creditor and preferred stockholder claims to the company's assets rank ahead of those of the common stockholders in case of liquidation. Because the common stock is generally the only stock carrying voting rights, it represents the means of controlling the corporation.

Preferred Stock

The second kind of stock, called **preferred stock,** may be issued so that the company can obtain money from investors who have different investment goals. Preferred stock has some preference over common stock, usually in the area of dividends. There may be several different classes of preferred stock, each with distinctive characteristics to attract different kinds of investors. Most preferred stock will have one or more of the following characteristics: preference as to dividends, preference as to assets of the business in liquidation, convertibility or nonconvertibility, callable option, and no voting rights.

Preference as to Dividends If a stock has preference as to dividends, the stockholders are entitled to a dividend before any payment can be made to the common stockholders. The dividend is usually stated in one of two ways. First, it may be stated as a specific dollar amount per share. For example, a corporation may issue a preferred stock and pay a yearly dividend of $4 per share. Second, the dividend may be expressed as a percentage of par value. For example, a corporation may issue a preferred stock of $100 par value and pay a yearly dividend of 6 percent of par value, which amounts to a $6 annual dividend.

The preferred stockholders have no guarantee of receiving dividends. They will be able to receive a dividend only when the board of directors

Objective 5
Calculate the
division of
dividends
between
common and
preferred stock-
holders

declares a dividend. Also, preferred stock may be either noncumulative or cumulative. In the case of **noncumulative preferred stock**, if a preferred dividend is not paid in a given year, it lapses and will never have to be paid. However, in any one year the preferred stockholders must be paid their dividend before the common stockholders receive a dividend. In the case of **cumulative preferred stock**, unpaid dividends accumulate over periods of time. So if all or a part of a yearly dividend is not paid in the year when it is due, it must be paid in a later year before dividends can be paid to common stockholders. Dividends that are not paid in the year they are due are called **dividends in arrears**. Assume that the preferred stock of a corporation is as follows: preferred stock, 5 percent cumulative, 10,000 shares, $100 par, $1,000,000. If in 19x1 no dividends were paid, at the end of that year there would be preferred dividends of $50,000 in arrears ($1,000,000 × 5% = $50,000). Thus if dividends are paid next year, the preferred stockholders' dividends in arrears plus the 19x2 preferred dividends must be paid before any dividends can be paid in 19x2 on common stock.

As an illustration, let us assume the following facts. On January 1, 19x1, a corporation issued 10,000 shares of $10 par, 6 percent cumulative preferred stock and 50,000 shares of common stock. The first year's operations resulted in income of only $4,000. The board of directors declared a $3,000 cash dividend to the preferred stockholders. The dividend picture at the end of 19x1 appears as follows:

19x1 dividends due preferred stockholders ($100,000 × 6%)	$6,000
19x1 dividends declared preferred stockholders	3,000
Preferred stock dividends in arrears	$3,000

Dividends can be declared only by the board of directors. Once the board declares a dividend, the corporation has a liability that should be recognized. The following entry is made when a dividend is declared:

Dec. 31	Dividends Declared	3,000
	Dividends Payable	3,000
	To record declaration of a	
	$3,000 cash dividend to pre-	
	ferred stockholders	

Dividends in arrears are not recognized as liabilities of a corporation because there is no liability until the board declares a dividend. A corporation cannot be sure of making a profit. So, of course, it cannot promise dividends to stockholders. However, if a company has dividends in arrears, they should be reported either in the body of the financial statements or in a footnote. It is important to give this information to the users of these statements. The following footnote appeared in a steel company's annual report a few years ago:

On January 1, 19xx, the company was in arrears by $37,851,000 ($1.25 per share) on dividends to its preferred stockholders. The company must pay all dividends in arrears to preferred stockholders before paying any dividends to common stockholders.

In 19x2, the company earned income of $30,000 and wished to pay dividends to both the preferred and the common stockholders. But the preferred stock is cumulative. So the corporation must pay the $3,000 dividends in arrears on the preferred stock, plus the current year's dividends, before the common stockholders can receive a dividend. For example, assume that the corporation's board of directors declared a $12,000 dividend to be distributed to the preferred and common stockholders. The distribution of the dividend would be as follows:

19x2 declaration of dividends	$12,000
Less 19x1 preferred stock dividends in arrears	3,000
	$ 9,000
Less 19x2 preferred stock dividend ($100,000 × 6%)	6,000
	$ 3,000
Less remainder to common stockholders	3,000
	—

The following entry is made when the dividend is declared:

Dec. 31 Dividends Declared	12,000	
Dividends Payable		12,000
To record declaration of a $9,000 cash dividend to preferred stockholders and a $3,000 cash dividend to common stockholders		

Preferred stock is called **nonparticipating** when its dividend is limited to the stated percentage or dollar amount per share. Preferred stock is called **participating** when the preferred stockholders may receive a larger proportion of the dividends than their stated dividend rate. For example, those who owned 6 percent participating preferred stock with a par value of $100 would be allowed a $6 dividend per share before the common stockholders received a dividend. The common stockholders would then be given a dividend equal to 6 percent of their stock's par value before any participation takes place. If any further dividends are declared after the common stockholders receive their 6 percent dividend, the common and preferred stockholders would share the rest in some stated ratio. Suppose that a corporation has 1,000 shares of 6 percent, $100 par value fully participating preferred stock and 50,000 shares of $10 par value common stock. The board of directors declares a $42,000 dividend for 19xx, and there are no dividends in arrears. The dividend for each class of stock is determined in three steps. First, each class is allocated an amount based on the percentage of the preferred stock dividend, as follows:

Dividend declared			$42,000		
Less 19xx preferred stock dividend ($100,000 × 6%)			6,000		
			$36,000		
Less 19xx common stock dividend ($500,000 × 6%)			30,000		
Remainder to be shared by preferred and common stockholders			$ 6,000		

Second, the $6,000 will be divided in some stated way between the preferred and common stockholders. One way is to divide the remaining dividend according to the relative total par values of the stock, as figured below.

Stock	Shares	Par Value	Total Par Value	Allocation Ratio	Amount
Preferred	1,000	$100	$100,000	$\frac{100,000}{600,000} = \frac{1}{6}$	$1,000
Common	50,000	10	500,000	$\frac{500,000}{600,000} = \frac{5}{6}$	5,000
			$600,000		$6,000

Third, the total dividends to each class are figured:

	Step 1 Amount	Step 2 Amount	Total Dividends Allocated
Preferred stock	$ 6,000	$1,000	$ 7,000
Common stock	30,000	5,000	35,000
	$36,000	$6,000	$42,000

If no limit is placed on the amount that the preferred stockholders can receive above their stated dividend, the stock is called fully participating preferred stock. If there is a limit on the additional dividends that the preferred stockholders can receive, the stock is called partially participating preferred stock.

Preference as to Assets Many preferred stocks have preference as to the assets of the corporation in the case of liquidation of the business. So when the business is ended, the preferred stockholders have a right to receive the par value of their stock or a larger stated liquidation value per share before the common stockholders receive any share of the company's assets. This preference may also include any dividends in arrears owed to the preferred stockholders.

Convertible Preferred Stock A corporation may make its preferred stock more attractive to investors by adding a convertible feature. Those who hold convertible preferred stock can exchange their shares of preferred stock, if they wish, for shares of the company's common stock at a ratio stated in the preferred stock contract. Convertibility is attractive to investors for two reasons. (1) Like all preferred stockholders, owners of convertible stock can be surer of regular dividends than can common stockholders. (2) If the market value of a company's common stock rises, the conversion feature will allow the preferred stockholders to share in this increase. The rise in value would come either through equal increases in the value of the preferred stock or through conversion to common stock.

For example, suppose that a company issues 1,000 shares of 8 percent, $100 par value convertible preferred stock for $100 per share. Each share of stock can be converted into five shares of the company's common stock at any time. The market value of the common stock is now $15 a share. In the past, the dividends on the common stock had been about $1 per share per year. The stockholder owning one share of preferred stock now holds an investment that is worth about $100 on the market, and the probability of dividends is higher than with common stock. Assume that in the next several years the corporation's earnings increase, and the dividends being paid to common stockholders also increase, to $3 per share. In addition, the market value of a share of common stock increases from $15 to $30. The preferred stockholders can convert each of their preferred shares into five common shares and increase their dividends from $8 on each preferred share to the equivalent of $15 ($3 on each of five common shares). Furthermore, the market value of each share of preferred stock will be close to the $150 value of the five shares of common stock because the share may be converted into the five shares of common stock.

Callable Preferred Stock   Most preferred stocks are **callable preferred stocks.** That is, they may be redeemed or retired at the option of the issuing corporation at a certain price stated in the preferred stock contract. The stockholder must surrender a nonconvertible preferred stock to the corporation when requested to do so. If the preferred stock is convertible, the shareholder may either surrender the stock to the corporation or convert it into common stock when the corporation calls the stock. The call price, or redemption price, is usually higher than the par value of the stock. For example, a $100 par value preferred stock might be callable at $103 per share. When preferred stock is called and surrendered, the stockholder is entitled to (1) the par value of the stock, (2) the call premium, (3) the dividends in arrears, and (4) a prorated (by the proportion of the year to the call date) portion of the current period's dividend.

There are several reasons why a corporation may call its preferred stock. The first is that the company may wish to force conversion of the preferred stock to common because the cash dividend to be paid on the equivalent common stock is less than the dividend being paid on the preferred shares. Second, it may be possible to replace the outstanding preferred stock on the current market with a preferred stock at a lower dividend rate or with long-term debt which may have a lower after-tax cost. Third, the company may simply be profitable enough to retire the preferred stock.

Retained Earnings   Retained earnings, the other component of stockholders' equity, represents the claim of stockholders to the assets of the company resulting from profitable operations. Chapter 17 focuses on the retained earnings section of the balance sheet.

Accounting for Stock Issuance

*Objective 6
Account for the
issuance of
common and
preferred stock
for cash and
other assets*

A share of capital stock is either a par or a no-par stock. If the capital stock is par stock, the corporation charter states the par value, and this value must be printed on each share of stock. Par value may be 10¢, $1, $5, $100, or any other amount worked out by the organizers of the corporation. The par values of common stocks tend to be lower than those of preferred stocks.

Par value is the amount per share that is entered into the corporation's Capital Stock account and makes up the legal capital of the corporation. The legal capital is the minimum amount that can be reported as contributed capital. A corporation may not declare a dividend that would cause stockholders' equity to fall below the legal capital of the firm. Therefore, the par value is a minimum cushion of capital that protects creditors. Any amount received in excess of par value from the issuance of stock is recorded as Paid-in Capital in Excess of Par Value and represents a portion of the company's contributed capital.

No-par stock is capital stock that does not have a par value. No-par stock may be issued with or without a stated value. The board of directors of the corporation issuing the no-par stock may place a stated value on each share of stock. The stated value can be any value set by the board, but some states do indicate a minimum value per share. The stated value may be set before or after the shares are issued if the state law does not specify this point.

When no-par stock is issued, the shares are recorded in the Capital Stock account at the stated value. Any amount received in excess of the stated value is recorded as Paid-in Capital in Excess of Stated Value. The excess of the stated value is a part of the corporation's contributed capital. However, the stated value is normally considered to be the legal capital of the corporation.

If a company issues a no-par stock without a stated value, then all proceeds of the stock's issuance are recorded in the Capital Stock account. This amount becomes the corporation's legal capital unless the amount is specified by state law. Because additional shares of the stock may be issued at different prices, the credit to the Capital Stock account will not be uniform per share. In this way it differs from par value stock or no-par stock with a stated value.

There are several reasons for issuing stock without a par value. One is that some investors have confused par value with book or market value of stock and have thus made poor investment decisions. Another reason is that when a par value stock is originally issued below par, it will normally carry a contingent liability upon the stockholders to creditors of the corporation in the amount of the difference between issue price and par value. This means, in the case of corporate liquidation, that the stockholders who purchased stock below its par value would have to pay the creditors the difference between par value and the purchase price if the company's assets are not sufficient to pay the creditors. Still another reason is that most states will not allow an original issuance of stock below par value and thereby limit a corporation's flexibility in obtaining capital.

Issuance of Par Value Stock

When a par value stock is issued, the Capital Stock account is credited for the par value (legal capital) regardless of whether the proceeds are more or less than the par value. For example, assume that Bradley Corporation is authorized to issue 20,000 shares of $10 par value common stock and actually issues 10,000 shares at $10 per share. The entry to record the issuance of the stock would be as shown below.

Jan. 1	Cash	100,000	
	Common Stock		100,000
	Issued 10,000 shares of $10 par value common stock for $10 per share		

Cash is debited for $100,000 (10,000 shares × $10), and Common Stock is credited for an equal amount because the stock was sold for par value (legal capital). If the stock had been issued for a price greater than par, the proceeds in excess of par would be credited to a capital account entitled Paid-in Capital in Excess of Par Value, Common. For example, assume that the 10,000 shares of Bradley common stock were sold for $12 per share. The entry to record the issuance of the stock would be as follows:

Jan. 1	Cash	120,000	
	Common Stock		100,000
	Paid-in Capital in Excess of Par Value, Common		20,000
	Issued 10,000 shares of $10 par value common stock for $12 per share		

Cash is debited for the proceeds of $120,000 (10,000 shares × $12), and Common Stock is credited at total par value of $100,000 (10,000 shares × $10). Paid-in Capital in Excess of Par Value, Common, is credited for the difference of $20,000 (10,000 shares × $2). The premium paid for the stock is a part of the corporation's contributed capital and will be added to Common Stock in the stockholders' equity section of the balance sheet. The stockholders' equity section for Bradley Corporation immediately following the stock issue would appear as follows:

Stockholders' Equity

Contributed Capital	
Common Stock—$10 par value, 20,000 shares authorized, 10,000 shares issued and outstanding	$100,000
Paid-in Capital in Excess of Par Value, Common	20,000
Total Contributed Capital	$120,000
Retained Earnings	—
Total Stockholders' Equity	$120,000

If a corporation issues stock for less than par, an account entitled Discount on Capital Stock should be debited for the discount. (The issuance of stock at a discount is illegal in many states and rarely occurs.) For example, assume that 10,000 shares of $10 par value common stock are sold for $9 per share, for a total of $90,000. The discount equals $10,000 ($100,000 par value minus $90,000 proceeds) and is recorded as follows:

Jan. 1	Cash	90,000	
	Discount on Common Stock	10,000	
	Common Stock		100,000
	Issued 10,000 shares of $10 par value common stock for $9 per share		

If a stock is issued at a discount, a contingent liability equal to the discount exists for those stockholders in case of corporate liquidation. This contingency is shown on the balance sheet by deducting the Discount on Common Stock as a contra account from Common Stock to arrive at contributed capital, as follows:

Contributed Capital	
Common Stock—$10 par value, 20,000 shares authorized, 10,000 shares issued and outstanding	$100,000
Discount on Common Stock	(10,000)
Total Contributed Capital	$ 90,000

Issuance of No-Par Stock

As mentioned earlier, stock may be issued without a par value. However, most states require that all or part of the proceeds from the issuance of no-par stock be designated as legal capital not subject to withdrawal, except in liquidation. The purpose is to protect the corporation's assets for the creditors.

For example, we will assume that the Bradley Corporation's capital stock is no-par common and that 10,000 shares are issued on January 1, 19xx, at $15 per share. The $150,000 (10,000 shares at $15) in proceeds would be recorded as shown in the following entry:

Jan. 1	Cash	150,000	
	Common Stock		150,000
	Issued 10,000 shares of no-par common stock at $15 per share		

Since the stock does not have a stated or par value, all proceeds of the issue are credited to Common Stock and are part of the company's legal capital.

Most states allow the board of directors to put a stated value on no-par stock, and this value represents the legal capital. Assume that Bradley's board puts a $10 stated value on its no-par stock. The entry to record the issue of 10,000 shares of no-par common stock for $15 per share would change from that in the last paragraph to the following:

```
Jan. 1   Cash                                       150,000
              Common Stock                                      100,000
              Paid-in Capital in Excess of Stated
              Value, Common                                      50,000
                  Issued 10,000 shares of no-par
                  common stock of $10 stated
                  value for $15 per share
```

Note that the legal capital credited to Common Stock is the stated value as decided by the board of directors. Note also that the account Paid-in Capital in Excess of Stated Value, Common, is credited for $50,000. The $50,000 is the difference between the proceeds ($150,000) and the total stated value ($100,000). Paid-in Capital in Excess of Stated Value, Common, is presented on the balance sheet in the same way as Paid-in Capital in Excess of Par Value, Common, is presented for par value stock.

Issuance of Stock for Noncash Assets

In many stock transactions, stock is issued for assets or services other than cash. As a result, a problem arises as to what dollar amount should be recorded for the exchange. The general rule for such a transaction is to record the transaction at the fair market value of what is given up—in this case, the stock. If the fair market value of the stock cannot be determined, the fair market value of the assets or services should be used to record the transaction. Transactions of this kind usually include the use of stock to pay for land or buildings or for services of attorneys and promoters.

Where there is an exchange of stock for noncash assets, the board of directors has the right to value the property. For example, when the Bradley Corporation was formed, it issued 100 shares of its $10 par value common stock to its attorney for services rendered. At the time of the issuance, the market value of the stock could not be determined. However, for similar services the attorney would have billed the company for $1,500. The entry to record the noncash transaction follows:

```
Jan. 1   Organization Costs                          1,500
              Common Stock                                        1,000
              Paid-in Capital in Excess of Par
              Value, Common                                         500
                  Issued 100 shares of $10 par
                  value common stock for attorney's
                  services
```

Assume further that the Bradley Corporation exchanged 1,000 shares of its $10 par common stock for a piece of land two years later. At the time of the exchange the stock was selling on the market for $16 per share and the value of the land could not be determined. The entry to record this exchange would be:

Jan. 1	Land	16,000	
	Common Stock		10,000
	Paid-in Capital in Excess of Par		
	Value, Common		6,000
	Issued 1,000 shares of $10 par value common stock for a piece of land; market value of the stock $16 per share		

Stock Subscriptions

Objective 7
Account for stock subscrip-tions

In some states, corporations may sell on a subscription basis. In a **stock subscription**, the investor agrees to pay for the stock on some future date or in installments at an agreed price. When a subscription is received, a contract exists and the corporation acquires an asset Subscriptions Receivable, which represents the amount owed on the stock, and a capital item Capital Stock Subscribed, which represents the par or stated value of the stock not yet fully paid for and issued. The Subscriptions Receivable account should be identified as either common or preferred stock. The Capital Stock Subscribed account should also be identified as either common or preferred stock. Whether or not the subscriber is entitled to dividends on the subscribed stock depends on the laws of the state in which the company is incorporated. In certain states, the stock is considered to be legally issued when a subscription contract is accepted, thereby making the subscriber a legal stockholder. However, in accounting for stock subscriptions, capital stock is not issued and recorded until the subscriptions receivable pertaining to the shares are collected in full and the stock certificate is delivered to the stockholder. Likewise, it may be assumed that dividends are not paid on common stock subscribed until it is fully paid for and the certificates issued.

To illustrate stock subscriptions, we will assume that on January 1, 19xx, the Bradley Corporation received subscriptions for 15,000 shares of $10 par value common stock at $15 per share. The entry to record the subscriptions would be as follows:

Jan. 1	Subscriptions Receivable, Common	225,000	
	Common Stock Subscribed		150,000
	Paid-in Capital in Excess of Par		
	Value, Common		75,000
	Received subscriptions for 15,000 shares of $10 par value common stock at $15 per share		

If the full subscription price for 10,000 shares was collected on January 21, 19xx, the entry for the collection of the subscription would be as follows:

```
Jan. 21   Cash                                        150,000
              Subscriptions Receivable, Common                  150,000
              Collected subscriptions in full
              for 10,000 shares of $10 par
              value common stock at $15 per
              share
```

Because the 10,000 shares are fully paid for, it is appropriate to issue the common stock, as shown here:

```
Jan. 21   Common Stock Subscribed                     100,000
              Common Stock                                      100,000
              Issued 10,000 shares of $10 par
              value common stock
```

Note that since the paid-in value in excess of par value was recorded in the January 1 entry, there is no need to record it again.

Assume that the financial statements are prepared on January 31, 19xx, before the remaining subscriptions are collected. The Subscriptions Receivable account of $75,000 ($225,000 − $150,000) would be classified as a current asset unless there was some reason why it would not be collected in the next year. The balance of $50,000 ($150,000 − $100,000) in the Common Stock Subscribed account represents the par value of the stock yet to be issued and is a temporary capital account. As such, it is properly shown as a part of stockholders' equity under Contributed Capital, as in the following illustration:

Stockholders' Equity

Contributed Capital		
Common Stock—$10 par value, 80,000		
shares authorized		
Issued and outstanding, 10,000 shares	$100,000	
Subscribed but not issued, 5,000 shares	50,000	$150,000
Paid-in Capital in Excess of Par Value,		
Common		75,000
Total Contributed Capital		$225,000

Assume that one-half payment of $37,500 is received on February 5 for the remaining subscriptions receivable. The entry for the collection would be as follows:

```
Feb. 5   Cash                                         37,500
              Subscriptions Receivable, Common                   37,500
              Collected one-half payment for
              subscriptions to 5,000 common
              shares
```

In this case, there is no entry to issue common stock because the subscription for the stock is not paid in full. If the subscriptions receivable are paid in full on February 20 the entries are as follows:

Feb. 20	Cash	37,500	
	Subscriptions Receivable, Common		37,500
	Collected subscriptions in full for 5,000 shares of $10 par value common stock for $15 per share		

Because the subscriptions are now paid in full, the common stock can be issued as follows:

Feb. 20	Capital Stock Subscribed, Common	50,000	
	Common Stock		50,000
	Issued 5,000 shares of $10 par value common stock		

Other Stockholders' Equity Transactions

Among other stockholders' equity transactions are the retirement of stock and donations of stock by stockholders and of assets by nonstockholders.

Retirement of Stock

*Objective 8
Account for the
retirement of
stock and
donations of
stock and other
assets*

A corporation may, with the approval of its stockholders, decide to purchase its stock to retire it. The company may undertake this action to buy out a shareholder, to adjust the structure of the company's stockholders' equity, or for other reasons favorable to the stockholders.

When stock is retired, all items related to that stock should also be removed from the related capital accounts. When stock is retired for a price that is less than the original contributed capital, the difference is recognized as Paid-in Capital, Retirement of Stock. However, if more is paid to retire the stock than was received when the shares were first issued, the difference is a reduction in stockholders' equity and is charged to Retained Earnings.

To illustrate the retirement of stock, we will assume that 100,000 shares of a corporation's preferred stock are being called and retired. The stock has a par value of $100 per share, is callable at $105, and was originally sold for $100 per share. The entry to record the retirement appears on the next page.

Preferred Stock	10,000,000	
Retained Earnings	500,000	
Cash		10,500,000

      Retirement of 100,000 shares
      of $100 par value preferred
      stock at call price of $105
      per share; original issue
      price $100 per share

This entry assumes that there is no previously recorded paid-in capital against which to charge the call premium.

Donation of Stock

When a company is having financial difficulties and the stock is owned by only a few people, the stockholders may vote to return a portion of their shares as a gift to the corporation. The stock can then be resold to raise additional working capital for the corporation. Because nothing has been paid for the donated stock, the company's assets, liabilities, and stockholders' equity are not affected. Therefore, donated stock should be recognized when received by a memorandum entry in the general journal. When the stock is resold, the company's assets and equities increase as they did when the stock was first issued.

Assume that a company has suffered losses for the last several years. The stockholders vote to donate 1,000 shares of their stock to the corporation for resale. The memorandum entry to record the donation follows:

Apr. 21   Received from the stockholders 1,000 shares
          of $5 par value common stock as a donation

Although the donation has not affected the assets, liabilities, or stockholders' equity, it is recognized on the balance sheet by affecting the number of shares outstanding, as shown below.

Stockholders' Equity

Contributed Capital		
Common Stock—$5 par value, 100,000 shares authorized,		
33,000 shares issued, 32,000 shares outstanding*		$ 165,000
Paid-in Capital in Excess of Par Value, Common		75,000
Total Contributed Capital		$ 240,000
Retained Earnings		838,200
Total Stockholders' Equity		$1,078,200

---

*There are 1,000 shares of treasury stock from stockholder donations.

To illustrate the resale of donated stock after conditions have improved, we will assume that the 1,000 shares are sold for $7 per share. The entry to record this transaction would be

```
May 10   Cash                                          7,000
              Paid-in Capital, Sale of Donated
              Stock                                                     7,000
                   Sold 1,000 shares of donated
                   stock for $7 per share
```

After sale of the stock, the stockholders' equity would appear as follows:

Stockholders' Equity

Contributed Capital	
Common Stock—$5 par value, 100,000 shares authorized,	
33,000 shares issued and outstanding	$ 165,000
Paid-in Capital in Excess of Par Value, Common	75,000
Paid-in Capital, Sale of Donated Stock	7,000
Total Contributed Capital	$ 247,000
Retained Earnings	838,200
Total Stockholders' Equity	$1,085,200

The sale of the stock has increased contributed capital and total stockholders' equity by $7,000. In addition, if the asset side of the balance sheet were presented, it would also show an increase in assets by the same amount.

Donations by Nonstockholders

Sometimes a corporation may receive a gift or donation from someone other than a stockholder. For example, many cities donate plant sites to corporations to persuade them to locate in their area. Such donations increase both the assets and the equity of the corporation. They are recorded at the fair market value of the asset received. For example, assume that Postville wanted to attract industry to provide new jobs. To do so, the city donated a plant site with a fair market value of $20,000 to a corporation. The donation would be recorded as follows:

```
Jan. 21   Land                                         20,000
              Paid-in Capital, Donated Plant Site                    20,000
                   To record the donation of a
                   plant site by the city of
                   Postville; fair value, $20,000
```

Many times donated assets have some restrictions as to their use. In such cases, it is often necessary to explain these restrictions in the notes to the financial statements.

Stock Values

The word *value* is associated with shares of stock in several ways. The terms *par value* and *stated value* have already been explained. They are each values per share that establish the legal capital of a company. Par value or stated value is arbitrarily set when the stock is authorized. Neither has any relationship to the book value or to the market value.

Book Value

*Objective 9
Calculate book
value per share,
and distinguish
it from market
value*

The **book value** of a company's stock represents the total assets of the company less liabilities. Thus it is simply the owners' equity of the company. The book value per share, therefore, represents the equity of the owner of one share of stock in the net assets of the corporation. This value, of course, does not necessarily equal the amount the shareholders would receive if the company were sold or liquidated. It is probably different, because most assets are recorded at historical cost, not at the current value at which they could be sold. To learn the book value per share when the company has only common stock outstanding, divide the total stockholders' equity by the total common shares outstanding plus shares subscribed but not issued. As an illustration, assume that a corporation has the following stockholders' equity:

Stockholders' Equity

Contributed Capital		
Common Stock—$10 par value, 20,000 shares authorized, 10,000 shares issued and outstanding	$100,000	
Paid-in Capital in Excess of Par Value, Common	50,000	$150,000
Retained Earnings		50,000
Total Stockholders' Equity		$200,000

The book value per share of common stock is figured in the following way:

$$\text{book value per share (BV)} = \frac{\text{total stockholders' equity}}{\text{total shares outstanding and subscribed}}$$

$$BV = \frac{\$200,000}{10,000}$$

$$BV = \$20 \text{ per share}$$

If a company has both preferred and common stock, the determination of book value per share is not so simple. The general rule is that the call value (or par value, if a call value is not specified) of the preferred stock plus any dividends in arrears is subtracted from total stockholders' equity to figure the equity pertaining to common stock. Suppose that a company reports its stockholders' equity as follows:

Stockholders' Equity

Contributed Capital		
Preferred Stock—$100 par value, 9% cumulative and nonparticipating, 2,000 shares authorized, issued, and outstanding		$ 200,000
Common Stock—$10 par value, 50,000 shares authorized, issued, and outstanding	$500,000	
Paid-in Capital in Excess of Par Value, Common	200,000	700,000
Total Contributed Capital		$ 900,000
Retained Earnings		100,000
Total Stockholders' Equity		$1,000,000

If there are no dividends in arrears and the preferred stock is callable at 105, the equity pertaining to common stock is figured as follows:

Total stockholders' equity	$1,000,000
Less equity allocated to preferred shareholders ($105 × 2,000 shares)	210,000
Equity pertaining to common shareholders	$ 790,000

The book values per share would be as follows:

Preferred Stock: $210,000 ÷ 2,000 shares = $105 per share
Common Stock: $790,000 ÷ 50,000 shares = $15.80 per share

If we assume the same facts except that two years of preferred stock dividends are in arrears, the stockholders' equity would be allocated as follows:

Total Stockholders' Equity		$1,000,000
Less: Call value of outstanding preferred shares	$210,000	
Dividends in arrears		
(9% × $200,000 × 2 years)	36,000	
Equity allocated to preferred shareholders		246,000
Equity pertaining to common shareholders		$ 754,000

The book values per share under this assumption are:

Preferred Stock: $246,000 ÷ 2,000 shares = $123 per share
Common Stock: $754,000 ÷ 50,000 shares = $15.08 per share

Undeclared preferred dividends fall into arrears on the last day of the fiscal year (the date when the financial statements are prepared). Also, dividends in arrears do not apply to unissued preferred stock.

Market Value

The book value per share often has little bearing on the market value per share. The **market value** is the price that investors are willing to pay for a share of stock on the open market. While the book value is based on historical cost, the market value is usually determined by investors' expectations for the particular company and general economic conditions. That is, what people expect about the company's future profitability and dividends per share, how risky they view the company and its current financial condition, as well as the state of the money market, all will play a part in determining the market value of a corporation's stock. For example, in April 1983 one major oil company, Texaco, had a market value per share of $32 compared with a book value per share of $55. At the same time, another large oil company, Shell, had a market value per share of $36 and a book value per share of $30.

Chapter Review

Review of Learning Objectives

1. Define a corporation and describe its basic organization and key personnel.

Corporations, whose ownership is represented by shares of stocks, are separate entities for both legal and accounting purposes. The stockholders own the corporation and elect the board of directors, whose duty it is to form corporate policy. The board appoints the corporate officers or management of the corporation. The officers are responsible for the operation of the business in accordance with the board's policy.

2. State the advantages and disadvantages of the corporate form of business.

The corporation is a separate legal entity having its own rights, privileges, and liabilities distinct from its owners. Like other forms of business entities, it has several advantages and disadvantages. The more common advantages are that (a) a corporation is a separate legal entity, (b) stockholders have limited liability, (c) it is easy to generate capital for a corporation, (d) stockholders can buy and sell shares of stock with ease, (e) there is a lack of mutual agency, (f) the corporation has a continuous existence, (g) authority and responsibility are centralized, and (h) it is run by a professional management team. Disadvantages of corporations include (a) a large amount of government regulation, (b) double taxation, (c) limited liability, and (d) the separation of ownership and control.

3. Account for organization costs.

The costs of organizing a corporation are recorded on a historical cost basis. As an intangible asset, organization costs are amortized over a reasonable period of time, usually five years.

4. Identify the components of stockholders' equity.

Stockholders' equity consists of contributed capital and retained earnings. Contributed capital may include more than one type of stock. Two of the most common types of stock are common stock and preferred stock. When only one type of security is issued, it is common stock. The holders of common stock have the right to elect the board of directors and vote on key issues of the corporation. In addition, common stockholders share in the earnings of the corporation, share in the assets of the corporation in case of liquidation, and maintain their percentage ownership.

Preferred stock is issued to investors whose investment objectives differ from those of common stockholders. To attract these investors, corporations give them a preference to certain items. Preferred stockholders' rights normally include the privilege of receiving dividends ahead of common shareholders, the right to assets in liquidation ahead of common shareholders, and convertibility to common stock.

Retained earnings, the other component of stockholders' equity, represents the claim of stockholders to the assets of the company resulting from profitable operations.

5. Calculate the division of dividends between common and preferred stockholders.

Most preferred stock is preferred as to dividends. This preference means that in allocating total dividends between common and preferred shareholders, the amount for the preferred stock is figured first. Then the remainder goes to common stock. If the preferred stock is cumulative and in arrears, the amount in arrears also has to be allocated to preferred before any allocation to common. If the preferred stock is participating, preferred stockholders share in additional dividends with common shareholders.

6. Account for the issuance of common and preferred stock for cash and other assets.

A corporation's stock will normally be issued for cash and other assets, or by subscription. The majority of states require that stock be issued at a minimum value called legal capital. Legal capital is represented by the par or stated value of the stock.

When stock is issued for cash or other assets, the par or stated value of the stock is recorded as common or preferred stock. When the stock is sold at an amount greater than the par or stated value, the excess is recorded as Paid-in Capital in Excess of Par or Stated Value.

Sometimes stock is issued for noncash assets. In these transactions, it is necessary to decide what value to use in recording the issuance of the stock. The general rule is to record the stock at the market value of the stock issued. If this value cannot be determined, then the fair market value of the asset received will be used to record the transaction.

7. Account for stock subscriptions.

When stock is not fully paid for at the time of sale, it is not issued. However, the transaction is recorded by debiting Subscriptions Receivable (a current asset) and crediting Capital Stock Subscribed (a stockholders' equity account). When the stock has been fully paid for and is issued, Capital Stock Subscribed is debited and Capital Stock is credited.

8. Account for the retirement of stock and donations of stock and other assets.

A company may decide to purchase its stock to retire it. When stock is retired, all the contributed capital associated with the retired shares must be removed from the accounts. If stock is retired for less than the original contributed capital, the difference should be recorded as Paid-in Capital, Retirement of Stock. If stock is retired for more than the contributed capital, the difference is a reduction in Retained Earnings.

Stockholders of a company may donate their stock to the company. Because the company does not pay for the shares, the donation should be recorded with a memorandum entry. When the stock is reissued, the company's assets and equity should increase as they did at the original issuance of the stock. The reissuance is recorded by a debit to the appropriate asset account and a credit to Paid-in Capital, Sale of Donated Stock. Other donated assets should be recorded at fair market value, and a credit should be made to Paid-in Capital, Donated Asset.

9. Calculate book value per share, and distinguish it from market value.

Book value per share is the owners' equity per share. It is calculated by dividing stockholders' equity by the number of common shares outstanding. When preferred stock exists, the call or par value plus any dividends in arrears are deducted first from total stockholders' equity before dividing by common shares outstanding. Market value per share is the price investors are willing to pay based on their expectations about the future earning ability of the company.

Review Problem
Stock Journal Entries, Stockholders' Equity, and Book Value Per Share

The Beta Corporation was organized in 19xx in the state of Arizona. The charter of the corporation authorized the issuance of 1,000,000 shares of $1 par value common stock and an additional 25,000 shares of 4 percent, $20 par value cumulative convertible preferred stock that is callable at $22 per share. Transactions that relate to the stock of the company for 19xx are shown below.

Feb. 12 Issued 100,000 shares of common stock for $125,000.
    20   Issued 3,000 shares of common stock for accounting and legal services. The services were billed to the company at $3,600.
Mar. 15 Issued 120,000 shares of common stock to Edward Jackson in exchange for a building and land, which had an appraised value of $100,000 and $25,000, respectively.
Apr. 2   Accepted subscriptions on 200,000 shares of common stock for $1.30 per share.
July 1   Issued 25,000 shares of preferred stock for $500,000.
Sept. 30 Collected in full subscriptions related to 60 percent of the common stock subscribed and issued the appropriate stock to subscribers.
Dec. 31 The company reported earnings of $40,000 for 19xx, and the board declared dividends of $20,000. Dividends include preferred stock cash dividend for one-half year.

Required

1. Prepare the journal entries necessary to record these stock-related transactions. Following the December 31 entry, show dividends payable for each class of stock.
2. Prepare the stockholders' equity section of the Beta Corporation balance sheet as of December 31.
3. Calculate book value per share for common and preferred stock.

Answer to Review Problem

1. Journal entries prepared:

Feb. 12	Cash	125,000	
	Common Stock		100,000
	Paid-in Capital in Excess of Par		
	Value, Common		25,000
	To record the sale of 100,000 shares of $1 par value common stock for $1.25 per share		

20	Organization Costs	3,600	
	Common Stock		3,000
	Paid-in Capital in Excess of Par		
	Value, Common		600
	To record issuance of 3,000 shares of $1 par value common stock for billed accounting and legal services of $3,600		

Mar. 15	Building	100,000	
	Land	25,000	
	Common Stock		120,000
	Paid-in Capital in Excess of Par		
	Value, Common		5,000
	To record issuance of 120,000 shares of $1 par value common stock for a building and tract of land appraised at $100,000 and $25,000		

Apr. 2	Subscriptions Receivable, Common Stock	260,000	
	Common Stock Subscribed		200,000
	Paid-in Capital in Excess of Par		
	Value, Common		60,000
	To record subscription for 200,000 shares of $1 par value stock at $1.30 a share		

July 1	Cash	500,000	
	Preferred Stock		500,000
	To record sale of 25,000 shares of $20 par value preferred stock for $20 per share		

Sept. 30	Cash	156,000	
	Subscriptions Receivable, Common Stock		156,000
	To record collection in full of 60 percent subscriptions receivable: $260,000 $\times$ .60 = $156,000		

30	Common Stock Subscribed	120,000	
	Common Stock		120,000
	To record issuance of common stock		

Dec. 31 Income Summary	40,000	
Retained Earnings		40,000
To record the transfer of net income to retained earnings		
31 Dividends Declared	20,000	
Dividends Payable		20,000
To record the declaration of a $20,000 cash dividend to preferred and common stockholders		

Preferred stock cash dividend
$$\$500,000 \times .04 \times \tfrac{1}{2} = \underline{\$10,000}$$

Common stock cash dividend:	
Total dividend	$20,000
Less preferred stock cash dividend	10,000
	$\underline{\underline{\$10,000}}$

2. Stockholders' equity section of balance sheet prepared:

Beta Corporation
Stockholders' Equity
December 31, 19xx

Contributed Capital		
4% Cumulative Convertible Preferred Stock—$20 par value, 25,000 shares authorized, issued, and outstanding, callable at $22 per share		$ 500,000
Common Stock—$1 par value, 1,000,000 shares authorized, 343,000 shares issued and outstanding	$343,000	
Common Stock Subscribed	80,000	
Paid-in Capital in Excess of Par Value, Common	90,600	513,600
Total Contributed Capital		$1,013,600
Retained Earnings		20,000
Total Stockholders' Equity		$1,033,600

---

3. Book value per share calculated:

Preferred stock:

$$\frac{\text{total call value} + \text{preferred dividends in arrears}}{\text{shares outstanding}} = \frac{(25,000 \times \$22 \text{ per share}) + 0}{25,000 \text{ shares}}$$

$$= \frac{\$550,000}{25,000} = \$22 \text{ per share}$$

Common stock:

$$\frac{\text{total stockholders' equity}}{\text{shares outstanding}} = \frac{\$1,033,600 - \$550,000}{343,000 \text{ shares}} = \frac{\$483,600}{343,000}$$
$$= \$1.41 \text{ per share}$$

Chapter Assignments

Questions

1. What is a corporation, and how is it formed?
2. What is the role of the board of directors in a corporation, and how does it differ from the role of management?
3. What are the typical officers in the management of a corporation and their duties?
4. What are several advantages of the corporate form of business? Explain.
5. What are several disadvantages of the corporate form of business? Explain.
6. What are organization costs of a corporation?
7. What is the proper accounting treatment of organization costs?
8. What are some of the rights accorded stockholders?
9. What is the legal capital of a corporation, and what is its significance?
10. How is the value determined for recording stock issued for noncash assets?
11. What are stock subscriptions, and how are Subscriptions Receivable and Common Stock Subscribed classified on the balance sheet?
12. What does it mean for preferred stock to be cumulative, participating, convertible, and/or callable?
13. What are dividends in arrears, and how should they be disclosed in the financial statements?
14. What is the proper classification of the following accounts on the balance sheet? (a) Organization Costs; (b) Common Stock; (c) Subscriptions Receivable, Preferred; (d) Preferred Stock Subscribed; (e) Paid-in Capital in Excess of Par Value, Common; (f) Paid-in Capital in Excess of Stated Value, Common; (g) Discount on Common Stock; (h) Retained Earnings.
15. Would you expect a corporation's book value per share to equal its market value per share? Why or why not?

Classroom Exercises

Exercise 16-1
Journal Entries and Stockholders' Equity
(L.O. 6)

The Gossage Hospital Supply Corporation was organized in 19xx. The company was authorized to issue 100,000 shares of no-par common stock with a stated value at $5 per share, and 20,000 shares of $100 par value, 6 percent noncumulative preferred stock. On March 1 the company sold 50,000 shares of its common stock for $12 per share and 5,000 shares of its preferred stock for $100 per share.

1. Prepare the journal entries to record the sale of the stock.
2. Prepare the company's stockholders' equity section of the balance sheet immediately after the common and preferred stock were issued.

Exercise 16-2
Stockholders' Equity
(L.O. 4)

The accounts and balances on the next page were taken from the records of Dunstan Corporation on December 31, 19xx.

Account Name	Balance Debit	Balance Credit
Common Stock—$10 par value, 60,000 shares authorized, 20,000 shares issued and outstanding		$200,000
Common Stock Subscribed		20,000
Preferred Stock—$100 par value, 9% cumulative, 10,000 shares authorized, 5,000 shares issued and outstanding		500,000
Paid-in Capital in Excess of Par Value, Common		170,000
Retained Earnings		12,000
Subscriptions Receivable, Common	$30,000	

Prepare a stockholders' equity section for Dunstan Corporation's balance sheet.

**Exercise 16-3
Preferred Stock
Dividends with
Dividends in
Arrears
(L.O. 5)**

The Morley Corporation has 10,000 shares of its $100, 8 percent cumulative preferred stock outstanding and 50,000 shares of its $1 par value common stock outstanding. In its first four years of operation, the board of directors of Morley Corporation paid cash dividends as follows: 19x1, none; 19x2, $140,000; 19x3, $140,000; 19x4, $140,000.

Determine the total cash dividends and dividends per share paid to the preferred and common stockholders during each of the four years.

**Exercise 16-4
Journal
Entries—Stated
Value Stock
(L.O. 6)**

The Richardson Corporation is authorized to issue 200,000 shares of no-par stock. The company recently sold 30,000 shares for $15 per share.

1. Prepare the journal entry to record the sale of the stock if there is no stated value.
2. Prepare the entry if a $5 stated value is authorized by the company's board of directors.

**Exercise 16-5
Book Value for
Preferred and
Common Stock
(L.O. 9)**

The stockholders' equity section of the Carlyle Corporation's balance sheet is shown below.

Stockholders' Equity

Contributed Capital		
Preferred Stock—$100 par value, 6% cumulative, 10,000 shares authorized, 100 shares issued and outstanding*		$10,000
Common Stock—$5 par value, 100,000 shares authorized, 10,000 shares issued and outstanding	$50,000	
Paid-in Capital in Excess of Par Value, Common	8,000	58,000
Total Contributed Capital		$68,000
Retained Earnings		15,000
Total Stockholders' Equity		$83,000

---

*The preferred stock is callable at $104 per share, and one year's dividends are in arrears.

Determine the book value per share for both the preferred and the common stock.

**Exercise 16-6
Preferred and
Common Stock
Dividends
(L.O. 5)**

The Knox Corporation pays dividends at the end of each year. The dividends paid for 19x1, 19x2, and 19x3 were $50,000, $20,000, and $80,000, respectively.

Calculate the total amount of dividends paid each year to the common and preferred stockholders if each of the following capital structures is assumed: (1) 10,000 shares of $100 par, 6 percent noncumulative preferred stock and 30,000 shares of $10 par common stock. (2) 5,000 shares of $100 par, 6 percent cumulative preferred stock and 30,000 shares of $10 par common stock. There were no dividends in arrears at the beginning of 19x1. (3) 5,000 shares of $100 par, 6 percent fully participating noncumulative preferred stock and 30,000 shares of $10 par common stock. (4) Same as 3, except partially participating up to a total of 8 percent of par value.

**Exercise 16-7
Organization
Costs Journal
Entries
(L.O. 3)**

The Plummer Corporation was organized during 19x7. The company incurred the following costs in organizing the company: (1) Attorney's fees, market value of services $2,000, acceptance of 1,500 shares of $1 par common stock. (2) Paid the state $1,000 for incorporation fees. (3) Accountant accepted 1,000 shares of $1 par value common stock for services that would normally be billed at $1,250.

Prepare the journal entries necessary to record these transactions and to amortize organization costs for the first year, assuming that the company elects to write off organization costs over five years.

**Exercise 16-8
Issuance of
Stock for
Noncash Assets
(L.O. 6)**

The Hammond Corporation issued 1,000 shares of its $10 par value common stock for some land. The land had a fair market value of $13,000.

Prepare the journal entries necessary to record the issuance of the stock for the land under each of the following conditions: (1) the stock was selling for $12 per share on the day of the transaction; and (2) management attempted to place a value on the common stock, but could not determine the value.

**Exercise 16-9
Stock Subscriptions
(L.O. 7)**

The Dalton Corporation sold 10,000 shares of its $5 par value common stock by subscription for $9 per share on February 15, 19xx. Cash was received in installments from the purchasers: 50 percent on April 1 and 50 percent on June 1.

Prepare the entries necessary to record these transactions.

**Exercise 16-10
Stock Transactions—Retirement and
Donation of
Stock
(L.O. 8)**

Record the following equity transactions of the Rollow Company during 19xx:

Mar. 14   Retired 10,000 shares of $100 par value preferred stock at call price of $110 per share. Stock was originally sold at par value.

May 5   Julia Barnes donated 5,000 shares of her $5 par value common stock to the company.

    6   Sold the 5,000 donated shares for $23 per share.

July 19   Charles Farmer donated land to the company as an incentive to move its subsidiary to Tullie. Farmer had purchased the land for $15,000, and the current value was $36,000.

**Published
Financial
Information:
United Technologies
Corporation
(L.O. 4)**

Interpreting Accounting Information

Over the years some companies have developed a very complex stockholders' equity section and engage in many different transactions affecting stockholders' equity each year. One such company is United Technologies Corporation, with $12 billion in sales, which designs, builds, and sells high-technology products. Among its best-known products are Pratt & Whitney Aircraft jet engines, Carrier air conditioners, Otis elevators, and Sikorsky helicopters. Instead of a simple statement of retained earnings, United Technologies has in its annual report a consolidated statement of changes in shareowners' equity. This statement explains the changes in all the components of stockholders' equity. In the year 1979 United Technologies engaged in a number of interesting stockholders' equity transactions, and its statement for that year is presented below (amounts are in thousands of dollars):

United Technologies Corporation
Consolidated Statement of Changes in Shareowners' Equity
For the Year Ended December 31, 1979

	$4.50 Preferred Stock	$2.55 Preferred Stock	$2.84 Preferred Stock	$3.875 Preferred Stock	$7.32 Preferred Stock	$8.00 Preferred Stock	Common Stock	Retained Earnings
Balance December 31, 1978	$ —	$ —	$1,214	$189,373	$106,962	$ 45,163	$607,081	$ 822,995
Issued in connection with acquisition of Carrier Corporation (40,000 and 21,444,361 shares)	4,000	536,109						
Issued on conversion of convertible debentures (229,497 preferred shares and 38,909 common shares)		6,466					1,441	
Issued on conversion of 228,746 shares of Preferred Stock (860,695 common shares and 12,198 preferred shares)		(8)	(1,041)	(22)	(938)	(15,116)	17,103	
Issued under employee incentive plans, and related tax benefit: 85,533 shares of Preferred Stock 169,190 shares of Common Stock		943		432	226		5,754	
Redemption and purchase of 46,531 shares of Preferred Stock	(476)		(173)	(1,743)				(242)
Net income								325,608
Dividends on: Common Stock ($2.20 per share) Preferred Stock								(91,699) (49,064)
Balance December 31, 1979	$3,524	$543,510	$ —	$188,040	$106,250	$ 30,047	$631,379	$1,007,598

All the preferred stock issues are preferred as to dividends, and all have par values of $100 per share except those that offer $2.55 per share and $3.875 per share dividends, which have par values of $25 and $50 per share, respectively. All are cumulative, and all are convertible into common stock except for the issue with a $4.50 per share dividend. The common stock has a par value of $5 per share. The column headed Common Stock includes both the par value of the stock issued and the paid-in capital in excess of par value.

Required

United Technologies' 1979 statement of changes in shareholders' equity has seven summary transactions. Show that you understand this statement by explaining each in one sentence. [You will have to use your judgment in this case because you have not studied all the kinds of transactions presented. Sometimes you will also have to make assumptions about an offsetting part of the entry. For example, assume that the company debits Investment in Carrier Corporation for the first entry, that there are no premiums or discounts on debentures (long-term debt), and that employees pay cash for stock purchased under employee incentive plans. You may want to look ahead to Chapter 18 on conversion of long-term bonds into capital stock.]

Problem Set A

Problem 16A-1
Stock Journal Entries and Stockholders' Equity
(L.O. 6)

On July 1, 19xx, Worthington, a new corporation, issued 15,000 shares of its common stock for a corporate headquarters building. The building had a fair market value of $155,000 and a book value of $130,000. Because the corporation is new, it is not possible to establish a market value for the common stock.

Required

1. Record the issuance of stock for the building, assuming the following conditions: (a) the par value of the stock is $9 per share, (b) the par value of the stock is $16 per share, (c) the stock is no-par stock, and (d) the stock is no-par stock, but has a stated value of $2 per share.
2. Prepare the stockholders' equity section of Worthington's balance sheet immediately after the issuance of the stock, assuming that the par value was $9 per share.

Problem 16A-2
Stock Journal Entries and Stockholders' Equity
(L.O. 6, 7)

The Fast Rail Company has been authorized by the state of Texas to issue 1,000,000 shares of $1 par value common stock. The company began issuing its common stock in July of 19xx. During July the company had the following stock transactions:

July 10 Issued 29,000 shares of stock for a building and land with fair market value of $22,000 and $7,000, respectively.
  15 Accepted subscriptions to 400,000 shares of its stock for $500,000.
  20 Collected full payment on 200,000 shares of the common stock subscribed on July 15. Issued the appropriate shares.
  23 Sold 15,000 shares of stock for $20,000 cash.
  27 Collected full payment on 100,000 shares of the common stock subscribed on July 15 and issued the shares.

Required

1. Prepare the journal entries to record the stock transactions of the Fast Rail Company for the month of July.
2. Prepare the stockholders' equity section of the Fast Rail Company's balance sheet as of July 31.

Problem 16A-3
Preferred and Common Stock Dividends
(L.O. 5)

The Seward Corporation had the following stock outstanding for 19x1 through 19x4:

Preferred stock—$50 par value, 4% cumulative, 10,000 shares authorized, issued, and outstanding

Common stock—$5 par value, 150,000 shares authorized, issued, and outstanding

The company paid $15,000, $15,000, $47,000, and $65,000 in dividends during 19x1, 19x2, 19x3, and 19x4, respectively.

Required

1. Determine the total amounts per share of dividends paid to common stockholders and preferred stockholders in 19x1, 19x2, 19x3, and 19x4.

2. Perform the same computations assuming that the preferred stock is noncumulative and fully participating.

Problem 16A-4
Preferred and Common Stock Book Values
(L.O. 9)

The stockholders' equity section of the Lancaster Company's balance sheet follows.

Stockholders' Equity

Contributed Capital		
Preferred Stock—$100 par value, 7% cumulative, 10,000 shares authorized, 7,000 shares issued and outstanding*		$ 700,000
Common Stock—$1 par value, 1,000,000 shares authorized, 800,000 shares issued and outstanding	$800,000	
Paid-in Capital in Excess of Par Value, Common	25,000	825,000
Total Contributed Capital		$1,525,000
Retained Earnings		2,230,000
Total Stockholders' Equity		$3,755,000

---

*The preferred stock is callable at $110 and one year's dividends are in arrears.

Required

1. Compute the preferred stock book value per share.

2. Compute the common stock book value per share.

Problem 16A-5
Comprehensive Stockholders' Equity Transactions and Book Value
(L.O. 6, 7, 8, 9)

In January 19xx, the Honey Corporation was organized and authorized to issue 2,000,000 shares of no-par common stock and 50,000 shares of 5 percent, $50 par value, noncumulative, fully participating preferred stock. The stock-related transactions of the first year's operations are presented below.

Jan. 19   Sold 15,000 shares of the common stock for $25,000. State law requires a minimum of $1 stated value per share.

26   Accepted subscriptions for 20,000 shares of the common stock for $2 per share.

Feb. 7   Issued 30,000 shares of common stock for a building that had an appraised value of $45,000.

Mar. 22   Collected full payment for 12,000 shares of the common stock subscribed on January 26, 19xx, and issued the stock.

April 19   Received a truck with a market value of $5,500, which was donated by a stockholder.

May 23   Received 5,000 shares of common stock, originally issued at $2 per share, as a donation from a stockholder. The stock is to be resold.

June 30   Closed the Income Summary account. Reported $80,000 income for the first six months of operations.

July 15   Sold and reissued the 5,000 donated shares of common stock at $3.

Sept. 1 Collected the full amount on the remaining 8,000 shares of common stock subscribed and issued the stock.

Oct. 30 Issued 4,000 shares of common stock for a piece of land. The stock is selling for $3 per share, and the land has a fair market value of $12,500.

Nov. 10 Accepted subscriptions for 10,000 shares of the common stock for $2.50 per share.

Dec. 15 Issued 2,200 shares of preferred stock for $50 per share.

31 Closed the Income Summary account. Reported $20,000 income for the last six months of operations.

Required

1. Prepare the journal entries to record only the stock-related transactions of Honey Corporation during 19xx.

2. Prepare the stockholders' equity section of Honey Corporation's balance sheet as of December 31, 19xx.

3. Figure the book value per share of preferred stock and common stock as of December 31, 19xx. The preferred stock is callable at $55 per share. For common stock, include common stock subscribed with outstanding shares.

Problem Set B

Problem 16B-1
Stock Journal
Entries and
Stockholders'
Equity
(L.O. 6)

Whitehall, a new corporation, issued 10,000 shares of its common stock on August 14, 19xx, for $80,000 cash and for building and equipment with fair market values of $40,000 and $20,000, respectively. A market value has not been established for the new corporation's stock.

Required

1. Record the issuance of the stock, assuming the following conditions: (a) the stock had a par value of $10 per share, (b) the stock had a par value of $15 per share, (c) the stock had no par value, and (d) the stock had no par value, but the stated value of the stock was $12 per share, set by the board of directors.

2. Prepare the stockholders' equity section of Whitehall's balance sheet immediately after the issuance of the stock, assuming that the par value was $10 per share.

Problem 16B-2
Stock Journal
Entries and
Stockholders'
Equity
(L.O. 6, 7)

The Blendon Woods Recreation Corporation recently received its charter from the state of New Mexico. This charter authorized the company to issue 500,000 shares of $5 par value common stock and 100,000 shares of $100 par value, 6 percent cumulative preferred stock. The company completed the following stock transactions prior to the opening of its recreational facilities.

Feb. 15 Sold 10,000 shares of its common stock for $60,000.

21 Issued 100,000 shares of its common stock for land at Blendon Woods, which had a fair market value of $575,000

23 Issued a total of 1,000 shares common stock for services by the company's accountants and lawyers in organizing the company. The services were billed to the company as $2,500 and $3,000, respectively.

25 Accepted subscriptions to 10,000 shares of its common stock for $5.75 per share and 10,000 shares of its preferred stock at $100 per share.

Mar. 10 Collected payment in full for 50 percent of stock subscriptions receivables recorded on February 25 and issued stock.

1. Prepare the journal entries to record the stock transactions of the corporation presented here.
2. Prepare the stockholders' equity section of the corporation's balance sheet as of March 11.

Problem 16B-3
Preferred and
Common Stock
Dividends
(L.O. 5)

The Parsons Corporation had 100,000 shares of its $10 par value common stock and 8,000 of its $100 par value, 6 percent noncumulative nonparticipating preferred stock outstanding for the years 19x1 through 19x4. Over the four-year period, the company's board of directors declared cash dividends of $100,000, $24,000, $60,000, and $150,000.

Required

1. Compute the total and per share dividends that would be paid to common and preferred stockholders in 19x1, 19x2, 19x3, and 19x4.
2. Perform the same computations, assuming that the preferred stock was cumulative instead of noncumulative.

Problem 16B-4
Preferred and
Common Stock
Book Values
(L.O. 9)

The Self Corporation's stockholders' equity as of December 31, 19xx, is presented below.

Stockholders' Equity

Contributed Capital
    Preferred Stock—$100 par value, 6% cumulative, 50,000

shares authorized, 20,000 shares issued and outstanding*	$2,000,000
Common Stock—$10 par value, 1,000,000 shares authorized,	
500,000 shares issued and outstanding	5,000,000
Paid-in Capital in Excess of Par Value, Common	110,000
Total Contributed Capital	$7,110,000
Retained Earnings	2,300,000
Total Stockholders' Equity	$9,410,000

---

*The preferred stock is callable at $106 and has $60,000 dividends in arrears.

Required

1. Compute the preferred stock book value per share.
2. Compute the common stock book value per share.

Problem 16B-5
Comprehensive
Stockholders'
Equity Transac-
tions and Book
Value
(L.O. 6, 7, 8, 9)

The Ogilvie Corporation was organized during 19xx, with authorization to issue 1,000,000 shares of $10 par value common stock and 100,000 shares of $100 par value, 9 percent noncumulative preferred stock that is callable at $105. Stock- and income-related transactions applicable to the first year are as follows:

Jan.   1   Issued 10,000 shares of $10 par value common stock for $110,000.
      24   Issued 100 shares of $10 par value common stock to an attorney for services associated with starting the corporation. Services were billed at $1,000.
Feb. 14   Accepted subscriptions to 30,000 shares of $10 par value common stock for $12 per share.

Mar. 15 Received full payment on 15,000 shares of the stock subscriptions received on February 14, 19xx. Issued the appropriate number of shares to the stockholders.

April 9 Dora Russell donated a building to the corporation so that it could expand its Marysville, Ohio, operations. Russell had paid $60,000 for the building originally, but its current value is $86,000.

June 30 Closed the Income Summary account. Reported income of $30,000 for the first six months of operations during 19xx.

July 20 Collected remaining amount due on the February 14 stock subscriptions and issued the remaining stock.

Aug. 26 Russell contributed 2,000 shares of her $10 par value common stock to the corporation. This action was taken so the company could resell the stock to obtain additional working capital. The stock was originally purchased at $12 per share.

Sept. 19 Sold the 2,000 shares of common stock shares donated by Dora Russell for $13 per share.

Nov. 1 Issued 500 shares of $100 par value noncumulative preferred stock for $100 per share.

Dec. 20 Accepted subscriptions for 8,000 shares of $10 par value common stock for $14 per share.

31 Closed the Income Summary account. Reported income of $40,000 for the last six months of operations during 19xx.

Required

1. Prepare journal entries to record the above transactions in 19xx.
2. Prepare the stockholders' equity section of Ogilvie Corporation's balance sheet on December 31, 19xx.
3. Compute book value per share of preferred stock and common stock as of December 31, 19xx. For common stock, include common stock subscribed with outstanding stock.

Financial Decision Case 16-1

Southwest Geotech Corporation (L.O. 4)

The companies offering services to the oil exploration industry are growing rapidly. Participating in this growth, Southwest Geotech Corporation has expanded rapidly in recent years. Because of its profitability, the company has been able to grow without obtaining external financing. This fact is reflected in its current balance sheet, which contains no long-term debt. The liability and stockholders' equity sections of the balance sheet are shown below.

Liabilities		
Current Liabilities		$ 500,000
Stockholders' Equity		
Common Stock, $10 par value, 100,000 shares		
issued and outstanding	$1,000,000	
Paid-in Capital in Excess of Par Value, Common	1,800,000	
Retained Earnings	1,700,000	
Total Stockholders' Equity		4,500,000
Total Liabilities and Stockholders' Equity		$5,000,000

The company is now faced with the possibility of doubling its size by purchasing the operations of a rival company for $4,000,000. If the purchase goes through, Southwest will become the top company in its specialized industry in the southwestern part of the country. The problem for management is how to finance the purchase. After much study and discussion with bankers and underwriters, management prepares three financing alternatives (see below) to present to the board of directors, which must authorize the purchase and the financing.

Alternative A: The company could issue $4,000,000 of long-term debt. Given the company's financial rating and the current market rates, it is believed that the company will have to pay an interest rate of 17 percent on the debt.

Alternative B: The company could issue 40,000 shares of 12 percent, $100 par value preferred stock.

Alternative C: The company could issue 100,000 additional shares of $10 par value common stock at $40.

Management explains to the board that the interest on the long-term debt is tax deductible and that the applicable income tax rate is 40 percent. The board members know that a dividend of $.80 per share of common stock was paid last year, up from $.60 and $.40 per share in the two years before that. The board has had a policy of regular increases in dividends of $.20 per share. The board feels that each of the three financing alternatives is feasible and now wishes to study the financial effects of each alternative.

Required

1. Prepare a schedule to show how the liability and stockholders' equity side of Southwest Geotech's balance sheet will look under each alternative, and figure the debt to equity ratio for each.

2. Compute and compare the cash needed to pay the interest or dividend for each kind of financing net of income taxes in the first year. How may this requirement change in future years?

3. Evaluate the alternatives, giving the arguments for and against each.

Learning Objectives

Chapter Seventeen

Retained Earnings and Corporate Income Statements

1. *Define and explain the significance of retained earnings.*

2. *Account for cash dividends, stock dividends, and stock splits.*

3. *Account for treasury stock transactions.*

4. *Define prior period adjustments and prepare a statement of retained earnings.*

5. *Account for the appropriation of retained earnings.*

6. *Define the basic terms of corporate income tax liability, and calculate corporate tax liability.*

7. *Describe the disclosure on the income statement of discontinued operations, extraordinary items, and accounting changes.*

8. *Compute primary and fully diluted earnings per share.*

This chapter continues the study of the stockholders' equity section of the balance sheet. It first covers the retained earnings of a corporation, transactions that affect them, and the statement of retained earnings. Then the rest of the chapter examines the components of the corporate income statement. After studying this chapter, you should be able to meet the learning objectives listed on the left.

Retained Earnings Transactions

Stockholders' equity, as presented earlier, has two parts: contributed capital and retained earnings. The retained earnings of a company are the part of the stockholders' equity that represents claims to assets arising from the earnings of the business. They equal the profits of a company since the date of its beginning less any losses, dividends to stockholders, or transfers to contributed capital. Figure 17-1 (next page) shows a statement of retained earnings of Caprock Corporation for 19xx. The beginning balance of retained earnings of $854,000 is increased by net income of $76,000 and decreased by cash dividends of $30,000, so that the ending balance is $900,000.

A credit balance in the Retained Earnings account is important because it shows the combined claims against total assets that have come from operations but have not been satisfied by payment of dividends to the company's stockholders. In most cases, the existence of retained earnings means that assets generated by operations have been kept in the company to help it grow or to meet other business needs. Note, however, that a credit balance in

Figure 17-1
A Simplified
Statement of
Retained
Earnings

Caprock Corporation Statement of Retained Earnings For the Year Ended December 31, 19xx	
Retained Earnings, Jan. 1	$854,000
Net Income, 19xx	76,000
Subtotal	$930,000
Less Cash Dividend, Common	30,000
Retained Earnings, Dec. 31	$900,000

*Objective 1
Define and
explain the
significance of
retained
earnings*

Retained Earnings does *not* mean that cash or any designated set of assets belongs directly to retained earnings. The fact that earnings have been retained means that assets as a whole have been increased.

Retained Earnings may carry a debit balance. Generally, this happens when a company's losses and distributions to stockholders are greater than its profits from operations. In such a case, the firm is said to have a **deficit** (debit balance) in retained earnings. This is shown in the stockholders' equity section of the balance sheet as a deduction from contributed capital.

Accountants have used different terms for the retained earnings of a business. One term is *surplus*, which implies that there are excess assets available for dividends, even though the company may have other business uses for the assets. Because of this possible misinterpretation, the American Institute of Certified Public Accountants has called for the use of more fitting terms, such as *retained income, retained earnings, accumulated earnings*, or *earnings retained for use in the business*.[1]

Several kinds of transactions affect the Retained Earnings account. These transactions are connected with (1) income and losses of a company, (2) dividend declarations, (3) treasury stock, and (4) prior period adjustments. Following the discussion of these events, a comprehensive statement of retained earnings is presented.

Income and Losses of a Corporation

At the end of the accounting period, the income or loss of a corporation is transferred from the Income Summary account to the Retained Earnings account by a closing entry. The reason for doing so is that the corporation by law must account to its owners—the stockholders—for the amount of earnings accumulated and available for distribution as dividends.

Dividends

As explained in Chapter 16, a **dividend** is a distribution of assets of a corporation to its stockholders. Each stockholder receives assets, usually

1. Committee on Accounting Terminology, *Accounting Terminology Bulletin No. 1*, "Review and Resume" (New York: American Institute of Certified Public Accountants, 1953), par. 69.

cash, in proportion to the number of shares of stock held. The board of directors has sole authority to declare dividends.

Dividends may be paid quarterly, semiannually, annually, or at other times decided on by the board. Most states do not allow the board to declare a dividend that exceeds retained earnings. Where such a dividend is declared, the corporation is essentially returning to the stockholders a part of their paid-in capital. This is called a **liquidating dividend** and is normally paid when a company is going out of business or is reducing its operations. However, having sufficient retained earnings does not in itself justify the distribution of a dividend. Cash or other readily distributable assets may not be available for distribution. In such a case the board of directors may elect to keep the assets in the business rather than declare a dividend.

There are three important dates associated with dividends. In order of occurrence, these are (1) the date of declaration, (2) the date of record, and (3) the date of payment. The date of declaration is the date the board of directors takes formal action declaring that a dividend will be paid. The date of record is the date on which ownership of the stock of a company, and therefore of the right to receive a dividend, is determined. Those individuals who own the stock on the date of record will be the ones to receive the dividend. The date of payment is the date the dividend will be paid to the stockholders of record.

For example, the board of the Caprock Corporation may declare a dividend of $1.50 per share of common stock on February 21 to those stockholders of record on March 10, payable on March 31. A dividend is recorded as a current liability on the date of declaration (February 21) because the board of directors has legally obligated the corporation to pay the dividend at that time. No entry is required on the date of record (March 10) because this date is used simply to determine the owners of the stock who will receive the dividends. No transaction occurs on that date. On the payment date (March 31), an entry is made to record the distribution of cash and to remove the dividend liability.

Cash Dividends To illustrate the accounting for cash dividends, we will assume that the Caprock Corporation has the following capital structure:

Preferred Stock—$100 par value, 6% cumulative, 1,000 shares authorized and outstanding	$100,000
Common Stock, $5 par value, 100,000 shares authorized and outstanding	500,000

The board of directors has decided that sufficient cash is available to pay a $56,000 cash dividend. The $56,000 will be distributed as a $6,000 annual dividend to the preferred stockholders and a 50¢ per share dividend to the common stockholders. The dividend is declared on February 21, 19xx, to be paid March 31, 19xx, to stockholders of record on March 10, 19xx. The entries to record the declaration and payment of the cash dividend follow:

Date of declaration

Feb. 21	Dividends Declared	56,000	
	Dividends Payable		56,000

To record the declaration of a
cash dividend, 6% of par value
to preferred stockholders and 50¢
per share to common stockholders
Preferred dividend
$100,000 \times 6\% = \$6,000$
Common dividend
100,000 shares $\times \$.50 = \$50,000$

Date of record

Mar. 10   No entry necessary

Date of payment

Mar. 31	Dividends Payable	56,000	
	Cash		56,000

To record the payment of cash
dividends of $56,000

Note that the obligation to pay the dividend was established on the date of declaration. No entry was required on the date of record, and the liability was liquidated, or settled, on the date of payment. At the end of the accounting period, the Dividends Declared account is closed by debiting Retained Earnings and crediting Dividends Declared. Retained earnings are thereby reduced by the total dividends declared during the period.

Some companies do not pay dividends very often. For one reason, the company may not have any earnings. For another, the company may be growing and thus the assets generated by the earnings are kept in the company for business purposes such as expansion of the plant. Investors in such growth companies expect a return on their investment in the form of an increased market value of their stock.

Stock Dividends   A stock dividend is a proportional distribution of shares of the company's stock to the corporation's stockholders. The distribution does not change the assets and liabilities of the firm as does a cash dividend. The board of directors may declare a stock dividend for several reasons:

1. It may wish to give stockholders some evidence of the success of the company without paying a cash dividend, which would affect the firm's working capital position.
2. The board's aim may be to reduce the market price of the stock by increasing the number of shares outstanding, though this goal is more often met by stock splits.
3. It may want to make a nontaxable distribution to stockholders. Stock

dividends that meet certain conditions are not considered income, so a tax is not levied on this type of transaction.

The total stockholders' equity is not affected by a stock dividend. The effect of a stock dividend is to transfer a dollar amount from the Retained Earnings account to the contributed capital section on the date of declaration. The amount to be transferred is the fair market value (usually market price) of the additional shares to be issued. The laws of most states state the minimum to be transferred under a stock dividend. This minimum is normally the minimum legal capital (par or stated value). However, generally accepted accounting principles state that market value reflects the economic effect of the stock distribution better than the minimum legal capital does. For this reason, the market price should be used for proper accounting of stock dividends.[2]

To illustrate the accounting for a stock dividend, we will assume that the Caprock Corporation has the stockholders' equity structure shown below.

Contributed Capital
    Common Stock—$5 par value, 100,000 shares

authorized, 30,000 issued and outstanding	$ 150,000
Paid-in Capital in Excess of Par Value, Common	30,000
Total Contributed Capital	$ 180,000
Retained Earnings	900,000
Total Stockholders' Equity	$1,080,000

Assume further that the board of directors declares a 10 percent stock dividend on February 24, distributable on March 31 to stockholders of record on March 15. The market price of the stock on February 24 was $20 per share. The entries to record the dividend declaration and distribution are as follows:

Date of declaration

Feb. 24	Retained Earnings	60,000	
	Common Stock Distributable		15,000
	Paid-in Capital in Excess of Par Value, Common		45,000

        To record the declaration of a
        10% stock dividend on common
        stock, distributable on March 31,
        to stockholders of record on
        March 15
        30,000 shares $\times$ 10% = 3,000 shares
        3,000 shares $\times$ $20/share = $60,000

Date of record

Mar. 15 No entry

2. *Accounting Research and Terminology Bulletin No. 43* (New York: American Institute of Certified Public Accountants, 1953), Chapter 7, Section B, par. 10.

Date of distribution

Mar. 31	Common Stock Distributable	15,000	
	Common Stock		15,000
	To record the distribution of		
	stock dividend of 3,000 shares		

The effect of the above stock dividend is to transfer permanently the market value of the stock, $60,000, from Retained Earnings to Contributed Capital and to increase the number of shares outstanding by 3,000. Common Stock Distributable is credited for the par value of the stock to be distributed (3,000 × $5 = $15,000). In addition, when the market value is greater than the par value of the stock, Paid-in Capital in Excess of Par Value must be credited for the amount that market value exceeds par value. In this case, total market value of the stock dividend ($60,000) exceeds the total par value ($15,000) by $45,000. No entry is required on the date of record. On the distribution date, the common stock is issued by debiting Common Stock Distributable and crediting Common Stock for the par value of the stock ($15,000).

Stock Dividends Distributable is not a liability, because there is no obligation to distribute cash or other assets. The obligation is to distribute additional shares of capital stock. If financial statements are prepared between the date of declaration and the distribution, Common Stock Distributable should be reported as part of Contributed Capital, as follows:

Contributed Capital	
Common Stock—$5 par value, 100,000 shares	
authorized, 30,000 issued and outstanding	$ 150,000
Common Stock Distributable, 3,000 shares	15,000
Paid-in Capital in Excess of Par Value, Common	75,000
Total Contributed Capital	$ 240,000
Retained Earnings	840,000
Total Stockholders' Equity	$1,080,000

Two points can be made from this example. First, the total stockholders' equity is unchanged before and after the stock dividend. Second, the proportionate ownership in the corporation of any individual stockholder is unchanged before and after the stock dividend. To illustrate these points, we will assume that a stockholder owns 1,000 shares before the stock dividend. After the 10 percent stock dividend is distributed, this stockholder would own 1,100 shares.

Stockholders' Equity	Before Dividend	After Dividend
Common Stock	$ 150,000	$ 165,000
Paid-in Capital in Excess of Par Value	30,000	75,000
Total Contributed Capital	$ 180,000	$ 240,000
Retained Earnings	900,000	840,000
Total Stockholders' Equity	$1,080,000	$1,080,000

Shares Outstanding	30,000	33,000
Book Value per Share	$36.00	$32.73

Stockholder's Investment

Shares owned	1,000	1,100
Percentage of ownership	$3\frac{1}{3}\%$	$3\frac{1}{3}\%$
Book value of investment ($3\frac{1}{3}\% \times \$1,080,000$)	$36,000	$36,000

Both before and after the stock dividend, the stockholders' equity totals $1,080,000 and the stockholder owns $3\frac{1}{3}$ percent of the company. Book value of the investment stays at $36,000.

All stock dividends have an effect on the market price of a company's stock. But some stock dividends are so large that they have a material effect on the price per share of the stock. For example, a 50 percent stock dividend would cause the market price of the stock to drop about 33 percent. The AICPA has arbitrarily decided that large stock dividends, those greater than 20 to 25 percent, should be accounted for by transferring the par or stated value of the stock on the date of declaration from Retained Earnings to Contributed Capital.[3]

Stock Splits A stock split occurs when a corporation increases the number of outstanding shares of stock and reduces the par or stated value proportionally. A company may plan a stock split when it wishes to lower the market value per share of its stock and increase the liquidity of the stock. This action may be necessary if the market value per share has become so high that it hinders the trading of the company's stock on the market. For example, suppose that the Caprock Corporation has 30,000 shares of $5.00 par value stock outstanding. The market value is $70.00 per share. The corporation plans a 2 for 1 split. This split will lower the par value to $2.50 and increase the number of shares outstanding to 60,000. If a stockholder previously owned 400 shares of the $5.00 par stock, he or she would own 800 shares of the $2.50 par stock after the split. When a stock split occurs, the market value tends to fall in proportion to the increase in outstanding shares of stock. For example, a 2 for 1 stock split would cause the price of the stock to drop by approximately 50 percent to about $35.00. The lower price plus the increase in shares tends to promote the buying and selling of shares.

A stock split does not, in itself, increase the number of shares authorized. Nor does it change the balances in the stockholders' equity section. It simply changes the par value and number of shares outstanding. Therefore, an entry is not necessary. However, it is appropriate to document the change by making a memorandum entry in the general journal. The change for the Caprock Corporation is shown below.

Before Stock Split

Contributed Capital
    Common Stock—$5 par value, 100,000 shares
    authorized, 30,000 issued and outstanding .... $ 150,000

3. Ibid., par. 13.

Paid-in Capital in Excess of Par Value, Common	30,000
Total Contributed Capital	$ 180,000
Retained Earnings	900,000
Total Stockholders' Equity	$1,080,000

After Stock Split

Contributed Capital

Common Stock—$2.50 par value, 100,000 shares authorized, 60,000 issued and outstanding	$ 150,000
Paid-in Capital in Excess of Par Value, Common	30,000
Total Contributed Capital	$ 180,000
Retained Earnings	900,000
Total Stockholders' Equity	$1,080,000

Treasury Stock Transactions

*Objective 3
Account for
treasury stock
transactions*

Treasury stock is capital stock, either common or preferred, that has been issued and reacquired by the issuing company but has not been reissued or retired. The company normally gets the stock back by purchasing the shares on the market or through donations by stockholders. There are several reasons why a company purchases its own stock. (1) It may want to have stock available to distribute to employees through stock option plans. (2) It may be trying to maintain a favorable market for the company's stock. (3) It may want to increase the company's earnings per share. (4) It may want to have additional shares of the company's stock available for such activities as purchasing other companies.

The effect of a treasury stock purchase is to reduce the assets and stockholders' equity of the company. The treasury stock is capital stock that has been issued but is no longer outstanding. Treasury shares may be held for an indefinite period of time, reissued, or canceled. Thus treasury stock is somewhat similar to unissued stock. That is, it has no rights until the stock is reissued. Treasury stock does not have voting rights, pre-emptive rights, rights to cash dividends, or rights to share in assets during liquidation of the company. However, there is one major difference between unissued shares and treasury shares. If a share of stock was originally issued at par value or greater and fully paid for, and then reacquired as treasury stock, it may be reissued at less than par value without a discount liability attaching to it.

Purchase of Treasury Stock When treasury stock is purchased, it is normally recorded at cost. The transaction reduces both the assets and stockholders' equity of the firm. For example, assume that the Caprock Corporation purchases 1,000 shares of its common stock on the market at a price of $50 per share. The purchase would be recorded as follows:

Sept. 15	Treasury Stock, Common	50,000	
	Cash		50,000
	Acquired 1,000 shares of company's common stock for $50 per share		

Note that the treasury shares were recorded at cost. Any par value, stated value, or original issue price of the stock was ignored.

The stockholders' equity section of Caprock's balance sheet would show the cost of the treasury stock as a deduction from the total of Contributed Capital and Retained Earnings. An example of this disclosure is given below. Note that the number of shares issued has not changed as a result of the treasury stock transaction.

Stockholders' Equity

Contributed Capital	
Common Stock—$5 par value, 100,000 shares authorized,	
30,000 shares issued, 29,000 shares outstanding	$ 150,000
Paid-in Capital in Excess of Par Value, Common	30,000
Total Contributed Capital	$ 180,000
Retained Earnings	900,000
Total Contributed Capital and Retained Earnings	$1,080,000
Less Treasury Stock, Common (at Cost)	50,000
Total Stockholders' Equity	$1,030,000

Reissuance of Treasury Stock The treasury shares may be reissued at cost, above cost, or below cost. When the stock is reissued at cost, the transaction is recorded by reversing the original entry. For example, assume that the 1,000 treasury shares of the Caprock Corporation are sold for $50 per share. The entry to record this transaction is

Nov. 15	Cash	50,000	
	Treasury Stock, Common		50,000
	Reissued 1,000 shares of treasury stock for $50 per share		

When treasury shares are sold for an amount greater than their cost, the excess of the sales price over cost should be credited to Paid-in Capital, Treasury Stock. No gain should be recorded. For example, suppose that the 1,000 treasury shares of the Caprock Corporation are sold for $60 per share. The entry for the reissue would be

Nov. 15	Cash	60,000	
	Treasury Stock, Common		50,000
	Paid-in Capital, Treasury Stock		10,000
	To record the sale of 1,000 shares of treasury stock for $60 per share; cost was $50 per share		

If the treasury shares are reissued below their cost, the difference should be deducted from Paid-in Capital, Treasury Stock. When this account does not exist or is insufficient to cover the excess of cost over reissuance price, Retained Earnings should absorb the excess. No loss should be recorded. For example, suppose that on September 15 the Caprock Corporation bought 1,000 shares of its common stock on the market at a price of $50 per share. The company sold 400 shares of its stock on October 15 for $60 per share and the remaining 600 shares on December 15 for $42 per share. The entries to record these transactions are presented below.

Sept. 15	Treasury Stock, Common	50,000	
	Cash		50,000
	To record the purchase of 1,000 shares of treasury stock at $50 per share		

Oct. 15	Cash	24,000	
	Treasury Stock, Common		20,000
	Paid-in Capital, Treasury Stock		4,000
	To record the sale of 400 shares of treasury stock for $60 per share; cost was $50 per share		

Dec. 15	Cash	25,200	
	Paid-in Capital, Treasury Stock	4,000	
	Retained Earnings	800	
	Treasury Stock, Common		30,000
	To record sale of 600 shares of treasury stock for $42 per share; cost was $50 per share		

In the December 15 entry, Retained Earnings is debited for $800 because the 600 shares were sold for $4,800 less than cost. That amount is $800 greater than the $4,000 of paid-in capital generated by the sale of the 400 shares on October 15.

STOP

Prior Period Adjustments

Prior period adjustments are events or transactions that relate to earlier accounting periods but were not determinable in the earlier period. The Financial Accounting Standards Board has identified only two kinds of prior period adjustments. The first would be to correct an error in the

Objective 4
Define prior
period adjust-
ments and
prepare a
statement of
retained
earnings

financial statements of a prior year. The second kind of adjustment would be needed if a company realized an income tax gain from carrying forward a preacquisition operating loss of a purchased subsidiary.[4] Prior period adjustments are, however, very rare in accounting.

The requirements for reporting prior period adjustments are described by the Accounting Principles Board as follows:

When financial statements for a single period only are presented, this disclosure should indicate the effects of such restatement on the balance of retained earnings at the beginning of the period and on the net income of the immediately preceding period. When financial statements for more than one period are presented, which is ordinarily the preferable procedure, the disclosure should include the effects for each of the periods included on the statements.[5]

As an illustration of this adjustment, suppose that the Caprock Corporation discovered in December 19x2 that it had failed to record depreciation of $50,000 on its office equipment in 19x1. It also found that the mistake would lower retained earnings by only $30,000 for that year because, being in the 40 percent tax bracket, the company would receive a $20,000 income tax refund when it amended its 19x1 tax return to include the $50,000 deduction. The entry to record this prior period adjustment would be as follows:

19x2			
Dec. 31	Retained Earnings	30,000	
	Income Taxes Refund Receivable	20,000	
	Accumulated Depreciation, Office Equipment		50,000
	To record the correction of an error in depreciation of prior years		

Statement of Retained Earnings

The statement of retained earnings is prepared as a summary of the changes in retained earnings during an accounting period. See the comprehensive example in Figure 17-2 (next page). In this statement, the retained earnings balance on January 1 is first restated for the prior period adjustment related to 19x1. Then the effects of 19x2 transactions are shown. Adding net income of $85,000 to the restated January 1 balance of $870,000 gives a subtotal of $955,000. The effects of cash and stock dividends as well as treasury stock transactions are listed. This total of $116,800 is deducted from the subtotal to arrive at the December 31 balance of $838,200.

4. *Statement of Financial Accounting Standards No. 16*, "Prior Period Adjustments" (Stamford, Conn.: Financial Accounting Standards Board, June 1977), par. 11.

5. Accounting Principles Board, *Opinion No. 9*, "Reporting the Results of Operations" (New York: American Institute of Certified Public Accountants, December 1966), par. 26; see also *Statement of Financial Accounting Concepts No. 3*, "Elements of Financial Statements of Business Enterprises" (Stamford, Conn.: Financial Accounting Standards Board, 1980), par. 56.

Figure 17-2
A Statement of
Retained
Earnings

Caprock Corporation Statement of Retained Earnings For the Year Ended December 31, 19x2		
Retained Earnings, Jan. 1, 19x2	$900,000	
Less Prior Period Adjustment, Correction of an Error (Net of Taxes), 19x1	30,000	
Retained Earnings, Jan. 1, 19x2, as Restated		$870,000
Net Income, 19x2		85,000
Subtotal		$955,000
Less:		
Cash Dividend, Common	$ 50,000	
Cash Dividend, Preferred	6,000	
Stock Dividend, Common	60,000	
Sale of Treasury Stock at Less than Cost (Net)	800	$116,800
Retained Earnings, Dec. 31, 19x2		$838,200

Appropriation of Retained Earnings

Objective 5
Account for the
appropriation of
retained
earnings

A corporation may wish to divide the Retained Earnings account into two parts: appropriated and unappropriated retained earnings. The reason for appropriating retained earnings is to separate a part of the Retained Earnings account on the balance sheet to give more information to the readers of the company's financial statements. When readers see **appropriated retained earnings** on the balance sheet, they know that some of the company's assets are to be used or set aside for purposes other than paying dividends.

Only the board of directors may appropriate retained earnings. The following are several reasons why it might do so:

1. A contractual agreement. For example, bond indentures may place a limitation on the dividends to be paid by the company. Such action is aimed at protecting the working capital position of the company so it can pay this debt.

2. State law. Many states will not allow dividends or the purchase of treasury stock to impair the capital of a company. So an appropriation may be necessary to show that a part of retained earnings must be maintained to preserve the company's capital.

3. Voluntary action by the board of directors. Many times a board will decide to retain assets in the business for future needs. For example, the company may be planning to build a new plant and may wish to show that dividends will be limited to save enough money for the building. Or the company may be facing settlement of a large lawsuit, with the outcome not known at the present time. The company may appropriate retained

earnings to show the possible future loss of assets resulting from the lawsuit.

There are two ways of reporting retained earnings appropriations to readers of financial statements. First, the appropriation of retained earnings may be shown by a journal entry that transfers the appropriated amounts from Retained Earnings to another stockholders' equity account that is more descriptive, such as Retained Earnings Appropriated for Plant Expansion. Second, the report of appropriated retained earnings may be made by means of a note to the financial statements.

The following case of the Caprock Corporation will show appropriation of retained earnings by transfer to a more descriptive account. The board of directors recognizes the need to expand the company's plant capacity in the next two years. After studying several ideas, the board chooses to expand by retaining assets generated by earnings in the amount of $300,000. It acts on July 1, 19x2, to appropriate retained earnings in this amount. The entry to record the board's action is as follows:

July 1	Retained Earnings	300,000	
	Retained Earnings Appropriated for Plant Expansion		300,000
	To record the appropriation of retained earnings for plant expansion according to action of the board of directors on July 1, 19x2		

This transaction does not change the total retained earnings or stockholders' equity of the company. It simply divides retained earnings into two parts, appropriated and unappropriated. The appropriated part shows that assets in that amount are being used or will be used for the expansion. The unappropriated amount represents earnings kept in the business that could be used for dividends and other purposes. The stockholders' equity section of Caprock's balance sheet below shows how retained earnings are divided.

Stockholders' Equity

Contributed Capital		
Common Stock—$5 par value, 100,000 shares authorized, 33,000 shares issued and outstanding		$ 165,000
Paid-in Capital in Excess of Par Value, Common		75,000
Total Contributed Capital		$ 240,000
Retained Earnings		
Appropriated for Plant Expansion	$300,000	
Unappropriated	538,200	
Total Retained Earnings		838,200
Total Stockholders' Equity		$1,078,200

The same facts about retained earnings appropriations could also be presented by reference to a note to the financial statements. For example:

Retained Earnings (Note 15) $838,200

Note 15:

Because of plans for expanding the capacity of the clothing division, the board of directors has restricted retained earnings available for dividends by $300,000.

When the conditions for the appropriation are no longer present, the amount of the restriction should be transferred back to Unappropriated Retained Earnings. In fact, the only charge to an appropriated retained earnings account is the one to transfer the balance back to Unappropriated Retained Earnings. For example, suppose that after two years Caprock finished the expansion of its plant at a cost of $325,000. The restriction of $300,000 on retained earnings is no longer needed. So the board acts on July 20, 19x3, to return the appropriated retained earnings to Unappropriated Retained Earnings. The entries to record the plant expansion and the transfer of retained earnings would be as follows:

July 20	Property, Plant, and Equipment	325,000	
	Cash		325,000
	To record the payment of $325,000 for plant expansion		
20	Retained Earnings Appropriated for Plant Expansion	300,000	
	Retained Earnings		300,000
	To eliminate appropriated retained earnings for plant expansion, according to the board of directors' action on July 20, 19x3		

Note that the appropriation of retained earnings does not restrict cash in any way. It simply explains to the readers of the financial statements that a certain amount of earnings will remain in the business for the purpose stated. It is still management's job to make sure that there is enough cash or assets on hand to satisfy the restriction.

Corporate Income Statements

This chapter and the one before it have shown how certain transactions are reflected in the stockholders' equity section of the corporate balance sheet and in the retained earnings statement. Chapter 19 deals with the statement of changes in financial position. The following sections will briefly describe some of the features of the corporate income statement.

The format of the income statement has not been specified by the accounting profession because flexibility has been considered more important than a standard income statement. Either the single-step or multistep form may be used (see Chapter 9). However, the accounting profession has taken the position that income for a period shall be an all-inclusive or comprehensive amount.[6] This rule means that income or loss for a period should include all revenues, expenses, gains, and losses of the period, except for prior period adjustments. This approach to the measurement of income has resulted in several items being added to the income statement. These items include discontinued operations, extraordinary items, and accounting changes. In addition, earnings per share figures should be disclosed. Figure 17-3 (next page) illustrates the corporate income statement and the disclosures required. The following sections discuss these components of the corporate income statement, beginning with income tax expense.

Income Tax Expense

Objective 6
Define the basic terms of corporate income tax liability, and calculate corporate tax liability

Except for certain classes of corporations such as banks, insurance companies, regulated investment companies, and cooperatives, most corporations determine their taxable income (the amount on which their taxes are figured) by subtracting allowable business deductions from includable gross income. The federal tax laws determine what business deductions are allowed and what revenues must be included in gross income.

As one would expect, corporations deduct cost of goods sold, operating expenses, and other costs from gross income in figuring taxable income. There are also certain features of finding a corporation's income tax liability that may not be so apparent. Some of the more important of these features are explained in the following paragraphs.

Dividends Received Deduction Corporations must include in gross income all dividends received on shares of stock in other corporations. However, they may subtract 85 percent of such dividends as a special deduction from gross income. This deduction means that the receiving corporation pays taxes on only 15 percent of the dividends.

Net Operating Loss Deduction This deduction lets corporations offset the losses of one year against the income of other years. In general, they may offset an operating loss of one year against the income of the three preceding years and, if unused losses still remain, against the income of fifteen future years.

Charitable Contributions Corporations may deduct charitable contributions from taxable income, but the deduction is limited to 10 percent of an amount equal to taxable income plus the contributions and the special deduction for dividends received (explained above). Contributions in excess of 10 percent in any given year may be carried forward to five subsequent years, subject to the 10 percent limitation of each of those years.

6. Ibid., par. 17–19.

Figure 17-3
A Corporate
Income
Statement

Junction Corporation
Income Statement
For the Year Ended December 31, 19xx

Revenues		$925,000
Less Costs and Expenses		500,000
Income from Continuing Operations Before Taxes		$425,000
Income Tax Expense		119,000
Income from Continuing Operations		$306,000
Discontinued Operations		
Income from Operations of Discontinued Segment (net of taxes $35,000)	$90,000	
Loss on Disposal of Segment (net of taxes $42,000)	(73,000)	17,000
Income Before Extraordinary Items and Cumulative Effect of Accounting Change		$323,000
Extraordinary Gain (net of taxes, $17,000)		43,000
Subtotal		$366,000
Cumulative Effect of a Change in Accounting Principle (net of taxes $5,000)		(6,000)
Net Income		$360,000
Earnings per Common Share:		
Income from Continuing Operations	$3.06	
Discontinued Operations	.17	
Income Before Extraordinary Items	3.23	
Extraordinary Gain (net of taxes)	.43	
Cumulative Effect of Accounting Change (net of taxes)	(.06)	
Net Income	3.60	

Capital Gains and Losses One effective means of tax planning is to arrange transactions involving certain types of assets in such a way that they qualify as capital gains and losses. These assets, called **capital assets**, usually include stocks and bonds owned by individuals and, in certain cases, buildings, equipment, and land used in businesses. Capital assets usually do not include receivables, inventories, certain government obligations, and rights to literary and other artistic works. If the capital assets being sold or exchanged have been held for more than one year, they are classified as long-term. The combined total of all gains and losses on short-term capital assets during the year is called **net short-term capital gain (or loss)**. The combined total of all gains and losses on long-term capital assets during a tax year is called **net long-term capital gain (or loss)**. If the net long-term capital gain exceeds any net short-term capital loss, the excess is called **net capital gain**. If the corporation has a net capital gain, it is taxed at a maximum rate of 28 percent. Net capital losses of corporations are not deductible from ordinary income. They are treated in a manner similar to the net operating losses described above. That is, corporations may offset such losses against capital gains in the three preceding years and five future years.

Corporate Tax Rates   The tax rates that apply to a corporation's taxable income are shown in Table 17-1. For example, a corporation with a taxable income of $70,000 would have a federal income tax liability of $14,250. This amount is figured by adding $8,250 (the income tax on the first $50,000 of taxable income) to $6,000 (30 percent times the $20,000 earned in excess of $50,000).

Investment Tax Credit and Other Tax Credits   In order to encourage spending that is related to the national goals, Congress allows special tax credits to businesses for certain kinds of expenditures that are judged to be in the national interest. Tax credits are subtractions from the computed tax liability. They should not be confused with deductions, which are subtracted from income to determine taxable income. Since tax credits reduce tax liability dollar for dollar, they are more helpful to the taxpayer than an equal dollar amount of deductions from taxable income. The most important one is the **investment tax credit**, which was adopted by Congress to encourage investment in plant assets. The investment tax credit is equal to 6 percent for assets with three-year cost recovery periods and 10 percent for assets with longer cost recovery periods. It is subject to certain limitations and other provisions beyond the scope of this book. However, it should be noted that the investment tax credit is an important means of reducing tax liability, especially for growing companies. Other tax credits apply to salaries and wages paid to employees in work incen-

Table 17-1
Tax Rate
Schedule for
Corporations

Taxable Income		Tax Liability	
Over	But Not Over		Of the Amount Over
—	$ 25,000	0 + 15%	—
25,000	50,000	$ 3,750 + 18%	$ 25,000
50,000	75,000	8,250 + 30%	50,000
75,000	100,000	15,750 + 40%	75,000
100,000	—	25,750 + 46%	100,000

tive programs, to new jobs formed, and to expenditures for certain building rehabilitations, pollution control, and vocational rehabilitation plans.

Corporate Tax Illustration Figure 17-4 illustrates the points described earlier by showing how tax liability is figured for the Junction Corporation. In this case, suppose that the company had a gross margin of $620,000, business expenses of $300,000, including charitable contributions of $50,000, and dividends from domestic corporations of $40,000. It has net long-term capital gains of $65,000, and a net capital loss carryforward of $15,000 from the year before. Junction may also take an investment tax credit that is equal to 10 percent of equipment purchases of $265,500. The resulting income tax expense of $119,000 is related to the corporation's income from continuing operations. There are other federal income tax effects related to the other portions of the income statement. They are discussed in the next section.

Net of Taxes

The phrase *net of taxes* is used in Figure 17-3 and in the discussion below. It means that the effect of applicable taxes (usually income taxes) has been considered when determining the overall effect of the item on the financial statements. The phrase is used on the corporate income statement when a company has items (such as those explained below) that must be disclosed on a separate section of the income statement. These items should be reported at net of income taxes to avoid distorting the net operating income figure. Let us use a simpler example than that shown in Figure 17-3. Assume that a corporation with $80,000 operating income before taxes has a total tax liability of $70,000 based on taxable income, including a capital gain of $100,000, on which a tax of $30,000 is due. The capital gain must be disclosed separately as an extraordinary gain. The proper presentation is as follows:

Operating Income Before Taxes	$ 80,000
Income Tax Expense (actual taxes are $70,000, of which $30,000 is applicable to extraordinary gain)	40,000
Income Before Extraordinary Item	$ 40,000
Extraordinary Gain (net of taxes) ($100,000 − $30,000)	70,000
Net Income	$110,000

If all the taxes payable were deducted from operating income before taxes, both the income before extraordinary items and the extraordinary gain would be distorted.

A company follows the same procedure in the case of an extraordinary loss. For example, assume the same facts as above except that total tax liability is only $10,000 because of a $100,000 extraordinary loss, which results in a $30,000 tax saving, as shown on the next page.

Figure 17-4
The Compu-
tation of
Corporate Tax
Liability

Junction Corporation
Summary of Federal Income Taxes Expense
For the Year Ended December 31, 19xx

Gross Margin			$620,000
Dividends from domestic corporations			40,000
Net long-term capital gain	$ 65,000		
Less net capital loss carry-forward	15,000		50,000
			$710,000
Less business expenses	300,000		
Less charitable contributions	50,000		250,000
Taxable income before deductions			$460,000
Deductions			
Charitable contributions, limited to 10% of $460,000		$ 46,000	
Dividends received deduction, 85% of $40,000		34,000	80,000
Taxable income			$380,000
Less excess of long-term gain over capital loss carry-forward to be taxed at 28% ($65,000 − $15,000)			50,000
Taxable at regular rates			$330,000
Calculation of Income Tax Expense:			
Regular tax			
On first $100,000		$ 25,750	
On next $230,000 at 46%		105,800	$131,550
Tax on excess of long-term gain over capital loss carry-forward, $50,000 at 28%			14,000
Tax liability before tax credit			$145,550
Less Investment tax credit (10% × $265,500)			26,550
Income tax expense			$119,000

Operating Income Before Taxes	$ 80,000
Income Tax Expense (actual taxes of $10,000 as a result of an extraordinary loss)	40,000
Income Before Extraordinary Item	$ 40,000
Extraordinary Loss (net of taxes) ($100,000 − $30,000)	(70,000)
Net Loss	$(30,000)

If we apply these ideas to Figure 17-3, the total of the income tax items is $124,000. This amount is allocated among five statement components, as follows:

Income Tax Expense	$119,000
Income Tax on Income of Discontinued Segment	35,000
Income Tax Saving on Loss on Disposal of Segment	(42,000)
Income Tax on Extraordinary Gain	17,000
Income Tax Saving on Cumulative Effect of Change in Accounting Principle	(5,000)
Total Income Taxes	$124,000

Discontinued Operations

Objective 7
Describe the
disclosure on
the income
statement of
discontinued
operations,
extraordinary
items, and
accounting
changes

Large companies in the United States usually have many segments. A segment of a business may be a separate major line of business or a separate class of customer. For example, a company that makes heavy drilling equipment may also have another line of business, such as mobile homes. These large companies may discontinue or otherwise dispose of certain segments of their business that are not profitable. **Discontinued operations** are segments that are no longer part of the ongoing operations of the business. Generally accepted accounting principles require that gains and losses from discontinued operations be reported separately in the income statement. The reasoning for the separate disclosure requirement is that the income statement will be more useful in evaluating the ongoing activities of the business if results from continuing operations are reported separately from discontinued operations. In Figure 17-3, the disclosure of discontinued operations has two parts. One part shows that the income from the segment of business that has been disposed of (or will be disposed of) to the decision date to discontinue was $90,000 (net of $35,000 taxes). The other part shows that the loss from disposal of the segment of business was $73,000 (net of $42,000 tax savings).

The computation of the gains or losses will be covered in more advanced accounting courses. The disclosure has been described, however, to give a complete view of the content of the corporate income statement.

Extraordinary Items

The Accounting Principles Board, in its *Opinion No. 30*, defines **extraordinary items** as those "events or transactions that are distinguished by their unusual nature *and* by the infrequency of their occurrence."[7] As stated in the definition, the major criteria for these items are that they must be unusual and must not happen very often. Unusual and infrequent occurrences are explained in the opinion as follows:

Unusual Nature—the underlying event or transaction should possess a high degree of abnormality and be of a type clearly unrelated to, or only incidentally related to, the ordinary and typical activities of the entity, taking into account the environment in which the entity operates.

7. Accounting Principles Board, *Opinion No. 30*, "Reporting the Results of Operations" (New York: American Institute of Certified Public Accountants, 1973), par. 20.

Infrequency of Occurrence—the underlying event or transaction should be of a type that would not reasonably be expected to recur in the foreseeable future, taking into account the environment in which the entity operates.[8]

Because these items are unusual and infrequent, they should be reported separately from continuing operations on the income statement. This disclosure will allow the reader of the statement to identify those gains or losses shown in the computation of income that would not be expected to happen again soon. Examples of extraordinary items are (1) uninsured losses from floods, earthquakes, fires, and theft; (2) gains and losses resulting from the passing of a new law; (3) expropriation (taking) of property by a foreign government; and (4) gains or losses from early retirement of debt. These items should be reported in the income statement after discontinued operations. Also, the gain or loss should be shown net of applicable taxes. In Figure 17-3, the extraordinary gain was $43,000 after applicable taxes of $17,000.

Accounting Changes

Consistency, one of the basic concepts of accounting, means that, for accounting purposes, companies apply the same accounting principles from year to year. However, a company is allowed to make accounting changes if current procedures are incorrect or inappropriate. For example, a change from the FIFO to the LIFO inventory method may be made if there is adequate justification for the change. Adequate justification usually means that, if the change occurs, the financial statements will better show the financial activities of the company. A company's desire to lower the amount of income taxes to be paid is not seen as an adequate justification for an accounting change. If justification does exist and an accounting change is made during an accounting period, generally accepted accounting principles require disclosure of the change. The following information must be in the financial statements:

1. The nature and justification of the accounting change should be disclosed in the notes to the financial statements.
2. The effect of the change on the current period's income and income before extraordinary items should be disclosed in the footnotes.
3. The effect of the change on earnings per share before extraordinary items and net income should be noted.
4. The cumulative effect of changing the principle should be shown on the income statement immediately after extraordinary items.[9]

The cumulative effect of an accounting change is the effect that the new accounting principle would have had on net income if it, instead of the old principle, had been applied in past years. For example, assume that the Junction Corporation has used the straight-line method in depreciating its machinery. The company changes to the sum-of-the-years'-digits method of depreciation this year. The following depreciation charges (net of taxes) were arrived at by the controller:

8. Ibid.
9. Accounting Principles Board, *Opinion No. 20,* "Accounting Changes" (New York: American Institute of Certified Public Accountants, July 1971).

Cumulative, 5-year sum-of-the-years'-digits depreciation	$16,000
Less cumulative, 5-year straight-line depreciation	10,000
Cumulative effect of accounting change	$ 6,000

The $6,000 difference (net of applicable income taxes) is the cumulative effect of the change in depreciation methods. It must be shown in the current year's income statement as a reduction in income (see Figure 17-3). Further study of accounting changes is left up to more advanced accounting courses.

Earnings per Share

Objective 8
Compute
primary and
fully diluted
earnings per
share

Readers of financial statements use earnings per share information to judge the performance of the company and to compare its performance with that of other companies. The Accounting Principles Board recognized the importance of this information in its *Opinion No. 15*. There it concluded that earnings per share of common stock should be presented on the face of the income statement.[10] As shown in Figure 17-3, the information is generally disclosed just below the net income figure. An earnings per share amount is always shown for (1) income from continuing operations, (2) income before extraordinary items and cumulative effect of accounting changes, (3) cumulative effect of accounting changes, and (4) net income. If the statement has a gain or loss from discontinued operations or a gain or loss on extraordinary items, earnings per share amounts may also be presented for these items.

A basic earnings per share amount is found when a company has only common stock and the same number of shares outstanding during the year. For example, it is assumed in Figure 17-3 that Junction Corporation, with a net income of $360,000, had 100,000 shares of common stock outstanding for the entire year. The earnings per share of common stock were figured as follows:

$$\text{earnings per share} = \frac{\text{net income } \textit{/ applicable to common}}{\text{shares outstanding}}$$

$$= \frac{\$360,000}{100,000 \text{ shares}}$$

$$= \$3.60 \text{ per share}$$

If, however, the number of shares outstanding changes during the year, it is necessary to figure a weighted-average number of shares outstanding for the year. Let us now suppose some different facts about Junction Corporation's outstanding shares. Let us assume that the common shares outstanding during various periods of the year were as follows: January–March, 100,000 shares; April–September, 120,000 shares; October–December, 130,000 shares. The weighted-average number of common shares outstanding and earnings per share would be found as shown on the next page.

10. Accounting Principles Board, *Opinion No. 15*, "Earnings per Share" (New York: American Institute of Certified Public Accountants, May 1969), par. 12.

100,000 shares $\times$ $\frac{1}{4}$ year	25,000
120,000 shares $\times$ $\frac{1}{2}$ year	60,000
130,000 shares $\times$ $\frac{1}{4}$ year	32,500
Weighted-average shares outstanding	117,500

$$\text{Earnings per share} = \frac{\$360,000}{117,500 \text{ shares}}$$

$$= \$3.06 \text{ per share}$$

If a company has nonconvertible preferred stock outstanding, the dividend for this stock must be subtracted from net income before figuring earnings per share for common stock. If we suppose that Junction Corporation has preferred stock on which the annual dividend is $23,500, earnings per share on common stock would be $2.86 [($360,000 − $23,500) ÷ 117,500 shares].

Companies with a capital structure in which there are no other bonds or stocks that could be converted into common stock are said to have a simple capital structure. The earnings per share for these companies are figured as shown above. Many companies, however, have a complex capital structure, which includes convertible stock and bonds. These convertible securities have the potential of diluting the earnings per share of common stock. Potential dilution means that a person's proportionate share of ownership in the company may be reduced by an increase in total shares outstanding through a conversion of stocks or bonds. For example, suppose that a person owns 10,000 shares of a company, which equals 2 percent of the outstanding shares of 500,000. Now suppose that holders of convertible bonds convert the bonds into 100,000 shares of stock. The person's 10,000 shares would then be only 1.67 percent (10,000 ÷ 600,000) of the outstanding shares. Also, the added shares outstanding would result in lower earnings per share and most likely a lower market price per share.

If, at the time of issuance, the value of convertible securities is close to their conversion value—that is, the value of the stock they could be converted into—they are said to be common stock equivalents. This classification means that they are roughly equal to common stock and should be considered as such in figuring the earnings per share.

When a company has a complex capital structure, a dual presentation of earnings per share is necessary. The company must report a primary earnings per share and a fully diluted earnings per share under the assumption that the stockholders should be aware of the potential effect of dilution of their ownership in the company. The formulas for finding these per share amounts are shown below.

anythin can be converte is core.

$$\text{primary earnings per share} = \frac{\text{net income applicable to common stock}}{\text{weighted-average common shares and common stock equivalents}}$$

$$\text{fully diluted earnings per share} = \frac{\text{net income applicable to common stock}}{\text{weighted-average common stock and common stock equivalents and other potentially dilutive securities}}$$

As an example of these computations, suppose that in 19x2, the Tampa Corporation had the following capital structure and net income:

1. There are 100,000 shares of $5 par value common stock outstanding for the whole year.
2. There are 10,000 shares of $10 par value cumulative, convertible preferred stock outstanding for the year. Each share is convertible into two shares of common, is a common stock equivalent, and has a dividend rate of $1 per share.
3. There are 5,000 shares of $20 par value cumulative, convertible preferred stock outstanding for the year. Each share is convertible into four shares of common stock. Though not a common stock equivalent at issuance, it has the potential to dilute common stock and has a $2 per share dividend rate.
4. Net income is $280,000.

The computation of earnings per share is shown below.

		Primary	Fully Diluted
Net income		$280,000	$280,000
Less dividend on $20 par value preferred stock (5,000 × $2)		10,000	
Income applicable to common stock		$270,000	$280,000
Common stock for primary earnings per share			
Weighted-average common stock	100,000		
Common stock equivalents—$10 par value preferred stock (10,000 × 2)	20,000	120,000	
Common stock for fully diluted earnings per share			
Common stock for primary	120,000		
Other dilutive securities—$20 par value preferred stock (5,000 × 4)	20,000		140,000
Earnings per share of common stock		$2.25	$2.00

Note that before you can figure the primary earnings per share, you must find out how much of the income is applicable to common stock. To do so, you subtract from net income the dividend on the preferred stock that is not a common stock equivalent. The earnings per share data as they would appear in Tampa Corporation's income statement for 19x1 and 19x2 (with assumed figures for 19x1) are as follows:

	19x2	19x1
Net Income	$280,000	$200,000
Earnings per Share of Common Stock		
Primary	$2.25	$1.58
Fully Diluted	$2.00	$1.43

Chapter Review

Review of Learning Objectives

1. Define and explain the significance of *retained earnings.*

Retained earnings are the part of stockholders' equity that comes from retaining assets earned in business operations. They are the claims of the stockholders against the assets of the company that arise from profitable operations. This account is different from capital stock, which represents the claims against assets brought about by the initial and later investments by the stockholders. Both are claims against the general assets of the company, not against any specific assets that may have been set aside. It is important not to confuse the assets themselves with the claims against the assets.

2. Account for cash dividends, stock dividends, and stock splits.

A dividend is a distribution of assets, usually cash, by a corporation to its stockholders in proportion to the number of shares of stock held by each owner. A summary of the key dates and accounting treatment of cash dividends and stock dividends follows:

Key Date	Cash Dividend	Stock Dividend
Declaration date	Debit Dividends Declared and credit Dividends Payable for the total amount of the dividend.	Debit Retained Earnings for the market value of the stock to be distributed and credit Common Stock Dividends Distributable (par value) and Paid-in Capital in Excess of Par Value for the excess of market value over the stock's par value.
Record date	No entry.	No entry.
Payment date	Debit Cash Dividends Payable and credit Cash.	Debit Common Stock Dividends Distributable and credit Common Stock for the par value of the stock that was distributed.

A stock split is usually undertaken to reduce the market value and improve the liquidity of a company's stock. Since there is normally a decrease in the par value of the stock proportionate to the number of additional shares issued, there is no effect on the dollar amounts in the stockholders' equity accounts. The split should be recorded in the general journal by a memorandum entry only.

3. Account for treasury stock transactions.

The treasury stock of a company is stock that has been issued and reacquired but not reissued or retired. A company acquires its own stock for reasons such as creating stock option plans, maintaining a favorable market for the stock, increasing earnings per share, and purchasing other companies. Treasury stock is similar to unissued stock in that it does not have rights until it is reissued. However, treasury stock can be resold at less than par value without incurring a discount liability. The accounting treatment for treasury stock is summarized below.

Treasury Stock Transaction	Accounting Treatment
Purchase of treasury stock	Debit Treasury Stock and credit Cash for the cost of the shares.
Reissuance of treasury stock at cost	Debit Cash and credit Treasury Stock for the cost of the shares.
Reissuance of treasury stock at an amount greater than the cost of the shares	Debit Cash for the reissue price of the shares and credit Treasury Stock for the cost of the shares and Paid-in Capital, Treasury Stock for the excess.
Reissuance of treasury stock at an amount less than the cost of the shares	Debit Cash for the reissue price; debit Paid-in Capital, Treasury Stock for the difference between reissue price and the cost of the shares; and credit Treasury Stock for the cost of the shares. If Paid-in Capital, Treasury Stock does not exist or is not large enough to cover the difference, Retained Earnings should absorb the difference.

4. Define prior period adjustments and prepare a statement of retained earnings.

Prior period adjustments are events or transactions that relate to earlier accounting periods but were not determinable in the earlier period. A correction of an error is an example. The statement of retained earnings will always show the beginning and ending balance of retained earnings, net income or loss, and cash dividends. It may also show prior period adjustments, stock dividends, and other transactions affecting retained earnings.

5. Account for the appropriation of retained earnings.

For reasons such as plant expansion, a company may need to retain a portion of its assets in the business rather than distribute them to the stockholders as dividends. Management may communicate the plans to stockholders and other users of the company's financial statements by appropriation of retained earnings. In this way a portion of Retained Earnings is transferred to an account such as Retained Earnings Appropriated for Plant Expansion. A more common way to disclose the appropriation is through a note to the financial statements. When the reason for the appropriation no longer exists, the appropriated amount can be returned to the Retained Earnings account or the note removed from the financial statements.

6. **Define the basic terms of corporate income tax liability, and calculate corporate tax liability.**

Corporate income tax liability is based on the taxable income of the corporation. Taxable income is figured by subtracting the allowable deductions from gross income. Factors that must be considered in figuring income tax liability are the dividends received deduction, the net operating loss deduction, charitable contributions, capital gains and losses, corporate tax rates, the investment tax credit, and other tax credits.

7. **Describe the disclosure on the income statement of discontinued operations, extraordinary items, and accounting changes.**

There are several accounting items that must be disclosed separately from continuing operations and net of income taxes on the income statement because of their unusual nature. These items include a gain or loss on discontinued operations, extraordinary items, and the cumulative effect of accounting changes.

8. **Compute primary and fully diluted earnings per share.**

Stockholders and other users of financial statements use earnings per share data to evaluate the performance of a company, estimate future earnings, and evaluate their investment opportunities. Therefore, earnings per share data are presented on the face of the income statement. Earnings per share amounts are figured for (1) income from continuing operations, (2) income before extraordinary items and cumulative effects of accounting changes, (3) cumulative effects of accounting changes, and (4) net income. They may also be computed for discontinued operations and for extraordinary items. The amounts are computed by dividing the income applicable to common stock by the common shares outstanding for the year. If the number of shares outstanding has varied during the year, then the weighted-average shares outstanding should be used in the computation. When the company has a complex capital structure, a dual presentation of primary and fully diluted earnings per share data must be disclosed on the face of the income statement. Formulas for the computation of primary and fully diluted earnings per share follow.

$$\frac{\text{primary earnings}}{\text{per share}} = \frac{\text{net income applicable to common stock}}{\text{weighted-average common shares and common stock equivalents}}$$

$$\frac{\text{fully diluted earnings}}{\text{per share}} = \frac{\text{net income applicable to common stock}}{\text{weighted-average common stock and common stock equivalents and other potential dilutive securities}}$$

Review Problem
Statement of Retained Earnings
and Corporate Income Statement

Two important corporate financial statements are presented in this chapter: the statement of retained earnings and the income statement. Review Figure 17-2 carefully for the format and components of the statement of retained earnings. Note that retained earnings are affected by prior period adjustments, net income, cash and stock dividends, and sale of treasury stock at less than cost.

Review the corporate income statement in Figure 17-3 carefully and identify the major components, which are indicated by color. They are income tax expense, discontinued operations, extraordinary gain, cumulative effect of a change in accounting principle, and earnings per common share. Be sure that you can describe the nature and content of each of these components.

Chapter Assignments

Questions

1. What are retained earnings, and how do they relate to the assets of a corporation?
2. When does a company have a deficit in retained earnings?
3. What items are identified by generally accepted accounting principles as prior period adjustments?
4. Describe the significance of the following dates as they relate to dividends: (a) date of declaration, (b) date of record, and (c) date of payment.
5. Distinguish between a cash dividend and a stock dividend, and describe the accounting treatment of each.
6. What is the difference between a stock dividend and a stock split? What is the effect of each on the capital structure of a corporation?
7. What is the purpose of appropriating retained earnings?
8. Define treasury stock. Why would a company purchase its own stock?
9. What are prior period adjustments and on what statement do they appear?
10. What is the importance of taxable income, capital gains, net operating loss deduction, and investment tax credit to the computation of corporate tax liability?
11. Explain the two major criteria for extraordinary items. How should extraordinary items be disclosed in financial statements?
12. How are earnings per share disclosed in financial statements?
13. When an accounting change occurs, what financial statement disclosures are necessary?
14. What is a common stock equivalent?
15. When does a company have a simple capital structure? a complex capital structure?
16. What is the difference between primary and fully diluted earnings per share?
17. Why should the gain or loss on discontinued operations be disclosed separately on the income statement?

Classroom Exercises

Exercise 17-1
Statement of Retained Earnings
(L.O. 1)

The Pound Corporation had a Retained Earnings balance on January 1, 19x2, of $130,000. During 19x2, the company reported a profit of $56,000 after taxes. In addition, the company located a $22,000 error that resulted in an overstatement of prior years' income and that meets the criteria of a prior period adjustment. During 19x2, the company declared cash dividends totaling $8,000.

Prepare the company's statement of retained earnings for the year ended December 31, 19x2.

Exercise 17-2
Journal Entries—Cash Dividends and Stock Dividends
(L.O. 2)

The Shelley Company has 20,000 shares of its $1 par value common stock outstanding.

Record the following transactions as they relate to the company's common stock:

July 1 Declared a 50¢ per share cash dividend on common stock to be paid on July 16 to stockholders of record on July 10.
     10 Record date.
     16 Paid the cash dividend declared on July 1.
     17 Declared a 10 percent stock dividend on common stock to be distributed on August 10. Market value of the stock was $5 per share on this date.
     31 Record date.
Aug. 10 Distributed the stock dividend declared on July 17.

Exercise 17-3
Stock Split
(L.O. 2)

The Rutherford Company currently has 100,000 shares of $1 par value common stock outstanding. The board of directors declared a 2 for 1 stock split on May 15, when the market value of the common stock was $2.50 per share. The Retained Earnings balance on May 15 was $700,000. Paid-in Capital in Excess of Par Value, Common Stock, on this date was $20,000.

Prepare the stockholders' equity section of the company's balance sheet before and after the stock split. What journal entry, if any, would be necessary to record the stock split?

Exercise 17-4
Appropriation of Retained Earnings
(L.O. 5)

The board of directors of the Gardiner Company has approved a major plant expansion during the coming year. The expansion should cost approximately $550,000. The board has taken action to appropriate retained earnings of the company in the amount of $550,000 on July 17, 19x1. On August 20, 19x2, the expansion was completed at a total cost of $525,000 and paid for with cash. Also, on that date, the appropriation of retained earnings was removed.

1. Prepare the necessary journal entries for July 17, 19x1, and August 20, 19x2.
2. If the company had unappropriated retained earnings of $976,000 immediately before the August 20, 19x2, entries, what were the total retained earnings immediately before and after August 20, 19x2?

Exercise 17-5
Treasury Stock Transactions
(L.O. 3)

Prepare the journal entries necessary to record the following stock transactions of the Javier Company during 19xx:

May 5   Purchased 200 shares of its own $1 par value common stock for $5.00, the current market price.

     17   Sold 75 shares of treasury stock purchased on May 5 for $5.50 per share.

     21   Sold 50 shares of treasury stock purchased on May 5 for $5.00 per share.

     28   Sold the remaining 75 shares of treasury stock purchased on May 5 for $4.75 per share.

Exercise 17-6
Computation of Corporate Income Tax Liability
(L.O. 6)

Using the corporate tax rate schedule in this chapter, figure the income tax liability for the following corporations:

Corporation	Taxable Income for Current Year Before Next Two Columns	Net Operating Loss Carry-forward	Capital Gain Taxable at 28% Rate	Amount Subject to 10% Tax Credit
A	$ 60,000	$20,000	$ 0	$ 40,000
B	130,000	40,000	150,000	90,000
C	280,000	0	100,000	250,000

Exercise 17-7
Income Statement
(L.O. 7)

Assume that the Hitchcock Furniture Company's chief financial officer gave you the following information: Net Sales, $1,500,000; Cost of Goods Sold, $700,000; Extraordinary Gain (applicable income tax on gain of $3,500), $16,000; Loss from Discontinued Operations (applicable income tax benefit of $30,000), $82,000; Loss on Disposal of Discontinued Operations (applicable income tax benefit of $13,000), $48,000; Selling Expenses, $50,000; Administrative Expenses, $40,000; Income Taxes Expense on Continuing Operations, $300,000.

From this information, prepare the company's income statement for the year ended June 30, 19xx. (Ignore earnings per share information.)

Exercise 17-8
Earnings per
Share
(L.O. 8)

During 19x1, the Potts Corporation reported a net income of $1,265,000. On January 1, Potts had 500,000 shares of common stock outstanding. The company issued an additional 300,000 shares of common stock on October 1. In 19x1, the company had a simple capital structure.

On January 1, 19x2, Potts issued 50,000 shares of 8 percent, $100 par value cumulative, convertible preferred stock. Each share of preferred stock is convertible into eight shares of common stock. During 19x2, there were no transactions involving common stock, and the company reported net income of $1,820,000.

1. Determine the weighted-average number of common shares outstanding each year.
2. Compute earnings per share for each year, including primary and fully diluted earnings per share, if appropriate, assuming that on the date of issue the preferred stock (a) qualified as a common stock equivalent and (b) did not qualify as a common stock equivalent.

Interpreting Accounting Information

Published
Financial
Information:
Lockheed
Corporation
(L.O. 7)

Presented below are several excerpts from an article that appeared in the February 2, 1982, *Wall Street Journal* entitled "Lockheed Had Loss in 4th Quarter, Year; $396 Million TriStar Write-Off Is Cited":

As expected, Lockheed Corp. took a $396 million write-off to cover expenses of its production phase-out of L-1011 TriStar commercial jets, resulting in a net loss of . . . $289 million for the year.

Roy A. Anderson, Lockheed Chairman, said he believed the company had "recognized all costs, including those yet to be incurred, that are associated with the phase-out of the TriStar program." He said he thinks the company now is in a sound position to embark on a program of future growth and earnings improvement.

Included in the $396 million total write-off are remaining deferred production start-up costs, adjustments for redundant inventories and provisions for losses and other costs expected to be incurred while TriStar production is completed. In addition to the write-off, discontinued operations include a $70 million after-tax loss associated with 1981 L-1011 operations. The comparable 1980 L-1011 loss was $108 million.

The $289 million 1981 net loss consists of the TriStar losses, reduced by the previously reported [extraordinary after-tax] gain of $23 million from the exchange of debentures. . . .

For the year, Lockheed had earnings from continuing operations of $154 million, a 14% gain from $135 million in 1980. In 1981 the company had a $466 million loss from discontinued operations, resulting in a net loss of $289 million. A year earlier, the concern had a $108 million loss from discontinued operations, resulting in a net profit of $28 million.

Required

1. Interpret the financial information from the *Wall Street Journal* by preparing a partial income statement for Lockheed for 1981, beginning with "income from continuing operations." Be prepared to explain the nature of each item on the income statement.
2. How do you explain the fact that on the New York Stock Exchange, Lockheed common stock closed at $50 per share, up 75 cents on the day after the quoted announcement of a net loss of $289 million and up from $41 per share two months earlier?

Problem Set A

**Problem 17A-1
Treasury Stock
Transactions
(L.O. 3)**

The following treasury stock transactions occurred during 19xx for the Detweiler Company: (a) Purchased 15,000 shares of its common stock on the market for $20 per share. (b) Sold 7,000 shares of the treasury stock for $21 per share. (c) Sold 6,000 shares of the treasury stock for $19 per share. (d) Purchased an additional 3,000 shares for $18 per share. (e) Sold all of the treasury stock remaining for $17 per share.

Required

Record these transactions in general journal form.

**Problem 17A-2
Stock and
Retained
Earnings
Transactions
(L.O. 2, 3, 4)**

A review of the stockholders' equity records of Gabler Cotton Mills disclosed the following transactions during 19xx:

Jan. 30 Purchased 5,000 shares of the company's $5 par value common stock for $10. The stock was originally sold for $9.

Mar. 5 The board of directors voted to appropriate $265,000 of retained earnings because of a contractual agreement to purchase cotton delinting equipment.

Apr. 16 Sold 1,000 shares of the company's stock purchased on January 30 for $12 per share.

May 15 The board of directors declared a $20,000 cash dividend to common stockholders.

June 15 Paid the cash dividend.

Aug. 17 Sold 1,000 shares of the company's stock purchased on January 30 for $9 per share.

Sept. 10 Purchased the cotton delinting equipment at a total cost of $285,000, including installation, and removed the appropriation of retained earnings in connection with the purchase contract.

Nov. 5 Sold 2,000 shares of the company's stock purchased on January 30 for $9 per share.

Dec. 31 Closed Net Income for the year of $65,000 from Income Summary to Retained Earnings.

Required

Record the above transactions of Gabler Cotton Mills in general journal form.

**Problem 17A-3
Taxable Income
and Tax
Liability for
Corporations
(L.O. 6)**

The following data come from the records of the Yates Corporation: sales, $1,355,440; dividends from other corporations, $87,000; beginning inventory, $52,800; ending inventory, $46,700; net purchases, $782,500; selling expenses, $271,300; general expenses, $96,400; contributions to charities, $27,500; long-term capital gains, $57,250; short-term capital losses, $14,650; operating loss carry-forward from previous years, $116,205. Yates is entitled to an investment tax credit equal to 10 percent of $180,000 in equipment purchases.

Required

1. Determine taxable income for Yates Corporation.
2. Determine the income tax liability for Yates Corporation, assuming a tax rate of 28 percent on net long-term capital gains.

Problem 17A-4
Dividend
Transactions
and Stock-
holders' Equity
(L.O. 2, 5)

The balance sheet of the Mota Clothing Company disclosed the following stockholders' equity as of September 30, 19x1:

Contributed Capital
Common Stock—$2 par value, 1,000,000 shares authorized, 250,000 shares issued and outstanding		$500,000
Paid-in Capital in Excess of Par Value, Common		60,000
Total Contributed Capital		$560,000
Retained Earnings		400,000
Total Stockholders' Equity		$960,000

The following stockholders' equity transactions were completed during the year in the order presented:

19x1
Dec. 17 Declared a 10 percent stock dividend to stockholders of record on January 1. The market value per share on the date of declaration was $4.

19x2
Jan. 20 Distributed the stock dividend.
Apr. 14 Declared a 25¢ per share cash dividend. Cash dividend payable May 15 to stockholders of record on May 1.
May 15 Paid the cash dividend.
June 17 Split its stock 2 for 1.
Sept. 14 Appropriated retained earnings for plant expansion in the amount of $95,000.
   15 Declared a cash dividend of $.10 per share payable October 10 to stockholders of record October 1.
   30 Closed Income Summary with a credit balance of $50,000 to Retained Earnings.
   30 Closed Dividends Declared to Retained Earnings.

Required

1. Record the above transactions in general journal form.
2. Prepare the stockholders' equity section of the company's balance sheet as of September 30, 19x2.

Problem 17A-5
Corporate
Income
Statement
(L.O. 7, 8)

Information concerning operations of the Jorgenson Shoe Company during 19xx is as follows: (a) Administrative Expenses, $100,000; (b) Cost of Goods Sold, $350,000; (c) Cumulative effect of an accounting change that increased income, change in depreciation methods (net of taxes $20,000), $42,000; (d) Extraordinary Item, Loss from Earthquake (net of taxes $46,000), ($60,000); (e) Sales (net), $800,000; (f) Selling Expenses, $80,000; (g) Income Taxes Expense applicable to continuing operations, $135,000.

Required

Prepare the company's income statement for the year ended December 31, 19xx, including earnings per share information. Assume a weighted average of 100,000 common stock shares outstanding during the year.

Problem 17A-6
Earnings per Share
(L.O. 8)

The Jeni Fey Corporation had the following capital structure during 19xx:

a. Common stock, $10 par value: (1) January–September, 200,000 shares outstanding; (2) October–December, 300,000 shares outstanding.
b. There are 20,000 shares of 6 percent, $100 par value convertible preferred stock outstanding for the entire year. The preferred shares are convertible into common stock at the rate of 2.5 shares of common stock for each share of preferred stock. The preferred stock shares are common stock equivalents.
c. There are 5,000 shares of $100 par value, convertible preferred stock outstanding for the entire year. The stock is convertible into common stock at the rate of 1 share of preferred to 5 shares of common, and it is not a common stock equivalent. The dividend rate is $2 per share.
d. Net income is $850,000.

Required

1. Figure the weighted-average number of shares outstanding in 19xx.
2. Figure the earnings-per-share amounts that must be disclosed by the Jeni Fey Corporation.

Problem 17A-7
Stockholders' Equity and Statement of Retained Earnings
(L.O. 1, 2, 3, 4)

On January 1, 19xx, the stockholders' equity section of the Galloway Company appeared as shown below.

Contributed Capital	
Common Stock—$4 par value, 100,000 shares authorized, 40,000 shares issued and outstanding	$ 160,000
Paid-in Capital in Excess of Par Value, Common	580,000
Total Contributed Capital	$ 740,000
Retained Earnings	316,000
Total Stockholders' Equity	$1,056,000

Selected transactions involving stockholders' equity are as follows: (a) During January, the board of directors obtained authorization for 20,000 shares of $20 par value preferred stock that carried an indicated dividend rate of $2 per share. The company sold 12,000 shares at $25 per share and issued another 2,000 in exchange for a building valued at $60,000. Also, during January, land valued at $10,000, on which the building was located, was donated to the company. (b) During March, the board of directors also declared a 2 for 1 stock split on the common stock. (c) In April, after the stock split, the company purchased 3,000 shares of common stock for the treasury at an average price of $6 per share; 1,000 of these shares were subsequently sold at an average price of $8 per share. (d) In May, 2,000 shares of the company's common stock were donated to the company through the will of a deceased stockholder. On the date the stock was received, its market value was $10 per share. It was subsequently sold for $13 in June. (e) During July, declared and paid a cash dividend of $2 per share on preferred stock and 20¢ per share on common stock. (f) The board of directors declared a 15 percent stock dividend in November when the common stock was selling for $10. The stock dividend had not been distributed by the end of the year. (g) Stock subscriptions for 4,000 common shares at an average price of $14 per share were received in December. Partial payments amounting to one-half the subscriptions were paid, but none of the stock was fully paid by the end of the year. (h) Also in December a prior period adjustment was made which reduced earnings by $15,000. No income taxes were involved. (i) Net loss for 19x1 was $115,000.

Required

1. Prepare journal entries to record the above transactions.
2. Prepare the company's statement of retained earnings for the year ended December 31.
3. Prepare the stockholders' equity section of the company's balance sheet as of December 31.

Problem Set B

Problem 17B-1
Treasury Stock
Transactions
(L.O. 3)

The Hanebrink Gem Company made the following stock transactions during 19xx:

Feb. 12   Purchased 20,000 shares of its common stock on the market at a cost of $10 per share and put it in the treasury.
May 2   Sold 5,000 shares of the treasury stock for $10 per share.
Aug. 4   Sold 6,000 shares of the treasury stock for $11 per share.
Sept. 15 Sold 5,000 shares of the treasury stock for $9 per share.
Nov. 19   Sold the remaining 4,000 shares of the treasury stock for $9 per share.

Required

Record the above transactions in general journal form.

Problem 17B-2
Stock and
Retained
Earnings
Transactions
(L.O. 2, 3, 5)

Holtzman Corporation has 105,000 shares of $10 par value common stock outstanding. It engaged in the following stockholders' equity transactions during 19xx:

Jan. 17   Purchased 10,000 shares of the company's own stock at $20 per share.
Mar. 22   Sold 1,000 shares of the company's stock purchased on January 17 for $25 per share.
Apr. 16   The board of directors voted to appropriate $125,000 of retained earnings for plant expansion. The board determined that the appropriation would not be adequately disclosed by footnote.
May 6   Sold 2,000 shares of the company's stock purchased on January 17 for $19 per share.
     29   Sold 2,000 shares of the company's stock purchased on January 17 for $16 per share.
June 30   Declared a cash dividend of 25¢ per share of common stock. The corporation had 100,000 shares of common stock outstanding.
July 25   Paid the cash dividend declared on June 30.
Dec. 10   Completed and paid the plant expansion at a cost of $130,000, and the board of directors voted to return the appropriated retained earnings to Unappropriated Retained Earnings.

Required

Prepare general journal entries to record the above transactions.

Problem 17B-3
Taxable Income
and Tax
Liability for
Corporations
(L.O. 6)

After two years of losses, DDT Corporation became profitable in the current year. In preparation for filing the company's tax return, the DDT accountant found that the company had a gross margin of $268,500 and business expenses of $110,000, including charitable contributions of $12,000. In addition, the company received dividends from other corporations of $27,000 and had a long-term capital gain of $20,000. It also had an operating loss carry-forward of $91,175 from the previous two years. DDT is entitled to an investment tax credit of 10 percent of $20,000 in equipment purchases.

Required

1. Determine taxable income for DDT Corporation.
2. Determine the income tax liability for DDT Corporation, assuming a tax rate of 28 percent on net long-term capital gains.

**Problem 17B-4
Dividend
Transactions
and Stock-
holders' Equity
(L.O. 2)**

The stockholders' equity of the Romano Manufacturing Company as of December 31, 19x0, was as follows:

Contributed Capital		
Common Stock—$1 par value, 500,000 shares authorized,		
400,000 shares issued and outstanding	$400,000	
Paid-in Capital in Excess of Par Value, Common	100,000	
Total Contributed Capital	$500,000	
Retained Earnings	230,000	
Total Stockholders' Equity	$730,000	

The following transactions were completed during 19x1:

Jan. 9   Declared a cash dividend of 10¢ per share of common stock, to be paid to stockholders of record on February 1. Date of payment is to be February 10.

Feb. 1   Date of record for cash dividend declared January 9.

10   Paid the cash dividend declared on January 9.

June 16   Declared a 5 percent stock dividend to be distributed on July 15. The market value of the stock was $7 per share.

July 15   Distributed the stock dividend declared on June 16.

Oct. 1   The board of directors voted a 2 for 1 stock split. At the same time, the number of shares authorized was doubled.

Dec. 10   Declared a cash dividend of $.05 per share of common stock, to be paid to stockholders of record January 1. Date of payment is to be January 10.

31   Net income for the year of $100,000 is closed to Retained Earnings.

31   Closed Dividends Declared to Retained Earnings.

Required

1. Record the above transactions in general journal form.
2. Prepare the stockholders' equity section of the company's balance sheet as of December 31, 19x1.

**Problem 17B-5
Corporate
Income
Statement
(L.O. 7)**

Balances from the general ledger of the Luzinski Manufacturing Company as of December 31 are presented below.

a. Administrative Expenses	$ 45,000
b. Cost of Goods Sold	300,000
c. Discontinued Operations	
(1) Profit from the Operations of Discontinued	
Segment (net of taxes $60,000)	63,000
(2) Gain on Disposal (net of taxes $50,000)	52,000
d. Extraordinary Loss, Expropriation of Plant by	
foreign government (net of taxes $40,000)	46,000
e. Income Tax Expense Applicable to Continuing Operations	95,000
f. Other Operating Expenses	145,000
g. Sales	750,000
h. Sales Commissions Expenses	75,000
i. Sales Returns and Allowances	5,000

Required

Prepare the income statement in good form for the company as of December 31, including earnings per share information. Assume weighted-average common shares of 100,000.

Problem 17B-6
Earnings per Share
(L.O. 8)

The Shellenback Corporation had the following capital structure during 19xx:

a. $5 par value common stock: (1) January–June, 100,000 shares outstanding; (2) July–September, 120,000 shares outstanding; (3) October–December, 140,000 shares outstanding.

b. There are 20,000 shares of $10 par value, cumulative, convertible preferred stock outstanding for the year. The stock is convertible into common stock at a rate of one share of preferred to two shares of common, and is a common stock equivalent. The dividend rate for the preferred stock is $1 per share.

c. There are 10,000 shares of $20 par value, cumulative, convertible preferred stock outstanding for the year. This stock is convertible into common stock at a rate of one share of preferred to three shares of common. The stock is not a common stock equivalent but if converted would dilute the earnings per share of common stock. The dividend rate is $1.25 per share.

d. Net income is $175,000.

Required

1. Compute the weighted-average number of common stock shares outstanding for 19x7.

2. Compute the earnings per share amounts necessary for proper disclosure for the Shellenback Corporation.

Problem 17B-7
Stockholders' Equity and Statement of Retained Earnings
(L.O. 1, 2, 3, 4)

The balance sheet of Holmes Developers presented the following stockholders' equity as of June 30, 19x7:

Contributed Capital		
Preferred Stock—$50 par value, 6% noncumulative, 100,000 shares authorized, 25,000 shares issued and outstanding		$1,250,000
Common Stock—$10 par value, 700,000 shares authorized, 400,000 shares issued and outstanding	4,000,000	
Paid-in Capital in Excess of Par Value, Common	600,000	4,600,000
Total Contributed Capital		$5,850,000
Retained Earnings		2,400,000
Total Stockholders' Equity		$8,250,000

The company's activities during the year included the following stockholders' equity transactions: (a) Net income was $650,000. (b) Purchased 20,000 shares of the company's common stock for $15 per share. (c) Sold 15,000 shares of the treasury stock for $16 per share. (d) Received a tract of land, with a market value of $100,000, which was donated to the company. (e) Declared and paid the indicated cash dividend to preferred stockholders for the year. (f) Declared and paid a cash dividend on common stock of 50¢ per share after the treasury stock transactions in b and c were completed. (g) After the above transactions, declared a 2 percent stock dividend on common stock, at which time the common stock was selling for $19 per share. The stock dividend had not been distributed at the end of the year. (h) Recorded a prior period adjustment net of taxes of $20,000. The adjustment was a correction of a depreciation error in 19x2. The depreciation for buildings was not recorded in 19x2, so depreciation was understated. (i) Accepted near the end of the year subscriptions on 5,000 shares of preferred stock at $54 per share. The subscriptions had not been paid at the end of the year.

Required

1. Prepare journal entries for the above transactions.
2. Prepare a statement of retained earnings for Holmes Developers for the year ended June 30, 19x8.
3. Prepare the stockholders' equity section of Holmes Developers' balance sheet as of June 30, 19x8.

Financial Decision Case 17-1

Metzger Steel Corporation
(L.O. 2, 3)

Metzger Steel Corporation (MSC) is a small specialty steel manufacturer located in northern Alabama, which has been owned by the Metzger family for several generations. Arnold Metzger III is a major shareholder in MSC by virtue of having inherited 200,000 shares of common stock in the company. Previously, Arnold has not shown much interest in the business because of his enthusiasm for archaeology, which takes him to far parts of the world. However, when he receives minutes of the last board of directors meeting, he questions a number of transactions involving the stockholders' equity of MSC. He asks you, as a person with a knowledge of accounting, to help him interpret the effect of these transactions on his interest in MSC.

First, you note that at the beginning of 19xx the stockholders' equity of MSC appeared as follows:

Metzger Steel Corporation	
Stockholders' Equity	
January 1, 19xx	

Contributed Capital	
Common Stock—$10 par value, 2,500,000 shares authorized, 1,000,000 shares issued and outstanding	$10,000,000
Paid-in Capital in Excess of Par Value, Common	25,000,000
Total Contributed Capital	$35,000,000
Retained Earnings	25,000,000
Total Stockholders' Equity	$60,000,000

Then, you read the relevant parts of the minutes of the December 15 meeting of the board of directors of MSC as they appear below:

Item A: A report by the president of the following transactions involving the company's stock during the last quarter:

October 15 Sold 300,000 shares of authorized common stock through the investment banking firm of A. B. Abbott at a net price of $50 per share.

November 1 Purchased 175,000 shares for the corporate treasury from Sharon Metzger at a price of $55 per share.

November 10 Received a donation from Mason Metzger of 25,000 shares of common stock.

November 15 Sold 10,000 of the shares purchased from Sharon Metzger and the 25,000 shares received from Mason Metzger at a net price of $60 per share.

December 1 Retired 65,000 of the shares received from Sharon Metzger. Sharon's father had originally purchased the shares with an investment in MSC of $20 per share.

Item B: The board declared a two-for-one stock split, followed by a 10 percent stock dividend. The board then declared the annual cash dividend of $2.00 per share on the resulting shares. All these transactions are applicable to stockholders of record on December 20 and are payable on January 10. The market value of Metzger stock on the board meeting date after the stock split was estimated to be $30.

Item C: The chief financial officer stated that he expected the company to report a net income for the year of $4,000,000.

Required

1. Prepare a stockholders' equity section of MSC's balance sheet as of December 31, 19xx, that reflects the status of the above transactions. (Hint: use T accounts to analyze transactions.)

2. Compute the book value per share and percent ownership of the company at the beginning and at the end of the year for Arnold's holdings. Explain the differences. Would you say that Arnold's position has improved or not during the year?

Learning
Objectives

Chapter
Eighteen

Long-Term
Liabilities

1. *Identify and contrast the major characteristics of bonds.*

2. *Record the issuance of bonds at face value, between interest dates, and at a discount or premium.*

3. *Amortize bond discount and premium by using the effective interest method, and make year-end adjustments.*

4. *Account for the retirement and conversion of bonds.*

5. *Compute sinking fund requirements, and prepare accounting entries associated with sinking fund bonds payable.*

6. *Explain the basic features of mortgages payable, long-term leases, and pensions as long-term liabilities.*

7. *Explain why income tax allocation is necessary, and account for the differences between accounting and taxable income.*

This chapter introduces long-term liabilities. It describes the nature of bonds and the accounting treatment for bonds payable, for other long-term liabilities such as mortgages, long-term leases, and pension liabilities, and for income tax allocation. After studying this chapter, you should be able to meet the learning objectives listed on the left.

A corporation has many sources of funds from which to finance operations and expansion. As you learned earlier, corporations acquire cash and other assets by having profitable operations, getting short-term credit, and issuing stock. Another source of funds for a business is long-term debt in the form of bonds or notes. When a company issues bonds or notes, it promises to pay the creditor periodic interest plus the principal of the debt on a certain date in the future. Notes and bonds are long-term if they are due more than one year from the balance sheet date. In practice, long-term notes can range from two to ten years to maturity and long-term bonds from ten to fifty years to maturity.

Nature of Bonds

A bond is a security representing money borrowed by a corporation from the public. (Other kinds of bonds are those used by the United States government, state and local governments, and foreign companies and countries to raise money.) Bonds must be repaid at a certain time and require periodic payments of interest. Interest is usually paid semiannually or twice a year. These bonds must not be confused with stocks. Because stocks are shares of ownership, stockholders are owners. Bondholders, however, are creditors. Bonds are promises to repay the amount borrowed, called the principal, and a certain rate of interest at specified future dates.

The holder of a bond receives a bond certificate as evidence of the company's debt to the bondholder. In most cases, the face value (denomination) of the bond is $1,000 or some multiple of $1,000. A bond issue is the total number of bonds that are issued at the same time. For example, a $1,000,000 bond issue may consist of a thousand $1,000 bonds. The issue may be bought and held by many investors. So the corporation usually enters into a supplementary agreement, called a bond indenture. The bond indenture defines the rights, privileges, and limitations of bondholders. The bond indenture will generally describe such things as the maturity date of the bonds, interest payment dates, interest rate, and characteristics of the bonds such as convertible or callable features. Repayment plans and restrictions are also usually covered.

The prices of bonds are stated in terms of 100s. If a bond issue is quoted at $103\frac{1}{2}$, this means that a $1,000 bond would cost $1,035 ($1,000 $\times$ $103\frac{1}{2}$%). When a bond sells at exactly 100, it is said to sell at face or par value. When it sells at above 100, it is said to sell at a premium and when below face value, at a discount. A $1,000 bond quoted at 87.62 would be selling at a discount and would cost the buyer $876.20.

A bond indenture can be written to fit the needs of an individual company and its financing needs. So the bonds being issued by corporations in today's financial markets have many different features. Several of the more important features are described below.

Secured or Unsecured Bonds

Bonds may be either secured or unsecured. If issued on the general credit of the company, they are unsecured bonds (also called debenture bonds). Secured bonds give the bondholders a pledge of certain assets of the company as a guarantee of repayment. The security identified by a secured bond may be any specific asset of the company or a general category such as property, plant, and equipment.

Term or Serial Bonds

When all the bonds of an issue mature at the same time, they are called term bonds. For example, a company may issue $1,000,000 worth of bonds, all due twenty years from the date of issue. If the maturity dates of a bond issue are spread over several maturity dates, the bonds are serial bonds. A company may issue serial bonds to make it easier to get together cash for retiring the bonds. An example of serial bonds would be a $1,000,000 issue that called for retiring $200,000 of the principal every five years. This arrangement means that after the first $200,000 payment is made, only $800,000 of the bonds would remain outstanding for the next five years. In other words, $1,000,000 is outstanding for the first five years, and $800,000 is outstanding for the second five years.

Registered or Coupon Bonds

Most bonds that are issued today are registered bonds. On registered bonds the name and address of the owner must be recorded with the issuing company. In this way the company keeps a register of the owners and pays interest by check to the bondholders of record on the interest payment date. Coupon bonds are generally not registered with the corporation but have interest coupons attached to them. Each coupon states the amount of interest due and the payment date. The coupons are removed from the bond on the interest payment dates and put in a bank for collection. In this way the interest is paid to the holder of the coupon.

Accounting for Bonds Payable[1]

Objective 2
Record the issuance of bonds at face value, between interest dates, and at a discount or premium

When the board of directors decides to issue bonds, it generally presents the proposal to the stockholders. If the stockholders agree to the issue, the company then prints the certificates and draws up a bond indenture. Finally, the bonds are authorized for issuance. It is not necessary to make a journal entry for the authorization, but most companies prepare a memorandum in the Bonds Payable account describing the issue. This note gives the amount of bonds authorized, interest rate, interest payment dates, and life of the bonds.

Once the bonds are issued, the corporation must pay interest to the bondholders during the life of the bonds (in most cases semiannually) and the principal of the bonds at maturity.

Balance Sheet Disclosure of Bonds

Bonds payable and either unamortized discount or premium (which will be explained later) are generally shown on a company's balance sheet as long-term liabilities. However, as explained in Chapter 12, if the maturity date of the bond issue is one year or less and the bonds will be retired by the use of current assets, bonds payable should be listed as current liabilities. If the issue is to be paid with segregated assets or replaced by another bond issue, then they should still be shown as long-term liabilities.

Important provisions of the bond indenture are reported in the notes to the financial statements, often with a list of all bond issues, the kind of bonds, interest rate, any security connected with the bonds, interest payment dates, maturity date, and effective interest rate.

Bonds Issued at Face Value

As an example, suppose that the Vason Corporation has authorized the issuance of $100,000 of 9 percent, five-year bonds on January 1, 19x0. Interest is to be paid on January 1 and July 1 of each year. Also suppose that the bonds are sold on January 1, 19x0, for their face value. The entry to record the issuance is as follows:

1. At the time this chapter is being written, the market interest rates on corporate bonds are quite volatile. Only the bold and reckless predict which way they will go. Therefore, the examples and problems in this chapter use a variety of interest rates that are convenient for demonstrating the concepts.

```
Jan. 1   Cash                                    100,000
              Bonds Payable                                    100,000
                  Sold $100,000 of 9%, 5-year
                  bonds at face value
```

As stated above, interest is paid on July 1 and January 1 of each year. Thus the corporation would owe the bondholders $4,500 interest on July 1, 19x0. The interest computation is shown below:

$$\text{interest} = \text{principal} \times \text{rate} \times \text{time}$$
$$= \$100,000 \times .09 \times \tfrac{1}{2} \text{ year}$$
$$= \$4,500$$

The interest paid to the bondholders on each semiannual interest payment date would be recorded as follows:

```
July 1   Bond Interest Expense                   4,500
              Cash (or Interest Payable)                       4,500
                  Paid (or accrued) semiannual
                  interest to bondholders of 9%,
                  5-year bonds
```

Sales of Bonds Between Interest Dates

Bonds may be issued on their interest date as in the example above, but many times they are sold between interest dates. The generally accepted method of handling bonds issued in this manner is to collect from the investor the interest that has accrued since the last interest payment date. Then when the next interest period arrives, the corporation pays the investor the interest for the entire period. Thus the interest collected when bonds are sold is returned to the investor on the next interest payment date. If a company were issuing bonds on several different days and did not collect the accrued interest, records would have to be maintained for each bondholder and date of purchase. In such a case, the interest due each bondholder would have to be computed on the basis of different time periods. It becomes clear that large bookkeeping costs would be incurred under this system. On the other hand, if accrued interest is collected when the bonds are sold, then on the interest payment date the corporation can pay the interest due for the entire period, eliminating the extra computations and costs.

For example, assume that the Vason Corporation sold $100,000 of 9 percent, five-year bonds for face value on April 1, 19x0, rather than on January 1, 19x0, the issue date. The entries to record the sale of the bonds and payment of interest on July 1, 19x0, follow:

```
Apr. 1   Cash                                    102,250
              Bond Interest Expense                            2,250
              Bonds Payable                                  100,000
                  Sold 9%, 5-year bonds at face
                  value plus 3 months' accrued
                  interest
                  $100,000 × .09 × ³⁄₁₂ = $2,250
```

As shown above, Cash is debited for the amount received, $102,250 (face value of $100,000 plus three months' accrued interest of $2,250). Bond Interest Expense is credited for the $2,250 of accrued interest, and Bonds Payable is credited for the face value of $100,000. When the first semiannual interest date arrives, the following entry is made:

July 1	Bond Interest Expense	4,500	
	Cash (or Interest Payable)		4,500
	Paid (or accrued) semiannual		
	interest		
	$100,000 \times .09\% \times \frac{1}{2} = \$4,500$		

Note that here the full half-year interest is both debited to Bond Interest Expense and credited to Cash. Also note that the actual interest expense for the six months is $2,250. This amount is the net balance of the $4,500 debit to Bond Interest Expense on July 1 less the $2,250 credit to Bond Interest Expense on April 1. We can see these steps clearly in the posted entries in the ledger account for Bond Interest Expense:

Bond Interest Expense						Account No. 723
					Balance	
Date	Item	Post. Ref.	Debit	Credit	Debit	Credit
19x0						
Apr. 1				2,250		2,250
July 1			4,500		2,250	

The Effect of the Market Rate of Interest on Bond Prices

The face value of a bond and its face interest rate are fixed. One hundred thousand dollars in bonds at 9 percent will pay $9,000 a year or $4,500 every six months until maturity. However, bonds are bought and sold by investors in the market every day, and interest rates in the market change from day to day. Vason Corporation can receive face value or $100,000 for the bonds, as shown above, only if the current market or effective rate of interest is 9 percent for bonds with the same conditions and quality. If the current market rate of interest on this kind of bond issue has gone up to 10 percent, Vason could receive less than $100,000 from the bond investor. In other words, given a market rate of interest of 10 percent, the wise investor will not pay $100,000 for a yearly interest payment of $9,000. On the other hand, if the market rate goes down to 8 percent, Vason Corporation will be able to issue the bonds for more than $100,000 because similar bonds will yield only 8 percent.

When issuing bonds, most companies try to set the face interest rate as close as possible to the market interest rate. However, a company must decide in advance what the face interest rate will be to allow time to file with regulatory bodies, publicize the issue, and print the certificates. So there is often a difference in the market or effective rate of interest and the face rate of interest on the issue date. The result is that the issue price of the bond does not equal the principal or face value of the bond. If the issue price is less than the face value, the bonds are said to be issued at a discount. The discount equals the excess of face value over issue price. If the issue price is more than the face value, the bonds are said to be issued at a premium. The premium is equal to the excess of the issue price over the face value.

Using Present Value to Value a Bond[2]

Present value is relevant here because the value of bonds is based on the present value of a series of fixed interest payments and the present value of a single payment at maturity. To determine the present value of a bond, therefore, use Tables B-3 and B-4 in Appendix B. The amount of interest that a bond pays is fixed over its life. During its life, however, the market rate of interest varies from day to day. Thus the amount that investors are willing to pay for the bond changes as well.

Assume, for example, that a particular bond has a face value of $10,000 and pays a fixed amount of interest of $450 (9 percent annual rate) every six months. The bond is due in five years. If the market rate of interest today is 14 percent, how much is the present value of the bond?

Because the compounding period is more than once a year, it is necessary to convert the annual rate to 7 percent (14% ÷ two six-month periods per year) and to use ten periods (five years × two six-month periods per year). Using this information, we compute the present value of the bond:

Present value of 10 periodic payments
  (from Table B-4): $450 × 7.024   = $3,160.80
Present value of a single payment
  (from Table B-3): $10,000 × 0.508   =   5,080.00
Present value of $10,000 bond   = $8,240.80

The market rate of interest has increased so much since the bond was issued (from 9 percent to 14 percent) that the value of the bond is only $8,240.80 today. This amount is all that investors would be willing to pay at this time for an income from this bond of $450 every six months.

Bonds Issued at a Discount

As a case of issuing bonds at a discount, suppose that the Vason Corporation issues its $100,000 of five-year, 9 percent bonds at 96.149 when the market rate of interest is 10 percent. The entry to record the issuance of the bonds at a discount is:

2. This section depends on a knowledge of present value concepts, which are introduced in Appendix A, and is optional.

```
Jan. 1   Cash                                          96,149
            Unamortized Bond Discount                   3,851
              Bonds Payable                                        100,000
                Sold $100,000 of 9%, 5-year
                bonds
```

```
                Face Amount of Bonds               $100,000
                Less Purchase Price of Bonds
                  ($100,000 × .96149)                 96,149
                Unamortized Bond Discount           $  3,851
```

As shown above, Cash is debited for the amount received ($96,149), Bonds Payable is credited for the face amount ($100,000) of the bond liability, and the difference ($3,851) is debited to Unamortized Bond Discount. If a balance sheet is prepared right after this issuance of bonds at a discount, the liability for bonds payable is as follows:

```
Long-Term Liabilities
  9% Bonds Payable, due 1/1/x5           $100,000
  Less Unamortized Bond Discount            3,851    $96,149
```

As can be seen, the Unamortized Bond Discount is deducted from the face amount of the bonds to arrive at the carrying value or present value of the bonds. The bond discount is described as unamortized because it will be amortized (written off) over the life of the bonds. For this reason, the carrying value of the bonds will gradually increase. By the time the maturity date of the bonds arrives, the carrying value of the bonds will equal their face value.

Calculation of Total Interest Cost

When bonds are issued at a discount, the effective interest rate paid by the company is greater than the face interest rate on the bonds. The reason is that the company must pay the bondholder an amount that is made up of the stated interest payments *plus* the amount of the bond discount. That is, the company did not receive the full face value of the bonds upon issue. So the difference between the issue price and the face value must be added to the interest payments to arrive at the actual interest expense. The full cost to the Vason Corporation of issuing the bonds at a discount is as follows:

```
Cash to be paid to bondholders
  Face value at maturity                              $100,000
  Interest payments ($100,000 × .09 × 5 years)          45,000
Total cash to bondholders                             $145,000
Cash received from bondholders                          96,149
Total interest cost                                   $ 48,851
```

Or alternatively

```
Interest payments ($100,000 × .09 × 5 years)          $ 45,000
Unamortized Bond Discount                                3,851
Total interest cost                                   $ 48,851
```

The total interest cost of $48,851 is made up of $45,000 in interest payments and the $3,851 of bond discount. So the bond discount increases the interest paid on the bonds from the stated to the effective interest rate.

The discount must be spread or allocated over the life of the bonds as an increase in the interest expense each period. This process of allocation is called amortization of the bond discount.

Amortizing the Bond Discount

Objective 3
Amortize bond
discount and
premium by
using the
effective interest
method, and
make year-end
adjustments

There are two ways of amortizing the discount: the straight-line method and the effective interest method. The straight-line method is the easier of the two and makes the amortization of the discount equal for each interest period. In this case, suppose that the interest payment dates for the Vason bond issue are January 1 and July 1. The bond discount is amortized and the interest cost is figured in four steps, as follows:

1. Total interest payments = interest payments per year $\times$ life of bonds
   $$= 2 \times 5$$
   $$= 10$$

2. Amortization of bond discount per interest payment
   $$= \frac{\text{bond discount}}{\text{total interest payments}} = \frac{\$3,851}{10} = \$385$$

3. Regular cash interest payment
   $$= \text{face value} \times \text{face interest rate} \times \text{time}$$
   $$= \$100,000 \times .09 \times \tfrac{1}{2}$$
   $$= \$4,500$$

4. Total interest cost per interest date
   $$= \text{interest payment} + \text{amortization of bond discount}$$
   $$= \$4,500 + \$385 = \$4,885$$

On July 1, 19x0, the semiannual interest date, the entry would be as follows:

July 1	Bond Interest Expense	4,885	
	Unamortized Bond Discount		385
	Cash (or Interest Payable)		4,500
	Paid (or accrued) semiannual interest to bondholders and amortized discount on 9%, 5-year bonds		

Note that the bond interest expense is $4,885, but the amount received by the bondholder is the $4,500 face interest payment. The difference of $385 is the credit to Unamortized Bond Discount. This will lower the debit balance of the Unamortized Bond Discount and so will raise the carrying value of the bonds payable by $385 each interest period. When the bond issue matures, there will be no balance in the Unamortized Bond Discount account, and the carrying value of the bonds payable will be $100,000. This is exactly equal to the amount due the bondholder.

Even though the straight-line method has long been used, it has a certain weakness. Because the carrying value goes up each period and the bond interest expense stays the same, the straight-line method leads to a decreasing rate of interest over time. Also, using the straight-line method to amortize a premium leads to a rising rate of interest over time. For this reason, the APB has ruled that the straight-line method can be used only where it does not lead to a material difference from the effective interest method.[3] As will be seen, the effective interest rate method supposes a constant rate of interest over the life of the bond. This rate will be constant if the total interest expense changes a little each interest period in response to the changing carrying value of the bond.

We will describe how to figure the interest and amortization of bond discount for each interest period under the **effective interest method**. One must apply a constant interest rate to the carrying value of the bonds at the beginning of the interest period. This rate would be the market rate (effective rate) at the time the bonds were issued. The amount to be amortized becomes the difference between the interest figured by using the constant rate (effective rate) and the actual interest paid to the bondholders.

As an example of this method, let us use the same facts as in the earlier case ($100,000 bond issue at 9 percent, five-year maturity, interest paid twice a year). The market or effective rate of interest at the time is 10 percent. The bonds were sold for $96,149, which means a discount of $3,851. The amounts of interest and amortization of the bond discount are shown in Table 18-1 (next page).

The following points should help to explain how the amounts in the table are figured:

Column A: The carrying value of the bonds is the face value of the bonds less unamortized bond discount ($100,000 − $3,851 = $96,149).

Column B: The interest expense to be recorded is the effective interest. It is found by multiplying the carrying value of the bonds by the effective interest rate for one-half year ($96,149 $\times$ .10 $\times$ $\frac{1}{2}$ = $4,807).

Column C: The interest paid in each period is the face value of the bonds multiplied by the interest rate for the bonds multiplied by the interest time period ($100,000 $\times$ .09 $\times$ $\frac{1}{2}$ = $4,500).

Column D: The discount amortized is the difference between the effective interest expense to be recorded and the interest to be paid on the interest payment date ($4,807 − $4,500 = $307).

Column E: The unamortized bond discount is the balance of the bond discount at the beginning of the period ($3,851) less the current period amortization of the discount ($307). The unamortized discount decreases each interest payment period because it is amortized as a portion of interest expense.

3. Accounting Principles Board, *Opinion No. 21*, "Interest on Receivables and Payables" (New York: American Institute of Certified Public Accountants, 1971), par. 15.

	A	B	C	D	E	F
Semi-annual Interest Period	Carrying Value at Beginning of Period	Semiannual Interest Expense at 10% to Be Recorded* (5% × A)	Semiannual Interest to Be Paid to Bondholders (4½% × $100,000)	Amortization of Discount (B − C)	Unamortized Bond Discount at End of Period	Carrying Value at End of Period (A + D)
0					$3,851	96,149
1	$96,149	$4,807	$4,500	$307	3,544	$96,456
2	96,456	4,823	4,500	323	3,221	96,779
3	96,779	4,839	4,500	339	2,882	97,118
4	97,118	4,856	4,500	356	2,526	97,474
5	97,474	4,874	4,500	374	2,152	97,848
6	97,848	4,892	4,500	392	1,760	98,240
7	98,240	4,912	4,500	412	1,348	98,652
8	98,652	4,933	4,500	433	915	99,085
9	99,085	4,954	4,500	454	461	99,539
10	99,539	4,961**	4,500	461	—	100,000

*Rounded to nearest dollar.
**Error due to rounding.

E + F always = 100,000

Table 18-1
Interest and Amortization of Bond Discount—Effective Interest Method

Column F: The carrying value of the bonds at the end of the period is the carrying value at the beginning of the period plus the amortization during the period ($96,149 + $307 = $96,456). Notice that the sum of the carrying value and unamortized discount (column E + column F) always equals the face value of the bonds ($96,456 + $3,544 = $100,000).

The entry to record the interest expense is exactly like the one shown when the straight-line method is applied. However, the amounts debited and credited to the various accounts are different. For example, the entry for July 1, 19x0, using the effective interest method, would be

July 1	Bond Interest Expense	4,807	
	Unamortized Bond Discount		307
	Cash (or Interest Payable)		4,500
	Paid (or accrued) semiannual interest to bondholders and amortized discount on 9%, 5-year bonds		

Note also that an interest and amortization table does not have to be prepared to determine the amortization of discount for any one interest payment period. It is necessary only to multiply the carrying value by the effective interest rate and subtract the interest payment from the result. For example, the amount of discount to be amortized in the seventh interest payment period equals $412 [($98,240 × .05) − $4,500].

Bonds Issued at a Premium

When bonds have a face interest rate that is above the market rate for similar investments, they will be issued at a price above the face value, or at a premium. For example, assume that the Vason Corporation issued $100,000 of bonds for $104,100 when the market rate of interest is 8 percent. This means that they will be purchased by investors at 104.1 percent of their face value. The entry to record their issuance would be as follows:

Jan. 1 Cash	104,100	
Unamortized Bond Premium		4,100
Bonds Payable		100,000
Sold $100,000 of 9%, 5-year bonds at 104.1		

Right after this entry is made, bonds payable would be presented on the balance sheet as follows:

Long-Term Liabilities
9% Bonds Payable, due 1/1/x5	$100,000	
Unamortized Bond Premium	4,100	$104,100

The carrying value of bonds payable is $104,100, which is equal to the face value of the bonds plus the unamortized bond premium. The cash received from the issuance of the bonds is also $104,100. This means that the purchasers were willing to pay a premium of $4,100 to get these bonds because the face interest on them was greater than the market rate. The $4,100 premium represents an amount that will not be paid back to the bondholders at maturity. For this reason, it is amortized over the life of the bonds as a decrease in Bond Interest Expense. Note in the calculation on the following page the difference from the amortization of bond discount, which raised interest expense. The bond premium, on the other hand, serves to lower total interest costs below the amount paid to bondholders.

Cash to be paid to bondholders	
Face value at maturity	$100,000
Interest payments ($100,000 × .09 × 5)	45,000
Total cash paid to bondholders	$145,000
Cash received from bondholders	104,100
Total interest costs	$ 40,900

Amortizing Bond Premium

When bonds are issued at a premium, the amount of the premium must be spread over the life of the bonds to lower the interest expense. As noted earlier in describing bond discounts, the effective interest method is the more acceptable way of amortizing bond premium. Using the same facts as above, the amortization of the bond premium under the effective interest method is shown in Table 18-2 (next page). This table is much like Table 18-1. The difference is that interest expense is being reduced

	A	B	C	D	E	F
Semi-annual Interest Period	Carrying Value at Beginning of Period	Semiannual Interest Expense at 8% to Be Recorded* (4% × A)	Semiannual Interest to Be Paid to Bondholders (4½% × $100,000)	Amortization of Premium (C − B)	Unamortized Bond Premium at End of Period	Carrying Value at End of Period (A − D)
0						
1	$104,100	$4,164	$4,500	$336	3,764	$103,764
2	103,764	4,151	4,500	349	3,415	103,415
3	103,415	4,137	4,500	363	3,052	103,052
4	103,052	4,122	4,500	378	2,674	102,674
5	102,674	4,107	4,500	393	2,281	102,281
6	102,281	4,091	4,500	409	1,872	101,872
7	101,872	4,075	4,500	425	1,447	101,447
8	101,447	4,058	4,500	442	1,005	101,005
9	101,005	4,040	4,500	460	545	100,545
10	100,545	3,955**	4,500	545	—	100,000

*Rounded to nearest dollar.
**Error due to rounding.

Table 18-2
Interest and Amortization of Bond Premium— Effective Interest Method

by the amortization of the premium. The first interest payment would be recorded as follows:

July 1	Bond Interest Expense	4,162	
	Unamortized Bond Premium	338	
	Cash (or Interest Payable)		4,500
	Paid (or accrued) semiannual interest to bondholders and amortize premium on 9%, 5-year bonds		

Note that the interest expense to be recorded each period decreases. It goes down because the carrying value to which the effective interest rate is applied becomes less in each period. Also note that the Unamortized Bond Premium drops to zero and the carrying value decreases to the face value over the life of the bond.

To find the amount of premium amortization in any one interest payment period, we subtract the effective interest expense (the carrying value times the effective interest rate) from the interest payment. So, in semiannual interest period 5, the amortization of premium equals $393 [($102,674 × .04) − $4,500].

Bond Issue Costs

Of course, there are costs connected with the issuance of bonds. Most bonds are sold through underwriters. The underwriters receive a fee for taking care of the details of marketing the issue or for taking a chance on getting the selling price. Since bond issue costs benefit the whole life of the bond issue, it makes sense to spread these costs over that period. It is acceptable practice to establish a separate account for bond issue costs and amortize them over the life of the bonds. However, issue costs decrease the amount of money received by the company for the bond issue. So they have the effect of raising the discount or lowering the premium on the issue. As a result, bond issue costs may be spread over the life of the bonds through the amortization of discount or premium. For this reason, it is assumed in the text and problems of this book that all bond issues at either a discount or premium are priced at the net of bond issue costs.

Year-End Accrual for Bond Interest Expense

It is not often that bond interest payment dates will correspond to a company's fiscal year. So an adjustment must be made at the end of the accounting period to accrue the interest expense on the bonds from the last payment date to the end of the fiscal year. Further, if there is any discount or premium on the bonds it must also be amortized for the fractional period. Remember that in the earlier example, Vason Corporation issued $100,000 in bonds on January 1 at 104.1. The company's fiscal year ends September 30, 19x0. In the period since the interest payment and amortization of premium on July 1, three months' interest has accrued, and the following adjusting entry must be made:

Sept. 30	Bond Interest Expense	2,075.50	
	Unamortized Bond Premium	174.50	
	Interest Payable		2,250.00
	Accrued interest on 9% bonds payable for three months and amortize one-half of the premium for second interest payment period		

This entry covers one-half of the second interest period. So the Unamortized Bond Premium is debited for $174.50, which is one-half of $349—the amortization of premium for the second period from Table 18-2. Accrued Interest Payable is credited for $2,250, for three months' face interest ($100,000 $\times$ .09 $\times$ $\frac{1}{4}$). The net debit figure of $2,075.50 ($2,250 − $174.50) is the Bond Interest Expense for the three-month period.

When the January 1, 19x1, payment date arrives, the entry to pay the bondholders and amortize the premium is as follows:[4]

---

4. This entry assumes that a reversing entry of the accrual was not made on October 1. Some firms may prefer to use reversing entries.

Jan. 1	Bond Interest Expense	2,075.50	
	Interest Payable	2,250.00	
	Unamortized Bond Premium	174.50	
	Cash		4,500.00
	Paid semiannual interest including that previously accrued and to amortize the premium for the period since the end of the fiscal year		

As shown above, one-half ($2,250) of the amount paid ($4,500) was accrued on September 30. The Unamortized Bond Premium is debited for the remaining amount from Table 18-2 to be amortized for the period ($349.00 − $174.50 = $174.50). The resulting Bond Interest Expense is the amount that applies to the three-month period from September 30 to January 1.

Bond discounts are recorded at year end in the same way as bond premiums. The difference is that the amortization of bond discounts will increase interest expense instead of decreasing it as a premium does.

Retirement of Bonds

Objective 4
Account for the retirement and conversion of bonds

Most bond issues provide for a call feature. This feature gives the corporation a chance to buy back and retire the bonds at a given price, usually above face value, before maturity. Such bonds are known as **callable bonds.** They give the corporation flexibility in financing its operations. If bond interest rates drop, the company can call its bonds and reissue debt at a lower interest rate. The bond indenture will state the time period and the prices at which the bonds can be redeemed.

As an illustration of this feature, assume that Vason Corporation may call or retire the $100,000 bond issue (the one issued at a premium) at 105 and that it decides to do so on July 1, 19x3. Because the bonds were issued on January 1, 19x0, the retirement takes place on the seventh interest payment date. Assume that the entry for the interest payment (which must be made) and the amortization of premium have been made. Then the entry to retire the bonds is as follows:

19x3			
July 1	Bonds Payable	100,000	
	Unamortized Bond Premium	1,447	
	Loss on Retirement of Bonds	3,553	
	Cash		105,000
	Retired 9% bonds at 105		

In this entry, the cash paid is the face value times the call price ($100,000 × 1.05 = $105,000). The Unamortized Bond Premium can be found in column E of Table 18-2. The loss on retirement of bonds occurs because the call price of the bonds is greater than the carrying value ($105,000 − $101,447 = $3,553). The loss is presented as an extraordinary item on the income statement, as explained in Chapter 17.

Conversion of Bonds into Stock

Bonds that may be exchanged for other securities of the corporation (in most cases common stock) are called **convertible bonds.** These bonds may be exchanged if the bondholder wishes. The conversion feature may be added to make the bonds more attractive to some investors. The convertible bond gives the investor a chance of making more money because if the market price of the common stock rises, the value of the bond rises. However, if the price of the common stock does not rise, the investor still holds the bond and receives the periodic interest payment as well as the principal at the maturity date.

When bonds are converted into common stock, the basic accounting rule is that the common stock is recorded at the carrying value of the bonds. The bond liability and associated unamortized discount or premium are written off the books. For this reason, no gain or loss is recorded on the transaction. For example, suppose that the bonds in the earlier case are not called on July 1, 19x3. Instead, Vason Corporation's stockholders decide to convert all the bonds to $8 par value common stock under a convertible provision of 40 shares of common stock for each $1,000 bond. The entry would be

19x3				
July 1	Bonds Payable		100,000	
	Unamortized Bond Premium		1,447	
	Common Stock			32,000
	Paid-in Capital in Excess of Par			
	Value, Common			69,447
	Converted 9% bonds payable			
	into common stock at a rate of			
	40 shares for each $1,000 bond			

The Unamortized Bond Premium is again found in Table 18-2. At a rate of 40 shares for each $1,000 bond, 4,000 shares will be issued at a total par value of $32,000 (4,000 × $8). The Common Stock account is credited for the amount of the par value of the stock issued. Another account, called Paid-in Capital in Excess of Par Value, Common, is credited for the difference between the carrying value of the bonds and the par value of the stocks issued ($101,447 − $32,000 = $69,447). No gain or loss is recorded on this transaction.

Bond Sinking Fund

*Objective 5
Compute
sinking fund
requirements,
and prepare
accounting
entries
associated with
sinking fund
bonds payable*

Many bond issues require that funds be set aside over the life of the issue. This is done to satisfy investors that money will be available to pay the bondholders at maturity. This segregation of assets is called a bond sinking fund. The bond indenture will usually state that the corporation will make periodic deposits over the life of the bonds. The trustee has control of the fund, and is charged with investing the deposits in income-producing securities. It is intended that the deposits plus the earnings on the investment be large enough to pay the bonds at maturity. Because the assets in the sinking fund cannot be used by the corporation for current operations, the sinking fund is classified as a long-term investment on the balance sheet.

When a corporation establishes a sinking fund, it must determine how much cash will be set aside each period to pay the bonds. The amount will depend on the estimated rate of return the investments can earn. Let us illustrate the accounting for a bond sinking fund. Assume that the Vason Corporation agrees with a trustee to set aside enough cash at the end of each year of its bond issue to accumulate the $100,000 maturity value. The trustee will be able to earn an 8 percent return on the investment of the cash deposited by the company. To pay the bonds in five years, the company must deposit $17,044.49 at the end of each year.[5] The investments will grow to a point where the sinking fund is equal to the principal at the maturity date, as shown in Table 18-3.

**Table 18-3
Growth of
Annual
Investments in
Sinking Fund**

End of Year	A Fund Balance at Beginning of Year	B Deposit	C Interest at 8% (8% × A)	D Fund Balance at End of Year (A + B + C)
1	$ —	$17,044.49	$ —	$17,044.49
2	17,044.49	17,044.49	1,363.55	35,452.53
3	35,452.53	17,044.49	2,836.20	55,333.22
4	55,333.22	17,044.49	4,426.65	76,804.36
5	76,804.36	17,044.49	6,144.34	99,993.19*

*Off $6.81 due to rounding.

The entry to record the creation of the sinking fund and the annual deposit would be as follows:

Dec. 31	Bond Sinking Fund	17,044.49	
	Cash		17,044.49
	Paid the annual deposit to the bond sinking fund		

5. This annual payment may be computed by using Table B-2 in Appendix B. Divide the principal by the future value of an annuity for five periods at 8 percent compound interest to find the amount of the annuity ($100,000 ÷ 5.867 = $17,044.49).

Every year the sinking fund trustee invests these funds to get the best return possible. The trustee collects interest and dividends and reports them to the corporation. As an illustration, assume that the cash set aside by the Vason Corporation earned the necessary $1,363.55 the second year. The earnings would be recorded as shown in the following entry:

Dec. 31	Bond Sinking Fund	1,363.55	
	Income from Bond Sinking Fund		1,363.55
	To record income from investment in the bond sinking fund		

The earnings of the sinking fund would appear on the income statement as Other Revenue.

If investments in the sinking fund are sold and result in a gain or loss, the transaction should be recognized by increasing or decreasing the bond sinking fund. For example, if the sale of an investment results in a $1,000 loss, the entry will be:

May 21	Loss on Sale of Sinking Fund Investment	1,000	
	Bond Sinking Fund		1,000
	To record loss on investment in bond sinking fund		

When the bonds mature, the trustee must sell the investments to obtain the cash to pay the bondholders. The amount earned in the fund over the years will rise and fall. So the actual cash realized is not likely to equal exactly the amount necessary to pay the bondholders. When excess cash is available, it should be transferred to Cash. If there is less cash than necessary to retire the bonds, the corporation must provide additional cash. For example, assume that at the bond maturity date the sinking fund contained a total of $99,600. The entry to pay the bonds follows:

Dec. 31	Bonds Payable	100,000	
	Bond Sinking Fund		99,600
	Cash		400
	To record the payment of bonds at maturity		

Other Long-Term Liabilities

A company may have long-term liabilities other than bonds. Three of the most common other long-term liabilities are mortgages payable, long-term leases, and pensions.

Table 18-4
Monthly
Payment
Schedule on
$50,000,
15 Percent
Mortgage

Payment Date	A Unpaid Balance at Beginning of Period	B Monthly Payment	C Interest for 1 Month at $1\frac{1}{4}\%$ on Unpaid Balance* $(1\frac{1}{4}\% \times A)$	D Reduction in Debt $(B - C)$	E Unpaid Balance at End of Period $(A - D)$
June 1					$50,000
July 1	$50,000	$900	$625	$275	49,725
Aug. 1	49,725	900	622	278	49,447
Sept. 1	49,447	900	618	282	49,165

*Rounded to nearest dollar.

Mortgages Payable

*Objective 6
Explain the
basic features
of mortgages
payable,
long-term leases,
and pensions as
long-term liabilities*

A **mortgage** is a type of long-term debt secured by real property. It is usually paid in equal monthly installments. Each monthly payment is partly interest on the debt and partly a reduction in the debt. To illustrate this point Table 18-4 shows the first three monthly payments on a $50,000, 15 percent mortgage. The mortgage was obtained on June 1 and the monthly payments are $900. According to the table, the entry to record the July 1 payment would be as shown below.

July 1	Mortgage Payable	275	
	Mortgage Interest Expense	625	
	Cash		900
	Made monthly payment on mortgage		

Note from the entry and from Table 18-4 that the July 1 payment represents interest expense of $625 ($50,000 $\times$ .15 $\times$ $\frac{1}{12}$) and a reduction in the debt of $275 ($900 − $625). So the unpaid balance is reduced by the $275 to $49,725 in July. Therefore the interest expense for August is slightly less than it was for July.

Long-Term Leases

There are different ways in which a company may get new operating assets. One way is to borrow the money and buy the asset. Another is to rent the equipment on a short-term lease. A third way is to obtain the equipment on a long-term lease. The first two methods cause no unusual accounting problems. In the first case, the asset and liability are recorded at the amount paid, and the asset is subject to periodic depreciation. In the second case, the lease is short-term or cancelable, and the risks of ownership lie with the lessor. So this type of lease is called an **operating lease**. It is proper accounting to treat operating lease payments as an expense and to debit the amount of each monthly payment to Rent Expense.

The third case, a long-term lease, is one of the fastest-growing ways of financing operating equipment in the U.S. economy. It has several advantages. For instance, it requires no immediate cash payment. The rental payment is deducted in full for tax purposes. And it costs less than a short-term lease. Acquiring the use of a plant asset under a long-term lease does cause several accounting problems, however. Often, such leases may not be canceled. Also, their length may be about the same as the useful life of the asset. Finally, they provide for the lessee to buy the asset at a nominal price at the end of the lease. The lease is much like an installment purchase because the risks of ownership lie with the lessee. The lessee company's available assets have increased and its legal obligations (liabilities) have increased because it must make a number of payments over the life of the asset. So this "off-the-balance-sheet financing" leads to a balance sheet that omits a material asset and a material liability.

Noting this problem, the Financial Accounting Standards Board has described such a long-term lease as a capital lease. This term reflects the terms of the lease, which make the transaction more like a purchase/sale on installment. The FASB has ruled that in the case of a capital lease, the lessee must record an asset and a long-term liability equal to the value of the total lease payments during the lease term. In doing so, the lessee must use the present value at the beginning of the lease.[6] In much the same way as the mortgage payments above, each lease payment becomes partly interest expense and partly a repayment of debt. Further, depreciation expense is figured on the asset and entered on the records.

Suppose, for example, that Isaacs Company enters into a long-term lease for a machine used in its manufacturing operations. The lease terms call for an annual payment of $4,000 for six years, which approximates the useful life of the machine. (See Table 18-5.) At the end of the lease period, the title to the machine passes to Isaacs. This lease is clearly a capital lease and should be recorded according to FASB *Statement No. 13*.

A lease is a periodic payment for the right to use an asset or assets. So present value techniques, explained in Appendix A, can be used to value the asset and the corresponding liability associated with a capital lease. The present value of the lease payments may be computed as follows, if Isaacs' usual interest cost is 16 percent:

periodic payment × factor (Table B-4) (16%, 6 years) = present value
$4,000   ×   3.685   = $14,740

The entry to record the lease contract is

Leased Asset, Equipment	14,740	
Lease Obligations		14,740

Each year, Isaacs must record depreciation on the leased asset. If we assume a six-year life and no salvage value, the entry will be

---

6. *Statement of Financial Accounting Standards No. 13*, "Accounting for Leases" (Stamford, Conn.: Financial Accounting Standards Board, 1976), par. 10.

Table 18-5
Payment
Schedule
on 16 Percent
Capital
Lease

Year	A Lease Payment	B Interest (16%) on Unpaid Obligation (D × 16%)	C Reduction of Lease Obligation (A − B)	D Balance of Lease Obligation
Beginning				$14,740.00
1	$ 4,000	$2,358.40	$ 1,641.60	13,098.40
2	4,000	2,095.74	1,904.26	11,194.14
3	4,000	1,791.06	2,208.94	8,985.20
4	4,000	1,437.63	2,562.37	6,422.83
5	4,000	1,027.65	2,972.35	3,450.48
6	4,000	549.52*	3,450.48	—
	$24,000	$9,260.00	$14,740.00	

*The last year's interest equals the lease payment minus the remaining balance of the lease obligation ($549.52 = $4,000 − $3,450.48) and does not exactly equal $552.08 ($3,450.48 × .16) because of cumulative rounding errors.

Depreciation Expense	2,456.67	
Accumulated Depreciation, Leased		
Equipment		2,456.67

The lease payments are recorded as follows:

Interest Expense (col. B, Table 18-5)	xxx	
Lease Obligations (col. C, Table 18-5)	xxx	
Cash		4,000

The amount of the interest expense for each year would be figured by multiplying the interest rate (16 percent) by the amount of the remaining lease obligation. Table 18-5 shows these calculations.

Pensions

Most employees who work for medium and large companies are covered by some sort of pension plan. A **pension plan** is a contract between the company and its employees under which the company agrees to pay benefits to employees after their retirement. Pension plans can take many forms. Most companies pay or contribute the full cost of the pension. Sometimes, however, the employees also pay a part of their salary or wages toward their pension. The contributions from both employer and employee are generally paid into a **pension fund**, and the benefits are paid out of this fund to retirees. In most cases, pension benefits consist of monthly payments to employees after retirement and other payments on death or disability.

Accounting for pension expense is hard. There is a bewildering array of pension plans and methods to accrue an expense whose final outcome will not be known for many years.[7] Two kinds of costs are connected with pension plans. The first kind is called the normal pension costs. Normal pension costs are the estimated retirement benefits for the employees who are working in the current year. The Employee Retirement Income Security Act of 1974 (ERISA) requires that the company pay these amounts into the pension fund in the current year. In the general journal, Pension Expense is debited and a current liability (or Cash) is credited for the amount of the expense. The major problem with normal pension costs is to figure out how much the expense should be. Estimating the expense is based on many complex factors such as the life expectancy of the employees, the age of the employees at retirement, and probable employee turnover. Gains and losses on pension fund investments, future salary levels of employees, pension benefits to be paid, and future levels of interest rates also enter into the estimate. In figuring the amount of the pension expense, compound interest tables are used to find the present value of the future payments for employees working this year.

The choice of the interest rate on which to compute the present value has an important impact on the amount of the pension expense. In general, given a specified level of future pension benefits, the choice of a lower interest rate will cause a larger expense than the choice of a higher interest rate. For example, Goodyear Tire & Rubber Company reported pension expense in 1980 of $148,578,000. Santa Fe Industries reported a pension expense of $109,400,000 in 1980. So it appears that Goodyear had about a $40,000,000 larger pension obligation. However, one should be careful in comparing the two amounts. In the notes to the financial statements Goodyear reports that it used a rate of 8.5 percent to find the present value. Santa Fe used a rate of 6 percent—a much more conservative rate than Goodyear's. Had they used the same rate, the difference between the two companies would have been even greater. A difference of 2.5 percent in pension fund earnings over a long period of time can mean a difference of millions of dollars in the current year's expense. Only time will tell which company, if either, made a wise estimate of the pension expense.

Past service costs are the second kind of costs connected with a pension plan. Since most pension plans are started after a company has been in business for a period of time, some employees of the company will normally qualify for the pension plan at the start-up date. Past service costs equal the present value of the estimated future pension benefits for these employees. The estimated costs are based on the number of employees who will probably reach retirement, the years remaining until their retirement, their expected retirement benefits, and their expected life span after retirement. The 1974 ERISA requires that these costs be paid into the

---

7. Accounting Principles Board, *Opinion No. 8,* "Accounting for the Cost of Pension Plans" (New York: American Institute of Certified Public Accountants, 1966); and *Interpretation No. 3,* "Accounting for the Cost of Pension Plans Subject to the Employee Retirement Income Security Act of 1974" (Stamford, Conn.: Financial Accounting Standards Board, 1974).

pension fund over a period of thirty or forty years depending on when the pension plan went into effect. Though the company must make these payments for the number of years specified, a pension liability is entered in the accounting records only if the amount paid into the pension fund in a particular year is less than the pension expense for that year.

Financial Reporting and Income Tax Allocation

Most small businesses find it convenient to keep their accounting records on the same basis as their tax records. This practice is usually acceptable when there is not a material difference between the tax treatment of an item and the proper accounting treatment of the same item. However, the purpose of accounting is to determine net income in accordance with generally accepted accounting principles, whereas the purpose of the tax code is to determine taxable income and tax liability. There can be important differences in results between the two. Therefore, accountants cannot let the tax procedures dictate the method of preparing reports if the result is misleading.

For example, consider the case of Mason Corporation, which has a before-tax accounting income of $100,000 in each of two years. Assume that Mason has an expense item of $30,000 that may be taken as a tax deduction in year 1 but should be deducted for accounting purposes in year 2. The company's accounting and taxable income, and the actual income taxes due (assuming a tax rate of 46%), are as follows:

	Year 1	Year 2
Before-tax accounting income	$100,000	$100,000
Taxable income	$ 70,000	$130,000
Income tax rate	×.46	×.46
Actual income taxes due	$ 32,200	$ 59,800

One alternative for Mason Corporation would be simply to report the actual taxes paid on its financial statements, with the following result:

	Year 1	Year 2
Before-tax accounting income	$100,000	$100,000
Actual income taxes paid	32,200	59,800
Net income	$ 67,800	$ 40,200

The astute reader of the above financial statements would surely question such a difference in tax expense when the accounting income is the

Objective 7
Explain why
income tax
allocation is
necessary, and
account for
the differences
between
accounting and
taxable income

same for both years. This problem is a serious one that the Accounting Principles Board addressed in its *Opinion No. 11*, "Accounting for Income Taxes." The APB's solution to the problem is an accounting technique called **income tax allocation**. The aim of income tax allocation is to accrue income tax expense on the basis of accounting income whenever there are differences in accounting and taxable income caused by the timing of revenues or expenses. Proponents of the income tax allocation procedure argue that it is in accordance with the matching rule, because the expense is directly related to the reported income for the period. For example, if the Mason Corporation uses income tax allocation, the income statements for the two years would appear as shown below.

	Year 1	Year 2
Before-tax accounting income	$100,000	$100,000
Income tax expense	46,000	46,000
Net income	$ 54,000	$ 54,000

The difference in accounting and taxable income may also result from different methods applied over a series of years. For example, the table below shows some possible alternatives.

	Accounting Method	Tax Method
Sales	Point of sale	Installment
Inventories	Average-cost	FIFO
Depreciation	Straight-line	Accelerated cost recovery system (see Chapter 13)

The journal entries to record Mason's income tax expense using the income tax allocation procedure are as follows:

Year 1	Income Tax Expense	46,000	
	Current Income Tax Payable		32,200
	Deferred Income Taxes		13,800
	To record current and deferred income taxes at 46% of accounting income of $100,000		

Year 2	Income Tax Expense	46,000	
	Deferred Income Taxes	13,800	
	Current Income Tax Payable		59,800
	To record current and deferred income taxes at 46% of accounting income of $100,000		

Note that in the entries given, the difference between the Income Tax Expense and the current Income Tax Payable accounts is called **Deferred Income Taxes**. The Deferred Income Taxes account has a credit balance for the first year. Whether or not the Deferred Income Taxes credit bal-

ance is classified as a current or long-term liability depends on the classification of the asset or liability that gave rise to the timing difference. For
example, if the timing difference was due to different inventory methods,
the deferred tax liability would be classified as a current liability, because
inventory is classified as a current asset on the balance sheet. If the difference arose from different depreciation methods of plant assets, it would be
a long-term liability, because plant assets are classified as long-term assets
on the balance sheet.[8] Some understanding of the importance of deferred
income taxes to financial reporting may be gained from studying the
financial statements of six hundred large companies surveyed in a recent
year. Of those companies, 90 percent reported some sort of deferred
taxes. Of these, about two-thirds reported Deferred Income Taxes with a
credit balance in the noncurrent liability section. About 20 percent
reported a debit balance in the current asset section. The rest were some
combination of current and noncurrent assets and liabilities.

There is controversy about whether deferred income taxes should even
be recorded and reported as a liability. Given management's desire to put
off the payment of taxes as long as possible and given the long-term
growth of the economy and inflation, there is evidence to support the
argument that deferred taxes for many companies will keep getting larger
year after year and will never have to be paid. AT&T, for example, had
almost $13 billion of deferred income taxes in 1978, equal to about 21.6
percent of total liabilities. By 1980, deferred income taxes had reached
almost $18 billion, or about 24.8 percent of total liabilities. These are huge
amounts. A liability represents "probable future sacrifices of economic
benefits arising from present obligations." There is a question as to
whether deferred income taxes are probable or are a present obligation.
The people who believe that deferred income taxes are not liabilities
would rather show income tax expense on the income statement at the
amount of taxes paid for that particular year. This view is held by a
minority, but it is still one that should be considered in interpreting
deferred income taxes.

Chapter Review

Review of Learning Objectives

1. Identify and contrast the major characteristics of bonds.

When bonds are issued, the corporation enters into a contract with the bondholders, called a bond indenture. The bond indenture identifies the major conditions of the bonds. A corporation may issue several types of bonds, each having
different characteristics. For example, a bond issue may require security or be
unsecured. It may be payable at a single time (term) or at several times (serial).
Also, it may be registered in the name of the holder, or the holder may be unidentified and have to return coupons to receive interest payable.

---

8. *Statement of Financial Accounting Standards No. 37*, "Balance Sheet Classifications of Deferred Income Taxes" (Stamford, Conn.: Financial Accounting Standards Board, 1980).

2. Record the issuance of bonds at face value, between interest dates, and at a discount or premium.

When bonds are issued, the bondholder will pay an amount equal to, greater than, or less than the face value of the bond. A bondholder will pay face value for the bonds when the interest rate on the bonds approximates the market rate for similar investments. The issuing corporation records the issuance of bonds as a long-term liability called Bonds Payable equal to the face value of the bonds.

If the bonds are sold on dates between the interest payment dates, the issuing corporation collects from the investor the interest that has accrued since the last interest payment date. When the next interest payment date arrives, the corporation pays the bondholder interest for the entire interest period.

Bonds are purchased at a rate less than the face value of the bonds when the bond interest rate is below the market rate for similar investments. The difference between face value and issue price is called a discount and is debited to Unamortized Bond Discount.

If the interest rate on bonds is greater than the return on similar investments, investors will be willing to pay more than face value for the bonds. The difference between the issue price and face value is called a premium and is credited to Unamortized Bond Premium.

3. Amortize bond discount and premium by using the effective interest method, and make year-end adjustments.

When bonds are sold at a premium or discount, the result is an adjustment of the interest rate on the bonds from the face rate to an effective rate that is close to the market rate when the bonds were issued. Therefore, bond premiums or discounts have the effect of increasing or decreasing the interest paid on the bonds over their life. Under these conditions, it is necessary to amortize the premium or discount over the life of the bonds in a way that will adjust the interest expense from the stated interest to the effective interest. The effective interest method is the accepted method for amortizing bond discount or premium.

The effective interest method results in a constant rate of interest on the carrying value of the bonds. To find interest and the amortization of premiums or discounts we apply the effective interest rate to the carrying value (face value plus premium or minus discount) of the bonds at the beginning of the interest period. The amount of premium or discount to be amortized is the difference between the interest figured by using the effective rate and that obtained by using the stated rate.

When the end of a corporation's fiscal year does not agree with interest payment dates, the corporation must accrue bond interest expense from the last interest payment date to the end of the company's fiscal year. This accrual results in the inclusion of the interest expense in the year incurred.

4. Account for the retirement and conversion of bonds.

Callable bonds may be retired before maturity at the option of the issuing corporation. The call price is usually an amount greater than the face value of the bonds. Thus the corporation must usually recognize a loss on the retirement of the bonds.

Convertible bonds allow the bondholder to convert the bond to stock of the issuing corporation. In this case, the common stock being issued is recorded at the carrying value of the bonds being converted. No gain or loss is recognized.

5. Compute sinking fund requirements, and prepare accounting entries associated with sinking fund bonds payable.

Some bond issues require the issuing corporation to segregate assets of the company over the life of the bonds so cash will be available to pay the bonds at maturity. The segregated assets are called a bond sinking fund. The corporation deposits cash in the fund over the life of the bonds. The deposits plus earnings on the deposits are planned so they will be sufficient to pay the face value of the bonds at maturity.

6. Explain the basic features of mortgages payable, long-term leases, and pensions as long-term liabilities.

A mortgage is a type of long-term debt secured by real property. It is usually paid in equal monthly installments. Each payment is partly interest expense and partly debt repayment. If a long-term lease is a capital lease, the risks of ownership lie with the lessee. For a capital lease, an asset and a long-term liability should be recorded. The liability should be equal to the present value at the beginning of the lease of the total lease payment during the lease term. Like a mortgage payment, each lease payment is partly interest and partly reduction of debt. The recorded asset is subject to depreciation. A company is also required to record pension expense in the current period. The expense should be equal to the present value of future benefits that are estimated to be paid to employees under a pension plan.

7. Explain why income tax allocation is necessary, and account for the differences between accounting and taxable income.

Income tax allocation is necessary when differences between accounting income and taxable income cause a material difference in income tax expense as shown on the income statement and the actual income tax liability. In such a case, the income tax allocation procedure should be used. This procedure accrues income taxes on the basis of accounting income whenever there are differences between accounting and taxable income. The difference between the accrued income taxes and the actual income taxes is debited or credited to an account called Deferred Income Taxes.

Review Problem
Interest and Amortization of Bond Discount, Bond Retirement, and Bond Conversion

The Merrill Manufacturing Company is currently expanding its metal window division in Utah. The company does not have enough capital for the expansion. Thus management has sought and received approval from the board of directors to issue bonds for this activity. The company plans to issue $5,000,000 of 8 percent, 5-year convertible bonds in 19x1. Interest is paid on December 31 and June 30 of each year. The bonds are callable at 104 and are convertible into $10 par value common stock at the rate of 40 shares per $1,000 bond. The bonds are sold on January 1, 19x1, at 96. The bonds have to be sold at a discount because the market rate for similar investments is 9 percent. The company plans to amortize the bond discount by using the effective interest method. On July 1, 19x3, one-half of the bonds were called and retired, and the other half were converted into common stock.

Required

1. Prepare an interest and amortization schedule for the first five interest payment dates.
2. Prepare the journal entries to record the sale of the bonds, the first two interest payments, the bond retirement, and the bond conversion.

Answer to Review Problem

1. Schedule for first five periods prepared.

Interest and Amortization of Bond Discount*

Semiannual Interest Payment	Carrying Value at Beginning of Period	Semi-annual Interest Expense (9% × ½)	Semi-annual Interest Paid per Period (8% × ½)	Amortiza-tion of Discount	Unamortized Bond Discount at End of Period	Carrying Value at End of Period
Jan. 1, 19x1					$200,000	
June 30, 19x1	$4,800,000	$216,000	$200,000	$16,000	184,000	$4,816,000
Dec. 31, 19x1	4,816,000	216,720	200,000	16,720	167,280	4,832,720
June 30, 19x2	4,832,720	217,472	200,000	17,472	149,808	4,850,192
Dec. 31, 19x2	4,850,192	218,259	200,000	18,259	131,549	4,868,451
June 30, 19x3	4,868,451	219,080	200,000	19,080	112,469	4,887,531

*Rounded to nearest dollar.

2. Journal entries prepared.

```
19x1
Jan.  1   Cash                                    4,800,000
          Unamortized Bond Discount                 200,000
             Bonds Payable                                      5,000,000
                Sold $5,000,000
                of 8% bonds at 96

June 30   Bond Interest Expense                   216,000
             Unamortized Bond Discount                             16,000
             Cash                                                 200,000
                Paid semiannual interest
                payment

Dec. 31   Bond Interest Expense                   216,720
             Unamortized Bond Discount                             16,720
             Cash                                                 200,000
                Paid semiannual interest
                payment

19x3
July  1   Bonds Payable                         2,500,000
          Loss on Retirement of Bonds Payable     156,235
             Unamortized Bond Discount                             56,235
             Cash                                               2,600,000
                Called $2,500,000 of
                8% bonds and retired them
                at 104
```

July 1	Bonds Payable	2,500,000	
	Unamortized Bond Discount		56,234
	Common Stock		1,000,000
	Paid-in Capital in Excess of Par		
	Value, Common		1,443,766

Converted $2,500,000 of 8% bonds into 100,000 shares of $10 par value common stock

Chapter Assignments

Questions

1. What is the difference between a bond certificate, a bond issue, and a bond indenture?

2. What is the essential difference between the bonds in the case of (a) secured versus debenture bonds, (b) term versus serial bonds, and (c) registered versus coupon bonds?

3. Napier Corporation sold $500,000 of 5 percent bonds on the interest payment date. What would the proceeds from the sale be if the bonds were issued at 95, at 100, at 102?

4. If you were buying a bond on which the face interest rate was less than the market interest rate, would you expect to pay more or less than par value for the bonds? Why?

5. Why does the amortization of a bond discount increase interest expense to an amount above the amount of interest paid? Why does a premium have the opposite effect?

6. When bonds are issued between interest dates, why is it necessary for the issuer to collect an amount equal to accrued interest from the buyer?

7. When the effective interest rate method of amortizing bond discount or premium is used, why does the amount of interest expense change from period to period?

8. Why would a company want to exercise the callable provision of a bond when it can wait longer to pay off the debt?

9. What are the advantages of convertible bonds to the company and to the investor?

10. The long-term investment section of the DeLoach Corporation balance sheet contains an account called Bond Sinking Fund. What is the purpose of this account?

11. What are the two components of a uniform monthly mortgage payment?

12. Under what conditions is a long-term lease called a capital lease? Why would such a lease result in recording both an asset and a liability?

13. What are normal pension costs and past service costs? What assumptions have to be made to account for them properly?

14. "Accounting income should be geared to the concept of taxable income because the public understands the concept of taxable income." Comment on this statement and tell why income tax allocation is necessary.

Classroom Exercises[9]

**Exercise 18-1
Bond Issue
Entries
(L.O. 2)**

Turnco is authorized to issue $400,000 in bonds on June 1. The bonds carry a face interest rate of 9 percent, which is to be paid on June 1 and December 1.

Prepare journal entries for the issue of the bonds by Turnco under the assumptions that (a) the bonds are issued on September 1 at 100 and (b) the bonds are issued on June 1 at 105.

**Exercise 18-2
Sale of Bonds
and Interest
Payments
(L.O. 2, 3)**

The Bedford Drapery Company sold $400,000 of its $9\frac{1}{2}$ percent, twenty-year bonds on April 1, 19xx, at 106. The semiannual interest payment dates are April 1 and October 1. The effective interest rate is approximately 8.9 percent. The company's fiscal year ends September 30.

Prepare journal entries to record the sale of these bonds on April 1, the accrual of interest and amortization of premium on September 30, and the first interest payment on October 1. Use the effective interest method to amortize the premium.

**Exercise 18-3
Bond
Conversion
Journal Entry
(L.O. 4)**

The McCloud Corporation has $500,000 of 6 percent convertible bonds outstanding. There is $20,000 of unamortized discount associated with these bonds. The bonds are convertible at the rate of 40 shares of $5 par value common stock for each $1,000 bond. On July 1, an interest payment date, bondholders presented $300,000 of the bonds for conversion.

Prepare the journal entry to record the conversion of the bonds.

**Exercise 18-4
Bond
Retirement
Journal
(L.O. 4)**

The Argosy Corporation has outstanding $700,000 of 8 percent bonds callable at 104. On September 1, a semiannual interest payment date, the unamortized bond discount equaled $21,000. On that date, $400,000 of the bonds were called and retired.

Prepare the entry to record the retirement of the bonds on September 1.

**Exercise 18-5
Journal Entries
for Interest and
Amortization of
Discount
(L.O. 3)**

On March 1, 19x1, the Polaris Corporation issued $600,000 of five-year, 10 percent bonds. The semiannual interest payment dates are March 1 and September 1. Because the market rate for similar investments was 11 percent, the bonds had to be issued at a discount. The discount on the issuance of the bonds was $24,335.

Prepare the journal entries to record the bond issue on March 1, 19x1, and the payments of interest and amortization of the discount on September 1, 19x1, and March 1, 19x2. Use the effective interest method. (Ignore year-end accruals.)

**Exercise 18-6
Journal Entries
for Interest
Payments
(L.O. 3)**

The long-term debt section of the Pierce Corporation's balance sheet at the end of its fiscal year, December 31, 1983, is shown below:

Long-Term Liabilities
Bonds Payable—8%, interest payable
1/1 and 7/1, due 12/31/98 $500,000
Unamortized Bond Discount   (40,000) $460,000

Prepare the journal entries relevant to the interest payments on July 1, 1984, December 31, 1984, and January 1, 1985. Assume an effective interest rate of 10 percent.

---

9. Bond interest rates are most often quoted in eighths of a percent. Some exercises and problems in this chapter quote the rates in tenths of a percent to ease the burden of computation.

Exercise 18-7
Mortgage
Payable
(L.O. 6)

Gardner Corporation purchased a building by signing a long-term $150,000 mortgage with monthly payments of $2,000. The mortgage carries an interest rate of 12 percent.

1. For the first three months, prepare a monthly payment schedule showing the monthly payment, the interest for the month, the reduction in debt, and the unpaid balance.
2. Prepare a journal entry to record the purchase and the first two monthly payments.

Exercise 18-8
Income Tax
Allocation
(L.O. 7)

The Watson Corporation reported the following before-tax accounting income, income tax expense, and net income for 19x2 and 19x3:

	19x2	19x3
Before-tax accounting income	$140,000	$140,000
Income tax expense	34,950	53,350
Net income	$105,050	$ 86,650

In 19x2, Watson deducted an item of $20,000 for income tax purposes. For accounting income purposes, the company did not deduct this item until 19x3. Watson has a marginal tax rate of 46 percent and does not use income tax allocation procedures.

1. Identify the distortions in Watson's income statements due to the failure to use income tax allocation procedures.
2. Show how the three income statement items would appear for both years using income tax allocation procedures.

Note: The next two exercises and the exercise in Interpreting Accounting Information require a knowledge of present value, which is dealt with in Appendix A and Tables B-3 and B-4 in Appendix B.

Exercise 18-9
Valuing Bonds
Using Present
Value
(L.O. 2)

XTR, Inc., is considering two bond issues. (a) One is a $200,000 bond issue that pays semiannual interest of $16,000 and is due in twenty years. (b) The other is a $200,000 bond issue that pays semiannual interest of $15,000 and is due in fifteen years. Assume that the market rate of interest for each bond is 12 percent.
    Calculate the amount that XTR, Inc., will receive if both bond issues occur. (Calculate the present value of each bond issue and sum.)

Exercise 18-10
Recording
Lease Obliga-
tions
(L.O. 6)

Tex-Tile Corporation has leased a piece of equipment that has a useful life of twelve years. The terms of the lease are $17,400 per year for twelve years. Tex-Tile is able to borrow money currently for a long-term interest rate of 15 percent.

1. Calculate the present value of the lease.
2. Prepare the journal entry to record the lease agreement.
3. Prepare the entry to record depreciation of the equipment for the first year.
4. Prepare the entries to record the lease payment for the first two years.

Interpreting Accounting Information

Published
Financial
Information:
J. C. Penney
(L.O. 2)

A bond or note with no interest sounds like a car with no motor. But some large companies are issuing this kind of bond. For example, in 1981, J. C. Penney Company advertised in the business press and sold $200,000,000 of zero coupon (no interest) bonds due in 1989. The price, however, was not $200,000,000 but only 33.247 percent of $200,000,000. In other words, the investor pays about $332,470 now and in eight years collects $1,000,000. The advantage to J. C. Penney is that it does not have to pay a cent of interest for eight years. It does, of course, have to come up with the full face value of the notes at the maturity date. For the investor, a return is guaranteed no matter what the market rate of interest may be over the next eight years, as long as J. C. Penney is able to pay off the notes at the maturity date. The J. C. Penney zero coupon can be contrasted with the financing transactions taking place at about the same time by two other companies of similar quality: Transamerica Corporation and Greyhound Corporation. Transamerica sold $200,000,000 (face value) 30-year bonds with a $6\frac{1}{2}$ percent coupon at a price at $480.67 per $1,000 bond. Greyhound issued $75,000,000 of 10-year notes carrying an interest rate of $14\frac{1}{4}$ percent at 100.

Required

1. Using Tables B-3 and B-4, compute the effective interest rate of the three debt issues. Which issue appears to be the most attractive to the investor?
2. Assume that the federal tax laws require the payment of income taxes on interest income that is amortized on low coupon bonds and notes (which they do) as well as on the interest that is actually paid. Would your answer to 1 change? What factors other than the effective interest rate and income taxes would you consider important to deciding which of these bonds to invest in?

Problem Set A

**Problem 18A-1
Bond Transactions**
(L.O. 2, 3)

Harvest Corporation has $5,000,000 of $9\frac{1}{2}$ percent, twenty-five-year bonds dated March 1, with interest payable on March 1 and September 1. The company's fiscal year ends on November 30, and it uses the effective interest method to amortize premium or discount.

Required

1. Prepare general journal entries for June 1, September 1, and November 30. Assume that the bonds were issued on June 1 at face value plus accrued interest.
2. Prepare general journal entries for March 1, September 1, and November 30. Assume that the bonds were issued at 102.5 on March 1, to yield an effective interest rate of 9.2 percent.
3. Prepare general journal entries for March 1, September 1, and November 30. Assume that the bonds were issued at 97.5 on March 1, to yield an effective interest rate of 9.8 percent.

**Problem 18A-2
Bonds Issued at
Discount and
Premium**
(L.O. 2, 3)

Zachary Corporation sold bonds twice during 19x2. A summary of the transactions involving these bonds is presented below.

19x2
Jan. 1 Issued $2,000,000 of its own $9\frac{9}{10}$ percent, ten-year bonds dated January 1, 19x2, with interest payable on December 31 and June 30. The bonds were sold at 102.6, a price that results in an effective interest rate of 9.4 percent.
Mar. 1 Issued $1,000,000 of its own $9\frac{1}{5}$ percent, ten-year bonds dated March 1, 19x2, with interest payable March 1 and September 1. The bonds were sold at 98.2, a price that results in an effective interest rate of 9.5 percent.
June 30 Paid the semiannual interest on the January 1 issue and amortized the premium, using the effective interest rate method.
Sept. 1 Paid the semiannual interest on the March 1 issue and amortized the discount, using the effective interest rate method.

Dec. 31   Paid the semiannual interest on the January 1 issue and amortized the premium, using the effective interest rate method.

31   Made an end-of-year adjusting entry to accrue the interest on the March 1 issue and amortize two-thirds of the discount applicable to the second interest period.

19x3
Mar. 1   Paid the semiannual interest on the March 1 issue and amortized the remainder of the discount applicable to the second interest period.

Required

Prepare the general journal entries to record the bond transactions.

Problem 18A-3
Bond and
Mortgage
Transactions
Contrasted
(L.O. 2, 3, 6)

Trillo Grocery Stores, Inc., is expanding its operations by buying a chain of four outlets in another city. To finance this purchase of land and buildings, Trillo is getting a $2,000,000 mortgage that carries an interest rate of 12 percent and requires monthly payments of $27,000. To finance the rest of the purchase, Trillo is issuing $2,000,000 of 12½ percent unsecured bonds due in twenty years, with interest payable December 31 and June 30. Selected transactions relating to these two financing activities are listed below.

Jan. 1   Issued the bonds for cash at 104 to yield an effective rate of 12 percent.
Feb. 1   Issued the mortgage bonds in exchange for land and buildings. The land represents 15 percent of the purchase price.
Mar. 1   Made the first mortgage payment.
31   Made the year-end adjusting entry to accrue interest on the bonds and amortize the premium, using the effective interest method.
Apr. 1   Made the second mortgage payment.
May 1   Made the third mortgage payment.
June 1   Made the fourth mortgage payment.
30   Made the first semiannual interest payment on the bonds and amortized the premium for the time period since the end of the fiscal year.
July 1   Made the fifth mortgage payment.
Dec. 1   Made the tenth mortgage payment.
31   Made the second semiannual interest payment on the bonds and amortized the premium for the time period since the last payment.

Required

1. Prepare a monthly payment schedule for the mortgage bonds for ten months with the following headings (round amounts to nearest dollar): Payment Date, Unpaid Balance at Beginning of Period, Monthly Payment, Interest for 1 Month at 1% on Unpaid Balance, Reduction in Debt, and Unpaid Balance at End of Period.
2. Prepare the journal entries for the selected transactions. (Ignore the mortgage payments of August 1 through November 1.)

Problem 18A-4
Bond Retire-
ments and
Conversions
(L.O. 4)

Hutchinson Corporation is authorized to issue $6,000,000 of unsecured convertible bonds, due March 31, 19x6. The bonds carry a face interest rate of 11⅗ percent, payable semiannually on March 31 and September 30. Each $1,000 bond is convertible into twenty-five shares of $20 par value common stock. The bonds are callable at 104 any time after March 31, 19x4.

All the bonds are issued on April 1, 19x1, at 102.261, a price that yields effective interest of 11 percent.

On April 1, 19x4, holders of one-half of the outstanding bonds present their bonds for conversion into common stock.

On October 1, 19x4, Hutchinson Corporation calls the remaining bonds and retires them.

Required

1. Prepare a table similar to Table 18-2 to show the interest and amortization of the bond premium for ten interest payment periods, using the effective interest method (round results to nearest dollar).
2. Prepare general journal entries for the bond issue, interest payments and amortization of bond premium, bond conversion, and bond retirement on the following dates: April 1, 19x1; September 30, 19x1; March 31, 19x4; April 1, 19x4; September 30, 19x4; and October 1, 19x4.

Problem 18A-5
Income Tax
Allocation
(L.O. 7)

Rayette Corporation has before-tax accounting income of $400,000 in each of two years, 19x3 and 19x4. Included in 19x3 income is a major expense item of $100,000 that is not deductible for tax purposes until 19x4.

Required

1. For each tax year, determine taxable income; actual income tax due, using the corporate tax rates in Table 17-1 on page 631; and net income. Assume no income tax allocation.
2. For each tax year, figure income tax expense, using the corporate tax rates in Table 17-1, and net income. Assume that the income tax allocation procedure is used.
3. Prepare journal entries to record income tax expense and income tax payable for each year. Assume that the income tax allocation procedure is used.

Problem 18A-6
Bond Issue
with a Bond
Sinking Fund
(L.O. 5)

Pollard Corporation is authorized to issue $6,000,000 of $9\frac{2}{5}$ percent, eight-year, sinking fund bonds on April 1, 19x0, the beginning of the company's fiscal year. Semiannual interest is payable on March 31 and September 30. The company is required to deposit $564,089 with a trustee at the end of each year for the life of the bond issue. It is assumed that the sinking fund investment will earn a return of 8 percent annually. Selected transactions related to the bond issue and its sinking fund are provided below.

19x0
Apr. 1   Sold the entire issue at 102.25, a price that gives the buyer a 9 percent annual return.
Sept. 30 Made the first semiannual interest payment and amortized the premium.

19x1
Mar. 31   Made the second semiannual interest payment and amortized the premium.
      31   Made the first sinking fund deposit.
Sept. 30 Made the third semiannual interest payment and amortized the premium.

19x2
Mar. 31   Made the fourth semiannual interest payment and amortized the premium.
      31   Made the second sinking fund deposit.
      31   Received a report from the sinking fund trustee indicating that the interest earned on the sinking fund for the first year was $45,127.

19x8

Mar. 31   Made the sixteenth semiannual interest payment and amortized the premium. (The carrying value on September 30, 19x7, was $6,011,483.)

31   Made the last sinking fund deposit.

31   Received a report from the trustee that (a) interest earned during the year on the sinking fund amounted to $403,200 and (b) a loss of $10,000 had been incurred on sinking fund transactions.

31   The trustee also requested and received a check from Pollard Corporation for $8,500 to make up the difference between the sinking fund balance and the bonds payable and paid the bonds.

Required

1. Prepare a table showing the growth of annual investments in the sinking fund (round amounts to the nearest dollar). The table should have the following headings: End of Year, Fund Balance at Beginning of Year, Deposit, Interest at 8%, and Fund Balance at End of Year.

2. Prepare general journal entries for the above transactions (round amounts to the nearest dollar).

Problem Set B

**Problem 18B-1
Bond Transactions**
(L.O. 2, 3)

Stanton Corporation has $10,000,000 of 10½ percent, twenty-year bonds dated June 1, with interest payment dates of May 30 and November 30. The company's fiscal year ends December 31, and it uses the effective interest method to amortize premium or discount.

Required

1. Prepare general journal entries for August 1, November 30, and December 31. Assume that the bonds are issued at face value plus accrued interest on August 1.

2. Prepare general journal entries for June 1, November 30, and December 31. Assume that the bonds were issued at 103 on June 1, to yield an effective interest rate of 10.1 percent.

3. Prepare general journal entries for June 1, November 30, and December 31. Assume that the bonds were issued at 97 on June 1, to yield an effective interest rate of 10.9 percent.

**Problem 18B-2
Bonds Issued at
Discount and
Premium**
(L.O. 2, 3)

Harper Corporation found it necessary to raise capital by issuing bonds twice during 19x1. The following transactions describe this financing activity:

19x1

Jan. 1   Issued $1,000,000 of its own 9⅕ percent, 10-year bonds dated January 1, 19x1, with interest payable on June 30 and December 31. The bonds were sold at 98.1, a price that results in an effective interest rate of 9.5 percent.

Apr. 1   Issued $1,000,000 of its own 9⅘ percent, 10-year bonds dated April 1, 19x1, with interest payable on March 31 and September 30. The bonds were sold at 102, a price that results in an effective interest rate of 9.5 percent.

June 30   Paid the semiannual interest on the January 1 issue and amortized the discount, using the effective interest rate method.

Sept. 30 Paid the semiannual interest on the April 1 issue and amortized the premium, using the effective interest rate method.

Dec. 31 Paid the semiannual interest on the January 1 issue and amortized the discount, using the effective interest rate method.

31 Made an adjusting entry to accrue the interest on the April 1 issue and amortize one-half of the premium applicable to the second interest period.

19x2

Mar. 31 Paid the semiannual interest on the April 1 issue and amortized the premium applicable to the second half of the second interest period.

Required

Prepare general journal entries to record the bond transactions.

Problem 18B-3
Bond and
Mortgage
Transactions
Contrasted
(L.O. 2, 3, 6)

Grace Manufacturing Company is expanding its operations by building and equipping a new plant. It is financing the building and land by issuing a $5,000,000, thirty-year mortgage that carries an interest rate of 12 percent and requires monthly payments of $59,000. The company is financing the equipment and working capital for the new plant by issuing $5,000,000, twenty-year bonds that carry a face interest rate of 11 percent, payable semiannually on March 31 and September 30. Selected transactions during 19x1 and 19x2 related to these two financing issues are as follows:

19x1

Jan. 1 Signed mortgage in exchange for land and building. Land represents 10 percent of total price.

Feb. 1 Made first mortgage payment.

Mar. 1 Made second mortgage payment.

31 Issued bonds for cash at 96, a price that results in an effective interest rate of 11.5 percent.

Apr. 1 Made third mortgage payment.

May 1 Made fourth mortgage payment.

June 1 Made fifth mortgage payment.

30 Made year-end adjusting entry to accrue interest on bonds and amortize the discount, using the effective interest method.

July 1 Made sixth mortgage payment.

Aug. 1 Made seventh mortgage payment.

Sept. 1 Made eighth mortgage payment.

30 Made first interest payment on bonds and amortized the discount for the time period since the end of the fiscal year.

19x2

Mar. 31 Made second interest payment on bonds and amortized the discount for the time period since the last interest payment.

Required

1. Prepare a monthly payment schedule for the mortgage bonds for ten months with the following headings (round amounts to the nearest dollar): Payment Date, Unpaid Balance at Beginning of Period, Monthly Payment, Interest for 1 Month at 1% on Unpaid Balance, Reduction in Debt, and Unpaid Balance at End of Period.
2. Prepare the journal entries for the selected transactions. (Ignore the mortgage payments between October 1, 19x1, and March 1, 19x2.)

**Problem 18B-4
Bond Retire-
ments and
Conversions**
(L.O. 4)

Hudson Corporation is authorized to issue $10,000,000 of six-year unsecured convertible bonds. The bonds carry a face interest rate of 9 percent, payable semiannually on June 30 and December 31. Each $1,000 bond is convertible into forty shares of $10 par value common stock. The bonds are callable at 105 any time after June 30, 19x4.

All the bonds are issued on July 1, 19x1, at 95.568, a price that yields effective interest of 10 percent.

On July 1, 19x4, when the common stock was selling for $30 per share, one-half of the bonds outstanding were converted into common stocks.

On January 1, 19x5, the remaining one-half of the bonds were called by the company and retired.

Required

1. Prepare a table similar to Table 18-1 to show the interest and amortization of bond discount for twelve interest payment periods. Use the effective interest method (round results to the nearest dollar).
2. Prepare general journal entries for the bond issue, interest payments and amortization of bond discounts, bond conversion, and bond retirement on the following dates: July 1, 19x1; December 31, 19x1; June 30, 19x4; July 1, 19x4; December 31, 19x4; and January 1, 19x5.

**Problem 18B-5
Income Tax
Allocation**
(L.O. 7)

Holstein Corporation has before-tax accounting income of $300,000 in each of two years, 19x1 and 19x2. Included in 19x1 income is a major revenue item of $80,000 that does not have to be reported for tax purposes until 19x2.

Required

1. For each tax year, determine taxable income; actual income tax due, using the corporate tax rates in Table 17-1 on page 631; and net income. Assume no income tax allocation.
2. For each tax year, determine income tax expense, using the corporate tax rates in Table 17-1, and net income. Assume that the income tax allocation procedure is used.
3. Prepare journal entries to record income tax expense and income tax payable for each year. Assume that the income tax allocation procedure is used.

Marquette Company, Inc., is authorized to issue $10,000,000 of $9\frac{3}{5}$ percent, ten-year sinking fund bonds on January 1, 19x0. Semiannual interest is payable on December 31 and June 30. The company is required to deposit $658,200 with a trustee at the end of each year for the life of the bond issue. It is assumed that the sinking fund investment will earn a return of 9 percent annually. Selected transactions involving this bond issue and its sinking fund are listed below:

19x0

Jan. 1   Sold the entire issue at 97.5, a price that gives the buyer a 10 percent annual return.

June 30   Made the first semiannual interest payment and amortized the discount.

Dec. 31   Made the second semiannual interest payment and amortized the discount.

      31   Made the first annual sinking fund deposit.

19x1

June 30   Made the third semiannual interest payment and amortized the discount.

Dec. 31   Made the fourth semiannual interest payment and amortized the discount.

      31   Made the second annual sinking fund deposit.

      31   Received a report from the sinking fund trustee indicating that interest earned on the sinking fund was $59,238 for 19x1.

19x9

June 30   Made the nineteenth semiannual interest payment and amortized the discount. (The carrying value of the bond payable on January 1 was $9,962,812.)

Dec. 31   Made the twentieth semiannual interest payment and amortized the discount.

      31   Made the final sinking fund deposit.

      31   Received a report from the sinking fund trustee indicating that the interest earned on the sinking fund in 19x9 was $774,500.

      31   Received from the trustee another report indicating that the bonds had been paid in full, together with a check for $7,300 representing the amount by which the final sinking fund balance exceeded the bonds payable.

Required

1. Prepare a table showing the growth of annual investments in the sinking fund (round amounts to the nearest dollar). The table should have the following headings: End of Year, Fund Balance at Beginning of Year, Deposit, Interest at 9%, and Fund Balance at End of Year.

2. Prepare general journal entries for the above transactions (round amounts to the nearest dollar).

Financial Decision Case 18-1

Gianni Chemical Corporation (L.O. 2, 6)

The Gianni Chemical Corporation is planning to build a new plant that will produce liquid fertilizer to sell to agricultural markets. The plant is expected to cost $200,000,000 and will be located in the southwestern part of the United States. The company's chief financial officer, Julio Bassi, has spent the last several weeks studying different means of financing the construction of the new plant. In talking with bankers and other financiers, he has decided that there are two basic choices. The plant can be financed through the issuance of long-term bonds or through a long-term lease. The two options can be summarized as follows:

a. Issuance of $200,000,000 of 25-year, 16 percent bonds that are secured by the new plant. Interest on the bonds is payable semiannually.
b. Signing of a 25-year lease calling for semiannual lease payments of $16,350,000.

Now that Bassi knows what the two basic choices are, he wants to look at the accounting effects of each choice on the financial statements. He estimates that the useful life of the plant is 25 years, at which time it is expected to have an estimated residual value of $20,000,000.

Required

1. Prepare the entries to record issuance of the bonds in exchange for the fertilizer plant. Assume that the transaction occurs on the first day of the fiscal year, which is July 1. Also prepare entries to pay the interest and to record depreciation on the plant during the first year. Assume that the straight-line method is used.

Describe the effects that these transactions will have on the balance sheet and income statement.

2. Prepare the entries required to treat the long-term lease as a capital lease. Assume that the plant is occupied on the first day of the fiscal year, July 1, and that an interest rate of 16 percent applies. Also prepare entries to record the lease payments and to record depreciation during the first year. Describe the effects that these transactions will have on the balance sheet and income statement. (A knowledge of present value, which is dealt with in Appendix A and Table B-4 in Appendix B, is necessary to do part 2.)

3. What factors would you consider important to deciding which alternative to choose? Contrast the annual cash requirement of each alternative.

Part Five

Special Reports and Analyses of Accounting Information

Because business organizations are so complex today, special reports are needed to present important information about their activities. In order to understand and evaluate financial statements, it is necessary to learn how to analyze them.

Part V deals with these important special reports and with the analysis of financial statements.

Chapter 19 presents the statement of changes in financial position, which explains the major financing and investing activities of a business. This chapter also presents the cash flow statement.

Chapter 20 attends to the problems of companies that expand in two ways. One is by investing in other companies, which often calls for consolidated financial statements. The other way of expanding is by operating in foreign markets.

Chapter 21 explains the key ideas and ratios of financial statement analysis.

Learning Objectives

Chapter Nineteen

Statement of Changes in Financial Position and Cash Flow Statement

1. *Distinguish cash from working capital as a concept of funds.*

2. *Identify the types of transactions that cause changes in working capital.*

3. *Identify common sources and uses of working capital.*

4. *Prepare a statement of changes in financial position work sheet.*

5. *Prepare a statement of changes in financial position including changes in components of working capital.*

6. *Prepare a cash flow statement.*

Earlier in this book, you studied the balance sheet, the income statement, and the statement of retained earnings. In this chapter, you will learn to prepare a fourth major financial statement: the statement of changes in financial position. You will also learn to prepare a cash flow statement. As a result of studying this chapter, you should be able to meet the learning objectives listed on the left.

The business enterprise engages in financing and investing activities to earn a profit. The balance sheet reveals the status of these activities at a particular time. Financing activities are represented as liabilities and owners' equity, and investment activities are shown as assets. The income statement reports on the progress of the business enterprise in earning a profit. However, neither of these statements answers the following questions: What new financing and investing activities did the company engage in during the year? How much of the new investment was provided by profitable operations and how much by increased liabilities or owners' equity? Why did the distribution of the assets change during the year? If liabilities were reduced, what was the source of the funds used to reduce the liabilities?

The purpose of the statement of changes in financial position is to answer questions such as those raised above. It shows each source of funds for the business and each use of funds by the business for the year. Even though its official name is **statement of changes in financial position,** it is often called simply the statement of changes.

Cash and Working Capital Funds Distinguished

*Objective 1
Distinguish
cash from
working capital
as a concept of
funds*

A common source of confusion is that the word *funds* can be defined in more than one way. Most people think that *funds* and *cash* are the same thing. This is not, however, the way in which most business people or accountants use this term. Instead, they use the term **funds** in the broader sense of working capital, because working capital (current assets minus current liabilities) is closely related to the operating cycle of the business. Cash, on the other hand, is obtained or its use delayed by making sales, issuing short-term notes, or using accounts payable and accrued liabilities. Once obtained, cash is used to pay expenses or to purchase inventory. The inventory in turn is sold for cash or turned into accounts receivable. There is a constant flow from cash to noncash assets and then back to cash. The executive and the accountant generally think of working capital as a pool of funds to be used in the smooth operation of the business.

As we will see later in this chapter, accountants, of course, can and do prepare cash flow statements. Such statements show the sources and uses of a firm's cash and are important in the hands of modern financial management. However, the statement of changes in financial position is broader in its view because it focuses on changes in working capital. It covers the whole range of a firm's liquid assets. The cash flow statement, on the other hand, concentrates on a single asset—cash. In short, the statement of changes in financial position tries to describe all of the changes in a firm's financial position that arise during a certain period of time.

Changes in Working Capital

*Objective 2
Identify the
types of trans-
actions that
cause changes
in working
capital*

Identifying changes in working capital requires an understanding of the effects of transactions on working capital. These effects are best illustrated by means of a balance sheet consisting of four parts:

A. Current Assets
C. Noncurrent Assets

B. Current Liabilities
D. Noncurrent Liabilities and
    Owners' Equity

Parts A and B are working capital accounts, and Parts C and D are non-working capital accounts. A transaction will affect (either increase or decrease) working capital if a part of the transaction involves working capital accounts and a part of it does not. For example, contrast the effects on working capital of borrowing cash by obtaining a short-term bank note and borrowing cash by issuing long-term bonds. In the first transaction, there is no effect on total working capital because both the debit and the credit involve working capital accounts. The debit to Cash (an increase in a working capital account) is offset by the credit to Notes Payable (a decrease in working capital). The net result is no change in total working capital. The second transaction, on the other hand, affects working capital

Figure 19-1
Effect of Trans-
actions on
Working
Capital

Debit Entry	Credit Entry	
	Current Account	Noncurrent Account
Current Account	No effect	Increase (source)
Noncurrent Account	Decrease (use)	No effect

because the debit is to a working capital account (Cash) and the credit (Bonds Payable) is not. The debit to Cash increases working capital, whereas the credit to Bonds Payable increases a noncurrent liability. The net result is an increase in total working capital. The effects of transactions on working capital are summarized in Figure 19-1.

We can apply the decision rules of Figure 19-1 to the four parts of the balance sheet as shown in Figure 19-2. When we do so we can distinguish ten types of transactions involving the four parts of the balance sheet (each line with arrows at both ends represents a type of transaction). Note that the horizontal line separates the current from the noncurrent balance sheet accounts. It is labeled the working capital line. Analysis of Figure 19-2 shows six types of transactions (1, 2, 3, 4, 5, 6) that do not cross the working capital line. These transactions, therefore, do not affect the amount of working capital. They may be summarized as follows:

Type of Transaction	Parts of Balance Sheet Affected	Examples
1	A, A	Collected an account receivable
2	A, B	Made a payment on an account payable
3	B, B	Issued a note payable to settle an account payable
4	C, C	Exchanged land for a building; no gain or loss recognized
5	C, D	Acquired a building by issuing a mortgage payable
6	D, D	Declared and issued a stock dividend

Further analysis of Figure 19-2 shows only four types of transactions (7, 8, 9, 10) that cross the working capital line. They are summarized below.

Type of Transaction	Parts of Balance Sheet Affected	Examples
7	A, C	Made a sale of long-term asset at book value; purchased computer with cash

Figure 19-2
Types of Trans-
actions Affect-
ing the Balance
Sheet

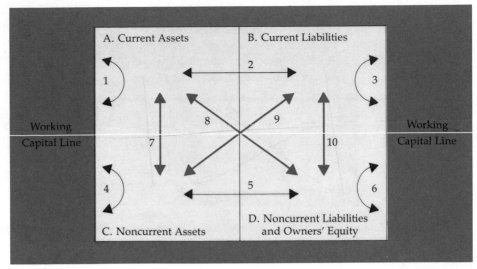

Source: Adapted from Robert J. Brill, "A Visual Aid for Explaining Sources and Applications of Funds," *The Accounting Review,* October 1964, p. 1015. Reprinted by permission of *The Accounting Review.*

8	A, D	Charged a customer for a sale on account; issued common stock for cash
9	B, C	Acquired equipment by issuing a short-term note payable
10	B, D	Purchased advertising on credit; exchanged a long-term note for a short-term note

Because part of each of these transactions is above the working capital line and part is below, each one affects the amount of working capital. The transactions involving income statement accounts may raise a question. Remember that the Sales account and the Advertising Expense account are nominal or temporary owners' equity accounts that at some point affect Retained Earnings. So a sale on account affects a working capital account (Accounts Receivable) and a nonworking capital account (Retained Earnings via Sales). A purchase of advertising on credit also affects a working capital account (Accounts Payable) and a nonworking capital account (Retained Earnings by way of Advertising Expense).

Effects of Transactions on Working Capital

After noting the transactions that affect working capital, it is important to determine what effects they have. A transaction that leads to a net increase in working capital is known as a **source of working capital**. A transaction that results in a net decrease in working capital is known as a **use of working capital**. Common sources and uses of working capital are

Figure 19-3
Common
Sources and
Uses of Work-
ing Capital

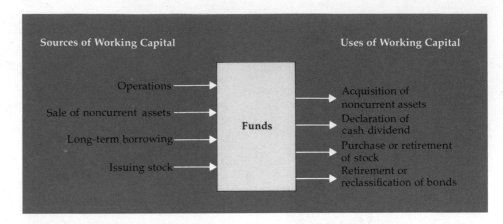

shown in Figure 19-3. Each source and use will be explained below to show its effect on working capital.

Sources of Working Capital

The most common sources of working capital are operations, sale of non-current assets, long-term borrowing, and issuance of capital stock.

Objective 3
Identify
common sources
and uses of
working capital

Operations The primary source of working capital is revenues. Similarly, the main use of working capital is expenses. Recall that revenues are generally recorded on the accrual basis and represent increases in current assets. The increase in current assets also increases working capital. This occurs, for example, when a merchandising transaction is recorded with a debit to the Accounts Receivable account (part A of the balance sheet) and a credit to the Sales account (part D of the balance sheet).

Expenses are also recorded on the accrual basis and generally represent decreases in working capital. There are, however, expenses that do not affect working capital. A familiar expense that does not bring about a decrease in working capital is depreciation. Recognition of depreciation expense in the accounts requires a debit to a depreciation expense account (part D of the balance sheet) and a credit to an accumulated depreciation account (part C of the balance sheet). Note that the recognition of depreciation expense does not involve a journal entry that crosses the working capital line.

To understand income from operations as a source of working capital, it is first necessary to analyze each of the revenue and expense items found on the income statement. For example, the following table shows how each item in the income statement (column 1) affects working capital (column 2).

	(1) Income Statement	(2) Items Affecting Working Capital
Sales	$1,000	$+1,000
Cost of Goods Sold	400	− 400
Gross Margin	$ 600	$ 600

Operating Expenses		
Wages Expense	$ 100	$— 100
Depreciation Expense	100	
Advertising Expense	50	— 50
Other Expenses	150	— 150
Total Operating Expenses	$ 400	$— 300
Net Income	$ 200	$+ 300

The analysis shows a $300 net increase in working capital from operations.

Using this approach to find funds from operations, then, we look carefully at each revenue and expense item shown on an income statement. Once we discover the nonfund items (depreciation in this case), we omit them from the income statement. Then we prepare an adjusted income statement to figure funds from operations. However, this method is not always easy to use. Notice that the income statement above was fairly simple. If a complicated income statement had been used, this way of determining funds from operations would not have been so easy.

Short-Cut Technique To make it easier to calculate funds from operations, accountants have devised a short cut. The short cut uses a formula for calculating funds from operations. One form of the formula is

Net income
Plus: Items decreasing income but not using working capital[1]
Equals: Working capital provided from operations

By using the data from the example in this formula, we arrive at the same $300 funds from operations:

Net income	$200
Plus items decreasing income but not using working capital—depreciation	100
Working capital from operations	$300

Unfortunately, the short-cut method makes depreciation appear to be a source of working capital. Clearly it is not. Depreciation is only added back to net income to arrive at funds from operations according to the short-cut formula. The $300 funds provided by operations came from revenues and expenses affecting working capital. Recognition of depreciation is necessary in determining income because it represents the allocation of the cost of a plant asset to the current accounting period. The expenditure for the plant asset occurred at the time it was purchased. As shown earlier, the journal entry recognizes that depreciation does not cross the working capital line and therefore is neither a source nor a use of working capital. Clearly, working capital from operations results from revenue and expense items *before* adding or deducting items that are neither sources nor uses of working capital. As proof of this point, note in

1. Items do exist that have the opposite effect—increasing income but not affecting working capital—but consideration of them is left up to more advanced courses.

the following that funds from operations do not change. Net income is reduced from $200 to $100 by deducting the additional $100 in depreciation, but there is no change in funds from operations. The short-cut formula supports this conclusion, as seen in the second computation.

	Income Statement	Items Affecting Working Capital
Sales	$1,000	$ + 1,000
Cost of Goods Sold	400	— 400
Gross Margin	$ 600	$ 600
Operating Expenses		
Wages Expense	$ 100	$ — 100
Depreciation Expense	200	
Advertising Expense	50	— 50
Other Expenses	150	— 150
Total Operating Expenses	$ 500	$ — 300
Net Income	$ 100	$ + 300

Short-cut technique

Net income	$100
Plus items decreasing income but not using working capital—depreciation	200
Working capital from operations	$300

Other expenses do not involve an outlay of funds and therefore must be added to net income to arrive at working capital provided by operations. Two of them are amortization of intangible assets and depletion of natural resources. An adjustment is also needed for gains and losses if the net income figure used in the statement of changes in financial position contains the gains and losses. The handling of such gains and losses is left up to more advanced courses.

Working capital is usually provided by operations. However, if a net operating loss is greater than the nonworking capital expenses, a decrease in working capital may result. When this happens, the decrease in working capital is placed either in the sources as a negative amount or in the uses.

Sale of Noncurrent Assets Noncurrent assets such as equipment or a long-term investment may be sold or exchanged for cash or some other current asset. When such a sale takes place, a company's working capital is increased by the amount of the cash or other current asset received. For example, if a machine is sold for a note receivable of $7,000 due within one year, the working capital provided by the transaction is $7,000. This statement is true regardless of the carrying value and whether there is a gain or loss. For example, assume that the following transaction reflects the facts:

May 15	Notes Receivable	7,000	
	Accumulated Depreciation, Machinery	8,000	
	Gain on Sale of Machinery		5,000
	Machinery		10,000
	Sale of machinery		

Note that only Notes Receivable is an above-the-line (working capital) account and is debited or increased. The other three accounts involved are below-the-line (noncurrent) accounts. Thus working capital is increased by $7,000. Also note that if the carrying value of the machinery were $9,000 ($17,000 − $8,000) instead of $2,000 ($10,000 − $8,000), with a resulting loss of $2,000 ($9,000 − $7,000), the working capital provided would still be $7,000.

Long-Term Borrowing When a firm borrows cash on a long-term basis, cash (a current asset) and long-term liabilities (noncurrent liabilities) are increased. Long-term liabilities are not a part of working capital (below the line) and cash is a part of working capital (above the line). So the borrowing of cash on a long-term basis is a source of working capital.

Issuance of Capital Stock The issuance of a company's stock for cash or other current assets is another source of funds. The results of such a transaction are to increase current assets (above the line) and owners' equity (below the line). Owners' equity is not a part of working capital. Thus the issuance of capital stock results in a source of working capital.

Uses of Working Capital

Some of the more common uses of working capital are acquisition of noncurrent assets, declaration of a cash dividend, purchase or retirement of stock, and retirement or reclassification of long-term debt.

Purchase of Noncurrent Assets Using current assets to purchase a noncurrent asset increases long-term assets (below the line) and decreases current assets (above the line). For example, suppose that the Hubbard Corporation bought a building for $200,000 cash. The entry to record the transaction would be:

Jan. 21	Buildings	200,000	
	Cash		200,000
	Purchase of building		

Note that the debit to Buildings increases a below-the-line nonworking capital account but the credit to Cash decreases an above-the-line working capital account. For this reason, a use of working capital of $200,000 results.

Declaration of a Cash Dividend An example of the entry to record the declaration of a cash dividend follows:

Oct. 30	Dividends Declared	10,000	
	Dividends Payable		10,000
	Declaration of cash dividend		

Note that the transaction involves both an above-the-line working capital account (Dividends Payable) and a below-the-line nonworking capital account (Dividends Declared). Because an increase in current liabilities reduces working capital, the declaration of a cash dividend is classified as a use of working capital. Note that the subsequent payment of the dividend is not a use of working capital because the transaction involves two working capital accounts: Dividends Payable and Cash.

Purchase or Retirement of Stock A company may use cash or other current assets to purchase treasury stock or to purchase and retire a part of its stock. Such transactions affect both current and noncurrent accounts and reduce current assets. So the amount of current assets given up is classified as a use of working capital on the statement of changes in financial position.

Retirement or Reclassification of Long-Term Debt The retirement or reclassification of a long-term debt may result in the use of a firm's working capital. If long-term debt is retired by using current assets, the transaction is much like the retirement of stock. There is a reduction both in the company's current assets (above the line) and in long-term debt (below the line). The amount of current assets used to retire the long-term debt is classified as a use of working capital.

When a portion of long-term debt comes due for payment during the current year, that portion of the debt must be reclassified as a current liability. This transaction results in an increase in the company's current liabilities (above the line) and in a decrease in long-term debt (below the line). Thus there is a decrease in working capital because of the increase in current liabilities. The reclassification is treated as a use of working capital.

Exchange Transactions

A company will occasionally exchange a long-term asset for a long-term liability. For example, assume that a $300,000 long-term mortgage is exchanged for $50,000 in land with a $250,000 building on it. The entry to record this transaction would be:

June 1	Land	50,000	
	Building	250,000	
	Mortgage Payable		300,000
	Exchange of mortgage payable for		
	land and building		

This **exchange transaction** involves parts C and D of the balance sheet and does not cross the working capital line. Therefore, it has no direct effect on working capital. It is, however, an important transaction—one about

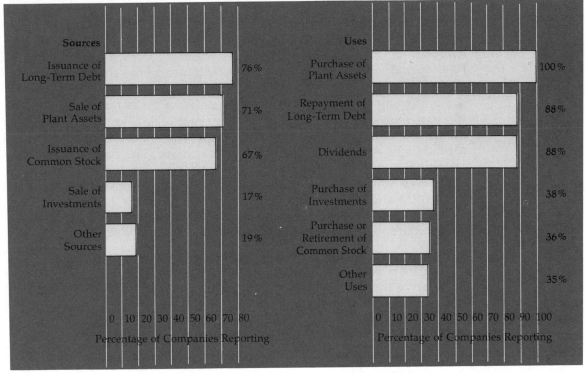

Sources		Uses	
Issuance of Long-Term Debt	76%	Purchase of Plant Assets	100%
Sale of Plant Assets	71%	Repayment of Long-Term Debt	88%
Issuance of Common Stock	67%	Dividends	88%
Sale of Investments	17%	Purchase of Investments	38%
Other Sources	19%	Purchase or Retirement of Common Stock	36%
		Other Uses	35%

Percentage of Companies Reporting · Percentage of Companies Reporting

Source: American Institute of Certified Public Accountants, *Accounting Trends and Techniques* (New York: AICPA, 1982).

**Figure 19-4
Sources of Capital and Uses Other than Operations Reported by 600 Companies**

which a statement user who was looking at the financial and investing activities of a business would want to know. For this reason, this exchange transaction may be viewed as two transactions: (1) the issuance of a mortgage payable for $300,000, and (2) the purchase of land for $50,000 and building for $250,000. As a result, the Accounting Principles Board, in its *Opinion No. 19*, requires that an **all financial resources** viewpoint be taken when the statement of changes in financial position is prepared.[2] The opinion means that significant exchange transactions must be treated as if they are both a source and use event. In this case, the issuance of the mortgage is shown as a source of working capital and the purchase of the land and buildings is shown as a use of working capital.

Other transactions that should be treated as exchange transactions are exchanges of capital stock for long-term assets and conversions of bonds payable or preferred stock into common stock. Figure 19-4 illustrates sources and uses of working capital reported by 600 companies.

Preparing the Statement of Changes in Financial Position

Once the transactions affecting working capital—that is, sources or uses of working capital—are determined, they are presented in the statement of

2. Accounting Principles Board, "Reporting Changes in Financial Position," *Opinion No. 19* (New York: American Institute of Certified Public Accountants, 1971), par. 8.

changes in financial position. The primary objective of this statement is to summarize the financing and investing activities of the company. These activities include the extent to which the enterprise has raised working capital from operations during an accounting period. This statement must be prepared whenever a balance sheet and an income statement are presented.[3]

The statement of changes in financial position has two major parts. The top part shows (1) the sources of working capital, including (a) from operations and (b) from other sources; (2) the uses of working capital; and (3) the increase (or decrease) in working capital. The bottom part of the statement shows the changes in the components of working capital. A completed statement and schedule are shown in Figures 19-8 and 19-9 (pages 713 and 714).

The important steps in preparing a statement of changes in financial position are as follows:

1. Determine the change in working capital for the year.
2. Prepare a work sheet.
3. Analyze the change in each noncurrent account to find out whether it was caused by a transaction that crosses the working capital line. If so, reclassify the change as a source or use of working capital.
4. Prepare the statement of changes in financial position.

The comparative balance sheets of Hubbard Corporation are used in Figure 19-5 to illustrate the preparation of the statement of changes in financial position.

Determining the Change in Working Capital for the Year

For the first step, find the change in working capital as shown in Figure 19-6 (on page 706) by comparing the working capital at the end of 19x2 with that at the end of 19x1. Because the total change in working capital for the Hubbard Corporation during 19x2 was a $3,000 increase, the sources of working capital should exceed the uses of working capital by $3,000 on the statement of changes in financial position.

Preparing the Work Sheet

Objective 4
Prepare a
statement of
changes in
financial
position work
sheet

After determining the change in working capital, analyze the noncurrent accounts to find the causes of the changes in financial position. Several methods are used to gather the data that bear on preparing the statement. The work sheet approach is used here because it is practical. It is also useful because, when complete, the lower part of the work sheet holds the information necessary to prepare the statement of changes in financial position.

The work sheet for the Hubbard Corporation is presented in Figure

3. Ibid., par. 7.

Chapter Nineteen

Figure 19-5
Comparative
Balance Sheet

Hubbard Corporation
Comparative Balance Sheet
December 31, 19x2, and December 31, 19x1

	19x2	19x1
Assets		
Current Assets		
Cash	$ 55,000	$ 30,000
Accounts Receivable (net)	40,000	45,000
Inventories	110,000	100,000
Prepaid Expenses	8,000	10,000
Total Current Assets	$213,000	$185,000
Property, Plant, and Equipment		
Land	$115,000	$115,000
Buildings	450,000	330,000
Accumulated Depreciation, Buildings	(54,000)	(44,000)
Equipment	150,000	60,000
Accumulated Depreciation, Equipment	(29,000)	(24,000)
Total Property, Plant, and Equipment	$632,000	$437,000
Total Assets	$845,000	$622,000
Liabilities		
Current Liabilities		
Accounts Payable	$ 50,000	$ 40,000
Accrued Liabilities	10,000	—
Current Portion of Bonds Payable	5,000	—
Total Current Liabilities	$ 65,000	$ 40,000
Long-Term Liabilities		
Bonds Payable	$345,000	$250,000
Total Liabilities	$410,000	$290,000
Stockholders' Equity		
Common Stock—$5 par value	$275,000	$200,000
Paid-in Capital in Excess of Par Value	25,000	—
Retained Earnings	135,000	132,000
Total Stockholders' Equity	$435,000	$332,000
Total Liabilities and Stockholders' Equity	$845,000	$622,000

Figure 19-6
Computation of
Change in
Working
Capital

Hubbard Corporation
Computation of Change in Working Capital
For the Year Ended December 31, 19x2

Current Assets	$213,000	
Current Liabilities	65,000	
Working Capital, December 31, 19x2		$148,000
Current Assets	$185,000	
Current Liabilities	40,000	
Working Capital, December, 31, 19x1		$145,000
Total Increase (Decrease) in Working Capital		$ 3,000

19-7. The following steps will serve as guidelines in work sheet preparation. Be sure to relate each step to Figure 19-7.

1. The work sheet should have a Description column (labeled A in Figure 19-7), and additional columns to the right with the following types of headings:
Column B: Account balances for the end of the prior year (19x1)
Column C: Analysis of transactions for the current year (19x2)
Column D: Account balances for the end of the current year (19x2)

2. Enter working capital on the first line in the Description column, and enter the amount of working capital at the end of the current and prior years in the proper columns ($145,000 and $148,000 in columns B and D). The difference of $3,000 between the columns must be the change in working capital for the current year as computed in Figure 19-6. Label the change with an (x) for the later reference in step 7 on page 708.

3. Immediately below the working capital in the Description column, put in all the noncurrent debits that appear on the comparative balance sheet. Then enter the amounts in the proper columns. Next total the debits for each of the two years. Note that the total debits for 19x1 and 19x2 in the illustration are $650,000 and $863,000, respectively.

4. List the noncurrent accounts with credit balances (including contra-asset accounts) from the comparative balance sheet. Enter the amounts in the proper column, and total the credits. The total credits for 19x1 and 19x2 in the illustration are $650,000 and $863,000, respectively. The total credits for each year must agree with the total debits.

5. Next drop down several lines on the work sheet and insert the title Sources of Working Capital. Then drop down several more lines and enter a second title, Uses of Working Capital. The reason for this step is that as the changes in noncurrent accounts are analyzed, they can be classified as a source or use. This step will help in preparing the statement of changes in financial position later.

6. Analyze the changes in noncurrent accounts that have occurred during the period. This is the most important step in the preparation of the work

Figure 19-7
Sample Work Sheet

Hubbard Corporation
Statement of Changes in Financial Position Work Sheet
For the Year Ended December 31, 19x2

A	B	C		D
		Analysis of Transactions for 19x2		
Description	Account Balances, 12/31/x1	Debit	Credit	Account Balances, 12/31/x2
Debits				
Working Capital	145,000	(x) 3,000		148,000
Land	115,000			115,000
Buildings	330,000	(d) 120,000		450,000
Equipment	60,000	(e) 100,000	(c) 10,000	150,000
Total Debits	650,000			863,000
Credits				
Accumulated Depreciation, Buildings	44,000		(b) 10,000	54,000
Accumulated Depreciation, Equipment	24,000	(c) 2,000	(b) 7,000	29,000
Bonds Payable	250,000	(f) 5,000	(e) 100,000	345,000
Common Stock	200,000		(g) 75,000	275,000
Paid-in Capital in Excess of Par Value	—		(g) 25,000	25,000
Retained Earnings	132,000	(h) 10,000	(a) 13,000	135,000
Total Credits	650,000	240,000	240,000	863,000
Sources of Working Capital				
Operations				
Net Income		(a) 13,000		
Depreciation, Buildings		(b) 10,000		
Depreciation, Equipment		(b) 7,000		
Other Sources				
Sale of Equipment		(c) 8,000		
Issuance of Bonds in Exchange for Equipment		(e) 100,000		
Issuance of Common Stock		(g) 100,000		
Uses of Working Capital				
Purchase of Building			(d) 120,000	
Purchase of Equipment by Exchanging Bonds			(e) 100,000	
Reclassification of Long-Term Debt			(f) 5,000	
Cash Dividend			(h) 10,000	
Total Sources & Uses of Working Capital		238,000	235,000	
Increase in Working Capital, 19x2			(x) 3,000	
Totals		238,000	238,000	

sheet because the transactions affecting noncurrent accounts are those that are likely to affect the sources and uses of working capital. For this reason, a separate analysis of each transaction is presented below.

7. Finally, add the debit and credit columns in both the top and bottom portions of the analysis section (column C). The debit and credit columns should balance in the top portion, and they should not balance in the bottom portion. If no errors have been made, the difference in the bottom portion should equal the increase or decrease in working capital. Add this difference to the lower column, and identify it as either an increase or a decrease in working capital. Label the change with an (x) and compare it with the change in working capital, also labeled (x), on the first line of the work sheet. The amounts should be equal.

After completing the work sheet, prepare the statement of changes in financial position. Because all the required information is listed under sources and uses of working capital, it is simply transferred and put in the proper format on the statement.

Analyzing the Changes in Noncurrent Accounts

The most crucial step in the preparation of the statement of changes in financial position, as mentioned earlier, is the analysis of the changes in noncurrent accounts that occurred during the year. To analyze the changes, the following additional information is needed:

a. Net income from operations for the year, $13,000.
b. Depreciation recorded on the building and equipment is $10,000 and $7,000, respectively.
c. Sold equipment that cost $10,000 and had accumulated depreciation of $2,000 for $8,000 cash.
d. Purchased a new building for $120,000 cash.
e. Issued $100,000 of bonds for new equipment.
f. Reclassified $5,000 of bonds payable as current.
g. Issued 15,000 shares of $5 par value common stock for $100,000.
h. Declared a $10,000 cash dividend.

The results of the analysis of the noncurrent accounts for the Hubbard Corporation are presented in column C of the work sheet in Figure 19-7. The explanations for these work sheet entries are presented in the following paragraphs. Keep in mind that the objective of each part of the analysis is to explain the change in a noncurrent account. When all changes in noncurrent accounts have been explained and classified, the change in working capital for the year as shown in the first line of the work sheet becomes clear.

a. The Hubbard Corporation reported net income for 19x2 of $13,000. Net income ultimately results in an increase in Retained Earnings (when Income Summary is closed to Retained Earnings at the end of the year). So it helps to account for the change in Retained Earnings for the year. Also, as already explained, net income is considered a source of working capital because it represents the excess of revenues over expenses. As a result, on the work sheet a credit is made to Retained Earnings for the increase in that account for the year. A corresponding debit is made to Net Income in the lower part of the work sheet under sources of working capital:

(a) Source of Working Capital: Net Income   13,000
        Retained Earnings   13,000

This entry is recorded on the work sheet in the analysis columns as entry **a**.

b. The depreciation expenses for building and equipment were $10,000 and $7,000, respectively. As explained earlier, though depreciation expense is included as a deduction in figuring net income, it does not involve an outlay of working capital. The amount of depreciation expense also helps to explain the change in the accumulated depreciation accounts for building and equipment. Thus the work sheet entry would be to credit the accumulated depreciation accounts and to debit the depreciation expense under sources of working capital on the lower part of the work sheet. In this way, depreciation expense is added back to net income:

(b) Increase in Working Capital: Building
     Depreciation   10,000
     Increase in Working Capital: Equipment
     Depreciation   7,000
        Accumulated Depreciation, Building   10,000
        Accumulated Depreciation, Equipment   7,000

c. The change in the Accumulated Depreciation, Buildings has been explained ($44,000 + $10,000 = $54,000). However, the change in Accumulated Depreciation, Equipment has not been completely explained. In other words, the beginning balance of $24,000 plus the credit of $7,000 does not equal the ending balance of $29,000. Neither has the change in Equipment been explained. Thus we must conclude that other transactions involving the account have taken place. The other information given reveals a sale of equipment that would be recorded as follows:

Cash   8,000
Accumulated Depreciation, Equipment   2,000
     Equipment   10,000
        Sale of equipment

An analysis of this transaction reveals that Cash, a working capital account, has increased by $8,000. The other two accounts are nonworking capital accounts. The work sheet entry is as follows:

(c) Source of Working Capital: Sale of
     Equipment   8,000
     Accumulated Depreciation, Equipment   2,000
        Equipment   10,000

With this entry the total change in Accumulated Depreciation, Equipment is accounted for ($24,000 − $2,000 + $7,000 = $29,000).

d. Among the noncurrent asset accounts, the changes in Buildings and Equipment remain to be explained. Turning to the Building account first, we find that the other data given above show the purchase of a building for $120,000 cash. The entry to record the purchase is as follows:

Building	120,000	
Cash		120,000

This business transaction reduces working capital by decreasing Cash. The entry on the work sheet is shown as

(d) Building	120,000	
Use of Working Capital: Purchase of Building		120,000

e. The supplemental information also reveals the issuance of an additional $100,000 of bonds for equipment. This event is an exchange transaction that fits the concept of all financial resources. The transaction as shown below does not change working capital because it involves two noncurrent accounts and is a transaction that does not cross the working capital line.

Equipment	100,000	
Bonds Payable		100,000
Issuance of bonds in exchange for equipment		

However, the transaction is viewed as an exchange transaction—that is, as both a source and a use of funds. The transaction is a short cut for issuing bonds for cash, which is the source of working capital, and then purchasing the equipment for cash, which is the use of working capital. To record this transaction properly on the work sheet, it should appear as follows:

(e) Equipment	100,000	
Source of Working Capital: Issuance of Bonds	100,000	
Bonds Payable		100,000
Use of Working Capital: Equipment Purchase		100,000

Note that after this transaction is recorded on the work sheet, the change in Equipment for the year is explained ($60,000 + $100,000 − $10,000 = $150,000). The changes in all noncurrent assets have now been explained.

f. Part of the change in Bonds Payable is yet to be accounted for. Item f reveals that, during the year, $5,000 of Hubbard Corporation's long-term debt became current and had to be reclassified as a current liability. The company could then make a formal entry to transfer $5,000 from Bonds

Payable to Current Portion of Long-Term Debt as follows:

Bonds Payable	5,000	
Current Portion of Long-Term Debt		5,000
To reclassify current portion of		
long-term debt as a current		
liability		

Part of this transaction is above the line (current liability) and part of it is below the line (noncurrent liability). The increase in Current Portion of Long-Term Debt results in an increase in current liabilities and in a reduction or use of working capital. The work sheet entry to show this use of working capital is presented below:

(f) Bonds Payable	5,000	
Use of Working Capital: Reclassi-		
fication of Long-Term Debt		5,000

Note that the total change in Bonds Payable in 19x2 has now been accounted for ($250,000 − $5,000 + $100,000 = $345,000).

g. The issuance of an additional 15,000 shares of $5 par value common stock for $100,000 would result in the following entry:

Cash	100,000	
Common Stock		75,000
Paid-in Capital in Excess of Par Value		25,000

When this transaction is analyzed, the increase in Cash causes an increase in working capital, but the increases in the equity accounts do not affect working capital. Thus the transaction results in an increase in working capital. The transaction below is recorded on the work sheet as entry **g.**

(g) Source of Working Capital: Issuance		
of Stock	100,000	
Common Stock		75,000
Paid-in Capital in Excess		
of Par Value		25,000

After this entry is recorded, the year's changes in Common Stock and Paid-in Capital in Excess of Par Value are accounted for.

h. The remaining account to be analyzed is Retained Earnings. Recall that in work sheet entry **a,** the recording of net income as a source of working capital resulted in a credit to Retained Earnings. The other entry to Retained Earnings during the year was the declaration of a $10,000 cash dividend by the Hubbard Corporation. The declaration of a cash dividend results in the following entry:

Dividends Declared	10,000	
Dividends Payable		10,000
Declaration of cash dividend		

This transaction contains one working capital account (Dividends Payable) and one nonworking capital account (Dividends Declared). The Dividends Declared account will reduce Retained Earnings when it is closed. Because an increase in a current liability results in a decrease in working capital, the entry is recorded on the work sheet as a use of working capital (credit) and a debit to Retained Earnings:

(h) Retained Earnings   10,000
        Use of Working Capital, Cash
            Dividends   10,000

The total change in Retained Earnings for the year has now been explained ($132,000 − $10,000 + $13,000 = $135,000).

x. After all the noncurrent transactions have been analyzed, the final step in the work sheet preparation is to total the debit and credit columns for the analysis of transactions for the top half and the bottom half of the work sheet. The two column totals for the top half should be equal. The difference in the two column totals for the bottom half will always equal the change in working capital for the year. Observe that in Figure 19-7 the bottom halves of the columns equal total sources of $238,000 and total uses of $235,000. The difference between these two is equal to the increase of $3,000 in working capital for the period. To complete the work sheet, the following entry should be made in the analysis columns:

(x) Working Capital   3,000
        Increase in Working Capital   3,000

Completing the Statement of Changes in Financial Position

Objective 5
Prepare a
statement of
changes in
financial
position
including
changes in
components of
working capital

Note that the transactions placed on the work sheet are *not* entered in the records of the company. The work sheet is merely a tool to assist accountants in preparing the statement of changes in financial position. When the work sheet is completed, it shows both the sources and the uses of working capital for the period. In addition, the sources and uses are listed according to type.

The information on the lower portion of the work sheet can now be used to prepare the major portion of the statement of changes in financial position. The completed statement for the Hubbard Corporation is shown in Figure 19-8 and consists of two parts. The top part of the statement shows the sources and uses of working capital as taken from the work sheet. The lower part of the statement is an analysis of working capital that shows the changes in the components of working capital. These changes can be determined from the comparative balance sheets as shown in the schedule illustrated in Figure 19-9 on page 714.

Preparing the Cash Flow Statement

Up to this point in the chapter, we have focused on the statement of changes in financial position on a working capital basis. By reporting the

Figure 19-8
Statement of
Changes in
Financial
Position

Hubbard Corporation
Statement of Changes in Financial Position
For the Year Ended December 31, 19x2

Sources of Working Capital

Operations

Net Income		$ 13,000	
Add Expenses Not Requiring Outlay of Working Capital in the Current Period			
Depreciation, Building	$10,000		
Depreciation, Equipment	7,000	17,000	
Working Capital Provided from Operations			$ 30,000
Other Sources of Working Capital			
Sale of Equipment		$ 8,000	
Issuance of Bonds in Exchange for Equipment		100,000	
Issuance of Common Stock		100,000	208,000
Total Sources of Working Capital			$238,000

Uses of Working Capital

Purchase of Building		$120,000	
Purchase of Equipment by Exchanging Bonds		100,000	
Reclassification of Long-Term Debt		5,000	
Cash Dividend		10,000	235,000
Increase in Working Capital			$ 3,000

Change in Components of Working Capital

Increase (Decrease) in Current Assets

Cash		$ 25,000	
Accounts Receivable (net)		(5,000)	
Inventories		10,000	
Prepaid Assets		(2,000)	$ 28,000

Decrease (Increase) in Current Liabilities

Accounts Payable		($ 10,000)	
Accrued Liabilities		(10,000)	
Current Portion of Long-Term Debt		(5,000)	
Total Uses of Working Capital			(25,000)
Increase (Decrease) in Working Capital			$ 3,000

Figure 19-9
Schedule of
Changes in
Working
Capital

Hubbard Corporation
Schedule of Changes in Working Capital
For the Year Ended December 31, 19x2

	19x2	19x1	Working Capital Increase	Working Capital Decrease
Current Assets				
Cash	$ 55,000	$ 30,000	$25,000	
Accounts Receivable (Net)	40,000	45,000		$ 5,000
Inventories	110,000	100,000	10,000	
Prepaid Expenses	8,000	10,000		2,000
Total Current Assets	$213,000	$185,000		
Current Liabilities				
Accounts Payable	$ 50,000	$ 40,000		10,000
Accrued Liabilities	10,000	—		10,000
Current Portion of Bond Payable	5,000	—		5,000
Total Current Liabilities	$ 65,000	$ 40,000	$35,000	$32,000
Working Capital	$148,000	$145,000		
Increase in Working Capital				3,000
			$35,000	$35,000

sources and uses of working capital during a given period, this statement gives management a broad view of the financing and investing activities of the company. However, management must also plan to have sufficient cash available to pay liabilities, dividends, and other obligations. A cash flow statement can provide management with this information. The cash flow statement is also useful to creditors in judging the liquidity of a company. In other words, it aids in determining whether a company can pay its liabilities and dividends and meet various requirements for business expansion.

The **cash flow statement** reports a company's sources and uses of cash during an accounting period. It may be prepared in the same format as a statement of changes in financial position on a working capital basis. The only difference is that it explains the increase or decrease in cash rather than in working capital. For purposes of the cash flow statement, most companies define cash as cash and short-term investments. The statement is normally a simple listing of sources of cash and uses of cash. The

Figure 19-10
Condensed
Income
Statement

Hubbard Corporation Condensed Income Statement For the Year Ended December 31, 19x2	
Net Sales	$650,000
Cost of Goods Sold	520,000
Gross Margin on Sales	$130,000
Operating Expenses	117,000
Net Income from Operations	$ 13,000

difference between the two amounts is identified as the increase or decrease in cash for the period. An example of a cash flow statement is presented in Figure 19-12 (page 718).

Cash Flow from Operations

The first step in preparing a cash flow statement is to determine the cash flow from operations. To do so, it is necessary to focus on the operating transactions affecting the Cash account.

Cash Receipts from Sales Sales are a source of cash for a company. Cash sales are increases in the cash flow of the company. Credit sales are originally recorded as accounts receivable. When they are collected, there is an inflow of cash. However, one should not assume that total sales are automatically a source of cash, because 100 percent of the accounts receivable are not necessarily collected in the current accounting period. A receivable may prove uncollectible, or it may be collected in a period after that of the sale. For example, for the $650,000 sales in Figure 19-10, assume that $50,000 were cash sales and $600,000 were credit sales. From the balance sheet in Figure 19-5, Accounts Receivable (net) decreased during the year by $5,000—that is, from $45,000 in 19x1 to $40,000 in 19x2. Because credit sales increase Accounts Receivable and collections reduce Accounts Receivable, collections must have exceeded credit sales by $5,000 during the year. The increase in cash from sales during the year then is $655,000 [$50,000 cash sales plus $605,000 ($600,000 + $5,000) collected from accounts receivable].

Cash Payments for Purchases The cost of goods sold amount on the income statement must be adjusted for changes in two balance sheet accounts to arrive at cash payments for purchases. First, cost of goods sold must be adjusted for changes in inventory to arrive at net purchases. Then, net purchases must be adjusted for the change in accounts payable to arrive at cash payments for purchases. These conclusions make sense. If a company is increasing its inventory, net purchases will be more than the cost of goods sold, and if a company is increasing its accounts payable, its cash payments for purchases will be less than its net purchases.

Cash Payments for Expenses Just as the cost of goods sold does not represent the amount of cash paid for purchases during an accounting period, operating expenses will not match the amount of cash paid. Two adjustments must be made in operating expenses to arrive at cash outflow. The first adjustment is related to the fact that in addition to arising from cash payments, expenses arise from the write-off of prepaid assets and the increase in accrued liabilities. If prepaid assets increase during the year, more cash will have been used than will appear as expense on the income statement. If prepaid assets decrease during the year, more expenses will appear on the income statement than cash spent. Also, if accrued liabilities increase during the year, expenses on the income statement will be more than cash spent. And if accrued liabilities decrease during the year, cash spent will be more than reported expenses. For this reason, operating expenses must be adjusted for changes in prepaid assets and accrued liabilities. The second adjustment relates to the fact that certain expenses do not call for a current outlay of cash. So they must be subtracted from the expense figure on the income statement to arrive at cash payments for expenses. Among these expenses are those for depreciation, amortization, and depletion.

Short-Cut Method Using the reasoning presented in the three paragraphs above, we can convert an income statement from the accrual to the cash basis. However, it is easier to find cash flow from operations by adjusting net income (which is the net result of sales, cost of goods sold, and operating expenses) for the changes in current assets (other than cash) and current liabilities. This principle is the same one used earlier in computing working capital from operations by adding back nonworking capital charges to net income. This short-cut method of finding cash flow from operations is shown below.

Net Income from Operations
Plus: Items reducing income but not using cash
      Decreases in current assets other than cash
      Increases in current liabilities

Less: Increases in current assets other than cash
      Decreases in current liabilities

Equals: Cash Flow from Operations

The changes in the various working capital accounts of Hubbard Corporation are found in the schedule of changes in working capital in Figure 19-9. In addition, the company had net income from operations of $13,000 (Figure 19-10) and depreciation of $10,000 on equipment and $7,000 on buildings. Cash flow from operations can thus be computed as shown in Figure 19-11.

Completing the Cash Flow Statement

In addition to operations, a company engages in other cash transactions during the year. For example, a company may buy or sell long-term assets; increase, reduce, or retire long-term debt; issue or purchase capital

Figure 19-11
Schedule of
Cash Flow from
Operations

Net Income from Operations			$13,000
Add			
Items reducing income but not using cash			
Depreciation, Equipment	$10,000		
Depreciation, Buildings	7,000	$17,000	
Decreases in current assets other than cash			
Accounts Receivable	$ 5,000		
Prepaid Expenses	2,000	7,000	
Increases in current liabilities			
Accounts Payable	$10,000		
Accrued Liabilities	10,000	20,000	$44,000
Subtotal			$57,000
Deduct			
Increases in current assets other than cash			
Inventories		$10,000	
Decreases in current liabilities		none	10,000
Cash flow from operations			$47,000

stock; or pay cash dividends. An analysis of previous information in the chapter for Hubbard Corporation indicated the following other cash transactions:

a. Sold equipment for $8,000 in cash.
b. Purchased a building for $120,000 in cash.
c. Issued 15,000 shares of $5 par value common stock for $100,000.
d. Paid a $10,000 cash dividend.

Also, Hubbard Corporation engaged in an exchange transaction of $100,000 of bonds for equipment that should be disclosed as both a source and a use of cash.

Using this information and the computation of cash flow from operations (Figure 19-11), we can prepare a cash flow statement as shown in Figure 19-12 (next page). Note that sources of cash provided cash receipts of $255,000 during the year and the uses of cash required cash disbursements of $230,000 during the year. The resultant increase in cash of $25,000 equals the change in cash for the year as shown in the balance sheet in Figure 19-5 and in the schedule in Figure 19-9. If the cash flow from operations had been negative, the amount would have been shown as a use of cash.

Figure 19-12
Cash Flow
Statement

Hubbard Corporation Cash Flow Statement For the Year Ended December 31, 19x2		
Sources of Cash		
Operations (see schedule)	$ 47,000	
Sale of Equipment	8,000	
Issuance of Bonds in Exchange for		
Equipment	100,000	
Issuance of Common Stock	100,000	
Total Sources of Cash		$255,000
Uses of Cash		
Purchase of Building	$120,000	
Purchase of Equipment by		
Exchanging Bonds	100,000	
Cash Dividends Paid	10,000	
Total Uses of Cash		230,000
Increase in Cash		$ 25,000

Chapter Review

Review of Learning Objectives

1. Distinguish cash from working capital as a concept of funds.

The analysis of cash as a concept of funds is limited to a study of the cash receipts and cash disbursements during the year. This analysis is useful for evaluating a limited aspect of liquidity (cash flow). However, working capital (current assets minus current liabilities) is a broader concept of funds. Its analysis takes in the operating cycle and the financing and investing activities of the business.

2. Identify the types of transactions that cause changes in working capital.

Transactions affect working capital if they result in a net increase or net decrease in working capital. The types of transactions that have these effects are those in which part of the transaction involves working capital accounts and part does not. Transactions involving only working capital accounts and those involving only noncurrent accounts do not have a net effect on the amount of working capital.

3. Identify common sources and uses of working capital.

Common sources of working capital are operations, sale of noncurrent assets, long-term borrowing, and issuance of common stock. Common uses of working capital are a negative flow from operations, acquisition of noncurrent assets, declaration of cash dividend, purchase or retirement of stock, and retirement or reclassification of long-term debt. Exchange transactions are the exchange of one noncurrent asset or liability for another noncurrent asset or liability. They result in both a source and a use of working capital.

4. Prepare a statement of changes in financial position work sheet.

A work sheet for the preparation of a statement of changes in financial position is useful. It is helpful in analyzing the changes that have occurred in each noncurrent account during the year and translating those changes into their effects (as sources and uses) on working capital. To carry out this step, the transactions involving noncurrent accounts are reconstructed. The working capital portion of those accounts is identified as a source or use of working capital. The difference between the total debits and credits of this transaction analysis should be equal to the change in working capital.

5. Prepare a statement of changes in financial position including changes in components of working capital.

The statement of changes in financial position is prepared from the information contained in the work sheet. The sources of working capital section should show working capital provided from operations separately from other sources. The other sources should be listed individually. The uses of working capital should also be listed separately. The change in working capital at the bottom of the statement should match the figure on an accompanying schedule of changes in working capital items. At the bottom of the statement, the change in each working capital item is listed with its effect on working capital.

6. Prepare a cash flow statement.

Preparation of a cash flow statement requires that cash flow from operations be determined and that other cash transactions be identified. The cash flow statement explains the change in the balance of cash from the beginning to the end of the year by showing the sources and uses of cash during the year.

Review Problem
Statement of Changes in Financial Position

The Double T Company's comparative balance sheet for the years 19x6 and 19x7 is shown on the following page.

The following additional information was taken from the company's general ledger:

a. Income from operations was $166,400.
b. Depreciation for the buildings and equipment was $12,000 and $5,300, respectively.
c. Amortization on intangible assets totaled $4,800 for 19x7.
d. Fully depreciated equipment that cost $7,500 was discarded.
e. Because of an opportunity to reinvest assets at a greater return, $50,000 of the long-term investment was sold at its book value.
f. Five acres of land were purchased for $25,000 to build a new parking lot.
g. The company reclassified $20,000 of bonds payable as current liabilities.
h. The preferred stock was converted to common stock, and the preferred stockholders received 10 shares of common stock for each share of preferred stock.

Required

1. Prepare a work sheet for the Double T Company's statement of changes in financial position.
2. From the work sheet and comparative balance sheet, prepare the statement of changes in financial position, including changes in the components of working capital.

Double T Company
Comparative Balance Sheet
December 31, 19x7, and December 31, 19x6

	19x7	19x6
Assets		
Cash	$ 173,650	$ 127,650
Short-Term Investments	25,000	25,000
Accounts Receivable (net)	296,000	314,500
Inventory	297,000	276,000
Long-Term Investments	36,000	86,000
Land	150,000	125,000
Building	462,000	462,000
Accumulated Depreciation, Building	(91,000)	(79,000)
Equipment	159,730	167,230
Accumulated Depreciation, Equipment	(43,400)	(45,600)
Intangible Assets	19,200	24,000
Total Assets	$1,484,180	$1,482,780
Liabilities and Stockholders' Equity		
Accounts Payable	$ 133,750	$ 233,750
Notes Payable (current)	75,700	145,700
Bonds Payable (current portion)	20,000	—
Accrued Liabilities	5,000	—
Bonds Payable	190,000	210,000
Mortgage Payable	350,000	350,000
Preferred Stock—$100 par value	—	100,000
Common Stock—$10 par value	400,000	300,000
Paid-in Capital in Excess of Par Value	50,000	50,000
Retained Earnings	259,730	93,330
Total Liabilities and Stockholders' Equity	$1,484,180	$1,482,780

Answer to Review Problem

Double T Company
Statement of Changes in Financial Position Work Sheet
For the Year Ended December 31, 19x7

Description	Account Balances, 12/31/x6	Analysis of Transactions for 19x7		Account Balances, 12/31/x7
		Debit	Credit	
Debits				
Working Capital	363,700	(i) 193,500		557,200
Long-Term Investments	86,000		(e) 50,000	36,000
Land	125,000	(f) 25,000		150,000
Building	462,000			462,000
Equipment	167,230		(d) 7,500	159,730
Intangible Assets	24,000		(c) 4,800	19,200
Total Debits	1,227,930			1,384,130
Credits				
Accumulated Depreciation, Building	79,000		(b) 12,000	91,000
Accumulated Depreciation, Equipment	45,600	(d) 7,500	(b) 5,300	43,400
Bonds Payable	210,000	(g) 20,000		190,000
Mortgage Payable	350,000			350,000
Preferred Stock	100,000	(h) 100,000		-0-
Common Stock	300,000		(h) 100,000	400,000
Paid-in Capital in Excess of Par Value	50,000			50,000
Retained Earnings	93,330		(a) 166,400	259,730
Total Credits	1,227,930	346,000	346,000	1,384,130
Sources of Working Capital				
Operations				
Net Income		(a) 166,400		
Depreciation Expense		(b) 17,300		
Amortization of Intangible Assets		(c) 4,800		
Other Sources				
Sale of Investment		(e) 50,000		
Issuance of Common Stock		(h) 100,000		
Uses of Working Capital				
Purchase of Land			(f) 25,000	
Reclassification of Bonds Payable			(g) 20,000	
Conversion of Preferred Stock to Common Stock			(h) 100,000	
Total Sources and Uses of Working Capital		338,500	145,000	
Increase in Working Capital, 19x7			(i) 193,500	
Totals		338,500	338,500	

Double T Company
Statement of Changes in Financial Position
For the Year Ended December 31, 19x7

Sources of Working Capital

Operations

Net Income		$166,400	
Add Expenses Not Requiring Working Capital			
Depreciation	$17,300		
Amortization of Intangible Assets	4,800	22,100	
Working Capital Provided from Operations			$188,500
Other Sources of Working Capital			
Sale of Investments		$ 50,000	
Issuance of Common Stock		100,000	150,000
Total Sources of Working Capital			$338,500

Uses of Working Capital

Purchase of Land		$ 25,000	
Reclassification of Bonds Payable		20,000	
Conversion of Preferred Stock to Common Stock		100,000	
Total Uses of Working Capital			145,000
Increase in Working Capital			$193,500

Changes in Components of Working Capital

Increase (Decrease) in Current Assets			
Cash		$ 46,000	
Short-Term Investments		0	
Accounts Receivable		(18,500)	
Inventory		21,000	$ 48,500
Decrease (Increase) in Current Liabilities			
Accounts Payable		$100,000	
Notes Payable		70,000	
Bonds Payable (Current Portion)		(20,000)	
Accrued Liabilities		(5,000)	145,000
Increase (Decrease) in Working Capital			$193,500

Chapter Assignments

Questions

1. What are the two concepts of funds that might be applied to the statement of changes in financial position? Which is preferable and why?

2. What is the objective of the statement of changes in financial position?

3. When should a statement of changes in financial position be presented as a major financial statement?

4. What is working capital, and what types of transactions do and do not affect the amount of working capital?

5. What are four or more sources of working capital?

6. What are four or more uses of working capital?

7. Why does the payment of accounts payable from cash not decrease working capital?

8. The Green-Ball Company had a net loss of $25,000 during 19xx, but working capital provided by operations was $5,000. What are some possible conditions that may have caused this situation?

9. What impact does write-off of an uncollectible account against an allowance account have on working capital?

10. Would the following items increase, decrease, or have no effect on working capital: (a) declaration of a cash dividend, (b) declaration of a stock dividend, (c) payment of an account payable with cash, (d) collection of an account receivable in cash?

11. What is an exchange transaction, and what is its impact on the statement of changes in financial position?

12. When a statement of changes in financial position that discloses working capital is prepared, are there any additional disclosure requirements?

13. The Stone Manufacturing Company reclassified $20,000 of its twenty-year, 6 percent bonds as current liabilities. What is the impact of the reclassification on the working capital of the company?

14. In preparing a cash flow statement, why must net income from operations be adjusted for changes in appropriate working capital accounts?

Classroom Exercises

**Exercise 19-1
Schedule of
Changes in
Working
Capital
(L.O. 5)**

From the comparative balance sheet of the Ferguson Corporation, prepare a schedule of changes in working capital similar to Figure 19-9 for the year ended December 31, 19x3.

**Ferguson Corporation
Comparative Balance Sheet
December 31, 19x3, and December 31, 19x2**

	19x3	19x2
Assets		
Cash	$ 10,000	$ 6,000
Accounts Receivable (net)	21,000	24,000
Inventory	42,000	36,000
Equipment	60,000	62,000
Other Assets	1,000	1,500
Total Assets	$134,000	$129,500

Liabilities and Stockholders' Equity

Accounts Payable	$ 22,000	$ 17,000
Notes Payable (60 days)	5,000	10,000
Bonds Payable	50,000	50,000
Common Stock	50,000	50,000
Retained Earnings	7,000	2,500
Total Liabilities and Stockholders' Equity	$134,000	$129,500

Exercise 19-2
Effect of
Transactions
on Working
Capital
(L.O. 2)

Analyze the following transactions, and indicate with an X in the appropriate column whether they resulted in a source of funds, a use of funds, or no impact on funds. The concept of funds to use is that of all financial resources.

		Effect on Working Capital		
	Transaction	Source	Use	Neither
a.	Sold $5,000 of merchandise above cost.			
b.	Collected $2,000 of accounts receivable.			
c.	Paid $4,000 of accounts payable.			
d.	Declared a $10,000 cash dividend.			
e.	Issued $100,000 par value common stock to retire at face value $100,000 of the company's long-term bonds.			

Exercise 19-3
Working
Capital
Provided by
Operations
(L.O. 2, 5)

The Merritt Corporation reported net income for the year ended December 31 as $120,000. At the end of the year, the following adjusting entries were made: (a) recorded depreciation expense, $15,600; (b) accrued interest on notes receivable, $750; (c) accrued interest on bonds payable, $2,000; (d) recorded uncollectible accounts expense, $2,000; (e) amortized prepaid insurance, $400; (f) amortized goodwill, $1,000.

Using the information presented above, determine the increase or decrease in working capital from operations during the year.

Exercise 19-4
Statement of
Changes in
Financial
Position
(L.O. 5)

A comparative balance sheet for the Hodges Corporation on September 30, 19x1 and 19x2, appears on the next page.

	19x2	19x1
Assets		
Cash	$ 45,500	$ 12,500
Accounts Receivable (net)	21,000	26,000
Inventory	46,000	51,000
Furniture	65,000	60,000
Accumulated Depreciation, Furniture	(9,000)	(5,000)
Total Assets	$168,500	$144,500
Liabilities and Stockholders' Equity		
Accounts Payable	$ 13,000	$ 14,000
Notes Payable (5 years)	30,000	30,000
Common Stock—$5 par value	95,000	90,000
Retained Earnings	30,500	10,500
Total Liabilities and Stockholders' Equity	$168,500	$144,500

Additional information: (a) issued $5,000 of stock at par value for furniture; (b) depreciation on the furniture during the year, $4,000; (c) cash dividends declared and paid, $10,000; (d) net income, $30,000.

Without using a work sheet, prepare a statement of changes in financial position including changes in the components of working capital.

Exercise 19-5
Cash Flow
Statement
(L.O. 6)

The condensed income statement for Hodges Corporation for the year ended September 30, 19x2, appears below.

Sales	$125,000
Cost of Goods Sold	80,000
Gross Margin on Sales	$ 45,000
Operating Expenses	15,000
Net Income	$ 30,000

Using the information above and in Exercise 19-4, and without using a work sheet, (1) compute cash flow from operations, and (2) prepare a cash flow statement.

Exercise 19-6
Conversion to
Cash Basis
Income
Statement
(L.O. 6)

The income statement for the Riley Corporation is on the next page.

Additional information: (a) All sales were on credit, and accounts receivable increased by $2,200 during the year. (b) All merchandise purchased was on credit. Inventories remained unchanged, and accounts payable increased by $7,000 during the year. (c) Accrued salaries increased by $500 during the year.

Compute cash flow from operations.

Riley Corporation
Income Statement
For the Year Ended June 30, 19xx

Sales		$50,000
Cost of Goods Sold		30,000
Gross Margin		$20,000
Other Expenses		
Salaries Expense	$16,000	
Depreciation Expense	1,000	17,000
Net Income		$ 3,000

Interpreting Accounting Information

**Published
Financial
Information:
Federal Express**
(L.O. 2)

Federal Express Corporation has become one of the fastest-growing companies in the United States. Using its integrated air-ground transportation system, it offers door-to-door delivery of packages and documents throughout the country overnight. From 1979 to 1981 its total assets almost doubled to $570 million dollars. About 65 percent of its total assets are plant and equipment, including airplanes, trucks, and ground services and handling facilities. Such expansion requires funds. Management's discussion and analysis of financial conditions and operations in the company's 1981 annual report address this need as follows:

The Company's ability to generate sufficient funds to meet its liquidity and capital expenditure requirements has increased significantly over the last three years, principally due to strong growth in profitable operations, three offerings of equity securities and several long-term borrowing arrangements. . . . Capital expenditures of $65.6 million in 1979, $176.0 million in 1980 and $171.1 million in 1981, principally related to the company's investment in DC-10 and 727 aircraft and related flight equipment, have been financed from the proceeds of loan agreements, equity offerings in 1980 and 1981 and internally generated funds.

On the next page is a part of Federal Express's statements of changes in financial position for the years ending May 31, 1979, 1980, and 1981 (amounts are in thousands of dollars).

Required

1. Verify management's assertion by showing that the sources mentioned in the report provide enough funds to finance capital expenditures for the three years.
2. Under "Funds Used for," there are three items related to preferred stock. Explain the transactions that would cause each of these items to be so placed. Also note than an item identical to one of them appears under "Funds Provided by." What kind of a transaction is it, and why does it appear in both places?

	1981	1980	1979
Funds Provided by:			
Net income	$ 59,340	$ 38,730	$ 21,423
Charges to income not requiring working capital:			
Depreciation and amortization	39,010	22,012	12,507
Deferred income taxes	7,412	7,176	2,807
Other	728	441	499
Working capital provided from operations	$106,490	$ 68,359	$ 37,236
Increase in long-term debt	86,125	206,813	58,724
Conversion of preferred stock into common stock	1,499	682	—
Proceeds from issuance of common stock	43,669	56,620	17,713
Disposition of property and equipment	36,538	92	1,067
Decrease in other assets	1,508	—	—
Total funds provided	$275,829	$332,566	$114,740
Funds Used for:			
Acquisition of property and equipment	171,096	175,962	65,605
Payment of dividends on preferred stock	1,284	1,343	942
Mandatory redemption of preferred stock	1,538	1,531	—
Conversion of preferred stock into common stock	1,499	682	—
Reduction of long-term debt	65,885	110,077	43,819
Increase in construction funds in escrow	162	19,568	—
Increase in other assets	—	5,632	3,095
Total funds used	$241,464	$314,795	$113,461
Increase in Working Capital	$ 34,365	$ 17,771	$ 1,279

3. Under "Funds Provided by," why are deferred income taxes treated in the same way as depreciation and amortization? (Hint: You may want to refer to Chapter 18 to refresh your memory about why deferred income taxes arise.)

Problem Set A

**Problem 19A-1
Effect of
Transactions
on Working
Capital**
(L.O. 2)

In the schedule on the next page, analyze the transactions presented and place an X in the appropriate column to identify the transaction as increasing, decreasing, or having no effect on working capital. Exchange transactions should be treated as affecting working capital.

Transaction	Effect on Working Capital		
	Increase	Decrease	No Effect
a. Recorded net income.			
b. Declared cash dividend.			
c. Issued stock for cash.			
d. Retired long-term debt by issuing stock.			
e. Paid accounts payable.			
f. Purchased inventory on credit.			
g. Purchased a one-year insurance policy.			
h. Purchased a long-term investment for cash.			
i. Sold marketable securities (at cost).			
j. Sold a machine for its book value (no gain or loss).			
k. Retired fully depreciated equipment.			

**Problem 19A-2
Working
Capital and
Cash Flow
from Operations**
(L.O. 5, 6)

The income statement for the Reece Hospital Supply Corporation is shown below.

**Reece Hospital Supply Corporation
Income Statement
For the Year Ended December 31, 19xx**

Sales		$500,000
Cost of Goods Sold		
Beginning Inventory	$220,000	
Purchases (net)	400,000	
Goods Available for Sale	$620,000	
Ending Inventory	250,000	
Cost of Goods Sold		370,000
Gross Margin on Sales		$130,000
Selling and Administrative Expenses		
Selling and Administrative Salaries Expense	$ 50,000	
Other Selling and Administrative Expenses	11,500	
Depreciation Expense	15,000	
Amortization Expense (Intangible Assets)	1,500	78,000
Net Income from Operations		$ 52,000

Additional information: (a) Accounts receivable (net) increased by $18,000, and accounts payable decreased by $26,000 during the year. (b) Accrued salaries payable at the end of the year were $7,000 more than last year. (c) The expired amount of prepaid insurance for the year is $500 and equals the decrease in the Prepaid Insurance account.

Required

1. Determine the working capital from operations for the Reece Hospital Supply Corporation for the year.
2. Determine the cash flow from operations for the Reece Hospital Supply Corporation for the year.

Problem 19A-3
Statement of Changes in Financial Position
(L.O. 4, 5)

The comparative balance sheet for the Winslow Company as of June 30, 19x1 and 19x2, is presented below.

Additional information concerning the company and transactions involving the noncurrent accounts that bear on preparing a statement of changes in financial position are as follows: (a) Net loss for the year was $35,500. (b) Depreciation expense recorded on the income statement was $10,000. (c) A fully depreciated fixture with an original cost of $1,000 was retired in August. (d) Bonds payable in the amount of $50,000 were exchanged for 2,000 shares of common stock.

	19x2	19x1
Assets		
Cash	$ 25,000	$ 25,000
Accounts Receivable (net)	105,000	100,000
Merchandise Inventory	175,000	225,000
Prepaid Rent	1,000	1,500
Furniture and Fixtures	71,000	72,000
Accumulated Depreciation, Furniture and Fixtures	(21,000)	(12,000)
Total Assets	$356,000	$411,500
Liabilities and Stockholders' Equity		
Accounts Payable	$ 92,400	$112,400
Bonds Payable	50,000	100,000
Common Stock—$10 par value	120,000	100,000
Paid-in Capital in Excess of Par Value	90,720	60,720
Retained Earnings	2,880	38,380
Total Liabilities and Stockholders' Equity	$356,000	$411,500

Required

1. From the information above, prepare a work sheet and the information for a statement of changes in financial position that discloses working capital changes. Exchange transactions are to be disclosed in the statement of changes in financial position.
2. Prepare a statement of changes in financial position including changes in the components of working capital.

Problem 19A-4
Statement of
Changes in
Financial
Position
(L.O. 4, 5)

Montoya Corporation had a net income of $12,700 during July, but working capital declined by $255,300. The owner, George Montoya, realizes the company has engaged in a number of important transactions during July but is worried about the large decrease in working capital. He has asked you to prepare a statement summarizing the monthly transactions in such a way as to explain why working capital decreased by so much. George gives you the balance sheet as of June 30, 19xx. The balance sheet for July 31, 19xx, is not available.

Montoya Corporation
Balance Sheet
June 30, 19xx

Assets

Cash	$ 147,000
Accounts Receivable	416,000
Inventory	587,000
Prepaid Assets	62,000
Long-Term Investments	150,000
Equipment	900,000
Accumulated Depreciation	(272,000)
Trademarks	180,000
Total Assets	$2,170,000

Liabilities and Stockholders' Equity

Accounts Payable	$ 217,000
Notes Payable (less than one year)	400,000
Notes Payable (due in five years)	500,000
Common Stock	200,000
Paid-in Capital in Excess of Par Value, Common	220,000
Retained Earnings	633,000
Total Liabilities and Stockholders' Equity	$2,170,000

In addition, George provides the following information from July's records: (a) net income for the month, $12,700; (b) depreciation on equipment, $9,000; (c) amortization of trademark, $3,000; (d) sale of long-term investment at carrying value, $50,000; (e) purchase of a 25 percent interest in another company as a long-term investment, $250,000; (f) purchase of equipment by issuing long-term notes, $200,000; (g) purchase of treasury stock, $75,000; (h) declaration and payment of cash dividend, $5,000.

Required

1. Prepare a work sheet for a statement of changes in financial position that explains the change in working capital. Exchange transactions should be disclosed on the statement of changes in financial position. (Hint: The July 31 account balances can be compiled when the transactions have been placed properly on the work sheet.)
2. From the work sheet, prepare a statement of changes in financial position. Exclude changes in the components of working capital.

**Problem 19A-5
Comprehensive
Statement of
Changes in
Financial
Position**
(L.O. 4, 5)

A comparative balance sheet for the Sharpe Corporation as of June 30, 19x1 and 19x2, is presented below.

The following information was developed by analyzing the company's operations and noncurrent accounts: (a) net loss for the year, $19,000; (b) depreciation expense for buildings and equipment, $15,000 and $3,000, respectively; (c) fully depreciated equipment with a carrying value of $2,000 was discarded and written off the records; (d) equipment purchases, $1,000; (e) amortization of patent, $2,000; (f) a building was purchased in September for $162,000; cash was paid in the amount of $12,000, and the remainder was paid by issuing a ten-year mortgage note; (g) the company issued 3,000 shares of $10 par value common stock for $50,000 cash; (h) a cash dividend of $18,000 was declared and paid in January.

Required

1. Prepare a work sheet for the statement of changes in financial position that explains the changes in working capital. Exchange transactions should be disclosed on the statement of changes in financial position.
2. Prepare a statement of changes in financial position including the changes in the individual working capital items.

	19x2	19x1
Assets		
Cash	$ 37,060	$ 27,360
Accounts Receivable (net)	102,430	75,430
Inventory	112,890	137,890
Prepaid Assets	—	20,000
Building	162,000	—
Accumulated Depreciation, Building	(15,000)	—
Equipment	33,000	34,000
Accumulated Depreciation, Equipment	(25,000)	(24,000)
Patent	4,000	6,000
Total Assets	$411,380	$276,680
Liabilities and Stockholders' Equity		
Accounts Payable	$ 30,750	$ 56,750
Notes Payable	10,000	—
Accrued Liabilities (current)	—	12,300
Mortgage Payable	150,000	—
Common Stock	180,000	150,000
Paid-in Capital in Excess of Par Value	57,200	37,200
Retained Earnings	(16,570)	20,430
Total Liabilities and Stockholders' Equity	$411,380	$276,680

**Problem 19A-6
Cash Flow
Statement**
(L.O. 6)

In addition to the comparative balance sheet and other information presented for Sharpe Corporation in Problem 19A-5, Sharpe's condensed income statement for the year ended June 30, 19x2, is as follows:

Sales		$259,000
Cost of Goods Sold		140,000
Gross Margin on Sales		$119,000
Operating Expenses		
Selling and Administrative Expenses	$118,000	
Depreciation Expense	18,000	
Patent Amortization	2,000	
Total Operating Expenses		138,000
Net Loss from Operations		($ 19,000)

Required

1. Compute cash flow from operations. (The balance sheets for Sharpe are in Problem 19A-5.)

2. Prepare a cash flow statement for Sharpe.

Problem Set B

**Problem 19B-1
Effects of
Transactions
on Working
Capital**
(L.O. 2)

In the schedule below, analyze the transactions presented, and place an X in the appropriate column to identify the transaction as increasing, decreasing, or having no effect on total working capital. Exchange transactions are to be treated as affecting working capital.

Transactions	Effect on Working Capital		
	Increase	Decrease	No Effect
a. Incurred a net loss.			
b. Declared a stock dividend.			
c. Paid a cash dividend previously declared.			
d. Collected accounts receivable.			
e. Purchased inventory for cash.			
f. Retired long-term debt for cash.			
g. Reclassified current portion of long-term debt as a current liability.			
h. Issued stock for equipment.			
i. Purchased a one-year insurance policy for cash.			
j. Purchased treasury stock for cash.			
k. Retired a fully depreciated truck (no gain or loss).			

Problem 19B-2
Working
Capital and
Cash Flow
from Opera-
tions
(L.O. 5, 6)

The income statement of Lopez Record Company is as follows:

Lopez Record Company Income Statement For the Year Ended June 30, 19xx		
Sales		$1,200,000
Cost of Goods Sold		
Beginning Inventory	$ 310,000	
Purchases (net)	760,000	
Goods Available for Sale	$1,070,000	
Ending Inventory	350,000	
Cost of Goods Sold		720,000
Gross Margin on Sales		$ 480,000
Operating Expenses		
Selling and Administrative Salaries Expense	$ 278,000	
Other Selling and Administrative Expenses	156,000	
Total Operating Expenses		434,000
Net Income from Operations		$ 46,000

Additional information: (a) Other selling and administrative expenses include depreciation expense of $26,000, amortization expense of $9,000. (b) At the end of the year, accrued liabilities for salaries were $6,000 less than the previous year, and prepaid expenses were $10,000 more than last year. (c) During the year, accounts receivable (net) increased by $72,000, and accounts payable increased by $57,000.

Required

1. Determine the working capital provided from operations for the Lopez Record Company for the year ended June 30, 19xx.
2. Determine the cash flow from operations for the Lopez Record Company for the year ended June 30, 19xx.

Problem 19B-3
Statement of
Changes in
Financial
Position
(L.O. 4, 5)

The comparative balance sheet of the Buchanon Corporation as of September 30, 19x6 and 19x7, is shown at the top of the next page.
Additional information concerning the company and transactions involving the noncurrent accounts that bear on preparing a statement of changes in financial position are as follows: (a) Net income for the year was $59,800. (b) Depreciation expense recorded on the income statement was $30,000. (c) Plant was increased in July by $50,000, and the mortgage was increased by the same amount. (d) The company paid $10,000 on the mortgage in September. (e) The notes payable were paid off, but the company borrowed an additional $15,000 under the same conditions in November. (f) A $30,000 dividend was declared and paid in November.

	19x7	19x6
Assets		
Cash	$ 80,000	$ 10,000
Accounts Receivable (net)	50,000	60,000
Finished Goods Inventory	90,000	110,000
Prepaid Insurance	300	500
Property, Plant, and Equipment	326,000	276,000
Accumulated Depreciation, Property, Plant, and Equipment	(100,000)	(70,000)
Total Assets	$446,300	$386,500
Liabilities and Stockholders' Equity		
Accounts Payable	$ 45,000	$ 30,000
Notes Payable (due in 90 days)	15,000	40,000
Mortgage Payable	180,000	140,000
Common Stock—$5 par value	100,000	100,000
Retained Earnings	106,300	76,500
Total Liabilities and Stockholders' Equity	$446,300	$386,500

Required

1. From the information given, prepare a work sheet and the information for a statement of changes in financial position that discloses working capital changes. Exchange transactions are to be disclosed in the statement of changes in financial position.

2. Prepare a statement of changes in financial position and a schedule showing the changes in the individual working capital items.

**Problem 19B-4
Statement of
Changes in
Financial
Position**
(L.O. 4, 5)

Suppose that the balance sheet account balances for only the year ended December 31, 19x2 (see next page), were given to you by Theresa Perry of Perry Enterprises.

The following transactions and other information relate to the month of January, 19x3: (a) Net income for the month was $1,200. (b) Depreciation amounts on the building and on furniture and fixtures were $1,000 and $600, respectively. One month's amortization of patent was also recorded in the amount of $100. (c) Issued $10,000 of bonds in exchange for new furniture. (d) Purchased a patent for $7,000. (e) Issued $20,000 of stock at par value for cash. (f) Additional long-term investments were purchased for $17,000. Payment is due to a broker and must be paid in five days.

	As of Dec. 31, 19x2
Assets	
Cash	$ 16,350
Accounts Receivable (net)	35,260
Merchandise Inventory	82,300
Prepaid Assets	2,500
Long-Term Investments	35,000
Building	78,000
Accumulated Depreciation, Building	(15,000)
Furniture and Fixtures	22,000
Accumulated Depreciation, Furniture and Fixtures	(4,000)
Total Assets	$252,410
Liabilities and Stockholders' Equity	
Accounts Payable	$ 35,420
Payable to Broker	17,000
Bonds Payable	80,000
Common Stock	100,000
Retained Earnings	19,990
Total Liabilities and Stockholders' Equity	$252,410

Required

1. Prepare a work sheet for a statement of changes in financial position that explains the change in working capital. Exchange transactions should be disclosed on the statement of changes in financial position. (Hint: The January 31 account balances can be computed when the transactions have been placed properly on the work sheet.)
2. From the work sheet, prepare a statement of changes in financial position. Exclude changes in the components of working capital.

Problem 19B-5 Comprehensive Statement of Changes in Financial Position (L.O. 4, 5)

The comparative balance sheet for the Harrington Paint Company for the years ending December 31, 19x2 and 19x3, is presented on the next page.

Additional information available concerning operations and transactions in the noncurrent accounts is as follows: (a) Net income for the year was $24,000. (b) Building and equipment depreciation expense amounts were $20,000 and $15,000, respectively. (c) Intangible assets were written off against net income in the amount of $5,000. (d) The company issued $60,000 of long-term bonds payable at par value. (e) In an exchange transaction, an additional building was purchased for $70,000 by increasing the mortgage payable by the same amount. (f) A cash dividend of $9,000 was declared and paid during the year.

	19x3	19x2
Assets		
Cash	$ 79,400	$ 76,400
Accounts Receivable (net)	184,700	189,700
Inventory	240,000	200,000
Prepaid Assets	3,700	6,700
Long-Term Investments	110,000	110,000
Land	80,300	80,300
Building	300,000	230,000
Accumulated Depreciation, Building	(60,000)	(40,000)
Equipment	120,000	120,000
Accumulated Depreciation, Equipment	(29,000)	(14,000)
Intangible Assets	5,000	10,000
Total Assets	$1,034,100	$969,100
Liabilities and Stockholders' Equity		
Accounts Payable	$ 117,700	$165,200
Notes Payable (current)	10,000	40,000
Accrued Liabilities	2,700	5,200
Mortgage Payable	270,000	200,000
Bonds Payable	250,000	190,000
Common Stock	300,000	300,000
Paid-in Capital in Excess of Par Value	20,000	20,000
Retained Earnings	63,700	48,700
Total Liabilities and Stockholders' Equity	$1,034,100	$969,100

Required

1. Prepare a work sheet to gather the information for preparing a statement of changes in financial position that discloses working capital.
2. From the work sheet, prepare the statement of changes in financial position and the accompanying schedule of changes in working capital.

Problem 19B-6
Cash Flow
Statement
(L.O. 6)

The condensed income statement for the Harrington Paint Company for the year ending December 31, 19x3, is presented at the top of the next page.
   Additional information related to Harrington is presented in Problem 19B-5.

Required

1. Compute cash flow from operations. (Balance sheet information is found in Problem 19B-5.)
2. Prepare a cash flow statement for Harrington.

Sales		$876,000
Cost of Goods Sold		502,000
Gross Margin on Sales		$374,000
Operating Expenses		
Selling and Administrative Expenses	$310,000	
Depreciation Expense, Building	20,000	
Depreciation Expense, Equipment	15,000	
Write-off of Intangible Assets	5,000	
Total Operating Expenses		350,000
Net Income from Operations		$ 24,000

Financial Decision Case 19-1

Estes Jewelers, Inc.
(L.O. 6)

William Estes, President of Estes Jewelers, Inc., is examining the statement of changes in financial position presented below, which has just been handed to him by his accountant, Robert Melvoin, CPA.

Estes Jewelers, Inc.
Statement of Changes in Financial Position
For the Year Ended December 31, 19x2

Sources of Working Capital		
Operations		
Net Income		$ 50,000
Add Expenses Not Requiring Outlay of Working Capital in the Current Period		
Depreciation		10,000
Working Capital Provided By Operations		$ 60,000
Other Sources of Working Capital		
Issuance of Mortgage Payable		180,000
Total Sources of Working Capital		$240,000
Uses of Working Capital		
Purchase of Building	$200,000	
Cash Dividend	24,000	
Total Uses of Working Capital		224,000
Increase in Working Capital		$ 16,000

After looking at the statement, Mr. Estes says to Mr. Melvoin, "Bob, this statement seems to be well done, but I already know that I purchased a building last year. What I need to know is why I don't have enough cash to pay my bills this month. According to this statement, shouldn't I have an additional $16,000?" Mr. Melvoin replies, "To answer your question, Bill, we have to look at the comparative balance sheets and prepare another type of statement. Here, take a look at these balance sheets." The statements handed to Mr. Estes are as follows:

Estes Jewelers, Inc.
Balance Sheet
December 31, 19x1 and 19x2

	19x2	19x1
Assets		
Cash	$ 2,000	$ 20,000
Accounts Receivable (net)	94,000	80,000
Inventory	120,000	90,000
Building	200,000	—
Accumulated Depreciation	(10,000)	—
Total Assets	$406,000	$190,000
Liabilities and Stockholders' Equity		
Accounts Payable	$ 60,000	$ 50,000
Mortgage Payable	180,000	—
Common Stock	100,000	100,000
Retained Earnings	66,000	40,000
Total Liabilities and Stockholders' Equity	$406,000	$190,000

Required

1. To what other type of statement is Mr. Melvoin referring? From the information given, prepare the additional statement.

2. Explain why Mr. Estes has a cash problem in spite of profitable operations and an increase in working capital.

Chapter
Twenty

Intercompany
Investments
and
International
Accounting

Corporations often find it profitable to expand their operations by investing in other companies or by extending their operations to other countries. One purpose of this chapter is to provide an overview of corporate investments in other corporations. Special emphasis is placed on the principles underlying consolidated financial statements. A second purpose of the chapter is to discuss some important problems of international accounting. As a result of studying this chapter, you should be able to meet the learning objectives listed on the left.

When management wants to expand a company's operations, it has several alternatives. The simplest method of expansion is to enlarge the present operation. Examples of this would be installing a new manufacturing process within the existing plant or adding a new section onto a retail store. If the company wants to appeal to new markets in other geographical locations, new branches or factories may be the answer. Leading companies that have expanded throughout the world are called **multinational,** or **transnational, corporations.**

Expansion requires increasing amounts of capital. Most companies begin as sole proprietorships or small partnerships and follow a trend of development similar to that pictured in Figure 20-1. As the business grows and requires more capital, a corporation may be formed. At this early stage of corporate life, the business may be a **closely held corporation**—one whose stock is owned by only a few individuals and whose securities are not publicly traded. If the company continues to grow and more capital is needed, it may wish to become a **publicly held corporation** by appealing to the public at large for capital. Such a corporation is registered with the Securities and Exchange Commission, and its securities are publicly traded. **Going public** involves meeting the SEC's strict requirements for protection of the public against fraud in the sale of the securities. If the company is successful, it may be able to spread throughout the world and become a large multinational corporation.

Figure 20-1
A Possible
Growth Pattern
for a Successful
Business

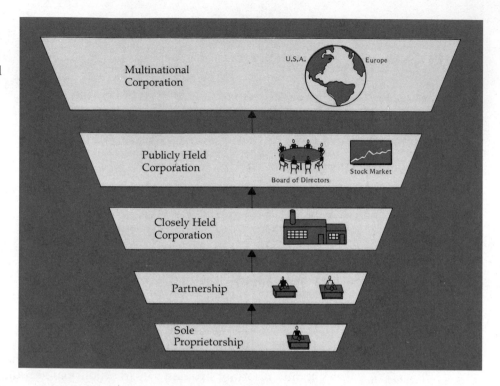

Because a corporation is a legal entity, it has the right to own property and thus may buy the shares of another corporation. In fact, investing in the shares of another corporation's stock is a popular method of expansion. There are many good reasons for expanding by this means. One is that the purchased company may have established customers or operations in an area where the buying company wants to expand. Another is that the purchased company may have access to raw materials needed in the buying company's manufacturing operation. In recent years, for example, some manufacturing companies, utilities, and chemical companies have been purchasing coal and gas companies to assure themselves of a supply of fuel in this age of energy shortages. Still another reason is that a company may need less capital to buy an interest in another company than to start a whole operation independently. In some states and many foreign countries, it is legally easier to buy or invest in a company than to start a new business. Sometimes there are tax advantages to investment in an existing business.

Classification of Long-Term Investments

One corporation may invest in another corporation by purchasing either bonds or stocks. These investments may be either short-term or long-term. In this chapter, we are concerned with long-term investments in stocks.

Objective 1
Apply the
lower-of-cost-or-
market method
and the equity
method to the
appropriate
situations in
accounting for
long-term invest-
ments

All long-term investments in stocks are recorded at cost, in accordance with generally accepted accounting principles. The later treatment of the investment in the accounting records depends on the extent to which the investing company can exercise significant influence or control over the operating and financial policies of the other company.

The Accounting Principles Board defined the important terms *significant influence* and *control* in its *Opinion No. 18.* **Significant influence** is the ability to affect the operating and financial policies of the company whose shares are owned, even though the investor holds less than 50 percent of the voting stock. Ability to influence a company may be shown by representation on the board of directors, participation in policy making, material transactions between the companies, exchange of managerial personnel, and technological dependency. To make accounting practice more uniform, the APB decided that unless there is proof to the contrary, an investment of 20 percent or more of the voting stock should lead to the presumption of significant influence. On the other hand, an investment of less than 20 percent of the voting stock would mean that the investor is not able to exercise significant influence.[1]

Control is defined as the ability of the investing company to decide the operating and financial policies of the other company. Control is said to exist when the investing company owns more than 50 percent of the voting stock of the company in which it has invested.

From the above definitions, it is possible to classify long-term investments in stock as follows: (1) Noninfluential and noncontrolling investment would be less than 20 percent ownership. (2) Influential but noncontrolling investment would be 20 percent to 50 percent ownership. (3) Controlling investment would be over 50 percent ownership. The accounting treatment for each kind of investment is described below.

Noninfluential and Noncontrolling Investment

The **cost method** of accounting for long-term investments applies when less than 20 percent of the voting stock is owned. Under the cost method, the investor records the investment at cost and recognizes income as dividends are received. The Financial Accounting Standards Board states that long-term investments in stock accounted for under the cost method should be valued at the lower of cost or market after acquisition.[2] At the end of each accounting period, the total cost and the total market value of these long-term stock investments must be figured. If the total market

---

1. The Financial Accounting Standards Board points out in its *Interpretation No. 35* (May 1981) that though the presumption of significant influence applies when 20 percent or more of the voting stock is held, the rule is not a rigid one. All relevant facts and circumstances should be judged in each case to find out whether or not significant influence exists. For example, the FASB notes five circumstances that may take away the element of significant influence: (1) The company files a lawsuit against the investor or complains to a government agency. (2) The investor tries and fails to become a director. (3) The investor agrees not to increase its holdings. (4) The company is operated by a small group that ignores the investor's wishes. (5) The investor tries and fails to obtain additional information from the company that is not available to other stockholders.
2. *Statement of Financial Accounting Standards No. 12,* "Accounting for Certain Marketable Securities" (Stamford, Conn.: Financial Accounting Standards Board, 1975).

value is less than the total cost, the difference must be credited to a contra-asset account called Allowance to Reduce Long-Term Investments to Market. The debit is to a contra-owners' equity account called Unrealized Loss on Long-Term Investment. If, at some later date, the market is greater than the valuation reported in the earlier period, the Long-Term Investment account is written up to the new market value, but not to more than the acquisition cost of the investments. When long-term investments in stock are sold, the difference between the sales price and what the stock cost is recorded and reported as a realized gain or loss on the income statement. Dividend income from such investments is recorded by a debit to Cash and a credit to Dividend Income in the amount received.

For example, assume the following facts about the long-term stock investments of Coleman Corporation:

June 1, 19x0   Paid cash for the following long-term investments: 10,000 shares Durbin Corporation common stock (representing 2 percent of outstanding stock) at $25 per share; 5,000 shares Kotes Corporation common stock (representing 3 percent of outstanding stock) at $15 per share.

Dec. 31, 19x0   Quoted market prices at year end: Durbin common stock, $21; Kotes common stock, $17.

Apr. 1, 19x1   A change in policy required the sale of 2,000 shares of Durbin Corporation common stock at $23.

July 1, 19x1   Received a cash dividend from Kotes Corporation equal to 20¢ per share.

Dec. 31, 19x1   Quoted market prices at year end: Durbin common stock, $24; Kotes common stock, $13.

Entries to record these transactions are shown below.

Investment

19x0

June 1   Long-Term Investments   325,000
            Cash   325,000
               To record investments in Durbin
               common stock (10,000 shares × $25 =
               $250,000) and Kotes common stock
               (5,000 shares × $15 = $75,000)

Year-end adjustment

19x0

Dec. 31   Unrealized Loss on Long-Term
              Investments   30,000
                 Allowance to Reduce Long-Term
                 Investments to Market   30,000
                    To record reduction of long-term
                    investment portfolio to market,
                    which is less than cost

Company	Shares	Market Prices	Total Market	Total Cost
Durbin	10,000	$21	$210,000	$250,000
Kotes	5,000	17	85,000	75,000
			$295,000	$325,000

Cost exceeds market by: $325,000 − $295,000 = $30,000

Sale

19x1			
Apr. 1	Cash	46,000	
	Loss on Sale of Investment	4,000	
	Long-Term Investments		50,000
	To record sale of 2,000 shares		
	of Durbin		
	2,000 × $23 = $46,000		
	2,000 × $25 = $50,000		

Dividend Received

July 1	Cash	1,000	
	Dividend Income		1,000
	To record receipt of cash		
	dividends from Kotes stocks		
	5,000 × 20¢ = $1,000		

Year-end Adjustment

Dec. 31	Allowance to Reduce Long-Term		
	Investments to Market	12,000	
	Unrealized Loss on Long-Term		
	Investments		12,000
	To record the adjustment in		
	long-term investment so it		
	is reported at lower of cost		
	or market		

The adjustment equals the previous balance ($30,000 from December 31, 19x0, entry) minus the new balance ($18,000), or $12,000. The new balance of $18,000 is the difference at the present time between the total market value and the total cost of all investments as a group. It is figured as follows:

Company	Shares	Market Prices	Total Market	Total Cost
Durbin	8,000	$24	$192,000	$200,000
Kotes	5,000	13	65,000	75,000
			$257,000	$275,000

Cost exceeds market by: $275,000 − $257,000 = $18,000

Influential but Noncontrolling Investment

As pointed out above, ownership of 20 percent or more of its voting stock is considered sufficient to influence the operations of another corporation. When this is the case, the investment in the stock of a controlled company should be accounted for by using the **equity method**. The three main features of this method are as follows:

1. The investor records the original purchase of the stock at cost.

2. The investor records its share of the investee's periodic net income as an increase in the Investment account. The investor must similarly record its share of the investee's periodic loss as a decrease in the Investment account.

3. When the investor receives a cash dividend, the asset account Cash should be increased and the Investment account decreased.

To illustrate the equity method of accounting, we will assume the following facts about an investment by the Vassor Corporation. Vassor Corporation, on January 1 of the current year, acquired 40 percent of the voting common stock of the Block Corporation for $180,000. With this share of ownership, the Vassor Corporation can exert significant influence over the operations of the Block Corporation. During the year, the Block Corporation reports net income of $80,000 and pays cash dividends of $20,000. The entries to record these transactions by the Vassor Corporation are presented below.

Investment

Investment in Block Corporation	180,000	
Cash		180,000
To record investment in Block Corporation common stock		

Recognition of Income

Investment in Block Corporation	32,000	
Income, Block Corporation Investment		32,000
To recognize 40% of income reported by Block Corporation		
40% × $80,000 = $32,000		

Receipt of Cash Dividend

Cash	8,000	
Investment in Block Corporation		8,000
To record cash dividend from Block Corporation		
40% × $20,000 = $8,000		

Controlling Investment

In some cases, an investor who owns less than 50 percent of the voting stock of a company may exercise such a powerful influence that for all

Table 20-1 Accounting Treatments of Long-Term Investments	Level of Ownership	Percentage of Ownership	Accounting Treatment
	Noninfluential and noncontrolling	Less than 20%	Cost method; value investment subsequent to purchase at lower of cost or market.
	Influential but noncontrolling	Between 20% and 50%	Equity method; value investment subsequently at cost plus the investor's share of income (or minus the loss) and minus the dividends received from the other company.
	Controlling	More than 50%	Consolidated financial statements are prepared.

practical purposes the investor "controls" the policies of the other company. Nevertheless, ownership of more than 50 percent of the voting stock is required for accounting recognition. When a controlling interest is owned, a parent and subsidiary relationship is said to exist, and it becomes necessary to consolidate the two financial statements. The investing company is known as the **parent company,** and the other company is the **subsidiary.** Because both corporations are separate legal entities, each prepares separate financial statements. However, owing to their special relationship, they are viewed for public financial reporting purposes as a single economic entity. For this reason, they must combine their financial statements into a single set of statements called **consolidated financial statements.**

Accounting for consolidated financial statements is very complex. It is usually the subject of an advanced-level course in accounting. However, most large public corporations have subsidiaries and must prepare consolidated financial statements. So it is important to have some understanding of accounting for consolidations.

The proper accounting treatments for long-term investment in stock are outlined in Table 20-1.

Consolidated Financial Statements

Objective 2
Explain when to prepare consolidated financial statements and describe their uses

Most major corporations find it convenient for economic, legal, tax, or other reasons to operate in parent-subsidiary relationships. When we speak of a large company such as Ford, RCA, or Texas Instruments, we generally think of the parent company, not of its many subsidiaries. When considering investment in one of these firms, however, the investor wants a clear financial picture of the total economic entity. The main purpose of consolidated financial statements is to give such a view of the parent and subsidiary firms by treating them as if they were one company. On a consolidated balance sheet, the Inventory account includes the inventory held by the parent and all its subsidiaries. Similarly, on the consolidated income statement, the Sales account is the total revenue from sales by the parent and all its subsidiaries. This overview is very useful to management and stockholders of the parent company in judging the company's progress in meeting its goals. Long-term creditors of the parent also find consolidated statements useful because of their interest in the long-range financial health of the whole corporation.

There are certain cases in which consolidated statements are not used. For example, they are not very useful to creditors and stockholders of the subsidiary companies because their interest in the business is limited to the subsidiary itself. Consolidated statements may also not be useful when the operations of the parent and subsidiary are totally different. For instance, a retailing company that owned a bank would usually not consolidate the financial statements even if it owned more than 50 percent of the bank because the two operations are so different. Finally, consolidated statements are sometimes not used when there are certain restrictions on the control of the parent. Subsidiaries in certain foreign countries and subsidiaries that are bankrupt usually would not be consolidated because of such restrictions. The Accounting Principles Board *Opinion No. 18* requires that the equity method described earlier be used in accounting for such unconsolidated subsidiaries.[3]

Methods of Accounting for Consolidations

Interests in subsidiary companies may be acquired by paying cash, exchanging shares of the parent's own unissued capital stock for the outstanding shares of the subsidiary's capital stock, issuing long-term bonds or other debt, or working out some combination of these forms of payment. For parent-subsidiary relationships that arise in these ways, it is mandatory to use the **purchase method,** which is explained below. For simplicity, our illustrations assume payment in cash. In the special case of establishing a parent-subsidiary relationship through an exchange of stock, the pooling of interests method may be appropriate. The pooling of interests method is the subject of more advanced courses.

Consolidated Balance Sheet

In preparing consolidated financial statements, similar accounts from the separate statements of the parent and the subsidiaries are combined. For this reason, it is important that certain **eliminations** be made. These eliminations avoid the duplication of accounts and reflect the financial position and operations from the standpoint of a single entity. Eliminations appear only on the work sheets used in preparing consolidated financial state-

3. Accounting Principles Board, *Opinion No. 18,* "The Equity Method for Accounting for Investment in Common Stock" (New York: Accounting Principles Board, 1971).

ments. They are never shown in the accounting records of either the parent or the subsidiary. There are no consolidated journals or ledgers.

Duplications are certain amounts that appear on both the parent and subsidiary books as a result of intercompany transactions and that, if combined, would result in a kind of double counting. A good example of this sort of duplication is the Investment in Subsidiary account in the parent's balance sheet and the stockholders' equity section of the subsidiary. When the balance sheets of the two companies are combined, these accounts must be eliminated to avoid duplicating these items in the consolidated financial statements.

To illustrate the preparation of a consolidated balance sheet, we will use the following balance sheets for Parent and Subsidiary companies:

Accounts	Parent Company	Subsidiary Company
Cash	$100,000	$25,000
Other Assets	760,000	60,000
Total Assets	$860,000	$85,000
Liabilities	$ 60,000	$10,000
Common Stock—$10 par value	600,000	55,000
Retained Earnings	200,000	20,000
Total Liabilities and Stockholders' Equity	$860,000	$85,000

Objective 3a
Prepare consolidated balance sheets at acquisition date for purchase at book value

100 Percent Purchase at Book Value Suppose that Parent Company purchases 100 percent of Subsidiary Company for an amount exactly equal to the Subsidiary's book value. The book value of Subsidiary Company is $75,000 ($85,000 − $10,000). Parent Company would record the purchase as follows:

Investment in Subsidiary Company	75,000	
Cash		75,000
To record 100 percent purchase of Subsidiary Company at book value		

It is helpful to use a work sheet like the one shown in Figure 20-2 in preparing consolidated financial statements. Note that the balance of Parent Company's Cash account is now $25,000 and that the Investment in Subsidiary Company is shown as an asset in Parent Company's balance sheet, reflecting the purchase of the subsidiary. To prepare a consolidated balance sheet, it is necessary to eliminate the investment in the subsidiary. This procedure is shown by elimination entry 1 in Figure 20-2. This elimination entry does two things. First, it eliminates the double counting that would take place when the net assets of the two companies are combined. Second, it eliminates the stockholders' equity section of the Subsidiary Company. The theory underlying consolidated financial statements is to view the parent and its subsidiary as a single entity. The stockholders' equity section of the consolidated balance sheet is the same

100%

Parent and Subsidiary Companies
Work Sheet for Consolidated Balance Sheet
As of Acquisition Date

Accounts	Balance Sheet Parent Company	Balance Sheet Subsidiary Company	Eliminations		Consolidated Balance Sheet
			Debit	Credit	
Cash	25,000	25,000			50,000
Investment in Subsidiary Company	75,000			(1) 75,000	
Other Assets	760,000	60,000			820,000
Total Assets	860,000	85,000			870,000
Liabilities	60,000	10,000			70,000
Common Stock—$10 par value	600,000	55,000	(1) 55,000		600,000
Retained Earnings	200,000	20,000	(1) 20,000		200,000
Total Liabilities and Stockholders' Equity	860,000	85,000	75,000	75,000	870,000

(1) Elimination of intercompany investment.

Figure 20-2
Work Sheet for Preparation of Consolidated Balance Sheet

as that of the Parent Company. So after eliminating the Investment in Subsidiary Company against the stockholders' equity of the subsidiary, we can take the information from the right-hand column in Figure 20-2 and present it in the following form:

Parent Company
Consolidated Balance Sheet
As of Acquisition Date

Cash	$ 50,000	Liabilities	$ 70,000
Other Assets	820,000	Common Stock	600,000
		Retained Earnings	200,000
		Total Liabilities and	
Total Assets	$870,000	Stockholders' Equity	$870,000

Less than 100 Percent Purchase at Book Value A parent company does not have to purchase 100 percent of a subsidiary to control it. If it purchases more than 50 percent of the voting stock of the subsidiary company, it will have legal control. In the consolidated financial statements, therefore, the total assets and liabilities of the subsidiary are combined with the assets and liabilities of the parent. However, it is still

Parent and Subsidiary Companies
Work Sheet for Consolidated Balance Sheet
As of Acquisition Date

Accounts	Balance Sheet Parent Company	Balance Sheet Subsidiary Company	Eliminations Debit	Eliminations Credit	Consolidated Balance Sheet
Cash	32,500	25,000			57,500
Investment in Subsidiary Company	67,500			(1) 67,500	
Other Assets	760,000	60,000			820,000
Total Assets	860,000	85,000			877,500
Liabilities	60,000	10,000			70,000
Common Stock—$10 par value	600,000	55,000	(1) 55,000		600,000
Retained Earnings	200,000	20,000	(1) 20,000		200,000
Minority Interest				(1) 7,500	7,500
Total Liabilities and Stockholders' Equity	860,000	85,000	75,000	75,000	877,500

(1) Elimination of intercompany investment. Minority interest equals 10 percent of subsidiary's stockholders' equity.

Figure 20-3
Work Sheet
Showing
Elimination of
Less than 100
Percent
Ownership

necessary to account for the interests of those stockholders of the subsidiary company who own less than 50 percent of the voting stock. These are the minority stockholders, and their **minority interest** must appear on the consolidated balance sheet at an amount equal to their percentage of ownership times the net assets of the subsidiary.

Suppose that the above Parent Company buys 90 percent of the Subsidiary Company's voting stock at a book value of $67,500 (90% × $75,000). The work sheet used for preparing the consolidated balance sheet appears in Figure 20-3. The elimination is made in the same way as in the case above except that the minority interest must be accounted for. All of the investment in Subsidiary Company ($67,500) is eliminated against all of Subsidiary's stockholders' equity ($75,000), and the difference ($7,500, or 10% × $75,000) is set as minority interest. There are two ways to classify minority interest on the consolidated balance sheet. One is to place it between long-term liabilities and stockholders' equity. The other is to consider the stockholders' equity section as consisting of (1) minority interest and (2) Parent Company's stockholders' equity:

Minority Interest	$ 7,500
Common Stock	600,000
Retained Earnings	200,000
Total Stockholders' Equity	$807,500

Objective 3b
Prepare consoli-
dated balance
sheets at acqui-
sition date for
purchase at
other than book
value

Purchase at More than or Less than Book Value The purchase price of a business depends on many factors, such as the current market price, the relative strength of the buyer's and seller's bargaining positions, and the prospects for future earnings. Thus it is only by chance that the purchase price of a subsidiary will equal the book value of the subsidiary's equity. Usually, it will not. Accounting for the difference is an important problem. For example, a parent company may pay more than the book value of a subsidiary to purchase a controlling interest if the assets of the subsidiary are understated. The recorded historical cost of the subsidiary's assets may not reflect current market values. The parent may also pay more than book value if the subsidiary has something that the parent wants, such as an important technical process, a new and different product, or a new market. On the other hand, the parent may pay less than book value for its share of the subsidiary's stock if the subsidiary's assets are not worth their original cost. Or the subsidiary may have suffered heavy losses, causing its stock to sell at rather low prices.

The Accounting Principles Board has provided the following guidelines for consolidating a purchased subsidiary and its parent:

First, all identifiable assets acquired . . . and liabilities assumed in a business combination . . . should be assigned a portion of the cost of the acquired company, normally equal to their fair values at date of acquisition.

Second, the excess of the cost of the acquired company over the sum of the amounts assigned to identifiable assets acquired less liabilities assumed should be recorded as goodwill.[4]

To illustrate the application of these principles, we will assume that the Parent Company purchases 100 percent of the Subsidiary Company's voting stock for $92,500, or $17,500 more than book value. Parent Company considered $10,000 of the $17,500 to be due to the increased value of Subsidiary's other assets and $7,500 of the $17,500 to be due to the overall strength that Subsidiary Company would add to Parent Company's organization. The work sheet used for preparing the consolidated balance sheet appears in Figure 20-4 (next page).

All of the Investment in Subsidiary Company ($92,500) has been eliminated against all of the Subsidiary Company's stockholders' equity ($75,000). The excess of cost over book value ($17,500) has been debited in the amounts of $10,000 to Long-Term Assets and $7,500 to a new account called **Goodwill**, or **Goodwill from Consolidation.** Goodwill appears as an asset on the consolidated balance sheet and represents the excess of cost of the investment over book value that cannot be allocated to any specific asset. Long-Term Assets appears on the consolidated balance sheet at the combined total of $830,000 ($760,000 + $60,000 + $10,000).

When the parent pays less than book value for its investment in the subsidiary, Accounting Principles Board *Opinion No. 16*, paragraph 87, requires that the excess of book value over cost of the investment be used to lower the carrying value of the subsidiary's long-term assets. The belief

4. Accounting Principles Board, *Opinion No. 16*, "Business Combinations" (New York: Accounting Principles Board, 1970), p. 318.

Chapter Twenty

Parent and Subsidiary Companies
Work Sheet for Consolidated Balance Sheet
As of Acquisition Date

Accounts	Balance Sheet Parent Company	Balance Sheet Subsidiary Company	Eliminations		Consolidated Balance Sheet
			Debit	Credit	
Cash	7,500	25,000			32,500
Investment in Subsidiary Company	92,500			(1) 92,500	
Long-Term Assets	760,000	60,000	(1) 10,000		830,000
Goodwill			(1) 7,500		7,500
Total Assets	860,000	85,000			870,000
Liabilities	60,000	10,000			70,000
Common Stock—$10 par value	600,000	55,000	(1) 55,000		600,000
Retained Earnings	200,000	20,000	(1) 20,000		200,000
Total Liabilities and Stockholders' Equity	860,000	85,000	92,500	92,500	870,000

(1) Elimination of intercompany investment. Excess of cost over book value ($92,500 — $75,000 — $17,500) allocated $10,000 to Long-Term Assets and $7,500 to Goodwill.

Figure 20-4 Work Sheet Showing Elimination Where Purchase Cost Is Greater than Book Value

here is that the least reliable estimates of market values are those applicable to long-lived assets (other than marketable securities) because a ready market does not normally exist for such assets. In other words, the APB advises against the use of negative goodwill except in very special cases.

Intercompany Receivables and Payables If either the parent or the subsidiary company owes money to the other, there will be a receivable on the creditor company's individual balance sheet and a payable on the debtor company's individual balance sheet. When a consolidated balance sheet is prepared, both the receivable and the payable should be eliminated because, from the viewpoint of the consolidated entity, neither the asset nor the liability exists. In other words, it does not make sense for a company to owe money to itself. The elimination entry would be made on the work sheet by debiting the payable and crediting the receivable for the amount of the intercompany loan.

Consolidated Income Statement

Objective 4 Prepare consolidated income statements for intercompany transactions

The consolidated income statement is prepared for a consolidated entity by combining the revenues and expenses of the parent and subsidiary companies. The procedure is the same as in preparing a consolidated balance sheet. That is, intercompany transactions are eliminated to prevent double counting of revenues and expenses. Several intercompany transactions affect the consolidated income statement. They are (1) sales and purchases of goods and services between parent and subsidiary (purchases for the buying company and sales for the selling company); (2) income and expenses on loans, receivables, or bond indebtedness between parent and subsidiary; and (3) income and expenses from intercompany transactions other than those listed in 1 and 2.

To illustrate the eliminating entries, we will assume the following transactions between a parent and its 100 percent owned subsidiary. Parent Company made sales of $120,000 in goods to Subsidiary Company, which in turn sold all the goods to others. Subsidiary Company paid Parent Company $2,000 interest on a loan from the parent.

The work sheet in Figure 20-5 (top of next page) shows how to prepare a consolidated income statement. The purpose of the eliminating entries is to treat the two companies as a single entity. Thus it is important to include in Sales only those made to outsiders and to include in Cost of Goods Sold only those purchases from outsiders. This goal is met with the first eliminating entry. This entry eliminates the $120,000 of intercompany sales and purchases by a debit of that amount to Sales and a credit of that amount to Cost of Goods Sold in the work sheet. As a result, only sales to outsiders ($510,000) and purchases from outsiders ($240,000) are included in the Consolidated Income Statement column. The intercompany interest income and expense is eliminated by a debit to Other Revenues and a credit to Other Expenses.

Other Consolidated Financial Statements

Public corporations also prepare consolidated statements of retained earnings and consolidated statements of changes in financial position. For examples of these statements, see Chapter 9.

Accounting for Bond Investments

Objective 5
Account for
bond investment
transactions

In Chapter 18, bond transactions and disclosures were discussed from the issuing corporation's viewpoint. Here, similar transactions will be presented from the investor's point of view. Sometimes a company buys a bond as a short-term investment to provide a return on idle cash until it is needed for operations. However, a company may buy a bond as a long-term investment for a number of reasons. For example, it may hold the bonds of a subsidiary or other company on a long-term basis. The company may invest money that it is accumulating over a long period of time for a major expenditure such as purchasing another company or building a factory. The classification and valuation problems related to short-term investments are presented in Chapter 10. Here, the focus is on transactions involving the purchase of the bonds, amortization of premium and discount and recording receipts for interest, and sale of the bonds. In each case, there are small differences in the accounting treatments for the same transactions by the issuer.

Parent and Subsidiary Companies
Work Sheet for Consolidated Income Statement
For the Year 19xx

Accounts	Income Statement Parent Company	Income Statement Subsidiary Company	Eliminations		Consolidated Income Statement
			Debit	Credit	
Sales	430,000	200,000	(1) 120,000		510,000
Other Revenues	60,000	10,000	(2) 2,000		68,000
Total Revenues	490,000	210,000			578,000
Cost of Goods Sold	210,000	150,000		(1) 120,000	240,000
Other Expenses	140,000	50,000		(2) 2,000	188,000
Total Deductions	350,000	200,000			428,000
Net Income	140,000	10,000	122,000	122,000	150,000

(1) Elimination of intercompany sales and purchases.
(2) Elimination of intercompany interest income and interest expense.

Figure 20-5
Work Sheet Showing Eliminations for Preparing a Consolidated Income Statement

Purchase of Bonds Between Interest Dates

The purchase price of bonds includes the price of the bonds plus the broker's commission. Also, when the bonds are purchased between interest dates, the purchaser must pay the interest that has accrued on the bonds since the last interest payment date. On the next payment date, the purchaser will receive a payment for the interest for the whole period. The payment for accrued interest should be recorded as a debit to Bond Interest Income to be offset later by a credit to Bond Interest Income when the semiannual interest is received.

Suppose that on May 1 Vason Corporation purchases twenty $1,000 MGR Corporation bonds that carry a face interest rate of 9 percent at 88 plus a broker's commission of $400 and accrued interest. The interest payment dates are January 1 and July 1. The following entry records this purchase transaction:

May 1	Investment in Bonds	18,000	
	Bond Interest Income	600	
	Cash		18,600

        To record purchase of MGR Corporation bonds at 88 plus $400 commission and accrued interest
$20,000 \times 9\% \times \frac{1}{3} = \$600$

Note that the purchase is recorded at cost, as are all purchases of assets. The debit to Investment in Bonds of $18,000 equals the purchase price of $17,600 ($20,000 × .88) plus the commission of $400. Because, in managing its investments, Vason Corporation will buy and sell as seems necessary and will not likely hold the bonds until maturity, the $20,000 face value of the bonds is not entered in the records. This case is very different from that of the issuing corporation, which must repay the bonds at the maturity date to anyone who holds them.

The debit to Bond Interest Income of $600 represents four months' interest (one-third year) from January 1 to May 1 paid to the seller of the bonds.

Amortization of Premium or Discount

Accounting Principles Board *Opinion No. 21* requires companies making long-term investments in bonds to amortize the difference between the cost of the investment and its maturity value over the life of the bond. The effective interest method, which results in a constant rate of return over the life of the investment, should be used.[5]

Because the investing company does not use separate accounts for the face value and any related discount or premium, the entry to amortize the premium or discount is made directly to the investment account. The amortization of a premium calls for a credit to the investment account to reduce the carrying value gradually to face value. The amortization of a discount calls for a debit to the investment account to increase the carrying value gradually to face value.

Returning to the case of Vason Corporation's purchase of bonds at a discount, we assume that the effective interest rate is $10\frac{1}{2}$ percent. Remember that the amount of amortization of a premium or discount is the difference between (1) the face interest rate times the face value and (2) the effective interest rate times the carrying value. On July 1, the first interest date after the purchase, two months will have passed. The amount of discount to be amortized is as follows:

Two months' effective interest:	
$18,000 × $10\frac{1}{2}$% × $\frac{1}{6}$	$315
Two months' face interest:	
$20,000 × 9% × $\frac{1}{6}$	300
Discount to be amortized	$ 15

The entry to record the receipt of an interest check on July 1 is:

July 1	Cash	900	
	Investment in Bonds	15	
	Bond Interest Income		915
	To record semiannual interest receipt, some of which was previously accrued, and to amortize discount		

5. Accounting Principles Board, *Opinion No. 21*, "Interest on Receivables and Payables" (New York: American Institute of Certified Public Accountants, 1971), par. 15.

In this entry, Cash is debited for the semiannual interest payment ($20,000 × 9% × $\frac{1}{2}$ = $900), Investment in Bonds is debited for the amortization of discount or $15, and Bond Interest Income is credited for the sum of the two debits or $915. Note that the net interest earned is $315, which is the net amount of the $600 debit on May 1 and the $915 credit on July 1 to Bond Interest Income. This amount of $315 is equal to the effective interest computed in the paragraph just above.

To continue the example, assume that Vason Corporation's fiscal year corresponds to the calendar year. Although the interest payment will not be received until January, it is necessary to accrue the interest and amortize the discount for the last six months since July 1 in accordance with the matching concept. The entry to record the accrual of interest on December 31 is as follows:

Dec. 31	Accrued Interest Receivable	$900.00	
	Investment in Bonds	45.79	
	Bond Interest Income		945.79
	To accrue interest earned and amortize discount on bond investment		

The period covered by this entry is six months. Therefore, the amounts to be debited and credited are as shown below.

Six months' effective interest:	
$18,015 × 10$\frac{1}{2}$% × $\frac{1}{2}$	$945.79
Six months' face interest:	
$20,000 × 9% × $\frac{1}{2}$	900.00
Discount to be amortized	$ 45.79

Note that the effective interest rate is applied to the new carrying value of $18,015 after the July 1 entry. The next time that the effective interest is calculated, the effective rate will be applied to $18,060.79 ($18,015 + $45.79).

Similar calculations are made when a company purchases bonds at premium. The difference is that Investment in Bonds is credited to reduce the carrying value. As a result, the interest earned is less than the face interest.

The entry on January 1 to record receipt of the interest payment check is as follows:[6]

Jan. 1	Cash	900	
	Accrued Interest Receivable		900
	To record receipt of interest on bonds		

6. This entry assumes that reversing entries are not made. Some companies may prefer to use reversing entries.

Sale of Bonds

The sale of a bond investment is recorded by debiting Cash for the amount received and crediting Investment in Bonds for the carrying value of the investment. Any difference in the proceeds from the sales and the carrying value of the bonds is debited or credited to loss or gain on sale of investments. If the sale is made between interest payment dates, the seller is entitled to the accrued interest from the last interest date, just as the company had to pay the accrued interest when the bonds were purchased. If we assume that Vason Corporation sells the bonds in our continuing example at 94 less commission of $400 on March 1, two entries are required. The first entry is necessary to amortize the discount for two months:

Mar. 1	Investment in Bonds	16.06	
	Bond Interest Income		16.06

To amortize 2 months' bond discount
Effective interest:
$18,060.79 \times 10\frac{1}{2}\% \times \frac{1}{6} = \$316.06$
Face interest:
$20,000 \times 9\% \times \frac{1}{6}$ =   300.00
Discount to be amortized $ 16.06

The second entry is to record the sale:

Mar. 1	Cash	18,700.00	
	Gain on Sale of Investments		323.15
	Investment in Bonds		18,076.85
	Bond Interest Income		300.00

To record sale of bonds at 94
less $400 commission plus
accrued interest

The cash received is the selling price of $18,800 ($20,000 \times .94) less commission of $400 plus the accrued interest for two months of $300 ($20,000 \times 9\% \times \frac{1}{6}$). The gain on sale of investments is the difference between selling price less commission ($18,400) and the carrying value of $18,076.85. The carrying value represents the assigned purchase plus all amortization of discounts:

May 1 purchase	$18,000.00
July 1 amortization	15.00
Dec. 31 amortization	45.79
Mar. 1 amortization	16.06
Carrying value of bond investment	$18,076.85

Table 20-2
Extent of
Foreign
Business for
Selected
Companies

Company	Country	Total Revenue (Millions)	Foreign Revenue as % of Total
Exxon	U.S.A.	$97,173	71.4
Mitsubishi	Japan	68,721	62.0
General Motors	U.S.A.	60,026	23.9
British Petroleum	Britain	51,353	82.0
International Business Machines (IBM)	U.S.A.	34,364	44.6
Volkswagenwerk	Germany	15,427	54.5
Bank America	U.S.A.	14,955	53.8
Nestlé	Switzerland	13,626	98.2
Procter & Gamble	U.S.A.	11,994	31.2
Xerox	U.S.A.	8,456	42.9

Source: Forbes, July 4, 1983, pp. 114, 118, and 124–125.

International Accounting

As businesses grow, it is natural for them to look for new sources of supply and new markets in other countries. Today, it is common for businesses, called multinational or transnational corporations, to operate in more than one country, and many of them operate throughout the world. Table 20-2 shows the extent of foreign business for a few multinational corporations. IBM, for example, has operations in eighty countries and receives about half of its sales and income from foreign operations. Nestlé, the giant Swiss chocolate and food products company, operates in fifteen countries and receives 98 percent of its sales from foreign operations. The economies of such industrial countries as the United States, Japan, Great Britain, West Germany, and France have given rise to large worldwide corporations. In addition, sophisticated investors no longer restrict their investment activities to their domestic securities markets. Many Americans invest in foreign securities markets, and non-Americans invest heavily in the stock market in the United States.

*Objective 6
Show how
changing
exchange rates
affect financial
reporting*

Such transactions have two major effects on accounting. First, most sales or purchases of goods and services in other countries involve different currencies. For this reason, one currency needs to be translated into another through the use of exchange rates. An exchange rate is the value of one currency in terms of another. For example, an English person who purchases goods from a U.S. company and has to pay in U.S. dollars must exchange the British pounds for U.S. dollars before making payment. In effect, the currencies are goods that can be bought and sold. Table 20-3 illustrates the exchange rates of several currencies in terms of dollars. It shows the exchange rate for British pounds as $1.46 per pound on a particular date. Like the price of any good or service, these prices change daily according to supply and demand for the currencies. For example, a year earlier the exchange rate for British pounds was $2.00.

Table 20-3
Partial Listing
of Foreign
Exchange Rates

Country	Prices in $ U.S.
Britain (pound)	1.49
Canada (dollar)	.81
France (franc)	.12
Italy (lira)	.0006
Japan (yen)	.0041
Mexico (peso)	.007
West Germany (mark)	.37

Source: The Wall Street Journal (Sept. 6, 1983).

Accounting for these price changes in recording foreign transactions and preparing financial statements for foreign subsidiaries is the subject of the next two sections.

The second major effect of international business on accounting is that financial standards are very different from country to country. This fact makes it hard for the international investor to compare performances of companies from different countries. Some of the obstacles to achieving better comparability and some of the progress in solving the problem are discussed later in this chapter.

Accounting for Transactions in Foreign Currencies

Among the first activities of an expanding company in the international market are the buying and selling of goods and services. For example, a maker of precision tools may try to expand by selling its product to foreign customers. Or it might try to lower its product cost by buying a less expensive part from a source in another country. In previous chapters, all transactions were recorded in dollars, and it was assumed that the dollar is a uniform measure in the same way that inches and centimeters are. In the international marketplace, a transaction may take place in Japanese yen, British pounds, or some other currency. The values of these currencies rise and fall daily in their relation to the dollar.

Foreign Sales When a domestic company sells merchandise abroad, it may bill either in its own country's currency or in the foreign currency. If the billing and the subsequent payment are both in the domestic currency, no accounting problem arises. For example, assume that the precision toolmaker sells $150,000 worth of tools to a British company and bills the British company in dollars. The entry to record the sale and payment is very familiar:

Date of sale:

Accounts Receivable, British company	150,000	
Sales		150,000

Date of Payment:

Cash	150,000	
Accounts Receivable, British company		150,000

However, if the U.S. company bills the British company in British pounds and accepts payment in pounds, the U.S. company may incur an exchange gain or loss. An exchange gain or loss will occur if the exchange rate of dollars to pounds changes between the date of sale and the date of payment. For example, assume that the sale of $150,000 above was billed as £100,000, reflecting an exchange rate of 1.50 (that is, $1.50 per pound) on the sale date. Now assume that by the date of payment, the exchange rate had fallen to 1.45. The entries to record the transactions are shown below.

Date of sale:

Accounts Receivable, British company (£100,000)	150,000	
Sales		150,000

Date of payment:

Cash (£100,000 × 1.45)	145,000	
Exchange Gain or Loss	5,000	
Accounts Receivable, British Company		150,000

The U.S. company has incurred an exchange loss of $5,000 because it agreed to accept a fixed number of British pounds in payment, and before the payment was made, the value of each pound went down in value. Had the value of the pound in relation to the dollar increased in value, the U.S. company would have made an exchange gain.

Foreign Purchases Purchases are the opposite of sales. So the same logic applies to them except that the relation of exchange gains and losses to the changes in exchange rates is reversed. For example, assume that the above maker of precision tools purchases $10,000 of a certain part from a Japanese supplier. If the purchase and subsequent payment are made in U.S. dollars, no accounting problem arises.

Date of purchase:

Purchases	10,000	
Accounts Payable, Japanese company		10,000

Date of payment:

Accounts Payable, Japanese company	10,000	
Cash		10,000

However, the Japanese company may bill the U.S. company in yen and be paid in yen. If so, the U.S. company will incur an exchange gain or loss if the exchange rate changes between the dates of purchase and payment. For example, assume that the transaction above is in yen and the exchange rates of the dates of purchase and payment are .0040 (that is, $.0040 per yen) and .0038, respectively. The entries are shown on the next page.

Date of purchase:
Purchases (Y2,500,000 × .004)	10,000	
Accounts Payable, Japanese company		10,000

Date of payment:
Accounts Payable, Japanese company	10,000	
Exchange Gain or Loss		500
Cash (Y2,500,000 × .0038)		9,500

In this case, the U.S. company received an exchange gain of $500 because it had agreed to pay a fixed Y2,500,000 and, between the dates of purchase and payment, the exchange value of the yen in relation to the dollar increased.

Realized Versus Unrealized Exchange Gain or Loss The above illustration dealt with completed transactions (in the sense that payment was completed), and the exchange gain or loss was recognized on the date of payment in each case. If financial statements are prepared between the sale or purchase and the subsequent receipt or payment, there will be unrealized gains or losses if the exchange rates have changed. The Financial Accounting Standards Board, in its *Statement No. 52*, requires that exchanges gains and losses "shall be included in determining net income for the period in which the exchange rate changes,"[7] including interim (quarterly) periods and whether or not the transaction is complete.

This ruling has caused much debate. Critics of the rule charge that it gives too much influence to temporary exchange rate changes, leading to random changes in earnings that hide long-run trends. Those who favor the ruling, on the other hand, feel that the use of current exchange rates on the balance sheet date to value receivables and payables is a major step toward economic reality (current values).

To show these effects, we will assume the following facts about the above case, in which a U.S. company buys parts from a Japanese supplier:

	Date	Exchange Rate ($ per Yen)
Date of purchase	Dec. 1	.0040
Balance sheet date	Dec. 31	.0035
Date of payment	Feb. 1	.0038

The only difference is that the transaction has not been completed by the balance sheet date and the exchange rate was $.0035 per yen on that date. The facts and entries can be shown as follows:

---

7. *Statement of Financial Accounting Standards No. 52*, "Foreign Currency Translation" (Stamford, Conn.: Financial Accounting Standards Board, 1981), par. 15.

Chapter Twenty

	Dec. 1	Dec. 31	Feb. 1
Purchase recorded in U.S. dollars (billed as Y2,500,000)	$10,000	$10,000	$10,000
Dollars to be paid to equal Y2,500,000	10,000	8,750	9,500
Unrealized gain (or loss)	—	$ 1,250	
Realized gain (or loss)			$ 500

Date	Account	Debit	Credit
Dec. 1	Purchases	10,000	
	Accounts Payable, Japanese company		10,000
Dec. 31	Accounts Payable, Japanese company	1,250	
	Exchange Gain or Loss		1,250
Feb. 1	Accounts Payable, Japanese company	8,750	
	Exchange Gain or Loss	750	
	Cash		9,500

In this case, the original sale was billed in yen by the Japanese company. Following the rules of *Statement No. 52*, an exchange gain of $1,250 is recorded on December 31, and an exchange loss of $750 is recorded on February 1. Even though the net effect of these large up-and-down changes is the rather small net exchange gain of $500 over the whole transaction, the effect on each year may be important.

Restatement of Foreign Subsidiary Financial Statements[8]

Objective 7
Restate a foreign subsidiary's financial statements in U.S. dollars

Growing companies often expand by setting up or buying foreign subsidiaries. If a foreign subsidiary is more than 50 percent owned and if the parent company exercises control, then the foreign subsidiary should be included in the consolidated financial statements. The consolidation procedure is the same as that for domestic subsidiaries except that the statements of the foreign subsidiary must be restated in the reporting currency before consolidation takes place. The **reporting currency** is the currency in which the consolidated financial statements are presented. Clearly, it makes no sense to combine the assets of a Mexican subsidiary stated in pesos with the assets of the U.S. parent company stated in dollars. For most U.S. companies present their financial statements in U.S. dollars. So the following discussion assumes that the U.S. dollar is the reporting currency.

The method of restatement depends on the foreign subsidiary's functional currency. The **functional currency** is the currency of the place where the subsidiary carries on most of its business. Generally, it is the currency in which a company mainly earns and spends its cash. The functional currency to be used depends on the kind of foreign operations in which the subsidiary takes part. There are two broad types of foreign

8. This section is based on the requirements of *Statement of Financial Accounting Standards No. 52*, "Foreign Currency Translation" (Stamford, Conn.: Financial Accounting Standards Board, 1981).

operations. Type I includes those that are fairly self-contained and integrated within a certain country or economy. Type II subsidiaries are those that are mainly a direct and integral part or extension of the parent company's business operations. As a general rule, Type I subsidiaries have as their functional currency the currency of the country in which they are located. Type II subsidiaries have as their functional currency the currency of the parent company. If the parent company is a U.S. company, the functional currency of a Type I subsidiary will be the currency of the country where the subsidiary carries on its business, and the functional currency of a Type II subsidiary will be the U.S. dollar. *Statement No. 52* makes an exception when a Type I subsidiary operates in a country such as Brazil or Argentina, where there is hyperinflation. (As a rule of thumb, this means more than 100 percent cumulative inflation over three years.) In this case, the subsidiary is treated as a Type II subsidiary, with the functional currency being the U.S. dollar.

After deciding what type the subsidiary is and what its functional currency is, the next step is to restate the subsidiary's financial statements in terms of the reporting currency. To do so, the subsidiary's statements based on the local currency must first be remeasured in terms of the functional currency and then translated into the reporting currency. This is easier than it may sound because in our cases only one kind of restatement is needed for each kind of subsidiary. In the case of Type I subsidiaries, financial statements must only be translated from the functional to the reporting currency, because the statements are already presented in terms of the functional currency. In the case of Type II subsidiaries, the statements that have been measured in the local currency must only be measured again in terms of the functional currency, because the functional and reporting currency are the same.

A distinction is made between translation and remeasurement because the rates used to restate are different. For this reason, the exchange difference is treated differently under the two methods. In translating the functional currency of a Type I subsidiary into the reporting currency, all balance sheet accounts except those for stockholders' equity must be translated into the reporting currency at the exchange rate on the balance sheet date. All income statement accounts are translated at the average exchange rate for the period. It will often happen that, just because of changes in exchange rates, the translation of financial statements will appear to make the value of the parent's investment in the foreign subsidiary go up and down from year to year. Changes that are due wholly to exchange rate fluctuations are called **translation adjustments.** Because these changes are judged not to affect net income, they are listed separately in the stockholders' equity part of the consolidated balance sheet.

In remeasuring the local currency of a Type II subsidiary in terms of the functional currency (which in this case is the U.S. dollar), the exchange rate on the balance sheet date is used only for monetary assets and liabilities. The historical exchange rate (the rate at the time of the transactions) is used for inventory, plant assets, and contributed capital. In general, the average exchange rate for the year is used to remeasure revenues and expenses. However, for depreciation, the same rate is used as for the related asset accounts. Since Type II subsidiaries are treated as an integral

Table 20-4
Restatement
Rates for
Foreign
Subsidiaries'
Financial
Statements

Accounts	Type I Translation Rate	Type II Remeasurement Rate
Monetary Assets	Current	Current
Inventories and Prepaid Expenses	Current	Historical
Plant Assets	Current	Historical
Liabilities	Current	Current
Contributed Capital	Historical	Historical
Retained Earnings	No Adjustment	No Adjustment
Revenues	Average	Average
Expenses (other than depreciation)	Average	Average
Depreciation	Average	Historical

part of the parent company, the effects of changes in the exchange rates are reported on the income statement as **translation gains or losses** and included in net income.

Restatement Rates   At this point, a short review may be helpful. The financial statements of Type I subsidiaries are translated from the functional currency (which is the same as the company's local currency) into the reporting currency (which is the U.S. dollar). The statements of Type II subsidiaries are remeasured from the local currency in terms of the functional currency (which is the same as the reporting currency, the U.S. dollar). The exchange rates used to translate or remeasure are shown in Table 20-4.

Example of Restatement   Suppose that Exmar Corporation has a 100 percent owned subsidiary in Mexico called Mexmar Corporation. Before year-end consolidated financial statements can be prepared, the statements of Mexmar must be restated in terms of U.S. dollars. Suppose also that the following exchange rates of pesos to dollars apply in this case: historical rates, .05 for inventories and .08 for plant assets and contributed capital; current rate, .025; average rate, .04.

The first step in the restatement, of course, is to determine if Mexmar is a fairly self-contained business or if it is an integral part of the parent company's operations. In other words, it is necessary to find out if it is a Type I or Type II subsidiary in order to know its functional currency. In the restatement of Mexmar's financial statements in Table 20-5, both alternatives are shown so as to compare the two approaches.

In converting the statements from pesos to dollars using the correct exchange rates as shown in the table, two calculations need to be explained further. First, exchange rates were not used for retained earnings. Retained earnings cannot be directly translated or remeasured because they are made up of several elements that have been translated or remeasured at different rates. For this reason, it is assumed in these cases that the beginning balances of the Retained Earnings account under Type I translation are $25,000 and that they are $72,000 under the Type II

	Pesos	Type I Translation		Type II Remeasurement	
		Exchange Rate	U.S. Dollars	Exchange Rate	U.S. Dollars

Balance Sheet

	Pesos	Exchange Rate	U.S. Dollars	Exchange Rate	U.S. Dollars
Cash	100,000	.025	$ 2,500	.025	$ 2,500
Accounts Receivable (net)	250,000	.025	6,250	.025	6,250
Inventories	400,000	.025	10,000	.05	20,000
Plant Assets (net)	1,500,000	.025	37,500	.08	120,000
Total Assets	2,250,000		$ 56,250		$148,750
Accounts Payable	150,000	.025	$ 3,750	.025	$ 3,750
Bonds Payable	600,000	.025	15,000	.025	15,000
Common Stock	500,000	.08	40,000	.08	40,000
Retained Earnings	1,000,000		41,000		90,000
Cumulative Translation Adjustment			(43,500)		
Total Liabilities and Stockholders' Equity	2,250,000		$ 56,250		$148,750

Income Statement

	Pesos	Exchange Rate	U.S. Dollars	Exchange Rate	U.S. Dollars
Sales	3,000,000	.04	$120,000	.04	$120,000
Cost of Goods Sold	1,400,000	.04	$56,000	.04	$ 56,000
Depreciation	200,000	.04	8,000	.08	16,000
Other Expenses	1,000,000	.04	40,000	.04	40,000
Translation Loss or (Gain)					(10,000)
Total Deductions	2,600,000		$104,000		$102,000
Net Income	400,000		$ 16,000		$ 18,000

Table 20-5
Restatement
of Types I
and II
Subsidiaries'
Financial
Statements

remeasurement. So retained earnings are figured in each case by adding net income from the income statement to the beginning balances of Retained Earnings. (It is also assumed that no dividends or other transactions affecting this account took place.)

Second, the cumulative translation adjustment in the Type I case may be determined by figuring the amount that is needed to make total liabilities and stockholders' equity equal to total assets. It reflects the translation adjustments used for earlier periods as well as for the current period. The calculations of the current year's translation adjustment for Type I subsidiaries and the translation gain or loss for Type II subsidiaries will be covered in more advanced accounting courses.

As you can see from this case, the results can be very different depending on whether a subsidiary is found to be Type I or II. First, total assets are much greater for the Type II subsidiary because the current exchange rate is much lower than the historical exchange rate used for remeasuring Type II inventory and plant assets. Over time the dollar has become stronger than the peso. Second, even though retained earnings are figured in both cases by adding net income from the income statement to the beginning balance of Retained Earnings, the nature of each balance is different. Retained earnings for Type II reflect the effects of changing exchange rates, because exchange gains and losses appear on the income statement and are later closed to Retained Earnings. For Type I, on the other hand, the effects of changing exchange rates are reflected in the cumulative translation adjustment on the balance sheet and so do not appear on the income statement or in Retained Earnings.

Before *Statement No. 52*, all foreign subsidiaries were treated as Type II. This older practice was criticized by corporations for increasing the volatility of earnings, because translation gains and losses due to changes in exchange rates were included in income. For Type II subsidiaries, which are closely connected with the parent company, the earlier approach did make sense. However, many subsidiaries are Type I (that is, independent and self-contained businesses). These companies are not very likely ever to realize any translation gains or losses. For this reason, removing these translation gains and losses from the income statement, and reporting a cumulative translation adjustment on the balance sheet will give a more realistic picture of Type I subsidiaries. Time and experience with the new rule are needed before useful conclusions can be drawn.

The Search for Uniformity of International Accounting Standards

Objective 8
Describe
progress toward
international
accounting
standards

International investors like to compare the financial position and results of operations of companies from different countries. At present, however, there are few recognized worldwide standards of accounting. A number of major problems stand in the way of setting such international standards. One is that accountants and users of accounting have not been able to agree on the goals of financial statements. Some other problems are the differences in the way in which the accounting profession has developed in various countries, differences in the laws regulating companies, and differences in the requirements of governments and other bodies. Still other difficulties are the failure to deal with differences among countries in basic economic factors affecting financial reporting, inconsistencies in practices recommended by the accounting professions in different countries, and the influence of tax laws on financial reporting.[9] In the last area noted, for example, a survey for a major accounting firm found widely differing requirements. In nine countries, strict adherence to tax accounting was required. In eleven countries, adherence to tax accounting was required in some areas. In four countries (including the United States), adherence to tax practice was mostly forbidden.[10]

9. *Accounting Standards for Business Enterprises Throughout the World* (Chicago: Arthur Andersen, 1974), pp. 2–3.
10. *Accounting Principles and Reporting Practices: A Survey in 38 Countries* (New York: Price Waterhouse International, 1973), sec. 233.

Some efforts have been made to reach greater international understanding and uniformity of accounting practice. The Accountants' International Study Group, formed in 1966 and consisting of the AICPA and similar bodies in Canada, England, Wales, Ireland, and Scotland, has issued reports that survey and compare accounting practices in the member countries.

Most likely the best hope for finding areas of agreement among all the different countries are the International Accounting Standards Committee (IASC) and the International Federation of Accountants (IFAC). The IASC was formed in 1973 as a result of an agreement by accountancy bodies in Australia, Canada, France, Germany, Japan, Mexico, the Netherlands, the United Kingdom and Ireland, and the United States. Professional accountancy bodies in about 50 countries are now members of IASC. The role of IASC is to contribute to the development and adoption of accounting principles that are relevant, balanced, and comparable throughout the world and to encourage their observance in the presentation of financial statements. The standards issued by IASC are generally followed by large multinational companies that are clients of international accounting firms. The IFAC, which was formed in 1977 and consists of approximately 80 accountancy organizations from 59 countries, fully supports the work of the IASC and recognizes the IASC as the sole body having responsibility and authority to issue pronouncements on international accounting standards. The IFAC, on the other hand, has the objective of developing international guidelines for auditing, ethics, education, and management accounting. Each five years an International Congress is held to judge the progress in achieving these objectives. The road to international harmony is a difficult one. However, there is reason for optimism because an increasing number of countries are recognizing the appropriateness of international accounting standards in international trade and commerce.

Chapter Review

Review of Learning Objectives

1. Apply the lower-of-cost-or-market method and the equity method to the appropriate situations in accounting for long-term investments.

Long-term stock investments fall into three categories. First are noninfluential and noncontrolling investments representing less than 20 percent ownership. To account for these investments, use the cost method, adjusting the investment to the lower of cost or market for financial statement purposes. Second are influential but noncontrolling investments representing 20 percent to 50 percent ownership. Use the equity method to account for these investments. Third are controlling interest investments representing more than 50 percent ownership. Account for them by using consolidated financial statement methods.

2. Explain when to prepare consolidated financial statements and describe their uses.

Consolidated financial statements are normally prepared when an investing company has legal and effective control over another company. Control usually exists when the parent company owns more than 50 percent of the voting stock of the subsidiary company. Consolidated financial statements are useful to investors and others because they treat the parent company and its subsidiaries realistically as an integrated economic unit.

3. Prepare consolidated balance sheets at acquisition date for purchase at (a) book value and (b) other than book value.

At the date of acquisition, a work sheet entry is made to eliminate the investment for the parent company's financial statements and the owners' equity section from the subsidiary's financial statements. The assets and liabilities of the two companies are combined. If the parent owns less than 100 percent of the subsidiary, minority interest will appear on the consolidated balance sheet equal to the percentage of the subsidiary not owned by the parent multiplied by the owners' equity of the subsidiary. If the cost of the parent's investment in the subsidiary is greater than the subsidiary's book value, an amount equal to the excess of cost above book value will appear on the consolidated balance sheet as goodwill. If the cost of the parent's investment in the subsidiary is less than the book value, the excess of book value over cost should be used to reduce the book value of the long-term assets (other than long-term marketable securities) of the subsidiary.

4. Prepare consolidated income statements for intercompany transactions.

When consolidated income statements are prepared, intercompany sales, purchases, interest income, and interest expense must be eliminated to avoid double counting of these items.

5. Account for bond investment transactions.

When a company invests in bonds, the bonds are recorded at cost, and no separate premium or discount is recorded. If the investment is long-term, the difference between the cost and face value of the investment is amortized, using the effective interest method.

6. Show how changing exchange rates affect financial reporting.

A domestic company may make sales or purchases abroad in either its own country's currency or the foreign currency. If a transaction (sale or purchase) and its resolution (receipt or payment) are made in the domestic currency, no accounting problem arises. However, if the transaction and its resolution are made in a foreign currency and the exchange rate changes between the time of the transaction and its resolution, an exchange gain or loss will occur and should be recorded.

7. Restate a foreign subsidiary's financial statements in U.S. dollars.

Foreign currencies are converted to U.S. dollars by multiplying the exchange rates by the amount in the foreign subsidiary's financial statements. The restatement rates to be used are specified in FASB *Statement No. 52*. In general, the rates that apply depend on whether the subsidiary is separate and self-contained (Type I) or an integral part of the parent company (Type II). In the Type I case, the resulting cumulative translation adjustment appears as part of the stockholders' equity section of the balance sheet. In the Type II case, the resulting translation gain or loss appears on the income statement.

8. Describe progress toward international accounting standards.

There has been some progress toward setting up international accounting standards, especially through the efforts of the International Accounting Standards Committee and the International Federation of Accountants. However, there still are serious inconsistencies in financial reporting among countries. These inconsistencies make the comparison of financial statements from different countries difficult.

Review Problem
Consolidated Balance Sheet Work Sheet

The balance sheet of Star Trip Corporation as of December 31, 19xx, is as follows:

Star Trip Corporation
Balance Sheet
December 31, 19xx

Assets		Liabilities and Stockholders' Equity	
Cash	$ 6,000,000	Accounts Payable	$ 500,000
Accounts Receivable	1,100,000	Bonds Payable	4,000,000
Inventory	1,400,000	Common Stock —	
Property, Plant, and		$10 par value	6,000,000
Equipment (net)	8,000,000	Retained Earnings	6,300,000
Other Assets	300,000		
		Total Liabilities and Stockholders'	
Total Assets	$16,800,000	Equity	$16,800,000

Because the company has been very successful recently, it now has a large amount of idle cash available. Therefore, management is looking at two alternatives for investing the idle cash. Alternative 1 is to purchase 75 percent of the outstanding voting stock of the Hilltop Company for $3,000,000. Alternative 2 is to purchase

	Hilltop Company	Remond Corporation
Assets		
Cash	$ 400,000	$ 800,000
Receivables	2,400,000	2,600,000
Inventory	2,000,000	3,100,000
Property, Plant, and Equipment (net)	1,500,000	2,000,000
Total Assets	$6,300,000	$8,500,000
Liabilities and Stockholders' Equity		
Accounts Payable	$1,000,000	$1,500,000
Long-Term Debt	1,300,000	3,400,000
Common Stock	3,250,000	3,000,000
Retained Earnings	750,000	600,000
Total Liabilities and Stockholders' Equity	$6,300,000	$8,500,000

60 percent of the outstanding voting stock of the Remond Corporation for $4,000,000. Since the cost of the investment exceeds book value, management determined that $250,000 was applicable to increased value of property, plant, and equipment. The balance sheets of Hilltop Company and Remond Corporation on the acquisition date are shown at the bottom of the previous page. Additional information: (a) Star Trip Corporation owes Hilltop Company $50,000, and (b) Remond Corporation owes Star Trip Corporation $100,000.

Required

Prepare a consolidated work sheet and balance sheet work sheet at the date of acquisition for each alternative.

Answer to Review Problem

Alternative 1

Star Trip Corporation and Hilltop Company
Work Sheet for Consolidated Balance Sheet
As of Acquisition Date

Accounts	Balance Sheet Star Trip Corporation	Balance Sheet Hilltop Company	Eliminations Debit	Eliminations Credit	Consolidated Balance Sheet
Cash	3,000,000	400,000			3,400,000
Accounts Receivable	1,100,000	2,400,000		(2) 50,000	3,450,000
Inventory	1,400,000	2,000,000			3,400,000
Investments	3,000,000			(1) 3,000,000	
Property, Plant, and Equipment	8,000,000	1,500,000			9,500,000
Other Assets	300,000				300,000
Total Assets	16,800,000	6,300,000			20,050,000
Accounts Payable	500,000	1,000,000	(2) 50,000		1,450,000
Bonds Payable	4,000,000	1,300,000			5,300,000
					812,500(M)
Common Stock	6,000,000	3,250,000	(1) 2,437,500		6,000,000
					187,500(M)
Retained Earnings	6,300,000	750,000	(1) 562,500		6,300,000
Total Liabilities and Stockholders' Equity	16,800,000	6,300,000	3,050,000	3,050,000	20,050,000

(1) Elimination of intercompany investment. Minority interest (M) equals $812,500 (25 percent × $3,250,000) and $187,500 (25 percent × $750,000).
(2) Elimination of intercompany receivables and payables.

**Star Trip and Remond Corporations
Work Sheet for Consolidated Balance Sheet
As of Acquisition Date**

Accounts	Balance Sheet Star Trip Corporation	Balance Sheet Remond Corporation	Eliminations		Consolidated Balance Sheet
			Debit	Credit	
Cash	2,000,000	800,000			2,800,000
Accounts Receivable	1,100,000	2,600,000		(2) 100,000	3,600,000
Inventory	1,400,000	3,100,000			4,500,000
Investments	4,000,000			(1) 4,000,000	
Property, Plant, and Equipment	8,000,000	2,000,000	(1) 250,000		10,250,000
Goodwill			(1) 150,000		150,000
Other Assets	300,000				300,000
Total Assets	16,800,000	8,500,000			21,600,000
Accounts Payable	500,000	1,500,000	(2) 100,000		1,900,000
Bonds Payable	4,000,000	3,400,000			7,400,000
Common Stock	6,000,000	3,000,000	(1) 3,000,000		6,000,000
Retained Earnings	6,300,000	600,000	(1) 600,000		6,300,000
Total Liabilities and Stockholders' Equity	16,800,000	8,500,000	4,100,000	4,100,000	21,600,000

(1) Elimination of intercompany investment. The $400,000 ($4,000,000 − $3,600,000) excess of purchase price over book value is allocated $250,000 to Property, Plant, and Equipment and $150,000 to Goodwill.
(2) Elimination of intercompany receivables and payables.

Chapter Assign- ments

Questions

1. Why are the concepts of significant influence and control important to a discussion of long-term investments?

2. For each of the following categories of long-term investments, briefly describe the applicable percentage of ownership and accounting treatment: (a) noninfluential and noncontrolling investment, (b) influential but noncontrolling investment, and (c) controlling investment.

3. What is meant by a parent-subsidiary relationship?

4. Would the stockholders of RCA Corporation be more interested in the consolidated financial statements of RCA than in the statements of its principal subsidiaries, such as NBC, Hertz Rent-A-Car, or the electronics division? Explain.

5. The annual report for United States Steel Corporation included the following statement in its Summary of Principal Accounting Policies: "*Principles applied in consolidation.*—Majority owned subsidiaries are consolidated, except for leasing and finance companies and those subsidiaries not considered to be material." Why were leasing and finance companies not consolidated?

6. Also from the annual report of United States Steel Corporation is the following statement in the Summary of Principal Accounting Policies: *"Investments.—* Investments in leasing and finance companies are at U.S. Steel's equity in the net assets and advances to such companies. Investments in other companies, in which U.S. Steel has significant influence in management and control, are also on the equity basis." What is the equity basis of accounting for investments, and why does United States Steel use it in this case?

7. Why may the price paid to acquire a controlling interest in a subsidiary company differ from the book value of the subsidiary?

8. Why should intercompany receivables, payables, sales, and purchases be eliminated in the preparation of consolidated financial statements?

9. The following item appears on a consolidated balance sheet: "Goodwill from Consolidation—$70,000." Explain how this item arose and where you would expect to find it on the consolidated balance sheet.

10. The following item appears on a consolidated balance sheet: "Minority Interest—$50,000." Explain how this item arose and where you would expect to find it on the consolidated balance sheet.

11. Subsidiary Corporation has a book value of $100,000, of which Parent Corporation purchases 100 percent for $115,000. What is the amount of goodwill from consolidation?

12. Subsidiary Corporation, a 100 percent owned subsidiary, has total sales of $500,000, $100,000 of which were made to Parent Corporation. Parent Corporation has total sales of $1,000,000, including sales of all items purchased from Subsidiary Corporation. What is the amount of sales on the consolidated income statement?

13. Why does the buying company record a bond investment at cost when the issuing company will record the same bond issue at face value and provide a separate account for any discount or premium?

14. What does it mean to say that the exchange rate of a French franc in terms of the U.S. dollar is .15? If a bottle of French perfume costs 200 francs, how much will it cost in dollars?

15. If an American firm does business with a German firm and all their transactions take place in German marks, which firm may incur an exchange gain or loss and why?

16. If you as an investor were trying to evaluate the relative performance of General Motors, Volkswagen, and Toyota Motors from their published financial statements, what problem might you encounter (other than language)?

17. What are some of the obstacles to uniform international accounting standards, and what efforts are being made to overcome them?

Classroom Exercises

**Exercise 20-1
Long-Term
Investments—
Cost and
Equity Methods**
(L.O. 1)

On January 1, Greenberg Corporation purchased, as a long-term investment, 10 percent of the voting stock of Starks Corporation for $200,000 and 40 percent of the voting stock of Lloyd Corporation for $1,000,000. During the year, Starks Corporation had earnings of $100,000 and paid dividends of $40,000. Lloyd Corporation had earnings of $300,000 and paid dividends of $200,000. The market value of neither investment declined during the year.

Which of these investments should be accounted for using the cost method? Which should use the equity method? At what amount should each investment be carried on the balance sheet at year end? Give a reason for each choice.

Exercise 20-2
Long-Term
Investments—
Lower-of-Cost-
or-Market
Method
(L.O. 1)

Angotti Corporation has the following portfolio of investments at year end:

Company	Percentage of Voting Stock Held	Cost	Year-End Market Value
A Corporation	3	$160,000	$200,000
B Corporation	11	750,000	500,000
C Corporation	4	60,000	90,000
Total		$970,000	$790,000

The Unrealized Loss on Long-Term Investments account and the Allowance to Reduce Long-Term Investments to Market account both currently have a balance of $80,000.

Prepare the year-end adjustment to reflect the above information.

Exercise 20-3
Long-Term
Investments—
Equity Method
(L.O. 1)

At the beginning of the current year, Noble Corporation acquired 45 percent of the voting stock of Tucker Corporation for $2,400,000 in cash, an amount sufficient to exercise significant influence over Tucker Corporation activities. During the year, Tucker Corporation paid dividends of $400,000 but incurred a net loss of $200,000.

Prepare journal entries to record the above information.

Exercise 20-4
Elimination
Entry for a
Purchase at
Book Value
(L.O. 3)

The Hillman Manufacturing Company purchased 100 percent of the common stock of the Rowe Manufacturing Company for $125,000. Rowe's stockholders' equity included common stock of $75,000 and retained earnings of $50,000.

Prepare the eliminating entry in general journal form that would appear on the work sheet for consolidating the balance sheets of these two entities as of the acquisition date.

Exercise 20-5
Elimination
Entry and
Minority
Interest
(L.O. 3)

The stockholders' equity section of the Ayers Corporation's balance sheet appeared as follows on December 31:

Common Stock—$5 par value, 40,000 shares authorized and issued	$200,000
Retained Earnings	24,000
Total Stockholders' Equity	$224,000

Assume that Blanton Manufacturing Company owns 90 percent of the voting stock of Ayers and paid $5.60 for each share.

In general journal form, prepare the entry (including minority interest) to eliminate Blanton's investment and Ayers's stockholders' equity that would appear on the work sheet used in preparing the consolidated balance sheet for the two firms.

Exercise 20-6
Consolidated
Balance Sheet
with Goodwill
(L.O. 3)

On September 1, G Company purchased 100 percent of the voting stock of K Company for $960,000 in cash. The separate condensed balance sheets immediately after the purchase are shown below.

	G Company	K Company
Other Assets	$2,206,000	$1,089,000
Investment in K Company	960,000	—
	$3,166,000	$1,089,000
Liabilities	$ 871,000	$ 189,000
Common Stock—$1 par value	1,000,000	300,000
Retained Earnings	1,295,000	600,000
	$3,166,000	$1,089,000

Prepare a work sheet for the consolidated balance sheet immediately after G Company acquired control of K Company. Assume that any excess of the cost of the investment in the subsidiary over book value acquired is attributable to goodwill from consolidation.

Exercise 20-7
Analyzing the Effects of Elimination Entries
(L.O. 3)

Some of the separate accounts from the balance sheets for A Company and B Company are shown just after A Company purchased 90 percent of B Company's voting stock for $810,000 in cash.

	A Company	B Company
Accounts Receivable	$1,300,000	$400,000
Interest Receivable, Bonds of B Company	7,200	—
Investment in B Company	810,000	—
Investment in B Company Bonds	180,000	—
Accounts Payable	530,000	190,000
Interest Payable, Bonds	32,000	20,000
Bonds Payable	800,000	500,000
Common Stock	1,000,000	600,000
Retained Earnings	560,000	300,000

The Accounts Receivable and Accounts Payable include the following: B Company owed A Company $50,000 for services rendered, and A Company owed B Company $66,000 for purchases of merchandise.

Determine the amount (including minority interest) that would appear in the consolidated balance sheet for each of the above accounts.

Exercise 20-8
Bond Investment Transactions
(L.O. 5)

On November 1, Fleming Corporation purchased one thousand $1,000 bonds for $1,050,000 plus accrued interest as a long-term investment. The bonds carried a face interest rate of $10\frac{1}{2}$ percent that is paid semiannually on July 1 and January 1.

Prepare journal entries to record the purchase on November 1 and the receipt of the interest check and amortization of premium on January 1, assuming an effective interest rate of $9\frac{1}{2}$ percent.

Exercise 20-9
Recording International Transactions— Fluctuating Exchange Rate
(L.O. 6)

U.S. Corporation purchased a special-purpose machine from German Corporation on credit for 30,000 DM (marks). At the date of purchase, the exchange rate was $.39 per mark. On the date of payment, which was made in marks, the value of the mark had increased to $.41.

Prepare journal entries to record the purchase and payment in the U.S. Corporation's accounting records.

Interpreting Accounting Information

Published Financial Information: U.S. Steel and Marathon Oil
(L.O. 3b)

In 1981 U.S. Steel Corporation fought Mobil Corporation for control of Marathon Oil Company. U.S. Steel won this battle of the giants by reaching an agreement to purchase all of Marathon's stock. The *Chicago Tribune* reported on March 12, 1982, that the $6 billion merger, as approved by the stockholders of Marathon, was the second-largest in history and created the twelfth-largest industrial corporation in the United States.

In a note to U.S. Steel's 1981 annual report the details of the purchase were revealed. U.S. Steel "purchased 30 million common shares of Marathon Oil Company for $125 per share . . . as the first step in its planned acquisition of the entire equity of Marathon." Additional Marathon shares would be purchased by issuing $100 principal amount of $12\frac{1}{2}$ percent notes due in 1994 for each share of stock. These notes are estimated by the financial press to have a fair market value of $80 per share. The total number of Marathon shares prior to these two transactions was 59.0 million.

On December 31, 1981, just before the merger, the condensed balance sheets of U.S. Steel and Marathon Oil appeared as follows (in millions):

	U.S. Steel	Marathon Oil
Assets		
Current Assets, Excluding Inventories	$ 4,214	$ 907
Inventories	1,198	576
Property, Plant, and Equipment (net)	6,676	4,233
Other Assets	1,228	278
Total Assets	$13,316	$5,994
Liabilities and Stockholders' Equity		
Current Liabilities	$ 2,823	$1,475
Long-Term Debt	2,340	1,368
Deferred Income Taxes	732	588
Other Liabilities	1,161	501
Total Liabilities	$ 7,056	$3,932
Stockholders' Equity	6,260	2,062
Total Liabilities and Stockholders' Equity	$13,316	$5,994

Further information in U.S. Steel's annual report indicates that when consolidated financial statements are prepared using the purchase method, management will adjust Marathon's assets and liabilities in the following manner. It will (a) increase inventory by $1,244 million; (b) increase current liabilities by $392 million; and (c) decrease deferred income taxes by $588. After these adjustments, any remaining excess of purchase price over book value of Marathon's shares will be attributed to property, plant, and equipment.

Required

1. Prepare the entry in U.S. Steel's journals to record the purchase of Marathon.
2. Prepare the eliminating entry, including the adjustments indicated, that would be made to consolidate U.S. Steel and Marathon.
3. Prepare a consolidated balance sheet for the merged companies.
4. Did U.S. Steel pay more or less than book value for Marathon? Why would U.S. Steel take this action? Did the purchase raise or lower U.S. Steel's book value per share?

Problem Set A

**Problem 20A-1
Long-Term
Investments—
Equity Method
(L.O. 1)**

The E. J. Cropp Corporation owns 40 percent of the voting stock of the Bottom Line Corporation. The investment account on the books of E. J. Cropp Corporation as of January 1, 19xx, was $360,000. During 19xx, the Bottom Line Corporation reported the following quarterly earnings and dividends:

Quarter	Earnings	Dividends Paid
1	$ 80,000	$ 50,000
2	120,000	50,000
3	60,000	50,000
4	(40,000)	50,000
	$220,000	$200,000

Because of the percentage of voting shares owned by the Cropp Corporation, it can exercise significant influence over the operations of Bottom Line. Under these conditions the Cropp Corporation must account for the investment by using the equity method.

Required

1. Prepare the journal entries that Cropp Corporation must make each quarter to record its share of earnings and dividends.
2. Prepare a ledger account for Cropp Corporation's investment in Bottom Line, enter the beginning balance, and post the relevant entries from 1.

Problem 20A-2
Long-Term
Investment
Transactions
(L.O. 1)

The Chisholm Company on January 2, 19x0, made several long-term investments in the voting stock of various companies. It purchased 10,000 shares of Crown at $2.00 a share, 15,000 shares of Gray at $3.00 a share, and 6,000 shares of Acme at $4.50 a share. Each investment represents less than 20 percent of the voting stock of the company. The remaining transactions of Chisholm in securities during 19x0 are as follows:

May 15 Purchased with cash 6,000 shares of Globe stock for $3.00 per share. This investment is less than 20 percent of the Globe voting stock.
July 16 Sold the 10,000 shares of Crown stock for $1.80 per share.
Sept. 30 Purchased with cash 5,000 additional shares of Gray for $3.20 per share.
Dec. 31 The market values per share of the stock in the Long-Term Investment account were as follows: Gray, $3.25; Acme, $4.00; and Globe, $2.00.

Chisholm's transactions in securities during 19x1 are as follows:

Feb. 1 Received a cash dividend from Gray of 10¢ per share.
July 15 Sold for cash the 6,000 Acme shares owned for $4.00 per share.
Aug. 1 Received a cash dividend of 10¢ per share from Gray.
Sept. 10 Purchased 3,000 shares of Lake for $7.00 per share.
Dec. 31 The market values per share of the stock in the Long-Term Investment account were as follows: Gray, $3.25; Globe, $2.50; and Lake, $6.50.

Required

Prepare the journal entries to record all the transactions of Chisholm Company in its long-term investments during 19x0 and 19x1.

Problem 20A-3
Consolidated
Balance Sheet—
Cost Exceeding
Book Value
(L.O. 3)

The balance sheets of Metz and Babbitt Corporations as of December 31, 19xx, are shown on the next page.

	Metz Corporation	Babbitt Corporation
Assets		
Cash	$ 600,000	$ 120,000
Accounts Receivable	700,000	600,000
Inventory	250,000	600,000
Investment in Babbitt Corporation	750,000	—
Property, Plant, and Equipment	1,350,000	850,000
Other Assets	20,000	50,000
Total Assets	$3,670,000	$2,220,000
Liabilities and Stockholders' Equity		
Accounts Payable	$ 750,000	$ 500,000
Salaries Payable	300,000	270,000
Bonds Payable	300,000	800,000
Common Stock	1,500,000	500,000
Retained Earnings	820,000	150,000
Total Liabilities and Stockholders' Equity	$3,670,000	$2,220,000

Required

Prepare a consolidated balance sheet work sheet for the two companies, assuming that Metz purchased 100 percent of the common stock of Babbitt for $750,000 immediately prior to December 31, 19xx, and that $60,000 of the excess of cost over book value is attributable to the increased value of Babbitt Corporation's inventory. The rest of the excess is considered goodwill.

**Problem 20A-4
Preparation of
Consolidated
Income
Statement
(L.O. 4)**

The Butcher Corporation has owned 100 percent of the Staufel Corporation since 19x0. The income statements of these two companies for 19x2 follow:

	Butcher Corporation	Staufel Corporation
Sales	$2,650,000	$900,000
Cost of Goods Sold	1,000,000	500,000
Gross Margin	$1,650,000	$400,000
Less: Selling Expenses	$ 800,000	$150,000
General and Administrative Expenses	200,000	50,000
Total Operating Expenses	$1,000,000	$200,000
Net Income from Operations	$ 650,000	$200,000
Other Income	18,000	—
Net Income	$ 668,000	$200,000

Additional information: (a) Staufel Corporation sold $200,000 of its goods to Butcher Corporation, all of which had been sold to Butcher's customers by December 31, 19x2. (b) Staufel Corporation purchased $100,000 of inventory items from the Butcher Corporation, all of which had been sold as of December 31, 19x2. (c) The Staufel Corporation rents delivery trucks from Butcher Corporation at the rate of $1,500 per month.

Required

Prepare a consolidated income statement work sheet for these companies for the year ended December 31, 19x2.

**Problem 20A-5
Consolidated
Balance
Sheet—Less
Than 100
Percent
Ownership
(L.O. 3)**

The Phelps Corporation purchased 70 percent of the outstanding voting stock of the McGuire Corporation for $718,200 in cash. The balance sheets of the two companies immediately after acquisition were as follows:

	Phelps Corporation	McGuire Corporation
Assets		
Cash	$ 150,000	$ 60,000
Accounts Receivable	360,000	200,000
Inventory	1,600,000	700,000
Investment in McGuire	718,200	—
Property, Plant, and Equipment (net)	2,500,000	1,000,000
Other Assets	100,000	40,000
Total Assets	$5,428,200	$2,000,000
Liabilities and Stockholders' Equity		
Accounts Payable	$ 400,000	$ 150,000
Salaries Payable	50,000	20,000
Taxes Payable	20,000	4,000
Bonds Payable	1,300,000	800,000
Common Stock	2,500,000	900,000
Retained Earnings	1,158,200	126,000
Total Liabilities and Stockholders' Equity	$5,428,200	$2,000,000

Additional information: (a) The Other Assets account on the McGuire balance sheet represents an investment in Phelps's Bonds Payable. (b) $60,000 of the Accounts Receivable of Phelps Corporation represent receivables due from McGuire.

Required

Prepare a work sheet as of the acquisition date for the preparation of a consolidated balance sheet.

Problem 20A-6
Bond
Investment
Transactions
(L.O. 5)

The transactions involving long-term bond investments made by Hagler Corporation are described below:

19x1

July 1 Purchased $500,000 of Seitz Corporation's $12\frac{1}{2}$ percent bonds at 104, a price that yields an effective interest rate of $11\frac{1}{2}$ percent. These bonds have semiannual interest payment dates of June 30 and December 31.

Nov. 1 Purchased $300,000 of Madden Company's 9 percent bonds, dated August 1, at face value plus accrued interest.

Dec. 31 Received a check from Seitz for semiannual interest and amortized the discount, using the effective interest method.

19x2

Feb. 1 Received a check from Madden for the semiannual interest.

June 30 Received a check from Seitz for the semiannual interest and amortized the discount, using the effective interest method.

30 Made a year-end adjusting entry to accrue the interest on the Madden bonds.

Aug. 1 Received a check from Madden for the semiannual interest.

Nov. 1 Sold the Madden bonds at 98 plus accrued interest.

Dec. 31 Received a check from Seitz for the semiannual interest and amortized the discount, using the effective interest method.

19x3

Jan. 1 Sold one-half of the Seitz bonds at 101.

Required

Prepare general journal entries to record the transactions.

Problem 20A-7
Conversion of
Balance Sheet
Using
Exchange Rates
(L.O. 7)

States Corporation owns 100 percent of Canadian Corporation, located in Ontario, Canada. To prepare consolidated financial statements for States Corporation and its subsidiary, the financial statements of Canadian Corporation must be converted from Canadian dollars into U.S. dollars. Canadian Corporation's balance sheet is presented on the next page.

The historical exchange rate is U.S. $.92 per Canadian dollar, the current rate is U.S. $.88 per Canadian dollar, and the average rate is U.S. $.90 per Canadian dollar. Canadian Corporation paid no dividends during 19xx.

Required

1. Convert the balance sheet of Canadian Corporation to U.S. dollars for consolidation purposes in each of two cases. (a) Canadian Corporation is a self-contained subsidiary operating wholly within Canada. Assume that net income in U.S. dollars for the year is $1,000,000 and that beginning Retained Earnings in U.S. dollars is $10,600,000. (b) Canadian Corporation is a direct and integral part of States Corporation.
2. How would you expect the converted income statements for the two cases in 1 to differ, and why?

Problem Set B

Problem 20B-1
Long-Term
Investments—
Equity Method
(L.O. 1)

The Hiatt Company owns 45 percent of the voting stock of the Curry Company. The investment account for this company on Hiatt Company's balance sheet had a balance of $150,000 on January 1, 19xx. During 19xx, Curry Company reported

Canadian Corporation
Balance Sheet
(in Canadian dollars)
December 31, 19xx

Assets

Cash	$ 1,350,000
Accounts Receivable	4,650,000
Inventory	10,100,000
Property, Plant, and Equipment	25,600,000
Total Assets	$41,700,000

Liabilities and Stockholders' Equity

Accounts Payable	$ 8,700,000
Taxes Payable	1,800,000
Common Stock	15,000,000
Retained Earnings	16,200,000
Total Liabilities and Stockholders' Equity	$41,700,000

the following quarterly earnings and dividends paid:

Quarter	Earnings	Dividends Paid
1	$20,000	$10,000
2	15,000	10,000
3	40,000	10,000
4	(10,000)	10,000
	$65,000	$40,000

Hiatt Company exercises significant influence over the operations of Curry Company and therefore uses the equity method to account for its investment.

Required

1. Prepare the journal entries that Hiatt Company must make each quarter in accounting for its investment in Curry Company.
2. Prepare a ledger account for the investment in common stock of Curry Company, enter the beginning balance, and post the relevant portions of the entries made in 1.

**Problem 20B-2
Long-Term
Investment
Transactions
(L.O. 1)**

Redden Corporation made the following transactions in its long-term investment account over a two-year period:

19x0

Apr. 1 Purchased with cash 20,000 shares of Hartry Company stock for $38 per share.

June 1 Purchased with cash 15,000 shares of Teague Corporation stock for $18.00 per share.

Sept. 1	Received a 50¢ per share dividend from Hartry Company.	
Nov. 1	Purchased with cash 25,000 shares of Dickens Corporation stock for $27.50 per share.	
Dec. 31	The market values per share of the shares held in the Long-Term Investment account were as follows: Hartry Company, $35.00; Teague Corporation, $8.00; and Dickens Corporation, $30.50.	

19x1

Feb. 1	Because of unfavorable prospects for the Teague Corporation, the Teague stock was sold for cash at $10.00 per share.	
May 1	Purchased with cash 10,000 shares of Witte Corporation for $56.00 per share.	
Sept. 1	Received a 50¢ per share dividend from Hartry Company.	
Dec. 31	The market values per share of the shares held in the Long-Term Investment account were as follows: Hartry Company, $40.00; Dickens Corporation, $35.00; and Witte Corporation, $50.00.	

Required

Prepare the entries to record the transactions above in Redden Corporation records, assuming that all investments represent less than 20 percent of the voting stock of the company whose stock was acquired.

Problem 20B-3
Consolidated
Balance
Sheet—Cost
Exceeding Book
Value
(L.O. 3)

The balance sheets of Scott and Penn Companies as of December 31, 19xx, are shown below.

	Scott Company	Penn Company
Assets		
Cash	$ 30,000	$ 20,000
Accounts Receivable	50,000	15,000
Investment in Penn Company	150,000	—
Other Assets	50,000	90,000
Total Assets	$280,000	$125,000
Liabilities and Stockholders' Equity		
Liabilities	$ 30,000	$ 15,000
Common Stock—$10 par value	200,000	100,000
Retained Earnings	50,000	10,000
Total Liabilities and Stockholders' Equity	$280,000	$125,000

Required

Prepare a consolidated balance sheet work sheet for the Scott and Penn Companies, assuming that the Scott Company purchased 100 percent of Penn's common stock immediately prior to the above balance sheet date and that $20,000 of the excess of cost over book value is attributable to Penn Company's Other Assets. The rest of the excess is considered to be goodwill.

Problem 20B-4
Preparation of
Consolidated
Income
Statement
(L.O. 3)

The Gaddis Company has owned 100 percent of the Combs Company since 19x0. The income statements of these two companies for the year ended December 31, 19x1, are shown at the top of the next page.

Chapter Twenty

	Gaddis Company	Combs Company
Sales	$1,500,000	$600,000
Cost of Goods Sold	750,000	400,000
Gross Margin	$ 750,000	$200,000
Less: Selling Expenses	$ 250,000	$ 50,000
General and Administrative Expenses	300,000	100,000
Total Operating Expenses	$ 550,000	$150,000
Net Income from Operations	$ 200,000	$ 50,000
Other Income	50,000	—
Net Income	$ 250,000	$ 50,000

Additional information: (a) The Combs Company purchased $300,000 of inventory from the Gaddis Company, all of which had been sold to Combs Company customers by the end of the year. (b) The Combs Company leased its building from the Gaddis Company for $50,000 per year.

Required

Prepare a consolidated income statement work sheet for the two companies for the year ended December 31, 19x1.

**Problem 20B-5
Consolidated
Balance
Sheet—Less
Than 100
Percent
Ownership**
(L.O. 3)

In a cash transaction, Timko Company purchased 80 percent of the outstanding stock of Pitts Company on June 30, 19xx. Immediately after the acquisition, the separate balance sheets of the companies appeared as follows:

	Timko Company	Pitts Company
Assets		
Cash	$ 80,000	$ 12,000
Accounts Receivable	130,000	60,000
Inventory	200,000	130,000
Investment in Pitts Company	169,600	—
Plant and Equipment (net)	300,000	220,000
Other Assets	10,000	40,000
Total Assets	$889,600	$462,000
Liabilities and Stockholders' Equity		
Accounts Payable	$170,000	$100,000
Long-Term Debt	200,000	150,000
Common Stock—$5 par value	400,000	200,000
Retained Earnings	119,600	12,000
Total Liabilities and Stockholders' Equity	$889,600	$462,000

Additional information: (a) Pitts Company's other assets represent a long-term investment in Timko Company's long-term debt. (b) Timko Company owes Pitts Company $15,000 for services rendered.

Required

Prepare a work sheet as of the acquisition date for the preparation of a consolidated balance sheet.

Problem 20B-6
Bond
Investment
Transactions
(L.O. 5)

Fortner Corporation follows the practice of purchasing bonds as long-term investments. Fortner's long-term bond investment transactions for 19x1 and 19x2 are described below.

19x1

Jan. 1 Purchased on the semiannual interest payment date $200,000 of Poole Company 10 percent bonds at 91, a price that yields an effective interest rate of 12 percent.

Apr. 1 Purchased $100,000 of Winfield Corporation 12 percent, twenty-year bonds dated March 1 at face value plus accrued interest.

July 1 Received a check from Poole Company for the semiannual interest and amortized the discount, using the effective interest method.

Sept. 1 Received a check from Winfield for the semiannual interest.

Dec. 31 Made year-end adjusting entries to accrue the interest on the Poole and Winfield bonds and to amortize the discount on the Poole bonds, using the effective interest method.

19x2

Jan. 1 Received a check from Poole for the semiannual interest.

Mar. 1 Received a check from Winfield Corporation for the semiannual interest.

July 1 Received a check from Poole for the semiannual interest and amortized the discount, using the effective interest method.

1 Sold one-half of the Poole bonds at 96.

Sept. 1 Received a check from Winfield for the semiannual interest.

Nov. 1 Sold the Winfield bonds at 98 plus the accrued interest.

Dec. 31 Made a year-end adjusting entry to accrue the interest on the remaining Poole bonds and to amortize the discount using the effective interest method.

Required

Prepare general journal entries to record the transactions.

Problem 20B-7
Conversion of
Balance Sheet
Using
Exchange Rates
(L.O. 7)

The balance sheet of Southern Leather Company, a 100 percent owned subsidiary of Northern Distributors, is shown on the next page. The subsidiary is in Mexico, and the statement is shown in pesos. As you prepare the consolidated financial statements for Northern Distributors, convert Southern Leather's balance sheet from pesos to U.S. dollars. The value of the peso has dropped dramatically in recent years through a series of devaluations. The historical exchange rate is $.04 per peso, the current rate is $.01 per peso, and the average rate is $.02 per peso. Southern Leather paid no dividends in 19xx.

Required

1. Convert the balance sheet of Southern Leather Company to U.S. dollars for consolidation purposes in each of two cases. (a) Southern Leather is a self-contained subsidiary operating wholly within Mexico. Assume that net income in U.S. dollars is $5,000 and beginning Retained Earnings in U.S. dollars is $9,000. (b) Southern Leather is an integral part of Northern Distributors' operations. 2. How would you expect the converted income statements for the two alternatives in 1 to differ, and why?

Southern Leather Company
Balance Sheet
(in pesos)
December 31, 19xx

Assets

Cash	100,000
Accounts Receivable	800,000
Inventory	1,600,000
Property, Plant, and Equipment (net)	2,500,000
Total Assets	5,000,000

Liabilities and Stockholders' Equity

Accounts Payable	250,000
Salaries Payable	200,000
Common Stock	4,000,000
Retained Earnings	550,000
Total Liabilities and Stockholders' Equity	5,000,000

Financial Decision Case 20-1

San Antonio Corporation (L.O. 1)

San Antonio Corporation is a successful oil and gas exploration business in the southwestern part of the United States. At the beginning of 19xx, the company made investments in three companies that perform services in the oil and gas industry. The details of each of these investments are presented in the next three paragraphs.

San Antonio purchased 100,000 shares in Levelland Service Corporation at a cost of $4 per share. Levelland has 1.5 million shares outstanding, and during 19xx paid dividends of $.20 per share on earnings of $.40 per share. At the end of the year, Levelland's shares were selling for $6 per share.

San Antonio also purchased 2,000,000 shares of Plainview Drilling Company at $2 per share. Plainview has 10,000,000 shares outstanding. In 19xx Plainview paid a dividend of $.10 per share on earnings of $.20 per share. During the current year the president of San Antonio was appointed to the board of directors of Plainview. At the end of the year Plainview's stock was selling for $3 per share.

In another action, San Antonio purchased 1,000,000 of Brownfield Oil Field Supplies Company's 5,000,000 outstanding shares at $3 per share. The president of San Antonio sought membership on the board of directors of Brownfield but was rebuffed by Brownfield's board when shareholders representing a majority of Brownfield's outstanding stock stated that they did not want to be associated with

San Antonio. Brownfield paid a dividend of $.20 per share and reported a net income of only $.10 per share for the year. By the end of the year, the price of its stock had dropped to $1 per share.

Required

1. What principal factors must you consider in order to determine how to account for San Antonio's investments? Should the investments be shown on the balance sheet as short-term or long-term investments? What factors affect this decision?

2. For each of the three situations make general journal entries for each of the following: (a) initial investment, (b) receipt of cash dividend, and (c) recognition of income (if appropriate).

3. What adjusting entry (if any) is required at the end of the year?

4. Assuming that San Antonio's investment in Brownfield is sold after the first of the year for $1.50 per share, what general journal entry would be made? Assuming that the market value of the remaining investments held by San Antonio are above cost at the end of this second year, what adjusting entry (if any) would need to be made?

Learning Objectives	Chapter Twenty-One	Financial Statement Analysis

This chapter presents a number of techniques intended to aid in decision making by highlighting important relationships in the financial statements. This group of techniques is called financial statement analysis. After studying this chapter, you should be able to meet the learning objectives listed on the left.

Effective decision making calls for the ability to sort out relevant information from a great many facts and to make adjustments for changing conditions. Very often, financial statements in a company's annual report run ten or more pages, including footnotes and other necessary disclosures. If these statements are to be useful in making decisions, decision makers must be able to find information that shows important relationships and helps them make comparisons from year to year and from company to company. The many techniques that together are called financial statement analysis accomplish this goal.

Objectives of Financial Statement Analysis

Those who use financial statements fall into two broad categories: internal and external. Management is the main internal user. The tools of financial analysis are, of course, useful in management's operation of the business. However, because those who run the company have inside information on operations, other techniques are available to them. So the main focus here is on the external use of financial analysis.

Creditors make loans in the form of trade accounts, notes, or bonds, on which they receive interest. They expect a loan to be repaid according to its terms. Investors buy capital stock, from

Objective 1
Describe and
discuss the
objectives of
financial
statement
analysis

which they hope to receive dividends and an increase in value. Both groups face risks. The creditor faces the risk that the debtor will fail to pay back the loan. The investor faces the risk that dividends will be reduced or not paid or that the price of the stock will drop. In each case, the goal is to achieve a return that makes up for the risk taken. In general, the greater the risk taken, the greater the return required as compensation.

Any one loan or any one investment can turn out badly. As a result, most creditors and investors put their funds into a **portfolio** or group of loans or investments. The portfolio allows them to average both the return and the risk. Nevertheless, the portfolio is made up of a number of loans or stocks, on which individual decisions must be made. It is in making these individual decisions that financial statement analysis is most useful. Creditors and investors use financial statement analysis in two general ways. (1) They use it to judge past performance and current position. (2) They use it to judge future potential and the risk connected with the potential.

Assessment of Past Performance and Current Position

Past performance is often a good indicator of future performance. Therefore, an investor or creditor is interested in the trend of past sales, expenses, net income, cash flow, and return on investment. These trends offer a means for judging management's past performance and are a possible indicator of future performance. In addition, an analysis of current position will tell where the business stands today. For example, it will tell what assets the business owns and what liabilities must be paid. It will tell what the cash position is, how much debt the company has in relation to equity, and how reasonable the inventories and receivables are. Knowing a company's past performance and current position is often important in achieving the second general objective of financial analysis.

Assessment of Future Potential and Related Risk

The past and present information is useful only to the extent that it bears on decisions about the future. An investor judges the potential earning ability of a company because that ability will affect the value of the investment (market price of the company's stock) and the amount of dividends the company will pay. A creditor judges the potential debt-paying ability of the company. The potentials of some companies are easier to predict than others, and so there is less risk associated with them. The riskiness of the investment or loan depends on how easy it is to predict future profitability or liquidity. If an investor can predict with confidence that a company's earnings per share will be between $2.50 and $2.60 next year, the investment is less risky than if the earnings per share are expected to fall between $2.00 and $3.00. For example, the potential associated with an investment in an established and stable electric utility, or a loan to it, is relatively easy to predict on the basis of the company's past performance and current position. The potential associated with a small minicomputer manufacturer, on the other hand, may be much harder to predict. For this reason, the investment or loan to the electric utility is less risky than the

Chapter Twenty-One

investment or loan to the small computer company. Often, in return for taking the greater risk, the investor in the minicomputer company will demand a higher expected return (increase in market price plus dividends) than the investor in the utility company. Also, a creditor of the minicomputer company will need a higher interest rate and possibly more assurance of repayment (a secured loan, for instance) than a creditor to the utility company. The higher interest rate is payment to the creditor for assuming a higher risk.

Standards for Financial Statement Analysis

Objective 2
Describe and
discuss the
standards for
financial
statement
analysis

In using financial statement analysis, decision makers must judge whether the relationships that they have found are favorable or unfavorable. Three standards of comparison that are often used are (1) rule-of-thumb measures, (2) past performance of the company, and (3) industry norms.

Rule-of-Thumb Measures

Many financial analysts and lenders use "ideal" or rule-of-thumb measures for key financial ratios. For example, it has long been thought that a current ratio (current assets divided by current liabilities) of 2:1 is acceptable. The credit-rating firm of Dun and Bradstreet, in its *Key Business Ratios,* offers these guidelines:

Current debt to tangible net worth. Ordinarily, a business begins to pile up trouble when this relationship exceeds 80%.

Inventory to net working capital. Ordinarily, this relationship should not exceed 80%.

Although such measures may suggest areas that need further investigation, there is no proof that they are the best for any one company. On the one hand, a company with a larger than 2:1 current ratio may have a poor credit policy (resulting in accounts receivable being too large), too much or out-of-date inventory, or poor cash management. On the other hand, another company may have a less than 2:1 ratio that resulted from excellent management in these three areas. For this reason, rule-of-thumb measures must be used with great care.

Past Performance of the Company

An improvement over the rule-of-thumb method is the comparison of financial measures or ratios of the same company over a period of time. This standard will at least give the analyst some basis for judging whether the measure or ratio is getting better or worse. It may also be helpful in showing possible future trends. However, since trends do reverse at times, such projections must be made with care. Another disadvantage is that the past may not be a good measure of adequacy. In other words, it may not be enough to meet present needs. For example, even if return on total investment improved from 3 percent last year to 4 percent this year, the 4 percent return may not be adequate.

Industry Norms

One way of making up for the limitations of using past performance as a standard is to use industry norms. This standard will tell how the company being analyzed compares with other companies in the same industry. For example, suppose that other companies in the same industry as the company in the paragraph above have an average rate of return on total investment of 8 percent. In such a case the 3 and 4 percent returns are probably not adequate. Industry norms can also be used to judge trends. For example, suppose that because of a downward turn in the economy, a company's profit margin dropped from 12 to 10 percent. A finding that other companies in the same industry had an average drop in profit margin from 12 to 4 percent would indicate that the company being analyzed did relatively well.

There are three limitations to using industry norms as standards. First, even though two companies may seem to be in the same industry, they may not be strictly comparable. For example, consider two companies that are said to be in the oil industry. The main business of one may be marketing through service stations oil products it buys from other producers. The other may be an international company that discovers, produces, refines, and markets its own oil products. The operations of these companies cannot be compared.

Second, most companies today operate in more than one industry. Some of these **diversified companies,** or **conglomerates,** operate in many unrelated industries. The individual segments of a diversified company generally have different rates of profitability and degrees of risk. In using the consolidated financial statements of these companies for financial analysis, it is often impossible to use industry norms as standards. There are simply no other companies that are closely enough related. One partial solution to this problem is a requirement by the Financial Accounting Standards Board in *Statement No. 14.* This requirement states that diversified companies must report revenues, income from operations, and identifiable assets for each of their operating segments. Depending on specific criteria, segment information may be reported for operations in different industries, in foreign markets, or to major customers.[1] An example of reporting for industry segments is given in Figure 21-1, which comes from Eastman Kodak's annual report. It is interesting to compare the two reported segments, photographic and chemicals. In 1982, photographic sales were about 4 times chemical sales ($8,935 million versus $2,151 million). But they produced about 8 times as much earnings from operations ($1,655 million versus $205 million).

Third, companies in the same industry with similar operations use different accounting procedures. That is, inventories may be valued by using different methods, or different depreciation methods may be used for

1. *Statement of Financial Accounting Standards No. 14,* "Financial Reporting for Segments of a Business Enterprise" (Stamford, Conn.: Financial Accounting Standards Board, 1976).

Chapter Twenty-One

	1982	1981	1980
Sales, including intersegment sales*			
Photographic	$ 8,935	$ 8,258	$ 7,904
Chemicals	2,151	2,349	2,070
Intersegment sales			
Photographic	(9)	(8)	(7)
Chemicals	(262)	(262)	(233)
Sales to unaffiliated customers	$10,815	$10,337	$ 9,734
Earnings from operations			
Photographic	$ 1,655	$ 1,771	$ 1,579
Chemicals	205	289	317
Earnings from operations	$ 1,860	$ 2,060	$ 1,896
Interest and other income (charges)			
Photographic	7	42	6
Chemicals	2	2	3
Corporate	92	143	104
Interest expense	(89)	(64)	(46)
Earnings before income taxes	$ 1,872	$ 2,183	$ 1,963
Assets			
Photographic	$ 7,887	$ 6,802	$ 5,894
Chemicals	2,001	1,680	1,549
Corporate (cash and marketable securities)	948	1,004	1,450
Intersegment receivables	(214)	(40)	(139)
Total assets at year end	$10,622	$ 9,446	$ 8,754
Depreciation expense			
Photographic	$ 474	$ 356	$ 311
Chemicals	101	96	88
Total depreciation expense	$ 575	$ 452	$ 399
Capital expenditures			
Photographic	$ 1,035	$ 874	$ 734
Chemicals	465	316	168
Total capital expenditures	$ 1,500	$ 1,190	$ 902

*The products of each segment are manufactured and marketed in the U.S. and in other parts of the world. The Photographic segment includes film, paper, equipment, and other related products. The Chemicals segment includes fibers, plastics, industrial and other chemicals. Sales between segments are made on a basis intended to reflect the market value of the products.

Figure 21-1
Segment
Information

assets that are alike. Even so, if little information is available about a company's prior performance, industry norms probably offer the best available standards for judging a company's current performance. They should be used with care.

Sources of Information

*Objective 3
State the
sources of
information
for financial
statement
analysis*

The external analyst is often limited to publicly available information about a company. The major sources of information about publicly held corporations are published reports, SEC reports, business periodicals, and credit and investment advisory services.

Published Reports

The annual report of a publicly held corporation is an important source of financial information. The major parts of this annual report are (1) management's analysis of the past year's operations, (2) the financial statements, (3) the notes to the statements, including the principal accounting procedures used by the company, (4) the auditor's report, and (5) a summary of operations for a five- or ten-year period. Also, most publicly held companies publish interim financial statements each quarter. These reports present limited information in the form of condensed financial statements, which may be subject to a limited review or a full audit by the independent auditor. The interim statements are watched closely by the financial community for early signs of important changes in a company's earnings trend.[2]

SEC Reports

Publicly held corporations must file annual reports, quarterly reports, and current reports with the Securities and Exchange Commission (SEC). All such reports are available to the public for a small charge. The SEC calls for a standard form for the annual report (Form 10-K). This report is fuller than the published annual report. Form 10-K is, for this reason, a valuable source of information. It is available, free of charge, to stockholders of the company. The quarterly report (Form 10-Q) presents important facts about interim financial performance. The current report (Form 8-K) must be filed within fifteen days of the date of certain major events. It is often the first indicator of important changes that may affect the company's financial performance in the future.

Business Periodicals and Credit and Investment Advisory Services

Financial analysts must keep up with current events in the financial world. Probably the best source of financial news is the *Wall Street Journal*, which is published daily and is the most complete financial newspaper. Some helpful financial magazines, published every week or every two weeks, are *Forbes, Barrons, Fortune,* and the *Commercial and Financial Chronicle.* For further details about the financial history of companies, the publi-

---

2. Accounting Principles Board, *Opinion No. 28*, "Interim Financial Reporting" (New York: American Institute of Certified Public Accountants, 1973); and *Statement of Financial Accounting Standards No. 3*, "Reporting Accounting Change in Interim Financial Statements" (Stamford, Conn.: Financial Accounting Standards Board, 1974).

Chapter Twenty-One

cations of such services as Moody's Investors Services and Standard and Poor's Industrial Surveys are useful. Data on industry norms, average ratios and relationships, and credit ratings are available from such agencies as Dun and Bradstreet, Inc. Dun and Bradstreet offers, among other useful services, an annual analysis using 14 ratios of 125 industry groups classified as retailing, wholesaling, manufacturing, and construction in its *Key Business Ratios*. Another important source of industry data is the *Annual Statement Studies*, published by Robert Morris Associates, which present many facts and ratios for 223 different industries. Also, a number of private services are available to the analyst for a yearly fee.

Tools and Techniques of Financial Analysis

Few numbers by themselves mean very much. It is their relationship to other numbers or their change from one period to another that is important. The tools of financial analysis are intended to show relationships and changes. Among the more widely used of these techniques are horizontal analysis, trend analysis, vertical analysis, and ratio analysis.

Horizontal Analysis

Objective 4
Apply
horizontal
analysis, trend
analysis, and
vertical analysis
to financial
statements

Generally accepted accounting principles call for presenting comparative financial statements that give the current year's and past year's financial information. A common starting point for studying such statements is **horizontal analysis,** which involves the computation of dollar amount changes and percentage changes from year to year. The percentage change must be figured to show how the size of the change relates to the size of the amounts involved. A change of $1 million in sales is not so drastic as a change of $1 million in net income, because sales is a larger amount than net income. Figures 21-2 and 21-3 (next two pages) present the comparative balance sheet and income statement, respectively, for Eastman Kodak, with the dollar and percentage changes shown. The percentage change is figured as follows:

$$\text{percentage change} = 100\left(\frac{\text{amount of change}}{\text{base-year amount}}\right)$$

The **base year** in any set of data is always the first year being studied. For example, from 1981 to 1982, Eastman Kodak's current assets increased by $226 million, from $5,063 million to $5,289 million, or by 4.5 percent, figured as follows:

$$\text{percentage increase} = 100\left(\frac{\$226 \text{ million}}{\$5,063 \text{ million}}\right) = 4.5\%$$

Care must be taken in the analysis of percentage change. For example, in analyzing the changes in the components of total assets in Figure 21-2, one might place equal weight on the 21.7 percent increases in both properties and long-term receivables. In dollar amount, though, properties increased by more than eighteen times as much as long-term receivables

Figure 21-2
Comparative
Balance Sheet
with Hori-
zontal Analysis

Eastman Kodak
Consolidated Balance Sheet
December 26, 1982 and December 27, 1981

	(In millions)		Increase (Decrease)	
	1982	1981	Amount	Percentage
Assets				
Current Assets				
Cash	$ 90	$ 163	$ (73)	(44.8)
Marketable securities	928	959	(31)	(3.2)
Receivables	1,829	1,709	120	7.0
Inventories	2,101	1,970	131	6.6
Prepaid expense and deferred charges	341	262	79	30.2
Total Current Assets	$ 5,289	$5,063	$ 226	4.5
Properties				
Land, buildings, machinery, and equipment less accumulated depreciation of $4,286 and $3,806	5,058	4,157	901	21.7
Long-term receivables and other noncurrent assets	275	226	49	21.7
Total Assets	$10,622	$9,446	$1,176	12.4
Liabilities				
Current Liabilities				
Payables	$ 1,670	$1,605	$ 65	4.0
Taxes	261	311	(50)	(16.1)
Dividends payable	215	203	12	5.9
Total current liabilities	$ 2,146	$2,119	$ 27	1.3
Debentures	341	66	275	416.7
Other long-term liabilities	148	142	6	4.2
Deferred income tax liabilities	446	349	97	27.8
Total Liabilities	$ 3,081	$2,676	$ 405	15.1
Ownership				
Common stock (par value)	$ 414	$ 407	$ 7	1.7
Additional paid-in capital	519	336	183	54.5
Retained earnings	6,608	6,027	581	9.6
Total Ownership	$ 7,541	$6,770	$ 771	11.4
Total Liabilities and Ownership	$10,622	$9,446	$1,176	12.4

Figure 21-3
Comparative
Income State-
ment with
Horizontal
Analysis

Eastman Kodak Consolidated Statement of Earnings For Years Ended December 26, 1982 and December 27, 1981				
	(In millions)		Increase (Decrease)	
	1982	1981	1982	1981
Sales	$10,815	$10,337	$ 478	4.6
Costs and Expenses				
Cost of goods sold	$ 6,830	$ 6,342	$ 488	7.7
Selling and administrative expenses	2,125	1,935	190	9.8
Total costs and expenses	$ 8,955	$ 8,277	$ 678	8.2
Earnings from Operations	$ 1,860	$ 2,060	$(200)	(9.7)
Other income and expenses including interest expense of $89 and $64	12	123	$(111)	(90.2)
Earnings Before Income Taxes	1,872	2,183	$(311)	(14.2)
Provision for income taxes	710	944	(234)	(24.8)
Net Earnings	$ 1,162	$ 1,239	$ (77)	(6.2)
Average number of common shares outstanding	163.2	161.7	1.5	.1
Net Earnings per Share	$ 7.12	$ 7.66	$ (.54)	(7.0)

($901 million versus $49 million). Dollar amounts and percentage increases must be considered together. On the liability side of the balance sheet, we can see that the company is relying more on long-term financing. This fact is shown by the increase in debentures of 416.7 percent ($275 million) at the same time that current liabilities went up by only $27 million or 1.3 percent.

In the income statement (Figure 21-3), the most important changes from 1981 to 1982 show a 4.6 percent growth in sales compared to an 8.2 percent rise in costs and expenses. When combined, these figures result in a 9.7 percent decrease in earnings from operations. Other income and expenses were also down a substantial 90.2 percent. Overall net earnings were down a more moderate 6.2 percent because the provision for income taxes decreased by 24.8 percent.

Trend Analysis

A variation of horizontal analysis is trend analysis, in which percentage changes are calculated for several successive years instead of between two years. Trend analysis is important because, with its long-run view, it may

Figure 21-4
Trend Analysis

Eastman Kodak
Summary of Operations
Selected Data
(Sales and Net Earnings in Millions)

	1982	1981	1980	1979	1978
Sales	$10,815	$10,337	$9,734	$8,028	$7,013
Net Earnings	1,162	1,239	1,154	1,001	902
Per Common Share					
Income	7.12	7.66	7.15	6.20	5.59
Dividends	3.55	3.50	3.20	2.90	2.33
Trend Analysis					
Sales	154.2	147.4	138.8	114.5	100.0
Net Earnings	128.8	137.4	127.9	111.0	100.0
Per Common Share					
Income	127.4	137.0	127.9	110.9	100.0
Dividends	152.4	150.2	137.3	124.5	100.0

point to basic changes in the nature of the business. Besides comparative financial statements, most companies give out a summary of operations and data on other key indicators for five or more years. Selected items from Eastman Kodak's summary of operations together with trend analysis are presented in Figure 21-4. Trend analysis uses an **index number** to show changes in related items over a period of time. For index numbers, one year, the base year, is equal to 100 percent. Other years are measured in relation to that amount. For example, the 1982 index of 154.2 for sales was figured as follows:

$$\text{index} = 100\left(\frac{\text{index year amount}}{\text{base year amount}}\right) = \left(\frac{\$10,815}{\$7,013}\right) = 154.2$$

An index number of 154.2 means that 1982 sales are 154.2 percent or 1.542 times 1978 sales. A study of the trend analysis in Figure 21-4 shows that sales grew more rapidly than net earnings over the five-year period. Sales had an index of 154.2 in 1982 versus 128.8 for net earnings. Income per common share closely paralleled net earnings (127.4 in 1982 versus 128.8), while dividends per share followed sales more closely (152.4 in 1982 versus 154.2). Apparently, the company felt it was important to keep up an increasing level of dividends in spite of the decrease in net earnings from 1981 to 1982.

Vertical Analysis

Vertical analysis uses percentages to show the relationship of the different parts to the total in a single statement. Vertical analysis sets a total figure in the statement equal to 100 percent and computes the percentage of each component of that figure. (This figure would be total assets or total liabilities and stockholders' equity in the case of the balance sheet, and revenues or sales in the case of the income statement.) The resulting statement of percentages is called a **common-size statement.** Common-size balance sheets and income statements for Eastman Kodak are shown in Figures 21-5 and 21-6 (next page). Generally, current assets and current liabilities are given only in total, because ratio analysis studies some of their components very carefully. Vertical analysis is useful for comparing the importance of certain components in the operation of the business. It is also useful for pointing out important changes in the components from one year to the next when comparative common-size statements are presented. For Eastman Kodak, the composition of assets in Figure 21-5 changed. More assets were in properties (47.6 percent versus 44.0 percent) and fewer were in current assets (49.8 percent versus 53.6 percent) in 1982 as opposed to 1981. Also, the part of total liabilities made up of current liabilities went down slightly, from 22.4 percent to 20.2 percent.

Figure 21-5
Common-Size
Balance Sheet

Eastman Kodak
Common-Size Balance Sheet
December 26, 1982 and December 27, 1981

	1982	1981
Assets		
Current Assets	49.8%	53.6%
Properties (less Accumulated Depreciation)	47.6	44.0
Long-Term Receivables and Other		
Noncurrent Assets	2.6	2.4
Total Assets	100.0%	100.0%
Liabilities		
Current Liabilities	20.2%	22.4%
Debentures	3.2	.7
Other Long-Term Liabilities	1.4	1.5
Deferred Income Tax Liabilities	4.2	3.7
Total Liabilities	29.0%	28.3%
Ownership		
Common Stock	3.9%	4.3%
Additional Paid-In Capital	4.9	3.6
Retained Earnings	62.2	63.8
Total Ownership	71.0%	71.7%
Total Liabilities and Ownership	100.0%	100.0%

Figure 21-6
Common-Size
Income
Statement

Eastman Kodak Common-Size Statement of Earnings For Years Ended December 26, 1982 and December 27, 1981		
	1982	1981
Sales	100.0%	100.0%
Cost and Expenses		
Cost of Goods Sold	63.2	61.4
Selling and Administrative Expenses	19.6	18.7
Total Costs and Expenses	82.8%	80.1%
Earnings from Operations	17.2	19.9
Other Income and Expenses	.1	1.2
Earnings Before Income Taxes	17.3%	21.1%
Provision for Income Taxes	6.6	9.1
Net Earnings	10.7%	12.0%

The difference was made up by the increase in debentures from .7 percent to 3.2 percent. The common-size income statement (Figure 21-6) shows the importance of the rise in costs and expenses from 80.1 to 82.8 percent of sales. This increase was the major cause of the decrease in earnings from operations from 19.9 to 17.2 percent of sales. The favorable change in income taxes is shown by the decrease in the provision for income taxes from 9.1 percent to 6.6 percent of sales.

Common-size statements are often used to make comparisons between companies. They allow an analyst to compare the operating and financing characteristics of two companies of different sizes in the same industry. For example, the analyst may want to compare Eastman Kodak to other companies in terms of the percentage of total assets financed by debt or the percentage of general administrative and selling expenses to sales and revenues. Common-size statements would show these relationships.

Ratio Analysis

Objective 5
Apply ratio
analysis to
financial state-
ments in the
study of an
enterprise's
liquidity, profit-
ability,
long-term
solvency, and
market tests

Ratio analysis is an important means of stating the relationship between two numbers. To be useful, a ratio must represent a meaningful relationship, but use of ratios cannot take the place of studying the underlying data. Ratios are guides or short cuts that are useful in evaluating the financial position and operations of a company and in comparing them to previous years or to other companies. The primary purpose of ratios is to point out areas for further investigation.

Ratios may be stated in several ways. For example, the ratio of net income of $100,000 to sales of $1,000,000 may be stated as (1) net income is 1/10 or 10 percent of sales; (2) the ratio of sales to net income is 10 to 1 (10:1) or 10 times net income, or (3) for every dollar of sales, the company has an average net income of 10 cents.

Survey of Commonly Used Ratios

In the following sections, ratio analysis is applied to four objectives: the evaluation of (1) liquidity, (2) profitability, (3) long-term solvency, and (4) market strength. Chapter 9 addressed the first two objectives in an introductory way. Here we expand the evaluation to bring in other ratios related to these objectives and to introduce the ratios related to two new objectives. Data for the analyses come from the financial statements of Eastman Kodak presented in Figures 21-2 and 21-3. Other data are presented as needed.

Evaluating Liquidity

The aim of liquidity is for a company to have enough funds on hand to pay bills when they are due and to meet unexpected needs for cash. The ratios that relate to this goal all have to do with working capital or some part of it, because it is out of working capital that debts are paid as they mature. Some common ratios connected with evaluating liquidity are the current ratio, the quick ratio, receivable turnover, and inventory turnover.

Current Ratio   The current ratio expresses the relationship of current assets to current liabilities. It is widely used as a broad indicator of a company's liquidity and short-term debt-paying ability. The ratio for Eastman Kodak for 1982 and 1981 is figured as follows:

Current Ratio	**1982**	**1981**
$\dfrac{\text{current assets}}{\text{current liabilities}}$	$\dfrac{\$5,289}{\$2,146} = 2.46$	$\dfrac{\$5,063}{\$2,119} = 2.39$

The current ratio for Eastman Kodak shows a slight increase from 1981 to 1982.

Quick Ratio   One of the current ratio's faults is that it does not take into account the make-up of current assets. They may appear to be large enough, but they may not have the proper balance. Clearly, a dollar of cash or even accounts receivable is more readily available to meet obligations than is a dollar of most kinds of inventory. The quick ratio is designed to overcome this problem by measuring short-term liquidity. That is, it measures the relationship of the more liquid current assets (cash, marketable securities or short-term investments, and receivables) to current liabilities. This ratio for Eastman Kodak for 1982 and 1981 is figured as follows:

Quick Ratio	**1982**	**1981**
$\dfrac{\text{cash + marketable securities + receivables}}{\text{current liabilities}}$	$\dfrac{\$90 + \$928 + \$1,829}{\$2,146}$	$\dfrac{\$163 + \$959 + \$1,709}{\$2,119}$
	$= \dfrac{\$2,847}{\$2,146} = 1.33$	$= \dfrac{\$2,831}{\$2,119} = 1.34$

This ratio shows almost no change from 1981 to 1982.

Financial Statement Analysis

Receivable Turnover The ability of a company to collect for credit sales in a timely way affects the company's liquidity. The **receivable turnover** ratio measures the relative size of a company's accounts receivable and the success of its credit and collection policies. This ratio shows how many times, on average, the receivables were turned into cash during the period. Turnover ratios usually consist of one balance sheet account and one income statement account. The receivable turnover is figured by dividing sales by average accounts receivable. Theoretically, the numerator should be credit sales, but the amount of credit sales is rarely made available in public reports. So we will use total sales. Further, in this ratio and others where an average is required, we will take the beginning and ending balances and divide by 2. If we had internal financial data, it would be better to use monthly balances to find the average, because the balances of receivables, inventories, and other accounts can vary widely during the year. In fact, many companies choose a fiscal year that begins and ends at a low period of the business cycle when inventories and receivables may be at the lowest levels of the year. Using a 1980 accounts receivable balance of $1,678 million, Eastman Kodak's receivable turnover is figured as follows:

Receivable Turnover	1982	1981
$\dfrac{\text{sales}}{\text{average accounts receivable}}$	$\dfrac{\$10,815}{(\$1,829 + \$1,709)\frac{1}{2}}$	$\dfrac{\$10,337}{(\$1,709 + \$1,678)\frac{1}{2}}$
	$= \dfrac{\$10,815}{\$1,769} = 6.11$ times	$= \dfrac{\$10,337}{\$1,693.5} = 6.10$ times

When the previous year's balance is not available for figuring the average, it is common practice to use the ending balance for the current year.

The higher the turnover ratio the better. With a higher turnover the company is turning receivables into cash at a faster pace. The speed at which receivables are turned over depends on the company's credit terms. Since a company's credit terms are usually stated in days, such as 2/10, n/30, it is helpful to convert the receivable turnover to **average days' sales uncollected.** This conversion is made by dividing the length of the accounting period (usually 365 days) by the receivable turnover (as computed above) as follows:

Average Days' Sales Uncollected	1982	1981
$\dfrac{\text{days in year}}{\text{receivable turnover}}$	$\dfrac{365 \text{ days}}{6.11} = 59.74$ days	$\dfrac{365 \text{ days}}{6.10} = 59.84$ days

In the case of Eastman Kodak, both the receivable turnover and the average days' sales uncollected were very stable from 1981 to 1982. The average accounts receivable was turned over about 6 times per year and Eastman Kodak had to wait on average about 60 days to receive payment for credit sales.

Inventory Turnover Inventory is two steps removed from cash (sale and collection). Inventory turnover measures the relative size of inventory and affects the amount of cash available to pay maturing debts. Of course, inventory should be maintained at the best level to support production and sales. In general, however, a smaller, faster-moving inventory means that the company has less cash tied up in inventory. It also means that there is less chance for the inventory to become spoiled or out of date. A build-up in inventory may mean that a recession or some other factor is preventing sales from keeping pace with purchasing and production. Using a 1980 inventory balance of $1,703, inventory turnover for 1982 and 1981 at Eastman Kodak is figured as follows:

Inventory Turnover	1982	1981
$\dfrac{\text{cost of goods sold}}{\text{average inventory}}$	$\dfrac{\$6,830}{(\$2,101 + \$1,970)\frac{1}{2}}$	$\dfrac{\$6,342}{(\$1,970 + \$1,703)\frac{1}{2}}$
	$= \dfrac{\$6,830}{\$2,035.5} = \dfrac{3.36}{\text{times}}$	$= \dfrac{\$6,342}{\$1,836.5} = \dfrac{3.45}{\text{times}}$

As with receivable turnover, there was little change in inventory turnover from 1981 to 1982.

Evaluating Profitability

A company's long-run survival depends on its being able to earn a satisfactory income. Investors become and remain stockholders only for a reason. They believe that the dividends and capital gains they will receive will be greater than the returns on other investments of about the same risk. An evaluation of a company's past earning power may give the investor a better understanding for decision making. Also, as pointed out in Chapter 9, a company's ability to earn an income usually affects its liquidity position. For this reason, evaluating profitability is important to both investors and creditors. In judging the profitability of Eastman Kodak, five ratios will be presented: profit margin, asset turnover, return on assets, return on equity, and earnings per share. All of these except asset turnover were introduced in Chapter 9.

Profit Margin The profit margin ratio measures the percentage of each revenue dollar that results in net income. It is figured for Eastman Kodak as follows:

Profit Margin[3]	1982	1981
$\dfrac{\text{net income}}{\text{sales}}$	$\dfrac{\$1,162}{\$10,815} = 10.7\%$	$\dfrac{\$1,239}{\$10,337} = 12.0\%$

The ratio confirms what was clear from the common-size income statement (Figure 21-6): that the profit margin decreased from 1981 (12.0 per-

3. In comparing companies in an industry, some analysts use net income before income taxes as the numerator to eliminate the effect of differing tax rates among the individual firms.

Financial Statement Analysis

cent) to 1982 (10.7 percent). The analysis of the common-size income statement showed that this decline was due mainly to an increase in costs and expenses as a percentage of total sales.

Asset Turnover Asset turnover is a measure of how efficiently assets are used to produce sales. It shows how many dollars in sales are produced by each dollar invested in assets. In other words, it tells how many times in the period assets were "turned over" in sales. The higher the asset turnover, the more concentrated is the use of assets. Using the data for Eastman Kodak from Figures 21-2 and 21-3 and 1980 total assets of $8,754 million, the asset turnovers for 1982 and 1981 are as follows:

Asset Turnover	**1982**	**1981**
$\dfrac{\text{revenues}}{\text{average assets}}$	$\dfrac{\$10,815}{(\$10,622 + \$9,446)\frac{1}{2}}$	$\dfrac{\$10,337}{(\$9,446 + \$8,754)\frac{1}{2}}$
	$= \dfrac{\$10,815}{\$10,034} = \dfrac{1.08}{\text{times}}$	$= \dfrac{\$10,337}{\$9,100} = \dfrac{1.14}{\text{times}}$

Compared to other industries, Eastman Kodak needs a large investment in assets for each dollar of sales. A retailer may have an asset turnover of between 4.0 and 6.0. In the case of Eastman Kodak, however, the turnover was only 1.14 in 1981 and 1.08 in 1982. This fact means that Eastman Kodak makes sales of a little more than one dollar for each dollar of assets. Or to put it another way, a dollar invested puts a little more than a dollar into sales.

Return on Assets The best overall measure of the earning power or profitability of a company is return on assets, which measures the amount earned on each dollar of assets invested. The return on assets for 1982 and 1981 for Eastman Kodak is as follows:

Return on Assets[4]	**1982**	**1981**
$\dfrac{\text{net income}}{\text{average assets}}$	$\dfrac{\$1,162}{\$10,034} = 11.6\%$	$\dfrac{\$1,239}{\$9,100} = 13.6\%$

Eastman Kodak's return on assets decreased from 13.6 percent in 1981 to 11.6 percent in 1982, an unfavorable change.

One reason why return on assets is a good measure of profitability is that it combines the effects of profit margin and asset turnover. The 1981 and 1982 results for Eastman Kodak can be analyzed as follows:

	Profit Margin		**Asset Turnover**		**Return on Assets**
Ratios:	$\dfrac{\text{net income}}{\text{sales}}$	$\times$	$\dfrac{\text{sales}}{\text{average total assets}}$	$=$	$\dfrac{\text{net income}}{\text{average total assets}}$

4. Some authorities would add interest expense to net income in the numerator because they view interest expense as a cost of acquiring capital, not a cost of operations.

| 1981 | 12.0% | × 1.14 | = 13.6% |
| 1982 | 10.7% | × 1.08 | = 11.6% |

From this analysis, it is clear that the decrease in return on assets in 1982 can be attributed to decreases in both profit margin and asset turnover. The poor economy together with inflation in 1982 led to lower profitability.

Return on Equity An important measure of profitability from the stockholders' standpoint is return on equity. This ratio measures how much was earned for each dollar invested by owners. For Eastman Kodak, this ratio for 1982 and 1981 is figured as follows (1980 owners' equity equals $6,028 million):

Return on Equity	**1982**	**1981**
$\dfrac{\text{net income}}{\text{average owners' equity}}$	$\dfrac{\$1,162}{(\$7,541 + \$6,770)\frac{1}{2}}$	$\dfrac{\$1,239}{(\$6,770 + \$6,028)\frac{1}{2}}$
	$= \dfrac{\$1,162}{\$7,155.50} = 16.2\%$	$= \dfrac{\$1,239}{\$6,399} = 19.4\%$

As might be expected from the analysis of other profitability ratios above, this ratio also went down from 1981 to 1982.

A natural question is, Why is there a difference between return on assets and return on equity? The answer lies in the company's use of leverage, or debt financing. A company that has interest-bearing debt is said to be leveraged. If the company earns more with its borrowed funds than it must pay in interest for those funds, then the difference is available to increase the return on equity. Because of Eastman Kodak's leverage, the decrease in return on assets from 1981 to 1982 of 13.6 to 11.6 percent resulted in a larger decrease in return on equity of 19.4 to 16.2 for the same two years. (The debt to equity ratio is presented later in this chapter.)

Earnings per Share One of the most widely quoted measures of profitability is earnings per share of common stock. Figure 21-4 shows that the primary earnings per share for Eastman Kodak fell from $7.66 to $7.12, reflecting the decrease in net income from 1981 to 1982. These disclosures must be made in financial statements; calculations of this kind were presented in Chapter 17.

Evaluation of Long-Term Solvency

Long-term solvency has to do with a company's ability to survive over many years. The aim of long-term solvency analysis is to point out early that a company is on the road to bankruptcy. Studies have shown that accounting ratios can show as much as five years in advance that a company may fail.[5] Declining profitability and liquidity ratios are key signs of possible business failure. Two other ratios that analysts often consider as indicators of long-term solvency are the debt to equity ratio and the interest coverage ratio.

Debt to Equity Ratio The existence of debt in a company's capital structure is thought to be risky. The company has a legal obligation to make interest payments on time and to pay the principal at the maturity date. And this obligation holds no matter what the level of the company's earnings is. If the payments are not made, the company may be forced into bankruptcy. In contrast, dividends and other distributions to equity holders are made only when the board of directors declares them. The **debt to equity ratio** measures the relationship of the company's assets provided by creditors to the amount provided by stockholders. The larger the debt to equity ratio, the more fixed obligations the company has and so the riskier the situation. This ratio is closely related to the capital structure ratio (debt to total assets) presented in Chapter 9 and to the common-size balance sheet in Figure 21-5. It is figured as follows:

Debt to Equity Ratio	1982	1981
$\dfrac{\text{total liabilities}}{\text{owners' equity}}$	$\dfrac{\$3,081}{\$7,541} = .41$	$\dfrac{\$2,676}{\$6,770} = .40$

From 1981 to 1982, the debt to equity ratio for Eastman Kodak went up from .40 to .41. This finding agrees with the analysis of the common-size balance sheet (Figure 21-5), which shows that the total debt of the company increased as a percentage of total assets in 1982.

Interest Coverage Ratio One question that usually arises at this point is, If debt is bad, why have any? The answer is that, as with many ratios, it is a matter of balance. In spite of its riskiness, debt is a flexible means of financing certain business operations. Also, because it usually carries a fixed interest charge, it limits the cost of financing. Thus if the company is able to earn a return on the assets greater than the cost of the interest, the company makes an overall profit.[6] However, the company runs the risk of not earning a return on assets equal to the interest cost of financing those assets, thereby incurring an overall loss. One measure of the degree of protection creditors have from a default on interest payments is the **interest coverage ratio**, computed as follows:

Interest Coverage Ratio	1982	1981
$\dfrac{\text{net income before taxes} + \text{interest expense}}{\text{interest expense}}$	$\dfrac{\$1,872 + \$89}{\$89}$	$\dfrac{\$2,183 + \$64}{\$64}$
	$= 22.03$ times	$= 35.11$ times

5. William H. Beaver, "Alternative Accounting Measures as Indicators of Failure," *Accounting Review* (January 1968); and Edward Altman, "Financial Ratios, Discriminant Analysis and the Prediction of Corporate Bankruptcy," *Journal of Finance* (September 1968).

6. In addition, as seen in Chapter 12, there are advantages to being a debtor in periods of inflation because the debt, which is fixed in dollar amount, may be repaid with cheaper dollars.

Chapter Twenty-One

Although interest coverage dropped during 1982, the interest payments are still well protected by a ratio of 22.03 times.

Market Test Ratios

The market price of a company's shares of stock is of interest to the analyst because it represents what investors as a whole think of a company at a point in time. Market price is the price at which people are willing to buy and sell the stock. It provides information about how investors view the potential return and risk connected with owning the company's stock. This information cannot be obtained by simply considering the market price of the stock by itself. Companies have different numbers of outstanding shares and different amounts of underlying earnings and dividends. So the market price must be related to the earnings per share, dividends per share, and prices of other companies' shares to get the necessary information. This analysis is done through the price/earnings ratio, the dividends yield, and market risk.

Price/Earnings Ratio   The price/earnings (P/E) ratio measures the ratio of the current market price of the stock to the earnings per share. Assuming a current market price of $85 and using the 1982 earnings per share for Eastman Kodak of $7.12 from Figure 21-4, we can figure the price/earnings ratio as follows:

$$\frac{\text{market price per share}}{\text{earnings per share}} = \frac{\$85}{\$7.12} = 11.9 \text{ times}$$

This ratio changes from day to day and from quarter to quarter as market price and earnings change. It tells how much the investing public as a whole is willing to pay for $1 of Eastman Kodak's earnings per share. At this time, Eastman Kodak's P/E ratio is 11.9 times the underlying earnings for that share of stock.

This ratio is very useful and widely applied because it allows companies to be compared. When a company's P/E ratio is higher than the P/E ratios for other companies, it usually means that investors feel that the company's earnings are going to grow at a faster rate than those of the other companies. On the other hand, a lower P/E ratio usually means a more negative assessment by investors. In this example, a P/E ratio of 11.9 for Eastman Kodak is about average for a successful and mature company in 1982. In comparison, the market was slightly less favorable toward General Mills (9.0 times earnings per share) and felt about the same toward IBM (11.0 times earnings per share).

Dividends Yield   The dividends yield is a measure of the current return to an investor in the stock. It is found by dividing the current annual dividend by the current market price of the stock. Assuming the same $85 per share and using the 1982 dividends of $3.55 per share for Eastman Kodak from Figure 21-4, we can figure the dividends yield as follows:

$$\frac{\text{dividends per share}}{\text{market price per share}} = \frac{\$3.55}{\$85} = 4.2\%$$

Thus an investor who owns Eastman Kodak stock at $85 had a return from dividends in 1982 of 4.2 percent. The dividends yield is only one part of the investor's total return from investing in Eastman Kodak. The investor must add or subtract from the dividends yield the percentage change (either up or down) in the market value of the stock.

Market Risk Earlier it was pointed out that besides assessing the potential return from an investment, the investor must also judge the risk associated with the investment. Many factors may be brought into assessing risk— the nature of the business, the quality of the business, the track record of the company, and so forth. One measure of risk that has gained increased attention among analysts in recent years is market risk. **Market risk** is the volatility of (or changes up and down in) the price of a stock in relation to the volatility of the prices of other stocks. The computation of market risk is complex, because it uses computers and sophisticated statistical techniques such as regression analysis. But the idea is simple. Consider the following data about the changes in the prices of the stocks of Company A and Company B and the average change in price of all stocks in the market:

Average Percentage Change in Price of All Stock	Percentage Change in Price of Company A's Stock	Percentage Change in Price of Company B's Stock
+10	+15	+5
−10	−15	−5

In this example, when the average price of all stocks went up by 10 percent, Company A's price increased 15 percent and Company B's increased only 5 percent. When the average price of all stocks went down by 10 percent, Company A's price decreased 15 percent and Company B's decreased only 5 percent. Thus, relative to all stocks, Company A's stock is more volatile than Company B's stock. If the prices of stocks go down, the risk of loss is greater in the case of Company A than in the case of Company B. If the market goes up, however, the potential for gain is greater in the case of Company A than in the case of Company B.

Market risk can be approximated by dividing the percentage change in price of the particular stock by the average percentage change in the price of all stocks, as follows:

$$\text{Company A} \quad \frac{\text{specific change}}{\text{average change}} = \frac{15}{10} = 1.5$$

$$\text{Company B} \quad \frac{\text{specific change}}{\text{average change}} = \frac{5}{10} = .5$$

These measures mean that an investor can generally expect the value of an investment in Company A to increase or decrease 1.5 times as much as the average increase or decrease in the price of all stocks. An investment in Company B can be expected to increase or decrease only .5 times as much as the price of all stocks.

Chapter Twenty-One

Analysts call this measure of market risk beta (β), after the mathematical symbol used in the formula for calculating the relationships of the stock prices. The actual betas used by analysts are based on several years of data and are continually updated. These calculations require the use of computers and are usually obtained from investment services.

The market risk or beta for U.S. Steel in a recent year was 1.01. This means that, other things being equal, a person who invests in the stock of U.S. Steel can expect its volatility or risk to be about the same as the stock market as a whole (which has a beta of 1.0). This makes sense when one considers that U.S. Steel is a mature company and the largest steel producer, with output closely related to the ups and downs in the economy as a whole.

If the investor's objective is to assume less risk than that of the market as a whole, other companies in the steel industry can be considered. The second largest steel company is Bethlehem Steel, but it can be eliminated because its beta of 1.25 makes it riskier than U.S. Steel. National Steel, the third largest steel processor, has been more stable over the years than its competitors, with a beta of only .75. It is a less risky stock in that there is less potential for loss in a "down" market, but there is also less potential for gain in an "up" market. The beta for National Steel is very low and compares favorably with that of a major regulated utility like American Telephone and Telegraph, which has a beta of .65.

Typically, growth stocks and speculative stocks are riskier than stocks in the market as a whole. Tandy Corporation (Radio Shack), a good example of a growth company, has had a beta of 1.45. It has rewarded investors' patience over the years but has been much more volatile and thus riskier than the average stock, which would have a beta of 1.00.

Investment decisions are not made on the basis of market risk alone, of course. First, other risk factors such as those indicated by the other ratios and analyses discussed in this chapter as well as by the industry, national, and world economic outlooks must be considered. Second, the expected return must be considered. Further, most investors try to own a portfolio of stocks whose average beta corresponds to the degree of risk they are willing to assume in relation to the average expected return of their portfolio.

Chapter Review

Review of Learning Objectives

1. Describe and discuss the objectives of financial statement analysis.

Creditors and investors use financial statement analysis to judge the past performance and current position of a company. In this way they also judge its future potential and the risk associated with this potential. Creditors use the information gained from analysis to help them make loans that will be repaid with interest. Investors use the information to help them make investments that provide a return that is worth the risk.

2. Describe and discuss the standards for financial statement analysis.

Three commonly used standards for financial statement analysis are rule-of-thumb measures, past performance of the company, and industry norms. Rule-of-thumb measures are weak because of the lack of evidence that they can be applied widely. The past performance of a company can offer a guideline for measuring improvement but is not helpful in judging performance relative to other companies. Although the use of industry norms overcomes this last problem, its disadvantage is that firms are not always comparable, even in the same industry.

3. State the sources of information for financial statement analysis.

The major sources of information about publicly held corporations are published reports such as annual reports and interim financial statements, SEC reports, business periodicals, and credit and investment advisory services.

4. Apply horizontal analysis, trend analysis, and vertical analysis to financial statements.

Horizontal analysis involves the computation of dollar amount changes and percentage changes from year to year. Trend analysis is an extension of horizontal analysis in that percentage changes are calculated for several years. The changes are usually computed by setting a base year equal to 100 and calculating the measures for subsequent years as a percentage of that base year. Vertical analysis uses percentages to show the relationship of the component parts to the total in a single statement. The resulting statements in percentages are called common-size statements.

5. Apply ratio analysis to financial statements in the study of an enterprise's liquidity, profitability, long-term solvency, and market tests.

The table below summarizes the basic information on ratio analysis.

Ratio	Components	Use or Meaning
Liquidity Ratios		
Current ratio	$\dfrac{\text{current assets}}{\text{current liabilities}}$	Measure of short-term debt-paying ability
Quick ratio	$\dfrac{\text{cash + short-term investments + receivables}}{\text{current liabilities}}$	Measure of short-term liquidity
Receivable turnover	$\dfrac{\text{sales}}{\text{average accounts receivable}}$	Measure of relative size of accounts receivable balance and effectiveness of credit policies
Average days' sales uncollected	$\dfrac{\text{days in year}}{\text{receivable turnover}}$	Measure of time it takes to collect an average receivable
Inventory turnover	$\dfrac{\text{cost of goods sold}}{\text{average inventory}}$	Measure of relative size of inventory

(continued)

Chapter Twenty-One

Ratio	Components	Use or Meaning
Profitability Ratios		
Profit margin	$\dfrac{\text{net income}}{\text{sales}}$	Income produced by each dollar of sales
Asset turnover	$\dfrac{\text{sales}}{\text{average total assets}}$	Measure of how efficiently assets are used to produce sales
Return on assets	$\dfrac{\text{net income}}{\text{average total assets}}$	Overall measure of earning power or profitability of all assets employed in the business
Return on equity	$\dfrac{\text{net income}}{\text{average owners' equity}}$	Profitabilty of owners' investment
Earnings per share	$\dfrac{\text{net income}}{\text{outstanding shares}}$	Means of placing earnings on a common basis for comparisons
Long-Term Solvency Ratios		
Debt to equity	$\dfrac{\text{total liabilities}}{\text{owners' equity}}$	Measure of relationship of debt financing to equity financing
Interest coverage	$\dfrac{\text{net income before taxes + interest expense}}{\text{interest expense}}$	Measure of protection of creditors from a default on interest payments
Market Test Ratios		
Price/earnings (P/E)	$\dfrac{\text{market price per share}}{\text{earnings per share}}$	Measure of amount the market will pay for a dollar of earnings
Dividends yield	$\dfrac{\text{dividends per share}}{\text{market price per share}}$	Measure of current return to investor
Market risk	$\dfrac{\text{specific change in market price}}{\text{average change in market price}}$	Measure of volatility of the market price of a stock in relation to that of other stocks

Review Problem
Comparative Analysis of Two Companies

Maggie Washington is considering an investment in one of two fast-food restaurant chains because she believes the trend toward eating out more often will continue. Her choices have been narrowed to Quik Burger and Big Steak, whose balance sheets and income statements are presented below.

Balance Sheets
(in thousands)

	Quik Burger	Big Steak
Assets		
Cash	$ 2,000	$ 4,500
Accounts Receivable (net)	2,000	6,500
Inventory	2,000	5,000
Property, Plant, and Equipment (net)	20,000	35,000
Other Assets	4,000	5,000
Total Assets	$30,000	$56,000
Liabilities and Stockholders' Equity		
Accounts Payable	$ 2,500	$ 3,000
Notes Payable	1,500	4,000
Bonds Payable	10,000	30,000
Common Stock ($1 par value)	1,000	3,000
Paid-in Capital in Excess of Par Value	9,000	9,000
Retained Earnings	6,000	7,000
Total Liabilities and Stockholders' Equity	$30,000	$56,000

Income Statements
(in thousands)

	Quik Burger	Big Steak
Sales	$53,000	$86,000
Cost of Goods Sold (including restaurant operating expense)	37,000	61,000
Gross Margin on Sales	$16,000	$25,000
General Operating Expenses		
Selling Expenses	$ 7,000	$10,000
Administrative Expenses	4,000	5,000
Interest Expense	1,400	3,200
Income Tax Expense	1,800	3,400
Total Operating Expenses	$14,200	$21,600
Net Income	$ 1,800	$ 3,400

In addition, dividends paid were $500,000 for Quik Burger and $600,000 for Big Steak. The market prices of the stock were $30 and $20, respectively. And the betas were 1.00 and 1.15. Information pertaining to prior years is not readily available to Maggie.

Required

Conduct a comprehensive ratio analysis of each company and compare the results. This analysis should be done in the following steps:

1. Prepare an analysis of liquidity.
2. Prepare an analysis of profitability.
3. Prepare an analysis of long-term solvency.
4. Prepare an analysis of market tests.
5. Compare the analysis of each company by inserting the ratio calculations from the preceding four steps in a table with the following columns: *Ratio Name, Quik Burger, Big Steak,* and *Company with More Favorable Ratio.* Indicate in the last column the company that apparently had the more favorable ratio in each case. (If ratios are within .1 of each other, consider them neutral.)
6. In what ways would having prior years' information aid this analysis?

Answer to Review Problem

Ratio Name	Quik Burger	Big Steak
1. Liquidity analysis		
a. Current ratio	$\dfrac{\$2{,}000 + \$2{,}000 + \$2{,}000}{\$2{,}500 + \$1{,}500}$	$\dfrac{\$4{,}500 + \$6{,}500 + \$5{,}000}{\$3{,}000 + \$4{,}000}$
	$= \dfrac{\$6{,}000}{\$4{,}000} = 1.5$	$= \dfrac{\$16{,}000}{\$7{,}000} = 2.3$
b. Quick ratio	$\dfrac{\$2{,}000 + \$2{,}000}{\$2{,}500 + \$1{,}500}$	$\dfrac{\$4{,}500 + \$6{,}500}{\$3{,}000 + \$4{,}000}$
	$= \dfrac{\$4{,}000}{\$4{,}000} = 1.0$	$= \dfrac{\$11{,}000}{\$7{,}000} = 1.6$
c. Receivable turnover	$\dfrac{\$53{,}000}{\$2{,}000} = 26.5$ times	$\dfrac{\$86{,}000}{\$6{,}500} = 13.2$ times
d. Average days' sales uncollected	$\dfrac{365}{26.5} = 13.8$ days	$\dfrac{365}{13.2} = 27.7$ days
e. Inventory turnover	$\dfrac{\$37{,}000}{\$2{,}000} = 18.5$ times	$\dfrac{\$61{,}000}{\$5{,}000} = 12.2$ times
2. Profitability analysis		
a. Profit margin	$\dfrac{\$1{,}800}{\$53{,}000} = 3.4\%$	$\dfrac{\$3{,}400}{\$86{,}000} = 4.0\%$
b. Asset turnover	$\dfrac{\$53{,}000}{\$30{,}000} = 1.8$ times	$\dfrac{\$86{,}000}{\$56{,}000} = 1.5$ times
c. Return on assets	$\dfrac{\$1{,}800}{\$30{,}000} = 6.0\%$	$\dfrac{\$3{,}400}{\$56{,}000} = 6.1\%$

d. Return on equity
$$\frac{\$1,800}{\$1,000 + \$9,000 + \$6,000}$$
$$= \frac{\$1,800}{\$16,000} = 11.3\%$$

$$\frac{\$3,400}{\$3,000 + \$9,000 + \$7,000}$$
$$= \frac{\$3,400}{\$19,000} = 17.9\%$$

e. Earnings per share
$$\frac{\$1,800,000}{1,000,000 \text{ shares}} = \$1.80$$

$$\frac{\$3,400,000}{3,000,000 \text{ shares}} = \$1.13$$

3. Long-term solvency

a. Debt to equity
$$\frac{\$2,500 + \$1,500 + \$10,000}{\$1,000 + \$9,000 + \$6,000}$$
$$= \frac{\$14,000}{\$16,000} = .9$$

$$\frac{\$3,000 + \$4,000 + \$30,000}{\$3,000 + \$9,000 + \$7,000}$$
$$= \frac{\$37,000}{\$19,000} = 1.9$$

b. Interest coverage
$$\frac{\$1,800 + \$1,800 + \$1,400}{\$1,400}$$
$$= \frac{\$5,000}{\$1,400} = 3.6 \text{ times}$$

$$\frac{\$3,400 + \$3,400 + \$3,200}{\$3,200}$$
$$= \frac{\$10,000}{\$3,200} = 3.1 \text{ times}$$

4. Market test analysis

a. Price/earnings ratio
$$\frac{\$30}{\$1.80} = 16.7$$

$$\frac{\$20}{\$1.13} = 17.7$$

b. Dividends yield
$$\frac{\$500,000 \div 1,000,000}{\$30} = 1.7\%$$

$$\frac{\$600,000 \div 3,000,000}{\$20} = 1.0\%$$

c. Market risk   1.00

1.15

5. Comparative analysis

Ratio	Quik Burger	Big Steak	Company with More Favorable Ratio*
1. Liquidity analysis			
a. Current ratio	1.5	2.3	Big Steak
b. Quick ratio	1.0	1.6	Big Steak
c. Receivable turnover	26.5 times	13.2 times	Quik Burger
d. Average days' sales uncollected	13.8 days	27.7 days	Quik Burger
e. Inventory turnover	18.5 times	12.2 times	Quik Burger
2. Profitability analysis			
a. Profit margin	3.4%	4.0%	Big Steak
b. Asset turnover	1.8 times	1.5 times	Quik Burger
c. Return on assets	6.0%	6.1%	Indeterminate
d. Return on equity	11.3%	17.9%	Big Steak
e. Earnings per share	$1.80	$1.13	Non-comparable†
3. Long-term solvency			
a. Debt to equity	.9	1.9	Quik Burger
b. Interest coverage	3.6 times	3.1 times	Quik Burger
4. Market test analysis			
a. Price/earnings ratio	16.7	17.7	Big Steak
b. Dividends yield	1.7%	1.0%	Quik Burger
c. Market risk	1.00	1.15	Quik Burger is less risky

*This analysis indicates the company with the apparently more favorable or unfavorable ratio. Class discussion may focus on conditions under which different conclusions may be drawn.

†Earnings per share is non-comparable because of the considerable difference in the number of common stockholders of the two firms. If information for prior years were available, it would be helpful in determining the earnings trend of each company.

6. Usefulness of prior years' information

The availability of prior years' information would be helpful in two ways. First, turnover and return ratios could be based on average amounts. Second, a trend analysis could be performed for each company.

Chapter Assign- ments

Questions

1. What differences and similarities exist in the objectives of investors and creditors in using financial statement analysis?

2. What role does risk play in making loans and investments?

3. What standards are commonly used to evaluate ratios, and what are their relative merits?

4. Where may an investor look to find information about a company in which he or she is thinking of investing?

5. Why would an investor want to do both horizontal and trend analyses of a company's financial statements?

6. What is the difference between horizontal and vertical analysis?

7. What does the following sentence mean: "Based on 1967 equaling 100, net income increased from 240 in 1980 to 260 in 1981"?

8. What is the purpose of ratio analysis?

9. Why would a financial analyst compare the ratios of Steelco, a steel company, to the ratios of other companies in the steel industry? What might cause such a comparison to be invalid?

10. In a period of high interest rates, why are receivable and inventory turnovers especially important?

11. The following statements were made on page 35 of the November 6, 1978, issue of *Fortune* magazine: "Supermarket executives are beginning to look back with some nostalgia on the days when the standard profit margin was 1 percent of sales. Last year the industry overall margin came to a thin 0.72 percent." How could a supermarket earn a satisfactory return on assets with such a small profit margin?

12. Circo Company has a return on assets of 12 percent and a debt to equity ratio of .5. Would you expect return on equity to be more or less than 12 percent?

13. Under what circumstances would a current ratio of 3 : 1 be good? Under what circumstances would it be bad?

14. Company A and Company B both have net incomes of $1,000,000. Is it possible to say that these companies are equally successful? Why or why not?

15. The market price of Company J's stock is the same as Company Q's stock. How might one determine whether investors are equally confident about the future of these companies?

16. Why is it riskier to own a stock whose market price is more changeable than the market price of other stocks?

17. "By almost any standard, Chicago-based Helene Curtis rates as one of America's worst-managed personal care companies. In recent years its return on equity has hovered between 10% and 13%, well below the industry average of 18% to 19%. Net profit margins of 2% to 3% are half that of competitors. . . . As a result, while leading names like Revlon and Avon are trading at three and four times book value, Curtis' trades at less than two-thirds book value."* Considering that

*Forbes, November 13, 1978, p. 154.

many companies are happy with a return on equity (owners' investment) of 10% and 13%, why is this analysis so critical of Curtis's performance? Assuming that Curtis could double its profit margin, what other information would you need to project the resulting return on owners' investment? Why does the writer feel that it is obvious that Revlon's and Avon's stocks are trading for more than Curtis's?

Classroom Exercises

Exercise 21-1
Trend Analysis
(L.O. 4)

Prepare a trend analysis of the data below, using 19x1 as a base year, and tell whether the situation shown by the trends is favorable or unfavorable. (Round your answers to one decimal point.)

	19x5	19x4	19x3	19x2	19x1
Sales	$12,650	$11,990	$12,100	$11,440	$11,000
Cost of Goods Sold	8,540	7,700	7,770	7,350	7,000
General and Administrative Expenses	2,640	2,592	2,544	2,448	2,400
Operating Income	1,470	1,698	1,786	1,642	1,600

Exercise 21-2
Horizontal Analysis
(L.O. 4)

Compute amount and percentage changes for the balance sheet below, and comment on the changes from 19x1 to 19x2. (Round the percentage changes to one decimal point.)

Meadows Company
Comparative Balance Sheets
December 31, 19x2 and 19x1

	19x2	19x1
Assets		
Current Assets	$ 19,200	$ 12,800
Property, Plant, and Equipment (net)	108,864	97,200
Total Assets	$128,064	$110,000
Liabilities and Stockholders' Equity		
Current Liabilities	$ 11,200	$ 3,200
Long-Term Liabilities	35,000	40,000
Stockholders' Equity	81,864	66,800
Total Liabilities and Owners' Equity	$128,064	$110,000

Exercise 21-3
Vertical Analysis
(L.O. 4)

Express the comparative income statements on the next page as common-size statements, and comment on the changes from 19x1 to 19x2. (Round computations to one decimal point.)

Meadows Company
Comparative Income Statement
For the Years Ended December 31, 19x2 and 19x1

	19x2	19x1
Sales	$212,000	$184,000
Cost of Goods Sold	127,200	119,600
Gross Margin on Sales	$ 84,800	$ 64,400
Selling Expenses	$ 53,000	$ 36,800
General Expenses	25,440	18,400
Total Operating Expenses	$ 78,440	$ 55,200
Net Operating Income	$ 6,360	$ 9,200

Exercise 21-4
Liquidity
Analysis
(L.O. 5)

Partial comparative balance sheet and income statement information for Moody Company appears below.

	19x2	19x1
Cash	$ 3,400	$ 2,600
Marketable Securities	1,800	4,300
Accounts Receivable (net)	11,200	8,900
Inventory	13,600	12,400
Total Current Assets	$30,000	$28,200
Current Liabilities	$10,000	$ 7,050
Sales	$80,640	$55,180
Cost of Goods Sold	54,400	50,840
Gross Margin on Sales	$26,240	$ 4,340

In addition, accounts receivable and inventories were $8,100 and $12,800, respectively, in 19x0. Figure the current ratio, quick ratio, receivable turnover, average days' sales uncollected, and inventory turnover for each year. Comment on the change in liquidity position from 19x1 to 19x2. (Round computations to one decimal point.)

Exercise 21-5
Profitability
Analysis
(L.O. 5)

Birch Company had total assets of $320,000 in 19x0, $340,000 in 19x1 and $380,000 in 19x2 and a debt to equity ratio of .67 in all three years. In 19x1, the company made a net income of $38,556 on revenues of $612,000. In 19x2, the company made a net income of $49,476 on revenues of $798,000. Figure the profit margin, asset turnover, return on assets, and return on equity for 19x1 and 19x2. Comment on the apparent cause of the increase or decrease in profitability. (Round the percentages and other ratios to one decimal point.)

Exercise 21-6
Long-Term
Solvency and
Market Test
Ratios
(L.O. 5)

An investor is considering investments in the long-term bonds and common stock of Companies J and K. Both companies operate in the same industry, but Company J has a beta of 1.0 and Company K has a beta of 1.2. In addition, both companies pay a dividend per share of $2, and the yield of both companies' long-term bonds is 10 percent. Other data for the two companies are presented below.

	Company J	Company K
Total Assets	$1,200,000	$540,000
Total Liabilities	540,000	297,000
Net Income Before Taxes	144,000	64,800
Interest Expense	48,600	26,730
Earnings per Share	1.60	2.50
Market Price on Common Stock	20	$23\frac{3}{4}$

Figure debt to equity ratios, interest coverage ratios, price/earnings (P/E) ratios, and dividend yield ratios, and comment on the results. (Round computations to one decimal point.)

Interpreting Accounting Information

Published Financial Information: Ford Motor Company
(L.O. 5)

Standard & Poor's Corporation (S & P) offers wide financial information services to investors. One of its services is rating the quality of bond issues of U.S. corporations. Its top bond rating is AAA, followed by AA, A, BBB, BB, B, and so forth. The lowest rating of C is reserved for companies that are in or near bankruptcy. *Business Week* reported on February 2, 1981, that S & P had downgraded the bond rating for Ford Motor Company, a leading U.S. automobile maker, from AAA to AA. The cause of the downgrading was a deterioration of Ford's financial strength as indicated by certain ratios considered important by S & P. These ratios, S & P's guidelines, and Ford's performance are summarized in the table below:

Ratio	S & P Guideline for AAA rating	Ford's Performance		
		1978	1979	1980
Interest Coverage	15 times	15.3 times	6.5 times	Deficit
Pretax Return on Assets	15% to 20%	13.4%	6.6%	Deficit
Debt to Equity	50%	34%	37.8%	63.4%
Cash Flow as a Percentage of Total Debt*	100%	152.6%	118.5%	9.1%
Short-Term Debt as a Percentage of Total Debt	25%	43.1%	48.3%	52.5%

*Cash flow includes net income plus noncash charges to earnings.

Required

1. Identify the objective (profitability, liquidity, long-term solvency) measured by each of the S & P ratios. Why is each ratio important to the rating of Ford's long-term bonds?
2. In the *Business Week* article, several actions were suggested for Ford to take to regain its previous status. Tell which of the ratios each of the following actions would improve: (a) "cutting operating costs"; (b) "scrapping at least part of its massive spending plans over the next several years"; (c) "eliminate cash dividends to stockholders"; (d) "sale of profitable nonautomobile-related operations such as its steelmaker, aerospace company, and electronic concerns."

Problem 21A-1
Analyzing the
Effects of
Transactions on
Ratios
(L.O. 5)

Problem Set A

Lowe Corporation engaged in the transactions listed in the first column of the table below. Opposite each transaction is a ratio and spaces to mark the effect of each transaction on the ratio.

| | Transaction | Ratio | Effect | | |
			Increase	Decrease	None
a.	Issued common stock for cash.	Asset turnover			
b.	Declared cash dividend.	Current ratio			
c.	Sold treasury stock.	Return on equity			
d.	Borrowed cash by issuing a note payable.	Debt to equity			
e.	Paid salary expense.	Inventory turnover			
f.	Purchased merchandise for cash.	Current ratio			
g.	Sold equipment for cash.	Receivable turnover			
h.	Sold merchandise on account.	Quick ratio			
i.	Paid current portion of long-term debt.	Return on assets			
j.	Gave a sales discount.	Profit margin			
k.	Purchased marketable securities for cash.	Quick ratio			
l.	Declared a 5% stock dividend.	Current ratio			

Required

Place an X in the appropriate column to show whether the transaction increased, decreased, or had no effect on the indicated ratio.

The condensed comparative income statement and selected comparative balance sheet data for O'Brian Corporation are presented at the top of the next page.

Required

1. Prepare a trend analysis for O'Brian Corporation, using 19x1 as the base year. (Round percentages to one decimal point.)
2. Comment on favorable and unfavorable trends shown in the analysis.

The condensed comparative statements of Blackhurst Corporation appear as shown on pages 816–817.

Required

(Round all ratios and percentages to one decimal point.)

1. Prepare a schedule showing amount and percentage changes from 19x1 to 19x2 for the comparative income statement and balance sheet.
2. Prepare a common-size income statement and balance sheet for 19x1 and 19x2.

Problem 21A-2 (*continued*)

O'Brian Corporation
Comparative Income Statement
For the Years Ended December 31, 19x5–19x1
(in thousands of dollars)

	19x5	19x4	19x3	19x2	19x1
Sales	$162,432	$118,195	$103,175	$91,152	$86,400
Cost of Goods Sold	78,600	59,500	50,700	46,600	42,600
Gross Margin on Sales	$ 83,832	$ 58,695	$ 52,475	$44,552	$43,800
Operating Expenses	56,100	43,000	41,000	36,000	34,000
Net Income	$ 27,732	$ 15,695	$ 11,475	$ 8,552	$ 9,800

Selected Balance Sheet Data

	19x5	19x4	19x3	19x2	19x1
Accounts Receivable	$24,500	$19,600	$17,200	$14,800	$12,800
Inventory	29,500	21,800	19,400	16,200	14,700
Current Assets	80,200	70,600	59,800	44,800	35,900
Current Liabilities	40,600	36,200	29,400	25,800	22,600

Problem 21A-3
(*continued*)

Blackhurst Corporation
Comparative Income Statement
For the Years Ended December 31, 19x2 and 19x1

	19x2	19x1
Sales	$791,200	$742,600
Cost of Goods Sold	454,100	396,200
Gross Margin on Sales	$337,100	$346,400
Operating Expenses		
Selling Expenses	$130,100	$104,600
Administrative Expenses	140,300	115,500
Interest Expense	25,000	20,000
Income Tax Expense	14,000	35,000
Total Operating Expenses	$309,400	$275,100
Net Income	$ 27,700	$ 71,300

Blackhurst Corporation
Comparative Balance Sheet
December 31, 19x2 and 19x1

	19x2	19x1
Assets		
Cash	$ 31,100	$ 27,200
Accounts Receivable (net)	72,500	42,700
Inventory	122,600	107,800
Property, Plant, and Equipment	577,700	507,500
Total Assets	$803,900	$685,200
Liabilities and Stockholders' Equity		
Accounts Payable	$104,700	$ 72,300
Notes Payable	50,000	50,000
Bonds Payable	200,000	150,000
Common Stock—$10 par value	300,000	300,000
Retained Earnings	149,200	112,900
Total Liabilities and Stockholders' Equity	$803,900	$685,200

3. Comment on the results found in **1** and **2** by identifying favorable and unfavorable changes in components and composition.

**Problem 21A-4
Ratio Analysis
(L.O. 5)**

Additional data for Blackhurst Corporation in 19x1 and 19x2 appear below. These data should be used in conjunction with the data in Problem 21A-3.

	19x2	19x1
Dividends Paid	$35,000	$35,000
Number of Common Shares	30,000	30,000
Market Price per Share	40	60
Beta	1.00	.90

Balances of selected accounts for 19x0 are Accounts Receivable (net), $52,700; Inventory, $99,400; Total Assets, $647,800; and Stockholders' Equity, $376,600. All of Blackhurst's Notes Payable are current liabilities; all the Bonds Payable are long-term liabilities.

Required

1. Prepare a liquidity analysis by calculating for 19x1 and 19x2 the (a) current ratio, (b) quick ratio, (c) receivable turnover, (d) average days' sales uncollected, and (e) inventory turnover. Indicate whether each ratio improved or not from 19x1 to 19x2 by using an F for favorable or U for unfavorable.
2. Prepare a profitability analysis by calculating for each year the (a) profit margin, (b) asset turnover, (c) return on assets, (d) return on equity, and (e) earnings per share. Indicate whether each ratio had a favorable (F) or unfavorable (U) change from 19x1 to 19x2.

3. Prepare a long-term solvency analysis by calculating for each year the (a) debt to equity ratio and (b) interest coverage ratio. Indicate whether each ratio had a favorable (F) or unfavorable (U) change from 19x1 to 19x2.

4. Conduct a market test analysis by calculating for each year the (a) price/earnings ratio, (b) dividends yield, and (c) market risk. Note the market risk measure, and indicate whether each ratio had a favorable (F) or unfavorable (U) change from 19x1 to 19x2.

Note: Round all answers to one decimal point, and consider changes of .1 or less to be neutral.

Problem 21A-5
Comprehensive
Ratio Analysis
of Two
Companies
(L.O. 5)

Wilma Daniels has decided to invest some of her savings in common stock. She feels that the chemical industry has good growth prospects and has narrowed her choice to two companies in that industry. As a final step in making the choice, she decided to make a comprehensive ratio analysis of two companies, Tanner and Nealy. Balance sheet and income statement data for the two companies appear below and on the next page.

During the year, Tanner paid a total of $140,000 in dividends, and the current market price per share of its stock is $20. Nealy paid a total of $600,000 in dividends during the year, and the current market price per share of its stock is $9. An investment service reports that the beta associated with Tanner's stock is 1.05 and that associated with Nealy's is .8. Information pertaining to prior years is not readily available. Assume that all Notes Payable are current liabilities and that all Bonds Payable are long-term liabilities.

	Tanner	Nealy
Assets		
Cash	$ 126,100	$ 514,300
Marketable Securities (at cost)	117,500	1,200,000
Accounts Receivable (net)	456,700	2,600,000
Inventories	1,880,000	4,956,000
Prepaid Expenses	72,600	156,600
Property, Plant, and Equipment (net)	5,342,200	19,356,000
Intangibles and Other Assets	217,000	580,000
Total Assets	$8,212,100	$29,362,900
Liabilities and Stockholders' Equity		
Accounts Payable	$ 517,400	$ 2,342,000
Notes Payable	1,000,000	2,000,000
Income Tax Payable	85,200	117,900
Bonds Payable	2,000,000	15,000,000
Common Stock—$1 par value	350,000	1,000,000
Paid-in Capital in Excess of Par Value	1,747,300	5,433,300
Retained Earnings	2,512,200	3,469,700
Total Liabilities and Stockholders' Equity	$8,212,100	$29,362,900

	y	Tanner	Nealy
Sales		$9,486,200	$27,287,300
Cost of Goods Sold		5,812,200	18,372,400
Gross Margin on Sales		$3,674,000	$ 8,914,900
Operating Expenses			
Selling Expenses		$1,194,000	$ 1,955,700
Administrative Expenses		1,217,400	4,126,000
Interest Expense		270,000	1,360,000
Income Tax Expense		450,000	600,000
Total Operating Expenses		$3,131,400	$ 8,041,700
Net Income		$ 542,600	$ 873,200

Required

Conduct a comprehensive ratio analysis of each company using the current end-of-year data. Compare the results. (Round all ratios and percentages to one decimal point.) This analysis should be done in the following steps:

1. Prepare an analysis of liquidity by calculating for each company the (a) current ratio, (b) quick ratio, (c) receivable turnover, (d) average days' sales uncollected, and (e) inventory turnover.
2. Prepare an analysis of profitability by calculating for each company the (a) profit margin, (b) asset turnover, (c) return on assets, (d) return on equity, and (e) earnings per share.
3. Prepare an analysis of long-term solvency by calculating for each company the (a) debt to equity ratio and (b) interest coverage ratio.
4. Prepare an analysis of market tests by calculating for each company the (a) price/earnings ratio, (b) dividends yield, and (c) market risk.
5. Compare the analysis of each company by inserting the ratio calculations from 1 through 4 in a table with the column heads *Ratio Name; Tanner; Nealy; Company with More Favorable Ratio*. In the right-hand column of the table indicate which company had the more favorable ratio in each case. (If the ratios are within .1 of each other, consider them neutral.)
6. How could the analysis be improved if prior years' data were available?

Problem 21A-6
Preparation of
Statements
from Ratios
and Incomplete
Data
(L.O. 5)

Presented on the next page are the income statement and balance sheet of Timbore Corporation with most of the amounts missing.

Additional information:

1. The company's common stock sells for $24 per share, and the price/earnings ratio is 8.   Stock 8 times its earnings   ~ 3#
2. The return on assets is 12 percent, and asset turnover is 1.6.
3. Interest coverage is 6 times.
4. The receivable turnover is 8, and the inventory turnover is 4.
5. The quick ratio is 1.1 and the current ratio is 2.3.
6. The debt to equity ratio is 2/3.
7. All ratios are based on the current year's figures.

Timbore Corporation
Income Statement
For the Year Ended September 30, 19xx
(in thousands of dollars)

Sales		$?
Cost of Goods Sold		?
Gross Margin on Sales		?
Operating Expenses		
Selling Expenses	$8,000	
Administrative Expenses	?	
Interest Expense	1,000	
Income Tax Expense	?	
Total Operating Expenses		13,000
Net Income		$ 3,000?

Timbore Corporation
Balance Sheet
September 30, 19xx
(in thousands of dollars)

Assets

Cash	$ 500	
Accounts Receivable (net)	?	
Inventories	?	
Total Current Assets		$?
Property, Plant, and Equipment (net)		?
Total Assets		$?

Liabilities and Stockholders' Equity

Current Liabilities	$?	
Bonds Payable	?	
Total Liabilities		$?
Capital Stock—$1 par value 1,000 shares	$1,000	
Paid-in Capital in Excess of Par Value	9,000	
Retained Earnings	?	
Total Stockholders' Equity		?
Total Liabilities and Stockholders' Equity		$?

Required

Complete the financial statements, using the information presented. Show supporting computations.

Problem 21B-1
Analyzing the
Effects of
Transactions on
Ratios
(L.O. 5)

Problem Set B

Davenport Corporation engaged in the transactions listed in the first column of the table below. Opposite each transaction is a ratio and spaces to mark the effect of each transaction on the ratio.

				Effect	
	Transaction	Ratio	Increase	Decrease	None
a.	Sold merchandise on account.	Current ratio			
b.	Sold merchandise on account.	Inventory turnover			
c.	Collected on account receivable.	Quick ratio			
d.	Write-off of an uncollectible account.	Receivable turnover			
e.	Paid on account payable.	Current ratio			
f.	Declaration of cash dividend.	Return on equity			
g.	Incurred advertising expense.	Profit margin			
h.	Issued stock dividend.	Debt to equity			
i.	Issued bond payable.	Asset turnover			
j.	Accrued interest expense.	Current ratio			
k.	Paid previously declared cash dividend.	Dividends yield			
l.	Purchased treasury stock.	Return on assets			

Required

Place an X in the appropriate column to show whether the transaction increased, decreased, or had no effect on the indicated ratio.

Problem 21B-2
Trend Analysis
(L.O. 4)

The condensed comparative income statement and additional selected data for Medford Corporation appear as follows:

	19x5	19x4	19x3	19x2	19x1
Sales	$1,061,500	$892,680	$972,840	$850,857	$784,200
Cost of Goods Sold	702,670	545,820	589,200	472,800	435,600
Gross Margin on Sales	$ 358,830	$346,860	$383,640	$378,057	$348,600
Operating Expenses	305,600	247,050	227,300	212,100	182,100
Net Income	$ 53,230	$ 99,810	$156,340	$165,957	$166,500

Additional selected data:

	19x5	19x4	19x3	19x2	19x1
Total Assets	$1,558,200	$1,552,700	$1,522,700	$1,486,200	$1,342,900
Total Liabilities	525,600	478,700	452,600	401,500	387,900
Earnings per Share	.52	.80	1.20	1.24	1.25
Dividends per Share	.30	.50	.70	.70	.70

Required

1. Prepare a trend analysis for Medford Corporation using 19x1 as the base year. (Round percentages to one decimal point.)
2. Comment on favorable and unfavorable trends shown in the analysis.

Problem 21B-3
Horizontal and Vertical Analysis
(L.O. 4)

The condensed comparative income statement and comparative balance sheet of Bowie Corporation follow. All figures are given in thousands of dollars.

Comparative income statement:

	19x2	19x1
Sales	$812,800	$786,600
Cost of Goods Sold	522,200	502,100
Gross Margin on Sales	$290,600	$284,500
Operating Expenses		
Selling Expenses	$119,200	$129,500
Administrative Expenses	111,800	105,800
Interest Expense	16,400	9,800
Income Tax Expense	15,600	14,200
Total Operating Expenses	$263,000	$259,300
Net Income	$ 27,600	$ 25,200

Comparative balance sheet:

	19x2	19x1
Assets		
Cash	$ 20,300	$ 10,200
Accounts Receivable (net)	58,900	57,300
Inventory	143,700	148,700
Property, Plant, and Equipment (net)	187,500	180,000
Total Assets	$410,400	$396,200

Liabilities and Stockholders' Equity

Accounts Payable	$ 66,900	$119,300
Notes Payable	50,000	100,000
Bonds Payable	100,000	—
Common Stock	100,000	100,000
Retained Earnings	93,500	76,900
Total Liabilities and Stockholders' Equity	$410,400	$396,200

Required

(Round percentages to one decimal point.)

1. Prepare a schedule showing amount and percentage changes from 19x1 to 19x2 for the corporate income statement and balance sheet.
2. Prepare a common-size income statement and balance sheet for 19x1 and 19x2.
3. Comment on the results found in **1** and **2** by identifying favorable and unfavorable changes in components and composition.

Problem 21B-4
Ratio Analysis
(L.O. 5)

Additional data for Bowie Corporation in 19x1 and 19x2 appear below. This information should be used along with the data in Problem 21B-3.

	19x2	19x1
Dividends Paid	$14,600,000	$ 8,600,000
Number of Common Shares	20,000,000	20,000,000
Market Price per Share	$9.00	$15.00
Beta	1.40	1.25

Balances of selected accounts for 19x0 are Accounts Receivable (net), $51,700,000; Inventory, $136,800,000; Total Assets, $366,400,000; and Stockholders' Equity, $160,300,000.

Required

1. Conduct a liquidity analysis by calculating for each year the (a) current ratio, (b) quick ratio, (c) receivable turnover, (d) average days' sales uncollected, and (e) inventory turnover. Indicate whether each ratio had a favorable (F) or unfavorable (U) change from 19x1 to 19x2.
2. Conduct a profitability analysis by calculating for each year the (a) profit margin, (b) asset turnover, (c) return on assets, (d) return on equity, and (e) earnings per share. Indicate whether each ratio had a favorable (F) or unfavorable (U) change from 19x1 to 19x2.
3. Conduct a long-term solvency analysis by calculating for each year the (a) debt to equity ratio and (b) interest coverage ratio. Indicate whether each ratio had a favorable (F) or unfavorable (U) change from 19x1 to 19x2.
4. Conduct a market test analysis by calculating for each year the (a) price/earnings ratio, (b) dividends yield, and (c) market risk. Note the market beta measures, and indicate whether each ratio had a favorable (F) or unfavorable (U) change from 19x1 to 19x2.

(Round percentages and ratios to one decimal point, and consider changes of .1 or less to be neutral.)

Problem 21B-5
Comprehensive
Ratio Analysis
of Two
Companies
(L.O. 5)

Rodney Ingram is considering an investment in the common stock of a chain of retail department stores. He has narrowed his choice to two retail companies, Miles Corporation and Talley Corporation, whose balance sheets and income statements are presented below.

	Miles Corporation	Talley Corporation
Assets		
Cash	$ 40,000	$ 96,200
Marketable Securities (at cost)	101,700	42,300
Accounts Receivable (net)	276,400	492,700
Inventory	314,900	626,700
Prepaid Expenses	27,200	57,000
Property, Plant, and Equipment (net)	1,456,800	3,276,000
Intangibles and Other Assets	276,600	72,400
Total Assets	$2,493,600	$ 4,663,300
Liabilities and Stockholders' Equity		
Accounts Payable	$ 172,000	$ 286,300
Notes Payable	75,000	200,000
Accrued Liabilities	25,100	36,700
Bonds Payable	1,000,000	1,000,000
Common Stock—$10 par value	500,000	300,000
Paid-in Capital in Excess of Par Value	304,900	1,784,300
Retained Earnings	416,600	1,056,000
Total Liabilities and Stockholders' Equity	$2,493,600	$ 4,663,300

	Miles Corporation	Talley Corporation
Sales	$6,280,000	$12,605,000
Cost of Goods Sold	3,071,000	7,417,000
Gross Margin on Sales	$3,209,000	$ 5,188,000
Operating Expenses		
Selling Expenses	$2,411,300	$ 3,554,100
Administrative Expenses	493,000	1,217,000
Interest Expense	97,000	114,000
Income Tax Expense	100,000	150,000
Total Operating Expenses	$3,101,300	$ 5,035,100
Net Income	$ 107,700	$ 152,900

During the year, Miles Corporation paid a total of $25,000 in dividends. The market price per share of its stock is currently $30. In comparison, Talley Corporation paid a total of $57,000 in dividends during the year, and the current market price per share of its stock is $38. An investment service indicated that the beta associated with Miles's stock is 1.20 and that associated with Talley's stock is .95. Information for prior years is not readily available.

Required

Conduct a comprehensive ratio analysis of each company using the available information, and compare the results. (Round percentages and ratios to one decimal point, and consider changes of .1 or less to be neutral.) This analysis should be done in the following steps:

1. Prepare an analysis of liquidity by calculating for each company the (a) current ratio, (b) quick ratio, (c) receivable turnover, (d) average days' sales uncollected, and (e) inventory turnover.
2. Prepare an analysis of profitability by calculating for each company the (a) profit margin, (b) asset turnover, (c) return on assets, (d) return on equity, and (e) earnings per share.
3. Prepare an analysis of long-term solvency by calculating for each company the (a) debt to equity ratio and (b) interest coverage ratio.
4. Prepare an analysis of market tests by calculating for each company the (a) price/earnings ratio, (b) dividends yield, and (c) market risk.
5. Compare the analysis of each company by inserting the ratio calculations from 1 through 4 in a table with the following column heads: *Ratio Name, Miles Corporation, Talley Corporation, Company with More Favorable Ratio.* Indicate in the right-hand column which company had the more favorable ratio in each case.
6. In what ways could the analysis be improved if prior years' information were available?

Problem 21B-6
Preparation of Statements from Ratios and Incomplete Data
(L.O. 5)

Presented below and on the next page are the income statement and balance sheet of Blocker Corporation with most of the amounts missing.

Blocker Corporation
Income Statement
For the Year Ended December 31, 19x1
(in thousands of dollars)

Sales		$9,000
Cost of Goods Sold		6,000
Gross Margin on Sales		3,000
Operating Expenses		
Selling Expenses	$1,772	
Administrative Expenses	117	
Interest Expense	81	
Income Tax Expense	310	
Total Operating Expenses		2,280 (3-720)
Net Income		$ 720

Blocker Corporation
Balance Sheet
December 31, 19x1
(in thousands of dollars)

Assets

Cash	$1,?00	
Accounts Receivable (net)	2,800	
Inventories	1,900	
Total Current Assets		4,500
Property, Plant, and Equipment (net)		2,700
Total Assets		$7,?00

Liabilities and Stockholders' Equity

Current Liabilities	$500	
Bond Payable, 9% interest	900	
Total Liabilities		$2?,00
Common Stock—$10 par value	$1,500	
Paid-in Capital in Excess of Par Value	1,300	
Retained Earnings	2,000	
Total Stockholders' Equity		$4,800
Total Liabilities and Stockholders' Equity		$7,200

Additional information: (a) the only interest expense is on long-term debt; (b) the debt to equity ratio is .5; (c) the current ratio is 3:1, and the quick ratio is 2:1; (d) the receivable turnover is 4.5, and the inventory turnover is 4.0; (e) the return on assets is 10 percent; (f) all ratios are based on the current year's information.

Required

Complete the financial statements using the information presented. Show supporting computations.

Financial Decision Case 21-1

Great Lakes Seafood Restaurant, Inc. (L.O. 2, 4)

Sam Slaski is the owner of Great Lakes Seafood Restaurant, Inc., which operates a 100-seat seafood restaurant in a suburb of a large midwestern city. Teresa Kelly, Sam's CPA, is going over with Sam the recently prepared income statement for last year, which is reproduced on the next page.

Sam is disturbed to see that the restaurant had a net loss for the year. "I honestly don't know what to do," Sam comments. "I think I run an efficient operation, and people say I have a good restaurant. Do you think I should try to cut costs or try to get more business?" Teresa replies, "Maybe it would be helpful

Great Lakes Seafood Restaurants, Inc.
Income Statement
For the Year Ended December 31, 19xx

Sales		
Food		$272,100
Beverage		98,400
Total Sales		$370,500
Cost of Goods Sold		
Food	$112,400	
Beverage	29,300	
Total Cost of Goods Sold		141,700
Gross Margin		$228,800
Operating Expenses		
Wages and Salaries Expense	$116,500	
Employee Benefits Expense	19,900	
Direct Operating Expenses	30,700	
Music and Entertainment Expenses	3,800	
Advertising and Promotion Expenses	8,300	
Utilities Expenses	11,900	
Administrative and General Expenses	22,800	
Repairs and Maintenance Expenses	6,200	
Rent, Property Taxes, and Insurance Expenses	22,800	
Depreciation Expense	12,900	
Interest Expense	5,100	
Total Operating Expenses		260,900
Net Loss Before Other Items		$ 32,100
Other Income and Expenses		
Other Income	$ 2,400	
Less: Other Expenses	1,200	
Net Other Income		1,200
Net Loss		$ 30,900

to compare your restaurant with other successful restaurants. I will try to see if any industry data are available."

One week later Teresa returns with the "Restaurant Industry Operations Report for 1984," published by the National Restaurant Association in cooperation with the international accounting firm of Laventhol & Horwath. "Sam, let's see how your restaurant compares. On page 23 is an income statement for restaurants in the United States that showed a profit last year. The amounts are on a per seat basis, so we can make a direct comparison with your restaurant." Data from the national survey (slightly rearranged) are shown on the next page.

Profitable Restaurants in the United States
Average Income Per Seat
For the Year Ended 1983

Sales

Food		$3,935
Beverage		1,457
Total Sales		$5,392

Cost of Goods Sold

Food	$1,608	
Beverage	377	
Total Cost of Goods Sold		1,985

Gross Margin $3,407

Operating Expenses

Wages and Salaries Expense	$1,410	
Employee Benefits Expense	237	
Direct Operating Expenses	290	
Music and Entertainment Expenses	40	
Advertising and Promotion Expenses	97	
Utilities Expenses	128	
Administrative and General Expenses	278	
Repairs and Maintenance Expenses	89	
Rent, Property Taxes, and Insurance Expenses	249	
Depreciation Expense	117	
Interest Expense	53	
Total Operating Expenses		2,988

Net Income Before Other Items $ 419

Other Income and Expenses

Other Income	$ 43	
Less: Other Expenses	16	
Net Other Income		27

Net Income Before Income Taxes $ 446

Required

1. Prepare comparative income statements on a per seat basis and common-size income statements for Great Lakes Seafood Restaurant, Inc., and the average profitable restaurant.

2. Identify and comment on the areas where Great Lakes is significantly different from the national average.

3. On the basis of your analysis, what would you say is Great Lakes' major problem? How would the items identified in **2** be affected if this problem were solved?

Part Six

Basic Concepts of Management Accounting

The first five parts of this book dealt primarily with the measurement and reporting problems pertaining to general-purpose financial statements used by people outside the business entity, such as bankers and stockholders. The basic concepts and practices of internal or management accounting are introduced in the final two parts of this text.

The focus in Part VI is on the basic tools of analysis used by managers. Specific types of information are needed by management to support day-to-day and long-term decisions. The management accountant provides these data. In Part VI you will be exposed to the development and accumulation of cost information for use in product or service costing, in the analysis of operating performance, and in reporting results of operations to management.

Chapter 22 introduces the field of management accounting, focusing on basic terminology used in accounting for internal operations. Reporting of manufacturing costs is also discussed and illustrated.

Chapters 23 and 24 involve two approaches to product costing. After defining the concept of absorption costing and describing the development and use of predetermined overhead rates, Chapter 23 focuses on product costing within the job order cost accounting system. Chapter 24 analyzes product costing in a process cost accounting environment.

Chapter
Twenty-Two

Manufacturing
Accounting:
Cost Elements
and Reporting

1. *Describe the field of management accounting.*

2. *Identify differences in accounting for manufacturing and merchandising companies.*

3. *State the differences among the three manufacturing cost elements: direct materials costs, direct labor costs, and factory (manufacturing) overhead costs.*

4. *Identify the source documents used to collect data on manufacturing cost accumulation.*

5. *Describe the nature, contents, and flow of costs through the Materials, Work in Process, and Finished Goods inventory accounts.*

6. *Prepare a statement of cost of goods manufactured.*

7. *Prepare the year-end work sheets, closing journal entries, and financial statements for a manufacturing company, using a periodic inventory approach. (See Work Sheet Analysis in the Working Papers.)*

This chapter introduces management accounting and its application to manufacturing operations. It focuses on managerial knowledge about operating costs needed to support day-to-day and long-term decisions. The chapter includes basic terms, the cost elements of manufacturing accounting, cost classification, the manufacturing inventory accounts, and preparation of the statement of cost of goods manufactured. As a result of studying this chapter, you should be able to meet the learning objectives listed on the left.

For manufacturers, as for merchandising companies, it is important to gather, interpret, and report financial information. Manufacturing companies (and companies that render services) are different because they *produce* products or services that are sold to other companies and individuals. Merchandising companies, on the other hand, *purchase* salable products for resale. For a merchandising company, arriving at the costs of products and inventory values involves simply finding the purchase price of the item in question (plus shipping and handling costs in some cases). A manufacturing company, however, must add up a series of production-related costs to arrive at the final cost of the manufactured product.

In this chapter, we focus on manufacturing firms. But you should be aware that service organizations such as hospitals, accounting firms, and banks are also interested in establishing the costs of their products (which are services). Many of the same internal accounting procedures discussed in this and future chapters can also be used by service organizations. Several of the decision cases in these last two parts of the book will also focus on data that support management decisions in service-oriented organizations.

A manufacturing company's financial statements look very much like those of a merchandising company. Each uses balance sheets with sections for assets, liabilities, and owners' equity. Revenues and expenses are reported in the income statement. Still, there are differences in the reports of the two types of companies, which will be explained later.

Besides the normal financial accounting structure described in earlier chapters, manufacturing companies must also maintain a cost accounting system. This system centers on the costs incurred in manufacturing each specific product. To account for production costs and to assign these costs to products, certain accounting principles and procedures have been developed. The cost accounting system is designed to handle all product-related costs. These basic cost elements are the costs of direct materials, direct labor, and factory overhead. This chapter introduces the three basic cost elements and the concept of unit cost—such as cost per textbook or per camera. We then reintroduce the perpetual inventory method and compare it with the periodic method used by most retail companies. Later in this chapter, we look at the flow of manufacturing costs through the Materials, Work in Process, and Finished Goods inventory accounts. All materials, labor, and factory overhead costs finally become part of the cost of a product. Then, once sold, they become part of the Cost of Goods Sold account balance. In addition, we analyze the statement of cost of goods manufactured. A special analysis in the Working Papers shows how to prepare work sheets and financial statements for a manufacturing company that uses a periodic inventory approach.

Management Accounting

Objective 1
Describe the
field of
management
accounting

Accounting for production and service-oriented enterprises is part of the field known as management accounting. Management accounting is often associated with large corporations, with many segments, engaged in manufacturing and assembly. These large corporations need more complex accounting and reporting systems than do small, one-owner businesses like a neighborhood grocery store or a shoe store. Even though large corporations need large *amounts* of information, small and medium-size businesses need certain *types* of financial information just as much as large corporations do. The types of data needed for efficient operating conditions do not depend entirely on an organization's size.

Three kinds of financial information are needed for effective management of a manufacturing company. They are (1) product costing information, (2) data for planning and control of operations, and (3) special reports and analyses that support management decisions. The field of management accounting consists of specific types of information gathering and reporting and appropriate accounting techniques and procedures. When collectively applied to a company's financial and production data, management accounting procedures will satisfy management's informational needs. Product costing is the first type of information. It uses cost accounting techniques to gather production information, assign specific costs to product batches, and calculate specific product costs. Product costing techniques are discussed in Chapters 23 and 24.

Data for planning and control, the second kind of information listed above, are organized in ways that help management plan production and its related costs. As production goes on, these expected costs are incurred. Then formal control procedures compare planned and actual costs to measure the effectiveness of operations and management. Chapters 25, 26, and 27 focus on these planning and control functions of management accounting.

The third kind of information helps management in decision making. All management decisions should be supported by analyses of alternative courses of action. The accountant is expected to supply information for management decisions. Several approaches used by the accountant are discussed in Chapter 28.

Merchandising Versus Manufacturing Operations

Objective 2
Identify the differences in accounting for manufacturing and merchandising companies

Much of this text has been about the merchandising organization. Thus it is important here to explain the differences in accounting for manufacturing firms and merchandising firms. Many kinds of businesses gather information on costs, but doing so is especially important in manufacturing. Figures 22-1 and 22-2 show how the computation of cost of goods sold differs between manufacturing and merchandising companies.

A merchandising company normally buys a product that is ready for resale when it is received. Nothing needs to be done to the product to make it salable except to prepare a special package or display. As shown in Figure 22-1, the total of the beginning merchandise inventory plus purchases is the basis for computing both the cost of goods sold and the ending merchandise inventory balances. Costs assigned to unsold items make up the ending inventory balance. The difference between the cost of goods available for sale and the ending inventory amount is the cost of goods sold during the period. The following example shows this computation:

Beginning merchandise inventory	$ 2,000
Plus total purchases of salable goods	8,000
Cost of goods available for sale	$10,000
Less ending merchandise inventory	(2,700)
Cost of goods sold	$ 7,300

This example and Figure 22-1 show how easy it is to figure the cost of goods sold for a merchandising company. The only expenditure occurs when salable goods are purchased. Any items unsold at year end make up the ending inventory balance. The remainder of the purchase costs (plus any balance in beginning merchandise inventory) are reported as Cost of Goods Sold.

Figuring the cost of goods sold for a manufacturing company is more complex. As shown in Figure 22-2, instead of one inventory account, a manufacturer maintains three different types of inventory accounts: Materials Inventory, Work in Process Inventory, and Finished Goods Inventory.

Purchased materials that are unused during the production process make up the year-end Materials Inventory balance. The cost of materials used plus the costs of labor services and factory overhead (utility costs, depreciation of factory machinery and building, and so forth) are moved

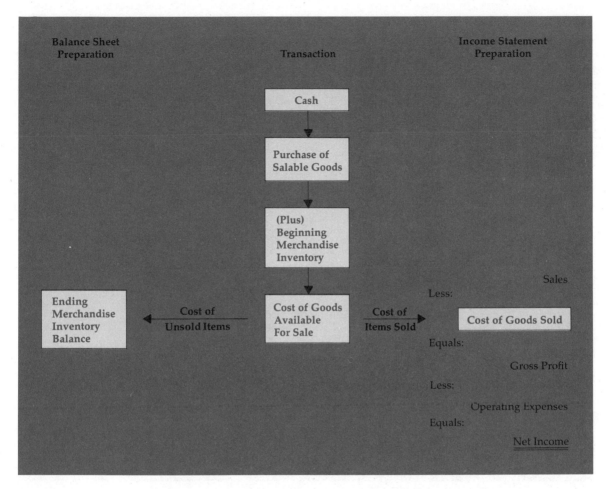

Figure 22-1
Cost of Goods
Sold: A
Merchandising
Company

to the Work in Process Inventory account when the material, service, or overhead item is used in the production process.

The three kinds of costs discussed earlier are often called simply materials, labor, and overhead (abbreviated M, L, and OH). These costs are accumulated in the Work in Process Inventory account during an accounting period. When a batch or order is completed, all manufacturing costs assigned to the completed units are moved to the Finished Goods Inventory account. Costs remaining in the Work in Process Inventory account belong to partly completed units. These costs make up the ending balance in the Work in Process Inventory account.

The Finished Goods Inventory account is set up in much the same way as the Merchandise Inventory account in Figure 22-1. Costs of completed goods are entered into the Finished Goods Inventory account. Then, as shown in Figure 22-2, costs attached to unsold items at year end make up the ending balance in the Finished Goods Inventory account. All costs related to units sold are added together and reported on the income statement as Cost of Goods Sold. To make the flow of costs clearer, the following section will discuss the three manufacturing cost elements—direct materials, direct labor, and factory (manufacturing) overhead.

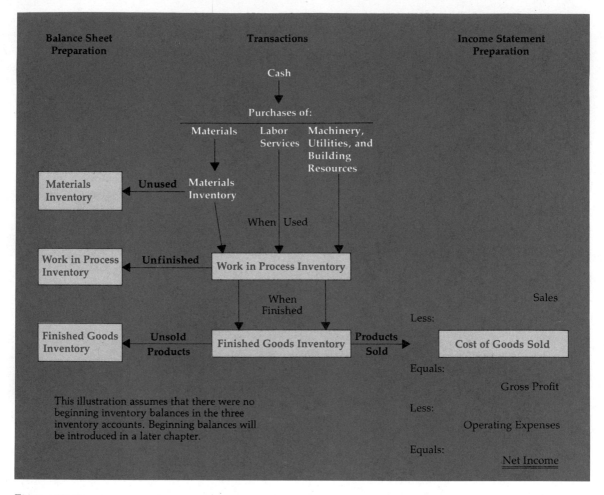

Balance Sheet Preparation

Transactions

Income Statement Preparation

Cash

↓

Purchases of:

Materials   Labor Services   Machinery, Utilities, and Building Resources

Materials Inventory   ← **Unused**   Materials Inventory

When Used

Work in Process Inventory   ← **Unfinished**   Work in Process Inventory

When Finished

Finished Goods Inventory   ← **Unsold Products**   Finished Goods Inventory   **Products Sold** →   Cost of Goods Sold

Sales

Less:

Equals:

Gross Profit

Less:

Operating Expenses

Equals:

Net Income

This illustration assumes that there were no beginning inventory balances in the three inventory accounts. Beginning balances will be introduced in a later chapter.

Figure 22-2
Cost of Goods Sold: A Manufacturing Company

Manufacturing Cost Elements

Objective 3
State the differences among the three manufacturing cost elements: direct materials costs, direct labor costs, and factory (manufacturing) overhead costs

Manufacturing costs can be classified in many different ways. Some costs can be traced directly to one product or batch of products. Other costs cannot be traced directly to products. In gathering information for business decisions, a particular cost may be important to one type of decision analysis and ignored in another. When we change from an external financial reporting approach (preparing financial statements for external users like stockholders) to an internal or management accounting approach, some costs take on different characteristics. In fact, manufacturing costs can be reclassified in many different ways depending on the goal of the cost analysis.

The most common classification scheme, as mentioned before, is to group manufacturing costs into one of three classes: direct materials costs, direct labor costs, and indirect manufacturing costs. This last class of costs is also often referred to as factory overhead. Direct costs can be

Chapter Twenty-Two

traced to specific products. **Indirect costs** must be assigned to products by some general plan for allocation.

Direct Materials Costs

All manufactured products are made of basic direct materials. The basic material may be iron ore for steel, sheet steel for automobiles, or flour for bread. These examples show the link between a basic raw material and a final product.

The way a company buys, stores, and uses materials is very important. Timely purchasing is important because, if the company runs out of materials, the manufacturing process will be forced to shut down. Shutting down production results in no products, unhappy customers, and loss of sales and profits. Buying too many direct materials, on the other hand, can lead to high storage costs.

Proper storage of materials will avoid waste and spoilage. Large enough storage space and orderly storage procedures are essential. Materials must be handled and stored properly to guarantee their satisfactory use in production. Proper records make it possible to find goods easily. They also reduce problems resulting from lost or misplaced items.

Direct materials are materials that become part of the finished product and can be conveniently and economically traced to specific product units. The costs of these materials are direct costs. In some cases, even though a material becomes part of a finished product, the expense of actually tracing the cost of the specific part is too great. Examples include nails in furniture, bolts in automobiles, and rivets in airplanes. These minor materials and other production supplies that cannot be conveniently or economically traced to specific products are accounted for as **indirect materials**. Indirect materials costs are included as part of factory overhead costs, which are discussed later in this chapter.

Direct Materials Purchases Direct materials are a sizable expenditure each year. So they call for special care in purchasing. A company must be careful to buy proper amounts and to make sure it has received quality goods. An efficient purchasing system uses several important documents to account for direct materials purchases. These documents were described in Chapter 8. The **purchase requisition** (or **purchase request**) is used to begin the materials purchasing process. This document starts in the production department. It describes the items to be purchased, and states the quantities needed. It must be approved by a qualified manager or supervisor.

From the information on the purchase requisition, the purchasing department prepares a formal **purchase order**. After a number of copies are made, some of the copies are sent to the vendor or supplier, and the remaining copies are kept for internal use. When the ordered goods are received, a **receiving report** is prepared. It is matched with the descriptions and quantities listed on the purchase order. Usually, the materials are inspected as soon as they arrive for inferior quality or damage. The purchasing process is complete when the company gets an invoice from the vendor and approves it for payment.

Objective 4
Identify the
source
documents used
to collect data
on manufac-
turing cost
accumulation

Direct Materials Usage Controlling direct materials costs does not end with the receipt and inspection of purchased goods. The materials must be stored in a safe place. They must be counted at regular intervals. And they should be issued into production only with the approval of a production supervisor. It is important to keep the materials storage areas clean and orderly and to lock up valuable items. Regular physical counts are necessary to see how many units are on hand and to test the inventory accounting system. Materials should be issued to production only when an approved **materials requisition** form is presented to the storeroom clerk. The materials requisition form, shown in Figure 22-3, is essential for controlling direct materials. Besides providing the supervisor's approval signature, the materials requisition describes the types and quantities of goods needed and received.

Direct Labor Costs

Labor services are, in essence, purchased from employees working in the factory. In addition, other types of labor are purchased from people and

Figure 22-3
The Materials
Requisition
Form

Gillies Manufacturing Company
Boston, Massachusetts

	Materials Requisition
	No. 49621

Charge to Job No. _____

Requested by _____   Date _____

Department _____

Part Number	Description	Quantity Requested	Quantity Issued	Unit Cost	Total Cost

Issued by _____   Date

Approved by _____   Received _____

Received by _____

organizations outside the company. However, the labor cost usually associated with manufacturing is that of factory personnel. These personnel include machine operators, maintenance workers, managers and supervisors, support personnel, and people who handle, inspect, and store materials. Because all of these people are connected in some way with the production process, their wages and salaries must be accounted for as production costs and, finally, as costs of products. However, it is difficult to trace many of these costs directly to individual products.

To help overcome this problem, the wages of machine operators and other workers involved in actually shaping the product are classified as direct labor costs. **Direct labor** costs include all labor costs for specific work performed on products that can be conveniently and economically traced to end products. Labor costs for production-related activities that cannot be connected with or conveniently or economically traced to end products are called **indirect labor** costs. These costs include the wages and salaries of such workers as machine helpers, supervisors, and other support personnel. Like indirect materials costs, indirect labor costs are accounted for as factory overhead costs.

Labor Documentation   Labor time records are important to both the employee and the company. The employee wants to be paid at the correct rate for all hours worked. The company does not wish to underpay or overpay its employees. In addition, company management wants a record kept of hours worked on particular products or batches of products made during the period. For these reasons, accounting for wages and salaries calls for careful attention.

The basic time record is called an employee **time card.** On each employee's time card, either the supervisor or a time clock records the employee's daily starting and finishing times. Normally, a company will use another set of labor cards to help verify the time recorded on the time cards and to keep track of labor costs per job or batch of goods produced. These documents, called **job cards,** record the time spent by an employee on a certain job. Each eight-hour period recorded on a time card may be supported by several job cards. Special job cards also record machine downtime, which may stem from machine repair or product design changes. Job cards verify the time worked by the employee and help control labor time per job.

Gross Versus Net Payroll   Accounting for direct and indirect labor costs often causes misunderstanding. People sometimes confuse gross payroll with net payroll. For internal cost accounting, gross wages and salaries are used. **Net payroll** is the amount paid to the employee after all payroll deductions have been subtracted from gross wages. Payroll deductions such as those for federal income taxes and social security taxes are paid by the employee. The employer just withholds them and pays them to the government and other organizations. **Gross payroll** is a measure of the total wages and salaries earned by employees, including payroll deductions. It is used to figure total manufacturing costs. The following example shows the difference between gross and net payroll.

Gross wages earned		
40 hours at $10/hour		$400.00
Less deductions		
Federal income taxes withheld	$82.50	
FICA taxes withheld	26.00	
U.S. government savings bond	37.50	
Union dues	12.50	
Insurance premiums	21.00	
Total deductions		179.50
Net wages paid (amount of check)		$220.50

The employee receives net wages of only $220.50, even though the company pays $400.00 in wages and deductions. The amounts withheld from the employee's gross wages are paid by the company to the taxing agencies, savings plan, union, and insurance companies. Gross payroll in this case is $400.00.

Labor-related Costs Other labor-related manufacturing costs fall into two categories: employee fringe benefits and employer payroll taxes. Fringe benefits are considered part of an employee's compensation package. They may include paid vacations, holiday and sick pay, and an employee pension plan. Other fringe benefits might be life and medical insurance, performance bonuses, profit sharing, and recreation facilities. Most of these costs vary in direct proportion to labor costs.

Besides the payroll taxes paid by the employee, there are also payroll-related taxes paid by the employer. For every dollar of social security (FICA) tax withheld from the paycheck, the employer usually pays an equal amount. The company must also pay state and federal unemployment compensation taxes. Agreements between management and labor, as well as government regulations, are sources of some labor-related costs. Company management may spend other money on a voluntary basis for the benefit of its employees.

Most labor-related costs are incurred in direct proportion to wages and salaries earned by the employees. As much as possible, labor-related costs that depend on direct labor costs and can be traced to them conveniently should be accounted for as part of direct labor. All other labor-related costs should be classified as factory overhead. However, because of the size and complexity of most payroll systems, labor-related costs are not traced to individual employees. Such costs are normally figured from wages and salaries by means of a predetermined rate based on past experience. For instance, a company may incur twelve cents of labor-related costs for every dollar of wages and salaries earned by employees. In this case, labor-related costs average 12 percent of labor costs. Therefore, if direct labor totaled $6,000 for a period of time, total direct labor cost would be $6,720 ($6,000 plus 12 percent, or $720, of labor-related costs). Total indirect labor cost would be computed in the same manner, as we will see in the next section.

Factory Overhead

The third manufacturing cost element is a catch-all for manufacturing costs that cannot be classified as direct materials or direct labor costs. **Factory overhead** costs are a varied collection of production-related costs that cannot be practically or conveniently traced to end products. This collection of costs has also been called manufacturing overhead, factory burden, and indirect manufacturing costs. Examples of the major classifications of factory overhead costs are listed below.

Indirect materials and supplies: nails, rivets, lubricants, small tools

Indirect labor costs: lift truck driver's wages, maintenance and inspection labor, engineering labor, machine helpers, supervisors

Other indirect factory costs: building maintenance, machinery and tool maintenance, property taxes, property insurance, pension costs, depreciation on plant and equipment

Although this list is not complete, it includes many common overhead costs and shows how varied they are.

Overhead Cost Behavior Cost behavior is an important concept in the field of management accounting. Manufacturing costs tend either to rise and fall with the volume of production or to stay the same within certain ranges of output. **Variable manufacturing costs** increase or decrease in direct proportion to the number of units produced. Examples include direct materials costs; direct labor costs; indirect materials and supply costs; heat, light, and power costs; and small-tool costs.

Production costs that stay fairly constant during the accounting period are called **fixed manufacturing costs.** Even with changes in productive output, these costs tend to stay the same. Examples of fixed manufacturing costs are fire insurance premiums, factory rent, supervisory salaries, and depreciation on machinery. Some costs are called semivariable, because part of the cost is fixed and part varies with usage. Telephone charges (basic charge plus long-distance charges) and utility bills are generally semivariable.

Cost behavior will be explored further in Chapter 25. In accounting for factory overhead costs, cost behavior analysis helps assign these indirect costs to units of output.

Overhead Cost Allocation A cost is classified as a factory overhead cost because it cannot be directly traced to an end product. Yet a product's total cost obviously includes factory overhead costs. Somehow, factory overhead costs must be identified with and assigned to specific products or jobs. Because direct materials and direct labor costs can be traced to products, assigning their costs to units of output is relatively easy. Factory overhead costs, however, have to be assigned to products by some cost allocation method. Such cost allocation is explained in Chapters 23 and 25.

Unit Cost Determination

Direct materials, direct labor, and factory overhead costs constitute total manufacturing costs for a period of time or for a batch of products. Product unit cost for each job completed is computed by dividing the total cost of materials, labor, and factory overhead for that job by the total units produced. For example, assume that Harold Products, Inc., produced 3,000 units of output for Job 12K. Costs for Job 12K included the following: direct materials, $3,000; direct labor, $5,400; and factory overhead, $2,700. The company's unit cost for Job 12K would be computed as follows:

Direct materials ($3,000/3,000 units)	$1.00
Direct labor ($5,400/3,000 units)	1.80
Factory overhead ($2,700/3,000 units)	.90
Total unit cost ($11,100/3,000 units)	$3.70

The unit cost described above was computed when the job was completed and all of the information was known. What about situations that call for this information a month before the job is started? Unit cost figures must then be estimated. Assume that accounting personnel developed the following estimates for another product: $2.50 per unit for direct materials, $4.50 per unit for direct labor, and 50 percent of direct labor cost for factory overhead. Then the unit cost would be as follows:

Direct materials	$2.50
Direct labor	4.50
Factory overhead (50% of $4.50)	2.25
Total unit cost	$9.25

This $9.25 unit cost is based on estimates. Still, it is useful for product pricing and job costing.

Product and Period Costs

Product costs and *period costs* are two terms commonly used in analyzing costs. **Product costs** consist of the three manufacturing cost elements: direct materials, direct labor, and factory overhead. They are incurred in making products that have not yet been sold. That is, product costs are associated with the materials, work in process, and finished goods inventories. They provide values for the ending balances of these inventories on year-end financial statements. Product costs are also considered unexpired costs because, as inventory balances, they are assets of the company. Assets, as we have seen in earlier chapters, are economic resources expected to benefit future operations.

Period costs (expenses) can have two meanings:

1. They are usually defined as all the expired costs of an accounting period, representing the resources used during the period. Any cost or expense item on an income statement is, in this sense, a period cost. Product costs become period costs when units of the product are sold.

2. Period costs can also be viewed in a narrower sense as costs that cannot be inventoried. Examples would include selling and administrative expenses, because the selling and administrative resources are used up in the same period in which they originate. Product costs, under this definition, would never be reclassified as period costs. And period costs under the second definition are linked to services consumed during a period and would never be used to determine product unit cost or to establish ending inventory balances.

Periodic Versus Perpetual Inventory Methods in Manufacturing Accounting

Cost flow in accounting for manufacturing costs depends on the way a company chooses to handle its inventories. In Chapter 11, we discussed the periodic and perpetual inventory methods. Because these methods are related to cost accounting systems, we also include a brief discussion here. A company using the periodic inventory method records materials purchases in a separate purchases account and assigns manufacturing costs to individual labor accounts and to various factory overhead cost accounts in the general ledger. Beginning inventory balances in the general ledger remain unchanged during the period. No costs flow through the Materials, Work in Process, and Finished Goods Inventory accounts during the accounting period (this is shown later in this chapter). Year-end inventory values are found by counting the items on hand and placing a cost on these goods. Inventory accounts are then adjusted to reflect the cost of the ending inventories.

If a company uses the perpetual inventory method, manufacturing costs flow through inventory accounts as goods and services are bought and used in the production process. Inventory account balances are updated perpetually. In this way it is possible to know these account balances at any point in time. Materials purchased are debited to the Materials Inventory account. The cost of materials used, direct labor, and factory overhead items are entered into the Work in Process Inventory account. The cost of completed units is debited directly to the Finished Goods Inventory account.

The perpetual inventory method is in common use. Greater accuracy and better inventory control are the major benefits of this approach. However, a perpetual inventory system is expensive to install and maintain. For this reason, many medium-size and small manufacturing companies use a periodic inventory approach.

Manufacturing Inventory Accounts

Accounting for inventories is the most difficult part of manufacturing accounting as compared to merchandising accounting. Instead of dealing with one account—Merchandise Inventory—we now must use *three* accounts: Materials Inventory, Work in Process Inventory, and Finished Goods Inventory.

Materials Inventory

*Objective 5
Describe the
nature, contents,
and flow of
costs through
the Materials,
Work in Process,
and Finished
Goods inventory
accounts*

The **Materials Inventory** account, also called the Stores and Materials Inventory Control account, is made up of the balances of materials and supplies on hand at a given time. This account is maintained in much the same way as the Merchandise Inventory account. The main difference is in the way that costs of items in inventory are assigned. For the merchandising company, goods taken out of inventory are items that have been sold. When a sale is made, an entry is needed to debit Cost of Goods Sold and to credit Merchandise Inventory for the cost of the item. Materials, on the other hand, are usually not purchased for resale but for use in manufacturing a product. Therefore, an item taken out of Materials Inventory and requisitioned into production is transferred to the Work in Process Inventory account (not Cost of Goods Sold). Figure 22-4 compares the accounting treatment for merchandise inventory with that for materials inventory.

Work in Process Inventory

All manufacturing costs that are incurred and assigned to products being produced are classified as **Work in Process Inventory** costs. This inventory account has no counterpart in merchandise accounting. A thorough understanding of the concept of Work in Process Inventory is vital in manufacturing accounting. Figure 22-5 (page 846) shows the various costs that become part of Work in Process Inventory and the way costs are transferred out of the account. Accounting for work in process (products in process) really began in Figure 22-4. The requisitioning of materials into production begins the production process. These materials must be cut, molded, assembled, or in some other way changed into a finished product. To make this change, people, machines, and other factory resources (buildings, electricity, supplies, and so on) must be used. All of these costs are manufacturing cost elements, and all of them enter into accounting for Work in Process Inventory.

Direct labor dollars earned by factory employees are also product costs. As these people work on specific products, their labor costs are assigned to those products by including the labor dollars earned as part of the Work in Process Inventory account. (Specific product costing is the topic of coming chapters. At this point, we will assume that all direct labor costs should be collected in the Work in Process Inventory account.)

Overhead costs are product costs and must be assigned to specific products. So they too are collected in the Work in Process Inventory account. As discussed earlier, there are too many overhead costs to account for on an individual basis. To reduce the amount of work needed to assign these costs to products, they are accumulated and accounted for under one account title: Factory Overhead. These costs may then be assigned to products by using a predetermined overhead rate. Using the predeter-

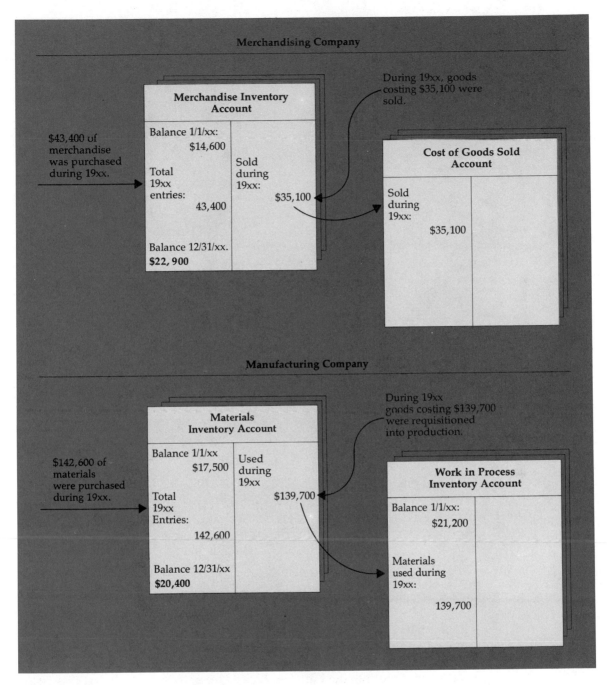

Figure 22-4
Materials
Inventory
Versus
Merchandise
Inventory
Accounting
(Perpetual)

mined overhead rate, costs are transferred from the Factory Overhead account to the Work in Process Inventory account. In our example in Figure 22-5, factory overhead costs of $156,200 were charged to the Work in Process Inventory account. The predetermined overhead rate will be discussed in Chapter 23.

As products are completed, they are put in the finished goods storage area. These products now have materials, direct labor, and factory over-

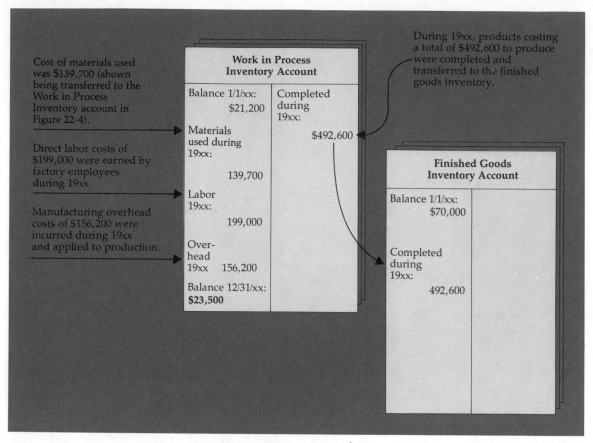

Cost of materials used was $139,700 (shown being transferred to the Work in Process Inventory account in Figure 22-4).

Direct labor costs of $199,000 were earned by factory employees during 19xx.

Manufacturing overhead costs of $156,200 were incurred during 19xx and applied to production.

During 19xx, products costing a total of $492,600 to produce were completed and transferred to the finished goods inventory.

Work in Process Inventory Account

Balance 1/1/xx: $21,200	Completed during 19xx: $492,600
Materials used during 19xx: 139,700	
Labor 19xx: 199,000	
Over-head 19xx: 156,200	
Balance 12/31/xx: **$23,500**	

Finished Goods Inventory Account

| Balance 1/1/xx: $70,000 | |
| Completed during 19xx: 492,600 | |

Figure 22-5
The Work in Process Inventory Account (Perpetual)

head costs assigned to them. When products are completed, these costs no longer belong to work (products) in process. Therefore, when the completed products are sent to the storage area, their costs are transferred from the Work in Process Inventory account to the Finished Goods Inventory account. The balance remaining in the Work in Process Inventory account ($23,500 in Figure 22-5) represents costs assigned to products partly completed and still in process at the end of the period.

Finished Goods Inventory

The **Finished Goods Inventory** account, like Materials Inventory, has some of the characteristics of the Merchandise Inventory account. We have already discussed how costs are moved from the Work in Process Inventory account to the Finished Goods Inventory account. At this point, Finished Goods Inventory takes on the characteristics of Merchandise Inventory. Compare the Merchandise Inventory account analysis in Figure 22-4 with the accounting for Finished Goods Inventory in Figure 22-6. The credit sides of both accounts are handled in the same way. Both examples show that when goods or products are sold, the costs of those goods are moved from the Finished Goods Inventory account to the Cost of Goods Sold account. However, the accounting procedures affecting the debit side of the Finished Goods Inventory account differ from those for

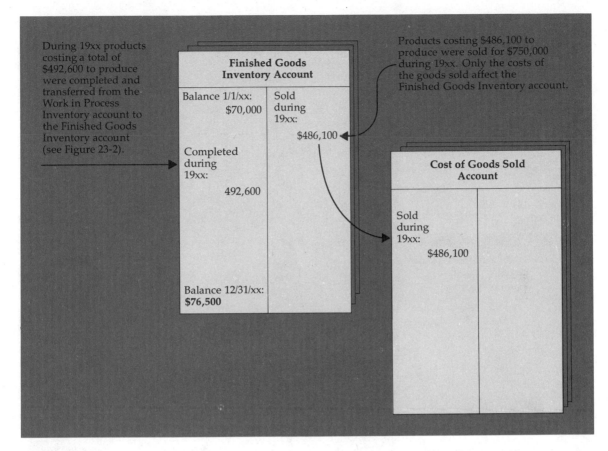

During 19xx products costing a total of $492,600 to produce were completed and transferred from the Work in Process Inventory account to the Finished Goods Inventory account (see Figure 23-2).

Products costing $486,100 to produce were sold for $750,000 during 19xx. Only the costs of the goods sold affect the Finished Goods Inventory account.

Finished Goods Inventory Account

Balance 1/1/xx: $70,000	Sold during 19xx: $486,100
Completed during 19xx: 492,600	
Balance 12/31/xx: **$76,500**	

Cost of Goods Sold Account

| Sold during 19xx: $486,100 | |

Figure 22-6
Accounting for
Finished Goods
Inventory
(Perpetual)

the Merchandise Inventory account. In a manufacturing firm, salable products are produced rather than purchased. All costs debited to Finished Goods Inventory represent transfers from the Work in Process Inventory account. At the end of an accounting period, the balance in the Finished Goods Inventory account is made up of the costs of products completed but not sold as of that date.

Manufacturing Cost Flow

Product costing, inventory valuation, and financial reporting depend on a defined, structured flow of manufacturing costs. This **manufacturing cost flow** was outlined in our discussion of the three manufacturing inventory accounts. Figure 22-7 (page 848) sums up the entire cost flow process as it relates to accounts in the general ledger. At this point, we do not need to worry about the actual journal entries needed to make this cost flow operational. These entries will be illustrated in Chapter 23.

Here, we will concentrate on the general pattern of manufacturing cost flow, as shown in Figure 22-8 (page 850). The cost flow begins with costs

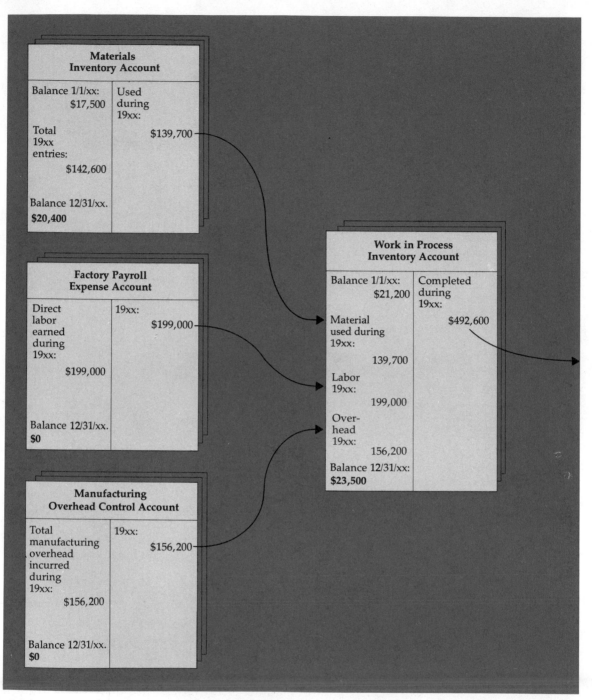

Figure 22-7
Manufacturing
Cost Flow: An
Example

being incurred. Manufacturing costs start in a number of ways. They may be cash payments, incurrence of liabilities, fixed asset depreciation, or the expiration of prepaid expenses. Once these costs have been incurred, they are recorded as being either direct materials, direct labor, or factory overhead costs. As the resources are used up, the company transfers their costs into the Work in Process Inventory account. When pro-

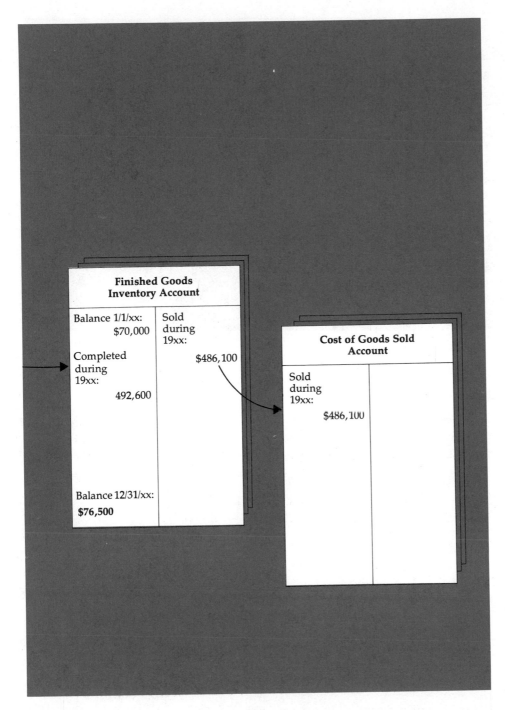

Figure 22-7
(*continued*)

duction is completed, costs assigned to finished units are transferred to the Finished Goods Inventory account. In much the same way, costs attached to units sold are transferred to the Cost of Goods Sold account. Before going on, compare the cost flow as it moves through the general ledger accounts in Figure 22-7 with the general pattern shown in Figure 22-8. Both figures show the same type of cost flow.

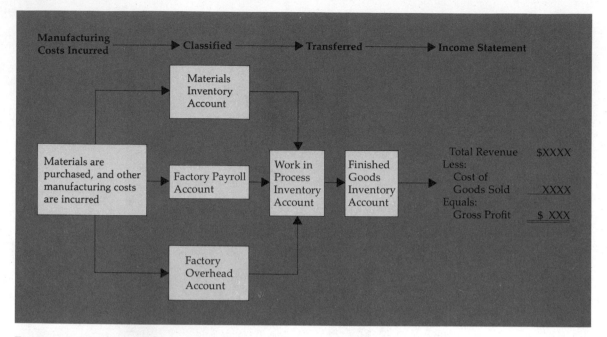

Total Revenue $XXXX
Less:
    Cost of
    Goods Sold   XXXX
Equals:
    Gross Profit $ XXX

Figure 22-8
Manufacturing
Cost Flow:
Basic Concepts

The Manufacturing Statements

Financial statements of manufacturing companies differ very little from those of merchandising companies. Depending on the industry, the account titles found on the balance sheet (statement of financial position) are the same in most corporations. (Examples are Cash, Accounts Receivable, Buildings, Machinery, Accounts Payable, and Capital Stock.) Even the income statements for the merchandiser and the manufacturer are very much alike. However, a closer look shows that the heading Cost of Goods Manufactured is used in place of Merchandise Purchases. Also, the Merchandise Inventory account is replaced by Finished Goods Inventory. Note these differences on the income statement of the Pedersen Company (Figure 22-9). The key to preparing an income statement for a manufacturing company is to determine the cost of goods manufactured. This dollar amount is the end result of a special manufacturing statement, the statement of cost of goods manufactured, which is prepared to support the figure on the income statement.

Statement of Cost of Goods Manufactured

Objective 6
Prepare a
statement of
cost of goods
manufactured

The flow of manufacturing costs, pictured in Figures 22-4 through 22-8, provides the basis for accounting for manufacturing costs. In this process, all manufacturing costs incurred are considered product costs. They are used to compute ending inventory balances and the cost of goods sold. The costs flowing from one account to another during the year have been combined into one number in the illustrations to help show the basic idea. In fact, hundreds of transactions take place during a year, and each

Figure 22-9
Income
Statement for a
Manufacturing
Company

Pedersen Company
Income Statement
For the Year Ended December 31, 19xx

Net Sales		$750,000
Cost of Goods Sold		
Finished Goods Inventory, Jan. 1, 19xx	$ 70,000	
Cost of Goods Manufactured (Figure 22-10)	492,600	
Total Cost of Finished Goods Available for Sale	$562,600	
Less Finished Goods Inventory, Dec. 31, 19xx	76,500	
Cost of Goods Sold		486,100
Gross Margin on Sales		$263,900
Operating Expenses		
Selling Expenses		
Salaries and Commissions	$46,500	
Advertising	19,500	
Other Selling Expenses	7,400	
Total Selling Expenses	$ 73,400	
General and Administrative Expenses		
Administrative Salaries	$65,000	
Franchise and Property Taxes	72,000	
Other G & A Expenses	11,300	
Total General and Administrative Expenses	148,300	
Total Operating Expenses		221,700
Income from Operations		$ 42,200
Less Interest Expense		4,600
Net Income Before Taxes		$ 37,600
Income Tax Expense		11,548
Net Income		$ 26,052

transaction affects part of the cost flow process. At the end of the year, the flow of all the manufacturing costs incurred during the year is summarized in the **statement of cost of goods manufactured.** This statement gives the dollar amount of costs for products completed and moved to Finished Goods Inventory during the year. The amount for cost of goods manufactured should be the same as the amount transferred from the Work in Process Inventory account to the Finished Goods Inventory account during the year.

The statement of cost of goods manufactured is shown in Figure 22-10. Even though it is rather complex, it can be pieced together in three steps.

Figure 22-10
Statement of
Cost of Goods
Manufactured

Pedersen Company
Statement of Cost of Goods Manufactured
For the Year Ended December 31, 19xx

Step One	Materials Used		
	Materials Inventory, Jan. 1, 19xx	$ 17,500	
	Materials Purchased	142,600	
	Cost of Materials Available for Use	$160,100	
	Less Materials Inventory, December 31, 19xx	20,400	
	Cost of Materials Used		$139,700
Step Two	Direct Labor		199,000
	Factory Overhead Costs		
	Indirect Labor	$ 46,400	
	Power	25,200	
	Depreciation Expense, Machinery and Equipment	14,800	
	Depreciation Expense, Factory Building	16,200	
	Small Tools Expense	2,700	
	Factory Insurance Expense	1,600	
	Supervision Expense	37,900	
	Other Factory Costs	11,400	
	Total Factory Overhead Costs		$156,200
Step Three	Total Manufacturing Costs		$494,900
	Add: Work in Process Inventory, January 1, 19xx		21,200
	Total Cost of Work in Process During the Year		$516,100
	Less Work in Process Inventory December 31, 19xx		23,500
	Cost of Goods Manufactured		$492,600

The first step is to compute the cost of materials used. Add the materials purchases for the period to the beginning balance in the Materials Inventory account. This step gives the cost of materials available for use during the year. Then subtract the balance of the ending Materials Inventory from the cost of materials available for use. The difference is the cost of materials used during the accounting period.

Computation of Cost of Materials Used

Beginning Balance: Materials Inventory	$ 17,500
Plus Materials Purchases	142,600
Cost of Materials Available for Use	$160,100
Less Ending Balance: Materials Inventory	20,400
Cost of Materials Used	$139,700

Before going to the next step, trace these numbers back to the Materials Inventory account in Figure 22-4 to see how that account is related to the statement of cost of goods manufactured.

Figuring total manufacturing costs for the year is the second step. As shown in Figure 22-6, we add the costs of materials used and direct labor to the total of all factory overhead costs incurred during the year. This step is shown below as well as in Figure 22-10.

Computation of Total Manufacturing Costs

Cost of Materials Used	$139,700
Plus Direct Labor Costs	199,000
Plus Total Factory Overhead Costs	156,200
Total Manufacturing Costs	$494,900

The third step shown in Figure 22-10 changes total manufacturing costs into total cost of goods manufactured for the year. Add the beginning Work in Process Inventory balance to total manufacturing costs for the period to arrive at the total cost of goods in process during the year. From this amount, subtract the ending Work in Process Inventory balance for the year to get the cost of goods manufactured.

Computation of Cost of Goods Manufactured

Total Manufacturing Costs	$494,900
Plus Beginning Balance: Work in Process Inventory	21,200
Total Cost of Goods in Process During the Year	$516,100
Less Ending Balance: Work in Process Inventory	23,500
Cost of Goods Manufactured	$492,600

The term *total manufacturing costs* must not be confused with the cost of goods manufactured. **Total manufacturing costs** are the total of materials used, direct labor, and factory overhead costs incurred and charged to production during an accounting period. **Cost of goods manufactured** consists of the total manufacturing costs attached to units of product *completed* during an accounting period. To understand the difference between these two dollar amounts, review the computation just shown. Total manufacturing costs of $494,900 incurred during the current year are added to the beginning balance in Work in Process Inventory. Costs of $21,200 in the beginning balance, by definition, are costs from an earlier period. We are now mixing costs of two different accounting periods to arrive at total cost of goods in process during the year of $516,100. The costs of ending products still in process ($23,500) are then subtracted from the total cost of goods in process during the year. The remainder of $492,600 is the cost of goods manufactured (completed) during the year. We assume that the items in beginning inventory were completed first. Costs attached to the ending Work in Process Inventory are part of the current period's total manufacturing costs. But they will not become part of the cost of goods manufactured until the next accounting period when the products are completed.

Cost of Goods Sold

Figures 22-9 and 22-10 demonstrate the relationship between the statement of cost of goods manufactured and the income statement. The total amount of cost of goods manufactured during the period is carried over to the income statement. There it is used to figure cost of goods sold. The cost of goods manufactured is added to the beginning balance of Finished Goods Inventory to get the total cost of goods available for sale during the period. Then cost of goods sold is figured by subtracting the ending balance in Finished Goods Inventory (cost of goods completed but unsold) from the total cost of goods available for sale. Cost of goods sold is considered an expense of the period in which the related products were sold.

Computation of Cost of Goods Sold

Beginning Balance: Finished Goods Inventory	$ 70,000
Plus Cost of Goods Manufactured	492,600
Total Cost of Finished Goods Available for Sale	$562,600
Less Ending Balance: Finished Goods Inventory	76,500
Cost of Goods Sold	$486,100

Note that the above computation is very much like the computation of cost of goods sold as shown in the income statement in Figure 22-9. The other parts of the income statement in Figure 22-9 should be familiar from earlier discussions in this text.

Chapter Review

Review of Learning Objectives

1. Describe the field of management accounting.

The field of management accounting consists of specific types of information gathering and reporting and appropriate accounting techniques and procedures. When collectively applied to a company's financial and production data, management accounting procedures will satisfy management's informational needs. These needs include (a) product costing information, (b) data for planning and control of operations, and (c) special reports and analyses that support management decisions.

2. Identify differences in accounting for manufacturing and merchandising companies.

Accounting methods used by a manufacturing company differ in important ways from those used by a merchandising company. Management or cost accountants of a manufacturing company must maintain an internal accounting system that classifies and assigns production and production-related costs to the products manufactured. The manufacturing accounting system uses three inventory accounts: Materials Inventory, Work in Process Inventory, and Finished Goods Inventory. Manufacturing costs (product costs) must flow through all three of the inventory accounts. This flow results in a more complex internal accounting system.

Merchandise accounting concentrates on the business as a whole rather than on specific products or processes. Only one account, Merchandise Inventory, is used to record and account for items in inventory. Because the items in merchandise inventory are purchased in salable condition, the cost flow from time of purchase to time of sale involves only three accounts: Cash or Accounts Payable, Purchases, and Cost of Goods Sold.

3. State the differences among the three manufacturing cost elements: direct materials costs, direct labor costs, and factory (manufacturing) overhead costs.

Direct materials are materials and parts that become part of the finished product and can be conveniently and economically traced to specific product units. Direct labor costs include all labor costs for specific work performed on products that can be conveniently and economically traced to end products. All other production-related costs are classified and accounted for as factory overhead costs. These costs cannot be practically or conveniently traced to end products. So they must be assigned to the products by some cost allocation method. Classifying manufacturing costs into the three elements described above is important for product costing purposes.

4. Identify the source documents used to collect data on manufacturing cost accumulation.

Purchase requisitions list the items or materials needed by the production departments. The purchasing department then uses the purchase order to order the items. When the items or materials come in from vendors, the receiving report is used to identify the items and is then matched against purchase orders to make sure the correct items were received. The materials requisition is used to request items, and it is also used to prove that items or materials were issued into the production process. Time cards record each employee's daily starting and finishing times. Job cards record time spent by each employee on each job. Job cards are matched against time cards to verify the time worked by each employee and to control labor time per job.

5. Describe the nature, contents, and flow of costs through the Materials Inventory, Work in Process Inventory, and Finished Goods Inventory accounts.

Cost flow through the inventory accounts begins when costs are incurred for materials, direct labor, and factory overhead. Materials costs flow first into the Materials Inventory account. This account is used to record the costs of materials when they are received and again when they are issued for use in a company's production process. All manufacturing-related costs—materials, direct labor, and factory overhead—are recorded in the Work in Process Inventory account as they enter the production process. When products are completed, their costs are transferred from the Work in Process Inventory account to the Finished Goods Inventory account. Costs remain in the Finished Goods Inventory account until the products are sold. At that time their costs are transferred to the Cost of Goods Sold account.

6. Prepare a statement of cost of goods manufactured.

Preparing a statement of cost of goods manufactured involves three steps. The first is to compute the cost of materials used. Total materials purchases are added to the beginning balance of Materials Inventory to arrive at the cost of materials available for use. From this amount, the ending Materials Inventory balance is subtracted to get the cost of materials used. The second step is to compute the total manufacturing costs for the period. Costs of direct labor and factory overhead are added to the cost of materials used to arrive at this amount. The third step is the actual computation of cost of goods manufactured. Total manufacturing costs and the beginning balance in the Work in Process Inventory account are added. Their sum is called total cost of goods in process during the year. By subtracting the ending Work in Process Inventory balance from total cost of goods in process, we get the total cost of goods manufactured.

7. Prepare the year-end work sheets, closing journal entries, and financial statements for a manufacturing company, using a periodic inventory approach.

Preparing the work sheet is the key to all year-end accounting procedures. (See the Work Sheet Analysis in the Working Papers.) Columns must be completed for the trial balance, year-end adjustments, adjusted trial balance, statement of cost of goods manufactured, income statement, and balance sheet. From this information, all year-end financial statements are prepared. Closing entries are then developed to complete the cycle.

Review Problem
Cost of Goods Manufactured—Three Fundamental Steps

In addition to the year-end balance sheet and income statement, the management of the Boca Raton Company requires the controller to prepare a statement of cost of goods manufactured. During 19x2, $309,414 of materials were purchased. Operating data and inventory account balances for 19x2 follow:

Account	Balance
Direct Labor (62,840 hours at $9.50 per hour)	$596,980
Plant Supervision	42,500
Indirect Labor (31,140 hours at $6.25 per hour)	194,625
Factory Insurance	8,100
Utilities	29,220
Depreciation, Factory Building	36,500
Depreciation, Equipment	42,800
Manufacturing Supplies	9,460
Repairs and Maintenance	11,720
Materials Inventory, Jan. 1, 19x2	$ 92,810
Work in Process Inventory, Jan. 1, 19x2	101,640
Finished Goods Inventory, Jan. 1, 19x2	126,260
Materials Inventory, Dec. 31, 19x2	96,174
Work in Process Inventory, Dec. 31, 19x2	98,990
Finished Goods Inventory, Dec. 31, 19x2	141,100

Required

To review the three basic steps for figuring cost of goods manufactured, do the following:

1. Prepare a schedule showing the calculation of the cost of materials used during the year.
2. Given the cost of materials used, develop an analysis to find total manufacturing costs for the year.

3. Given total manufacturing costs for the year, prepare an analysis to find the cost of goods manufactured during the year.

Answer to Review Problem

1. Computation of cost of materials used:

Beginning Balance: Materials Inventory	$ 92,810
Plus Materials Purchases	309,414
Cost of Materials Available for Use	$ 402,224
Less Ending Balance: Materials Inventory	96,174
Cost of Materials Used	$ 306,050

2. Computation of total manufacturing costs:

Cost of Materials Used		$ 306,050
Plus Direct Labor Costs		596,980
Plus Factory Overhead Costs:		
Plant Supervision	$ 42,500	
Indirect Labor	194,625	
Factory Insurance	8,100	
Utilities	29,220	
Depreciation, Factory Building	36,500	
Depreciation, Equipment	42,800	
Manufacturing Supplies	9,460	
Repairs and Maintenance	11,720	
Total Factory Overhead		374,925
Total Manufacturing Costs		$1,277,955

3. Computation of cost of goods manufactured:

Total Manufacturing Costs	$1,277,955
Plus Beginning Balance: Work in Process Inventory	101,640
Total Cost of Goods in Process During the Year	$1,379,595
Less Ending Balance: Work in Process Inventory	98,990
Cost of Goods Manufactured	$1,280,605

Chapter Assignments

Questions

1. Describe the field of management accounting, including the three kinds of information needed by management.

2. What is the difference between a merchandising company and a manufacturing company? Include in your answer a description of inventory cost flows for each type of company.

3. Does the size of a business dictate the types or amount of financial information needed by management? Explain your answer.

4. What are the three kinds of costs included in product cost?

5. What is the difference between a period cost and a product cost?

6. Define a direct cost. How is it different from an indirect cost?

7. Define direct materials.

8. Describe the following: purchase requisition (request), purchase order, and receiving report.

9. How is direct labor different from indirect labor?
10. What are the two kinds of labor-related costs? Discuss each one.
11. What characteristics identify a cost as being part of factory overhead?
12. What is meant by cost behavior?
13. How does the periodic inventory method differ from the perpetual inventory method?
14. Identify and describe the three inventory accounts used by a manufacturing company.
15. What is meant by manufacturing cost flow?
16. Describe how to compute the cost of materials used.
17. How do total manufacturing costs differ from the cost of goods manufactured?
18. How is the cost of goods manufactured used in computing the cost of goods sold?
19. "Computing the cost of goods sold for a merchandising company is not as complex as computing the same balance for a manufacturing company." Is this statement true? Explain your answer.

Classroom Exercises

**Exercise 22-1
Cost Classification
(L.O. 3)**

The following is a list of typical costs incurred by a garment maker: (a) gasoline and oil for salesperson's automobile; (b) telephone charges; (c) dyes for yardage; (d) seamstresses' regular hourly labor; (e) thread; (f) president's subscription to *The Wall Street Journal;* (g) sales commissions; (h) business forms used in the office; (i) buttons and zippers; (j) depreciation of sewing machines; (k) property taxes, factory; (l) advertising; (m) brand labels; (n) administrative salaries; (o) interest on business loans; (p) starch and fabric conditioners; (q) patterns; (r) hourly workers' vacation pay; (s) roof repair, office; (t) packaging.

1. At the time these costs are incurred, which ones will be classified as period costs? Which ones will be treated as product costs?
2. Of the costs identified as product costs, which are direct costs? Which are indirect costs?

**Exercise 22-2
Cost of
Materials Used
(L.O. 6)**

Data for the cost of materials for the month ended August 31, 19xx, are as follows: Materials Inventory on August 1, 19xx, $20,700; Materials Inventory on August 31, 19xx, $15,700; purchases of materials during August, $20,500.
    Compute the cost of materials used during August 19xx.

**Exercise 22-3
Computing
Total Manufac-
turing Costs
(L.O. 6)**

The partial trial balance of Katherine Millinery, Inc., is shown below. Inventory accounts still reflect balances at the beginning of the period. Period-end balances are $67,200, $96,400, and $47,600 for Materials Inventory, Work in Process Inventory, and Finished Goods Inventory, respectively.

	Debit	Credit
Accounts Receivable	$147,420	
Materials Inventory	58,400	
Work in Process Inventory	98,400	
Finished Goods Inventory	36,900	
Accounts Payable		$ 79,450
Sales		828,940
Purchases	297,600	
Direct Labor	184,200	
Operating Supplies Expense, Factory	17,700	
Depreciation Expense, Machinery	54,100	

Fire Loss	62,000
Insurance Expense, Factory	10,700
Indirect Labor Expense	46,900
Supervisory Salaries, Factory	32,700
President's Salary	39,900
Property Tax Expense, Factory	9,400
Other Indirect Manufacturing Expenses	16,500

From the above information, prepare a schedule (in good form) to compute total manufacturing costs for the period ending May 31, 19xx.

Exercise 22-4
Periodic Versus Perpetual Inventory Methods
(L.O. 3)

1. In as much detail as possible, discuss the differences between the periodic and the perpetual inventory methods. Be sure to describe the kinds of businesses that might use each method.
2. Would the periodic or perpetual inventory method be more suitable for each business listed below? Be able to defend your answers.

a. Major home appliance retailer
b. Grocery store
c. Hardware store
d. Retailer of fine jewelry
e. Sporting goods store
f. Grain elevator
g. Discount department store
h. Auto parts store

i. Furniture store
j. Paper manufacturer
k. Fertilizer manufacturer
l. Tire manufacturer
m. Cosmetics outlet for exclusive distributorship
n. Car dealer
o. Office supplies store

Exercise 22-5
Concept of Three Types of Inventories
(L.O. 5)

"For manufacturing companies, the concept of inventories must be expanded to include three types: Materials Inventory, Work in Process Inventory, and Finished Goods Inventory."

Briefly explain how the three inventory accounts function and how they relate to each other.

Exercise 22-6
Manufacturing Cost Flow
(L.O. 5)

Using the ideas shown in Figures 22-7 and 22-8 and expressed in this chapter, describe in detail the flow of materials costs through the recording process of a cost accounting system. Include in your answer all general ledger accounts affected and all recorded documents used. Prepare your answer in proper order.

Exercise 22-7
Statement of Cost of Goods Manufactured
(L.O. 6)

Information on the manufacturing costs incurred by the Kiger Company for the month ended May 31, 19xx, is as follows:

Purchases of materials during May were $39,000.
Direct labor was 10,400 hours at $4.75 per hour.
The following factory overhead costs were incurred: Utilities, $1,870; Supervision, $18,600; Indirect Supplies, $4,000; Depreciation, $3,200; Insurance, $830; Miscellaneous, $500.
Inventories on May 1 were as follows: Materials, $48,600; Work in Process, $53,250; Finished Goods, $60,500.
Inventories on May 31 were as follows: Materials, $50,100; Work in Process, $47,400; Finished Goods, $62,450.

From the information given, prepare a statement of cost of goods manufactured.

Exercise 22-8
Computing Cost of Goods Sold
(L.O. 5)

Sherrie Distilleries, Inc., produces a deluxe line of wines and beverages. During 19xx, the company operated at record levels, with sales totaling $695,000. The accounting department has already determined that total manufacturing costs for the period were $255,500. Operating expenses for the year were $229,740.

Assume a 50 percent tax rate. You discover that inventory balances were as follows:

	Jan. 1, 19xx	Dec. 31, 19xx
Materials Inventory	$25,490	$18,810
Work in Process Inventory	57,400	41,980
Finished Goods Inventory	84,820	69,320

From the above information, prepare an income statement for the year ended December 31, 19xx.

Exercise 22-9 Definitions of Management Accounting (L.O. 1)

There are many definitions and descriptions of the field of management accounting. The National Association of Accountants, in Statement No. 1A of its series of Statements on Management Accounting, defined management accounting as

. . . the process of identification, measurement, accumulation, analysis, preparation, and communication of financial information used by management to plan, evaluate, and control within the organization and to assure appropriate use and accountability for its resources. Management accounting also comprises the preparation of financial reports for nonmanagement groups such as shareholders, creditors, regulatory agencies, and tax authorities.

In *The Modern Accountant's Handbook,* edited by Edwards and Black (Dow Jones-Irwin, 1976, p. 830), management (managerial) accounting is described as follows:

Managerial accounting, although generally anchored to the financial accounting framework, involves a broader information-processing system. It deals in many units of measure and produces a variety of reports designed for specific purposes. Its scope encompasses the past, the present, and the future. Its purposes include short- and long-range planning, cost determination, control of activities, assessment of objectives and program performance, and provision of basic information for decision making.

1. Compare these two statements about management accounting.
2. "It is impossible to distinguish where financial accounting ends and management accounting begins." Explain this statement.

Interpreting Accounting Information

Internal Management Information: Rusty Manufacturing Company (L.O. 6, 7)

Rusty Manufacturing Company manufactures sheet metal products for heating and air conditioning installations. For the past several years its income has been declining, and this past year 19x6 was particularly poor. The company's statement of cost of goods manufactured and its income statement for 19x5 and 19x6 are shown below. You have been asked to comment on why the company's profit situation has deteriorated.

**Rusty Manufacturing Corporation
Statement of Cost of Goods Manufactured
For the Years Ended December 31, 19x6 and 19x5**

	19x6		19x5	
Materials used				
Materials Inventory, January 1	$ 89,660		$ 92,460	
Materials Purchased	789,640		760,040	
Cost of Materials Available for Use	$879,300		$852,500	
Less Materials Inventory, December 31	94,930		89,660	
Cost of Materials Used		$ 784,370		$ 762,840

	19x6	19x6	19x5	19x5
Direct Labor		871,410		879,720
Factory Overhead Costs				
Indirect Labor	$ 82,660		$ 71,980	
Power Expense	34,990		32,550	
Insurance Expense	22,430		18,530	
Supervision	125,330		120,050	
Depreciation Expense	75,730		72,720	
Other Factory Expenses	41,740		36,280	
Total Factory Overhead Costs		382,880		352,110
Total Manufacturing Costs		$2,038,660		$1,994,670
Add Work in Process Inventory, January 1		148,875		152,275
Total Cost of Goods in Process During the Year		$2,187,535		$2,146,945
Less Work in Process Inventory, December 31		146,750		148,875
Cost of Goods Manufactured		$2,040,785		$1,998,070

Rusty Manufacturing Corporation
Income Statements
For the Years Ended December 31, 19x6 and 19x5

	19x6	19x6	19x5	19x5
New Sales		$3,442,960		$3,496,220
Cost of Goods Sold				
Finished Goods Inventory, January 1	$ 192,640		$ 184,820	
Cost of Goods Manufactured	2,040,785		1,998,070	
Total Cost of Finished Goods Available for Sale	$2,233,425		$2,182,890	
Less Finished Goods Inventory, December 31	186,630		192,640	
Cost of Goods Sold		2,046,795		1,990,250
Gross Margin on Sales		$1,396,165		$1,505,970
Operating Expenses				
Sales Salaries and Commissions Expense	$ 494,840		$ 429,480	
Advertising Expense	216,110		194,290	
Other Selling Expenses	82,680		72,930	
Administrative Expenses	342,600		295,530	
Total Operating Expenses		1,136,230		992,230
Income from Operations		$ 259,935		$ 513,740
Other Revenues and Expenses				
Interest Expense		54,160		56,815
Net Income Before Taxes		$ 205,775		$ 456,925
Income Tax Expense		102,887		228,462
Net Income		$ 102,888		$ 228,463

Required

1. In preparing your comments, compute the following ratios for each year:
   a. Ratios of cost of materials used to total manufacturing costs, direct labor to total manufacturing costs, and total factory overhead costs to total manufacturing costs.
   b. Ratios of gross margin on sales to sales, operating expenses to sales, and net income to sales.
2. From your evaluation of the ratios computed in 1, state the probable causes of the decline in net income.
3. What other factors or ratios do you believe should be considered?

Problem Set A

**Problem 22A-1
Unit Cost
Computation
(L.O. 3)**

Carol Industries has recently finished production of Job CG-28. The corporation's cost accountant is ready to calculate the unit cost for this order. Relevant information for the month ended March 31, 19xx, is as follows: The number of units produced was 38,480. Cost information for Department B-14 included 2,210 liters at $2.00 per liter for direct materials used, 168 hours at $7.50 per hour for direct labor incurred, and $1,270 of factory overhead. Cost data for Department C-12 included 800 liters at $4.57 per liter for direct materials used, 400 hours at $6.80 per hour for direct labor incurred, and $5,440 of factory overhead. Cost data for Department D-15 included 1,005 liters at $4.00 per liter for direct materials used, 320 hours at $7.00 per hour for direct labor incurred, and $3,360 of factory overhead. Each unit produced was processed through the three departments, B-14, C-12, and D-15, in that order. There was no ending work in process inventory as of March 31, 19xx.

Required

1. Compute the unit cost for each of the three separate departments.
2. Compute the total unit cost.
3. Order CG-28 was specially made for the New London Company for a selling price of $30,784. Determine whether the selling price was appropriate. List the assumptions or computations on which you base your answer. What advice, if any, would you offer the management of Carol Industries on the pricing of future orders to the New London Company?

**Problem 22A-2
Direct
Materials—Cost
Flow
(L.O. 3, 5)**

A solid working knowledge of direct materials cost is important for understanding the elements, purpose, and operation of a cost accounting system.

Required

1. Name the characteristics of (a) direct materials and (b) indirect materials.
2. Give at least two examples for each of the two cost categories listed in 1.
3. Prepare a diagram of the flow of all materials costs for a manufacturing concern. Show which documents are used to record materials costs, and relate these documents to specific parts of the cost flow diagram.
4. If a direct materials invoice for $600 is dated September 2, with terms of 2/10, n/30, how much should be paid if the invoice is paid on September 8? On September 29?

**Problem 22A-3
Cost of Goods
Manufac-
tured—Three
Fundamental
Steps
(L.O. 6)**

Victoria Metallurgists, Inc., is a large manufacturing firm that prepares financial statements on a quarterly basis. Assume that you are working in the firm's Accounting Department. Preparing a statement of the cost of goods manufactured is one of your regular quarterly duties. Account balances were as follows for the quarter ended March 31, 19xx:

Office Supplies Expense	$ 1,870
Depreciation Expense, Plant and Equipment	14,230
President's Salary	25,000
Property Taxes, Office	850
Equipment Repairs Expense, Factory	1,290
Plant Supervisors' Salaries	18,750
Insurance Expense, Plant and Equipment	1,040
Direct Labor	146,310
Utilities Expense, Plant	3,420
Indirect Labor	15,000
Manufacturing Supplies Expense	3,760
Small Tools Expense	800
Materials Inventory, Jan. 1, 19xx	596,950
Materials Inventory, Mar. 31, 19xx	514,030
Work in Process Inventory, Jan. 1, 19xx	829,840
Work in Process Inventory, Mar. 31, 19xx	815,560
Finished Goods Inventory, Jan. 1, 19xx	675,010
Finished Goods Inventory, Mar. 31, 19xx	702,840
Purchases of Materials During the Quarter	1,525,330

Required

Highlight the three basic steps in preparing the statement of cost of goods manufactured by doing the following:

1. Prepare an analysis that calculates the cost of materials used during the quarter.
2. Using the figure calculated in **1**, prepare a schedule that determines the total manufacturing costs for the quarter.
3. From the figure arrived at in **2**, prepare a final schedule that derives cost of goods manufactured for the quarter.

**Problem 22A-4
Statement of
Cost of Goods
Manufactured**
(L.O. 6)

Sebastian and Maria operate a large vineyard in California that produces a full line of varietal wines. The company, whose fiscal year begins on November 1, has just completed a record-breaking year ending October 31, 19x4. Production figures for this period are as follows:

Account	Nov. 1, 19x3	Oct. 31, 19x4
Materials Inventory	$ 4,956,200	$ 5,203,800
Work in Process Inventory	8,371,000	7,764,500
Finished Goods Inventory	11,596,400	11,883,200

Materials purchased during the year amounted to $3,500,000. Direct labor hours incurred totaled 342,500, at an average labor rate of $4.20 per hour. The following factory overhead costs were incurred during the year: Depreciation Expense, Plant and Equipment, $985,600; Operating Supplies Expense, $607,300; Property Tax Expense, Plant and Equipment, $514,200; Material Handlers' Labor Expense, $1,113,700; Small Tools Expense, $82,400; Utilities Expense, $2,036,500; Employee Fringe Benefits Expense, $846,100.

Required

Using proper form, prepare a statement of cost of goods manufactured from the information provided.

Problem 22A-5
Year-End Work
Sheet and
Financial
Statement
Analysis
(L.O. 7)

(Before working this problem, see the illustrative Work Sheet Analysis in the Working Papers.)

Rosman Metal Fabricators, Inc., manufactures a diversified line of metal pipe. The corporation's trial balance as of December 31, 19xx, is shown below.

	Debit	Credit
Cash	$ 14,920	
Accounts Receivable	35,020	
Materials Inventory, Jan. 1, 19xx	26,240	
Work in Process Inventory, Jan. 1, 19xx	19,100	
Finished Goods Inventory, Jan. 1, 19xx	42,110	
Manufacturing Supplies Inventory, Jan. 1, 19xx	6,930	
Prepaid Factory Insurance	4,800	
Machinery and Equipment	238,425	
Accumulated Depreciation, Machinery and Equipment		$102,640
Accounts Payable		22,220
Notes Payable ($5,000 due each year)		60,000
Common Stock		50,000
Retained Earnings, Jan. 1, 19xx		25,170
Sales		678,190
Materials Purchases	171,080	
Direct Labor	122,610	
Plant Supervision Expense	51,000	
Factory Utilities Expense	12,910	
Factory Rent Expense	26,000	
Indirect Labor	32,625	
Repairs Expense	9,220	
Factory Property Tax Expense	6,910	
Selling Expenses, Control	48,630	
Administrative Expenses, Control	69,690	
	$938,220	$938,220

Year-end adjustment information for Rosman is as follows: (a) prepaid factory insurance on Dec. 31, 19xx, $2,400; (b) machinery and equipment depreciation for the year, $9,537; (c) manufacturing supplies used during the year, $2,300; (c) accrued salaries and wages payable on Dec. 31, 19xx, including Direct Labor, $9,120; Indirect Labor, $1,760; Plant Supervision, $2,040; (e) estimated federal income taxes, $60,000; (f) ending inventory balances for Materials Inventory, $30,480; Work in Process Inventory, $26,950; Finished Goods Inventory, $40,690.

The company uses the periodic inventory method.

Required

1. Prepare a twelve-column work sheet, and enter the trial balance amounts. Make year-end adjusting entries from the information given, post the entries to the work sheet, and compute the adjusted trial balance.
2. Extend all amounts to the proper columns for the statement of cost of goods manufactured, the income statement, and the balance sheet.
3. Complete the work sheet, and prepare formal year-end financial statements, including a statement of cost of goods manufactured.
4. Prepare closing entries.

Problem Set B

**Problem 22B-1
Unit Cost
Computation**
(L.O. 3)

Order 8477 has just been completed, and the assistant controller of Fritzemeyer Corporation is about to compute the order's unit cost. The number of units produced was 14,690. Cost information for Department 12 included 44,070 grams at $.50 per gram for direct materials used, 7,340 hours at $6.50 per hour for direct labor, and $29,360 of factory overhead. Cost information for Department 24 included 14,670 grams at $1.20 per gram for direct materials used, 22,035 hours at $7.00 per hour for direct labor, and $308,490 of factory overhead. Cost information for Department 36 included no direct materials used, 58,760 hours at $6.00 per hour for direct labor, and $58,760 of factory overhead. Each unit produced was processed through all three departments in order, and there were no units in the work in process inventory at the end of the period.

Required

1. Compute the unit cost of processing the product through each of the three departments.
2. What is the total unit cost?
3. The entire order was sold to the O'Donald Company for $1,057,680. Was the selling price adequate? List the assumptions or computations on which you base your answer. What suggestions would you make to the assistant controller on the pricing of future orders?

**Problem 22B-2
Direct Labor—
Cost Flow**
(L.O. 3, 5)

A thorough knowledge of direct labor costs is essential to understanding the elements, purpose, and operation of a cost accounting system.

Required

1. Name the characteristics of (a) direct labor and (b) indirect labor.
2. List two examples of each cost category listed in **1**.
3. Diagram the flow of all labor costs in a manufacturing environment. List the documents used to record these costs, and link them with specific parts of the cost flow diagram.
4. The SBAE Company has just issued the weekly payroll. Ms. Cox, whose wage rate is $7.25 per hour, worked fifty-two hours (this includes twelve hours overtime at time and a half). Deductions for the current pay period on her pay check were as follows: $42.05 for federal income tax, $20.00 for state income tax, $28.60 for FICA taxes, $17.50 for bond deduction, $10.00 for union dues, and $12.25 for insurance premium. What is the amount of gross wages? Net wages? Which amount should be charged to production? Why?

**Problem 22B-3
Cost of Goods
Manufac-
tured—Three
Fundamental
Steps**
(L.O. 6)

As she was preparing year-end financial statements, Sue Anderson, controller of HRA Enterprises, was asked to present a formal statement of cost of goods manufactured to management. Account balances were as follows: Materials Inventory, Jan. 1, $64,540; Work in Process Inventory, Jan. 1, $81,050; Finished Goods Inventory, Jan. 1, $100,040; Materials Inventory, Dec. 31, $62,820; Work in Process Inventory, Dec. 31, $84,590; Finished Goods Inventory, Dec. 31, $88,880; Direct Labor (4,900 hours at $11.50 per hour), $56,350; Indirect Labor Expense (6,200 hours at $6.90 per hour), $42,780; Heat, Light, and Power Expense, $3,940; Operating Supplies, $7,610; Supervision Expense, Factory, $18,400; Repairs Expense, $6,820; Depreciation Expense, Plant and Equipment, $7,915; Property Tax Expense, Plant and Equipment, $2,185; Insurance Expense, Plant, $690.

During the year, $264,290 of materials were purchased.

Required

1. Prepare a schedule showing the calculation of materials used during the year.
2. Given the amount of materials used, determine total manufacturing costs for the year. Show your analysis.
3. Given the total manufacturing costs for the period, derive the cost of goods manufactured during the year. Show your analysis.

Problem 22B-4
Statement of
Cost of Goods
Manufactured
(L.O. 6)

The Texas Food Company has been in business for several years. The information below was taken from its records on June 30, 19x6, the last day of the company's fiscal year. Inventory balances on July 1, 19x5, were as follows: Materials, $95,800; Work in Process, $192,700; Finished Goods, $96,500. Inventory balances on June 30, 19x6, were: Materials, $96,400; Work in Process, $162,490; Finished Goods, $97,400.

Materials were purchased during the year for $214,600. Direct labor totaled 18,420 hours at $5.50 per hour plus 4,850 hours at $4.80 per hour for the twelve-month period. Factory overhead costs incurred during the year were as follows: Indirect Labor, $12,830; Employee Fringe Benefits, $4,720; Janitorial and Maintenance Service, $1,640; Plant Security Service, $1,260; Depreciation Expense, Machinery and Equipment, $850; Depreciation Expense, Building, $600; Insurance Expense, $880; Property Tax Expense, $1,320; Small Tools Used in the Factory, $250; Heat, Light, and Power, $990; Quality Control, Factory, $1,110.

Required

Using the information provided above, prepare a statement of cost of goods manufactured for the fiscal year ended June 30, 19x6.

Problem 22B-5
Year-End
Work Sheet
and Financial
Statement
Analysis
(L.O. 7)

(Before working this problem, see the illustrative Work Sheet Analysis in the Working Papers.)

The trial balance of the Temecula Manufacturing Company as of December 31, 19xx, appeared as follows:

	Debit	Credit
Cash	$ 19,500	
Accounts Receivable	14,240	
Materials Inventory, Jan. 1, 19xx	18,450	
Work in Process Inventory, Jan. 1, 19xx	22,800	
Finished Goods Inventory, Jan. 1, 19xx	28,840	
Manufacturing Supplies Inventory, Jan. 1, 19xx	2,700	
Prepaid Factory Insurance	3,400	
Machinery and Equipment	145,600	
Accumulated Depreciation, Machinery and Equipment		$ 14,560
Small Tools	4,720	
Accounts Payable		21,200
Note Payable ($10,000 per year)		40,000
Common Stock		125,000
Retained Earnings		16,110
Sales		387,540
Materials Purchases	72,150	
Direct Labor	80,420	
Factory Supervision Expense	26,960	
Indirect Labor Expense	16,750	
Heat, Light, and Power Expense, Factory	9,310	

Factory Rent Expense	36,000	
Repairs and Maintenance Expense, Factory	12,650	
Property Tax Expense, Machinery and Equipment	4,500	
Selling Expenses, Control	38,900	
Administrative Expenses, Control	46,520	
	$604,410	$604,410

Year-end adjustment information is as follows: (a) depreciation for 19xx on machinery and equipment, $7,280; (b) factory insurance expired, $1,400; (c) small tools used during 19xx, $1,700; (d) manufacturing supplies consumed, $900; (e) accrued salaries and wages payable, including Direct Labor, $1,200; Indirect Labor, $890; Factory Supervision, $1,400; (f) estimated federal income taxes, $4,765; (g) ending inventory balances for Materials Inventory, $21,490; Work in Process Inventory, $24,210; Finished Goods Inventory, $29,680.

The company uses the periodic inventory method.

Required

1. Prepare a twelve-column work sheet, and enter the trial balance amounts. Make year-end adjusting entries from the information given, post the entries to the work sheet, and compute the adjusted trial balance.
2. Extend all amounts to the proper columns for the statement of cost of goods manufactured, the income statement, and the balance sheet.
3. Complete the work sheet, and prepare formal financial statements, including a statement of cost of goods manufactured.
4. Prepare closing entries.

Management Decision Case 22-1

Noreen Municipal Hospital
(L.O. 2, 3)

Hospitals exist in a very competitive environment, and they rely heavily on cost data to keep their pricing structures in line with those of competitors. Noreen Municipal Hospital is a case in point. Located in a large city, the hospital offers three broad kinds of service. *General services* (dietary, housekeeping, maintenance, patient care coordination, and general and administrative services) are the first kind of service. *Ancillary services* (anesthesiology, blood bank, central and sterile supply, electrodiagnosis, laboratory, operating and recovery room, pharmacy, radiology, and respiratory therapy) are the second kind. And *nursing care services* (acute or intensive care units, intermediate care units, neonatal [newborn] nursery, and nursing administration) are the third kind.

The hospital's controller is Peter Facione. He is reviewing the billing procedure for patients using the thirty intensive care units (ICUs) in the facility. Each unit contains a regular hospital bed and a great deal of special equipment. This includes special suction equipment, oxygen flowmeters at bedside, endotracheal tubes to assist breathing, a portable respirator, back-up suction machinery, and multiple IVs (intravenous feeding lines) with automatic drip counters. An H.P. Swan Ganz machine has a cardiac catheter tube that, when inserted into the heart, constantly monitors the pressure inside the heart chambers. One of the most important pieces of equipment at each bedside in the ICU is the cardiac monitor that displays the patient's heartbeat. A set of central monitors at the nurses' station helps nurses watch for instances of tachycardia (excessively rapid heartbeat), arrhythmia (irregular heartbeat), or bradycardia (abnormally slow heartbeat). An alarm system attached to the monitor warns the nurses when the patient's heartbeat is over or under acceptable limits. To equip an ICU today costs in the neighborhood of $85,000 per room. Use of the equipment is billed to the patient at a rate of $150 per day. This includes a 25 percent markup to cover hospital overhead and profit.

Other ICU patient costs include the following:

Doctors' care	2 hours per day @ $150 per hour (actual)
Special nursing care	8 hours per day @ $25 per hour (actual)
Regular nursing care	24 hours per day @ $8 per hour (average)
Medicines	$27 per day (average)
Medical supplies	$24 per day (average)
Room rental	$40 per day (average)
Food and service	$30 per day (average)

For billing these costs, as with the equipment charge, the hospital adds 25 percent to all costs to cover its operating costs and profit.

Required

1. From the costs listed, identify the direct costs in determining the "cost per patient day" for an ICU.
2. Compute the cost per patient day.
3. Compute the billing per patient day using the hospital's existing markup rate to cover operating expenses and profit.
4. Many hospitals use separate markup rates for each cost when preparing billing statements. Industry averages revealed the following markup rates:

Doctors' care	30%
Special nursing care	40%
Regular nursing care	50%
Medicines	50%
Medical supplies	50%
Room rental	20%
Food and service	25%
Equipment	30%

Using these rates, recompute the billing per patient day for an ICU.
5. Using the information in 3 and 4, which billing procedure would you recommend to the hospital's director? Why?

Learning Objectives

Chapter Twenty-Three

Product Costing: The Job Order System

Determining a product's unit cost is one of the basic functions of a cost accounting system. Business success depends on product costing information in several ways. First, unit costs are an important element in determining an adequate, fair, and competitive selling price. Second, product costing information often forms the basis for forecasting and controlling operations and costs. Finally, product unit costs are needed to arrive at ending inventory balances. As a result of studying this chapter, you should be able to meet the learning objectives listed on the left.

One important reason for having a cost accounting system is to figure out the cost of manufacturing an individual product or batch of products. Such cost accounting systems are different from one company to another. But each system is designed to give information that company management feels is important. In this chapter, we apply the basic information on manufacturing accounting discussed in Chapter 22 to a traditional product costing system: the job order costing system. A job order is a customer order for a specific number of specially designed, made-to-order products. We also learn to figure product costs in job order situations. Then we link these costs to units completed and transferred to the finished goods inventory.

However, before we can discuss a specific product cost accounting system, we need more background information. In the first part of this chapter we compare the two most common product costing systems—job order costing and process costing. Next we explain the concept of absorption costing. Then we discuss predetermined overhead rates and their application to specific jobs or products. The last objective for this chapter is covered in a special analysis in the Working Papers. (In Chapter 22, you will recall, a similar analysis was done for a company that used the periodic inventory method.)

Job Order Versus Process Costing

Job order costing and process costing are the two traditional, basic approaches to product cost accounting systems. Actual cost accounting systems may differ widely. However, all are based

*Objective 1
Describe the
difference
between job
order costing
and process
costing*

on one of these product costing concepts. They are then adjusted to fit a particular industry, company, or operating department. The objective of the two systems is the same. They are both meant to provide product unit cost information for product pricing, cost control, inventory valuation, and income statement preparation. End-of-period values for the Cost of Goods Sold, the Work in Process Inventory, and the Finished Goods Inventory accounts are figured by using product unit cost data.

Characteristics of Job Order Costing

A **job order cost accounting system** is a product costing system used in making one-of-a-kind or special-order products. In such a system, direct materials, direct labor, and factory overhead costs are assigned to specific job orders or batches of products. In figuring unit costs, the total manufacturing costs for each job order are divided by the number of good units produced for that order. Industries that use a job order cost accounting system include those that make ships, airplanes, large machines, and special orders.

The primary characteristics of a job order cost system are as follows: (1) It collects all manufacturing costs and assigns them to specific jobs or batches of product. (2) It measures costs for each completed job, rather than for set time periods. (3) It uses just one Work in Process Inventory account in the general ledger. This account is supported by a subsidiary ledger of job order cost sheets for each job still in process at period end.

Characteristics of Process Costing

A **process cost accounting system** is a product costing system used by companies that make a large number of similar products or have a continuous production flow. In either case, it is more economical to account for product-related costs for a period of time (a week or a month) than to try to assign them to specific products or job orders. Unit costs are computed by dividing total manufacturing costs assigned to a particular department or work center during a week or month by the number of good units produced during that time period. If a product is routed through four departments, four unit cost amounts are added together to find the product's total unit cost. Companies producing paint, oil and gas, automobiles, bricks, or soft drinks use some form of a process costing system.

The main characteristics of a process cost accounting system are as follows: (1) Manufacturing costs are grouped by department or work center, with little concern for specific job orders. (2) It emphasizes a weekly or monthly time period rather than the time it takes to complete a specific order. (3) It uses several Work in Process Inventory accounts—one for each department or work center in the manufacturing process. Process costing will be discussed in detail in Chapter 24.

The Concept of Absorption Costing

Objective 2
Describe the
concept of
absorption
costing

Product costing is possible only when the accounting system can define the types of manufacturing costs to be included in the analysis. For instance, should all factory overhead costs be considered costs of making the product, or only the variable factory overhead costs? Usually, we assume that product costing is governed by the concept of absorption costing. **Absorption costing** is an approach to product costing that assigns *all* types of manufacturing costs to individual products. The costs of direct materials, direct labor, variable factory overhead, and fixed factory overhead are all assigned to products. The product costing systems we discuss in this chapter and in Chapter 24 apply the absorption costing concept.

Direct materials and direct labor costs are not difficult to handle for product costing because they can be conveniently and economically traced to products. Factory overhead costs, on the other hand, are not as easy to trace directly to products. For example, for a company making lawn and garden equipment, how much machine depreciation should be assigned to a single lawnmower? How about the costs of electrical power and indirect labor? One solution would be to wait until the end of the accounting period. We could then add up all the variable and fixed factory overhead costs incurred. Then we could just divide this amount by the number of units produced during the period. This procedure would be an acceptable method of computing a unit cost under only two conditions. (1) All products would have to be alike and require the same manufacturing operations. (2) We would have to be able to wait until the end of the period to learn the product unit costs. Such a situation is seldom found in industry. A company usually makes many different products. And it needs product costing information to set prices for goods before they are produced. Therefore, under absorption costing, we must use a predetermined overhead rate to allocate factory overhead costs to products.

Predetermined Overhead Rates

Objective 3
Compute a
predetermined
overhead rate,
and use this
rate to apply
overhead costs
to production

Factory overhead costs are a problem for the management accountant. How can these costs be estimated and assigned to certain products or jobs before the end of the accounting period? The most common way is to use a **predetermined overhead rate** for each department or other operating unit. We can define this rate as an overhead cost factor used to assign factory overhead costs to specific products or jobs. It is based on *estimated* overhead costs and production levels for the period. The rate is computed in three steps:

1. **Estimate factory overhead costs.** Using cost behavior analysis, estimate all factory overhead costs. Do so for each production department in the coming accounting period. (Cost behavior analysis will be discussed in Chapter 25.) Add the totals for all the production departments. For exam-

ple, suppose that the total costs of rent, utilities, insurance, and so on for the coming year are expected to be $450,000.

2. **Select a basis for allocating costs.** We must find a way to connect overhead costs to the products produced. Common measures of production activity are labor hours, dollars of direct labor cost, machine hours, or units of output. The particular basis chosen attempts to link the overhead cost to the product produced in a meaningful way. For instance, if an operation is more labor-hour than machine-hour intensive (as in the typical assembly line), then labor hours would be a good basis to use for overhead allocation. In our example, let us suppose that overhead per hour of direct labor would be the most useful measure. Management believes that 25,000 hours of direct labor will be used during the year.

3. **Divide the total overhead costs that are estimated for the period by the total estimated basis (hours, dollars, or units).** The result is the predetermined overhead rate. The computation for our example is as follows:

$$\frac{\text{predetermined overhead rate}}{\text{per direct labor hour}} = \frac{\text{total estimated overhead costs}}{\text{total direct labor hours}}$$

$$= \frac{\$450,000}{25,000 \text{ hours}}$$

$$= \$18 \text{ of overhead per direct labor hour}$$

Overhead costs are then applied to each product using this rate. For example, let us say it takes one-half hour of direct labor to produce one unit. The overhead rate is $18 per direct labor hour. So that unit is assigned $9 of factory overhead cost. This amount is then added to the direct materials and direct labor costs already assigned to the product. The sum is the total unit cost.

Importance of Good Estimates

The whole process of overhead cost allocation depends for its success on two factors. One is a careful estimate of the total amount of overhead. The other is a good forecast of production activity used as the allocation basis.

Estimating total overhead costs is critical. If this estimate is wrong, the overhead rate will be wrong. The result will be that either too much or too little overhead cost will be assigned to the products produced. Therefore, in developing this estimate, the management accountant must be careful to include all factory overhead items and make forecasts of their costs accurately.

Overhead costs are generally estimated as part of the normal budgeting process. Expected overhead costs are gathered from all departments involved directly or indirectly with the production process. The accounting department receives and totals each department's cost estimates. Costs of supporting service departments, such as maintenance or electrical departments, have only an indirect connection with products. Therefore, these costs must be distributed among the production departments. In this way they can be included as part of total manufacturing overhead when figuring the predetermined overhead rate for the period.

Figure 23-1
Overhead Cost
Allocation

Forecasting production activity is also critical to the success of overhead cost allocation. First, we must ask which activity base is most appropriate—hours, dollars, or units of output. The basis chosen should be one that relates to the overhead cost in a causal or beneficial way. For example, a greater number of machine hours would cause higher electricity costs and depreciation charges. Therefore, departments that are equipment intensive (say, for example, one person running twenty-five or thirty machines by remote control) would use machine hours as the allocation basis. The object is to pick the one activity base that varies most with total overhead costs. Selecting an inappropriate activity base will mean that the amounts of overhead costs assigned to individual jobs or products will not be correct.

Figure 23-1 sums up the whole process of overhead cost allocation. In the first phase we figure the predetermined overhead rate. To do so, we estimate total overhead costs and total production activity. In the second phase we use the predetermined overhead rate to figure the amount of overhead costs to be applied to products or jobs during the period.

Underapplied or Overapplied Overhead

Objective 4
Dispose of
underapplied or
overapplied
overhead

A lot of time and effort may be put into estimating and allocating factory overhead costs. Still, actual overhead costs and actual production activities will seldom agree with these estimates. Something will happen to cause a difference (or variance) to occur. Differences in either area will cause factory overhead to be **underapplied** or **overapplied**. That is, the amount of overhead costs assigned to products will be less or more than the actual amount of overhead costs incurred. We must account for these actual overhead costs by making a quarterly or annual adjustment.

Monthly differences between actual overhead incurred and overhead costs applied are normally not adjusted. In many cases, monthly differences tend to offset one another, leaving only a small adjustment to be made at year end.

An example will illustrate the accounting problems of using predetermined overhead rates. Assume that the accounting records of the Fertakis Company show the overhead transactions below. Also assume that all overhead costs are debited to one general ledger controlling account—the Factory Overhead Control account—instead of to individual overhead accounts.

May 25 Paid utility bill for three months, $1,420.
27 Recorded usage of indirect materials and supplies, $940.
June 21 Paid indirect labor wages, $2,190.
Aug. 12 Paid property taxes on factory building, $620.
Sept. 9 Recorded expiration of prepaid insurance premium, $560.
Nov. 27 Recorded depreciation of machinery and equipment for the year, $1,210.

These transactions resulted in the following entries:

May 25	Factory Overhead Control	1,420	
	Cash		1,420
	To record payment of 3-month utility bill		
May 27	Factory Overhead Control	940	
	Materials (or Supplies) Inventory		940
	To record usage of indirect materials and supplies		
June 21	Factory Overhead Control	2,190	
	Factory Payroll		2,190
	To distribute indirect labor from factory payroll		
Aug. 12	Factory Overhead Control	620	
	Cash		620
	To record payment of property taxes on factory building		
Sept. 9	Factory Overhead Control	560	
	Prepaid Insurance		560
	To record expiration of insurance premiums		
Nov. 27	Factory Overhead Control	1,210	
	Accumulated Depreciation, Machinery and Equipment		1,210
	To record depreciation for the year		

The entries above record actual overhead expenses. However, they do not help in assigning these costs to products. Nor do they help transfer costs to the Work in Process Inventory account. Such a transfer must take place before product unit costs can be computed.

Here the predetermined overhead rate is useful. Assume that the predetermined overhead rate for the period was $2.50 per direct labor hour. The following list of jobs completed during the period shows the number of direct labor hours for each job. It also shows the overhead cost that was applied to each one.

Job	Direct Labor Hours	×	Rate	=	Overhead Applied
16-2	520		$2.50		$1,300
19-4	718		2.50		1,795
17-3	622		2.50		1,555
18-6	416		2.50		1,040
21-5	384		2.50		960
	2,660				$6,650

A journal entry like the one below was used to record the application of predetermined overhead costs to each job worked on during the period. This entry transfers estimated overhead costs from the Factory Overhead Applied account to the Work in Process Inventory account. (Normally it is made when payroll is recorded, since overhead costs can be applied only after the number of labor hours is known. But in our example weekly and monthly labor data are not available. Thus we apply estimated overhead to the entire job.)

Mar. 2	Work in Process Inventory	1,300	
	Factory Overhead Applied		1,300
	To record application of		
	overhead costs to Job 16-2		

Similar entries would be prepared for each job worked on during the period.

After posting all the actual overhead transactions discussed earlier, we can compare overhead costs applied against actual overhead costs. The resulting general ledger account entries and balances are shown below.

Factory Overhead Control (Incurred)			Factory Overhead Applied	
5/25	1,420		Job 16-2	1,300
5/27	940		Job 19-4	1,795
6/21	2,190		Job 17-3	1,555
8/12	620		Job 18-6	1,040
9/9	560		Job 21-5	960
11/27	1,210		Bal.	6,650
Bal.	6,940			

At year end, these records of the Fertakis Company show that overhead has been *under*applied by $290 ($6,940 − $6,650). More actual overhead costs were incurred than were applied to products. The predetermined overhead rate was a little low. That is, it did not apply all of the overhead costs incurred to the products produced. The $290 must now be added to the production costs of the period.

Two courses of action are available. First, if the $290 difference is considered small, or if most of the items worked on during the year have been sold, the entire amount can be charged to Cost of Goods Sold. This approach is the most common one because it is easy to apply. The adjusting entry would be as follows:

Factory Overhead Applied	6,650	
Cost of Goods Sold	290	
Factory Overhead Control		6,940
To close out overhead accounts and		
to charge underapplied overhead		
to the Cost of Goods Sold account		

Another method is used if the amount of the adjustment is large or if a large number of the products worked on during the year are unsold at year end. Using this approach, underapplied or overapplied overhead is divided at year end among the Work in Process Inventory, Finished Goods Inventory, and Cost of Goods Sold accounts. For example, assume that at year end the products that the Fertakis Company worked on during the year were located as follows: 30 percent in Work in Process Inventory, 20 percent in Finished Goods Inventory, and 50 percent sold. In such cases, the following entry would be made:

Factory Overhead Applied	6,650	
Cost of Goods Sold (50% of $290)	145	
Work in Process Inventory (30% of $290)	87	
Finished Goods Inventory (20% of $290)	58	
Factory Overhead Control		6,940
To close out overhead accounts and to		
account for underapplied factory		
overhead		

The breakdown of the $290 among the three accounts would be based on either the number of units worked on during the period or the direct labor hours incurred and attached to units within the three accounts. The Review Problem at the end of this chapter offers more guidance in accounting procedures for underapplied or overapplied overhead.

Product Costing and Inventory Valuation

One of the main goals of cost accounting is to supply management with information about production costs. This information is useful in many ways. It assists internal decision making. It helps the accountant control

*Objective 5
Explain the
relationship
between product
costing and
inventory
valuation*

costs. And, through inventory valuation, it forms the link between financial accounting and management accounting.

All manufacturing costs incurred during a period must be accounted for in the year-end financial statements. However, not all of these costs will appear on the income statement. Only those costs assigned to units sold will be reported on the income statement. Costs assigned to units sold have "expired." They were used up in producing revenue. Costs assigned to unsold units (ending inventory) are "unexpired," or unused, costs. They are classified as assets and included in either the Work in Process Inventory or the Finished Goods Inventory on the balance sheet. Product unit cost information is needed to figure end-of-period balances in the Work in Process Inventory and the Finished Goods Inventory, as well as to figure the cost of goods sold.

The Job Order Cost Accounting System

As we have seen, a job order cost system is designed to gather manufacturing costs for a specific order or batch of products and to aid in figuring product unit costs. Price-setting decisions, production scheduling, and other management tasks depend on information from a company's cost accounting system. For these reasons, it is necessary to maintain a system that gives timely, correct data about product costs. In Chapter 22, we discussed the three main cost elements—materials, labor, and factory overhead. Here we see how these costs are accounted for in a job order cost system.

Incurrence of Materials, Labor, and Factory Overhead Costs

A basic part of a job order cost system is the set of procedures and journal entries used when the company incurs materials, labor, and factory overhead costs. To help control these costs, businesses use various documents for each transaction. The effective use of these procedures and documents promotes accounting accuracy. It also makes for a smooth, efficient flow of cost information through the accounting record system. Note that all inventory balances in a job order cost system are kept on a perpetual basis.

Materials Careful use of materials improves a company's overall efficiency. It conserves production resources and can bring about large cost savings. At the same time, good records ensure accountability and cut down waste. Controlling the physical materials and keeping good records enhances profits.

To help record and control materials costs, accountants rely heavily on a connected series of cost documents. These documents include the purchase request, purchase order, receiving report, inventory records, and materials requisition. Each of these documents was discussed in Chapter

22 and is an important link in accounting for materials costs. Direct materials costs are traced to specific jobs or products. Costs of indirect materials and supplies are charged to factory overhead.

Labor Labor is one production resource that cannot be stored and used later. So it is very important to link labor costs with each job or product. Labor time cards and job cards are used to record labor costs as they are incurred. Indirect labor costs are routed through the Factory Overhead account.

Factory Overhead All indirect manufacturing costs are classified as factory overhead. Unlike materials and direct labor, overhead costs do not call for special documents. Vendors' bills support most payments. Factory depreciation expenses and usage of prepaid expenses are charged to the Factory Overhead account through journal entries. Overhead costs may be accounted for in separate accounts, but that is not done in a job order cost system. Because factory overhead costs are linked to certain products, they are all debited to a Factory Overhead Control account.

A control account, you will recall, sums up several similar account balances to reduce accounting detail. A separate subsidiary account is also kept for each type of factory overhead cost. These separate accounts make up a subsidiary ledger to the Factory Overhead Control account. In general, a subsidiary ledger is kept for each control account. It is made up of the individual accounts included in the control account balance.

Factory overhead costs, by nature, cannot be traced directly to jobs or products. For this reason, an estimate of factory overhead costs is applied to products by means of the predetermined overhead rate. This process was discussed earlier, and it will be illustrated later in this chapter.

The Work in Process Inventory Account

*Objective 6
Describe the
cost flow in a
job order cost
accounting
system*

Job order costing focuses on the flow of costs through the Work in Process Inventory account. All manufacturing costs incurred and charged to production are routed through the Work in Process Inventory. Figure 23-2 shows cost flow in a job order cost system. Materials costs are debited to Work in Process Inventory. But indirect materials and supplies are debited to the Factory Overhead Control account. All labor costs that can be traced to specific jobs are debited to Work in Process Inventory. But indirect labor costs are charged against the Factory Overhead Control account balance. By means of a predetermined overhead rate, we apply overhead costs to specific jobs by debiting Work in Process Inventory and crediting Factory Overhead Applied.

Attaching costs of direct materials, direct labor, and factory overhead to specific jobs and products is not an automatic process. Even though all manufacturing costs are debited to Work in Process Inventory, we need a separate accounting procedure to link those costs to specific jobs. For this purpose we use a subsidiary ledger made up of **job order cost cards.** There is one job order cost card for each job being worked on, and all costs of that job are recorded on it. As costs are debited to Work in

Figure 23-2
Job Order Cost
Flow

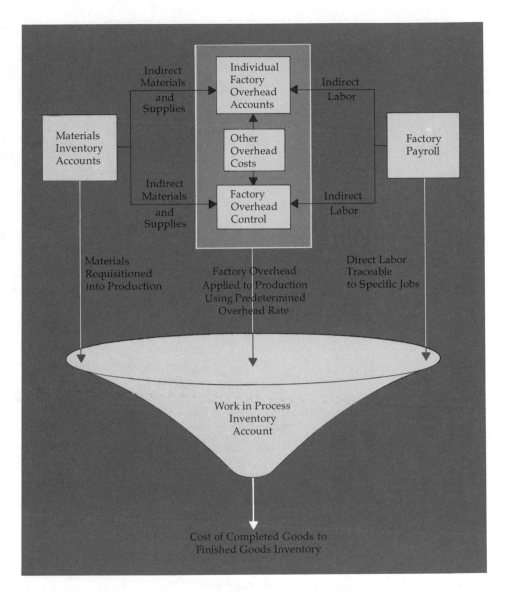

Process Inventory, we must reclassify them by job and add them to their job order cost cards.

A typical job order cost card is shown in Figure 23-3. Each card has space for materials, direct labor, and factory overhead costs. There is also space to write the job order number, product specifications, name of customer, date of order, projected completion date, and summary cost data. Job order cost cards for incomplete jobs make up the subsidiary ledger for the Work in Process Inventory Control account. To make sure the ending balance in the Work in Process Inventory Control account is right, we compare it with the total of the costs shown on the job order cost cards.

Figure 23-3
Job Order Cost
Card

Job Order

No. _16F_   Great Boat Company
Azusa, California

Product Specs: *Model GB30 - Mark I : 30-foot fiberglass sailing sloop with full galley*

Customer:	Materials:	
Hinds Yachts, Inc.	Dept. 1.	$48,210
	Dept. 2.	11,850
Date of Order:	Dept. 3.	-0-
February 10, 19X8	Total	$60,060
Date of Completion:	Direct Labor:	
October 28, 19X8	Dept. 1.	$21,720
	Dept. 2.	30,480
	Dept. 3.	20,200
Cost Summary:	Dept. 4.	
Materials $60,060	Dept. 5.	
Direct Labor 72,400	Total	$72,400
Factory Overhead 61,540	Applied Factory Overhead:	
Total $194,000	Dept. 1.	$18,462
	Dept. 2.	25,908
Units Completed 11 (eleven)	Dept. 3.	17,170
	Dept. 4.	
Cost per Unit $17,636.36	Dept. 5.	
	Total	$61,540

Accounting for Finished Goods

When a job has been completed, all costs assigned to that job order are moved to Finished Goods Inventory. We accomplish this in the accounting records by debiting the Finished Goods Inventory account and crediting the Work in Process Inventory account. When this entry is made, the job order cost card should be removed from the subsidiary ledger file. It is then used to help update the Finished Goods Inventory records.

When goods are shipped, the order for them is recorded as a sale. We debit Accounts Receivable and credit Sales for the entire selling price. But we also need to account for the cost of the goods shipped. The proper procedure is to debit Cost of Goods Sold and to credit Finished Goods Inventory for the cost of the goods shipped.

To learn the mechanics of operating the system just described, you really need to go through an analysis of transactions and related journal entries. While studying the journal entry analysis that follows, review the preceding paragraphs. Try to keep in mind the cost flow concept shown in Figure 23-2.

Journal Entry Analysis

Objective 7
Journalize
transactions in
a job order cost
accounting
system

Because a job order cost system emphasizes cost flow, we need to understand the journal entries that record the various costs as they are incurred. We also need to know the entries that transfer costs from one account to another. In fact, these entries, along with job order cost cards and other subsidiary ledgers for materials and finished goods inventories, are a major part of the job order cost system. As we cover each area in our analysis of the Great Boat Company, we will first describe the related transaction. We will follow with the journal entry needed to record the transaction. We will finish each section with a discussion of the unique features of the transaction or the accounts being used. Figure 23-4 (next page) shows the entire job order cost flow through the general ledger. Supporting subsidiary ledgers are also shown. As each entry is discussed, trace its number and related debits or credits to Figure 23-4.

Materials Purchased In recording direct materials purchases, we will see the differences between journal entries used in the perpetual inventory approach and those used for periodic inventories. For example, Great Boat Company purchased the following materials: Material 5X for $28,600 and Material 14Q for $17,000. Materials purchases are recorded at cost in the Materials Inventory Control account.

Entry 1:	Materials Inventory Control	45,600	
	Accounts Payable (or Cash)		45,600
	To record purchase of $28,600 of Material 5X and $17,000 of Material 14Q		

This procedure differs in several ways from the recording of purchases discussed before in this text. First, the debit is to an inventory account instead of a purchases account because the inventory system is perpetual. All costs of materials flow through the inventory account. A second difference in our entry above is the use of a **control** or **controlling account.** The term *control* means that the account is an accumulation of several individual account balances. Some companies have hundreds of items in inventory. To keep a separate account for each item in the general ledger would make the ledger crowded and hard to work with. A control account is used in each area where several similar items are being accounted for and only one cumulative total appears in the general ledger. Each control account is supported by a subsidiary ledger that holds all the individual account balances. At the time that entry 1 is posted to the general ledger, the individual accounts in the materials ledger are also updated (see Figure 23-4).

Purchase of Supplies The following transaction and entry are for the purchase of supplies for production. The company purchased $4,100 of operating supplies for the manufacturing process.

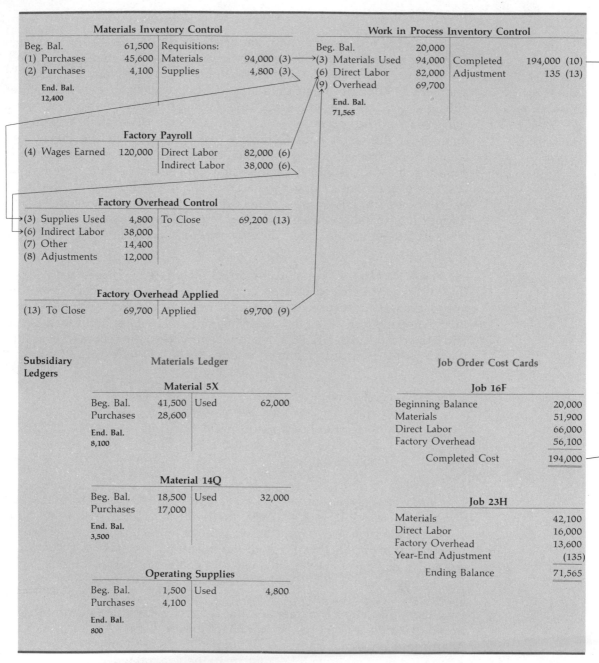

Figure 23-4
The Job Order
Cost System

Entry 2:   Materials Inventory Control   4,100
                Accounts Payable (or Cash)   4,100
                      To record the purchase of
                      operating supplies

The procedures used to account for the purchase of supplies are much like those used to record direct materials purchases. Supplies Inventory, in our example, is assumed to be one subsidiary account making up the total Materials Inventory Control account. If the supplies inventory is large, a

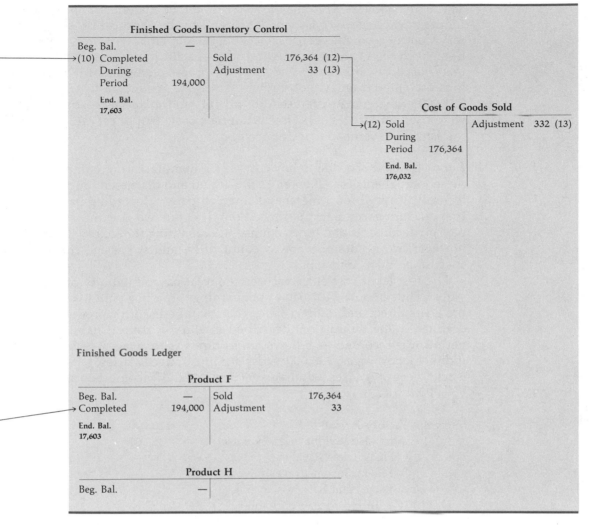

Finished Goods Inventory Control

Beg. Bal.	—	Sold	176,364 (12)	
→(10) Completed During Period	194,000	Adjustment	33 (13)	
End. Bal. 17,603				

Cost of Goods Sold

→(12) Sold During Period	176,364	Adjustment	332 (13)
End. Bal. 176,032			

Finished Goods Ledger

Product F

Beg. Bal.	—	Sold	176,364
→Completed	194,000	Adjustment	33
End. Bal. 17,603			

Product H

Beg. Bal.	—

Figure 23-4
(*continued*)

separate general ledger account may be used. No matter what method is selected, the accountant should be able to give reasons to support the approach taken and should then follow this approach consistently.

Requisitioning of Materials and Supplies   Upon receipt of a properly prepared materials requisition form, the following direct materials and supplies are issued from inventory to production: Material 5X for $62,000, Material 14Q for $32,000, and operating supplies for $4,800.

Entry 3:	Work in Process Inventory Control	94,000	
	Factory Overhead Control	4,800	
	Materials Inventory Control		98,800
	To record issuance of $62,000 of Material 5X, $32,000 of Material 14Q, and $4,800 of operating supplies into production		

The entry above shows that $94,000 of direct materials and $4,800 of indirect materials were issued. The debit to the Work in Process Inventory Control account records the cost of direct materials issued to production. Such costs can be directly traced to specific job orders. As the direct materials costs are charged to work in process, amounts for individual jobs are entered on the job order cost cards. As shown in Figure 23-4, $51,900 of materials were used on Job 16F, and materials costing $42,100 were used on Job 23H. Indirect materials costs (supplies) are debited to the Factory Overhead Control account.

Labor Costs Recording labor costs for a manufacturing company takes three journal entries. Chapter 12 illustrated and discussed journal entries to record payroll for a merchandising company. Recording payroll for a manufacturing company is more complex, but we use the same basic payroll documents and transactions. In accounting for factory labor costs, however, we need some new account titles, and we assign the costs to specific products and jobs.

The first labor cost entry records the total payroll liability of the company. Though only $107,640 of net earnings are to be paid to employees, the gross direct and indirect labor costs will be used for product and job costing. In the transaction, described in entry 4, payroll liability for the period was recorded as follows: gross direct labor wages, $82,000; gross indirect labor wages, $38,000; gross administrative salaries, $36,000; FICA (social security) taxes withheld, $9,360; federal income taxes withheld, $39,000.

Entry 4:	Factory Payroll	120,000	
	Administrative Salaries Expense	36,000	
	FICA Taxes Payable		9,360
	Federal Income Taxes Payable		39,000
	Wages and Salaries Payable		107,640
	To record payroll liability		
	for the period		

A follow-up entry is now needed to account properly for labor costs. This entry, entry 5, will record the payment of the payroll liability established in entry 4. In this transaction, payroll checks for the period were prepared and given to the employees.

Entry 5:	Wages and Salaries Payable	107,640	
	Cash		107,640
	To record payment of payroll		

The total payroll dollars of factory personnel first debited to the Factory Payroll account must now be moved to the production accounts. This step takes two entries. Gross direct labor costs are debited to Work in Process Inventory Control. Total indirect wages (including factory supervisory salaries) are debited to Factory Overhead Control.

```
Entry 6:   Work in Process Inventory Control        82,000
           Factory Overhead Control                 38,000
               Factory Payroll                                   120,000
                   To record the distribution of
                   factory payroll to production
                   accounts
```

In addition, the direct labor costs are recorded by job on the individual job order cost cards. This distribution of $66,000 to Job 16F and $16,000 to Job 23H is shown in Figure 23-4.

Other Factory Overhead Costs   As factory overhead costs other than indirect materials and labor charges are incurred, the sum of these costs is charged (debited) to the Factory Overhead Control account. Each cost itself is identified in the explanation of the journal entry. In our example, factory overhead costs were paid as follows: electricity, $3,100; maintenance and repair, $8,400; insurance, $1,300; and property taxes, $1,600.

```
Entry 7:   Factory Overhead Control                 14,400
               Cash                                              14,400
                   To record incurrence of the
                   following overhead costs:
                   electricity, $3,100; maintenance
                   and repair, $8,400; insurance
                   expense, $1,300; and property
                   taxes, $1,600
```

From the information in the journal entry's explanation, individual subsidiary ledger accounts are updated. Because of the amount of information already included in Figure 23-4, the subsidiary ledger for the Factory Overhead Control account is not shown. However, the subsidiary ledger would include an individual account for each type of factory overhead cost. The costs would be accounted for in much the same way as described for the materials ledger and the job order cost cards.

The next transaction is an adjusting entry needed to record depreciation on factory equipment for the period.

```
Entry 8:   Factory Overhead Control                 12,000
               Accumulated Depreciation, Equipment              12,000
                   To record depreciation on
                   factory equipment for the
                   period
```

This entry is out of order, since we usually prepare adjusting entries after all transactions for the period have been recorded. But we introduce it at this point because depreciation of factory equipment is a part of total factory overhead cost. The actual Depreciation Expense account will be part of the overhead subsidiary ledger.

Factory Overhead Applied   We apply factory overhead by using a predetermined overhead rate and an allocation base (direct labor hours, direct labor dollars, machine hours, or units of output). In this transaction, factory overhead costs were applied to production by using a rate of 85 percent of direct labor dollars.

Entry 9:   Work in Process Inventory Control   69,700
           Factory Overhead Applied   69,700
               To apply factory overhead
               costs to production

The amount of overhead charged to production is found by multiplying the overhead rate by the units of the base. In our example, we multiplied 85 percent times the direct labor dollars ($82,000), which gave us $69,700 ($82,000 × .85). This amount was debited to the Work in Process Inventory Control account. Because the overhead application is related to direct labor dollars, we can update the job order cost cards by the same procedure. Job 16F is assigned $56,100 of overhead costs ($66,000 × .85). Job 23H receives a charge of $13,600 ($16,000 × .85). These amounts have been posted to the job order cost cards in Figure 23-4.

Accounting for Completed Units As various job orders are completed, their costs are moved to the Finished Goods Inventory Control account. In this case, goods costing $194,000, for Job 16F, were completed and transferred to finished goods inventory.

Entry 10:   Finished Goods Inventory Control   194,000
           Work in Process Inventory Control   194,000
               To record transfer of completed
               goods for Job 16F from work
               in process inventory to
               finished goods inventory

When a job is completed, its job order cost card is pulled from the Work in Process subsidiary ledger. The card is then used to help update the Finished Goods ledger. Specifically, costs recorded on the job order cost card are used to figure unit costs and to determine the amount of the transfer entry.

Accounting for Units Sold The final phase of manufacturing cost flow is the transfer of costs from the Finished Goods Inventory Control account to the Cost of Goods Sold account. At this point, a major batch of Job 16F was shipped to the customer. The selling price for the goods shipped was $260,000. The cost to manufacture these products totaled $176,364.

Entry 11:   Accounts Receivable   260,000
           Sales   260,000
               To record sale of portion of
               Job 16F

Entry 12:   Cost of Goods Sold   176,364
           Finished Goods Inventory Control   176,364
               To record the transfer of the

cost of the shipped goods for
Job 16F from Finished Goods
Inventory to Cost of Goods Sold

Both the entry to record the sale and the entry to establish the cost of the goods sold are shown here. Entry 12 is made at the same time that the sale is recorded. When we transfer the costs of the product sold out of the Finished Goods Inventory Control account, we should also update the finished goods ledger (subsidiary ledger), as shown in Figure 23-4.

Overhead Disposition At the end of an accounting period, we total the Factory Overhead Control account and the Factory Overhead Applied account. Then we make an entry to close these accounts and dispose of any underapplied or overapplied overhead.

Entry 13:	Factory Overhead Applied	69,700	
	Work in Process Inventory		
	Control		135
	Finished Goods Inventory		
	Control		33
	Cost of Goods Sold		332
	Factory Overhead Control		69,200
	To close out factory overhead account balances and to dispose of the overapplied balance		

In this transaction, we see that factory overhead has been overapplied by $500. So, as we closed the Factory Overhead Control and Factory Overhead Applied accounts, we distributed the $500 difference among Work in Process Inventory Control, Finished Goods Inventory Control, and Cost of Goods Sold. We did so on the basis of each account's balance before the adjustment. The following analysis shows how we arrived at these figures.

First, we use T accounts to summarize the overhead account balances before entry 13. Numbers in parentheses refer to earlier journal entries.

Factory Overhead Control			Factory Overhead Applied	
(3)	4,800		(9)	69,700
(6)	38,000			
(7)	14,400			
(8)	12,000			
	69,200			69,700

Overhead has been overapplied by $500 ($69,700 − $69,200). This amount can be either credited to the Cost of Goods Sold account or distributed among the Work in Process Inventory Control, Finished Goods Inventory Control, and Cost of Goods Sold accounts. We assume that the amount is significant, and so we distribute it among the three accounts on the basis of their ending balances (see Figure 23-4). The following table shows how the distribution amounts were figured:

Account	Ending Balance	Percentage of Each to Total	×	Amount to Be Allocated	=	Allocation of Overapplied Overhead
Work in Process Inventory Control	$ 71,700	27.0		$500		$135
Finished Goods Inventory Control	17,636	6.6		500		33
Cost of Goods Sold	176,364	66.4		500		332
Totals	$265,700	100.0				$500

After entry 13 has been posted to the general ledger, the accounts affected will look like those in Figure 23-4. In addition, all subsidiary ledgers affected by the overhead adjustment must be updated. In our example, the entire $135 of adjustment to Work in Process was credited to Job 23H. Because Job 16F had been completed, its share of the adjustment was assigned to the Finished Goods Inventory Control and the Cost of Goods Sold accounts.

Computing Product Unit Costs

*Objective 8
Compute
product unit
cost for a
specific job
order*

The process of computing product unit cost is fairly simple in a job order costing system. All costs of materials, direct labor, and factory overhead for each job are recorded on its job order cost card as the job progresses to completion. When the job is finished, all costs on the job order cost card are totaled. The unit cost is then figured by dividing total manufacturing costs for the job by the number of good units produced. Job 16F was completed in the journal entry analysis we just finished. The cost data for this job are shown on the job order cost card in Figure 23-3. Eleven sailing sloops were produced at a total cost of $194,000. This worked out to a cost of $17,636.36 per sloop before adjustments. Note in Figure 23-4 that only ten of the sloops were actually shipped during the year. One still remains in Finished Goods Inventory Control.

Fully and Partly Completed Products

In a job order costing system, as we have seen, manufacturing costs are accumulated, classified, and reclassified several times. As products near completion, all manufacturing costs for their production are linked to them. These costs then follow the products first to Finished Goods Inventory Control and then to Cost of Goods Sold. Figure 23-4 illustrated the accounting procedures and cost flows of units worked on during the period. Dollar amounts in that figure came from posting the journal entries just discussed.

At period end, some costs remain in the Work in Process Inventory Control and the Finished Goods Inventory Control accounts. The ending balance of $71,565 in Work in Process Inventory Control is from costs attached to partly completed units in Job 23H. These costs can be traced to the specific job order cost cards for partly completed jobs in the subsidiary ledger. Finished Goods Inventory Control also has an ending balance. Of all units completed during the period, one sloop costing $17,603 (after the adjustment) from Job 16F has not been sold or shipped. Its cost now appears as the ending balance in Finished Goods Inventory Control.

Chapter Review

Review of Learning Objectives

1. Describe the difference between job order costing and process costing.

Both job order costing and process costing are basic, traditional approaches to product cost accounting. However, they have different characteristics. A job order costing system is used for unique or special-order products. In such a system, materials, direct labor, and factory overhead costs are assigned to specific job orders or batches of products. In figuring unit costs, the total manufacturing cost assigned to each job order is divided by the number of good units produced for that order. A process costing system is used by companies that produce a large number of similar products or have a continuous production flow. These companies find it more economical to account for product-related costs for a period of time (week or month) than to assign them to specific products or job orders. Unit costs in a process costing system are found by dividing total manufacturing costs for a department or work center during a week or month by the number of good units produced.

2. Describe the concept of absorption costing.

Absorption costing is an approach to product costing that assigns a representative portion of *all* manufacturing costs to individual products. The costs of direct materials, direct labor, variable factory overhead, and fixed factory overhead are all assigned to products.

3. Compute a predetermined overhead rate, and use this rate to apply overhead costs to production.

A predetermined overhead rate is computed by dividing total estimated overhead costs for a period by the total activity basis expected for that same time period. Factory overhead costs are applied to a job order by multiplying the predetermined overhead rate by the amount of the activity base (such as labor hours) used for that job order.

4. Dispose of underapplied or overapplied overhead.

If there is any difference between the balances in the Factory Overhead Control and Factory Overhead Applied accounts at year end, there are two ways to get rid of the difference. If the difference is small, it should be adjusted to the Cost of Goods Sold account. Often, however, the amount of the adjustment is large, or the costs of the products worked on during the period are spread among the Work in Process Inventory, Finished Goods Inventory, and Cost of Goods Sold accounts. In such cases, the difference should be assigned proportionately to these three accounts.

5. Explain the relationship between product costing and inventory valuation.

Product costing techniques are necessary to attach costs to job orders or units of product worked on during a given time period. At period end, when financial statements are prepared, these product costs are used in costing the Work in Process and Finished Goods Inventories.

6. Describe the cost flow in a job order cost accounting system.

A job order cost accounting system generally follows the concept of absorption costing. It also uses the perpetual approach to inventory maintenance and valuation. Within these limits, materials and supplies costs are first debited to the Materials Inventory Control account. Labor costs are debited to the Factory Payroll account. And the various factory overhead costs are debited to the Factory Overhead Control account. As the products are being manufactured, costs of materials and direct labor are transferred to the Work in Process Inventory Control account. Factory overhead costs are applied and charged to the Work in Process Inventory Control account by using a predetermined overhead rate. These overhead cost charges are credited to the Factory Overhead Applied account. When products or jobs are completed, the costs assigned to them are transferred to the Finished Goods Inventory Control account. These same costs are transferred to the Cost of Goods Sold account when the products are sold and shipped.

7. Journalize transactions in a job order cost accounting system.

Mastery of a job order costing system requires that the user be able to prepare journal entries for each of the following transactions: (a) purchase of materials, (b) purchase of operating supplies, (c) requisition of materials and supplies into production, (d) recording of payroll liability, (e) payment of payroll to employees, (f) distribution of factory payroll to production accounts, (g) cash payment of overhead costs, (h) recording of noncash overhead costs such as depreciation of factory and equipment, (i) application of factory overhead costs to production, (j) transfer of costs of completed jobs from the Work in Process Inventory Control account to the Finished Goods Inventory Control account, (k) sale of products and transfer of related costs from the Finished Goods Inventory Control account to the Cost of Goods Sold account, and (l) disposition of underapplied or overapplied factory overhead.

8. Compute product unit cost for a specific job order.

Product costs in a job order costing system are computed by first totaling all the manufacturing costs accumulated on a particular job order cost card. This amount is then divided by the number of good units produced for that job to find the individual unit cost for the order. Unit cost information is entered on the job order cost card and used for inventory valuation purposes.

9. Prepare the year-end work sheets, closing journal entries, and financial statements for a manufacturing company, using a perpetual inventory approach.

Preparing the work sheet is the key to all year-end accounting procedures. (See the Work Sheet Analysis in the Working Papers.) Columns must be completed for the trial balance, year-end adjustments, adjusted trial balance, income statement, and balance sheet. From this information, all year-end financial statements are prepared. Closing entries are then developed to complete the cycle. Be sure to study the Work Sheet Analysis in the Working Papers before trying to do Practice Set III: Aluma-Cylinder Company, Inc.

Review Problem
Journal Entry Analysis—Job Order Costing System

The McBride Manufacturing Company produces "uniframe" desk and chair assemblies and study carrels for libraries. The firm uses a job order cost system and a current factory overhead application rate of 220 percent of direct labor dollars. The following transactions and events took place during September 19xx:

Sept. 4 Received direct materials costing $9,540. Purchased on account.
  7 The production department requisitioned $2,700 of materials and $650 of operating supplies.
  14 Gross factory payroll of $16,000 was paid to factory personnel. Of this amount, $11,500 represents direct labor and the remaining amount is indirect labor. (Prepare only the entry to distribute factory payroll to production accounts.)
  14 Factory overhead costs were applied to production.
  16 Received supplies costing $3,500 and direct materials costing $17,000. Both were ordered on 9/11/xx and purchased on account. Both can be inventoried.
  20 Requisitioned $9,000 of direct materials and $1,750 of supplies for production.
  26 Paid the following overhead costs: heat, light, and power, $1,400; repairs by outside firm, $1,600; and property taxes, $2,700.
  28 Gross factory payroll of $15,600 was earned by factory personnel. Of this amount, indirect wages and supervisory salaries totaled $6,400. Prepare only the entry to distribute factory payroll to production accounts.
  28 Factory overhead costs were applied to production.
  29 Completed units costing $67,500 were transferred to Finished Goods Inventory.
  30 Depreciation of plant and equipment for September was $24,000. During the same period, $1,200 of prepaid fire insurance expired.
  30 Library carrel units costing $32,750 were shipped to a customer for a total selling price of $53,710.

Required

1. Record the journal entries for all of the above transactions and events.
2. Assume that the beginning balance in Materials Inventory Control was $4,700. The beginning balance in Work in Process Inventory Control was $6,200. And the beginning balance in Finished Goods Inventory Control was $9,000. Compute the ending balances in these inventory accounts.
3. Determine the amount of underapplied or overapplied overhead.
4. If 131 carrels were included in the order sold and shipped on September 30, compute the cost and selling price per carrel shipped.

Answer to Review Problem

1. Journal entries:

Sept.	4	Materials Inventory Control	9,540	
		Accounts Payable		9,540
		To record purchase of direct materials on account		
	7	Work in Process Inventory Control	2,700	
		Factory Overhead Control	650	
		Materials Inventory Control		3,350
		To record requisition of direct materials and supplies into production		

14	Work in Process Inventory Control	11,500	
	Factory Overhead Control	4,500	
	Factory Payroll		16,000
	To distribute payroll to		
	production accounts		
14	Work in Process Inventory Control	25,300	
	Factory Overhead Applied		25,300
	To apply factory overhead costs		
	to production ($11,500 × 220%)		
16	Materials Inventory Control	20,500	
	Accounts Payable		20,500
	To record purchase of $3,500 of		
	operating supplies and $17,000		
	of direct materials		
20	Work in Process Inventory Control	9,000	
	Factory Overhead Control	1,750	
	Materials Inventory Control		10,750
	To record requisition of direct mate-		
	rials and supplies into production		
26	Factory Overhead Control	5,700	
	Cash		5,700
	To record payment of the		
	following overhead costs: heat,		
	light, and power, $1,400; out-		
	side repairs, $1,600; property		
	taxes, $2,700		
28	Work in Process Inventory Control	9,200	
	Factory Overhead Control	6,400	
	Factory Payroll		15,600
	To distribute payroll to		
	production accounts		
28	Work in Process Inventory Control	20,240	
	Factory Overhead Applied		20,240
	To apply factory overhead costs		
	to production ($9,200 × 220%)		
29	Finished Goods Inventory Control	67,500	
	Work in Process Inventory Control		67,500
	To transfer costs of completed		
	goods to Finished Goods		
	Inventory		
30	Factory Overhead Control	25,200	
	Accumulated Depreciation,		
	Plant and Equipment		24,000
	Prepaid Insurance		1,200
	To charge Factory Overhead		
	Control with expired asset		
	costs		

			30	Accounts Receivable	53,710	

        30   Accounts Receivable   53,710
                 Sales   53,710
                     To record sales for September

        30   Cost of Goods Sold   32,750
                 Finished Goods Inventory Control   32,750
                     To record transfer of costs from
                     Finished Goods Inventory to
                     Cost of Goods Sold

2. Ending balances of inventory accounts:

Materials Inventory Control

Beg. Bal.	4,700	9/7	3,350
9/4	9,540	9/20	10,750
9/16	20,500		
	34,740		14,100
Bal.	20,640		

Work in Process Inventory Control

Beg. Bal.	6,200	9/29	67,500
9/7	2,700		
9/14	11,500		
9/14	25,300		
9/20	9,000		
9/28	9,200		
9/28	20,240		
	84,140		67,500
Bal.	16,640		

Finished Goods Inventory Control

Beg. Bal.	9,000	9/30	32,750
9/29	67,500		
	76,500		32,750
Bal.	43,750		

3. Underapplied or overapplied overhead:

Factory Overhead Control

9/7	650	
9/14	4,500	
9/20	1,750	
9/26	5,700	
9/28	6,400	
9/30	25,200	
Bal.	44,200	

Factory Overhead Applied

	9/14	25,300
	9/28	20,240
	Bal.	45,540

Factory overhead is overapplied by $1,340 ($45,540 − $44,200).

4. Cost and selling price per unit:

Cost per unit: $32,750 ÷ 131 = $250 per unit
Selling price per unit: $53,710 ÷ 131 = $410 per unit

Chapter Assignments

Questions

1. What is the common goal of a job order cost accounting system and a process cost accounting system?
2. Explain the concept of absorption costing.
3. What is the connection between manufacturing cost flow and the perpetual inventory method?
4. Describe the steps used to arrive at a predetermined overhead rate based on direct labor hours.
5. What are the factors for success in applying overhead to products and job orders?
6. What is meant by underapplied or overapplied overhead?
7. Describe two ways to adjust for underapplied or overapplied overhead.
8. "Some costs of direct materials, direct labor, and factory overhead used during a period will be reported in the company's income statement. Others will be reported in the company's balance sheet." Discuss the accuracy of this statement.
9. What are the differences between a job order cost system and a process cost system? (Focus on the characteristics of each system.)
10. In what way is timely purchasing a "do or die" function?
11. How does materials usage influence the efficiency of operations?
12. "Purchased labor resource services cannot be stored." Discuss this statement.
13. Discuss the role of the Work in Process Inventory account in a job order cost system.
14. What is the purpose of a job order cost card? Name the types of information recorded on such a card.
15. Define the terms *control account* and *subsidiary ledger*. How are they related?
16. Cost and management accounting are often overshadowed by financial accounting, since it is better publicized. Describe the importance of a product costing system to (a) the preparation of financial statements and (b) profitability.

Classroom Exercises

**Exercise 23-1
Overhead Rate
Determination**
(L.O. 3)

Overhead costs of Pappas Enterprises, Inc., for the upcoming accounting period have been arrived at through cost behavior analysis. They are expected to be $35,000. The allocation basis selected by management for assigning overhead costs is direct labor dollars. Total direct labor charges for 19xx are expected to be 640 hours at $7 per hour plus 280 hours at $9 per hour.

1. Figure the predetermined overhead rate, using direct labor dollars as the allocation base.
2. Figure the predetermined overhead rate, using direct labor hours as a base.

**Exercise 23-2
Concept of
Absorption
Costing**
(L.O. 2)

Using the absorption costing concept, determine product unit cost from the following costs incurred during March: $2,500 in Liability Insurance, Factory; $1,900 in Rent Expense, Sales Office; $3,100 in Depreciation Expense, Factory Equipment; $19,650 in Materials Used; $2,480 in Indirect Labor, Factory; $980 in Factory Supplies; $1,410 in Heat, Light, and Power, Factory; $1,600 in Fire Insurance, Factory; $3,250 in Depreciation Expense, Sales Equipment; $2,850 in Rent Expense, Factory; $27,420 in Direct Labor; $2,100 in Manager's Salary, Factory; $4,800 in President's Salary; $7,250 in Sales Commissions; $1,975 in Advertising Expense. The Inspection Department reported that 150,800 good units were produced during March.

Exercise 23-3
Overhead
Application
Rate
(L.O. 3)

Deborah Datatrans specializes in the analysis and reporting of complex inventory costing projects. Materials costs are minimal, consisting entirely of operating supplies such as data processing cards, inventory sheets, and other recording tools. Labor is the highest single expense item, totaling $785,500 for 120,700 hours of work in 19x4. Factory overhead costs for 19x4 were $766,445, and this amount was applied to specific jobs on the basis of labor hours worked.

In 19x5, the company anticipates a 25 percent increase in overhead costs. The number of hours worked during 19x5 is expected to increase 30 percent.

1. Determine the total amount of factory overhead anticipated by the company in 19x5.
2. Compute the predetermined overhead rate for 19x5. (Round your answer to the nearest penny.)
3. During April 19x5, the following jobs were completed, with the related hours worked: Job 16A4, 1,490 hours; Job 21C2, 6,220 hours; and Job 17H3, 3,270 hours. Prepare the journal entry required to apply overhead costs to operations for April.

Exercise 23-4
Disposition of
Underapplied
Overhead
(Extension of
Exercise 23-3)
(L.O. 4)

At the end of 19x5, Deborah Datatrans had compiled a total of 156,250 hours worked. The actual overhead incurred was $964,800 during the year.

1. Using the predetermined overhead rate computed in Exercise 23-3, determine the total amount of overhead applied to operations during 19x5.
2. Compute the amount of underapplied overhead for the year.
3. Prepare the journal entry to close out the overhead accounts and to dispose of the underapplied overhead amount for 19x5. Assume that the amount is not significant.

Exercise 23-5
Disposition of
Overapplied
Overhead
(L.O. 4)

The Vocovich Manufacturing Company ended the year with a total of $13,400 of overapplied overhead. Because management feels that this amount is significant, this favorable difference should be distributed among the three appropriate accounts in proportion to their ending balances. The ending account balances are Materials Inventory Control, $195,400; Work in Process Inventory Control, $167,760; Finished Goods Inventory Control, $438,040; Cost of Goods Sold, $326,200; Factory Overhead Control, $174,500; and Factory Overhead Applied, $187,900.

Using good form, close out the factory overhead accounts, and dispose of the overapplied overhead. Show your work in journal entry form. Separately, give supporting computations.

Exercise 23-6
Cost System—
Industry
Linkage
(L.O. 1)

Which of the following types of manufactured products would normally be produced using a job order costing system? Which would be produced using a process costing system? (a) paint, (b) automobiles, (c) 747 jet aircraft, (d) bricks, (e) large milling machines, (f) liquid detergent, (g) aluminum compressed-gas cylinders of standard size and capacity, (h) aluminum compressed-gas cylinders with a special fiberglass overwrap for a Mount Everest expedition, (i) nails from wire, (j) television sets, (k) printed wedding invitations, (l) a limited edition of lithographs, (m) flea collars, (n) high-speed lathes with special-order thread drills, (o) breakfast cereal, (p) an original evening gown.

Exercise 23-7
Job Order Cost
Flow
(L.O. 6)

The three manufacturing cost elements—direct materials, direct labor, and factory overhead—flow through a job order cost system in a structured, orderly fashion. Specific general ledger accounts, subsidiary ledgers, and source documents are used to verify and record the cost information. In paragraph and diagram form, describe cost flow in a job order cost accounting system.

Exercise 23-8
Journal
Entries—
Completed
Units
(L.O. 7)

A special order of 344 units costing $84,624 was completed on June 16, and the costs were moved to the Finished Goods Inventory Control account. On June 30, these same goods were shipped to a customer, who was billed for a total of $113,520.

1. Using good journal entry form, record these June transactions.
2. Compute the unit cost and the unit selling price.

Exercise 23-9
Work in
Process
Inventory
Account—
Journal Entry
Analysis
(L.O. 7)

On June 1, there was a $26,430 beginning balance in the Work in Process Inventory account of the Lash Specialty Company. Production activity for June was as follows: (a) Materials costing $126,200, along with $15,820 of operating supplies, were requisitioned for production. (b) Total factory payroll for June was $167,490, of which $39,990 was payments for indirect labor. (Assume that payroll has been recorded but not distributed to production accounts.) (c) Factory overhead was applied at a rate of 80 percent of direct labor cost.

1. Prepare journal entries to record the materials, labor, and overhead costs for June.
2. Compute the ending balance in the Work in Process Inventory Control account. Assume a transfer of $346,800 to the Finished Goods Inventory Control account during the period.

Exercise 23-10
Predetermined
Overhead Rate
Computation
(L.O. 3)

The overhead costs used by Rhodes Industries, Inc., to compute its predetermined overhead rate for 19x2 were as follows:

Indirect Materials and Supplies	$ 46,200
Repairs and Maintenance	18,900
Outside Service Contracts	37,300
Indirect Labor	89,100
Factory Supervision	62,900
Depreciation, Machinery	75,000
Factory Insurance	28,200
Property Taxes	17,500
Heat, Light, and Power	21,700
Miscellaneous Factory Overhead	9,040
	$405,840

A total of 45,600 direct labor hours was used as the 19x2 allocation base.

In 19x3, all overhead costs except depreciation and property taxes are expected to increase by 10 percent. Depreciation should increase by 5 percent, and a 25 percent increase in property taxes is expected. Plant capacity in terms of direct labor hours used will increase by 3,800 hours in 19x3.

1. Figure the 19x2 predetermined overhead rate.
2. Figure the predetermined overhead rate for 19x3.

Interpreting Accounting Information

Internal
Management
Information:
Brown
Company and
Green Corpo-
ration
(L.O. 3)

Both Brown Company and Green Corporation use predetermined overhead rates for product costing, inventory pricing, and sales quotations. The two businesses are about the same size, and they compete in the corrugated box industry. Brown Company's management believes that since the predetermined overhead rate is an estimated measure, the controller's department should spend little effort in developing the rate. The company figures the rate once a year based on trend analysis of last year's costs. It does not monitor the accuracy of the rate.

Green Corporation takes a much more sophisticated approach. One person in the controller's office is assigned the responsibility of developing predetermined overhead rates on a monthly basis. All cost inputs are checked out carefully to make sure the estimates are realistic. Accuracy checks are a routine procedure during each monthly closing analysis. Foreseeing normal business changes is part of the overhead rate analyst's regular performance evaluation by his or her supervisor.

1. Describe the advantages and disadvantages of each company's approach to overhead rate determination.
2. Which company has taken the most cost-effective approach in developing predetermined overhead rates? Defend your answer.
3. Is an accurate overhead rate most important for product costing, inventory valuation, or sales quotations? Why?

Problem Set A

**Problem 23A-1
Application of
Factory
Overhead
(L.O. 3, 4)**

Christine Cosmetics Company applies factory overhead costs on the basis of direct labor dollars. The current predetermined overhead rate is computed by using data from the two prior years, in this case 19x5 and 19x6, adjusted to reflect expectations for the current year, 19x7. The controller prepared the overhead rate analysis for 19x7, using the information below.

	19x5	19x6
Direct labor dollars	$115,000	$138,000
Factory overhead costs		
Indirect labor	$ 46,200	$ 60,060
Employee fringe benefits	38,000	43,700
Manufacturing supervision	29,600	32,560
Utilities	18,700	26,180
Factory insurance	20,000	27,000
Janitorial services	18,000	22,500
Depreciation, factory and machinery	15,500	18,600
Miscellaneous manufacturing expenses	9,500	10,450
Total overhead	$195,500	$241,050

For the year 19x7, each item of factory overhead cost is expected to increase by the same percentage as from 19x5 to 19x6. Direct labor expense is expected to total $165,600 for the year 19x7.

Required

1. Compute the overhead rate for 19x7.
2. The company actually surpassed its sales and operating expectations. Jobs completed during 19x7 and the related direct labor dollars were as follows: Job 2214, $28,000; Job 2215, $32,000; Job 2216, $22,000; Job 2217, $36,000; Job 2218, $44,000; Job 2219, $18,000. The total was $180,000. Determine the amount of factory overhead to be applied to each job and to total production during 19x7.
3. Prepare the journal entry needed to close the overhead accounts and to dispose of the underapplied or overapplied overhead. Assume that $320,490 of factory overhead was incurred in 19x7. Also assume that the difference between actual and applied overhead costs is considered to be insignificant.

Problem 23A-2
Job Order Cost Flow
(L.O. 6)

April 1 inventory balances of Deukmejian House, manufacturers of high-quality men's clothing, were as follows:

Materials Inventory Control	$31,360
Work in Process Inventory Control	15,112
Finished Goods Inventory Control	17,120

Additional information concerning operating events in April is summarized below.

Job order cost cards for jobs in process as of April 30, 19x4, revealed the following:

Job No.	Materials	Direct Labor	Factory Overhead
4A	$496	$390	$351
4B	392	480	432
4C	784	960	864
4D	408	760	684

Materials purchased and received in April:

April 4	$13,120
April 16	8,600
April 22	11,920

Direct labor costs for April:

April 15 payroll	$23,680
April 29 payroll	25,960

Predetermined overhead rate: 110 percent of direct labor dollars

Materials requisitioned into production during April:

April 6	$17,240
April 23	18,960

Finished goods with a 75% markup over cost were sold during April for $238,000.

Required

1. Reconstruct the transactions for April and determine the ending inventory balances.
2. Figure the cost of units completed during the period.
3. What was the total cost of units sold during April?

Problem 23A-3
Job Order Costing—Unknown Quantity Analysis
(L.O. 6)

Partial operating data for the Angelo Tire Company for October and November are given below. Management has decided on an overhead rate of 120 percent of direct labor dollars for the current year.

	October	November
Beginning Materials Inventory Control	(a)	(e)
Beginning Work in Process Inventory Control	$ 89,505	(f)
Beginning Finished Goods Inventory Control	79,764	$ 67,660
Materials Requisitioned	48,025	(g)
Materials Purchased	47,090	50,116
Direct Labor Costs	38,760	44,540
Factory Overhead Applied	(b)	(h)
Cost of Units Completed	(c)	219,861
Cost of Goods Sold	155,805	(i)
Ending Materials Inventory Control	33,014	28,628
Ending Work in Process Inventory Control	(d)	(j)
Ending Finished Goods Inventory Control	67,660	30,515

Using the data provided, compute the amount of each lettered unknown. Show your computations.

Problem 23A-4
Job Order
Costing—
Journal Entry
Analysis and
T Accounts
(L.O. 7)

Fukuda Manufacturing, Inc., produces electric shopping carts. These carts are special-order items, and so a job order cost accounting system is needed. Factory overhead is applied at the rate of 70 percent of direct labor cost. Below is a listing of events and transactions for March.

Mar. 1 Materials costing $186,400 were purchased on account.
  2 $28,500 of operating supplies were purchased on account.
  4 Production personnel requisitioned materials costing $174,200 and operating supplies costing $22,100 into production.
  10 Paid the following overhead costs: utilities, $3,400; factory rent, $2,500; and maintenance charges, $1,800.
  15 Payroll was distributed to employees. Gross wages and salaries were as follows: direct labor, $128,000; indirect labor, $42,620; sales commissions, $22,400; and administrative salaries, $28,000.
  15 Overhead was applied to production.
  19 Operating supplies costing $27,550 and materials listed at $200,450 were purchased on account.
  21 Materials costing $192,750 and operating supplies costing $29,400 were requisitioned into production.
  26 Production completed during the month was transferred to Finished Goods Inventory Control. Total costs assigned to these jobs were $463,590.
  31 The following gross wages and salaries were paid to employees: direct labor, $142,000; indirect labor, $46,240; sales commissions, $21,200; and administrative salaries, $28,000.
  31 Overhead was applied to production.
  31 Products costing $394,520 were shipped to customers during the month. Total selling price of these goods was $526,800, and these sales should be recorded at month end.
  31 The following overhead costs are to be recorded: prepaid insurance expired, $3,900; property taxes (payable at year end), $3,200; and depreciation, machinery, $52,500.

Required

1. Record the journal entries for all March transactions and events. For the payroll entries, concern yourself only with the distribution of factory payroll to the production accounts.
2. Post the entries prepared in 1 to T accounts, and determine the partial account balances.
3. Figure the amount of underapplied or overapplied factory overhead at March 31.

Problem 23A-5
Job Order
Costing—
Comprehensive
Journal Entry
Analysis
(L.O. 7)

The Howard Manufacturing Company maintains a job order cost accounting system. The company is currently using an overhead application rate of 120 percent of direct labor cost.

Accounting records on August 1 showed that the Materials Inventory Control account balance was $83,390 and the materials subsidiary ledger balances were $39,800 for Mixing Fluid, $34,610 for MX Powder, and $8,980 for Operating Supplies. The Work in Process Inventory Control account balance was $95,060 and the subsidiary ledger job order cost card balances were $74,910 for Job 20-4, $13,730 for Job 30-5, and $6,420 for Job 50-6. The Finished Goods Inventory

Control account balance was $57,850 and the finished goods subsidiary ledger balances were: none for Product 20, $26,240 for Product 30, and $31,610 for Product 50.

The Factory Payroll, Factory Overhead Control, and Factory Overhead Applied accounts have no balances carried forward from July because these accounts are closed at the end of each month. The following transactions and events took place during August:

Aug. 1   Operating supplies totaling $13,650 were requisitioned into production.

    4   Received $51,650 of mixing fluid and $32,720 of MX powder, purchased on account.

    6   Paid the following factory overhead costs in cash: factory rent, $1,850; heat, light, and power, $1,790; repairs and maintenance, $6,240; and outside contractual services, $8,525.

    9   The following semimonthly payroll liability was recorded: gross direct labor wages (Job 20-4, $21,640; Job 30-5, $6,800; Job 50-6, $4,810), $33,250; gross indirect labor wages, $17,420; gross administrative salaries, $8,250; FICA taxes withheld, $3,535; federal income taxes withheld, $15,320.

    9   Factory payroll was distributed to the production accounts.

    9   Factory overhead costs were applied to production.

  12   Purchased and received $14,120 of operating supplies, on account.

  13   Requisitioned $35,280 of mixing fluid and $19,960 of MX powder into production for Job 30-5.

  14   Payroll checks for the liability recorded on August 9 were prepared and distributed to the employees.

  15   Paid property taxes of $4,100, chargeable to factory overhead.

  18   Job 20-4 was completed and transferred to Finished Goods Inventory.

  20   Requisitioned $21,890 of mixing fluid and $16,770 of MX powder into production for Job 50-6.

  23   The following semimonthly payroll liability was recorded: gross direct wages (Job 30-5, $19,410; Job 50-6, $11,810), $31,220; gross indirect labor wages, $18,140; gross administrative salaries, $8,250; FICA taxes payable, $3,460; federal income taxes withheld, $14,980.

  23   Factory payroll was distributed to the production accounts.

  23   Factory overhead costs were applied to production.

  26   A major portion of Job 20-4 was sold and shipped to a customer. Four thousand liters were shipped at a cost of $23 per liter. This shipment sold for $139,840.

  28   Payroll checks for the liability recorded on August 23 were prepared and distributed to the employees.

  30   Depreciation on machinery of $7,940 for the month was recorded.

  30   The Factory Overhead Control and the Factory Overhead Applied accounts were closed out, and the difference was distributed to the Cost of Goods Sold account.

Required

1. Prepare the journal entries for all of the above transactions and events.

2. Prepare T accounts for all of the general ledger and subsidiary ledger accounts relevant to the job order costing system. Enter the beginning balances where applicable and post the journal entries prepared in **1** to these accounts.

3. To check the accuracy of ending inventory control account balances, compare them with the totals of their subsidiary ledger accounts.

Problem Set B

Problem 23B-1
Application of
Factory
Overhead
(L.O. 3, 4)

Poluzzi Tool and Die Company applies factory overhead costs to production on the basis of direct labor dollars. The firm figures its current predetermined overhead rate by using data from the two preceding operating quarters, adjusted to reflect expectations for the current quarter. During the first ten days of July, the controller used the following information to prepare the overhead rate analysis for the third quarter:

	First Quarter	Second Quarter
Direct labor dollars	$65,200	$ 67,525
Factory overhead costs		
Manufacturing supplies	$19,000	$ 20,900
Materials-handling costs	11,500	12,650
Indirect labor	22,800	25,080
Factory supervision	28,000	30,800
Heat, light, and power	4,800	6,000
Fire insurance	1,600	2,000
Depreciation, plant and equipment	3,400	3,400
Other	6,700	7,370
Total overhead	$97,800	$108,200

For the third quarter of the year, each item of factory overhead costs is expected to increase by the same percentage as from the first to the second quarter. Direct labor dollars are expected to total $79,920 for the three-month period ending September 30.

Required

1. Compute the overhead rate for the third quarter of the year.
2. Actual operations for the third quarter exceeded the expectations of Poluzzi management. Job orders worked on during the third quarter and related direct labor dollars are as follows: Job 632, $12,400; Job 710, $10,750; Job 698, $9,800; Job 726, $14,650; Job 914, $11,900; Job 852, $8,600; Job 574, $13,100. Determine the amount of factory overhead applied to each job and to total production during the three-month period ending September 30.
3. Prepare the journal entry to close the overhead accounts for the third quarter and to dispose of the underapplied or overapplied overhead. Assume that $120,750 of factory overhead costs were incurred during the third quarter. Assume also that the difference between actual and applied costs is felt to be insignificant.

Problem 23B-2
Job Order Cost
Flow
(L.O. 6)

American Enterprises, makers of fine cookware, uses a job order cost system. They had the following beginning inventory balances in July:

Materials Inventory Control	$28,700
Work in Process Inventory Control	19,890
Finished Goods Inventory Control	26,900

A summary of transactions and related information for July is shown below. Job order cost cards for jobs in process on July 31 revealed the following:

Job	Materials	Direct Labor	Factory Overhead
7C	$720	$590	$531
7E	590	700	630
7G	1,080	1,300	1,170
7H	610	1,060	954

Materials purchases for July:

July 7	$18,400
July 20	12,750
July 27	16,900

Direct labor costs for July:

July 14	$32,600
July 28	36,450

Predetermined factory overhead rate: 90 percent of direct labor cost

Materials requisitioned into production during July:

July 10	$23,550
July 23	25,700

Finished goods with an 80% markup over cost were sold during July for $388,080.

Required

1. Reconstruct the transactions for July and determine the ending inventory balances.
2. Figure the cost of units completed during the period.
3. What was the total cost of units sold during July?

Problem 23B-3
Job Order Costing— Unknown Quantity Analysis
(L.O. 6)

Fragments of the operating data for Texas Business Forms Company for May and June are shown below. The company uses an overhead rate of 150 percent of direct labor cost.

	May	June
Beginning Materials Inventory Control	(a)	(e)
Beginning Work in Process Inventory Control	$ 52,650	(f)
Beginning Finished Goods Inventory Control	46,920	$ 39,800
Direct Labor Charges	22,800	26,200
Factory Overhead Applied	(b)	(g)
Materials Requisitioned	28,250	(h)
Cost of Goods Sold	101,650	(i)
Materials Purchased	27,700	29,480
Ending Materials Inventory Control	19,420	16,840
Ending Work in Process Inventory Control	(c)	(j)
Ending Finished Goods Inventory Control	39,800	17,950
Cost of Completed Units	(d)	129,330

Required

From the information given, compute the amount of each lettered unknown. Show your computations.

Problem 23B-4
Job Order Costing— Journal Entry Analysis and T Accounts
(L.O. 7)

Sneed Manufacturing Company, which makes patio furniture, began operations in April. The company uses a job order cost system and a current overhead application rate of 160 percent of direct labor dollars. The following transactions and events took place in April:

Apr. 2 Materials totaling $207,250 were purchased on account.

4 Requisitioned $180,000 of materials and $22,000 of operating supplies for production.

14 Factory personnel earned gross payroll of $210,304. Of this amount, $163,000 represented direct labor, and the balance was indirect labor.

15 Overhead costs were applied to production.

17 Received supplies (purchased on account) costing $18,160 and materials costing $90,000 from vendor.

18 Requisitioned $75,000 of materials and $15,250 of operating supplies into production.

20 Paid the following overhead costs: insurance premium on plant, $207,500; property taxes, $9,230; maintenance contract, $112,000; utilities, $3,460.

28 Factory personnel earned gross payroll of $202,620. Of this amount, $157,000 represented direct labor, with the balance being allocated as indirect labor.

29 Overhead costs were applied to production.

30 Completed furniture costing $744,000 was transferred to Finished Goods Inventory Control.

30 Depreciation of factory building and machinery was $46,000. Miscellaneous factory overhead expenses amounted to $83,411 and were paid on this date.

30 Patio furniture costing $680,000 was shipped to customers on account for total selling price of $1,226,000.

Required

1. Record the journal entries for all of the April transactions and events. For the payroll entries, concern yourself only with the distribution of factory payroll to the production accounts.
2. Post the entries prepared in **1** to T accounts, and determine the partial account balances.
3. Determine the amount of underapplied or overapplied overhead on April 30.

Problem 23B-5
Job Order
Costing—
Comprehensive
Journal Entry
Analysis
(L.O. 7)

On March 1, the accounting records of Gereau Manufacturing Company revealed that the inventory control account balances were as follows: $75,700 in Materials, $96,440 in Work in Process, and $63,100 in Finished Goods. On the same date, subsidiary ledger balances were as follows: The materials subsidiary ledger had $37,880 for Sheet Steel, $31,610 for Pipe, and $6,210 for Operating Supplies. The job order cost cards revealed $82,640 for Job AA1, $11,200 for Job BB3, and $2,600 for Job DD6. The finished goods subsidiary ledger had no balance for Product AA, $20,500 for Product BB, and $42,600 for Product CC.

The Cost of Goods Sold balance was $190,000. The Factory Payroll, Factory Overhead Control, and Factory Overhead Applied accounts have no balances carried forward from February because these accounts are closed at the end of each month. The company employs an overhead application rate of 80 percent of direct labor cost. During March, the following transactions and events took place:

Mar. 2 Received $46,200 of sheet steel and $29,850 of pipe, purchased on account.

3 Operating supplies totaling $2,940 were requisitioned into production.

8 Paid the following factory overhead costs in cash: electricity bill, $490; gas and oil bill, $520; repairs and maintenance, $850; and outside labor services, $1,710.

Mar. 10   Requisitioned $28,100 of sheet steel and $14,850 of pipe into production for Job BB3.

     10   The following semimonthly payroll liability was recorded: gross direct labor wages (Job AA1, $11,000; Job BB3, $6,500; Job DD6, $4,100), $21,600; gross indirect labor wages, $13,200; gross administrative salaries, $6,750; FICA taxes withheld, $2,493; federal income taxes withheld, $10,803.

     10   Factory payroll was distributed to the production accounts.

     10   Factory overhead costs were applied to production.

     12   Purchased and received $3,250 of operating supplies, on account.

     15   Payroll checks for the liability recorded on March 10 were prepared and distributed to the employees.

     16   Paid factory rent of $1,400, chargeable to factory overhead.

     20   Job AA1 was completed and transferred to Finished Goods Inventory.

     22   Requisitioned $16,400 of sheet steel and $11,110 of pipe into production for Job DD6.

     24   The following semimonthly payroll liability was recorded: gross direct labor wages (Job BB3, $14,200; Job DD6, $8,200), $22,400; gross indirect labor wages, $14,600; gross administrative salaries, $6,750; FICA taxes withheld, $2,625; federal income taxes withheld, $11,375.

     24   Factory payroll was distributed to the production accounts.

     24   Factory overhead costs were applied to production.

     26   A major portion of Job AA1 was sold and shipped to the customer. Fifty products were shipped at a unit cost of $1,660. The entire shipment sold for $132,800.

     29   Payroll checks for the liability recorded on March 24 were prepared and distributed to the employees.

     30   Depreciation of machinery of $2,800 for the month was recorded.

     30   The Factory Overhead Control and Factory Overhead Applied accounts were closed out and the difference distributed to the Cost of Goods Sold account.

Required

1. Prepare the journal entries for all of the above transactions and events.

2. Prepare T accounts for all of the general ledger and subsidiary ledger accounts relevant to the job order costing system. Enter the beginning balances where applicable and post the journal entries prepared in **1** to these accounts.

3. Check the accuracy of ending inventory control account balances by reconciling them with the totals of their respective subsidiary ledger accounts.

Management Decision Case 23-1

Holmes Manufacturing Company
(L.O. 5, 6, 8)

Holmes Manufacturing Company is a small family-owned business that makes specialty plastic products. Since it was started, three years ago, the company has grown quickly and now employs ten production people. Because of its size, the company uses a job order cost accounting system that was designed around a periodic inventory method. Work sheets and special analyses are used to account for manufacturing costs and inventory valuations.

Two months ago, the company's accountant quit. You have now been called in to assist management. The following information has been given to you:

Beginning inventory balances (1/1/x7):

Materials	$10,420
Work in Process (Job K-2)	59,100
Finished Goods (Job K-1)	71,700

Materials requisitioned into production during 19x7:

Job K-2	$ 9,000
Job K-4	28,800
Job K-6	48,000

Direct labor for year:

Job K-2	$27,300
Job K-4	36,480
Job K-6	65,600

The company purchased materials only once during the year and all jobs use the same material. Purchases totaled $76,500. For the current year, the company has been using an overhead application rate of 125 percent of direct labor dollars. So far in 19x7, two jobs, K-2 and K-4, have been completed. Jobs K-1 and K-2 have been shipped to customers. Job K-1 was made up of 3,000 units. Job K-2 contained 5,500 units. Job K-4 had 4,800 units.

Required

1. Reconstruct the job order cost sheets for each job worked on during the period. What were the unit costs for jobs K-1, K-2, and K-4?

2. From the information given and using T-account analysis, compute the current balances in the three inventory accounts and the cost of goods sold.

3. The president has asked you to analyze the current job order cost accounting system. Should the system be changed? How? Why? Prepare an outline of your response to the president.

Learning
Objectives

Chapter
Twenty-Four

Product
Costing: The
Process Cost
Accounting
System

1. *Explain the role of the Work in Process Inventory account(s) in a process cost accounting system.*

2. *Describe product flow and cost flow through a process cost accounting system.*

3. *Compute equivalent production for situations with and without units in the beginning work in process inventory.*

4. *Compute product unit cost for a specific time period (unit cost analysis schedule).*

5. *Prepare a cost summary schedule that assigns costs to units completed and transferred out of the department during the period, and find the ending Work in Process Inventory balance.*

6. *Make the journal entry(ies) needed to transfer costs of completed units out of the Work in Process Inventory account.*

A major goal of any cost accounting system is to find product unit costs and to set ending values for Materials, Work in Process, and Finished Goods inventories. Continuous product flows (liquids) and long production runs of identical or standard products generally call for a process cost accounting system. With this system, manufacturing costs are not traced to specific products or job orders. Instead, they are averaged over the units produced in each period of time. As a result of studying this chapter, you should be able to meet the learning objectives listed on the left.

Process costing depends on three schedules: (1) the schedule of equivalent production, (2) the unit cost analysis schedule, and (3) the cost summary schedule. From the information in these three schedules, we can tell what costs to attach to units that are completed and transferred out of the department. Then we use a journal entry to transfer these costs out of the Work in Process Inventory account. Those costs remaining in the Work in Process Inventory account belong to units still in process at period end. This chapter will analyze the process cost accounting system and explain how to figure product unit costs. It will also show how to compute and verify the period-end balance for the Work in Process Inventory and the costs assigned to units completed. These units will have been transferred either to the next department or to the Finished Goods Inventory account.

In Chapter 23, we compared the characteristics of job order product costing and process costing. You will remember that a process cost accounting system is used by companies like those in the paint, oil, fastener (screws and bolts), gas, and beverage industries. Such companies produce large amounts of similar products or have a continuous production flow. A process costing system has the following characteristics: (1) Cost data are collected by department or work center, with little concern for specific job orders. (2) A weekly or monthly time period is emphasized, rather than the time it takes to complete a specific order. (3) The accounting system uses several Work in Process Inventory accounts—one for each department or work center in the manufacturing process.

Cost Flow Through Work in Process Inventory Accounts

Accounting for the costs of materials, direct labor, and factory overhead does not differ much between job order costing and process costing. Under both systems, costs must be recorded and eventually charged to production. Materials and supplies must be purchased and requisitioned into production. Direct labor wages must be paid to the employees and charged to production accounts. And costs of various kinds of factory overhead are assigned to production. Journal entries like those described in Chapter 23 record these transactions and events. So we see that the flow of costs *into* the Work in Process Inventory account is very much the same in the two product costing systems.

The major difference between job order cost accounting and process cost accounting is the way costs are assigned to products. In a job order cost system, costs are traced to specific jobs and products. However, in a process cost system, an averaging technique is used. For figuring unit cost in the process cost system, all products worked on during a specific time period (a week or a month) are used as the output base. Total costs of materials, direct labor, and factory overhead that have been accumulated in the Work in Process Inventory account (or accounts) are divided by the units worked on during the period. This procedure may seem clear enough. But technical aspects make it more difficult than it first appears. These aspects are discussed below.

Work in Process Inventory Accounts

Objective 1
Explain the role
of the Work in
Process
Inventory
account(s) in a
process cost
accounting
system

The Work in Process Inventory account is the focus of process costing. Unlike the job order approach, a process cost system is not limited to one Work in Process Inventory account. In fact, process costing uses as many Work in Process Inventory accounts as there are departments or steps in the production process. The process shown in Figure 24-1 (next page) has two departments. Finished units of Department 1 become the direct materials input of Department 2. As shown in this figure, the three cost elements flow into the Work in Process Inventory account of Department 1. The total unit cost of each completed product from Department 1 moves to Department 2 along with the completed unit. In Department 2, the products from Department 1 are processed further. No more materials are needed in Department 2 but, as shown in Figure 24-1, more labor is used and factory overhead is assigned. Usually it is assigned on the basis of labor cost or hours.

When the completed products are finished, they are transferred from work in process inventory (Department 2) to finished goods inventory. At that point each unit cost amount is made up of five cost inputs. Three are from Department 1 and two from Department 2. A detailed breakdown is shown on the next page, using *hypothetical* dollar amounts.

Figure 24-1
Cost Elements
and Process
Cost Accounts

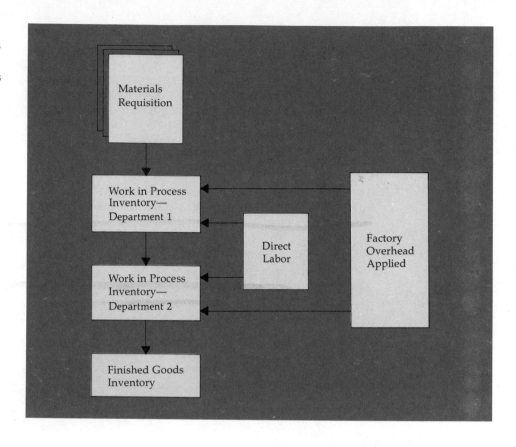

Total Unit Cost

Department 1		
Materials	$1.40	
Direct labor	1.10	
Factory overhead	.55	
Total, Department 1		$3.05
Department 2		
Direct labor	$1.90	
Factory overhead	2.09	
Total, Department 2		3.99
Total unit cost (to Finished Goods Inventory)		$7.04

Production Flow Combinations

There are hundreds of possible ways that product flows can combine with department or production processes. Two basic structures are illustrated in Figure 24-2. Example 1 shows a *series* of three processes or departments. The completed product of one department becomes the direct materials input of the next department. (Figure 24-1 also showed a series of departments.) The number of departments in a series can be anywhere

Figure 24-2
Cost Flow for
Process Costing

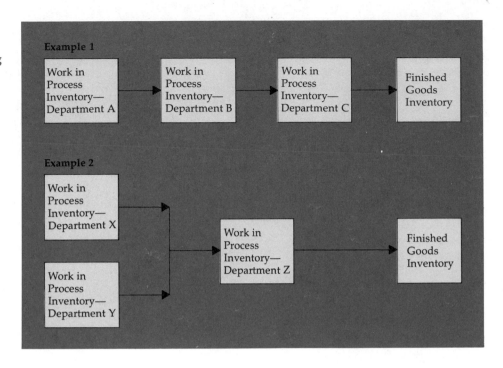

Objective 2
Describe
product flow
and cost flow
through a
process cost
accounting
system

from two to over a dozen. The important point to remember is that product unit cost is the sum of the cost elements used in all of the departments.

Example 2 in Figure 24-2 shows a different kind of production flow. Again there are three departments. In this example, however, the product does not flow through all departments in a simple 1-2-3 order. Here, two separate products are developed, one in Department X and another in Department Y. Both products then go to Department Z, where they are joined with a third direct material input. The possible combinations are again limitless. The unit cost that is transferred to Finished Goods Inventory when the products are completed includes cost elements from Departments X, Y, and Z.

Note: The three-schedule cost analysis that is to be shown in this chapter must be prepared for *each* department for *each* time period. Thus a company with three production departments and two monthly time periods must prepare six *sets* of the three-schedule analysis.

The Concept of Equivalent Production

A key feature of a process cost accounting system is the idea of computing equivalent units of production for each accounting period. This computation is needed to arrive at product unit costs.

Remember that in process costing, an averaging approach is used. All manufacturing costs incurred by a department or production process are divided by the units produced during the period. There are several

Objective 3
Compute
equivalent
production for
situations with
and without
units in the
beginning work
in process
inventory

important questions: How many units were produced? Do we count only those units completed during the period? What about partly completed units in the beginning work in process inventory? Do we count them even if only part of the work needed to complete them was done during this period? What about products in ending work in process inventory? Is it proper to focus only on those units started and completed during the period?

The answers to all of these questions are linked to the concept of equivalent production. **Equivalent production** (also called **equivalent units**) is a measure of units produced in a period of time. This measure is expressed in terms of fully completed or equivalent whole units produced. Partly completed units are restated in terms of equivalent whole units. The number of equivalent units produced must be found. It is equal to the sum of (1) total units started and completed during the period and (2) an amount for partly completed products. This amount is a restatement of these units in terms of equivalent whole units. A "percentage of completion" factor is used to figure the number of equivalent whole units. Figure 24-3 illustrates the equivalent unit computation. Three automobiles were started and completed during February. In addition, one-half (.5) of Car A is completed in February and three-quarters (.75) of Car E is completed. We find the total equivalent units for the month by adding together those units started and completed (3.0) and those units partly completed (.5 and .75). Therefore, equivalent production for February for direct labor and factory overhead is 4.25 units.

Once we know the number of equivalent units produced, we can figure unit costs for materials and conversion costs for each department in the production process. **Conversion costs** are the combined total of direct labor and factory overhead costs incurred by a production department. The equations for figuring the unit cost amounts appear below. (Note the role of equivalent units.)

$$\text{unit cost for materials} = \frac{\text{total materials costs}}{\text{equivalent units—materials}}$$

$$\text{unit cost for conversion costs} = \frac{\text{total labor and factory overhead costs}}{\text{equivalent units—conversion costs}}$$

Figuring the equivalent units of production for materials usually differs from the way they are figured for conversion costs. As shown in Figure 24-3, materials are usually all added in at the beginning of a process. Therefore, materials for Car A were added in January and do not influence equivalent units for materials in February. However, materials for Car E were *all* added to production in February. We add 3.0 (units started and completed—Cars B, C, and D) and 1.0 (unit started but not completed—Car E) to get the equivalent units of production for materials for February (4.0 units).

No Beginning Work in Process Inventory

To begin our detailed analysis for figuring equivalent production, we will assume that there are no units in beginning work in process inventory.

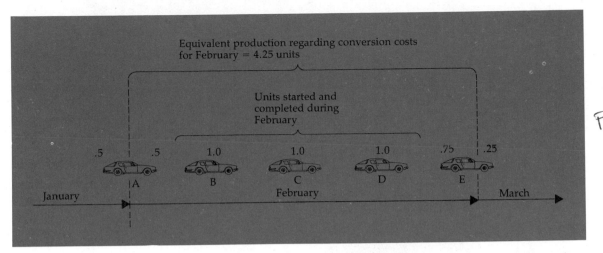

Equivalent production regarding conversion costs
for February = 4.25 units

Units started and
completed during
February

.5 | .5 | 1.0 | 1.0 | 1.0 | .75 | .25

A   B   C   D   E

January   February   March

Fifo

**Figure 24-3
Equivalent Unit
Computation**

Facts: Conversion costs (those for direct labor and factory overhead) are incurred uniformly as each car moves through production. Equivalent production for February is 4.25 units as to conversion costs. But materials costs are all added to production at the beginning of the process. Since four cars entered production in February (cars B, C, D, and E), equivalent production for the month is 4.0 units as to materials costs.

So we need to consider only (1) units started and completed during the period and (2) units started but not completed. By definition, units started but not completed are the balance in the ending work in process inventory. Equivalent product production is figured in parts as follows:

Part 1: Units started and completed = (number of units) × 100 percent
Part 2: Equivalent units in ending work in process inventory = (number of units) × (percentage of completion)

The *sum* of these two amounts gives us the equivalent whole units completed during the period. Percentage of completion figures are learned from supervisors in the production departments.

Earlier we noted an important point about computing unit cost. That is that direct labor and factory overhead costs are usually lumped together and called conversion costs. The reason is that both of these costs are usually incurred uniformly throughout the production process. Combining them is convenient. Materials costs are generally not incurred uniformly throughout the process. They are normally incurred either at the beginning of the process (materials input) or at the end of it (packing materials). Because of this difference, the equivalent unit amount for materials will not be the same as that for conversion costs. Separate computations are necessary.

For example, assume that the records of Jansson Clothing, Inc., for January 19xx show the following information: (a) 47,500 units were started during the period. (b) 6,200 units were partly complete at period end. (c) Units in ending work in process inventory were 60 percent complete. (d) Materials were added at the *beginning* of the process. (e) Conversion costs were incurred *uniformly* throughout the process. (f) No units were lost or spoiled during the month.

In the **schedule of equivalent production,** equivalent production is

Figure 24-4
Equivalent
Units—No
Beginning
Inventory

Jansson Clothing, Inc.
Schedule of Equivalent Production
For the Month Ended January 31, 19xx

Units—Stage of Completion	Units to Be Accounted For	Equivalent Units	
		Materials Costs	Conversion Costs
Beginning inventory—units completed in this period	—	—	—
Units started and completed in this period	41,300	41,300	41,300
Ending inventory— units started but not completed in this period	6,200		
(Materials—100% complete)		6,200	
(Conversion costs—60% complete)			3,720
Totals	47,500	47,500	45,020

figured for the period for both materials and conversion costs. This schedule is shown for Jansson Clothing in Figure 24-4. Because there were no units in beginning work in process inventory, dashes are entered in that row. We see that 41,300 units were started and completed during the period (47,500 units started less 6,200 units not completed). All 41,300 have received 100 percent of the materials, labor, and overhead effort needed to complete them. Therefore, 41,300 equivalent units are recorded in both the Materials and Conversion Costs columns.

Accounting for equivalent units in ending inventory is a bit more complicated. These 6,200 units have received all materials inputs because materials were added to each product as it entered the production process. Therefore, in the Materials column, 6,200 equivalent units are entered. However, as we know, conversion costs are added uniformly as the products move through the process. The 6,200 units in ending inventory are only 60 percent complete. So we can obtain the number of equivalent whole units by multiplying the number of actual units by the percentage completed. In Figure 24-4, the amount of equivalent units for conversion costs of ending inventory is 6,200 units × 60% completion = 3,720 equivalent units. As a result of these computations for January, we have 47,500 equivalent units for materials costs. And we have 45,020 equivalent units for conversion costs.

With Beginning Work in Process Inventory

A situation with no beginning work in process inventory is almost never found in industry. By definition, process costing techniques are used in industries where production flows continuously or where there are long runs of identical products. In these cases, there is always something in process at month end. So there are always units in beginning Work in Process Inventory in the next period. We now turn to this situation, expanding the example used above.

During February 19xx, unit production facts for Jansson Clothing, Inc., were as follows: (a) 6,200 units in beginning Work in Process Inventory; (b) 60 percent completion of beginning inventory; (c) 57,500 units started during the period; (d) 5,000 units partly complete at period end; and (e) 45 percent completion of ending Work in Process Inventory.

Beginning inventories make it a little harder to figure equivalent units. Before doing so, we must go back to the concept of first-in, first-out (FIFO) product flow. Process costing is normally associated with a continuous production flow. So products in process at the beginning of the period are assumed to be the first products completed. After they are finished, new units are worked on and completed.   .

February operations of Jansson Clothing, Inc., involve both beginning and ending balances in Work in Process Inventory. To figure equivalent units for February, we must be careful to account only for the work done in February. Units in beginning inventory were 60 percent complete as to conversion costs. They were 100 percent complete as to materials. These costs were assigned to the products during the preceding period (January). Therefore, for these units, no equivalent units of materials were applicable to February, and only 40 percent of the conversion costs were needed in February to complete the units. As shown in Figure 24-5, completing the units in beginning inventory required no raw materials and only 2,480 equivalent units of conversion costs (6,200 units times 40 percent, the remaining percentage of completion).

Computations for units started and completed and for units in ending inventory are also shown in Figure 24-5. These computations are like those used in the January illustration. Units started and completed received the full amount of materials and conversion costs. Therefore, the resulting equivalent units equal 52,500 (57,500 started minus the 5,000 not completed) for both materials and conversion costs. Ending inventory is 100 percent complete as to materials (5,000 units). It is 45 percent complete as to conversion costs (5,000 × 45% = 2,250). The end result is that February produced 57,500 equivalent units that used materials and 57,230 equivalent units that had conversion costs. Note that our illustrations cover only two of the hundreds of possible process costing situations that could arise with varying percentages of completion.

The "Average" Cost Flow Assumption

The idea of equivalent production is basic to process costing. However, the computations we have just performed are rather cumbersome. Therefore, a way around them has been developed.

As stated earlier, products flow in a first-in, first-out (FIFO) manner in a process costing environment. We assume that beginning inventory items are completed before new ones are brought into the production process. Unit costs, like the actual units, can also be accounted for on a FIFO basis.

Figure 24-5
Equivalent
Units—With
Beginning
Inventory
(FIFO)

		Equivalent Units	
Units—Stage of Completion	Units to Be Accounted For	Materials Costs	Conversion Costs
Beginning inventory—units completed in this period (Materials—100% complete) (Conversion costs—60% complete)	6,200	—	2,480
Units started and completed in this period	52,500	52,500	52,500
Ending inventory— units started but not completed in this period (Materials—100% complete) (Conversion costs—45% complete)	5,000	5,000	2,250
Totals	63,700	57,500	57,230

**Jansson Clothing, Inc.
Schedule of Equivalent Production
For the Month Ended February 29, 19xx**

However, because of its cumbersome aspects, FIFO process costing has given way to the average process costing method. *The average process costing method assumes that the items in beginning Work in Process Inventory were started and completed during the current period.* Although a bit less accurate, this method is much easier to understand and work with. It is illustrated below. We will use it for all computations in the remaining sections of this chapter.

The equivalent unit computations shown in Figure 24-5 are based on the FIFO approach. We must now change the Schedule of Equivalent Production for average costing. You will note that the average method is a short cut, and very practical. Remember, though, that the FIFO method is more accurate and realistic.

Figure 24-6 is the same as Figure 24-5 except that it follows the average costing approach. Remember, in average costing you treat all the units in beginning work in process inventory as if they were both started and completed in this one period. Therefore, *all* materials and conversion costs are assumed to be added during the current period. All units in beginning inventory are treated as equivalent whole units. The computations for units started and completed and ending Work in Process Inventory are the same as in Figure 24-5. Because of the change in cost flow assumptions, equivalent units are 63,700 for materials costs and 60,950 for conversion costs. Note that there is no change in the way we

Figure 24-6
Equivalent
Units—With
Beginning
Inventory
(Average
Costing
Approach)

Jansson Clothing, Inc.
Schedule of Equivalent Production
For the Month Ended February 29, 19xx

| Units—Stage of Completion | Units to Be Accounted For | Equivalent Units | |
		Materials Costs	Conversion Costs
Beginning inventory—units completed in this period	6,200	6,200	6,200
Units started and completed in this period	52,500	52,500	52,500
Ending inventory— units started but not completed in this period (Materials—100% complete)	5,000	5,000	
(Conversion costs—45% complete)			2,250
Totals	63,700	63,700	60,950

figure equivalent units for ending Work in Process Inventory. Only the units for beginning inventory are different. The equivalent units computed in Figure 24-4 for January do not have to be recomputed, because the only area treated differently between the FIFO and average methods is the *beginning* inventory units. January had no beginning inventory. So the amount of equivalent units in our example is the same under the two methods.

Cost Analysis Schedules

*Objective 4
Compute
product unit
cost for a
specific time
period (unit cost
analysis
schedule)*

So far, we have emphasized accounting for *units* of productive output. In the schedule of equivalent production, we found the total units to be accounted for. Then we figured equivalent units for materials costs and conversion costs. Once we have sorted out the unit information and arrived at equivalent unit figures, we can turn to the dollar information. Now we bring manufacturing costs, cost per equivalent unit, and inventory costing into our analysis.

Unit Cost Analysis Schedule

The **unit cost analysis schedule** is the second of the three schedules used in process costing. It does two things. (1) It adds all costs charged to the Work in Process Inventory account of each department or production process. (2) It computes cost per equivalent unit for materials and conversion costs. A unit cost analysis schedule is pictured in Figures 24-7 and 24-9, both discussed later in this chapter. We arrive at unit costs in two steps. First, the schedule summarizes all costs for the period. These costs are made up of costs of materials, conversion costs, and the costs included in the beginning Work in Process Inventory. (The Total Costs to Be Accounted For column later serves as a check figure for the third schedule—the cost summary schedule.)

The second step in the unit cost analysis is to divide the costs by the number of equivalent units. Total costs for materials are divided by the equivalent units for materials. In the same way, total conversion costs are divided by the equivalent units for conversion costs. When we use the average cost flow assumption, units and costs in beginning inventory are included in figuring this period's costs per equivalent unit.

Cost Summary Schedule

*Objective 5
Prepare a cost
summary
schedule that
assigns costs to
units completed
and transferred
out of the
department
during the
period, and find
the ending
Work in Process
Inventory
balance*

The final phase of the process costing analysis is to distribute the total costs accumulated during the period among all the units of output. Some costs may stay in ending Work in Process Inventory. Others will go with the units completed and transferred out of the department. Costs are assigned by means of the **cost summary schedule**. Information in this schedule comes from the schedule of equivalent production and the unit cost analysis schedule.

It is fairly easy to figure the total costs to be transferred out of the department. Suppose that 16,500 units were completed during the period and moved to Finished Goods Inventory. Cost per equivalent unit was found to be $3.30. Therefore, $54,450 (16,500 × $3.30) is transferred out of the Work in Process Inventory through a journal entry. All costs remaining in Work in Process Inventory after costs of completed units have been transferred out represent the cost of ending units in process.

To complete the analysis, we add together the total cost of units transferred and the costs that belong to ending Work in Process Inventory. Then we compare the total with the total costs to be accounted for in the unit cost analysis schedule. If the two totals are not equal, there has been an arithmetic error (sometimes due to rounding).

Illustrative Analysis

To fully explain the form and use of the cost schedules, we will expand the Jansson Clothing, Inc., example. Besides the equivalent unit information we discussed earlier, the company has the following cost data:

January, 19xx	
Beginning Work in Process Inventory	—
Cost of materials used	$154,375
Conversion costs for the month	258,865
February, 19xx	
Cost of materials used	$190,060
Conversion costs for the month	319,930

Figure 24-7
Unit Cost
Determi-
nation—No
Beginning
Inventories

| Jansson Clothing, Inc. |
| Unit Cost Analysis Schedule |
| For the Month Ended January 31, 19xx |

Total Costs	Costs from Beginning Inventory	Costs from Current Period	Total Costs to Be Accounted For
Materials	—	$154,375	$154,375
Conversion costs	—	258,865	258,865
Totals	—	$413,240	$413,240

Equivalent Unit Costs	Total Costs to Be Accounted For ÷	Equivalent Units =	Cost per Equivalent Unit
Materials	$154,375	47,500	$3.25
Conversion costs	258,865	45,020	5.75
Totals	$413,240		$9.00

From these data, we will figure equivalent unit costs, total costs transferred to Finished Goods Inventory, and the ending balance in Work in Process Inventory for January and February 19xx.

January The unit cost analysis schedule for January is shown in Figure 24-7. Total costs to be accounted for are $413,240. Of this amount, costs for materials are $154,375 and conversion costs are $258,865. When we divide these costs by the equivalent unit amounts (computed in Figure 24-4), we get costs per equivalent unit of $3.25 for materials ($154,375 ÷ 47,500) and $5.75 for conversion costs ($258,865 ÷ 45,020). Total unit cost for the period is $9.00. The per unit cost amounts are then used in the cost summary schedule to compute costs transferred to Finished Goods Inventory and the cost of ending Work in Process Inventory.

Jansson's cost summary schedule for January is shown in Figure 24-8. No units were in process at the beginning of January, so no costs are entered for beginning inventory. (Even though there was no beginning inventory for January, the headings are included so that the form can be used for any process costing situation.) Units transferred to Finished Goods Inventory in January are made up entirely of units started and completed, since there were no units in beginning inventory. These 41,300 units cost $9.00 each to produce (total cost per equivalent unit). So $371,700 must be transferred to Finished Goods Inventory.

We debited $413,240 to Work in Process Inventory during January and just transferred $371,700 of that amount to Finished Goods Inventory. The difference of $41,540 remaining in the account is the ending Work in

Figure 24-8
Ending
Inventory
Computation—
No Beginning
Inventories

	Jansson Clothing, Inc. Cost Summary Schedule For the Month Ended January 31, 19xx	
	Cost of Goods Transferred to Finished Goods Inventory	Cost of Ending Work in Process Inventory
Beginning inventory None	—	
Units started and completed* 41,300 units × $9.00 per unit	$371,700	
Ending inventory* Materials: 6,200 units × $3.25		$ 20,150
Conversion costs: 3,720 units × $5.75		21,390
Totals	$371,700	$ 41,540
Check of computations Costs to Finished Goods Inventory		$371,700
Cost of ending Work in Process Inventory		41,540
Total costs to be accounted for (unit cost analysis schedule)		$413,240

*Note: Unit figures come from schedule of equivalent production for January (Figure 24-4).

Process inventory balance. This amount is verified in Figure 24-8 as follows. Using the ending inventory amounts from the schedule of equivalent production in Figure 24-4 and the costs per equivalent unit from the cost analysis schedule in Figure 24-7, we make the following computations:

Materials costs: 6,200 equivalent units × $3.25 per unit	$20,150
Conversion costs: 3,720 equivalent units × $5.75 per unit	21,390
Ending Work in Process Inventory balance	$41,540

The check of computations at the bottom of Figure 24-8 makes sure that all the arithmetic is right. Total costs figured in Figure 24-7 have been accounted for.

February The cost analysis for February is a bit more difficult because we must consider units and costs in beginning Work in Process Inventory. February operating results are analyzed in Figures 24-9 and 24-10. Total costs to be accounted for in February are $551,530. Included in this amount are the beginning inventory balance of $41,540 (see Figure 24-8)

Figure 24-9
Unit Cost
Determi-
nation—With
Beginning
Inventories

Jansson Clothing, Inc.
Unit Cost Analysis Schedule
For the Month Ended February 29, 19xx

Total Costs	Costs from Beginning Inventory	Costs from Current Period	Total Costs to Be Accounted For
Materials	$20,150	$190,060	$210,210
Conversion costs	21,390	319,930	341,320
Totals	$41,540	$509,990	$551,530

Equivalent Unit Costs	Total Costs to Be Accounted For ÷	Equivalent Units =	Cost per Equivalent Unit
Materials	$210,210	63,700	$3.30
Conversion costs	341,320	60,950	5.60
Totals	$551,530		$8.90

Figure 24-10
Ending
Inventory
Computation—
With
Beginning
Inventories

Jansson Clothing, Inc.
Cost Summary Schedule
For the Month Ended February 29, 19xx

	Cost of Goods Transferred to Finished Goods Inventory	Cost of Ending Work in Process Inventory
Beginning inventory*		
6,200 units × $8.90 per unit	$ 55,180	
Units started and completed*		
52,500 units × $8.90 per unit	467,250	
Ending inventory*		
Materials: 5,000 units × $3.30		$ 16,500
Conversion costs:		
2,250 units × $5.60		12,600
Totals	$522,430	$ 29,100
Check of computations		
Costs to Finished Goods Inventory		$522,430
Costs to ending Work in Process Inventory		29,100
Total costs to be accounted for (unit cost analysis schedule)		$551,530

*Note: Unit figures come from schedule of equivalent production (Figure 24-6).

plus current costs from February of $190,060 and $319,930 for materials and conversion costs, respectively. We add these costs to the materials and conversion costs carried over from January in the Work in Process Inventory account. The total costs to be accounted for are then divided by the equivalent unit figures computed in Figure 24-6. February's $8.90 cost per equivalent unit includes $3.30 per unit for materials and $5.60 per unit for conversion costs.

We finish the February cost analysis by preparing the cost summary schedule (Figure 24-10). Costs transferred to Finished Goods Inventory total $522,430. This amount includes costs of $55,180 for the 6,200 units in beginning inventory and the costs for 52,500 units started and completed during February.

The ending Work in Process Inventory balance of $29,100 is made up of $16,500 of materials costs and $12,600 of conversion costs. At the bottom of the cost summary schedule, we do a check to make sure that no arithmetic errors were made.

Journal Entry Analysis

Objective 6
Make the journal entry(ies) needed to transfer costs of completed units out of the Work in Process Inventory account

Our major emphasis has been on the schedules for equivalent production, unit cost analysis, and cost summary. However, none of the schedules offers a direct way to transfer costs in the accounting records. All three schedules deal mostly with the Work in Process Inventory account. The goal of the whole process costing analysis is to figure the dollar totals for goods completed and transferred to Finished Goods Inventory and for partly completed products that stay in the Work in Process Inventory account. However, the three schedules alone do not cause costs to flow through accounts in the general ledger. They only give the information needed for journal entries. It is the journal entries that actually move costs from one account to another.

The final step in a process costing analysis, then, is a journal entry to transfer costs of completed products out of Work in Process Inventory. Remember that all of the entries analyzed in Chapter 23 are also necessary in a process costing system. Only one entry is highlighted here, however, because it is involved directly with the transfer of costs of completed goods. To transfer the costs of units completed, we debit Finished Goods Inventory (or the Work in Process Inventory of a subsequent department) and credit Work in Process Inventory. The amount of the cost transfer was figured in the cost summary schedule.

In the example of Jansson Clothing, Inc., the following entries would be made at the end of each time period:

Jan. 31	Finished Goods Inventory	371,700	
	Work in Process Inventory		371,700
	To transfer cost of units completed in January to Finished Goods Inventory		

Feb. 29	Finished Goods Inventory	522,430	
	Work in Process Inventory		522,430
	To transfer cost of units		
	completed in February to		
	Finished Goods Inventory		

After the entries are posted, the Work in Process Inventory account would appear as follows on February 29, 19xx:

Work in Process Inventory

Balance	—	Transferred to Finished	
Jan. materials	154,375	Goods in Jan.	371,700
Jan. conversion costs	258,865		
Balance 1/31/xx	**41,540**		
Feb. materials	190,060	Transferred to Finished	
Feb. conversion costs	319,930	Goods in Feb.	522,430
Balance 2/29/xx	**29,100***		

*This amount is confirmed by the cost summary schedule in Figure 24-10.

In our analysis of Jansson Clothing, Inc., we assumed that the company had only *one* production department, and we centered on two consecutive monthly accounting periods. Because only one production department was used, only one Work in Process Inventory account was needed. The following example deals with *two* production departments in a series. The product passes from the first to the second department and then to Finished Goods Inventory. This production flow is like Example 1 of Figure 24-2. When the production process requires two departments, the accounting system must maintain two separate Work in Process Inventory accounts, one for each department. This situation calls for more work, but the computations are the same. The key point is to treat *each* department and related Work in Process Inventory account in a separate analysis. The three schedules must be prepared for *each* department. Departments should be analyzed in the same order in which they appear in the series.

Illustrative Problem: Two Production Departments

Jackson Manufacturing Company produces a liquid chemical for converting salt water to fresh water. The production process involves the Mixing Department and the Cooling Department. Every unit produced must be processed by both departments. Cooling is the final operation.

In the Mixing Department, a basic chemical powder, Material BP, is added to water, heated to 88° Celsius, and mixed for two hours. Assume that no evaporation takes place and that Material BP is added at the beginning of the process. Conversion costs are incurred uniformly throughout the process. Operating data for the Mixing Department for April 19xx are as follows:

Beginning Work in Process Inventory		
Units (30% complete)		1,450 liters
Costs:	Materials	$13,050
	Conversion costs	$ 1,760
Ending Work in Process Inventory		
All units 60% complete		
April operations		
Units started		55,600 liters
Costs:	Materials used	$488,990
	Conversion costs	$278,990
Units completed and transferred to		
the Cooling Department		54,800 liters

Required

1. Using good form, prepare (a) a schedule of equivalent production, (b) a unit cost analysis schedule, and (c) a cost summary schedule.
2. From information in the cost summary schedule, prepare the proper journal entry to transfer costs of completed units for April out of the Mixing Department.

Solution

1. Before doing the three schedules and preparing the journal entry, it is necessary to make a special analysis of the units (liters) worked on during April. To complete the schedule of equivalent production, we must first find the number of units started and completed and the number of units in ending Work in Process Inventory. These amounts were not given above, but they can easily be computed.

Units started and completed:		
	Units completed and transferred (given)	54,800 liters
Less:	Units in beginning inventory (given)	1,450 liters
Equals:	Units started and completed	53,350 liters
Units in ending inventory:		
	Units started during April (given)	55,600 liters
Less:	Units started and completed (above)	53,350 liters
Equals:	Units in ending inventory	2,250 liters

Now that we know the number of units started and completed and the number of units in ending work in process inventory, we can prepare the three schedules in the cost analysis (shown on the next two pages).
2. The costs of completed units for April are now ready to be transferred from the Mixing Department to the Cooling Department. The required journal entry would be as follows:

Jackson Manufacturing Company
Mixing Department
Process Costing Schedules
For the Month Ended April 30, 19xx

1a. Schedule of Equivalent Production

Units—Stage of Completion	Units to Be Accounted For	Equivalent Units	
		Materials Costs	Conversion Costs
Beginning inventory	1,450	1,450	1,450
Units started and completed in this period	53,350	53,350	53,350
Ending inventory—units started but not completed in this period	2,250		
(Materials—100% complete)		2,250	
(Conversion costs—60% complete)			1,350 (60% of 2,250)
Totals	57,050	57,050	56,150

1b. Unit Cost Analysis Schedule

Total Costs	Costs from Beginning Inventory	Costs from Current Period	Total Costs to Be Accounted For
Materials	$13,050	$488,990	$502,040
Conversion costs	1,760	278,990	280,750
Totals	$14,810	$767,980	$782,790

Equivalent Unit Costs	Total Costs to Be Accounted For ÷	Equivalent Units =	Cost per Equivalent Unit
Materials	$502,040	57,050	$ 8.80
Conversion costs	280,750	56,150	5.00
Totals	$782,790		$13.80

(continued)

Work in Process—Cooling Department	756,240	
Work in Process—Mixing Department		756,240
To transfer cost of units completed in April from Mixing Department to Cooling Department		

Note that the $756,240 is being transferred from one Work in Process Inventory account to another. The $756,240 attached to the units transferred into the Cooling Department during April would be accounted for

Jackson Manufacturing Company
Mixing Department
Process Costing Schedules (continued)
For the Month Ended April 30, 19xx

1c. Cost Summary Schedule

	Cost of Goods Transferred to Cooling Department	Cost of Ending Work in Process Inventory
Beginning inventory		
1,450 units × $13.80 per unit	$ 20,010	
Units started and completed		
53,350 units × $13.80 per unit	736,230	
Ending inventory		
Materials: 2,250 units × $8.80		$19,800
Conversion costs:		
1,350 units × $5.00		6,750
Totals	$756,240	$26,550
Check on computations:		
Costs to Cooling Department	$756,240	
Costs in ending Work in Process Inventory	26,550	
Total costs to be accounted for (unit cost analysis schedule)	$782,790	

in the same way as materials used in the Mixing Department. All other procedures and schedules illustrated in the Mixing Department example would be used again for the Cooling Department. See the special problem at the end of this chapter for the accounting treatment of the Cooling Department (page 926).

Cost-based Pricing of Products

Product cost information is not used only for inventory pricing. Companies also depend on it for setting the selling price of a product. Setting a selling price is an art rather than a science. There is no magic formula that will pump out consistently valid prices for a company's products. One approach is to charge whatever the buying public will bear. Another is to use your competition's prices to help in setting your own prices. A third approach is to use product cost information. Most successful companies probably use a combination of these approaches. Cost-based pricing is a conservative, yet wise route to setting prices. First the product's manufacturing costs are figured. Then an amount is usually added in to cover the operating and selling costs of the business. Finally, a factor is added for profit.

The cost-based price, however, is just the starting point in selecting an effective price. Knowing the competition and using your intuition are also important. Years of experience go into good price development. Remember, though, that the basic number on which to adjust and build is product cost. A cost-based price is the life-line of a business.

Chapter Review

Review of Learning Objectives

1. Explain the role of the Work in Process Inventory account(s) in a process cost accounting system.

The Work in Process Inventory account is the heart of the process cost accounting system. Each production department or operating unit has its own Work in Process Inventory account. All costs charged to that department flow into this inventory account. Special analysis, using three schedules, is needed at period end to determine the costs flowing out of the account. All special analyses in process cost accounting are related to costs in the Work in Process Inventory account.

2. Describe product flow and cost flow through a process cost accounting system.

Products in a process costing environment are liquids or long production runs of identical products. Therefore, products flow in a FIFO fashion (first in, first out). Once a product is started into production, it flows on to completion. Manufacturing costs are handled in a different way. Current costs of materials, direct labor, and factory overhead are added to costs in beginning inventory when figuring unit costs. The unit costs are then assigned either to completed units or to units in ending Work in Process Inventory.

3. Compute equivalent production for situations with and without units in the beginning work in process inventory.

The number of equivalent units is found with the aid of a schedule of equivalent production. Units worked on during the period are classified as being (a) in beginning inventory (started last period) and completed this period, (b) started and completed this period, or (c) started this period and still in process at period end. Percentage of completion data are used to figure equivalent units separately for materials and conversion costs.

4. Compute product unit cost for a specific time period (unit cost analysis schedule).

Unit costs are found with the aid of a unit cost analysis schedule. Materials costs for units in beginning inventory and costs of the current period are added together. The same is done for conversion costs. Next, the total cost of materials is divided by the equivalent unit amount for materials. The same procedure is followed for conversion costs. Then unit cost for materials and unit cost for conversion are added to reach final unit cost.

5. Prepare a cost summary schedule that assigns costs to units completed and transferred out of the department during the period, and find the ending Work in Process Inventory balance.

The first part of the cost summary schedule helps compute costs assigned to units completed and transferred out during the period. This part is done in two steps: (a) Costs attached to units in beginning inventory are computed. (b) Units started and completed during the current period are assigned a full share of production costs. The total of these two calculations represents costs attached to units completed and transferred out during the period. The second part of the cost summary schedule assigns costs to units still in process at period end. Unit costs for materials and conversion costs are multiplied by their respective equivalent units. The total of these two dollar amounts represents the ending Work in Process Inventory balance for the period.

6. Make the journal entry(ies) needed to transfer costs of completed units out of the Work in Process Inventory account.

The first part of the cost summary schedule is completed (the part that assigns costs to units completed and transferred out during the period). Now a journal entry should be prepared to transfer these costs out of the Work in Process Inventory account. A credit is made to the inventory account for the whole amount. The debit can be either to Finished Goods Inventory or to another Work in Process Inventory account, depending on the network of production departments in the process.

Special Problem: Costs Transferred In

This problem will review the three-schedule analysis used in process costing. It will also introduce two new situations common in process costing.

1. Costs transferred in   Accounting for the second in a series of Work in Process Inventory accounts is very much like accounting for the first department's costs. The only difference is that instead of accounting for current materials costs, we are dealing with *costs transferred in* during the period. All procedures used to account for costs transferred in are exactly the same as those used for materials costs and units. *When accounting for costs and units transferred in, treat them as you would materials added at the beginning of the process.*

2. Rounding of numerical answers   Unlike the problems discussed so far in this chapter, most real-world unit costs do not work out to even-numbered dollars and cents. The concept of rounding helps deal with this problem. Remember these three simple rules: (a) Round off all unit cost computations to three decimal places. (b) Round off cost summary data to the nearest dollar. (c) On the cost summary schedule, any difference caused by rounding should be added to or subtracted from the amount being transferred out of the department before the journal entry is prepared.

The purpose of this review problem is to illustrate the accounting approach for the second in a series of production departments and to show how to use cost rounding. We will go on with the example of the Jackson Manufacturing Company's Cooling Department. Operating data for the Cooling Department for April 19xx are shown below. No new materials are added in this department. Only conversion costs are added in the cooling process.

Beginning Work in Process Inventory
Units (40% complete)	2,100 liters
Costs: Transferred in	$29,200
Conversion costs	2,654

Ending Work in Process Inventory
    All units 60% complete
April operations
    Units transferred in   54,800 liters
    Costs: Transferred in $756,240
            Conversion costs   172,130
    Units completed and transferred
        to Finished Goods Inventory   54,450 liters

Required

1. Using good form, prepare (a) a schedule of equivalent production, (b) a unit cost analysis schedule, and (c) a cost summary schedule.
2. From the cost summary schedule, prepare the journal entry to transfer costs of completed units for April to Finished Goods Inventory.

Answer to Special Problem

1. Before doing the three-schedule analysis, we again must first analyze the unit information.

Units started and completed:
	Units completed and transferred (given)	54,450 liters
Less:	Units in beginning inventory (given)	2,100 liters
Equals:	Units started and completed	52,350 liters

Units in ending Work in Process Inventory:
	Units transferred in during April (given)	54,800 liters
Less:	Units started and completed (above)	52,350 liters
Equals:	Units in ending inventory	2,450 liters

With this unit information, we can now prepare the three schedules.

Jackson Manufacturing Company
Process Cost Analysis—Cooling Department
For the Month Ended April 30, 19xx

1a. Schedule of Equivalent Production

Units—Stage of Completion	Units to Be Accounted For	Equivalent Units Transferred In	Equivalent Units Conversion Costs
Beginning inventory—units completed in this period	2,100	2,100	2,100
Units started and completed in this period	52,350	52,350	52,350
Ending Inventory—units started but not completed in this period	2,450		
(Transferred in—100% complete)		2,450	
(Conversion costs—60% complete)			1,470
Totals	56,900	56,900	55,920

1b. Unit Cost Analysis Schedule

Total Costs	Costs from Beginning Inventory	Costs from Current Period	Total Costs to Be Accounted For
Transferred-in costs	$29,200	$756,240	$785,440
Conversion costs	2,654	172,130	174,784
Totals	$31,854	$928,370	$960,224

Equivalent Unit Costs	Total Costs to Be Accounted For ÷	Equivalent Units =	Cost per Equivalent Unit
Transferred-in costs	$785,440	56,900	$13.804*
Conversion costs	174,784	55,920	3.126*
Totals	$960,224		$16.930

1c. Cost Summary Schedule

	Cost of Goods Transferred to Finished Goods Inventory	Cost of Ending Work in Process Inventory
Beginning inventory 2,100 units × $16.930 per unit	$ 35,553	
Units started and completed		
52,350 units × $16.930 per unit	886,286†	
Ending Inventory		
Transferred-in costs: 2,450 units × $13.804		$33,820†
Conversion costs: 1,470 units × $3.126		4,595†
Totals	$921,839	$38,415

Check on computations:

Costs to Finished Goods Inventory	$921,839
Costs in ending Work in Process Inventory	38,415
Error due to rounding—subtract from costs transferred to Finished Goods Inventory	(30)
Total costs to be accounted for (unit cost analysis schedule)	$960,224

*Answer is rounded to three decimal places.   †Answer is affected by the use of rounded unit cost amounts.

2. The costs of completed units for April are now ready to be transferred from the cooling department to Finished Goods Inventory. The proper journal entry is:

Finished Goods Inventory	921,809	
Work in Process—Cooling Department		921,809
To record the transfer of cost of completed units in April from the Cooling Department to Finished Goods Inventory		

Chapter Assignments

Questions

1. What kinds of production are suited to a process cost accounting system?
2. "For job order costing, *one* Work in Process Inventory account is used. However, in process costing we often find *several* Work in Process Inventory accounts in use." Explain.
3. Define equivalent units.
4. Why do actual unit data need to be changed to equivalent unit data for product costing purposes in a process costing system?
5. Define *conversion costs.* Why is this concept used in process costing computations?
6. What are the three schedules used in process costing analysis?
7. Why is it easier to compute equivalent units without units in beginning inventory than with?
8. What is the difference between the FIFO approach and the average costing approach in figuring equivalent units?
9. In figuring equivalent production for conversion costs under the FIFO approach, units in ending inventory are multiplied by the percentage of completion. But in the same computation for beginning inventory, the opposite of the percentage of completion—that is, the percentage *not* completed—is used. Why?
10. What are the purposes of the unit cost analysis schedule?
11. What are the two important dollar amounts that come from the cost summary schedule? How do they relate to the year-end financial statements?
12. Describe how to check the accuracy of the results in the cost summary schedule.
13. What is the significance of the journal entry used to transfer costs of completed products out of the Work in Process Inventory account?
14. What is a "transferred-in" cost? Where does it come from? Why is it handled like materials added at the beginning of the process?

Classroom Exercises

Exercise 24-1 Process Cost Flow Diagram (L.O. 2)

Plummer Paint Company uses a process costing system for its costs in making paint. Production of Quality Brand starts in Department QB1, where materials AH and C24 are added to a water base. The solution is heated to 70° Celsius and then transferred to Department QB2. There it is mixed for one hour. Then the paint goes to Department QB3, where it is cooled and put into 4-liter cans. Direct labor and factory overhead charges are incurred uniformly throughout each part of the process.

In a diagram, show the product flow for Quality Brand paint.

Exercise 24-2 Equivalent Units— Beginning Inventories (FIFO) (L.O. 3)

Graber Enterprises makes Rainwater Shampoo for professional hair stylists. On January 1, 26,400 liters of shampoo were in process, 60 percent complete as to conversion costs and 100 percent complete as to materials. During the year, 142,500 liters of materials were put into production. Data for work in process inventory on December 31 were as follows: shampoo, 7,500 liters; stage of completion, 70 percent of conversion costs and 100 percent of materials content.

From this information, prepare a schedule of equivalent production for the year. Use the FIFO approach.

Exercise 24-3 Equivalent Units—

The Antoinette Company, a major producer of liquid vitamins, uses a process cost accounting system. During January, 45,000 gallons of Material B-4 and 10,000 gallons of Material NAA were put into production. Beginning work in process

Beginning Inventories (Average Costing Method) (L.O. 3)

inventory was 17,500 gallons of product, 80 percent complete as to labor and overhead. Ending Work in Process Inventory was made up of 13,000 gallons, 25 percent complete as to conversion costs. All materials are added at the beginning of the process.

From the above information, prepare a schedule of equivalent production for January using the average costing approach.

Exercise 24-4 Unit Cost Determination (L.O. 4)

Tulsa Kitchenwares, Inc., manufactures heavy duty cookware. Production has just been completed for July. Beginning Work in Process Inventory: materials, $40,200; conversion costs, $46,800. Cost of materials used in July was $123,475. Conversion costs for the month were $206,349. During July, 35,190 units were started and completed. A schedule of equivalent production for July has already been prepared. It shows 64,910 equivalent units as to conversion costs, and 65,470 equivalent units as to materials.

With this information, prepare a unit cost analysis schedule for July. Use the average costing approach.

Exercise 24-5 Cost Summary Schedule (L.O. 5)

The Family Bakery uses a process cost system for internal recordkeeping. Production for August was as follows:

a. Beginning inventory of 22,900 units included costs from the preceding period of materials at $74,000 and conversion costs at $166,000.   *average*
b. Units started and completed totaled 118,600 units at $12.00 per unit.
c. Ending Work in Process Inventory was as follows: materials, 12,000 equivalent units at $3.70 each; conversion costs, 6,500 equivalent units at $8.30 each.

Using the information given, compute the cost of goods transferred to Finished Goods Inventory, the cost of ending Work in Process Inventory, and the total costs to be accounted for. Use the average costing approach.

Exercise 24-6 Cost Transfer— Journal Entry Required (L.O. 3, 6)

The cost summary schedule below was prepared for the Reichardt Paste Company for the year ended July 31, 19xx.

1. From the information given, prepare the journal entry for July 31, 19xx.
2. Draw up the company's schedule of equivalent production. Assume that materials are added at the beginning of the process.

	Cost of Goods Transferred to Finished Goods Inventory	Cost of Ending Work in Process Inventory
Beginning inventory		
13,140 units at $2.10	$ 27,594	
Units started and completed:		
84,960 units at $2.10	178,416	
Ending inventory		
Materials: 6,400 units at $1.20		$ 7,680
Conversion costs: 3,200 units at $.90		2,880
Totals	$206,010	$10,560

Interpreting Accounting Information

Internal Management Information: Tennessee Tire
(L.O. 4)

Tennessee Tire Corporation makes several lines of car and truck tires. The company operates in a competitive marketplace, and so it relies heavily on cost data from its process cost accounting system. It uses this information to set prices for its most competitive tire lines. The company's "Gray Radial" line has lost market share during each of the past four years. Management has decided that the price breaks allowed by the three competitors are the major reason for the decline in sales.

The company controller, Pam Donalson, has been asked to review the product costing information that supports price decisions on the Gray Radial line. In preparing her report, she collected the following data related to 19x6, the last full year of operations.

	Units	Dollars
Equivalent units: Materials costs	48,540	
Conversion costs	46,590	
Manufacturing costs: Materials		$1,018,640
Direct labor		415,278
Factory overhead applied		830,556
Unit cost data: Materials		22
Conversion costs		27
Work in Process Inventory: Beginning		
(30% complete)	2,240	
Ending (50% complete)	3,900	

There were 42,400 units started and completed during 19x6. The costs attached to the year's beginning Work in Process Inventory were materials costs, $49,240, and conversion costs, $12,096.

During her review, Donalson found that very little spoilage had taken place. And the proper cost allowance for spoilage had been included in the predetermined overhead rate of $2.00 per direct labor dollar. Careful study of the direct labor cost, however, revealed that $139,770 had been charged a second time in error to the period's production.

So far in 19x7, the Gray Radial has been selling for $79 per tire. This price was based on the 19x6 unit cost data plus 40 percent to cover operating costs and 15 percent of the total unit cost for profit. During 19x7, the three competitors' prices have been about $70 per tire.

In the company's process costing system, all materials are added at the beginning of the process, and conversion costs are incurred uniformly throughout.

Required

1. Point out the various effects that such a cost charging error can have on the company.
2. Prepare a revised unit cost analysis schedule for 19x6. Use the average costing approach.
3. What should have been the minimum selling price per tire in 19x7?
4. Suggest ways to the controller for preventing such errors in the future.

Problem Set A

Problem 24A-1 Process Costing–

The California Candy Company, which produces several flavors of bubble gum, began production of a new banana-flavored gum on June 1, 19xx. Two basic materials, gum base and banana-flavored sweetener, are blended at the beginning

No Beginning Inventories
(L.O. 3)

of the process. Direct labor and factory overhead costs are incurred uniformly throughout the blending process. During June, 135,000 kilograms of gum base were used and 270,000 kilograms of banana additive, at costs of $324,000 and $162,000, respectively. Direct labor charges were $1,441,240, and factory overhead costs applied during June were $425,000. The ending work in process inventory was 21,600 kilograms. All materials have been added to these units, and 25 percent of the conversion costs have been assigned.

Required

1. Using proper form, prepare for the Blending Department for June: (a) a schedule of equivalent production, (b) a unit cost analysis schedule, and (c) a cost summary schedule.
2. From the cost summary schedule, prepare the journal entry to transfer costs of completed units for June from the Blending Department to the Forming and Packing Department.

**Problem 24A-2
Process
Costing—With
Beginning
Inventories**
(L.O. 3, 4, 5, 6)

The Bess Wafer Company makes high-vitamin, calorie-packed wafers used by professional sports teams to supply quick energy to players. The company uses a process costing system based on the average costing approach to cost flow. Production of these thin white wafers is through a continuous product flow process. The company recently purchased several automated machines so that the wafers can be produced in a single department. The materials are all added at the beginning of the process. The costs for the machine operator's labor and production-related overhead are incurred uniformly throughout the process.

In March, a total of 231,200 liters of materials were put into production. The average cost of the materials was $1.60 per liter. Two liters of materials are used to produce one unit of output (one unit = 144 wafers). Labor costs for March were $124,500. Factory overhead was $187,620. Beginning Work in Process Inventory on March 1 was 56,000 units. The units were 100 percent complete as to materials and 40 percent complete as to conversion costs. The total cost of beginning inventory was $244,400, with $177,200 assigned to the cost of materials. The ending Work in Process Inventory of 48,000 units is fully complete as to materials, but only 30 percent complete as to conversion costs.

Required

1. Using good form and an average costing approach and assuming no loss due to spoilage, prepare (a) a schedule of equivalent production, (b) a unit cost analysis schedule, and (c) a cost summary schedule.
2. From the cost summary schedule, prepare a journal entry to transfer costs of completed units in March to Finished Goods Inventory.

**Problem 24A-3
Process
Costing—With
Beginning
Inventories**
(L.O. 3, 4, 5, 6)

Abdulwahed Bottling Company makes and sells several kinds of soft drinks. Materials (sugar syrup and artificial flavor) are added at the beginning of production in the Mixing Department. Direct labor and factory overhead costs are applied to products throughout the process. The following information is for the Fruit Punch product for August. Beginning Work in Process Inventory (60 percent complete) was 2,400 liters. Ending inventory (50 percent complete) was 3,600 liters. Production data showed 90,000 liters started. A total of 88,800 liters was completed and transferred to the Bottling Department. Beginning inventory data showed $600 for materials and $576 for conversion costs. Current period costs were $22,500 for materials and $35,664 for conversion costs.

Required

1. Using good form and an average costing approach, prepare the following schedules for the Mixing Department for August: (a) a schedule of equivalent production, (b) a unit cost analysis schedule, and (c) a cost summary schedule.
2. From the cost summary schedule, prepare a journal entry to transfer the cost of completed units to the Bottling Department.

Problem 24A-4
Process
Costing—One
Process and
Two Time
Periods
(L.O. 3, 4, 5, 6)

The Diefenderfer Company owns thousands of beehives and produces organic honey for sale to health food stores. Before raw honey can be sold, it must pass through several filterings to remove things like pieces of the honeycomb and dust. No materials other than the honey from the hives are used. The production operation is a simple one in which the impure honey is added at the beginning of the process. A series of filterings follows, leading to a pure finished product. Production data for April and May are shown below.

	April	May
Beginning Work in Process Inventory		
Units	28,400 liters	49600
Costs: Materials	$ 33,128	?
Conversion costs	23,856	?
Production during the period		
Units started	776,000 liters	820,000 liters
Current period costs		
Materials	$ 465,600	$ 492,000
Conversion costs	1,046,752	1,137,304
Ending Work in Process Inventory		
Units	49,600 liters	67,600 liters

For the incomplete inventory figures, assume that all materials have already been added. April beginning inventory was 60 percent complete as to conversion costs, and ending inventory was 20 percent complete. Ending inventory for May was 30 percent complete for conversion costs. Costs of labor and factory overhead are incurred uniformly throughout the filtering process. Assume that there was no loss from spoilage or evaporation.

Required

1. Using good form and an average costing approach, prepare the following schedules for the month of April: (a) a schedule of equivalent production, (b) a unit cost analysis schedule, and (c) a cost summary schedule.
2. From the cost summary schedule, prepare a journal entry to transfer costs of completed units in April to Finished Goods Inventory.
3. Repeat requirements 1 and 2 above for May.

Problem 24A-5
Process
Costing—With
Beginning
Inventories and
Two Depart-
ments
(L.O. 3, 4, 5, 6)

Canned fruits and vegetables are the main products of Cheng Foods, Inc. In preparing canned peaches, all basic materials are put in at the beginning of the Mixing Department's process. When completely mixed, the solution goes to the Cooking Department. There it is heated to 100° Celsius and left to simmer for twenty minutes. When cooled, the mixture goes to the Canning Department for final processing. Throughout the operations of the Mixing and Cooking Departments, direct labor and factory overhead costs are incurred uniformly. No materials are added in the Cooking Department.

Cost data and other information for January are shown on the next page.

Production Cost Data

	Materials	Conversion Costs
Mixing Department		
Beginning inventory	$ 14,400	$ 2,400
Current period costs	216,000	91,200

	Transferred-in	Conversion Costs
Cooking Department		
Beginning inventory	$ 31,500	$ 6,660
Current period costs	?	335,520
Work in Process Inventories		
Beginning Inventories		
Mixing Department (40% complete)		12,000 liters
Cooking Department (20% complete)		18,000 liters
Ending Inventories		
Mixing Department (70% complete)		16,000 liters
Cooking Department (80% complete)		20,000 liters

Unit Production Data

	Mixing Department	Cooking Department
Units started during January	180,000 liters	176,000 liters
Units transferred out during January	176,000 liters	174,000 liters

Assume that no spoilage or evaporation loss took place during January.

(Before completing this problem, refer to the Special Problem on page 926.)

Required

1. Using proper form and an average costing approach, prepare the following schedules for the Mixing Department for January: (a) a schedule of equivalent production, (b) a unit cost analysis schedule, and (c) a cost summary schedule.
2. From the cost summary schedule, prepare a journal entry to transfer costs of completed units for January from the Mixing Department to the Cooking Department.
3. Prepare the same schedules for the Cooking Department that were requested in 1. Also prepare a journal entry to transfer costs of completed units from the Cooking Department to the Canning Department.

Problem Set B

**Problem 24B-1
Process
Costing—No
Beginning
Inventories**
(L.O. 3)

The Clapp Chemical Corporation produces compounds used in the synthesis of an antibiotic. It has just completed its first month of operation. The production process involves two operating departments: the Compounding Department, in which direct labor, factory overhead, and all materials are added; and the Centrifuging Department, in which only conversion costs are added. Each unit produced must be processed by both departments. No significant evaporation occurs in either department. The following operating information was provided by the Accounting Department as of July 31, 19xx: During July, 152,400 units were started. Costs of materials used were $1,981,200, and conversion costs were $797,160. A total of 88,200 units were completed and transferred to the Centrifuging Department. In ending Work in Process Inventory, all units in the Compounding Department on July 31 were 40 percent complete as to conversion costs. All materials are added at the beginning of the process.

Required

1. Using good form, prepare the following schedules for the Compounding Department: (a) a schedule of equivalent production, (b) a unit cost analysis schedule, and (c) a cost summary schedule.
2. From the cost summary schedule, prepare the journal entry to transfer costs of completed units for July to the Centrifuging Department.

Problem 24B-2
Process Costing—With Beginning Inventories
(L.O. 3, 4, 5, 6)

The main product of the Bakken Britches Company is a line of corduroy jeans for infants. All operations are performed by a series of automated machines in one process. Corduroy material is introduced at the beginning of the process. Conversion costs are uniform throughout the process.

During August, 462,500 square meters of material were put into production. Average unit cost was $2.80 per square meter. August labor costs were $229,568, and overhead was $92,775. Work in Process Inventory on August 1 was made up of 3,700 units (pairs of pants), which were 100 percent complete as to materials and 80 percent complete as to conversion costs. The beginning inventory value was $6,216. Of that, $5,180 represents the cost of materials.

The ending Work in Process Inventory of 6,800 units is complete as to materials costs. But it is only 30 percent complete as to conversion costs. Note that one square meter of corduroy makes *two* units of output.

Required

1. Using good form and an average costing approach, prepare (a) a schedule of equivalent production, (b) a unit cost analysis schedule, and (c) a cost summary schedule.
2. From the cost summary schedule, prepare a journal entry to transfer costs of completed units in August to Finished Goods Inventory.

Problem 24B-3
Process Costing—With Beginning Inventories
(L.O. 3, 4, 5, 6)

Ultrasonics, Inc., makes fuse assemblies for guided missiles. The painting operation is only one of many production processes. The assemblies are painted at the beginning of the process, and conversion costs are added as the units pass through the Painting Department. After being dried and polished, the assemblies are sent to the Inspection Department.

The beginning Work in Process Inventory for the Painting Department for the month of May consists of 2,900 units (60 percent complete). Costs of materials were $10,600. Conversion costs were $3,520.

During the month, 111,200 units were started. Costs of materials were $1,556,800. Conversion costs were $546,050. There were 109,600 units completed and sent to the Inspection Department.

In ending Work in Process Inventory, all fuse assemblies remaining in the Painting Department on May 31 were 30 percent complete as to conversion costs.

Required

1. Using good form and an average costing approach, prepare the following for the Painting Department for May: (a) a schedule of equivalent production, (b) a unit cost analysis schedule, and (c) a cost summary schedule.
2. From the cost summary schedule, prepare a journal entry to transfer costs of completed fuse assemblies for May to the Inspection Department.

Problem 24B-4
Process Costing—One Process and Two Time Periods
(L.O. 3, 4, 5, 6)

Making and selling an inexpensive dry red wine is the specialty of the Andor Tizson Winery. Materials include a water base, fresh grape juice, sugar, and an aging ingredient. All are added at the beginning of the process. The aging ingredient results in a rapid, artificial aging process so that the wine can be considered a finished product right after the production process. Data for February and March are shown on the next page.

	February	March
Beginning Work in Process Inventory		
Units	7,100 liters	?
Costs: Materials	$ 5,112	?
Conversion costs	1,917	?
Production during the period		
Units started	194,000 liters	205,000 liters
Current period costs		
Materials	$139,680	$149,650
Conversion costs	84,114	101,545
Ending Work in Process Inventory Units	12,400 liters	16,900 liters

For all partly completed inventories, all materials have been added. The February beginning inventory was 60 percent complete as to conversion costs, and the ending inventory was 20 percent complete. Ending inventory for March was 30 percent complete as to conversion costs. Costs of labor and factory overhead are incurred uniformly throughout the process. Assume no loss from spoilage or evaporation.

Required

1. Using good form and an average costing approach, prepare the following schedules for the month of February: (a) a schedule of equivalent production, (b) a unit cost analysis schedule, and (c) a cost summary schedule.
2. From the cost summary schedule, prepare a journal entry to transfer costs of completed units in February to Finished Goods Inventory.
3. Repeat the requirements in **1** and **2** above for the month of March.

Problem 24B-5
Process Costing—With Beginning Inventories and Two Departments
(L.O. 3, 4, 5, 6)

The G & W Company has been making breakfast cereals for three generations. The production of bean flakes involves several processes. Two of them are blending and baking. Materials are added at the beginning of the blending process. None are added in the baking process. Conversion costs are incurred uniformly throughout both processes. After the baking process is finished, the units of product are sent to the Packaging Department. Production has just been completed for March. The Accounting Department has provided the month's production data as shown below.

Beginning Work in Process inventories for the Blending Department were made up of 6,200 units (25 percent complete). Costs of materials were $43,400. Conversion costs were $9,300. Beginning Work in Process inventories for the Baking Department were 5,800 units (40 percent complete). Transferred-in costs were $72,500. Conversion costs were $20,880.

During March the Blending Department started 23,000 units. Costs for materials were $161,000. Conversion costs were $130,260. There were 18,400 units completed and transferred to the Baking Department. The Baking Department started these 18,400 units, but transferred-in costs must be computed. Conversion costs were $197,400. A total of 22,000 units was completed and transferred to the Packaging Department.

In ending Work in Process inventories for the Blending Department, all units were 45 percent complete as to conversion costs. For the Baking Department, all units were 60 percent complete as to conversion costs.

Before completing this problem, you may need to refer to the Special Problem on page 926.

Required

1. Using proper form and an average costing approach, prepare the following schedules for the Blending Department for March: (a) a schedule of equivalent

production, (b) a unit cost analysis schedule, and (c) a cost summary schedule.
2. From the cost summary schedule, prepare a journal entry to transfer costs of completed units for March from the Blending Department to the Baking Department.
3. Repeat requirement **1** for the Baking Department and prepare an entry to transfer costs of completed units for March from the Baking Department to the Packaging Department.

Management Decision Case 24-1

Opry Cola, Inc.
(L.O. 3, 4)

For the past four years, three companies have dominated the soft drink industry, holding a combined 85 percent of market share. Opry Cola, Inc., ranks second nationally in soft drink sales with gross revenues last year of $27,450,000. Management is thinking about introducing a new low-calorie drink called Slimit Cola.

Soft drinks at Opry are completely processed in a single department. All materials are added at the beginning of the process. Fluids are bottled at the end of the process into bottles costing two cents each. Direct labor and factory overhead costs are applied uniformly throughout the process.

Corporate controller Sal Forzano believes that costs for the new cola will be very much like those for the company's Cola Plus drink. Last year, the following data related to Cola Plus:

	Units	Costs
Work in Process Inventory		
January 1, 19x5[1]	6,420	
Materials costs		$ 10,280
Conversion costs		3,876
December 31, 19x5[2]	8,900	
Materials costs		14,240
Conversion costs		7,476
Units started during the year	459,380	
Costs for 19x5		
Liquid materials added		735,000
Direct labor		344,925
Factory overhead applied		206,955
Bottles		219,312

[1]50% complete   [2]70% complete   Note: Each unit is a 24-bottle case

Variable operating and selling costs are $1.10 per unit. Fixed operating and selling costs are assigned to products at the rate of $.50 per unit. Its two major competitors have already introduced a diet cola into the marketplace. Company A's product sells for $6.00 per unit and that of Company B for $5.90.

All costs in 19x6 are expected to increase by 10 percent over 19x5 costs. The company tries to earn a profit of at least 12 percent.

Required

1. What factors should the company consider in setting a selling price for Slimit Cola?
2. Using the average costing approach, compute (a) the total production cost per unit and (b) the total cost per unit of Cola Plus for 19x5.
3. What is the expected total cost per unit of Slimit Cola for 19x6?
4. Recommend a unit selling price range for Slimit Cola and give your reason(s).
5. Would your answer to **4** change if the competitors' average price was $5.40 per unit? Why?

Part Seven

Accounting for Management Decision Making

Part VI exposed you to the field of management accounting, focusing on the development of useful manufacturing cost information for product costing and management reporting purposes. Emphasis was placed on the first of three aspects of management accounting: management's need for product or service costing information.

In Part VII we analyze the final two aspects of the field of management accounting: management's need for (1) data used for planning and control of operations, and (2) special reports and analyses used to support management decisions.

Chapter 25 introduces cost planning and control, specifically focusing on cost behavior patterns, cost-volume-profit relationships, and responsibility accounting.

In Chapter 26 the cost planning tools described in Chapter 25 are used to implement the planning function of the budgetary control process. Emphasis is placed on budgeting principles and preparation, including the cash budget.

Chapter 27 concludes your study of the budgetary control process. Standard costing is analyzed by first looking at the nature, purpose, and development of standard costing information. Then variance analysis is introduced to aid in management's control of operations.

Chapter 28 deals with ways of developing and providing relevant information, including variable costing, contribution reporting, and incremental analysis. These approaches to information reporting are then applied to operating decisions involving capital expenditures analysis, make or buy alternatives, special product orders, and sales mix analyses.

Learning Objectives

Chapter Twenty-Five

Basic Cost Planning and Control Tools

1. *Define and classify variable costs, semivariable costs, and fixed costs.*

2. *Compute the breakeven point in units of output and in sales dollars.*

3. *Use contribution margin analysis to estimate levels of sales that will produce planned profits.*

4. *State the role of cost objectives in the cost allocation process.*

5. *Assign costs of supporting service functions to production departments.*

6. *Allocate common manufacturing costs to joint products.*

7. *Describe a responsibility accounting system.*

Cost planning and control are vital to the on-going life of a company. Good cost planning results in efficient production, and cost control contributes to profits. Knowledge of cost behavior patterns, cost-volume-profit relationships, and the responsibility accounting system all help a company achieve good cost planning and control. In this chapter we also discuss the role of cost allocation in accounting for total costs incurred. Cost allocation techniques are used not only to assign costs after they have been incurred; they are also useful in planning future activities. As a result of studying this chapter, you should be able to meet the learning objectives listed on the left.

Cost Behavior

Before estimating a future cost or preparing a budget, a manager must know the basic behavior patterns of costs. We can define cost behavior as how costs respond to changes in activity or volume. To understand cost behavior, we need to look at the basic characteristics and the accounting classifications of costs. This knowledge is useful for predicting future costs and analyzing past cost performance.

Variable and Fixed Costs

Almost any cost can be classified as either a variable cost or a fixed cost. Some cost totals increase or decrease along with increases or decreases in productive output. Others costs remain constant. (Though we focus on cost behavior as it relates to production, we

Objective 1
Define and
classify variable
costs, semivar-
iable costs, and
fixed costs

should realize that some costs are *not* measured in terms of production. Sales commissions, for example, depend on sales revenue, and not on production measures.)

Total costs that change in direct proportion to productive output or any other volume measure changes are called **variable costs.** To see how variable costs work, consider the example of an auto maker. Each new car has four tires, and each tire costs $38. Thus the total tire cost (four tires per automobile) is $152 for one automobile, $304 for two, $456 for three, $608 for four, $760 for five, $1,520 for ten, and $15,200 for one hundred. In manufacturing automobiles, total tire cost is a variable cost. On a per unit basis, a variable cost remains constant. In this case, tire cost per automobile is $152 ($38 × 4) whether one car is produced or one hundred cars.

In discussing variable costs, we have assumed that there is a linear relationship between cost and volume. Figure 25-1 shows this relationship. In this example, each unit of output requires $2.50 of labor cost. Total labor costs grow in direct proportion to the increase in units of output.

However, not all variable costs behave in this way. Electricity rates, for instance, go down as the use of electricity goes up. Although variable in some ways, this cost pattern is more like that of semivariable costs, which are discussed in the next section of this chapter. For now, we will assume that variable costs have a linear relationship to volume, as shown in Figure 25-1.

Fixed costs behave in an entirely different manner. Total **fixed costs** remain constant within a relevant range of volume or activity. A **relevant range** of activity is the range within which actual operations are likely to occur. Supervisory salaries are a good example of a fixed cost. Assume that a local manufacturing company needs one supervisor for an eight-hour work shift. Production can range from 0 to 500,000 units per month

Figure 25-1
A Common
Cost Behavior
Pattern:
Variable Cost

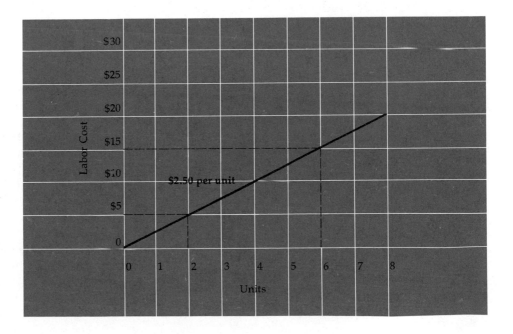

per shift. The supervisor's salary is $2,000 per month, and the relevant range is 0 to 500,000 units. The cost behavior analysis is as follows:

Units of Output	Total Supervisory Salaries per Month
100,000	$2,000
200,000	2,000
300,000	2,000
400,000	2,000
500,000	2,000
600,000	4,000

As noted, a maximum of 500,000 units can be produced per shift. So any output over 500,000 units calls for another work shift and another supervisor.

On a per unit basis, fixed costs go down as volume goes up. In our example, supervisory costs per unit would change as follows:

Volume of Activity	Cost per Unit
100,000 units	$2,000/100,000 = $.02
200,000 units	$2,000/200,000 = $.01
300,000 units	$2,000/300,000 = $.0067
400,000 units	$2,000/400,000 = $.005
500,000 units	$2,000/500,000 = $.004
600,000 units	$4,000/600,000 = $.0067

The per unit cost increased at the 600,000 unit level because the volume was not within the relevant range and another supervisor was hired.

Total fixed costs stay the same for all levels of activity within the relevant range. A graphic view of this fixed overhead cost is shown in Figure 25-2. Fixed overhead costs of $2,000 are needed for the first 500,000 units of production. Fixed costs hold steady at $2,000 for any level of output within the relevant range. But output over 500,000 units calls for another supervisor, and the cost level jumps to $4,000.

Semivariable and Mixed Costs

Some costs cannot be classified as either variable or fixed. A **semivariable cost** acts like both a variable cost and a fixed cost. Part of the cost is fixed, and part changes with the volume of output. Telephone expense is an example. Monthly telephone charges are made up of a service charge plus extra charges for extra telephones and long-distance calls. The service charge and the cost of extra telephones are fixed costs. But the long-distance charges are variable because they depend on monthly use.

Mixed costs also act like both variable and fixed costs. **Mixed costs** result when more than one kind of cost is charged to the same general ledger account. The Repairs and Maintenance account is a good example of an account balance made up of mixed costs. Labor charges to this account may vary in proportion to the amount of repairs done. However, only one repair and maintenance worker may be employed on a full-time basis (a fixed cost), and extra help is hired only when needed (a variable

Figure 25-2
A Common
Cost Behavior
Pattern: Fixed
Cost

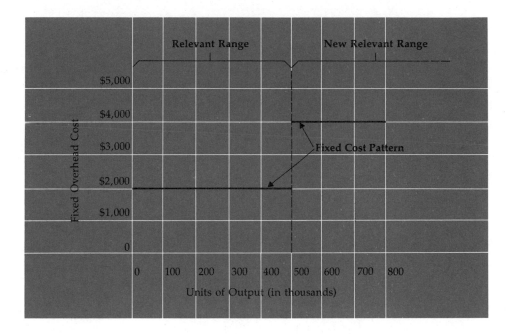

cost). Depreciation costs for repair and maintenance machinery are also a fixed cost, but costs of repair supplies depend on use. *For purposes of cost planning and control, semivariable and mixed costs must be divided into their respective variable and fixed cost parts.* They can then be grouped with other variable and fixed costs for analysis.

Operating Capacity: Definition and Cost Influence

Operating capacity plays an important part in our study of cost behavior and in budgetary control. Operating capacity is the upper limit on production output and related costs. So it is essential information when predictions are being made. Because variable costs increase or decrease in direct proportion to expected volume or output, it is important to know what is meant by the term *operating capacity*. **Theoretical** or **ideal capacity** is the maximum productive output a department or a company could reach for a given period if all machinery and equipment were operated at optimum speed without any interruptions. Theoretical capacity is useful in thinking about maximum production levels. However, it has little value for day-to-day operations. No company operates at ideal capacity. **Practical capacity** is theoretical capacity reduced by normal and expected work stoppages. Production may be interrupted by machine downtime for retooling, repair and maintenance, or employee work breaks. These normal interruptions and the resulting lower output should be thought of when measuring capacity.

Seldom does a company operate at either ideal or practical capacity. **Excess capacity** is extra machinery and equipment kept on hand on a stand-by basis. Such extra equipment may be used when regular equipment is being repaired. Or during a slow season, a company may use only part of its equipment. Or it may work just one or two shifts instead of around the clock. Because of these circumstances, normal capacity, rather than ideal or practical capacity, is often used for planning. **Normal capacity** is the average annual level of operating capacity that is needed to meet expected sales demand. This demand figure is adjusted for seasonal changes and for business and economic cycles. Therefore, normal capacity is a realistic measure of what *is likely* to be produced, rather than what *can* be produced, by an operating unit.

Cost-Volume-Profit Relationships

Cost behavior patterns underlie the relationships among costs, volume of output, and profit. These relationships are studied through **cost-volume-profit analysis** (or **C-V-P analysis**). They are useful for predicting future operating results. A company may use C-V-P analysis as a planning tool when the sales volume is known and management needs to find out how much profit will result. Another way of planning is to begin with a target profit. Then, through C-V-P analysis, a company can decide the level of sales needed to reach that profit.

For cost control purposes, C-V-P analysis is a way to measure how well different departments in the company are doing. At the end of a period, the company analyzes sales volume and related actual costs to find actual profit. It measures performance by comparing actual costs with expected costs. These expected costs are computed by applying C-V-P analysis to the actual sales volume. The result is a performance report on which management can base the control of operations. This process is explained further in Chapter 27.

C-V-P Analysis: Break-even Point and Profit Planning

Cost-volume-profit analysis is based on the relationships among operating costs, sales volume, sales revenue, and target net income. Before starting C-V-P analysis, we must first classify costs as either variable costs (VC) or fixed costs (FC). Sales (S) are computed by multiplying units sold by the selling price per unit. Target net income (NI) is decided by management. The usual formula for C-V-P analysis is

sales revenue = variable costs + fixed costs + net income

Or, more simply,

$$S = VC + FC + NI$$

If we move the variable costs (VC) and fixed costs (FC) over to the left side of the equals sign and change these signs from positive to negative, this same equation begins to look like the income statement:

$$S - VC - FC = NI$$

Break-even Point The **break-even point** is that point where total revenue equals total costs incurred. Thus it is the point at which a company begins

*Objective 2
Compute the
break-even point
in units of
output and in
sales dollars*

to earn a profit. When planning new ventures or product lines, you can quickly measure the likelihood of success by finding the project's break-even point. If, for instance, break-even is 50,000 units and the total market is only 25,000, the idea should be promptly abandoned. When finding a company's or a product's break-even point, only sales (S), variable cost (VC), and fixed cost (FC) are used. There is no net income (NI) when a company breaks even. The goal is to find the level of activity where sales revenue equals the sum of all variable and fixed costs. Break-even data can be stated in break-even sales units or break-even sales dollars. The general equations for finding the break-even point are

$$S = VC + FC \quad \text{or} \quad S - VC - FC = 0$$

An example will show how the equation can be used to find break-even units and dollars. Sterling Products, Inc., makes wooden stands for portable television sets. Variable costs are $25 per unit, and fixed costs average $20,000 per year. Each wooden stand sells for $45. Given this information, we can figure the break-even point for this product in sales units and dollars.

Break-even point in sales units (represented by x):

$$S = VC + FC$$
$$\$45x = \$25x + \$20,000$$
$$\$20x = \$20,000$$
$$x = 1,000 \text{ units}$$

Break-even point in sales dollars:

$$\$45/\text{unit} \times 1,000 \text{ units} = \$45,000$$

We can also make a rough estimate of the break-even point by using a graph. This method is less exact, but it does yield meaningful data. Figure 25-3 shows a break-even analysis for Sterling Products. This standard break-even chart has five parts: (1) a horizontal axis in volume or units; (2) a vertical axis in dollars; (3) a horizontal line for the upper limit of fixed costs ($20,000); (4) a total cost line beginning at a point where the fixed cost line crosses the vertical axis and sloping upward to the right (the slope of the line depends on the variable costs per unit); and (5) a total revenue line beginning at the origin of the vertical and horizontal axes and sloping upward to the right (the slope depends on the selling price per unit). At the point where the total revenue line crosses the total cost line, revenues will equal total costs. The break-even point, stated in either units or dollars of sales, can be found by extending lines from this point to the axes. As shown in Figure 25-3, Sterling Products will break even when 1,000 television stands have been made and sold for $45,000 in sales.

Profit Planning The break-even process can be extended easily to include profit planning. Assume that Sterling Product's president, Myra Miles, has set a $10,000 profit as the goal for the year. If all the previous data stay the same, how many television stands must Sterling Products make and sell to reach the target profit? The answer is figured below (x = number of units).

Figure 25-3
Graphic Break-
even Analysis:
Sterling
Products, Inc.

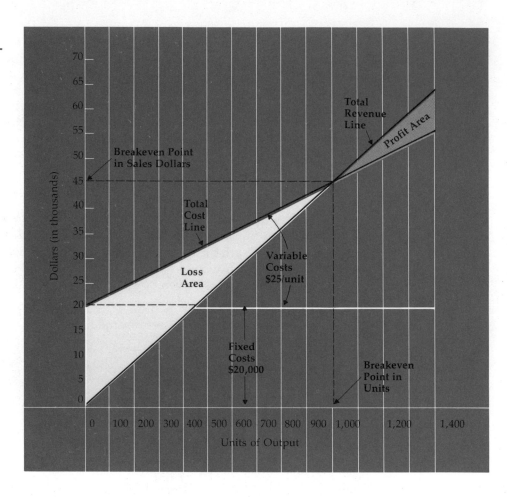

$$S = VC + FC + NI$$
$$\$45x = \$25x + \$20,000 + \$10,000$$
$$\$20x = \$30,000$$
$$x = 1,500 \text{ units}$$

To check the accuracy of this answer, put all the known data into the equation for an income statement:

$$S - VC - FC = NI$$
$$(1,500 \text{ units} \times \$45) - (1,500 \times \$25) - (\$20,000) = \$10,000$$
$$\$67,500 - \$37,500 - \$20,000 = \$10,000$$

Contribution Margin Concept

Our analysis of cost-volume-profit relationships is not complete until we add a new concept to our discussion. **Contribution margin** is the excess of revenues over all variable costs related to a particular sales volume. A product line's contribution margin represents its net contribution to paying off fixed costs and to profits. Net income for Sterling Products, Inc., figured by using the contribution approach, is shown on the next page.

| | Units Produced and Sold | |
	1,000	1,500
Sales revenue ($45 per unit)	$45,000	$67,500
Less variable costs ($25 per unit)	25,000	37,500
Contribution margin	$20,000	$30,000
Less fixed costs	20,000	20,000
Net income	—	$10,000

Objective 3
Use contri-
bution margin
analysis to
estimate levels
of sales that
will produce
planned profits

Adding contribution margin into C-V-P analysis changes the make-up of the equations as well as the format of the income statement. The equation now becomes

$$S - VC = CM - FC = NI$$

Contribution margin (CM) is what remains after variable costs have been subtracted from total sales. So the break-even point (BE) can be expressed as the point where contribution margin (CM) minus total fixed costs (FC) equals zero. That is, break-even occurs when $CM - FC = 0$. In terms of units of product, the break-even point equation is changed as follows:

$$(CM/unit \times BE\ units) - FC = 0$$

At this point we need to develop an equation that isolates the expression, BE units. The equation above can be rearranged as follows:

1. Move FC to the right side of the equation:

$$CM/unit \times BE\ units = FC$$

2. Divide both sides of the equation by CM/unit:

$$\frac{CM/unit \times BE\ units}{CM/unit} = \frac{FC}{CM/unit}$$

3. After canceling terms, the end result is

$$BE\ units = \frac{FC}{CM/unit}$$

For profit planning, the equation is adjusted to include target net income as follows:

$$target\ unit\ sales = \frac{FC + NI}{CM/unit}$$

To illustrate the use of these equations, we will put in the data given earlier for Sterling Products.

$$BE\ units = \frac{FC}{CM/unit} = \frac{\$20,000}{\$45 - \$25} = \frac{\$20,000}{\$20} = 1,000\ units$$

$$\text{target unit sales} = \frac{FC + NI}{CM/\text{unit}} = \frac{\$20,000 + \$10,000}{\$20} = \frac{\$30,000}{\$20} = 1,500 \text{ units}$$

Once mastered, the use of the contribution margin simplifies finding the break-even point and planning for profits.

Assumptions Underlying C-V-P Analysis

Cost-volume-profit figures are useful only when certain assumptions hold true and certain conditions exist. If one or more of these assumptions and conditions are absent, the results of the analysis may be misleading. These assumptions and conditions are as follows:

1. Behavior of variable and fixed costs can be measured accurately.
2. Costs and revenues have close linear approximation. For example, if costs rise, revenues will rise proportionately.
3. Efficiency and productivity will hold steady within the relevant range of activity.
4. Cost and price variables will also hold steady during the period being planned for.
5. The product sales mix will not change during the planning period.
6. Production and sales volume will be about equal.

Illustrative Problem: Profit Planning—
Contribution Margin Approach

Producing college textbooks is made up of many complex steps. All of them add to the cost of published materials. Good paper and binding materials add much to the cost as well as to the useful life of a book. Barton Publishing Company is taking a very careful look at a new manuscript on management information systems. Early estimates are that variable costs per book will be $6.80 and that total fixed costs will be $60,000. The company plans to market the book wholesale at $12.80 per copy.

Required

1. Using the contribution margin approach, compute how many copies of the book the company must sell to earn a profit of $30,000.
2. Using the same approach and assuming that fixed costs are cut to $50,000, figure the number of copies that must be sold to earn a target profit of $61,000.
3. Given the original information and assuming that 21,000 copies of the book can be sold, find the selling price that the company must set to earn profits of $80,700.
4. The company's marketing director says that the most optimistic sales estimate for the book would be 36,000 copies. Assume that the highest possible price that the company can charge is $13.20 and that variable costs per unit cannot be reduced below $6.80. How much more can be spent on fixed advertising costs if the new target profit is $40,000?

Chapter Twenty-Five

Solution

1. Target units computed

$$\text{Unit sales} = (\text{FC} + \text{NI}) \div \text{CM per unit}$$
$$= (\$60,000 + \$30,000) \div (\$12.80 - \$6.80)$$
$$= \$90,000 \div \$6$$
$$= \underline{15,000} \text{ copies}$$

2. Units computed for higher profit and lower costs

$$\text{Unit sales} = (\text{FC} + \text{NI}) \div \text{CM per unit}$$
$$= (\$50,000 + \$61,000) \div (\$12.80 - \$6.80)$$
$$= \$111,000 \div \$6$$
$$= \underline{18,500} \text{ copies}$$

3. Selling price determined

$$\text{Unit sales} = (\text{FC} + \text{NI}) \div \text{CM per unit}$$
$$21,000 = (\$60,000 + \$80,700) \div (x - \$6.80)$$

Multiplying both sides of the equation by $(x - \$6.80)$, we get

$$21,000(x - \$6.80) = \$140,700$$
$$21,000x - \$142,800 = \$140,700$$
$$21,000x = \$283,500$$
$$x = \underline{\$13.50}$$

4. Increased amount for advertising determined

$$\text{Unit sales} = (\text{FC} + \text{NI}) \div \text{CM per unit}$$
$$36,000 = (x + \$40,000) \div (\$13.20 - \$6.80)$$
$$36,000 = (x + \$40,000) \div \$6.40$$

Multiplying both sides of the equation by $6.40, we get

$$\$6.40(36,000) = x + \$40,000$$
$$\$230,400 = x + \$40,000$$
$$x = \$230,400 - \$40,000$$
$$x = \$190,400$$

Total fixed costs allowed	$190,400
Less original fixed cost estimate	60,000
Additional dollars available for advertising	$130,400

Cost Allocation

Cost allocation, or assignment, is very important to every part of management accounting, including the finding of unit costs for products and services. Some operating costs (direct costs) can be easily traced and assigned to products or services. But other costs (indirect costs) must be assigned by using some form of allocation method. The need for cost allocation goes beyond just identifying product or service costs. Every report that a company's accountants prepare requires some form of cost allocation. Depreciation expense on a building, for example, is often allocated to the different departments housed in that building. Depreciation expense itself is originally established by allocating an investment's total cost to various time periods. Even the president's salary is allocated to the various divisions in a company.

In accounting for operating costs, each cost must be assigned to products, services, departments, or jobs before accounting reports can be prepared. Without proper cost allocation techniques, management accountants could not do their work. Management accountants have three major tasks in preparing internal accounting documents: (1) They must find product or service unit costs. (2) They must work out cost budgets and cost controls for management. (3) They must prepare reports to aid and support management decisions. Each task requires proper cost allocation procedures.

Several terms are unique to the concept of cost allocation and should be discussed further. For instance, the terms *cost allocation* and *cost assignment* are often used interchangeably, although *cost allocation* is the more popular of the two. For our purposes, **cost allocation** is the process of assigning a specific cost to a specific cost objective.[1] Understanding such terms as *cost center, cost objective, direct cost,* and *indirect cost* is also vital to the study of cost allocation.

A **cost center** is any organizational segment or area of activity for which there is a reason to accumulate costs. Examples of cost centers include the company as a whole, corporate divisions, specific operating plants, departments, and even specific machines or work areas. Once a cost center has been selected, methods can be worked out that will assign costs accurately to that cost center. No accounting report about a cost center can be prepared until all the proper cost allocation methods have been carried out.

A **cost objective** is the destination of an assigned cost.[2] If the purpose of a certain cost analysis is to evaluate the operating performance of a division or department, the cost objective would be that department or division (cost center). But if product costing is the reason for accumulating costs, a specific product, order, or an entire contract could be the cost objective. The important point is that cost classification and cost allocation results differ, depending on the cost objective being analyzed.

Objective 4
State the role of cost objectives in the cost allocation process

Now we can expand the definitions of direct and indirect costs that were used earlier in relation to product costing. A direct cost is any cost that can be conveniently and economically traced to a specific cost objective. Direct materials costs and direct labor costs are normally thought of as

1. Cost Accounting Standard 402, promulgated by the Cost Accounting Standards Board in 1972, defined the term *allocate* as follows: "To assign an item of cost, or group of items of cost, to one or more cost objectives. This term includes both direct assignment of cost and the reassignment of a share from an indirect cost pool."
2. Cost Accounting Standard 402, promulgated by the Cost Accounting Standards Board in 1972, defined the term *cost objective* as follows: "A function, organizational subdivision, contract or other work unit for which cost data are desired and for which provision is made to accumulate and measure the cost to processes, products, jobs, capitalized projects, etc."

direct costs. However, costs considered to be direct will vary with individual cost objectives. In general, the number of costs classified as direct increases with the size of the cost objective. If the cost objective is a large division of a company, then electricity, maintenance, and special tooling costs of the division may be classified as direct costs. An indirect cost is any cost that cannot be conveniently or economically traced and assigned to a specific cost objective. In an actual situation, any production cost not classified as a direct cost is an indirect cost.

Allocation of Manufacturing Costs

All manufacturing costs can be traced or assigned to a company's divisions, departments, or units of productive output. Direct costs, such as the cost of direct materials, can be assigned to specific products, departments, or jobs. Many manufacturing costs, however, are indirect costs that are incurred for the benefit of more than one product or department. These costs should be allocated to the departments and those products that benefited from incurring the cost. For example, electricity cost is incurred for the benefit of all departments or divisions of a company. This cost must be allocated to all the work done during a week or a month. Assigning all of it to one department would not give a true picture of events. This benefit theory and the methods used to distribute costs are basic to cost allocation.

The cost allocation process is shown in Figure 25-4. All three cost elements are included: materials, labor, and factory overhead. Costs of lumber and the cabinet maker's wages are direct costs of the product. Factory overhead costs include depreciation of the table saw, clean-up and janitorial services, and nails. All factory overhead costs are indirect costs of the product and must be assigned by means of an allocation method. In this example, the cost objective is the product. Various cost classifications and cost allocation methods are used when a different cost objective is being analyzed.

Figure 25-4
Cabinet
Making:
Assigning
Manufacturing
Costs to the
Product

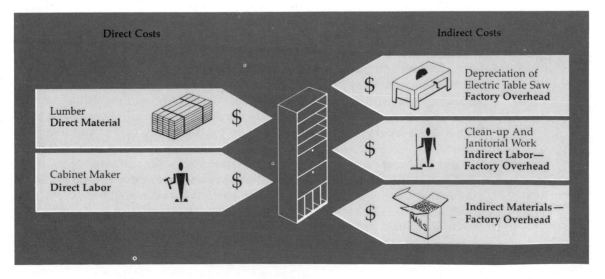

To summarize, allocation of production costs calls for assigning direct and indirect manufacturing costs to specific cost objectives. A cost may be a direct cost to a large cost objective (a large division) but an indirect cost to a smaller cost objective (a product). In each case, all manufacturing costs are assigned to the specific cost objectives being analyzed as either direct or indirect costs.

The Role of Cost Assignment in Corporate Reporting

Accounting reports are prepared for all levels of management, from the president down to the department manager or supervisor. The president is responsible for all costs of the company. A department manager, on the other hand, is responsible for only the costs connected to that one department. Reports must be prepared for all cost centers including the company as a whole, each division, and all departments within each division. The same costs shown in departmental reports will appear again in divisional and corporate reports, but perhaps in summary form.

As focus shifts from one cost center or cost objective to another, so does the ease with which costs can be traced. Here is where cost allocation comes into the picture. The different types of accounting reports can be prepared only with the aid of cost allocation techniques. As costs are reclassified and assigned to smaller cost centers or cost objectives, they become more difficult to trace. More costs are accounted for as indirect when emphasis shifts from divisional to departmental reporting. When the size of the cost objective is reduced to focus on a single product, only direct materials and direct labor costs can be directly traced. All other costs are classified as indirect and must be parceled out to the different products. This distribution calls for special procedures.

Table 25-1 shows how three manufacturing costs are traced differently as cost objectives change. Direct materials costs can be traced directly to any level of cost objective shown. They are a direct cost at the divisional, departmental, and product levels. All 40,000 pounds of sugar were issued to Division A. So they can be traced directly to that division. Only half (20,000 pounds) of the division's sugar was used by Department XZ. So only that amount can be traced directly to that department. At the product level, every unit of Product AB requires one-half pound of sugar. The cost of that one-half pound is a direct cost that can be traced to the product. Depreciation of Factory Building G, which is used entirely by Division A, can be traced directly to Division A. For any smaller cost objectives, though, it becomes an indirect cost. Building depreciation expense must be shared by the various cost centers in the building. Such costs must be allocated to departmental or product cost objectives using an allocation base such as space occupied. Depreciation costs of Machine 201 can be traced directly to either Division A or Department XZ. When Product AB is the cost objective, however, depreciation of machinery is considered an indirect manufacturing cost. It is accounted for as a factory overhead cost. Factory overhead costs are accumulated and then allocated to the products produced in Department XZ, as we saw in previous chapters. The principles of classifying and tracing costs we have discussed here play a part in all internal accounting reports.

Costs	Cost Objectives		
	Division A	Department XZ	Product AB
Direct Materials	*Direct cost:* 40,000 pounds of sugar issued from inventory specifically for Division A.	*Direct cost:* 20,000 of the 40,000 pounds of sugar issued from inventory were used by Department XZ (can be directly traced).	*Direct cost:* Every unit of Product AB requires one-half pound of sugar.
Depreciation of Factory Building G	*Direct cost:* Factory Building G is used entirely by Division A. Therefore, all depreciation charges from usage of Factory Building G can be directly traced to Division A.	*Indirect cost:* Department XZ is one of four departments in Factory Building G. Depreciation of Factory Building G is allocated to the four departments according to square footage used by each department.	*Indirect cost:* Depreciation of Factory Building G is an indirect product cost. It is allocated to individual products as part of factory overhead charges applied to products using direct labor hours as a base.
Depreciation of Machine 201	*Direct cost:* Machine 201 is located within Department XZ and is used exclusively by Division A (can be directly traced).	*Direct cost:* Machine 201 is used only by Department XZ. Therefore, its depreciation charges can be directly traced to Department XZ.	*Indirect cost:* Depreciation of Machine 201 cannot be directly traced to individual products it produces. Such depreciation charges are accounted for as part of factory overhead costs.

Table 25-1
Cost Classification and Traceability

*Objective 5
Assign costs of supporting service functions to production departments*

Assigning Costs of Supporting Service Functions

Every company and manufacturing process depends on the aid of many supporting service functions or departments. A **supporting service function** is not directly involved in production, but it is an operating unit or department that is needed for the overall operation of the company. Examples include a repair and maintenance department, a production scheduling department, a central power department, an inspection department, and materials storage and handling.

Labor costs and various indirect operating costs are accumulated for each service function. The costs of these supporting departments are incurred for the purpose of producing a product. So the costs incurred by supporting service functions are product costs. They should be treated as indirect manufacturing costs and assigned to products through the Factory Overhead account. This type of cost allocation is done in two steps. First, the supporting service function's costs are allocated to the departments or cost centers that benefited from the services. After this step, the assigned costs are included in the production department's Factory Overhead account and allocated to the end product.

Allocating factory overhead costs to products was discussed in Chapter 23. Here we will concentrate on assigning supporting service department costs to production departments. A service function must benefit other departments to justify its existence. It is on this concept of benefit that supporting service department costs are assigned to production departments. Benefit must be measured on some basis that shows how the service performed relates to the department that received the service.

Table 25-2 gives examples of bases used to allocate costs of supporting service functions. Each should be used when there is a benefit relationship between the service function and the production departments. Each request may represent an equal amount of benefit or service to the receiving department. In that case the number of service requests can be the basis. Or total benefit may be measured by the number of labor hours needed to complete the service. Then labor hours can be the basis. Similar relationships justify the use of kilowatt hours or the number of materials requisitions as the allocation basis. The following problem will help you understand the process of assigning supporting service department costs.

Illustrative Problem: Assigning Service Department Costs

Hartline Metal Products Company has six production departments. The company also has three supporting service departments. One is the Repairs and Maintenance (R & M) Department. Costs of the R & M

Table 25-2 Cost Allocation Bases for Assigning Costs of Supporting Service Functions	Possible Allocation Basis	When to Use It
	1. Number of service requests	Used when each service takes the same amount of time or when a record of service requests is maintained and no other basis is available
	2. Labor hours	Used when service labor hours are recorded for each service performed; a very good basis when the different services take different amounts of time
	3. Kilowatt hours used	Used to distribute the costs of a central power department maintained by the company
	4. Number of materials requisitions	Used to allocate costs of a materials storage area

Chapter Twenty-Five

Department are assigned to the six production departments on the basis of the number of service requests that each department makes. Costs incurred and charged against the R & M Department during February are as follows:

Supplies and parts	
Small tools	$ 1,850
Lubricants and supplies	940
Replacement parts	2,100
Labor	
Repair and maintenance	3,910
Supervision	1,600
Depreciation	
Equipment	1,290
Machinery	1,620
Other operating costs	2,440
Total costs for February	$15,750

The production departments made the following numbers of service requests during February: 16 requests by the Cutting Department, 21 by the Extruding Department, 8 by the Shaping Department, 31 by the Threading Department, 24 by the Polishing Department, and 25 by the Finishing Department.

Required

1. Using the number of service requests, prepare a schedule allocating the R & M Department's operating costs for February to the six production departments.
2. Name and discuss another possible allocation basis for assigning the R & M Department's costs to the six production departments.

Solution

1. The goal of this part of the problem is to see what portion of February R & M costs should be assigned to each production department. The specific dollar amounts are found by using a ratio of the benefits that each production department received to total benefits rendered by the R & M Department. Using the number of service requests as the cost allocation basis, we can approach this problem in two ways:

a. Find the average cost per request and multiply this amount by each department's number of service requests:

$$\frac{\text{total cost}}{\text{total service requests}} = \frac{\$15,750}{125} = \$126 \text{ per request}$$

R & M Department cost allocation for February:

To Cutting Department (16 × $126)	$ 2,016
To Extruding Department (21 × $126)	2,646
To Shaping Department (8 × $126)	1,008
To Threading Department (31 × $126)	3,906

To Polishing Department (24 × $126)	3,024
To Finishing Department (25 × $126)	3,150
Total costs allocated	$15,750

b. The other approach is to take the ratio of each department's requests to the total number of requests and multiply by the total costs to be allocated. R & M Department cost allocation for February:

To Cutting Department (16/125) ($15,750)	$ 2,016
To Extruding Department (21/125) ($15,750)	2,646
To Shaping Department (8/125) ($15,750)	1,008
To Threading Department (31/125) ($15,750)	3,906
To Polishing Department (24/125) ($15,750)	3,024
To Finishing Department (25/125) ($15,750)	3,150
Total costs allocated	$15,750

The allocations are the same by method **b** as by method **a**, as they should be.

2. Labor hours used would be another possible allocation basis. Time records can be kept for each service call. Then costs can be allocated by finding the average R & M Department cost per labor hour. This cost is then multiplied by the number of service labor hours used by each production department.

Accounting for Joint Production Costs

Objective 6
Allocate
common
manufacturing
costs to joint
products

Joint or common costs present a special need for cost allocation. A **joint cost** (or common cost) is one that relates to two or more products produced from a common input or raw material and that can be assigned only by means of arbitrary cost allocation after the products become identifiable. Joint products cannot be identified as separate products during most of the production process. Only at a particular point in the manufacturing process, called the **split-off point**, do separate products evolve from a common processing unit. Joint products are often found in industries such as petroleum refining, wood processing, and meat packing. In all these cases, more than one end product arises from a single kind of input.

In the beef processing industry, the final cuts of meat (steaks, roasts, hamburger) do not appear until the end of the process. However, the cost of the steer, transportation costs, storage and hanging costs, and labor costs have been incurred to get the side of beef ready for final butchering. How do we assign these joint costs to specific cuts of beef? This type of cost allocation is the objective of accounting for joint costs.

Figure 25-5 shows a joint production situation and the accounting problem of joint costs. The joint costs of $420,000 can be assigned to Product AAA and Product BBB in several ways. We outline the two most commonly used methods in the following paragraphs.

Figure 25-5
Joint
Production Cost
Allocation

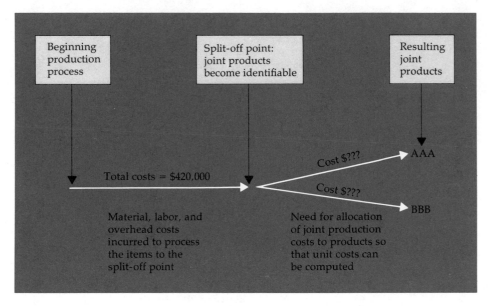

Physical Volume Method

One way to allocate joint production costs to specific products is called the **physical volume method.** This approach uses a measure of physical volume (units, pounds, liters, grams) as the basis for joint cost allocation. An example will show how the physical volume method applies to the problem in Figure 25-5.

Assume that the Leo Company makes two grades of paint from the same mixture of substances. During August, 75,000 liters of various ingredients were put into the production process. The final output for the month was 25,000 liters of Product AAA and 50,000 liters of Product BBB. Total joint production costs for August were $420,000. They were made up of $190,000 for direct materials, $145,000 for direct labor, and $85,000 for factory overhead. The joint products cannot be identified until the end of the production process. Product AAA sells for $9 per liter and Product BBB for $6 per liter.

Now let us use the physical volume method of assigning joint costs. We take total liters as the allocation basis. Then we apply a ratio of the physical volume of each product to total physical volume.

	Total Liters	Allocation Ratio	Joint Cost Allocation	
Product AAA	25,000	$\frac{25,000}{75,000}$ or $\frac{1}{3}$	$140,000	($420,000 × $\frac{1}{3}$)
Product BBB	50,000	$\frac{50,000}{75,000}$ or $\frac{2}{3}$	$280,000	($420,000 × $\frac{2}{3}$)
Totals	75,000		$420,000	

Product AAA generates $225,000 in revenues (25,000 liters at $9 per liter). Thus the net income for this product line will be $85,000. We compute this by subtracting $140,000 of assigned joint costs from the total revenues of $225,000. Product BBB sells for a total of $300,000 (50,000 liters at $6 per liter) and will show only a $20,000 profit ($300,000 minus $280,000 of assigned joint costs).

The physical volume method is easy to use. However, it often seriously distorts net income. This distortion results because the physical volume of joint products may not be in proportion to each product's ability to generate revenue. In our example, Product BBB's net income suffered because its high-volume content attracted two-thirds of the production costs even though its selling price was much less than Product AAA.

Relative Sales Value Method

A different way to allocate joint production costs depends on the relative sales value of the products. The **relative sales value method** allocates joint production costs to products in proportion to each product's ability to generate revenue. Extending the Leo Company data, we can make the following analysis. (Costs are assigned to joint products on the basis of their relative sales value when they first become identifiable as specific products—that is, at the split-off point.)

	Liters Produced	$\times$ Selling Price	= Sales Value at Split-off	Allocation Ratio	Joint Cost Allocation
Product AAA	25,000	$9.00	$225,000	$\dfrac{\$225,000}{\$525,000}$ or $\frac{3}{7}$	$180,000 ($420,000 $\times$ $\frac{3}{7}$)
Product BBB	50,000	6.00	300,000	$\dfrac{\$300,000}{\$525,000}$ or $\frac{4}{7}$	240,000 ($420,000 $\times$ $\frac{4}{7}$)
Totals	75,000		$525,000		$420,000

Product AAA has a relative sales value of $225,000 at split-off, and Product BBB's relative sales value totals $300,000. The resulting cost allocation ratios are 3/7 and 4/7, respectively, for Products AAA and BBB. Applying these ratios to the total joint cost of $420,000, we assign $180,000 to Product AAA and $240,000 to Product BBB.

If we compare the two joint cost allocation methods, we see a wide difference in gross income for the two product lines.

	Product AAA		Product BBB	
	Physical Volume Method	Relative Sales Value Method	Physical Volume Method	Relative Sales Value Method
Sales	$225,000	$225,000	$300,000	$300,000
Cost of sales	140,000	180,000	280,000	240,000
Gross profit	$ 85,000	$ 45,000	$ 20,000	$ 60,000
Gross profit as percent of sales	37.8%	20%	6.7%	20%

The major advantage of the relative sales value method is that it allocates joint costs according to a product's ability to absorb the cost. For this reason, equal gross profit percentages will always result when products are valued at the split-off point. Our example shows that under the relative sales value method, gross profit as a percentage of sales is 20 percent for both Product AAA and Product BBB.

As mentioned earlier, these approaches to assigning joint production costs are arbitrary. The reason for using arbitrary approaches is that it is difficult to determine just how the end products (cost objectives) specifically benefited from the incurrence of the cost. These approaches—whether the physical volume method or the relative sales value method—should be used only when it is impossible to tell how the cost benefited the cost objective. Most cost assignment methods used for determining product unit costs are based on a benefit relationship.

Responsibility Accounting

*Objective 7
Describe a
responsibility
accounting
system*

Reporting operating costs calls for special report formats and reporting techniques. The goal of the statement of cost of goods manufactured is to translate manufacturing cost data into information that can be used for inventory valuation, profit measurement, and external reporting purposes. As discussed in Chapter 22, all costs of materials, direct labor, and factory overhead are used to compute the cost of goods manufactured. However, management needs more than the data included in the statement of cost of goods manufactured. It also needs information and costs on many day-to-day activities. Budget preparation, revenue and cost recording, cost control, and managerial performance evaluation all call for a special system for collecting and reporting information.

Responsibility accounting provides for classifying and comparing reports of financial data according to specific areas of responsibility in a company. It is also called **activity accounting** or **profitability accounting**. A **responsibility accounting system** personalizes accounting reports. It classifies and reports cost and revenue information according to the defined responsibility areas of specific managers or management positions. Even though a company uses a responsibility accounting system, it still needs to collect normal cost and revenue data. It uses all the same recording practices, the same debit and credit entries, a general ledger, special journals, and a defined chart of accounts. However, responsibility accounting centers on the reporting—not the recording—of operating cost and revenue data. Once the financial data from daily operations have been recorded, specific costs and revenues can be reclassified and reported for specific areas of managerial responsibility.

Organizational Structure and Reporting

A responsibility accounting system is made up of several reporting centers. There is one for each area or level of managerial responsibility. The reports for each center include only those cost and revenue items that can be controlled by the manager of that center. If the manager cannot influence the amount of a certain cost or revenue item, that item is not included in the report. Because there is a report for each manager, and because lower-level managers report to higher-level managers, the same costs will appear in several reports. So lower-level operating data are included in reports to higher-level managers.

A look at a corporate organization chart and a series of reports will show us how a responsibility accounting system works. Figure 25-6 (below) shows a typical management hierarchy with three vice presidents under the corporate president. We have condensed the organization chart in the sales and finance areas to expand the manufacturing area. The production managers of Divisions A and B report to the vice president of manufacturing. Within Division B, the managers of the Stamping Department, Painting Department, and Assembly Department report to the division's production manager.

Figure 25-6
Organization
Chart Emphasizing the
Manufacturing
Area

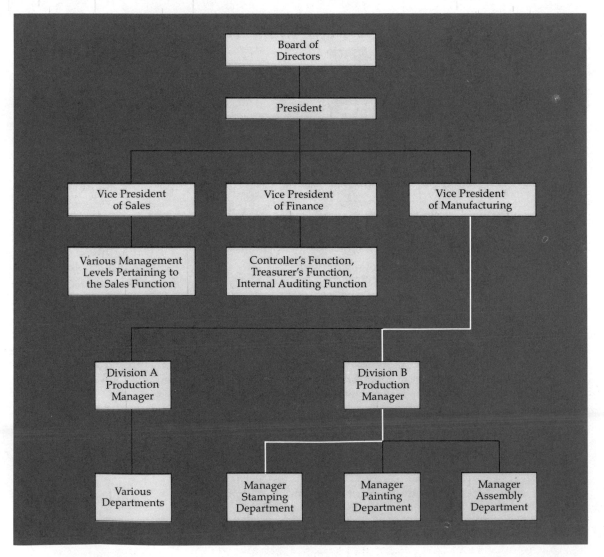

Chapter Twenty-Five

In responsibility accounting, operating reports for each level of management are tailored to individual needs. They focus on the cost and revenue items over which each manager has control. Figure 25-7 (next page) shows how the responsibility reporting network is tied together. At department level, the report gives a detailed listing of cost items under the control of the manager and compares expected (or budgeted) costs with actual costs to measure operating performance. The manager who receives the departmental report in Figure 25-7 should be particularly concerned with direct materials cost and maintenance salaries because they are so much over budget.

The production manager of Division B is responsible for the three operating departments plus the controllable division-wide costs. The production manager's report includes a summary of results from the Stamping Department as well as from all other areas of responsibility. However, at the division level, the report does not present detailed cost items. Only departmental totals appear. The data are even more condensed in the vice president's report. Only corporate and summarized divisional data on costs that can be controlled by the vice president are included. Note that the actual supplies cost at the departmental level is a part of the vice president's report (in the $399,400), but like all costs reported at higher levels, specific identity has been lost.

Cost and Revenue Controllability

Management wants the lowest possible costs and the highest possible profits. To accomplish these goals, management must know the origin of a cost or revenue item and be able to identify the person responsible for it. From a list of traceable costs that originate in a particular part of the company, responsibility accounting focuses on those costs that can be controlled by the individual manager.

A manager's **controllable costs** are those costs that result from his or her actions and decisions. If the manager can regulate or influence a cost or revenue item, the item is controllable at that level of operation. If managers have the authority to acquire or supervise the use of a certain resource or service, they control its cost.

Controllability is the key to a successful responsibility accounting system. By nature, it means that every cost incurred by a company can be traced to and controlled by at least one manager. Identifying controllable costs at lower management levels is often difficult. At lower levels, managers seldom have full authority to acquire or supervise the use of resources and services. They have only partial control and influence over costs. For this reason, managers themselves should help identify the costs for which they will be held accountable in their performance reviews. If cost and revenue items are controlled by the person responsible for the area where they originate, then an efficient, meaningful reporting system can be designed for measuring operating performance and pinpointing trouble spots.

Figure 25-7
Reporting
Within a
Responsibility
Reporting
System

Manufacturing: Vice President		Monthly Report: November	
Amount Budgeted	Controllable Cost	Actual Amount	Over (Under) Budget
	Central production		
$ 281,400	scheduling	$ 298,100	$16,700
179,600	Office expenses	192,800	13,200
19,800	Operating expenses	26,200	6,400
	Divisions		
339,500	A	348,900	9,400
→426,200	B	399,400	(26,800)
$1,246,500	Totals	$1,265,400	$18,900

Division B: Production Manager		Monthly Report: November	
Amount Budgeted	Controllable Cost	Actual Amount	Over (Under) Budget
	Division expenses		
$101,800	Salaries	$96,600	$ (5,200)
39,600	Utilities	39,900	300
25,600	Insurance	21,650	(3,950)
	Departments		
→46,600	Stamping	48,450	1,850
69,900	Painting	64,700	(5,200)
142,700	Assembly	128,100	(14,600)
$426,200	Totals	$399,400	$(26,800)

Stamping Department: Manager		Monthly Report: November	
Amount Budgeted	Controllable Cost	Actual Amount	Over (Under) Budget
$22,500	Direct materials	$23,900	$1,400
14,900	Factory labor	15,200	300
2,600	Small tools	1,400	(1,200)
5,100	Maintenance salaries	6,000	900
1,000	Supplies	1,200	200
500	Other costs	750	250
$46,600	Totals	$48,450	$1,850

Chapter Review

Review of Learning Objectives

1. Define and classify variable costs, semivariable costs, and fixed costs.

Variable costs are total costs that change in direct proportion to changes in productive output. Direct materials and direct labor are examples of variable costs. Semivariable costs act like both variable and fixed costs. That is, part of the cost is fixed and part changes with the volume of output. Examples are power costs and telephone charges. Total fixed costs remain constant within a relevant range of volume or activity. Examples of fixed costs include supervisory salaries and depreciation charges.

2. Compute the break-even point in units of output and in sales dollars.

The break-even point is that point where total revenue equals total costs incurred. In formula form, break-even occurs when $S = VC + FC$ (sales equals variable costs plus fixed costs). In terms of contribution margin, the formula is

$$BE \text{ units} = \frac{FC}{CM/unit}$$

Once the number of break-even units is known, it can be multiplied by the product's selling price to get the break-even point in dollars of sales.

3. Use contribution margin analysis to estimate levels of sales that will produce planned profits.

The addition of projected net income (NI) to the break-even equation makes it possible to plan levels of operation that yield target profits. The formula in terms of contribution margin is

$$\text{target unit sales} = \frac{FC + NI}{CM/unit}$$

4. State the role of cost objectives in the cost allocation process.

A cost objective is the destination of an assigned cost. The cost objective varies according to the focus of a particular report. It may range from the entire company or a division down to one particular product. Cost allocation is the process of assigning a specific cost to a specific cost objective. Cost objectives provide a target for the allocation process.

5. Assign costs of supporting service functions to production departments.

Costs incurred by supporting service departments must be accounted for as indirect manufacturing costs. They are allocated to production departments on a benefit basis—a beneficial relationship of cost to cost objective. Several allocation bases exist. Each is suitable for a certain relationship between the service used and the production department receiving the service.

6. Allocate common manufacturing costs to joint products.

Joint products evolve from a common processing unit. They cannot be identified as specific products until the split-off point in the process. All manufacturing costs incurred prior to the split-off point are shared by all the joint products. After the split-off point, costs are assigned to individual products by either the physical volume method or the relative sales value method.

7. Describe a responsibility accounting system.

Responsibility accounting classifies and compares reports of financial data according to specific areas of responsibility in a company. It is also called activity or profitability accounting. A responsibility accounting system personalizes accounting reports. It classifies and reports cost and revenue information according to the defined responsibility areas of specific managers or management positions. A responsibility accounting system is made up of several reports, one for each area of managerial responsibility.

Review Problem
Break-even/Profit Planning Analysis

Ortiz Organs, Inc., is a major producer of large pipe organs. Model SAM is a two-manual organ with a large potential market. Data from 19x3 operations for Model SAM are summarized below.

Variable costs per unit
Direct materials	$ 3,700
Direct labor	5,200
Factory overhead	2,600
Selling expenses	2,500

Total fixed costs
Factory overhead	$390,000
Advertising	110,000
Administrative expenses	136,000
Selling price per unit	$ 29,900

Management is pondering alternative courses of action for 19x4. Each alternative should be treated as an independent action and not tied to the other alternatives.

Required

1. Compute the 19x3 break-even point in units.
2. Calculate the amount of net income generated if 45 SAM models were sold in 19x3.
3. For 19x4:

    a. Calculate the number of units that must be sold to generate a $190,800 profit. Assume that costs and selling price remain constant.

    b. Calculate the net income if the company increases the number of units sold by 20 percent and cuts the selling price by $900 per unit.

    c. Figure the number of units that must be sold to break even if advertising is increased by $47,700.

    d. If variable costs are cut by 10 percent, find the number of units that must be sold to generate a profit of $315,500.

Answer to Review Problem

1. Break-even point in units computed for 19x3:

Variable costs per unit	$ 14,000
Contribution margin per unit:	
$29,900 − $14,000	15,900
Total fixed costs	$636,000

$$\text{Break-even point} = \frac{FC}{CM/unit} = \frac{\$636,000}{\$15,900} = 40 \text{ units}$$

2. Net income for 45 units calculated:

Units sold	45
Units required to break even	40
Units over break-even	5

19x3 net income = $15,900 per unit × 5 = $79,500

Contribution margin equals sales minus all variable costs. CM/unit equals the amount of sales dollars remaining, after variable costs have been subtracted, to cover fixed costs and provide a profit for the company. If all fixed costs have been absorbed by the time break-even is reached, the whole contribution margin of each unit sold in excess of break-even represents profit.

3. a. Number of units calculated to generate a given profit:

$$\text{unit sales} = \frac{FC + NI}{CM/\text{unit}}$$

$$= \frac{\$636,000 + \$190,800}{\$15,900} = \frac{\$826,800}{\$15,900} = 52 \text{ units}$$

3. b. Net income calculated under specified conditions:

Units to be sold = 45 × 120% = 54 units
New selling price = $29,000
Contribution margin = $29,000 − $14,000 = $15,000

$$\text{BE units} = \frac{\$636,000}{\$15,000} = 42.4 \text{ units}$$

Units to be sold in excess of break-even:

$$54 - 42.4 = 11.6 \text{ units}$$

Projected net income:

$$11.6 \text{ units} \times \$15,000/\text{unit} = \$174,000$$

3. c. Number of break-even units calculated under specified conditions:

$$\text{BE units} = \frac{\$636,000 + \$47,700}{\$15,900}$$

$$= \frac{\$683,700}{\$15,900} = 43$$

3. d. Number of units calculated to generate a given profit:

Variable costs per unit = $14,000 × .9 = $12,600
Contribution margin per unit = $29,900 − $12,600 = $17,300

$$\text{Unit sales} = \frac{\$636,000 + \$315,500}{\$17,300} = \frac{\$951,500}{\$17,300} = 55 \text{ units}$$

Chapter Assignments

Questions

1. What makes variable costs different from other costs?
2. "Fixed costs remain constant in total but decrease per unit as output increases." Explain this statement.
3. What is meant by the relevant range of activity?
4. Why is a telephone charge considered a semivariable cost?
5. What is the difference between practical capacity and ideal capacity?
6. Why does a company seldom operate at either ideal or practical capacity? What other expression of capacity is more relevant and useful? Why?
7. What is the relationship between cost-volume-profit analysis and the concept of cost behavior?
8. Define what the break-even point is. State why information on break-even is useful to management.

9. How does a corporate organization chart help in designing a responsibility accounting system?

10. Define controllable cost, and describe its role in a responsibility accounting system.

11. Define contribution margin. How is this concept useful?

12. State the equation that determines target unit sales, using the elements of fixed costs, net income, and contribution margin.

13. What conditions must be met for cost-volume-profit computations to be accurate?

14. What is a cost objective, and what is its role in cost accounting?

15. "As the size of the cost center or cost objective goes down, the ability to trace cost and revenue becomes more limited." Explain this statement.

16. What is a supporting service department? Give examples.

17. What is a joint manufacturing cost?

18. Describe the physical volume method of allocating joint costs to products. List the advantages and disadvantages of the physical volume method.

19. Should joint costs be allocated to a product on the basis of the product's ability to generate revenue? Explain your answer.

Classroom Exercises

**Exercise 25-1
Determination
of Fixed and
Variable Costs**
(L.O. 1)

From the following list of costs of productive output, indicate which are usually considered variable costs and which are fixed costs: (1) packing materials for stereo components, (2) real estate taxes, (3) gasoline for a delivery truck, (4) property insurance, (5) depreciation expense of buildings (straight-line method), (6) supplies, (7) indirect materials used, (8) bottles used in the sale of liquids, (9) license fees for company cars, (10) wiring used in radios, (11) machine helper's wages, (12) wood used in bookcases, (13) city operating license, (14) employer's share of social security payments, (15) machine operators' wages, (16) cost of required outside inspection on each unit produced. Could any of these costs be considered a semivariable cost? Explain.

**Exercise 25-2
Break-even
Analysis**
(L.O. 2)

Rivers Manufacturing Company makes head covers for golf clubs. The company expects to make a profit next year. It anticipates fixed manufacturing costs to be $97,000 and fixed general and administrative expenses to be $116,920 for the year. Variable manufacturing and selling costs per set of head covers will be $4.65 and $1.25, respectively. Each set will sell for $11.50.

1. Compute the break-even point in sales units.
2. Compute the break-even point in sales dollars.

**Exercise 25-3
Profit Planning**
(L.O. 2)

Short-term automobile rentals are the specialty of Carbondale Auto Loans, Inc. Average variable operating expenses have been $7.25 per day per automobile. The company owns thirty cars. Fixed operating costs for the next year are expected to be $75,050. Average daily rental revenue per automobile is expected to be $18.75. Management would like to earn $25,000 during the year.

1. Calculate the number of total *daily* rentals that the company must have during the year to earn the target profit.
2. On the basis of your answer to **1,** figure the number of days on the average that each automobile must be rented.
3. Find the total rental revenue for the year that is needed to earn the $25,000 profit.

Exercise 25-4
Contribution
Margin/Profit
Planning
(L.O. 3)

Basi Ballistics, Ltd., makes undersea missiles for nuclear submarines. The management has just been offered a government contract that may result in a profit for the company. The contract purchase price is $30,000 per unit, but the number of units to be purchased has not yet been decided. The company's fixed costs are budgeted at $3,975,000, and the variable costs per unit are $18,500.

Compute the number of units at the stated contract price that the company should agree to make to earn a target income of $15,000,000.

Exercise 25-5
Cost Allocation
Basis
(L.O. 4)

A plan for cost assignment is vital to corporate reporting, product costing, and inventory valuation. Examples of costs and related cost objectives are listed below.

Cost	Cost Objective
Materials-handling costs	Product
Plant depreciation costs	Division
Repair and maintenance department costs	One of five production departments served
Corporate president's salary	Division

1. Which costs would be direct costs of the related cost objective? Which would be indirect costs?
2. For each indirect cost, choose a cost allocation basis that provides a logical relationship between the cost and the cost objective. Defend your answers.

Exercise 25-6
Cost Reclassifi-
cation—Direct
Versus Indirect
(L.O. 4)

Classifying a cost as direct or indirect depends on the cost objective. Depreciation of a factory building is a direct cost when the plant is the cost objective. But when the cost objective is a product, the depreciation cost becomes indirect.

For the costs listed below, indicate for each cost objective whether it would be an indirect cost (I) or a direct cost (D). Be able to defend your answers.

	Cost Objective		
	Division	Department	Product
Direct labor			
Departmental supplies			
Division head's salary			
President's salary			
Department manager's salary			
Direct materials			
Fire insurance on specific machine			
Property taxes, division plant			
Department repairs and maintenance			

Exercise 25-7
Service
Department
Cost Allocation
(L.O. 5)

National Polygraphics, Inc., has six departments that must share the services of a single central computer. Management has decided that the best basis for cost allocation is the minutes of computer time used by each department. Usage by department for the first week in June was as follows: 1,548 minutes for Department A, 2,064 for Department B, 2,280 for Department C, 1,032 for Department

D, 516 for Department E, and 2,580 for Department F. The total for all departments was 10,020 minutes. The total cost of operating the computer during the month was $4,650.

Determine the computer expense to be assigned to each department for the one-week period.

Exercise 25-8
Joint Cost
Allocation—
Physical
Volume
Method
(L.O. 6)

Molasses and refined sugar are joint products made from a common material, the juice extracted from sugar cane. The Maui Corporation makes both products at the same time. It has decided to use the physical volume method to assign the common or joint costs to the two products. The allocation base is liters. During February, Maui Corporation put 620,000 liters of sugar cane juice into the production process. The final products from this input were 93,000 liters of molasses and 527,000 liters of refined sugar. The following joint product costs were incurred during the month of February: $1,820 for materials, $4,620 for direct labor, and $5,760 for factory overhead. So total joint costs amounted to $12,200.

Assuming no loss through evaporation, assign a portion of joint production costs to each product.

Exercise 25-9
Joint Cost
Allocation—
Relative Sales
Value Method
(L.O. 6)

In the processing of pulp for making paper, two distinct grades of wood pulp come out of a common crushing and mixing process. Peoria Paper Products, Inc., produced 22,000 liters of pulp during January. Direct materials inputs cost the company $43,000. Labor and overhead costs for the month were $28,000 and $18,000, respectively. Output for the month was as follows:

Product	Quantity	Market Value at Split-off
Grade A pulp	14,000 liters	$7.00 per liter
Grade B pulp	8,000 liters	$5.25 per liter

Using the relative sales value method, allocate the production costs to Grade A pulp and Grade B pulp.

Interpreting Accounting Information

Internal
Management
Information:
Godeke Food
Products
(L.O. 7)

The Food Packing and Storage Department at Godeke Food Products Company is run by Joan Samsvick. A responsibility accounting system has recently been installed, and a performance report is prepared monthly for each of the company's cost centers.

Ms. Samsvick's performance report for May is shown on the next page. Top management sees that the overage of $2,935 is 8.04 percent over budget, far above the 4 percent tolerance that was agreed upon. Amounts allocated to the Food Packing and Storage Department were figured by means of appropriate allocation bases.

Required

1. Using the concept of controllable costs, identify the costs that should not be in Ms. Samsvick's performance report.
2. Recast the performance report using only those costs controllable by the department's supervisor.
3. How should Ms. Samsvick respond to top management?

Godeke Food Products Company
Performance Report
Food Packing and Storage Department
For the Month Ended May 31, 19xx

Amount Budgeted	Cost Item	Actual Amount	Over (Under) Budget
$ 3,500	Packing materials	$ 3,600	$100
1,800	Packing supplies	1,700	(100)
8,240	Wages—packing	8,110	(130)
5,680	Wages—storage	5,820	140
4,500	Salaries—packing and storage	4,500	—
1,600	Salaries—Vice President's staff	3,100	1,500
1,840	Depreciation, packing machinery	1,820	(20)
3,200	Depreciation, storage warehouse	3,200	—
1,250	Depreciation, company-wide office building	2,500	1,250
870	Electric power—packing and storage	910	40
490	Electric power—main office	580	90
575	Heating—packing and storage	600	25
380	Heating—main office	420	40
780	Equipment rental—packing	750	(30)
410	Equipment rental—main office	450	40
290	Insurance expense—packing and storage	290	—
160	Insurance expense—total company	180	20
460	Equipment maintenance expense— packing and storage	440	(20)
220	Lift truck expense—packing and storage	200	(20)
250	Miscellaneous expense	260	10
$36,495	Totals	$39,430	$2,935

Problem Set A

**Problem 25A-1
Break-even
Analysis
(L.O. 2)**

The accounting department of High Intensity, Ltd., must find the point every year at which projected sales revenue will equal total budgeted variable and fixed costs. The company makes custom-made, durable seals for aircraft and space vehicles. Each seal sells for an average of $369. Variable costs per unit are $205. Total fixed costs are estimated to be $164,000.

Required

1. Compute the break-even point in sales units.
2. Compute the break-even point in sales dollars.

3. Find the new break-even point in sales units if the fixed costs should go up by $4,920.

4. Using the original figures, compute the break-even point in sales units if the selling price decreases to $365 per unit, fixed costs go up by $17,400, and variable costs decrease by $19 per unit.

Problem 25A-2
Allocation
Process—
Cost-Base
Relationship
(L.O. 4)

Below are five types of costs for a typical manufacturing company. Each cost is allocated to a cost objective.

Type of Cost	Cost Objective
1. Cost of corporate computer center	Production departments
2. Depreciation of division factory buildings	Production departments
3. Tool and die making cost (service department)	Production departments
4. Material storage costs	Products
5. Repairs and maintenance department costs	Production departments

A number of allocation bases could be used to assign the costs listed above to their respective cost objectives. They include (a) direct labor dollars, (b) direct labor hours, (c) machine hours, (d) facility or service usage hours, (e) direct materials costs, (f) square footage, and (g) number of service requests.

Required

1. For each of the five types of costs, select the allocation base that best expresses the beneficial relationship between the cost and the cost objective. State the reasons for your answers.

2. What would be wrong with including all these costs in one overhead cost pool and allocating them to production departments on the basis of direct labor dollars? What would be the advantage of such an approach?

Problem 25A-3
Profit
Planning—
Contribution
Margin
Approach
(L.O. 3)

Jewel Cobb is president of the Fullerton Plastics Division of CSU Industries. Management is considering a new product line that features a large elephant posed in a running posture. Called "Ramblin Titan", this product is expected to have worldwide market appeal and become the mascot for many high school and university athletic teams. Expected variable unit costs are as follows: direct materials, $4.45; direct labor, $2.74; production supplies, $.21; selling costs, $1.90; other, $1.45. The following are annual fixed costs: depreciation, building and equipment, $13,000; advertising, $32,500; other, $5,755. The company plans to sell the product for $27.50.

Required

1. Using the contribution margin approach, compute the number of products the company must sell to (a) break even and (b) earn a profit of $35,175.

2. Continuing with the same approach, compute the number of products that must be sold to earn a target profit of $70,115 if advertising costs rise by $20,000.

3. Assuming the original information and sales of 10,000 units, compute the new selling price that the company must use to make $65,745 profit.

4. According to the vice president of marketing, Irene Lange, the most optimistic annual sales estimate for the product would be 25,000 items. How much more can be spent on fixed advertising costs if the highest possible selling price that the company can charge is $23.25, if the variable costs cannot be reduced, and if target net income for 25,000 unit sales is $125,500?

Problem 25A-4
Service
Department
Expense
Allocation
(L.O. 5)

Hausmaninger Community Hospital has one respirator that must be shared by the hospital's six departments. To judge efficiency and to aid in future budgeting, each department's operating income or loss is figured separately each month. Before these calculations can be made, expenses that are considered "common" expenses must be allocated to each of the departments. Depreciation and maintenance expenses connected directly to the respirator are allocated to the departments according to hours of usage.

The costs for upkeep of the respirator for October are as follows: Depreciation was $550 on the respirator and $120 on supplemental machinery. Labor costs were $3,000 for the operator and $900 for maintenance. Materials costs were $1,600 for oxygen, $240 for small replacement parts, $480 for supplies, and $310 for other operating costs. Thus total costs for October were $7,200.

The respirator usage by department for October was as follows: 86.5 hours for the Oncology Department, 16.3 hours for the Orthopedic Department, 44.1 hours for the Nephrology Department, 36.9 hours for the Geriatric Department, 18.7 hours for the Pediatric Department, and 37.5 hours for the Maternity Department.

Required

1. Assign the respirator costs for October to each of the six departments according to hourly usage.
2. Explain other bases of allocation that could be used to assign costs in this case. Discuss the advantages and disadvantages of each allocation basis.

Problem 25A-5
Joint Cost
Allocation
(L.O. 6)

Three distinct grades of ice cream are made by the High Cal Ice Cream Company. The initial ingredients for all three grades of ice cream are first blended together. After this blending, other ingredients are added to produce the three separate grades. The Extra-Rich blend sells for $2.10 per liter. The Quality blend sells for $1.80 per liter. And the Regular blend sells for $1.50 per liter. In July, 744,000 liters of ingredients were put into production, with output as follows: 163,680 liters of Extra-Rich blend, 297,600 liters of Quality blend, and 282,720 liters of Regular blend. Joint costs for the period are made up of $150,600 for direct materials, $123,000 for direct labor, and $98,400 for factory overhead. Assume that there were no beginning or ending inventories and that there was no loss of input during production.

Required

1. Using the physical volume method, allocate joint costs to the three ice cream blends.
2. Using the relative sales value method, allocate joint costs to each of the three blends.
3. Prepare a schedule that compares the gross profit at split-off point that results from the two allocation methods for the three products. Compute gross profit both in total dollars and as a percentage of sales.
4. Additional processing costs could be incurred after split-off for a special ingredient for the Extra-Rich blend that would push up its selling price. If the company incurred $40,920 for this ingredient in this period, it is felt that the selling price could be increased to $2.50 per liter. Following these assumptions, how much profit would be earned from Extra-Rich sales? Should the company add the extra ingredient?

Problem Set B

**Problem 25B-1
Break-even
Analysis
(L.O. 2)**

Making plastic pipes for sprinkler systems involves mixing chemicals and mold-ing the pipes. Deborah Products, Inc., makes pipes of different diameters, all in 5-meter lengths. The 1.9-centimeter pipe has variable costs per 5-meter section of $.08 for raw materials, $.06 for direct labor, and $.05 for factory overhead costs. Total variable costs are thus $.19. Fixed costs for the 1.9-centimeter pipe are expected to be $67,855 for the year. The projected selling price is $.60 per 5-meter section.

Required

1. Compute the break-even point in sales units.
2. Compute the break-even point in sales dollars.
3. Find the unit break-even point if management could cut fixed costs by $2,665 while maintaining the same selling price.
4. Using the original information, figure the break-even point in units if the sell-ing price were $.70 per unit, fixed costs fell by $7,855, and variable costs per unit fell by $.02.

**Problem 25B-2
Allocation
Process—
Cost-Base
Relationship
(L.O. 4)**

Below are four kinds of costs for a typical manufacturing company. Each cost is allocated to a cost objective.

Type of Cost	Cost Objective
1. Materials handling costs Labor costs of truck drivers, depreciation on trucks and other equip-ment, fuel costs, operating supplies.	Production department
2. Departmental overhead costs Each employee runs one machine, and all employees earn similar wages.	Product
3. Departmental overhead costs Each employee runs 20 to 25 machines at the same time.	Product
4. Departmental overhead costs Each employee runs one machine, and there are wide differences in hourly wage rates.	Product

The allocation bases that might be used to assign these costs to cost objectives are (a) direct labor dollars, (b) machine hours, (c) materials costs, (d) direct labor hours, and (e) square footage.

Required

1. For each of the four cost categories, choose the allocation base that best expresses the beneficial relationship between the cost and the cost objective. Discuss your reasoning.
2. Some companies group all of the costs listed above in one factory overhead cost "pool" and allocate them to products using just one allocation base such as direct labor dollars. What are the advantages and disadvantages of this approach?

**Problem 25B-3
Profit
Planning—
Contribution
Margin
Approach
(L.O. 3)**

St. Louis Industries makes portable microwave ovens. The ovens are costly to produce because of their intricate parts and the skilled craftsmanship needed to assemble them. A less expensive, slightly different model is being considered to reach the lower-income market. The estimates are as follows: variable costs per oven of $90, total fixed costs of $330,000, and a tentative selling price per oven of $260.

Required

1. Using the contribution margin approach, find the number of ovens the company will need to sell to make a profit of $97,000.

2. Continuing with the same approach and raising fixed costs to $420,000, find the number of ovens that must be sold to reach the target profit of $105,000.

3. Assuming the original information and sales of 4,200 ovens, compute the new selling price that the company should use to make a $426,000 profit.

4. The marketing vice president says that maximum sales for the new, less expensive ovens are likely to be 19,800 units. If the highest possible selling price that the company can charge is $290, if variable costs per unit cannot be reduced below the original estimates, and if the new target profit is $140,000, how much more can be spent on fixed advertising costs?

Problem 25B-4
Service Department Expense Allocation
(L.O. 5)

Melcher Appliance Company owns and maintains a company aircraft. The company has six divisions, each operated as an independent unit. To aid in judging performance, net income is figured monthly for each division. Before doing that, common corporate expenses must be allocated to the six divisions. Maintenance and depreciation costs for the aircraft are assigned to the various divisions according to the hours of usage.

The aircraft department is a supporting service. Its costs in March are as follows: Depreciation costs were $2,500 for aircraft, $2,100 for building, and $700 for machinery. Labor costs were $2,400 for supervision and $8,000 for maintenance. Materials costs were $650 for small tools, $490 for supplies, and $2,160 for parts. Fuel cost was $6,800. Other operating costs amounted to $1,500. Total costs for March came to $27,300.

Divisional usage of the aircraft in March was as follows: 8.6 hours for the TV Division, 10.9 for the Refrigerator Division, 0.8 for the Stove Division, 42.4 for the Oven Division, 19.0 for the Dishwasher Division, and 9.3 for the Stereo and CB Division.

Required

1. Using hours of usage, allocate the aircraft department's operating costs for March to the six divisions.

2. Discuss other cost allocation bases that could be used to assign costs in this case. Discuss the merits and disadvantages of each allocation basis.

Problem 25B-5
Joint Cost Allocation
(L.O. 6)

The chemicals used by the Winnebago County Ink Company to produce three grades of printer's ink are first mixed together in a common production process. After four hours of mixing, the solution separates into three distinct grades of ink. Grade AA sells for $25 per liter, Grade BB sells for $20 per liter, and Grade CC sells for $10 per liter. During September, 48,000 liters of chemical were put into production. With no loss of materials, output for the month was 6,000 liters of Grade AA, 18,000 liters of Grade BB, and 24,000 liters of Grade CC. Cost data for September are $290,000 for direct materials, $205,000 for direct labor, and $65,000 for factory overhead. Thus total joint costs were $560,000 for the month. Assume that there were no beginning or ending work in process inventories. All three products are ready for sale at the split-off point.

Required

1. Using the physical volume method, figure the amount of joint costs to be assigned to each of the three product groups.

2. Using the relative sales value method, allocate the joint costs to the three product groups.

3. Compare the gross profits (both in total dollars and as a percentage of sales) resulting from the two allocation methods for each product group.

4. Product CC can either be sold at split-off or processed further. For the period under review, the product could have sold for $14 per liter if the company had incurred $72,000 more in processing costs. Should the company have processed Product CC beyond split-off? Defend your answer.

Management Decision Case 25-1

American State Bank (L.O. 5, 7)

Rockford Bancorp is the parent corporation for two regional banks, American State Bank and National State Bank. The American State Bank is the responsibility of its president, Mr. Harry Richards. Four senior vice presidents report to him and coordinate the activities of Marketing, Operations, Commercial Loans, and Investments. In addition, the Internal Audit Division reports directly to the Board of Directors. Within the Operations area, there are five departments, as follows:

Departments	Functions
Controller's Department:	General ledger maintenance Assistant Controller Special cost and revenue analyses
Data Processing Department:	Programming Systems Design Data Entry Computer Operators Systems Maintenance
Customer Service Department:	Tellers New account representatives Customer concerns
Bookkeeping Department:	Customer statement preparation Telephone and wire dollar transfers Service and vault charges
Proof Department:	Proving of bulk deposits Internal check clearinghouse

The Customer Service Department is considered the primary department of this division, with the remaining four being supporting service departments.

According to the controller's department, fixed costs of the division are shared by all five departments and should, therefore, be grouped together in a fixed overhead cost pool and allocated based on total salary dollars. During 19xx, the entire division expects to pay $600,000 in salaries. Projected costs to be charged to the fixed overhead cost pool include:

Depreciation, furniture & fixtures	$12,900
Telephone charges	$320/month plus $100/month for long-distance calls
Property taxes	$9,620
Electricity expense	$410/month plus $.001 per kilowatt hour of usage[1]
Rent, buildings	$18,000
Insurance expense	$5,980

Gas heating expense	$520/month plus $.005 per cubic foot of gas consumption[2]	
Equipment leasing expense	$82,500	

1. 46,400,000 kilowatt hours are expected to be used.
2. 1,640,000 cubic feet of gas are expected to be consumed.

Required

1. Compute the fixed overhead cost rate for the Operations Division for 19xx.
2. During 19xx, the departments incurred the following salary costs:

Controller's	$118,240
Data Processing	186,460
Customer Service	139,700
Bookkeeping	83,200
Proof	68,500

Determine the amount of fixed overhead costs that were allocated to each department during the year.
3. Ms. K. A. Anderson, manager of the Data Processing Department, received a performance report for the year ending December 31, 19xx, as shown below. How good was Ms. Anderson's performance? Critique the performance report as part of your answer.

The American State Bank
Operations Division
Data Processing Department
Performance Report
For the Year Ended December 31, 19xx

Budget	Cost/Expense Item	Actual	Over (Under) Budget
$ 48,000	Salaries, programmers	$ 47,530	$ (470)
48,000	Salaries, system designers	42,540	(5,460)
60,000	Salaries, computer operators	63,910	3,910
32,000	Salary, manager	32,480	480
12,810	Salaries, bank administration	18,760	5,950
82,500	Equipment leasing	86,440	3,940
15,000	Computer supplies	14,210	(790)
40,000	Software purchases	36,740	(3,260)
3,000	Data storage diskettes	3,280	280
2,460	Depreciation, furniture & fixtures	2,460	—
45,120	Fixed divisional overhead	55,938	10,818
13,500	Back-up data file maintenance	12,770	(730)
5,000	Bank-wide overhead	5,250	250
2,000	Miscellaneous expenses	1,640	(360)
$409,390	Totals	$423,948	$14,558

Chapter
Twenty-Six

Budgetary
Control:
The Planning
Function

1. *Identify the five
groups of budgeting
principles, and explain
the principles in each
group.*
2. *Define the concept of
budgetary control.*
3. *Identify the compo-
nents of a master
budget, and describe
how they are related to
each other.*
4. *Prepare a period
budget.*
5. *Describe the purpose
and make-up of a cash
budget.*
6. *Prepare a cash
budget.*
7. *Describe the unique
aspects of the budgeting
process in not-for-profit
and public-sector
organizations.*

The budgetary control process includes cost planning and cost control. In this chapter the focus is on cost planning. We outline the principles of budgeting, which deal with long-term and short-term goals, human responsibilities, housekeeping, and follow-up. Using these principles along with a number of cost accounting tools explained earlier in the book, we describe the preparation of period budgets, the master budget, and the cash budget.

To plan effectively and to meet goals, both profit-oriented and not-for-profit organizations must prepare budgets. A special section at the end of this chapter deals with budgeting for organizations in the public sector (federal, state, and municipal governments) and not-for-profit organizations such as clubs, charities, and private schools. As a result of studying this chapter, you should be able to meet the learning objectives listed on the left.

Basic Principles of Budgeting

The preparation of an organization's budget is the single most important aspect of its success. First, it forces management to look ahead and try to see the future of the organization, in terms of both long-term and short-term goals and events. Second, it requires that the whole management team, from the lowest-level supervisor to the chairman of the board of directors, work together to make and carry out the yearly plans. Finally, by comparing the budget with actual results it is possible to review performance at all levels of management. The principles of effective budgeting are summarized in Figure 26-1. Each group of principles will be explained further to show how closely connected all of the principles are to the whole budgeting process.

Long-Range Goals Principles

Annual operating plans cannot be made unless those responsible for preparing the budget know the direction that top management expects for the organization. Long-range goals must be set by top

Figure 26-1
Principles of
Effective
Budgeting

Group A: Long-Range Goals Principles
1. Develop long-range goals for the enterprise.
2. Convert the long-range goals into statements about long-range plans for product lines or services offered and associated profit plans in broad quantitative terms.

Group B: Short-Range Goals and Strategies Principles
3. Restate the long-range plan in terms of short-range plans for product lines or services available and a detailed profit plan.
4. Prepare a set of budget development plans and a specific timetable for the whole period.

Group C: Human Responsibilities and Interaction Principles
5. Identify the budget director and staff.
6. Identify all participants in budget development.
7. Practice participative budgeting.
8. Obtain the full support of top management and communicate this support to budget participants.
9. Practice full communications during entire budgeting process.

Group D: Budget Housekeeping Principles
10. Practice realism in the preparation of all budgets.
11. Require that all budget preparation deadlines be met.
12. Use flexible application procedures.

Group E: Follow-up Principles
13. Maintain a continuous budgeting process and monitor the budget through out the period.
14. Develop a system of periodic performance reports that are linked to assigned responsibilities.
15. Review problem areas to be studied before further planning takes place.

*Objective 1
Identify the five
groups of
budgeting
principles, and
explain the
principles in
each group*

management. Statements about the expected quality of products or services and about growth rates and percentage-of-market targets are among the long-range goals. Economic and industry forecasts, employee-management relationships, and the structure and role of top management in leading the organization also bear on these goals.

It is necessary to name those responsible for achieving the long-term goals and to set actual targets and expected timetables. For example, Fairways Corporation has, as one of its long-term goals, the control of 15 percent of its product's market. At present the company holds only 4 percent of the market. The company's long-term goals may state that the vice president of marketing is to develop plans and strategies so that the company controls 10 percent of the market in five years and increases its share to 15 percent by the end of ten years.

Once all of the organization's goals have been developed, they should be brought together into a total long-range plan. This plan should state a broad range of targets and goals and give direction to management in trying to reach them. Specific statements about long-term goals, then, are the basis for preparing the annual budget.

Short-Range Goals and Strategies Principles

Using long-range goals, management must prepare yearly operating plans and targets. The short-range plan or budget involves every part of the enterprise and is much more detailed than are the long-range goals. The first order of business each year is to restate the long-range goals in terms of what should be accomplished during the year. Statements must be made about sales targets by product or service line, profit expectations by division or product line, personnel needs and expected changes, and plans for introducing new products or services. Budget statements must also cover materials and supplies needs, forecasts of overhead costs such as electric power needs and expected costs of property taxes and insurance, and all capital expenditures such as new buildings, machinery, and equipment. These short-range targets and goals are woven together to form the organization's operating budget for the year.

A very important part of the process described above is the approach to collecting and processing the information that goes into the annual budget. Once the short-range goals are set by management, the controller or budget director takes charge of preparing the budget. He or she designs a complete set of budget development plans and a timetable with deadlines for all levels and parts of the year's operating plan. Specific people must be named to carry out each part of the budget's development and their responsibilities, targets, and deadlines clearly described. The last step in the budget's development is to clearly communicate the plan to the participants. It may seem all too obvious that everyone should be fully aware of the need for and importance of budget development. But do not forget that each of the participants in the budgeting process has another job in the organization. The production supervisor, for instance, is most interested in what is happening on the production floor. Thinking about the next year's activities does not help to meet the current month's production targets. The same can be said for the district sales managers, financial and cost accounting people, and the rest of the staff. It is the budget director's responsibility to organize all of the budget information, and a key part of that process is making sure each participant knows what he or she is expected to do and when the information is due.

Human Responsibilities and Interaction Principles

Budgeting success or failure is, in large part, determined by how well the human aspects of the process are handled. From top management down to the lowest-level supervisor in the organization, *all* appropriate people must take part actively and honestly if the process is to be successful. To get this kind of cooperation, each person must feel very much like an important link in the organizational chain.

Choosing a budget director (and staff if necessary) is very important to an effective budgeting system. This person must be able to communicate well with the people both above and below in the organization. Top management gives the budget targets and organizational goals to the budget director. This person in turn assigns those targets and goals to managers at various levels. The managers then try to put into operation the goals and targets that have been assigned to them. Problem areas found by the managers are communicated to the budget director who, after careful analysis, must pass the information on to top management. The targets and goals are then reassessed, restructured, and passed back to the budget director, and the process begins all over again. Since the budget director acts as an information-gathering center and clearing house for the budgeting process, this person is the key to its success.

All participants in the budget development process should be identified and told early of their responsibilities in the program. The identification process begins with high-level managers. These people must then identify lower-level managers under their supervision who will actually prepare the data. At the lower levels, the organization's main activities take place, whether they are production, sales, health care, or education. From these managers, the information must flow through all the supervisory levels up to the top management. Each one of these people plays a part in developing the budget and putting it to work. It is the budget director's job to coordinate all of the budgeting activities of the different managers.

Participative budgeting means that all levels of supervisory and data input personnel take part in the budgeting process in a meaningful, active way. If every manager has had significant input into the goals and expectations of his or her unit, personal motivation has been woven into the budgeting process. This sort of interaction and cooperation is what participative budgeting is all about.

Top management's role is also very important to the budgeting process. If top management simply dictates and sends down targets and goals for others to carry out, participative budgeting is not being practiced. Such dictated targets are often hard to attain and do not motivate lower-level managers to try to reach them. Similarly, if top management simply lets the budget director handle everything, the other managers are likely to feel that budgeting has a low priority and may not take it seriously. To have an effective budgeting program, top management must communicate its support and enthusiasm to all levels of management and allow the managers to take part in a meaningful way. If this happens, the principle of practicing full communication has also been followed.

Budget Housekeeping Principles

In terms of "housekeeping," the budget process depends heavily on three things. First, a realistic approach must be taken by the participants. Second, all deadlines must be met. Third, the organization must use flexible application procedures.

Realism is a two-way street. Top management must first suggest realistic targets and goals. Then each manager must provide realistic information and not place departmental goals ahead of the goals of the whole organization. Inflated expenditure plans or deflated sales targets in one or two cases may make life easier for a manager's unit. However, they can cause the entire budget to be inaccurate and hard to use as a guide and control mechanism for the organization as a whole.

The reason for having and meeting budget development deadlines is clear. Budget preparation depends on the timely cooperation of many people. If one or two people ignore a deadline for submitting information to their supervisor or to the budget director, the budget will not be ready on time. Top management should communicate the importance of the budget development timetable to all participants and should review timely budget data submission as part of each manager's performance evaluation.

Budgets are important guides to the actions of management. However, they should always be treated as "guides" and not as "absolute truths." Remember that budgets are prepared almost a year in advance of the actual operating cycle. During that time, certain unexpected changes may take place. A manager cannot simply ignore these changes just because they were not a part of the budget. Instead, a means of dealing with revenue and expenditure changes should be worked out as part of budget implementation. A procedure for notifying the budget director of a change and receiving approval for it takes care of the matter and does not upset the performance of the manager's operating unit.

Follow-up Principles

Budget follow-up is really part of the control aspect of budgetary control and will be explained further in Chapter 27. The follow-up principles play an important role in budgeting. Since we are dealing with projections and estimates as the budget is being developed, it is important that the budget be checked continuously and corrected whenever necessary. If a budget is found to be in error, it makes more sense to correct the error than to work with a less accurate guide.

Organizational or departmental expectations can also be unrealistic. Such problems are found when performance reports are used to compare actual results with budgeted or planned operating results. These reports are the backbone of the responsibility accounting system presented in Chapter 25. The budgeting cycle is complete when problems are identified in the performance evaluation of the last budgeting cycle and are analyzed and restructured to become targets or goals of the next budgeting cycle.

The Need for Budgetary Control and Planning

Objective 2
Define the
concept of
budgetary
control

Planning and control of costs and operations are the keys to good management. The process of (1) developing plans for a company's expected operations and (2) controlling operations to help carry out those plans is known as **budgetary control.** In Chapter 25, you studied cost behavior patterns and cost-volume-profit analysis, which are two of the tools used in developing a company's annual budget and profit goals. Profit planning is very important to all successful profit-oriented companies as part of their budgeting program. In this chapter we will deal mainly with the planning element.

A successful business does not reap the benefits of effective budgetary control by operating in a haphazard way from day to day. The company must set quantitative goals, define the roles of individuals, and set intermediate operating targets. These are the first steps in the planning process. Companies begin by making both long-term and short-term operating plans.

First, they must prepare and maintain a long-term plan covering a five- or ten-year period. Such plans are general. They usually describe product line changes, expansion of plant and facilities, machinery replacement, and changes in marketing strategies. Long-term plans are important because they provide broad goals to work toward through yearly operations.

Yearly operating plans do not automatically grow out of long-term plans. Even though long-term plans provide broad goals, they do not contain specific instructions on how to get the expected results through annual production and sales efforts. Given the five- or ten-year plan, management must translate long-term objectives into more specific goals for each year. Once the goals have been defined for the next accounting period, various levels of managers must work out in detail the operations needed to meet them. This task centers on a one-year time period and stated targets.

Short term or one-year plans are generally formulated in a set of period budgets (also known as detailed operating budgets). A **period budget** is a forecast of a year's operating results for a segment of a company. It is a quantitative expression of planned activities. Period budgets are prepared by the whole management team. They require timely information and careful coordination. This process converts unit sales and production forecasts into revenue and cost estimates for each of the many operating segments of the company. Everyone involved in budgeting should take care to make these forecasts as accurate and realistic as possible.

Period budget preparation relies heavily on several management accounting tools already discussed. Knowledge of cost behavior patterns and the use of cost-volume-profit analysis help management project departmental or product-line revenue and cost amounts. Profit planning, in itself, is possible only after all cost behavior patterns have been identified. Responsibility accounting, with its network of managerial responsibilities and information flows, provides a blueprint for the structure of the budget-data gathering process. These tools, together with the concepts of cost allocation and cost accumulation, provide the foundation for preparing an organization's budget.

The Master Budget

A **master budget** is a combined set of departmental or functional period budgets that have been consolidated into forecasted financial statements

Objective 3
Identify the
components of a
master budget,
and describe
how they are
related to each
other

for the whole company. Each of the separate budgets gives the projected costs and revenues for that part of the company. When they are combined, these budgets show all anticipated transactions of the company for a future accounting period. With this information, the anticipated results of the company's operations can be put together with the beginning general ledger balances to prepare forecasted statements of the company's net income and financial position for the time period.

Three steps lead up to the completed master budget. (1) The period budgets are prepared. (2) The forecasted income statement is prepared. (3) The forecasted balance sheet is prepared. After describing each of these components, we will explain how the budgets are prepared.

Relationships Among the Period Budgets

Period budgets are generally prepared for each departmental or functional cost and revenue producing segment of a company. These budgets are usually the following: (1) sales (in units), (2) production (in units), (3) selling expenses, (4) direct materials purchases, (5) direct materials usage, (6) labor hour requirements, (7) direct labor dollars, (8) factory overhead, (9) general and administrative (G&A) expenses, and (10) capital expenditures.

These budgets are closely related to each other. Following the sales unit forecast, the production budget can be prepared. The selling expense budget also depends on the sales forecast. Direct materials usage and resulting purchase requirements are related to the production forecast. The production budget also leads to the labor and factory overhead budgets. In most cases, plans for general and administrative expenses and capital expenditures are made by top management. However, much of this information may be gathered at the departmental level and included in these period budgets. The key point to remember is that the whole budgeting process begins with the sales unit forecast. Figure 26-2 shows how these period budgets set the stage for determining the effects of planned operations on the company's financial position.

Forecasted Income Statement

Once the period budgets have been prepared, the controller or the budget director can begin to put all the information together. He or she prepares a cost of goods sold forecast from data in the direct materials, direct labor, and factory overhead budgets. Revenue information is figured from the unit sales budget. Using the expected revenue and cost of goods sold data, and adding the information from the selling expense and general and administrative expense budgets, the controller can prepare the forecasted income statement. This step is also shown in Figure 26-2.

Financial Position Forecast

The last step in the master budget process is to prepare a financial position forecast or projected balance sheet for the company, assuming that planned activities actually take place. As Figure 26-2 shows, all budgeted

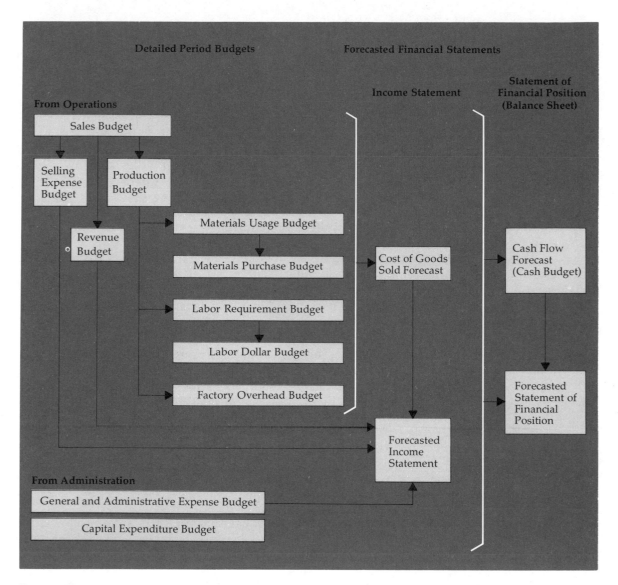

Income Statement   Statement of Financial Position (Balance Sheet)

From Operations

Sales Budget

Selling Expense Budget

Production Budget

Revenue Budget

Materials Usage Budget

Materials Purchase Budget

Labor Requirement Budget

Labor Dollar Budget

Factory Overhead Budget

Cost of Goods Sold Forecast

Cash Flow Forecast (Cash Budget)

Forecasted Statement of Financial Position

Forecasted Income Statement

From Administration

General and Administrative Expense Budget

Capital Expenditure Budget

Figure 26-2
Preparation of
Master Budget

data are used in this process. The controller prepares a cash flow forecast or cash budget from all planned transactions requiring cash inflow or expenditure. A more detailed explanation of cash budgeting follows later in this chapter. In preparing the forecasted statement of financial position, the budget director must know the projected cash balance and must have determined the net income and amount of capital expenditures. All of the expected transactions shown in the period budgets must be classified and posted to the different accounts in the general ledger. The projected financial statements are the end product of the budgeting process. At this point, management must decide to accept the proposed master budget, as well as the planned operating results, or else ask the budget director to change the plans and do parts of the budget over again.

Budget Implementation

Budget implementation is the responsibility of the budget director. Two important things determine the success of this process. The first is proper communication of budget expectations and production and profit targets to all key persons in the company. All persons involved in the operations of the business must know what is expected of them and receive directions on how to reach their goals. Second, and equally important, is support and encouragement by top management. No matter how sophisticated the budgeting process is, it will succeed only if middle- and lower-level managers can see that top management is truly interested in the final outcome and willing to reward people for meeting the budget goals.

Illustrative Problem: Budget Preparation

*Objective 4
Prepare a
period budget*

Period budget preparation and the make-up of the master budget will vary from one company to another. Therefore, it is impossible to cover all procedures found in actual practice. Our problem will show only one approach to preparing period budgets. However, by applying the tools of cost behavior, C-V-P analysis, and responsibility accounting to a particular case, one can prepare any kind of budget.

Stallman Steelworks, Inc., manufactures cans from 4-by-8-foot sheets of steel of different thicknesses. The number of cans produced from each sheet of steel depends on the height and diameter of the cans. During 19xx, the company expects the following sales and unit changes in inventory:

Can Size	Unit Sales	Unit Change in Finished Goods Inventory
6″ × 3″	1,250,000	100,000 (increase)
8″ × 4″	710,000	8,000 (decrease)

Direct materials requirements for these two products are as follows:

Can Size	Sheet Steel Type	Average Usable Cans per Sheet	Average Usable Lids per Sheet
6″ × 3″	No. 16	90	500
8″ × 4″	No. 22	45	270

Usage is the same over a twelve-month period. On the first day of each operating quarter, 25 percent of the year's direct materials requirements will be purchased, starting January 1. Assume no changes in the balances of the Materials Inventory and Work in Process Inventory accounts.

Required

Prepare a direct materials usage budget and a direct materials purchases budget for 19xx. Expected prices for the year are $10.20 per sheet for No. 16 and $13.40 per sheet for No. 22.

Solution

Before preparing the required budgets, we must compute the total number of cans (including lids for tops and bottoms) to be produced per sheet of steel. The following relationships were supplied by the Engineering Department.

6″ × 3″ can: 450 cans (plus 900 lids) require 6.8 sheets of steel, so you can manufacture 66.176 cans and necessary lids per sheet of steel

8″ × 4″ can: 135 cans (plus 270 lids) require 4 sheets of steel, so you can manufacture 33.75 cans and necessary lids per sheet of steel

---

Stallman Steelworks, Inc.
Materials Usage Budget
For the Year Ended December 31, 19xx

6″ × 3″ Can	Number of Cans
Expected sales	1,250,000
Plus increase in inventory	100,000
Total to be produced	1,350,000

No. 16 sheets to be used:

$$\frac{\text{units to be produced}}{\text{cans per sheet}} = \frac{1{,}350{,}000 \text{ cans}}{66.176 \text{ cans/sheet}} = 20{,}400.15 \text{ or } 20{,}400 \text{ sheets}$$

8″ × 4″ Can	
Expected sales	710,000
Less decrease in inventory	8,000
Total to be produced	702,000

No. 22 sheets to be used:

$$\frac{\text{units to be produced}}{\text{cans per sheet}} = \frac{702{,}000 \text{ cans}}{33.75 \text{ cans/sheet}} = 20{,}800 \text{ sheets}$$

Stallman Steelworks, Inc.
Materials Purchases Budget
For the Year Ended December 31, 19xx

Sheet Steel Type	Unit Cost/Sheet	Sheets to Be Purchased Quarterly*	Total Quarterly Purchase Cost	Annual Cost
No. 16	$10.20	5,100	$52,020	$208,080
No. 22	13.40	5,200	69,680	278,720
Total Purchases Budget				$486,800

*Purchases of one-fourth of annual usage on January 1, April 1, July 1, October 1.

Budgetary Control: The Planning Function

Cash Budgeting

Cash flow is one of the most important aspects of the operating cycle of a business. Within the master budget preparation cycle, the cash budget is developed after all period budgets are final and the forecasted income statement is complete. A **cash flow forecast** or **cash budget** is a projection of the cash receipts and cash payments for a future period of time. It sums up the cash results of planned transactions in all phases of a master budget. Generally, it shows the company's projected ending cash balance and the cash position for each month of the year. So periods of high and low cash availability can be anticipated. Very large cash balances mean that funds of the company may not have been used to earn the best possible rate of return. Low cash reserves may mean that the company will not be able to make current payments on amounts it owes. Therefore, to prevent either of these problems, careful cash planning is necessary.

The cash budget has two main parts—forecasted cash receipts and forecasted cash disbursements. Sales budgets, cash or credit sales data, and accounts receivable collection data are used to figure the expected cash receipts for the period. Other sources of cash such as the sale of stock, the sale of assets, or loans also enter into cash receipts planning.

Expected cash disbursements are taken from the different period budgets. The person preparing the cash budget must know how the direct materials, labor, and other goods and services are going to be purchased. That is, are they to be paid for with cash immediately or purchased on account with the cash payment delayed for a period of time? When dealing with accounts payable, it is important to know the company's payment policies. Besides the regular operating expenses, cash is also used for buying equipment and paying off loans and other long-term liabilities. All of this information must be available before an accurate cash budget can be prepared.

Cash Budgeting: Purposes and Nature

*Objective 5
Describe the
purpose and
make-up of a
cash budget*

The cash budget serves two purposes. First, it shows the ending cash balance, which is needed to complete the projected balance sheet. Second, it highlights periods of excess cash reserves or cash shortages. The first purpose focuses on the role of the cash budget in the master budget preparation cycle. The second purpose reflects its important use as a tool of cash management, which is key to any business. Without cash, a business cannot function. Too much cash on hand means that the company is not getting the best return possible on this asset. By comparing projected cash receipts and cash payments, the budget director can advise financial executives of the months when the company will need extra short-term financing because of cash shortages. Similarly, the budget director can point out times when excess cash will be available for short-term investments.

A cash budget combines information from several different period budgets. All elements of cash flow, both cash inflows (cash receipts) and cash outflows (cash disbursements or payments) are brought together to

| | | | | April– | |
	January	February	March	December	Totals

Bengtson Toys, Inc.
Cash Budget
For the Year Ending December 31, 19xx

	January	February	March	April–December	Totals
Cash receipts					
Sales—previous month (38%*)	$ 10,773	$ 7,182	$ 10,773	$ 14,364	$ 43,092
Sales—current month (60%*)	11,340	17,010	22,680	368,928	419,958
Total receipts	$ 22,113	$24,192	$ 33,453	$383,292	$463,050
Cash disbursements					
Direct materials	$ 7,146	$ 7,146	$ 7,622	$ 72,434	$ 94,348
Operating supplies	237	—	—	710	947
Direct labor	3,700	3,850	4,220	34,940	46,710
Factory overhead	3,440	3,480	3,750	32,580	43,250
Selling expenses	8,585	10,000	11,420	109,870	139,875
General and administrative expenses	4,500	4,500	4,500	40,500	54,000
Capital expenditures	4,200	—	7,920	14,780	26,900
Income taxes	—	—	22,640	—	22,640
Interest expense	6,000	—	—	8,920	14,920
Total disbursements	$ 37,808	$28,976	$ 62,072	$314,734	$443,590
Cash increase (decrease)	$(15,695)	$ (4,784)	$(28,619)	$ 68,558	$ 19,460
Beginning cash balance	36,275	20,580	15,796	(12,823)	36,275
Ending cash balance	$ 20,580	$15,796	$(12,823)	$ 55,735	$ 55,735

*2% of sales result in bad debt expense.

Figure 26-3
Typical
Cash Budget

show expected cash flows of the company. The cash budget of Bengtson Toys, Inc., is shown in Figure 26-3. To highlight the first quarter of the year, detailed cash inflows and outflows have been shown for January, February, and March. The remaining nine months have been lumped together in this annual cash forecast.

Now let's explore the relationship of the cash budget shown in Figure 26-3 to the parts of the master budget shown in Figure 26-2. Somewhere in all business transactions, cash has to come into the picture. Since the master budget is a summary of all expected transactions for a future time period, it also must be the key to all expected cash transactions. To prepare the cash budget, then, one must analyze the master budget in terms of cash inflows and outflows. Figure 26-4 focuses on the relationships between the master budget and the cash budget and explains how the cash budget for Bengtson Toys, Inc., shown in Figure 26-3, is created. For the next year, the company expects cash receipts only from sales. Note that 60 percent of all sales are for cash. Thirty-eight percent are credit sales collected in the following month. All of the necessary cash inflow information would come from the sales and sales revenue budgets.

Figure 26-4
Master Budget
and Cash
Budget Inter-
relationships

Elements of the Cash Budget	Sources of the Information
Cash Receipts	
Cash sales	Sales budget (cash sales)
Cash collections of previous sales	Sales budget (credit sales) plus collection record—percent collected in first month, second month, etc.
Proceeds from sale of assets	Forecasted income statement
Loan proceeds	Previous month's information on cash budget
Cash Disbursements	
Direct materials	Materials purchase budget
Operating supplies	Factory overhead budget and materials purchase budget
Direct labor	Labor dollar budget
Factory overhead	Factory overhead budget
Selling expenses	Selling expense budget
General and administrative expenses	General and administrative expense budget
Capital expenditures	Capital expenditure budget
Income taxes	Estimated from previous year's income statement and current year projections
Interest expense	Forecasted income statement
Loan payments	Loan record

Note: Other sources of cash receipts and possible cash disbursements exist. The above analysis covers only the most common types of cash inflows and outflows.

Information supporting cash disbursement forecasts comes from several different sources. Cash used to purchase direct materials and operating supplies is determined by changing the materials purchase budget into a cash flow analysis. Materials are generally purchased on account. Every company should have a policy about payment on account as part of its cash management. If the company's policy is to pay everything within the discount period, cash flow would take place in 10 or 20 days, if the terms of the purchase were 2/10, n/30 or 3/20, n/60. If, however, the company wants to hold its cash for the maximum time, cash payments would not be made for 30 or 60 days. In most cases, direct labor cash flow, for obvious reasons, is delayed very little. Information from the labor dollar budget is used to support the cash payments for both direct and indirect labor services. Cash payments for all factory overhead other than operating supplies and indirect labor are figured by using the factory overhead budget.

Cash requirements for selling expenses, general and administrative expenses, and capital expenditures are determined from their respective budgets. Again, the timing of the cash exchange is important. Selling expenses such as gasoline purchases and sales brochures may be made on credit, and the actual payment may be postponed for thirty days or more.

The same may be true for large capital expenditures. When preparing a cash budget, one must concentrate on the time of actual cash flow, not the time of the original sale or purchase transaction.

The final two cash disbursements shown in Figure 26-3 are for income taxes and interest expense. Corporations usually make quarterly tax payments, which are applied against an estimate of the current year's tax liability. Any excess owed at year end is due on the fifteenth day of the third month following the close of the company's fiscal year. Interest expense payments may be made monthly, quarterly, semiannually, or annually, depending on the terms of the loan agreement. This information can be found in the organization's loan record.

Once the cash receipts and cash disbursements have been established, the cash increase or decrease for the period is computed. The resulting increase or decrease is added to the period's beginning cash balance to arrive at the projected cash balance at period end. In the case of Bengtson Toys, the first three months will put a heavy drain on cash reserves, but positive cash flow returns during the last nine months of the year. The company seems to have a favorable cash position for the year, except at the end of March. Depending on cash payment patterns, the company would want to plan on taking out a small loan to take care of the cash shortage and protect itself in case a large unexpected payment becomes due. On the other hand, a $55,735 balance in cash at year end may be too much extra cash. So management may want to make plans for investing this money in short-term securities.

Illustrative Problem

Objective 6
Prepare a cash budget

Chen Information Processing Company provides word-processing services for its clients. Chen uses state-of-the-art computerized information processing equipment. It employs five keyboard operators, who each average 120 hours of work a month. The following information was developed by the budget officer:

	Actual—19x5		Forecast—19x6		
	November	December	January	February	March
Client billings (sales)	$25,000	$35,000	$25,000	$20,000	$40,000
Selling expenses	4,500	5,000	4,000	4,000	5,000
General and administrative expenses	7,500	8,000	8,000	7,000	7,500
Operating supplies purchased	2,500	3,500	2,500	2,500	4,000
Factory overhead	3,200	3,500	3,000	2,500	3,500

The company has a bank loan of $12,000 at a 12 percent annual interest rate. Interest is paid monthly, and $2,000 of the principal of the loan is due on February 28, 19x6. No capital expenditures are anticipated for the first quarter of the coming year. Income taxes for calendar year 19x5 of

$4,550 are due and payable on March 15, 19x6. The company's five employees earn $7.50 an hour, and all payroll-related labor benefit costs are included in factory overhead.

For the revenue and cost items included in the chart just given, assume the following conditions:

Client billings:	60% are cash sales that are collected during the current period
	30% are collected in the month following the sale
	10% are collected in the second month following the sale
Operating supplies:	Paid in the month purchased
Selling expenses, general and administrative expenses, & factory overhead:	Paid in the month following the cost's incurrence

The beginning cash balance on January 1, 19x6 is expected to be $13,840.

Required

Prepare a monthly cash budget for the Chen Information Systems Company for the three-month period ending March 31, 19x6.

Solution

The three-month cash budget for the Chen Information Processing Company is shown in Figure 26-5. Details supporting the individual computations are shown below.

	January	February	March
Client billings			
Current month = 60%	$15,000	$12,000	$24,000
Previous month = 30%	10,500	7,500	6,000
Month before last = 10%	2,500	3,500	2,500
Totals	$28,000	$23,000	$32,500
Operating supplies			
All paid in the month purchased	$ 2,500	$ 2,500	$ 4,000
Direct labor			
5 employees × 120 hours/month × $7.50/hour	$ 4,500	$ 4,500	$ 4,500
Factory overhead			
Paid in the following month	$ 3,500	$ 3,000	$ 2,500
Selling expenses			
Paid in the following month	$ 5,000	$ 4,000	$ 4,000
General and administrative expenses			
Paid in the following month	$ 8,000	$ 8,000	$ 7,000

Interest expense
  January and February =
    1% of $12,000 $ 120 $ 120
    March = 1% of $10,000 $ 100
Loan payment   — $ 2,000   —
Income tax payment   —   — $ 4,550

The ending cash balances of $18,220, $17,100, and $22,950 for January, February, and March, 19x6, respectively, appear to be comfortable but not too large for the company.

<table>
<tr><td>Figure 26-5
Example of a
Period Budget</td><td colspan="5">Chen Information Processing Company
Monthly Cash Budget
For the Three-Month Period Ending March 31, 19x6</td></tr>
<tr><td></td><td></td><td>January</td><td>February</td><td>March</td><td>Totals</td></tr>
<tr><td></td><td>Cash receipts</td><td></td><td></td><td></td><td></td></tr>
<tr><td></td><td> Client billings</td><td>$28,000</td><td>$23,000</td><td>$32,500</td><td>$83,500</td></tr>
<tr><td></td><td>Cash disbursements</td><td></td><td></td><td></td><td></td></tr>
<tr><td></td><td> Operating supplies</td><td>$ 2,500</td><td>$ 2,500</td><td>$ 4,000</td><td>$ 9,000</td></tr>
<tr><td></td><td> Direct labor</td><td>4,500</td><td>4,500</td><td>4,500</td><td>13,500</td></tr>
<tr><td></td><td> Factory overhead</td><td>3,500</td><td>3,000</td><td>2,500</td><td>9,000</td></tr>
<tr><td></td><td> Selling expenses</td><td>5,000</td><td>4,000</td><td>4,000</td><td>13,000</td></tr>
<tr><td></td><td> General and administrative
    expenses</td><td>8,000</td><td>8,000</td><td>7,000</td><td>23,000</td></tr>
<tr><td></td><td> Interest expense</td><td>120</td><td>120</td><td>100</td><td>340</td></tr>
<tr><td></td><td> Loan payment</td><td>—</td><td>2,000</td><td>—</td><td>2,000</td></tr>
<tr><td></td><td> Income tax payment</td><td>—</td><td>—</td><td>4,550</td><td>4,550</td></tr>
<tr><td></td><td>   Total disbursements</td><td>$23,620</td><td>$24,120</td><td>$26,650</td><td>$74,390</td></tr>
<tr><td></td><td>Cash increase (decrease)</td><td>$ 4,380</td><td>$(1,120)</td><td>$ 5,850</td><td>$ 9,110</td></tr>
<tr><td></td><td>Beginning cash balance</td><td>13,840</td><td>18,220</td><td>17,100</td><td>13,840</td></tr>
<tr><td></td><td>Ending cash balance</td><td>$18,220</td><td>$17,100</td><td>$22,950</td><td>$22,950</td></tr>
</table>

Budgeting in Not-for-Profit Organizations

The major difference between not-for-profit organizations and those that are profit oriented is the overall goal of the organization. On the one hand, some enterprises must make a profit in order to exist, so making a profit must be their major objective. On the other hand, the not-for-profit

*Objective 7
Describe the
unique aspects
of the budgeting
process in not-
for-profit and
public-sector
organizations*

organization is meant to serve some function or purpose other than making a profit. This purpose can be served, however, only if the organization carefully controls its funds and their use. For this reason, organizations that are not profit oriented depend heavily on budgeting to maintain control over their funds as well as to help in carrying out their goals. Budgeting is a major project for large governmental organizations at the federal, state, and municipal levels. Public officials are charged with the safety and wise use of the public's money. Careful preparation of the annual budget plays an important role in this process. The same concerns are faced by officials of organizations such as professional groups, civic organizations, clubs, charitable organizations, and student fraternities and sororities.

Except for the profit element, the budgeting principles illustrated in Figure 26-1 also apply to not-for-profit and public-sector organizations. These entities must have long-term objectives as well as short-term goals and operating strategies. Human responsibilities and interaction principles are as much a part of the budgeting process in the public sector as they are in the private sector. Budget housekeeping rules apply as well as the follow-up principles. In other words, making a profit is not the only reason for participating in the budgeting function.

However, governmental units and other not-for-profit organizations need budgeting data on anticipated changes in fund balances rather than amounts of profit or loss. Such organizations rely heavily on cash budgeting techniques, since their budgets are related to expected fund changes. The budgeted amount of each cost or expense item or grouping is the maximum expenditure approved for the period. Any changes in such an amount must have official approval.

Figure 26-6 describes the budgeting procedure used by the government of the United States. Preparing the country's annual budget is an enormous undertaking that involves hundreds of people and agencies. The steps of the process shown in Figure 26-6 take almost a whole year. Note that the process begins with the president submitting a complete budget proposal to Congress for study and approval. Thousands of hours have already been spent to put this proposal together. This early stage adds several more months to the U.S. budgeting process.

Congress and the president control the country's purse strings through budgeting. Emphasis is placed on trying to cut down overspending and waste and to prevent misuse of the taxpayers' money. Not-for-profit organizations generally operate with a board of directors having the same sort of responsibilities as the Congress or the legislature have in the government.

To present a more detailed picture of the budgeting process of a not-for-profit organization, we will turn to Beta Alpha Psi, the national accounting fraternity for honor students. Beta Alpha Psi was founded to recognize honor students in accounting and to expose them to professional issues while they are still in school. Its size makes its budgeting procedures much easier to analyze than those of the federal government.

Beta Alpha Psi's budget for the year ending June 30, 1982, and related actual expenditures are shown in Figure 26-7 (page 994). The budget is prepared by the director of administration during the spring. The director

Figure 26-6
Congressional
Budget Process
Timetable

Suggested Deadlines	Action to Be Completed
On or before:	
November 10	President submits current services budget
Fifteenth day after Congress meets [Jan. 15]	President submits his budget
March 15	Committees and joint committees submit reports to Budget Committees
April 1	Congressional Budget Office submits report to Budget Committees
April 15	Budget Committees report first concurrent resolution on the budget to their houses
May 15	Committees report bills and resolutions authorizing new budget authority
May 15	Congress completes action on first concurrent resolution on the budget
7th day after Labor Day	Congress completes action on bills and resolutions providing new budget authority and new spending authority
September 15	Congress completes action on second required concurrent resolution on the budget
September 25	Congress completes action on reconciliation bill or resolution, or both, implementing second required concurrent resolution
October 1	Fiscal year begins

Source: Title III, U.S. Code Congressional and Administrative News, §300, 93rd Cong., 2d Sess., 1974, p. 336.

first gets input from the other five directors and the national president. Past expenditure patterns and expected future events are used as the basis for projecting each revenue and expense item. An early draft of the budget is sent to board members before the organization's spring meeting. Then certain items are questioned at the meeting, and the revised budget is submitted for the board's approval around the first of June.

Actual results will, of course, be different from the budgeted figures. To control cost overruns, the board of directors should set up a policy that calls for board approval before any increases are funded. A small overrun does not call for such action. Only the significant increases must be controlled. Since cost control is the subject of Chapter 27, the control of expenditures of not-for-profit and government organizations will be covered there in greater detail.

Figure 26-7
Typical
Not-for-Profit
Budget

National Council of Beta Alpha Psi
(The National Accounting Fraternity)
Statements of Revenue, Expenditures, and Changes in Fund Balance
For the Year Ended June 30, 1982

	Actual	Budget
Revenues		
Initiation fees	$164,982	$160,000
Associates program contributions	78,000	60,000
Scholarship contributions	44,000	44,000
Publication contributions	7,000	7,000
Outstanding faculty vice-president awards contributions	4,000	4,000
Charter fees	4,500	4,500
Membership insignia royalties	996	1,000
Interest on investments	13,725	10,000
Other	1,641	1,000
Total Revenues	$318,844	$291,500
Expenditures		
National council:		
Annual, mid-year and spring meetings	$ 30,097	$ 29,800
Chapter installations and visitations	6,999	5,000
National chapter:		
Annual banquet and student meeting	10,398	14,000
Faculty vice-president and student expense reimbursements	16,900	24,000
Local chapter:		
Membership certificates	10,147	9,800
Banners and miscellaneous	1,288	900
Performance awards	5,924	6,000
Case competition awards	1,864	10,000
Directory	–0–	11,000
Administration:		
Supplies	2,559	2,000
Postage and telephone	7,153	6,000
Miscellaneous	4,323	6,000
Special projects:		
Faculty vice-president awards	4,000	4,000
Regional meetings	29,660	35,000
Manuscript awards	8,801	6,000
Student seminar	9,059	12,000
Publications	23,320	36,000
Beta Alpha Psi history project	282	1,500
Superior chapter scholarship awards	44,000	44,000
Accountant for the public interest awards	220	–0–

Central office costs	20,923	25,000
Honoraria	1,000	1,000
Total Expenditures	$238,917	$289,000
Revenue over (under) Expenditures	$ 79,927	$ 2,500
Fund Balance, Beginning of Year	78,746	78,746
Fund Balance, End of Year	$158,673	$ 81,246

Chapter Review

Review of Learning Objectives

1. Identify the five groups of budgeting principles, and explain the principles in each group.

The five groups of budgeting principles are (1) long-range goals principles, (2) short-range goals and strategies principles, (3) human responsibilities and interaction principles, (4) budget housekeeping principles, and (5) follow-up principles. Every organization needs to set long-range goals and convert them into plans for product line or service offerings. Short-range goals and strategies must be restated in terms of the annual product line or service offerings and associated profit plans. The budget development plans and timetable must also be set up. The human side includes identifying a budget director, staff, and participants. These people must be informed of their duties and responsibilities. It is essential to practice participative budgeting, obtain the full support of top management, and make sure of full and open communication among all participants. Being realistic, requiring that all deadlines be met, and using flexible application procedures are the housekeeping principles of budgeting. Finally, budget follow-up includes maintaining a continuous budgeting process and using a system of period reports to measure performance of the operating segments. Problems are identified for analysis and inclusion in the next period's planning activities.

2. Define the concept of budgetary control.

The budgetary control process consists of the cost planning function and the cost control function. Cost planning and control are key functions leading to effective management. Budgetary control is the total process of (1) developing plans for a company's expected operations and (2) controlling operations to help carry out those plans.

3. Identify the components of a master budget, and describe how they are related to each other.

A master budget is a combined set of departmental or functional period budgets that have been consolidated into forecasted financial statements for the whole company. First the detailed operating or period budgets are prepared. These are the sales budget, production budget, selling expense budget, materials purchases budget, materials usage budget, labor hour requirements budget, direct labor dollars budget, factory overhead budget, general and administrative expenses budget, and capital expenditures budget. The selling expense budget and the production budget are computed from the sales budget data. Materials usage, labor hour and dollars, and factory overhead budgets arise from the production budget. Materials purchases can be pinned down only after materials use is known. General and administrative expenses and proposed capital expenditures are determined by top management. Once these budgets have been prepared, a forecasted income statement, a forecasted cash flow statement (cash budget), and a forecasted balance sheet can be prepared, assuming that all planned activities actually take place.

4. Prepare a period budget.

A period budget, also known as an operating budget, is a forecast of a year's operating results for a segment of a company. It is a quantitative expression of planned activities. For examples of period budgets, see the illustrative problems on pages 984 and 989. The period budgeting process converts unit sales and production forecasts into revenue and cost estimates for each of the many operating segments of the company.

5. Describe the purpose and make-up of a cash budget.

The cash budget's purposes are (1) to disclose the firm's projected ending cash balance and (2) to show the cash position for each month of the year so that periods of excess cash or cash shortages can be planned for. Cash management is critical to the success of an organization, and the cash budget is a major tool used in that process. The cash budget begins with the projection of all expected sources of cash (cash receipts). Next all expected cash disbursements or payments are found by analyzing all other period budgets within the master budget. The difference between these two totals is the cash increase or decrease anticipated for the period. This total combined with the period's beginning cash balance yields the ending cash balance.

6. Prepare a cash budget.

A cash budget or cash flow forecast is a projection of the cash receipts and payments for a future period of time. It summarizes the cash results of planned transactions in all parts of a master budget. For an example, see Figure 26-3.

7. Describe the unique aspects of the budgeting process in not-for-profit and public-sector organizations.

The not-for-profit aspect of these organizations makes their budgeting process unique. Their budgeting process yields anticipated changes in fund balances rather than amounts of profits or losses. Revenues and expenditures are projected by line item or item groupings. The budgeted amount for each of the cost or expense categories represents the maximum expenditure approved for the period. Additional expenditures must have the approval of the board of directors or legislature, whatever the case may be. For the most part, however, the budgeting principles for profit-oriented companies also apply to not-for-profit or public-sector organizations.

Additional Illustrative Problem

Gilman Richard is president of Hough Travel Services, Inc. Last year's forecasted income statement for the company is shown on the next page.

Hough Travel Services, Inc.
Forecasted Income Statement
For the Year Ending December 31, 19x4

Revenues		
Travel receipts	$246,500	
Special tours	137,800	
Total revenues		$384,300
Operating expenses		
Airline costs	$111,400	
Cruise costs	62,100	
Bus costs	12,800	
Salaries: agents	60,000	
executives	80,000	
Rent—building	6,400	
Depreciation of equipment	3,900	
Utilities	1,800	
Supplies	2,100	
Brochure printing	3,500	
Computer services	6,700	
Miscellaneous	900	
Total operating expenses		351,600
Income before taxes		$ 32,700
Federal income taxes (50%)		16,350
Net income after taxes		$ 16,350

During 19x5, the following changes are anticipated:

a. Travel receipts and special tour revenues are both expected to increase by 20 percent.

b. Airline costs are scheduled for a 30 percent increase in January, 19x5.

c. Cruise and bus costs will rise 10 percent.

d. All salaries will be increased by 20 percent.

e. Rent, depreciation, and utility expenses are expected to stay the same throughout next year.

f. Supplies costs will decrease by 10 percent.

g. Brochure printing costs will rise by 40 percent.

h. Computer services costs will double because of expanded services.

i. Miscellaneous expenses should total $1,000 in 19x5.

Required

Prepare the forecasted income statement for 19x5.

Solution

Hough Travel Services, Inc.
Forecasted Income Statement
For the Year Ending December 31, 19x5

Revenues		
Travel receipts ($246,500 × 1.2)	$295,800	
Special tours ($137,800 × 1.2)	165,360	
Total revenues		$461,160
Operating expenses		
Airline costs ($111,400 × 1.3)	$144,820	
Cruise costs ($62,100 × 1.1)	68,310	
Bus costs ($12,800 × 1.1)	14,080	
Salaries: agents ($60,000 × 1.2)	72,000	
executives ($80,000 × 1.2)	96,000	
Rent—building	6,400	
Depreciation of equipment	3,900	
Utilities	1,800	
Supplies ($2,100 × .9)	1,890	
Brochure printing ($3,500 × 1.4)	4,900	
Computer services ($6,700 × 2)	13,400	
Miscellaneous	1,000	
Total operating expenses		428,500
Income before taxes		$ 32,660
Federal income taxes (50%)		16,330
Net income after taxes		$ 16,330

Chapter Assignments

Questions

1. Describe the concept of budgetary control.
2. Distinguish between long-term plans and yearly operating plans.
3. What is a period budget?
4. How does responsibility accounting help in period budget preparation?
5. What is a master budget?
6. Why is the preparation of a forecasted cash flow statement or cash budget so important to a company?
7. Name the three main phases of the budget preparation cycle.
8. Identify and discuss the relationships among detailed operating budgets.
9. What are the long-range goals principles of budgeting?
10. One of the budgeting principles we listed was "Restate the long-range plan in terms of short-range plans for product lines or services available and a detailed profit plan." What is the purpose of this principle?
11. Why is it necessary to identify all participants in budget development?

12. Describe participative budgeting.

13. State the budget housekeeping principles.

14. Why use a continuous budgeting process?

15. What is the connection between periodic performance reports and responsibility accounting?

16. In the budget preparation cycle, what steps must precede the preparation of the cash budget?

17. How are the areas of sales and purchases on account handled when drawing up the cash budget?

18. Do not-for-profit organizations require budgets just as profit-oriented enterprises do? Explain your answer.

19. How do budgets help control costs for public-sector and not-for-profit organizations?

Classroom Exercises

**Exercise 26-1
Budgeting
Principles
(L.O. 1)**

Long-range goals principles and short-range goals and strategies principles are critical to a successful budgeting system. Assume that you work in the accounting department of a small wholesale warehousing business. The president has just returned from an industry association meeting where he attended a seminar on the values of a budgeting system. He wants to develop a budgeting system and has asked you to direct it.

State the points that you should communicate to the president about the initial development steps of the process. Concentrate on the two sets of principles mentioned above.

**Exercise 26-2
Production
Budget
Preparation
(L.O. 4)**

The FEI Garage Door Company's forecast of unit sales for 19x3 is as follows: January, 30,000; February, 40,000; March, 50,000; April, 60,000; May, 50,000; June, 40,000; July, 30,000; August, 40,000; September, 50,000; October, 60,000; November, 70,000; December, 50,000.

The forecast of unit sales for January 19x4 is 40,000. Beginning finished goods inventory on January 1, 19x3 contained 5,000 doors. Company policy states that minimum finished goods inventory is 5,000 units and that the maximum is one-half of the following month's sales. Maximum productive capacity is 55,000 units per month.

Using the information given above, prepare a monthly production budget stating the number of units to be produced. Keep in mind that the company wants to have a fairly constant productive output so that a constant work force can be maintained. How many units will be in finished goods inventory on December 31, 19x3?

**Exercise 26-3
Direct
Materials
Purchases
Budget (Linked
to Exercise
26-2)
(L.O. 4)**

Refer to the data for the FEI Garage Door Company in Exercise 26-2. Prepare a direct materials purchases budget for January, February, and March 19x3, assuming the following breakdown of parts needed:

Hinges	4 sets/door	$ 8.00/set
Door panels	4 panels/door	$17.00/panel
Other hardware	1 lock/door	$11.00/lock
	1 handle/door	$ 2.50/handle
	2 rollers tracks/door	$22.00/set of two roller tracks
	8 rollers/door	$ 1.00/roller

All direct materials are purchased in the month before their use in production.

Car Team, Inc., is an automobile maintenance and repair organization with outlets throughout the midwestern United States. Ms. Musick, budget director for the home office, is beginning to assemble next quarter's operating cash budget. Sales are projected as follows:

	On Account	Cash
October	$642,000	$165,800
November	580,000	150,000
December	710,500	179,400

Past collection results for sales on account indicate the following pattern:

Month of sale	40%
1st month following sale	30%
2nd month following sale	28%
Uncollectible	2%

Sales on account during August and September were $746,000 and $495,000, respectively.

Compute the amount of cash to be collected from sales during each month of the last quarter.

Peking Cosmetics, Inc., is collecting information for its comprehensive 19x4 master budget. The company manufactures three products (U, S, and C), and each product requires units of different direct materials input. Planned unit production of each product in 19x4 is 10,000 for U, 30,000 for S, and 20,000 for C. The materials requirements for one unit of each product are summarized below:

Unit Materials Requirements

Product	Materials			
	A	B	C	D
U	2	—	1	—
S	1	2	—	3
C	3	1	2	4

Unit cost and inventory for each item of direct materials are:

	A	B	C	D
19x4 unit cost	$2.00	$3.50	$4.00	$1.00
Inventory in units				
Jan. 1, 19x4	10,000	5,000	3,000	10,000
Dec. 31, 19x4	8,000	2,000	6,000	30,000

Direct materials unit prices as budgeted are the delivered unit costs experienced by Peking Cosmetics in 19x3.

Prepare a direct materials purchase budget for 19x4.

Exercise 26-6
Budgeting for
Not-For-Profit
Organizations
(L.O. 7)

The Board of Directors of the Apple County Animal Shelter has been discussing budget strategy for several months. Recently, Ms. Jonathan was appointed budget director. She is now putting together the cash expenditure budget for 19x6. Below is a listing of 19x5 expenditures:

Salaries and wages	$ 80,900
Employee benefits expense	25,430
Truck expenses	6,540
Medical lab expenses	26,400
Medical supplies expense	12,600
Repairs and maintenance expense	7,260
Heating costs	2,800
Electricity expense	3,400
Water charges	200
Insect control costs	260
Building rent expense	3,500
Animal food costs	4,200
Miscellaneous expenses	620
Total	$174,110

During 19x6, salaries, wages, and related employee benefits are expected to rise by 10 percent. Medical lab and supplies expenses will go up 20 percent next year. All other expenses should be 5 percent higher in 19x6.

Prepare the cash expenditure budget for the Apple County Animal Shelter for 19x6.

Exercise 26-7
Cash Budget
Preparation—
Expenditures
(L.O. 6)

Cabernet Corporation relies heavily on its cash budget to predict periods of high or low cash. The company considers proper cash management to be its primary short-range strategy for achieving higher profits. All materials and supplies are purchased on account, with terms of either 2/10, n/30 or 2/30, n/60. Discounts are taken whenever possible, but payment is not made until the final day of the discount period. Purchases for the next quarter are expected to be as follows:

Date	Terms	Gross Amount	Date	Terms	Gross Amount
July 10	2/10, n/30	$ 6,400	Aug. 31	2/10, n/30	$ 6,800
July 16	2/30, n/60	8,200	Sept. 4	2/10, n/30	9,400
July 18	2/10, n/30	8,600	Sept. 6	2/30, n/60	9,600
July 24	2/30, n/60	7,400	Sept. 9	2/10, n/30	8,100
July 31	2/10, n/30	9,800	Sept. 15	2/30, n/60	6,200
Aug. 6	2/10, n/30	6,200	Sept. 18	2/10, n/30	7,500
Aug. 12	2/30, n/60	10,400	Sept. 20	2/10, n/30	10,400
Aug. 18	2/30, n/60	10,500	Sept. 24	2/30, n/60	9,400
Aug. 24	2/10, n/30	12,400	Sept. 26	2/10, n/30	12,600
Aug. 30	2/10, n/30	11,600	Sept. 29	2/10, n/30	4,900

Three purchases in June affected July cash flow: June 6, 2/30, n/60, $14,200; June 21, 2/30, n/60, $10,400; and June 24, 2/10, n/30, $6,400.

From the information given, compute total cash outflow for July, August, and September resulting from the purchases identified above.

Rutemiller Metals Company manufactures three products in a single plant with four departments: Cutting, Grinding, Polishing, and Packing. The company has estimated costs for products J, K, and M and is currently analyzing direct labor hour requirements for the budget year 19xx. The routing sequence and departmental data are presented below.

Unit of Product	Estimated Hours per Unit				Total Estimated Direct Labor Hours/Unit
	Cut	Grind	Polish	Pack	
J	.3	.5	.2	.1	1.1
K	.5	—	1.4	.3	2.2
M	.8	1.5	—	.2	2.5
Hourly labor rate	$8	$6	$5	$4	
Annual DLH capacity	450,000	600,000	624,000	180,000	

The annual direct labor hour capacity for each department is based on a normal two-shift operation. Hours of labor in excess of capacity are provided by overtime labor at 150 percent of normal hourly rates. Budgeted unit production in 19xx for the products is 210,000 of J, 360,000 of K, and 300,000 of M.

Prepare a monthly direct labor hour requirements schedule for 19xx and the related direct labor cost budget. Assume that direct labor hour capacity is the same each month and that production should be as close as possible to constant each month.

Interpreting Accounting Information

**Internal
Management
Information:
Rudolph
Corporation**
(L.O. 1, 3)

Rudolph Corporation is a manufacturing company with annual sales of $15,000,000. The controller, Mr. Randolph, appointed Mr. Roland as budget director. After much difficulty, Mr. Roland created the following budget formulation policy based on a calendar-year accounting period:

May 19x4   Meeting of corporate officers and budget director to discuss corporate plans for 19x5.

June 19x4   Meeting(s) of division managers, department heads, and budget director to communicate 19x5 corporate objectives. At this time, relevant background data are distributed to all managers and a time schedule is established for development of 19x5 budget data.

July 19x4   Managers and department heads continue to develop budget data. Complete 19x5 monthly sales forecasts by product line, and receive final sales estimates from sales vice president.

Aug. 19x4   Complete 19x5 monthly production activity and anticipated inventory level plans. Division managers and department heads should communicate preliminary budget figures to budget director for coordination and distribution to other operating areas.

Sept. 19x4   Development of preliminary 19x5 master budget. Revised budget data from all functional areas to be received. Budget director will coordinate staff activities, integrating manpower requirements, direct materials and supplies requirements, unit cost estimates, cash requirements, and profit estimates into 19x5 master budget.

Oct. 19x4   Meeting with corporate officers to discuss preliminary 19x5 master budget; any corrections, additions, or deletions to be communicated to budget director by corporate officers; all authorized changes to be incorporated into the 19x5 master budget.

Nov. 19x4   Submit final draft of 19x5 master budget to corporate officers for approval. Publish approved budget and distribute to all corporate officers, division managers, and department heads.

Required

1. Comment on the proposed budget formulation policy.
2. What changes in the policy would you recommend?

Problem Set A

Problem 26A-1
General and
Administrative
Expense Budget
(L.O. 4)

Bandy Metal Products, Inc., has four divisions and a centralized management structure. The home office is located in Hugo, Oklahoma. General and administrative expenses of the corporation for 19x7 and expected percentage increases for 19x8 are presented below:

Expense Categories	19x7 Expenses	Expected Increase in 19x8
Administrative salaries	$250,000	20%
Facility depreciation	74,000	10%
Operating supplies	49,000	20%
Insurance and taxes	12,000	10%
Computer services	400,000	40%
Clerical salaries	110,000	15%
Miscellaneous	25,000	10%
Total	$920,000	

To determine divisional profitability, all general and administrative expenses except for computer services are allocated to divisions on a total labor dollar basis. Computer service costs are charged directly to divisions on the basis of usage time. Computer charges and direct labor costs in 19x7 were as follows:

	Computer Charges	Direct Labor
Division A	$100,000	$150,000
Division B	88,000	100,000
Division C	72,000	125,000
Division D	60,000	125,000
Home Office	80,000	
Total	$400,000	

Required

1. Prepare the general and administrative expense budget for Bandy Metal Products, Inc., for 19x8.

2. Prepare a schedule of budgeted computer service cost charges to each division and the home office, assuming that percentages of usage time and cost distribution in 19x8 will be the same as in 19x7.

3. Determine the amount of general and administrative expense to be allocated to each division in 19x8, assuming the same direct labor cost distribution percentages as in 19x7.

Problem 26A-2
Budget
Preparation
(L.O. 4)

The principal item made by Hedlund Enterprises, Inc., is a multipurpose hammer that carries a lifetime guarantee. The manufacturing process has combined production steps by using modern, automated equipment. A list of cost and production information about the production of the Hedlund hammer is given below.

Direct materials
  Anodized steel: 2 kilograms per hammer at $.30 per kilogram
  Leather strapping for handle: $\frac{1}{2}$ square meter per hammer at $2.40 per square meter
  Packing materials are returned to the manufacturer and thus are not included as part of cost of goods sold.
Direct labor
  Forging operation: $10.50 per direct labor hour; 6 minutes per hammer
  Leather-wrapping operation: $8.00 per direct labor hour; 12 minutes per hammer
Factory overhead
  Forging operation: rate = 70% of department's direct labor dollars
  Leather-wrapping operation: rate = 50% of department's direct labor dollars

For the three months ended December 31, 19xx, management expects to produce 38,000 hammers in October, 32,000 hammers in November, and 30,000 hammers in December.

Required

1. For the three-month period ending December 31, 19xx, prepare monthly production cost information for the manufacture of the Hedlund hammer. In your budget analysis, show a detailed breakdown of all costs involved and the computation methods used.

2. Prepare a quarterly production cost budget for the hammer. Show monthly cost data and combined totals for the quarter for each cost category.

Problem 26A-3
Divisional
Budget
Preparation
(L.O. 4)

Mona Lisa is budget director for Galley Spectaculars, Inc., a division of Diversified, Ltd., a multinational company based in New England. Galley Spectaculars organizes and coordinates art shows and auctions throughout the world. Budgeted and actual costs and expenses for 19x4 are compared in the table on the next page. For 19x5, the following fixed costs have been budgeted:

Salaries: executives	$400,000
Advertising expense	95,000
Insurance: merchandise	20,000
liability	34,000
Total	$549,000

Additional information follows.

a. Net receipts are expected to be $2,600,000 in 19x5.
b. Staging salaries will increase 50% over 19x4 actual figures.

| | 19x4 Amounts | |
Expense Item	Budget	Actual
Salaries expense: staging	$ 120,000	$ 136,400
executive	380,000	413,600
Travel costs	210,000	226,010
Auctioneer services	160,000	114,910
Space rental costs	125,500	123,290
Printing costs	66,000	71,250
Advertising expense	84,500	91,640
Insurance: merchandise	22,400	18,650
liability	12,000	13,550
Home office costs	94,600	89,940
Shipping costs	12,500	16,280
Miscellaneous	2,500	1,914
Total	$1,290,000	$1,317,434
Net receipts	$2,500,000	$2,734,600

c. Travel costs are expected to be 11% of net receipts.
d. Auctioneer services will be billed at 9.5% of net receipts.
e. Space rental costs will go up 20% from 19x4 budgeted amounts.
f. Printing costs are expected to be $75,000 in 19x5.
g. Home office costs are budgeted for $125,000 in 19x5.
h. Shipping costs are expected to rise 20% over 19x4 budgeted amounts.
i. Miscellaneous expenses for 19x5 will be budgeted at $3,000.

Required

1. Prepare the division's budget for 19x5. Assume that only services are being sold and that there is no cost of sales. (Net receipts equal gross margin.) Use a 50 percent federal income tax rate.
2. Should the budget director be worried about the trend of the company's operations? Be specific.

**Problem 26A-4
Cash Budget
Preparation**
(L.O. 6)

Mount Hawk Ski Resort, Inc., located in central Oregon, has been in business for twenty-two years. Although the skiing season is difficult to predict, the company operates under the assumption that all of its revenues will be generated during the first three months of the calendar year. Routine maintenance and repair work is done during the remaining nine-month period. The following projections were developed by Laura DeLay, company budget director, for 19x6:

Cash Receipts
Lift tickets:
January, 24,800 people @ $19; February, 22,400 people @ $20; March, 24,800 people @ $21.
Food sales:
January, $62,000; February, $56,000; March, $62,000.

Skiing lessons:

January, $248,000; February, $224,000; March, $248,000.

Equipment sales and rental:

January, $992,000; February, $896,000; March, $992,000.

Liquor sales:

January, $124,000; February, $112,000; March, $124,000.

Cash Disbursements

Salaries:

Ski area:

Lift operators—20 people at $2,000 per month for January, February, March (first quarter).

Ski patrol—12 people at $2,400 per month for first quarter.

Equipment sales and rental—24 people at $1,200 per month for first quarter.

Instruction—35 people at $3,000 per month for first quarter.

Maintenance:

$33,000 per month for first quarter, and $94,000 for the rest of the year.

Customer service:

Parking control—20 people at $1,200 per month for first quarter.

Shuttle bus drivers—10 people at $1,200 per month for first quarter.

Medical:

Nurses—12 people at $2,400 per month for first quarter.

Paraprofessionals—6 people at $4,000 per month for first quarter.

Food service:

Waiters—12 people at $800 per month for first quarter.

Cooks—6 people at $1,800 per month for first quarter.

Cleanup—18 people at $600 per month for first quarter.

Purchases:

Food: $20,000 per month for the first quarter.

Ski equipment: purchases of $440,000 in both January and February plus a $600,000 purchase in December 19x6.

Clothing for personnel: $145,000 payment in January for purchase in December 19x5 on account.

Liquors: $40,000 in each month of the first quarter.

Tickets and supplies: $50,000 in January, $40,000 in February, and $80,000 in December 19x6.

Advertising: $30,000 in January, $20,000 in February, and $80,000 from April through the end of the year.

Insurance:

Fire: semiannual premium payments of $3,000 in January and July.

Liability: Annual premium of $10,000 due in January.

Medical facility costs: $5,000 in January, $5,000 in February, and $10,000 in December 19x6.

Utilities: $3,000 per month for the first quarter and $1,000 per month for the rest of the year.

Lift maintenance: $15,000 per month for the first quarter and $10,000 per month for the rest of the year.

Property taxes: $280,000 due in June.

Federal income taxes: 19x5 taxes of $564,000 due in March.

The beginning cash balance for 19x6 is anticipated to be $40,000.

Chapter Twenty-Six

Required

Required

Prepare a cash budget for Mount Hawk Ski Resort, Inc., for 19x6, using the following column headings:

| Item | January | February | March | April–December | Total |

Problem 26A-5
Master Budget
Preparation
(L.O. 3)

Located in Washington, D.C., the accounting firm of Abel, Adams, and Sacks, CPA's, specializes in providing accounting services to defense contractors. Mr. Sacks, the budget officer, is in the process of putting the 19x8 master budget together.

Abel, Adams, and Sacks' 19x7 monthly income statement is shown below.

Month (% of fees)	Fees	Personnel Cost (50%)	Firm Operating Overhead (5% + $5,000)*	General and Administrative Expenses (6% + $7,000)**	Net Income
January	$ 71,600	$ 35,800	$ 8,580	$ 11,296	$ 15,924
February	82,000	41,000	9,100	11,920	19,980
March	94,000	47,000	9,700	12,640	24,660
April	125,000	62,500	11,250	14,500	36,750
May	74,000	37,000	8,700	11,440	16,860
June	66,500	33,250	8,325	10,990	13,935
July	59,600	29,800	7,980	10,576	11,244
August	56,100	28,050	7,805	10,366	9,879
September	72,600	36,300	8,630	11,356	16,314
October	76,700	38,350	8,835	11,602	17,913
November	79,200	39,600	8,960	11,752	18,888
December	84,200	42,100	9,210	12,052	20,838
Totals	$941,500	$470,750	$107,075	$140,490	$223,185

*Fixed expenses include $3,000 of depreciation.
**Fixed expenses include $4,000 of depreciation.

The firm's 19x7 year-end balance sheet appears on the next page.
Additional information needed to prepare the 19x8 master budget follows.

a. Accounts payable are paid on the first day of the following month and represent purchases of supplies from the current month. The amount of the accounts payable is expected to remain constant during 19x8.
b. There are no federal income taxes for the organization since it is a partnership and the individual partners must pay federal income taxes on their share of the firm's net income.
c. Salaries payable are one-half of the current month's personnel costs and are paid as part of the first payroll of the following month.
d. Fees are collected as follows:

20 percent in the current month
40 percent in the first month following billing
40 percent in the second month following billing

Abel, Adams, and Sacks
Certified Public Accountants
Balance Sheet
As of December 31, 19x7

Current Assets		
Cash	$ 17,450	
Accounts Receivable	101,960	
Supplies	23,200	
Prepaid Assets	7,940	
Total Current Assets		$150,550
Long-Term Assets		
Equipment	$466,720	
Furniture and Fixtures	291,600	
Total	$758,320	
Less Accumulated Depreciation	(324,500)	
Total Long-Term Assets		433,820
Total Assets		$584,370
Current Liabilities		
Accounts Payable	$ 6,000	
Salaries Payable	21,550	
Total Current Liabilities		$ 27,550
Long-Term Debt (10 year, 9% note)		234,000
Partners' Equity		
Beginning Balance	$296,040	
Current Year's Net Income	223,185	
Less Partners' Withdrawals	(196,405)	
Ending Balance		322,820
Total Liabilities and Partners' Equity		$584,370

Fees for November and December 19x7 were $82,500 and $86,200, respectively.
e. Supplies inventory and prepaid asset account balances are expected to remain constant during the upcoming year.
f. No purchases of equipment, furniture, or fixtures are expected in 19x8.
g. Fees are expected to increase by 10 percent in 19x8.
h. The firm's fixed operating overhead, other than depreciation, which will remain constant, will increase by 20 percent in 19x8.
i. All fixed general and administrative expenses will remain constant throughout 19x8.
j. All expenses are paid in the month incurred unless otherwise indicated.
k. Monthly partners' withdrawals for 19x8 will be as follows:

Abel: $6,000 per month
Adams: $4,000 per month
Sacks: $10,000 per month

l. The company maintains a minimum cash balance of $15,000. Temporary borrowing should be in $1,000 increments (ignoring interest on these short-term loans) and will be paid back as soon as possible.

m. Interest on the existing ten-year note is due and paid on the last day of each quarter. The note was executed at the end of 19x7.

Required

1. Prepare a forecasted monthly income statement for 19x8.
2. Prepare a quarterly cash budget for 19x8.
3. Prepare a forecasted balance sheet for the firm as of December 31, 19x8.

Problem Set B

Problem 26B-1
Factory
Overhead
Expense Budget
(L.O. 4)

Eubanks Manufacturing Company has a central office and three operating divisions. The central office houses the top management personnel, including all accounting functions. The factory overhead costs incurred during 19x4 are summarized below.

Expense Categories	Division AB	Division CD	Division EF	Total	Expected Increase in 19x5
Indirect labor	$24,500	$28,600	$30,200	$ 83,300	10%
Indirect materials	4,800	5,200	6,000	16,000	20%
Supplies	3,900	3,900	4,000	11,800	10%
Utilities	6,200	7,400	7,100	20,700	10%
Computer services	20,400	26,900	28,600	75,900	—
Insurance	3,400	3,500	3,600	10,500	10%
Repairs and maintenance	5,600	6,000	5,400	17,000	20%
Miscellaneous	1,100	1,200	1,300	3,600	10%
Totals	$69,900	$82,700	$86,200	$238,800	

Expected percentage increases for 19x5 are shown for all categories except computer services. These services will increase by different amounts for each division: Division AB, 25%; Division CD, 30%; and Division EF, 40%. In 19x4, the central office was charged with $42,500 of computer service costs, and this amount is expected to rise by 25 percent in 19x5. During 19x5, the company will rent a new software package at an annual cost of $60,000.

Required

1. Find the total expected cost for computer services for 19x5 for the three divisions and the central office.
2. Assume that the new software package rental charge is allocated to computer service users on the basis of their normal use costs as a percentage of total service charges. Compute the allocation of the rental charges to the three divisions and the central office. (Use the 19x5 amounts computed in 1 above, and round to two decimal places.)

3. Prepare the divisional factory overhead expense budget for Eubanks Manufacturing Company for 19x5.

Problem 26B-2
Budget
Preparation
(L.O. 4)

One of the products manufactured by Hubbard Corporation is a heavy-duty construction nail. Because of modern technology, many of the production steps have been combined through the use of labor-saving equipment. Below is the cost and production information relevant to this construction nail.

Direct materials needed are steel wire (5,000-foot coil at $29 per coil; 20,000 nails per coil), and packing material (bulk packing at $.10 per 1,000 nails). Direct labor for the cut-blank-head operation is figured at $9.60 per direct labor hour, and 10 minutes are required per 1,000 nails; for the point-polish-pack operation the rate should be $9.00 per direct labor hour, and 5 minutes are required per 1,000 nails. Factory overhead for the cut-blank-head operation is figured at a rate of 80 percent of the department's direct labor dollars, and for the point-polish-pack operation at a rate of 60 percent of the department's direct labor dollars.

For the three-month period ending March 31, 19xx, management is anticipating the following monthly unit production figures: 3,600,000 nails in January, 4,800,000 nails in February, and 6,000,000 nails in March.

Required

1. For the three-month period ending March 31, 19xx, prepare monthly production cost information for the manufacture of the construction nails. Show a detailed breakdown of all costs involved and computation methods used.
2. Prepare a quarterly production cost budget for the construction nails. Show monthly cost data and combined totals for the quarter for each cost category.

Problem 26B-3
Selling Expense
Budget
Preparation
(L.O. 4)

Dean Company uses a cost accounting system for its various products and prepares comprehensive period budgets for planning and control. The vice president of sales is responsible for approving the 19x7 selling expense budget. Budgeted and actual selling expenses for 19x6 are compared below.

	19x6 Amounts	
Expense Item	Budget	Actual
Advertising	$ 200,000	$ 190,000
Commissions	1,600,000	1,554,000
Shipping and billing	500,000	530,000
Administrative salaries	600,000	620,000
Travel—commercial	400,000	380,000
Travel—auto fleet	100,000	107,000
Printing	50,000	54,000
Premiums expense	40,000	43,000
Warranty expense	110,000	102,000
Bad debts	500,000	525,000
Total	$4,100,000	$4,105,000
Total sales (in thousands)	$ 200,000	$ 210,000
Cost of sales	(120,000)	(132,300)
Gross margin	$ 80,000	$ 77,700

Fixed costs are budgeted as follows for 19x7:

Advertising	$ 220,000
Administrative salaries	660,000
Travel—commercial	440,000
Printing	60,000
Total	$1,380,000

Variable and semivariable costs are estimated as follows:

Commissions: 2 percent of estimated gross margin
Shipping and billing: $300,000 + .1 percent of sales
Bad debts: $\frac{1}{4}$ percent of sales
Travel—auto fleet: $80,000 + $.20 mile

Expected fleet auto travel in 19x7 is 120,000 miles. Premiums and warranty expenses are expected to increase 20 percent each during 19x7.

Required

1. Prepare a selling expense budget for 19x7 based on expected sales of $240,000,000 and cost of goods sold at 60 percent of sales. Indicate whether each expense is fixed, variable, or semivariable.
2. An assistant to the vice president of sales has suggested simplifying the system by budgeting the selling expenses at 2.1 percent of sales. Without attention to detailed expense categories, the assistant says that being able to spend budgeted funds as needed within the overall 2.1 percent limit will motivate personnel and improve sales volume. Discuss the potential dangers of following the assistant's recommendation.

Problem 26B-4
Cash Budget
Preparation
(L.O. 6)

For the most part, Big Sky Condominiums, Inc., relies on seasonal condo rentals. Located in the desert region of the far southwestern United States, Big Sky operates over a dozen condo complexes. It earns its highest revenues during the warm winter months and the lowest in summer, when temperatures reach 120°F almost daily. Cash budget preparations for 19x2 are currently under way. To date, the following information has been gathered:

Cash Receipts
Rentals:
Year-round: $20,000 per month.
Monthly: $180,000 in January, $200,000 in February, $220,000 in March, and $10,000 monthly for the rest of the year.
Weekly: January, $75,000; February, $80,000; March, $90,000; and $3,000 per month for the remaining months.
Daily: January, $6,000; February, $7,000; March, $8,000; and $1,000 per month for the rest of the year
Telephone reimbursements: $1,000 in January; $1,100 in February; $1,200 in March; and $100 per month for the remaining months
Cleaning deposits: January, $6,000; February, $6,500; March, $7,000; and $200 per month for the rest of the year.
Cash Disbursements
First mortgages: $30,000 monthly
Second mortgages: $10,000 monthly
Land lease expense: $2,000 monthly
Condo maintenance expense: $10,000 monthly
Advertising: $500 in January; $300 in February; and $2,000 in December

Rental commissions: 10% of rental collections per month

Electricity service: January, $6,000; February, $7,000; March, $8,000; and $2,000 per month thereafter

Gas service: January, $4,000; February, $4,500; March, $6,000; and $1,500 per month thereafter

Water and sanitation service: January, $1,500; February, $1,600; March, $1,700; and $100 per month thereafter

Cable TV expense: $3,000 every other month beginning in January

Pest control expense: $1,800 in January

Repairs: January, $2,000; February, $3,000; March, $4,000; and $1,500 per month thereafter

Telephone service: January, $1,800; February, $2,000; March, $2,200; and $300 per month thereafter

Taxes:
  Property—$22,000 in June
  Income—$56,500 in March

Insurance:
  Fire—$6,500 in January and July
  Liability—$14,000 in January

Seasonal landscaping: January, $4,000; February, $3,000; and $5,000 in December

Postage: $120 monthly

Carpet and drape cleaning: January, $800; February, $600; and $1,000 in December

Bank charges: $100 monthly

Deposit refunds: January, $200; February, $6,000; March, $6,500; April, $7,000; and $200 per month thereafter

Miscellaneous: $200 monthly

The company anticipates a $20,000 beginning cash balance on January 1, 19x2.

Required

Prepare a cash budget for Big Sky Condominiums, Inc., for 19x2, using the following column headings:

Item	January	February	March	April–December	Total

**Problem 26B-5
Budget
Preparation—
Not-for-Profit
Organization
(L.O. 7)**

Hayward College is a small liberal arts school with an enrollment of around 2,500 students. The college was founded in 1860 by a missionary and his wife and has become well known over the years. Graduates of the school have been very successful and include senators, corporate presidents, military leaders, famous academic and research personnel and even two state governors.

The college's development program has been in operation for fifty years and is now under the direction of Dr. Jay Tontz. During the past twelve years, the college's endowment has grown from $15,500,000 to an expected $165,450,000 at the close of operation on December 31, 19x6. The breakdown of that amount is as follows (information in parentheses shows how each part of the endowment is invested and its current yield).

Unrestricted
  Corporate "silver plate" program
    (12% money market fund) $ 23,400,000
  Alumni open donation account
    (10% corporate bonds)   14,900,000
  Alumni/college beneficiary insurance proceeds
    (14% certificate of deposit)   46,850,000
  Friends of the College fund
    (12% money market fund)   7,280,000

    Total unrestricted $ 92,430,000

Restricted
  Endowed professorships:
    Science—6 at $1,000,000 $ 6,000,000
    Business—3 at $1,000,000   3,000,000
    Religion—1 at $800,000   800,000
    History—1 at $600,000   600,000
      (10% corporate bonds and preferred stock)
  Alumni student scholarship fund
    (12% certificate of deposit)   4,900,000
  Building maintenance program
    (14% second mortgage loans)   16,850,000
  Capital facility expansion fund
    (12% government securities)   40,870,000

    Total restricted $ 73,020,000
Total college endowment $165,450,000

After careful analysis, Dr. Tontz anticipates the following additions to the endowment next year:

Corporate "silver plate" program	$ 640,000
Alumni open donation	110,000
Alumni/college beneficiary insurance proceeds	1,500,000
Friends of the College	410,000
Endowed professorships:	
One in science	1,000,000
One in social science	400,000
Alumni student scholarship fund	550,000
Building maintenance program	310,000
Capital facility expansion fund	2,500,000

Note: The endowed professorship in science and the addition to the capital facility expansion fund will be received in January. Assume that the other endowment additions earn half the normal interest for the year.

Required

1. Prepare the complete projected college endowment budget as of December 31, 19x7.

2. Compute the projected interest income for the year from each part of the endowment.

3. The interest income from the unrestricted part of the endowment must first be used to cover expenses of $2,460,000 for the development program operation. Explain what kinds of uses the college could make of the remaining funds. Give at least four examples.

Management Decision Case 26-1

Walkman Enterprises
(L.O. 1, 4)

During the past ten years, Walkman Enterprises has practiced participative budgeting all the way from the maintenance personnel to the president's staff. Gradually, however, the objectives of honesty and decisions made in the best interest of the company as a whole have given way at the divisional level to division-benefiting decisions and budgets biased in favor of divisional interests. Ms. Beck, corporate controller, has asked Mr. Christopher, budget director, to carefully analyze this year's divisional budgets before incorporating them into the company's master budget.

The FM Division was the first of the six divisions to submit its 19x4 budget request to the corporate office. Its summary income statement and accompanying notes are presented on the next page.

Required

1. Recast the FM Division's Forecasted Income Statement into the following format (round percentages to two decimal places):

	Budget—12/31/x3		Budget—12/31/x4	
Account	Amount	Percent of Sales	Amount	Percent of Sales

2. Actual results for 19x3 revealed the following information about revenues and cost of goods sold:

	Amount	Percent of Sales
Sales: radios	$ 760,000	43.30
appliances	560,000	31.91
telephones	370,000	21.08
miscellaneous	65,000	3.71
Total revenues	$1,755,000	100.00
Less cost of goods sold	763,425	43.50
Gross margin	$ 991,575	56.50

On the basis of this information and your analysis in **1**, what should the budget director say to officials of the FM Division? Mention specific areas of the budget that need to be revised.

Walkman Enterprises
FM Division
Forecasted Income Statement
For the Years Ending December 31, 19x3 and 19x4

	Budget 12/31/x3	Budget 12/31/x4	Increase (Decrease)
Revenues			
Sales: Radios	$ 840,000	$ 900,000	$ 60,000
Appliances	690,000	750,000	60,000
Telephones	265,000	300,000	35,000
Miscellaneous	82,400	100,000	17,600
Total Revenues	$1,877,400	$2,050,000	$172,600
Less Cost of Goods Sold	750,960	717,500[1]	(33,460)
Gross Margin	$1,126,440	$1,332,500	$206,060
Operating Expenses			
Wages: Warehouse	$ 84,500	$ 92,250	$ 7,750
Purchasing	67,800	74,000	6,200
Delivery/Shipping	59,400	64,780	5,380
Maintenance	32,650	35,670	3,020
Salaries: Supervisory	60,000	92,250	32,250
Executive	120,000	164,000	44,000
Purchases, supplies	17,400	20,500	3,100
Merchandise Moving Equipment:			
Maintenance	72,400	82,000	9,600
Depreciation	62,000	71,750[2]	9,750
Building Rent	96,000	102,500	6,500
Sales Commissions	187,740	205,000	17,260
Insurance: Fire	12,670	20,500	7,830
Liability	18,200	20,500	2,300
Utilities	14,100	15,375	1,275
Taxes: Property	16,600	18,450	1,850
Payroll	26,520	41,000	14,480
Miscellaneous	4,610	10,250	5,640
Total Operating Expenses	$ 952,590	$1,130,775	$178,185
Net Income Before Taxes	$ 173,850	$ 201,725	$ 27,875

Notes: (1) Less expensive merchandise will be purchased in 19x4 to boost profits.
(2) Depreciation is increased because of a need to buy additional equipment to handle increased sales.

Learning
Objectives

Chapter
Twenty-Seven

Cost Control
Using
Standard
Costing

1. *Describe the nature and purpose of standard costs.*

2. *Identify the six elements of a standard unit cost, and describe the factors to consider in developing each element.*

3. *Compute a standard unit cost.*

4. *Prepare a flexible budget.*

5. *Describe management by exception.*

6. *Compute and evaluate direct materials, direct labor, and factory overhead variances.*

7. *Prepare journal entries involving variances from standard costs.*

8. *Describe the basic techniques used by public sector and not-for-profit organizations to control costs of operations.*

After planning, which was discussed in the last chapter, the second part of the budgetary control process is to monitor operations so that operating plans and targets can be achieved. Most of the management accounting tools used in this process are performance evaluation techniques. By this we mean any procedure that analyzes past performance, including cost control techniques. As we will see later in the chapter, public-sector or not-for-profit organizations, just like businesses, need to control costs along with other aspects of their performance.

A standard cost accounting system is a very common approach to cost control and performance evaluation. In this chapter, we will first look at the nature and purpose of standard costs. We will discuss ways of developing standard costs and then show how they can be used. Finally, after an introduction to flexible budgeting, we will move on to standard cost variance analysis, which is at the center of cost control using standard costs. As a result of studying this chapter, you should be able to meet the learning objectives listed on the left.

Standard Cost Accounting

Standard cost accounting is a tool used by management for cost planning and cost control purposes. When a company uses standard costs, all costs affecting the inventory accounts and the Cost of Goods Sold account are stated in terms of standard or predetermined costs rather than actual costs incurred. A standard cost system is used along with an existing job order or process costing system. It is not a full cost accounting system in itself. Together with cost behavior relationships and the various cost-volume-profit analyses, the use of standard costs in a cost accounting system provides the foundation for budgetary control. Standard costs are useful for (1) evaluating the performance of workers and management, (2) preparing budgets and forecasts, and (3) helping to decide on appropriate selling prices. Because the topic of standard costs is so important and represents such a major change in costing concepts, our discussion will be divided into two parts. First we will look at the nature and purpose of standard costs—their make-up, how they are developed, their use in product costing, and related journal entries. Then we will analyze their primary use as a cost control tool.

Nature and Purpose of Standard Costs

*Objective 1
Describe the
nature and
purpose of
standard costs*

Standard costs are realistically predetermined costs for direct materials, direct labor, and factory overhead. They are usually expressed as cost per unit of finished product. Predetermined overhead costs, which we discussed in Chapter 23, are different from standard costs. The concept of standard costing focuses on total unit cost, which includes all three manufacturing cost elements. It goes beyond factory overhead cost. And more care and effort are given to figuring standard costs.

Predetermined overhead costing and standard costing do, however, share two very important elements. (1) Both forecast dollar amounts to be used in product costing. (2) Both depend on expected costs of budgeted items. But this is where the similarity ends. Standard costs are based on engineering estimates, forecasted demand, worker input, time and motion studies, and direct materials types and quality. Standard costs depend on more than the simple projections of past costs that are used to develop predetermined overhead rates. However, we should not play down the role of the predetermined overhead rate. It provides some of the same data as the standard overhead rate. And standard costing is both sophisticated and expensive. If a company cannot afford to add standard costing to its cost system, then it should go on using predetermined overhead rates.

Standard costing is a total cost concept. It is made up of costs for direct materials, direct labor, and factory overhead. In a fully integrated standard cost system, all actual manufacturing cost data are replaced by standard (or predetermined) cost data. Accounts such as Direct Materials Inventory, Work in Process Inventory, Finished Goods Inventory, and Cost of Goods Sold are all stated in terms of standard costs. All debit and credit entries made to these accounts are in terms of standard costs, not actual costs. All inventory balances are figured by using standard unit costs. Separate records of actual costs are kept to compare standard costs (what should have been spent) with actual costs. The two are usually compared at the end of each accounting period, whether weekly, monthly, or quarterly. If large differences (variances) exist, the cost accountant looks for the causes of the differences. This process, known as variance analysis, is one of the most effective cost control tools. We discuss it later in this chapter.

Standard costs are introduced into a cost accounting system for several reasons. Standard costs are useful for preparing operating budgets. They make it easier to pinpoint production costs that need to be controlled.

They help in setting realistic prices. And they basically simplify cost accounting procedures for inventories and product costing. Although expensive to set up and maintain, a standard cost accounting system can save a company a lot of money by reducing waste.

Development of Standard Costs

Objective 2
Identify the six
elements of a
standard unit
cost, and
describe the
factors to
consider in
developing each
element

A standard unit cost has six parts: (1) direct materials price standard, (2) direct materials quantity standard, (3) direct labor time standard, (4) direct labor rate standard, (5) standard variable factory overhead rate, and (6) standard fixed factory overhead rate. To develop a standard unit cost, we must identify and analyze each of these items.

Standard Direct Materials Cost The **standard direct materials cost** is found by multiplying the standard price for direct materials by the standard quantity for direct materials. If the price standard for a certain item is $2.75 and a specific job calls for eight of these items, the standard direct materials cost for that job is $22.00 (8 × $2.75).

The **direct materials price standard** is a careful estimate of the cost of a certain type of direct material in the next accounting period. Possible price increases, changes in quantities available, and new supplier sources must all be taken into account. Any of these could influence the price standard. A company's purchasing agent is responsible for developing price standards for all direct materials. The purchasing agent also follows through with actual purchases at the projected standard prices.

The standard use of direct materials is one of the most difficult standards to forecast. The **direct materials quantity standard** is an estimate of expected quantity use. It is influenced by product engineering specifications, quality of direct materials, age and productivity of machinery, and the quality and experience of the workforce. Production managers are usually responsible for establishing and policing direct materials quantity standards. However, many people provide input into the development of these standards.

Standard Direct Labor Cost The **standard direct labor cost** for a product, task, or job order is figured by multiplying the standard hours of direct labor by the standard wage for direct labor. Assume that a product takes 1.5 standard direct labor hours to produce and that the standard labor rate is $8.40 per hour. Even if the person actually making the product is paid only $7.90 per hour, $12.60 ($8.40 × 1.5) of standard direct labor cost would be charged to the Work in Process Inventory account.

Current time and motion studies of workers and machines and past employee and machine performance are the basic input for a **direct labor time standard.** Such standards express the time it takes for each department, machine, or process to complete production on one unit or batch of output. In many cases, standard time per unit will be a small fraction of an hour. Meeting time standards is the responsibility of the department manager or supervisor. These standards should be revised whenever a machine is replaced or the quality of workers changes.

Labor rates are either set by labor contracts or defined by the company. So standard labor rates are fairly easy to develop. **Direct labor rate standards** are the hourly labor cost that is expected to prevail during the next accounting period for each function or job classification. Though rate ranges are established for each type of worker and rates vary within these ranges, an average standard rate is developed for each task. Problems arise when a highly paid worker performs a low-level task. For instance, a machine operator making $9.25 per hour may actually perform the work of a set-up person earning $4.50 per hour. Here, the actual cost for the work will be at variance with the standard direct labor rate.

Standard Factory Overhead Cost Basically, the **standard factory overhead cost** is an estimate of variable and fixed overhead in the next accounting period. The variable overhead cost and the fixed overhead cost depend on standard rates computed in very much the same way as the predetermined overhead rate we discussed in Chapter 23. There are only two differences. First, the standard overhead rate is made up of two parts, the rate for variable costs and the rate for fixed costs. Second, more time and effort are put into figuring standard overhead rates.

The reason for computing the variable rate and the fixed rate separately is that different application bases are generally appropriate. The **standard variable overhead rate** is usually figured on the basis of *expected* direct labor hours. (Other bases may be used if direct labor hours are not a good barometer of variable costs.) The formula is as follows:

$$\frac{\text{standard variable}}{\text{overhead rate}} = \frac{\text{total budgeted variable overhead costs}}{\text{expected number of standard direct labor hours}}$$

The **standard fixed overhead rate,** on the other hand, is most often figured on the basis of **normal operating capacity.** This basis is expressed in the same terms as those used to compute the variable overhead rate.

$$\frac{\text{standard fixed}}{\text{overhead rate}} = \frac{\text{total budgeted fixed overhead costs}}{\text{normal capacity in terms of standard direct labor hours}}$$

By using normal capacity as the application basis, all fixed overhead costs should be applied to units produced by the time normal capacity is reached.

If actual output (standard hours allowed) is more than normal capacity, a favorable situation exists because more fixed overhead has been applied than was actually incurred. But if actual output is less than normal capacity, then not all of the expected fixed overhead costs have been applied to production units—an unfavorable condition. The difference (variance) between factory overhead incurred and factory overhead applied will be discussed later in the chapter.

Using Standards for Product Costing

Using standard costs does away with the need to figure unit costs from actual cost data every week or month, or for each batch. Once standards are developed for direct materials, direct labor, and factory overhead, a total standard unit cost can be computed at any time.

Standard cost elements can be used to find the following: (1) cost of purchased direct materials entered into Materials Inventory, (2) cost of goods requisitioned out of Materials Inventory and into Work in Process Inventory, (3) cost of direct labor charged to Work in Process Inventory, (4) cost of factory overhead applied to Work in Process Inventory, (5) cost of goods completed and transferred to Finished Goods Inventory, and (6) cost of units sold and charged to the Cost of Goods Sold account. In other words, all transactions (entries) affecting the three inventory accounts and Cost of Goods Sold will be expressed in terms of standard costs, no matter what the actual costs incurred. An illustrative problem will show how this concept works.

Illustrative Problem: Use of Standard Costs

*Objective 3
Compute a
standard unit
cost*

Ike Industries, Inc., uses standard costs in its Denison, Texas, division. Recently, the company changed the standards for its line of automatic pencils to agree with current costs for the year 19xx. New standards include the following:

Direct materials price standards are $7.20 per square foot for casing material and $1.25 for each movement mechanism. Direct materials quantity standards are .125 square foot of casing material per pencil and one movement mechanism per pencil. Direct labor time standards are .01 hour per pencil for the Stamping Department and .05 hour per pencil for the Assembly Department. Direct labor rate standards are $6.00 per hour for the Stamping Department and $7.20 per hour for the Assembly Department. Standard factory overhead rates are $18.00 per direct labor hour for the standard variable overhead rate and $12.00 per direct labor hour for the standard fixed overhead rate.

Required

Compute the standard manufacturing cost of one automatic pencil.

Solution

Standard cost of one pencil computed:

Direct materials costs	
Casing ($7.20/sq ft × .125 sq ft)	$ .90
One movement mechanism	1.25
Direct labor costs	
Stamping department (.01 hr/pencil × $6.00/hr)	.06
Assembly department (.05 hr/pencil × $7.20/hr)	.36
Factory overhead	
Variable overhead (.06 hr/pencil × $18.00/hr)	1.08
Fixed overhead (.06 hr/pencil × $12.00/hr)	.72
Total standard cost per pencil	$4.37

Journal Entry Analysis

Recording standard costs is much like recording actual cost data. The only major difference is that any amount for direct materials, direct labor, or factory overhead being entered into the Work in Process Inventory account is stated at standard cost. This means that the Work in Process Inventory account is stated entirely at standard cost. Any transfer of units to Finished Goods Inventory or to the Cost of Goods Sold account will automatically be at standard unit cost. When actual costs for direct materials, direct labor, and factory overhead are different from standard costs, the difference is recorded in a variance account. (We will discuss such accounts in the next section.) In the following analysis, we will assume that all costs incurred are at standard cost. Again, we use Ike Industries as an example.

Transaction: Purchased 400 square feet of casing material at standard cost.

Entry: Materials Inventory   2,880
                Accounts Payable   2,880
                    To record purchase of 400 sq ft of
                    casing material at $7.20/sq ft

(It does not matter if the actual purchase price is higher or lower than the standard price. The same $2,880 standard cost is still entered into the Materials Inventory account. See also the journal entry for purchases on page 1032.)

Transaction: Requisitioned 60 square feet of casing material and 240 movement mechanisms into production.

Entry: Work in Process Inventory   732
                Materials Inventory   732
                    To record requisition of 60 sq ft of
                    casing material (at $7.20/sq ft)
                    and 240 movement mechanisms
                    (at $1.25 each) into production

Transaction: At period end, 300 pencils were completed and transferred to Finished Goods Inventory.

Entry: Finished Goods Inventory   1,311
                Work in Process Inventory   1,311
                    To record the transfer of 300
                    completed units to finished
                    goods inventory (300 pencils ×
                    $4.37/pencil)

The above analysis shows only a few examples of the journal entries used in recording standard cost information. The examples given later in this chapter are more realistic because they are joined with the analysis of variances. Our purpose here is just to show that when a standard cost accounting system is being used, standard costs, rather than actual costs, flow through the production and inventory accounts.

Cost Control Through Variance Analysis

Performance evaluation is an important part of cost control. Emphasis is on comparing "what did happen" with "what was expected (budgeted) to happen." Our discussion will focus on the differences between (1) actual costs and budgeted costs, and (2) actual costs and standard costs. Performance evaluation is usually associated with cost variances in the manufacturing process. But standard costs for evaluating selling and other functions in a company are equally important for profitability and operating efficiency.

Evaluating Performance

Performance is measured by comparing actual with budgeted results. This process has several aspects, some involving company policies and others involving human factors.

An effective control program includes policies or procedures for (1) preparing operational plans, (2) establishing responsibility for performance, (3) communicating operational plans to key personnel, (4) evaluating each area of responsibility, and (5) if variances exist, learning the causes and making needed corrections.

Company policies are important but, alone, will not lead to effective control of operations. The human aspect is the most important part of trying to meet corporate goals. People do the planning, people perform the manufacturing operations, and people evaluate or are evaluated.

Some basic guidelines regarding people must be part of any cost control system. First, those who are responsible for an operating area must have direct input into the goal-setting process. Incentive to perform is a key factor in meeting goals. If a manager believes that an operating target is unrealistic, or if plans are developed without the participation of department-level personnel, the desire to reach those goals may fall. Second, management must clearly communicate every goal or plan to all the people involved, spelling out each person's exact responsibilities. Failure to communicate is a common cause of inefficient operating performance. The third guideline is to give responsible individuals feedback on their performance. Management should praise good performance and not take it for granted. Silence does not imply good performance; it means bad management. If performance is poor or substandard, the responsible individual should have the chance to defend any actions taken. There may be a good reason for variance from the standard that was set. Perhaps the cause is beyond the person's control. In any case, management should develop appropriate policies and follow sound behavioral guidelines when setting up a performance evaluation process.

Figure 27-1
Performance
Analysis:
Comparison of
Actual and
Budgeted Data

Killham Industries, Inc. Performance Report—Michigan Division For the Year Ended December 31, 19xx			
Cost Item	Budget*	Actual†	Difference Under (Over) Budget
Direct materials	$ 42,000	$ 46,000	$(4,000)
Direct labor	68,250	75,000	(6,750)
Factory overhead			
Variable			
Indirect materials	10,500	11,500	(1,000)
Indirect labor	14,000	15,250	(1,250)
Utilities	7,000	7,600	(600)
Other	8,750	9,750	(1,000)
Fixed			
Supervisory salaries	19,000	18,500	500
Depreciation	15,000	15,000	—
Utilities	4,500	4,500	—
Other	10,900	11,100	(200)
Totals	$199,900	$214,200	$(14,300)

*Budget based on expected productive output of 17,500 units.
†Actual cost of producing 19,100 units.

Flexible Budgets

Budgets were emphasized in Chapter 26, which focused on the planning process. Why, then, you might ask, should we introduce the concept of flexible budgets as part of cost control rather than as a planning tool? We do so because a flexible budget (also called a variable budget) is primarily a cost control tool that helps to evaluate performance. A **flexible budget** is a summary of expected costs for a range of activity levels; it is geared to changes in the level of productive output. The budgets we discussed as part of the planning function are called static or fixed budgets because they describe just one level of expected sales and production activity. Period budgets are usually prepared for an expected or normal level of output.

For budgeting or planning purposes, a set of static budgets based on a single level of output is good enough for management needs. These budgets show management the desired picture of operating results. They also provide a target for managers to use in developing monthly and weekly operating plans. However, these budgets often prove inadequate for judging operating results. Figure 27-1 presents data for Killham Industries, Inc. Actual costs exceed budgeted costs by $14,300, or 7.2 percent. Such an overrun is felt to be significant by most managers. But was there really

Figure 27-2
Flexible Budget
Preparation

Killham Industries, Inc.
Flexible Budget Analysis—Michigan Division
For the Year Ended December 31, 19xx

Cost Item	Unit Levels of Activity			Variable Cost per Unit*
	15,000	17,500	20,000	
Direct materials	$ 36,000	$ 42,000	$ 48,000	$2.40
Direct labor	58,500	68,250	78,000	3.90
Variable factory overhead				
Indirect materials	9,000	10,500	12,000	.60
Indirect labor	12,000	14,000	16,000	.80
Utilities	6,000	7,000	8,000	.40
Other	7,500	8,750	10,000	.50
Total variable costs	$129,000	$150,500	$172,000	$8.60
Fixed factory overhead				
Supervisory salaries	$ 19,000	$ 19,000	$ 19,000	
Depreciation	15,000	15,000	15,000	
Utilities	4,500	4,500	4,500	
Other	10,900	10,900	10,900	
Total fixed costs	$ 49,400	$ 49,400	$ 49,400	
Total costs	$178,400	$199,900	$221,400	

Flexible budget formula:
(variable cost per unit × number of units produced) + budgeted fixed costs
= ($8.60 × units produced) + $49,400

Note: Activity expressed in units was used as the basis for this analysis. When units are used, direct material and direct labor costs are included in the analysis. Flexible budgets commonly are restricted to overhead costs. In such a situation, direct labor hours are used in place of units produced.
*Computed by dividing the dollar amount in any column by the respective level of activity.

a cost overrun? As explained in the notes to Figure 27-1, the budgeted amounts are based on expected output of 17,500 units, but actual output was 19,100 units.

Before analyzing the performance of the Michigan Division, we must change the budgeted data to reflect output of 19,100 units. In this example, the static budget for 17,500 units is of no use for judging performance. The role of a flexible budget is to provide forecasted data that can be adjusted automatically for changes in the level of output. Figure 27-2 presents a flexible budget for Killham Industries, Inc., with budgeted data for 15,000, 17,500, and 20,000 units of output. The important part of this illustration is the flexible budget formula shown at the bottom. The $8.60 variable cost per unit is computed in the upper right column, and the $49,400 is found in the fixed-cost section of the analysis. Using this formula, we can draw up a budget for the Michigan Division at any level of output.

Figure 27-3
Performance
Analysis Using
Flexible Budget
Data

	Killham Industries, Inc. Performance Report—Michigan Division For the Year Ended December 31, 19xx		
Cost Item (Variable Unit Cost)	Budget Based on 19,100 Units Produced	Actual Costs at 19,100- Unit Level	Differences Under (Over) Budget
Direct materials ($2.40)	$ 45,840	$ 46,000	$(160)
Direct labor ($3.90)	74,490	75,000	(510)
Factory overhead			
Variable			
Indirect materials			
($.60)	11,460	11,500	(40)
Indirect labor ($.80)	15,280	15,250	30
Utilities ($.40)	7,640	7,600	40
Other ($.50)	9,550	9,750	(200)
Fixed			
Supervisory salaries	19,000	18,500	500
Depreciation	15,000	15,000	—
Utilities	4,500	4,500	—
Other	10,900	11,100	(200)
Totals	$213,660	$214,200	$(540)

In Figure 27-1, budgeted data would have to be adjusted for expected costs at the 19,100-unit level before they could be compared with actual dollar amounts. Figure 27-3 shows a performance report using flexible budget data. Unit variable cost amounts have been multiplied by 19,100 units to arrive at total budgeted figures. Fixed overhead information has been carried over from the flexible budget developed in Figure 27-2. As the new performance report shows, costs exceeded budgeted amounts during the year by only $540, or two-tenths of one percent. Using the flexible budget concept, we find that the performance of the Michigan Division is almost on target. Performance has now been measured and analyzed accurately.

Variance Determination

We can evaluate operating performance by comparing actual results with either budgeted data or standard cost data. Budgeted data tend to be less precise than standard cost data, but both provide cost goals. In this section of the chapter we will focus on performance evaluation based on standard costs. The first step is to find out if a cost variance exists. Variance determination helps to locate areas of operating efficiency or inefficiency so that corrective steps can be taken if needed. But the key to effective control of

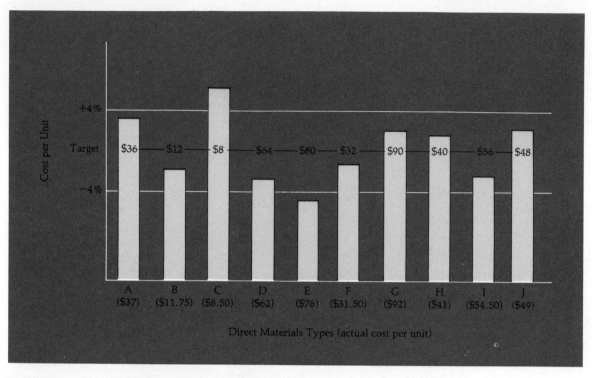

Figure 27-4
The Management by Exception Technique

Objective 5
Describe management by exception

operations is not just in finding the amount of the variance. Finding the reason for the variance is essential. Once the reason is known, steps can be taken to correct the trouble spot.

Management needs a system for analyzing operations. Many companies are so big that it is impossible to review all areas of operations. Locating and analyzing only the areas of unusually good or bad performance is called **management by exception.** Variance analysis is the major cost accounting tool in management by exception. Let's assume that management decides that performance with ±4 percent of budget or target is acceptable. When reviewing performance reports, only cost areas where differences exceed these limits will be analyzed for cause. In Figure 27-4, only direct materials C and E are outside the 4 percent limits, and their purchasing practices will be analyzed.

We can figure variances for whole cost categories, such as total direct materials cost, or we can find variances for each item of direct materials. The more refined and detailed the analysis, the more effective it is for cost control purposes. The rest of this chapter uses standard cost variance analysis in simplified cost areas. In practice, variance analyses are much more involved, taking into account all facets of the production and distribution functions. However, the technique shown here is the basis for the more complicated situations.

Direct Materials Variances To discover direct materials variances, we compare standard amounts for price and quantity with actual prices and materials use. Let us assume, for example, that Billings Company makes leather chairs. Each chair should use 4 yards of leather (standard quantity),

Chapter Twenty-Seven

Objective 6
Compute and
evaluate direct
materials, direct
labor, and
factory
overhead
variances

and the standard price of leather is $6.00 per yard. During August, 760 yards of leather costing $5.90 per yard were purchased and used to produce 180 chairs. The total direct materials cost variance is figured below.

Actual cost

actual quantity × actual price =
760 yd at $5.90/yd = $4,484

Standard cost

standard quantity × standard price =
(180 chairs × 4 yd/chair) at $6.00/yd =
720 yd at $6.00/yd = $4,320

Total direct materials cost variance $ 164(U)

The "U" following the dollar amount indicates an unfavorable situation. (A favorable situation would be indicated by an "F.") The special problem facing the Billings Company is that part of this variance is caused by price differences and part is caused by direct materials usage. To find the area or people responsible for these variances, the total direct materials cost variance must be broken down into two parts: the direct materials price variance and the direct materials quantity variance.

The **direct materials price variance** is the difference between the actual price and the standard price, multiplied by the actual quantity purchased. For the Billings Company, it would be figured as follows:

Actual price	$5.90
Less standard price	6.00
Difference	$ .10(F)

price variance = difference in price × actual quantity
= .10(F) × 760 yards
= $76(F)

The **direct materials quantity variance** is the difference between the actual quantity used and the standard quantity that should have been used, multiplied by the standard price.

Actual quantity	760 yd
Less standard quantity (180 chairs × 4 yd/chair)	720 yd
Difference	40 yd(U)

quantity variance = difference in quantity × standard price
= 40 yd(U) × $6/yd
= $240(U)

As a check of these answers, the sum of the price variance and the quantity variance should equal the total direct materials cost variance.

Price variance	$ 76(F)
Quantity variance	240(U)
Total direct materials cost variance	$164(U)

Normally, the purchasing agent is responsible for price variances and the production department supervisors are accountable for quantity variances. In cases like this one, however, the cheaper materials may have been of such poor quality that higher scrap rates resulted. Each situation must be evaluated according to specific circumstances and not in terms of general guidelines.

Direct Labor Variances The approach to finding variances in direct labor costs parallels the approach to finding direct materials variances. Total direct labor variance is the difference between the actual labor cost and standard labor cost for the good units produced. Expanding the Billings Company example, we find that each chair requires 2.4 standard labor hours and the standard labor rate is $8.50 per hour. During August, 450 direct labor hours were used to make 180 chairs at an average pay rate of $9.20 per hour. The total direct labor cost variance is figured as shown below.

Actual cost
      actual hours × actual rate = 450 hr × $9.20/hr = $4,140
Standard cost
            standard hours allowed × standard rate =
            (180 chairs × 2.4 hr/chair) × $8.50/hr =
                  432 hr × $8.50/hr =   3,672
Total direct labor cost variance $ 468(U)

The actual hours per chair and the actual labor rate both varied from standard. For effective cost control, management must know how much of the total cost arose from different labor rates and how much from varying labor hour usage. This information is found by figuring the labor rate variance and the labor efficiency variance separately.

The **direct labor rate variance** is the difference between the actual labor rate and the standard labor rate, multiplied by the actual hours worked.

Actual rate $9.20
Less standard rate   8.50
   Difference $ .70(U)

            rate variance = difference in rate × actual hours
                          = .70(U) × 450 hours
                          = $315(U)

The **direct labor efficiency variance** is the difference between actual hours worked and standard hours allowed for the good units produced, multiplied by the standard labor rate.

Actual hours worked   450 hr
Less standard hours allowed (180 chairs × 2.4 hr/chair)   432 hr
   Difference   18 hr(U)

$$\text{efficiency variance} = \text{difference in hours} \times \text{standard rate}$$
$$= 18\ \text{hr(U)} \times \$8.50/\text{hr}$$
$$= \underline{\$153\text{(U)}}$$

The following check shows that the variances have been computed correctly.

Rate variance	$315(U)
Efficiency variance	153(U)
Total direct labor cost variance	$468(U)

Labor rate variances are generally the responsibility of the personnel department. A rate variance often happens when a person is hired at an incorrect rate or performs the duties of a higher- or lower-paid employee. Labor efficiency variances can be traced to departmental supervisors. As with direct materials variances, an unfavorable labor efficiency variance can occur if an inexperienced, lower-paid person is assigned to a task requiring greater skill. Management should judge each situation only after looking at all the circumstances.

Factory Overhead Variances Controlling overhead costs is more difficult than controlling direct materials and direct labor costs because responsibility for overhead costs is hard to pin down. But if variable overhead costs can be linked to operating departments, some control is possible. Most fixed costs are not controlled by specific departmental managers.

Analyses of factory overhead variances vary in sophistication. The basic approach is to figure the total overhead variance and then divide this amount into two parts: the controllable overhead variance and the overhead volume variance. Other, more involved approaches are possible, but we will use this one. In our example, the Billings Company budgeted standard variable overhead costs of $5.75 per direct labor hour plus $1,300 of fixed overhead costs for August. Normal capacity was set at 400 direct labor hours per month. The company incurred $4,100 of actual overhead costs in August.

Before finding the overhead variances, we must calculate the total overhead rate. The total standard overhead rate has two parts. One part is the variable rate of $5.75 per direct labor hour. The other is the standard fixed overhead rate, which is found by dividing budgeted fixed overhead ($1,300) by normal capacity. This works out to $3.25 per direct labor hour ($1,300 ÷ 400 hours). So the total standard overhead rate is $9.00 per direct labor hour ($5.75 + $3.25). The total fixed overhead costs divided by normal capacity provides a rate that assigns fixed overhead costs to products in a way that is consistent with expected output. The total overhead variance for the Billings Company is figured below.

Actual overhead costs incurred	$4,100
Standard overhead costs applied to good units produced	
$9.00/direct labor hour × (180 chairs × 2.4 hr/chair)	3,888
Total overhead variance	$ 212(U)

The **controllable overhead variance** is the difference between the actual overhead incurred and the factory overhead budgeted for the level of production reached. Thus the controllable variance for the Billings Company for August would be as follows:

Actual overhead costs incurred		$4,100
Less budgeted factory overhead		
(flexible budget) for 180 chairs:		
Variable overhead cost		
(180 chairs × 2.4 hr/chair)		
× $5.75/direct labor hour	$2,484	
Budgeted fixed overhead cost	1,300	
Total budgeted factory overhead		3,784
Controllable overhead variance		$ 316(U)

The **overhead volume variance** is the difference between the factory overhead budgeted for the level of production achieved and the overhead applied to production using the standard overhead rate. Continuing with the Billings Company example, we have

Budgeted factory overhead (see above)	$3,784	
Less factory overhead applied		
(180 chairs × 2.4 hr/chair)		
× $9.00/direct labor hour	3,888	
Overhead volume variance	$ 104(F)	

Checking the computations, we find that the two variances do equal the total overhead variance.

Controllable overhead variance	$316(U)
Overhead volume variance	104(F)
Total overhead variance	$212(U)

In this example, the company spent more than it should have, so the controllable variance is unfavorable.

Use of existing facilities and capacity is measured by the overhead volume variance. A volume variance will occur only if more or less capacity than normal is actually used. In the example, 400 direct labor hours is the measure of normal use of facilities. In producing 180 chairs, the company should have used 432 standard direct labor hours (standard hours allowed). Fixed overhead costs are applied on the basis of standard hours allowed. In the example, overhead would be applied on the basis of 432 hours, but the fixed overhead rate was figured by using 400 hours (normal capacity). Thus more fixed costs would be applied to products than were budgeted. Because the products can absorb no more than actual costs incurred, this level of production would tend to lower unit cost. When more than expected capacity is used, the result is a favorable overhead volume variance. When less than normal capacity is used, not all of the fixed overhead costs will be applied to units produced. It is then necessary to add the amount of underapplied fixed overhead to the cost of

Figure 27-5
Overhead
Variance
Analysis

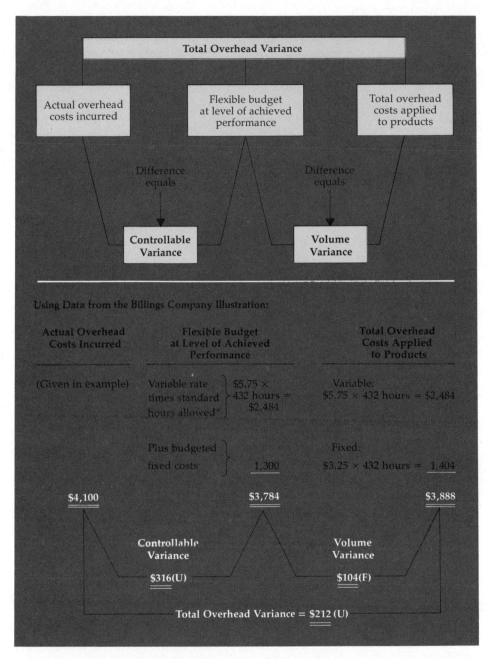

*Standard hours allowed (achieved performance level) is computed by multiplying good units produced times required standard time per unit. Here the computation is as follows:

180 chairs produced × 2.4 hours per chair = 432 standard hours allowed

the good units produced, thereby increasing their unit cost. This condition is unfavorable.

Figure 27-5 sums up our discussion of overhead variance analysis. All procedures shown are exactly the same as those explained above. To figure the controllable variance, subtract the budgeted overhead amount (using a flexible budget) for the level of output achieved from actual overhead costs incurred. A positive answer means an unfavorable variance, because actual costs were greater than those budgeted. The controllable variance is favorable if the difference is negative. Subtracting total overhead applied from overhead budgeted at the level of output achieved produces the volume variance. As before, a positive answer means an unfavorable variance, and a negative answer means a favorable variance. The data from the Billings Company example are shown in the lower part of Figure 27-5. Carefully check the solution in the figure with that given earlier.

Variances in the Accounting Records

When variances from standard costs develop, special journal entries are needed. A few simple rules will make this recording process easier to remember:

Objective 7
Prepare journal entries involving variances from standard costs

1. As stated earlier, *all* inventory balances are recorded at standard cost.
2. Separate accounts are created for each type of variance.
3. *Unfavorable* variances are *debited* to their accounts, and *favorable* variances are *credited*.

With these rules in mind, we will now record all the transactions of the Billings Company described earlier.

(Note that it is possible to operate a standard cost system without putting the variances into the records with journal entries. Variances are figured on work sheets, and actual costs are run through the accounts. This approach is less costly to operate. However, it loses the advantages of consistent pricing of products and inventories. It also makes it harder to record product cost flow.)

Journal Entries for Direct Materials Transactions

a. Purchases:

Materials Inventory (760 yds @ $6)	4,560	
Direct Materials Price Variance		76
Accounts Payable (actual cost)		4,484
To record purchase of direct		
materials and resulting variance		

There are two key points in this transaction. (1) The increase in Materials Inventory is recorded at the actual quantity purchased but priced at standard cost. (2) Accounts Payable is stated at the actual cost (actual quantity purchased times actual price per unit) to record the proper liability.

b. Requisition:

Work in Process Inventory (720 yds @ $6)	4,320	
Direct Materials Quantity Variance	240	
Materials Inventory (760 yds @ $6)		4,560
To record usage of direct materials		
and resulting variance		

Note the important aspects of this entry. (1) Everything in the Work in Process Inventory is recorded at standard cost, which here means standard quantity times standard price. (2) Actual quantity at standard price must come out of Materials Inventory because that is the way it was at first recorded. Remember that quantities purchased may actually be used in smaller amounts. In our example, the entire amount of the purchase was used during the period.

Journal Entry for Direct Labor Transactions

Work in Process Inventory (432 hr @ $8.50/hr)	3,672	
Direct Labor Rate Variance	315	
Direct Labor Efficiency Variance	153	
Factory Payroll (450 hr @ $9.20/hr)		4,140
To charge labor cost to		
Work in Process and to identify		
the resulting variances		

When recording labor costs, the same rules hold true as for recording the requisition of materials. (1) Work in Process Inventory is charged with standard labor cost—standard hours allowed times standard labor rate. (2) Factory Payroll must be credited for the actual labor cost of the workers—actual hours worked times the actual labor rate earned. The variances, if figured properly, will balance out the difference between these two amounts.

Journal Entries for Application of Factory Overhead

Work in Process Inventory		
(432 direct labor hours @ $9/direct labor hour)	3,888	
Factory Overhead Applied		3,888
To apply factory overhead costs		
to Work in Process at standard		
cost		
Factory Overhead Applied	3,888	
Controllable Overhead Variance	316	
Overhead Volume Variance		104
Factory Overhead Control		4,100
To close out Factory Overhead		
Control and Applied accounts and		
record resulting variances		

Recording factory overhead variances differs in timing and technique from recording variances related to direct materials and direct labor. First, the factory overhead (the total of variable and fixed amounts) is charged to Work in Process Inventory at standard cost (direct labor hours allowed times standard variable and fixed rates). Then the variances are identified when Factory Overhead Applied and Factory Overhead Control accounts are closed out at period end.

Journal Entry for Transfer of Completed Units to Finished Goods Inventory

We now have $11,880 of standard costs recorded in the Work in Process Inventory account. Assuming that these 180 chairs have been completed, the following entry would be made:

Finished Goods Inventory		
(180 chairs @ $66/chair)	11,880	
Work in Process Inventory		11,880
To record transfer of completed units		
to Finished Goods Inventory		

The standard unit price of $66 was computed as follows:

Direct materials:	
4 yards @ $6	$24.00
Direct labor	
2.4 hours @ $8.50	20.40
Factory overhead	
2.4 hours @ $9	21.60
Total Standard Unit Cost	$66.00

All costs went into the Work in Process Inventory account at standard cost, so standard cost is also used when costs are transferred out of the account.

Journal Entry to Transfer Cost of Units Sold to Cost of Goods Sold Account

Assume that the 180 chairs completed were sold on account for $169 per chair and shipped to a customer:

Accounts Receivable (180 chairs @ $169)	30,420	
Sales		30,420
To record sale of 180 chairs		
Cost of Goods Sold	11,880	
Finished Goods Inventory		11,880
To record transfer of standard		
cost of units sold to Cost of		
Goods Sold account		

Journal Entry to Dispose of End-of-Period Variance Account Balances

The balances in the variance accounts at the end of the period are disposed of much as over- or underapplied overhead was earlier. Here we will continue to assume that all units worked on were completed and sold. If so, a period-end journal entry will be made to close all variances to Cost of Goods Sold:

Cost of Goods Sold	844	
Direct Materials Price Variance	76	
Overhead Volume Variance	104	
Direct Materials Quantity Variance		240
Direct Labor Rate Variance		315
Direct Labor Efficiency Variance		153
Controllable Overhead Variance		316
To close all variance account balances to Cost of Goods Sold		

If balances still exist at period end in Work in Process Inventory and Finished Goods Inventory, the net amount of the variances ($844 here) should be divided among Work in Process Inventory, Finished Goods Inventory, and Cost of Goods Sold, in proportion to their balances.

Performance Reports Using Standard Costs

Figure 27-6
Performance
Report Using
Variance
Analysis

Performance reports should be tailored to responsibilities. The report should be accurate and clearly stated, and it should only contain cost items that can be controlled by the manager receiving the report. Figure 27-6 shows a performance report using the variance data in the Billings

---

Billings Company
Production Department Performance Report—Cost Variance Analysis
For the Month Ended August 31, 19xx

400 hours: Normal capacity (direct labor hours)
432 hours: Capacity performance level achieved (standard hours allowed)
180 chairs: Good units produced

Cost Analysis

	Costs		Variance	
	Budgeted	Actual	Amount	Type
Direct materials used (leather)	$ 4,320	$ 4,560	$240(U)	Quantity variance
Direct labor usage	3,672	3,825	153(U)	Efficiency variance
Factory overhead	3,784	4,100	316(U)	Controllable overhead variance
Totals	$11,776	$12,485	$709(U)	

Reasons for Variances

Direct materials quantity variance: (1) inferior quality-control inspection, and (2) cheaper grade of direct materials caused excessive scrap

Direct labor efficiency variance: (1) inferior direct materials, and (2) new, inexperienced employee

Controllable overhead variance: (1) excessive indirect labor usage, (2) changes in employee overtime, and (3) unexpected price changes

---

Company problem that pertain only to the production department supervisor. The production supervisor is responsible for direct materials used (and the related direct materials quantity variance), direct labor hours used (and the related direct labor efficiency variance), and the cost areas used to compute the controllable overhead variance. Dollar figures in Figure 27-6 have been limited to these costs. It is important to leave enough space on performance reports for managers to write the reasons for the variances. The report shown here is simpler than most. Normally such a report would show several items of direct materials, two or more direct labor classifications, and many items of overhead cost.

Cost Control—Public-Sector and Not-for-Profit Organizations

*Objective 8
Describe the
basic techniques
used by public
sector and
not-for-profit
organizations to
control costs of
operations*

The way to approach effective cost control in public-sector and not-for-profit organizations is through the budgeting process. These organizations rely heavily on expected revenues for the coming period, and their budgets are linked closely with this figure. For public-sector organizations such as the federal government, a state university, or a municipal government unit, revenues would be the funds *appropriated* for that period of time. Sometimes dollars can be shifted from one operating fund to another during the period, but the total appropriation sets the upper limit on spending. A not-for-profit organization like a charitable group or a professional organization (the National Association of Accountants, for example) depends on the forecast of charitable contributions or membership dues for its spending limit.

Expenditure budgets for public-sector and not-for-profit enterprises are usually developed independently of the revenue projection for the period. Once both budgets are completed, the budgeted expenditures normally need to be trimmed to match the spending limit set in the revenue forecast. Budgets approved by the legislature, city council, board of trustees, or board of directors then become the standard against which all expenditures are judged.

Public-Sector Organizations

For public-sector organizations, an appropriation means that expenditures have been formally approved and dollars have been set aside for specific purposes. When those dollars are gone, expenditures must cease. Therefore, administrative control over the use of these funds becomes extremely important. Each public-sector unit has at least two main uses for its funds: (1) to carry out its mission and (2) to cover its day-to-day operations.

Operating costs such as salaries, supplies, and equipment are distributed to each operating department or unit as part of the budgeting process. Each manager must then account for the specific uses of funds within his or her unit and is held responsible for any deviation from the budget. Since revenues are limited, any increase in cost over budgeted amounts must be formally requested and approved by the organization's governing body.

Expenditures used to carry out the intended mission of a public-sector organization are controlled in a different manner. Let's compare cost control techniques for two types of public-sector units, the Department of Defense and a municipal street department. Both these units contract with outside, profit-oriented companies for specific projects such as building a new jet fighter or paving a street. The contract itself is the cost control mechanism used by many public-sector organizations. Types of contracts range from "firm fixed price" contracts to so-called "cost plus a fee" varieties.

If at all possible, a firm fixed price contract should be obtained. With this kind of contract, the public-sector unit establishes an upper expenditure limit, above which the contractor must absorb all costs and still complete the project. All costs and profit are included in the firm fixed price. Most of the projects of a municipal street department will be under firm fixed price contracts, but the Department of Defense can make only limited use of this kind of contract. Why? Because it is easy to forecast costs for paving a street, as it is for building one hundred more tanks. But what about designing and building a new jet fighter or a nuclear submarine? Imagine the amount of uncertainty involved in projecting costs for such projects. Because of this uncertainty, profit-oriented companies will not take on such a project under a firm fixed price contract. For these situations, a cost plus fixed or variable fee contract is used. Such a contract shifts the risks from the contractor to the public-sector unit. These risks and uncertainties often cause cost overruns that become targets of the news media. Without such contracts, however, no profit-oriented company would accept risky projects, and the Department of Defense would have to build its own factories for new defense projects. The government to date has been unwilling to compete with the private sector in this way. Since the Department of Defense, like the municipal street department, must operate within set spending limits, any cost overrun that cannot be absorbed by other units within the department must come before Congress for approval. Such a procedure—submitting excess costs to a governing body for approval—is another type of cost control for public-sector organizations.

Not-for-Profit Organizations

Many of the cost control procedures used by not-for-profit enterprises have already been discussed in general terms. We will now show how these procedures might be used in a church. The United Church has a budget committee charged with the task of developing the church's operating budget each year. The Board of Deacons of the church then approves the budget after making adjustments for events unforeseen by the budget committee. Last year, the board approved a budget with the following items: Building Repairs, $6,500; Utilities Costs, $3,450; and New Hymnals, $1,200. A hot water heater explosion, increased utility rates, and an unexpected new edition of the hymnal caused all three cost categories to be questioned during the year. Since donations and member offerings were not expected to increase much even with these unusual needs, the board had to decide how to keep costs within the set limits and still keep the church operating.

Building repairs after the explosion amounted to $10,000, $6,000 of which was covered by insurance. The $4,000 difference brought the total building repairs for the year to $7,200. Utility bills shot up 15 percent, and actual utility bills totaled $3,970. New hymnals for the church would cost $4,500. The board, after discussing these events, decided that the building repairs and payment of utility bills were necessary for the continued operation of the church. Therefore, the purchase of new hymnals was put off until the following year. The current year's appropriation of $1,200 for hymnals was diverted to Building Repairs ($700) and Utility Costs ($500) to help cover the increases. It took formal approval of the Board of Deacons to make these cost overrun payments. Cost control takes many forms in not-for-profit organizations, but all are connected with the budget and the approval/review process of the governing body.

Chapter Review

Review of Learning Objectives

1. Describe the nature and purpose of standard costs.

Standard costs are realistically predetermined costs for direct materials, direct labor, and factory overhead. They are usually expressed as a cost per unit of finished product. They are introduced into a cost accounting system to help in the budgetary control process. Standard costs are useful for evaluating performance and preparing operating budgets. They also help in identifying areas of the production process that require cost control measures, in deciding on realistic prices, and basically in simplifying cost accounting procedures for inventories and product costing.

2. Identify the six elements of a standard unit cost, and describe the factors to consider in developing each element.

The six elements of a standard unit costs are (1) the direct materials price standard, (2) the direct materials quantity standard, (3) the direct labor time standard, (4) the direct labor rate standard, (5) the standard variable factory overhead rate, and (6) the standard fixed factory overhead rate. The direct materials price standard is found by carefully considering expected price increases, changes in quantities available, and possible new supplier sources. The direct materials quantity standard is an expression of forecasted or expected quantity usage. It is affected by product engineering specifications, quality of direct materials used, age and productivity of the machines being used, and the quality and experience of the machine operators and set-up people. The direct labor time standard is based on current time and motion studies of workers and machines and past employee and machine performance. Labor union contracts and company personnel policies lead to direct labor rate standards. Standard variable and fixed factory overhead rates are found by taking total budgeted or forecasted variable and fixed factory overhead costs and dividing by an appropriate application base such as standard direct labor hours or normal capacity.

3. Compute a standard unit cost.

A product's total standard unit cost is computed by adding together the following costs: (1) direct materials cost (equals direct materials price standard times direct materials quantity standard), (2) direct labor cost (equals direct labor time standard times direct labor rate standard), and (3) factory overhead cost (equals standard variable and standard fixed factory overhead rate times standard direct labor hours allowed per unit).

4. Prepare a flexible budget.

A flexible budget is a summary of anticipated costs prepared for a range of activity levels. It is geared to changes in the level of productive output. Variable and fixed costs are given for several levels of capacity or output, with each column showing the total expected cost for a different output level. Once prepared, the flexible budget is used to determine the flexible budget formula. This formula, which can be applied to any level of productive output, is a key tool in evaluating performance of individuals and departments.

5. Describe management by exception.

Management by exception is a performance evaluation technique used to highlight significant variances from budgeted or planned operations and to analyze their causes. Variances within specific limits set by management are not analyzed. This technique is especially useful for companies attempting to control a large number of cost centers or cost categories.

6. Compute and evaluate direct materials, direct labor, and factory overhead variances.

Cost variances, or differences between actual and standard manufacturing costs, can be computed for direct materials, direct labor, and factory overhead. The direct materials price and quantity variances help explain differences between actual and standard direct materials costs. Direct labor cost differences are analyzed through the direct labor rate variance and the direct labor efficiency variance. The controllable overhead variance and the overhead volume variance help explain differences in overhead costs. Each variance results from specific causes, and these causes help pinpoint reasons for the differences between actual and standard costs.

7. Prepare journal entries involving variances from standard costs.

Journal entries are used to integrate standard cost variance information into the accounting records. Unfavorable variances will create debit balances, and favorable variances will be credited. General ledger accounts are maintained for direct materials price variance, direct materials quantity variance, direct labor rate variance, direct labor efficiency variance, controllable overhead variance, and overhead volume variance. At the close of an accounting period, balances in these accounts are disposed of by either (1) closing them to Cost of Goods Sold if the balances are small or if most or all of the goods produced during the period were sold, or (2) dividing the net variance balance among Work in Process Inventory, Finished Goods Inventory, and Cost of Goods Sold in proportion to their balances.

8. Describe the basic techniques used by public-sector and not-for-profit organizations to control costs of operations.

Budgets are the key to effective cost control by public-sector and not-for-profit organizations. Revenues or cash inflows are restricted either by appropriations for governmental bodies, or by dues and contributions for not-for-profit organizations. The budget, once approved by the legislature or governing board, identifies expenditure categories and maximum spending amounts. Any significant deviation from these spending limits must be approved by the same people who approved the original budget. In addition, firm fixed price and cost plus fee contracts play a major role in cost control in public-sector organizations.

Review Problem: Variance Analysis

DKA Manufacturing Company has a standard cost system and keeps all cost standards up to date. The company's main product is heating pipe, which is made in a single department. The standard variable costs for one unit of finished pipe are

Direct materials (two square meters at $1.50)	$ 3.00
Direct labor (1.5 hours at $7.00)	10.50
Variable overhead (1.5 hours at $4.00)	6.00
Standard variable cost per unit	$19.50

Normal capacity is 18,000 direct labor hours, and budgeted fixed overhead costs for the year were $36,000. During the year, 12,200 units were produced and sold. Related transactions and actual cost data for the year were as follows: Direct materials consisted of 24,500 square meters purchased and used; unit purchase cost was $1.40 per meter. Direct labor consisted of 18,200 direct labor hours worked at an average labor rate of $7.20 per hour. Factory overhead incurred consisted of variable overhead cost of $73,500 and fixed overhead cost of $36,000.

Required

Using the data above, compute the following:

1. Standard hours allowed
2. Standard fixed overhead rate
3. Direct materials price variance
4. Direct materials quantity variance
5. Direct labor rate variance
6. Direct labor efficiency variance
7. Controllable overhead variance
8. Overhead volume variance

Answer to Review Problem

1. Standard hours allowed = good units produced × standard direct labor hours per unit.

$$12,200 \text{ units} \times 1.5 \text{ hours/unit} = \underline{\underline{18,300 \text{ hours}}}$$

2. Standard fixed overhead rate = $\dfrac{\text{budgeted fixed overhead cost}}{\text{normal capacity}}$

$$= \frac{\$36,000}{18,000 \text{ hours}}$$

$$= \underline{\underline{\$2.00 \text{ per direct labor hour}}}$$

3. Direct materials price variance:

Price difference: Actual price paid	$1.40/meter
Less standard price	1.50/meter
Difference	$ .10(F)

Direct materials price variance = difference in price × actual quantity
= .10(F) × 24,500 square meters
= $2,450(F)

4. Direct materials quantity variance:

Quantity difference: Actual quantity used		24,500 meters
Less standard quantity		
(12,200 units × 2 meters)		24,400 meters
Difference		100(U)

Direct materials quantity variance = difference in quantity × standard price
= 100(U) × $1.50/meter
= $150(U)

5. Direct labor rate variance:

Rate difference: Actual labor rate	$7.20/hour
Less standard labor rate	7.00/hour
Difference	$ .20(U)

Direct labor rate variance = difference in rate × actual hours
= .20(U) × 18,200 hours
= $3,640(U)

6. Direct labor efficiency variance:

Difference in hours: Actual hours worked	18,200 hours
Less standard hours allowed	18,300 hours
Difference	100(F)

Direct labor efficiency variance = difference in hours × standard rate
= 100 hours (F) × $7.00/hour
= $700(F)

7. Controllable overhead variance:

Actual overhead incurred		$109,500
Less budgeted factory overhead for 18,300 hours		
Variable overhead cost		
(18,300 hours at $4.00/hour)	$73,200	
Budgeted fixed factory overhead	36,000	
Total budgeted factory overhead		109,200
Controllable overhead variance		$ 300(U)

8. Overhead volume variance:

Total budgeted factory overhead (see **7**)		$109,200
Less factory overhead applied		
Variable: 18,300 hours at $4/hour	$73,200	
Fixed: 18,300 hours at $2/hour	36,600	
Total factory overhead applied		109,800
Overhead volume variance		$ 600(F)

Cost Control Using Standard Costing

Chapter Assignments

Questions

1. What is a standard cost?
2. What do predetermined overhead costing and standard costing have in common? How are these costing approaches different?
3. "Standard costing is a total cost concept in that standard unit costs are determined for direct materials, direct labor, and factory overhead." Explain.
4. Name the six elements used to compute total standard unit cost.
5. What three factors could affect a direct material price standard?
6. "Standard labor cost rests on the degree of efficiency and unionization." Is this a true statement? Defend your answer.
7. What general ledger accounts are affected by a standard cost system?
8. "Performance is evaluated or measured by comparing what did happen with what should have happened." What is meant by this statement? Relate your comments to the budgetary control process.
9. What is a variance?
10. How can a variance help management achieve effective control of operations?
11. What is the formula for computing a direct materials price variance?
12. How would you interpret an unfavorable direct materials price variance?
13. What is the difference between the controllable overhead variance and the overhead volume variance?
14. What is a flexible budget? What is its purpose?
15. What are the two parts of a flexible budget formula? How are they related?
16. If standard hours allowed are more than normal hours, will the period's overhead volume variance be favorable or unfavorable? Explain your answer.
17. Can an unfavorable direct material quantity variance be caused, at least in part, by a favorable direct material price variance? Explain.
18. What are the three rules that underlie the recording of standard cost variances?
19. "Contracts with outside contractors is a common means of cost control for public-sector organizations." Explain this statement.
20. In not-for-profit organizations, how are potential cost overruns handled? Why is this action necessary?

Classroom Exercises

**Exercise 27-1
Standard Unit
Cost Analysis**
(L.O. 3)

Accountants and engineers of the Mykkanen Manufacturing Company have developed the following cost, usage, and time standards for a small chain saw, one of the company's main products. Direct materials required are a saw motor casing at $4.75, an operating chain at $3.50, a 3-horsepower motor at $19.90, and a chain housing at $6.25. Direct labor consists of .5 hour from a materials inspector at $5.50 per hour, .5 hour from an assembler at $7.00 per hour, and .25 hour from a product tester at $6.00 per hour. Factory overhead charges are figured at a variable rate of $8.00 per labor hour, and at a fixed rate of $7.40 per labor hour.

Compute the total standard manufacturing cost of one chain saw.

**Exercise 27-2
Flexible Budget
Preparation**
(L.O. 4)

Fixed overhead costs for the Wickramaratne Company for 19xx are expected to be as follows: depreciation, $42,000; supervisory salaries, $38,000; property taxes and insurance, $12,000; and other fixed overhead, $6,000. Total fixed overhead is thus expected to be $98,000. Variable costs per unit are expected to be as follows: direct materials, $2.50; direct labor, $3.75; operating supplies, $.75; indirect labor, $1.00; and other variable overhead costs, $.50.

Prepare a flexible budget for 16,000 units, 18,000 units, and 20,000 units. What is the flexible budget formula for 19xx?

Exercise 27-3
Standard Unit Cost Computation
(L.O. 3)

Aerodynamics, Inc., makes electronically equipped weather balloons for university meteorology departments. Generally rising prices nationwide have caused the company to recompute its standard costs.

New direct materials price standards are $620 per set for electronic parts and $4 per square meter for heavy-duty canvas. Direct materials quantity standards include one set of electronic parts and 120 square meters of heavy-duty canvas per balloon. Direct labor time standards are 14.5 hours per balloon for the Electronics Department and 12.0 hours per balloon for the Assembly Department. Direct labor rate standards are $9.00 an hour for the Electronics Department and $6.50 an hour for the Assembly Department. Standard factory overhead rates are $12.00 per direct labor hour for the standard variable overhead rate and $7.00 per direct labor hour for the standard fixed overhead rate.

Compute the standard manufacturing cost of one weather balloon.

Exercise 27-4
Direct Materials Price Variance
(L.O. 6)

The Asilomar Tree Farm uses vermiculite to fortify the soil around trees bearing rare fruit, as the trees are the company's main product. The price standard used is $2.50 per 10-pound sack of vermiculite. During the current year, the actual purchase price averaged $2.65 per sack, according to the company's purchasing agent. The company purchased and used 1,470 sacks of vermiculite during the year.

Compute the direct materials price variance.

Exercise 27-5
Direct Materials Quantity Variance
(L.O. 6)

The Lowbid Elevator Company manufactures small hydroelectric elevators with a maximum capacity of ten passengers each. One of the direct materials used by the production department is heavy-duty carpeting for the floors of the elevators. The direct materials quantity standard used for the month ended April 30, 19xx, was 6 square yards per elevator. The purchasing agent was able to get this carpeting at $8 per square yard, which equaled the price standard. During April, 82 elevators were completed and sold, and the production department used 5.6 yards of carpet per elevator.

Calculate the direct materials quantity variance for April 19xx.

Exercise 27-6
Direct Labor Rate and Efficiency Variances
(L.O. 6)

Park Foundry, Inc., manufactures castings used by other companies in the production of machinery. For the past two years, the largest-selling product has been a casting for an eight-cylinder engine block. Standard direct labor hours per engine block are 1.8 hours. The labor contract requires that $7.50 per hour be paid to all direct labor employees. During June, 16,500 engine blocks were produced. Actual direct labor hours and cost for June were 30,000 hours and $228,000, respectively.

1. Compute the direct labor rate variance for June for the engine block product line.
2. Using the same data, figure the direct labor efficiency variance for June for the engine block product line. [Check your answer, assuming that total direct labor variance is $5,250(U).]

Exercise 27-7
Factory Overhead Variances
(L.O. 6)

The Stenberg Company produces handmade lobster pots that are sold to distributors throughout New England. The company incurred $6,100 of actual overhead costs in May. Budgeted standard overhead costs were $4 of variable overhead costs per direct labor hour plus $1,250 in fixed overhead costs for May. Normal capacity was set at 1,000 direct labor hours per month. In May, the company was able to produce 400 lobster pots. The time standard is 3 direct labor hours per lobster pot.

Compute the controllable overhead variance, the overhead volume variance, and the total overhead variance for May.

Bush Battery Manufacturing Company produces batteries for automobiles, motorcycles, and mopeds. Transactions for direct materials and direct labor for March were as follows:

1. Purchased 1,000 type A battery casings for $6.50 each on account; standard cost, $7.00 per casing.
2. Purchased 5,000 type 10C lead battery plates for $2.40 each on account; standard cost, $2.25 per plate.
3. Requisitioned 32 type A battery casings and 128 type 10C lead plates into production. Order No. 476 called for 30 batteries each using a standard quantity of four plates per casing.
4. Direct labor costs for Order No. 476 were as follows:

Department H
  Actual labor   26 hours @ $5/hour
  Standard labor   24 hours @ $5/hour
Department J
  Actual labor   10 hours @ $6.50/hour
  Standard labor   12 hours @ $7.00/hour

Prepare journal entries for the four transactions described above.

Interpreting Accounting Information

Not-for-Profit
Organization:
The National
Association of
Accountants
(L.O. 8)

The National Association of Accountants (NAA), originally called the National Association of Cost Accountants, was created to assist in the development of the management accounting profession. Its primary purpose is continued education of its members, even though its more than 300 local chapters engage in some activities that are not strictly educational. The NAA publishes many items including *Management Accounting,* a monthly professional magazine. Through its sister organization, the Institute of Management Accounting (IMA), the organization promotes and administers the Certificate in Management Accounting (CMA) examination and program.

The NAA operates through an executive committee of 33 members and a large board of directors. Included on the executive committee are the national president, the chairman of the association, twelve national vice presidents, the treasurer, the past president, eleven chairpersons of standing committees, and six appointed members. The annual budget is developed by several people and committees during the year. Then it is pulled together by the Finance Committee and presented to the Board of Directors for approval at the June meeting. On the next page is the Association's Budget and Statement of Revenues and Expenses and Changes in Fund Balance for 1981–1982. After studying it carefully, respond to the following questions:

1. What concerns should the NAA have about revenues?
2. What expenses should be questioned and analyzed for the next budget cycle?
3. What overall thoughts do you have about the financial direction of the association?

Problem Set A

A planned change in the employee labor rate structure has caused the Utah Salt Company to develop a new standard direct labor cost for its product. Standard direct labor costs per 100 pounds of salt in 19x4 were .5 hour in the Sodium

National Association of Accountants
Statement of Revenues and Expenses and Changes in Fund Balance—Current Operating Fund
For the Year Ended June 30, 1982

	Budget	Actual
Revenues		
Membership dues	$5,195,000	$5,135,790
Continuing education program—registration fees and sales of material	1,152,000	1,069,237
Annual and international conferences—registration fees	275,000	391,517
Advertising and sales of publications	869,000	949,323
Institute of Management Accounting—registration and examination fees	597,000	631,752
Interest and dividends on reserve fund investments	260,000	408,007
Interest on current operating fund investments	280,000	331,600
(Loss) on security sales	—	(19,920)
Research fund contributions applied	180,000	95,314
Miscellaneous	6,000	70,601
	$8,814,000	$9,063,221
Expenses		
Chapter services		
Payment to chapters	$1,022,000	$1,030,408
Other	500,000	522,515
Technical publications	1,380,000	1,345,947
Marketing		
Membership and new chapter development	340,000	325,261
Public relations and promotion	200,000	179,583
Meeting arrangements	180,000	216,930
Technical services		
Continuing education program	1,310,000	1,149,361
Research fund expenditures	300,000	287,313
Other	160,000	246,209
Administration	650,000	810,440
Finance		
Accounting	140,000	300,423
Data processing	303,000	333,593
Administrative services		
General office and office services	670,000	689,657
Occupancy costs	420,000	408,922
Word processing and administrative support	380,000	405,998
Institute of Management Accounting	550,000	606,270
Annual and international conferences	300,000	389,947
	$8,805,000	$9,248,777
Excess (deficiency) of revenues to cover expenses	$ 9,000	$ (185,556)
Fund balance (deficit), beginning of year	(210,355)	(210,355)
Fund balance (deficit), end of year	$ (201,355)	$ (395,911)

Preparation Department at $8.40 per hour, .8 hour in the Chloride Mixing Department at $9.00 per hour, and .4 hour in the Cleaning and Packaging Department at $6.50 per hour. Labor rates are expected to increase in 19x5 by 10 percent in the Sodium Preparation Department, 5 percent in the Chloride Mixing Department, and 12 percent in the Cleaning and Packaging Department. New machinery in the Chloride Mixing Department will lower the direct labor time standard by 25 percent per 100 pounds of salt. All other time standards are expected to remain the same.

Required

Complete each of the following separately.

1. Compute the standard direct labor cost per 100 pounds of salt in 19x5.
2. Management has a plan to improve productive output by 20 percent in the Sodium Preparation Department. If such results are achieved in 19x5, determine (a) the effect on the direct labor time standard and (b) the resulting total standard direct labor cost per 100 pounds of salt.
3. Unskilled labor can be hired to staff all departments in 19x5, with the result that all labor rates paid in 19x4 would be cut by 60 percent in the new year. Such a change in labor skill would cause the direct labor time standards to increase by 50 percent over their anticipated 19x5 levels using skilled labor. Compute the standard direct labor cost per 100 pounds of salt if this change takes place.

**Problem 27A-2
Materials and
Labor Variances**
(L.O. 6)

The Unique Fruit Packaging Company makes plastic berry baskets for food wholesalers. Each basket is made of 1.6 grams of liquid plastic and 1.2 grams of an additive that provides the color and hardening agents. The standard prices are $.004 per gram of liquid plastic and $.005 per gram of additive.

Labor is of three kinds: molding, trimming, and packing. The labor time standard per 1,000-box batch and the rate standards are as follows: molding, .4 hour per batch at an hourly rate of $10; trimming, .4 hour per batch at an hourly rate of $8; packing, .2 hour at $5 per hour.

During 19xx, the company produced 4,225,000 berry baskets. Actual materials used were 6,637,000 grams of liquid plastic, at a total cost of $33,185; and 5,492,000 grams of additive, which cost $27,460. Direct labor included 1,710 hours for molding, at a total cost of $16,758; 1,700 hours for trimming, which came to $13,532; and 850 hours for packing, which cost $4,080.

Required

1. Compute the direct materials price and quantity variances for both the liquid plastic and the additive.
2. Compute the direct labor rate and efficiency variances for the molding, trimming, and packing processes.

**Problem 27A-3
Developing and
Using Standard
Costs**
(L.O. 2, 3, 7)

The Otani Supplies Company manufactures swimming pool equipment and accessories. To make swimming pool umbrellas, waterproof canvas is first sent to the cutting department. In the assembly department, the canvas is stretched over the umbrella's ribs on the center pole and opening mechanism. Then the umbrella is mounted on a heavy base before being packed for shipment.

The company uses a standard cost accounting system. Direct labor and factory overhead standards for each pool umbrella for 19x6 are as follows: Direct labor consists of .2 hour charged to the Cutting Department at $7.00 per hour and of .8 hour charged to the Assembly Department at $8.50 per hour. Variable overhead is 140 percent, and fixed overhead is 120 percent of total direct labor dollars.

During 19x5 the company used the following direct materials standards: Waterproof canvas was $1.30 per square yard for 4 square yards per umbrella. The standard for a unit consisting of pole, ribs, and opening mechanism was $8.50 per unit. The base was $5.40 per unit.

Quantity standards are expected to remain the same during 19x6. However, the following price changes are likely: The cost of waterproof canvas will increase by 20 percent. The pole, ribs, and opening mechanism will be purchased from three vendors. Vendor A will provide 10 percent of the total supply at $8.60 per unit. Vendor B will provide 60 percent at $8.80. Vendor C will supply 30 percent at $9.00. The cost of each base will increase 20 percent.

Required

1. Compute the total standard direct materials cost per umbrella for 19x6.
2. Using your answer from 1 and information from the problem, compute the 19x6 standard manufacturing cost of one pool umbrella.
3. Using your answers from 1 and 2, prepare journal entries for the following transactions:

Jan. 20   Purchased 4,500 square yards of waterproof canvas at standard cost on account.
Feb. 1   Requisitioned 525 pole, rib, and opening mechanism assemblies into production to complete a job calling for 515 umbrellas.
Mar. 15   Transferred 350 completed pool umbrellas to finished goods inventory.

**Problem 27A-4
Direct
Materials,
Direct Labor,
and Factory
Overhead
Variances**
(L.O. 6)

Cheng Footwear Company has a Sandal Division that produces a line of all-vinyl thongs. Each pair of thongs calls for .4 meter of vinyl material that costs $1.00 per meter. Standard direct labor hours and cost per pair of thongs are .25 hour and $1.75 (.25 hour × $7.00 per hour), respectively. The division's current standard variable overhead rate is $.60 per direct labor hour, and the standard fixed overhead rate is $1.40 per direct labor hour.

In August, the Sandal Division manufactured and sold 30,000 pairs of thongs. During the month, 12,200 meters of vinyl material were used up, at a total cost of $11,590. The total actual overhead costs for August were $15,600. The total number of direct labor hours worked were 7,450, and August's factory payroll for direct labor was $52,895. Monthly normal capacity for the year has been set at 25,000 pairs of thongs.

Required

Compute (1) direct materials price variance, (2) direct materials quantity variance, (3) direct labor rate variance, (4) direct labor efficiency variance, (5) controllable overhead variance, and (6) overhead volume variance.

**Problem 27A-5
Standard Cost
Journal Entry
Analysis**
(L.O. 7)

Ridge Bottle Company makes wine bottles for many of the major wineries in California's Napa and Sonoma valleys as well as for wineries in the grape growing regions around Cupertino and Santa Cruz, California. Constance Hillis, as controller of the company, has installed the following cost, quantity, and time standards for 19x6:

Direct materials: 2 five-gallon pails of a special silicon dioxide and phosphorus pentoxide based compound per one gross (144) of bottles; cost, $6 per pail
Direct labor: Forming Department—.2 hour per gross at $6.80 per direct labor hour; Finishing/Polishing Department—.1 hour per gross at $5.40 per direct labor hour
Factory overhead: variable—$1.20 per direct labor hour; fixed—$1.80 per direct labor hour

The direct materials are added at the beginning of the forming process. Much of the machinery is automated, and the compound is heated, mixed, and poured into molds in a very short time. Once cooled, the new bottles move via conveyor belt to the Finishing/Polishing Department. Again the process is highly automated. Machines scrape off excess material on the bottles and then polish all the outside and inside surfaces. After polishing, the bottles are fed into large cartons for shipping to customers.

During March, 19x6, the following selected transactions took place:

March 2 Purchased 12,000 pails of compound at $5.80 per pail on account.
3 Requisitioned 2,612 pails of compound into production for an order calling for 1,300 gross of wine bottles.
6 Requisitioned 5,880 pails of compound into production for an order of 2,900 gross of wine bottles.
12 Transferred 3,400 gross of bottles to Finished Goods Inventory.
15 Requisitioned 4,630 pails of compound into production for an order calling for 2,300 gross of wine bottles.
16 For the two-week period ending March 14, actual labor costs included 860 direct labor hours in the Forming Department at $6.50 per hour and 410 direct labor hours in the Finishing/Polishing Department at $5.50 per hour. During the pay period, 4,200 gross of good bottles were produced.
16 Factory overhead was applied to units worked on during the previous two weeks.
18 Purchased 9,000 pails of compound at $6.10 per pail on account.
20 Requisitioned 6,960 pails of compound into production for an order of 3,500 gross of wine bottles.
28 Transferred 6,000 gross of bottles to Finished Goods Inventory.
30 For the two-week period ending March 28, actual labor costs included 1,040 direct labor hours in the Forming Department at $7.00 per hour and 550 direct labor hours in the Finishing/Polishing Department at $5.50 per hour. During the pay period, 5,300 gross of good bottles were produced.
30 Factory overhead was applied to units worked on during the two-week period.
31 During March, 9,800 gross of wine bottles were sold on account and shipped to customers. Selling price for these bottles was $26 per gross.

Actual factory overhead for February was $3,500 of variable and $5,300 of fixed overhead. These amounts were recorded in the Factory Overhead Control account. Budgeted fixed factory overhead is $5,000 for March. Beginning inventory information included: Materials Inventory, $21,300; Work in Process Inventory, $10,064; Finished Goods Inventory, $17,760.

Required

1. Compute the standard cost per gross of wine bottles.
2. Prepare the entries necessary to record the above transactions (show calculations for each variance). For the direct labor entries, assume that everything has already been recorded except the distribution of Factory Payroll to Work in Process Inventory.
3. Analyze the factory overhead accounts, and compute the controllable and volume variances.
4. Prepare the entry to dispose of the overhead accounts and record the overhead variances.
5. Close all variance account balances to the Cost of Goods Sold account.

Problem Set B

Problem 27B-1
Development of
Standards:
Direct
Materials
(L.O. 2)

Kara Johan & Co. manufactures an electronic gadget called a Taxputer. This device stores financial data and computes a person's taxable income on a perpetual input basis. Parts of the assembly of the gadget in 19x6 include the following standard costs: housing at $6.00 per unit, electronic mechanism at $9.50 per unit, and wires, circuits, and so forth, at $4.50 per unit.

In 19x7, housings are to be bought from two sources: 40 percent at $7.00 from Supplier A and 60 percent at $7.50 from Supplier B. All electronic mechanisms will be purchased from Supplier C at a 30 percent increase over the 19x6 cost. Per-unit prices of wire, circuits, and so on, are expected to increase 20 percent over 19x6 amounts.

Required

Complete each of the following separately.

1. Compute the total standard materials cost per unit for 19x7.
2. If the company purchased the housings and electronic mechanisms in lots of 1,000, it would receive a 20 percent price reduction from 19x6 prices. Wire, circuits, and so on, will still increase by 20 percent. Find the resulting standard direct materials unit cost.
3. Substandard housings can be purchased at $5.50, but 20 percent of them will be unusable and cannot be returned. Compute the standard direct materials unit cost if the company follows this procedure, assuming the original facts of the case for the remaining data. The cost of the defective direct materials will be spread over good units produced.

Giles T. Brown, Ltd., specializes in tailor-made suits produced from imported fabrics. An average suit requires 3 meters of suit fabric and 1 meter of lining material. The standard price of suit fabric is $28 per meter, and lining material is $16 per meter.

Labor is classified under three separate functions: cutting, tailoring, and cleaning. The standard times and labor rates per suit for 19xx were as follows:

	Labor Time Standard	Labor Rate Standard
Cutting	.5 hr	$6/hr
Tailoring	5.0 hr	$9/hr
Cleaning	.2 hr	$4/hr

During 19xx, the company produced 2,900 suits. Actual operating data are shown below.

Materials usage and cost		Total Cost
Suit fabric	9,000 meters	$247,500
Lining materials	2,850 meters	51,300

Direct labor usage and cost		
Cutting	1,500 hours	$ 9,000
Tailoring	14,500 hours	131,950
Cleaning	600 hours	2,550

Required

1. Compute the materials price and quantity variances for both the suit fabric and the lining material.

2. Compute the labor rate and efficiency variances for the cutting, tailoring, and cleaning functions.

Problem 27B-3
Developing and Using Standard Costs
(L.O. 2, 3, 7)

Orlando Lawn and Garden Company makes and sells chemical fertilizers for home and business use. In addition, the company assembles and markets a line of gardening tools and accessories. For these items, the company purchases all of the necessary parts, assembles them in the Assembly Department, and transfers the products to the Painting and Packing Department for final processing. One of the main items in this line of tools and accessories is a lawn chemical spreader. Labor and overhead standards for the spreader for the coming year, 19x4, are as follows: Direct labor is .5 hour in the Assembly Department at $7.80 per hour and .2 hour in the Painting and Packing Department at $9.00 per hour. The standard for variable overhead is 220 percent of all direct labor dollars, and for fixed overhead is 160 percent of all direct labor dollars.

Direct materials price standards for 19x4 have not yet been developed. Price standards for 19x3 are $1.60 per set of wheels, $3.70 per casing, $2.40 per handle assembly, and $1.20 for paint per spreader. After careful analysis, the following changes are expected in direct materials prices for 19x4: The cost of wheels will increase 20 percent per set. Thirty percent of the casings will be purchased from Vendor A at $3.80 per unit and 70 percent will be purchased from Vendor B at $4.00 per unit. The handle unit will increase 30 percent in price, and paint prices will go up 10 percent.

Required

1. Compute the total standard direct materials cost per spreader for 19x4.
2. Using your answer from **1** and information from the problem, compute the 19x4 standard manufacturing cost of one lawn chemical spreader.
3. Using your answers from **1** and **2**, prepare journal entries for the following transactions:

Jan. 31 Purchased 700 sets of wheels at standard cost on account.
Feb. 20 Requisitioned 460 spreader casings into production to complete an order calling for 450 spreaders.
Mar. 31 Transferred 190 completed spreaders to Finished Goods Inventory.

Problem 27B-4
Direct Materials, Direct Labor, and Factory Overhead Variances
(L.O. 6)

A forged socket wrench is the product made by Dependable Sockets, Inc. Each socket wrench should use 2 kilograms of liquid steel at a standard cost of $1.90 per kilogram. Each wrench requires .4 standard direct labor hour at a standard rate of $7.50 per hour. The standard variable overhead rate is $4.20 per direct labor hour, and normal capacity is set at a monthly level of 30,000 hours of direct labor. Fixed overhead costs of $75,600 were budgeted for June.

In June, the firm actually produced 80,000 socket wrenches, using 164,000 kilograms of liquid steel at a total cost of $295,200. A total of 25,200 direct labor hours were used at an expense of $201,600. Total overhead expenses came to $181,360.

Required

Compute (1) direct materials price variance, (2) direct materials quantity variance, (3) direct labor rate variance, (4) direct labor efficiency variance, (5) controllable overhead variance, and (6) overhead volume variance.

Problem 27B-5
Comprehensive Variance Analysis
(L.O. 6)

Diamond Head Specialty Products Company produces various lines of gardening tools. The company's long-handled spade is considered a superior product. A stamping operation is required to cut and shape the blade of the spade and the neck of the assembly. The firm purchases wooden handles in lots of 1,000 from a local woodworking shop. Quantity, time, and cost standards for this product are listed below.

Direct materials needed are sheet metal (1 × 2-meter sheets at $10.80 per sheet; 18 blades and 18 necks should be produced from each sheet), and wooden handles at $380 per 1,000 handles. Direct labor is expected to include stamping blade and neck sets (180 sets per hour at a labor rate of $9.00 per hour), and assembly (60 units per person per hour at a labor rate of $8.40 per hour). Factory overhead for stamping is set at a variable rate of $5.60 per direct labor hour and at a fixed rate of $6.30 per direct labor hour. Factory overhead for assembly will consist of a variable rate of $4.20 per direct labor hour and a fixed rate of $2.10 per direct labor hour. Normal capacity is 300,600 units per year. Budgeted fixed factory overhead is $10,521 for each of the two departments, Stamping and Assembly, for the year.

The company manufactured 291,600 spades during the year. Company records showed the following:

Direct materials	Usage	Cost
Sheet metal	16,300 sheets	$11/sheet
Wooden handles	292,200 handles	$390/1,000 handles

Direct labor		
Stamping	1,600 hours	$9.00/hr
Assembly	4,900 hours	$8.50/hr

Factory overhead		
Stamping:	Variable	$ 9,600
	Fixed	10,100
Assembly:	Variable	20,500
	Fixed	10,300

Required

Compute (1) standard hours allowed for the stamping and assembly departments for the year, (2) direct materials price variances, (3) direct materials quantity variances, (4) direct labor rate variances, (5) direct labor efficiency variances, (6) controllable overhead variances, and (7) overhead volume variances.

Management Decision Case 27-1

Scandinavian Atlantic Corporation (L.O. 6)

Scandinavian Atlantic Corporation produces water sports gear including safety cushions, water skis, towing lines, goggles, and snorkeling equipment. Much of the operation involves the assembly of parts purchased from outside vendors. However, all rubber parts are produced by the company in the Shaping Department. Face masks and goggles are assembled in the Face Wear Department, using purchased clear plastic lenses and fastener devices. Rubber mask casings and head straps are transferred in from the Shaping Department. Bengt Johansson is in charge of the Shaping Department, and Irene Nilsson supervises the Face Wear Department.

At the end of April, 19x5, the Accounting Department developed the performance reports for the two departments that are shown on the next page.

When asked to comment on his performance, Johansson stated, "Compared with the Face Wear Department, my performance is very good. Most of the $1,670(U) net variance arose because of two new inexperienced workers who

Report #1

Scandinavian Atlantic Corporation
Shaping Department
Performance Report—Cost Variance Analysis
For the Month Ended April 30, 19x5

Supervisor: Bengt Johansson

	Costs		Variance	
	Standard	Actual	Amount	Type
Direct materials used	$17,800	$18,000	$ 200(U)	Quantity variance
Direct labor usage	9,640	10,120	860(F)	Rate variance
			1,340(U)	Efficiency variance
Factory Overhead	6,400	7,390	990(U)	Controllable variance
Totals	$33,840	$35,510	$1,670(U)	

Report #2

Scandinavian Atlantic Corporation
Face Wear Department
Performance Report—Cost Variance Analysis
For the Month Ended April 30, 19x5

Supervisor: Irene Nilsson

	Costs		Variance	
	Standard	Actual	Amount	Type
Direct materials used	$12,600	$16,450	$3,850(U)	Quantity variance
Direct labor usage	8,200	11,580	20(F)	Rate variance
			3,400(U)	Efficiency variance
Factory overhead	5,460	7,220	1,760(U)	Controllable variance
Totals	$26,260	$35,250	$8,990(U)	

reduced the average labor rate for the department. Since overhead is applied based on direct labor hours, an unfavorable controllable variance was expected."

Ms. Nilsson was quite upset at Mr. Johansson's comments. She said, "First of all, one of the variances is in error. The standard for direct labor usage should be $9,020 since 1,100 standard hours allowed were earned at an $8.20 standard labor rate. Also, the additional 100 standard hours allowed would cause the controllable variance to decrease by $420 because of the $4.20 per direct labor hour standard variable overhead rate." She continued, "Now let's focus on the large unfavorable quantity and efficiency variances. All my production problems can be traced to the poor quality of mask casings coming from the Shaping Department. Poor workmanship meant dozens of spoiled mask assemblies, and my people had to work overtime to meet the customer orders for the period. If we had had decent mask casings, we would have had an overall favorable performance for the period. Either the quality of the mask casings improves, or I will ask to have them purchased from an outside vendor in the future!"

Required

1. Recompute the variances and the performance report for the Face Wear Department, assuming that Ms. Nilsson's information is correct.
2. Which supervisor's performance should be further analyzed? Why?
3. If you were Vice President of Production, what steps would you take to correct the situation? Develop a plan of action.

Learning Objectives

Chapter Twenty-Eight

Capital Budgeting and Other Management Decisions

1. Define and identify relevant decision information.

2. Describe the steps in the management decision cycle.

3. Calculate product costs, using variable costing procedures.

4. Prepare an income statement, using the contribution reporting format.

5. Develop decision data, using the incremental analysis technique.

6. Describe the purpose of a minimum desired rate of return, and explain methods for arriving at this rate.

7. Evaluate capital expenditure proposals, using (a) accounting rate of return method, (b) payback method, and (c) present value method.

8. Prepare decision alternative evaluations for (a) make or buy decisions, (b) special order decisions, and (c) sales mix analyses.

9. Analyze capital expenditure decision alternatives that incorporate the effects of income taxes.

Top management very often depends on the management accountant for information that is needed for decision making. To evaluate decision alternatives, the accountant uses special analyses and reporting techniques. Decisions about long-term capital expenditures are the most complex. However, day-to-day operating decisions call for accurate evaluation too. As a result of studying this chapter, you should be able to meet the learning objectives listed on the left.

Three kinds of accounting information that management uses are product costing for pricing and inventory valuation, cost analyses for operational planning and control, and special analyses to support management decision making. This chapter emphasizes the third kind of accounting information. After exploring the management decision cycle and describing various approaches to decision analysis, we will analyze several kinds of important management decisions. We also explain income tax effects on capital expenditure decisions.

Relevant Information for Management

The management decision process calls for comparing two or more possible solutions to a problem and deciding which one is the best under the circumstances. Supplying relevant information to management for each alternative is the responsibility of the management accountant. Members of top management should evaluate the possible solutions to a particular problem. To do so, they should not have to wade through pages and pages of data to find out how each alternative will affect the operations of the business. Many of the facts may be the same for each alternative. For instance, total sales may not be affected by a cost-saving proposal. If there are three possible courses of action and total sales are the same in each case, the sales data would not influence the decision. Also, the accountant often uses past data in preparing cost estimates of the decision alternatives. However, it is the cost estimates that are relevant to the decision, not the historical data. **Relevant decision information** is future cost, revenue, or resource usage data that will be different for the various

Objective 1
Define and
identify
relevant
decision infor-
mation

alternatives being evaluated. A decision must be made on the basis of the alternatives available. So information that is alike for those alternatives, or costs or transactions that have already happened, will not be helpful in picking out the one best alternative. Relevant information is limited to future data that differ among the possible alternatives.

Management Decision Cycle

The decision-making process is an unstructured area of responsibility. Many decisions are unique and do not lend themselves to strict rules, steps, or timetables. However, certain events accompany each kind of management decision analysis. Figure 28-1 shows the events that make up the management decision cycle. Following the discovery of a problem or resource need, the accountant should seek out all possible courses of action that are open to management and will solve the problem or meet the need. After identifying the alternatives, the accountant prepares a complete analysis for each action, showing its total cost, cost savings, or financial effects on business operations. Each type of decision calls for different information. When all the information has been gathered and organized in a meaningful way, management can decide on or choose the one best course of action. After the decision has been carried out, the accountant should prepare a post-decision audit analysis to see if the decision was correct. If further action is needed, the decision cycle begins all over again. If not, this particular decision process has been completed.

Figure 28-1
The Management
Decision Cycle

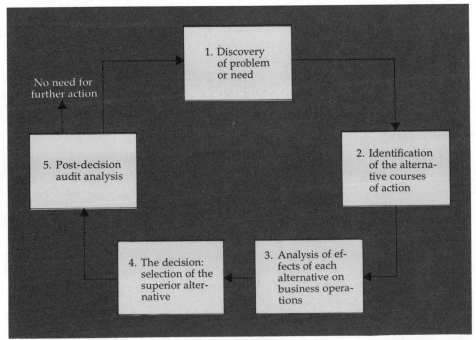

Accounting Tools and Reports
for Decision Analysis

The accountant usually plays the role of data supplier in the management decision process. Certain accounting tools and reports are used for this purpose. Management expects decision information to be accurate, timely, refined, and presented in a readable way. For this reason, the accountant must be concerned not only with the information itself but with the reporting form as well.

Variable costing and incremental analysis are the two most common decision tools used by the accountant. Each technique helps to identify information relevant to a particular decision. Each technique also provides the accountant with a special decision-reporting format.

Variable Costing

Variable costing (also called direct costing) is primarily an approach to product costing. Unlike absorption costing, which assigns all manufacturing costs to products, **variable costing** uses only the variable manufacturing costs for product costing and inventory valuation. Direct materials costs, direct labor costs, and variable factory overhead costs are the only cost elements used to figure product costs. Fixed factory overhead costs are considered costs of the current accounting period.

Support for variable costing stems from the fact that a factory will have fixed manufacturing costs whether it operates or not. For this reason, those who favor variable costing argue that such costs do not have a direct relationship to the product and should not be used to find the product unit cost. Fixed manufacturing costs are linked more closely with time than with productive output. Opponents of variable costing say that without the fixed manufacturing costs, production would stop. Therefore, such costs are an integral part of product costs.

Whatever side you are on, two points are certain. The first is that variable costing is *very* useful for internal management decision purposes. The second is that neither the Internal Revenue Service nor the American Institute of Certified Public Accountants accepts variable costing for external reporting purposes. They reject it because fixed costs are not included in inventory and cost of goods sold. Therefore, this approach cannot be used for figuring federal income taxes or for reporting the results of operations and financial position to stockholders and others outside the company.

*Objective 3
Calculate
product costs,
using variable
costing proce-
dures*

Product Costing For product costing, variable costing treats fixed manufacturing costs differently from costs that vary with output. A point that is often overlooked is that fixed manufacturing costs are also left out of all inventories. For this reason, the value of inventories arrived at by means of variable costing is lower than the value of those figured by means of absorption costing.

An example will help to explain the differences between these two product costing approaches. Granoff Industries, Inc., produces grills for outdoor cooking. During 19xx, the company put a new disposable grill into production. A summary of 19xx cost and production data for the grill follows: direct materials cost, $59,136; direct labor, $76,384; variable factory overhead, $44,352; and fixed factory overhead, $36,960. There were 24,640 units completed and 22,000 units sold during 19xx. There were no beginning or ending work in process inventories.

Using the above data, we can find the unit cost as well as the ending inventory and cost of goods sold amounts for 19xx under a variable costing approach and under an absorption costing approach. This information is summarized in Figure 28-2. Unit production cost under variable costing is $7.30 per grill, whereas unit cost is $8.80 working with absorption costing. Ending Finished Goods Inventory balances are not the same because of the $1.50 difference in unit cost. Because fewer costs remain in inventory at year end with variable costing amounts, it is logical that greater costs will appear on the income statement. As shown in Figure 28-2, $197,560 of current manufacturing costs are considered period costs, to be subtracted from revenue in the variable costing income statement. Only $193,600 is shown as Cost of Goods Sold when absorption costing is

Figure 28-2
Variable
Costing
Versus
Absorption
Costing

Granoff Industries, Inc. Unit Cost and Ending Inventory Values For the Year Ended December 31, 19xx		
	Variable Costing	Absorption Costing
Unit Cost		
Direct materials ($59,136 ÷ 24,640 units)	$2.40	$2.40
Direct labor ($76,384 ÷ 24,640 units)	3.10	3.10
Variable factory overhead ($44,352 ÷ 24,640 units)	1.80	1.80
Fixed factory overhead ($36,960 ÷ 24,640 units)	—	1.50
Total unit cost	$7.30	$8.80
Ending Finished Goods Inventory		
2,640 units at $7.30	$ 19,272	
2,640 units at $8.80		$ 23,232
Cost of Goods Sold for 19xx		
22,000 units at $7.30	$160,600	
22,000 units at $8.80		$193,600
Plus fixed factory overhead	36,960	
Costs appearing on 19xx income statement	$197,560	$193,600
Total costs to be accounted for	$216,832	$216,832

used. The difference of $3,960 (2,640 units in inventory $\times$ $1.50 fixed costs per unit) is shown as inventory under absorption costing.

Objective 4 Prepare an income statement, using the contribution reporting format

Performance Analysis: The Income Statement The use of variable costing leads to differences in financial reporting as well as in product costing. Putting together concepts of contribution margin and variable costing results in an entirely new form of income statement. This new form emphasizes cost variability and segment or product line contributions to income. Costs are no longer classified as either manufacturing or non-manufacturing costs. Instead, attention is focused on separating variable costs from fixed costs.

Adding further to the Granoff Industries example will help to explain this point. Assume the following additional information for 19xx: Selling price per grill is $24.50. Variable selling costs per grill are $4.80. Fixed selling expenses are $48,210, and fixed administrative expenses are $82,430. Net income under both variable costing and absorption costing procedures is compared in Figure 28-3. The contribution format is presented first. Note that the term *gross margin* is replaced by the term *contribution margin* and that only variable costs (including variable selling costs) are subtracted from sales to get the contribution margin. This is the amount that each segment or product line is contributing to the fixed costs and profits of the company. Net income figured by using the conventional statement is shown in the lower part of Figure 28-3. Note that net income is different under the two methods. This difference, $3,960, is the same amount noted earlier. It is the part of fixed manufacturing overhead cost that is inventoried when absorption costing is used.

Contribution Reporting and Decisions Variable costing and the contribution approach to reporting are used a great deal in decision analysis. Their most common use is in deciding whether or not to continue a segment, division, or product line. Other uses are in the evaluation of new product lines and in sales mix studies. Decisions about the contribution of sales territories also use the contribution approach to income reporting. We will explain these uses later when we look at certain kinds of decisions.

Incremental Analysis

Objective 5 Develop decision data, using the incremental analysis technique

Incremental analysis, an approach often used in decision reporting, compares different alternatives by looking only at informational differences. Only decision data that differ among alternatives are of concern and, for decision purposes, only future data are included. As a result, incremental analysis is based on information relevant to the decision at hand. By focusing on the differences among alternatives, incremental analysis helps to highlight the important points. It makes the evaluation easier for the decision maker. And it reduces the time needed to choose the best course of action.

As an illustration, assume that the Wilson Company is trying to decide which one of two machines, P and D, to buy. Management has been able to collect the following annual operating estimates on the two machines:

Figure 28-3
The Income
Statement—
Contribution
Versus Conven-
tional Formats

Granoff Industries, Inc.
Disposable Grill Division
Income Statement
For the Year Ended December 31, 19xx

Sales		$539,000
Variable Manufacturing Cost of Goods		
Produced	$179,872	
Less Ending Inventory	19,272*	
Variable Cost of Goods Sold	$160,600*	
Plus Variable Selling Costs		
(22,000 units at $4.80)	105,600	266,200
Contribution Margin		$272,800
Less Fixed Costs		
Fixed Manufacturing Costs	$ 36,960	
Fixed Selling Expenses	48,210	
Fixed Administrative Expenses	82,430	167,600
Net Income (before taxes)		$105,200
Sales		$539,000
Cost of Goods Sold		
Cost of Goods Manufactured	$216,832*	
Less Ending Inventory	23,232*	193,600*
Gross Margin on Sales		$345,400
Selling Expenses		
Variable	$105,600	
Fixed	48,210	
Administrative Expenses	82,430	236,240
Net Income (before taxes)		$109,160

*Detailed computations are found in Figure 28-2.

	Machine P	Machine D
Increase in revenue	$16,200	$19,800
Increase in annual operating costs		
Direct materials	2,800	2,800
Direct labor	4,200	6,100
Variable factory overhead	2,100	3,050
Fixed factory overhead		
(depreciation included)	5,000	5,000

The best method of comparing these two decision alternatives is to prepare an analysis that will show the amount of increase in the revenues and costs that are relevant to the decision. This analysis is shown on the next page.

Wilson Company
Incremental Decision Analysis

	Machine P	Difference in Favor of Machine D	Machine D
Increase in revenues	$16,200	$3,600	$19,800
Increase in operating costs			
Direct materials	$ 2,800	—	$ 2,800
Direct labor	4,200	1,900	6,100
Variable factory overhead	2,100	950	3,050
Fixed factory overhead	5,000	—	5,000
Total operating costs	$14,100	$2,850	$16,950
Resulting increase in net income	$ 2,100	$ 750	$ 2,850

If we assume that the purchase price and useful life of the two machines are the same, the analysis shows that Machine D will generate $750 more in net income than Machine P. Thus the decision would be to purchase Machine D.

Special Reports

Qualitative as well as quantitative data are useful in decision making. When only quantitative data are being considered, most problems of choosing between alternatives can be solved by using either contribution reporting or incremental analysis. However, in some decisions there are many different alternatives, each of which is the best one in certain circumstances. One may be more profitable, but another may further diversify a company's product line. A third alternative may help prevent a huge layoff of personnel in some part of the country, thus bolstering the company's goodwill there. Even though many equally good qualitative decision alternatives may be available, management must choose only one course of action. In cases such as those described above, the accountant must use imagination and prepare the special decision report that is best under the circumstances. There is no set structure for these special decision reports. They are created by skilled, experienced accountants to fit individual situations.

The Capital Expenditure Decision

Among the most important kinds of decisions facing management are those about when and how much to spend on capital facilities for the company. These are called **capital expenditure decisions**. Also under this heading are decisions about installing new equipment, replacing old equipment, expanding the production area by adding to an existing building, buying or building a new factory, or acquiring another company. All of these major spending decisions call for careful analysis by the accountant and generally involve comparative analysis of two or more alternatives.

Capital Budgeting: A Cooperative Venture

Capital budgeting is the process of identifying the need for a facility, analyzing different courses of action to meet that need, preparing the reports for management, choosing the best alternative, and rationing capital expenditure funds among competing resource needs. This process calls for input from people in every part of the business organization. Finance people are expected to supply a target cost of capital or desired rate of return for the decision analysis and an estimate of how much money can be spent on any one project. Without this kind of information, a decision cannot be reached. Marketing people identify areas of the business that need plant and facility expansion through their predictions of future sales trends. Management people at all levels help to identify facility needs and often prepare preliminary cost estimates of the desired facility. These same people help in carrying out capital expenditure decisions by trying to keep actual results within the cost and revenue estimates.

The accountant gathers and organizes the decision information into workable, readable form. Generally, he or she applies one or more evaluation methods to the information gathered for each alternative. The most common capital expenditure proposal evaluation methods are (1) the accounting rate of return method, (2) the payback method, and (3) the present value method. Once these methods have been applied, management can make a choice based on the criteria used for the decision. We are now going to look at the desired rate of return of a capital investment. Then the rest of this part of the chapter centers on the accountant's evaluation of the proposal using these methods and describes the final selection process.

Desired Rate of Return on Investment

Choosing the best capital expenditure alternative is not always the approach taken in the decision-making process. Most companies have a set minimum rate of return, below which the expenditure request is automatically refused. If none of the capital expenditure requests is expected to meet the minimum desired rate of return, all requests will be turned down.

*Objective 6
Describe the
purpose of a
minimum
desired rate of
return, and
explain the
methods used to
arrive at this
rate*

Why do companies use such a cutoff point? The idea is that if an expenditure request falls below the minimum rate of return, the funds can be used more profitably in another part of the company. Supporting poor-return proposals now will lower the whole company's profitability later.

Deciding on a company's minimum desired rate of return is no simple matter. Each of the measures that can be used to set a cutoff point has certain advantages. The most common measures used are (1) cost of capital, (2) corporate return on investment, (3) industry average return on investment, and (4) bank interest rate. We will describe how to find the cost of capital in some detail. Then we will explain briefly the use of the other measures.

Cost of Capital Measures Of all the measures for desired rates of return listed above, cost of capital measures are the most widely used and discussed. The goal is to find the cost of financing the company's activities. However, to finance its activities, a company borrows funds and issues preferred and common stock, and also tries to operate at a profit. Each of these financing alternatives has a different cost rate. Further, each company uses a different mix of these sources to finance current and future operations.

To set a desired cutoff rate of return, management can use cost of debt, cost of preferred stock, cost of equity capital, or cost of retained earnings. In many cases, a company will average these cost results to establish an **average cost of capital** measure. Sophisticated methods are used to compute these financial return measures.[1] But our purpose here is simply to identify measures used. Thus we will present only a brief description of each kind of cost of financing.

Cost of debt is the ratio of loan charges to net proceeds of the loan. The effects of income taxes and the present value of interest charges must be taken into account, but the rate is essentially the ratio of costs to loan proceeds. **Cost of preferred stock** is the stated dividend rate of the individual stock issue. Tax effects are not important in this case, because dividends are not a deductible expense like interest charges. **Cost of equity capital** is the rate of return to the investor and is what makes stock valuable in the market. It is not just the dividend rate to the stockholder, because the dividend rate can be raised or lowered almost at will by management. This concept is very complex but has sound authoritative financial support.[2] **Cost of retained earnings** is the opportunity cost or the dividends given up by the stockholder. Such a cost is linked closely with the cost of equity capital just described. The point is that a firm's cost of capital is very hard to compute because it is a weighted average of the cost of the various financing methods. However, this figure is the best estimate of a minimum desired rate of return.

Weighted average cost of capital is computed by first finding the cost rate for each source or class of capital-raising instrument. The second part

1. See James C. Van Horne, "Cost of Capital of the Firm," in *Financial Management and Policy,* 6th ed. (Englewood Cliffs, N.J.: Prentice-Hall, Inc., 1983), Chapter 8, pp. 213–227.
2. Ibid.

of the computation is to figure the percentage of each source of capital to the total debt and equity financing of the company. Weighted average cost of capital is the sum of the products of each financing source's percentage multiplied by its cost rate. For example, assume that the Leventhal Company's financing structure is as follows:

Cost Rate	Source of Capital	Amount	Capital Mix (Percentage of Each to Total)
10%	Debt financing	$150,000	30
8%	Preferred stock	50,000	10
12%	Common stock	200,000	40
14%	Retained earnings	100,000	20
	Totals	$500,000	100

Weighted average cost of capital of 11.4 percent would be computed in the following way:

Source of Capital	Cost Rate	×	Ratio of Capital Mix	=	Portion of Weighted Average Cost of Capital
Debt financing	.10		.30		.030
Preferred stock	.08		.10		.008
Common stock	.12		.40		.048
Retained earnings	.14		.20		.028
Weighted average cost of capital					.114

Other Cutoff Measures If cost of capital information is not available, management can use one of three less accurate but still useful amounts as the minimum desired rate of return. The first is average total corporate return on investment. The reasoning used to support such a measure is that any capital investment that produced a return lower than an amount earned historically by the company would have a negative effect on future operations. A second method is to use industry averages of the cost of capital. Most sizable industry associations supply such information. As a last resort, a company might use the current bank lending rate. But because most companies are both debt and equity financed, this rate seldom reflects an accurate rate of return.

Accounting Rate of Return Method

Among the methods used to measure the estimated performance of a capital investment, the **accounting rate of return method** is a crude but easy approach to understand and use. With this method, we measure expected performance by using two variables: estimated annual after-tax net income from the project and the average investment cost. The basic equation is as follows:

Objective 7a
Evaluate capital
expenditure
proposals, using
the accounting
rate of return
method

$$\text{accounting rate} \atop \text{of return} = \frac{\text{project's average annual after-tax net income}}{\text{average investment cost}}$$

To compute average annual after-tax net income, we use the revenue and expense data prepared for evaluating the project. Average investment in the proposed capital facility is figured as follows:[3]

$$\text{average investment} = \frac{\text{total investment} + \text{salvage value}}{2}$$

For example, assume that the Kollias Company is interested in purchasing a new bottling machine. Only projects that promise to yield more than a 16 percent return are acceptable to management. Estimates for the proposal include an increase in revenues of $17,900 a year and operating cost increases of $8,500 a year (including depreciation). The cost of the machine is $51,000. Its salvage value is $3,000. The company's income tax rate is 50 percent. Should the company invest in the machine? To answer the question, we figure the accounting rate of return as follows:

$$\text{accounting rate of return} = \frac{(\$17,900 - \$8,500) \times .50}{(\$51,000 + \$3,000) \div 2}$$

$$= \frac{\$4,700}{\$27,000} = \underline{17.4\%}$$

The projected rate of return is higher than the 16 percent minimum desired rate of return. So management should think seriously about making the investment.

Because this method is easy to understand and apply, it is widely used. However, it is important to know the disadvantages of the accounting rate of return method. First, the use of averages tends to equalize all information, leading to errors in annual income and investment data. Second, the method is hard to use if estimated annual net incomes differ from year to year. Finally, the time value of money is not considered in the computations. Thus future and present dollars are treated as being equal.

Cash Flow and the Payback Method

Instead of measuring the rate of return on investments, many managers would rather estimate the cash flow to be generated by a capital investment. In such cases, the goal is to determine the minimum length of time it may take to get back the initial amount of the investment. If two investment alternatives are being studied, the choice will be the investment

---

3. The procedure of adding salvage value to the numerator may not seem logical. However, a fixed asset is never depreciated below its salvage value. Average investment is computed by determining the midpoint of the depreciable portion of the asset and adding back the salvage value. Another way of stating the above formula would be

$$\text{average investment} = \frac{\text{total investment} - \text{salvage value}}{2} + \text{salvage value}$$

which reduces to the formula used above.

Objective 7b
Evaluate capital
expenditure
proposals, using
the payback
method
which pays back its initial amount in the shortest time. This period of time is known as the payback period, and the capital investment evaluation approach is called the **payback method.**

We compute the payback period as follows:

$$\text{payback period} = \frac{\text{cost of investment}}{\text{annual net cash inflow}}$$

To apply the payback method to the proposed capital investment of the Kollias Company discussed earlier, we need some further information. We need to determine the net cash flow. To do so, we find and eliminate the effects of all the noncash revenue and expense items included in the analysis of net income. In our case, we will assume that the only noncash expense or revenue amount is machine depreciation. To figure this amount, we must know the asset life and the depreciation method. Suppose that the Kollias Company uses the straight-line depreciation approach, and the new bottling machine will have a ten-year estimated service life. Using this information and the facts given earlier, we compute the payback period as shown below.

$$\text{annual depreciation} = \frac{\text{cost} - \text{salvage value}}{10 \text{ (years)}}$$

$$= \frac{\$51,000 - \$3,000}{10}$$

$$= \underline{\$4,800} \text{ per year}$$

$$\text{payback period} = \frac{\text{cost of machine}}{\text{cash revenue} - \text{cash expenses} - \text{taxes}}$$

$$= \frac{\$51,000}{\$17,900 - (\$8,500 - \$4,800) - \$4,700}$$

$$= \frac{\$51,000}{\$9,500}$$

$$= \underline{5.368} \text{ years}$$

If the company's desired payback period is six years or less, the capital investment proposal would be approved.

Payback has the advantage of being easy to compute and understand and is widely used for this reason. However, the disadvantages of this approach far outweigh the advantages. First, the method does not measure profitability. Second, the present value of cash flows from different periods is not recognized. Finally, emphasis is on the time it takes to get out of the investment rather than on the long-run return on the investment.

Present Value Method[4]

*Objective 7c
Evaluate capital
expenditure
proposals, using
the present
value method*

Today there are a great many opportunities to do something with investment capital other than purchase fixed assets. As a result, management expects a reasonable return from an asset during its useful life. Capital expenditure decision analysis calls for the evaluation of estimates for several time periods in the future. Cash flows from different periods do not have the same values when measured in current dollars. For this reason, to treat all future income flows alike ignores the time value of money. Both the accounting rate of return and payback evaluation methods have this disadvantage.

The concept of **discounted cash flow** helps to overcome the disadvantages of the accounting rate of return and payback methods in evaluating capital investment alternatives. By using the present value tables found in Appendix B, it is possible to discount future cash flows back to the present. This approach to capital investment analysis is called the **present value method.** Multipliers used to find the present value of a future cash flow are found in the present value tables. Which multipliers to use is figured by connecting the minimum desired rate of return and the life of the asset or length of time for which the amount is being discounted. Each element of cash inflow and cash outflow to be realized over the life of the asset is discounted back to the present. If the present value of all expected future net cash inflows is greater than the amount of the current investment, the expenditure meets the minimum desired rate of return, and the project should be carried out.

The present value method is used in different ways, depending on whether annual cash flows are equal or unequal. If all annual cash flows (inflows less outflows) are equal, the discount factor to be used will come from Table B-4 in Appendix B. This table gives multipliers for the present value of $1 received *each period* for a given number of time periods. One computation will cover the cash flows of all time periods involved. If, however, expected cash inflows and outflows differ from one year to the next, each year's amount has to be discounted back to the present. Discount factors used in this kind of analysis are found in Table B-3 in Appendix B. Multipliers in Table B-3 are used to find the present value of $1 to be received (or paid out) at the end of a given number of time periods.

An example will help to show the difference in the present value analysis of expenditures with equal and unequal cash flows. Suppose that the Burrows Metal Products Company is trying to decide which of two stamping machines to buy. The Red Machine has equal expected annual net cash inflows, and the Green Machine has unequal annual amounts. Information on the two machines follows.

	Red Machine	Green Machine
Purchase price: January 1, 19x4	$16,500	$16,500
Expected life	5 years	5 years

4. This section is based on the concept of present value. Appendixes A and B explain this concept and provide tables of multipliers for computations.

Chapter Twenty-Eight

Estimated net cash inflows: *annuity*

19x4	$5,000	$6,000
19x5	$5,000	$5,500
19x6	$5,000	$5,000
19x7	$5,000	$4,500
19x8	$5,000	$4,000

The company's minimum desired rate of return is 16 percent. Which—if either—of the two alternatives should be chosen?

The evaluation process is shown in Figure 28-4. An analysis involving equal annual cash flows is easier to prepare. Present value of net cash inflows for the five-year period for the Red Machine is figured by multiplying $5,000 by 3.274. The multiplier, 3.274, is found in Table B-4 in Appendix B by using the 16 percent minimum desired rate of return and the five-year life of the Red Machine. Present value of the total cash inflows from the Red Machine is $16,370. When we compare this figure with the $16,500 purchase price, the result is a *negative* net present value of $130.

Analysis of the Green Machine alternative gives a different result. As shown in Figure 28-4, unequal net cash inflows cause more work. Multipliers for this part of the analysis are found by using the same 16 percent rate. But five different multipliers, one for each year of the life of the asset, must be used. Table B-3 in Appendix B applies here, because each annual amount must be individually discounted back to the present. For the Green Machine, the $16,851.50 present value of net cash inflows is more than the $16,500.00 purchase price of the machine. So there is a positive net present value of $351.50.

Figure 28-4
Present Value
Analysis:
Equal Versus
Unequal Cash
Flows

Burrows Metal Products Company
Capital Expenditure Analysis
19x3

Red Machine

Present value of cash inflows	$5,000 × 3.274 =	$16,370.00
Less purchase price of machine		16,500.00
Negative net present value *didn't earn 16%*		($ 130.00)

Green Machine

Present value of cash inflows:

19x4	($6,000 × .862)	$ 5,172.00
19x5	($5,500 × .743)	4,086.50
19x6	($5,000 × .641)	3,205.00
19x7	($4,500 × .552)	2,484.00
19x8	($4,000 × .476)	1,904.00
Total		$ 16,851.50
Less purchase price of machine		(16,500.00)
Positive net present value		$ 351.50

A positive net present value figure means that the return on the asset exceeds the 16 percent minimum desired rate of return. A negative figure means that the rate of return is below the minimum cutoff point. In the Burrows Metal Products case, the right decision would be to purchase the Green Machine.

Incorporating the time value of money in the evaluation of capital expenditure proposals is the major advantage of the present value method. This method also deals mainly with total cash flows from the investment over its useful life so it brings total profitability into the analysis as well. The major disadvantage of the present value method is that many managers do not trust or understand the procedure. They prefer the payback or the accounting rate of return method because the computations are easier.

Other Operating Decisions of Management

Management depends on the accountant to supply relevant information for many kinds of decisions other than those involving capital expenditures. We will now turn to the data relevant to the make or buy decision, the special order decision, and the sales mix analysis.

Make or Buy Decisions

Objective 8a
Prepare decision
alternative
evaluations for
make or buy
decisions

One common group of decision analyses centers on the many parts used in product assembly operations. Management is faced continually with the decision as to whether to make or to buy some or all of the parts. The goal of the **make or buy decision** is to identify those cost and revenue elements relevant to this kind of decision. Below is the information to be considered.

To Make	**To Buy**
Need for expensive machinery	Purchase price of item
Other variable costs of making the item	Rent or net cash flow to be generated from vacated space in factory
Repair and maintenance expenses	Salvage value of new machinery

To illustrate a make or buy decision, we present the case of the Marini Electronics Company. The firm has been purchasing a small transistor casing from an outside supplier for the past five years at a cost of $1.25 per casing. However, the supplier has just informed Marini Electronics that the price will be raised by 20 percent, effective immediately. The company has idle machinery that could be used to produce the casings. Also, management has found that the costs of producing the casings would be $84 per 100 casings for direct materials, six minutes of labor per casing at $4 per direct labor hour, and variable factory overhead at $2 per direct labor hour. Fixed factory overhead would include $4,000 of depreciation per year and $6,000 of other fixed costs. Annual production and usage would be 20,000 casings. The space and machinery to be used would not be usable if the part were purchased. Should Marini Electronics Company make or buy the casings?

From the information given, the company should make the casings. An incremental cost analysis of the two decision alternatives is presented in Figure 28-5. All costs connected with the decision are shown in the analysis. Because the machinery has already been bought and neither the machinery nor the required factory space has any other use, the fixed factory overhead costs are the same for both alternatives. For this reason they are not relevant to the decision. The costs of making the needed casings (leaving out the fixed overhead costs) are $28,800. The cost of buying 20,000 casings will be $30,000 at the increased purchase price. It is clear, then, that $1,200 will be saved if the casings are made within the company.

Using incremental analysis is a good approach to the make or buy decision. This approach allows the analyst to use all decision data available and quickly identify anything that is irrelevant to the final decision.

Special Product Orders

Management is often faced with **special order decisions**, about whether or not to accept special product orders. These orders are normally for large

Figure 28-5
Incremental
Analysis:
Make or Buy
Decision

Marini Electronics Company Incremental Decision Analysis Current Year—Annual Usage			
	Make	Difference in Favor of Make	Buy
Raw materials (20,000 ÷ 100 × $84)	$16,800	$(16,800)	—
Direct labor (20,000 ÷ 10 × $4)	8,000	(8,000)	—
Variable factory overhead (20,000 ÷ 10 × $2)	4,000	(4,000)	—
Fixed factory overhead			
Depreciation*	4,000	—	4,000
Other*	6,000	—	6,000
To purchase completed casings 20,000 × $1.50	—	30,000	30,000
Totals	$28,800	$ 1,200	$30,000

*Irrelevant because these amounts are the same for both decision alternatives. Amounts have not been included in totals.

Objective 8b
Prepare deci-
sion alternative
evaluations
for special
order decisions

numbers of similar products to be sold at prices below those listed in advertisements. Because management would not have expected such orders, the orders would not have been included in any annual cost or sales estimates. Generally, these orders are one-time events and should not be included in estimates of subsequent years' operations. (Because standard products are sold to the public at stated prices, legal advice on federal price discrimination laws should be obtained before accepting special orders.)

To illustrate special order analysis, consider Moustafa Sporting Goods, Inc., which manufactures a complete line of sporting equipment. Bailey Enterprises operates a large chain of discount stores and has approached the Moustafa company with a special order. The order calls for 30,000 deluxe baseballs, to be shipped with bulk packaging of 500 baseballs per box. Bailey is willing to pay $2.45 per baseball.

The following data were developed by the Moustafa accounting department: annual expected production, 400,000 baseballs; current year's production, 410,000 baseballs; maximum production capacity, 450,000 baseballs. Additional data are presented below.

Unit cost data	
Direct materials	$ .60
Direct labor	.90
Factory overhead	
Variable	.50
Fixed ($100,000 ÷ 400,000)	.25
Packaging per unit	.30
Advertising ($60,000 ÷ 400,000)	.15
Other fixed selling and admin-	
istrative costs ($120,000 ÷ 400,000)	.30
Total	$3.00
Unit selling price	$4.00
Total estimated bulk packaging costs	
(30,000 baseballs: 500 per box)	$2,500

Should Moustafa Sporting Goods, Inc., accept the Bailey offer?

A profitability analysis reveals that the special order from Bailey Enterprises should be accepted. Figure 28-6 contains a comparative analysis based on the contribution reporting format. Net income before taxes is computed for the Baseball Division for operations both with and without the Bailey order.

The only costs affected by the order are for direct materials, direct labor, variable factory overhead, and packaging. Materials, labor, and overhead costs are shown for sales of 410,000 and 440,000 baseballs, respectively. Sales data were computed using these same unit amounts. Packaging costs will increase, but only by the amount of the added bulk packaging costs. All other costs will remain the same in each case. The net result of accepting the special order is an $11,000 increase in contribution margin (and net income before taxes). This amount can be verified by the following computations:

net gain = [(unit selling price − unit variable mfg. costs) × units] −
        bulk pack costs
      = [($2.45 − $2.00) 30,000] − $2,500
      = $13,500 − $2,500 = $11,000

For special order analysis, both the comparative contribution reporting approach and incremental analysis can be used. In the above case, we chose contribution reporting because of the misleading fixed cost data given in the problem. Contribution reporting highlights the effect of variable cost changes on contribution margin and net income.

Sales Mix Analysis

Objective 8c
Prepare deci-
sion alternative
evaluations
for sales
mix analyses

Profit analysis and maximization are possible only when the profitability of all product lines is known. The question is, Which product or products contribute the most to company profitability in relation to the amount of capital assets or other scarce resources needed to produce the item(s)? To answer this question, the accountant must measure the contribution margin of each product. The next step is to determine a set of ratios of contribution margin to the required capital equipment or other scarce resources. Once this step is completed, management should request a

Figure 28-6
Contribution
Reporting:
Special Product
Order

	Moustafa Sporting Goods, Inc. Comparative Decision Analysis Special Product Order—Baseball Division	
	Without Bailey Order	With Bailey Order
Sales	$1,640,000	$1,713,500
Less variable costs		
Direct materials	$ 246,000	$ 264,000
Direct labor	369,000	396,000
Variable factory overhead	205,000	220,000
Packaging costs	123,000	125,500
Total variable costs	$ 943,000	$1,005,500
Contribution margin	$ 697,000	$ 708,000
Less fixed costs		
Factory overhead	$ 100,000	$ 100,000
Advertising	60,000	60,000
Selling and administrative	120,000	120,000
Total fixed costs	$ 280,000	$ 280,000
Net income before taxes	$ 417,000	$ 428,000

marketing study to set the upper limits of demand on those products that are most profitable. If product profitability can be computed and market demand exists for these products, management should shift production to the more profitable products.

Many kinds of decisions can be related to the approach described here. **Sales mix analysis** means determining the most profitable combination of product sales when a company produces more than one product. Closely connected with sales mix analysis is the product line profitability study designed to discover which products are losing money for the company. The same decision approach is used, but the goal is to eliminate the unprofitable product line(s). Another decision area is that of corporate segment analysis. The contribution margin approach is again used, with the goal of isolating production costs to identify the unprofitable segment(s). If corrective action is not possible, management should eliminate the noncontributing segment(s). Even though not all of these decision areas will be discussed, it is important to remember that the same kind of analysis can be used for product line profitability studies and corporate segment analyses.

An example of this kind of analysis will aid understanding. The management of Don Schweitzer and Family, Inc., is in the process of analyzing its sales mix. The company manufactures three products—C, S, and U—using the same production equipment for all three. The total productive capacity is being used. Below are the product line statistics.

	Product C	Product S	Product U
Current production and sales (units)	20,000	30,000	18,000
Machine hours per product	2	1	2.5
Selling price per unit	$24.00	$18.00	$32.00
Unit variable manufacturing costs	$12.50	$10.00	$18.75
Unit variable selling costs	$ 6.50	$ 5.00	$ 6.25

Should the company try to sell more of one product and less of another?

Because total productive capacity is being used, the only way to expand the production of one product is to reduce the production of another product. The sales mix analysis of Don Schweitzer and Family, Inc., is shown in Figure 28-7. Though contribution reporting is used here, contribution margin per product is not the important figure for a decision about shifts in sales mix. In the analysis, Product U has the highest contribution margin. However, all products use the same machinery and all machine hours are filled. So machine hours become the scarce resource.

The analysis in Figure 28-7 goes one step beyond the computation of contribution margin per unit. A sales mix decision such as this one should use two decision variables: contribution margin per unit and machine hours required per unit. For instance, Product C requires two machine hours to generate $5 of contribution margin. But Product S would generate $6 of contribution margin using the same two machine hours. For this reason, we have figured contribution margin per machine hour. Based on

Figure 28-7
Contribution
Reporting: Sales
Mix Analysis

Don Schweitzer and Family, Inc.
Sales Mix Analysis
Contribution Reporting Format

	Product C	Product S	Product U
Sales price	$24.00	$18.00	$32.00
Variable costs			
Manufacturing	$12.50	$10.00	$18.75
Selling	6.50	5.00	6.25
Total	$19.00	$15.00	$25.00
Contribution margin (A)	$ 5.00	$ 3.00	$ 7.00
Machine hours required per unit (B)	2	1	2.5
Contribution margin per machine hour (A ÷ B)	$ 2.50	$ 3.00	$ 2.80

this information, management can readily see that it should produce and sell as much of Product S as possible. Next, it should push Product U. If any productive capacity remains, it should produce Product C.

Income Taxes and Business Decisions

Tax Effects on Capital Expenditure Decisions

Objective 9
Analyze capital
expenditure
decision alterna-
tives that
incorporate the
effects of
income taxes

Income taxes are an important cost of doing business, and they often have an important impact on business decisions. The aim of capital budgeting evaluation techniques such as payback period and net present value is to measure and compare the relative benefits of proposed capital expenditures. These measurements focus on cash receipts and payments for a given project. For profit-oriented companies, income taxes are important in capital budgeting analyses because they affect the amount and timing of cash flows. For this reason, capital expenditure evaluation analysis must take tax effects into account.

Corporate income tax rates range from 15 percent for low incomes to 46 percent on income over $100,000.

Taxable Income	Tax Rate
$0 to $25,000	15%
$25,000 to $50,000	$ 3,750 + 18% of amount over $25,000
$50,000 to $75,000	$ 8,250 + 30% of amount over $50,000
$75,000 to $100,000	$15,750 + 40% of amount over $75,000
$100,000 and over	$25,750 + 46% of amount over $100,000

Because of different tax rates and because of changes from year to year, we will show the effects of income taxes on cash flow by simply using a corporate tax rate of 46 percent of taxable income. Suppose that a project makes the following contribution to annual net income:

Cash revenues	$400,000
Cash expenses	(200,000)
Depreciation	(100,000)
Income before taxes	$100,000
Income taxes at 46%	(46,000)
Income after taxes	$ 54,000

Annual cash flow for this project can be determined by two different procedures:

1. Cash flow—receipts and disbursements

Revenues (cash inflow)	$400,000
Cash expenses (outflow)	(200,000)
Income taxes (outflow)	(46,000)
Net cash inflow	$154,000

2. Cash flow—income adjustment procedure

Income after taxes	$ 54,000
Add: Noncash expenses (depreciation)	100,000
Less: Noncash revenues	—
Net cash inflow	$154,000

In both computations, the net cash inflow is $154,000, and the total effect of income taxes is to lower the net cash flow by $46,000.

Revenues and gains from the sale of equipment both raise taxable income and tax payments. When dealing with cash inflows, you must make the distinction between a gain on the sale of an asset and the proceeds received from the sale. *Gains* are the amount received that is over and above the book value of the asset, whereas the *proceeds* include the whole sales price and represent the cash inflow. Gains are not cash flow items, but they do raise tax payments. If equipment with a book value of $80,000 is sold for $180,000 in cash, the gain is $100,000. Assuming that this gain is taxable at the capital gains tax rate of 28 percent, we analyze the cash flow as follows:

Proceeds from sale		$180,000
Gain on sale	$100,000	
Capital gains tax rate	× .28	
Cash outflow (tax increase)		(28,000)
Net cash inflow		$152,000

As the cash flows from the receipt of revenues and proceeds from the sale of assets are reduced because of income taxes, so too are the amounts of potential expenses (cash outflows). Cash expenses lower net income and result in cash outflows only to the extent that they exceed the related tax reductions. This generalization is true for both cash operating expenses and losses on the sale of fixed assets. The following examples show the cash flow effects of increases in cash and noncash expenses and losses on the sale of equipment:

Cash expenses:

Increase in cash operating expenses	$100,000
Less: tax reduction at 46%	(46,000)
Net increase in cash outflow	$ 54,000

Noncash expenses:

Annual depreciation expense	$200,000
Corporate tax rate	× .46
Tax reduction = cash savings	$ 92,000

Loss on the sale of an asset:

Proceeds from sale		$150,000
Loss on sale	$100,000	
Capital gains tax rate	× .28	
Reduction of taxes and cash outflow		28,000
Total cash inflow resulting from sale		$178,000

Depreciation expense is not a cash flow item itself, but it does provide a cash benefit equal to the amount of the reduction in taxes. Losses on the sale of fixed assets also are not cash flow items, but they provide a cash benefit by reducing the amount of taxes to be paid in cash. For illustrations of the above ideas, see the review problem for this chapter (page 1077).

Minimizing Taxes Through Planning

In operating a business, there are many ways to plan for keeping the tax liability as low as possible. One of the most important is the timing of business transactions. For example, a corporation that is nearing $50,000 of taxable income for the year may want to put off an income-producing transaction until just after the end of the year to avoid the higher tax rate. Or it may speed up making certain expenditures for the same reason.

Another important way to reduce tax liability through operating decisions is by the timing of transactions involving depreciable business assets and land. For example, if at all possible, no such asset should be sold at a gain less than twelve months from date of purchase. Also, a corporation may be holding depreciable business assets, some of which have gains and some of which have losses. It may be possible to sell the assets with losses in one year and deduct them from ordinary income, and to put off selling the assets with gains until the next year, when the capital gains will be taxed at a lower rate.

It is always good management to try to take advantage of provisions of the tax law that allow preferential treatment. For example, the tax law has often been used to encourage investment in areas thought to be important for national goals. Because these goals change over the years, the tax law has been used to promote everything from emergency war equipment to pollution control devices. For example, the IRS currently gives a corporation a business energy credit for purchasing equipment that will reduce energy use. Corporations also are urged to spend money on research and development. In addition to the regular deduction for these expenses, the tax law gives a company a research and development tax credit for a part of them. Special credits are also allowed for certain spending that lowers unemployment or encourages the hiring of under-employed groups such as the handicapped.

Chapter Review

Review of Learning Objectives

1. Define and identify relevant decision information.

Any future cost, revenue, or resource usage data used in decision analyses that will be different for the decision's alternative courses of action are considered relevant decision information. Recognition of relevant data comes from development of a comparative analysis of the decision alternatives.

2. Describe the steps in the management decision cycle.

The decision cycle begins with the discovery of a problem or resource need. Then, the various alternative courses of action to solve the problem or meet the need are identified. Next, a complete analysis to determine the effects of each alternative on business operations is prepared. With this supporting data, the decision maker chooses the best alternative. After the decision has been carried out, the accountant should do a post-audit to see if the decision was correct or if other needs have arisen.

3. Calculate product costs, using variable costing procedures.

Variable costing uses only variable manufacturing costs for product costing and inventory valuation. Direct materials costs, direct labor costs, and variable factory overhead costs are the only elements used to compute product costs. Fixed factory overhead costs are considered costs of the current period and are not included in inventories.

4. Prepare an income statement, using the contribution reporting format.

Unlike the conventional form of income reporting, which depends on the absorption costing concept, the contribution form is based on variable costing procedures. Variable costs of goods sold and variable selling expenses are subtracted from sales to arrive at contribution margin. All fixed costs, including those from manufacturing, selling, and administration, are subtracted from contribution margin to determine net income (before taxes).

5. Develop decision data, using the incremental analysis technique.

Incremental analysis is a form of decision reporting in which the various decision alternatives are identified and differences in information about them are examined. When all revenue and cost data are examined in this way, the data relevant to the decision are highlighted, since they are the ones where differences exist. Revenue and cost items that are the same under the various alternatives are not relevant to the decision.

6. Describe the purpose of a minimum desired rate of return, and explain the methods used to arrive at this rate.

The purpose of establishing a minimum desired rate of return is to create a decision point below which the related capital expenditure request is refused automatically. By means of such an approach to decision making, many unprofitable requests are turned away without a great deal of wasted executive time. Among the measures used for desired rates of return are cost of capital, corporate return on investment, industry average return on investment, and bank interest rates. Weighted average cost of capital and average return on investment are the most widely used approaches to setting a minimum desired rate of return.

7. Evaluate capital expenditure proposals, using (a) the accounting rate of return method, (b) the payback method, and (c) the present value method.

When using the accounting rate of return method to evaluate two or more capital expenditure proposals, the alternative that yields the highest ratio of net income after taxes to average cost of investment is chosen. When using the payback method to evaluate a capital expenditure proposal, the emphasis is placed on the shortest time period needed to recoup in cash the original amount of the investment. The present value method depends very much on the time value of money. Present values of future cash flows are studied to see if they are more than the current cost of the capital expenditure being evaluated.

8. Prepare decision alternative evaluations for (a) make or buy decisions, (b) special order decisions, and (c) sales mix analyses.

Make or buy decision analysis helps management decide whether to buy a part used in product assembly or to make the part inside the company. This analysis centers on an incremental view of the costs of each alternative. Special order decisions have to do with unused capacity and finding the lowest acceptable selling price of a product. In most cases, fixed costs are irrelevant to the decision because they have been covered by regular operations. Contribution margin is a key decision yardstick. Sales mix analysis is used to learn the most profitable combination of product sales when a company makes more than one product using a common scarce resource. A similar approach can be used for decisions connected with identifying profitable sales territories or profitable corporate segments. Comparative analyses using the contribution reporting format are important in all of these studies.

9. Analyze capital expenditure decision alternatives that incorporate the effects of income taxes.

Income taxes affect the results of all capital expenditure analyses. Care must be taken to look at both sides of income taxes effects. Revenues and gains on the sale of assets increase taxes, and increased expenditures, noncash expenditures, and losses from the sale of assets decrease taxes. Tax-related inflows result from capital losses, increased expenses, and noncash expenditures, while tax-related cash outflows arise when a company has capital gains from the sale of fixed assets or from increased sales revenue.

Review Problem: Tax Effects on a Capital Expenditure Decision

The Hugo Construction Company specializes in the development of large shopping centers. The company is considering the purchase of a new earthmoving machine and has gathered the following information:

Purchase price	$600,000
Salvage value	$100,000
Useful life	4 years
Effective tax rate	40%

Depreciation method	Straight-line
Desired before-tax payback period	3 years
Desired after-tax payback period	5 years
Minimum before-tax rate of return	15%
Minimum after-tax rate of return	9%

The before-tax cash flow estimates are as follows:

Year	Revenues	Expenses	Net Cash Flow
1	$ 500,000	$260,000	$240,000
2	450,000	240,000	210,000
3	400,000	220,000	180,000
4	350,000	200,000	150,000
Totals	$1,700,000	$920,000	$780,000

Required

1. Using before-tax information, analyze the Hugo Construction Company's investment in the new earthmoving machine. In your analysis use (a) the accounting rate of return method, (b) the payback period method, and (c) the present value method.
2. Repeat part 1 using after-tax information.

Answer to Review Problem

1. Before-tax calculations

The increase in net income is as follows:

Year	Before-tax Net Cash Flow	Depreciation	Income Before Taxes
1	$240,000	$125,000	$115,000
2	210,000	125,000	85,000
3	180,000	125,000	55,000
4	150,000	125,000	25,000
Totals	$780,000	$500,000	$280,000

1a. (Before-tax) Accounting rate of return method:

$$\text{accounting rate of return} = \frac{\text{average annual net income}}{\text{average investment cost}}$$

$$= \frac{\$280,000 \div 4}{(\$600,000 + \$100,000) \div 2} = \frac{\$70,000}{\$350,000} = 20\%$$

1b. (Before-tax) Payback period method:

Total cash investment		$600,000
Less cash flow recovery		
Year 1	$240,000	
Year 2	210,000	
Year 3 ($\frac{5}{6}$ of $180,000)	150,000	(600,000)
Unrecovered investment		—

Payback period $2\frac{5}{6}$ years or 2.833 years or 2 years, 10 months

1c. (Before-tax) Present value method (multipliers are from Table B-3):

Year	Net Cash Flow	Present Value Multiplier	Present Value
1	$240,000	.870	$208,800
2	210,000	.756	158,760
3	180,000	.658	118,440
4	150,000	.572	85,800
4	100,000 (salvage)	.572	57,200

Total present value	$629,000
Cost of original investment	(600,000)
Positive net present value	$ 29,000

2. After-tax calculations

The increase in net income after taxes is as follows:

Year	Before-tax Net Cash Flow	Depreciation	Income Before Taxes	Taxes	Income After Taxes
1	$240,000	$125,000	$115,000	$ 46,000	$ 69,000
2	210,000	125,000	85,000	34,000	51,000
3	180,000	125,000	55,000	22,000	33,000
4	150,000	125,000	25,000	10,000	15,000
Totals	$780,000	$500,000	$280,000	$112,000	$168,000

The after-tax cash flow is as follows:

Year	Net Cash Flow Before Taxes	Taxes	Net Cash Flow After Taxes
1	$240,000	$ 46,000	$194,000
2	210,000	34,000	176,000
3	180,000	22,000	158,000
4	150,000	10,000	140,000
Totals	$780,000	$112,000	$668,000

2a. (After-tax) Accounting rate of return method:

$$\text{accounting rate of return} = \frac{\text{average annual after-tax net income}}{\text{average investment cost}}$$

$$= \frac{\$168,000 \div 4}{(\$600,000 + \$100,000) \div 2} = \frac{\$42,000}{\$350,000} = 12\%$$

2b. (After-tax) Payback period method:

Total cash investment		$600,000
Less cash flow recovery		
Year 1	$194,000	
Year 2	176,000	
Year 3	158,000	
Year 4 (.514 × $140,000)	72,000	(600,000)
Unrecovered investment		—

Payback period 3.514 years

2c. (After-tax) Present value method (multipliers are from Table B-3):

Year	Net Cash Inflow After Taxes	Present Value Multiplier	Present Value
1	$194,000	.917	$177,898
2	176,000	.842	148,192
3	158,000	.772	121,976
4	140,000	.708	99,120
4	100,000 (salvage)	.708	70,800
Total Present Value			$617,986
Cost of Original Investment			(600,000)
Positive Net Present Value			$ 17,986

Hugo Construction Company: Summary of decision analysis

	Before-tax		After-tax	
	Desired	Predicted	Desired	Predicted
Accounting rate of return	15%	20%	9%	12%
Payback period	3 yrs	2.833 yrs	5 yrs	3.514 yrs
Present value	—	$29,000	—	$17,986

Based on the calculations for parts 1 and 2, the Hugo Company's proposed investment in the earthmoving machine meets all the company's criteria for such investments. Given these results, the company should invest in the machine.

Chapter Assignments

Questions

1. What is meant by the term *relevant decision information?* What are the two important characteristics of such information?

2. Describe and discuss the five steps of the management decision cycle.

3. Describe the concept of variable costing. How does variable costing differ from absorption costing?

4. Is variable costing used for financial reporting purposes? Defend your answer.

5. What is the connection between variable costing and the contribution approach to reporting?

6. What are the purposes of incremental analysis?

7. Discuss and illustrate some of the qualitative inputs into decision analysis.

8. What is a capital expenditure? Give illustrations of different types of capital expenditure decisions. Define capital budgeting.

9. What is a crude but easy method for evaluating capital expenditures? List the advantages and disadvantages of this method.

10. What is the formula used for determining payback period? Is this decision measure accurate? Defend your answer.

11. "To treat all future income flows alike ignores the time value of money." Discuss this statement.

12. What is the objective of using the concept of discounted cash flows?

13. Why is it important to consider income taxes when evaluating a capital expenditure proposal?

14. Company Q has net cash inflow from operations for 19x6 of $42,000, noncash expenditures of $8,000, and a sale of an asset that netted $36,000 in proceeds and involved a $10,000 capital gain. Using the 46 percent tax rate for normal income and 28 percent for capital gains, compute the company's tax liability.

15. How does one determine the data relevant to a make or buy decision?

16. Identify and discuss information that bears on special product orders.

17. What question must be answered in trying to make the most of product line profitability? Give some examples of approaches to the solution of this question.

Classroom Exercises

**Exercise 28-1
Relevant Data
and Incre-
mental Analysis**
(L.O. 1, 5)

Mr. Martin, business manager for Roush Industries, must select a new typewriter for his secretary. Rental of Model H, which is like the typewriter now being used, is $300 per year. Model G is a deluxe typewriter that rents for $400 per year, but it will require a new desk for the secretary. The annual desk rental charge is $150. The secretary's salary of $400 per month will not change. If Model G is rented, $130 in training costs will be incurred. Model G has greater capacity and is expected to save $450 per year in part-time secretarial wages. Upkeep and operating costs will not differ between the two models.

1. Identify the relevant data in this problem.
2. Prepare an incremental analysis for the business manager to aid him in his decision.

**Exercise 28-2
Income
Statement—
Contribution
Reporting Form**
(L.O. 4)

The income statement in the conventional reporting format for Beatrice Products, Inc., for the year ended December 31, 19xx, appeared as shown on page 1082.

Fixed manufacturing costs of $17,600 and $1,850 are included in Cost of Goods Available for Sale and Ending Inventory, respectively. Total fixed manufacturing costs for 19xx were $16,540. There were no beginning or ending work in process inventories. All administrative expenses are considered to be fixed.

From the above information, prepare an income statement for Beatrice Products, Inc., for the year ended December 31, 19xx, using the contribution reporting form.

**Exercise 28-3
Variable
Costing: Unit
Cost Compu-
tation**
(L.O. 3)

Kapalua Enterprises produces a full line of energy-tracking devices. These devices can detect and track all forms of thermochemical energy-emitting space vehicles. The following cost data are provided: Direct materials cost $485,000 for four units. Direct labor for assembly is 590 hours per unit at $11.50 per hour. Variable factory overhead is $15.00 per direct labor hour, and fixed factory overhead is $792,000 per month (based on an average production of 128 units per month). Packaging materials come to $7,200 for four units, and packaging labor is

Beatrice Products
Income Statement
For the Year Ended December 31, 19xx

Sales		$296,400
Cost of Goods Sold		
Cost of Goods Available for Sale	$125,290	
Less Ending Inventory	12,540	112,750
Gross Margin on Sales		$183,650
Less Operating Expenses		
Selling Expenses		
Variable	$ 49,820	
Fixed	26,980	
Administrative Expenses	37,410	114,210
Net Income Before Taxes		$ 69,440

11.5 hours per unit at $8.20 per hour. Advertising and marketing cost $96,750 per month, and other fixed selling and administrative costs are $87,680 per month.

1. From the cost data above, find the unit production cost, using both the variable costing and the absorption costing methods.
2. Assume that the current month's ending inventory is twelve units. Compute the inventory valuation under both variable and absorption costing methods.

Exercise 28-4
Capital
Expenditure
Decision—
Accounting
Rate of Return
Method
(L.O. 7a)

Costa Mesa Corporation manufactures metal hard hats for on-site construction workers. Recently, management has tried to raise productivity to meet the growing demand from the real estate industry. The company is now thinking about a new stamping machine. Management has decided that only projects that will yield a 20 percent return before taxes will be accepted. The following projections for the proposal are given: The new machine will cost $105,000. Revenue will increase $45,600 per year. The salvage value of the new machine will be $5,000. Operating cost increases (including depreciation) will be $34,600.

Using the accounting rate of return method, decide whether the company should invest in the machine. (Show all computations to support your decision, and ignore income tax effects.)

Exercise 28-5
Using the
Present Value
Tables
(L.O. 7)

For each of the following situations, identify the correct multiplier to use from the tables in Appendix B, and compute the appropriate present value.

a. Annual net cash inflow of $10,000 for five years, discounted at 16%
b. An amount of $25,000 to be received at the end of ten years, discounted at 12%
c. The amounts of $12,000 to be received at the end of two years and $6,000 to be received at the end of years four, five, and six, discounted at 10%
d. Annual net cash inflow of $22,500 for twelve years, discounted at 14%
e. The following five years of cash inflows, discounted at 10%:

Year 1	$25,000
Year 2	20,000

Year 3	30,000
Year 4	40,000
Year 5	50,000

f. The amount of $60,000 to be received at the beginning of year seven, discounted at 14% - money could earn if in bank

Exercise 28-6
Capital
Expenditure
Decision—
Payback
Method
(L.O. 7b)

Classic Vibes, Inc., manufacturers of stereo speakers, is thinking about adding a new injection molding machine. This machine can produce speaker parts that the company now buys from outsiders. The machine has an estimated life of fourteen years and will cost $82,000. Gross cash revenue from the machine will be about $167,500 per year, and related cash expenses should total $126,750. Taxes on income are estimated at $18,000 a year. The payback period as set by management should be four years or less.

On the basis of the data given, use the payback method to figure out whether the company should invest in this new machine. Show your computations to support your answer.

Exercise 28-7
Capital
Expenditure
Decision—
Present Value
Method
(L.O. 7c)

Dennis Berg and Associates is thinking of buying an automatic extruding machine. This piece of equipment would have a useful life of six years, would cost $38,250, and would increase annual after-tax net cash inflows by $9,630. Assume that there is no salvage value at the end of six years. The company's minimum desired rate of return is 14 percent.

will have in future

Using the present value method, prepare an analysis to determine whether or not the company should purchase the machine.

Exercise 28-8
Minimum
Desired Rate of
Return
(L.O. 6)

The controller of Jessie Corporation is trying to establish a minimum desired rate of return and would like to use a weighted average cost of capital. Current data about the corporation's financing structure are as follows: debt financing, 50 percent; preferred stock, 20 percent; common stock, 20 percent; retained earnings, 10 percent. After-tax cost of debt is 8 percent. Dividend rates on the preferred and common stock issues are 6 and 10 percent, respectively. Cost of retained earnings is 12 percent.

Compute the weighted average cost of capital.

Exercise 28-9
Make or Buy
Decision
(L.O. 8a)

One of the parts for a radio assembly being produced by Callis Audio Systems, Inc., is being purchased at present for $85 per 100 parts. Management is studying the possibility of manufacturing these parts. Cost and production data are as follows: Annual production (usage) is 50,000 units. Fixed costs (all of which remain unchanged whether the part is made or purchased) are $18,000. Variable costs are $.35 per unit for direct materials, $.22 per unit for direct labor, and $.23 per unit for manufacturing overhead.

Using incremental decision analysis, decide whether the company should make the part or continue to purchase it from an outside vendor.

Exercise 28-10
Special Order
Decision
(L.O. 8b)

Lamp Domes, Inc., produces antique-looking lampshades. Management has just received a request for a special design order and must decide whether or not to accept it. The special order calls for 12,000 shades to be shipped in a total of 100 bulk pack cartons. Shipping costs of $80 per carton will replace normal packing and shipping costs. The purchasing company is offering to pay $16 per shade plus packing and shipping expenses.

The following information has been provided by the accounting department: Annual expected production is 150,000 shades, and the current year's production (before special order) is 160,000 shades. Maximum production capacity is 180,000 shades. Unit cost data include $4.20 for direct materials, $6.00 for direct labor, variable factory overhead of $3.80, and fixed factory overhead of $2.50 ($375,000 ÷ 150,000). Normal packaging and shipping costs per unit come to $1.50, and advertising is $.20 per unit ($30,000 ÷ 150,000). Other fixed administrative costs are $.80 per unit ($120,000 ÷ 150,000). Total normal cost per unit is thus $19.00, with per unit selling price set at $26.00. Total estimated bulk packaging costs ($80 per carton × 100 cartons) are $8,000.

Figure out whether this special order should be accepted.

Exercise 28-11
Sales Mix
Analysis
(L.O. 8c)

Greek Enterprises is analyzing its sales mix to find out if it is making the best possible profits. The company produces three similar items: Alpha, Tau, and Omega. All three of these products are made with the same equipment, and maximum productive capacity measured in machine hours is now being used. Product line statistics are as follows:

	Alpha	Tau	Omega
Current production and sales (units)	70,000	105,000	63,000
Machine hours per unit	14	7	17.5
Selling price per unit	$84.00	$63.00	$112.00
Unit variable manufacturing costs	$43.75	$35.00	$65.62
Unit variable selling costs	$22.75	$17.50	$21.88

Determine whether the existing sales mix is the most profitable one possible. If your answer is no, offer your suggestion to improve the sales mix.

Interpreting Accounting Information

Internal
Management
Information:
Altamonte
Springs Federal
Bank
(L.O. 7c)

Automatic round-the-clock tellers are the newest thing in the banking industry. Several companies have developed these computerized money machines and are bombarding bank managers with advertising brochures and sales people. Altamonte Springs Federal Bank is planning to install such a device and has narrowed the choice to the CGA machine. Mr. Clarence, the controller, has prepared the decision analysis shown on the next page. He has recommended the purchase of the machine based on the positive net present value shown in the analysis.

The CGA machine has an estimated life of five years and an expected salvage value of $20,000. Its purchase price would be $220,000. Two existing teller machines, each having a book value of $17,500, would be sold for a total of $45,000 to a neighboring bank. Annual operating cash inflow is expected to increase in the following manner:

Year 1	$35,000
Year 2	40,000
Year 3	45,000
Year 4	50,000
Year 5	60,000

The bank uses straight-line depreciation. Before-tax minimum desired rate of return is 16 percent, and a 10 percent rate is used for interpreting after-tax data. Assume a 46 percent tax rate for normal operations and a 28 percent tax rate for capital gains items.

1. Analyze the work of Mr. Clarence. What changes need to be made in his capital expenditure decision analysis?
2. What would be your recommendation to bank management about the CGA machine purchase?

Altamonte Springs Federal Bank
Capital Expenditure Decision Analysis
Before-Tax Net Present Value Approach
March 21, 19x3

Year	Net Cash Inflows	Present Value Multipliers	Present Value
1	$35,000	.909	$ 31,815
2	40,000	.826	33,040
3	45,000	.751	33,795
4	50,000	.683	34,150
5	60,000	.621	37,260
5 (salvage)	20,000	.621	12,420
Total present value			$182,480
Initial investment		$220,000	
Less proceeds from the sale of existing teller machines		45,000	
Net capital investment			175,000
Positive Net Present Value			$ 7,480

Problem Set A

Problem 28A-1
Variable
Costing—
Contribution
Approach to
Income
Statement
(L.O. 3, 4)

Roofing tile is the major product of the Barton Corporation. The company had a particularly good year in 19x9, as is shown by the following operating data: It produced 72,650 cases (units) of tile and sold 68,400 cases. Direct materials used cost $319,660, direct labor was $210,685, variable factory overhead was $217,950, fixed factory overhead was $145,300, variable selling expenses were $102,600, fixed selling expenses were $114,325, and fixed administrative expenses were $89,750. Selling price was $20 per case. There were no partially completed jobs in process at the beginning or the end of the year. Finished goods inventory had been used up at the end of the previous year, 19x8.

Required

1. Compute the unit cost and ending finished goods inventory value, using (a) variable costing procedures and (b) absorption costing procedures.
2. Prepare the year-end income statement for the Barton Corporation, using (a) the contribution form based on variable costing data and (b) the conventional form based on absorption costing data.

Problem 28A-2
Capital
Expenditure
Decision—
Present Value
Method
(L.O. 7c)

The management of Las Vegas Plastics has recently been looking at a proposal to purchase a new plastic injection-style molding machine. With the new machine, the company would not have to buy small plastic parts to use in production. The estimated life of the machine is fifteen years, and the purchase price including all set-up charges is $160,000. Salvage value is estimated to be $10,000. The net addition to the company's cash inflow due to the savings from making the plastic parts within the company is estimated to be $26,000 a year. Management has decided on a minimum desired before-tax rate of return of 14 percent.

Required

1. Using the present value method to evaluate this capital expenditure, determine whether the company should purchase the machine. Support your answer.
2. If management had decided on a minimum desired rate of return of 16 percent, should the machine be purchased? Show all computations to support your answers.
3. Assuming straight-line depreciation, a 46 percent tax rate, and an after-tax minimum desired rate of return of 8 percent, should the company purchase the machine? Show your computations.

Problem 28A-3
Sales Mix
Analysis
(L.O. 8c)

The vice president of finance for Madison Machine Tool, Inc., is evaluating the profitability of the company's four product lines. During the current year, the company will operate at full machine-hour capacity. The following production data have been compiled:

Product	Current Year's Production (Units)	Total Machine Hours Used
14E	30,000	75,000
27M	50,000	100,000
19S	20,000	20,000
30T	90,000	45,000

Sales and operating cost data are as follows:

	Product 14E	Product 27M	Product 19S	Product 30T
Selling price per unit	$30.00	$40.00	$50.00	$60.00
Unit variable manufacturing cost	12.00	30.00	35.00	50.00
Unit fixed manufacturing cost	6.00	4.00	3.00	2.00
Unit variable selling costs	3.00	2.00	8.00	5.50
Unit fixed administrative costs	4.00	2.00	4.00	1.50

Required

1. Compute the machine hours needed to produce one unit of each product type.
2. Determine the contribution margin of each product type.
3. Which product line(s) should be pushed by the company's sales force? Why?

Problem 28A-4
Make or Buy
Decision
(L.O. 8a)

The Azusa Refrigerator Company has been buying and installing defrost clocks in its products. The clocks cost $381.60 per case, and each case contains thirty-six clocks. The supplier recently gave advance notice that, effective in thirty days, the price will rise by 50 percent. The company has idle equipment that could be used to produce similar defrost clocks with only a few changes in the equipment.

The following cost estimates have been prepared under the assumption that the company could make the product itself. Direct materials would cost $216 per 36 clocks. Direct labor required would be 10 minutes per clock at a labor rate of $9.00 per hour. Variable factory overhead would be $3.50 per clock. Fixed factory overhead (which would be incurred under either decision alternative) would be $86,400 a year for depreciation and $129,600 a year for other expenses. Production and usage are estimated to be 72,000 clocks a year. (Assume that the idle equipment could not be used for any other purpose.)

Required

1. Prepare an incremental decision analysis to figure out whether the defrost clocks should be made within the company or purchased from the outside supplier at the higher rate.

2. Compute the unit cost to make one clock and to buy one clock.

Problem 28A-5
Special Order
Decision
(L.O. 8b)

On November 15, 19xx, Rowe Sporting Equipment, Inc., received a special order for 6,000 three-wood golf sets. These golf clubs will be marketed in Europe. Denmark Imports, Ltd., the purchasing company, wants the clubs bulk packaged and is willing to pay $68 per set for the clubs.

Mr. Selester, president of Rowe Sporting Equipment, Inc., has gathered the following product costing information about the set of woods being discussed: Direct materials (wood) cost $800 per 100 sets, direct materials (metal shafts) are $1,200 per 100 sets, and direct materials (grips) are $200 per 100 sets. Direct labor is $27 per set. Variable manufacturing costs are $16 per set, and fixed manufacturing costs are 20 percent of direct labor dollars. Variable selling expenses are $14 per set, and variable shipping costs are $9 per set. Fixed general and administrative costs are figured at 30 percent of direct labor dollars. Bulk shipping costs will total $12,000, thus eliminating both variable selling and variable shipping costs from consideration. The company did not expect this order and will reach planned production capacity for the year, leaving enough plant capacity for the special order.

Required

1. Prepare an analysis for Mr. Selester to use in deciding whether to accept or reject the offer by Denmark Imports, Ltd. What decision should be made?

2. What is the lowest possible price that Rowe Sporting Equipment could charge per set of woods and still make a $10,000 profit on this order?

Problem 28A-6
Capital
Expenditure
Decision—
Comprehensive
(L.O. 7, 9)

The Hermansson Manufacturing Company, based in St. Cloud, Minnesota, is one of the fastest-growing companies in its industry. According to Mr. Hjalmer, the company's production vice president, keeping up with technological changes is what makes the company a leader in the industry.

Mr. Hjalmer feels that a new machine introduced recently would fill an important need of the company. The machine has an expected useful life of four years, a purchase price of $108,000 and a salvage value of $18,000. The company controller's estimated operating results, using the new machine, are summarized below. The company uses straight-line depreciation for all its machinery. Mr. Hjalmer uses a 12 percent minimum desired rate of return and a 2.5 year payback period for capital expenditure evaluation purposes (before-tax decision guidelines).

	Cash Flow Estimates		
	Cash Revenues	Cash Expenses	Net Cash Inflow
Year 1	$150,000	$100,000	$50,000
Year 2	150,000	110,000	40,000
Year 3	150,000	120,000	30,000
Year 4	150,000	130,000	20,000

Required

1. Ignore income taxes. Analyze the purchase of the machine, and decide if the company should purchase it. Use the following evaluation approaches in your analysis: (a) the accounting rate of return method, (b) the payback period method, and (c) the present value method.

2. Rework part **1,** assuming a 46 percent tax rate and after-tax guidelines of an 8 percent minimum desired rate of return and a 4.5 year payback period. Does the decision change when after-tax information is used?

Problem Set B

Problem 28B-1
Variable
Costing—
Contribution
Approach to
Income
Statement
(L.O. 3, 4)

On December 31, 19xx, Jerome Industries completed its first full year of operation. A summary of cost and production data for 19xx follows: $141,570 for direct materials; $81,510 for direct labor; $60,060 for variable factory overhead; $47,190 for fixed factory overhead; 42,900 units completed; 41,600 units sold; selling price per unit of $22; variable selling expenses per unit of $7; fixed selling expenses of $62,550; fixed administrative expenses of $98,900. There were no beginning or ending work in process inventories and no beginning Finished Goods Inventory.

Required

1. Compute the unit cost and ending Finished Goods Inventory value, using (a) variable costing procedures and (b) absorption costing procedures.
2. Prepare the year-end income statement for Jerome Industries, using (a) the contribution form based on variable costing data and (b) the conventional form based on absorption costing data.

Problem 28B-2
Capital
Expenditure
Decision—
Present Value
Method
(L.O. 7c)

Foot-rite, Inc., is considering the purchase and use of a new machine to speed up the manufacture of its only product, arch support inserts. This new machine has an estimated twenty-year life and will cost $12,000 in cash plus a five-year note of $20,000, due at the end of the fifth year. Estimated salvage value is $2,000. The increased annual net cash inflows generated by the increased output should be about $3,000 a year. The minimum desired before-tax rate of return has been determined to be 14 percent.

Required

1. Ignore income taxes. Using the present value method to evaluate this capital expenditure, decide whether the company should purchase the new machine. (Ignore the interest on the $20,000 note.)
2. If the minimum desired rate of return were 10 percent, would your answer in **1** be different? Show all computations to support your answers.
3. Assuming straight-line depreciation, a 46 percent tax rate, and an after-tax minimum desired rate of return of 8 percent, should the company purchase the machine? Show your computations.

Problem 28B-3
Minimum
Desired Rate of
Return
(L.O. 6)

Capital investment analysis is the main function of Marilyn Hunt, special assistant to the controller of UCF Manufacturing Company. During the previous twelve-month period, the company's capital mix and respective costs (after tax) were as follows:

	Percentage of Total Financing	Cost of Capital (Percent)
Debt financing	30	5
Preferred stock	20	8
Common stock	40	12
Retained earnings	10	12

Plans for the current year call for a shift in total financing of 10 percent from common stock financing to debt financing. Also, the after-tax cost of debt is expected to increase to 6 percent, though the cost of the other types of financing will remain the same.

Ms. Hunt has already anaylzed several proposed capital expenditures. She expects that the return on investment for each capital expenditure would be as follows: 7.5 percent on project A; 8.5 percent on equipment item B; 15.0 percent on product line C; 6.9 percent on project D; 9.0 percent on product line E; 11.9 percent on equipment item F; 8.0 percent on project G.

Required

1. Compute the weighted average cost of capital for the previous year.
2. Using the expected adjustments to cost and capital mix, compute the weighted average cost of capital for the current year.
3. Identify the proposed capital expenditures that should be implemented, based on the minimum desired rate of return calculated in part 2.

Problem 28B-4
Make or Buy
Decision
(L.O. 8a)

The Anthony Athletic Equipment Company is presently buying the rubber valves needed to inflate its basketballs. The valves have been purchased at a cost of $115.20 per ten cases, and each case holds 144 valves. Management has just been informed that the price of these valves is to increase 50 percent, effective with the next shipment. Anthony has idle machinery that it could easily convert to produce similar rubber valves. The company's cost analyst has estimated the cost to produce the part using the idle machinery. Direct materials would cost $8.64 per 144 valves and direct labor required would be five minutes per 40 valves at $9.60 per hour. Variable factory overhead would be $.03 per valve. Fixed factory overhead, which would be incurred under either decision alternative, would be $1,150 a year for depreciation and $2,850 a year for other expenses. Annual production and use will be 849,600 valves. Assume that the idle machinery cannot be used for any other purpose.

Required

1. Prepare an incremental decision analysis to find out whether the company should continue to buy the valves at the higher rate or should begin production of its own valves.
2. Figure unit costs to make one valve or to buy one valve.

Problem 28B-5
Special Order
Decision
(L.O. 8b)

McClaron Resorts, Ltd., has approached Diversified Printers, Inc., with a special order to produce 300,000 two-page brochures. Most of the work done by Diversified consists of recurring short-run orders. McClaron Resorts is offering a one-time order, but Diversified Printers does have the capacity to handle the order over a two-month period.

McClaron's management has stated that the company would not be willing to pay more than $38 per thousand brochures. The following cost data were assembled by Diversified's controller for this decision analysis: Direct materials (paper) would be $22.50 per thousand brochures. Direct labor costs would be $4.80 per thousand brochures. Direct materials (ink) would be $2.40 per thousand brochures. Variable production overhead would be $4.20 per thousand brochures. Machine maintenance (fixed cost) is $1.00 per direct labor dollar. Other fixed production overhead amounts to $2.40 per direct labor dollar. Variable Packing costs would be $4.30 per thousand brochures. Also, the share of general and administrative expenses (fixed costs) to be allocated would be $5.25 per direct labor dollar.

Required

1. Prepare an analysis for Diversified's management to use in deciding whether to accept or reject the offer by McClaron Resorts, Ltd. What decision should be made?

2. What is the lowest possible price that Diversified Printers could charge per thousand and still make a $6,000 profit on the order?

**Problem 28B-6
Capital
Expenditure
Decision—
Comprehensive**
(L.O. 7c, 9)

Alice Bengtson is director of Capital Facilities for Benet Enterprises, an international land development company. Recently, an equipment manufacturer marketed a new kind of earth-moving machine called the Payloader. Ms. Bengtson is interested in purchasing one of the machines and has compiled the following data:

| | Cash Flow Estimates | | |
	Cash Revenues	Cash Expenses	Net Cash Inflow
Year 1	$260,000	$200,000	$60,000
Year 2	280,000	210,000	70,000
Year 3	300,000	220,000	80,000
Year 4	320,000	230,000	90,000

Benet Enterprises uses the straight-line method in depreciating its equipment. The expected useful life of the equipment is four years. The Payloader has a purchase price of $240,000 and a salvage value of $40,000. Ms. Bengtson uses a 16 percent minimum desired rate of return and a 2.5 year or less payback period for capital expenditure evaluation purposes (before-tax decision guidelines).

Required

1. Ignore income taxes. Analyze the purchase of the equipment, and decide if Benet Enterprises should purchase it. Use the following evaluation approaches in your analysis: (a) accounting rate of return method, (b) payback period method, and (c) present value method.

2. Rework part 1, assuming a 46 percent tax rate and after-tax decision guidelines of an 8 percent minimum desired rate of return and a 4.5 year payback period. Does your decision change when you use after-tax information?

Management Decision Case 28-1

Van Trease Hotel Syndicate
(L.O. 7c, 9)

The Van Trease Hotel Syndicate owns four resort hotels in Southern Florida and the Bahamas. Because their St. Louis Park, Florida, operation (Hotel 3) has been booming over the past three years, management has decided to add a new wing that will increase capacity by 50 percent.

A construction firm has bid on the proposed new wing. The building would have a 20-year life with no salvage value, and the company uses straight-line depreciation.

Deluxe accommodations are highlighted in this contractor's proposal. The new wing would cost $30,000,000 to construct, with the following estimates of cash flows:

	Increase in Cash Inflows From Room Rentals	Increase in Cash Operating Expenses
Years 1–7	$37,900,000	$30,400,000
Year 8	40,000,000	32,000,000
Year 9	42,100,000	33,600,000
Years 10–20	44,200,000	35,200,000

Capital investment projects must generate a 12 percent after-tax minimum desired rate of return to qualify for consideration. Assume a 40 percent tax rate for normal operations.

Required

Evaluate the proposal from the contractor using present value analysis, and make a recommendation to management.

Learning Objectives

Appendix A

The Use of Future Value and Present Value in Accounting

1. *Distinguish simple interest from compound interest.*

2. *Use compound interest tables to compute (a) the future value of a single invested sum at compound interest, and (b) the future value of an ordinary annuity.*

3. *Use present value tables to compute (a) the present value of a single sum due in the future, and (b) the present value of an ordinary annuity.*

4. *Apply the concept of present value to some simple accounting situations.*

Interest is an important cost to the debtor and an important revenue to the creditor. Because interest is a cost associated with time, and "time is money," it is also an important consideration in any business decision. For example, an individual who holds $100 for one year without putting that $100 in a savings account has forgone the interest that could have been earned. Thus there is a cost associated with holding this money equal to the interest that could have been earned. Similarly, a business person who accepts a noninterest-bearing note instead of cash for the sale of merchandise is forgoing the interest that could have been earned on that money. These examples illustrate the point that the timing of the receipt and payment of cash must be considered in making business decisions.

Simple Interest and Compound Interest

Interest is the cost associated with the use of money for a specific period of time. Simple interest is the interest cost, for one or more periods, if we assume that the amount on which the interest is computed stays the same from period to period. Compound interest is the interest cost, for two or more periods, if we assume that after each period the interest of that period is added to the amount on which interest is computed in future periods. In other words, compound interest is interest earned on a principal sum that is increased at the end of each period by the interest of that period.

Example: Simple Interest Joe Sanchez accepts an 8 percent, $30,000 note due in 90 days. How much will he receive in total at that time? Remember the formula for calculating simple interest, which was presented in Chapter 10, on notes receivable:

interest = principal × rate × time
interest = $30,000 × 8/100 × 90/360
interest = $600

The total that Sanchez will receive is computed as follows:

$$\text{total} = \text{principal} + \text{interest}$$
$$\text{total} = \$30{,}000 + \$600$$
$$\text{total} = \$30{,}600$$

Example: Compound Interest   Ann Clary deposits $5,000 in a savings account that pays 6 percent interest. She expects to leave the principal and accumulated interest in the account for three years. How much in total will be in her account at the end of three years? Assume that the interest is paid at the end of the year and is added to the principal at that time and that this total in turn earns interest. The amount at the end of three years can be figured as follows:

(1) Year	(2) Principal Amount at Beginning of Year	(3) Annual Amount of Interest (col. 2 × .06)	(4) Accumulated Amount at End of Year (col. 2 + col. 3)
1	$5,000.00	$300.00	$5,300.00
2	5,300.00	318.00	5,618.00
3	5,618.00	337.08	5,955.08

At the end of three years, Clary will have $5,955.08 in her savings account. Note that the annual amount of interest increases each year by the interest rate times the interest of the previous year. For example, between year 1 and year 2, the interest increased by $18 ($318 − $300), which exactly equals .06 times $300.

Future Value of a Single Sum Invested at Compound Interest

Another way to ask the question in the example of compound interest above is, What is the future value of a single sum ($5,000) at compound interest (6 percent) for three years? **Future value** is the amount that an investment will be worth at a future date if invested at compound interest. A businessperson often wants to know future value, but the method of finding the future value shown above takes too much time in practice. Imagine how long the calculation would take if the example were ten years instead of three. Fortunately, there are tables that make problems involving compound interest much simpler and quicker to solve. Table A-1, showing the future value of $1 after a given number of time periods, is an example. It is actually part of a larger table, B-1, in Appendix B. Suppose that we want to solve the problem of Clary's savings account above. We simply look down the 6 percent column in Table A-1 until we reach period 3 and find the factor 1.191. This factor when multiplied by $1 gives the future value of that $1 at compound interest of 6 percent for three periods (years in this case). Thus we solve the problem:

$$\text{principal} \times \text{factor} = \text{future value}$$
$$\$5{,}000 \quad \times 1.191 = \quad \$5{,}955$$

Except for a rounding error of $.08, the answer is exactly the same. Another example will illustrate this simple technique again.

Example: Future Value of a Single Invested Sum at Compound Interest   Ed Bates invests $3,000, which he believes will return 5 percent interest compounded over a five-year period. How much will Bates have at the end of five years? From Table

Periods	1%	2%	3%	4%	5%	6%	7%	8%	9%	10%	12%	14%	15%
1	1.010	1.020	1.030	1.040	1.050	1.060	1.070	1.080	1.090	1.100	1.120	1.140	1.150
2	1.020	1.040	1.061	1.082	1.103	1.124	1.145	1.166	1.188	1.210	1.254	1.300	1.323
3	1.030	1.061	1.093	1.125	1.158	1.191	1.225	1.260	1.295	1.331	1.405	1.482	1.521
4	1.041	1.082	1.126	1.170	1.216	1.262	1.311	1.360	1.412	1.464	1.574	1.689	1.749
5	1.051	1.104	1.159	1.217	1.276	1.338	1.403	1.469	1.539	1.611	1.762	1.925	2.011
6	1.062	1.126	1.194	1.265	1.340	1.419	1.501	1.587	1.677	1.772	1.974	2.195	2.313
7	1.072	1.149	1.230	1.316	1.407	1.504	1.606	1.714	1.828	1.949	2.211	2.502	2.660
8	1.083	1.172	1.267	1.369	1.477	1.594	1.718	1.851	1.993	2.144	2.476	2.853	3.059
9	1.094	1.195	1.305	1.423	1.551	1.689	1.838	1.999	2.172	2.358	2.773	3.252	3.518
10	1.105	1.219	1.344	1.480	1.629	1.791	1.967	2.159	2.367	2.594	3.106	3.707	4.046

Source: Henry R. Anderson and Mitchell H. Raiborn, *Basic Cost Accounting Concepts* (Boston: Houghton Mifflin, 1977), excerpt from Table 1, p. 552. Reprinted by permission.

Table A-1
Future Value of $1 after a Given Number of Time Periods

A-1, the factor for period 5 of the 5 percent column is 1.276. Therefore, we calculate as follows:

$$\text{principal} \times \text{factor} = \text{future value}$$
$$\$3,000 \times 1.276 = \$3,828$$

Bates will have $3,828 at the end of five years.

Future Value of an Ordinary Annuity

Another common problem involves an **ordinary annuity,** which is a series of equal payments made at the end of equal intervals of time, with compound interest on these payments.

Example: Future Value of an Ordinary Annuity Assume that Ben Katz deposits $200 at the end of each of the next three years in a savings account that pays 5 percent interest. How much money will he have in his account at the end of the next three years? One way of computing the amount is shown in the following table:

(1) Year	(2) Beginning Balance	(3) Interest Earned (5% × col. 2)	(4) Periodic Payment	(5) Accumulated at End of Period (col. 2 + col. 3 + col. 4)
1	$ —	$ —	$200	$200.00
2	200.00	10.00	200	410.00
3	410.00	20.50	200	630.50

Katz would have $630.50 in his account at the end of three years, made up of $600 in periodic payments and $30.50 in interest.

This calculation can also be simplified by using Table A-2. We look down the 5 percent column until we reach period 3 and find the factor 3.153. This factor when multiplied by $1 gives the future value of a series of three $1 payments

Periods	1%	2%	3%	4%	5%	6%	7%	8%	9%	10%	12%	14%	15%
1	1.000	1.000	1.000	1.000	1.000	1.000	1.000	1.000	1.000	1.000	1.000	1.000	1.000
2	2.010	2.020	2.030	2.040	2.050	2.060	2.070	2.080	2.090	2.100	2.120	2.140	2.150
3	3.030	3.060	3.091	3.122	3.153	3.184	3.215	3.246	3.278	3.310	3.374	3.440	3.473
4	4.060	4.122	4.184	4.246	4.310	4.375	4.440	4.506	4.573	4.641	4.779	4.921	4.993
5	5.101	5.204	5.309	5.416	5.526	5.637	5.751	5.867	5.985	6.105	6.353	6.610	6.742
6	6.152	6.308	6.468	6.633	6.802	6.975	7.153	7.336	7.523	7.716	8.115	8.536	8.754
7	7.214	7.434	7.662	7.898	8.142	8.394	8.654	8.923	9.200	9.487	10.09	10.73	11.07
8	8.286	8.583	8.892	9.214	9.549	9.897	10.26	10.64	11.03	11.44	12.30	13.23	13.73
9	9.369	9.755	10.16	10.58	11.03	11.49	11.98	12.49	13.02	13.58	14.78	16.09	16.79
10	10.46	10.95	11.46	12.01	12.58	13.18	13.82	14.49	15.19	15.94	17.55	19.34	20.30

Source: Henry R. Anderson and Mitchell H. Raiborn, *Basic Cost Accounting Concepts* (Boston: Houghton Mifflin, 1977), excerpt from Table 2, p. 553. Reprinted by permission.

Table A-2
Future Value of $1 Paid in Each Period for a Given Number of Time Periods

(years in this case) at compound interest of 5 percent. Thus we solve the problem:

$$\text{periodic payment} \times \text{factor} = \text{future value}$$
$$\$200 \qquad \times 3.153 = \quad \$630.60$$

Except for a rounding error of $0.10, this result is the same as the one above.

Present Value

Suppose that you had the choice of receiving $100 today or one year from today. Without even thinking about it, you would choose to receive the $100 today. Why? You know that if you have the $100 today, you can put it in a savings account to earn interest and will have more than $100 a year from today. Therefore, we can say that an amount to be received in the future (future value) is not worth as much today as an amount to be received today (present value) because of the cost associated with the passage of time. In fact, present value and future value are closely related. **Present value** is the amount that must be invested now at a given rate of interest to produce a given future value.

Example: Present Value Sue Dapper needs $1,000 one year from now. How much should she invest today to achieve that goal if the interest rate is 5 percent? From earlier examples, the following equation may be established:

$$\text{present value} \times (1.0 + \text{interest rate}) = \text{future value}$$
$$\text{present value} \times \qquad 1.05 \qquad = \$1,000$$
$$\text{present value} \qquad\qquad\qquad = \$1,000 \div 1.05$$
$$\text{present value} \qquad\qquad\qquad = \$952.38$$

Thus to achieve a future value of $1,000, a present value of $952.38 must be invested. Interest of 5 percent on $952.38 for one year equals $47.62, and these two amounts added together equal $1,000.

Present Value of a Single Sum Due in the Future

When more than one time period is involved, the calculation of present value is more complicated. Consider the following example.

Example: Present Value of a Single Sum in the Future Don Riley wants to be sure of having $4,000 at the end of three years. How much must he invest today in a

The Use of Future Value and Present Value in Accounting

5 percent savings account to achieve this goal? Adapting the above equation, we compute the present value of $4,000 at compound interest of 5 percent for three years in the future.

Year	Amount at End of Year	Divide by			Present Value at Beginning of Year
3	$4,000.00	÷	1.05	=	$3,809.52
2	3,809.52	÷	1.05	=	3,628.12
1	3,628.12	÷	1.05	=	3,455.35

Riley must invest a present value of $3,455.35 to achieve a future value of $4,000 in three years.

This calculation is again made much easier by using the appropriate table. In Table A-3, we look down the 5 percent column until we reach period 3 and find the factor 0.864. This factor when multiplied by $1 gives the present value of that $1 to be received three years from now at 5 percent interest. Thus we solve the problem:

$$\text{future value} \times \text{factor} = \text{present value}$$
$$\$4,000 \quad \times 0.864 = \quad \$3,456$$

Except for a rounding error of $0.65, this result is the same as the one above.

Present Value of an Ordinary Annuity   It is often necessary to find the present value of a series of receipts or payments. When we calculate the present value of equal amounts equally spaced over a period of time, we are computing the present value of an ordinary annuity.

Example: Present Value of an Ordinary Annuity   Assume that Kathy Foster has sold a piece of property and is to receive $15,000 in three equal annual payments

Table A-3
Present Value of $1 to Be Received at the End of a Given Number of Time Periods

Periods	1%	2%	3%	4%	5%	6%	7%	8%	9%	10%
1	0.990	0.980	0.971	0.962	0.952	0.943	0.935	0.926	0.917	0.909
2	0.980	0.961	0.943	0.925	0.907	0.890	0.873	0.857	0.842	0.826
3	0.971	0.942	0.915	0.889	0.864	0.840	0.816	0.794	0.772	0.751
4	0.961	0.924	0.888	0.855	0.823	0.792	0.763	0.735	0.708	0.683
5	0.951	0.906	0.883	0.822	0.784	0.747	0.713	0.681	0.650	0.621
6	0.942	0.888	0.837	0.790	0.746	0.705	0.666	0.630	0.596	0.564
7	0.933	0.871	0.813	0.760	0.711	0.665	0.623	0.583	0.547	0.513
8	0.923	0.853	0.789	0.731	0.677	0.627	0.582	0.540	0.502	0.467
9	0.914	0.837	0.766	0.703	0.645	0.592	0.544	0.500	0.460	0.424
10	0.905	0.820	0.744	0.676	0.614	0.558	0.508	0.463	0.422	0.386

Source: Henry R. Anderson and Mitchell H. Raiborn, *Basic Cost Accounting Concepts* (Boston: Houghton Mifflin, 1977), excerpt from Table 3, p. 554. Reprinted by permission.

of $5,000, beginning one year from today. What is the present value of this sale, assuming a current interest rate of 5 percent? This present value may be computed by calculating a separate present value for each of the three payments (using Table A-3) and summing the results, as shown below.

Future Receipts (Annuity)			Present Value Factor at 5 percent (from Table A-3)		Present Value
Year 1	Year 2	Year 3			
$5,000			× 0.952	=	$ 4,760
	$5,000		× 0.907	=	4,535
		$5,000	× 0.864	=	4,320
Total Present Value					$13,615

The present value of this sale is $13,615. Thus there is an implied interest cost (given the 5 percent rate) of $1,385 associated with the payment plan that allows the purchaser to pay in three installments.

We can make this calculation by using Table A-4. We look down the 5 percent column until we reach period 3 and find factor 2.723. This factor when multiplied by $1 gives the present value of a series of three $1 payments (spaced one year apart) at compound interest of 5 percent. Thus we solve the problem:

$$\text{periodic payment} \times \text{factor} = \text{present value}$$
$$\$5,000 \times 2.723 = \$13,615$$

This result is the same as the one computed above.

Table A-4
Present Value of $1 Received Each Period for a Given Number of Time Periods

Time Periods

In all the examples above and in most other cases, the compounding period is one year, and the interest rate is stated on an annual basis. However, in each of the

Periods	1%	2%	3%	4%	5%	6%	7%	8%	9%	10%
1	0.990	0.980	0.971	0.962	0.952	0.943	0.935	0.926	0.917	0.909
2	1.970	1.942	1.913	1.886	1.859	1.833	1.808	1.783	1.759	1.736
3	2.941	2.884	2.829	2.775	2.723	2.673	2.624	2.577	2.531	2.487
4	3.902	3.808	3.717	3.630	3.546	3.465	3.387	3.312	3.240	3.170
5	4.853	4.713	4.580	4.452	4.329	4.212	4.100	3.993	3.890	3.791
6	5.795	5.601	5.417	5.242	5.076	4.917	4.767	4.623	4.486	4.355
7	6.728	6.472	6.230	6.002	5.786	5.582	5.389	5.206	5.033	4.868
8	7.652	7.325	7.020	6.733	6.463	6.210	5.971	5.747	5.535	5.335
9	8.566	8.162	7.786	7.435	7.108	6.802	6.515	6.247	5.995	5.759
10	9.471	8.983	8.530	8.111	7.722	7.360	7.024	6.710	6.418	6.145

Source: Henry R. Anderson and Mitchell H. Raiborn, *Basic Cost Accounting Concepts* (Boston: Houghton Mifflin, 1977), excerpt from Table 4, p. 556. Reprinted by permission.

four tables the left-hand column refers, not to years, but to periods. This wording is used because there are compounding periods of less than one year. Savings accounts that record interest quarterly and bonds that pay interest semiannually are cases in point. To use the tables in such cases, it is necessary to (1) divide the annual interest rate by the number of periods in the year, and (2) multiply the number of periods in one year by the number of years.

Example: Time Periods Assume that a $6,000 note is to be paid in two years and carries an annual interest rate of 8 percent. Compute the maturity (future) value of the note, assuming that the compounding period is semiannual. Before using the table, it is necessary to compute the interest rate that applies to the compounding period and the number of periods. First, the interest rate to use is 4 percent (8% annual rate ÷ 2 periods per year). Second, the number of compounding periods is 4 (2 periods per year × 2 years). From Table A-1, therefore, the maturity value of the note may be computed as follows:

$$\text{principal} \times \text{factor} = \text{future value}$$
$$\$6,000 \quad \times \quad 1.170 = \quad \$7,020$$

The note will be worth $7,020 in two years.

This procedure for determining the interest rate and the number of periods when the compounding period is less than one year may be used with all the tables.

Applications of Present Value to Accounting

The concept of present value is used widely in accounting. Here, the purpose is to show its usefulness in some simple applications. In-depth study of present value is left up to more advanced courses.

Imputing Interest on Non-Interest-Bearing Notes

Clearly there is no such thing as an interest-free debt, regardless of whether the interest rate is explicitly stated. The Accounting Principles Board has declared that when a long-term note does not explicitly state an interest rate (or if the interest rate is unreasonably low), a rate based on the normal interest cost of the company in question should be assigned, or imputed.[1] The next example applies this principle.

Example: Imputing Interest on Noninterest-Bearing Notes On January 1, 19x8, Gato purchases merchandise from Haines by making an $8,000 noninterest-bearing note due in two years. Gato can borrow money from the bank at 9 percent interest. Gato pays the note in full after two years. Prepare journal entries to record these transactions.

Note that the $8,000 note represents partly a payment for merchandise and partly a payment of interest for two years. In recording the purchase and sale, it is necessary to use Table A-3 to determine the present value of the note. The calculation follows.

$$\text{future value} \times \text{present value factor (9\%, 2 years)} = \text{present value}$$
$$\$8,000 \quad \times \quad 0.842 \quad = \quad \$6,736$$

The imputed interest cost is $1,264 ($8,000 − $6,736). The entries necessary to record the purchase in the Gato records and the sale in the Haines records are shown below.

1. Accounting Principles Board, *Opinion No. 21,* "Interest on Receivables and Payables" (New York: American Institute of Certified Public Accountants, June 1, 1982), par. 13.

	Gato Journal			Haines Journal	
Purchases	6,736		Notes Receivable	8,000	
Prepaid Interest	1,264		Discount on		
Notes Payable		8,000	Notes Receivable		1,264
			Sales		6,736

On December 31, 19x8, the adjustments to recognize the interest expenses and interest earned will be:

	Gato Journal			Haines Journal	
Interest Expense	606.24		Discount on Notes		
Prepaid			Receivable	606.24	
Interest		606.24	Interest Earned		606.24

The interest is found by multiplying the original purchase by the interest for one year ($6,736 × .09 = $606.24). When payment is made on December 31, 19x9, the following entries will be made in the respective journals:

	Gato Journal			Haines Journal	
Interest			Discount		
Expense	657.76		on Notes		
Notes Payable	8,000.00		Receivable	657.76	
Prepaid			Cash	8,000.00	
Interest		657.76	Interest		
Cash		8,000.00	Earned		657.76
			Notes		
			Receivable		8,000.00

The interest entries represent the remaining interest to be expensed or realized ($1,264 − $606.24 = $657.76). This amount approximates (because of rounding errors in the table) the interest for one year on the purchases plus last year's interest [($6,736 + $606.24) × .09 = $660.80].

Valuing an Asset

An asset is recorded because it will provide future benefits to the company that owns it. This future benefit is the basis for the definition of an asset. Usually, the purchase price of the asset represents the present value of these future benefits. It is possible to evaluate a proposed purchase price of an asset by comparing that price with the present value of the asset to the company.

Example: Valuing an Asset Sam Hurst is thinking of buying a new labor-saving machine that will reduce his annual labor cost by $700 per year. The machine will last eight years. The interest rate that Hurst assumes for making managerial decisions is 10 percent. What is the maximum amount (present value) that Hurst should pay for the machine?

The present value of the machine to Hurst is equal to the present value of an ordinary annuity of $700 per year for eight years at compound interest of 10 percent. From Table A-4, we compute the value as follows:

$$\text{periodic savings} \times \text{factor} = \text{present value}$$
$$\$700 \times 5.335 = \$3,734.50$$

Hurst should not pay more than $3,734.50 for the new machine.

Other Accounting Applications

There are many other applications of present value to accounting. Examples of its application to bond valuation, finding the amount of mortgage payments, and accounting for leases are presented in Chapter 18. Others are the recording of pension obligations; the determination of premium and discount on debt;

accounting for depreciation of plant, property, and equipment; analysis of the purchase price of a business; evaluation of capital expenditure decisions; and generally any problem where time is a factor.

Exercises

Tables B-1 to B-4 in Appendix B may be used to solve these exercises.

Exercise A-1
Future Value
Calculations
(L.O. 2)

Naber receives a one-year note that carries a 12 percent annual interest rate on $1,500 for the sale of a used car.

Compute the maturity value under each of the following assumptions: (1) The interest is simple interest. (2) The interest is compounded semiannually. (3) The interest is compounded quarterly. (4) The interest is compounded monthly.

Exercise A-2
Future Value
Calculations
(L.O. 2)

Find the future value of (1) a single payment of $10,000 at 7 percent for ten years, (2) ten annual payments of $1,000 at 7 percent, (3) a single payment of $3,000 at 9 percent for seven years, and (4) seven annual payments of $3,000 at 9 percent.

Exercise A-3
Present Value
Calculations
(L.O. 3)

Find the present value of (1) a single payment of $12,000 at 6 percent for twelve years, (2) twelve annual payments of $1,000 at 6 percent, (3) a single payment of $2,500 at 9 percent for five years, and (4) five annual payments of $2,500 at 9 percent.

Exercise A-4
Future Value
Calculations
(L.O. 2)

Assume that $20,000 is invested today. Compute the amount that would accumulate at the end of seven years when the interest is (1) 8 percent annual interest compounded annually, (2) 8 percent annual interest compounded semiannually, and (3) 8 percent annual interest compounded quarterly.

Exercise A-5
Future Value
Calculations
(L.O. 2)

Calculate the accumulation of periodic payments of $500 for four years, assuming (1) 10 percent annual interest compounded annually, (2) 10 percent annual interest compounded semiannually, (3) 4 percent annual interest compounded annually, and (4) 16 percent annual interest compounded quarterly.

Exercise A-6
Future Value
Applications
(L.O. 2)

a. Two parents have $10,000 to invest for their child's college tuition, which they estimate will cost $20,000 when the child enters college twelve years from now.

Calculate the approximate rate of annual interest that the investment must earn to reach the $20,000 goal in twelve years. (Hint: Make a calculation; then use Table B-1.)

b. Bill Roister is saving to purchase a summer home that will cost about $32,000. He has $20,000 now, on which he can earn 7 percent annual interest.

Calculate the approximate length of time he will have to wait to purchase the summer home. (Hint: Make a calculation; then use Table B-1.)

Exercise A-7
Working
Backwards from
a Future Value
(L.O. 2)

May Marquez has a debt of $45,000 due in four years. She wants to save money to pay it off by making annual deposits in an investment account that earns 8 percent annual interest.

Calculate the amount she must deposit each year to reach her goal. (Hint: Use Table B-2; then make a calculation.)

Exercise A-8
Present Value
of a Lump-Sum
Contract
(L.O. 3)

A contract calls for a lump-sum payment of $30,000. Find the present value of the contract, assuming that (1) the payment is due in five years, and the current interest rate is 9 percent; (2) the payment is due in ten years, and the current interest rate is 9 percent; (3) the payment is due in five years, and the current interest rate is 5 percent; and (4) the payment is due in ten years, and the current interest rate is 5 percent.

Exercise A-9
Present Value
of an Annuity
Contract
(L.O. 3)

A contract calls for annual payments of $600. Find the present value of the contract, assuming that (1) the number of payments is seven, and the current interest rate is 6 percent; (2) the number of payments is fourteen, and the current interest rate is 6 percent; (3) the number of payments is seven, and the current interest rate is 8 percent; and (4) the number of payments is fourteen, and the current interest rate is 8 percent.

Exercise A-10
Noninterest-
Bearing Note
(L.O. 4)

On January 1, 19x8, Olson purchases a machine from Carter by signing a two-year, noninterest-bearing $16,000 note. Olson currently pays 12 percent interest to borrow money at the bank.

Prepare journal entries in Olson's and Carter's records to (1) record the purchase and the note, (2) adjust the accounts after one year, and (3) record payment of the note after two years (on December 31, 19x9).

Exercise A-11
Valuing an
Asset for the
Purpose of
Making a
Purchasing
Decision
(L.O. 4)

Kubo owns a service station and has the opportunity to purchase a car wash machine for $15,000. After carefully studying projected costs and revenues, Kubo estimates that the car wash will produce a net cash flow of $2,600 annually and will last for eight years. Kubo feels that an interest rate of 14 percent is adequate for his business.

Calculate the present value of the machine to Kubo. Does the purchase appear to be a correct business decision?

Exercise A-12
Determining
an Advance
Payment
(L.O. 2)

Ellen Saber is contemplating paying five years' rent in advance. Her annual rent is $4,800. Calculate the single sum that would have to be paid now for the advance rent, if we assume compound interest of 8 percent.

Appendix B

Compound Interest and Present Value Tables

Table B-1
Future Value of $1 After a Given Number of Time Periods

Periods	1%	2%	3%	4%	5%	6%	7%	8%	9%	10%	12%	14%	15%
1	1.010	1.020	1.030	1.040	1.050	1.060	1.070	1.080	1.090	1.100	1.120	1.140	1.150
2	1.020	1.040	1.061	1.082	1.103	1.124	1.145	1.166	1.188	1.210	1.254	1.300	1.323
3	1.030	1.061	1.093	1.125	1.158	1.191	1.225	1.260	1.295	1.331	1.405	1.482	1.521
4	1.041	1.082	1.126	1.170	1.216	1.262	1.311	1.360	1.412	1.464	1.574	1.689	1.749
5	1.051	1.104	1.159	1.217	1.276	1.338	1.403	1.469	1.539	1.611	1.762	1.925	2.011
6	1.062	1.126	1.194	1.265	1.340	1.419	1.501	1.587	1.677	1.772	1.974	2.195	2.313
7	1.072	1.149	1.230	1.316	1.407	1.504	1.606	1.714	1.828	1.949	2.211	2.502	2.660
8	1.083	1.172	1.267	1.369	1.477	1.594	1.718	1.851	1.993	2.144	2.476	2.853	3.059
9	1.094	1.195	1.305	1.423	1.551	1.689	1.838	1.999	2.172	2.358	2.773	3.252	3.518
10	1.105	1.219	1.344	1.480	1.629	1.791	1.967	2.159	2.367	2.594	3.106	3.707	4.046
11	1.116	1.243	1.384	1.539	1.710	1.898	2.105	2.332	2.580	2.853	3.479	4.226	4.652
12	1.127	1.268	1.426	1.601	1.796	2.012	2.252	2.518	2.813	3.138	3.896	4.818	5.350
13	1.138	1.294	1.469	1.665	1.886	2.133	2.410	2.720	3.066	3.452	4.363	5.492	6.153
14	1.149	1.319	1.513	1.732	1.980	2.261	2.579	2.937	3.342	3.798	4.887	6.261	7.076
15	1.161	1.346	1.558	1.801	2.079	2.397	2.759	3.172	3.642	4.177	5.474	7.138	8.137
16	1.173	1.373	1.605	1.873	2.183	2.540	2.952	3.426	3.970	4.595	6.130	8.137	9.358
17	1.184	1.400	1.653	1.948	2.292	2.693	3.159	3.700	4.328	5.054	6.866	9.276	10.76
18	1.196	1.428	1.702	2.026	2.407	2.854	3.380	3.996	4.717	5.560	7.690	10.58	12.38
19	1.208	1.457	1.754	2.107	2.527	3.026	3.617	4.316	5.142	6.116	8.613	12.06	14.23
20	1.220	1.486	1.806	2.191	2.653	3.207	3.870	4.661	5.604	6.728	9.646	13.74	16.37
21	1.232	1.516	1.860	2.279	2.786	3.400	4.141	5.034	6.109	7.400	10.80	15.67	18.82
22	1.245	1.546	1.916	2.370	2.925	3.604	4.430	5.437	6.659	8.140	12.10	17.86	21.64
23	1.257	1.577	1.974	2.465	3.072	3.820	4.741	5.871	7.258	8.954	13.55	20.36	24.89
24	1.270	1.608	2.033	2.563	3.225	4.049	5.072	6.341	7.911	9.850	15.18	23.21	28.63
25	1.282	1.641	2.094	2.666	3.386	4.292	5.427	6.848	8.623	10.83	17.00	26.46	32.92
26	1.295	1.673	2.157	2.772	3.556	4.549	5.807	7.396	9.399	11.92	19.04	30.17	37.86
27	1.308	1.707	2.221	2.883	3.733	4.822	6.214	7.988	10.25	13.11	21.32	34.39	43.54
28	1.321	1.741	2.288	2.999	3.920	5.112	6.649	8.627	11.17	14.42	23.88	39.20	50.07
29	1.335	1.776	2.357	3.119	4.116	5.418	7.114	9.317	12.17	15.86	26.75	44.69	57.58
30	1.348	1.811	2.427	3.243	4.322	5.743	7.612	10.06	13.27	17.45	29.96	50.95	66.21
40	1.489	2.208	3.262	4.801	7.040	10.29	14.97	21.72	31.41	45.26	93.05	188.9	267.9
50	1.645	2.692	4.384	7.107	11.47	18.42	29.46	46.90	74.36	117.4	289.0	700.2	1,084

Source: All tables in Appendix B are from Henry R. Anderson and Mitchell H. Raiborn, *Basic Cost Accounting Concepts* (Boston: Houghton Mifflin, 1977), pp. 552–557. Reprinted with permission.

Table B-1 provides the multipliers necessary to find the future value of a *single* cash deposit made at the *beginning* of year 1. Three factors must be known before the future value can be figured: (1) time period in years, (2) stated annual rate of interest to be earned, and (3) dollar amount invested or deposited.

Example Find the future value of $5,000 deposited now that will earn 9 percent interest compounded annually for five years. From Table B-1, the necessary multiplier for five years at 9 percent is 1.539, and the answer is:

$$\$5,000(1.539) = \underline{\$7,695}$$

Situations requiring the use of Table B-2 are similar to those requiring Table B-1 except that Table B-2 is used to find the future value of a *series* of *equal* annual deposits.

**Table B-2
Future Value
of $1 Paid in
Each Period
For a Given
Number of
Time Periods**

Example What will be the future value at the end of thirty years if $1,000 is deposited each year on January 1, assuming 12 percent interest compounded annually? The required multiplier from Table B-2 is 241.3, and the answer is:

$$\$1,000(241.3) = \underline{\$241,300}$$

Periods	1%	2%	3%	4%	5%	6%	7%	8%	9%	10%	12%	14%	15%
1	1.000	1.000	1.000	1.000	1.000	1.000	1.000	1.000	1.000	1.000	1.000	1.000	1.000
2	2.010	2.020	2.030	2.040	2.050	2.060	2.070	2.080	2.090	2.100	2.120	2.140	2.150
3	3.030	3.060	3.091	3.122	3.153	3.184	3.215	3.246	3.278	3.310	3.374	3.440	3.473
4	4.060	4.122	4.184	4.246	4.310	4.375	4.440	4.506	4.573	4.641	4.779	4.921	4.993
5	5.101	5.204	5.309	5.416	5.526	5.637	5.751	5.867	5.985	6.105	6.353	6.610	6.742
6	6.152	6.308	6.468	6.633	6.802	6.975	7.153	7.336	7.523	7.716	8.115	8.536	8.754
7	7.214	7.434	7.662	7.898	8.142	8.394	8.654	8.923	9.200	9.487	10.09	10.73	11.07
8	8.286	8.583	8.892	9.214	9.549	9.897	10.26	10.64	11.03	11.44	12.30	13.23	13.73
9	9.369	9.755	10.16	10.58	11.03	11.49	11.98	12.49	13.02	13.58	14.78	16.09	16.79
10	10.46	10.95	11.46	12.01	12.58	13.18	13.82	14.49	15.19	15.94	17.55	19.34	20.30
11	11.57	12.17	12.81	13.49	14.21	14.97	15.78	16.65	17.56	18.53	20.65	23.04	24.35
12	12.68	13.41	14.19	15.03	15.92	16.87	17.89	18.98	20.14	21.38	24.13	27.27	29.00
13	13.81	14.68	15.62	16.63	17.71	18.88	20.14	21.50	22.95	24.52	28.03	32.09	34.35
14	14.95	15.97	17.09	18.29	19.60	21.02	22.55	24.21	26.02	27.98	32.39	37.58	40.50
15	16.10	17.29	18.60	20.02	21.58	23.28	25.13	27.15	29.36	31.77	37.28	43.84	47.58
16	17.26	18.64	20.16	21.82	23.66	25.67	27.89	30.32	33.00	35.95	42.75	50.98	55.72
17	18.43	20.01	21.76	23.70	25.84	28.21	30.84	33.75	36.97	40.54	48.88	59.12	65.08
18	19.61	21.41	23.41	25.65	28.13	30.91	34.00	37.45	41.30	45.60	55.75	68.39	75.84
19	20.81	22.84	25.12	27.67	30.54	33.76	37.38	41.45	46.02	51.16	63.44	78.97	88.21
20	22.02	24.30	26.87	29.78	33.07	36.79	41.00	45.76	51.16	57.28	72.05	91.02	102.4
21	23.24	25.78	28.68	31.97	35.72	39.99	44.87	50.42	56.76	64.00	81.70	104.8	118.8
22	24.47	27.30	30.54	34.25	38.51	43.39	49.01	55.46	62.87	71.40	92.50	120.4	137.6
23	25.72	28.85	32.45	36.62	41.43	47.00	53.44	60.89	69.53	79.54	104.6	138.3	159.3
24	26.97	30.42	34.43	39.08	44.50	50.82	58.18	66.76	76.79	88.50	118.2	158.7	184.2
25	28.24	32.03	36.46	41.65	47.73	54.86	63.25	73.11	84.70	98.35	133.3	181.9	212.8
26	29.53	33.67	38.55	44.31	51.11	59.16	68.68	79.95	93.32	109.2	150.3	208.3	245.7
27	30.82	35.34	40.71	47.08	54.67	63.71	74.48	87.35	102.7	121.1	169.4	238.5	283.6
28	32.13	37.05	42.93	49.97	58.40	68.53	80.70	95.34	113.0	134.2	190.7	272.9	327.1
29	33.45	38.79	45.22	52.97	62.32	73.64	87.35	104.0	124.1	148.6	214.6	312.1	377.2
30	34.78	40.57	47.58	56.08	66.44	79.06	94.46	113.3	136.3	164.5	241.3	356.8	434.7
40	48.89	60.40	75.40	95.03	120.8	154.8	199.6	259.1	337.9	442.6	767.1	1,342	1,779
50	64.46	84.58	112.8	152.7	209.3	290.3	406.5	573.8	815.1	1,164	2,400	4,995	7,218

Periods	1%	2%	3%	4%	5%	6%	7%	8%	9%	10%	12%
1	0.990	0.980	0.971	0.962	0.952	0.943	0.935	0.926	0.917	0.909	0.893
2	0.980	0.961	0.943	0.925	0.907	0.890	0.873	0.857	0.842	0.826	0.797
3	0.971	0.942	0.915	0.889	0.864	0.840	0.816	0.794	0.772	0.751	0.712
4	0.961	0.924	0.888	0.855	0.823	0.792	0.763	0.735	0.708	0.683	0.636
5	0.951	0.906	0.883	0.822	0.784	0.747	0.713	0.681	0.650	0.621	0.567
6	0.942	0.888	0.837	0.790	0.746	0.705	0.666	0.630	0.596	0.564	0.507
7	0.933	0.871	0.813	0.760	0.711	0.665	0.623	0.583	0.547	0.513	0.452
8	0.923	0.853	0.789	0.731	0.677	0.627	0.582	0.540	0.502	0.467	0.404
9	0.914	0.837	0.766	0.703	0.645	0.592	0.544	0.500	0.460	0.424	0.361
10	0.905	0.820	0.744	0.676	0.614	0.558	0.508	0.463	0.422	0.386	0.322
11	0.896	0.804	0.722	0.650	0.585	0.527	0.475	0.429	0.388	0.350	0.287
12	0.887	0.788	0.701	0.625	0.557	0.497	0.444	0.397	0.356	0.319	0.257
13	0.879	0.773	0.681	0.601	0.530	0.469	0.415	0.368	0.326	0.290	0.229
14	0.870	0.758	0.661	0.577	0.505	0.442	0.388	0.340	0.299	0.263	0.205
15	0.861	0.743	0.642	0.555	0.481	0.417	0.362	0.315	0.275	0.239	0.183
16	0.853	0.728	0.623	0.534	0.458	0.394	0.339	0.292	0.252	0.218	0.163
17	0.844	0.714	0.605	0.513	0.436	0.371	0.317	0.270	0.231	0.198	0.146
18	0.836	0.700	0.587	0.494	0.416	0.350	0.296	0.250	0.212	0.180	0.130
19	0.828	0.686	0.570	0.475	0.396	0.331	0.277	0.232	0.194	0.164	0.116
20	0.820	0.673	0.554	0.456	0.377	0.312	0.258	0.215	0.178	0.149	0.104
21	0.811	0.660	0.538	0.439	0.359	0.294	0.242	0.199	0.164	0.135	0.093
22	0.803	0.647	0.522	0.422	0.342	0.278	0.226	0.184	0.150	0.123	0.083
23	0.795	0.634	0.507	0.406	0.326	0.262	0.211	0.170	0.138	0.112	0.074
24	0.788	0.622	0.492	0.390	0.310	0.247	0.197	0.158	0.126	0.102	0.066
25	0.780	0.610	0.478	0.375	0.295	0.233	0.184	0.146	0.116	0.092	0.059
26	0.772	0.598	0.464	0.361	0.281	0.220	0.172	0.135	0.106	0.084	0.053
27	0.764	0.586	0.450	0.347	0.268	0.207	0.161	0.125	0.098	0.076	0.047
28	0.757	0.574	0.437	0.333	0.255	0.196	0.150	0.116	0.090	0.069	0.042
29	0.749	0.563	0.424	0.321	0.243	0.185	0.141	0.107	0.082	0.063	0.037
30	0.742	0.552	0.412	0.308	0.231	0.174	0.131	0.099	0.075	0.057	0.033
40	0.672	0.453	0.307	0.208	0.142	0.097	0.067	0.046	0.032	0.022	0.011
50	0.608	0.372	0.228	0.141	0.087	0.054	0.034	0.021	0.013	0.009	0.003

Table B-3
Present Value
of $1 to Be
Received at
the End of a
Given Number
of Time
Periods

14%	15%	16%	18%	20%	25%	30%	35%	40%	45%	50%	Periods
0.877	0.870	0.862	0.847	0.833	0.800	0.769	0.741	0.714	0.690	0.667	1
0.769	0.756	0.743	0.718	0.694	0.640	0.592	0.549	0.510	0.476	0.444	2
0.675	0.658	0.641	0.609	0.579	0.512	0.455	0.406	0.364	0.328	0.296	3
0.592	0.572	0.552	0.516	0.482	0.410	0.350	0.301	0.260	0.226	0.198	4
0.519	0.497	0.476	0.437	0.402	0.328	0.269	0.223	0.186	0.156	0.132	5
0.456	0.432	0.410	0.370	0.335	0.262	0.207	0.165	0.133	0.108	0.088	6
0.400	0.376	0.354	0.314	0.279	0.210	0.159	0.122	0.095	0.074	0.059	7
0.351	0.327	0.305	0.266	0.233	0.168	0.123	0.091	0.068	0.051	0.039	8
0.308	0.284	0.263	0.225	0.194	0.134	0.094	0.067	0.048	0.035	0.026	9
0.270	0.247	0.227	0.191	0.162	0.107	0.073	0.050	0.035	0.024	0.017	10
0.237	0.215	0.195	0.162	0.135	0.086	0.056	0.037	0.025	0.017	0.012	11
0.208	0.187	0.168	0.137	0.112	0.069	0.043	0.027	0.018	0.012	0.008	12
0.182	0.163	0.145	0.116	0.093	0.055	0.033	0.020	0.013	0.008	0.005	13
0.160	0.141	0.125	0.099	0.078	0.044	0.025	0.015	0.009	0.006	0.003	14
0.140	0.123	0.108	0.084	0.065	0.035	0.020	0.011	0.006	0.004	0.002	15
0.123	0.107	0.093	0.071	0.054	0.028	0.015	0.008	0.005	0.003	0.002	16
0.108	0.093	0.080	0.060	0.045	0.023	0.012	0.006	0.003	0.002	0.001	17
0.095	0.081	0.069	0.051	0.038	0.018	0.009	0.005	0.002	0.001	0.001	18
0.083	0.070	0.060	0.043	0.031	0.014	0.007	0.003	0.002	0.001		19
0.073	0.061	0.051	0.037	0.026	0.012	0.005	0.002	0.001	0.001		20
0.064	0.053	0.044	0.031	0.022	0.009	0.004	0.002	0.001			21
0.056	0.046	0.038	0.026	0.018	0.007	0.003	0.001	0.001			22
0.049	0.040	0.033	0.022	0.015	0.006	0.002	0.001				23
0.043	0.035	0.028	0.019	0.013	0.005	0.002	0.001				24
0.038	0.030	0.024	0.016	0.010	0.004	0.001	0.001				25
0.033	0.026	0.021	0.014	0.009	0.003	0.001					26
0.029	0.023	0.018	0.011	0.007	0.002	0.001					27
0.026	0.020	0.016	0.010	0.006	0.002	0.001					28
0.022	0.017	0.014	0.008	0.005	0.002						29
0.020	0.015	0.012	0.007	0.004	0.001						30
0.005	0.004	0.003	0.001	0.001							40
0.001	0.001	0.001									50

Table B-3
(continued)

Table B-3 is used to find the value today of a *single* amount of cash to be received sometime in the future. To use Table B-3, you must first know: (1) time period in years until funds will be received, (2) annual rate of interest, and (3) dollar amount to be received at end of time period.

Example What is the present value of $30,000 to be received twenty-five years from now, assuming a 14 percent interest rate? From Table B-3, the required multiplier is 0.038, and the answer is:

$$\$30,000(0.038) = \underline{\$1,140}$$

Periods	1%	2%	3%	4%	5%	6%	7%	8%	9%	10%	12%
1	0.990	0.980	0.971	0.962	0.952	0.943	0.935	0.926	0.917	0.909	0.893
2	1.970	1.942	1.913	1.886	1.859	1.833	1.808	1.783	1.759	1.736	1.690
3	2.941	2.884	2.829	2.775	2.723	2.673	2.624	2.577	2.531	2.487	2.402
4	3.902	3.808	3.717	3.630	3.546	3.465	3.387	3.312	3.240	3.170	3.037
5	4.853	4.713	4.580	4.452	4.329	4.212	4.100	3.993	3.890	3.791	3.605
6	5.795	5.601	5.417	5.242	5.076	4.917	4.767	4.623	4.486	4.355	4.111
7	6.728	6.472	6.230	6.002	5.786	5.582	5.389	5.206	5.033	4.868	4.564
8	7.652	7.325	7.020	6.733	6.463	6.210	5.971	5.747	5.535	5.335	4.968
9	8.566	8.162	7.786	7.435	7.108	6.802	6.515	6.247	5.995	5.759	5.328
10	9.471	8.983	8.530	8.111	7.722	7.360	7.024	6.710	6.418	6.145	5.650
11	10.368	9.787	9.253	8.760	8.306	7.887	7.499	7.139	6.805	6.495	5.938
12	11.255	10.575	9.954	9.385	8.863	8.384	7.943	7.536	7.161	6.814	6.194
13	12.134	11.348	10.635	9.986	9.394	8.853	8.358	7.904	7.487	7.103	6.424
14	13.004	12.106	11.296	10.563	9.899	9.295	8.745	8.244	7.786	7.367	6.628
15	13.865	12.849	11.938	11.118	10.380	9.712	9.108	8.559	8.061	7.606	6.811
16	14.718	13.578	12.561	11.652	10.838	10.106	9.447	8.851	8.313	7.824	6.974
17	15.562	14.292	13.166	12.166	11.274	10.477	9.763	9.122	8.544	8.022	7.120
18	16.398	14.992	13.754	12.659	11.690	10.828	10.059	9.372	8.756	8.201	7.250
19	17.226	15.678	14.324	13.134	12.085	11.158	10.336	9.604	8.950	8.365	7.366
20	18.046	16.351	14.878	13.590	12.462	11.470	10.594	9.818	9.129	8.514	7.469
21	18.857	17.011	15.415	14.029	12.821	11.764	10.836	10.017	9.292	8.649	7.562
22	19.660	17.658	15.937	14.451	13.163	12.042	11.061	10.201	9.442	8.772	7.645
23	20.456	18.292	16.444	14.857	13.489	12.303	11.272	10.371	9.580	8.883	7.718
24	21.243	18.914	16.936	15.247	13.799	12.550	11.469	10.529	9.707	8.985	7.784
25	22.023	19.523	17.413	15.622	14.094	12.783	11.654	10.675	9.823	9.077	7.843
26	22.795	20.121	17.877	15.983	14.375	13.003	11.826	10.810	9.929	9.161	7.896
27	23.560	20.707	18.327	16.330	14.643	13.211	11.987	10.935	10.027	9.237	7.943
28	24.316	21.281	18.764	16.663	14.898	13.406	12.137	11.051	10.116	9.307	7.984
29	25.066	21.844	19.189	16.984	15.141	13.591	12.278	11.158	10.198	9.370	8.022
30	25.808	22.396	19.600	17.292	15.373	13.765	12.409	11.258	10.274	9.427	8.055
40	32.835	27.355	23.115	19.793	17.159	15.046	13.332	11.925	10.757	9.779	8.244
50	39.196	31.424	25.730	21.482	18.256	15.762	13.801	12.234	10.962	9.915	8.305

**Table B-4
Present Value
of $1 Received
Each Period
for a Given
Number of
Time Periods**

Table B-4 is used to find the present value of a *series* of *equal* annual cash flows.

Example Arthur Howard won a contest on January 1, 1984, in which the prize was $30,000, payable in fifteen annual installments of $2,000 every December 31, beginning in 1984. Assuming a 9 percent interest rate, what is the present value of Mr. Howard's prize on January 1, 1984? From Table B-4, the required multiplier is 8.061, and the answer is:

$$\$2,000(8.061) = \underline{\underline{\$16,122}}$$

14%	15%	16%	18%	20%	25%	30%	35%	40%	45%	50%	Periods
0.877	0.870	0.862	0.847	0.833	0.800	0.769	0.741	0.714	0.690	0.667	1
1.647	1.626	1.605	1.566	1.528	1.440	1.361	1.289	1.224	1.165	1.111	2
2.322	2.283	2.246	2.174	2.106	1.952	1.816	1.696	1.589	1.493	1.407	3
2.914	2.855	2.798	2.690	2.589	2.362	2.166	1.997	1.849	1.720	1.605	4
3.433	3.352	3.274	3.127	2.991	2.689	2.436	2.220	2.035	1.876	1.737	5
3.889	3.784	3.685	3.498	3.326	2.951	2.643	2.385	2.168	1.983	1.824	6
4.288	4.160	4.039	3.812	3.605	3.161	2.802	2.508	2.263	2.057	1.883	7
4.639	4.487	4.344	4.078	3.837	3.329	2.925	2.598	2.331	2.109	1.922	8
4.946	4.772	4.607	4.303	4.031	3.463	3.019	2.665	2.379	2.144	1.948	9
5.216	5.019	4.833	4.494	4.192	3.571	3.092	2.715	2.414	2.168	1.965	10
5.453	5.234	5.029	4.656	4.327	3.656	3.147	2.752	2.438	2.185	1.977	11
5.660	5.421	5.197	4.793	4.439	3.725	3.190	2.779	2.456	2.197	1.985	12
5.842	5.583	5.342	4.910	4.533	3.780	3.223	2.799	2.469	2.204	1.990	13
6.002	5.724	5.468	5.008	4.611	3.824	3.249	2.814	2.478	2.210	1.993	14
6.142	5.847	5.575	5.092	4.675	3.859	3.268	2.825	2.484	2.214	1.995	15
6.265	5.954	5.669	5.162	4.730	3.887	3.283	2.834	2.489	2.216	1.997	16
6.373	6.047	5.749	5.222	4.775	3.910	3.295	2.840	2.492	2.218	1.998	17
6.467	6.128	5.818	5.273	4.812	3.928	3.304	2.844	2.494	2.219	1.999	18
6.550	6.198	5.877	5.316	4.844	3.942	3.311	2.848	2.496	2.220	1.999	19
6.623	6.259	5.929	5.353	4.870	3.954	3.316	2.850	2.497	2.221	1.999	20
6.687	6.312	5.973	5.384	4.891	3.963	3.320	2.852	2.498	2.221	2.000	21
6.743	6.359	6.011	5.410	4.909	3.970	3.323	2.853	2.498	2.222	2.000	22
6.792	6.399	6.044	5.432	4.925	3.976	3.325	2.854	2.499	2.222	2.000	23
6.835	6.434	6.073	5.451	4.937	3.981	3.327	2.855	2.499	2.222	2.000	24
6.873	6.464	6.097	5.467	4.948	3.985	3.329	2.856	2.499	2.222	2.000	25
6.906	6.491	6.118	5.480	4.956	3.988	3.330	2.856	2.500	2.222	2.000	26
6.935	6.514	6.136	5.492	4.964	3.990	3.331	2.856	2.500	2.222	2.000	27
6.961	6.534	6.152	5.502	4.970	3.992	3.331	2.857	2.500	2.222	2.000	28
6.983	6.551	6.166	5.510	4.975	3.994	3.332	2.857	2.500	2.222	2.000	29
7.003	6.566	6.177	5.517	4.979	3.995	3.332	2.857	2.500	2.222	2.000	30
7.105	6.642	6.234	5.548	4.997	3.999	3.333	2.857	2.500	2.222	2.000	40
7.133	6.661	6.246	5.554	4.999	4.000	3.333	2.857	2.500	2.222	2.000	50

Table B-4
(continued)

Table B-4 applies to *ordinary annuities*, in which the first cash flow occurs one time period beyond the date for which present value is to be computed. An *annuity due* is a series of equal cash flows for N time periods, but the first payment occurs immediately. The present value of the first payment equals the face value of the cash flow; Table B-4 then is used to measure the present value of $N - 1$ remaining cash flows.

Example Find the present value on January 1, 1984, of twenty lease payments; each payment of $10,000 is due on January 1, beginning in 1984. Assume an interest rate of 8 percent:

$$\text{present value} = \text{immediate payment} + \left\{ \begin{array}{l} \text{present value of 19} \\ \text{subsequent payments of 8\%} \end{array} \right.$$

$$= \$10,000 + [10,000(9.604)]$$

$$= \underline{\underline{\$106,040}}$$

Appendix C

Overview
of Income
Taxes for
Individuals

1. *Explain and differentiate some basic concepts related to income taxes and accounting.*

2. *Identify the major components used in determining the income tax liability of individuals.*

The United States Congress first passed a permanent income tax law in 1913, after the Sixteenth Amendment to the Constitution gave legality to such a tax. Its original goal was to provide revenue for the U.S. government, and today the income tax is still a major source of revenue. Of course, most states and many cities also have an income tax. Because these tax laws are in many cases much like those in the federal tax system, the discussion in this appendix is limited to the federal income tax.

Though it is still an important purpose of the federal income tax laws to produce revenue, Congress has also used its taxing power as an instrument of economic policy. Among the economic goals proposed by Congress are a fairer distribution of income, stimulation of economic growth, full employment, encouragement of exploration for oil and minerals, control of inflation, and a variety of social changes.

All three branches of the federal government have a part in the federal income tax system. The Internal Revenue Service (IRS), which is an agency of the Treasury Department, administers the system. The income tax law is based on over fifty revenue acts and other related laws that have been passed by Congress since 1913. Also, the IRS issues regulations that interpret the law. It is the federal court system, however, that must uphold these important regulations and that has final authority for interpreting the law.

The income tax has had important effects on both individuals and businesses. In 1913, an individual who earned $30,000 paid only $300 or $400 in income taxes. Today, an individual who earns the same amount may pay as much as $5,000 or more, and corporations may pay almost half of their income in taxes. Clearly, the income tax is an important cost of doing business today.

Some Basic Concepts Related to Federal Income Taxes

To understand the nature of federal income taxes, it is important to distinguish between taxable income and accounting income, between tax planning and tax evasion, between cash basis and accrual basis, and among classifications of taxpayers.

Taxable Income and Accounting Income

The government assesses income taxes on **taxable income**, which usually is gross income less various exemptions and deductions specified by the law and the IRS regulations. Taxable income is generally found by referring to information in the accounting records. However, it is very unlikely that taxable income and accounting income for an entity will be the same, because they have different purposes. The government levies income taxes to obtain revenue from taxpayers and to carry out economic policies totally unrelated to the measurement of economic income, which is the purpose of accounting.

Tax Planning and Tax Evasion

The arrangement of a taxpayer's affairs in such a way as to incur the smallest legal tax is called **tax planning**. For almost every business decision, alternative courses of action are available that will affect taxable income in different ways. For example, the taxpayer may lease or buy a truck, may use LIFO, FIFO, or average cost to account for inventories, or may time an expenditure to be accounted for in one accounting period or another. Once the taxpayer chooses and acts upon an alternative, however, the IRS will usually treat this alternative as the final one for income tax determination. Therefore, in tax planning it is important to consider tax-saving alternatives before putting decisions into effect.

It is the natural goal of any taxable entity to pay as small a tax as possible; both the tax law and the IRS hold that no entity should pay more than is legally required. The best way to accomplish this goal is by careful tax planning. It is, however, illegal to evade paying taxes by concealing actual tax liabilities. This is called **tax evasion**.

Cash Basis and Accrual Basis

In general, taxpayers may use either the cash basis or the accrual basis to arrive at their taxable income. Most individuals use the **cash basis**—the reporting of items of revenue and expense when they are received or paid—because it is the simplest method. Employers usually report their employees' income on a cash basis, and companies that pay dividends and interest on a cash basis must also report them in this way.

Professional and other service enterprises such as those of accountants, attorneys, physicians, travel agents, and insurance agents also typically use the cash basis in determining taxable income. One advantage of this method is that fees charged to clients or customers are not considered to be earned until payment is received. Thus it is possible to defer the taxes on these revenues until the tax year in which they are received. However, the government does not allow a deduction for estimated uncollectible accounts in this case because these losses will simply show up as reduced revenues (cash receipts). Similarly, expenses such as rent, utilities, and salaries are recorded when they are paid. Thus a business can work at tax planning by carefully timing its expenditures. Still, this method does not apply to expenditures for buildings and equipment used for business purposes. Such items are treated in accordance with the accelerated cost recovery system discussed in Chapter 13.

Businesses that engage in production or trading of inventories must use the **accrual basis** of accounting rather than the cash basis. In other words, they must report revenues from sales in the period in which they sold the goods, regardless of when they received the cash. And they must record purchases in the year of purchase rather than in the year of payment. They must follow the usual accounting for beginning and ending inventories in determining cost of goods sold. However, the tax laws do not require a strict accrual method in the accounting sense for manufacturing and merchandising concerns. Various modified cash and accrual bases are possible as long as they yield reasonable and consistent results from year to year.

Classifications of Taxpayers

The federal tax law recognizes four classes of taxpayers: individuals, corporations, estates, and trusts. Members of each class must file tax returns and pay taxes on taxable income. This appendix discusses only individuals. Taxation of corporations is covered in Chapter 17. Taxation of estates and trusts is left for a more advanced course.

Although they are business entities for accounting purposes, sole proprietorships and partnerships are not taxable entities. Instead, a proprietor must include the business income on an individual income tax return. Similarly, each partner in a business must include his or her share of the partnership income on an individual return. Each partnership, however, must file an information return showing the results of the partnership's operations and how each partner's share of the income was determined.

In contrast, corporations are taxable entities that must file tax returns and are taxed directly on their earnings. If, after paying its income tax, the corporation distributes some of its earnings to its stockholders, the stockholders must report the dividend income as part of their gross income. This rule has led to the claim that corporate income is subject to double taxation—once when it is earned by the company and once when it is paid to the owners of the company's stock.

Income Tax for Individuals

It is important to study income tax for individuals for several reasons. First, most persons who earn taxable income must file a tax return. Second, all persons who operate proprietorships or partnerships must report the income from their businesses on their individual tax returns. Third, many of the same tax terms are used for both individuals and corporations.

The Internal Revenue Code establishes the method of calculating taxable income for individuals. The starting place for figuring taxable income is finding gross income. The next step is to find the amount of adjusted gross income by subtracting deductions from gross income. Under this heading are the expenses of running a business or profession and certain other specified expenses. Then, from adjusted gross income one subtracts a second kind of deductions, called deductions from adjusted gross income, to arrive at taxable income. Under this second heading come (1) certain business and personal expenses and (2) allowances known as exemptions. These procedures can be outlined as follows:

Gross income	$xxx	
Less deductions from gross income	xxx	
Adjusted gross income		$xxx
Less deductions from adjusted gross income:		
a. Excess of itemized expenses over zero bracket amount plus the direct charitable deduction	$xxx	
b. Exemptions	xxx	xxx
Taxable income		$xxx

Gross Income	The Internal Revenue Code defines **gross income** as income from all sources, less allowable exclusions. Under this heading are wages, salaries, bonuses, fees, tips, interest, dividends, pensions, and annuities. Rents, royalties, alimony, prizes, profits or shares of profits from business, and gains on sale of property or stocks are also included. Income from illegal sources also must be reported as gross income.

Deductions from Gross Income

The calculation of **adjusted gross income** is important to the individual because it serves as the basis for certain personal deductions in figuring taxable income. These **deductions from gross income** are meant to give people a fairer base than gross income. For example, some people may have a high gross income but may have had many business expenditures to gain that gross income. So it is fair to let them deduct the amount spent in earning the gross income. Also, employees who have expenses connected with their jobs should be allowed to deduct them from gross income. Such a case is the automobile expenses of salespeople who must use their own automobiles.

Deductions from Adjusted Gross Income

Deductions from adjusted gross income fall under three headings: (1) excess itemized deductions, if any, (2) exemptions, and (3) direct charitable deductions. In the first case, every taxpayer is allowed to deduct the excess of itemized deductions over the zero bracket amount. The **zero bracket amount** is the amount of income on which there is no tax. It is called by this name because taxpayers who earn less than the zero bracket amount pay no taxes. For a single person or unmarried head of household, the zero bracket amount in a recent year was $2,300. For married couples filing jointly, the amount was $3,400. If a taxpayer can prove that he or she spent more than the zero bracket amount on certain items, the taxpayer may deduct the excess of these items over the zero bracket amount. Of course, it is an advantage to the taxpayer to itemize deductions if possible. The itemized deductions allowed are medical and dental expenses, interest expense, taxes, charitable contributions, casualty losses, and miscellaneous deductions such as professional or union dues.

Besides the itemized deductions or the zero bracket amount, a taxpayer is allowed a second kind of deduction called an **exemption.** For each exemption, the taxpayer may deduct $1,000 from adjusted gross income. A taxpayer is allowed a personal exemption for himself or herself, plus one for each dependent. To qualify as a dependent, a person (1) must be closely related to the taxpayer or have lived in the taxpayer's house for the whole year, (2) must have received over half of his or her support from the taxpayer during the year, (3) must not file a joint return with his or her spouse (if married), (4) must have had less than $1,000 of gross income during the year (unless he or she is a child of the taxpayer and is either under 19 or a student), and (5) must be a U.S. citizen or a resident of the United States, Canada, or Mexico. Other exemptions are allowed if the taxpayer is over sixty-five years of age or blind. If husband and wife file a joint return, they may combine their exemptions.

Computing Tax Liability

In general, the income tax is a **progressive tax,** which means that the rate becomes larger as the amount of taxable income becomes larger. In other words, the higher a person's taxable income, the larger the proportion of it that goes to pay taxes.[1] Different rate schedules apply to single taxpayers, married taxpayers who file joint returns, married taxpayers who file separate returns, and single taxpayers

1. In contrast to a progressive tax rate, a **regressive tax** rate becomes less as one's income rises. An example of a regressive tax is the social security (FICA) tax, which is levied on incomes only up to a certain amount. A **proportional tax** is one in which the rate is the same percentage regardless of income. Examples are most sales taxes and the income taxes of some states, such as Illinois.

who qualify as heads of households. Any of these taxpayers can find their tax liability by referring to the tax table for their category. Part of the 1982 tax table is reproduced in Figure C-1. This table takes into account the zero bracket amount and applies to taxpayers whose taxable income is less than $50,000. For example, a single taxpayer with two exemptions earning $13,275 would have a tax liability of $1,490, as shown in the tax table in Figure C-1.

Taxpayers whose taxable income exceeds these limits must use the tax rate schedules, two of which are reproduced in Figure C-2. By looking at this schedule, one can easily see the progressive nature of the income tax. For example, a single taxpayer with taxable income between $23,500 and $28,800 pays $4,837 plus 35 percent of the amount over $23,500. A single taxpayer with

Figure C-1
Excerpt from
the 1982 Tax
Table

If line 37 (taxable income) is—		And you are—			
At least	But less than	Single	Married filing jointly *	Married filing separately	Head of a household
		Your tax is—			
10,750	10,800	1,380	1,054	1,637	1,313
10,800	10,850	1,391	1,062	1,650	1,323
10,850	10,900	1,402	1,070	1,662	1,333
10,900	10,950	1,413	1,078	1,675	1,343
10,950	11,000	1,424	1,086	1,687	1,353
11,000					
11,000	11,050	1,435	1,094	1,700	1,363
11,050	11,100	1,446	1,102	1,712	1,373
11,100	11,150	1,457	1,110	1,725	1,383
11,150	11,200	1,468	1,118	1,737	1,393
11,200	11,250	1,479	1,126	1,750	1,403
11,250	11,300	1,490	1,134	1,762	1,413
11,300	11,350	1,501	1,142	1,775	1,423
11,350	11,400	1,512	1,150	1,787	1,433
11,400	11,450	1,523	1,158	1,800	1,443
11,450	11,500	1,534	1,166	1,812	1,453
11,500	11,550	1,545	1,174	1,825	1,463
11,550	11,600	1,556	1,182	1,837	1,473
11,600	11,650	1,567	1,190	1,850	1,483
11,650	11,700	1,578	1,198	1,862	1,493
11,700	11,750	1,589	1,206	1,875	1,503
11,750	11,800	1,600	1,214	1,887	1,513
11,800	11,850	1,611	1,222	1,900	1,524
11,850	11,900	1,622	1,230	1,912	1,535
11,900	11,950	1,633	1,239	1,925	1,546
11,950	12,000	1,644	1,248	1,937	1,557
12,000					
12,000	12,050	1,655	1,258	1,950	1,568
12,050	12,100	1,666	1,267	1,962	1,579
12,100	12,150	1,677	1,277	1,975	1,590
12,150	12,200	1,688	1,286	1,987	1,601
12,200	12,250	1,699	1,296	2,000	1,612
12,250	12,300	1,710	1,305	2,012	1,623
12,300	12,350	1,721	1,315	2,026	1,634
12,350	12,400	1,732	1,324	2,040	1,645
12,400	12,450	1,743	1,334	2,055	1,656
12,450	12,500	1,754	1,343	2,069	1,667
12,500	12,550	1,765	1,353	2,084	1,678
12,550	12,600	1,776	1,362	2,098	1,689
12,600	12,650	1,787	1,372	2,113	1,700
12,650	12,700	1,798	1,381	2,127	1,711
12,700	12,750	1,809	1,391	2,142	1,722

Figure C-2
Excerpt from
the 1982 Tax
Rate Schedules

Schedule X

Single Taxpayers

Use this Schedule if you checked **Filing Status Box 1** on Form 1040—

If the amount on Form 1040, line 37 is: Over—	But not Over—	Enter on Form 1040, line 38	of the amount over—
$0	$2,300	—0—	
2,300	3,400	............12%	$2,300
3,400	4,400	$132+14%	3,400
4,400	6,500	272+16%	4,400
6,500	8,500	608+17%	6,500
8,500	10,800	948+19%	8,500
10,800	12,900	1,385+22%	10,800
12,900	15,000	1,847+23%	12,900
15,000	18,200	2,330+27%	15,000
18,200	23,500	3,194+31%	18,200
23,500	28,800	4,837+35%	23,500
28,800	34,100	6,692+40%	28,800
34,100	41,500	8,812+44%	34,100
41,500	....	12,068+50%	41,500

Schedule Y

Married Taxpayers and Qualifying Widows and Widowers

Married Filing Joint Returns and Qualifying Widows and Widowers

Use this schedule if you checked **Filing Status Box 2 or 5** on Form 1040—

If the amount on Form 1040, line 37 is: Over—	But not Over—	Enter on Form 1040, line 38	of the amount over—
$0	$3,400	—0—	
3,400	5,500	............12%	$3,400
5,500	7,600	$252+14%	5,500
7,600	11,900	546+16%	7,600
11,900	16,000	1,234+19%	11,900
16,000	20,200	2,013+22%	16,000
20,200	24,600	2,937+25%	20,200
24,600	29,900	4,037+29%	24,600
29,900	35,200	5,574+33%	29,900
35,200	45,800	7,323+39%	35,200
45,800	60,000	11,457+44%	45,800
60,000	85,600	17,705+49%	60,000
85,600	....	30,249+50%	85,600

Married Filing Separate Returns

Use this schedule if you checked **Filing Status Box 3** on Form 1040—

If the amount on Form 1040, line 37 is: Over—	But not Over—	Enter on Form 1040, line 38	of the amount over—
$0	$1,700	—0—	
1,700	2,750	............12%	$1,700
2,750	3,800	$126.00+14%	2,750
3,800	5,950	273.00+16%	3,800
5,950	8,000	617.00+19%	5,950
8,000	10,100	1,006.50+22%	8,000
10,100	12,300	1,468.50+25%	10,100
12,300	14,950	2,018.50+29%	12,300
14,950	17,600	2,787.00+33%	14,950
17,600	22,900	3,661.50+39%	17,600
22,900	30,000	5,728.50+44%	22,900
30,000	42,800	8,052.50+49%	30,000
42,800	....	15,124.50+50%	42,800

taxable income between $28,800 and $34,100 pays $6,692 plus 40 percent of the amount over $28,800. The 35 percent and the 40 percent in this example are known as the **marginal tax rates** because they apply to the last increment of taxable income. The average tax rate is much lower because the lower levels of income were taxed at lower rates.

From Figure C-2 it is clear that the marginal tax rate can go as high as 50 percent. A single taxpayer whose taxable income is in excess of $41,500 and married taxpayers filing jointly whose taxable income is in excess of $85,600 are therefore taxed proportionally on such excess taxable income. The law also provides a tax break for taxpayers whose income fluctuates widely from year to year. They are allowed to use a formula called **income averaging**, which averages their taxable income over five years.

Capital Gains and Losses	One effective means of tax planning is to arrange transactions involving certain types of assets in such a way that they qualify for special treatment as capital gains and losses. These assets, called **capital assets**, usually include stocks and bonds owned by individuals and, under certain circumstances, buildings, equipment, and land used in businesses. Capital assets usually do not include receivables, inventories, and literary or artistic works held by taxpayers whose personal efforts created this property. If the capital assets being sold or exchanged have been held for one year or less, they are classified as short-term. If they have been held for more than one year, they are classified as long-term. The combined total of all gains and losses on short-term capital assets during a tax year is called **net short-term capital gain (or loss)**. The combined total of all gains and losses on long-term capital assets during a tax year is called **net long-term capital gain (or loss)**. If the net long-term capital gain exceeds any net short-term capital loss, the excess is called the **net capital gain**.

Net Capital Gain The effect of the above classification of assets on the resulting net capital gain is to limit the tax, because 60 percent of any net capital gain is deducted from gross income in arriving at adjusted gross income.

Net Capital Loss When a taxpayer's transactions involving capital assets for a year result in a net capital loss, the amount of the loss that may be deducted in any one year is limited. The taxpayer can use the loss to reduce gross income only by as much as $3,000. Any excess of net capital loss over $3,000 must be carried over to be deducted in future years.

By timing the holding period for capital gains and losses during the year in which the capital transactions take place, an individual can greatly change the amount of tax he or she pays. For example, suppose the taxpayer must take a loss in a stock investment. It may be wise to sell the stock just before the end of the twelve-month holding period in order to incur a short-term loss, which is fully deductible up to $3,000. If the taxpayer has a gain, on the other hand, it may be best to wait until just beyond the twelve-month period to sell the stock and recognize the gain because it will receive preferential treatment. Near the end of the tax year, it is sometimes a good idea to sell securities in order to recognize gains and offset losses incurred earlier in the year, or vice versa.

Credits Against the Tax Liability	Tax credits are subtractions from the computed tax liability and should not be confused with deductions that are subtracted from income to determine taxable income. Since tax credits reduce tax liability dollar for dollar, they are more beneficial to the taxpayer than an equal dollar amount of deductions from taxable income. A tax credit is allowed for one-half the contributions made to candidates for public office, subject to a $50 maximum (or $100 if filing jointly). There are also tax credits for the elderly, for dependent care expenses, for a percentage of certain investments, for income taxes paid in foreign countries, for wages paid in work incentive programs, and for jobs given to members of certain groups. Homeowners and renters are entitled to a tax credit for a percentage of their energy-saving expenditures as well.

Withholding and Estimated Tax	For most individuals the tax year ends on December 31, and their return is due three and one-half months later, on April 15. If they are wage earners or salaried employees, their employer is required to withhold an estimated income tax from their pay during the year and remit it to the Internal Revenue Service. The employer reports this withholding to the employee on form W-2 on or before January 31 for the preceding year (see Chapter 12 for a discussion of payroll procedures). Taxpayers who have income beyond a certain amount that is not

subject to withholding must report a Declaration of Estimated Tax and pay an **estimated tax**, less any amount expected to be withheld, in four installments during the year. When taxpayers prepare their tax returns, they deduct the amount of estimated tax withheld and the amount paid in installments from the total tax liability to find the amount they must pay when they file the tax return.

Questions

1. What is the difference between tax planning and tax evasion?
2. What are the four classes of taxpayers?
3. J. Vickery's sole proprietorship had a net income of $37,500 during the taxable year. During the same year, Vickery withdrew $24,000 from the business. What income must Vickery report on his individual tax return?
4. Which of the two methods of accounting, cash or accrual, is more commonly used by individual taxpayers?
5. Why is it sometimes claimed that corporate income is subject to double taxation?
6. Figure C-2 indicates that a single taxpayer with a taxable income (after deduction for exemption) of $20,000 owes $3,752 in federal income taxes. What is this taxpayer's average tax rate and his or her marginal tax rate?
7. If a friend of yours turned down the opportunity to earn an additional $500 of taxable income because it would put him or her in a higher tax bracket, would you consider this action rational? Why?

Exercise C-1

Computation of Tax Liability

From Figures C-1 and C-2, figure the income tax before-tax credit for each of the following: (1) single individual with taxable income of $12,500, (2) single individual with taxable income of $59,000, (3) married couple filing jointly with taxable income of $11,250, (4) married couple filing jointly with taxable income of $59,000.

Glossary

Note: The number in parentheses after each definition refers to the chapter where the term is first discussed.

Absorption costing: an approach to product costing that assigns a representative portion of *all* manufacturing costs to individual products. (23)

Accelerated cost recovery system (ACRS): requires that a cost recovery allowance be computed on the unadjusted cost of the property being recovered. (13)

Accelerated methods: methods of depreciation that allocate relatively large amounts of the depreciable cost of the asset to earlier years and reduced amounts to later years. (13)

Account: the basic storage unit for data in accounting systems; consists of one for each asset, liability, component of owner's equity, revenue, and expense. (3)

Accountant's report (or auditor's report): a report by an independent public accountant that accompanies the financial statements and contains the accountant's opinion regarding the fairness of presentation of the financial statements. (9)

Account balance: the difference in total dollars between the total debit footing and the total credit footing of an account. (3)

Accounting: an information system that measures, processes, and communicates financial information about an identifiable economic entity to permit users of the system to make informed judgments and decisions. (1)

Accounting cycle: all steps in the accounting process including analyzing and recording transactions, posting entries, adjusting and closing the accounts, and preparing financial statements; accounting system. (5)

Accounting equation, see Balance sheet equation

Accounting period problem: the difficulty of assigning revenues and expenses to short periods of time such as months or years; related to the periodicity assumption. (4)

Accounting practice: the procedures employed in accounting to measure, process, and communicate information. (1)

Accounting rate of return method: a method used to measure the estimated performance of a capital investment that yields an accounting rate of return computed by dividing the project's average after-tax net income by the average cost of the investment over its estimated life. (28)

Accounting system, see Accounting cycle

Accounting theory: the theoretical framework which underlies the actions or practice of accountants. (1)

Accounts receivable: short-term liquid assets that arise from sales on credit to customers at either the wholesale or the retail level. (10)

Accounts receivable aging method: a method of estimating uncollectible accounts expense based on the assumption that the probability of collecting accounts receivable at the end of the period will depend on the length of time individual accounts are past due. (10)

Accrual: the recognition of an expense or revenue that has arisen but has not yet been recorded. (4)

Accrual accounting: all the techniques developed by accountants to apply the matching rule. (4)

Accrual basis: the reporting of revenues from sales in the period in which they are sold, regardless of when the cash is received, and the reporting of expenses in the period of purchase, regardless of when payment is made. (Appendix C)

Accrued expense: an expense that has been incurred but is not recognized in the accounts, necessitating an adjusting entry; unrecorded expense. (4)

Accrued revenue: a revenue for which the service

has been performed or the goods have been delivered but that has not been recorded in the accounts; unrecorded revenue. (4)

Accumulated depreciation: a contra-asset account used to accumulate the total past depreciation on a specific long-lived asset. (4)

Activity accounting, see Profitability accounting

Addition: an expenditure resulting from an expansion of an existing plant asset. (14)

Adjusted gross income: gross income minus deductions from gross income. (Appendix C)

Adjusted trial balance: a trial balance prepared after all adjusting entries have been reflected in the accounts. (4)

Adjusting entry: entry made to apply accrual accounting to transactions that span more than one accounting period. (4)

Aging of accounts receivable: the process of listing each customer in accounts receivable according to the due date of the account. (10)

All financial resources (concept of funds): the concept of funds used in preparation of the statement of changes in financial position when exchange transactions are considered as both a source and a use of working capital. (19)

Allowance for uncollectible accounts: a contra accounts receivable account in which appears the estimated total of the as yet unidentified accounts receivable that will not be collected. (10)

American Institute of Certified Public Accountants (AICPA): the professional association of CPAs. (1)

Amortization: the periodic allocation of the cost of an intangible asset over its useful life. (13)

Annual report: a corporation's yearly financial report to its stockholders, sent as part of management's responsibility to report to the owners of the company; also filed with the SEC. (9)

Appropriated retained earnings: a restriction of retained earnings that indicates that a portion of a company's assets are to be used for purposes other than paying dividends. (17)

Arithmetic/logic unit: the part of the central processor in a computer system that performs the computing and decision-making functions. (8)

Articles of incorporation: a contract between the state and the incorporators forming the corporation. (16)

Asset: an economic resource owned by a business that is expected to benefit future operations. (2)

Asset turnover: a ratio that measures how efficiently assets are used to produce sales. (21)

Audit committee: in the organization of a corporation, a committee with several outside directors which ensures that the board of directors will be objective in judging management's performance. (16)

Audit trail: the sequence of written approval by key individuals supporting an expenditure in a voucher system. (8)

Auditing: the principal and most distinctive function of a certified public accountant; the process of examining and testing the financial statements of a company in order to render an independent professional opinion as to the fairness of their presentation; also called the attest function. (1)

Auditor's report, see Accountant's report

Authorized stock: the maximum number of shares a corporation may issue without changing its charter with the state. (16)

Average-cost method: an inventory costing method under which each item of goods sold and of inventory is assigned a cost equal to the average cost of all goods purchased. (11)

Average cost of capital: a minimum desired rate of return on capital expenditures computed by finding the average of the cost of debt, cost of preferred stock, cost of capital equity, and cost of retained earnings. (28)

Average days' sales uncollected: a ratio that measures how many days it takes before the average receivable is collected. (21)

Balance sheet: a financial statement that shows the financial position of a business at a particular date. (2)

Balance sheet equation: algebraic expression of financial position; assets = liabilities + owner's equity; also called the accounting equation. (2)

Bank reconciliation: the process of accounting for the differences between the balance appearing on the bank statement and the balance of cash according to the depositor's records. (8)

Bank statement: a monthly statement of the transactions related to a particular bank account. (8)

Base year: the first year to be considered in any set of data. (21)

Batch processing: a type of computer system design in which separate computer jobs such as purchasing, inventory control, payroll, production scheduling, and so forth are processed individually but in a carefully coordinated way. (7)

Beginning inventory: merchandise on hand for sale to customers at the beginning of the accounting period. (6)

Beta: the measure of market risk. (21)

Betterment: an expenditure resulting from an improvement to but not an enlargement of an existing plant asset. (14)

Bond: a security, usually long-term, representing money borrowed by a corporation from the investing public. (18)

Bond certificate: the evidence of a company's debt to the bondholder. (18)

Bond indenture: a supplementary agreement to a bond issue that defines the rights, privileges, and limitations of bondholders. (18)

Bonding: investigating an employee and insuring the company against any theft by that individual. (8)

Bond issue: the total number of bonds that are issued at one time. (18)

Bond sinking fund: a fund established by the segregation of assets over the life of the bond issue to satisfy investors that money will be available to pay the bondholders at maturity. (18)

Bonus: in partnership accounting, an amount that accrues to the original partners when a new partner pays more to the partnership than the interest received or that accrues to the new partner when the amount paid to the partnership is less than the interest received. (15)

Bookkeeping: the means by which transactions are recorded and records are kept; a process of accounting. (1)

Book value: total assets of a company less total liabilities; owners' equity. (16)

Break-even point: that point in financial analysis at which total revenue equals total cost incurred and at which a company begins to generate a profit. (25)

Budgetary control: the total process of (1) developing plans for a company's anticipated operations and (2) controlling operations to aid in accomplishing those plans. (26)

Business transaction: an economic event that affects the financial position of a business entity. (2)

Callable bonds: bonds that a corporation has the option of buying back and retiring at a given price, usually above face value, before maturity. (18)

Callable preferred stock: preferred stock that may be redeemed and retired by the corporation at its option. (16)

Capital assets: certain types of assets that qualify for special treatment when gains and losses result from transactions involving the assets. (17, Appendix C)

Capital budgeting: the combined process of identifying a facility need, analyzing alternative courses of action to satisfy that need, preparing the reports for management, selecting the best alternative, and rationing available capital expenditure funds among competing resource needs. (28)

Capital expenditure: an expenditure for the purchase or expansion of plant assets. (14)

Capital expenditure decision: the decision to determine when and how much money to spend on capital facilities for the company. (28)

Capital lease: long-term lease that is in effect an installment purchase of assets; recorded by entering on the books an asset and a corresponding liability at the present value of the lease payments; each lease payment is partly a repayment of debt and partly an interest payment on the debt. (18)

Carrying value: the unexpired portion of the cost of an asset; sometimes called book value. (13)

Cash basis of accounting: a basis of accounting under which revenues and expenses are accounted for on a cash received and cash paid basis. (4, 14, Appendix C)

Cash disbursements journal, see Cash payments journal

Cash flow forecast: a forecast or budget that shows the firm's projected ending cash balance and the cash position for each month of the year so that periods of high or low cash availability can be anticipated; also called a cash budget. (26)

Cash flow statement: a financial statement that shows a company's sources and uses of cash during an accounting period. (19)

Cash over or short: an account used to record small shortages or overages that result from the handling of cash. (8)

Cash payments journal: a multicolumn special-purpose journal in which disbursements of cash are recorded; also called cash disbursements journal. (7)

Cash receipts journal: a multicolumn special-purpose journal in which transactions involving receipts of cash are recorded. (7)

Central processor: a piece of hardware in which the actual computing in the computer system is done; consists of the control unit, the arithmetic/logic unit, and the storage units. (7)

Certified public accountant (CPA): public accountants who have met stringent licensing requirements. (1)

Chart of accounts: a numbering scheme that assigns a unique number to each account to facilitate finding the account in the ledger. (3, 9)

Check: a negotiable instrument used to pay for goods and services. (8)

Check authorization: a document prepared by the accounting department authorizing the payment of the invoice; supported by a purchase order, invoice, and receiving report. (8)

Check register: a special-purpose journal used in a voucher system to record each expenditure made by check. (8)

Classification problem: the difficulty of assigning all the transactions in which a business engages to the appropriate account or accounts. (3)

Classified financial statements: financial statements divided into useful subcategories. (9)

Clearing entries, see Closing entries

Closely held corporation: a corporation whose stock is owned by a few individuals and whose securities are not publicly traded. (20)

Closing entries: journal entries made at the end of the accounting period that set the stage for the next accounting period by closing the expense and revenue accounts of the balances and transferring the net amount to the owner's capital account or retained earnings; clearing entries. (5)

Common-size statement: a statement in which all components of the statement are shown as a percentage of a total in the statement; results from applying vertical analysis. (21)

Common stock: the stock representing the most basic rights to ownership of a corporation. (16)

Common stock equivalents: convertible securities that, at the time of issuance, have a value that is closely related to their conversion value, that is, the value of the stock into which they could be converted. (17)

Comparability: the qualitative characteristic of accounting information that presents information in such a way that the decision maker can recognize similarities, differences, and trends over time and/or make comparisons with other companies. (9)

Comparative financial statements: financial statements in which data for two or more years are presented in adjacent columnar form. (9)

Compatability principle: a principle of systems design that holds that the design of a system must be in harmony with organizational and human factors of a business. (7)

Compensating balance: a minimum amount that a bank requires a company to keep in its bank account as part of a credit-granting arrangement. (10)

Complex capital structure: a capital structure with additional securities (convertible stocks and bonds) that can be converted into common stock. (17)

Compound entry: a journal entry that has more than one debit and/or credit entry. (3)

Compound interest: the interest cost for two or more periods, if one assumes that after each period the interest of that period is added to the amount on which interest is computed in future periods. (Appendix A)

Comprehensive income: the change in equity (net assets) of an entity during a period from transactions and other events and circumstances from nonowner sources except those changes resulting from investments by owners and distributions to withdrawals by owners. (9)

Computer: an electronic tool for the rapid collection, organization, and communication of large amounts of information. (1)

Computer operator: the person who runs the computer. (7)

Condensed financial statements: presents only the major categories of the financial statement. (9)

Conglomerate: a company that operates in more than one industry; a diversified company. (21)

Conservatism: an accounting convention that means when accountants are faced with major uncertainties as to which alternative accounting procedure to apply, they tend to exercise caution and choose the procedure that is least likely to overstate assets or income. (9)

Consistency: an accounting convention that requires that a particular accounting procedure, once adopted, will not be changed from period to period. (9)

Consolidated financial statements: the combined financial statements of a parent company and its subsidiaries. (20)

Constant dollar accounting: the restatement of historical cost statements for general price level changes with the result that all amounts are stated in dollars of uniform general purchasing power. (14)

Contingent liability: a potential liability that can develop into a real liability if a possible subsequent event occurs. (10, 12)

Continuity problem: the difficulty associated with the indefinite life of business enterprises; related to the going concern assumption. (4)

Contra account: an account whose balance is subtracted from an associated account in the financial statements. (4)

Contributed or paid-in capital: that part of owners' equity representing the amounts of assets invested by stockholders. (16)

Contribution margin: the excess of revenues over all variable costs related to a particular sales volume. (25)

Control: the process of seeing that plans are carried out. (1)

Control (of parent over subsidiary): in connection with long-term investments, the ability of the investing company to determine the operating and financial policies of the investee company. (20)

Controllable costs: those costs that result from a particular manager's actions and decision and over which he or she has full control. (25)

Controllable overhead variance: the difference between actual overhead costs incurred and factory overhead budgeted for the level of production achieved. (27)

Controlling (or control) account: an account in the general ledger that summarizes the total balance of a group of related accounts in a subsidiary ledger. (7, 23)

Control principle: a principle of systems design that holds that an accounting system must provide all the features of internal control needed to safeguard assets and ensure the reliability of data. (7)

Control unit: the part of the central processor in a computer system that directs and coordinates all parts of the computer. (7)

Conversion costs: the combined total of direct labor and factory overhead costs incurred by a production department or other work center. (24)

Convertible bonds: bonds that may be exchanged for other securities of the corporation, usually common stock. (18)

Convertible preferred stock: stock that can be converted into common stock. Bonds may also have this feature. (16)

Copyright: an exclusive right granted by the federal government to the possessor to publish and sell literary, musical, and other artistic materials. (14)

Corporation: a body of persons granted a charter legally recognizing them as a separate entity having its own rights, privileges, and liabilities distinct from those of its members. (1, 16)

Cost: exchange price associated with a business transaction at the point of recognition; original cost; historical cost. (3)

Cost allocation (assignment): the process of assigning a specific cost or pool of costs to a specific cost objective or cost objectives. (25)

Cost behavior: the manner in which costs respond to changes in activity or volume. (25)

Cost-benefit principle: a principle of systems design that holds that the value or benefits from a system and its information output must be equal to or greater than its cost. (7, 9)

Cost center: any organizational segment or area of activity for which there is a reason to accumulate costs. (25)

Cost flow: the association of costs with their assumed flow within the operations of a company. (11)

Cost method: a method of accounting for long-term investments when the investor has neither significant influence nor control of the investee; the investor records the investment at cost and recognizes dividends as income when they are received. (20)

Cost objective: the destination of an assigned cost. (25)

Cost of debt: the ratio of loan charges to net proceeds of the loan. After-tax considerations and present value of interest charges should be acknowledged in the computation. (28)

Cost of equity capital: the rate of return to the investor that maintains the stock's value in the marketplace. (28)

Cost of goods manufactured: a term used in the statement of cost of goods manufactured that represents the total manufacturing costs attached to units of product completed during an accounting period. (22)

Cost of goods sold: item on income statement that is computed by subtracting the merchandise inventory at the end of the year from the goods available for sale; deducted from revenue to give gross profit. (6)

Cost of preferred stock: the stated dividend rate of the individual stock issue. (28)

Cost of retained earnings: the opportunity cost or dividends forgone by the stockholder. (28)

Cost summary schedule: a process costing schedule in which total manufacturing costs accumulated during the period are distributed to units completed and transferred out of the department or the units in ending Work in Process Inventory. (24)

Cost-volume-profit (C-V-P) analysis: an analysis based on the relationships among operating cost, sales volume and revenue, and target net income; used as a planning device to predict one of the factors when the other two are known. (25)

Coupon bonds: bonds whose owners are not registered with the issuing corporation but that have interest coupons attached. (18)

Credit: the right side of an account. (3)

Crossfooting: horizontal addition and subtraction of rows in adjacent columns. (5)

Cumulative preferred stock: preferred stock on which unpaid dividends accumulate over time and must be satisfied in any given year before a dividend may be paid to common stockholders. (16)

Current assets: cash or other assets that are reasonably expected to be realized in cash or sold during a normal operating cycle of a business or within one year if the operating cycle is shorter than one year. (9)

Current liabilities: obligations due to be paid within the normal operating cycle of the business or within a year, whichever is longer. (9, 12)

Current ratio: a measure of liquidity; current assets divided by current liabilities. (9, 21)

Current value accounting: a method of accounting that would recognize the effects of specific price changes in the financial statements. (14)

Data processing: the means by which the accounting system collects data, organizes them into meaningful forms, and issues the resulting information to users. (7)

Debenture bonds, See Unsecured bonds

Debit: the left side of an account. (3)

Debt to equity ratio: a ratio that measures the relationship of assets provided by creditors to the amount provided by stockholders. (9, 21)

Declining-balance method: an accelerated method of depreciation. (13)

Deductions from gross income: certain personal deductions allowed in computing taxable income. (Appendix C)

Deferral: the postponement of the recognition of an expense already paid or of a revenue already received. (4)

Deferred Income Taxes: the difference between the Income Taxes Expense and the current Income Taxes Payable accounts. (18)

Deferred revenues: obligations for goods or services that the company must deliver in return for an advance payment from a customer. (12)

Deficit: a debit balance in the Retained Earnings account. (17)

Definitely determinable liability: a liability that is determined by contract or statute and can be measured precisely. (12)

Deflation: a decrease in the general price level. (14)

Depletion: the proportional allocation of the cost of a natural resource to the units removed; the exhaustion of a natural resource through mining, cutting, pumping, or otherwise using up the resource. (13)

Deposits in transit: deposits mailed or taken to the bank but not received by the bank in time to be recorded before preparation of the monthly statement. (8)

Deposit ticket: a document used to make a deposit in a bank. (8)

Depreciable cost: the cost of an asset less its residual value. (13)

Depreciation (depreciation expense): the periodic allocation of the cost of a tangible long-lived asset over its estimated useful life. (4, 13)

Direct charge-off method: a method of accounting for uncollectible accounts by debiting expenses directly when bad debts are discovered instead of using the allowance method; a method that is unacceptable because it violates the matching rule. (10)

Direct cost: a manufacturing cost that is traceable to a specific product or cost objective. (22)

Direct labor: all labor costs for specific work performed on products that are conveniently and economically traceable to end products. (22)

Direct labor efficiency variance: the difference between actual hours worked and standard hours allowed for the good units produced, multiplied by the standard labor rate. (27)

Direct labor rate standards: the hourly labor cost per function or job classification that is expected to exist during the next accounting period. (27)

Direct labor rate variance: the difference between the actual labor rate paid and the standard labor rate, multiplied by the actual hours worked. (27)

Direct labor time standard: an hourly expression of the time it takes for each department, machine, or process to complete production on one unit or one batch of output; based on current time and motion studies of workers and machines and past employee/machine performances. (27)

Direct materials: materials that become an integral part of the finished product and are conveniently and economically traceable to specific units of productive output. (22)

Direct materials price standard: a carefully derived estimate or projected amount of what a particular type of material will cost when purchased during the next accounting period. (27)

Direct materials price variance: the difference between the actual price paid for materials and the standard price, multiplied by the actual quantity purchased. (27)

Direct materials quantity standard: an expression of forecasted or expected quantity usage that is influenced by product engineering specifications, quality of materials used, and productivity of the machines being used, and the quality and experience of the machine operators and set-up people. (27)

Direct materials quantity variance: the difference between the actual quantity of materials used and the standard quantity that should have been used, multiplied by the standard price. (27)

Discontinued operations: segments of a business that are no longer part of the ongoing operations of the company. (17)

Discount: *verb:* to take out the interest on a promissory note in advance; *noun:* the amount of the interest deducted. (10, 18)

Discounted cash flow: the process of discounting future cash flows back to the present using an anticipated discount rate. (28)

Dishonored note: a promissory note that the maker cannot or will not pay at the maturity date. (10)

Disposal value, see Residual value

Dissolution: a change in the original association of the partners in a partnership resulting from such events as the admission, withdrawal, or death of a partner. (15)

Diversified company, see Conglomerate

Dividend: a distribution of assets of a corporation to its stockholders. (17)

Dividends in arrears: the accumulated unpaid dividends on cumulative preferred stock from prior years. (16)

Dividends yield: a ratio that measures the current return to an investor in a stock. (21)

Double-declining balance method: an accelerated method of depreciation, related to the declining-balance method, under which the fixed rate used in the method is double the straight-line rate; this rate is the maximum allowable for income tax purposes. (13)

Double-entry system: a system of recording business transactions requiring that each transaction have equal debit and credit totals, thereby maintaining a balance within the accounts taken as a whole. (3)

Double taxation: a term referring to the fact that earnings of a corporation are taxed twice, both as the net income of the corporation and as the dividends distributed to the stockholders. (Appendix C)

Duration of note: length of time in days between the making of a promissory note and its maturity date. (10)

Earnings per (common) share: item on corporate income statements that shows the net income earned on each share of common stock; net income divided by the weighted average number of common shares and common share equivalents outstanding; also called net income per share. (9, 17)

Effective interest method: a method of determining the interest and amortization of bond discount or premium for each interest period that requires the application of a constant interest rate to the carrying value of the bonds at the beginning of the period. (18)

Eliminations: adjustments that appear on work sheets in the preparation of consolidated financial statements that are intended to reflect the financial position and operations from the standpoint of a single entity. (20)

Employee earnings record: a record of earnings and withholdings for a single employee. (12)

Ending inventory: merchandise on hand for sale to customers at the end of the accounting period. (6)

Equity: the residual interest in the assets of an entity that remains after deducting its liabilities. (2)

Equity method: a method of accounting for long-term investments under which the investor records the initial investment at cost and records its proportionately owned share of subsequent earnings and dividends of the investee as increases or decreases, respectively, in the investment account. (20)

Equivalent units: a measure of productive output of units for a period of time, expressed in terms of fully completed or equivalent whole units produced; partially completed units are restated in terms of equivalent whole units; also called equivalent production. (24)

Estimated liability: a definite obligation of the firm, the exact amount of which cannot be determined until a later date. (12)

Estimated tax: an amount paid in advance by a taxpayer in anticipation of income not subject to withholding. (Appendix C)

Estimated useful life: the total number of service units expected from a long-term asset. (13)

Evaluation: the process of scrutinizing the entire decision system for the purpose of improving it. (1)

Excess capacity: machinery and equipment purchased in excess of needs so that extra capacity is available on a stand-by basis during peak usage periods or when other machinery is down for repair. (25)

Exchange rate: the value of one currency in terms of another. (20)

Exchange transaction: when used in connection with the statement of changes in financial position, an exchange of a long-term asset for a long-term liability. (19)

Exemption: a type of deduction from adjusted gross income based on personal characteristics and number of dependents. (Appendix C)

Expenditure: a payment or incurrence of an obligation to make a future payment for an asset or service rendered. (14)

Expenses: the costs of the goods and services used up in the process of obtaining revenue; expired cost. (4)

Extraordinary items: events or transactions that are distinguished by their unusual nature and the infrequency of their occurrence. (17)

Extraordinary repairs: repairs that affect the estimated residual value or estimated useful life of an asset. (14)

Factory (manufacturing) overhead: a diverse collection of production-related costs that are not practically or conveniently traceable to end products and must be assigned by some allocation method. (22)

FIFO product and cost flow: first products to be introduced into a production process are the first products to be completed. Costs attached to those first products are the first costs to be transferred out of the particular production center or department. (25)

Financial accounting: accounting information reported to and used by those outside the organization. (1)

Financial Accounting Standards Board (FASB): body that has responsibility for developing and issuing rules on accounting practice; issues Statements of Financial Accounting Standards. (1)

Financial position: the collection of resources belonging to a company and the sources of these resources or claims on them at a particular point in time; shown by a balance sheet. (2)

Financial statement analysis: the collective term used for the techniques that show significant relationships in financial statements and that facilitate comparisons from period to period and among companies. (21)

Financial statements: the means by which accountants communicate to information users; financial reports. (2)

Finished goods inventory: an inventory account unique to the manufacturing or production area to which the costs assigned to all completed products are transferred. The balance at period-end represents all manufacturing costs assigned to goods completed but not sold as of that date. (22)

First-in, first-out (FIFO) method: an inventory costing method under which the cost of the first items purchased are assigned to the first items sold and the costs of the last items purchased are assigned to the items remaining in inventory. (11)

Fiscal year: any twelve-month accounting period used by a company. (4)

Fixed assets: another name, no longer in wide use, for long-term nonmonetary assets. (13)

Fixed cost: a cost that remains constant in total within a relevant range of volume or activity. (25)

Fixed manufacturing costs: production-related costs that remain relatively constant in amount during the accounting period and vary little in relation to increases or decreases in production. (22)

Flexibility principle: a principle of systems design that holds that the accounting system should be sufficiently flexible to accommodate growth in the volume of transactions and organizational changes in the business. (7)

Flexible budget: a summary of anticipated costs prepared for a range of different activity levels and geared to changes in the level of productive output. (27)

FOB destination: term relating to transportation charges meaning that the supplier bears the transportation costs to the destination. (6)

FOB shipping point: term relating to transportation charges meaning that the buyer bears the transportation costs from the point of origin. (6)

Footing: a memorandum total of a column of numbers; to foot, to total a column of numbers. (3)

Freight in: transportation charges on merchandise purchased for resale; transportation in. (6)

Full costing: a method of accounting for oil and gas development and exploration under which the costs associated with both successful and unsuccessful explorations are capitalized and depleted over the useful life of the producing resources. (13)

Full disclosure: an accounting convention requiring that financial statements and their accompanying footnotes contain all information relevant to the user's understanding of the situation. (9)

Fully diluted earnings per share: net income applicable to common stock divided by the sum of the weighted-average common stock and common stock equivalents and other potentially dilutive securities. (17) See also Earnings per common share.

Functional currency: currency of the country where the subsidiary carries on most of its business. (20)

Funds: equivalent to working capital when used in connection with the statement of changes in financial position. (19)

Future value: the amount that an investment will be worth at a future date if invested at compound interest. (Appendix A)

General journal: the simplest and most flexible type of journal. (3)

Generally accepted accounting principles (GAAP): the conventions, rules, and procedures necessary to define accepted accounting practice at a particular time. (1)

General price level: a price level that reflects the price changes of a group of goods or services. (14)

General-purpose external financial statements: means by which the information accumulated and processed in the financial accounting system is periodically communicated to those persons, especially investors and creditors, who use it outside the enterprise. (9)

Going concern: the assumption that unless there is evidence to the contrary the business will continue to operate for an indefinite period. (4)

Going public: the process by which a corporation offers its shares to the public. (20)

Goods flow: the actual physical movement of inventory goods in the operations of a company. (11)

Goodwill: the excess of the cost of a group of assets (usually a business) over the market value of the assets individually. (14, 20)

Government Accounting Standards Board (GASB): issues accounting standards for state and local governments. (1)

Gross income: income from all sources, less allowable exclusions. (Appendix C)

Gross payroll: a measure of the total wages or salary earned by an employee before any deductions are subtracted. This amount is also used to determine total manufacturing labor costs. (22)

Gross margin: difference between revenue from sales and cost of goods sold; also called gross margin from sales. (6)

Gross profit method: used to estimate the value of inventory; assumes that the ratio of gross margin for a business is relatively stable from year to year. (11)

Gross sales: total sales for cash and on credit for a given accounting period. (6)

Group depreciation: the grouping of items of similar plant assets together for purposes of calculating depreciation. (13)

Hardware: all the equipment needed for the operation of a computer data processing system. (7)

Horizontal analysis: the computation of dollar amount changes and percentage changes from year to year. (21)

Imprest system: a petty cash system in which a petty cash fund is established at a fixed amount of cash and is periodically reimbursed for the exact amount necessary to bring it back to the fixed amount. (8)

Income averaging: a formula that allows taxpayers whose income fluctuates widely to average their income over five years. (Appendix C)

Income from operations: the excess of gross profit from sales over operating expenses. (9)

Income statement: a financial statement that shows the amount of income earned by a business over an accounting period. (2)

Income summary: a nominal account used during the closing process in which are summarized all revenues and expenses before the net amount is transferred to the capital account or retained earnings. (5)

Income tax allocation: an accounting method designed to accrue income taxes on the basis of accounting income whenever there are differences in accounting and taxable income. (18)

Income tax expense, see Provision for income taxes

Incremental analysis: a decision analysis format that highlights only relevant decision information or the differences between costs and revenues under two or more alternative courses of action. (28)

Index number: a number constructed by setting the base year equal to 100 percent and calculating other years in relation to the base year. (21)

Indirect cost: a manufacturing cost that is not traceable to a specific product or cost objective and must be assigned by some allocation method. (22)

Indirect labor: labor costs for production-related activities that cannot be associated with, or are not conveniently and economically traceable to, end products and must be assigned by some allocation method. (22)

Indirect materials: less significant materials and other production supplies that cannot be conveniently or economically assigned to specific products and must be assigned by some allocation method. (22)

Inflation: an increase in the general price level. (14)

Installment accounts receivable: accounts receivable that are payable in periodic payments. (10)

Intangible assets: long-term assets that have no physical substance but have a value based on rights or privileges accruing to the owner. (9, 13, 14)

Interest: the cost associated with the use of money for a specific period of time. (10, Appendix A)

Interest coverage ratio: a ratio that measures the protection of creditors from a default on interest payments. (21)

Interest earned: payment by a bank of interest earned on a company's average balance which is reported by the bank on the bank statement. (8)

Interim financial statements: financial statements prepared on a condensed basis for an accounting period of less than one year. (9, 21)

Internal accounting controls: the controls employed primarily to protect assets and ensure the accuracy and reliability of the accounting records. (8)

Internal administrative controls: controls established to ensure operational efficiency and adherence to managerial policies; related to the decision processes leading to management's authorization of transactions. (8)

Internal control: the plan of organization and all of the coordinate methods and measures adopted within a business to safeguard its assets, check the accuracy and reliability of its accounting data, promote operational efficiency, and encourage adherence to prescribed managerial policies. (8)

Internal Revenue Service (IRS): federal agency that interprets and enforces the U.S. tax laws governing the assessment and collection of revenue for operating the government. (1)

Inventory cost: cost recorded upon purchase of inventory; includes invoice price less cash discounts plus freight and transportation in and applicable insurance, taxes, and tariffs. (11)

Inventory turnover: a ratio that measures the relative size of inventory. (21)

Investments: assets, generally of a long-term nature, that are not used in the normal operation of a business and that management does not intend to convert to cash within the next year. (9)

Investment tax credit: a special tax credit allowed to businesses by Congress to encourage investment in plant assets. (17)

Invoice: a document prepared by a supplier requesting payment for goods or services provided. (8)

Issued stock: shares of stock sold or otherwise transferred to the stockholders. (16)

Item-by-item method: a method of applying the lower-of-cost-or-market rule to inventory pricing. (11)

Job card: a labor card supplementing the time card, on which each employee's time on a specific job is recorded; used to support an employee's daily time recorded on the time card and to assign labor costs to specific jobs or batches of products. (22)

Job order: a customer order for a specific number of specially designed, made-to-order products. (23)

Job order cost card: a document maintained for each job or work order in process, upon which all costs of that job are recorded and accumulated as the job order is being worked on. These cards make up the subsidiary ledger of the Work in Process Inventory Control account. (23)

Job order cost system: a product costing system used in the manufacturing of unique or special-order products in which direct materials, direct labor, and manufacturing overhead costs are assigned to specific job orders or batches of products. (23)

Joint cost: a cost that collectively applies or relates to several products or cost objectives and can be assigned to those cost objectives only by means of arbitrary cost allocation; also called common cost. (25)

Journal: a chronological record of all transactions; place where transactions are first recorded. (3)

Journal entry: a separate entry in the journal, that records a single transaction. (3)

Journalizing: the process of recording transactions in a journal. (3)

Last-in, first-out (LIFO) method: an inventory costing method under which the costs of the last items purchased are assigned to the first items sold and the cost of the inventory is composed of the cost of items from the oldest purchases. (11)

Leasehold: a payment made to secure the right to a lease. (14)

Leasehold improvement: an improvement to leased property that becomes the property of the lessor at the end of the lease. (14)

Ledger: a book or file of all of a company's accounts, arranged as in the chart of accounts. (3)

Ledger account form: a form of the account that has four columns, one for debit entries, one for credit entries, and two columns (debit and credit) for showing the balance of the account; used in the general ledger. (3)

Legal capital: the minimum amount that can be reported as contributed capital; usually equal to par value or stated value. (16)

Leverage: the use of debt financing. (21)

Liability: a debt of the business; an amount owed or an obligation to perform a service to creditors, employees, government bodies, or others; a claim against assets. (2, 12)

Limited life: the characteristic of a partnership shown when certain events such as the admission, withdrawal, or death of a partner can terminate the partnership. (15)

Liquidating dividend: a dividend that exceeds retained earnings. (17)

Liquidation: the process of ending a business; entails selling assets, paying liabilities, and distributing any remaining assets to the partners. (15)

Liquidity: the position of having enough funds on hand to pay a company's bills when they are due and provide for unanticipated needs for cash. (1, 9)

Long-term liabilities: debts of a business that fall due more than one year ahead, beyond the normal operating cycle, or are to be paid out of noncurrent assets. (9, 12)

Long-term nonmonetary assets: assets that (1) have a useful life of more than one year, (2) are acquired for use in the operation of the business, and (3) are not intended for resale to customers; fixed assets. (11, 13)

Lower-of-cost-or-market (LCM) rule: a method of inventory pricing under which the inventory is priced at cost or market, whichever is lower. (11)

Major category method: a method of applying the lower-of-cost-or-market method to inventory pricing. (11)

Make or buy decision: a decision commonly faced by management as to whether to make the item, product, or component or to purchase it from outside sources. (28)

Management: the group of people in a business with overall responsibility for achieving the company's goals. (1)

Management accounting: the aspect of accounting that consists of specific information gathering and reporting concepts and accounting procedures that, when applied to a company's financial and production data, will satisfy internal management's needs for product costing information, data used for planning and control of operations, and special reports and analyses used to support management's decisions. (1, 22)

Management advisory services: consulting services offered by public accountants. (1)

Management by exception: a review process whereby management locates and analyzes only the areas of unusually good or bad performance. (27)

Management information system: the interconnected subsystems that provide the information necessary to operate a business. (1)

Manual data processing: a system of data processing in which recording, posting, and other bookkeeping procedures are done by hand. (7)

Manufacturing cost flow: the defined or structured flow of direct materials, direct labor, and manufacturing overhead costs from their incurrence through the inventory accounts and finally to the Cost of Goods Sold account. (22)

Marginal tax rates: the tax rate that applies to the last increment of taxable income. (Appendix C)

Market: in inventory valuation, the current replacement cost of inventory. (11)

Marketable securities: investment in securities which are readily marketable; short-term investments. (10)

Market risk: the volatility or fluctuation of the price of a stock in relation to the volatility or fluctuation of the prices of other stocks. (21)

Market value: the price investors are willing to pay for a share of stock on the open market. (16)

Master budget: an integrated set of departmental or functional period budgets that have been consolidated into forecasted financial statements for the entire company. (26)

Matching rule: the rule of accounting that revenue must be assigned to the accounting period in which the goods were sold or the services performed, and expenses must be assigned to the accounting period in which they were used to produce revenue; the rule underlying accrual accounting. (4)

Materiality: an accounting convention that refers to the relative importance of an item. (9)

Materials inventory: an inventory account made up of the balances of materials and supplies on hand at a given time; also called the Stores and materials inventory control account. (22)

Materials requisition: a document that must be completed and approved before raw materials are issued to production. This form is essential to the control of raw materials and contains such information as the types and quantities of raw materials and supplies needed and the supervisor's approval signature. (22)

Maturity date: the due date of a promissory note. (10)

Maturity value: the total proceeds of a promissory note including principal and interest at the maturity date. (10)

Merchandise inventory: goods on hand and available for sale to customers. (6)

Minority interest: the percentage of ownership attributable to minority stockholders times the net assets of the subsidiary, an amount which appears in the stockholders' equity section of a consolidated balance sheet. (20)

Miscellaneous charges and credits: bank charges for services such as collection and payment of promissory notes, stopping payment on checks, and printing checks. (8)

Mixed cost: a cost category that results when more than one type of cost is charged to the same general ledger account. The Repairs and Maintenance account is an example of a mixed cost account. (25)

Monetary assets: consists of cash and other assets representing the right to receive a specific amount of cash. (11)

Money measure: a concept in accounting that requires that business transactions be measured in terms of money. (2)

Mortgage: a type of long-term debt secured by real property that is paid in equal monthly installments. (18)

Multinational corporations: corporations that do business or operate in more than one country; also, transnational corporation. (20)

Multistep form: form of the income statement that arrives at net income in steps. (9)

Mutual agency: the authority of partners to act as agents of the partnership within the scope of normal operations of the business. (15)

Natural resources: long-term assets purchased for the physical substance that can be taken from them and used up rather than for the value of their location. (13)

Net capital gain: the excess of net long-term capital gain over any net short-term capital loss. (17, Appendix C)

Net income: the net increase in owner's equity resulting from the profit seeking operations of a company; net income = revenue − expenses. (4, 6)

Net income per share, see Earnings per common share

Net long-term capital gain (or loss): the combined total of all gains and losses on long-term capital assets during a tax year. (17, Appendix C)

Net payroll: the amount paid to the employee (cash or check) after all payroll deductions have been subtracted from gross wages. (22)

Net realizable value (NRV): the established selling price of an item in the ordinary course of business less reasonable selling costs. (14)

Net short-term capital gain (or loss): the combined total of all gains and losses on short-term assets during a tax year. (17, Appendix C)

Neutrality: carrying out generally accepted accounting principles as faithfully as possible, the main concern being relevance and reliability of the accounting information rather than the effect on a particular interest. (9)

Nominal accounts: temporary accounts showing the accumulation of revenue and expenses only for an accounting period; at the end of the accounting period, these account balances are transferred to owner's equity. (4)

Noncumulative preferred stock: preferred stock on

which the dividend may lapse and does not have to be paid if not paid within a given year. (16)

Nonmonetary assets: assets that represent unexpired costs that will become expenses in future accounting periods. (11)

Nonparticipating preferred stock: preferred stock on which the dividend is limited to the indicated amount or rate per share. (16)

No-par stock: capital stock that does not have a par value. (16)

Normal balance: the balance one would expect an account to have; the usual balance of an account. (5)

Normal capacity: the average annual level of operating capacity that is required to satisfy anticipated sales demand; adjusted to reflect seasonal business factors and operating cycles. (5, 27)

Normal pension costs: the estimated retirement benefits for the employees who are working in the current fiscal year. (18)

Notes to the financial statements: a section of a corporate annual report that contains notes that aid the user in interpreting some of the items in the financial statements. (9)

Notice of protest: a sworn statement that a promissory note was presented to the maker for payment and the maker refused to pay. (10)

NSF (not sufficient funds) check: a check that is not paid when the depositor's bank presents it for payment to the maker's bank. (8)

Obsolescence: the process of becoming out of date; a contributor, together with physical deterioration, to the limited useful life of tangible assets. (13)

On-line processing: a type of computer system design in which input devices and random-access storage files are tied directly to the computer, enabling transactions to be entered into the records as they occur and data to be retrieved as needed. (7)

Operating expenses: expenses other than cost of goods sold incurred in the operation of a business; especially selling and administrative expenses. (6)

Operating lease: periodic payment for the right to use an asset or assets, recorded in a manner similar to the way in which rent expense payments are recorded. A short-term cancelable lease for which the risks of ownership lie with the lessor. (18)

Opinion section (of accountant's report): the portion of the report that tells the results of the accountant's audit of the financial statements. (9)

Ordinary annuity: a series of equal payments made at the end of equal intervals of time, with compound interest on these payments. (Appendix A)

Ordinary repairs: expenditures, usually of a recurring nature, that are necessary to maintain an asset in good operating condition. (14)

Organization costs: the costs of forming a corporation. (16)

Other revenues and expenses: any revenues and expenses unrelated to normal business operations such as revenues from investments (dividends and interest from stocks, bonds, and savings accounts), interest earned on credit or from notes extended to customers, and interest expense and other expenses that result from borrowing money or from credit being extended to the company. (9)

Outstanding checks: checks issued and recorded by the depositor but not yet presented to the bank for payment. (8)

Outstanding stock: the shares of a corporation's stock held by stockholders. (16)

Overhead volume variance: the difference between the factory overhead budgeted for the level of production achieved and the overhead applied to production using the standard overhead rate. (27)

Owner's equity: the resources invested by the owner of the business; assets − liabilities = owner's equity; also called residual equity. (2)

Parent company: a company that owns a controlling interest in another company. (20)

Participating preferred stock: preferred stock on which stockholders may receive a dividend higher than the indicated rate if common stockholders receive a dividend. (16)

Participative budgeting: all levels of supervisory and data input personnel take part in the budgeting process in a meaningful, active way. (26)

Partners' equity: the owners' equity section of the balance sheet in a partnership. (15)

Partnership: an association of two or more persons to carry on as co-owners a business for profit. (1, 15)

Partnership agreement: the contractual relationship between partners that identifies the details of the partnership; agreement should clarify such things as name of the business, duties of partners, partner investments, profit and loss ratios, and procedures for admission and withdrawal of partners. (15)

Par value: the amount printed on each share of stock, which must be recorded in the capital stock accounts; used in determining the legal capital of a corporation. (16)

Patent: an exclusive right granted by the federal government to make a particular product or use a specific process. (14)

Payback method: a method used to evaluate a capital expenditure proposal that focuses on the cash flow of the project and determines the payback period or the time required to recoup the original investment through cash flow from the item or project. (28)

Payroll register: a detailed listing of a firm's total payroll, prepared each payday. (12)

Pension fund: contributions from both employer and employee out of which benefits to retirees are paid. (18)

Percentage of net sales method: a method of estimating uncollectible accounts expense based on the assumption that a certain percentage of total net sales will not be collectible. (10)

Period budget: a forecast of annual operating results for a segment or functional area of a company that represents a quantitative expression of planned activities. (26)

Period costs (expenses): expired costs of an accounting period that represent dollars attached to resources used or consumed during the period; any cost or expense item on an income statement. (22)

Periodic inventory method: a method of accounting for inventory under which the cost of goods sold is determined by adding the net cost of purchases to beginning inventory and subtracting the ending inventory. (6, 11, 22)

Periodicity: the assumption that the measurement of net income for any period less than the life of the business is necessarily tentative, but nevertheless a useful approximation. (4)

Perpetual inventory method: a method of accounting for inventory under which the sales and purchases of individual items of inventory are recorded continuously, therefore allowing cost of goods sold to be determined without taking a physical inventory. (6, 11, 22)

Petty cash fund: a small fund established by a company to make small payments of cash. (8)

Petty cash system, see Imprest system

Petty cash voucher: a document that supports each payment made out of a petty cash fund. (8)

Physical inventory, see Taking a physical inventory

Physical volume method: an approach to the problem of allocating joint production costs to specific products that is based on or uses some measure of physical volume (units, pounds, liters, grams, etc.) as the basis for joint cost allocation. (25)

Planning: the process of formulating a course of action. (1)

Point-of-sale basis: a basis of revenue recognition that recognizes revenue at the point when title passes to the buyer, usually the delivery date. (14)

Portfolio: a group of loans or investments designed to average the return and risks of a creditor or investor. (21)

Post-closing trial balance: a trial balance prepared after all adjusting and closing entries have been posted and just before the next period as a final check on the balance of the ledger. (5)

Posting: the process of transferring journal entry information from the journal to the ledger. (3)

Practical capacity: theoretical capacity reduced by normal and anticipated work stoppages. (25)

Predetermined overhead rate: an overhead cost factor that is used to assign manufacturing (factory) overhead costs (all indirect manufacturing costs) to specific units, jobs, or cost objectives. (23)

Predictive value: usefulness of information to the decision maker in making a prediction, not that it is itself a prediction; a qualitative characteristic of accounting information. (9)

Preferred stock: a type of stock that has some preference over common stock, usually including dividends. (16)

Premium: the amount by which the issue price of a stock or bond exceeds the face value. (18)

Prepaid expenses: expenses paid in advance that do not expire during the current accounting period; an asset account. (4)

Present value: the amount that must be invested now at a given rate of interest to produce a given future value. (Appendix A)

Present value method: a discounted cash flow approach to measure the estimated performance of a capital investment. The value of all future cash flows discounted back to the present (present value) must exceed the initial investment if a positive decision is to be made. (28)

Price/earnings (P/E) ratio: a ratio that measures the relationship of the current market price of a stock to the earnings per share. (21)

Price index: a series of numbers, one for each period, that represents an average price for a group of goods and services, relative to the average price of the same group of goods and services at a beginning date. (14)

Primary earnings per share: net income applicable to common stock divided by the sum of the weighted-average common shares and common stock equivalents. (9, 17) See also Earnings per (common) share.

Prior period adjustments: events or transactions that relate to an earlier accounting period but were not determinable in the earlier period. (17)

Proceeds from discounting: the amount received by the borrower when a promissory note is discounted; proceeds = maturity value − discount. (10)

Process cost system: a product costing system used by companies that produce a large number of similar products or have a continuous production flow where manufacturing costs are accumulated by department or process rather than by batches of products. (23)

Product cost: costs identified as being either direct

materials, direct labor, or manufacturing overhead, traceable or assignable to products; they become part of a product's unit manufacturing cost, and are in inventories at period end. (22)

Production method: a method of depreciation that bases the depreciation charge for a period of time solely on the amount of use of the asset during the period of time. (13)

Profit: imprecise term for the earnings of a business enterprise. (4)

Profitability: the ability of a business to earn a satisfactory level of profits and to attract investor capital. (1, 9)

Profit margin: a measure of profitability; the percentage of each sales dollar that results in net income; net income divided by sales. (9, 21)

Program: the means by which a computer is instructed; consists of a sequence of instructions that, when carried out, will produce a desired result. (7)

Programmer: the person who writes the programs that instruct the computer based on the specifications of the systems analyst. (7)

Progressive tax: a tax based on a rate structure that increases the rate of tax as the amount of taxable income becomes larger. (Appendix C)

Promissory note: an unconditional promise to pay a definite sum of money on demand or at a future date. (10)

Property, plant, and equipment: tangible assets of a long-term nature used in the continuing operation of the business. (9)

Protest fee: the charge made by a bank for preparing and mailing a notice of protest. (10)

Provision for income taxes: the expense for federal and state income tax shown on the income statement; income tax expense. (9)

Proxy: a legal document, signed by the stockholder, giving another party the authority to vote his or her shares. (16)

Public accounting: the field of accounting that offers services in auditing, taxes, and management advising to the public for a fee. (1)

Publicly held corporation: a corporation registered with the Securities and Exchange Commission; its securities are traded publicly. (20)

Purchase method: a method of preparing consolidated financial statements. (20)

Purchase order: a document prepared by the accounting department authorizing a supplier to ship specified goods or provide specified services. (8, 22)

Purchase requisition (request): a document, used to begin the raw materials purchasing function, that originates in the production department and identifies the items to be purchased, states the quantities

required, and must be approved by a qualified manager or supervisor. (8, 22)

Purchases: an account used under the periodic inventory system in which the cost of all merchandise bought for resale is recorded. (6)

Purchases discounts: allowances made for prompt payment for merchandise purchased for resale; a contra purchases account. (6)

Purchases journal: a type of special-purchase journal in which are recorded credit purchases of merchandise (if it is a single-column journal) or credit purchases in general (if it is a multicolumn journal). (7)

Purchases returns and allowances: account used to accumulate cash refunds and other allowances made by suppliers on merchandise originally purchased for resale; a contra purchases account. (6)

Purchasing power: the ability of a dollar at a point in time to purchase goods or services. (14)

Purchasing power gains and losses: gains and losses that occur as a result of holding monetary items during periods of inflation or deflation. (14)

Qualitative characteristics: criteria for judging the information accountants provide to decision makers; the primary criteria are relevance and reliability. (9) See also Standards of quality.

Quick ratio: a ratio that measures the relationship of the more liquid current assets (cash, marketable securities, and accounts receivable) to current liabilities. (21)

Ratio analysis: a means of stating a meaningful relationship between two numbers. (21)

Real accounts: balance sheet accounts; accounts whose balances can extend past the end of an accounting period. (4)

Receivable turnover: a ratio that measures the relative size of accounts receivable. (21)

Receiving report: a document prepared when ordered goods are received, the data of which are matched with the descriptions and quantities listed on the purchase order to verify that the goods ordered were actually received. (8, 22)

Recognition problem: the difficulty of deciding when a business transaction occurs; usually determined to be the point in a sale when title is transferred. (3)

Registered bonds: bonds for which the name and address of the bond owner are recorded with the issuing company. (18)

Relative sales value method: an approach to the problem of allocating joint production costs to specific products that is based on or uses the product's revenue-producing ability (sales value) as the basis for joint cost allocation. (25)

Relevance: standard of quality requiring that accounting information bear directly on the economic decision for which it is to be used; one of the primary qualitative characteristics of accounting information. (9)

Relevant decision information: future cost, revenue, or resource usage data used in decision analyses that differ among the decision's alternative courses of action. (28)

Relevant range: a range of productive activity that represents the potential volume levels within which actual operations are likely to occur. (25)

Reliability: standard of quality requiring that accounting information be faithful to the original data and that it be verifiable; one of the primary qualitative characteristics of accounting information. (9) See also Representational faithfulness and Verifiability.

Replacement cost: an entry value that represents the cost to buy (or replace), in the normal course of business, new assets of equivalent operating or productive capacity. (14)

Reporting currency: currency in which the consolidated financial statements involving foreign subsidiaries are presented. (20)

Representational faithfulness: the agreement of information with what it is supposed to represent. (9)

Reserve recognition accounting: a method of accounting for oil and gas reserves proposed by the Securities and Exchange Commission under which new proved reserves would be recognized immediately in the accounting records at their estimated current value. (13)

Residual equity: the common stock of a corporation. (16)

Residual value: the estimated net scrap, salvage, or trade-in value of a tangible asset at the estimated date of disposal; also called salvage value or disposal value. (13)

Responsibility accounting system: an accounting system that personalizes accounting reports by classifying and reporting cost and revenue information according to defined responsibility areas of specific managers or management positions; also called activity accounting or profitability accounting. (25)

Retail method: a method of estimating inventory at cost in a retail enterprise. (11)

Retained earnings: the stockholders' equity that has arisen from retaining assets from earnings in the business; the accumulated earnings of a corporation from its inception minus any losses, dividends, or transfers to contributed capital. (9, 17)

Return on assets: a measure of profitability that shows how efficiently a company is using all its assets; net income divided by total assets. (9, 21)

Return on equity: a measure of profitability related to the amount earned by a business in relation to the owners' investment in the business; net income divided by owners' equity. (9, 21)

Revenue: a measure of the asset values received from customers during a specific period of time; equals the price of goods sold and services rendered during that time. (4)

Revenue expenditure: an expenditure necessary to maintain and operate plant and equipment; charged to expense because the benefits from the expenditure will be used up in the current period. (14)

Revenues from sales: revenues arising from sales of goods by the merchandising company. (6)

Reversing entries: entries made after the closing of records for one accounting period that reverse certain adjusting entries; designed to aid in routine bookkeeping the next accounting period. (5)

Salaries: compensation to employees who are paid at a monthly or yearly rate. (12)

Sales discounts: discounts given to customers for early payment for sales made on credit; a contra sales account. (6)

Sales journal: a type of special-purpose journal used to record credit sales. (7)

Sales mix analysis: an analysis to determine the most profitable combination of product sales when a company produces more than one product. (28)

Sales returns and allowances: account used to accumulate amount of cash refund granted to customers or other allowances related to prior sales; a contra sales account. (6)

Salvage value, see Residual value

Schedule of equivalent production: a process costing schedule in which equivalent production is computed for the period for both materials and conversion costs. (24)

Scope section (of accountant's report): the portion of the accountant's report that tells the extent of the accountant's audit of the financial statements. (9)

Secured bonds: bonds that give the bondholders a pledge of certain assets of the company as a guarantee of repayment. (18)

Securities and Exchange Commission (SEC): an agency of the federal government that has the legal power to set and enforce accounting practices for firms reporting to it. (1)

Semivariable cost: a cost that possesses both variable and fixed cost behavior characteristics in that part of the cost is fixed and part varies with the volume of output. (25)

Separate entity: a concept in accounting that requires a business to be treated as separate from its creditors, customers, and owners. (2)

Serial bonds: a bond issue with several different maturity dates. (18)

Service charge: a charge made by banks for various functions they perform for a depositor. (8)

Share of stock: a unit of ownership in a corporation. (16)

Short-term investments (marketable securities): investments intended to be held only until needed to pay a current obligation. (10)

Short-term liquid assets: assets such as cash, temporary investments, accounts receivable, and notes receivable that derive their usefulness from their relative availability for the payment of current obligations; these assets are not used in the productive functions of the enterprise. (10)

Short-term nonmonetary assets: current assets such as inventory, supplies, and prepaid expenses. (11)

Signature card: a card, maintained by a bank, that contains the signatures authorized to sign a depositor's checks. (8)

Significant influence (of investor over investee company): ability of an investor to affect operating and financial policies of an investee company, even though the investor holds less than 50 percent of the voting stock of the investee. (20)

Simple capital structure: a capital structure with no other securities (either stocks or bonds) that can be converted into common stock. (17)

Simple interest: the interest cost for one or more periods, if one assumes that the amount on which the interest is computed stays the same from period to period. (Appendix A)

Single-step form: form of the income statement that arrives at net income in a single step. (9)

Social accounting: field of accounting devoted to the evaluation through cost-benefit analysis of government and other human service programs and projects. (1)

Software: comprises the programs, instructions, and routines that make possible the use of computer hardware. (7)

Sole proprietorship: a business formed by one person. (1)

Source of working capital: a transaction that results in net increase in working capital. (19)

Special order decision: a type of decision faced by management in which a customer wishes to purchase a large number of similar or identical products at prices below those listed in brochures or advertisements. If capacity exists to produce the order while not disturbing the regular production process, the company can consider the order; also called special product order decision. (28)

Special-purpose journal: an input device in an accounting system that is used to record a single type of transaction. (7)

Specific-identification method: an inventory costing method under which the actual cost of specific items is used for determining cost of goods sold. (11)

Specific price level: a price level that reflects the price changes of a specific commodity or item. (14)

Split-off point: a particular point in a manufacturing process where a joint product splits or divides and two or more separate products emerge. (25)

Standard costs: realistically predetermined costs for direct materials, direct labor, and factory overhead that are usually expressed as a cost per unit of finished product. (27)

Standard direct labor cost: a standard cost computed by multiplying the direct labor time standard by the direct labor rate standard. (27)

Standard direct materials cost: a standard cost computed by multiplying the direct materials price standard by the direct materials quantity standard. (27)

Standard factory overhead cost: a standard cost computed by multiplying the standard variable overhead rate and the standard fixed overhead rate by the appropriate application base. (27)

Standard fixed overhead rate: an overhead application rate computed by dividing the total budgeted fixed overhead costs by the normal capacity for the period. (27)

Standards of quality: criteria for judging the information accountants provide to decision makers. (9) See also Qualitative characteristics.

Standard variable overhead rate: an overhead application rate computed by dividing the total budgeted variable overhead costs by the application base being used by the company. (27)

Stated value: a value assigned by the board of directors to no-par stock. (16)

Statement of changes in financial position: a major financial statement that summarizes the financing and investing activities of a business. (2, 19)

Statement of cost of goods manufactured: formal statement summarizing the flow of all manufacturing costs incurred during a period; yields the dollar amount of costs of products completed and transferred to Finished Goods Inventory in that period. (22)

Statement of owner's equity: a financial statement that shows the changes in the owner's capital account during the year. (2)

Statement of retained earnings: a statement summarizing the changes in retained earnings during an accounting period. (17)

Stock certificate: a document issued to a stockholder in a corporation indicating the number of shares of stock owned by the stockholder. (16)

Stock dividend: a proportional distribution of shares of a corporation's stock to the corporation's stockholders. (17)

Stockholders' equity: the owners' equity section of a corporation's balance sheet. (16)

Stock split: an increase in the number of outstanding shares of stock accompanied by a proportionate reduction in the par or stated value. (17)

Stock subscription: an issuance of stock where the investor agrees to pay for the stock on some future date or in installments at an agreed price. (16)

Storage units: the part of the central processor in a computer system where programs and data are retained until needed. (7)

Straight-line method: a method of depreciation that assumes that depreciation is dependent on the passage of time and that allocates an equal amount of depreciation to each period of time. (13)

Subsidiary: a company whose stock is more than 50 percent owned by another company. (20)

Subsidiary ledger: a ledger separate from the general ledger; contains a group of related accounts the total of whose balances equals the balance of a controlling account in the general ledger. (7)

Successful efforts accounting: a method of accounting for oil and gas development and exploration costs under which the costs of successful exploration are capitalized and depleted over the useful life of the producing resources and the costs of unsuccessful explorations are expensed immediately. (13)

Summary of significant accounting policies: section of a corporate annual report that discloses which generally accepted accounting principles the company has followed in preparing the financial statements. (9)

Sum-of-the-years'-digits method: an accelerated method of depreciation. (13)

Supporting service function: an operating unit or department not directly involved in production but needed for the overall operation of the company. (25)

System design: a phase of system installation whose purpose is to formulate the new system or changes in the existing system. (7)

System implementation: a phase of system installation whose purpose is to put in operating order a new system or change in an existing system. (7)

System investigation: a phase of system installation whose purpose is to determine the requirements of a new system or to evaluate an existing system. (7)

Systems analyst: the person who, in a computer system, carries out the functions of systems investigation and systems design. (7)

T account: a form of an account which has a physical resemblance to the letter T; used to analyze transactions. (3)

Taking a physical inventory: the act of making a physical count of all merchandise on hand at the end of an accounting period. (6)

Tangible assets: long-term assets that have physical substance. (13)

Taxable income: the amount on which income taxes are assessed. (Appendix C)

Tax credits: deductions from the computed tax liability. (17, Appendix C)

Tax evasion: the illegal concealment of actual tax liabilities. (Appendix C)

Tax liability: the amount of tax that must be paid based on taxable income and the applicable tax table. (Appendix C)

Tax planning: the arrangement of a taxpayer's affairs in such a way as to incur the smallest legal tax. (Appendix C)

Tax services: services offered by public accountants in tax planning, compliance, and reporting. (1)

Term bonds: bonds of a bond issue that all mature at the same time. (18)

Theoretical capacity: the maximum productive output of a department or a company if all machinery and equipment were operated at optimum speed without any interruptions in production for a given time period; also called ideal capacity. (25)

Time card: a basic time record document of an employee upon which either the supervisor or a time clock records the daily starting and finishing times of the person. (22)

Timeliness: the qualitative characteristic of accounting information that reaches the user in time to help in making a decision. (9)

Total inventory method: a method of applying the lower-of-cost-or-market method to inventory pricing. (11)

Total manufacturing costs: a term used in the statement of cost of goods manufactured that represents the total of direct materials used, direct labor, and manufacturing overhead costs incurred and charged to production during an accounting period. (22)

Trade credit: credit to customers at either the wholesale or the retail level. (10)

Trademark: a registered symbol that gives the holder the right to use it to identify a product or service. (14)

Translation adjustments: changes in the financial

statement due wholly to the exchange rate fluctuations. (20)

Translation gains or losses: the effects of changes in the exchange rates as reported on the income statement. (20)

Transportation in, see Freight in

Treasury stock: capital stock of a company, either common or preferred, that has been issued and reacquired by the issuing company but has not been reissued or retired. (17)

Trend analysis: the calculation of percentage changes for several successive years; a variation of horizontal analysis. (21)

Trial balance: a listing of accounts in the general ledger with their debit or credit balances in respective columns and a totaling of the columns; used to test the equality of debit and credit balances in the ledger. (3)

2/10, n/30: credit terms enabling the debtor to take a 2 percent discount if the invoice is paid within ten days after the invoice date; otherwise, the debtor must pay the full amount within thirty days. (6)

Uncollectible accounts: accounts receivable from customers who cannot or will not pay. (10)

Underapplied or overapplied overhead: the difference resulting when the amount of factory overhead costs applied to products during an accounting period is more or less than the actual amount of factory overhead costs incurred in that period. (23)

Understandability: the qualitative characteristic of accounting information that is presented in a form and in terms that its user can understand. (9)

Unearned revenue: a revenue received in advance for which the goods will not be delivered or the services performed during the current accounting period; a liability account. (4)

Unit cost: the amount of manufacturing costs incurred in the completion or production of one unit of product; usually computed by dividing total production costs for a job or period of time by the respective number of units produced. (23)

Unit cost analysis schedule: a process costing statement used to (1) accumulate all costs charged to the Work in Process Inventory account of each department or production process, and (2) compute cost per equivalent unit for materials and conversion costs. (24)

Unlimited liability: each partner has a personal liability for all debts of the partnership. (15)

Unsecured bonds: bonds issued on the general credit of a company; debenture bonds. (18)

Use of working capital: a transaction that results in a net decrease in working capital. (19)

Valuation problem: the difficulty of assigning a value to a business transaction; in general, determined to be original, or historical, cost. (3)

Variable cost: a cost that changes in total in direct proportion to productive output or any other volume measure. (25)

Variable costing: an approach to product costing in which only variable manufacturing costs are assigned to products for product costing and inventory valuation purposes; also called direct costing. (28)

Variable manufacturing costs: types of manufacturing costs that increase or decrease in direct proportion to the number of units produced. (22)

Verifiability: the qualitative characteristic of accounting information that can be confirmed or duplicated by independent parties using the same measurement techniques. (9)

Vertical analysis: the calculation of percentages to show the relationship of the component parts of a financial statement to the total in the statement. (21)

Voucher: a written authorization prepared for each expenditure in a voucher system. (8)

Voucher check: a check specifically designed for use in a voucher system. (8)

Voucher register: a special-purpose journal in which vouchers are recorded after they have been properly approved. (8)

Voucher system: any system providing documentary evidence of and written authorization for business transactions, usually associated with expenditures. (8)

Wages: compensation for employees at an hourly rate or on a piecework basis. (12)

Wasting assets: another term for natural resources. (13)

Working capital: the amount by which total current assets exceed total current liabilities. (9)

Working papers: documents prepared and used by the accountant that aid in organizing the accountant's work and provide evidence to support the basis of the financial statements. (5)

Work in process inventory: an inventory account unique to the manufacturing or production area to which all manufacturing costs incurred and assigned to products are charged. The balance at period-end represents all costs assigned to goods partially completed at that particular time. (22)

Work sheet: a type of working paper that is used as a preliminary step and aid to the preparation of financial statements. (5)

Zero bracket amount: an amount of gross income equal to the amount on which no income tax liability would result. (Appendix C)

Index